Jimmy Swaggart Bible Commentary

John

JIMMY SWAGGART BIBLE COMMENTARY

- Genesis [639 pages 11-201]
- Exodus [639 pages 11-202]
- Leviticus [435 pages 11-203]
- Numbers
  Deuteronomy [493 pages 11-204]
- Joshua
  Judges
  Ruth [329 pages 11-205]
- I Samuel
  II Samuel [528 pages 11-206]
- I Kings
  II Kings [560 pages 11-207]
- I Chronicles
  II Chronicles [528 pages 11-226]
- Ezra
  Nehemiah
  Esther [288 pages 11-208]
- Job [320 pages 11-225]
- Psalms [672 pages 11-216]
- Proverbs [311 pages 11-227]
- Ecclesiastes
  Song Of Solomon [238 pages 11-228]
- Isaiah [688 pages 11-220]
- Jeremiah
  Lamentations [456 pages 11-070]
- Ezekiel [508 pages 11-223]
- Daniel [403 pages 11-224]
- Hosea
  Joel
  Amos [496 Pages 11-229]
- Obadiah
  Jonah
  Micah
  Nahum
  Habakkuk
  Zephaniah [545 pages 11-230]
- Haggai
  Zechariah
  Malachi [449 pages 11-231]
- Matthew [888 pages 11-073]
- Mark [606 pages 11-074]
- Luke [736 pages 11-075]
- John [532 pages 11-076]
- Acts [697 pages 11-077]
- Romans [536 pages 11-078]
- I Corinthians [632 pages 11-079]
- II Corinthians [589 pages 11-080]
- Galatians [478 pages 11-081]
- Ephesians [550 pages 11-082]
- Philippians [476 pages 11-083]
- Colossians [374 pages 11-084]
- I Thessalonians
  II Thessalonians [498 pages 11-085]
- I Timothy
  II Timothy
  Titus
  Philemon [687 pages 11-086]
- Hebrews [831 pages 11-087]
- James
  I Peter
  II Peter [730 pages 11-088]
- I John
  II John
  III John
  Jude [377 pages 11-089]
- Revelation [602 pages 11-090]

For prices and information please call: 1-800-288-8350
Baton Rouge residents please call: (225) 768-7000
Website: www.jsm.org • E-mail: info@jsm.org

JIMMY SWAGGART BIBLE COMMENTARY

John

WORLD
EVANGELISM
PRESS

ISBN 978-1-941403-17-4

11-076 • COPYRIGHT © 2015 Jimmy Swaggart Ministries®
P.O. Box 262550 • Baton Rouge, Louisiana 70826-2550
Website: www.jsm.org • E-mail: info@jsm.org
(225) 768-8300
19 20 21 22 23 24 25 26 27 28 / Sheridan / 15 14 13 12 11 10 9 8 7 6
All rights reserved. Printed and bound in U.S.A.
No part of this publication may be reproduced in any form or by any means
without the publisher's prior written permission.

TABLE OF CONTENTS

1. John Introduction v

2. John 1

3. Index 695

INTRODUCTION

JOHN WAS A FISHERMAN

As is known, John was not of the aristocracy of Israel; consequently, as part of the laboring class, he had little, if any, opportunity to sit at the feet of the great teachers of that day. When Jesus called him and his brother, James, these sons of Zebedee were toiling in the occupation in which they had been raised, the fishing business, which was conducted on the Sea of Galilee. It seems that without hesitation, he and his brother instantly responded to the Clarion Call. It was to be the greatest day of their lives. It also seems that they even went with the blessings of their father, who was, no doubt, left short-handed as a result of their response. However, it is possible that Zebedee felt, and even somewhat understood, the moment of this occasion respecting Jesus.

John's mother's name was Salome and is the third woman who is said to have accompanied the two Mary's to the Tomb (Mat. 27:56; Mk. 16:1).

Some think that Salome may have been the sister of Mary, the Mother of Jesus. If this is correct, then John would have been first cousin to Jesus on his mother's side.

JOHN, A DISCIPLE OF JOHN THE BAPTIST

John has often been identified as the unmade Disciple of John the Baptist, who, with Andrew, was directed by the Baptist to Jesus as the Lamb of God (Jn. 1:35-37). So, if that is correct, his hunger for God is pronounced even before he met Christ.

SONS OF THUNDER

The brothers, James and John, were nicknamed *"Sons of Thunder"* by Jesus. Perhaps this was because they were high-spirited, with their zeal undisciplined and sometimes misdirected (Lk. 9:49).

Of the Twelve, it seems that John, along with his brother James, and Peter, were selected for a more intimate relationship with Christ, despite their impetuosity. So, despite the brusque outward expression, the Lord saw something in him and knew it could be molded into the Image of the Heavenly. And so it was!

HOSTILITY!

It seems that both John and Peter had to bear the main brunt of Jewish hostility regarding the early Christian Church (Acts 4:13; 5:33, 40). Both men showed a boldness of speech and action, which astounded the Jewish authorities, who regarded them as uneducated men (Acts 4:13).

It is said that John played a leading part in the Church at Jerusalem. He was said by Paul to be a *"pillar"* of the Jerusalem Church at the time when Paul visited the city some 14 years after Paul's Conversion (Gal. 2:9).

It is not known when John left Jerusalem or where he went after his departure.

It is assumed that he was at Ephesus when he was banished to Patmos *"on account of the Word of God, and the Testimony of Jesus"* (Rev. 1:9); however, the date of this exile is uncertain.

He is supposed to have died at about 100 years of age, actually, the only Apostle of the Original Twelve, it is said, who died a natural death.

Jerome says that after Patmos, John tarried at Ephesus to an extreme old age. He records that when John had to be carried to the meetings, due to being unable to walk, he would repeat again and again, *"Little children, little children, love one another."*

It is thought that he wrote the Gospel which bears his name in about A.D. 90; however, exactly where it was written is not known.

THE LAST ONE

It is said that he was the last one who knew, heard, and actually touched the Lord Jesus Christ.

He lamented that when he was gone, there would be no eyes who had seen that Face, ears which had heard those Words, or hands which had touched that Sacred Form.

PROFOUND

Even though but a fisherman, he is said by some to have written the most profound account of any of the Books of the Bible. Whether that is correct, only the Holy Spirit would know. However, the depths which he plumbed, and I speak of his account of the Person and the Ministry of Christ, are unequaled, I think, by any other. Such only testifies to his closeness to Christ and the Work of the Holy Spirit within his heart.

It is said that to the close of his life, John was a man of fiery enthusiasm and severe judgment on those who blasphemed and resisted the Authority of the Lord. It is also said that once, upon entering a public bath but ascertaining that a certain individual by the name of Cerinthus was within, John leaped out of the place and fled from the door. He would not endure to enter under the same roof with Cerinthus because he considered this man to be an enemy of Truth. He exhorted those with him to do the same, saying, *"Let us flee, lest the bath fall in, as long as Cerinthus, the enemy of Truth, is within."*

AN ANALYSIS OF THIS GOSPEL

The Holy Spirit in the Book of Matthew cried, *"Behold your King!"*

Mark said, in essence, *"Behold your Servant!"*

Luke, in essence, exclaimed, *"Behold your Man!"*

However, in this fourth Book, John cries, *"Behold your God!"* (Isa. 40:9); for his purpose in this Gospel is to present the Lord Jesus as God.

Thus, this Gospel is necessarily distinct from the other three. They present His Perfect Humanity and are called synoptic because of this common purpose.

This fundamental distinction between the first three Gospels and the fourth demands the many differences in literary style and in other features particular to this Book.

DIFFERENCES

This is why such matters as the Temptation in the Wilderness, the Agony in the Garden, etc., are omitted. It is because they are out of harmony with the purpose of the Book.

For a similar reason, the Transfiguration is omitted. That concerned our Lord's Physical Glory while the great subject of this fourth Book is His Moral Glory.

In this Gospel, His Person is presented rather than His Actions, and Jerusalem is the center rather than Galilee, as in the other three.

Words, terms, and incidents revealing His Attributes as God are particular, therefore, to John, as distinguished from the other Evangelists; hence, they form a group apart by themselves. In them, the Lord is presented as *"praying"* to the Father; in this Gospel of John, as *"speaking"* to Him. In the synoptic Books (Matthew, Mark, and Luke), His Praying on eight occasions is recorded, but not once is He so presented in John's Gospel. Moreover, in this Gospel alone, He *"lays down"* His Life — no one takes it from Him (Jn. 10:17).

THAT WHICH WAS WRITTEN

John wrote five Books of the New Testament, that is, if one is to call I, II, and III John *"Books."* Concerning the New Testament, only Paul and Luke contributed more to the Bible. As well, John would have the privilege of closing out the Canon of Scripture, which had begun nearly 1,600 years earlier with Moses. The Holy Spirit will use *"the one whom Jesus loved"* to close it out on a barren atoll by the name of Patmos, imprisoned there by Caesar. We speak, of course, of the Book of Revelation. But, what a conclusion!

John would close it all by giving a description of the Vision God had given him of the *"New Jerusalem"* (Rev., Chpts. 21-22).

So, the Word of God, the only revealed Truth in the world, began with Moses, who had been brought up in the palace of Pharaoh, and concluded with John the Beloved, a lowly fisherman, but touched by the Holy Spirit possibly in a way as no other man. He had been with Jesus!

Thus was John, and thus is John!

"On Calvary's hill of sorrow,
"Where sin's demands were paid,
"And rays of hope for tomorrow,
"Across our path were laid."

"Today no condemnation,
"Abides to turn away,
"My soul from His Salvation,
"He's in my heart to stay."

"When gloom and sadness whisper,
"You've sinned no use to pray,
"I look away to Jesus,
"And He tells me to say:"

"And when we reach the portal,
"Where life forever reigns,

*"The ransomed hosts' grand final,
"Will be this glad refrain."*

*"I see a crimson stream of Blood,
"It flows from Calvary,
"Its waves which reach the Throne of God,
"Are sweeping over me."*

THE BOOK OF JOHN

NOTES

(1) "IN THE BEGINNING WAS THE WORD, AND THE WORD WAS WITH GOD, AND THE WORD WAS GOD."

The diagram is:

1. The Bible cannot be understood by the unredeemed, at least as far as its spiritual content and intent are concerned. This means that it is not carnally discerned (I Cor. 2:14).

2. The idea is that it is the Holy Spirit Alone Who abides within us, and Who helps us understand the Word of God.

3. The Word of God is so important that the Scripture plainly tells us that God *"has magnified His Word above all His Name"* (Ps. 138:2).

IN THE BEGINNING WAS THE WORD

The phrase, *"In the beginning was the Word,"* refers to the Incarnate Christ but speaks of His Existence before the Incarnation.

The word *"beginning"* does not imply that He had a beginning because, as God, He had no beginning, but it refers to the time of Creation and corresponds with Genesis 1:1.

Williams says, *"As speech reveals the mind, so Jesus as the Word reveals God. But to reveal God He must Himself be God, for only God could reveal God."*[1]

It is extremely interesting that the Holy Spirit through John describes Jesus as the *"Word,"* i.e., *"The Eternal Logos."* This can refer to an expression of thought but is never used by New Testament writers in that fashion. They always use it in the realm of *"speech," "utterance,"* or *"word,"* or so the Greek scholars claim.

For instance, in the record of the Creation in Genesis, Chapter 1, the proclamation of Creation is described eight times by the expression, *"And God said."* The *"Word"* which was uttered was so powerful that it could only come from the Omnipotent Word.

As an example, the Jewish translators and commentators had so thoroughly grasped the idea that they were accustomed to substituting the phrase, *"Memra-Jah," "The Word of the Lord,"* for the Name of the Most High.

They seemed to feel that the Lord could be better understood in the form of this expression, which proclaimed, at least in their minds, His Eternal and Absolute Being.

As well, the Eternal Word, or *"Logos,"* was not placed in suspension during the thirty-three and one-half years of the Incarnation of Christ. Even though He was very Man, still, He was very God. Consequently, He was the *"Word"* and, therefore, was before the Incarnation and carried through the Incarnation. Thus, He never ceased to exercise the functions that belonged to His Eternal Glory.

Reynolds said:

"He was 'in the beginning,' and therefore existed before all Creation. He did not 'become.' He was not 'made.' He 'was!'"[2]

AND THE WORD WAS WITH GOD

The phrase, *"And the Word was with God,"* expresses the idea of the Trinity.

This tells us that Jesus, i.e., *"The Word,"* was ever-existing (*"was"*), and that He had a Personal existence, for He was with God.

The Greek scholars say that this statement as given by John is difficult to translate.

It is equivalent to, *"Was in relationship with God,"* or, *"Stood over against,"* not in space or time, but eternally and constitutionally. In other words, it is more than just merely being with God, as we think of such a term. It is actually having the same relation, which the next phrase declares.

AND THE WORD WAS GOD

The phrase, *"And the Word was God,"* does not mean that before the Incarnation Jesus was God but ceased to be during the Incarnation, but it rather means the opposite. He *"was"* God before the Incarnation; He *"was"* God during the Incarnation; He *"was"* God after the Incarnation; and, He *"was"* and *"is"* God from eternity past to eternity future.

Williams says, *"In His existence Eternal, in His Person distinct, in His Nature Divine, so that His Personality was not of time, for prior to Creation He was with God (Jn. 17:5; Col. 1:17; Heb. 1:2). Thus He existed before the world began to exist; and this existence — being a conscious Personal One as distinct from the Father — necessitated His Personal Glory as God, i.e., 'Son of God'; and so, being God, that relationship was in its nature eternal."*[3]

JESUS CHRIST AND THE BIBLE

The phrase, *"And the Word was God,"* means that Jesus, in a sense, or one might even say, in essence, is in every Book of the Bible, every Chapter in every Book, every Verse in every Chapter, and every Word in every Verse. Actually, the Story of the Bible is the Story of *"Jesus Christ and Him Crucified."* It began immediately after the Fall with the First Family. Although driven from the Garden, they were told by the Lord that despite their fallen condition, a way had been made for them to have forgiveness of sins and communion with the Lord. This would be by virtue of the slain lamb. That slain lamb would be a Type of the Coming Redeemer. So, the Cross of Christ was set out immediately as the Means. We might say it like this:

• Jesus Christ is the Source of all things we receive from God (Jn. 1:1-3, 14, 29; Col. 2:10-15).

• The Cross of Christ is the Means, and the only Means, by which all of these things are given to us (I Cor. 1:17-18, 21, 23; 2:2).

• With Jesus Christ being the Source and the Cross being the Means, our Faith must always have as its Object Jesus Christ and what He did for us at the Cross. That, in essence, is having Faith in the Word (Rom. 6:1-14; I Cor. 1:17; Gal. 6:14).

• With our Faith anchored properly in Christ and the Cross, the Holy Spirit, Who works exclusively within the parameters, so to speak, of the Finished Work of Christ, will then work mightily on our behalf. We must remember that what needs to be done, we within ourselves cannot do. We have to have the Help, the Leading, the Guidance, and the Empowerment of the Holy Spirit. That is all made possible by the Cross. It is the Cross of Christ that made it legal for the Holy Spirit to permanently abide within the hearts and lives of all Believers. Without the Cross of Christ ever being the Object of our Faith, the Holy Spirit cannot properly work (Rom. 8:1-11; Eph. 2:13-18).

(2) "THE SAME WAS IN THE BEGINNING WITH GOD."

The overview is:

1. *"The same,"* i.e., this very Person, was in eternity with God. The Holy Spirit emphasizes this in order to declare His Eternal Relationship as the Son with the Father.

2. However, there is no indication that the Logos was a second God or merely Divine or God-like, nor is He described as proceeding out of or from God, and neither is He to be called, *"The God absolute,"* as opposed to all of His Manifestations. The *"Logos"* is said to be *"God"* — God in His Nature and Being. He stands over and against the Eternal God in mutual communion with the Absolute and Eternal (Reynolds).[4]

3. To attempt to understand the Trinity, the *"Father"* is *"God"* but not *"First God."*

The *"Son"* is *"God"* but not *"Second God."*

The *"Holy Spirit"* is *"God"* but not *"Third God."*

There is only One God, but that doesn't mean that They are One in number, but rather One in Essence. God is manifested in Three Persons, God the Father, God the Son, and God the Holy Spirit.

4. As God, They had no beginning and have no ending. As God, They are Uncaused, Unformed, and Unmade. As God, They always were and always shall be. As God, They are Self-sufficient and have need of nothing.

(3) "ALL THINGS WERE MADE BY HIM; AND WITHOUT HIM WAS NOT ANY THING MADE THAT WAS MADE."

The exegesis is:

1. It is absolutely impossible to exhaust the potential of the Word.

2. In some mysterious way, the Word of God is the written form of the Living Christ.

3. As such, it is energized at all times by the Holy Spirit, which means that in some mysterious way, the Holy Spirit literally inhabits the Word.

THE CREATOR

The phrase, *"All things were made by Him,"* tells us that all things came into being through Him, and without Him, not one single thing came into being.

This denies the theory of the eternity of matter, which was held by some in ancient times, and continues to be claimed by some.

Also, absolute distinction, therefore, exists between Jesus and Creation.

As well, the pronoun, *"Him,"* referring to Jesus, makes it distinct that the *"Word"* is a Person (Williams).[5]

The two words, *"All things,"* refer to every item of Creation one by one, rather than all things regarded in totality. This tells us, at least according to the limit of our comprehension, that Jesus painstakingly saw to the end of the individual Creation of each being, plant, planet, star, etc., and as Paul said, *"For by Him were all things created, that are in Heaven, and that are in Earth, visible and invisible, whether they be thrones, or dominions, or principalities, or powers: all things were created by Him, and for Him"* (Col. 1:16).

JESUS AND DEMON SPIRITS

Did Jesus create demon spirits and some of the awful beings that we read about in the Ninth Chapter of Revelation? No!

Everything that the Lord has ever created has been, and is, good (Gen. 1:10, 12, 21, 25, 31).

NOTES

So, if God did not create these creatures, where did they come from?

It is not a question of where they came from, but rather that they fell from their lofty estate and became what they are presently.

Some Bible scholars claim that these creatures we presently know as demon spirits were once a Creation that did only good and actually served under Lucifer, who we now know as Satan, which was before the Fall. They threw in their lot with Lucifer in his revolution against God and became disembodied spirits; however, they were not created in this fashion.

We look at the Ninth Chapter of Revelation, and we see creatures with grotesque appearances. It says, *"And the shapes of the locusts were like unto horses prepared unto battle; and on their heads were as it were crowns like gold, and their faces were as the faces of men. And they had hair as the hair of women, and their teeth were as the teeth of lions."*

It goes on to say, *"And they had breastplates, as it were breastplates of iron; and the sound of their wings was as the sound of chariots of many horses running to battle. And they had tails like unto scorpions, and there were stings in their tails: and their power was to hurt men five months."*

It continues, *"And they had a king over them, which is the Angel of the bottomless pit, whose name in the Hebrew tongue is Abaddon, but in the Greek tongue has his name Apollyon"* (Rev. 9:7-11).

Now, we know that God did not make these creatures in that fashion, but that they rather became this way over a period of time.

Once again, they became this way because they threw in their lot with Lucifer and his revolution against God.

Looking on the righteous side of that scale, so to speak, we see creatures in Heaven who are unlike anything on this Earth. These creatures have four heads and faces, one might say, *"like a lion. . . , like a calf. . . , like a man. . . , like a flying eagle."* As well, they have six wings, and they are full of eyes. They stand before the Throne saying, *". . . Holy, Holy, Holy, Lord God Almighty, which was, and is, and is to come*" (Rev. 4:6-8).

No, God has never created anything specifically evil, but some things became that way because of their throwing in their lot with Satan in his revolution against God.

In Verse 1, we are told how God created all things. It was by the *"Logos,"* or *"Word,"* which is the organ or instrument by which everything, one by one, was made.

CREATION

And yet, this only gives us the manner in which everything was created; it really doesn't tell us how. In fact, the Lord never really tells us how that He created all things, but rather that He did. In essence, the Lord devoted only one sentence to Creation when He said, *"In the beginning God created the heaven and the Earth"* (Gen. 1:1).

However, when it came to the description of the Tabernacle, which was built by men appointed by Moses and was God's First Dwelling Place on Earth among men, so to speak, we find that the Holy Spirit devoted some 50 Chapters to it. If we count the Book of Hebrews and that given in the Pentateuch, it comes to some 50 Chapters that God devoted to this subject. In other words, He counted that, His dwelling among men, far, far more important than the Creation. Actually, the Tabernacle is referred to in Scripture as *"the tent of meeting,"* and is done so 144 times. It is called this simply because the Lord desires to meet with His Children, which is brought about by prayer and worship on the part of Believers, etc.

HE MADE ALL THINGS

The phrase, *"And without Him was not anything made that was made,"* says the same thing as the first phrase, but in an opposite manner, in order to stress the emphasis of Jesus as Creator.

The words, *"Without Him,"* mean that independently of His Cooperation and Volition, nothing, not even one single thing, was made.

When one considers the order of Creation, how it functions according to set Laws, and never varies from these Laws, continuing to fulfill the Creative Order, one cannot help but be totally awed.

For instance, when the astronauts go into space, in order to go into orbit, they have to go in at a certain time, and they have to come back at a certain time. They are depending on this Planet being faithful to the zenith degree, regarding its revolutions. If not, they would be stranded in space forever.

Other than the absolute absurdity and stupidity which characterizes the vapid philosophy of evolution, the sheer affront to God as Creator by the propagation of this lie is the greatest insult of all. Actually, evolution is an insult to intelligence in any capacity. The idea that something on its own can be brought out of nothing is the beginning of this lie. As well, the thought, which is the very heart of evolution, that something can gradually come from disorganized matter into a well-ordered structure is the very opposite of that which really happens. If left unattended and uncultivated, there is always a *"regression"* instead of a *"progression."* That is the reason the Lord told Adam and Eve, *"Be fruitful, and multiply, and replenish the Earth, and subdue it: and have dominion over the fish of the sea, and over the fowl of the air, and over every living thing that moves upon the Earth"* (Gen. 1:28).

Even though we have given the following elsewhere in these Volumes, in view of the significance of this subject, we will give it again in abbreviated form:

EVOLUTION: FACT OR FICTION

Evolution is now taught in our schools and colleges as a science when, in reality, it meets none of the criteria for true science. So, the teachers who peddle this fabrication to gullible students, whether in grade school or college, are, in effect, violating all the rules of true science.

All science is basically formulated from the foundation of mathematics. In other words, two plus two equals four, which means that two plus three doesn't equal four, and neither does one plus six, etc.

We will show in the following statements that the theory of evolution doesn't even remotely approach true science. In fact, it cannot even honestly be called a theory. Pure and simple, it is a fabrication.

THE BIBLE

The Bible declares in no uncertain terms that God is the First Cause of everything and the Last Cause.

In the original Creation as formulated by God and given to us in the first two Chapters of Genesis, Creation contains no hint of foreboding for the future, for everything has the seal of affection stamped on it. Until the fall and declension of man and woman from pristine Grace, the prospect for the future was one of continuous and untrammeled fellowship with God. When sin entered the human experience, it cast a blemish upon all created life (Hos. 4:7; Rom. 8:21-22), and threatened the future of man by separating his personality from God.

Therefore, it became necessary for the Creator to make specific provisions for human spiritual needs. It was first by the Promise of One Who would effectively break the power of the Tempter (Gen. 3:15), then by the provision of a Sacrificial system, which would enable the penitent worshipper to renew his fellowship with God, and finally, by revealing that at some specific point in history the Creator's Purpose would be entirely realized and a New Heaven and Earth would replace the existing order of things. All of this is and shall be realized in Jesus Christ.

CREATION CANNOT PRODUCE SOMETHING GREATER THAN ITSELF

That being the case, this blows to pieces all the claims of evolution.

In fact, all things that are created actually degenerate if left on their own. While species can be improved upon by a careful cultivation, no new species can be produced by such a law.

The idea of evolution is that over a tremendous period of time, everything became and becomes better and better. Every single shred of evidence proves the very opposite of that. In fact, as stated, if left on its own, there is a degeneration in everything instead of a generation. That is patently obvious all over the world and for all time.

AFTER ITS KIND

Emphatically, in Genesis, Chapter 1, the Bible declares over and over that everything created by God reproduces *"after its kind,"* which means the following:

The squirrel has always been a squirrel, as the horse has always been a horse. There is no record in history, or is there any presently, that there has been a reproduction of anything except by *"their own kind."*

The evolutionists would have us believe that the entire chain of this false philosophy is intact with the exception of the so-called *"missing link."* However, the truth is, the entire chain is missing.

The phrase, *"After its kind,"* is remarkable when we consider that there are over 2,000,000 species of plant and animal life. None of these have ever broken out of the mold and reproduced something that is different. Once again, this totally debunks the idea of evolution.

REPRODUCTION

The power of reproduction is not in that which is produced, but in that which does the producing. The question has ever been asked as to which came first, the hen or the egg. The answer is very simple:

The chicken alone could produce the egg, so the chicken came first.

DEAD MATTER

Science has itself proven that life cannot be brought out of dead matter. In fact, they have tried to do it many times now but, of course, with no success.

When the Lord originally created life, and He is the Source of all life, He created it in the sense of lower forms of life depending on higher forms of life. In other words, the simple depends on the complex, the powerless upon the powerful, etc.

However, let us not forget that even though this is so as it regards the lower forms depending on the higher forms, we must never forget that all life ultimately depends on God as Creator.

A COMMON ANCESTOR

In the study of evolution, despite all the claims of *"natural selection"* and the *"survival of the fittest,"* both have proven to be false.

The very foundation of evolution is that

of a slow and tedious process, played out over millions and millions of years, and perhaps even longer.

The truth is, all of Creation passes through various stages of growth very rapidly, completely debunking the theories of evolution.

It is amazing that despite their theories of *"natural selection"* and the *"survival of the fittest,"* the teachers of evolution have never found one single example of evolution from one species to another.

So, the next best thing for the evolutionists is *"similarity"*; however, similarity only proves similarity, and nothing else.

I am wearing a watch; it is a mechanical device, the same as a 747 airliner is a mechanical device. In that it is mechanical, it has similarities to the 747 in a minor way, but, to be sure, it will never evolve into a 747. So, the teaching that all life comes from a common ancestor is basely false.

DEGENERATION

Degeneration, as should be obvious, is the very opposite of evolution. The theory of this false science teaches that things evolve into higher and higher forms of life. Nature teaches the very opposite. In fact, it teaches degeneration instead of generation, as previously stated.

It's a common thing for us to say that nature is full of life; however, in reality, it is full of death.

Using the physical body of man as an example, the same 6,000 years of recorded history proclaim no evolving process. In other words, despite all the modern medicine and technology, the human lifespan is little more today than it was a thousand, or several thousand years ago. In fact, the Bible tells us that for the first 1,000 years, men lived for several centuries, with Methuselah living some 969 years (Gen. 5:27). Let the reader understand that these are not idle tales, but, in reality, these men actually lived that long.

In fact, God originally created man to live forever. Due to the Fall, spiritual death was brought on, which ultimately occasioned physical death, i.e., degeneration. Abraham lived to be 175, with Jacob, his grandson, dying at 147 years old. By the time of David, about 800 years after Jacob, David died at 70 years of age. Looking at the entirety of the world, 70 years of age is about the average lifespan.

The only way this degeneration can be suspended is through the Lord Jesus Christ. Actually, were it not for His Intervention, which He did at the Cross, the lifespan of humanity would gradually decrease, despite modern technology. Ultimately, Christ will put an end to the entirety of the process of sin and its companion, death (I Cor., Chpt. 15; Rev., Chpts. 19-22).

GEOLOGY

Some have tried to prove evolution by geology, but their efforts have proved fruitless.

It is now believed by many that such mighty canyons, as the Grand Canyon and others similar, were, in fact, carved out in a matter of hours or days at the most. The evolutionists claim millions of years, but there is no proof of that.

In opening some of the floodgates on the Hoover Dam, the force of the water rushing through carved out several feet of solid rock in a matter of hours. To be sure, the force and pressure of that particular water outlet is nothing by comparison to what happened during the Flood, and we speak of Noah's Flood, when these things probably occurred.

There is no proof whatsoever of evolution in geology.

JUDGMENT AND RECREATION

Evolution teaches that everything is growing better and better, always evolving into a higher process, despite the fact that there is absolutely no physical proof of such and, in fact, never has been.

There is evidence now that the whole world is moving toward a climax of Judgment and re-creation.

In chemistry, which is possibly the closest study of the forces of inanimate matter and life, there is no evidence of a surge upward, but rather the very opposite.

True science tells us that *"the tendency of atoms of higher atomic weight to break* up into other atoms of lower weight seem to be the universal tendency of all matter." This is also true in the vegetable and animal kingdoms. This, as stated, blows to pieces the evolutionary theory.

CONTRADICTION

Tyndale said that the world had its beginning in a *"fire-mist,"* which contracted as it became cold.

Spence says it was a *"cold-cloud"* that became heated and contracted.[2]

Evolution teaches that all forms of life, whatever they may presently be, have gradually evolved from lower forms of life, which has been a process of millions of years.

However, again we state, there is no record whatsoever of the *"in-between"* species. Common sense tells us that if evolution was a reliable science, then there would be all types of vegetation, animals, and men in various stages of progression, but that doesn't exist in even one single example.

In other words, despite searching the world over, they have never found Bigfoot, and will never find Bigfoot. As well, as we've stated, evolution has absolutely no idea as to the first cause. Let me state the following:

The idea that God is the First Cause, with the evolutionary process taking up thereafter, is totally unbiblical. The theory of evolution in all of its forms has no relationship to fact and has no relationship to the Word of God. In other words, one simply cannot believe in evolution and the Biblical account of Creation at the same time.

So, I'm sorry! The Pope is dead wrong when he claims that he believes that God created all things but has done it by the means of evolution. Nothing could be more contradictory.

THE FOOLISHNESS OF EVOLUTION

If it is to be noticed, there is a bitter hatred by evolutionists of God and the Bible. Consequently, they manufacture multiplied drawings of supposed human beings rising from a molecule through a monkey to the present man, and pass it off as fact when, in reality, it is fiction, pure and simple. They foster all of this off on young children in school and teach it as the truth when, in reality, there is no truth in evolution whatsoever.

As well, if the evolutionists have their way, they not only demand that evolution alone be taught in the public school system but, as well, that the Biblical account of Creation not be taught at all. If they are so sure of their *"theory,"* why do they fear the Word of God?

A PERSONAL EXAMPLE

Back when the Soviet Union was in existence, of course, their main education of courses were psychology, evolution, etc. Being atheistic, they claimed there is no God.

At any rate, in a biology class and in their teaching of evolution, one young man in the class disagreed with the teaching, stating that God was the Creator, etc. Of course, he was laughed to scorn, put down, and ridiculed.

On one particular day after the teacher and all the students had left, he lingered behind and out of paper and pasteboard, he made an excellent replica of the Universe. He placed it on the teacher's desk.

The next morning when class started, the teacher immediately saw this reproduction of the Universe on her desk and remarked how excellent that it was. She then asked as to who did it. No one raised a hand. She insisted, and still no one raised a hand.

She then said, *"Come on now, somebody in this class did this; it didn't just happen."*

Then the young man stood to his feet and said, *"Teacher, that's what I've been trying to tell you all along. It didn't just happen; there had to be a Creator, and that Creator is God."*

MAN AND BIBLICAL CREATION

There is a personal relationship that exists between God and His Creation. Consequently, there can be no room in Scripture for the idea of the *"nature"* as an autonomous power set in motion by a first cause. In the Word of God and in Creation itself, which is obvious, God is depicted as being at all times in control of the world (Job 38:33; Jer. 5:24). As such, it needs His Continual

Undergirding, and, to be sure, it has His Continual Undergirding.

While the world was intended to display the Glory of God, it was also fashioned as the dwelling place for man (Isa. 45:18), incidentally, the crown of Divine Creation.

While everything was created originally by God, we find that man is the direct product of created activity and is dignified in a special manner by being the recipient of the *"Living Breath"* of God. Stress is laid upon the nature of man as the highest form of created life by man being described as made in the Divine Image (Gen. 1:26-27). This can only mean that man, in his complete bodily existence, was patterned after the Image of God.

SPIRIT, SOUL, AND BODY

Genesis 2:7 speaks of man becoming a *"living soul."* It would probably have been better for the Hebrew words, *"Neps hayyah,"* to have been translated, *"Personality,"* since it is the totality of man which is here in view. Hebrew thought consistently viewed man as a personality, and the numerous Old Testament references to the relationship between emotions and bodily changes demonstrated concern for the integration of the personality of the individual. Man is not just a *"body"* into which a *"soul"* has been placed. Instead, he is a living personality, which has physical extension in time and place.

When living by Divine Law, he is neither *"body"* nor *"soul,"* but a unified being in which all aspects of existence are designed to function in an integrated manner to the Glory of God. Even though man was created *"spirit, soul, and body,"* the Hebrews always looked at man as one indigenous personality, and rightly so.

THE LIVING IMAGE OF GOD

Because man is, in effect, the living Image of God upon Earth, he is given the task of serving as the Divine representative and ordering the ways of those aspects of Creation which are put under his control (Gen. 1:28). Though he has been made in the Image of God, man is still vastly inferior to the Deity and Stature of God (Ps. 8:6-8). Nevertheless, he is crowned with glory and honor because he has been made especially to enjoy fellowship with the Creator.

Unlike the animal creation, which has to obey instinctive impulses and laws, man has been given a freedom of will as part of his Spiritual heritage. While his prime vocation is to serve God and the world of nature, he is unique in being the only creature which can respond to God in disobedience as well as in Faith and Trust. He can revile God as well as praise Him, and can separate himself from the Divine Presence just as easily as he can have fellowship with God.

Certainly the latter was the clear Intention of the Creator since no other species can articulate the Divine Praises.

Thus, man was made to communicate meaningfully and intelligently with God, an ideal which is subsequently attributed to the Nation in Covenant relationship with Him, namely Israel (Isa. 43:21).

Incidentally, man is not merely a higher form of animal life. In fact, man is not an animal at all, but rather, as stated, one created in the Image of God.

THE NEW CREATION IN CHRIST

The New Testament authors agreed with Judaism that God Alone was the Creator of the world through His Word. However, in the light of the fuller Revelation of God in Christ, they viewed the process of Creation Christologically. In Jesus, all things cohered (Col. 1:17), and the unity of Creation in Him was demonstrated further as part of the Divine Purpose in history (Eph. 1:9-10). It is He Who upholds the Universe by His Powerful Word (Heb. 1:3) and brings meaning to the historical process as the Saviour and Redeemer of the world.

In the light of this conviction, it was possible for those who were associated with the Early Church to assert their human Salvation as predestined in Christ before the founding of the world (Mat. 25:34; Eph. 1:4; I Pet. 1:20). Everything centers upon the Firstborn of all Creation, Who is Christ (Col. 1:15). This means that He is the Creator of all things since it has been created through Him and unto Him, Who is the Beginning and the End.

IN CHRIST

The New Testament authors were insistent that the new Kingdom of Grace, long promised by Prophecy, had already appeared with the Incarnate Christ. The New Creation was actually a promise of future glory (Eph. 1:14; Rev. 21:1-4), when all redeemed creatures would laud their Creator (Rev. 4:8-11; 5:13). Christ was the New Man whom Adam foreshadowed (Rom. 5:12-14; 1 Cor. 15:21-22), the Image of the invisible God (Col. 1:15), Whose Death would redeem the world from bondage to sin and make individual Salvation possible. In the Work of Calvary, Christ has paid the penalty for human iniquity and has opened the way for renewal of the individual personality through confession, surrender, and the acceptance of God's Saving Grace by Faith (Rom. 10:9-10, 13; Eph. 2:8-9). When one has identified himself completely with the Work of Calvary and has received cleansing and pardon, he is *"in Christ."* The Saviour has restored the human pattern which God planned at the first, and those who are His are themselves New Creations by Divine Grace.

(4) "IN HIM WAS LIFE; AND THE LIFE WAS THE LIGHT OF MEN."

The composition is:

1. God always honors His Word, and Satan always respects God's Word because He has no choice.

2. Christians attempting to live a victorious life outside of Faith in the Cross always meet with failure.

3. Satan does not respect our efforts as it regards our own *"works."* He only respects the Word of God, which, in effect, proclaims the Sacrifice of Christ.

IN HIM WAS LIFE

The phrase, *"In Him was Life,"* presents Jesus, the Eternal Logos, as the First Cause.

While it is true that Creation exists in Him, still, to use the term only in that manner is error. Life exists in Him, which brought about the Creation. As well, this brought Him into relation with a special part of His Creation, which is man, with whom was all His Delight.

Many men can create things, even as God, albeit on a much lower scale. But yet, man has to create things out of that which already exists. He cannot create things out of nothing as God can. Inasmuch as man contains no life solely derived within himself, whatever he creates is dependent on the first cause, Who is God.

As an example, when man created the airplane, or anything else for that matter, he had to power that invention by some type of source which only comes from God, and which is dependent, as well, on other Laws created by God.

However, the *"Life"* which is in Christ is derived solely from Him, with Him dependent on nothing outside of Himself.

MAN'S TERRIBLE DILEMMA

Actually, this is the reason for man's terrible dilemma. At the Fall, he lost the *"Life"* imparted to him by God and has nothing left but death. Consequently, man is born dying. As well, death inculcates itself in all of Creation in this world simply because of the Fall. The Life it had derived from God was lost; consequently, inasmuch as there is no other Life, man must die as well as all he touches.

THE LIFE WAS
THE LIGHT OF MEN

The phrase, *"And the Life was the Light of men,"* proclaims two things:

1. Before the Fall, Jesus was the *"Light of men,"* which means there is no other life or no other light.

Reynolds said, *"The Life which was in the Logos 'was,' has always been, is now, will ever be, 'the Light of men.'"*[6]

When men fell from that Light Source, they had to fall into darkness because there was no other Light; consequently, there could be no other *"Light."* The *"Life"* and *"Light"* are exclusively in Him.

2. When the *"Light"* at the Fall was lost due to the *"Light"* being rejected, God immediately set about to restore the *"Life,"* which would automatically bring the *"Light."*

LIFE

There is *"Life"* in Creation, with men attempting to worship that *"Life,"* not realizing or believing that it is derived from God. That is why Paul said, *"Professing themselves to be wise, they became fools,*

"And changed the glory of the uncorruptible God into an image made like to corruptible man, and to birds, and four-footed beasts, and creeping things."

He then said, *"Who changed the Truth of God into a lie, and worshipped and served the creature more than the Creator, Who is blessed forever. Amen"* (Rom. 1:22-23, 25).

LIGHT OF MEN

The phrase, *"Light of men,"* is an extremely interesting statement. This *"Light"* cannot be unless it is derived from the *"Life"* which is in Jesus. And yet, men attempt to find *"Light"* in various other places. This is because of the way man fell. Satan told man a lie and was successful in getting him to believe it. He told Adam and Eve, *". . . then your eyes shall be opened, and you shall be as gods, knowing good and evil"* (Gen. 3:5).

However, their eyes were not opened, but rather closed, i.e., the *"Light"* was gone!

As well, by disobeying God and, in effect, rebelling against Him, they did not gain godhood as promised by Satan, but rather fell to the level of demonhood. This is the reason that demon spirits make their abode in the bodies and minds of much of humanity, either through direct possession or through influence and oppression.

THE FALL

As well, the Fall was of such magnitude and to such a degree that there is no way man can fully comprehend its extent. He cannot tell how far he has fallen because he has no idea of his original state; consequently, there is no way to make a comparison. Man knows that something is wrong, but due to having no *"Light,"* he does not know exactly what it is. He continues to think it can be corrected by education, money, or various different philosophies; hence, he opts for modern psychology even though it does not work, and he knows it does not work.

He thinks he is only slightly maladjusted and can be quickly rehabilitated. Consequently, he talks about the *"psychology of life,"* which is man's answer to man's dilemma, or *"the strength from within,"* as if he can solve his own problems. However, this he cannot do, despite the fact of thousands of years of trying.

Into this torment of failure, and failure it is, God became Man and came into this world as the *"Last Adam."* As such, He brought back *"Life,"* which the first Adam lost, and with it the *"Light."* Outside of Christ there is no *"Light of men."*

(5) "AND THE LIGHT SHINES IN DARKNESS; AND THE DARKNESS COMPREHENDED IT NOT."

The exegesis is:

1. Satan respects the Cross of Christ as nothing else. It was there that he was defeated.

2. He also knows that the Holy Spirit backs up the Cross in its entirety. In other words, the Holy Spirit works entirely within the parameters, so to speak, of the Finished Work of Christ.

3. The Word of God demands a choice on our part. Our choice to obey and to trust may mean that the sharp sword of the Word may sever the dearest of ties. It is designed to cut away that which is unholy and to separate us from all that is unscriptural.

THE SHINING LIGHT

The phrase, *"And the Light shines in darkness,"* speaks of the Incarnation of Christ and His Coming into this world. His *"Light,"* because it is derived from His *"Life,"* drives out *"darkness."* As we have repeatedly said, that *"Light"* is Jesus. There is no other, not Joseph Smith, Buddha, Karl Marx, Confucius, Muhammad, etc. All others are false, and He Alone is the Light.

This is at least one of the reasons that the Gospel of Jesus Christ must be taken to all points of the world, even as Jesus said, *"Unto the uttermost part of the Earth"* (Acts 1:8). The reason is obvious: there is no other light.

If Jesus is presented, the Light will *"shine,"* if not, the darkness will remain.

That is the reason we plead for funds to air our television programming, which we feel must, without delay, go to every city in the world.

A PERSONAL EXPERIENCE

On July 1, 1985, on a Monday morning, I drove in my car to a place about a mile from our house where I generally went every morning during those particular times. There, I would study the Word for a little bit and then walk down a railroad track, seeking the Face of the Lord. Then, it afforded privacy, with no houses, businesses, etc. That has all changed now.

I had been seeking the Face of the Lord for a few minutes as I walked down the track, and then, all of a sudden, His Presence literally enveloped me. What transpired I personally believe was a Vision.

I saw in every direction cotton stalks heavily laden with fluffy bolls of cotton. It stretched over the horizon in every direction. In fact, the harvest was very great, with every stalk literally laden over with cotton, with not a green leaf on any of the stalks.

For a few moments, I was mesmerized looking at this expanse of cotton that had to be harvested immediately. In the distance I could see two or three mechanical pickers, and my immediate thoughts were, *"There is going to have to be a greater effort."*

Then I looked to my left, which is actually the east, and I saw the most hideous storm that was coming down upon this great harvest. The heavens were as black as ink, and jagged forks of lightning were piercing through the skies. Of course, my immediate thoughts were, *"If this harvest is not gathered, and gathered quickly, the storm will destroy it all."*

THE WORD OF THE LORD

Then the Lord began to speak to me. He told me, *"I want you to put the television programming in every city in the world that will open its door."* He then said, *"I will hold back the storm for a period of time until this thing can be done."* At that time, I believed, and I still do, that the storm represented the coming Great Tribulation that's going to be the worst time, Jesus said, this world has ever known (Mat. 24:21).

The Lord then said to me, *"Don't fail Me. I have called other Ministries for localities, but this Ministry alone for the entirety of the world."*

In the time that followed, I thought, *"Oh Lord, I have failed. I am unable to do what You called me to do."*

THE SONLIFE BROADCASTING NETWORK

Then, in 2010, the Lord instructed us to begin *"The SonLife Broadcasting Network."* We were to air the programming 24 hours a day, seven days a week. It was a monumental task, but the Lord opened door after door.

At the time of this writing (March, 2012), we are now airing in 60 million plus homes in America, 24 hours a day, seven days a week. We are airing in some 17 million homes in the United Kingdom, plus another 30 or 40 million in Europe, Asia, Africa, Central and South America, and the islands of the sea. However, we must do much, much more.

At any rate, in 2010, while in prayer one afternoon, the Lord spoke to me again. He took me back to that day in 1985. In effect, I relived it all over again. He then said to me:

"When I gave you the Commission in 1985 to put the television programming in every city in the world that would open its door to you, I knew what the future held. I knew there would be tremendous problems. But I am speaking to you now, to tell you that the Commission I gave you at that time still holds. I am still holding back the storm that this Work may be accomplished."

That's the reason that God has helped us as He has, and there is one other thing I must say about this.

THE GREAT HARVEST OF SOULS

I believe the Lord has told me, as well, that we are about to see the greatest harvest of souls on a worldwide basis that the world or the Church has ever known. I believe the Lord has informed me that millions are going to come into the Kingdom of God. As well, I believe that He has said that this will be the last great Move on a worldwide basis before the coming Great Tribulation.

At this particular time, technology has made it possible to take the Gospel of Jesus Christ to the entirety of the world in a matter of days, if not less. We must do it! By the Grace of God, we must not fail!

YOU!

And yet, there is no way that I can even remotely carry out this task without your help. Please understand, to every one of you who turns on one of our radio programs, sees the television programming, or watches us on the Internet, you are not just a bystander, but rather Called of God to be where you are. In other words, you have been chosen to be a part of the greatest Move of God, regarding souls being Saved, that the world has ever known. Believe that! Understand that! Conduct yourself accordingly!

In answer to this, many would say, *"But Brother Swaggart, what can I do?"*

You can do three things:

1. You can pray for us even on a daily basis. We solicit your prayers! We ask for your prayers! We plead for your prayers, even as Paul said that the Gospel might have free course.

2. You can tell others about THE SONLIFE BROADCASTING NETWORK. It would be the greatest favor you ever did that person, whomever it or they might be. Thank God, so many of you are already doing this.

3. As well, you can support us financially, which without, we cannot do what God has called us to do. What a privilege it is to support something that's touching the entirety of the world for the Cause of Christ. You are an integral part of this. Always understand that and never forget it.

THE CHURCH

Sadly and regrettably, most of that which calls itself *"Church,"* may, in fact, be church, but not that which belongs to God. Satan has a *"church,"* as well! It looks very similar to the real thing, which is Satan's intention, but its real purpose is to corrupt the Gospel. Satan realizes that he cannot stop the Gospel per se. What Jesus did at Calvary's Cross is a fact of history. It cannot be denied. So, he does the next best thing; he seeks to corrupt or pervert the Message. Listen to Paul:

"I marvel that you are so soon removed from Him *(the Holy Spirit)* **Who called you into the Grace of Christ** *(made possible by the Cross)* **unto another gospel** *(anything which doesn't have the Cross as its Object of Faith)***:**

"Which is not another *(presents the fact that Satan's aim is not so much to deny the Gospel, which he can little do, as to corrupt it)*; **but there be some who trouble you, and would pervert the Gospel of Christ** *(once again, to make the object of Faith something other than the Cross)*.**"**

Paul went on to say, **"But though we** *(Paul and his associates)*, **or an Angel from Heaven, preach any other gospel unto you than that which we have preached unto you** *(Jesus Christ and Him Crucified)*, **let him be accursed** *(eternally condemned; the Holy Spirit speaks this through Paul, making this very serious)*.

"As we said before, so say I now again *(at some time past, he had said the same thing to them, making their defection even more serious)*, **If any *man* preach any other gospel unto you** *(anything other than the Cross)* **than that you have received** *(which saved your souls)*, **let him be accursed** *('eternally condemned,' which means the loss of the soul)*.

"For do I now persuade men, or God? *(In essence, Paul is saying 'Do I preach man's doctrine, or God's?')* **or do I seek to please men?** *(This is what false apostles do.)* **for if I yet pleased men, I should not be the Servant of Christ** *(one cannot please both men and God at the same time)*" **(Gal. 1:6-10).**

The truth is, only a small part of that which refers to itself as Gospel can truthfully be said to be Gospel. We speak of churches, entire religious denominations, and that which refers to itself as Christian radio or Christian television. In other words, what is proclaimed will not help anybody, will not save any souls, will not heal anyone, and will not draw anyone to Christ. It is merely the religion business, and it is the biggest business in the world.

THE DARKNESS COMPREHENDED IT NOT

The phrase, *"And the darkness comprehended it not,"* would have been better translated, *"And the darkness apprehended it not."*

The Greek word for *"comprehended"* is, *"Katalambano,"* and means, *"To seize upon; to beat down or under; to stop."*

It has reference to the fact that Satan did everything within Hell's power to stop the *"Light from shining,"* but in that, he failed. He did not overcome the Word, but in truth, the Word overcame him, and the Cross spoiled all satanic powers (Col. 2:10-15).

As well, this is not something to be done in the future, but something, in fact, which is already done. *"For this purpose the Son of God was manifested, that He might destroy the works of the Devil"* (I Jn. 3:8).

LIGHT

From the time of Christ and because of the entrance of the *"Light,"* which comes from His *"Life,"* the world has improved in many ways.

Had it not been for the Dark Ages, which was brought about by Satan's church, the advancement would have been made much sooner. I speak of the Catholic church, which, for hundreds of years, successfully hid the Bible, i.e., *"Light,"* from man. Regrettably, much of the Protestant world is likewise following in the same train.

Even most of the Pentecostal denominations, at least those in America and Canada, which claim to know and have the Holy Spirit, have by and large turned their backs on the Holy Spirit and the Word of God. In other words, sad to say, that Light has gone out. It is not a question of the church heading toward apostasy. In truth, the church has already apostatized.

As such, and in fact, they have become Satan's church. They do all they can to stop the Gospel instead of proclaiming the Gospel. That is a serious indictment, but it happens to be true!

Nevertheless, wherever the *"Light"* shines, the powers of darkness are destroyed, and man is bettered in every conceivable way possible.

Through the years, I, and other preachers, as well, have seen multiple tens of thousands of people delivered by the mighty Power of God of the worst and vilest of sins and bondages. I speak of acute alcoholics set free and drug addicts delivered, even in the last stages. I speak, as well, of those delivered from the terrible bondage of religion, which, in many cases, is worse than all other bondages. Only Jesus Christ can do such a thing and not man or his efforts, irrespective as to what they may be.

(6) "THERE WAS A MAN SENT FROM GOD, WHOSE NAME WAS JOHN."

The exposition is:

1. The great Sacrifice of Christ is the Word of God being portrayed in action as it refers to Redemption.

2. As well, every particle of the Word and every nuance of the Word in some way point to this Finished Work.

3. I really cannot see how anyone can interpret the Bible otherwise, especially if he reads it in the Light of the Cross.

A MAN SENT FROM GOD

The phrase, *"There was a man sent from God,"* speaks of the place and purpose of John's mission. God sent him for one reason and one reason only, to prepare the Way for the *"Logos"* and to present Him, which he did!

John was the last of the Old Testament Prophets. In truth, he was *"more than a Prophet"* simply because he alone was able to present the *"Logos"* Incarnate, while the Prophets of old were only able to point into the future to His Coming. They said, *"He is coming,"* while John said, *"He is here,"* i.e., *"Behold, the Lamb of God. . . ."*

Because of this, the privilege of being the one Called by God to introduce Christ, there would be no one greater who had been born of woman.

The Mission of Jesus was to fulfill the past, of which John was its close, and bring the future. That He did!

WHOSE NAME WAS JOHN

The phrase, *"Whose name was John,"* refers to John the Baptist.

All the Gospels contain a report of the Ministry of this Prophet. His name was derived not from his Message but from a striking new practice he instituted: John baptized in the waters of the river Jordan those who responded to his preaching by believing his Message.

He called for the people of Israel to repent and to turn to God wholeheartedly as a preparation for the Coming of the Messiah, Whose Day was rapidly approaching. Those who accepted John's Message were called on to acknowledge their commitment publicly. As John preached Repentance, those who went into the waters to be baptized acknowledged their sins and made a commitment to live righteously.

Ever blunt, the stern John warned them to *"produce fruit in keeping with Repentance"* (Lk. 3:8). The ritual itself had no merit. It must be the changed lives of those baptized that testify to the inner sincerity of their hearts.

This was the man God sent to introduce the *"Living Word."*

(7) "THE SAME CAME FOR A WITNESS, TO BEAR WITNESS OF THE LIGHT, THAT ALL MEN THROUGH HIM MIGHT BELIEVE."

The structure is:

1. Physical healing is part of the Redemptive Work of Christ (Isa. 53:5; Mat. 8:17).

2. Jesus suffered a physical beating, which, in the Mind of God, paid for the healing of our physical bodies.

3. Concerning healing and the Cross, the Scripture says, *"Who His Own Self bear our sins in His Own Body on the tree, that we, being dead to sins, should live unto Righteousness: by Whose stripes you were healed"* (I Pet. 2:24).

THE WITNESS

The phrase, *"The same came for a witness,"* speaks of the mission of the Prophet. The word, *"Witness,"* means that John not only proclaimed the Truth of his Message but, as well, the Power of that Truth. He had one business, one mission, and one urgency on this Earth, and that was to carry out exactly what God had called him to do. His whole demeanor, nature, character, and person testifies to that Calling. It is as follows:

ALONE

He lived almost as a recluse, having little fellowship with his fellow countrymen. This proclaims that Israel, despite their claims to the contrary, was too immersed in the things of this world.

HIS DIET

His diet was very Spartan, containing as its basics wild locusts and honey, showing that Israel had become too taken up with a rich lifestyle.

HIS RAIMENT

His raiment was that of camel's hair, with a leather girdle about his loins, which was basically worn only by the poor. The rich used girdles of silk or linen, decorated with gold, silver, and precious stones. As his diet, his dress portrayed the opposite of the rich lifestyle of Israel, who had become very taken up with the things of the world. How similar to the present time.

THE WILDERNESS

His Ministry, for the most part, was carried out in the wilderness, which testified through its stark barrenness of Israel's present Spiritual condition.

HIS MESSAGE

His Message was *"Repentance,"* saying, *"Repent you: for the Kingdom of Heaven is at hand"* (Mat. 3:2). In other words, before the Advent of Christ, Israel was called upon to repent because they desperately needed to do so.

John the Baptist came in the Spirit and Power of Elijah, who will, as well, call Israel to Repentance the last half of the coming Great Tribulation (Mal. 4:5-6; Rev. 11:3-12).

WATER BAPTISM

He came baptizing people in water, which was new to Israel and the world, and was really not a part of the Law of Moses, except for the washings, which had to do with the sacrifices, etc. However, that little resembled what John was doing, which, in effect, introduced the New Covenant.

Every Preacher of the Gospel should take a lesson from John the Baptist. Even though the purpose of his Message was slightly different than that of fellow Preachers, still, there are many similarities, and above all, his lifestyle should say something to us.

THE LIGHT

The phrase, *"To bear witness of the Light,"* spoke of Jesus and only Jesus.

Too often, modern preachers bear witness of their denomination or of their own agenda. As John, all Believers, and especially Ministers of the Gospel, have but one purpose, and that is to lift up Jesus.

Our business is not economics, science, psychology, sociology, or 100 other things that could be named, but Jesus and Jesus Alone! Sadly, this coming Sunday morning, most of the pulpits in America, and the rest of the world for that matter, will bear witness to many things but little of *"The Light."*

The phrase, *"That all men through Him might believe,"* presents Jesus, not only for Israel, but rather for the entirety of the world, *"for all men."*

THROUGH HIM

The words, *"Through Him,"* tell us that Salvation is exclusively by and through Jesus Christ.

It is *"by Him"* because He paid the price at Calvary's Cross for man's Redemption.

It is *"through Him,"* and *"Him"* alone, that men can reach the Father (Jn. 14:6).

Consequently, this means that all who are trying to reach God through Muhammad, Joseph Smith, Buddha, or any other fake luminary, will not be heard at all. It is through Jesus and Jesus Alone. The world blanches at that.

Why?

Inasmuch as Jesus paid the price for man's Redemption, it should be easily understood and easily accepted that He Alone is the Way to the Father. When men pay the utility company for the power they have used in their homes or businesses, they pay the one who provided the power, which is readily understandable. However, men do not desire to use the same rationale with God as they do other things.

They balk at accepting Jesus Christ as the only Way to the Father simply because men love to originate their own salvation. It makes them feel important, and it appeals to their self-righteousness. Above all, it is because of deception. Men are deceived easily because it was by deception that man fell in the Garden of Eden.

(8) "HE WAS NOT THAT LIGHT, BUT WAS SENT TO BEAR WITNESS OF THAT LIGHT."

The construction is:

1. Preaching philosophy, the latest book report, or any other such foolishness will have little effect on anyone. Preaching the Cross will save the souls of men (I Cor. 1:18).

2. While the preaching of the Cross might be foolishness to the world, still, that's what we must preach because it alone is the solution (I Cor. 1:23).

3. The Cross of Christ is the dividing line between the true Church and the apostate church. In fact, it has always been that way but is more so now than ever because we are nearing the end of the Church Age (Gal. 6:14).

THE LIGHT OF MAN

The phrase, *"He was not that Light,"* simply means that John the Baptist was not the Light.

This means that the *"Light"* of men has a higher Source and wider range of operation than that of any prophetic man. So, as we have stated, that eliminates all the luminaries who claim to have *"Light"* but actually have none at all.

However, this statement, as written by John the Beloved, goes much further than the personalities to which we may allude. It also speaks of anything man does, even in the realm of Christendom, which displaces Christ in any capacity. In other words, it speaks of the Pope and all priests simply because these individuals claim to serve as mediators between God and men. As well, scores of so-called Protestant religious leaders fall into the same category.

BEARING WITNESS OF THE LIGHT

Even though the so-called Protestant religious leaders do not openly come out saying they are the Light, still, the man-devised religious offices they occupy, and above all, the manner in which they are occupied, testify to the same error.

They claim to be Spiritual Authority, and

as such, they must be obeyed in whatever it is they demand.

WHAT IS SPIRITUAL AUTHORITY?

Every Believer on the face of the Earth has Spiritual Authority. The Scripture plainly says, *"And these signs shall follow them who believe"* (Mk. 16:17). It places no designation whatsoever, only that we are Believers.

The authority here given, which every Believer possesses, is never over other human beings, but only over Satan himself, fallen Angels, and demon spirits (Mk. 16:17-18; Eph. 6:12; Col. 2:10-19).

Now, it is certainly true that those who are called to be *"Apostles, Prophets, Evangelists, Pastors, and Teachers,"* at times, may have more authority than others, but still, it is only over spirits of darkness and never over individuals (Eph. 4:11).

The only allegiance that one Believer owes another is to love my brother and sister in the Lord (Rom. 13:8). This is true irrespective as to what type of religious office one may hold, even an office which is legitimate, such as Apostle, Prophet, etc.

In Romans 13:1-7, Paul speaks of the allegiance that we owe civil authorities, but when it comes to those in the Church, in other words, fellow Believers, we only owe them love. This foolishness about men having Spiritual Authority which must be obeyed, irrespective as to what they tell us to do, is not in the Word of God. In fact, untold millions are in Hell right now because they believed such stupidity and bowed to such, which caused them to lose their soul.

A PERSONAL EXPERIENCE

A pastor acquaintance of mine related the following information to one of my associates.

He received a phone call from one of the officials in a particular Pentecostal denomination. During the course of the conversation by phone, the official told him that there was something that he had to do, which my friend instantly knew was unscriptural. He kindly said to the man, *"I cannot do that, it's not scriptural."* The man retorted by saying, *"You are to obey me, whatever it is I demand. If it's unscriptural, I'll answer for it and not you."*

Immediately upon hanging up the phone, he spoke to his wife about the situation. She told him that surely he had misunderstood the man because, as she knew, such was obviously wrong. She asked him to get him back on the phone and make certain that the matter was cleared up.

He did what his wife stated, and the man answered him, *"No, you did not misunderstand me, you must obey me, whatever it is I say."*

As I have previously stated, there are untold millions in Hell at this moment who did obey such and died eternally lost because of it. Please understand, whenever we stand before the Lord, we will not be able to pass the buck, so to speak. In other words, we won't be able to say to the Lord, *"But so and so told me I had to do this, and I obeyed him because he had Spiritual Authority."* That's not going to cut any ice with the Lord. Every Believer is going to answer to God for what we have done, not what somebody else told us we had to do. To be sure, the Word of God is the criterion, and the only criterion.

Individuals are fond of throwing around the statement, *"He or she is rebelling against Spiritual Authority,"* etc. Let me say it again.

Every Believer in the world has Spiritual Authority, but that authority can be exercised, and is meant to be exercised, only over Satan, fallen Angels, and demon spirits. It is never to be exercised over other human beings. James addressed this, as well, by saying:

"There is one Lawgiver, Who is able to save and to destroy (presents God as the Only One Who can fill this position)**: who are you who judges another?** (The Greek actually says, 'But you — who are you?' In other words, 'Who do you think you are?')**" (James 4:12).**

Anything that any Believer asks me to do, providing it's Scriptural and applies to me, that I will do; however, if it is unscriptural, that I will not do. Even if such is Scriptural, but it does not apply to me and, in fact, cannot apply to me, that, as well, I will not do.

Every Believer on the face of the Earth is

going to be judged according to the Word of God, and not according to what other people say. As somebody has well said, and rightly so, *"People say things about me, and God says things about me. It's only what God says that counts."*

THE HEADSHIP OF CHRIST

Christ must never, in any capacity, be abrogated as the Head of the Church. If that position is infringed upon to the slightest degree, and it is infringed upon constantly, that segment of the church, whether local, national or international, will be bereft of the Holy Spirit. As men can add nothing to their Salvation, likewise, they can add nothing to the Headship of Christ. Please remember, Christ is an active Head and not merely a passive Head.

The phrase, *"But was sent to bear witness of that Light,"* presents the sum total that man can do. All that he or any Apostle, Prophet, Evangelist, Pastor, or Teacher can do is to *"bear witness of that Light."*

The Prophets, from Moses to John, plus all the Preachers of the New Covenant, derived and derive all their Power, their sanction, and the corroboration of their Message from the Logos — Light shining through conscience and blazing through providential events and burning up the stubble of human action with unquenchable fire.

(9) "THAT WAS THE TRUE LIGHT, WHICH LIGHTS EVERY MAN WHO COMES INTO THE WORLD."

The exposition is:

1. The Word of God serves as a mirror for the Child of God, showing him what he is, what he ought to be, and what he can be in Christ.

2. That's the reason that daily Bible study must be a part of our everyday life and living.

3. It is a shame when many Christians, if not most, have never even read the Bible through once. In fact, the Bible should be read completely through at least once a year, every year.

THE TRUE LIGHT

The phrase, *"That was the True Light,"* has reference to two things:

NOTES

1. The Greek word for *"Light"* is *"Photizo,"* and means, *"To enlighten,"* and in this case, *"Spiritual Enlightenment."* It is the *"Light"* which alone shows the true meaning of all things; however, Jesus and the Light are One. To accept the Light is to accept Jesus. To refuse Jesus is to refuse the Light. That is the problem in the entirety of the world: they have rejected the Light, and so there is nothing left but darkness.

2. The Word, *"True,"* tells us that the Evil One is constantly attempting to deceive man into accepting a false light. Paul mentioned this when he said, *"For Satan himself is transformed into an Angel of Light."*

He also said, *"Therefore it is no great thing if his ministers* (Satan's ministers) *also be transformed as the ministers of righteousness; whose end shall be according to their works"* (II Cor. 11:14-15).

So, the false light not only resides in the religions of this world, but also in some, or even much, of that which goes under the guise of *"Christendom."*

EVERY MAN

The phrase, *"Which lights every man who comes into the world,"* would have been better translated, *"which lights every man who was ever coming into the world."*

This tells us several things:

• This *"True Light"* enlightens all men without distinction, be they Jew or Gentile, and irrespective of race.

• This *"Light"* is shown to every man on the Earth in some manner, although much more to some than others.

Paul said, *"For the invisible things of Him from the creation of the world are clearly seen, being understood by the things that are made, even His Eternal Power and Godhead; so that they are without excuse"* (Rom. 1:20).

This speaks of Creation, which is a witness of that Light, constantly telling man by its ordered precision that Creation must have a Creator.

• No man is left without some direct communication of Light from the Father of Lights. That Light may be quenched, the eye of the soul may be blinded, and the folly of the world may obscure it as a cloud disperses the direct rays of the sun; but a fundamental fact remains — the veritable Light illumines every man.

• This *"Light"* is a continual coming into the world.

In the Garden of Eden, it came to the fallen pair by the Lord giving instructions concerning the sacrifices (Gen. 4:6-7).

The sacrifices, which were Types of our Saviour, continued as the way to reach God even up to Moses and, consequently, served as the *"Light."* With Moses, the *"Light"* was greatly enlarged in that a pattern for living was given through the Law, which was a greater shining of that *"Light."* As well, and even more so, this Light did shine through the Patriarchs and Prophets of old. Of course, when Jesus came, Very Light Himself, and to Whom the Prophets had pointed, it now lightens the whole world.

In an even greater way, this Light will expand at the Second Coming until it illuminates all of mankind, thereby, driving out darkness until this evil remains not at all in the world. *"For the Earth shall be filled with the knowledge of the Glory of the LORD, as the waters cover the sea"* (Hab. 2:14).

THE SONLIFE BROADCASTING NETWORK

At this moment, as it regards the television satellites, plus the signals that go out to the Internet, the Message of Redemption in Christ Jesus, which we preach and proclaim, can be heard, if a little effort is made, by virtually the entirety of the world. As well, the programming is translated into Spanish, which covers all of Mexico and Central and South America. We are also on satellite, covering all of India and China, which together constitutes nearly two and one-half billion people. India is an English speaking country. About one-half of the people in China, as well, speak English. The satellite is designed to go into people's homes. Actually, it is referred to as a *"free to home satellite."* In other words, we are doing everything within our power, going through every door that the Lord opens, to proclaim the greatest Message that man has ever known, the grandest Story ever told, to a lost and dying world. As well, the Lord has given us the Message, which can be, and is, anointed by the Holy Spirit. This I believe:

While we are seeing many souls Saved, for which we give the Lord all the praise and all the glory, I personally believe that the greatest harvest of souls the world has ever known is about to take place. I also believe the Lord has told me that it will be the last great worldwide Move before the coming Great Tribulation. I personally believe that millions will be swept into the Kingdom of God.

WHAT ABOUT THOSE WHO HAVE NEVER HEARD THE GOSPEL?

This Ninth Verse of the First Chapter of John tells us that every man who has ever been born, and every person who is alive at present, in some way, must be given an opportunity to accept Christ. While, sadly and regrettably, most reject Him, still, they must have the opportunity. It is our responsibility to see that that opportunity presents itself, at least as far as lies within our power.

As it regards those who have never had the opportunity to hear, in other words, they haven't been given the opportunity to say, *"Yes,"* or, *"No,"* those we will have to leave to the Lord. As Abraham said of the Lord so long, long ago, *"Shall not the Judge of all the Earth do right?"* (Gen. 18:25)

Why is it that men will accept a lie, and we speak of false religions such as Catholicism, Mormonism, Hinduism, Islam, etc., long before they will accept the Truth?

That's a good question!

In America today, there is probably more animosity against the Lord Jesus Christ and the Bible than there is the religion of Islam, despite the fact that the religion of Islam is responsible for nearly 4,000 Americans dying violently with the destruction of the twin towers in New York City. Why is that? How could that be? How is it that our political leaders will bend over backward so as not to offend Muslims, despite the fact that the world of Islam has vowed our destruction? They hate us and openly say so, but our leaders still bow before them. Why? The reason is because of the following:

Jesus Christ is real, and the Bible is real, also. All these other religions are false, actually given birth by demon spirits. It goes back to that said by the Lord immediately after the Fall of Adam and Eve in the Garden of Eden. He said to Satan, but spoke through the serpent, **"And I will put enmity** *(animosity)* **between you and the woman** *(presents the Lord now actually speaking to Satan, who had used the serpent; in effect, the Lord is saying to Satan, 'You used the woman to bring down the human race, and I will use the woman as an instrument to bring the Redeemer into the world, Who will save the human race')*, **and between your seed** *(mankind which follows Satan)* **and her Seed** *(the Lord Jesus Christ)*; **it** *(Christ)* **shall bruise your head** *(the Victory that Jesus won at the Cross [Col. 2:14-15])*, **and you shall bruise His Heel** *(the sufferings of the Cross)*" **(Gen. 3:15).**

These political and educational leaders who greatly oppose Jesus Christ, and who make allowances for the religion of Islam, all come from the same source. In other words, the religion of Islam comes from the powers of darkness and operates accordingly, and so does everyone in the world who hasn't accepted Jesus Christ as their Saviour and Lord. So, it is easy for them to make allowances for Islam simply because they all serve the same master — Satan.

The weaker the church, the weaker the nation! Tragically, the church is weaker at this hour than it has been at any time since the Reformation. That is sad but true! To be frank, the Message that we are attempting to bring to the world, THE MESSAGE OF THE CROSS, just might be the only thing holding back the tides of darkness. In fact, the Cross of Christ is the only thing standing between mankind and eternal Hell. Now, that's quite a statement, and the reader should study it very carefully.

(10) "HE WAS IN THE WORLD, AND THE WORLD WAS MADE BY HIM, AND THE WORLD KNEW HIM NOT."

The synopsis is:

1. The phrase, *"He was in the world,"* speaks of the Eternal Logos being in the world through His Creation. As stated, Paul referred to this in Romans 1:19-32. Of course, the phrase also speaks of the Incarnation of Christ. However, this, as wonderful as it was, was only an enlargement of what had been all along.

2. As well, this Creation, above all, includes man. Inasmuch as man was created in the Image of God, certain attributes of that Image remained despite the Fall. Since that is true, unregenerate man can do some good things, but they do not affect his lack of Salvation at all. As well, spiritual blindness is so deep and so total that, due to the Fall, man, within himself, cannot be awakened to his need for God except through the Person and Agency of the Holy Spirit, Who always functions in some manner according to the Word of God. As stated, this is true even though man is made in the Image of God.

3. In other words, without the Word being preached in some manner, as brief as it might be, even in a song or on a pamphlet, the Holy Spirit cannot bring the lost soul to the realization of a need for God (Rom. 10:17). This is what makes the carrying out of the Great Commission so very, very important (Mat. 20:18-20; Mk. 16:15-20; Lk. 24:47; Rom. 10:14-17).

4. *"And the world was made by Him,"* does not speak of the world as it now is, but rather the way it was originally created by Him. Since the Fall, this Planet has suffered great abuse. In fact, its system is totally and completely of Satan.

5. *"And the world knew Him not,"* means, as Paul said, *"The world by wisdom knew not God"* (I Cor. 1:21). Of course, this is speaking of worldly wisdom, which is *"earthly, sensual, devilish"* (James 3:15). This means that the world does not know God the Father, God the Son, or God the Holy Spirit, and, as stated, by the wisdom of this world, cannot know Him, irrespective of how intelligent they may be.

6. In fact, this is the reason for the tragic perversions of His Glorious Perfection, which every heathenism and cult, and even every philosophy, have perpetrated (Acts 17:21).

(11) "HE CAME UNTO HIS OWN, AND HIS OWN RECEIVED HIM NOT."

The exegesis is:

1. The Word of God passes Judgment on man's feelings and on his thoughts.

2. Nothing evades the scope of this Word.

3. What man holds as most secret, he finds subject to its scrutiny and Judgment. Because it is the Word of God, it never makes a mistake.

JESUS AND THE JEWS

The phrase, *"He came unto His Own,"* refers to the world in general but, more specifically, to the Jews. These were the people He had raised up from the loins of Abraham for a special purpose in the world. As we have said many times in these Volumes, they were to do the following:

• Give the world the Word of God, which they did. With the exception of possibly Luke, every other writer in the Bible was Jewish. It is my contention that Luke was Jewish as well.

• Israel was to serve as the Womb of the Messiah, which they did, also.

• They were to evangelize the world. In a sense, they failed, and in a sense, they succeeded. Paul, as is obvious, was Jewish. He was the masterbuilder of the Church, and under the tutelage of the Holy Spirit, laid the foundation of the entirety of the Church for all time and all ages. But yet, the greater part of Israel, by far the greater part, rejected Christ.

However, it must be recognized that every vestige of the Knowledge of God which this world may have, and, in fact, ever has had, with the exception of the few who lived before Abraham, has come through the Jewish people. Paul asked the question, *"What advantage then has the Jew?"*

He then answered, *"Much every way: chiefly, because that unto them were committed the Oracles of God"* (Rom. 3:1-2).

As well, when Jesus came into this world, He came as a Jew. Born of the Virgin Mary, of the Tribe of Judah and of the House of David, He, in effect, was Heir to the Throne of David, should that lineage have continued, which it did not, at least at that time. However, it will be picked up again and exercised at the Second Coming.

REJECTION

"And His Own received Him not," means that He came as the Heir unto His Own Possessions (Mat. 21:38), but His Own Servants did not receive Him; on the contrary, they killed Him.

Sadly enough, the Lord was rejected by His Own People, many of His Own Disciples, by the religious hierarchy of Israel, and by the Sanhedrin. He was, as well, rejected by the populace who chose Barabbas over Christ, even though Barabbas was a robber. We might quickly add, Israel has been robbed ever since.

Regrettably, the sum total of the history of Israel, with some few exceptions, is a continuous repudiation of the Leading of the Lord.

Reynolds said, *"They rejected the Lord, they fell in the wilderness, they were turned unto other gods, they went a-whoring after their own inventions. They knew not that God had healed them. The great things of His Law were accounted strange things to them."*

Reynolds went on to say, *"The same kind of treatment has continually been given by the world, and even by those who have boasted of standing in the special lines of His Grace."*[7]

Even as I write these words, my own heart grieves at the failures and the times, even with hot tears, that I have had to ask for His Mercy and Grace, regrettably, even as all others. And yet, His Love has never weakened or waned, nor has His Grace ever faltered for one second.

What a loving God we serve!

Someone has said that this Eleventh Verse is one of the saddest statements ever uttered, and so it is!

(12) "BUT AS MANY AS RECEIVED HIM, TO THEM GAVE HE POWER TO BECOME THE SONS OF GOD, EVEN TO THEM WHO BELIEVE ON HIS NAME."

The exposition is:

1. The Lord knows all things about all things which He has created.

2. Therefore, it is impossible to hide anything from God in any capacity. Nothing in all Creation remains invisible to God.

3. Consequently, it was foolish for Adam and Eve to attempt to hide themselves from the Presence of the Lord (Gen. 3:8).

RECEIVING CHRIST

The phrase, *"But as many as received Him,"* refers to two things. They are:

1. Despite the rejection of His Own, and the majority of the world, there have been some who have received Him, and continue to do so unto this hour. To be sure, it has been that few who have brought about the changes for God that this world presently enjoys. However, it must quickly be said that it is not so much them, as such, but Christ within them.

Of these who have mostly been maligned and mistreated, or at least sorely criticized, the Holy Spirit says, *"Of whom the world was not worthy"* (Heb. 11:38).

2. Those who truly receive Him do so as the Eternal Logos, the full Revelation of the Essence, Character, and Activity of God.

Millions have received Him as a great Teacher or Miracle Worker, but that is not what the Holy Spirit here intended. Jesus must be received as God, Which and Who He actually is. He must be received, as well, as God manifest in the flesh, hence, the Incarnation, and as the Perfect Sacrifice offered at Calvary for the sin of man, thereby, satisfying Heavenly Justice and taking the full penalty of the Law in our place. Faith in Him and what He did is an absolute requirement for Salvation (Jn. 3:16).

POWER

The phrase, *"To them gave He Power to become the sons of God,"* constitutes one of the greatest Promises in the Word of God.

Within himself, irrespective of his education or ability, man has no power to effect a spiritual change within his life. However, upon receiving Jesus as one's Saviour, by His Power and Authority, one becomes a Child of God. To believe upon Him is to receive Him.

This is the Miracle of the New Birth and is an absolute requirement for one to enter the Kingdom of God.

FAITH

The phrase, *"Even to them who believe on His Name,"* proclaims Him, the Lord Jesus Christ, as the Author and Developer of our Faith (Heb. 12:2).

People have always been Saved through Jesus Christ, and more particularly, what He did at Calvary. Those who were Saved before He came were Saved by looking forward to what He would do at Calvary. This was symbolized by the offering of the sacrifices, which was more perfectly outlined in the Law of Moses.

Since Calvary, all have been Saved by looking backward to that moment in history. In other words, all have been Saved in the same manner, through the shed Blood of Jesus Christ at Calvary's Cross.

His *"Name"* is *"Jesus,"* which means, *"Saviour,"* and *"Christ,"* which means, *"Anointed,"* and for a specific purpose, to effect the Salvation of man.

When one accepts Christ as Saviour, thereby, accepting Who He Is (God) and What He is (Saviour), He then becomes *"Lord"* to that person, i.e., *"Lord Jesus Christ"* (Ruler).

(13) "WHICH WERE BORN, NOT OF BLOOD, NOR OF THE WILL OF THE FLESH, NOR OF THE WILL OF MAN, BUT OF GOD."

The structure is:

1. The phrase, *"Which were born, not of blood,"* means that men become God's Children, not by natural birth. It also refers to the fact that irrespective as to the wealth, place and position, or status of one's family, such affords no salvation whatsoever. The billionaire must come the same way as the pauper, the intellectual as the simple, the popular as the unpopular, and the good as the bad.

THE WILL OF THE FLESH

The phrase, *"Nor of the Will of the flesh,"* refers to personal resolution. Most of the world, whether they believe in God or not, attempt to merit Spiritual favor by certain things they do or certain things they don't do. In other words, it is a works religion, which God will not and, in fact, cannot accept.

No one is born as a little baby into Salvation, irrespective as to whom and what their parents may be. In fact, every individual has to be *"Born-Again"* (Jn. 3:3).

WHAT IS THE FLESH?

The flesh is that which is indicative to a human being. I speak of one's willpower, talent, education, intellect, ability, etc. Within themselves, these things aren't wrong; however, God cannot use any of it. He can only use that which He totally and completely provides. That goes for the unredeemed and the Redeemed as well. That's one of the hardest things for the Believer to understand. It's difficult for the Believer to come to the conclusion that there is nothing he can provide that God wants or desires, or can accept. Everything must originate with the Holy Spirit. The ingredient for receiving all that God has is simple Faith, and we are referring to Faith in Christ and what Christ has done for us at the Cross. The Cross of Christ must ever be the Object of our Faith. God honors no other faith in any capacity whatsoever (I Cor. 1:17, 18, 23; 2:2; Gal. 6:14; Col. 2:10-15).

THE WILL OF MAN

The phrase, *"Nor of the will of man,"* refers to priestly action, whether Catholics or Protestants acting as such. Catholics claim that if one is faithful to the Catholic church, one will be Saved. Many Protestant denominations follow suit, claiming that alignment with their organization either affords Salvation or at least plays a part thereof. Let it be understood, there is no salvation in any church, religious rituals, religious ceremonies, or even true Ordinances, such as Water Baptism or the Lord's Supper.

The short phrase, *"But of God,"* simply means that Salvation is not at all of man but altogether of God. Faith in Jesus Christ is the criterion, and the criterion alone (Gal. 3:26).

This one Verse, although brief, shuts out all religions and all man-devised efforts and holds up God and His Way alone as the road to Eternal Life. Consequently, the reader ought to ask himself (or herself) if his (or her) trust is in natural birth, personal resolution, priestly action, or any part thereof?

Many claim to be trusting Jesus for their Salvation, as the Judaizers of Acts, Chapter 15, but, in fact, add something to Faith in Him, such as Church membership, Water Baptism, the Lord's Supper, good works, etc., in effect, nullifying their Faith. If anyone attempts to add anything to the Grace of God (and we mean anything), Paul said, *"Christ is become of no effect unto you, whosoever of you are justified by the Law* (or a law of ones own making)*; you are fallen from Grace"* (Gal. 5:4).

As far as Redemption is concerned, Verse 13 could well be the most important collection of words ever uttered!

(14) "AND THE WORD WAS MADE FLESH, AND DWELT AMONG US, (AND WE BEHELD HIS GLORY, THE GLORY AS OF THE ONLY BEGOTTEN OF THE FATHER,) FULL OF GRACE AND TRUTH."

The synopsis is:

1. The Catholic church says that the Word of God is what the church says it is, making themselves superior to the Word.

2. I remind all and sundry that the Word of God is what Christ says it is, for He is the Living Word (Jn. 1:1).

3. The Word of God is a perfect instrument for exposing and judging the most secret emotions of the heart and nature.

THE WORD WAS MADE FLESH

The phrase, *"And the Word was made flesh,"* refers to the Incarnation. However, it should be understood, this *"flesh"* of the Son of God was totally different than the *"flesh"* of Verse 13. The flesh of the Saviour was perfect in every respect, meaning that it was not fallen.

Jesus, born of the Virgin Mary, means that He did not take upon Himself original sin as did all others. In fact, that's the reason He had to be Virgin born. Man had absolutely nothing to do with His Birth, with the exception of Mary providing a house for the nine-month gestation period. This means that Jesus did not carry any of the characteristics of Joseph or Mary. This means, as well, that He did not look like his brothers, sisters, etc. Mary was actually made pregnant by decree. In other words, the Holy Spirit decreed her pregnancy, meaning that He said, *"Let it be,"* and it was.

That God, the *"Eternal Word,"* and all of His Wondrous Glory as the Creator of all things, which is beyond the comprehension of man, would become *"flesh,"* portrays a type of love which cannot be imagined by mere mortals. As well, he would retain this *"flesh"* forever, albeit in Glorified Form.

This made Jesus God's Son, for Sonship in connection with Jesus Christ always refers to humanity and never to Deity. He was always the *"Word"* but not always *"flesh"*! However, He did not cease to be the *"Word"* even when He became *"flesh."*

THE INCARNATION

When Jesus *"became flesh,"* His moral Glory brought back to the human family the very Image of God. Man departed from God and lost His Image. So, the True Image of God came to dwell with man in order that the Holy Spirit could dwell in man that man might dwell in God.

Man has never observed man as God originally made him, other than when men observed Jesus Christ. Man, who has fallen from his lofty state, has no idea as to what he was before the Fall. There was and is no way he could know, except in Jesus. Jesus was, even in His Consummate Flesh, the Perfect Man, *"The Man Christ Jesus"* (I Tim. 2:5). Sadly, man does not desire to accept God's Standard of Perfection and continues to try to produce his own, which always fails. The very idea of Redemption, as portrayed in Verse 12, is to make men *"Sons of God,"* in effect, in the Image of Christ, Who is the Image of God.

DWELT AMONG US

The phrase, *"And dwelt among us,"* refers to Jesus, although Perfect, not holding Himself aloof from all others, as many or most of the self-appointed greats of the world do, but rather lived, even as a Peasant. His Mother and Foster Father, at least as far as the economic sense was concerned, were of the poor. In fact, at the time of Christ, there was no such thing as the *"middle class,"* as it is presently. There were only the abject poor and the obscene rich. Our Lord fell into the category of the *"abject poor."*

Joseph, His Foster Father, so to speak, was a carpenter, and it seems that he raised Jesus in this same occupation, for tradition says that Jesus, as a young man, mostly made ploughs and yokes. Consequently, as *"flesh,"* He knew exactly how most of the world lives, laboring to earn a bare existence. As a result, He is *"touched with the feeling of our infirmities"* (Heb. 4:15).

HIS GLORY

The phrase, *"And we beheld His Glory,"* speaks of His Deity, although hidden from eyes which were merely curious. Someone has said that in the Incarnation, Christ laid aside the expression of His Deity while never losing possession of His Deity.

His *"Glory"* was represented not only in Who He was but, as well, in what He did. His Miracle-working Power, which He used to heal literally thousands, was, in a sense, a transferring of a tiny part of His Glory from Himself to the needy soul. The same could be said for Miracles and Deliverances.

The Greek word for *"beheld"* in Verse 14 is *"theaomai,"* and means, *"A careful and deliberate vision which interprets its object."* It is more than merely seeing but has the idea in mind of an object, in this case a Person, displaying a certain aura or attribute which causes one to see something far above the ordinary. Such was Christ! Consequently, the Pharisees and religious leaders of Israel had no excuse for their actions inasmuch as this *"Glory"* was obvious to all. There is none so blind as those who refuse to see, even though plainly obvious to them.

In fact, as stated, His *"Glory"* manifested itself constantly, and it was obvious to all as He healed the worst cases of sickness, cleansed the lepers, and even raised the dead.

THE ONLY BEGOTTEN OF THE FATHER

The phrase, *"The Glory as of the Only Begotten of the Father,"* presents Jesus, Who is, and was, and always will be *"The Only Begotten Son of God."*

Men never will be *"begotten"* or *"born"* in the same sense as Jesus was (Mat. 1:18-25; Lk. 1:34-35), for our sonship is on a different basis — that of adoption, not an actual begetting and coming into existence (Rom. 8:15; 9:4; Gal. 4:5; Eph. 1:5).

The phrase, *"Full of Grace and Truth,"*

proclaims with the word, *"Full,"* His Deity, for only God is *"Full of Grace and Truth,"* as *"flesh"* proclaimed His Humanity.

So, the Glory in which He was seen was that of an Only Son with the Father, the One Sole Object of the Father's Delight. Such are the two Glories displayed in these Verses — His Glory as the Word, Who was with God in Eternity, and His Glory on Earth as the Only Son of the Father.

If one is to notice, there is no pedigree in this Gospel, for how could Deity have a pedigree? In Mark, as well, there is also no pedigree, for a servant needs none; he only needs a character.

(15) "JOHN BORE WITNESS OF HIM, AND CRIED, SAYING, THIS WAS HE OF WHOM I SPOKE, HE WHO COMES AFTER ME IS PREFERRED BEFORE ME: FOR HE WAS BEFORE ME."

The synopsis is:

1. The phrase, *"John bore witness of Him,"* speaks of the essence of His Ministry, which, in fact, was His Ministry. John was raised up by God for this purpose and when this was done, the introduction of Jesus Christ, the preparation of the Way, John's Ministry, was finished, and the Lord took him home. While Herod was his executioner and would and will give account for such, still, he carried out this terrible act only with the Permission of the Lord, whether he realized it or not.

2. *"And cried, saying, This was He of Whom I spoke,"* concerns the Ministry of John regarding the Person of Jesus, but more particularly speaks of His Introduction when John baptized Him in water as recorded in John, Chapter 1, Verse 29.

3. *"He Who comes after me is preferred before me,"* testifies to the eternity of the Being of Christ.

4. John's Testimony in the first three Gospels mainly concerns Christ's Earthly Relationships, but in this Gospel, His Heavenly Relationships. He testified to the fullness of the Deity of Christ (Jn. 1:34) and the sufficiency of His Atonement (Jn. 1:29). The Lord Jesus declared that his Testimony was true (Jn. 5:32).

5. The word, *"Preferred,"* should have been translated, *"Existed,"* as *"He Who comes after me existed before me."*

6. The phrase, *"For He was before me,"* means He came before John in existence but after John in public earthly Ministry (Mat. 3:11; Lk. 3:16; Jn. 1:31-33).

(16) "AND OF HIS FULLNESS HAVE ALL WE RECEIVED, AND GRACE FOR GRACE."

The pattern is:

1. The phrase, *"And of His Fullness have all we received,"* tells us two things:

• John has told us Who Jesus is, i.e., *"The Eternal Word."* Now he tells us What He does. It speaks of the Grace and Truth, which alone is in Christ, and that everything man needs is here given.

• Christ is *"All in All"* because He provides *"All in All!"* He is the Provider of Salvation, Divine Healing, the Baptism with the Holy Spirit, Deliverance, and every need. None need look apart from Christ, and in truth, there is nothing apart from Christ.

2. The phrase, *"And Grace for Grace,"* actually says, *"Grace upon Grace."*

3. This is the provision of His Love heaped one upon another in this supply of His People's needs. Not Truth upon Truth, but Grace upon Grace; for Truth is simple and declarative while Grace is manifold (I Pet. 4:10) and executive.

(17) "FOR THE LAW WAS GIVEN BY MOSES, BUT GRACE AND TRUTH CAME BY JESUS CHRIST."

The composition is:

1. All who ignore the Word of God and its binding precepts are naked to the Judgment of God.

2. When the Scripture says of Adam and Eve after the Fall, *"And they knew that they were naked,"* it refers to far more than a lack of covering regarding clothing. It actually meant that they were naked or exposed to the Judgment of God (Gen. 3:7).

3. It is a fearful thing to realize that almost all of the world, and for all time, lays naked and exposed to Judgment!

THE LAW OF MOSES

The phrase, *"For the Law was given by Moses,"* refers to it being given to the people. It was given to Moses by God, and as such, was Truth.

The Hebrew word for *"Law"* is, *"Torah,"* and means, *"To teach or instruct."* It focuses on how one should live.

The Old Testament looks in wonder at the fact that God stooped to instruct Israel. If we have thought of God's Law as some cold, rigid set of rules, brutally applied, we miss the heart and soul of what Law was really about.

Moses reveals the warm heart of Law in Deuteronomy, Chapter 4, when He said to an expectant new generation about to enter the Promised Land:

"See, I have taught you decrees and Laws, even as the LORD my God commanded me, so that you may follow them in the land you are entering to take possession of it. Observe them carefully, for this will show you wisdom and understanding to the nations, who will hear about all these Decrees and say, 'Surely this great Nation is a wise and understanding people.' What other nation is so great as to have their gods near them the way the LORD our God is near us whenever we pray to Him? And what other nation is so great as to have such righteous decrees and laws as the body of Laws I am setting before you today?" (Deut. 4:5-8).

THE LAW AND THE LIFE OF ISRAEL

The Law covered every aspect of Israel's personal and national life. It was the moral, ceremonial, and civil way of life God ordained for His Old Testament People.

To be sure, there had been laws in the world before the Law of Moses, but they had been laws devised by man and were consequently seriously flawed, very flawed. Because it originated with God, the Law of Moses was totally superior in every respect to all other Laws, and in a grand manner. In other words, there was no comparison! It was totally fair, just, and honest with all people, treating all alike, and dealing, as stated, with every aspect of life, be it moral or civil.

Unfortunately, Israel added hundreds of other laws to the original Law of Moses, which many of them concluded to be even more important than the original Law. As such, it eventually became a load grievous to be borne. So, by the time of Christ, the Law of Moses was little referred to as such anymore simply because, due to man's additions, it had been completely changed.

WHAT THE LAW INCLUDED

In this sense, the Law consists of all the Statutes, Ordinances, Precepts, Commandments, and Testimonies given by God to guide His People. However, the Mosaic Law — those teachings included in the first five Books of the Old Testament — includes even more.

It includes Moses' review of an interpretation of history, his record of God's Mighty Acts, and his report of Creation.

In time, *"the Law"* came to indicate everything that God revealed through Moses, and in one sense, it indicates the entirety of the Pentateuch.

When we read the word, *"Law,"* in the Old Testament, it is helpful to remember that it may have many references. It may refer to God's Revelation in a general way. It may point to a specific set of instructions — e.g. the Law of Passover or the Ten Commandments. It may indicate the moral or ceremonial codes or the writings of Moses.

What is clear, however, is that whatever a particular use of *"Law"* points to, the Old Testament views as Divine Instruction. The Law was God's Gift, which was intended to show Israel how to live a Holy and happy life in this world.

Regrettably, Israel never lived up to the Law and finally fell so far away from its precepts that the curse of the Law ultimately destroyed them.

Only Jesus fully lived and kept the Law, and He did it in perfection. Consequently, He became the Representative Law-keeper for all who trust in His Name, with His Perfect Law-keeping given to all who believe in His Name (Jn. 3:16).

NOT FOR SALVATION

Even though the Law was Truth, there was no Salvation in the Law simply because it was never intended to save; it could not save. As stated, it was to show Israel how to live, respecting her personal and national life. In this, it would also show Israel her inadequacy due to the weakness of the flesh. The will of man is too far enslaved for it to yield spontaneously to the Majesty of the Law-Giver or to feel the attractions of obedience. The Law condemns — it is incapable of justifying the ungodly; the Law terrifies — it never reconciles. The Law even provokes the sin and excites the passions, which it punishes. And yet, the Law was a Gift, a Divine bestowment of entirely unspeakable value to those who were ignorant of the Mind and Will of God. But yet, as stated, it could not save! That alone could come through Jesus, to Whom the sacrifices pointed, and Who now has paid the price, proclaiming since that day at the Cross that sacrifices are now no longer necessary.

GRACE AND TRUTH

The phrase, *"But Grace and Truth came by Jesus Christ,"* proclaims Him as the Representative Law-keeper for all humanity, i.e. to all who will believe.

The Law was *"given,"* but Grace and Truth *"came."* The Law manifested men — full of wickedness; the Son manifested God — full of goodness. The Law demands from man the Righteousness which he cannot furnish; Grace gives to man the Righteousness which he needs. Christ is both Grace and Truth; for if Grace were not in Him, He would not be the *"Truth"*; and He *"gives"* Grace and Glory. When He came, Grace and Truth came because He is *"Grace and Truth."*

If one is to notice, Grace precedes Truth because Truth cannot be applied until Grace is first received.

This Scripture does not mean that there was no Law before Moses or Grace and Truth before Jesus Christ. The Law itself is Truth, and the New Testament, in one sense of the word, is Law.

The idea is that the fullness of Grace came by Jesus Christ. One can get today in fullness what men received only in part in Old Testament times.

(18) "NO MAN HAS SEEN GOD AT ANY TIME; THE ONLY BEGOTTEN SON, WHICH IS IN THE BOSOM OF THE FATHER, HE HAS DECLARED HIM."

NOTES

The order is:

1. Man can either accept the Sacrifice of Christ, which means that He took the Judgment on our behalf, or else, we will take the Judgment ourselves.

2. This means that the entirety of mankind for all time will either face Jesus as the Saviour or the Judge, but face Him, all will!

3. The Cross of Christ is the centrality of the Gospel. As such, it stands at the very center of human history.

GOD

The phrase, *"No man has seen God at any time,"* would have been better translated, *"No man has ever comprehended or experienced God at any time in all His Fullness, save the Only Begotten Son... He has declared Him."*

The word, *"Seen,"* not only means to see with the eyes but also means to comprehend fully or understand clearly. Actually, God has been seen by men with the eyes a number of times (Gen. 18:2, 33; 32:24-30; Ex. 24:10; 33:11; Josh. 5:13; Isa., Chpt. 6; Ezek. 1:26-28; Dan. 7:9-14; 10:5-6; Acts 7:56-59; Rev. 4:2-5; 5:1-7).

The phrase, *"The Only Begotten Son,"* refers to Jesus Christ in the Incarnation, Who Alone could perfectly declare the Father.

"Which is in the Bosom of the Father," proclaims the most intimate and loving fellowship with the Father as the Only Begotten.

"He has declared Him," means that the Incarnation was not only to provide a Perfect Sacrifice as the Sin Offering in order to redeem humanity but, as well, to declare the Heavenly Father to man.

This was done in several ways:

• In essence, Jesus was the Personification of the Father. He said to Philip when the Apostle asked, *"Lord, show us the Father, and it suffices us."*

Jesus said unto him, "Have I been so long with you, and yet have you not known Me, Philip? He who has seen Me has seen the Father" (Jn. 14:8-9).

This speaks of such union that the Father and the Son are of the same essence.

• Israel had known God by many Names but not as *"Father."*

GOD AS THE FATHER

Even though at times God did speak of Himself as a *"Father"* to Israel, that relationship was corporate rather than individual. God was the Father of Israel, the Covenant people, for *"is He not your Father, your Creator, Who made you and formed you?"* (Deut. 32:6). It is in this distinctive sense of Originator, the One Who called Israel into being as a people, that God was Father to His Old Testament People (Isa. 63:16; 64:8; Jer. 39:9; Mal. 1:6; 2:10).

However, it is not until Jesus came that we discover the wonder of the relationship introduced by Christ that God has planned for those who come to Him in Faith.

It was a shock to Israel, who was steeped in Old Testament Doctrine, to hear Jesus refer to God as His Own Personal Father.

Jesus also revealed God as our Father in a way that Israel had not known, implying intimate relationship, which would come as a result of the Born-Again experience.

God is revealed as the Father in His Intrinsic Relationship within the Trinity, in which Jesus is the Son. God is revealed as Father in the stunning relationship He establishes with Believers.

THE TRINITY

The Passages in which God is spoken of as the Father are typically Trinitarian in character. They focus on the First Person of the Trinity, either in His Relationship with Jesus, or in distinction from the other members of the Trinity. Despite the fact that Jesus and the Father, together with the Spirit, are One God (Jn. 10:30; 14:10-11), the Father is said by Jesus to be greater than He (Jn. 14:28).

When Jesus was on the Earth, only the Father knew the day and hour of Jesus' Return or the schedule of the end of this Dispensation (Mat. 24:36; Mk. 13:32; Acts 1:7).

DIFFERENCES?

The exact character of the differences between the Persons of the Trinity are, and will remain, a mystery, at least as far as total knowledge is concerned. However, the First Person of the Trinity has from eternity been *"The Father,"* and the Second has been *"The Son,"* at least according to our measure of understanding. And yet, there are some who claim that Jesus as the Son became such only at the Incarnation, and that is possible! However, it must be understood that Jesus has always been God, is God presently, and ever shall be God, but His Designation as *"Son,"* as stated, was strictly an affair of the Incarnation. In other words, He became such in order to go to the Cross.

Thankfully, the New Testament contributes much toward a greater understanding of God, especially in identifying God as Father.

SOME THINGS UNIQUELY THE FATHER'S

Although the Bible does not go into detail on distinctives within the Trinity, some things are specified as uniquely the Father's. John says that all those who come to Jesus come because the Father has enabled them to do so (Jn. 6:37, 44, 65).

Colossians 1:12-13 says that it is the Father Who qualifies us to share in the inheritance of the Saints, and it is He Who rescues us from the dominion of darkness by bringing us into the Kingdom of the Son, Whom He loves.

Ephesians 1:4-5 portrays the Father as the Architect of the Plan of Salvation. He *"chose us in Him before the creation of the world"* and *"predestined us to be adopted as His Sons through Jesus Christ,"* which speaks, of course, of those who willingly accept Him. It is the Plan of God which is predestined, and those who conform to that Plan, for Salvation is offered to all, are predestined to receive all that the Plan affords.

Despite the theological significance of the use of *"Father"* to distinguish the First Person of the Trinity respecting the others, the overwhelming personal impact of the Name in the First Century cannot be overestimated. The distant God of the Fathers was suddenly shown in a new light. The awesome One, Whose Name Yahweh, the Pious Jew would never pronounce (and even the writing of Whose Name by a Scribe called immediately for a ritual bath), was now presented to humankind in the most intimate and loving way. Even today, if we pause to consider, we must hear Jesus' Words in awe and wonder, *"When you pray, say, 'Our Father'"* (Lk. 11:2).

GOD AS THE FATHER OF JESUS

The Revelation of God as Father is introduced by Jesus. He often spoke of God as *"My Father in Heaven,"* (only recorded in Mat. 7:21; 10:32-33; 12:50; 15:13; 16:17; 18:10, 19, 35). In addition, in His Public and Private Prayers, Jesus addressed God as Father (Mat. 11:25-26; 26:39, 42; Mk. 14:36; Lk. 10:21; 22:42; 23:34; Jn. 11:41; 12:27-28).

This claim that He had a Father-Son relationship with God was shocking, as stated, to the religious leaders of the First Century. When Jesus spoke of God as His Father, the Jews (John's term for the religious leaders) *"tried all the harder to kill Him."* Jesus not only violated their traditions, *"But He was even calling God His Own Father, making Himself equal with God"* (Jn. 5:18).

THE RELATIONSHIP BETWEEN THE FATHER AND THE SON

Many of the things Jesus taught explored the relationship between the Father and the Son. When Jesus claimed, *"I and My Father are One"* (Jn. 10:30), He aroused hostility. Rather than accept His Claim, the Jews made attempts to stone Jesus because, they told Him, *"You, a mere Man, claim to be God"* (Jn. 10:33).

Yet, the Claims of Jesus were authenticated over and over again. The Oneness existing between Jesus and the Father was expressed in Christ's Words and in His Miraculous Works (Jn. 14:10-11). God the Father was at work in all Jesus did so that Christ perfectly expressed the Will and Character of the Father (Jn. 5:17-23).

The Father and Jesus were One in Authority and Power. Jesus has the Divine Right to judge and the Divine Power to give Life (Jn. 5:21-22). Preexistent as God with the Father (Jn. 1:1-5; 8:56-58), the Son is One with the Father as the Object of our love and worship (Jn. 14:21-23).

The statements made by Jesus and recorded in the Gospels affirm the Son's Identity with the Father. Jesus could say, *"Anyone who has seen Me has seen the Father"* (Jn. 14:9), *"For I am in the Father, and the Father is in Me"* (Jn. 14:10). Jesus fully and perfectly expresses the very Character of God the Father. And yet, Jesus remains as the Second Person of the Trinity, distinct from the Father.

Jesus said the Father is greater than He (Jn. 14:28), portrayed Himself as sent by the Father (Jn. 5:36-37; 6:57; 8:16, 18, 42; 12:49), and lived His Life on Earth according to the Father's Will (Mat. 26:39-42; Jn. 5:36; 12:49).

ONE GOD

While the existence of One God as a Trinity of Father, Son, and Holy Spirit involves concepts beyond our understanding, what is more important is that in the coming of the Son, we have a stunning Revelation of the fact that God is the Father. This could come only through Jesus. As Christ said, *"No one knows the Son except the Father, and no one knows the Father except the Son and those to whom the Son chooses to reveal Him"* (Mat. 11:27; Lk. 10:21-22; Jn. 14:1-13). In presenting himself as Son, Jesus presented an aspect of God completely unknown before the Incarnation. He spoke of God as His Father — the One they claimed as their God — saying to the Jewish leaders, *"Though you do not know Him, I know Him"* (Jn. 8:54-55).

Only in Jesus do we learn that God is Father. Only in seeing God as Father do we begin to realize the intimacy of the relationship that can exist between the Believer and the Lord.

GOD IS OUR FATHER

Jesus used the term, *"Father,"* carefully. He spoke of *"My Father,"* and to the Disciples He referred to God as *"Your Father."* He never used the phrase, *"Our Father,"* in a way that would link Himself with them: the relationship of Jesus with the Father is unique. While He is our Father by adoption, He is the Father of Jesus by eternal generation, and through Jesus, human beings have been welcomed into a family relationship with God the Father.

In their introductions and in other formulas, the New Testament authors who wrote the Epistles typically remind Believers constantly of their position as Children of God. The family language of the Bible shows us that our relationship with God and with one another is rooted in the fact that God is Father of a family that encompasses all whom Faith makes His Children.

OUR RELATIONSHIP WITH GOD

What are the implications of a relationship with a God Who is now revealed to be the Father by His Very Nature, as well as our Father by Redemption?

The Gospels in particular suggest a number of ways in which God acts as our Father. He rewards us (Mat. 6:1) and disciplines us (Jn. 15:2; Heb. 12:7-11). God the Father listens to our prayers (Mat. 6:6; 18:19). He knows, and He meets our needs (Mat. 6:8; Lk. 12:30), thus fulfilling the Father's Obligation to provide for His Family.

God has lavished love on us (I Jn. 3:1; Jude, Vs. 1) and has given us good gifts (Mat. 7:11; Lk. 11:13). He numbers the very hairs of our heads and remains in such total command of the Universe that not even a sparrow can fall without His Permission (Mat. 10:29-30).

As our Father, God is merciful (Lk. 6:36) and is pleased to give the Kingdom to Jesus' Disciples (Lk. 12:32). Yet, though our Father loves us (Jn. 16:27), He also judges each person's work (I Pet. 1:17).

WE ARE TO BE LIKE OUR FATHER

Jesus, Revealer of God as our Father, spells out other implications of this relationship. A father sets the pattern for his children; thus, we are to be like our Heavenly Father in showing love, even to our enemies (Mat. 5:43-48). The father in the earthly pattern accepts responsibility to meet the needs of his family. Our Heavenly Father does the same thing; thus we are released from anxiety and from the necessity of focusing our energies on attaining material things. We must seek God and His Kingdom first of all (Mat. 6:25-34; Lk. 12:22-31) and be free to share our possessions with those in need (Lk. 12:32-34). When we seek His Kingdom first, He has promised that all our material needs will be met, etc.

NOTES

We have confidence in our new relationship with God, for we have access to His Presence at any time (Heb. 4:16). When we come into the Presence of the Lord of the Universe, we are free to address Him as *"Our Father"* (Mat. 6:9).

(Most of the thoughts on God the Father were derived from Dr. Lawrence O. Richards.)

(19) "AND THIS IS THE RECORD OF JOHN, WHEN THE JEWS SENT PRIESTS AND LEVITES FROM JERUSALEM TO ASK HIM, WHO ARE YOU?"

The form is:

1. The phrase, *"And this is the record of John,"* proclaims a part of his Ministry not mentioned by Matthew, Mark, or Luke. So, John the Beloved, regarding John the Baptist, takes up where the others leave off.

2. When the Baptism of Jesus was accomplished, and the Spirit had led Him away into the wilderness, John stood, much as Elisha might have done (in the very same region) when Elijah went heavenward in the train of a chariot of fire. However, John proceeded to testify new and strange things about Jesus.

3. The question, *"When the Jews sent Priests and Levites from Jerusalem to ask Him, Who are you?"* was posed accordingly because there was a widespread impression that John the Baptist could be the Christ of their popular expectation.

4. This was at the time of John's highest popularity. His Ministry had produced the most amazing excitement among the people. They had flocked to his side and to his Baptism, confessing their sins. They had heard his summons to Repentance. They had trembled under his threats of Judgment.

5. His Prophetic indignation against their selfishness and greed, their formalism, and their boast of covenanted immunity from the consequences of moral fault had roused the conscience into an uncommon activity.

6. It must be remembered, John the Baptist was the first Prophetic voice heard by Israel since Malachi, a timespan of some 400 years.

(20) "AND HE CONFESSED, AND DENIED NOT; BUT CONFESSED, I AM NOT THE CHRIST."

The pattern is:

1. The phrase, *"And he confessed, and denied not,"* has somewhat of a double meaning:

• *"And he confessed"*: this means there was absolutely no hesitation in his confession regarding who he actually was, and above all, his mission.

• *"And denied not"*: he did not deny that some were calling him *"Christ."* However, to not even the slightest degree did he encourage this and, in fact, grandly repudiated the rumor.

2. The phrase, *"But confessed, I am not the Christ,"* in the Greek actually says, *"I, for my part, am not the Christ,"* and is said with emphasis.

3. Not only does his statement emphatically proclaim his denial, but even more, it says that he knows another to be the Christ. Consequently, he gave the Priests more than they asked.

(21) "AND THEY ASKED HIM, WHAT THEN? ARE YOU ELIJAH? AND HE SAID, I AM NOT. ARE YOU THAT PROPHET? AND HE ANSWERED, NO."

The diagram is:

1. It is stated that Jerusalem is at the exact center of the Earth. If so, this means that the Cross stood, as well, at the exact center of this Earth, meaning that there is equal access to all!

2. The Cross of Christ was a Finished Work. Nothing needed to be added because nothing could be added.

3. This means that the Cross of Christ must be the Object of Faith for every Believer, and the only Object of Faith.

ARE YOU ELIJAH?

The question, *"And they asked him, What then? Are you Elijah?"* referred, as is obvious, to Elijah the Tishbite.

The Prophet Malachi (4:5) had predicted the coming again from Heaven of Elijah the Prophet.

In a sense, and which Jesus informed His Disciples, John was the fulfillment of Malachi's prediction in that John came in the spirit and power of Elijah.

John, in the spirit of that Prophet, had attempted to get Israel ready for the Messiah, Who, sadly, they would not accept. In that sense, he could have been Elijah if they had only accepted the Lord, but they would not!

Consequently, Israel will have to undergo such sorrow in the coming Great Tribulation as no people has ever undergone before. Then, Elijah will truly come, fulfilling the prediction of Malachi, and preaching Repentance exactly as John the Baptist (Rev. 11:3-13). In fact, Elijah and Enoch, two men who have never died, will minister powerfully from Jerusalem the last half of the Great Tribulation.

A CATEGORICAL NEGATIVE

The phrase, *"And he said, I am not,"* presents a categorical negative, and for reason.

The Jews were not asking if he had come in the spirit and power of Elijah, which he actually had, but rather that he was the actual reincarnation of that Prophet.

Tradition said that Elijah was expected *"three days before the Messiah,"* and that he would come in the mountains of Israel, weeping over the people, saying, *"O land of Israel, how long will you remain arid and desolate?"*

John had come preaching in the wilderness, with a Message that greatly resembled this unscriptural tradition. Given that he was not Christ, they mused that he must be a reincarnation of Elijah. In that sense, he answered with an emphatic, *"No!"*

John the Baptist was the natural son of Zecharias and Elisabeth (Lk. 1:24, 57). As stated, he came in the spirit and power of Elijah to do for Israel before the First Advent what Elijah will do before the Second Advent (Mal. 4:5-6; Lk. 1:17).

The question, *"Are you that Prophet?"* spoke of the Prophet mentioned by Moses in Deuteronomy 18:15-18. This was the Messiah, as predicted by Moses, and presents the Jews going back to their first question concerning John being Christ.

Perhaps they did not interpret Moses' Prophecy as referring to the Messiah, or maybe they were just trying another tactic with John.

The phrase, *"And he answered, No,"* presents a curt reply to their inquiry.

He wants there to be absolutely no doubt as to what he is saying, and evidently weary with their repetition, he bluntly answers.

(22) "THEN SAID THEY UNTO HIM, WHO ARE YOU? THAT WE MAY GIVE AN ANSWER TO THEM WHO SENT US. WHAT DO YOU SAY OF YOURSELF?"

The overview is:

1. The expiatory and vicarious Work of Christ on the Cross was accepted by God in the heavens, which means it is irrefutable.

2. His being in the Heavens means that He has opened the door to Heaven by what He accomplished as our Great High Priest.

3. Jesus as the Son of God is vastly superior to all the earthly Priests of Israel, who, in effect, were mere symbols of Him.

WHO ARE YOU?

The question, *"Then said they unto him, Who are you?"* pinpoints, as they demand, exactly who he is and exactly what his mission is. Inasmuch as John was the first Prophet since Malachi, a time frame of approximately 400 years, this question was most important.

However, had these religious leaders known and understood the Word of God, as they certainly should have, they would have known who John was. In fact, John will answer them from the Book of Isaiah, as we shall see.

This is amazing! These men were a part of the religious structure of Israel, with the Bible supposedly as its foundation, and yet, they came to the single most important event in history, which is amply predicted in the Word of God, and they had no idea as to the identification of John the Baptist.

However, I am concerned that the same scene is being played out presently. The Rapture of the Church is imminent, and most of the church world knows nothing about it, or else, expresses no confidence in the Doctrine.

THE ANSWER

The phrase, *"That we may give an answer to them who sent us,"* tells us more than meets the eye.

They were not really seeking information or the truth about the matter, but rather desired that he claim something of which they could accuse him. If they were opposed to Christ, and they certainly were, then they would be opposed to John the Baptist, for he testified of Christ. In fact, even though the people flocked to John by the thousands, for the obvious reasons, there is no record that any of the religious hierarchy of Israel, or most of the Pharisees, followed suit. They were evil, despite their religious show, and would oppose that of God.

TWO TYPES OF UNRIGHTEOUSNESS

1. The unrighteousness of sin inculcates itself in all unbelievers and, unfortunately, in some Believers. This is the reason that man must be *"Born-Again."* In fact, it is not too difficult for the Holy Spirit to convict of this type of unrighteousness.

2. There is a religious unrighteousness, which amounts to self-righteousness, that is another story altogether. The Holy Spirit is very seldom able to penetrate this barrier simply because those with this type of unrighteousness seldom believe or recognize such.

HYPOCRISY

Jesus called these types, *"Hypocrites,"* (Mat., Chpt. 23) which they certainly were, even though they would not recognize that in themselves.

Hypocrisy, as it is known to most, refers to an individual playing a part, somewhat like an actor, which they really do not possess in reality. As well, those who practice this type of hypocrisy are well aware of what they are doing.

However, the type of hypocrisy practiced by the Pharisees was totally different. These individuals, at least for the most part, had mouthed their lie of religious profession for so long that they had come to the place that they believed it themselves. They were very religious, wrapping themselves in a mantle of religious ceremony and outward show, which caused others to think very highly of them, consequently professing something they really did not have. However, they were so deceived and blinded that they were not aware of their spiritual poverty.

Consequently, when they heard John the Baptist, they in no way placed themselves in the position of needing his Message.

They threw it over their shoulders, or else, pointed to others as needful of this remedy.

However, all religion of this nature sees any and every true Move of God as a threat which must be silenced; hence, they would send emissaries to John, hoping to trap him into making some type of wild claim.

The question, *"What do you say of yourself?"* is a revealing question.

In effect, they did not even agree that he was a Prophet, much less the Messiah, but they wanted to know what he claimed of himself. His answer is extremely revealing!

(23) "HE SAID, I AM THE VOICE OF ONE CRYING IN THE WILDERNESS, MAKE STRAIGHT THE WAY OF THE LORD, AS SAID THE PROPHET ISAIAH."

The pattern is:

1. The phrase, *"He said, I am the voice of one crying in the wilderness,"* is taken from Isaiah 40:3.

2. Those who questioned John had read this Passage innumerable times and knew exactly what it meant. Consequently, when John came preaching in the wilderness, they should have known instantly that he was the fulfillment of this Prophecy. This is especially true considering that it was accompanied greatly by the Moving and Operation of the Holy Spirit.

3. As well, the Holy Spirit had carefully used the word, *"Voice,"* which denoted that John was not the Messiah but only the *"Crier,"* who would introduce the Messiah.

4. *"Make straight the Way of the Lord, as said the Prophet Isaiah,"* proclaims his *"mission,"* as the first phrase proclaimed his *"identity."*

5. Malachi, as well, proclaimed the same Message in abbreviated form (Mal. 3:1).

6. These Passages, in both Isaiah and Malachi, also point to the Second Advent of Christ when Elijah and Enoch will serve in the capacity of preparation.

(24) "AND THEY WHICH WERE SENT WERE OF THE PHARISEES."

The composition is:

1. The Holy Spirit is careful to delineate the source of these questions, which tells us, as well, that this opposition that here begins will flower into full bloom against Christ. They did not love Christ, so they would not love the one who pointed to Christ!

2. Jesus said two things about this:

• *"If the world hate you, you know that it hated Me before it hated you"* (Jn. 15:18). In other words, all of those who hate Jesus will also hate His True Followers!

• *"If they have kept My Saying, they will keep yours also"* (Jn. 15:20). He is, in effect, saying, *"If men truly love Me, they will truly love you."*

3. This should carry over to the fact that men cannot claim to be of God and, at the same time, oppose that which is of God!

(25) "AND THEY ASKED HIM, AND SAID UNTO HIM, WHY DO YOU BAPTIZE THEN, IF YOU BE NOT THAT CHRIST, NOR ELIJAH, NEITHER THAT PROPHET?"

The structure is:

1. The phrase, *"And they asked him, and said unto him,"* poses the framing of a question, which, in essence, meant the same thing as they would later ask Christ, *"Tell us, by what authority do You these things? or who is he who gave You this authority?"* (Lk. 20:2).

2. The question, *"Why do you baptize then, if you are not that Christ, nor Elijah, neither that Prophet?"* in effect, as stated, is asking the source of his authority.

3. It alluded to the fact that Jews were accustomed to making converts by ceremonial cleansing, but never without an order from the Sanhedrin or before three magistrates or doctors of the Law.

4. They, therefore, were indignant that John not only baptized without Jewish authority, but baptized Jews contrary to the practice of the Pharisees.

5. In other words, he had not asked or sought their permission, nor did it seem that he cared whether they agreed or not!

6. Regrettably, the action of these men has continued in others of similar spirit from that moment until now.

7. Incidentally, *"Christ"* means, *"The Anointed,"* and was not looked at as a proper name. However, it did refer to the Messiah.

(26) "JOHN ANSWERED THEM, SAYING, I BAPTIZE WITH WATER: BUT THERE STANDS ONE AMONG YOU, WHOM YOU KNOW NOT."

The exposition is:

1. The phrase, *"John answered them, saying, I baptize with water,"* was of far greater implication than this brief answer given by John. At least part of the reason for his brevity is that he felt they should know and not have to ask. Several things are said here:

2. The Lord calls men to do certain things, and He does not seek first the approval of some religious hierarchy. If it is truly ordained of God, it will be according to the Word of God and will bring forth the appropriate results or fruit. Jesus said, *"By their fruits you shall know them"* (Mat. 7:20).

3. The fruit of John's Ministry was evident and obvious. In fact, Israel had not seen such a stir by the Lord in many centuries. So, the Pharisees could not speak ill of the results, only that he was doing this outside of their authority. Of course, with God, they had no authority.

4. Even though the Jewish washings, especially the ritual washings of the Pharisees, had some remote similarity to John's Baptism, still, even though there was no Scriptural precedent, there was a Scriptural Promise. Actually, this *"Promise"* was wrapped up in the entirety of the Old Testament, with all sacrifices, rituals, feasts, and Laws pointing to that which was to come, namely Christ.

5. So, Water Baptism was a Spiritual sign, and a very appropriate one, to say the least, symbolizing the Born-Again experience, which was soon to come to pass.

6. Jesus Himself would be baptized, not because of sin, but as a portrayal of His Death, Burial, and Resurrection and, thereby, to fulfill all Righteousness. It spoke of a Newness of Life, which was far removed from the Law of old. The Old Covenant was cold because it was written on stone. The New Covenant is warm because, in effect, Jesus is the New Covenant. Also, it is written on the hearts of men and women and is best of all symbolized outwardly by Water Baptism.

7. The phrase, *"But there stands One among you,"* in effect, points to their spiritual ignorance. He was in their very midst, and of that, they did not know!

NOTES

8. *"Whom you know not,"* has a far deeper meaning than the mere lack of recognition. They did not know Him simply because they were not serving the One He represented. His Father was not their Father.

(27) "HE IT IS, WHO COMING AFTER ME IS PREFERRED BEFORE ME, WHOSE SHOE'S LATCHET I AM NOT WORTHY TO UNLOOSE."

The exegesis is:

1. The phrase, *"He it is,"* in effect, says, *"The Messiah is already here, even though you do not know Him, and He, as stated, is not me."*

2. I wonder what the thoughts of these men were upon hearing this from John.

3. *"Who coming after me,"* refers to himself as the forerunner for the actual purpose of introducing Christ. The phrase also speaks of Jesus' Coming as being imminent, even at the moment. In effect, he is saying, *"You won't have long to wait."*

4. *"Is preferred before me,"* simply means that John's Ministry, as exciting as it was to Israel, was but a prelude for that which was now at hand, the Ministry of Christ. As well, even though John the Baptist, in the Words of Jesus, was the greatest Prophet born of woman, still, such was of small moment in comparison to Jesus Christ, the Eternal Logos, the Son of the Living God.

5. The phrase, *"Whose shoe's latchet I am not worthy to unloose,"* adequately describes the comparison, and if true of John, the greatest Prophet born of woman, how much more is it true for all others!

6. As well as the comparison which John makes, his portrayal of humility also proclaims that attribute as the basic requirement for being baptized with the Holy Spirit. Even though John the Beloved did not link these statements together in his account (humility) of being baptized with the Spirit, Matthew, Mark, and Luke did (Mat. 3:11; Mk. 1:7-8; Lk. 3:16).

(28) "THESE THINGS WERE DONE IN BETHABARA BEYOND JORDAN, WHERE JOHN WAS BAPTIZING."

The structure is:

1. *"Bethabara"* was probably on the other side of the Jordan River, not too far from Jericho. The wilderness to which Jesus

went after His Baptism is believed by many to be that which is near Jericho.

2. I have personally been to Jericho many times. However, on the last trip to that ancient city, our guide took us on the old road from Jericho towards Jerusalem, actually, the same route Jesus would have travelled. Along that route, which is extremely mountainous, I had the opportunity to observe this wilderness in far greater detail, whereas previously I had only seen it from afar.

3. In its own way, it is beautiful, but yet, it is wilderness, to be sure. When one thinks that this is where Jesus spent 40 days and 40 nights facing the powers of darkness, and fasting this entire time, as well, then the area takes on new meaning altogether.

4. As well, this was probably the area in which most of John's Ministry was conducted. The people came from all over Israel to hear him, and inasmuch as this wilderness was very near the Jordan River, it stands to reason that this would have been the place.

(29) "THE NEXT DAY JOHN SEES JESUS COMING UNTO HIM, AND SAID, BEHOLD THE LAMB OF GOD, WHICH TAKES AWAY THE SIN OF THE WORLD."

The construction is:

1. The Incarnation, the Temptation, the Death, and the High Priestly Ministry of Jesus have always stood out as seriously unique.

2. Paul never made any attempt to prove the humanity of Christ. He accepted it as a fact, as it was!

3. As well, there is no attempt made to justify the Suffering of Christ by philosophical argument.

JESUS

The phrase, *"The next day John sees Jesus coming unto him,"* is, no doubt, after the Baptism of Jesus and the wilderness experience. Consequently, the information John will now give is after the fact.

"The next day," refers to the day after John had been questioned by the emissaries from the Sanhedrin.

According to the following statements, John, upon seeing Jesus coming toward him, is given a Revelation by the Holy Spirit, which sheds greater Light on everything and, above all, opens up the coming Work of Christ to redeem humanity, thereby, liberating fallen mankind.

When John saw Jesus, he saw something that neither he nor anyone else had seen previously.

The shepherds saw a Baby; the Magi, a Child; the Scribes, a Boy; the Nazarites, a Carpenter; and the Greeks, a Street-Preacher. However, in some way, John saw Jesus' Glory. He saw Him as the Redeemer of mankind. In fact, so did the aged Simeon (Lk. 2:32) and, as well, all whose eyes are open by Faith.

He was the God of Glory and the Great Light when in the manger as much as He was when on the Mount (Mat. 17:2), and in truth, the shepherds and the Magi worshipped him as such.

THE LAMB OF GOD

Why did the Holy Spirit through John proclaim Jesus as the *"Lamb of God"*?

He did so simply because all, without exception, of the millions of lambs, which were offered up to Jehovah the past 4,000 years, were symbolic of the Lord Jesus Christ, Who would ultimately come, and now has come. Every one of those lambs symbolized the Cross of Christ, what Jesus would there do, and the great Victory that He would there win, meaning that the Cross of Christ is the Means by which all things are given to us by the Lord. In fact, were it not for the Cross, the Lord could not even look at us, much less have communion with us, and above all, forgiveness of sins.

The phrase, *"Lamb of God,"* proclaims Jesus as the Sacrifice for sin, in fact, the Sin Offering, Whom all the millions of offered lambs had represented. It is well nigh impossible for anyone to adequately comprehend how the Eternal Logos would come down to this world, become Man, live in abject poverty, opposed and humiliated by almost all, and die for lost humanity. But He did!

As well as the fulfilling of all that the offered lambs represented down through the many centuries, this statement by John fulfilled, at least when carried to conclusion, the Promise made to Abraham by the Lord concerning the Name given to the Lord by that Patriarch — *"Jehovah-Jireh,"* i.e., *"The Lord will provide."* Jesus as the *"Lamb of God"* was the Provision of which Abraham spoke and God promised (Gen. 22:1-14).

TO TAKE AWAY THE SIN OF THE WORLD

The phrase, *"Who takes away the sin of the world,"* presents a startling Truth, so startling, in fact, that it would change God's Dealings with man entirely. It is found in the words, *"Takes away."*

Heretofore, the sins of even the greatest Believers, such as Abraham, Isaac, Jacob, Isaiah, David, etc., were not taken away, only *"covered."* The Scripture plainly says, *"For it is not possible that the blood of bulls and goats should take away sins"* (Heb. 10:4).

To be sure, all have ever been Saved, even from the very beginning, by Faith and trust in Christ, to Whom the sacrifices pointed in the future, as all since Calvary now look backward. However, it has ever been Christ and His Shed Blood, for there is no other way that one can be Saved.

Before Calvary and the Resurrection, even though Believers were just as Saved then as now, they were not privileged to enjoy all the fruits of their Salvation. This was because Jesus had not yet been glorified (Jn. 7:38-39).

For instance, when Believers died before Calvary, they were not then able to go directly to Heaven, the Residence of God, but rather to paradise, which was in the heart of the Earth (Lk., Chpt. 16). This was because their sins had not been taken away but merely covered by Atonement, which was brought about by the sacrifice of certain innocent animals.

As well, Believers in Old Testament times could not be baptized with the Holy Spirit even though the Holy Spirit did help them in many and varied ways. He even occupied some to help them carry out their mission; however, when that mission was finished, the Holy Spirit would leave out, and, as stated, that was only for a few.

When Jesus died and rose again, thereby, *"taking away the sin of the world,"* Paradise was emptied and, in fact, is used no more. Upon death, Believers now instantly go to be with Christ (Phil. 1:23), all because of what Jesus did at the Cross.

As well, at the moment of Conversion, due to the Cross, the Holy Spirit now comes into the hearts and lives of all Believers, there to abide forever (Jn. 14:16-17).

Also, Believers can now be baptized with the Holy Spirit with the evidence of speaking with other Tongues. All of this is given, plus a far greater communion with our Heavenly Father, due to the fact that our sins are *"taken away."* In other words, since Jesus paid the price, these sins cannot be charged against any Believer ever again! As well, God judges and looks at all Believers, not according to their own merit, but according to the merit of Christ.

GLORIFIED

However, even though Jesus has now taken our sins away, with all its attendant Blessings and with far greater magnitude than the Old Covenant, still, there are some things the Believer does not yet have, even in some sense, as in Old Testament times. For instance, even though the Believer is presently washed, sanctified, and justified, we are not yet glorified, with all the attendant Blessings which will come about at that particular time (Rom. 8:17-18; I Cor. 6:11).

This, the Saints being *"glorified,"* will take place at the First Resurrection (I Cor. 15:42, 51-57). If one is to notice, the word, *"Sin,"* is used in the singular, which refers to all sin. Consequently, exponentially, in the Mind of God, every single sin for all time has been removed, past, present, and future; however, it remains for the sinners to take advantage of this great Gift of God! If not, their sins will not be *"taken away,"* but rather remain *"against them."* When Jesus died, He died for the entirety of the world, not just for Jews, etc. (Jn. 3:16).

As well, the following should be noted:

• During the time of Cain and Abel, the Lord demanded a sacrifice for each person (Gen. 4:4).

• At the time of the Deliverance from Egypt, it was a sacrifice for each family (Ex. 12:3).

• During the time of the Law, it was a sacrifice for the entirety of the Nation of Israel. It was called the Great Day of Atonement (Lev., Chpt. 16).

• Now Jesus will offer Himself as a Sacrifice for the entirety of the *"world"* (Jn. 3:16).

Note the progression: a person, a house, a Nation, and finally, the entirety of the world.

WHOSOEVER WILL

This means that all may be Saved, and, in fact, the Great Invitation says, *"Whosoever will!"* (Rev. 22:17). The only thing that is required is a simple Faith in Christ (Rom. 10:9-10, 13).

Deep is the joy caused by the knowledge of forgiveness of sin through the Sacrifice that He perfected as the Lamb of God on the Altar of Calvary. Deeper is the joy that results from a knowledge of what He is in Himself — the unsearchable riches of Grace, Love, Pity, and Power dwelling in Him in infinite fullness and displaying themselves in His Offices and Ministries. However, deepest will be the joy resulting from fellowship with Him and likeness to Him in His Future Glory. Then the total result and fruit of one's Salvation will appear.

(30) "THIS IS HE OF WHOM I SAID, AFTER ME COMES A MAN WHICH IS PREFERRED BEFORE ME: FOR HE WAS BEFORE ME."

The synopsis is:

1. The phrase, *"This is He of Whom I said,"* proclaims John making a positive identification. It is the One Who *"takes away the sin of the world."*

2. *"After me comes a Man Who is preferred before me,"* proclaims a Testimony affirming the actual Humanity of Jesus of Nazareth.

3. The phrase, *"For He was before me,"* affirms His Essential Deity.

4. Consequently, for all who heard John say this, and there could have been hundreds, or even more, Jesus Christ is plainly proclaimed as the long looked for Messiah.

5. Did they understand what he was saying?

With John proclaiming Jesus as *"The Lamb of God,"* there was no reason for them to misunderstand. Everything was clear, open, Scriptural, and above speculation. As well, when Jesus began His Ministry, He fulfilled every single Scriptural prediction, which left the religious leaders of Israel without excuse.

6. The only reason they did not know Who He was is because they did not want to know. In this state, there is absolutely no amount of proof, irrespective of how revealing it may be, which would change their minds. It was a willful, spiritual blindness and deafness, which left God no alternative or choice but to bring a willful Judgment, which He did!

(31) "AND I KNEW HIM NOT: BUT THAT HE SHOULD BE MADE MANIFEST TO ISRAEL, THEREFORE AM I COME BAPTIZING WITH WATER."

The composition is:

1. Jesus served as the Substitute for all of mankind. In fact, He was referred to as the *"Second Man"* and the *"Last Adam"* (I Cor. 15:45-47).

2. As the Redeemer, Christ must not only come in the flesh, but He also must suffer and be tempted as man.

3. By this suffering, Christ Jesus would fully take our place, thereby, becoming the Perfect Mediator and High Priest.

RECOGNITION

The phrase, *"And I knew Him not,"* does not mean that John was not acquainted with Jesus, especially considering how close Mary and Elisabeth were (Lk. 1:39-45).

From Luke 1:36, many conclude that John and Jesus were cousins. However, the Greek word used in this Scripture for *"cousin"* is, *"Suggenes,"* which means, *"Countryman,"* and not necessarily a cousin, as in the sense of blood kin.

Zechariah and Elisabeth, the parents of John the Baptist, were from the Tribe of Levi, which Zechariah had to be in order to be a Priest. Joseph and Mary were from the Tribe of Judah through David.

That they were cousins in the sense of blood relationship is possible but not likely.

THE HOLY SPIRIT

John meant that up until this present Revelation by the Holy Spirit, which began at the Baptism of Jesus and included the *"Lamb of God"* Revelation, he was not absolutely certain that Jesus was indeed the Promised Messiah. There is no doubt that Elisabeth discussed with her son many times the visit of Mary at the Conception of Jesus, with many things at that time also discussed concerning the visit of the Angel Gabriel and the things he said to Mary (Lk. 1:26-56). However, it seems that John did not boldly announce Who Jesus really was until it was pointedly revealed to him by the Holy Spirit, which left absolutely no doubt. Before this Revelation, he was not sure, but now, he is absolutely certain!

It seems that the Holy Spirit dealt with John during all these preparation years, guiding him as to exactly what he would say and do, with the announcement of the Purpose and Person of Jesus to be done only at a certain time. I think the record is clear that the Holy Spirit had prepared John for this very time, consequently, leading him accordingly.

The phrase, *"But that He should be made manifest to Israel,"* means that at a certain time, and not before, Jesus was to be introduced to Israel as the Messiah, which John carried out exactly as led.

"Therefore am I come baptizing with water," proclaims that which the Holy Spirit told him to do, which he had been doing for sometime, and which would occasion this great Revelation to John, which it did! Matthew 3:13-17 clearly bears this out.

(32) "AND JOHN BEAR RECORD, SAYING, I SAW THE SPIRIT DESCENDING FROM HEAVEN LIKE A DOVE, AND IT ABODE UPON HIM."

The pattern is:

1. If the Son was to properly represent man before God, then it was necessary that Christ be Man.

2. Here Paul touches on the need of the Incarnation and the Virgin Birth (Heb. 4:14).

3. One Who stands between God and man is himself both human and Divine, conceived by the Holy Spirit, yet is the Seed of a woman (Gen. 3:15).

THE RECORD

The phrase, *"And John bear record,"* means that this is exactly what the Holy Spirit said would happen, concerning the identity of Jesus as the Messiah. Actually, there are seven witnesses which did bear record to the identity of the Messiah, all given in the Gospel according to John the Beloved:

1. The Father (5:30-38; 8:13-18).
2. The Son (5:17-27; 8:14; 18:37).
3. The Holy Spirit (15:26; 16:13-15).
4. The Written Word (1:45; 5:38, 45).
5. Divine Works (5:17, 36; 10:25; 14:11; 15:24).
6. John the Baptist (1:7, 32-34; 5:33-35).
7. Disciples (15:27; 19:35; 21:24).

THE SPIRIT DESCENDING

The phrase, *"Saying, I saw the Spirit descending from Heaven like a dove,"* tells us several things:

• This is what the Holy Spirit said would happen and which would identify the Messiah. John was to wait for this before making a public announcement.

• The Revelation came in unmistakable form from Heaven, actually from the Throne of God, which characterizes all such Revelations.

• John plainly said that he *"saw the Spirit,"* which tells us, at least in some fashion, that the Holy Spirit can be seen, and that He consequently has some type of Spirit Body. Some may claim that this is nothing more than an anthropomorphism. This means it's something or someone Who is not human, as God is not human, but is explained in human terms in order that man may have a greater understanding. However, that which says too much says nothing!

As well, John did not say the Holy Spirit looked like a dove, but rather *"descending in a bodily shape like a dove upon Him,"* meaning Jesus (Lk. 3:22), with the gentleness of a dove.

The Holy Spirit is definitely not a *"dove,"* with that being used by John in a symbolical sense, explaining the manner in which the Holy Spirit came. However, that He does have a *"bodily shape,"* as expressed by John, must, I think, be taken at face value.

• These Passages are a clear reference to the Trinity. The Son, John did not know;

the Father, he did know; and the Spirit, he saw coming from the Father upon the Son (Mat. 3:16-17; Lk. 3:22).

THE BEGINNING OF THE MINISTRY OF CHRIST

The phrase, *"And it abode upon Him,"* refers to the Holy Spirit. The Greek word for *"abode"* is, *"Meno,"* and means, *"To abide, dwell, and remain."* The coming of the Spirit upon Him signaled the beginning of His Ministry. That should be a lesson to us. In fact, He could not begin His Ministry until the infilling of the Holy Spirit. That is meant to be the same presently. Without the Holy Spirit, nothing for the Lord is going to be done. Unfortunately, over half of the modern church doesn't even believe in the Baptism with the Holy Spirit with the evidence of speaking with other Tongues. Worse yet, the half that claims the Baptism with the Holy Spirit, sadly, is depending on Him less and less.

If Jesus, as a Man in the Incarnated State, could do nothing for God without the Holy Spirit, even though Perfect in every way, where does that leave us? That's the reason that Jesus commanded His Followers *"that they should not depart from Jerusalem, but wait for the Promise of the Father, which, said He, you have heard of Me.*

"For John truly baptized with water; but you shall be baptized with the Holy Spirit not many days hence" (Acts 1:4-5). I remind the reader that this is a *"command"* and not a suggestion. Let me say it again:

If Jesus, as a Man in the Incarnated State, could do nothing for God without the Holy Spirit, even though Perfect in every way, where does that leave us?

Exactly as with Christ, so it is with all others. We must have the Holy Spirit in order to carry out that which God wants done. In other words, without the Holy Spirit, absolutely nothing is done on this Earth in the Spiritual realm, at least that which is Righteous.

Also, I am not speaking of the Entrance of the Holy Spirit in His Work of Regeneration respecting the Born-Again experience, as necessary as that is, but rather the Baptism with the Holy Spirit, which is always accompanied by speaking with other Tongues, and is outlined in Acts 2:4, etc.

This means that these preachers, and laymen for that matter, who do not believe that the Acts 2:4 experience is for us today are going to do absolutely nothing for the Lord Jesus Christ. While it is true that much religious activity may be carried out, it will all be man-made because it is man-devised. Everything done for God must be done by Jesus Christ through the Person, Ministry, and Agency of the Holy Spirit.

DEPENDENT ON THE SPIRIT

As well, having the Acts 2:4 experience does not necessarily mean that things will be done for the Lord. Believers must learn to be totally dependent upon the spirit, thereby, allowing ourselves to be channels through which the Holy Spirit can work. Regrettably, the Holy Spirit is allowed little latitude in the lives of many, if not most, Spirit-filled Believers. The flesh is too predominant in most. The Spirit of God being in the heart and life is one thing (I Cor. 3:16). His being allowed to carry forth the Will of God is something else entirely! Regrettably, only a precious few fall into the latter category.

(33) "AND I KNEW HIM NOT: BUT HE WHO SENT ME TO BAPTIZE WITH WATER, THE SAME SAID UNTO ME, UPON WHOM YOU SHALL SEE THE SPIRIT DESCENDING, AND REMAINING ON HIM, THE SAME IS HE WHICH BAPTIZES WITH THE HOLY SPIRIT."

The order is:

1. By woman, Satan plunged the human race into spiritual oblivion.

2. By woman, God will ultimately elevate the human race back to what He originally intended.

3. What love that God would become Man, step down from His Royal Throne of Creation, walk down the starry steps from Heaven, and be born of a woman in a stable, and be raised in the home of a carpenter.

TO BAPTIZE WITH WATER

The phrase, *"And I knew Him not,"* is used the second time by John with purpose. The Holy Spirit wants all to know that

John's introduction of Jesus as the Messiah was not according to the flesh, i.e., personal knowledge, circumstances, observation, etc., but rather by Revelation from on High. Likewise, no one can truly know Jesus unless revealed by the Holy Spirit, and to all who will, such Revelation will definitely be afforded.

The phrase, *"But He Who sent me to baptize with water,"* tells us, as well, that this act of Water Baptism, which was completely new to Israel and the world, was not John's idea at all, but rather given by Revelation from God.

So, we see how the Lord told John exactly what to do, and how the religious hierarchy was not happy at all because it was done without their approval. However, it was not the Will of God that John present his Ministry to the Sanhedrin for approval, or else, the Lord would have told him to do so. In fact, had he done so, they would have been extremely disapproving and would have stopped him.

LED BY MEN

Regrettably, most of the preachers in the world today are little led by the Holy Spirit, as John, but rather by men. Consequently, little, if anything, is done for the Lord, at least in those circles.

The Scriptural ideal is that the individual consecrate himself (or herself) before the Lord, and that the Lord speak to that person, giving Guidance and Direction, with him carrying out that which the Lord wants and desires. Does that type of Spirit-led individual ask permission? No! Faith never asks permission, especially considering that the individual believes he has heard from Heaven. If, in fact, that is the case, he must obey God, irrespective of what others may say.

While it is perfectly proper and, at times, even necessary that one submit what he believes God has given him to proper individuals, the question of obeying God must never be in doubt. Obedience is never open for discussion, while the proposed Vision may meet much discussion.

When Mary was visited by the Angel Gabriel, given the greatest Message that any maiden had ever heard, Luke said she went immediately to the home of Zechariah and Elisabeth, the soon-to-be parents of John the Baptist (Lk. 1:26-56). With something so weighty, this was a proper thing for her to do. However, we must make certain, as Mary, that we visit one of like Faith, and not submit what we believe God has given us to unbelievers. In the case of John the Baptist, the religious Sanhedrin of Israel, no matter their lofty religious position and authority, was looked at by God as unbelievers, as should be obvious. Regrettably, many, if not most, in positions of leadership in organized religion are classified accordingly.

UPON WHOM YOU SHALL SEE THE SPIRIT DESCENDING

The phrase, *"The same said unto me, Upon Whom you shall see the Spirit descending, and remaining on Him,"* was to be the Revelation from God that John was to heed, which he did.

So, the Introduction of Jesus Christ as the Messiah was designed and given by Revelation from God, which completely ignored the religious hierarchy of Israel. God doesn't consult with man about His Actions; man is supposed to consult with God.

HE WHO BAPTIZES WITH THE HOLY SPIRIT

The phrase, *"The same is He Who baptizes with the Holy Spirit,"* proclaims that which Jesus would do after His Death, Resurrection, and Ascension.

As well, these Passages tell us that *"no man can say that Jesus is the Lord* (Jehovah), *but by the Holy Spirit"* (I Cor. 12:3). Therefore, neither John the Baptist nor Simon Peter could recognize Jesus as Jehovah till thus illuminated, though they might recognize Him as the Messiah of Jewish expectation, and *"after the flesh"* (II Cor. 5:16).

Salvation is God's Greatest Gift to man and is given for many purposes; however, the main purpose of Salvation is that the Believer may be *"an habitation of God through the Spirit"* (Eph. 2:22). God desires to dwell with man!

Before Calvary, the nearest that God, in essence, could come to man was to dwell in the Tabernacle and later the Temple. Due to sin and rebellion, He was forced to leave the Temple (Ezek. 11:22-23). Since Calvary and the Resurrection, God can dwell directly in the Believer, making the Believer the *"Temple of God"* (I Cor. 3:16).

WAIT FOR THE PROMISE OF THE FATHER

If the Spirit of God is not allowed this habitation, all that Salvation means and does simply cannot be carried out. That is the reason Jesus commanded His Followers to *"wait for the Promise of the Father"* (Acts 1:4). It was not a suggestion!

I am positive that by this time the reader is equating my statements with being baptized with the Holy Spirit with the evidence of speaking with other Tongues (Acts 2:4). That is exactly what I am saying!

Even though such, within itself, does not pertain to Salvation, with that coming by Faith alone in Christ, still, the end result of Salvation cannot be fully realized, as stated, without the Believer going on and being baptized with the Holy Spirit. Even though the Blood of Jesus certainly cleanses one from all sin and needs nothing added to it, still, growth in the Lord and service for the Lord are all tied to the Holy Spirit.

(34) "AND I SAW, AND BEAR RECORD THAT THIS IS THE SON OF GOD."

The diagram is:

1. The phrase, *"And I saw,"* presents the greatest Testimony there is, that of an eyewitness.

2. *"And bear record that this is the Son of God,"* is said by Revelation from God. Therefore, the record is twofold:

- John, as stated, was an eyewitness.
- That which was done and which he saw was exactly what God told him it would be and, therefore, seals the Testimony.

(35) "AGAIN THE NEXT DAY AFTER JOHN STOOD, AND TWO OF HIS DISCIPLES."

The overview is:

1. At this time, these two Disciples were followers of John the Baptist, in other words, his Disciples. We know that one was Andrew, and the other was probably John the Beloved, the writer of this Gospel.

2. So, this tells us that these men, by following John the Baptist, were hungry for God and, consequently, were being prepared to be Followers of the Lord even though, at that time, they would not have been aware of such.

3. This *"day"* in question was to prove to be the greatest day of their lives.

(36) "AND LOOKING UPON JESUS AS HE WALKED, HE SAID, BEHOLD THE LAMB OF GOD!"

The exegesis is:

1. The phrase, *"And looking upon Jesus as He walked,"* takes us back to Verse 29, for both Verses speak of the same incident.

2. *"He* (John the Baptist) *said, Behold the Lamb of God,"* is used here again in order to develop the time frame for the account about to be given.

3. The basis of God's First Relationship to the Earth was that of innocence. Sin destroyed that foundation. The *"Lamb of God"* — the Lamb Whom God Alone could furnish — took away the sin of the world. In doing so, He established a new Foundation, the eternal basis of God's Present Relations with both Heaven and Earth (Williams).[8]

(37) "AND THE TWO DISCIPLES HEARD HIM SPEAK, AND THEY FOLLOWED JESUS."

The composition is:

1. The phrase, *"And the two Disciples heard him speak,"* refers to what John said about Jesus.

2. *"And they followed Jesus,"* means that John's statement made a profound impression upon them.

3. From this statement, they probably recognized Jesus at the time as the Messiah. However, their knowledge of Him was imperfect, but His knowledge of them was perfect (Williams).[9]

(38) "THEN JESUS TURNED, AND SAW THEM FOLLOWING, AND SAID UNTO THEM, WHAT DO YOU SEEK? THEY SAID UNTO HIM, RABBI, (WHICH IS TO SAY, BEING INTERPRETED, MASTER,) WHERE DO YOU DWELL?"

The structure is:

1. The question, *"Then Jesus turned, and saw them following, and said unto them, What do you seek?"* presents the first words spoken by the Lord in this Gospel.

2. The words, *"Saw them following,"* according to the Greek Text, represents an intense gaze. There was absolutely nothing about this *"gaze"* that was harsh or negative, but rather the very opposite. It was *"august and wonderful."* And yet, it was a *"gaze"* which looked deep inside these two men.

3. At the moment, what their thoughts were concerning Jesus as the Messiah could not have had much depth. Above all, they little knew or understood that the One staring intently at them was the Lord of Glory, the Saviour of all mankind, and the Creator of all things.

4. The question, *"They said unto Him, Rabbi, (which is to say, being interpreted, Master,) where do You dwell?"* was that of far greater import than they could ever begin to realize, at least now.

5. They were speaking of an earthly abode, while the full answer to that question incorporated a dimension that was beyond the comprehension of any mere mortal. His actual dwelling place was the Throne of God, with this excursion on Earth representing the first time in human history that God had come down to dwell with man, at least in this fashion.

6. The manner in which John explained what the title, *"Rabbi,"* meant shows us that this Gospel was written primarily for Gentiles.

(39) "HE SAID UNTO THEM, COME AND SEE. THEY CAME AND SAW WHERE HE DWELT, AND ABODE WITH HIM THAT DAY: FOR IT WAS ABOUT THE TENTH HOUR."

The structure is:

1. The phrase, *"He said unto them, Come and see,"* presents His Answer to their question.

2. Once again, their thoughts would have concerned only the present tense. However, His Invitation was of far greater magnitude. The journey on which they began that day has not stopped even unto this hour. It would catapult them to a dizzying height of glory that they could not even begin to imagine. In fact, the entirety of the Twelve Apostles will have their names inscribed forever in the foundations of New Jerusalem (Rev. 21:14), with Matthias having taken the place of Judas. If that isn't enough, they will sit on thrones, judging the Twelve Tribes of Israel, which will be in the coming Kingdom Age (Lk. 22:30).

3. *"They came and saw where He dwelt,"* represented a place, undoubtedly, not very far from where He was baptized in the river Jordan. It would have been temporary and something very humble. Of that, one can be assured.

4. Understanding this and knowing where He had originally dwelt for a period beyond time, in unimaginable splendor, such love can only be approached with amazement, for it is beyond understanding.

5. *"And abode with Him that day: for it was about the tenth hour,"* has been debated for centuries regarding the time. Normally, the *"tenth hour,"* as Jews reckoned time, would have referred to 4 p.m. However, the evidence seems to conclude that John was not using Jewish time, but rather Roman time. That being the case, it would have been 10 a.m.

6. This seems to be correct in that the Text says that they *"abode with Him that day,"* implying much more than just two or three hours, which would have been the case if John were reckoning by Jewish time.

(40) "ONE OF THE TWO WHICH HEARD JOHN SPEAK, AND FOLLOWED HIM, WAS ANDREW, SIMON PETER'S BROTHER."

The structure is:

1. It is believed that John wrote this Gospel when he was about 90 years old. That being the case, both Andrew and Peter had long since gone to dwell with Jesus permanently. In writing this, how so much the Apostle must have lingered over these phrases, recalling the scene as the Holy Spirit vividly imprinted it upon his mind. No doubt, it had seemed like such a long time ago, and yet, it must have burned in his heart as fresh as if it had happened yesterday. Those who come in contact with Jesus are never the same again. He will take them, if allowed to do so, to such sublime heights that it beggars description.

2. The manner in which *"Andrew"* is addressed, as the brother of *"Simon Peter,"* tells us that Peter's name was now

recognized to a greater degree than any of the other Apostles.

3. Even as I write these words, I sense the Presence of the Lord. Even though Peter had had some hard times, and even some failures, as is glaringly obvious, still, his association with Jesus, and by the Power of the Holy Spirit, would make of him one of the greatest Men of God who ever lived.

4. From every indication, Andrew would have been very proud to have been addressed as *"Simon Peter's brother."* As well, John the Beloved would make this reference without the faintest touch of deprecation. Such was Peter's name now respected.

(41) "HE FIRST FOUND HIS OWN BROTHER SIMON, AND SAID UNTO HIM, WE HAVE FOUND THE MESSIAH, WHICH IS, BEING INTERPRETED, THE CHRIST."

The exposition is:

1. The phrase, *"He first found his own brother Simon,"* presents Andrew first of all looking for his brother, and when finding him, bringing him to Jesus.

2. Some have likened Andrew's efforts as a true sign of one who is newly and truly converted. However, every evidence is that Andrew had long since been a Believer, that is, as the word would have been used at that time.

3. No! Andrew's eagerness was wrapped up more in what he saw in Jesus than anything else.

4. *"And said unto him, We have found the Messiah, which is, being interpreted, the Christ,"* was entirely the cause of Andrew's eagerness and excitement.

5. Evidently, and as the Scripture seems to portray, Andrew and John the Beloved overheard John the Baptist proclaim Jesus as the *"Lamb of God, Who takes away the sin of the world."* That, along with all the other things said by John, and above all, the accompanying Moving of the Holy Spirit, which was, no doubt, present, instantly spoke to these men that Jesus was, in fact, the long-awaited *"Messiah."* That is the reason they followed Jesus, with Him inviting them to His Abode.

6. A Revelation from God, which is what these two experienced, is of such magnitude that one needs no further convincing.

NOTES

7. *"Christ"* means *"Anointed"* and is used as a synonym of the Messiah in the Old Testament. Actually, the word, *"Anointed,"* as it referred to the Messiah, was first used by Hannah (I Sam. 2:10, 35; Ps. 2:2; 45:7; Isa. 61:1; Dan. 9:25-26; Jn. 1:41; 4:25).

(42) "AND HE BROUGHT HIM TO JESUS. AND WHEN JESUS BEHELD HIM, HE SAID, YOU ARE SIMON THE SON OF JONAH: YOU SHALL BE CALLED CEPHAS, WHICH IS BY INTERPRETATION, A STONE."

The synopsis is:

1. Under the Law, an imperfect Priest could only offer imperfect sacrifices (Heb. 9:11-14; 10:1-4).

2. Therefore, both the Covenant on which his Priesthood is based (Heb. 8:6), and the Holy Place in which it is performed (Heb. 9:11), are imperfect.

3. Finally, the net result is imperfect, as would be obvious. Consequently, the old system *"can never . . . make perfect those who draw near"* (Heb. 10:1). Only Jesus can make perfect, which He did by the Means of the Cross (Gal. 6:14).

HE BROUGHT HIM TO JESUS

The phrase, *"And he brought him to Jesus,"* was, no doubt, an exciting moment for both, especially considering that Andrew believed Jesus to be the Messiah, which He was!

It seems, as well, that Peter was there to hear John and may have even been one of his Disciples also. All of this shows a deep hunger in their hearts for the things of God, which, no doubt, occasioned Jesus selecting them, even though humble fisherman, for the highest Spiritual positions on the face of the Earth. They hungered and thirsted for Righteousness, and Righteousness they would find in the Person of Jesus Christ.

WHEN JESUS BEHELD HIM

The phrase, *"And when Jesus beheld him,"* refers to far more than just observation.

The Greek word for *"beheld"* is, *"Emblepo,"* and means, *"To earnestly look."*

However, it also has reference to the Greek word, *"Blepo,"* which means, *"An intent, earnest contemplation."*

So, Jesus was enabled by the Holy Spirit to look into the very soul of Peter, seeing what he was and what He could make of him.

SIMON THE SON OF JONAH

The phrase, *"He said, You are Simon the son of Jonah,"* is used in this manner by Jesus for a particular purpose.

The name, *"Simon,"* means, *"Hearing,"* and means that Peter was named after *"Simeon,"* the second son of Jacob and Leah (Gen. 29:32-33).

In Biblical cultures, a name did more than identify. It communicated something of the essence, the character, or the reputation of the person or thing named.

In Jewish culture, except on rare occasions, the mother had the privilege of naming the newborn child. Whatever the name, it was meant to convey what she wanted the child to be, felt it would be, or because of some situation negative or positive that had happened, or a name received by Revelation from the Lord.

Names were at times changed by the Lord, as He did with *"Abraham,"* which means, *"Father of the multitudes,"* from *"Abram,"* which means, *"Exalted father."*

CEPHAS

The phrase, *"You shall be called Cephas, which is by interpretation, A stone,"* proclaims the ability of Christ to change men fundamentally and characteristically — or rather to recreate men. There is a tremendous lesson here to be learned.

Even though Jesus would give Peter a new name, which proclaims what the Holy Spirit will make of him, as we study the Gospels, we find this is not done easily or quickly. Simon was not to bear this new name until he was deserving of it. Jesus actually never called him anything but Simon (Mat. 17:25; Mk. 14:37; Lk. 22:31; Jn. 21:15-17).

However, Paul called him by the names of Peter and Cephas, proclaiming that the Holy Spirit had done and was doing His Office Work in Peter's life.

Jacob is another example! Through a tremendous Revelation from the Lord, which instigated a struggle, Jacob's name was changed to *"Israel,"* which means, *"Prince or Soldier of God."*

JACOB AND ISRAEL

However, if one is to notice, the Holy Spirit, in referring to Jacob throughout the rest of his life, as is recorded in the remaining Chapters of Genesis, uses both names, *"Jacob"* and *"Israel."* When Jacob's Faith waned and weakened, he would be referred to by his old name. However, when the flesh was weak and the Spirit was strong, he would be addressed as *"Israel."*

As one notices the balance of Jacob's life, it becomes obvious that he is referred to more and more as *"Israel,"* noting that, little by little, the flesh is being subdued, with the Spirit becoming stronger. As stated, this was not done easily or quickly (Gen. 32:24-32).

The name *"Cephas,"* in the Aramaic, means, *"Stone."* In the Greek, it is *"Petros,"* denoting *"a piece of a rock."*

In I Corinthians 10:4, Jesus is referred to as a *"Petra,"* which denotes a *"mass of rock."* Consequently, this destroys the Catholic theory of Peter being the massive rock of Matthew 16:18, on which the Church is built. The *"Rock"* of which Jesus spoke in that Verse speaks of Himself, on which the Church stands, and not Peter.

(43) "THE DAY FOLLOWING JESUS WOULD GO FORTH INTO GALILEE, AND FOUND PHILIP, AND SAID UNTO HIM, FOLLOW ME."

The composition is:

1. The phrase, *"The day following Jesus would go forth into Galilee,"* seems to insinuate that His Journey from the place of His Water Baptism and Wilderness Temptation, the latter which John does not mention, will now commence toward Galilee. Luke said, *"And Jesus returned in the Power of the Spirit into Galilee: and there went out a fame of Him through all the region round about"* (Lk. 4:14).

2. Actually, the far greater majority of the Ministry of Christ was carried out in this region. Isaiah had prophesied some 800 years earlier, *". . . Beyond Jordan, in Galilee of the nations. The people who walked in darkness have seen a great light: they who*

dwell in the land of the shadow of death, upon them has the light shined" (Isa. 9:1-2).

3. *"And found Philip, and said unto him, Follow Me,"* does not exactly tell us where this happened. However, this is some small indication that it was back in Galilee.

4. In the lists of the Apostles in Matthew 10:3; Mark 3:18; and Luke 6:14, Philip is placed fifth in order, with Bartholomew sixth: Acts 1:13 places him fifth but puts Thomas in the sixth place, that is, if that really matters. The only other references to him in the New Testament tell of his inability to suggest to Jesus how to supply the food for the 5,000 (Jn. 6:5), his bringing the Greeks to Jesus (Jn. 12:21), and his request of Jesus to see the Father (Jn. 14:8).

(44) "NOW PHILIP WAS OF BETHSAIDA, THE CITY OF ANDREW AND PETER."

The pattern is:

1. This town was located on the northern shore of the Sea of Galilee, actually, on the east of the Jordan River, which flowed into the lake.

2. It seems, as well, that this had been the home of both Andrew and Peter before moving to Capernaum, about six miles distance.

3. These places became famous only because of Jesus. As stated, this would be where He would carry out most of His Ministry.

(45) "PHILIP FOUND NATHANAEL, AND SAID UNTO HIM, WE HAVE FOUND HIM, OF WHOM MOSES IN THE LAW, AND THE PROPHETS, DID WRITE, JESUS OF NAZARETH, THE SON OF JOSEPH."

The order is:

1. All of the Old Testament system was an imperfect system, which it only could be (Heb. 9:9-10).

2. Therefore, the Old was only a Type (a shadow) of the Real Who was to come, namely Jesus (Heb. 9:23-24; 10:1).

3. Jesus Christ is the New Covenant, and, therefore, this Covenant is perfect and will never need amending, deleting, or changing in any manner (Heb. 13:20).

PHILIP FINDS NATHANAEL

The phrase, *"Philip found Nathanael,"* presents this man who was from Cana of Galilee. *"Nathanael"* is also called *"Bartholomew."*

Philip's action in finding Nathanael, especially that which he said, presents one who has no doubt as to what he has found, namely *"The Messiah."*

WE HAVE FOUND HIM

The phrase, *"And said unto him, We have found Him, of Whom Moses in the Law, and the Prophets, did write,"* proclaims Philip as being a student of the Word. In his mind, which was definitely correct, Jesus met the criterion of the Word of God. If the Bible is not the Anchor and Foundation of all that we believe, then what is?

Sadly, many Christians base what they believe on what someone tells them, or just because that's what their *"church"* believes. When all stand before God, whether the *"Judgment Seat of Christ"* or the *"Great White Throne Judgment,"* it will not really matter what other people said, but what the Word of God proclaims. That and that alone will be the basis of Judgment.

JESUS OF NAZARETH, THE SON OF JOSEPH

The phrase, *"Jesus of Nazareth, the Son of Joseph,"* actually says several things:

"Jesus of Nazareth": as we shall see, Nazareth was not exactly a place held in high repute by much of Israel.

Nazareth lay very close to several main trade routes for easy contact with the outside world, which brought frowns from much of the religious hierarchy of Israel. As well, it is thought that a Roman garrison was located nearby, which further sullied the place, at least in the thinking of most Jews.

So, from this, we learn that the Holy Spirit chose this town where Jesus would be raised and would live a little longer than 30 years. From this and many other things, it is easy to see that the Holy Spirit did absolutely nothing which would make Jesus look good in any capacity of the flesh.

A PEASANT

First of all, Jesus was a Peasant, which placed Him on the lowest possible rung of the social scene. It must be understood that there was no middle class in the Israel of Jesus' Day. There were only the obscene rich and the abject poor. Christ fell into the latter.

Secondly, Jesus lived with a stigma of His Virgin Birth all of His Life when, in fact, His Birth was the only truly legitimate Birth that ever was.

Thirdly, He did not have the approval whatsoever of any of the religious hierarchy of Israel. Actually, they opposed him greatly and ultimately crucified Him.

So, as Isaiah prophesied, *"When we shall see Him, there is no beauty that we should desire Him"* (Isa. 53:2).

SON OF JOSEPH?

Jesus really was not the son of Joseph, due to the Virgin Birth, but was referred to in that manner for the obvious reasons. Joseph, in fact, was His Foster Father, while Jesus was Joseph's Foster Son, one might say.

Nevertheless, Jesus bore this stigma of His Birth all His Life. Due to the Fall, all other babies, with none excluded, were and are born in sin. However, due to Jesus having no earthly father, for it's the father through whom the seed passes, He was born without sin.

Despite what people saw concerning His Circumstances, which, within themselves, contained no wrong or wrongdoing, He fit the Prophecies of the Word of God in totality, which is the only criterion that really matters.

(46) "AND NATHANAEL SAID UNTO HIM, CAN THERE ANY GOOD THING COME OUT OF NAZARETH? PHILIP SAID UNTO HIM, COME AND SEE."

The form is:

1. Christ is the ultimate Priest because by His Death, He ratified a New Covenant (Heb. 9:15-22), toward which the Old Testament itself had looked (Heb. 8:8-13).

2. Moreover, God had promised that the Messianic King would also be *"a Priest forever after the order of Melchizedek"* (Ps. 110:4). Such a promise indicates the imperfection of the Old Aaronic Order (Heb. 7:11-14).

3. It is Jesus Alone Who perfectly *"fulfills"* this Promise.

NOTES

NAZARETH

The question, *"And Nathanael said unto him, Can there any good thing come out of Nazareth?"* seems to smack of sarcasm; however, I think we will see that such was not the intention of Nathanael. So, what was he thinking at this time?

It seems that Philip's claim concerning Jesus startled Nathanael, especially considering that he referred to Him as the long-awaited Messiah. As well, Philip sounds so sure but seemingly without the investigation that Nathanael demands. What he does not realize is that the Presence of Christ, which he will soon experience just as Philip, will answer all questions, even those the most inquisitive soul may have, at least if it is honest.

As well, his denigrating question concerning *"Nazareth"* may have well referred to its lack of fame and something which seemed to have been of a personal nature with Nathanael, whatever that may have been.

In fact, the entire district of Galilee was looked at with disdain by Jerusalem as being of somewhat an unsophisticated area. However, that would have mattered little to Nathanael, considering that he, as well, was from Cana, also of Galilee.

Places carried much weight with the Jews of Jesus' Time. Each famous place was linked with a great Biblical happening or person, which gave it fame. As an example, although small, Beth-lehem was famous because it was the birthplace of David, the greatest king of Israel. Ramah was the birthplace of Samuel. Shiloh was where the Tabernacle once stood. However, *"Nazareth"* is not even mentioned in the Old Testament, much less as being a place of some prominence. Nathanael, aware of this, would have been startled by the possibility of a carpenter's Son, in a spot utterly undistinguished, being the Messiah of Whom their sacred writers spoke.

COME AND SEE

The phrase, *"Philip said unto him, Come and see,"* proclaims within itself the basic thrust of Christianity.

While Preachers of the Gospel, and all

Believers for that matter, do our best to extol His Greatness and Glory, still, until one actually comes to see for himself, thereby, accepting the Lord as Saviour and Redeemer, he cannot know Who Jesus really is. In fact, probably one could explain the Gospel by the following term better than anything else.

"Who Jesus is, the Son of the Living God, God manifest in the flesh, actually the Word made flesh, and what Jesus did, which refers to the Cross of Christ, which satisfied the demands of the broken Law in every capacity, and which, by the giving of Himself in Sacrifice, atoned for all sin, past, present, and future, at least for all who will believe, and, thereby, defeated Satan, all fallen Angels, and every demon spirit," proclaims, I think, the Gospel more so than anything else which could be said (Col. 2:10-15; Rom. 6:1-14; 8:1-11; I Cor. 1:17, 18, 23; 2:2; Gal. 6:14).

As stated, for one to truly know, there must be a Revelation of Christ to the soul, which can only be done by the Holy Spirit. While men are capable of telling about Jesus, and can even be anointed by the Holy Spirit to do so, that within itself, although awakening the need in the heart of the unbeliever, only seeks to open the door, which now must be entered. If men will *"Come and see,"* it will be shown them.

(47) "JESUS SAW NATHANAEL COMING TO HIM, AND SAID OF HIM, BEHOLD AN ISRAELITE INDEED, IN WHOM IS NO GUILE!"

The diagram is:

1. Melchizedek appeared and disappeared in the Old Testament without *"beginning of days nor end of life,"* simply meaning that it wasn't recorded, thus prefiguring the Eternal Son of God (Heb. 7:3).

2. Jesus is a Priest *"forever"* in contrast to the Aaronic Priests, who *"were prevented by death from continuing in office"* (Heb. 7:23).

3. This is Paul's main interest in Jesus' Humanity. Other Priests could not continue because of sin, but Jesus, though *"made like His Brethren in every respect,"* was sinless. Therefore, He is the Perfect and Eternal High Priest (Heb. 2:17; 4:15; 5:7-10; 7:23-28; 9:14).

NOTES

JESUS AND NATHANAEL

The phrase, *"Jesus saw Nathanael coming to Him,"* speaks of a Faith that is feeble and intelligence which is defective, and yet, the Reception of Jesus in any capacity is the reception of all that He is.

This is a fact of the greatest interest and consolation. At the dawn of the Christian Life, He may be believed upon as a Saviour that forgives sin and delivers from the wrath to come. However, in response to that limited Faith, He gives Himself to the Believer in all His Plentitude as God and Saviour.

TWO GREAT PRINCIPLES, FIRST THE CENTER

There is but one Center of gathering in the world — Christ. No Prophet or Servant of God could claim, or ever did claim, to be such. Christ is the One Divine Center around which His People gather.

He accepted this place. The world was under sentence of death and without God. The Election was to be taken out of it and gathered around Him Who was the Object of God's Perfect Affection.

THE PATH

Next, He pointed out the Path in which the Redeemed were to walk — *"Follow Me."* Man needed no path in Eden, for all was innocence, but in a world of sin, there can be no rest or certain path, so Christ gives a Divinely-ordered Path out of it. In Heaven, there will be no path because one is not needed. It will be a realm of perfect peace and rest because there will be no sin there. So, as Nathanael went to Jesus, he was going to the only Light in the world and, in fact, ever has been, i.e., *"Center and Path."*

WITHOUT GUILE

The phrase, *"And said of him, Behold an Israelite indeed, in whom is no guile!"* does not say that Jesus said such to him, but *"of"* him, which is vastly different. However, Nathanael overheard the statement, as did the others.

Jesus did not say that this man was sinless, but *"guileless,"* which means, *"To be without deceit."* It speaks of one who is full and free in his confession, knowing himself, and sheltering himself under no devices or seeming shows.

The Publican was without guile when he cried, *"God be merciful to me a sinner!"* (Lk. 18:13). The Pharisee was steeped in self-deception and guile when he said, *"God, I thank You, that I am not as other men"* (Lk. 18:11).

Concerning Nathanael, sincerity, openness of eye, simplicity of speech, and no wish to appear other than what he is before God and man, affirms his guilelessness.

As well, Jesus calling him an *"Israelite indeed"* is an accolade of the highest order, for it means, *"Friend with God."*

(48) "NATHANAEL SAID UNTO HIM, FROM WHERE DO YOU KNOW ME? JESUS ANSWERED AND SAID UNTO HIM, BEFORE THAT PHILIP CALLED YOU, WHEN YOU WERE UNDER THE FIG TREE, I SAW YOU."

The exegesis is:

1. The question, *"Nathanael said unto Him, From where do You know me?"* proclaims this potential Disciple as being startled.

2. *"Jesus answered and said unto him, Before that Philip called you, when you were under the fig tree, I saw you,"* proclaims immediately the proof of what Philip had said.

3. Many people think that Jesus did these things because He was God, which He certainly was. However, all things of this nature, plus Healings and Miracles, even as grand as they were, were not done by Jesus as God but as a Man filled with the Holy Spirit. In looking at this as one of the Gifts of the Spirit as outlined in I Corinthians 12:8-10, this would have been the Word of Knowledge.

4. All of the Gifts of the Spirit naturally worked in the Life and Ministry of Jesus, with the exception of Tongues and Interpretation of Tongues, which had not yet been given (Jn. 7:39).

5. These Gifts, as outlined in the Word of God, are meant to be a part of the Body of Christ, and operative in Spirit-filled Believers. Even though no Believer can even remotely rise to the status of Christ, still, mighty things are meant to be done through the Body in the Name of Jesus and by the Power and Person of the Holy Spirit. Jesus Himself said, *"Verily, verily, I say unto you, He who believes on Me, the Works that I do shall he do also; and greater Works than these shall he do; because I go unto My Father"* (Jn. 14:12).

6. Actually, the Body of Christ is meant to be filled with the Spirit that it may continue *"all that Jesus began both to do and teach"* (Acts 1:1).

7. The need in the modern church is the Supernatural Power of God. However, this comes only through the Person and Agency of the Holy Spirit, which most of the modern church little has and little believes. Consequently, even though there is much religious machinery, very little is actually done for the Lord.

(49) "NATHANAEL ANSWERED AND SAID UNTO HIM, RABBI, YOU ARE THE SON OF GOD; YOU ARE THE KING OF ISRAEL."

The exegesis is:

1. The phrase, *"Nathanael answered and said unto Him,"* proclaims an answer which is the result of Revelation. Again and again, it must be emphasized that God cannot be learned, or even approached by the intellect or education, but only by Faith. Only then will the Lord reveal Himself. As Philip, Nathanael, in a moment's time, comes to Faith.

2. *"Rabbi, You are the Son of God; You are the King of Israel,"* presents the great confession of Nathanael. Jesus is not *"A Son of God"* but *"The Son of God."*

3. Luthard said, *"Nathanael's Faith will never possess more than it embraces at this moment."*[10]

4. Godet adds, *"The gold-seeker puts his hand on an ingot; when he has coined it, he has it better, but not more."*[11]

5. The idea of Divine Sonship comes from the Old Testament Prophecies, which have their roots in Psalms 2 and 72.

6. As well, the Divine Sonship is the basis on which Nathanael rears his further Faith that He is the *"King of Israel."* He is the Messiah-King because He is *"The Son of God."* Consequently, the true Israelite recognizes his King (Mat. 2:2; 12:23; Lk. 1:32).

7. When Nathanael looked upon Jesus, he saw God. When the Pharisees looked upon Jesus, they saw nothing! Such is the world!

8. A few see Him as He really is, while most, as the Pharisees, see everything, but yet, nothing.

(50) "JESUS ANSWERED AND SAID UNTO HIM, BECAUSE I SAID UNTO YOU, I SAW YOU UNDER THE FIG TREE, DO YOU BELIEVE? YOU SHALL SEE GREATER THINGS THAN THESE."

The exposition is:

1. The question, *"Jesus answered and said unto him, Because I said unto you, I saw you under the fig tree, do you believe?"* is meant to be answered in the affirmative.

2. *"You shall see greater things than these,"* tells us that Faith begets Faith. If the Lord is believed, greater things are then given. To the contrary, the Pharisees would not believe, and even what little they had was lost!

3. One is here observing the ingredient of Faith in God. More automatically brings more while less automatically brings less. *"Believing"* brings *"greater things."*

4. If this lesson, which Jesus taught Nathanael on that day of so long ago, can be learned by even the weakest Believer, there is no limit to what can be done in God. Even as I dictate these words, I sense the Presence of the Lord! To believe is to receive! To doubt is to fail!

5. For a truth, Nathanael did see *"greater things."* He had the privilege of seeing the greatest Miracles, as performed by Jesus, as the world had never seen. To be sure, in the world to come, it shall continue unabated.

(51) "AND HE SAID UNTO HIM, VERILY, VERILY, I SAY UNTO YOU, HEREAFTER YOU SHALL SEE HEAVEN OPEN, AND THE ANGELS OF GOD ASCENDING AND DESCENDING UPON THE SON OF MAN."

The exposition is:

1. The phrase, *"And He said unto him, Verily, verily, I say unto you,"* occurs some 25 times in John's Gospel. This particular form is peculiar to this Gospel, although used in an abbreviated manner in the others.

In its purest form, it means, *"Truth, Truth!"*

2. The phrase, *"Hereafter you shall see Heaven open,"* has to do with Jacob's dream (Gen. 28:11-13) and it being fulfilled in Jesus, as it could only be fulfilled in Jesus. He Alone could open Heaven because He Alone is the Way to God. There is no other!

3. Not only did He open Heaven, but it remains open unto this moment, and will remain so forever, all because of what He did at Calvary.

4. Even though these words are little understood, this which Jesus said is one of the singular, most important things that has ever happened to the human family. Heretofore, Heaven had been closed because of man's terrible sin. However, as someone said:

"Jesus opened up the Way,
"The Way to Heaven's Gate."

5. *"And the Angels of God ascending and descending upon the Son of Man,"* is that which constantly happened while Jesus was on Earth.

6. Angels ministered unto Him during the temptation in the wilderness (Mat. 4:11), and again during the Passion in Gethsemane (Lk. 22:43). At the Resurrection, Angels were at the Tomb (Lk. 24:4) and, no doubt, were present all through the Ministry of Jesus, although unseen. Actually, Jesus told Peter at the time of His Arrest that if desired, He could pray to the Father and be given *"Twelve Legions of Angels"* (about 72,000) (Mat. 26:53).

7. Even though Jesus used the phrase, *"Son of Man,"* concerning Himself a number of times, He was never addressed by the Apostles in this fashion.

8. Also, Jesus told Nathanael that he would see *"Heaven open,"* but He did not necessarily say that he would see the Angels, with them invisible most of the time, or else, appearing when the Apostles were not present.

"Amazing Grace how sweet the sound,
"That saved a wretch like me,
"I once was lost, but now am found,
"Was blind, but now I see."

CHAPTER 2

(1) "AND THE THIRD DAY THERE WAS

A MARRIAGE IN CANA OF GALILEE; AND THE MOTHER OF JESUS WAS THERE."

The diagram is:

1. The phrase, *"And the third day,"* speaks of the amount of time which had lapsed since Jesus left the Wilderness of Temptation to begin His public Ministry. However, as stated, His Ministry began with the incoming of the Holy Spirit upon His Person, which took place when He was baptized of John in the Jordan. This could have been approximately 43 days earlier.

2. The phrase, *"There was a marriage in Cana of Galilee,"* occasions the site of His very first Miracle.

3. On this day, the poor water of man's efforts will be changed into the rich wine of God's Provision. This tells us that the Millennial Kingdom will be the Father's House of Wine, and the joy of that house will be the joy and love of an eternal marriage feast (Williams).[1]

4. In that day, Cana was a small town, probably about the size of Nazareth, and was situated about seven miles north of that city. It was called Cana of Galilee to distinguish it from Cana of Ashur.

5. *"And the mother of Jesus was there,"* indicates that she was already there and maybe had been for several hours, or even a day or two, before Jesus came with His Disciples. Marriage feasts in those days lasted a week or more.

(2) "AND BOTH JESUS WAS CALLED, AND HIS DISCIPLES, TO THE MARRIAGE."

The overview is:

1. There is some indication in the Greek tense that Jesus and His Disciples were invited at the last moment. At any rate, to be invited to such a feast and not attend was an insult to the host.

2. Religion and asceticism, which refers to the practicing of strict self-denial as a measure of personal spiritual discipline, are often associated in the carnal mind.

3. Such has been popular down through the centuries, and has even been an earmark of particular religious denominations in the not too distant past. However, we see that Jesus had no sympathy with isolation, unsocialbleness, or austerity. It must ever be remembered that the Biblical demand for separation from the world is not isolation from the world.

4. Actually, Jesus frequented all kinds of human society. He dined with Pharisees and with Publicans, with these two being a world apart, with an impartial sociability. He does not seem to have refused many invitations, if any, to partake of hospitality, from whatever quarter it might come. Actually, it was a complaint brought against Him by the formalists, that He was *"gluttonous, a winebibber, and a friend of Publicans and sinners."* This was grossly untrue, but it points to a truth, that our Lord had no aversion to social gatherings.

(3) "AND WHEN THEY WANTED WINE, THE MOTHER OF JESUS SAID UNTO HIM, THEY HAVE NO WINE."

The structure is:

1. Melchizedek appeared and disappeared in the Old Testament without *"beginning of days, nor end of life,"* simply meaning that it wasn't recorded, thus prefiguring the Eternal Son of God (Heb. 7:3).

2. The clearest evidence that the blood of bulls and goats was inadequate was that such offerings had to be continually repeated (Heb. 10:1-4).

3. By offering Himself, Jesus offered a Perfect Sacrifice *"once for all,"* one that need not be repeated (Heb. 9:23-28).

WAS THE WINE OF THIS MIRACLE ALCOHOLIC WINE?

The phrase, *"And when they wanted wine,"* means they had run out of wine.

This illustration, as given by John the Beloved, has been debated, I suppose, since it was written, as to whether this was grape juice or alcoholic wine.

I believe it was grape juice, and I will explain why:

If this wine is understood to be intoxicating wine, our Lord is automatically placed in the position of providing men, who had already *"well drunk"* (Jn. 2:10), with more wine. If it was alcoholic wine, the Lord then would have been breaking His Own Law against temperance.

The total amount of water turned to wine was approximately 150 gallons. If this had been an intoxicating beverage, it would have served as an invitation to drink. It would have placed our Lord in the unsavory position of providing a flood of intoxicants for the people who had already consumed a considerable amount, as is obvious.

GOOD WINE

The word, *"Good,"* was used to describe what the Lord had miraculously brought about (Jn. 2:10).

The word, *"Good,"* in the Greek Text is *"kalos,"* and is defined in *"Vine's Expository Dictionary of New Testament Words"* as denoting what is *"intrinsically good."*[2] Now, the pure, sweet juice of the grape could rightly be denoted as *"intrinsically good,"* but the rotted, fermented, decayed, spoiled, and intoxicating kind of wine could hardly be called *"good."* It is easy to think of the term, *"Good,"* in describing whatever the Lord makes. For example, in describing the Creation, Moses said, *"And God saw everything that He had made, and, behold, it was very good"* (Gen. 1:31).

It is unthinkable that our Lord would have made corrupted, fermented wine at Cana, the kind which would make one drunk, and call it *"good."*

Fermentation, which is a part of the alcohol process, is a kind of decomposition, just as is putrefaction and decay. It would be almost blasphemous to call that *"good"* in connection with Jesus.

Pliny, an ancient Greek scholar said that *"good wine"* was a term used to denote the Jews destitute of spirit.

Albert Barnes says, *"The wine referred to here was doubtless such as was commonly drunk in the Israel of that day."*[3] That was the pure juice of the grape. It was not branded or drugged wine, and neither was it wine compounded of various substances, such as people drink presently. The common wine of that day which was drunk in Israel was the simple juice of the grape.

WINE IN BIBLICAL TIMES

There are several words in the Bible that describe wine. However, in the New Testament, the Greek word, *"Oinos,"* is used more frequently and can mean either fermented or unfermented wine.

NOTES

Dr. Ferrar Fenton, a Biblical translator (The Holy Bible in Modern English), lists six different meanings for the word, *"Oinos,"* as used in the Greek New Testament. They are:
1. Grapes, as fresh fruit
2. Raisins
3. Thick grape syrup
4. A thick jam
5. Fresh grape juice
6. Fermented grape juice. The last type will make one drunk.

Dr. Lyman Abbott said that fermented wine in Bible times was the least common of all wines. Even in the fermented kind, the percentage of alcohol was small.

In the Old Testament, the Hebrew word most used for wine is *"yayin."* That word is found about 141 times in the Old Testament and is used interchangeably, depending on the context.

More importantly, it is unthinkable that Jesus would have broken His Own Word:

He said, *"Wine is a mocker, strong drink is raging: and whosoever is deceived thereby is not wise . . . Who has woe? who has sorrow? who has contentions? who has babbling? who has wounds without cause? who has redness of eyes?*

"They who tarry long at the wine; they who go to seek mixed wine.

"You must not look upon the wine when it is red, when it gives his color in the cup, when it moves itself aright.

"At the last it bites like a serpent, and stings like an adder" (Prov. 20:1; 23:29-32).

THE FIRST MIRACLE OF JESUS

I think it would be tantamount to blasphemy to suppose that the first Miracle that Christ performed after being filled with the Holy Spirit (Mk. 1:9-12; Lk. 4:1) was an act of creating intoxicating wine for a crowd of celebrants, the kind of wine that would make them drunk. Such is unthinkable!

Another fact from the record in John, Chapter 2, is this:

Those men, who had already drunk a considerable amount, praised the bridegroom for having kept the *"good wine"* until the last.

It is a simple fact that alcohol drunk to any excess will deaden the taste buds of the drinker. If the wine in Cana of Galilee, of which the guests had already been partaking, was intoxicating wine (they had already partaken of quite a bit at this point), then when the wine that Jesus had miraculously made was given to them, they could not have detected its taste. Their taste buds would have been deadened.

To be honest, they would have been drunk by this time, or almost so. Only if they had been drinking the form of the vine's fruit that we know as *"grape juice,"* and then had been provided some fresh grape juice, would the governor of the feast been able to make the observation that he did.

SUFFICIENT PROOF

I think the reasons given, both from practicality and from the Word of God, are sufficient proof that Jesus did not change water to the kind of wine that would make one drunk. Instead, it was a sweet, pure grape juice.

The Word of God, not social mores, culture, or conventional wisdom, is always to be the criterion for what we believe. Also, proper interpretation of the Word of God is to compare Scripture with Scripture. If it is *"rightly divided,"* there will be no contradiction, with the meaning being plainly clear throughout the entirety of the Text.

Looking at the entirety of the teaching of the Bible concerning *"strong drink,"* I think it is obvious that the Holy Spirit is saying (and He is the Author of the Bible) that this water Jesus miraculously changed did not become intoxicating beverage, but rather, as stated, sweet, pure grape juice.

BEFORE PROHIBITION

Before prohibition, *"wine"* was considered to be exactly as it was in Bible times. At that time, it could be referred to as grape juice or intoxicating beverage. However, when prohibition was enacted in 1929, the term had to be defined more closely. Consequently, *"wine"* was designated to mean something that will make one drunk.

The other kind of non-intoxicating beverage was called by whatever name desired, grape juice or whatever. Consequently, many people today confuse the simple word,

NOTES

"Wine," as it was used in the Bible, with our present understanding of that word. However, that is wrong!

Again, let us say, we believe Jesus' First Miracle was not the making of wine that would make one drunk, but rather pure, sweet, fresh grape juice. I believe that Scripturally, scientifically, and legally we have proven that.

The phrase, *"The mother of Jesus said unto Him, They have no wine,"* presents the Passage used by many to support their erroneous doctrine of the value of the intercession of Mary the Mother of Jesus. However, the facts here recorded destroy that doctrine.

WAS THE INTERCESSION OF MARY HELPFUL?

It is somewhat evident from Verse 5 that the servants had engaged Mary to intercede for them with Jesus. She did so and was met with a rebuke, *"What have I to do with you?"*

This formula occurs some eight times in the Scriptures (II Sam. 16:10; 19:22; I Ki. 17:18; II Ki. 3:13; Mat. 8:29; Mk. 1:24; Lk. 4:34; and Jn. 2:4). An examination of these Passages proves that the answer is, *"Nothing."*

THE CONTRAST BETWEEN THE CARNAL NATURE AND THE HOLY SPIRIT

In every instance of the Word of God, at least concerning this conflict, the contrast is between the carnal nature, which is sinful, and the Holy Spirit. The Spiritual Kingdom has no contact with the carnal. There is an impassable abyss between them. There could, therefore, be no union between the Sinless Nature of Christ and the sinful nature of Mary, at least in this context.

Neither could He admit her authority. This is declared in the words, *"My hour is not yet come,"* that is, *"The moment for Me to act will be revealed by My Father, and His Voice is the only One to which I hearken."*

MARY, BY HER OWN ACTION DISPROVES THE CATHOLIC DOCTRINES

With great intelligence, Mary recognized her error and stepped at once aside from between these needy people and the Almighty Giver of every good and perfect gift, telling the servants to turn from her to Him. When she was out of the way, He spoke directly to the men in charge, and in a moment, the water was wine! So long as she stood between Jesus and these needy sinners, there was no wine!

MARY AND ISRAEL

Mary here represents Israel. The Messiah was born of that Nation, but because of unbelief, Israel became, in the words of Hosea, *"Lo-ammi,"* hence, He refused to recognize her (Hos. 1:9). However, in John 19:26, He committed Israel, as again represented by His Mother, to the Apostles, as personated by John, who represents the Church. As John was to care for Mary, likewise, the Church is to stand behind Israel, at least whenever and wherever possible.

At the Second Coming, Israel will no longer be *"Lo-ammi,"* which means, *"You are not My People, and I will not be your God,"* but rather, *"Ammi,"* which means, *"You are My People, and I am your God."* Then Israel will be recognized by Jesus as His Mother.

It was when Mary looked upon Him as pierced that she fully believed, and in this, she symbolizes the Nation when it will look upon Him as pierced and will repent (Zech. 13:6).

LEARN THE LESSON?

Whether these people that day at the marriage feast of Cana learned the lesson permanently, that the Lord Jesus is to be appealed to directly and not through an intermediary, is more than doubtful, for to this day, man has not learned it. And so, millions pray to Mary, although she is dead (Williams).[4]

Even when she was alive, the thief on the Cross, coming down to his last dying moments, ignored her, even though she was only a few yards away, and turned rather to Jesus directly (Lk. 23:39-43).

He was rewarded with Paradise but would have received nothing had he appealed to Mary, which is exactly what all receive who appeal to her.

This is not meant to denigrate Mary in any capacity, but rather to set the Biblical Doctrine straight.

(4) "JESUS SAID UNTO HER, WOMAN, WHAT HAVE I TO DO WITH YOU? MY HOUR IS NOT YET COME."

The overview is:

1. Desperation generally always precedes Revelation, of which the Seventh Chapter of Romans is an excellent example.

2. The modern church is in a terrible spiritual condition primarily because it has strayed from the Foundation of the Cross of Christ.

3. Regrettably, the church anymore little preaches the Cross, but rather preaches psychology.

WHAT DID JESUS SAY?

The phrase, *"Jesus said unto her,"* constitutes the answer to which the Catholic church should take heed.

It's not what the church says that matters, but rather what the Lord says. Men are not going to be judged by God according to their church, or whatever, only according to the Word of God. The great question should always be, *"Is it Scriptural?"*

When men stray from the Bible, then whatever it is they are preaching is constituted as no more than religion.

Religion is that which is conceived by man and, thereby, devised by man, which claims to reach God or to better oneself in some way. It is not of God and, in fact, has never been of God. Anything that is sanctioned by the Lord must be conceived by the Lord, given birth by the Lord, instituted by the Lord, and proclaimed by the Lord. In other words, it's all of God and none of man.

It is very difficult for man to understand, even redeemed man, that he cannot produce anything within himself that God can accept. It is the hardest for redeemed man to admit this and, thereby, look to the Lord for Leading. In fact, this is the reason for all the trouble in the church and among Christians. We try to devise our own religious methods, and it is always that which God cannot accept. Go to His Word, see what He says about the matter, and then follow His Word. Then, one will find Victory.

WOMAN, WHAT HAVE I TO DO WITH YOU?

The question, *"Woman, what have I to do with you?"* does not pose a question of disrespect, nor is it meant to do so. *"Woman,"* as then used, was basically the same as our present use of *"madam"* (Mat. 15:28; Jn. 4:21; 19:26; 20:15).

However, while there is no disrespect, there is definitely a line drawn as to Whom He obeys, and it is not her, but rather His Heavenly Father (Jn. 5:19-20).

The language implies that the period of subjection to Joseph and Mary was now at an end. He is now *"The Servant of Jehovah,"* and His Work as the Messiah has at last begun. Once again, the answer, as given by Jesus, completely destroys the Roman Catholic myth of Mary as mediator between Christ and man.

In truth, the Believer is not really supposed to even pray to Jesus, but rather to the Heavenly Father, and do so by the Name of Jesus. By using the Name of Jesus in this respect, our petition will be granted by our Father in Heaven (Jn. 16:23-24). In fact and truth, Jesus is the Mediator and Intercessor to the Heavenly Father on our behalf (Jn. 16:26; I Tim. 2:5).

MY HOUR IS NOT YET COME

The phrase, *"My hour is not yet come,"* refers to when and what He will do according to directions from His Father. Only God gave Him directions, and only from God His Father did He take direction.

If one is to notice, throughout the four Gospels, with some few exceptions, about everything said to Him by other men and women was contrary to the Will of God. Regrettably, that ratio still holds!

Jesus came to do the Will of the Father, which is evident in everything He did, and is proclaimed strongly even at the outset of His Ministry. That must be the criterion of the Believer as well!

However, the *"hour"* of which He specifically speaks here is that which pertains to the very reason for which God became Man, the reason for His Coming, which is the Cross. Everything led up to the Cross! Everything pointed to the Cross! In fact,

NOTES

Peter rebuked Christ when Jesus said that *"He must go unto Jerusalem, and suffer many things of the Elders and Chief Priests and Scribes, and be killed, and be raised again the third day."*

Peter said to Him, *"Be it far from You, Lord: this shall not be unto You."*

Jesus turned and said unto Peter:

"You get behind Me, Satan: you are an offense unto Me: for you savor not the things that be of God, but those that be of men" (Mat. 16:21-23).

The Cross was so very, very important that anything that would seek to deter Him from the Cross, even one of His Most Trusted Disciples, Simon Peter, would be rebuked in the sternest of terms.

In fact, this Miracle of Cana, His turning the water to wine, would be His Very First. There were many, many Miracles, even to the raising of the dead. However, every Miracle led to one thing, and that was what He would do to redeem the fallen sons of Adam's lost race. We continue to speak of the Cross.

(5) "HIS MOTHER SAID UNTO THE SERVANTS, WHATSOEVER HE SAYS UNTO YOU, DO IT."

The composition is:

1. On top of the Ark of the Covenant in the Holy of Holies of both the Tabernacle and the Temple sat the *"Mercy Seat."* Thank God that it was not the Judgment Seat.

2. Before the Cross, God dwelt between the Mercy Seat and the Cherubim in the Holy of Holies. Since the Cross, He can now abide permanently within the heart and life of each and every Believer, which He does (Jn. 14:16-17).

3. Abel's lamb redeemed one man; the Paschal Lamb, one family; the Day of Atonement Lamb, one Nation; and the Lamb of Calvary, the whole world (Jn. 1:29).

THE MOTHER OF CHRIST

The phrase, *"His Mother said unto the servants,"* may imply, as thought by some, that Mary had something to do with the responsibilities of this marriage feast, hence, her coming to Jesus. In other words, she had helped to organize it. However, that is only speculation!

Our Catholic friends derive from this their praying to Mary, hence, the little bumper sticker, *"Cannot find Jesus, try His Mother!"* Now, if we are to go to God through Mary, then it seems strange that the words, *"Whatsoever He says unto you, do it,"* would be her last recorded words.

No! Praying to Mary is grossly unscriptural.

When she made the statement, *"Whatsoever He says unto you, do it,"* she promptly stepped aside, in effect, telling the servants to turn from her to Him.

When leaving the error of the Catholic church, regarding Mary, the Gospels tell us very little about her. It seems that she never really identified herself with Jesus and His Disciples until Acts 1:14. Especially considering that Jesus' Half-brothers were opposed to Him, at least during His Earthly Ministry (Jn. 7:5), this placed Mary in a very awkward position. However, is it not possible that everyone is placed in an awkward position regarding Christ?

And yet, the advice she gave to the servants concerning the obeying of Jesus was exactly that which should have been. In effect, she was saying that they should not try to understand His Commands, at least, should He give any, but just do what He said!

(6) "AND THERE WERE SET THERE SIX WATERPOTS OF STONE, AFTER THE MANNER OF THE PURIFYING OF THE JEWS, CONTAINING TWO OR THREE FIRKINS APIECE."

The composition is:
1. The six waterpots of stone.
2. The purifying of the Jews.
3. The limit of these waterpots.

SIX WATERPOTS OF STONE

The phrase, *"And there were set there six waterpots of stone,"* represents Jesus using these vessels for a purpose.

First of all, the number, *"Six,"* represents the number of man, which always falls short of perfection, with perfection represented by the number, *"Seven,"* called, *"God's Number."*

As well, the material of *"stone"* represented the Law (Ex. 34:1).

It is very hard for man to realize that no matter what he does, he cannot produce anything that God can use. Even the godliest among us proves oneself to be woefully inadequate in this regard. That's the problem of the church and, in fact, always has been. It keeps producing man-devised plans, which never work. If it is to be used of God, the following must be done:

The Holy Spirit must conceive the idea, whatever it is, must give birth to the effort, must empower the effort, and must guide and direct. Only then can the Lord use man as man functions in the capacity of a willing instrument.

Religious man is ever coming up with schemes and efforts, all to no avail. Take Abraham for example. This man was one of the godliest who ever lived. He and Sarah were to bring a little boy into this world, and, of course, Sarah, as the Bible student knows, was barren. So, seeing time slip away, Sarah and Abraham concocted a scheme that they thought would solve the problem. The Egyptian girl, Hagar, would serve as a surrogate, and the child born would serve the purpose, or so they thought. Ishmael was the result, and the world is paying for that mistake even unto this hour.

God could not accept Ishmael, and to be frank, before the Lord could use Abraham and Sarah to bring Isaac into the world, all hope of the flesh had to die. In other words, Abraham and Sarah had to exhaust their personal efforts before the Lord could take control and bring it all to pass, which He ultimately did.

Man was created on the sixth day, so the number, *"Six,"* is man's number, but always falls short of the number, *"Seven,"* which is God's Number.

THE PURIFYING OF THE JEWS

The phrase, *"After the manner of the purifying of the Jews,"* had to do mostly with oral laws, which were not originally given by God and, therefore, man-devised. There were many washings of the *"hands, cups, brazen vessels, and tables"* (Mat. 15:2). Sadly, all of this ritual actually purified nothing! And so it is for man's personal efforts to gain Righteousness. The only thing he succeeds in doing is to produce self-righteousness. That's the problem with the modern church, and to be factual, that's the problem with every one of us. We try to do, by our own ingenuity, religious ability, and personal efforts, what only the Holy Spirit can do. It's difficult for man, as stated, even godly men, to come to the understanding that we cannot do anything that God can accept. This is where the modern church goes wrong. It tries to bring up something that will take the place of the Cross. It claims to believe in the Cross, but yet, it ignores what the Cross did and keeps trying to insert its own plans and schemes.

And then, on the other hand, before the Lord can finally use us, whomever we may be, all hope of the flesh, as we have previously stated, must die. That means we have to come to the end of ourselves, realizing that what's got to be done, we simply cannot do it. It's not that some of us can do it and others cannot, but it's that none of us can do it. What we have to have is the Work of the Holy Spirit alone, and He works exclusively within the parameters of the Finished Work of Christ, i.e., *"the Cross."* So, this means that our Faith must be exclusively in Christ, which means we've come to the end of ourselves. Jesus said so (Lk. 9:23).

MORE IS BETTER?

The phrase, *"Containing two or three firkins apiece,"* referred to approximately 20 gallons each. Consequently, these waterpots were quite large.

When man begins to devise religion, he ultimately thinks that more is better. That's the reason that in some churches, rules abound!

So, this Miracle will portray the difference in man's religion and Christ's Redemption! Even the Law of Moses, as given to Moses by God, could not save. Actually, it could only curse, for there was no Salvation in its command (Salvation came by trusting in Who and What the sacrifices represented, namely, Jesus and what He would do at the Cross of Calvary).

So, if the true Law of Moses, which was given by God, could not save, and it couldn't, where did that leave these little, insignificant, man-devised, religious laws, symbolized by these waterpots?

NOTES

That's a good question!

(7) *"JESUS SAID UNTO THEM, FILL THE WATERPOTS WITH WATER. AND THEY FILLED THEM UP TO THE BRIM."*

The exegesis is:

1. The Word of the Lord.

2. They did all they could do, which was provide the water.

3. Thankfully, they had enough Faith to *"fill them up to the brim."*

JESUS SAID UNTO THEM

The phrase, *"Jesus said unto them, Fill the waterpots with water,"* simply means that His Hour had come, and He had been given instructions from His Heavenly Father as to what He should do.

About 450 years had now elapsed since the last public Miracle of the Old Testament. It was that of Daniel, Chapter 6.

Regarding this episode, we will find out that Jesus made all the difference. Without Him, the wine would not have been replenished. Without Him, the hosts of the wedding would have been grossly embarrassed. Without Jesus, there was nothing anyone could do. It was not a catastrophe, as should be obvious, but it was a special day for the bride and the groom. To be sure, it was to be far more special than they could ever begin to dare realize. Think about it! Jesus Christ would perform His very first Miracle, which would be the first of many, and it was done at the wedding feast of this young couple. How privileged they were! How blessed they were!

I wonder if they had even a fathom of understanding as it regards what was done? Also, I wonder if we do not fall into the same category?

OBEDIENCE

Jesus told them, *"Fill the waterpots with water."*

As they were filling these waterpots, I wonder what their thoughts were. He had told them to do it, and they obeyed. I don't think they even remotely thought that He would turn the water to wine, or that He could do so! This would have been beyond their contemplation. However, thank the Lord, they did obey as it regarded filling the waterpots.

In the great Plan of God, our part as Believers is very small. But yet, it is very important, as small as it may be, that we do our part. This shows Faith! It shows obedience!

FILL THEM UP TO THE BRIM

Filling these pots to the brim presented all that man could do. The balance was left up to Jesus.

This is a source of tremendous encouragement to those who work for the Lord. He is able to do great and mighty things. The key is in listening for His Voice and then doing what He says do, believing that He will perform the necessary Miracle, irrespective of what it takes. Even though I have related the following in another Volume, I think it would be profitable to recount it again.

MIRACLES!

Sometime back, while writing Commentary on the Gospel according to Mark, I believe it was, the Lord, I believe, gave me a greater insight into this subject of *"Miracles."* Regrettably, most of the modern church doesn't even believe in Miracles anymore, claiming they passed away with the Ministry of Christ, stopped with the death of the original Apostles, or ceased when John finished the Canon of Scripture in the writing of the Book of Revelation. As well, many Pentecostals and Charismatics have been subtly led away from the God of the Bible, Who is a God of Miracles, to the psychological way, which is the way of man. I think one would have to admit that Faith in God for great things to happen, in whatever capacity, is not as strong as it ought to be.

I will not forget that moment that the Lord touched my mind as it regards the subject of Miracles. I pushed my chair back from the desk where I was dictating notes for the Commentary, feeling in my spirit that there was something here I was missing as it regarded Miracles. The following is what I believe the Lord spoke to my heart.

AN EXPLANATION!

He said, *"You have not been looking at this subject as you should. In truth, I am performing Miracles constantly for those who believe Me."*

He then went on to say, *"Any time a Believer asks Me to do something and asks in Faith believing, and it is My Will, at that moment, I begin to perform Miracles. While it is true that most of these Miracles cannot be seen, still, that makes them no less real."*

The Lord then finished by saying, *"The moment I begin to intervene in answer to prayer, Miracles begin to happen. At that time, I cause events, persons, or things to do what is needed, in one way or the other, in order to bring to pass that which is desired."*

Even though what I have just said may not seem to be a great Revelation, still, knowing and understanding the magnitude of what the Lord actually does on behalf of His Children in answering prayer and meeting needs will help the Believer to place such acts in proper perspective. As stated, most of the time, the Lord has to perform one or more Miracles, although unseen, in the carrying out of His Divine Intervention. So, one could say, and not be exaggerating, that the Lord is performing Miracles every day for those who truly believe Him and are asking Him to direct their lives and work.

The terrible truth is, as previously stated, most of the modern church does not even believe that God answers prayer anymore, much less performs Miracles. However, despite the unbelief of most, *"the people who do know their God shall be strong, and do exploits"* (Dan. 11:32).

(8) "AND HE SAID UNTO THEM, DRAW OUT NOW, AND BEAR UNTO THE GOVERNOR OF THE FEAST. AND THEY BEAR IT."

The synopsis is:

1. Restoration has to be one of the most beautiful words in any language. It means that which seems to have been forever lost has been regained.

2. The Cross alone makes possible Restoration. Nothing else can!

3. The Cross of Christ is the Means by which the Lord gives us all things. It was at the Cross that all sin was atoned, past, present, and future, at least for all who will believe (Jn. 3:16).

WHAT DID JESUS DO?

The command, *"And He said unto them, Draw out now, and bear unto the governor of the feast,"* presents all that was done. Jesus said nothing and did nothing, at least that was visible or obvious.

I wonder what went through the minds of these individuals upon hearing this Command.

At the moment Jesus gave the Command, had the water already been turned into wine, or did it do so as they took it to the governor?

Whichever, it does not really matter, inasmuch as it took Faith on the part of these people to obey.

THEY DID WHAT HE TOLD THEM TO DO

The phrase, *"And they bear it,"* proclaims their obedience. In a sense of the word, this action of the servants is a portrayal of all who labor for the Lord in any manner.

The *"water"* was all these people had; however, with Jesus on the scene, and that is the key, great and mighty things happen. He can take whatever we have, and if we do what He says do, He will turn it into whatever is needed. Again, the Secret is Jesus.

The water is like the Gospel. As the preacher prepares to deliver it to thirsty souls, it seems at first to be so little and, furthermore, to be woefully inadequate for the gargantuan task ahead. However, once the Anointing of the Holy Spirit comes upon it, it is changed into the *"Wine of the Joy of the Lord."*

MARY

We should commend Mary for going to Jesus concerning this need.

Actually, why did she go to Jesus? He had not begun His Public Ministry yet, meaning that He had not performed a single Miracle of any nature up to that time. Probably all that one could say is that she had a feeling in her heart, no doubt, prompted by the Holy Spirit. She knew Who He was although, still, there was a multitude of questions unanswered.

To be sure, what He would do, change the water to wine, I personally think never one time entered her mind. So this means, if, in fact, that is the case, she just obeyed the Promptings of the Holy Spirit. I have absolutely no doubt that the Holy Spirit was very much involved in all of this.

No great thing was at stake regarding this young wedding couple running out of wine. The worst that could happen to them would be embarrassment. However, what Jesus did shows us that He is concerned about our small needs, as well, and that we should take everything to Him.

All of this lets us know how much Jesus actually desires to be a part of our everyday lives and living, even those things that we may think are not spiritual, such as this incident. Serving Jesus is 24 hours a day, with Him actually wanting total involvement in everything we do. The crowning sin of man is that he thinks he can do without the Lord. The truth is, we desperately need the Lord in every function of our lives. He Who notes the sparrow's fall and even numbers the very hairs of our heads strongly desires that He be allowed this latitude. If allowed, the Believer will find *"more Abundant Life."*

(9) "WHEN THE RULER OF THE FEAST HAD TASTED THE WATER THAT WAS MADE WINE, AND KNEW NOT FROM WHERE IT CAME: (BUT THE SERVANTS WHICH DREW THE WATER KNEW;) THE GOVERNOR OF THE FEAST CALLED THE BRIDEGROOM."

The order is:

1. The Cross of Christ is the dividing line between the true Church and the apostate church.

2. It has always been that way, beginning with the Fourth Chapter of Genesis. However, due to the fact that we're coming close to the end, I think it is more pronounced now than ever.

3. The foray of the church into humanistic psychology is a slap in the Face of Christ, in effect, a repudiation of the Cross.

FROM WHERE DID IT COME?

The phrase, *"When the ruler of the feast had tasted the water that was made wine, and knew not from where it came,"* proclaims that he had no idea what had been done. Evidently, this scenario had taken place only in the presence of a few people.

The ruler of the wedding feast did not know of Mary directing attention to Jesus, or that Jesus had told them to fill the waterpots with water. He was without knowledge regarding all of this. He knew they had run out of wine but had no idea whatsoever as to how the problem had been addressed this quickly.

THE TURN OF EVENTS

As governor of the wedding feast, he was responsible for everything that took place. So, in effect, people were looking to him respecting this lack. As such, the bridegroom stood to be embarrassed because of what looked like improper planning.

Almost immediately after he had been given the news of this problem and was instantly concerned as to how it could be rectified, if at all, the servants came to him with containers of wine. He immediately tasted it, thinking surely that this was a very poor product, hence, used only in an emergency. He would taste it to see if it was fit to give to the guests.

He could hardly believe what he was tasting and would exclaim such to the bridegroom immediately.

David had written so long before, *"O taste and see that the LORD is good"* (Ps. 34:8).

THE WINE OF SALVATION

It is sad, but most of the world looks at the *"Wine of Salvation"* offered to them and never bother to taste its flavor. They have formed an opinion based on ignorance, or else, desire to continue in their sin, not realizing that its wages is death. However, for the few who do taste this grand elixir of life, they will always find, and without exception, exactly as David said, *"Taste and see that the LORD is good."* Worse yet are the hundreds of millions who have no opportunity to taste. The servants (workers for the Lord) never bother to bring it to them.

What would have happened that day had Jesus performed this great Miracle, with the servants not bothering to dispense this product?

Should that have happened, which, of course, it did not, I think these servants would have been in terrible trouble. Due to this very thing, I wonder now if many of the Servants of the Lord, in fact, are in great trouble.

Jesus can perform the Miracle of changing men's lives. It is up to us to take this *"Wine of Salvation"* to a lost world.

THE SONLIFE BROADCASTING NETWORK

The Lord has commissioned us (Jimmy Swaggart Ministries) to take the Gospel of Jesus Christ, more particularly, *"Jesus Christ and Him Crucified,"* to the entirety of the world. That's our Calling, our Commission, and what God has told us to do. It's a big task, but we serve a big God. At the same time, we aren't operating merely on the premise of something that needs to be done, but rather that which the Lord has called us to do.

Never before in history has it been possible to reach untold millions of people, even with a single service. We speak of television and the Internet. We are broadcasting 24 hours a day, seven days a week. We believe we have the Message which the Holy Spirit is saying to the Churches. It is *"The Message of the Cross."* We must not be disobedient to that Heavenly Vision.

(10) "AND SAID UNTO HIM, EVERY MAN AT THE BEGINNING DOES SET FORTH GOOD WINE; AND WHEN MEN HAVE WELL DRUNK, THEN THAT WHICH IS WORSE: BUT YOU HAVE KEPT THE GOOD WINE UNTIL NOW."

The exposition is:

1. The ancient Mosaic Law taught the offerer to closely associate the death and sufferings of the slain lamb with the message for which he gave thanks.

2. It teaches men today the same lesson. To disassociate worship and thanksgiving from the Anguish and Blood-shedding of the Lord Jesus, in other words, to separate all of this from the Cross, is to offer to God an abomination and to bring death into the soul and into the church.

3. The Cross is the answer for sin, and the Cross alone is the answer for sin!

AN UNBIASED TESTIMONY

The governor of the marriage feast was

pleasantly surprised when he found that this newly-made wine was better than any they had had all day. Actually, as stated, he had no knowledge of what had taken place regarding Jesus performing this Miracle, which meant that his Testimony was completely unbiased.

Incidentally, the words, *"Well drunk,"* simply mean they had *"drunk freely,"* and not that all were drunk, as some suppose.

As we have already explained at the beginning of this Chapter, and I think with convincing explanation, this was not the kind of wine that makes one drunk. In fact, it was grape juice.

It certainly would be natural to understand that the very best of anything, especially in a situation of this nature, is always given first. If more is needed, the second best will be provided, that is, if available. The governor is amazed because this rule does not seem to have been followed, but, of course, he was wrong; it had been followed.

Jesus had stepped in and had created wine, and, of course, whatever He creates is the absolute best.

THE BEST WAS SAVED UNTIL THE LAST

The phrase, *"But you have kept the good wine until now,"* in effect, says that the *"best was saved until the last."*

I personally believe this has a wide Spiritual application as well. It is twofold:

1. With the world, all good things come during the times of youth, with old age generally bringing the very opposite. However, with the Believer, serving Jesus just gets better and better as we get older. Consequently, the best is saved for the last.

2. As well, I believe that during these last days, the Spirit of God is going to be poured out even to a greater degree than ever before. In Joel, Chapter 2, the Prophet speaks of a *"former"* and *"latter rain."* The insinuation is that the *"latter rain"* will have a greater visitation even than the former (Joel 2:21-32).

Actually, the Early Church, as is recorded in the Book of Acts and the Epistles, constitutes the *"former rain."*

The *"latter rain"* has to do with these last days and actually began, I believe, at about the turn of the Twentieth Century. Since that time, multiple millions have been Saved and baptized with the Holy Spirit. All of this is the *"latter rain."* However, at the very end of the *"latter rain,"* I believe that God is going to do something special. I believe He has told me the following:

THE LAST GREAT MOVE

The Forty-first Chapter of Genesis records the two Dreams given by the Lord to Pharaoh. Of course, Pharaoh had no idea that it was the Lord Who gave him these Dreams, but the Lord did it this way for a purpose. Joseph was called out of prison in order to interpret the Dreams.

The first Dream had to do with seven cattle that were fat-fleshed, which came up out of the river. Then, seven other cattle came up after them out of the river, ill-favored and lean-fleshed, which consumed the seven fat cattle.

As Joseph would interpret this Dream, the seven fat cattle symbolized seven years of harvest such as Egypt had never known. That seven years of plenty would be followed by the seven years of famine, symbolized by the lean-fleshed cattle. It was fulfilled exactly as Joseph said it would in the interpretation.

Then, in the second Dream, the monarch dreamed there were seven ears of grain, which were healthy and full, but then, seven thin ears of grain came up after them and devoured them.

I believe the Lord has told me that this second part to Pharaoh's Dream has not yet been fulfilled. We'll take the latter first.

I believe the seven thin ears symbolize the coming Great Tribulation, which will last for seven years. However, I also believe the seven full ears of grain represent the greatest harvest of souls that the world has ever seen.

The only thing that Joseph said about the second Dream was, *"And for that the Dream was doubled unto Pharaoh twice; it is because the thing is established by God, and God will shortly bring it to pass"* (Gen. 41:32).

THE MEANING OF THE SECOND DREAM

The interpretation, as given by Joseph, and which greatly concerned Pharaoh, was to take place in the immediate future. However, due to the fact of the Dream being doubled, the second part, I believe, has an Endtime meaning, as well. It will be of far greater magnitude than that which would take place in Joseph's day. It is as follows:

We know that this terrible famine, which would follow the seven years of plenty, would ultimately bring Joseph's brothers to him, along with his father, Jacob. In a sense, as Joseph is a Type of Christ, this represents Israel coming to Christ, which they shall do at the conclusion of the seven-year Great Tribulation Period. So, the seven years of famine of the second Dream point to the coming seven-year Great Tribulation Period prophesied by Daniel and foretold by our Lord (Dan. 9:27; Mat. 24:21).

As well, the *"east wind"* mentioned in Genesis 41:27 localizes the Great Tribulation Period that is coming, which will affect the entire Earth but will have its beginning in the Middle East.

As it regards the seven years of plenty, which immediately precede the seven years of famine, looking at it in the prophetic sense, we can take the number, *"Seven,"* in two different ways.

The number, *"Seven,"* which is God's Number of Perfection, could pertain to the Church, it being completed, and then taken out of the world immediately before the seven years of Great Tribulation. Or, even as the seven years of famine correspond exactly to the coming seven years of Great Tribulation, the seven years of plenty could refer to a tremendous harvest of souls immediately preceding the Rapture, which I feel is definitely the case, and which will be followed by the Great Tribulation.

However, the great harvest of souls is that which I want to key in on. I believe the Lord has told me this will be the last great harvest before the coming Great Tribulation. It could result in the Salvation of millions of souls. As well, I believe that Jimmy Swaggart Ministries is going to play a great part in this great harvest. Now, with television and the Internet, it is possible to reach millions of souls with one particular Service or program. With the Spirit of God moving in a great and powerful way, it could quite well be possible to see thousands, if not tens of thousands, of people Saved as the result of the Moving and Operation of the Holy Spirit in a single program. This, I believe, the Lord is going to do. In other words, I believe the Lord is saving the best for the last.

I cannot feature the Lord not making a great Move, especially in the time of spiritual declension, with the modern church weaker than it has ever been since the Reformation.

I'm not saying that a great revival is coming. In fact, from the Word of God, I do not see a revival in these last of the last days. However, I do see a harvest, and with modern technology, it can be a great harvest. In order for this to be done, there is going to have to be a Moving of the Holy Spirit in a fashion and in a way that the world has never known before. In other words, the Preachers used by the Lord will have to experience an Anointing of the Holy Spirit as never before. As well, there has got to be the Convicting Power of the Holy Spirit as never before. The Lord is able!

(11) "THIS BEGINNING OF MIRACLES DID JESUS IN CANA OF GALILEE, AND MANIFESTED FORTH HIS GLORY; AND HIS DISCIPLES BELIEVED ON HIM."

The exegesis is:

1. The changing of the water to wine at the little village of Cana of Galilee was the first Miracle performed by our Lord at the beginning of His Ministry.

2. This first Miracle manifested His Glory. In other words, He began His Ministry with a Miracle.

3. His Disciples believed that He was the Son of God and, as well, Israel's Messiah.

THE BEGINNING OF MIRACLES

The phrase, *"This beginning of Miracles did Jesus in Cana of Galilee,"* means that this was the first Miracle He performed. Consequently, this tells us that all of the so-called miracles that He performed in His Childhood, as recorded in the apocryphal books, are false.

For instance, these accounts claim that when Jesus was a Teenager, He stretched lumber to the desired length; made one grain of wheat grow 800 bushels; made birds and animals of clay and gave life to them, etc.

Actually, as here stated, Jesus did no miracle until after His Anointing with the Spirit (Mat. 3:16-17). So, Cana had the distinction of being the location for the beginning of the Ministry of the Son of God and the Redemption of mankind, which was, to date, by far the greatest event in human history.

WHY DID THE HOLY SPIRIT THROUGH CHRIST CHOOSE THE CHANGING OF WATER TO WINE AS HIS FIRST MIRACLE?

To think about this, one would think that the first Miracle would have been the opening of blind eyes, the healing and cleansing of a leper, or even the raising of the dead, but changing water to wine?

One thing is certain: the Lord does nothing by accident. This which Jesus did was exactly what the Holy Spirit wanted done, and perhaps the following will give us a clue:

MARRIAGE BETWEEN A MAN AND A WOMAN

First of all, it should be obvious that by changing the water to wine at the marriage feast of Cana, Jesus placed the highest seal of approval upon the institution of marriage. Of course, this had already been done, even from the very beginning (Gen. 2:24). Nevertheless, this action by Christ placed even greater emphasis on this all-important social fabric.

As well, I think it should be very obvious as to the abomination carried out respecting so-called same-sex marriages. As is obvious, the homosexual lobby is working day and night that Congress would legitimize such action; however, Congress is one thing, while God Almighty is something else altogether. It really doesn't matter if Congress does approve of such, God never will, and it's to God that man will ultimately have to answer.

The fabric of a nation is the home. If that is destroyed, the sinew of the nation is destroyed. It is the nuclear family, which consists of a husband, wife, and children, that the Lord has designed and, consequently, blesses.

As the late Senator Byrd of Virginia said concerning this proposal of Congressional legitimacy, *"Regarding this issue of same-sex marriages, America is being weighed in the balances."* He then went on to say, *"Irrespective of whether we legitimize it, God will not, and we will be 'found wanting.'"*

That such would even be considered by the legislative branch of our government only shows to what depths this nation has fallen.

THE POWER TO CHANGE THINGS

Among other reasons, this Miracle was performed by Christ to proclaim His Power to change things, whether man, situations, or events. The Lord is letting us know by His changing the water to wine that no matter how bad our situation might be, He can change it. That is a monumental statement. Everyone has things that need to be changed. The Lord can do it, and, in fact, He is the only One Who can do such.

Then, the greatest of all, the Lord can change the character, the lifestyle, and the very personality of an individual. In other words, He can make a new Creation out of any person, irrespective as to whom he might be. To be sure, that is the greatest Miracle of all. The changing of a heart, the changing of a life, and the changing of an eternity, Christ alone can do such. He has done it untold millions of times and is doing it now, and He will do it for you if you will only believe Him.

A PART OF EVERYTHING

This Miracle, in what might be concluded a mundane matter, shows us that the Lord is desirous of being a part of everything we do as His Children, even the small, mundane matters. This Miracle portrays that.

His changing the water to wine was not a life or death situation. As is obvious, one might even say it was mundane. However, the Lord wants to be involved, not only in the large things in our lives, but the small things as well. He wants total control, but it is control that we must freely give Him. He will never force the issue, always waiting upon our compliance.

HE CAN MAKE SOMETHING OF NOTHING

The Lord made wine out of water. This means that He can take what we consider to be nothing and can make something beautiful out of it. To be sure, if we give Him full control of our lives, He most definitely will make something beautiful of that which seems to be nothing.

So, the meaning of Jesus turning the water to wine as His First Miracle carried with it tremendous reasons.

THE MANIFESTING OF HIS GLORY

The phrase, *"And manifested forth His Glory,"* proclaims to us several great Truths:

• If one is to notice, it says, *"His Glory,"* instead of His Power! While it certainly took Power to do this Miracle, it was Power used in a way that is totally opposite from most of the world. When men gain power, they usually use it for themselves. Jesus used it for others, hence, *"His Glory."*

• The Greek word for *"Glory"* is, *"Doxa,"* and means, *"The nature and acts of God in self-manifestation, i.e., what He essentially is and does, as exhibited in whatever way He reveals Himself in these respects, and particularly in the Person of Christ, in Whom essentially His Glory has ever shown forth and ever will do."*

In this particular comment, it has to do exclusively with the positive. In other words, Jesus did not make anyone to be blind but made many to see. He did not cause anyone with this great Power to have leprosy, but rather He healed them of their leprosy. At this time, He did not use His Power to judge mankind or to bring Judgment, but rather the very opposite. Therefore, it was *"Glory."*

• The word, *"Manifested,"* means, at least in this case, to manifest or proclaim something openly so that there be no doubt as to its origin. Such was this Miracle at Cana, and such were all His Miracles. This was done, at least in part, that His detractors might not be able to accuse Him of trickery; consequently, everything was done openly.

FAITH

The phrase, *"And His Disciples believed on Him,"* does not mean that they had formerly disbelieved Him, but that their Faith was increased due to the manifestation of His Glory in the changing of the water to wine.

For those who are truly God-Called and have a particular mission to perform, at least one of their greatest needs is to have people around them who truly and sincerely believe in them.

If one is to notice, the Apostle Paul surrounded himself with such individuals. They believed that God had called him for world Evangelism. They believed also in the Message he preached, which was the great Gospel of Grace, i.e., *"the Cross."* This was especially significant considering that many, even some in Jerusalem, held his views suspect, or at the least gave them little, if any, support.

Of course, it was not very difficult for the Disciples of Christ to believe on Him, especially considering that the Miracles He performed were constant and obvious. Actually, that should have been the case with all, including the religious leaders of Israel; however, seemingly, it was not enough. Actually, willful blindness cannot see because it does not desire to see.

At the same time, a Divine Faith must be based on the Scriptures and not things which can be observed alone.

(12) "AFTER THIS HE WENT DOWN TO CAPERNAUM, HE, AND HIS MOTHER, AND HIS BRETHREN, AND HIS DISCIPLES: AND THEY CONTINUED THERE NOT MANY DAYS."

The form is:

1. Capernaum was to be the headquarters for the Earthly Ministry of Christ.

2. His Mother, His Brethren, and His Disciples went with Him. Evidently, Joseph, His Foster Father, was now passed away.

3. They didn't stay in Capernaum very long because the Passover was to commence very shortly.

CAPERNAUM

The phrase, *"After this He went down to Capernaum,"* has to do with this city being of lower elevation than Cana, which, in fact, was approximately 700 feet higher in altitude.

"Capernaum" would become His Headquarters in His three and one-half years of public Ministry. It was a very energetic trading center and was quite large in size. It prospered greatly from the fishing business

on the Sea of Galilee, and the great trade routes, which ran near from the north, east, and south. Actually, it was probably one of, if not the most, prosperous areas in the whole of Israel.

As well, it seems that Peter had by now made this city his place of abode rather than Bethsaida (Jn. 1:44).

THE FAMILY OF CHRIST

The phrase, *"He, and His Mother, and His Brethren, and His Disciples,"* provides a most interesting Text.

No mention is made of Joseph, so it must be assumed that he has died. As well, no mention is made of the half-sisters of Jesus inasmuch as they possibly were married and living in Nazareth.

The Catholic church claims that *"His Brethren"* mentioned here are actually His Cousins. They also claim that Mary remained a perpetual virgin.

However, such is totally unscriptural. Mary did not remain a virgin, nor were these mentioned the cousins of Jesus, but rather His Half-brothers.

It is plainly stated in Scripture that Jesus had four brothers (half-brothers), James, Joseph, Simon, and Jude. He had at least two or three half-sisters, also, even though the exact number is not stated, using only the words, *"Are not His Sisters here with us?"* These are referred to as *"His Own Kin"* and *"His Own House."*

As well, Jesus is called Mary's *"Firstborn"* (Mat. 1:25; Lk. 2:7), and the natural inference is that she had other children. The Greek *"prototokos"* is used in Romans 8:29; Colossians 1:15-18; Hebrews 1:6; 11:28; 12:23; and Revelation 1:5, and means, *"The first of others."* Had Jesus been her only son, the word would have been, *"Monogenes,"* which occurs in Luke 7:12; 8:42; and 9:38.

It was also predicted by God that Mary would have other children, and the Messiah would have brothers. *"I am become a stranger unto my brethren, and an alien unto my mother's children"* (Ps. 69:8-9).

As well, in this Text, it tells us of Mary going with Jesus to Capernaum, and it also speaks of *"His Brethren."* The children of some other woman would not be following Mary as *"His Brethren."*

HIS BRETHREN

The natural meaning of *"His Brethren"* would never have been questioned but for the fact of pagan corruption in the church — in seeking to raise Mary from a mere *"handmaid of the Lord"* (Lk. 1:38) to that of Mother of God, and to invest her with Divine Powers as a goddess.

Thus, the way was prepared for identifying her with the goddess of paganism, who is supposed to be the mother of a divine son, and who is yet a virgin, a deity known in Egypt as Isis, the mother of Horus; in India, Isi; in Asia, Cybele; in Rome, Fortuna; in Greece, Ceres; in China, Shing Moo; and in other lands by different names, but always with a son in arms.

So, it is said that Mary had no other children and that His Brethren were cousins by another Mary and Cleophas, that Joseph was too old to have children of Mary, or that he had children by a former marriage.

All of this is false as nothing is mentioned in Scripture or history about these claims. If Joseph did have children before Jesus was born, then Jesus could not be the legal heir to David's Throne, which, by Law, went to the firstborn.

Concerning *"His Brethren"* going with Him to Capernaum, the evidence is that they had not yet taken the stand against Christ which they would later take. While we do not have information on all of the half-brothers, we do know that James and Jude became great pillars in the Early Church, and even wrote two short Epistles which bear their names and are included in the Canon of Scripture. However, it seems that they did not come to Faith until after the Resurrection. John will later record the sad statement, *"For neither did His Brethren believe in Him"* (Jn. 7:5).

WHY DID NOT HIS BRETHREN BELIEVE IN HIM?

Of course, the complete answer to that question can only be given by the Lord; however, some things are obvious.

They probably had great difficulty in

believing that Jesus was the Son of God, the Messiah of Israel, especially considering that they had been raised with Him, and during the formative years, saw no sign of such, even though they would be forced to admit that His Life was impeccable.

As well, a little later in the Ministry of Christ, the Pharisees and religious leaders of Israel would become more and more openly hostile toward Jesus. What type of effect this had on His Immediate Family is not known. However, especially considering that the townspeople of Nazareth had rejected Jesus out of hand, this probably caused some hardship on the family.

Also, there may have been some envy or jealousy present in that He did not choose any of them to be His Closest Disciples.

Irrespective as to the excuse, self-will was the mitigating factor, which cheated them out of the greatest Blessing they could ever have. To have had the privilege to be the Half-brothers of Jesus and, as well, to be a part of His Ministry, which they certainly could have been, would be the greatest thing that could ever happen to anyone. However, these four brothers missed this glorious opportunity, which they would ever regret.

Some have said that this is the reason James, at the beginning of his Epistle, did not call himself an *"Apostle,"* but rather a *"Servant of God."* Jude, as well, addressed himself accordingly as the *"Servant of Jesus Christ, and brother of James."* Due to their rejection of Him during His Earthly Ministry, they felt they were not worthy to claim more.

THE PASSOVER

The phrase, *"And they continued there not many days,"* referring to Capernaum, has reference to the *"Passover,"* which was to commence shortly. As was their custom, they would attend this Passover in Jerusalem, which would be the first since Jesus had begun His Public Ministry. To be sure, and as we shall see, He would stir up quite a bit of controversy.

(13) "AND THE JEWS' PASSOVER WAS AT HAND, AND JESUS WENT UP TO JERUSALEM."

The pattern is:

1. The Jews' Passover.
2. Jesus went up to Jerusalem.

THE JEWS' PASSOVER

The phrase, *"And the Jews' Passover was at hand,"* has significance as to its phrasing.

It had been Jehovah's Passover, but corruption had proceeded apace, and it was now *"the Jews' Passover."*

This is the same with many modern religious denominations. They begin well and are truly Called and Anointed by the Holy Spirit; however, little by little, corruption sets in until that which once belonged to God and was greatly used of God no longer is.

The basic reason for these happenings has to do with man, little by little, usurping authority over God. In other words, the Government of God, which is the Word of God, is replaced by man. That's what ultimately caused the spiritual wreckage of the Early Church. After the Apostles and those who knew them passed on, little by little, the spirituality of the Church began to deteriorate. Little by little, the Word of God was replaced with man's inventions, whatever that was. It finally morphed into what is now known as the Catholic church. Actually, it was only in the early Seventh Century that the Bishop of Rome came to be called the *"Pope."* The deterioration continued from then until now, at least as it regards the Catholic church. When man's word is substituted for God's Word, catastrophe is always the end result.

JESUS AND JERUSALEM

The phrase, *"And Jesus went up to Jerusalem,"* proclaims Him making this trip, although, as events will relate, not with enthusiasm.

Actually, there is no record that Jesus spent a single night in Jerusalem during His Public Ministry, with the exception of the night of His Trial. He would always retire, it seems, to Bethany or to the Mount of Olives. Jerusalem, as the center of Judaism, and, as well, having turned its back on God, would prove to be very hostile toward the Ministry of Christ. In fact, they rejected Him out of hand!

Years ago, we preached meetings in

churches and then, finally, in auditoriums. Whenever we went to a city that was the headquarters of a particular denomination, and it really didn't matter which, it seemed to always be the most difficult place to see a Move of God. Most of the time, the spirits of darkness would be so prominent in the services that it was almost impossible to have Church.

What was this?

In many religious denominations, religious spirits abound. These are demon spirits that are proficient in the art of religion, which purposely steer in the wrong direction. Of course, they are totally opposed to the Lord and His Word. As stated, these denominations become filled with these spirits because of leaving the Word of God and instituting their own Word. In fact, as I dictate these notes on June 27, 2012, it is my personal thought that all who are in these denominational churches, whatever they might be, should get out of these churches. I am speaking only of the United States and Canada. Even the ones which might be labeled as *"good"* still are supporting the direction of that denomination, which is not according to the Word of God. For the Spiritual welfare of the individual, it would be far better to be out of it than in it.

What I'm about to say sounds self-serving, but the Lord knows I say it only for one's Spiritual benefit.

Several years ago, we at Jimmy Swaggart Ministries began FAMILY WORSHIP CENTER MEDIA CHURCH. We encourage those who desire to join this church, irrespective as to where they might live. The only requirement is to be Born-Again. Are there obligations? Only three which we request. In other words, it is a request and not a command.

1. Pray for us daily or as the Lord brings us to your mind.

2. Tell others about THE SONLIFE BROADCASTING NETWORK.

3. Support the Network with your tithes and offerings as you are led by the Lord. A Believer should support that which feeds him. As I dictate these notes, we are having over 100 people a week that are joining.

As it regards the Services that originate at Family Worship Center in Baton Rouge,

NOTES

Louisiana, USA, these people worship with us wherever they are. Please believe me, you'll be far better off worshipping in this respect, in other words, joining with us, as multiple thousands do all over the world, than hearing some false doctrine, etc.

Spiritually speaking, we are living in perilous times. One cannot be Spiritually nourished unless one is being properly fed, and that means according to the Word of God.

And yet, if a good Church is nearby, which preaches the Cross, you should be associated with that.

To join Family Worship Center Media Church, all one has to do is call the office and tell the operator what you desire to do. It's just that simple. A certificate will be sent to you, and, as well, Frances, Donnie, or Gabe will read your first name and the state or the country of your domicile. We do it this way to protect your privacy.

(14) "AND FOUND IN THE TEMPLE THOSE WHO SOLD OXEN AND SHEEP AND DOVES, AND THE CHANGERS OF MONEY SITTING."

The pattern is:

1. The manner in which the Temple was being used.

2. All of this commerce was probably taking place in the Court of the Gentiles but carried out by Jews.

3. The changers of money.

THE TEMPLE

The phrase, *"And found in the Temple,"* spoke of the place where God was supposed to reside between the Mercy Seat and the Cherubim; however, there is no record that this had been the case for the last 600 years. Ezekiel actually saw the Lord depart from this edifice, to which He had not yet returned. He would only return in the Person of Jesus during the time of His Earthly Ministry but, as we shall see, not with blessing (Ezek. 11:22-23).

In fact, there had not even been an Ark of the Covenant in the Holy of Holies since Solomon's Temple had been destroyed by Nebuchadnezzar. That was in the year 586 B.C. What happened to the Ark, no one knows! So, the Holy of Holies in Herod's

Temple, which Jesus entered, was such in name only.

Since Jesus has paid the price on Calvary's Cross for the Redemption of humanity, the Lord no longer dwells in a house made with hands, but rather in the hearts and lives of Believers (I Cor. 3:16). So, the question might well be asked, *"As Jesus searched out that Temple, what does He find in our Temple?"*

OXEN, SHEEP, AND DOVES

The phrase, *"Those who sold oxen and sheep and doves,"* probably, as stated, refers to the Court of the Gentiles.

The three animals here mentioned were those most frequently required for sacrifices. Jews, arriving from all over the Roman Empire, especially during the three great Feast times during the year, would doubtlessly need some market where these could be obtained, and the sufficient guarantee of their freedom from blemish be secured.

Consequently, it doesn't seem to be the selling of the animals to which Jesus objected, but to where they were being sold. One can well imagine the din and racket caused by these proceedings, with Jews attempting to shout each other down, that they had the best deal, etc.

MONEY CHANGERS

The phrase, *"And the changers of money sitting,"* referred to those who exchanged acceptable coins for those bearing the image of Caesar, or any foreign prints, for that matter.

Once again, it was not the practice which Jesus condemned, but rather where it was being conducted. From this Text, many have attempted to equate modern church buildings with the ancient Temple. They falsely assume that it is wrong to have a kitchen, a bookstore, etc., in a church building; however, the modern church building has little in common with the Temple of old.

As we have stated, the Lord no longer resides in a building. He resides in men's hearts, at least those who have accepted Him as Saviour and Lord. Consequently, no building should be looked at as the Temple of old.

I realize that many Believers are accustomed to referring to a church building as *"The House of God"*; however, such is an incorrect statement.

While it is certainly proper to dedicate a church building to the Lord, that's as far as it ought to go. Actually, Believers should dedicate everything they have to the Lord.

Christians should quit being so concerned over buildings and take stock of their own immediate hearts and lives, which are the true Temples (I Cor. 3:16).

During the time of the Early Church, which we read about in the Book of Acts and the Epistles, there were no church buildings. People worshipped the Lord in homes, in caves, out in the forest, etc. Rome would not allow church buildings to be constructed. We should understand that Church is really not a building. It's an attitude of the heart, with Believers coming together to worship the Lord, and it can be carried forth anywhere.

(15) "AND WHEN HE HAD MADE A SCOURGE OF SMALL CORDS, HE DROVE THEM ALL OUT OF THE TEMPLE, AND THE SHEEP, AND THE OXEN; AND POURED OUT THE CHANGERS' MONEY, AND OVERTHREW THE TABLES."

The order is:

1. Jesus used a scourge to drive out the moneychangers.

2. He also drove out the sheep and the oxen.

3. He then overturned all of the money tables of the moneychangers.

THE SCOURGE

The phrase, *"And when He had made a scourge of small cords,"* represents the Lord's First Cleansing of the Temple. The second and last cleansing was that of Matthew 21:12. Here He was a Son over His Father's House; in Luke 2:46, He was a Son in His Father's House. It ceased to be such on His leaving it (Mat. 23:38; 24:1).

The situation must have been bad, very bad, for the Lord to take the steps that He did, realizing that His Action would greatly infuriate the High Priesthood. In fact, it would show them up for what they really were. God's House, where He was supposed to dwell between the Mercy Seat and the Cherubim, had been turned into that which was little more than a brothel. In fact, spiritual adultery was the sin constantly being committed.

HE DROVE THEM OUT

The phrase, *"He drove them all out of the Temple, and the sheep, and the oxen,"* proclaimed Him taking a very serious step indeed!

According to Josephus, over 250,000 animals were sacrificed each Passover, so the market must have been great. The Chief Priests of the Temple sold licenses to the vendors, so this profanation must have been a large source of revenue to these religious leaders. Now, let us say it again. The Lord was not condemning the sale of the animals or even the changing of the money. What He was condemning was where it was being done.

If Jesus is to be our Example, we should note the lengths to which He went in order to uphold the Scripture. I am positive that His Action in the cleansing of the Temple would be little applauded by most modern religious denominations, that is, if the scene was reenacted now.

As well, it must be understood that Jesus is the only One Who can cleanse the Temple. I get amazed at mere men who think they can do such. What self-righteous men generally do, in carrying out their self-righteous acts, is throw out the Holy Spirit instead.

It should be quickly added that when Jesus *"drove them all out of the Temple,"* very shortly, the religious officials drove Him out. However, when they did so, they destroyed their reason for being. Consequently, the Temple would be totally destroyed in A.D. 70 by the Romans. They could have Him, or they could have the money which came from the sale of the animals in the Temple, but they could not have both.

THE MONEY CHANGERS

The phrase, *"And poured out the changers' money, and overthrew the tables,"* must have presented quite a sight. One can see this *"scourge"* as it lightly lashed the backs of these animals, and them stamping out the doors. With the money tables being overturned, coins scattering all over the floor, and people scampering after them, one could probably say that bedlam broke loose. Several things are said here:

• What He did, as we shall see, was Scriptural (Ps. 69:9). The Scriptures must be our guide as well!

• He did not at all seek or ask for any type of compromise simply because the Word of God cannot be compromised. Consequently, we, as Preachers of the Gospel, must follow suit.

• The zeal of the Lord exhibited should be our zeal as well; however, Jesus did this only as His Father told Him to do so. As well, we too must be led strictly by the Lord. To do otherwise, especially in matters of this nature, is to invite disaster.

• However, it should also be noted that even though something is done in the Will of God, with one being totally led by the Spirit, that does not mean that there will not be repercussions. There were with Jesus, and there will be with us as well. In other words, be prepared to suffer the consequences.

(16) "AND SAID UNTO THEM WHO SOLD DOVES, TAKE THESE THINGS HENCE; MAKE NOT MY FATHER'S HOUSE AN HOUSE OF MERCHANDISE."

The composition is:

1. The Word of the Lord to them who sold doves.

2. Jesus told them, *"Take these things outside."*

3. *"Do not make My Father's House an house of merchandise."*

THE WORD OF THE LORD TO THEM WHO SOLD DOVES

The phrase, *"And said unto them who sold doves, Take these things hence,"* does not mean that He was less physical with these, but that they were most likely caged. Tradition says that He opened the cages, letting the doves loose, with them flying away over the heads of the people, etc.

It should be noted that Jerusalem and the Temple were crowded with pilgrims, due to it being the Passover season. So, the news of what He did would have spread over the city like proverbial wildfire.

MY FATHER'S HOUSE

The phrase, *"Make not My Father's House an house of merchandise,"* presents a startling statement. He said, *"My Father's House,"* not, *"Our Father's House,"* therefore, claiming especially to be the Son of God Most High. The Eternal, the Holy One of Israel, stands in this mysterious relationship to Him.

I'm sure the Priests in the Temple that day heard and noted what He said, and I'm also certain that it was delivered to the High Priest very quickly.

And yet, after the second cleansing of the Temple, He used the term, *"Your house,"* and then added, *"is left unto you desolate"* (Mat. 23:38).

Actually, the Temple was to be a Type of the Lord Jesus Christ. All its duties carried out were symbolic of what Jesus would do in His Life and Living, in other words, what He actually was, as well as what He would do at Calvary and the Resurrection. So, three things are said here:

1. When they rejected him, they were rejecting all for which the Temple was supposed to stand. The truth was, they had long since forgotten What and Whom the Temple represented. They had made a religion out of its ritual, not understanding anymore to Whom it pointed.

2. When Jesus paid the price at Calvary for the Redemption of man, the Temple, which was a mere Type, was no longer needed. Jesus had become the Sacrifice; consequently, the offering up of animals must come to an end.

3. The duty of the Priests who served as mediators between God and men was now no longer necessary. Due to the claims of Heavenly Justice being satisfied by Calvary, Jesus now serves as our *"Great High Priest"* and as *"Mediator"* between God and men (I Tim. 2:5; Heb., Chpt. 9).

THE GREAT DAY OF ATONEMENT

Then, the Holy of Holies could only be entered once a year, and that by the High Priest, where he would offer up blood on the Mercy Seat. It was called, *"The Great Day of Atonement."* However, this actually had not been done for nearly 600 years, as stated, due to the loss of the Ark of the Covenant on which sat the Mercy Seat.

Due to Jesus having shed His Own Blood at Calvary's Cross, now any Believer can enter *"boldly unto the Throne of Grace, that we may obtain Mercy, and find Grace to help in time of need"* (Heb. 4:16).

So, upon completion by Christ of what the Temple represented, which He did in His Life and Living, and above all, in His Work of Atonement on the Cross, it then ceased to be of use and was consequently destroyed.

(17) "AND HIS DISCIPLES REMEMBERED THAT IT WAS WRITTEN, THE ZEAL OF YOUR HOUSE HAS EATEN ME UP."

The structure is:

1. His Disciples instantly remembered what the Bible said concerning what Jesus was now doing regarding the cleansing of the Temple.

2. The Word of God stated, *"The zeal of Your House has eaten Me up."*

HIS DISCIPLES

The phrase, *"And His Disciples remembered that it was written,"* indicates that this was present tense, in other words, immediately after He had cleansed the Temple, and not something they later recalled.

If they had continued to follow the Word as they did here, much misunderstanding concerning the Mission of Christ would have been avoided.

There is evidence that His Own Personal Disciples, whom He had Personally chosen, little understood Him or His Mission. This is especially true regarding when He told them that the religious leaders of Israel would kill Him, and that He would rise from the dead on the third day. It totally bypassed them. The Scripture says:

"Then Peter took Him, and began to rebuke Him, saying, Be it far from You, Lord: this shall not be unto You.

"But Jesus turned, and said unto Peter, You get behind Me, Satan: you are an offense unto Me: for you savor not the things that be of God, but those that be of men" (Mat. 16:21-23).

Actually, despite Him telling them any number of times that He would be resurrected on the third day, when they saw Him die on the Cross, not a single Disciple believed that He would be resurrected.

I realize it is easy for us to criticize the Disciples, I suppose, feeling if we had been there, we would have believed Him. We would be wise not to think such.

THE ZEAL OF YOUR HOUSE

The phrase, *"The Zeal of Your House has eaten Me up,"* is taken from Psalm 69:9. This is a foreshadowing of the reproach and agony which will befall the Righteous Servant of God in His Passion for God's Honor.

The idea is that His Holy Zeal for God's House would bring the wrath of the religious authorities upon His Head and ultimately consume Him, i.e., *"eat Him up!"*

(18) "THEN ANSWERED THE JEWS AND SAID UNTO HIM, WHAT SIGN DO YOU SHOW US, SEEING THAT YOU DO THESE THINGS?"

The construction is:

1. The Jews now questioned Him regarding His Action.

2. These Jews wanted a sign. In fact, they were always wanting signs, yet totally ignoring the most miraculous signs that had ever been carried out on Earth in the healing of the sick of every description.

THE BEGINNING OF THE OPPOSITION

The phrase, *"Then answered the Jews and said unto Him,"* concerns itself with the beginning of the opposition, which would only grow in intensity. Ultimately, they would murder the Lord of Glory. The tragedy is, they did not recognize their own Messiah when He came, despite incontrovertible evidence. The fact is, unbelief simply cannot see, no matter how much evidence is presented.

THE SIGN

The question, *"What sign do You show us, seeing that You do these things?"* tells us that by their mere questioning of Him, they sensed His Great Power and Authority. Anyone else, who would have done such a thing as He had done in cleansing the Temple, would have been arrested on the spot, if not stoned. Even though John does not mention it here, it seems from Verse 23 that Jesus had already begun to perform Miracles, which, as well, added authenticity to His Claims.

With the great crowds who gathered to His Miracles, and no wonder, coupled with the authority with which He spoke, these religious authorities knew that He was completely out of the ordinary. So, they merely asked for a *"sign!"*

He had, no doubt, been overheard claiming God as His Father and His Father as the Owner of this *"House."* As God's Son, the *"House"* technically was His, with Him consequently having the authority to do in His House what He so desired.

By their question, they had rejected this out of hand but were still faced with His Power, His Authority, and His Miracles.

As well, the proper translation of this Scripture should have been, *"What sign do You show unto us that You are the Messiah, seeing that You do these things?"*

(19) "JESUS ANSWERED AND SAID UNTO THEM, DESTROY THIS TEMPLE, AND IN THREE DAYS I WILL RAISE IT UP."

The diagram is:

1. Jesus answered their question.

2. He said unto them, *"Destroy this Temple, and in three days I will raise it up."*

3. He was speaking of His Physical Body, regarding His Death and Resurrection, and not this Temple made of stone.

JESUS ANSWERED

The phrase, *"Jesus answered and said unto them, Destroy this Temple,"* referred to His Physical Body, and not the structure built by Herod. As well, when He said this, He probably pointed to His Body, so there would be no misinterpretation. However, people see what they want to see and hear what they want to hear!

As well, this was the first time that He mentioned His Coming Death, and the manner in which He would die, i.e., *"His Body would be destroyed by Crucifixion."* Inasmuch as He now knew what would happen concerning His Life, it stands to reason that He had known it for quite some time, possibly even as far back as when He was 12 years old (Lk. 2:49).

RESURRECTION

The phrase, *"And in three days I will raise it up,"* spoke of His Resurrection and exactly when it would be, three days after His Death. So, the *"sign"* they demanded would be that of His Resurrection. However, even though it was the grandest *"sign"* ever known in the annals of human history, it was a sign that they, regrettably, would not accept.

(20) "THEN SAID THE JEWS, FORTY AND SIX YEARS WAS THIS TEMPLE IN BUILDING, AND WILL YOU RAISE IT UP IN THREE DAYS?

The exegesis is:

1. The Jews answered Jesus.

2. They pointed to the Temple in which they were now standing.

3. Then they said to Him, *"Will you raise it up in three days?"*

THE CONSTRUCTION OF THE TEMPLE

The phrase, *"Then said the Jews, Forty and six years was this Temple in building,"* refers to that which was commenced by Herod the Great in 20 B.C. He tore down Zerubbabel's Temple, which had stood on the same spot for nearly 400 years, in order to build this Temple, which was far larger and more extravagant. Actually, work was continuing even unto this very moment, and would continue until A.D. 64 under Herod Agrippa, the great grandson of Herod the Great.

Herod built this Temple, attempting to ingratiate himself with his Jewish subjects; however, he was of Edomite descent, consequently, a Gentile. In fact, he was never accepted, but rather hated!

WILL YOU RAISE IT UP IN THREE DAYS?

The question, *"And will You raise it up in three days?"* is spoken in sarcasm.

Even though Jesus may have pointed to Himself when He said, *"Destroy this Temple, and in three days I will raise it up,"* His detractors would not have known His meaning.

The enemies of Jesus remembered His Words and perverted them; His Disciples remembered them and profited by them.

(21) "BUT HE SPOKE OF THE TEMPLE OF HIS BODY."

The diagram is:

1. Even at the outset of His Ministry, our Lord predicted His Death and Resurrection.

2. The very purpose for the Incarnation, God becoming Man, was to go to the Cross.

3. The entire preparation of the Incarnation was for the Cross. It was there that every Victory was won.

(22) "WHEN THEREFORE HE WAS RISEN FROM THE DEAD, HIS DISCIPLES REMEMBERED THAT HE HAD SAID THIS UNTO THEM; AND THEY BELIEVED THE SCRIPTURE, AND THE WORD WHICH JESUS HAD SAID."

The construction is:

1. After His Resurrection, the Disciples of Jesus recalled that He had foretold this great event.

2. In fact, Jesus was giving them the Word of God.

3. They probably were referring to Psalm 16:10.

HIS DISCIPLES REMEMBERED

The phrase, *"When therefore He was risen from the dead, His Disciples remembered that He had said this unto them,"* seems to say that all the things He had said during His Public Ministry, at least that which had been noted or remembered, was scrupulously analyzed after the Resurrection. Then, many things became much clearer and would have been clear when they said them if they, at that time, had only analyzed them by the Scriptures, as they would later do.

THEY BELIEVED

The phrase, *"And they believed the Scripture, and the Word which Jesus had said,"* portrays them comparing what He had said with what had already been written in the Old Testament. Actually, this was the only Bible they had at that time. Perhaps, as previously stated, they were referring here to Psalm 16:10. A Divine Faith is always based upon the Scriptures.

(23) "NOW WHEN HE WAS IN JERUSALEM AT THE PASSOVER, ON

THE FEAST DAY, MANY BELIEVED IN HIS NAME, WHEN THEY SAW THE MIRACLES WHICH HE DID."

The pattern is:

1. Due to the Miracles, many believed in His Name.

2. How anyone could have followed the Ministry of Jesus at His First Advent and not immediately detected that He was the Son of God, the Messiah, is beyond understanding.

3. But yet, individuals who are persuaded by Miracles do not last very long. Faith in the Word Alone makes the Believer.

THE PASSOVER

The phrase, *"Now when He was in Jerusalem at the Passover, on the Feast Day,"* speaks of the same time in which He had cleansed the Temple.

Basically, Christ began His Ministry by cleansing the Temple and, in a sense, closed His Ministry by cleansing the Temple. Immediately, He incurred the wrath of the religious establishment, which never slacked until they ultimately put Him on a Cross. It did not matter at the Power of His Miracles. It did not matter that they were astounding, even to the raising of the dead. It did not matter that such had never been done in human history. Still, they never would accept Him as the Messiah. And yet, some believed, even as we shall see.

BELIEF IN HIS NAME

The phrase, *"Many believed in His Name, when they saw the Miracles which He did,"* proclaims Him healing the sick and, no doubt, casting out demons during this visit. As stated previously, the Jews, who were questioning Him and very upset about the cleansing of the Temple, would have been faced with this Miracle-working Power. No doubt, thousands of people were gathered around Him at every opportunity. Consequently, the religious authorities were very reluctant to press the issue beyond the questioning stage.

(24) "BUT JESUS DID NOT COMMIT HIMSELF UNTO THEM, BECAUSE HE KNEW ALL MEN."

The order is:

NOTES

1. Jesus Christ is the Source of all things we receive from God.

2. The Cross of Christ is the Means by which all of these wonderful things are given to us.

3. The Cross of Christ must be the Object of our Faith at all times.

JESUS DID NOT COMMIT HIMSELF

The phrase, *"But Jesus did not commit Himself unto them,"* means that He paid little attention to their praises, which were occasioned by the Miracles. Their faith was a shallow faith and was rooted not necessarily on the Scriptures, but rather on outward observances. In other words, it could quickly turn on the proverbial dime.

The shallow mouthed faith, which is skin deep, so to speak, the Lord will never honor. He will commit Himself to Faith which is anchored in the Cross of Christ and that alone. Let's say it again:

God will not honor faith that's in anything else other than the Cross of Christ. Millions of Christians call themselves having Faith in the Word while they ignore the Cross. Such is not to be. The Story of the Bible is the Story of *"Jesus Christ and Him Crucified."* So, if one says he understands the Bible and has little or no understanding of the Cross of Christ relative to our Sanctification, such a person really does not understand the Word.

Millions understand the Cross of Christ as it refers to Salvation, and rightly so. Thank God for that. However, they have no understanding at all of the Cross of Christ relative to Sanctification. One must understand, ninety-nine percent of the Bible is given over to telling Believers how to live for God. If it weren't a complicated process, I do not think that all of the time and attention allotted thusly would have been forthcoming. The Cross of Christ is the Means by which the Lord gives us all things, which demands our constant Faith. In other words, the Cross of Christ must be the Object of our Faith, and must remain the Object of our Faith for all of our lives.

BECAUSE HE KNEW ALL MEN

The phrase, *"Because He knew all men,"*

refers to the fickleness of men, especially those whose Faith is misplaced, as these.

The Faith of these individuals was based upon evidence, i.e., *"Miracles,"* and involved no consciousness of sin and its eternal doom. It was, consequently, a worthless faith.

Tragically, this type of faith characterizes too much of the modern church. It runs hither and yon after religious phenomenon, and if it is loud or garrulous enough, it is eagerly accepted.

The acceptable fruit of a Christ-centered Ministry, such as souls being Saved, bondages being broken, lives being changed, and Believers being baptized with the Holy Spirit, is little accepted in the modern church, or even given any credence. Whenever Believers meet Testimonies of glorious Deliverances by the Power of God with no more than a yawn, something is terribly amiss.

By this example, Jesus shows us where true Faith must reside.

TRUE FAITH

It must be anchored in the Scriptures and must not be swayed by outward circumstances.

This is more amazing still when one considers that Jesus is speaking of His Own Ministry. The Healings and Miracles were genuine. People were gloriously healed and delivered. And yet, He knew that the acceptance of Him by these people was not for the right reasons. While some of them may have even heralded Him as the Messiah, it was strictly because of the sensation of the moment. So Jesus little responded to their accolades of praise. What a lesson for us!

The following should be noted:

• Upon observing His Great Power, the people probably assumed it would be used to deliver them from Rome, hence, they praised Him. However, they were wanting to use Jesus, instead of Jesus using them, even as do many in the modern church, i.e., *"the greed gospel."*

• The Believer not only must be careful to respond only to that which is Scriptural but, as well, respond correctly. For instance, what Jesus was doing was certainly Scriptural, but the manner of the people's response was unscriptural. As stated, they wanted Deliverance from Rome, which is why they were probably praising Him, but not Deliverance from sin, which they desperately needed.

• In the modern church, our response to what God does must be in the following order:

1. The Salvation of souls must be the occasion of our greatest praise. All other things done by the Lord certainly should elicit praise, but properly so.

2. If Believers are more excited over peripheral things, even though of God, than that which is paramount with the Lord, such portrays spiritual immaturity.

3. Whenever Believers will travel hundreds, if not thousands, of miles to participate in phenomenon, such as *"holy laughter,"* or some other such thing, but show little interest in the Salvation of souls, such action portrays that which is contrary to the Word of God, even though the former may possibly be of God.

4. If the Believer is where he should be with the Lord, that which excites the Lord most will excite him accordingly. For instance, Jesus said, *"I say unto you, that likewise joy shall be in Heaven over one sinner who repents, more than over ninety and nine just persons, which need no repentance"* (Lk. 15:7).

Our Lord doesn't say there is joy in Heaven over anything else that takes place, as good as it might be in its own right. The joy in Heaven is elicited only as it regards sinners being Saved. That should tell us something!

5. As well, if the Believer continues to respond wrongfully, as the people in Jerusalem, the Lord will ultimately discontinue *"committing Himself to them,"* exacerbating the spiritual slide downward.

(25) "AND NEEDED NOT THAT ANY SHOULD TESTIFY OF MAN: FOR HE KNEW WHAT WAS IN MAN."

The pattern is:

1. Defilement is cleansed by the *"Blood"* (I Jn. 1:7), which, of course, speaks of the Cross.

2. Defilement is cleansed also by *"the Spirit"* (Titus 3:3-5).

3. Defilement is also cleansed by the *"Word"* (Eph. 5:26), all working together, in a sense, as one.

ONLY THE LORD KNOWS THE HEART OF MAN

The phrase, *"And needed not that any should testify of man,"* means that He Alone properly discerned the true nature of man.

What is that true nature?

As a result of the Fall, man is distorted, twisted, perverted, and spiritually blind. Pertaining to the Things of the Lord, he has little more spiritual perception than a little child who grabs at something simply because it sparkles or shines. That's the reason so much faith, especially in the Pentecostal and Charismatic realms, is based on surface attraction alone and has no Scriptural or lasting strength.

To think that He knew this, and He certainly did, and yet came to this world anyway in order to redeem the few who would actually receive Him is strictly beyond the comprehension of mere mortals. Charles Wesley wrote, *"O love that will not let me go."*

He knew what was in man.

The phrase, *"For He knew what was in man,"* does not draw a pretty picture, and yet, He died for man, even though in the natural, there seemed to be little worth saving.

What is in man?

Due to the fact that man fell in the Garden of Eden through pride, deception, and unbelief, these three maladies continue to plague him.

DECEPTION

Man is deceived and, consequently, can be further deceived very easily.

Along with the deception, man is riddled with unbelief, which causes him to automatically hold God suspect.

If that isn't enough, he is eaten up with pride, which induces self-righteousness; consequently, he runs to do evil.

The phrase, *"Total depravity,"* is used by some to explain what and who man really is. In effect, the statement says that in no way can man desire God on his own, which means to be without the Help of the Holy Spirit. Within himself, he not only has no desire for God, but actively opposes God. So, the Holy Spirit must break through this shell, which He Alone can do, and does so on the proclaimed Word of God. Actually, Jesus will explain this very thing to Nicodemus, as given in the next Chapter.

We will learn that entrance into the human family is by natural birth and into the Divine Family by Spiritual Birth (Jn. 3:3, 16). As it is impossible to enter the human family except by physical birth, so is it impossible to enter the Divine Family without the New Birth. This is the great Doctrine of the upcoming Chapter.

> "When Jesus comes to reward His Servants,
> "Whether it be noon or night,
> "Faithful to Him will He find us watching,
> "With our lamps all trimmed and bright?"
>
> "If, at the dawn of the early morning,
> "He shall call us one by one,
> "When to the Lord we restore our talents,
> "Will He answer you, 'Well done'?"
>
> "Have we been true to the trust He left us?
> "Do we seek to do our best?
> "If in our hearts there is naught condemns us,
> "We shall have a glorious rest."
>
> "Blessed are those whom the Lord finds watching,
> "In His Glory they shall share;
> "If He shall come at the dawn or midnight,
> "Will He find us watching there?"

CHAPTER 3

(1) "THERE WAS A MAN OF THE PHARISEES, NAMED NICODEMUS, A RULER OF THE JEWS."

The order is:

1. Justification assures Salvation from the guilt of sin.

2. Sanctification effects separation from the filth of sin.

3. Superficial views of sin would lead men to imagine that a sin done in ignorance is not a guilty thing. God says differently because He looks into the heart and discerns the deep-seated source.

NICODEMUS

Nicodemus is said to have been one of the three richest men in Jerusalem. He is mentioned only in this fourth Gospel, where, as we shall see, he seems to have been an earnest man attracted by the Character and Teaching of Jesus, as well as the Miracles, but seemingly somewhat afraid to allow this interest to be known by his fellow Pharisees.

He is mentioned again in John 7:50-52, where he shows more courage in protesting against the Condemnation of Christ without giving Him a hearing.

The final reference is in John 19:39, where he is said to have brought a lavish gift of spices to anoint the Body of Christ, where he seems to have boldly taken a stand for Jesus, but only at the Crucifixion.

Evidently, Nicodemus was one of the men who, seeing the Miracles, was convinced by them, but he and the other carnal Believers remained in a moral night; for he seems to not have been able to understand the things Jesus told him.

THE PHARISEES

It is thought that Ezra might have been the founder of the Pharisees. If so, they most definitely began right. Actually, the word, *"Pharisees,"* means, *"The separated ones."*

It is said that they suffered heavily under Antipater and Herod and evidently learned that spiritual ends could not be attained by political means, for after Herod's death, we find some of them petitioning for direct Roman rule.

The Pharisees were always a minority group. Actually, during the time of Christ, they probably numbered no more than approximately 6,000. They were what one might call the fundamentalists of that day, those who claimed to believe all the Bible, etc.

They were the greatest enemies of Christ during His Ministry. Actually, they were the ones who led the effort for His Crucifixion. Their worship of God during the time of Christ had degenerated to where it was no more than mere legalism. They claimed to be sticklers for the Law, but Jesus bluntly told them that they did not keep the Law, whereas, under Ezra, they started well, but, sadly and regrettably, they ended poorly.

(2) "THE SAME CAME TO JESUS BY NIGHT, AND SAID UNTO HIM, RABBI, WE KNOW THAT YOU ARE A TEACHER COME FROM GOD: FOR NO MAN CAN DO THESE MIRACLES THAT YOU DO, EXCEPT GOD BE WITH HIM."

The composition is:

1. When the church leaves the Cross, the church has just left the Bible.

2. The Story of the Bible is the Story of *"Jesus Christ and Him Crucified."*

3. In fact, one cannot properly understand the Bible unless one understands the Cross of Christ. The two are synonymous.

NICODEMUS CAME TO JESUS BY NIGHT

The phrase, *"The same came to Jesus by night,"* should not be exaggerated, but neither should it be ignored.

The possibility definitely exists that he could not get an audience with Jesus during the day simply because of Him ministering to thousands of people. Therefore, he came by night. It could have meant, as well, that he was obligated during the day, therefore, having no opportunity, and came when opportunity presented itself.

However, the opposition against Christ from the vaunted Sanhedrin, the ruling body of Israel, had already begun. With his being a member of this particular body, it is also possible that he felt that his fellow rulers would have taken a very dim view of him meeting with Jesus at any time, so he did so when he was not likely to be noticed.

RABBI?

The phrase, *"And said unto Him, Rabbi, we know that You are a Teacher come from God,"* even though partially right and partially wrong, was still a great admission from this man.

The class distinction in Israel at this time was great. Considering the fact that

Jesus was a Peasant, for this man, a member of the Sanhedrin, to come to Jesus at all shows that he had been greatly moved by the things Jesus had said and the Miracles performed. However, in no way does he recognize Christ, at least at this juncture, as the Messiah, but rather a great *"Teacher,"* and, as well, that He is of God, and more particularly, has *"come from God."* Also, by the use of the pronoun, *"We,"* it is possible that Nicodemus represented several members of the Sanhedrin.

While Jesus definitely was the *"Teacher"* of all teachers, and He truly came from God, He, as well, was God, the Messiah of Israel, and the Creator of all things. Therefore, Nicodemus addressed Him only as a Man, which is somewhat the thinking of much of the world presently.

The world has to admit that Jesus lived because the evidence of such is overwhelming. Many will even admit that He was a great Teacher and even a Miracle Worker. Some might even say that He came from God. However, none of this admission, as true as it might be, at least as far as it goes, will save anyone.

Jesus must be addressed as God manifest in the flesh (Isa. 7:14), that He Alone is the Door to Salvation, and, in fact, paid the price for man's Redemption on Calvary's Cross. This, Nicodemus would ultimately do, which all must do, if they are to be Saved.

MIRACLES

The phrase, *"For no man can do these Miracles that You do, except God be with him,"* is exactly right.

The key is found in the words, *"These Miracles!"* While it is true that Satan can perform some types of miracles (Rev. 13:14-15; 16:13-14), they will in no way be the type of Miracles performed here by Jesus. Anything Satan does is done to deceive.

For instance, the so-called healings at the Catholic shrine of Lourdes, are, for the most part, bogus. However, it is certainly possible that some few genuine Healings may take place, with Satan removing the sickness or disease he actually originated, all done in order to deceive people. This is done to make people believe this thing is of God, when it really isn't. How do we know that?

If it's not Scriptural, then it is wrong, irrespective of what it may sound or look like. At Lourdes, as with most Catholic shrines, Mary is lauded instead of Jesus. That is not Scriptural; consequently, what is done, irrespective of what happens, is not of God.

PROPER RESPONSE

Unless our Faith is in Christ and what He did for us at the Cross, Paul labels such direction as *"another Jesus"* (II Cor. 11:4). The phrase, *"Another Jesus,"* pertains to Christ Who is worshipped outside of the Cross. In other words, the Cross has no part in such thinking, but this is worship and faith that God will not honor.

The Work performed by Christ at Calvary, which was to atone for all sin, is what affords Salvation, the Baptism with the Holy Spirit, Divine Healing, Deliverance from bondages of darkness, the Fruit of the Spirit, the Gifts of the Spirit, and, in fact, anything and everything given to us by the Lord. It is the Cross of Christ that makes it all possible.

The sad truth is, the modern church gives little shift to the Cross of Christ. Please understand, when we speak of the Cross, we aren't speaking of a wooden beam on which Christ died, but what He there accomplished.

IS IT WHO HE WAS OR WHAT HE DID?

It is both!

No one else could have paid the price at Calvary's Cross. That's why Jesus had to be born of the Virgin Mary. Had He been born like all other babies, He would have been born in original sin, which would have instantly made Him unacceptable.

But yet, we must understand that despite the fact that He was and is God, which means that He was unformed, unmade, uncreated, always was, always is, and always shall be, still, that alone, as necessary as it was, would not have Saved anyone. Jesus has always been God, but as God, without the Cross, no one would have been Saved.

To be sure, simply because God is Almighty, He could have Saved individuals without the Cross. However, to do that, He would have had to have gone against His Nature, His Character, and His Righteousness, and that He will not do. In other words, God would not treat sin in a cavalier fashion. The full price had to be paid, that is, if the Holiness and Righteousness of God was to be satisfied. So, to do this, He had to go to the Cross.

Therefore, it was both Who He was and What He did.

(3) "JESUS ANSWERED AND SAID UNTO HIM, VERILY, VERILY, I SAY UNTO YOU, EXCEPT A MAN BE BORN AGAIN, HE CANNOT SEE THE KINGDOM OF GOD."

The pattern is:

1. Without the Cross, there is no Salvation.

2. Without the Cross, there is no Baptism with the Holy Spirit.

3. Without the Cross, there is no Heaven for the simple reason that the blood of bulls and goats could not take away sins. The Cross alone can and did do that (Heb. 10:4).

THE ANSWER GIVEN BY CHRIST

The phrase, *"Jesus answered and said unto him,"* presents something totally different than what this ruler of the Jews was anticipating.

In fact, Jesus ignored the statement given by Nicodemus as it regarded the Miracles, etc. He went straight to the heart of the real problem. And yet, despite Nicodemus being one of the religious leaders of Israel, he didn't have any idea as to what Jesus was talking about.

In the few words given, Jesus would address Israel's great error as well as proclaim a fundamental Truth, actually the most important Truth of all.

THE NEW BIRTH

The phrase, *"Verily, verily, I say unto you, Except a man be born again,"* refers to the basic Foundation of the Gospel, which one must experience if one is to be Saved. As stated, it addressed Israel's error and man's need:

Israel had come to the place of a nationalistic salvation, meaning that her religious leaders believed that simply being born an Israelite constituted Salvation. However, they did believe that one could apostatize, such as the Publicans, and, thereby, be lost. Actually, what they called *"apostasy"* regarding the Publicans, Jesus did not address as such. They hated the Publicans, who were tax-collectors for Rome, simply because they felt this was high treason against their national position as the People of God; hence, they concluded them to be lost. Jesus repudiated these actions because tax-collecting was not a sin unless it was done dishonestly. He even chose a Publican, Matthew, to be one of His Disciples.

In fact, John the Baptist, when addressing Israel, was addressing a nationalistic salvation when he said, *"And think not to say within yourselves, We have Abraham to our father: for I say unto you, that God is able of these stones to raise up children unto Abraham"* (Mat. 3:9).

They felt that simply being a child of Abraham and, therefore, a true Jew, constituted Salvation. Both John and Jesus told them differently!

So, Jesus addresses this error in the thinking of Nicodemus.

Here Jesus addresses the greatest need of the human family, the need to be *"Born-Again,"* which constitutes Redemption. In effect, Jesus is saying that this applies to all, even the Jews, no matter that they are the children of Abraham.

ORIGINAL SIN

As well, this means that all men are sinners, actually having been born in sin, which is referred to as, *"Original sin."* This was brought about due to the fall of man in the Garden of Eden.

The term, *"Born-Again,"* means that man has already had a natural birth but now must have a Spiritual birth, which comes by Faith in Christ and is available to all (Jn. 3:16; Rev. 22:17).

This Spiritual birth is totally of God and none of man. This means that man's good works, religious rituals, and ceremonies play no part whatsoever in the *"Born-Again"* experience. *"For by Grace are you Saved through Faith; and that not of yourselves:*

it is the Gift of God:

"*Not of works, lest any man should boast*" (Eph. 2:8-9).

As Jesus will tell Nicodemus, the Miracle of the New Birth takes place as the individual exhibits Faith, which comes about by the Word of God in what Christ did at Calvary. At the very beginning, the Lord showed man this Way of Salvation through the sacrifices, which served as a Type of the One Who was to come (Gen. 3:21; 4:4).

SACRIFICES?

The writer of Hebrews, whom I believe was Paul, made it abundantly clear that the sacrifices within themselves had no power to save anyone (Heb. 10:4), but What, and more particularly, Who they represented, namely Jesus Christ, could save. All that was required was Faith. Consequently, before Calvary, men were Saved by looking forward to that event, and they are now Saved by looking backward to that event. All has ever been in Jesus, as all will ever be in Jesus.

Even though Nicodemus only recognized Jesus, at least at this time, as a "*Rabbi,*" or "*Teacher,*" still, Jesus will portray to him in no uncertain terms that He, in fact, is the Son of God, the Saviour of mankind.

THE MORAL QUESTION

In doing this, Jesus at once raised the moral question with Nicodemus. He immediately stopped the religious discussion by telling this most religious man and professed Believer that he was so sinful, so hopelessly corrupt and fallen as to be incapable of Reformation, and so darkened morally that he could neither recognize nor experience Spiritual phenomenon unless born from above. This fundamental Truth is obnoxious to man, especially religious man, for it humbles him.

The Lord here unveils what man really is. He is a sinner, having responsibility but no life. He is lost and must seek life and pardon outside of himself, that is, in Christ, Who meets his failure and responsibility and gives him Eternal Life, that is, if man will truly believe (Jn. 3:16).

Of course, the question begs to be asked,

NOTES

"*Was Nicodemus truly Saved at this time, although somewhat confused on the issue, with Jesus taking this opportunity to explain Salvation more perfectly, or was he spiritually lost?*"

Despite being one of the rulers in Israel as a member of the Sanhedrin, and consequently, extremely religious, the evidence shows that this "*good man*" was lost. To be sincere as Nicodemus was is not necessarily to be Saved! There are multiple hundreds of millions, especially if they are overly religious, as Nicodemus, who think surely their place and position in life affords them Salvation. However, Jesus completely shot all of these things down, proclaiming in no uncertain terms that they effected nothing toward one's Salvation. To be Saved, one must be "*Born-Again,*" which can only be done by Faith, and more particularly, Faith in Christ and what He has done for us at the Cross. To experience a Spiritual birth, as we shall see, one must be "*born from above.*"

THE SPIRITUAL REBIRTH

This experience, sometimes referred to as a "*Spiritual rebirth,*" which man must experience, does not come through any natural process. God is the Actor or Person Who effects the New Birth in those who believe and receive the Son (Jn. 1:12-13). The New Birth makes us Children of God and leads to moral transformation. In fact, a glorious change is always effected!

For instance, one who is born of God does what is right (what is Scriptural) (I Jn. 2:29). While the Believer may fail at times, no one born of God "*practices sinning,*" which means to "*keep on sinning,*" thinking one can do such and be Saved at the same time. God's Life is planted within our reborn personality, and now, if we are a true Christian, we hate sin (I Jn. 3:6, 9; 5:18).

Another expression of the New Life we receive from God is found in our love for one another (I Jn. 4:7; 5:1-2). Love and purity of life are sure to follow the New Birth, for God's Own Life swells within the twice born. We who have become God's Children by Grace through Faith are destined to grow into Jesus' Likeness, for that is the purpose of the New Birth — to be like Jesus.

THE KINGDOM OF GOD

The phrase, *"He cannot see the Kingdom of God,"* actually means that without the New Birth, one cannot understand or comprehend the *"Kingdom of God."*

This is the reason that those who are truly Born-Again have a completely different world view than those who aren't. The Believer sees things through the Word of God and judges accordingly. He knows and understands, or certainly should, the Plan of God through the Lord Jesus Christ and by the Cross for the human family, and the entirety of the world for that matter. The Believer knows that the present scheme of things is temporal. He knows the world is in rebellion against God and is filled with evil because of that rebellion. He knows the Only Answer is Jesus Christ.

JESUS IS COMING AGAIN

In this realm of Salvation, afforded by God, brought about by Jesus Christ and what He did for us at the Cross, and, thereby, empowered by the Holy Spirit, the Believer knows Jesus is coming again and will ultimately rule this world (Rev., Chpt. 19).

Those who are not *"Born-Again"* have no knowledge of Spiritual things. They walk in spiritual darkness; therefore, they have no comprehension or understanding of things as they really are. Actually, every good thing that has happened to this world, in whatever capacity, has been brought about not by the efforts of darkened humanity, but rather by Jesus working in the hearts and lives of Born-Again Believers. Believers are *"salt"* and *"Light"* simply because we have Jesus within our hearts and, as a result, serve as *"preservative"* and *"illumination"* for the world. We are busy promoting the *"Kingdom of God"* rather than the kingdoms of this world.

We admit that the totality of the *"Kingdom of God"* has not yet come to this world, as is overly obvious, hence, the continuing of sin, war, sickness, pain, and suffering. Consequently, Believers continue to pray, *"Your Kingdom come, Your Will be done in Earth, as it is in Heaven"* (Mat. 6:10). To be sure, as stated, this *"Kingdom"* will come into totality when the King comes, Who is Jesus Christ.

(4) "NICODEMUS SAID UNTO HIM, HOW CAN A MAN BE BORN WHEN HE IS OLD? CAN HE ENTER THE SECOND TIME INTO HIS MOTHER'S WOMB, AND BE BORN?"

The synopsis is:

1. It is the Cross alone that makes possible the Born-Again experience.

2. Those who claim the Cross is not enough, blaspheme!

3. It is at the Cross where Redemption was totally completed. When Jesus atoned for all sin, past, present, and future, at least for those who will believe, nothing was left undone.

4. While the Resurrection was of supreme significance, as should be obvious, still, it did not take the Resurrection, the Ascension, or the Exaltation of Christ to complete the Redemption process. In fact, and as stated, because Jesus atoned for all sin, past, present, and future, the Resurrection was not in doubt. One might say that the Resurrection ratified what Jesus did at the Cross, but Salvation was complete with the Cross when Jesus said, *"It is finished. Father, into Your Hands I commit My Spirit."*

HOW CAN A MAN BE BORN AGAIN?

The question, *"Nicodemus said unto Him, How can a man be born when he is old?"* proclaims this Spiritual leader of Israel having no knowledge at all of what Jesus was saying. By his question, he portrayed that he had no understanding of Spiritual things. He was thinking in natural terms while Jesus was speaking in Spiritual terms. Had he truly been *"Born-Again,"* he would have understood these terms.

The question, *"Can he enter the second time into his mother's womb, and be born?"* proclaims a double ignorance as he has asked a double question.

THE CIRCUMCISION OF THE HEART

Did he not know the language of the Prophets concerning circumcision of the heart (Deut. 30:6; Jer. 4:4) and concerning a hard heart and right spirit (Ps. 51:10; Ezek. 36:26-27)?

He should have known, even as Jesus would soon say, but like most of Israel, he had drifted away from the Word of God, with a gradual shift toward Salvation by natural birth as a Jew, good works, and religious ritual. He was not unlike much of the world presently!

The Scripture plainly says that Nicodemus was a Pharisee, which meant that he subscribed to the myriad of man-devised, oral, religious laws, which had been added to the Law of Moses. However, when men begin to forsake the Word of God, thereby, adding their own words, as Nicodemus, they cease to understand Spiritual things, even though continuing to be very religious. So, Nicodemus would respond foolishly to the Statement of Christ.

(5) "JESUS ANSWERED, VERILY, VERILY, I SAY UNTO YOU, EXCEPT A MAN BE BORN OF WATER AND OF THE SPIRIT, HE CANNOT ENTER INTO THE KINGDOM OF GOD."

The overview is:

1. Outside of the Cross of Christ there is no salvation.

2. Outside of the Cross of Christ there is no victory over sin.

3. Outside of the Cross of Christ there is no real understanding of the Word of God.

TRUTH

The phrase, *"Jesus answered, Verily, verily, I say unto you,"* is the same thing as saying, *"Truth, truth,"* or, *"Truly, truly!"*

Despite being very religious, Nicodemus was about to hear the Truth for the first time in his life. He wouldn't understand it simply because he was unredeemed; nevertheless, the Truth he would hear.

Jesus addressed him in this fashion simply because as one of the religious leaders of Israel, he should have had at least a modicum of understanding respecting what our Lord was addressing. Sadly, he didn't have a clue, despite his religiosity. As such, he was and is like most in the modern church presently. They are religious but lost!

BORN OF WATER AND OF THE SPIRIT

The phrase, *"Except a man be born of water and of the Spirit,"* has been the source of great controversy. The phrase, *"Born of water,"* speaks of the natural birth, of which Jesus speaks in the next Verse, and pertains to a baby being born. Being *"born of the Spirit"* speaks of the Holy Spirit and a Spiritual birth, which is brought about by God Alone.

It does not speak of Water Baptism, as many believe, simply because there is no Salvation in water. For instance, the Baptism of John was not held up at all as containing any type of Saving Grace. In other words, the act of Water Baptism did not save anyone. John, by this Baptism, did not give Repentance or Remission of sins to the people. Water Baptism was the result of a Finished Work brought about in the hearts and lives of Believers who had already repented. It was the result and not the occasion.

Nothing but the Blood and Spirit of Christ could convey either Remission or Repentance to the souls of men. John preached the Baptism of Repentance unto Remission but could confer neither. He taught the people to look to the One Who should come after him.

As well, he sharply discriminated the Baptism with water from the Baptism with the Spirit (Mat. 3:11).

WATER BAPTISM

There was no regenerating efficacy in the Water Baptism of John, nor is there any in Christian Baptism as well! Even though Christian Baptism definitely serves a purpose, just as did the Baptism of John, that purpose has nothing to do with one's Salvation, which comes exclusively by Faith in Christ (Eph. 2:8-9).

Christian Baptism is meant to serve as a symbol of the Death, Burial, and Resurrection of Christ, carried out in the heart and life of the Believer upon Conversion. As well, the Believer is baptized not in order to be Saved, but as a result of having been Saved. Likewise, Water Baptism is a symbol of the death of the old man of sin, the burial of that old man, and the Resurrection of the New (Rom. 6:3-5). This is symbolized by the person being immersed totally in water and then brought out. It is to fulfill all Righteousness and the answer of a good conscience toward God (Mat. 3:15; I Pet. 3:21).

NO CEREMONIAL RITE

Actually, there is no proof at all that the Apostles of Christ were ever baptized with water unless it was at the hands of John or during the early Ministry of Jesus, which is when it probably occurred (Jn. 4:2). Consequently, considering the plain teaching of the Word of God, we know that the Lord was not making any ceremonial rite indispensable for entrance into the Kingdom.

The idea of this statement by Christ is that before a person can *"enter into the Kingdom of God,"* he must first of all be born as a human being, which is the natural birth, and illustrated by the phrase, *"Born of water,"* and then he must be *"Born-Again,"* which speaks of being *"born of the Spirit."* The very statement, *"Born-Again,"* automatically means that one has already had a birth, in this case, the natural birth.

(6) "THAT WHICH IS BORN OF THE FLESH IS FLESH; AND THAT WHICH IS BORN OF THE SPIRIT IS SPIRIT."

The exposition is:

1. What Jesus did at the Cross answers the sin question and provides the solution, which it alone can do.

2. In truth, we are encouraged to come into a knowledge that sin is a much larger matter than that of which we are conscious.

3. Despite the power of sin, it is within the reach and grasp of our Lord's Atoning Power, which is made possible by the Cross.

BORN OF THE FLESH

The phrase, *"That which is born of the flesh is flesh,"* has to do with the natural birth and is illustrated by the phrase, *"Born of water."* As stated, it does not have any reference to Water Baptism, but, unfortunately, untold millions down through the centuries have placed Salvation in the ceremonial rite of Water Baptism, thinking it saves. Let it be understood, there is nothing that man can produce, such as water, ceremonies, rituals, rites, etc., that can provide Salvation. Salvation does not lie within the grasp of man, not at all. It is all in Christ and what He has done for us at the Cross (Jn. 3:16; Eph. 2:8-9; Rev. 22:17).

BORN OF THE SPIRIT

The phrase, *"And that which is born of the Spirit is spirit,"* has to do with that which is solely of God. The one (flesh) has no relationship to the other (Holy Spirit) and cannot be joined. Actually, this is the great problem every Christian faces. It is the constant struggle between the *"flesh and the Spirit,"* i.e., *"Holy Spirit."* If the *"flesh"* is mixed with the *"Spirit,"* great difficulties ensue.

As one comes into the Kingdom of God by being *"born of the Spirit,"* likewise, one has victory over the flesh by following *"after the Spirit"* (Rom. 8:4).

WHAT DOES IT MEAN TO WALK AFTER THE SPIRIT?

It has nothing to do with the doing of Spiritual things. Regrettably, most think that is the answer, but it isn't.

Walking after the Spirit (Rom. 8:1-11) refers to walking after the Holy Spirit, in other words, how He works.

To *"walk after the Spirit,"* the Saint of God must place his or her Faith exclusively in Christ and what Christ did for us at the Cross (Rom. 6:1-14; 8:1-11). Placing our Faith exclusively in Christ and the Cross, and maintaining it exclusively in Christ and the Cross, is walking after the Spirit, which gives the Holy Spirit great liberty and latitude to work within our lives. In fact, this is God's Prescribed Order of Victory.

Perhaps the following diagram can be of help:

• Jesus Christ is the Source of all things we receive from God (Jn. 1:1-2; 14:6; Col. 2:10).

• The Cross of Christ is the Means by which all of these wonderful things are given unto us (I Cor. 1:17, 18, 23; 2:2; Col. 2:10-15).

• Jesus being the Source and the Cross being the Means, the Object of our Faith must ever be the Cross of Christ (I Cor. 1:17-18; Col. 2:14-15; Gal. 6:14).

• With Jesus being the Source and the Cross being the Means, and the Cross ever being the Object of our Faith, then the Holy Spirit, Who works exclusively within the parameters of the Finished Work of Christ, so to speak, will then have liberty and latitude within our lives, giving us victory over the world, the flesh, and the Devil (Rom. 8:1-11; Eph. 2:13-18). This is the way the Holy Spirit works, and He will not work outside of these parameters.

(7) "MARVEL NOT THAT I SAID UNTO YOU, YOU MUST BE BORN AGAIN."

The exposition is:

1. Justification by Faith is based squarely on the Cross of Christ.

2. In fact, the Cross of Christ is the Foundation of all Bible Doctrine, actually formulated in the Mind of God from before the foundation of the world (I Pet. 1:18-20).

3. All false doctrine, whatever it might be, is because of an improper understanding of the Cross, an ignoring the Cross, or an outright denial of the Cross.

DO YOU MARVEL?

The phrase, *"Marvel not that I said unto you,"* evidently addresses itself to the surprise which must have been registered on the countenance of Nicodemus.

These short statements as given by Christ took the heart out of all that Nicodemus had been taught and firmly believed. In a few moments' time, he found that the old ideas of national privilege, sacramental purification, and of soundly taught principles and habits meant nothing at all to the Lord.

Could this be a dress rehearsal for that which will happen to hundreds of millions of others when they stand before God one day and find out that all of their good works, ritual religion, and beautiful ceremonies had absolutely nothing to do with being right with God?

The phrase, *"You must be born again,"* says it all! This and this alone will be recognized by the Creator of the ages.

Entrance into the human family is by natural birth and into the Divine Family by Spiritual birth. As it is impossible to enter the human family except by natural birth, so it is impossible to enter the Divine Family except by Spiritual birth. This is the great Doctrine that Jesus is proclaiming.

NOTES

(8) "THE WIND BLOWS WHERE IT LISTS, AND YOU HEAR THE SOUND THEREOF, BUT CANNOT TELL FROM WHERE IT COMES, AND WHERE IT GOES: SO IS EVERY ONE WHO IS BORN OF THE SPIRIT."

The form is:

1. Sin defiles, and there is only one answer, and that is the Cross.

2. Any direction other than the Cross of Christ always and without exception leads to self-righteousness.

3. Sadly and regrettably, due to the fact that the Cross of Christ has been so little preached in the last few decades, this modern church is the most self-righteous church ever, at least since the Reformation.

THE WIND?

The phrase, *"The wind blows where it lists, and you hear the sound thereof, but cannot tell from where it comes, and where it goes,"* is the way in which Jesus explains the *"Born-Again"* experience. He likens it to the wind which comes and goes but is impossible to tell exactly how. What causes it to blow in the first place? What causes it to blow in certain directions, and exactly where does it originate? All of that is past finding out.

The idea is that one cannot deny its presence because it can readily be felt; however, its coming and going is a mystery.

Why did the Lord use this type of explanation?

He used it simply because the Born-Again experience, which is all of God and none of man, is beyond our comprehension. If the Lord bothered to explain all of it to us, we simply would not understand it. So, He explains it to Nicodemus, and to you and me, in this fashion in order to tell us that even though we cannot answer many questions as it regards the *"wind,"* nevertheless, we know that it's real; likewise, the Born-Again experience.

The phrase, *"So is everyone who is born of the Spirit,"* proclaims the manner in which it is done, but, as stated, which is beyond the pale of human comprehension.

One knows that God is the Author of Salvation, and that He carries it out by the Power of the Holy Spirit according to Faith evidenced in Jesus and what He did at Calvary. We also know it is a Gift of God. However, the manner in which the Lord does this, the changing of a human heart immediately upon Faith in Christ, is as the wind, indiscernible.

(9) "NICODEMUS ANSWERED AND SAID UNTO HIM, HOW CAN THESE THINGS BE?"

The order is:

1. The Cross of Christ is God's Way and, in fact, His only Way.

2. Due to the Fall, the world is geared in an entirely different direction — the direction of self.

3. Unfortunately, the clinging vines of self cling even to the dedicated Believer, which is a source of constant difficulties. The answer to that as given by Jesus is, *"We should deny ourselves and take up the Cross daily and follow Him"* (Lk. 9:23).

HOW CAN THESE THINGS BE?

Once again, Nicodemus is startled by this Revelation and asks the question, *"How can these things be?"* He is still thinking in the natural because that's really the only way he can think. Not being *"Born-Again"* at this particular time, despite his vast intelligence in other areas, he has no understanding of this great Truth.

One must wonder exactly how much he had studied the Word of God! However, not knowing the Lord, the Scriptures would not have been open to him. His man-devised religion, as with most of Israel at this time, coupled with a lack of the New Birth, only exacerbated the problem.

In other words, it is bad enough not to be saved, but for one to be immersed in religion, thereby, thinking he is Saved, only adds to the problem.

And yet, his question shows that he wants more explanation, which Jesus will readily give him.

(10) "JESUS ANSWERED AND SAID UNTO HIM, ARE YOU A MASTER OF ISRAEL, AND KNOW NOT THESE THINGS?"

The pattern is:

1. Scripture interprets Scripture.

2. This means that to properly understand a Bible subject, we are to look at all the Passages in the Word that relate to that particular subject and then interpret them accordingly.

3. The Scripture will never contradict itself.

A MASTER OF ISRAEL

This question, as posed by Jesus to Nicodemus, *"Are you a master of Israel,"* is extremely probing and of extreme significance, as should be obvious. As well, it is addressed to all in similar circumstances.

The term, *"A Master of Israel,"* means that Nicodemus was held in very high regard as one of the Spiritual leaders of Israel. He was, as stated, a member of the Sanhedrin. However, he was looked upon even in a more superior light than just being a member of that body, which within itself was of the greatest privilege. And yet, he knew the Word of God so little that he really did not know how to be Saved. This is the tragedy, and it fits hundreds of millions in the world at present and, in fact, always has.

Actually, very few in Israel at that time would have thought of this man as anything but a Spiritual giant, and yet, he was not only not a spiritual giant, but actually not even saved.

This means that *"association"* with Spiritual things does not bring Salvation. It also means that *"participation"* in Spiritual things contains no Saving Grace. It, as well, means a correct Spiritual *"environment"* does not equal Salvation.

Multiple tens of millions belong to a church and profess Salvation but, in reality, do not know the Lord and are totally and completely lost, as all unsaved are!

Almost all in what is referred to as *"Seeker Sensitive churches"* are, in fact, lost. Actually, almost all in the *"Purpose Driven Life churches"* fall into the same category. All of this is Salvation by works, by doing good things, by *"being good,"* whatever that means, by other means of ceremonies and rituals, etc. Jesus said:

"Enter in at the straight gate: for wide is the gate, and broad is the way, that leads to

destruction, and many there be which go in thereat:

"Because straight is the gate, and narrow is the way, which leads unto life, and few there be who find it" (Mat. 7:13-14).

DO YOU NOT KNOW THESE THINGS?

The conclusion of the question, *"Do you not know these things?"* means that he should have known the Way of Salvation, but the sad fact was, he didn't.

Why?

As we have stated, he was not being led by the Word of God, but rather by other things. The erroneous teaching of the Pharisees had inculcated its error into his heart. He had the idea that being born a Jew and, therefore being a good Jew, a child of Abraham, so to speak, constituted Salvation. After all, were they not the People of God? Were they not the people of the Prophets? To these Prophets, had not the Word of God been given? This meant that Israel was the only people on the face of the Earth who had this great privilege.

As wonderful as all of that was, none of it had anything to do with Salvation, and that was very hard for Nicodemus or any Jew to hear.

As well, Nicodemus was very rich, which Israel equated with the Blessings of God and, thereby, Salvation, for that matter. They felt that rich men were Saved and poor men were not or, at the least, had the frown of God upon them for some reason, which translated into their poverty.

In the midst of all of this, every evidence is that Nicodemus little studied the Word of God. It was talked about a lot but, evidently, read with the idea of making it conform to his beliefs instead of him conforming to its teaching. He did not allow the Word to be a mirror, as it was intended to be; consequently, the Holy Spirit had little opportunity to speak to his heart. As well, this blind position of religion is probably the hardest for the Holy Spirit to penetrate. The simple reason is these people think they are Saved and even conclude themselves as greatly spiritual.

THE WORD OF GOD

However, in the midst of all of this, Jesus reveals the Word of God as it ought to have

NOTES

been revealed, which was probably the first time Nicodemus had ever really heard the Truth. Consequently, the Spirit of God dealt with him greatly, which, no doubt, made him see his spiritual lack, with him seeking an audience with Jesus.

If Nicodemus were sat down in the midst of the modern church, especially considering that he was rich and religious, he would probably be sought after far and wide. He would probably appear on just about every Christian television talk show and be held in high regard and respected as one of the great Spiritual leaders of our day. However, in the Eyes of God, he was *"wretched, and miserable, and poor, and blind, and naked"* (Rev. 3:17).

I wonder how many this actually applies to at present, and I speak of those called *"Spiritual leaders,"* such as Nicodemus.

From the way that Jesus asked, *"Do you not know these things?"* we learn there is no excuse for not knowing them. The Word of God, at least in most countries, is available to all. Our problem is, even though we greatly claim the Lord Jesus Christ, the truth is, we little know Him or His Book. So, millions think they are Saved when they really aren't! Others believe false doctrines, which greatly weaken their Spiritual experience. Others make decisions totally contrary to the Word of God — all because we *"know not these things."*

(11) "VERILY, VERILY, I SAY UNTO YOU, WE SPEAK THAT WE DO KNOW, AND TESTIFY THAT WE HAVE SEEN; AND YOU RECEIVE NOT OUR WITNESS."

The composition is:

1. The blood poured out at the bottom of the Altar, as portrayed in the Old Testament, typified the Blood of Jesus that would be shed at Calvary.

2. The little animal then being slain testified to the Death of Christ. This animal was innocent, and so was Christ.

3. No Bible Passage speaks of Christ as reconciling God to man, but rather man to God. It is man's sin which has caused the enmity.

WE SPEAK THAT WE DO KNOW

The phrase, *"Verily, verily, I say unto*

you, *We speak that we do know,*" has confused many because Jesus used the plural pronouns, *"We"* and *"Our."*

Jesus was speaking of the Triune Godhead and, as well, of all the *"Apostles and Prophets."* The Holy Spirit through Paul said:

"And are built (meaning the Church) *upon the Foundation of the Apostles and Prophets, Jesus Christ Himself being the Chief Corner Stone."*

He then said:

"In Whom also you are built together for an habitation of God through the Spirit" (Eph. 2:20, 22).

In essence, Jesus is speaking of the Word of God and is directing Nicodemus to that Source instead of tradition. He is saying, in effect, *"We speak what We know!"* It is the sure Word of the Lord, not the word of man.

When Preachers preach the Bible, they are preaching that which is certain; however, they have to *"know"* the Word before they can properly *"speak"* the Word!

THE TESTIMONY

The phrase, *"And testify that We have seen,"* means that one can actually *"see"* the fruit or benefits of this *"Testimony,"* i.e., the Word of God, i.e., *"Miracles."*

No religion in the world can compare with this. It *"knows"* what it speaks about, and the results can be *"seen"* in changed lives and situations.

The phrase, *"And you receive not our witness,"* had to do with the Jewish Sanhedrin, the religious leadership of Israel. As it did not then, it does not now!

Actually, two members of that 70 man ruling order did accept Christ, Nicodemus and Joseph of Arimathea. However, it seems that it was only at the Crucifixion that these two men fully and openly accepted Christ. Otherwise, this religious clique of Israel opposed Jesus from the very beginning. They made no investigation of His Claims, nor did His Ministry of Healing and Miracles or Message of Redemption move them in the slightest.

It was because they were *"of their father the Devil, and the lusts of their father they would do"* (Jn. 8:44).

NOTES

The same holds true presently and always has. The majority of those who call themselves *"Believers,"* and the majority of those who are referred to as Spiritual leaders, *"Receive not Our* (His) *witness."*

(12) "IF I HAVE TOLD YOU EARTHLY THINGS, AND YOU BELIEVE NOT, HOW SHALL YOU BELIEVE, IF I TELL YOU OF HEAVENLY THINGS?"

The synopsis is:

1. The only thing standing between mankind and eternal Hell is the Cross of Christ (Jn. 3:16).

2. The only thing standing between the Church and apostasy is the Cross of Christ (I Cor. 2:2).

3. The only answer for sin is the Cross of Christ (Heb. 9:28).

EARTHLY THINGS

The phrase, *"If I have told you earthly things, and you believe not,"* refers to the earthly types and events in the Bible, such as the sacrifices and Feast Days, Circumcision, etc., which Nicodemus, no doubt, read many times in the Bible, but was so blind that he did not see or believe its lessons. These things had no spiritual meaning for his heart or conscience. So it is with multitudes of professing Christians presently.

The truth is, the religious leaders of Israel had so perverted the Word of God, so added to the Word of God, or had taken away from the Word of God that its original intent had long since been lost. That being the case, it was very difficult for anyone to be Saved simply because Salvation then rested in the Cross the same as it rests today in the Cross. What do we mean by that?

All of the sacrifices offered up were Types of the Lord Jesus Christ and what He would do on the Cross to redeem humanity, which was to atone for all sin, past, present, and future, at least for all who will believe. While the sacrifices themselves could not save anyone, what they represented, namely our Lord and His Offering of Himself, definitely could save and, in fact, did save. Every single person who had been Saved from the time of Adam and Eve was Saved as a result of putting their Faith in that which the sacrifices represented. To be sure, their understanding of all of this was very dim, but, still, their Faith saved them. It was Faith then and Faith now. To be more specific, it was Faith then in the Cross of Christ, which was typified by the sacrifice, and it is Faith now in the Cross of Christ that affords Salvation.

UNBELIEF

Unbelief is the crowning sin of humanity. Actually, it is *"unbelief"* of which the Holy Spirit convicts (Jn. 16:8-9). More specifically, it is unbelief pertaining to Jesus. Men do not desire to believe that He is the Son of God, the Creator of the ages, and the Saviour of mankind, the One Who paid the price for man's Redemption and, in fact, the only Way to the Father (Jn. 10:7-9; 14:6).

I think I can say without exaggeration that the pivot point of all unbelief is directed toward Christ. For one to properly understand the Bible, one must have a proper knowledge of Jesus Christ, Who He is, the Son of the Living God, God manifest in the flesh, and What He has done for us at Calvary and the Resurrection. Actually, His Life and Ministry can be summed up in four parts:

1. Jesus is the Saviour (Jn. 3:3, 16; Rev. 22:17).
2. Jesus is the Baptizer with the Holy Spirit (Mat. 3:11).
3. Jesus is the Healer (Jn. 15:7; James 5:14-15).
4. Jesus is coming again to establish His Kingdom on this Earth (Rev. 19:11-21).

In essence, if one understands the Cross of Christ, then one will properly understand these points just given. In fact, it is well nigh impossible to properly understand the Bible unless one understands the Cross of Christ, not only respecting Salvation but, as well, Sanctification. In other words, we are speaking of how we live for God, how we order our behavior, how we grow in Grace and the Knowledge of the Lord, and how we have victory over the world, the flesh, and the Devil. Actually, all false doctrine begins with an improper understanding of the Cross of Christ, an ignoring the Cross of Christ, or an outright denial of the Cross of Christ.

HEAVENLY THINGS

The conclusion of the question, *"How shall you believe, if I tell you of heavenly things?"* in effect, tells us that if we are to know Jesus as God (heavenly things) we must first know Jesus in the Incarnation (earthly things). It must be remembered that Nicodemus has addressed Jesus as merely a *"Teacher"*; so, until he understands God becoming flesh and dwelling among men (Jn. 1:14), he will not understand heavenly things.

A PROPER UNDERSTANDING

Basically, concerning Jesus, most unbelief by all men is wrapped up in the Incarnation, which translates into the Cross. Most simply cannot, or else, refuse to understand that One Who lived as a Peasant is the Son of God, the Creator of all things (Jn. 1:1-2). Even though many in the world may speak of Him in a positive sense, it is mostly with the idea of Him being a *"Good Man,"* a *"Great Teacher,"* or even a *"Miracle Worker,"* but not the Son of God! Not understanding that He is the Eternal Logos, and because of unbelief, and a willful unbelief, we may quickly add, it takes the Holy Spirit to break through that shell and bring them to acceptance of Christ.

As it regards Believers, many have problems understanding the Cross of Christ regarding Sanctification, i.e., how we live for God. The truth is, most modern Believers simply do not know how to live for God.

HOW TO LIVE FOR GOD

When we make a statement such as we have just made, that most modern Believers simply do not know how to live for God, it raises all kinds of flags. Most would retort with, *"What do you mean, I don't know how to live for God?"* But the truth is, most don't. How do I know that?

I know it simply because to properly live for God, to be what we ought to be in Christ, to have victory over the world, the flesh, and the Devil, and to properly grow in Grace and the knowledge of the Lord, one has to understand the Cross of Christ as it relates to our Sanctification. Most modern

Christians draw a blank when you tell them that the Cross has literally everything to do with their victory, with their life and living, etc. They know and realize that it has everything to do with their Salvation, at least, most do, but when it comes to our Sanctification, how we live for the Lord, most don't have the foggiest idea as to what you are talking about. Please note carefully the following simple diagram:

• The only Way to God the Father is through Jesus Christ (Jn. 14:6).

• The only Way to Jesus Christ is through the Cross of Christ (Lk. 9:23).

• The only Way to the Cross is a denial of self (Lk. 9:23; 14:27).

(13) "AND NO MAN HAS ASCENDED UP TO HEAVEN, BUT HE WHO CAME DOWN FROM HEAVEN, EVEN THE SON OF MAN WHICH IS IN HEAVEN."

The construction is:

1. The effect of all Scripture to one's own soul when properly interpreted, which is done directly by the Power of the Holy Spirit, is to lead us out of self to Christ.

2. Wherever we see our fallen nature, at whatever stage of its history we've contemplated it — whether in its conception, at its birth, or at any point along its whole career, from the womb to the coffin — it wears the double stamp of infirmity and defilement (Mackintosh).[1]

3. The Cross of Christ was the Eternal Destination of Christ, actually, the reason for the Incarnation.

ASCENDING UP TO HEAVEN

Some have thought that Jesus ceased speaking with the Twelfth Verse, with John the Beloved picking up with the Thirteenth Verse; however, I feel that Jesus Personally continues speaking through the Twenty-first Verse of this Third Chapter of John.

This Thirteenth Verse could be translated, *"The same Man Who will ascend up to Heaven is He Who came down from Heaven, even the Son of Man Whose abode is in Heaven."*

The phrase, *"And no man has ascended up to Heaven,"* refers to the fact that He will complete His Mission, which refers to going to the Cross, which He will later mention, and will do so victorious in every capacity. In other words, He would not be able to *"ascend up to Heaven"* if He were unable to carry out the task assigned to Him, which is the Redemption of the fallen sons of Adam's lost race.

HE CAME DOWN FROM HEAVEN

The phrase, *"But He Who came down from Heaven,"* speaks of the Incarnation, God becoming flesh and dwelling among men (Jn. 1:14).

He came down from Heaven for a distinct purpose. That was to redeem mankind from the power of sin, which He did by going to the Cross. There He paid the price in totality, which was accepted fully by God. His Mission was to redeem man, which He did, which was done at the Cross.

THE SON OF MAN WHICH IS IN HEAVEN

The phrase, *"Even the Son of Man which is in Heaven,"* is referring to the fact that only One from Heaven could carry out this task, meaning no one on Earth could do so.

If Jesus Christ were a mere man but ever so talented, ever so knowledgeable, ever so powerful, ever so charismatic, and even a Miracle-Worker, that would be one thing. However, if He is the Son of the Living God, meaning that He is God, the Creator of the Ages (Jn. 1:1-3), then that's something else altogether. To reject a man is one thing, but to reject a Man Who is at the same time God is something else.

We must always remember, while God became Man, He never ceased to be God, not for a moment. While Jesus laid aside the expression of His Deity, He never for a moment laid aside the possession of His Deity. While He never used the Powers of Deity in His Work and Ministry on Earth, doing all things rather by the Power of the Holy Spirit, still, He was always God. There is one thing that man must understand:

We will face Jesus Christ today, and I speak of the Cross of Calvary where our sins can be washed clean by His Precious Blood, or we will face Him at the Great White Throne Judgment, but face Him we will.

(14) "AND AS MOSES LIFTED UP THE SERPENT IN THE WILDERNESS,

EVEN SO MUST THE SON OF MAN BE LIFTED UP."

The exposition is:

1. The serpent lifted up on the pole proclaims the fact that the Cross would be where Satan would be totally defeated.

2. This was fulfilled by the Lord Himself being lifted up on the Cross.

3. The purpose of the Cross of Christ was to defeat sin in every capacity. Jesus did this by atoning for all sin, past, present, and future, at least for all who will believe (Jn. 3:16).

4. By atoning for all sin, this defeated Satan, all fallen Angels, and all demon spirits.

THE LIFTING UP OF THE SERPENT IN THE WILDERNESS

The phrase, *"And as Moses lifted up the serpent in the wilderness,"* has reference to Numbers 21:9. It speaks of the Children of Israel, while in the wilderness, murmuring against God and Moses concerning their difficulties in that place, and the Lord sending fiery serpents among the people, with many being bitten and dying.

The Lord told Moses in answer to his prayer for the people, *"Make you a fiery serpent, and set it upon a pole: and it shall come to pass, that everyone who is bitten, when he looks upon it, shall live"* (Num. 21:5-9).

THE PLACE OF REDEMPTION AND THE MANNER OF REDEMPTION

It was to Abraham that the Lord showed the place of Redemption, which was *"Moriah,"* actually, where the Temple later would be built. As well, it is said that the Holy of Holies of the Temple was situated over the exact spot where Abraham was to offer up Isaac but was stopped at the last moment (Gen. 22:2). Abraham understood that it would be by death that God would redeem humanity, actually, the Death of God's Only Son, typified by Isaac. However, He did not show Abraham the manner of that death, which would be the Cross. That information was given to Moses, to which Jesus alludes. Of course, the manner was and is the Cross.

THE SON OF MAN LIFTED UP

As Jesus speaks of Himself being *"lifted up"* on the Cross, in John 12:32, He says, *"And I, if I be lifted up from the Earth, will draw all men unto Me."*

Consequently, even in both cases, the Lord was speaking not merely of being lifted up from the Earth on a Roman Cross but, as well, of being *"lifted up out of the Earth altogether."* That includes His Cross, His Death, Burial, Resurrection, and Ascension. In John 3:14, the Cross only is in view, and for the reason that only the Atonement is mentioned there. However, in John 12:32, the drawing Power of our Lord Jesus is spoken of as well!

A dead Christ on a Cross can draw no sinner to Himself. It takes a Crucified, Risen, Ascended, Glorified God-Man in the Glory to draw sinners to Himself. Thus does Jesus preach the Gospel to Nicodemus.

THE SACRIFICE FOR SIN

Jesus speaks of Himself as the Sacrifice for sin to which all the Old Testament sacrifices pointed. He tells Nicodemus by this that the Levitical system will soon be set aside in favor of the actual Redemption for sin which God will offer, and that the Redemption will be Himself dying on a Roman Cross, which atoned for all sin.

Actually, the New Testament only mentions the Atonement one time (Rom. 5:11). In reality, it should have been translated, *"Reconciliation."*

Jesus explains to the spiritually blind Jewish teacher that Faith in Him as the Substitutionary Sacrifice results in the Salvation of the individual. This is exactly what the sacrifices taught, all the way from Genesis 3:21, where the Lord God made coats of skins and clothed Adam and Eve, through the Levitical system, and up till the time when Jesus was speaking these Words. He was stating that the sinner during those times should look ahead to a Sacrifice that would be offered for him by God, which was in Jesus. Since the Judaism of the First Century was a mere ethical cult, having lost that Supernatural Revelation of the Sacrifice for sin in its teachings, Nicodemus was blind to all this. However, as we have stated, there is evidence to the fact that this Jewish leader did ultimately accept Christ as his Saviour.

AN ETHICAL CULT

Regrettably and sadly, the modern church follows suit in that, anymore, it is no more than a *"mere ethical cult."* It has lost the Revelation of the Cross, and, therefore, sin is not really addressed. The only cure for sin is the Cross, and if sin is to be ignored, you don't need the solution, hence, the Cross being laid aside as old-fashioned and not needed anymore in the modern religious climate.

The truth is, the Cross of Christ is just as old-fashioned as yesterday and as modern as tomorrow. The idea that poor, pitiful, pathetic man has so advanced spiritually that he no longer needs the Cross is ridiculous, to say the least. However, that's where the modern church is. Let us say it again; it is a *"mere ethical cult."* The way to Salvation presently, at least in the minds of most, is that we do good things for the community. Once again, we are ignoring man's real problem, which is sin, and, thereby, ignoring the only solution for sin, which is the Cross.

The word, *"Atonement,"* is used very little in the New Testament, only one time, with other words taking its place, words such as *"Reconciliation," "Redemption," "Salvation,"* etc. However, what Jesus did at the Cross was to atone for all sin, as previously stated, past, present, and future, at least for all who will believe.

The need for Atonement is brought about by three things:

1. The universality of sin.
2. The seriousness of sin.
3. Man's inability to deal with sin.

We find that man cannot deal with the situation of sin. He is not able to keep his sin hidden, and he cannot cleanse himself of it. No deeds of Law will ever enable man to stand before God justified (Rom. 3:20; Gal. 2:16). If he must depend on himself, then man will never be saved. Perhaps the most important evidence of this is the very fact of the Atonement. If the Son of God came to Earth to save men, then men were sinners and their plight serious indeed.

From the Old Testament, we learn certain things concerning the Atonement. Some of them are:

NOTES

• We learn that the victim, the innocent lamb, must always be unblemished because it typified the coming Redeemer. In fact, this indicated the necessity for perfection.

• Of course, as should be obvious, the victims, the lambs, cost something, for Atonement is not cheap, and sin is never to be taken lightly.

• The death of the victim was the important thing. There had to be death, or there could not be a sacrifice. As well, it is clear that in the Old Testament, it was recognized that death was the penalty for sin (Ezek. 18:20), and that God graciously permitted the death of a sacrificial victim, once again, a lamb, to substitute for the death of the sinner. So clear is the connection that the writer of the Epistle to the Hebrews can sum it up by saying, *"Without the shedding of blood there is no forgiveness of sins"* (Heb. 9:22).

THE CROSS

The Cross is absolutely central to the New Testament and, indeed, to the whole Bible. All before leads up to it; all after looks back to it.

THE DEATH OF CHRIST

It should be understood up front that the Death of Christ was a death for sin. It was not simply that certain wicked men rose up against Him. It is not that His Enemies conspired against Him, and He was not able to resist them. In fact, His Death was not actually an execution or an assassination. It was a Sacrifice. Christ came to this world for one supreme purpose, and that was to go to the Cross. He came especially to die for our sins. His Blood was shed *"for many for the forgiveness of sins"* (Mat. 26:28). He *"made purification for our sins"* (Heb. 1:3). He *"bore our sins in His Body on the tree"* (I Pet. 2:24). He is *"the propitiation* (another word for Atonement) *for our sins"* (I Jn. 2:2). The Cross of Christ will never be understood unless it is seen that thereon the Saviour was dealing with the sins of all mankind.

OUR REPRESENTATIVE MAN

It is agreed by most Bible students that Christ's Death was vicarious. In one sense,

He died *"for sin,"* in another, He died *"for us."* *"Vicarious"* is a term which may mean much or little. It means that the Death of Christ is representative. It is not that Christ died and somehow the benefits of that death became available to men. It is rather that He died specifically for us. He was our Representative as He hung on the Cross. This is expressed succinctly in II Corinthians 5:14, *"One died for all; therefore all have died."* The Death of the Representative counts as the death of those He represents. When Christ is spoken of as our *"Advocate with the Father"* (another name for Atonement) (I Jn. 2:1), there is the plain thought of representation. As the Passage immediately goes on to deal with His Death for sin, it is relevant to our purpose. The Epistle to the Hebrews has as one of its major themes that of Christ as our Great High Priest. In fact, the thought is repeated over and over. Now, whatever else may be said about a High Priest, he represents men. The thought of representation may thus be said to be very strong in this Epistle.

Paul saw in the Cross the Way of Deliverance. Men naturally are enslaved to sin (Rom. 6:17; 7:14), but in Christ, men are free (Rom. 6:14, 22).

How are we free?

We are free by virtue of the fact that Jesus Christ, as stated, atoned for all sin at the Cross of Calvary, at least for those who will believe, and, thereby, removed the legal right that Satan had to hold man captive. He has no more legal right to do such. If he does such, it's because that we do not take advantage of what Christ has done for us.

The Believer is to understand that the Cross of Christ pertains not only to one's Salvation but, as well, to one's Sanctification. In fact, virtually all of the teaching in the entirety of the Bible has to do with the Cross of Christ, referring to Believers. Of course, there are some Passages devoted to Salvation, but only a few. The reason should be obvious: the Bible is not written for unbelievers, but rather for Believers.

The Believer is to understand that all Victory is in the Cross, and I mean all Victory. In fact, there is no victory outside of the Cross. Therefore, we must place our Faith constantly in the Cross of Christ, and maintain it constantly in the Cross of Christ (Lk. 9:23-24). Placing our Faith exclusively in Christ and the Cross then gives the Holy Spirit latitude and liberty to work within our hearts and lives, which only He can do, thereby, bringing about victory in every capacity. While the Bible does not teach sinless perfection, it most definitely does teach that *"sin is not to have dominion over us"* (Rom. 6:14).

"Dominion" is a strong word. The sad truth is the vast majority of modern Christians, and we speak of those who truly love the Lord, are being dominated by sin (the sin nature) in some way. It is because they do not understand the part the Cross plays in our Sanctification, how we live for God, etc.

Regrettably, the modern church is doing everything within its power to go the opposite direction of the Cross. In fact, it has sold out to humanistic psychology. Please understand, either one, the Cross of Christ or humanistic psychology, cancels out the other. You cannot have both. So, these preachers who claim to believe in the Cross and have, as well, embraced humanistic psychology are, proverbially speaking, trying to force the square peg into the round hole. It won't work. It is the Cross! The Cross! The Cross!

(15) "THAT WHOSOEVER BELIEVES IN HIM SHOULD NOT PERISH, BUT HAVE ETERNAL LIFE.

The exegesis is:

1. If the Son of God came to Earth to save men, and He most definitely did, then men were sinners and their plight serious indeed.

2. The sacrifices of the Old Testament point us to certain truths concerning the Cross.

3. For instance, the animal had to be unblemished inasmuch as it was a Type of the coming Redeemer, Who would be perfect in every respect.

WHOSOEVER

The word, *"Whosoever,"* means that all are lost, and, consequently, all can be Saved.

"Whosoever" destroys the erroneous hyper-Calvinistic explanation of predestination, that some are predestined to be Saved

while all others are predestined to be lost, and the person has nothing to say about it.

"Whosoever" means exactly what it says! None are excluded as being lost, and none are excluded from being Saved. The great Word of the Gospel always has been, is now, and ever shall be, *"Whosoever will!"* (Rev. 22:17).

BELIEVE IN HIM

It is not enough to merely *"believe,"* as do multiple millions in all sorts of things religious, but one must believe in *"Him,"* i.e., the Lord Jesus Christ.

What does it mean to believe in Him?

The word, *"Believe,"* contains the idea of entrusting oneself or something else into the custody and safe keeping of another.

When these words refer to the Faith which a lost sinner must place in the Lord Jesus in order to be Saved, they include the following idea:

• The individual must believe that Jesus Christ is the Son of the Living God, in fact, that Christ is God (Jn. 1:1-4, 14, 29).

• One must believe that Jesus Christ went to the Cross in order to redeem humanity. He did so by the giving of Himself as a Sacrifice (Jn. 3:16; Heb. 7:27).

• The person must believe that the only Way to the Father is through Jesus Christ (Jn. 14:6).

All of this means a definite taking of oneself out of one's own keeping and entrusting oneself into the Keeping of the Lord Jesus.

To believe in Jesus does not mean to merely believe that He lived. Even though there are many things that one must believe concerning Christ, the main ingredient as expressed here, concerns what He did at Calvary. It is the Doctrine of Substitution and Identification. Jesus became our Substitute, and upon identifying with what He did, one is Saved.

SHOULD NOT PERISH

This tells us that all are perishing, whether moral or immoral, good or bad, sincere or insincere — unless Christ is accepted as Lord and Saviour.

The word *"perish"* means the loss of the soul in eternal Hell (Lk. 12:5; 16:23). Let's say it another way:

Unless a person receives Jesus Christ as his Saviour and his Lord, he will *"perish,"* which means to be lost in eternal Hell forever and forever. Yes, the Bible teaches that there is a Hell (Lk. 16:19-31).

ETERNAL LIFE

The *"life"* here addressed pertains to that which was lost by the Fall in the Garden of Eden.

Life is properly the Life of God, the Ever-Living One (Rom. 5:21; Rev. 4:9), Who has Life in Himself, and Alone has immortality (Jn. 5:26; I Tim. 6:16).

The Life of God is manifest in Jesus Christ. In the Gospels, Jesus simply assures His Followers of a Resurrection Life (Mat. 25:46; Mk. 8:34; 9:41; 10:29) and evidences His Power to bestow it.

One might refer to *"Eternal Life"* as *"Resurrection Life,"* when, at that time, the Believer would receive the full quality of such life, even as now we possess such.

In Jesus' Resurrection, immortal life has been actualized on the plain of history. His Resurrection becomes the basis for all Resurrection, and all Resurrection is to be understood in terms of His Resurrection (I Cor., Chpt. 15; Col. 3:4; I Jn. 3:2).

Resurrection Life is imparted and sustained by God's Creative Word. Man has no control over it. He may receive it and, thereby, enter it, but it is totally of Christ.

Eternal Life is instantly granted at Salvation, which refers to being *"Born-Again."* It will be realized fully only in the coming Resurrection. Let us say it again:

This is something, Eternal Life, that one has now, at least upon Faith in Christ, and not something which would be granted in the future.

(16) "FOR GOD SO LOVED THE WORLD, THAT HE GAVE HIS ONLY BEGOTTEN SON, THAT WHOSOEVER BELIEVES IN HIM SHOULD NOT PERISH, BUT HAVE EVERLASTING LIFE."

The synopsis is:

1. As we previously stated, there are some who claim that this conversation between Jesus and Nicodemus ended with Verse 12, while others claim it goes through

Verse 15, with John picking up in either case and elaborating on what Jesus has said.

2. However, there is no concrete proof either way.

3. Having read the arguments, it is still my thought and contention that this conversation between the Master and the Jewish ruler continued through Verse 21.

LOVE

The phrase, *"For God so loved the world,"* presents to us a type of love heretofore unknown in the world.

Understanding God as Omnipotent, which means that He is All-powerful, meaning He can do anything, Omniscient, meaning that He knows all things, past, present, and future, and Omnipresent, meaning that He is everywhere, one must wonder as to exactly why the Crucifixion had to be.

It was not the Justice of God which required the Son to pay the penalty of sin. God, in perfect Righteousness, could have required sinful man to pay his own penalty for his wrongdoing. The broken Law would have been satisfied, for the wages of sin is death; however, to have done so would have destroyed man in every way, with the race ceasing to exist.

It was the Love of God for a race of lost sinners that was the necessity in the nature of the case, which required that a substitute be found to pay for man's sin. That Substitute is the Lord Jesus Christ.

When John wrote the words, *"God so loved the world,"* as had been uttered by Jesus, he was writing in Greek. He was now faced with a problem of finding the exact word in the Greek language that would speak of the Love of God for a lost race. Here was a Love that loved not only the unlovely and unlovable, but one's enemies even to the point of total self-sacrifice, where the person gives all that he has for the benefit of the one loved.

FOUR WORDS IN THE GREEK LANGUAGE FOR LOVE

1. The first word is *"Erao"* or *"Eros."* It refers to a love based upon passion, either good or bad, according to the context. To be frank, this is the type of love most dominant in the world and, sadly, even in the church.

In other words, a person is loved if he is useful, whether rich, famous, or talented; however, if he ceases to be any of this, the love then stops. I think it is obvious as to the selfishness of such love. Actually, this is the very opposite of that which is the Love of God.

2. Another Greek word is *"Stergo,"* and speaks of a natural love, such as love of parents for children. However, the unsaved are not Children of God and, therefore, this word would not suffice.

3. There is a third Greek word called, *"Phileo,"* and refers to a love called out of one's heart by the pleasure one takes in the object loved. However, God takes no pleasure in the wicked and, therefore, this is not a fitting word.

4. The fourth Greek word is *"Agapao."* This is a love called out of one's heart by the preciousness of the object loved. In effect, it is a God kind of Love, of which the Greeks had some small knowledge but no examples. This is the kind of love of which Jesus was speaking.

THE WORLD

God's Love for a lost race, the fallen sons of Adam's lost race, was called out of His Heart by the preciousness of each lost soul. It is precious because He finds in that lost soul His Own Image, though that Image is marred by sin, and precious because that lost soul is made of material that God through Salvation can transform into the very Image of Christ.

As well, the word, *"World,"* has to do with the entirety of all men.

This means that as in Adam, all were lost; in Christ, all can be Saved.

As well, the lostness of man is to a far greater degree than man even remotely understands. The *"spiritual death"* suffered by man at the Fall was a death so complete in every way, physical, mental, domestic, and, above all, spiritual, that there was no way that man, at least within his own efforts, could be Saved. Consequently, the teaching here is that man in his totally depraved condition cannot be improved. Reformation will not change him into a fit subject for the Kingdom of God.

THE NEW NATURE

The flesh is so incurably wicked, which was brought on by the Fall (Rom. 8:10), that it cannot be changed by any process, at least by human means, so as to produce a righteous life. When we speak of the flesh, we are referring to that which is indicative of human beings, such as talent, education, ability, self-will, willpower, etc. What the person needs, Jesus says, is a new nature, a Spiritual nature which will produce a life pleasing to God, and which will be a life fit for the Kingdom of God. This is found only in the *"Born-Again"* experience by the Means of the Cross, and only by the Means of the Cross.

This is what Jesus was addressing when He said, *"That which is born of the Spirit is spirit"* (Jn. 3:6), and as a result, remains spiritual in nature. That is, the New Birth is a permanent thing, producing a permanent change in the life of the individual, making him a fit subject for the Kingdom of God.

When Jesus used the word, *"World,"* of necessity, it included Israel and meant, as well, that Israel was just as much in need of this Salvation as the pagans.

He had already stated to Nicodemus, *"Marvel not"* (Jn. 3:7), no doubt, because of seeing the startled expression on the face of the Jewish ruler.

As well, in the Seventh Verse, when He said, *"You must be born again,"* in the Greek, the word, *"You,"* is plural and stands out very plainly.

THE SANHEDRIN

Consequently, in using the pronoun, *"You,"* in the plural, Jesus evidently had several things in mind. First, He recognized the fact that Nicodemus belonged to the Sanhedrin and maybe represented the position of that body with reference to Himself.

Secondly, He was making it plain to Nicodemus that not only was it necessary for him to be Born-Again, but that all his associates in that venerated body of men also needed to be regenerated.

Thirdly, there is also the implication in the use of this pronoun that Jesus was suggesting to Nicodemus that he take this word back to the Sanhedrin itself.

As a result, Jesus made it plain that almost all of Israel was lost, including its religious leaders, and especially its religious leaders. Consequently, it comes as a shock to this member of the Sanhedrin.

THE WHOLE WORLD IS INCLUDED

During Jesus' Day, there were precious few people in the entirety of the world who were truly Saved, even among the Jews. The truth is, it has always been that way and remains so today, even though the number of true *"Born-Again"* Believers is vastly larger at present, but still small in comparison to the whole.

Actually, there are just two races of individuals in the world, those having the first Adam as their federal head, and those having the Last Adam as their Federal Head.

The first race stood in the first Adam before he fell, and thus possessed spiritual life in him. However, the first Adam fell into sin, lost the Spiritual Life for himself and for the human race, and plunged it into a totally depraved and lost condition, and under the Wrath of God.

The second race, composed of those who are in the Last Adam, the Lord Jesus Christ, as our Federal Head, are members of the Kingdom of God. To be a member of the Kingdom of God means that the individual must have a nature that produces in him a righteous life, which is fitting to those who are in the Kingdom of God. This constitutes the necessity of the New Birth and the nature of the case.

So, when Jesus used the word, *"World,"* especially considering that it be coupled with all else that was said, Nicodemus was stripped of all he held so dear and was made to realize his lost condition, as well as his contemporaries.

THAT WHICH THE FATHER DID TO REDEEM THE WORLD

The phrase, *"That He gave His Only Begotten Son,"* speaks of the *"Love"* held by God for the human family in that He would put into action that which He is. To talk about this type of Love is one thing, but to put it into action is something else altogether.

This type of Love gives itself in total Sacrifice for the benefit of the person loved, that person being unlovely and unlovable and, in fact, a bitter enemy. This kind of Love was not, at that time, known in the world, even though the Greeks knew the word.

God the Father gave His Son as a Substitutionary Sacrifice for sin, satisfying His Justice, maintaining His Divine Government, and, thereby, opening the floodgates of Mercy to a Hell-deserving race of sinners.

Jesus came to this world for one particular purpose, and that was to serve as that *"Substitutionary Sacrifice."* Consequently, the desire of the Disciples and the populace as a whole, that He then be the King of Israel, thereby, overthrowing Rome, was in direct contradiction to the very reason He came. Satan placed this carnal thought in the hearts of even Jesus' Closest Disciples, attempting to persuade Jesus to this line of thought. Of course, Satan was not only unsuccessful in this, but really had no chance at all of succeeding.

JESUS IS THE INTERSECTION

The phrase, *"That whosoever believes in Him,"* places Christ as the Focal Point of everything, and I mean everything.

Consequently, the entirety of the human family for all time stands in the place of the first fallen Adam or in the place of the Last Victorious Adam, the Lord Jesus Christ, Who purchased back with His Own Blood that which the first Adam lost.

The animosity leveled at Jesus by almost the entirety of the world, and for all time, cannot be explained in a rational sense. Why or how could someone such as Jesus be hated? He did nothing but heal people, deliver people, set people free, and give them Eternal Life!

If one is to notice, there is very little anger expressed toward the teaching of Muhammad, even though it is a religion of murder and responsible for much, if not most, of the terrorism in the world today. Why is that so?

ISLAM

Sometimes the news media in America will report the terrorist activities of the religion of Islam against Americans but will seldom, if ever, define what Islam really is. It is a religion from Hell, openly vowing to do anything possible to destroy America, calling it the *"Great Satan."* In truth, if the Muslims had the power, there would not be a single American left alive in the world. They do not do such only because they are not powerful enough to do so.

Sometime back, over CBS News, they ran a very favorable five minute piece on the qualities of Islam, etc. Even though it was not labeled as such, still, that's what it was.

They extolled the tremendous growth of the Muslim religion in America, especially among the blacks. They played down the inflammatory rhetoric coming from Louis Farrakhan, the self-appointed leader of Muslims in America, who hates Jews and anyone in particular who is not black and Muslim.

The reason the news media little sees the terrible danger of Islam is because the same spirit which propels Islam also propels the news media. Although in different directions, it is all from the same source, and I speak of the kingdom of darkness, with Satan at its head. As Jesus plainly said, which is obviously true, Satan does not cast out Satan (Mat. 12:26).

So, the same spirit in Islam and other religions, which opposes Christ, is in the entirety of this world's system as well!

MAN IS INCURABLY RELIGIOUS

Whether Islam or other religions, association requires no regeneration. Its worship, as characterizes all religions, consists of external rites. The conscience is not touched. The individual is allowed to go on in his sin, just as long as he observes certain outward rules.

Man, being incurably religious, demands the exercises of religion. Consequently, the religions of the world satisfy this longing, and at the same time, allow its devotees to continue the way of life which they love. It gives people what they want and caters to their evil natures.

However, as such, it has no *"life"* and, therefore, brings no peace or joy to its followers, irrespective of what nature it may be.

The reason for the terrible opposition against Christ and all those who truly follow Him is because His Righteousness is a rebuke to the unrighteousness of the world. His Perfection is a rebuke to its imperfections.

He is Light, and the world is in darkness, i.e., *"spiritual darkness."* Consequently, it opposes Him.

Also, Jesus is Truth, while every other religion in the world is a lie. Actually, Bible Christianity is not a religion, but rather a relationship with a Person, the Man Christ Jesus. In other words, God the Father, God the Son, and God the Holy Spirit, and the Bible, are real, while everything else is a lie, actually nurtured by demon spirits. In fact, for people to be Saved, the Holy Spirit has to break through this shell of darkness as the Word of God is preached, thereby, bringing the sinner under conviction and, hopefully, to an acceptance of Christ.

SHOULD NOT PERISH

The phrase, *"Should not perish,"* means that without Christ, the whole world is perishing, irrespective of its education, race, culture, place, or position.

In simple terms, this means that every person in the world, who has not received Jesus as his Saviour, is at this moment *"perishing."*

The Greek word for *"perish"* is, *"Apollumi,"* and means, *"To be ruined."* The idea is not extinction, for the soul will never cease to exist.

It means that outside of Christ, one cannot even remotely come up to his full potential, not even close, and that such a soul, if remaining in that condition, will die eternally lost, living forever in the place called, *"The Lake of Fire"* (Rev. 20:11-15).

EVERLASTING LIFE

The phrase, *"But have Everlasting Life,"* is the same as *"Eternal Life."*

Outside of Jesus, there is no *"life,"* and in Jesus Alone, there is *"Everlasting Life."*

This, as should be obvious, has the opposite meaning of *"perish,"* and refers to one realizing his full potential in Christ and, as well, living with Him forever in His Eternal Kingdom (Rev., Chpts. 21-22).

NOTES

In the Greek Text, in the phrase, *"Should not perish, but have Everlasting Life,"* there is a radical change in the tenses. The contrast is one between the final utter ruin and lost state of the unbeliever, and the possession of Eternal Life as an enduring experience on the part of the Believer. The entire Verse taken straight from the Greek Text is as follows:

"For in this manner God loved the world, so that His Son, the Only Begotten One, He gave, in order that everyone who places his trust in Him might not perish but might be constantly having Life Eternal" (Wuest).[2]

ETERNAL

As well, we should quickly add that the words, *"Eternal"* and *"Everlasting,"* apply to the *"Life"* which comes from Christ and not necessarily from the individual who has this *"Life."* From these Texts, some have attempted to assume that once a person is Saved, no matter what he does thereafter, he cannot be lost because his Salvation is *"Eternal and Everlasting."*

While it is certainly true that as long as a Believer continues to trust Christ, he or she cannot be lost, if one wants to leave Christ, as some few foolishly do, one can do so, for one's free will is never abrogated by the acceptance of Christ.

As well, if one desires to constantly practice sin, one cannot have both Christ and that lifestyle at the same time, as many attempt to do.

It is the *"Life"* itself which is eternal, and not man's possession of it. It is eternal whether man ever gets it or not. It is still eternal whether man loses it or not.

So, one's Salvation certainly is eternal, that is, if he continues to trust and follow Christ.

Even though the following has been given elsewhere in these Volumes, due to the manner in which Commentaries are normally studied and the seriousness of this matter, we felt it would be profitable to include it again at this juncture.

THE DOCTRINE OF UNCONDITIONAL ETERNAL SECURITY

Basically, there are two schools of

thought on the matter of security for the Believer. One is Calvinism and the other is Arminianism. Both are based somewhat on Scripture, but their conclusions diverge dramatically.

Calvinism emphasizes the Sovereignty of God and His Divine Prerogative. Arminianism stresses man's free will and responsibility.

The Doctrine of Unconditional Eternal Security accepts the Calvinist perspective and states that once a person has been Saved and accepts the Atoning Blood of Jesus Christ, he can never be lost afterward, no matter what he might do.

The Armenian view is that man has a free will, and it is the free will of man which determines his condition — even to the point of constant vacillation between positions of Salvation and of being lost.

Perhaps there is some truth and error in both views.

In order to come to full understanding of both of these positions, I feel they should be analyzed together. Without question, God is Sovereign and this Sovereignty allows Him full latitude in any area whatsoever. At the same time, God will always be consistent. We can, therefore, determine His Predictable Reaction by reviewing Scripture. Any doctrine demanding capricious or arbitrary action by God contrary to other areas in the Word can be assumed to be error.

In order to properly evaluate this issue, we will attempt to investigate four questions:

1. Can a Saved person be lost?
2. Is our Salvation dependent on works or Faith?
3. What happens when a Believer sins?
4. What are the fruits of the Doctrine of Unconditional Eternal Security?

CAN A SAVED PERSON BE LOST?

No, a Saved person cannot be lost.

Sometime back, I read two sermons which asked the same question. One asked, *"Can a Christian be lost?"* and the other asked, *"Can a Born-Again Believer be lost?"* As stated, the answer is, *"No,"* to both questions.

The motive behind these sermons was promotion of the doctrine of Unconditional Eternal Security. What were the conclusions of both of the preachers? It was that a Born-Again Believer, a Christian, cannot be lost. As stated, that is exactly right.

Unfortunately, these preachers didn't go the one step further necessary to complete their investigation of this matter. They should have also asked the question of whether a Born-Again Christian can cease being a Born-Again Christian. The answer to that question is, *"Yes, a Believer can stop believing; a Christian, through his own free will, can stop being a Christian; and the Born-Again can turn his back on Salvation, if he so desires, and once again revert to the status of being 'lost.'"*

It is Faith in Christ and what He did for us at the Cross that got us in, and it is Faith in Christ and what He did for us at the Cross which keeps us in.

What about the sinning Christian?

What about the Christian who denies the Cross?

We will address both of these questions ultimately in the body of this Volume.

EXAMPLES

• Lucifer was once without sin and walked perfectly within the Grace of God. Read Ezekiel 28:12-19, where the fall from Grace of Lucifer is so poignantly described and his ultimate end so graphically revealed.

• Then, there are the unaccounted millions of Angels created by God. Of these, one-third rebelled and chose to follow Lucifer in his insurrection against God (Rev. 12:4). At that moment, every one of these became destined to join Lucifer at some point in time in the fiery pit (Mat. 25:41).

• Adam and Eve were once created in God's Grace and Favor (Gen. 1:26-31). What happened? They fell from Grace and lost the eternal residence they would have enjoyed if only they had obeyed God and walked in His Statutes. Adam was a Son of God (Lk. 3:38), but he lost his sonship through transgression. No specific mention is made anywhere within the Word of God of Adam and Eve's subsequent Salvation from sin. Actually, there is some small Scriptural evidence that they did not return to God.

- Nadab and Abihu were sons of Aaron, God's Anointed, who served as the first Priests of the Children of Israel after Deliverance from Egypt. Actually, Nadab would have been the next High Priest after his father Aaron died, but for his rebellion. As recounted in Leviticus 10:1-2, they disobeyed God. What was their instantaneous end? They were destroyed by fire from God.
- Korah, Dathan, and Abiram rebelled against God. Korah was a Levite, a Priest, an incense bearer before God in the worship services of the Israelites. What happened to him and his fellow rebels? They were cast into the pit and lost their souls because of their decision to turn away from God.
- Just the other day, I read the answer of a preacher who was asked whether Saul, Israel's first king, was Saved when he died? The preacher's answer: *"Yes, Saul was Saved,"* he said, *"And went to Heaven."*

Of course, this preacher was a devotee of the doctrine of Unconditional Eternal Security. If this doctrine were valid, of course, his answer would be correct, but what does the Bible say about Saul's fate?

"So Saul died for his transgression which he committed against the LORD, even against the Word of the LORD, which he kept not, and also for asking counsel of one who had a familiar spirit, to enquire of it;

"And enquired not of the LORD: therefore He killed him, and turned the kingdom unto David the son of Jesse" (I Chron. 10:13-14).

If that sounds like the account of a faithful Child of God being taken home to be with the Lord, I must be reading a different Version of the Bible than that used by the preacher quoted above. It seems obvious to me from this Scripture that Saul was not saved when he died, nor did he go to Heaven.

THE NEW TESTAMENT

- Turning to the New Testament, we find in John 6:66 that many of the faithful — the very Disciples who walked personally with our Lord — turned away from His Grace and walked with Him no more. In Luke 8:13, the Words of our Saviour Himself tell us that many, in times of temptation, fall away after receiving the Word.
- Just the other day, a radio preacher stated that Ananias and Sapphira were Saved and, even though they lost fellowship with God, they still went to Heaven upon their deaths. This preacher was, as well, a proponent of the Unconditional Eternal Security doctrine.

To accept the concept that Ananias and Sapphira died Saved just doesn't conform to God's Principles as laid out in the balance of His Word.

THE WORD OF GOD

It is stated unequivocally in Acts 5:3-4 and 9 that they lied to God and the Holy Spirit. What is the fate of liars according to God's Word? In Revelation 21:8, we are told that liars are to be cast into the Lake of Fire. What happens to those cast into the Lake of Fire? Revelation 20:10 says, *"They shall be tormented day and night forever and forever."* According to God's Word, the fate of Ananias and Sapphira is quite different from that described by the radio preacher.

PAUL

In I Timothy 1:19-20, Paul refers in passing to Hymenaeus and Alexander. He states that they, though once being in the Faith, have made their faith shipwrecked by putting it away.

REPENTANCE

We are admonished in many places throughout the Bible to avoid the special wrath God has reserved for those who turn away after coming to know the Light. In the Old Testament (Ex. 32:33), the Lord said, *". . . Whosoever has sinned against Me, him will I blot out of My Book."* This means one who refuses to repent.

In Ezekiel 3:20-21, we are told, *"When a righteous man turns from his Righteousness, and commits iniquity . . . he shall die in his sin. . . ."* Of course, that speaks, as well, of one refusing to repent.

Jesus spoke of the salt that had lost its savor (Mat. 5:13). What is it good for? It is good only to be cast out.

In John 8:31, the Lord said, *"If you continue in My Word, you are My Disciples. . . ."*

PAUL AND PETER

• In Galatians 5:4, Paul accused some in the churches of Galatia of having *"fallen from Grace."* In I Timothy 4:1, he said expressly that some will depart from the Faith, *"giving heed to seducing spirits, and doctrines of demons."*

Peter said, *"Give diligence to make your Calling and Election sure: for if you do these things, you shall never fall:"* (II Pet. 1:10). He also said, *"If after they have escaped the pollutions of the world through the knowledge of the Lord and Saviour Jesus Christ, they are again entangled therein, and overcome, the latter end is worse . . . than the beginning"* (II Pet. 2:20-22).

Those who do not overcome will have their names blotted out of the Book of Life (Ex. 32:32-33; Ps. 69:28; Rev. 3:5).

HEBREWS

• Paul, in Hebrews 6:4-6, tells us that it is *"impossible to renew again unto Repentance those who were once enlightened; who have tasted of the Heavenly Gift; who were partakers of the Holy Spirit; and who have tasted the good Word of God; but who have fallen away."* This means they refuse to obey the Word of God and actually cease to believe that Jesus Alone is the Saviour of sinners.

There is no mistaking the meaning of this Scripture. Anyone trying to subvert its meaning by saying it refers to a sinner under conviction is guilty of ignoring the obvious and substituting the obscure for the evident.

The remainder of this particular Passage in Hebrews tells us that those who do fall away after coming to know the Truth, *"Crucify to themselves afresh the Son of God, and put Him to an open shame."* It is very difficult to apply this phrase to the actions of a Born-Again Believer or of a sinner merely under conviction.

THE GREEK SCHOLAR

In my opinion, Kenneth Wuest was one of the greatest Greek scholars of the Twentieth Century. He is now with the Lord. He had, I think, tremendous insight into the Scriptures and was a devotee to Unconditional Eternal Security. It was very interesting regarding his *"take"* on Hebrews 6:4-6 and Hebrews 10:26-29.

He stated, and I paraphrase his answer, *"The Greek language is crystal clear in these Passages. These Jews had once been Saved but then reverted back to a position of being unsaved."*

Now, having admitted the Truth of the Greek Text, how did he square this with his belief regarding Unconditional Eternal Security? His explanation was very interesting.

As stated, he admitted that these Jews had most definitely been Saved but if staying in that position of unbelief, they then died eternally lost.

He then stated that it was only Jews who could have done this and only Jews who lived in that particular generation.

I hold Kenneth Wuest in high regard as a Bible scholar; however, I cannot go along with him as it regards his explanation. It is just simply wrong.

TRUSTING CHRIST

So, persons who were once Saved can lose their Salvation. Once they do, they are, of course, no longer Christians, Born-Again, or Believers. So, it is impossible for a Born-Again Believer to lose his Salvation; but it is not impossible for a Born-Again Christian to stop believing, that is, if he so desires. Then, as such, he is no longer *"Born-Again."* Once in that position, such a person is lost.

As long as one continues to trust Christ, one is Saved; however, there is no such thing as one trusting Christ in sin, but rather He forgives and cleanses from all sin.

There are no perfect Believers! All of us, at one time or the other, have had to go before the Lord, in fact, many, many times, and ask forgiveness for things we have done which are wrong. He is always Faithful and Just to forgive and cleanse (I Jn. 1:9). However, it is foolish to think that God keeps one who habitually practices sin and, in effect, desires to do so. One cannot have sin and the Saviour at the same time. Such completely negates the entire purpose and reason for all that Christ has done to redeem sinners. As stated, He didn't come to save in sin but from sin.

ARE WE SAVED AND KEPT BY WORKS OR BY FAITH?

The Bible clearly states that we are Saved by Grace (the Goodness of God) through Faith (Faith in Christ and the Cross) (Eph. 2:8). We are further told that the just shall live by Faith in Christ and the Cross (Heb. 10:38). Salvation is given to the Believer, not by works or by so-called acts of Righteousness, but as a gift through the act of Faith. It is, of course, maintained in exactly the same way.

Our status as Saved Christians is not a matter of works but of Faith. Please understand, it always must be Faith in Christ and the Cross, or else, it's a Faith that God will not recognize. Even though a sinner does good works, he does not become acceptable to God on the basis of those works. We can only become acceptable to God through Grace on the basis of Faith, and as soon as we do, works become of no account.

With our acceptance, through Faith, of the fact that Jesus Christ died for our sins, and with acceptance of His Sacrifice as Atonement for our sins, we receive forgiveness and cleansing by God's Grace (Eph. 2:8-9).

The sinner accepts Jesus' Sacrifice by Faith, and by Faith he throws himself on the Mercy of God, knowing that God will accept His Son's Sacrifice as payment in full for those sins.

The sinner then sees himself, through Faith, clothed with the Righteousness of God. This is a *"standing"* imputed to the sinner through no intrinsic merit — it is strictly a Gift of God (Jn. 3:16; Eph. 2:8-9; Rev. 22:17).

STANDING AND STATE

The Believer's *"state"* must not be confused with his *"standing."* He stands clothed in the Righteousness of God, whatever his *"state."* This *"standing"* with God is a result of Grace through Faith — God's Grace and the Believer's Faith. Beyond this, of course, Righteousness in the Believer's life is a matter of Spiritual Growth, a progressive Sanctification by obedience to and cooperation with God's Holy Spirit (Rom. 6:12; II Pet. 1:5-7).

Is the Christian then perfect? In Christ, yes! In practice, no! In fact, the Christian will sin from time to time. He need not, however, doubt his Salvation as long as he has Faith in Jesus Christ and what He did for us at the Cross as the Author of his Salvation, and continues to trust Him accordingly. As long as he has Faith that God will not repudiate His Word, the Believer cannot doubt his Salvation because it is certain and sure.

WHAT HAPPENS WHEN A BELIEVER SINS?

Sadly, it seems clear that both through experience and through Scripture, Christians do sin. When the Christian does sin, his recourse is forgiveness through Christ. Our Lord sits continually at the Right Hand of the Father, making intercession for us (Rom. 8:34; I Jn. 1:8-9; 2:1-2). In fact, His very Presence at the Throne of God guarantees this intercession.

There is a great difference, however, between inadvertent sin and consciously choosing to sin. In fact, no true Christian wants to sin. Every true Christian hates sin with a passion. So, it is un-Biblical, un-Christlike, and unnatural for a Born-Again Believer to sin habitually and deliberately. This means to practice sin and to do so simply because one desires to do so. As stated, every true Believer hates sin. While the flesh may want something that is wrong and, in fact, often does, the *"inward man"* of the Believer does not want anything that is unscriptural, i.e., *"sin"* (Rom. 7:22).

We are told in God's Word that *"he who practices sin is of the Devil, and whosoever is born of God does not practice sin."* In other words, a Christian neither embraces situations that lead to sin nor feels comfortable in situations conducive to sin (I Jn. 3:8-9).

NO CONDEMNATION

The Apostle Paul, speaking under the Anointing of the Holy Spirit, states in Romans 8:1 that the Child of God is free from condemnation, that is, if he walks *"after the Spirit"* and not after *"the flesh."*

Therefore, God does not demand that a person become free of sin before he seeks Salvation or perfect afterward. We all have flaws and shortcomings of one kind or another. In other words, there is a Perfect Christ and a Perfect Salvation, but, sadly, there aren't any perfect Christians. However, once we become Christians, we begin to be conscious of our shortcomings as we seek the Face of God and begin to work toward the goal of improving ourselves through the Grace of God.

Without question, we don't lose all of our worldly tendencies and inclinations the instant we become Christians. In truth, even though the Believer is Saved from sin, the sin nature remains. However, we recognize these old leanings for what they are, and we are repulsed by them.

Sin is foreign to the new nature, so when the old nature occasionally reappears, the new nature recognizes the situation and reacts to it. Now we are repelled by sin and its temptations, rather than being drawn to them.

Let's look now at the sin nature.

THE SIN NATURE

What is the sin nature?

The sin nature is the nature of man that's been taken over by sin. This is what happened to Adam and Eve when they fell. Wherein they had total God-consciousness before the Fall, after the Fall, they now had total self-consciousness, with no God-consciousness at all. Their very nature was that of sin, meaning that everything they did was constituted as sin. Inasmuch as Adam was the federal head of the human race, this means that whatever happened to him has passed down through the natural birth to every human being who has ever lived, with the exception of the Lord Jesus Christ.

If you, as a Believer, will look back at your life before Redemption, you will have to admit that everything you did and everything you were was sin. Even the so-called good things had the wrong motive.

The sin nature in the modern church is addressed in one of five ways. Of necessity, I will have to be brief.

1. IGNORANCE: regrettably, despite the fact that this is one of the most important subjects in the entirety of the Bible, most Christians have no idea whatsoever as to what it is. They function in ignorance and, thereby, fall prey to the great hurt of the sin nature.

2. DENIAL: many preachers deny the fact that a Christian has a sin nature. My answer to that is simple. If there is no sin nature in the Believer, why did the Holy Spirit go to all the trouble of explaining it in Romans, Chapter 6? The truth is, every Believer has a sin nature. Momentarily, we will show you how to have victory over the *"old man."*

3. LICENSE: some few Believers do understand that we have a sin nature, and they, thereby, claim that due to this fact, they can't help but sin. Paul answered that by saying, *"What shall we say then? Shall we continue in sin, that Grace may abound? God forbid. How shall we, who are dead to sin, live any longer therein?"* (Rom. 6:1-2)

4. STRUGGLE: many Christians believe that this is something we have to struggle with all the days of our lives. While there definitely is a struggle in this Christian experience, it's always with our Faith and not something else. If the Believer is struggling with the sin nature, such produces a miserable experience. It's God's Will that we have perpetual victory over this thing, which we will address momentarily.

5. GRACE: the Grace of God is the only legitimate means, thereby, to address the sin nature.

When the believing sinner comes to Christ, at that moment, the sin nature is made dormant. It is not removed for disciplinary reasons, but it is rendered inactive. So, what is it that activates it once again?

It's not actually sin that does this, but rather the Object of our Faith being wrong. In other words, when we begin to place our faith in anything except Christ and the Cross, this is faith that God will not honor, which then gives the sin nature the right, so to speak, to have a resurrection. Regrettably, because virtually the entirety of the modern church, and we speak of those who truly love the Lord, have their faith placed in anything and everything except Christ and the

Cross, this means that the sin nature is ruling most Believers.

The Believer is to place his Faith constantly in Christ and the Cross, and maintain it constantly in Christ and the Cross, and that being done, *"the sin nature will no longer have dominion over us"* (Rom. 6:14).

PAUL

Some in Paul's time had questioned Paul's teaching on the subject of Grace and had attempted to claim that he was saying that God is willing to forgive sin as fast as a man commits sin.

Paul's answer is, *"God forbid, away with the thought, let not such a thing occur"* (Rom. 6:2).

A second answer is, *"How is it possible for such as we, who have once for all been separated from the power of the sin nature, to live any longer in its grip?"* (Rom. 6:5-7).

Paul speaks of the Christian as being dead to sin. This death is not extinction but separation.

The Christian has died to sin in the sense that God, in supernatural Grace, while leaving the sin nature in the Believer, has separated him from it. There has been a definite cleavage, a disengagement of the person from the evil nature. The evil nature is a dethroned monarch even though it still remains in the Believer.

Before Salvation, the sin nature was the master of the individual. Since Salvation, the Believer is its master. When the Believer begins to see this Truth, he has isolated this sinful nature, identified it and its proper character, and has within his grasp the remedy for it. It is the unknown and unseen enemy which is hard to fight. The Christian who has not isolated the evil nature fights sin in the dark, and ignorant of the fact that the sinful nature is no longer his master, continues to obey it, more or less, because he has no knowledge of how to gain victory over it.

We have here the Emancipation Proclamation issued by God in which the Christian has been released from slavery to the evil nature. However, like many slaves after the Civil War who were ignorant of Abraham Lincoln's Emancipation Proclamation, and who continued in the service of the slave master, so Christians who are ignorant of Romans, Chapter 6, continue to be slaves of the indwelling sinful nature to the extent that they are not gaining consistent victory over sin.

PAUL AND THIS VERY SITUATION OF THE SINFUL NATURE

After the Apostle Paul was Saved on the road to Damascus, and not knowing God's Prescribed Order of Life and Living, which is the Cross of Christ, he tried to live for God by the means of keeping Commandments. In fact, there was no one else at that time who knew this Divine Order either. This great Truth was, in fact, given to the Apostle Paul, which the great Apostle gave to us in his 14 Epistles. The truth is, Paul lived in this state of defeat for several years, which the Seventh Chapter of Romans bears out. He said:

"I am carnal, sold under sin. For that which I do I do not understand: for what I would, that I do not, but what I hate, that I do" (Rom. 7:14-15). Paul knew he was Saved, but he did not understand, at least not at this time, his Christian experience.

The very thing he wished to do, namely good, he did not do, and the very thing he did not want to do, namely sin, that is what he did. He was struggling in his own strength to keep from sinning and to do what was right; however, he found that human endeavor was not equal to the task. Many Christians are in a similar situation.

ROMANS, CHAPTER 6

The Truth which Paul gave us in Romans, Chapter 6, enables the Believer to gain consistent victory over the indwelling sinful nature. No, while the Bible does not teach sinless perfection, it most definitely does teach that sin is not to have dominion over us (Rom. 6:14). The very fact that Paul brings out in this Sixth Chapter is that the sin nature has had its power over the Believer broken by the Power of Christ. Before Salvation, the Believer was absolutely the slave, as we have stated, of the sin nature. However, since Grace has separated him from its power, he does not need to obey these sinful impulses. When he learns this, he learns that he has the Power in Christ to not yield. This is one great step in the battle which he wages against indwelling sin. The beautiful thing about it all is that the more he trusts in Christ, the easier it is to withstand these temptations, until it becomes a habit with him to trust Christ over this sinful nature.

Thus, it is a matter of trusting Christ, with the understanding that all victory over sin was won by Christ at the Cross and was done so for you and me.

THE DIVINE NATURE

In addition to breaking the power of the sin nature, God imparts His Own Divine Nature to us (II Pet. 1:4). In Romans 6:4, we have New Life imparted to us, and this new nature gives the Christian both the desire and the power to do God's Will, but only if we keep our Faith exclusively in Christ and the Cross. Actually, the reason for the Lord allowing the sin nature to remain is that we may learn how to trust Christ and not ourselves. Only trust and continued trust in Him gives us the victory.

So, it is a matter of not only having Faith to be Saved but, as well, to continue to have Faith to live a victorious, overcoming Christian Life.

Even though the Believer continues to trust Christ, regrettably, at times, that trust weakens, and the Believer finds unexpected incursions of sin in his Christian life. We should immediately turn to the Lord Jesus Christ at that time, Who is the Propitiation for our sin, but not as we did as unbelievers seeking Salvation.

The lost sinner turning to God does so as an *"outsider"* seeking a new status within the Family of God. We, with occasional failings, come before Christ knowing we are Children of the Most High God with Christ as our Advocate before the Father. We don't have to question our *"standing."* We know God isn't going to suddenly change His Mind about our Salvation. The critical question is, *"Do we want to live for God and walk in the light?"*

If the answer is, *"Yes,"* there can be no question as to our Salvation — with or without an inadvertent sin in our life.

THE FREE WILL OF HUMAN BEINGS

All human beings have a free will. As well, our free will is not lost to us upon coming to Christ. It is through our free will that we come to God, and through that same free will, we can reject God after coming to Him, if we so desire. If we do elect to turn away from God, according to Scripture, we will be lost.

Free will is our passport to Salvation, i.e., *"whosoever will,"* even as Jesus said (Jn. 3:15; Rev. 22:17). Free will is our foundation in Salvation; and free will is our ticket out of Salvation if one would be so foolish as to desire that latter course.

It is through our free will that we maintain our Salvation, by our simple Faith and Trust in Christ. As long as we maintain our commitment to the Lord, we have nothing to fear. God will not let us fall.

Many proponents of the "always saved, regardless of what one may do" doctrine, base their belief on a faulty interpretation of John 10:28. The Lord said in this Verse, *"And I give unto them Eternal Life; they shall never perish, neither shall any man pluck them out of My Hand."*

In the preceding Verse, we are told that we are Christ's Sheep. The "regardless, always saved" supporters contend that if we are His Sheep now, we must always be His Sheep. *"Once a sheep, always a sheep,"* they say.

However, the problem is: the Scripture actually says we are Christ's Sheep *"if we hear His Voice, and if we follow Him"* (Jn. 10:27). If we don't follow Him, we, of course, stop being His Sheep, and the whole theory goes down the drain, so to speak.

Try as you will, you won't find (no matter how hard you search) any Promise of Salvation in the Bible to those who stop listening for His Voice and who stop following Him. The Scripture says that if we stray from the fold, we turn from being *"His Sheep"* to being *"lost sheep"* (Lk. 15:6).

ALWAYS THE FATHER'S SON?

Another argument used to promote this doctrine is that in the natural, no matter how recalcitrant the child, he still remains his father's son. This is expanded to the theory that anyone who is once a Child of God must eternally remain a Child of God. It doesn't matter the degree to which such a person might mire himself in sin and unbelief, he is still God's Child, they say, and, therefore, an heir to Salvation.

The trouble is, Scripture reports that Jesus was God the Father's Only Begotten Son. We, in fact, are adopted sons (Rom. 8:15; 9:4; Gal. 4:5; Eph. 1:5). We, therefore, as adopted sons, are well capable of falling back into the sinful state, losing our inheritance, and forfeiting our position as adopted sons, that is, if we seek to attempt to maintain Christ and sin at the same time.

At one time, Adam was a Son of God. Through sin, he lost this position. He never repented and, therefore, remained lost. We can do the same thing if we don't constantly reaffirm our sonship through Faith.

WHAT ABOUT THE CHRISTIAN WHO IS STRUGGLING WITH A CONTINUOUS SIN?

That's an excellent question!

Due to the fact that the church is so little preaching the Cross at this particular time, virtually the entirety of Christendom, and we speak of those who truly love the Lord, are, in fact, being controlled by the sin nature, thereby, daily struggling with this problem, with an *"O wretched man that I am! Who shall deliver me from the body of this death?"* (Rom. 7:24).

They are in the state the Apostle Paul was in before the Lord gave him the victory through the understanding of the Cross of Christ. The following is what he said concerning this subject. We will include our notes from THE EXPOSITOR'S STUDY BIBLE as well.

"For I was alive without the Law once *(Paul is referring to himself personally and his Conversion to Christ; the Law, he states, had nothing to do with that Conversion; neither did it have anything to do with his life in Christ)***: but when the Commandment came** *(having just been Saved and baptized with the Holy Spirit, but not understanding the Cross of Christ, he tried to live for God by keeping the Commandments through his own strength and power; in his defense, and as stated, no one else at that time understood the Cross; in fact, the meaning of the Cross, which is actually the meaning of the New Covenant, would be given to the Apostle Paul)*, **sin revived** *(the sin nature will always, without exception, revive under such circumstances, which results in failure)*, **and I died** *(he was not meaning that he physically died, as would be obvious, but that he died to the Commandment; in other words, he failed to obey no matter how hard he tried; let all Believers understand that if the Apostle Paul couldn't live for God in this manner, neither can you!)*.

DECEPTION

"And the Commandment, which *was* ordained to life *(refers to the Ten Commandments)*, **I found *to be* unto death** *(means that the Law revealed the sin, as it always does, and its wages which are death; in other words, there is no victory in trying to live by Law; we are to live by Faith, referring to Faith in Christ and the Cross)*.

"For sin *(the sin nature)*, **taking occasion by the Commandment** *(in no way blames the Commandment, but that the Commandment actually did agitate the sin nature and brought it to the fore, which it was designed to do)*, **deceived me** *(Paul thought, now that he had accepted Christ, by that mere fact alone, he could certainly obey the Lord in every respect; but he found he couldn't, and neither can you, at least in that fashion)*, **and by it killed me** *(despite all of his efforts to live for the Lord by means of Law-keeping, he failed; and again, I say, so will you!)*.

DON'T UNDERSTAND . . .

"For that which I do *(the failure)* **I allow not** *(should have been translated, 'I understand not'; these are not the words of an unsaved man, as some claim, but rather a Believer who is trying and failing)*: **for what I would, that do I not** *(refers to the obedience he wants to render to Christ, but rather fails; why? as Paul explained, the Believer is married to Christ but is being unfaithful to Christ by spiritually *cohabiting with the Law, which frustrates the Grace of God; that means the Holy Spirit will not help such a person, which guarantees failure [Gal. 2:21])*; **but what I hate, that do I** *(refers to sin in his life which he doesn't want to do and, in fact, hates, but finds himself unable to stop; unfortunately, due to the fact of not understanding the Cross as it refers to Sanctification, this is the plight of most modern Christians)"* **(Rom. 7:9-11, 15).**

WILLPOWER

While willpower is very important, hence, *"whosoever will,"* still, within itself, it cannot bring about victory. And yet, about all that a Believer can give to the Lord which He can use is *"a willing mind and an obedient heart."* However, the truth is, willpower within itself, although, as stated, necessary, is not enough to bring about the victory that one must have over the powers of darkness.

The Believer must understand what we are facing in the spirit world as Christians. Paul said this:

"For we wrestle not against flesh and blood, but against principalities, against powers, against the rulers of the darkness of this world, against spiritual wickedness in high places" (Eph. 6:12).

The Greek scholars tell us that *"principalities," "powers,"* and *"rulers of the darkness of this world"* all three refer to powerful fallen Angels. These are Angels that threw in their lot with Lucifer when he led his revolution against God in the dateless past.

The last designation, *"Spiritual wickedness in high places,"* refers to demon spirits.

And then, when we look into the Ninth Chapter of Revelation, we see demon spirits described such as we have never seen before. They had *"faces like the faces of men,"* but *"were like unto horses prepared unto battle; and they had hair as the hair of women, and their teeth were as the teeth of lions"* (Rev. 9:7-11).

At any rate, whatever it is that we are facing in the spirit world, it is so far beyond the powers of man, which should be explicitly understood. So, if we are to walk in victory, we have to do this thing God's Way. His Way

NOTES

is not willpower, as important as that attribute is.

The only way that willpower can be successfully used is to choose the Way of the Lord. We have the privilege of choosing God's Way or the Way of man, with the latter proving to be hopeless. The Way of the Lord is the Way of the Cross, i.e., *"Jesus Christ and Him Crucified"* (I Cor. 1:23).

Regrettably, virtually the entirety of the modern church world, and again we are speaking of those who truly love the Lord, is trying to live for God by the means of willpower alone. Once again we go back to Paul, and I quote totally from THE EXPOSITOR'S STUDY BIBLE.

"For I know that in me (that is, in my flesh,) dwells no good thing *(speaks of man's own ability, or rather the lack thereof in comparison to the Holy Spirit, at least when it comes to spiritual things)*: **for to will is present with me** *(Paul is speaking here of his willpower; regrettably, as stated, most modern Christians are trying to live for God by means of willpower alone, thinking falsely that since they have come to Christ, they are now free to say 'no' to sin; that is the wrong way to look at the situation; the Believer cannot live for God merely by the strength of willpower; while the will is definitely important, it alone is not enough; the Believer must exercise Faith in Christ and the Cross, and do so constantly; then he will have the ability and strength to say 'yes' to Christ, which automatically says 'no' to the things of the world)*; **but *how* to perform that which is good I find not** *(outside of the Cross, it is impossible to find a way to do good)"* **(Rom. 7:18).**

Let me say it again:

The only place where sin can be dealt with is the Cross of Christ. Through and by the Cross alone, the Believer can have victory over the powers of darkness. Satan doesn't care at all how much we come against him by the means of the flesh, that which is indicative to human beings, but he certainly doesn't want us placing our Faith exclusively in Christ and the Cross because that's where he and all of his minions of darkness were totally and completely defeated.

THE CROSS OF CHRIST

Paul said:

"**And you, being dead in your sins and the uncircumcision of your flesh** (*speaks of spiritual death [i.e., 'separation from God'], which sin does!*), **has He quickened together with Him** (*refers to being made spiritually alive, which is done through being 'Born-Again'*), **having forgiven you all trespasses** (*the Cross made it possible for all manner of sins to be forgiven and taken away*);

"**Blotting out the handwriting of Ordinances that was against us** (*pertains to the Law of Moses, which was God's Standard of Righteousness, which man could not reach*), **which was contrary to us** (*Law is against us simply because we are unable to keep its precepts, no matter how hard we try*), **and took it out of the way** (*refers to the penalty of the Law being removed*), **nailing it to His Cross** (*the Law with its decrees was abolished in Christ's Death, as if crucified with Him*);

"***And*** **having spoiled principalities and powers** (*Satan and all of his henchmen were defeated at the Cross by Christ atoning for all sin; sin was the legal right Satan had to hold man in captivity; with all sin atoned, he has no more legal right to hold anyone in bondage*), **He** (*Christ*) **made a show of them openly** (*what Jesus did at the Cross was in the face of the whole Universe*), **triumphing over them in it.** (*The triumph is complete, and it was all done for us, meaning we can walk in power and perpetual victory due to the Cross*)" **(Col. 2:13-15).**

HOW DID JESUS DEFEAT SATAN AT THE CROSS?

Forget about any type of physical confrontation. Satan wants nothing to do with Jesus Christ whatsoever. If the Lord tells him to jump, the only retort that Satan gives is, *"How high?"* So, what exactly did Jesus do that defeated Satan and all of his minions of darkness?

At the Cross, Jesus atoned for all sin, past, present, and future, at least for all who will believe (Jn. 3:16). He did so by the giving of Himself as a Perfect Sacrifice, which God the Father totally accepted as payment in full. That means the ransom was paid, with nothing left owing. For us to receive the benefits of what Jesus there did, all we have to do is to have Faith in Him and His Finished Work.

Sin is the legal means that Satan has to hold man captive. With all sin removed, which it was at the Cross, this leaves Satan with no legal right to hold anyone in bondage. So, the reason all unredeemed are totally in bondage is because they will not accept what Jesus Christ has done. This goes for Believers as well!

Sadly and regrettably, most Christians, and again we speak of those who truly love the Lord, understand the Cross of Christ as it refers to Salvation but have no understanding whatsoever of how the Cross refers to Sanctification, i.e., how we live for God, how we have victory over the world, the flesh, and the Devil, how we order our behavior, etc. Not understanding this all-important Truth, the result is failure. While most do not lose their soul, still, their lives are miserable. Being dominated by the sin nature is an awful thing, but it is that which characterizes virtually all Christians presently simply because they do not know God's Prescribed Order of Victory, which is the Cross of Christ.

Yes, while willpower is definitely important, it is important only in our making the decision to live this life by God's Manner and Way. Otherwise we fail.

Many Christians erroneously believe that once they come to Christ, the Lord gives them a super willpower to where they can say, *"No,"* to the powers of darkness. Nothing like that is correct. You have the same will in you now as you did before you were Saved. If willpower is the key to victory, then that means that the individual will receive the glory, which none of us deserve. If the Cross is the reason for victory, then the Lord Jesus Christ receives the Glory, which He totally deserves.

THE FRUITS OF THE DOCTRINE OF UNCONDITIONAL ETERNAL SECURITY

Millions of souls are now residing in Hell because they were told that having received Salvation, they could mire themselves in sin to whatever degree they chose, and they would not lose their Salvation. The preachers responsible for spreading this error, and error it is, will have to answer before Christ someday for the souls lost as a result of their preaching and teaching.

Many today are wallowing in sin and confidently rebelling against God because, at some point in their lives, they made some kind of tepid commitment to Christ. They have been told that they cannot lose their Salvation under any circumstances; consequently, they continue on that path.

I believe in Eternal Security, but I believe in Eternal Security as it is taught in the Word of God.

ETERNAL SECURITY

Christians can have Eternal Security if they claim it on God's terms, not on the terms of man. Any hope of Salvation, while living in rebellion against God, is futile. Any teaching that holds out a promise of Salvation and Eternal Security while living in sin against God is false and satanic.

To be sure, God does not casually remove His Hands from any life; consequently, when the person passes the point of no return, he can only be judged by the Lord. We should, therefore, leave the matter of judging such situations in the Hands of our Omniscient God.

One thought should always be kept in mind. If God doesn't hesitate to extend effort in the hope of bringing the prodigal home, neither should His Church. All too often, people write off individuals when God has not written them off.

FORFEITING SALVATION?

The Bible documents the possibility of our forfeiting our Salvation, but it also extends continuing hope for anyone who wants to respond to the Call of the Holy Spirit. Thank God for that! The Master's Invitation comes without qualification.

"Come unto Me, all you who labor and are heavy laden, and I will give you rest." These Words of our Lord Jesus are quoted in Matthew 11:28.

The Bible also states in Romans 10:13, *"Whosoever shall call upon the Name of the Lord shall be saved."*

"Whosoever" covers a broad tapestry. I hope anyone who has placed his or her Salvation in jeopardy will recommit his life today and start living a Christian life. Jesus is waiting and willing to help all who will submit to Him and follow Him accordingly.

Once again, however, we must remember that the Lord does not save in sin, but rather from sin (Rom. 10:13).

(17) "FOR GOD SENT NOT HIS SON INTO THE WORLD TO CONDEMN THE WORLD; BUT THAT THE WORLD THROUGH HIM MIGHT BE SAVED."

The construction is:

1. The Atonement was not cheap, and sin is never to be taken lightly.

2. It is clear that in the Old Testament, it was recognized that death was the penalty for sin (Ezek. 18:20).

3. However, God graciously permitted the death of a sacrificial victim, namely a lamb, to substitute for the death of the sinner.

NO CONDEMNATION

The phrase, *"For God sent not His Son into the world to condemn the world,"* means that the object of Christ's Mission was to save, but the issue to those who reject Him must, and can only be, condemnation. The acceptance of Christ takes away all condemnation; however, the rejection of Christ brings acute condemnation. This problem of condemnation, i.e., *"guilt,"* is, no doubt, the cause of much sickness, fear, depression, emotional disturbances, etc.

The Greek word for *"condemn"* is *"krino"* and means *"to judge."* So, upon the First Advent, Jesus came to save; however, at the Second Advent, it will be to judge (Mat. 16:27; 5:31-46).

If it is to be noticed, Jesus did not *"condemn the world,"* i.e., the unsaved. However, He did, in fact, condemn, and sharply so, those who called themselves the people of God but actually were not. I speak of the religious leadership of Israel. A cursory glance at Matthew, Chapter 23, portrays to us a scathing denunciation and condemnation.

As one studies the four Gospels, the contempt the religious leadership had for Jesus is overly obvious, even to the point of ultimately murdering Him. This hatred was so severe because it originated with Satan. As we have previously stated, Satan's greatest efforts in the damning of eternal souls are always in the realm of religion. There is no hatred like religious hatred!

ETERNALLY LOST

There are well over 100,000,000 people in America who claim to be Born-Again; however, if the truth be known, the true number is probably shockingly small. So, Satan has been very adept at getting people to believe something that does not exist. As with Nicodemus, tens of millions think they are Saved but, in reality, are not. Actually, their Righteousness does not even come up to the level of that religious leader of long ago.

When one couples Buddhism, Islam, Shintoism, Confucianism, Catholicism, Mormonism, etc., with the parts of Christianity which are apostate, at least three-quarters of the present population is covered in that summation, and eternally lost, we might quickly add.

So, while Jesus had scathing words of condemnation for apostate religion, He had nothing but kindness and graciousness for the sinner who made no pretense at Salvation.

This means He healed every single one who came to Him, irrespective of their spiritual condition. Likewise, He helped all who came to Him, again, irrespective of their spiritual condition. He never told anyone who came for healing that they were not living right and could, therefore, not be healed, which I am certain could have applied to many, if not most. He healed them all, irrespective of their spiritual condition. As well, he healed any religious leaders who came to Him, and without question, but, sadly, there were few who actually came.

SALVATION

The phrase, *"But that the world through Him might be Saved,"* proclaims to us several things.

- Jesus Christ is the only Salvation for the world. There is no other!
- He would effect Salvation by taking upon Himself the curse of the broken Law, which He did at Calvary's Cross, thereby, satisfying the claims of Heavenly Justice against man. In other words, He would settle the account, which was extremely large, and as the song says, *"Growing everyday."* Since Calvary, to the Believer, no sin can be charged to his account, either past, present, or future, that is, if he continues to trust Christ.
- Since the fall of man, the only thing that has saved this world from total sinful destruction has been the few who have Christ, and who do follow Christ. Before Noah, a time span of approximately 1,600 years, it is recorded that only two people actually lived for God during this time. These two were Abel, who was murdered by his brother Cain, and Enoch, who was translated before he died. That was about 1,000 years after Abel (Gen. 4:8; 5:21-24).

TOTAL CORRUPTION

During this period of time (before the Flood, a time frame of about 1,600 years), the Earth became so corrupt that the Scripture says, *"And God saw that the wickedness of man was great in the Earth, and that every imagination of the thoughts of his heart was only evil continually"* (Gen. 6:5). The only thing that saved this Earth from total destruction was Noah and his family. The Scripture says, *"But Noah found Grace in the eyes of the LORD"* (Gen. 6:8-10).

Due to the fact that *"all flesh had corrupted his way upon the Earth,"* there was nothing left to do, that is, if the human family was to be Saved, but to destroy all on the Earth. This God did by sending a flood of worldwide proportions. As stated, this was about 1,600 years after Adam.

ABRAHAM

Even though knowledge is scant, there is some small evidence that Shem, Noah's son, lived for God after the Flood, and may have even been the one who testified to Abraham. At any rate, when God called Abraham out of Ur of the Chaldees, this was the only family on Earth who was truly living for God, with the exception possibly of Shem and those with Melchizedek. Actually, some even think that Shem may have been the

Melchizedek of Genesis 14:18.

From the loins of Abraham came the Jewish people, made up of Thirteen Tribes, and consisting of the heirs of the sons of Jacob. Consequently, this small group of people were the only ones on Earth who kept the Judgment of God from destroying the entirety of the world. Without Israel and the Church, and more perfectly, Jesus in Israel and the Church, the world would have long since perished. Even now, as then, it has only been a stopgap measure. However, the Second Coming of the Lord will climax all these many years of preparation, and will institute Righteousness at long last on the Earth because the Son of Righteousness will rule Personally.

So, were it not for Jesus, the world would have been destroyed a long, long time ago.

(18) "HE WHO BELIEVES ON HIM IS NOT CONDEMNED: BUT HE WHO BELIEVES NOT IS CONDEMNED ALREADY, BECAUSE HE HAS NOT BELIEVED IN THE NAME OF THE ONLY BEGOTTEN SON OF GOD."

The exegesis is:

1. The Cross of Christ is absolutely central to the New Testament and, indeed, to the whole Bible.

2. All before the Cross leads up to it. All after the Cross looks back to it.

3. We must all understand that the Atonement proceeds from the Love of God.

BELIEVING ON HIM

The phrase, *"He who believes on Him is not condemned,"* constitutes a statement that is flat out in its proclamation.

The only way that one can rid oneself of condemnation, i.e., *"guilt,"* is by the acceptance of Jesus Christ as one's Saviour and Lord. That automatically strikes all condemnation.

There is an enmity between God and man, and, to be sure, it is God Who has been wronged and not man. So, God feels this animosity far more than does man. Nevertheless, the condemnation is there just the same.

When a person comes to Christ, which means to be Born-Again, he literally becomes a New Creation, with *"old things having passed away, and all things becoming new"* (II Cor. 5:17). Then the animosity between God and man is removed. However, we must understand, a tremendous price had to be paid to make all of this possible. It was a price so gargantuan that man could not pay such. So, if it was to be paid, God would have to pay it Himself, which He did. I speak of the Cross of Christ.

This is what makes Salvation so remarkable. What was owed, man could not pay, and I mean flat out, could not pay. So, God paid it in the form of the giving of His Only Son as a Sacrifice. To be clear of all debt, and we speak of spiritual debt, all sin, all transgression, and all iniquity, all one has to do is exhibit Faith in Christ and what Christ did for us at the Cross. That being done, all condemnation instantly ceases.

CONDEMNATION

The phrase, *"But he who believes not is condemned already,"* simply means that believing Christ is the only remedy for this affliction, not in Buddha, Muhammad, Confucius, Joseph Smith, or any other fake luminary.

Theologically, condemnation can be avoided only by trusting in Jesus, Who bears our sin and thus removes us from the position of prisoners before the bar of Divine Justice.

The reason the Believer cannot be condemned (Rom. 8:1) is because there is no charge against the Child of God. Jesus has *"taken away"* all sin, having, thereby, paid the price for all who believe. So, when Paul said, *"There is therefore now no condemnation to them which are in Christ Jesus,"* this refers to past, present, and future, but only as one continues to trust Christ.

I personally believe that much sickness, emotional disturbances, fear, and depression, in other words, outright misery, is caused by condemnation. As we have stated, the only cure for such, and I mean the only cure, is Jesus Christ and what He did for us at the Cross.

THE ONLY BEGOTTEN SON OF GOD

The phrase, *"Because he has not believed in the Name of the Only Begotten Son of*

God," actually refers to the Name Jesus, which means, *"Saviour."*

This means that believing in Jesus as a *"Good Man," "Miracle-Worker,"* or even as a *"Prophet,"* will not suffice. One must believe in and accept Him as Saviour.

The short phrase, *"Only Begotten Son of God,"* referred to the Incarnation and what God had to do in order to redeem man. He actually had to become Man, although never ceasing to be God. In effect, He became the Last Adam, thereby, purchasing for lost humanity what the first Adam had lost. Several things are here implied:

• The sinner must believe that Jesus was Virgin Born in order that He be free from the contamination of sin, for that was an absolute requirement of the Incarnation.

• One must believe that Jesus is the Saviour, and the Only Saviour, for that matter, and in order to Save me, He had to die on Calvary and rise from the dead on the third day.

• The simple phrase, as given by Jesus, constitutes the Doctrine of *"Substitution and Identification."* Jesus became our Substitute, we identify with Him by Faith, and, consequently, we are Saved.

(19) "AND THIS IS THE CONDEMNATION, THAT LIGHT IS COME INTO THE WORLD, AND MEN LOVED DARKNESS RATHER THAN LIGHT, BECAUSE THEIR DEEDS WERE EVIL."

The pattern is:

1. The Atonement shows us the Love of the Father just as it does the Love of the Son.

2. The Death of Christ was no accident, and neither was it an execution or assassination. It was a Sacrifice.

3. As well, the Death of Christ was no accident in that it was rooted in a compelling Divine necessity.

THE BASIS OF JUDGMENT

The phrase, *"And this is the condemnation, that Light is come into the world,"* refers to Jesus as the *"Light."* There is no other!

The word, *"Condemnation,"* as it is here used, in the Greek Text is *"krisis,"* and means, *"Judgment or basis of judgment, not the result of it."* In other words, the world is judged not because of mere rejection of the *"Light,"* but that their rejection of the Light is the result of the Judgment, i.e., *"condemnation."* The sin and its inculcated darkness, and man's love of it, is why man is condemned.

Many have the erroneous concept in their minds that those who have never heard of Jesus and, consequently, have had no opportunity to accept or reject him, will not be lost. However, men are lost already, whether they hear of Jesus or not, and will be judged or condemned on that basis.

THE LOVE OF DARKNESS

The phrase, *"And men loved darkness rather than light, because their deeds were evil,"* proclaims that the great penalty of sin is sinful desire. The love of darkness is the consequence of man's wicked ways.

The rejection of Jesus Christ is not the occasion of man's lostness, but rather the result of it. So, the primary reason men do not accept Jesus Christ as Saviour, i.e., the Light, is because they love *"darkness,"* i.e., their sins. They don't want to change their way of living, which is evil, so they reject the *"Light"* that offers to save them from the terrible results of sin, which is death. Being deceived, and because of the darkness, there is a great measure of unbelief attached to their love for their sin.

In every generation, and even as we have addressed referring to Unconditional Eternal Security, men have tried to find a way to have the Salvation the *"Light"* brings while, at the same time, continuing in their darkness. Such cannot be! It is either *"Light"* or *"Darkness!"* Both are not possible!

(20) "FOR EVERY ONE WHO DOES EVIL HATES THE LIGHT, NEITHER COMES TO THE LIGHT, LEST HIS DEEDS SHOULD BE REPROVED."

The order is:

1. In His Death on the Cross, Jesus fulfilled all that the old sacrifices had foreshadowed.

2. Jesus Himself referred to His Blood as *"Blood of the Covenant"* (Mk. 14:24).

3. John the Baptist said of Christ, *"Behold the Lamb of God, Who takes away the sin of the world"* (Jn. 1:29). He is the Only One Who could have done this.

HATERS OF THE LIGHT

The phrase, *"For everyone who does evil hates the Light,"* presents a striking rebuke to Nicodemus with a keen thrust of the sharp sword, saying to him that evildoers chose the darkness, so why did he, a Pharisee, come by night?

So, in this phrase, we find the reason for the hatred of the world toward Jesus and all who follow Him. They *"hate the Light,"* irrespective of where it may be. There is only One *"Light,"* and that is Jesus.

As well, religious men will have a tendency to hate the True Light and all who truly follow that Light. They try, with their religiosity, to make up a light of their own, which, of course, God will never recognize. So, if there is anything in opposition to that fabricated light, religious men will take any measure to extinguish the True Light.

WILL NOT COME TO THE LIGHT

The phrase, *"Neither comes to the Light,"* now offers Nicodemus hope because all who come to the Light desire the Light. Nicodemus, by his coming to the Light, proved that his heart hungered for that which he did not have. He had made a great profession of religion but none of Faith, up to now.

The idea of *"doing evil"* means that the person desires to continue to do evil and wants nothing to hinder the continuance of these evil deeds.

However, to those who do not desire to continue this *"evil,"* they, as Nicodemus, will *"come to the Light,"* i.e., Jesus.

The idea expresses itself of those who have had the opportunity and privilege of hearing the Gospel. At that time, because of the Power and Revelation of the Holy Spirit upon the Word of God, they must make the decision that they want to continue in their evil or rid themselves of the evil.

THE REVELATION AND CONDEMNATION OF EVERY EVIL WAY

The phrase, *"Lest his deeds should be reproved,"* presents the crisis point for the world. To truly come to Jesus means the Revelation and condemnation of every evil way, which is totally unlike the religions of the world, which reveal nothing. The *"Light"* automatically reveals what is hidden by the darkness. If the Gospel is truly preached under the Anointing of the Holy Spirit, it will always expose sin. At that time, one must make a decision if one desires to remain in the darkness or come to the Light.

If one wants to remain in the darkness, one will reject the Light. If one desires the Light, one will have one's life gloriously and wondrously changed by the Power of the Holy Spirit. It is done upon simple Faith in Jesus Christ, which will also grant the Believer Eternal Life.

(21) "BUT HE WHO DOES TRUTH COMES TO THE LIGHT, THAT HIS DEEDS MAY BE MADE MANIFEST, THAT THEY ARE WROUGHT IN GOD.

(22) "AFTER THESE THINGS CAME JESUS AND HIS DISCIPLES INTO THIS LAND OF JUDAEA; AND THERE HE TARRIED WITH THEM, AND BAPTIZED."

The construction is:

1. It must be obvious in our thinking that Jesus died specifically for us. He was our Representative as He hung on the Cross.

2. The Death of the Representative counts as the death of those He represents.

3. When Christ is spoken of as our *"Advocate with the Father"* (I Jn. 2:1), there is the plain thought of representation.

JESUS AND HIS DISCIPLES

The phrase, *"After these things came Jesus and His Disciples into this land of Judaea,"* simply means that Jesus and His Disciples left the metropolis of Jerusalem where the hostility was already beginning to mount, especially considering His cleansing of the Temple. Consequently, He went out to the countryside. Exactly where, the Scripture does not say.

WATER BAPTISM

The phrase, *"And there He tarried with them, and baptized,"* could very well have been near or where He was baptized by John in the river Jordan.

He actually did not do any baptizing Himself. It was done by His Disciples but, no doubt, under His Direction.

JOHN 3:23-25

The Scripture is not clear exactly how long His Disciples practiced the Water Baptism of followers, but it seems not to have been too very long. Actually, Matthew, Mark, and Luke do not mention this part of the Ministry of Christ. However, there is a reason that Jesus did this, which seemed to stop after John's death.

To give authenticity to John's Ministry and to sanction him as the great forerunner, by the rite of Water Baptism, He allied His Ministry with that of John's. Consequently, the Water Baptism of Jesus corresponded in significance with the Water Baptism of John. They were one and the same ordinance, predictive, symbolic, and anticipatory of the Baptism with the Spirit, which was yet to come. As John exercised the Baptism of Repentance, so did Jesus (Lk. 3:3).

JOHN THE BAPTIST

There could be no greater honor paid the Baptist than for Jesus, the Lord of Glory, the Saviour of mankind, and the Baptizer with the Holy Spirit, to practice the same rite as His Forerunner. As stated, this sanctioned everything John said and did and authenticated his Introduction and Preparation of the One he said was *"greater than he."* Perhaps what was asked of John the Baptist, to which we will momentarily refer, has never been asked of another man. He was greater than all the Prophets who had gone before him because of the One Whom he introduced, still, *"to whom much is given, much is required!"* (Lk. 12:48).

(23) "AND JOHN ALSO WAS BAPTIZING IN AENON NEAR TO SALIM, BECAUSE THERE WAS MUCH WATER THERE: AND THEY CAME, AND WERE BAPTIZED."

The composition is:

1. As to the exact location in the phrase, *"And John also was baptizing in Aenon near to Salim, because there was much water there,"* it seems to be lost to most present Bible expositors. However, it is believed to have been located about 50 miles north of Jerusalem in Samaria.

2. The phrase, *"And they came, and were baptized,"* refers to crowds continuing to come to John, but yet, smaller than previously.

NOTES

3. The question, I suppose, must be asked as to why John continued his own Ministry up to this point, especially considering he had finished what God had originally called him to do. It was:
- To prepare the way for the Messiah.
- To introduce the Messiah.

4. These things John had done wondrously and admirably so! The next Verses, I believe, will tell us exactly what John was doing, and that he was exactly in the center of God's Will.

(24) "FOR JOHN WAS NOT YET CAST INTO PRISON."

The overview is:

1. That of which John the Beloved writes concerns John being placed in prison for his statement regarding the wife of Herod.

2. So, the Holy Spirit is telling us by this Twenty-fourth Verse that John's Ministry is about to conclude.

3. The great Prophet had done exactly what the Lord had called him to do. May we be as faithful!

(25) "THEN THERE AROSE A QUESTION BETWEEN SOME OF JOHN'S DISCIPLES AND THE JEWS ABOUT PURIFYING."

The diagram is:

1. It is agreed by most Bible students that Christ's Death on the Cross was vicarious, i.e., *"substitutionary."*

2. In one sense, He died *"for sin,"* and in another, He died *"for us."*

3. The Epistle to the Hebrews has as one of its major themes that of Christ as our Great High Priest (Heb. 5:5-6).

THE QUESTION

The phrase, *"Then there arose a question,"* in the Greek Text pertains to a very angry debate, which, in effect, was useless. It is the unending argument over matters of religion, which profits nothing.

Having ministered over radio and television for years, and many times opening the lines to any and all who would like to call, I have always been amazed at the number of people trying to promote some pet theory or doctrine, and in a contentious spirit. This is the type of spirit held by these *"Jews"* who came to John.

A discussion of the Word of God is one thing while a contentious spirit is something else altogether.

THE MATTER OF PURIFYING

The phrase, *"Between some of John's Disciples and the Jews about purifying,"* is said by the expositors to refer to one of two things:

1. There were all types of *"purifying"* processes in the oral laws made up by the Pharisees, which spoke of many washings, etc. As all religion, these Jews thought that such purified one from sin. However, those *"washings"* did not and neither did the Baptism of John, nor was it meant to do so. Only the Blood of Jesus can cleanse from sin.

However, this argument rages unto this very hour, with many people actually thinking that certain things, such as *"The Lord's Supper," "Water Baptism,"* other religious ceremonies, or certain actions actually do purify from sin.

The truth is, it doesn't and never has.

2. Some believe, which the next Verse seems to imply, that these Jews were attempting to pit Jesus against John, claiming His Baptism was greater than John's, or disavowing both.

John, baptizing on the one hand, and Jesus, baptizing on the other (His Disciples), enabled the Pharisees, through their spokesman, who was, no doubt, prompted by Satan, to raise a dissension to the moral and religious value of these two Baptisms.

The Pharisees, by hinting that these two Baptisms, one by John and one by Jesus, were in rivalry could excuse themselves from submitting to either. However, John enrolled Disciples in order to pass them on to Jesus, for he declared that he was not the Messiah, that he was only the friend of the Divine Bridegroom, that he rejoiced greatly at hearing of the fame of Jesus; and that he was satisfied that all of his Disciples were leaving him and going to Jesus.

This had to be, to which we have alluded, one of the noblest and most affecting utterances that ever came from the lips of man.

(26) "AND THEY CAME UNTO JOHN, AND SAID UNTO HIM, RABBI, HE WHO WAS WITH YOU BEYOND JORDAN, TO WHOM YOU BEAR WITNESS, BEHOLD, THE SAME BAPTIZES, AND ALL MEN COME TO HIM."

The order is:

1. The phrase, *"And they came unto John,"* proclaims the opposition of the religious leadership of Israel deepening, even at this early stage. They had no interest in John or in Jesus, except that their place and position in the hierarchy of Israel was threatened, or at least they thought.

2. The phrase, *"And said unto Him, Rabbi, He Who was with you beyond Jordan, to Whom you bear witness,"* proclaims clearly that the religious hierarchy of Israel knew that John had introduced Jesus as the Messiah. Consequently, they were confronted with proof on every side.

3. John was the first Prophet since Malachi, a period of about 400 years. As well, it was very obvious that the very nature of John's Ministry signaled something great.

4. Also, they knew from Daniel's Prophecies that the Messiah was to make His Appearance at about this time (Dan. 9:25-26).

5. They were also very well aware that Jesus fit the profile exactly concerning the Messiah. Had the Davidic Dynasty continued, Joseph would have been king when Jesus was born, with Jesus now assuming the throne inasmuch as He was the Firstborn and that Joseph, it seems, was now dead. Through Joseph, even though he was only the Foster Father of Jesus, the Genealogy of Jesus went back to David through Solomon. Through Mary, the Genealogy of Jesus went back to David through Nathan, another son of David. So, as stated, His Genealogy was perfect, and they knew all of this. They had no excuse!

6. The phrase, *"Behold, the same baptizes, and all men come to Him,"* seems that their intention was to demean John. However, his answer was from Heaven, just as his Ministry had been from Heaven.

(27) "JOHN ANSWERED AND SAID, A MAN CAN RECEIVE NOTHING, EXCEPT IT BE GIVEN HIM FROM HEAVEN."

The overview is:

1. John's Ministry was from God and, therefore, from Heaven, and Jesus' Ministry was from God and, therefore, from Heaven.

2. John had been told by God to do what he was doing, and Jesus had been told by His Heavenly Father to do what He was doing. So, the fact that both were baptizing presents no problem as both were in the Will of God.

3. These things pertaining to God and Ministry and its direction are ordained by God and not man. Hence, John was telling these Pharisees that they had no authority over him or Jesus.

4. As such, neither the religious hierarchy of Israel, nor any other man-devised hierarchy, can bestow anything of God on anyone. The Lord does not work through intermediaries as it regards those whom He calls, but rather directly from Himself to the person in question. Actually, this is what angers religious hierarchy so much; they cannot control that which God does, nor are they meant to control it. Sadly and regrettably, as here, about all that religious hierarchy can do is to try to stop the Gospel instead of preaching the Gospel. It is sadder still when one realizes that entire religious denominations presently fall into this category. The entirety of their resources is used to hinder the spread of the Gospel instead of its promotion. As the Pharisees of old, if it is not of their doing, they will oppose it. Consequently, opposition to the Gospel pretty well makes up their existence.

5. What is given by God to men must be recognized by other men. In other words, failure to recognize that which God truly is doing is tantamount to opposing God, a battle which no one can hope to win. Actually, this is the cause of most of the conflict in the church. Men refuse to recognize that which is truly of God. Religious men want to control other men, and, of course, that which is of God cannot be controlled, at least by men.

(28) "YOU YOURSELVES BEAR ME WITNESS, THAT I SAID, I AM NOT THE CHRIST, BUT THAT I AM SENT BEFORE HIM."

The diagram is:

1. The phrase, *"You yourselves bear me witness,"* means that the possibility at least exists that some of these now questioning John may have been the same ones who questioned John at the beginning (Jn. 1:19).

NOTES

2. The phrase, *"That I said, I am not the Christ,"* means that he is subservient and submissive to the One Who is actually the Christ, i.e., *"The Anointed."*

3. *"But that I am sent before Him,"* proclaims the fact that John knows that He is under the Authority of Jesus and not the authority of the Pharisees or any part of the religious hierarchy of Israel. To be sure, this greatly angered these Pharisees.

(29) "HE WHO HAS THE BRIDE IS THE BRIDEGROOM: BUT THE FRIEND OF THE BRIDEGROOM, WHICH STANDS AND HEARS HIM, REJOICES GREATLY BECAUSE OF THE BRIDEGROOM'S VOICE: THIS MY JOY THEREFORE IS FULFILLED."

The exposition is:

1. On the Cross, God, for our sake, *"Made Jesus to be sin, Who knew no sin"* (II Cor. 5:21).

2. In His Death, He took our place, and His Holy Soul shrank from this identification with sinners. In essence, one might say that God made Jesus to be the *"Sin Offering,"* which means that He took the penalty for our sin, which was death.

THE BRIDEGROOM

As John uttered the phrase, *"He Who has the Bride is the Bridegroom,"* it is not meant by the Holy Spirit to establish a doctrine.

He is merely saying that all the souls he had been winning, in reality, belong to Jesus and not him because Jesus is the *"Bridegroom."* Consequently, he takes no umbrage at the great crowds now going to Jesus, which had originally come to him.

The phrase, *"But the friend of the Bridegroom,"* is that of which John concludes himself to be. He has done everything to make the marriage ready. In fact, that was his mission, and he carried it out very well. The Ministry of Jesus is proof of that!

HEARING CHRIST

"Which stands and hears Him," refers to the Ministry of Christ, which exceeds all that John could ever have surmised.

The word, *"Stands,"* refers back to John 1:35-36, where it speaks of John standing and introducing Christ as the *"Lamb of God."*

"Rejoicing greatly because of the Bridegroom's Voice," refers to the beginning of Jesus' Ministry.

Actually, John the Baptist was the last Prophet, even of a long line of Prophets, who functioned under the Old Covenant. The others spoke of the One coming, but John had the privilege of introducing Him. The others saw Him only in shadow while John actually heard His *"Voice."*

"This my joy therefore is fulfilled," equates with Paul's statement, *"I have fought the good fight, I have finished my course, I have kept the Faith"* (II Tim. 4:7).

John had finished what God had called him to do; consequently, he had not only *"fulfilled"* his mission, but he, as well, was *"fulfilled."* Rather than being hurt because the popularity was now shifting to Jesus, it had brought him great *"joy."*

What a Testimony!

(30) "HE MUST INCREASE, BUT I MUST DECREASE."

The structure is:

1. The phrase, *"He must increase,"* not only pertained to what John must do (decrease), but all others as well! Jesus must ever *"increase,"* not men, denominations, religious offices, the Virgin Mary, Apostles, etc.

2. *"But I must decrease,"* as well, pertained not only to John's Ministry, but all others.

3. The Ministers of the New Testament all take up the same note of Divine Praise and of self-depletion as they prepare the Way of the Lord to human hearts. They hide themselves behind the greater Glory of their Lord. However, considering their powers, they are serviceable only as they contribute to the Glory and succeed in unveiling the Face of our Lord.

(31) "HE WHO COMES FROM ABOVE IS ABOVE ALL: HE WHO IS OF THE EARTH IS EARTHLY, AND SPEAKS OF THE EARTH: HE WHO COMES FROM HEAVEN IS ABOVE ALL."

The form is:

1. The phrase, *"He Who comes from above is above all,"* refers to the fact that the Messiah was not a mere man, but rather had His Origin in Heaven.

NOTES

2. In fact, after Calvary and the Resurrection, the Father gave all Power to the Son *"in Heaven and in Earth"* (Mat. 28:18).

3. It had been His equally with the Father and Holy Spirit before becoming Man, but He had become limited while being a Man (Lk. 2:40, 52; Jn. 8:28; Phil. 2:7). At that time, the time of the Resurrection, His Full Glory was restored.

4. *"He who is of the Earth is earthly, and speaks of the Earth,"* refers to all men, even the great Prophets, and are of necessity limited.

5. *"He Who comes from Heaven is above all,"* places Christ in a category above all men, which He certainly is.

6. The Jews, it seems, were attempting to make Jesus as no more than another Prophet, a mere Man. While He certainly was a Man, and fully Man, above all, He was, at the same time, God, and, consequently, above all. This they did not believe or recognize.

7. Consequently, they had no success in attempting to raise dissention.

(32) "AND WHAT HE HAS SEEN AND HEARD, THAT HE TESTIFIES; AND NO MAN RECEIVES HIS TESTIMONY."

The order is:

1. The phrase, *"And what He has seen and heard, that He testifies,"* referred to that which Jesus received from the Father, which testified of Him and He of it.

2. *"And no man receives His Testimony,"* actually means that no man contributed to His Testimony, but that it was all from God.

3. Everything about Jesus was all of God and none whatsoever of man.

(33) "HE WHO HAS RECEIVED HIS TESTIMONY HAS SET TO HIS SEAL THAT GOD IS TRUE."

The pattern is:

1. The phrase, *"He who has received His Testimony,"* refers to all who have believed on His Name and accepted Him as Lord and Saviour.

2. *"Has set to His Seal that God is true,"* has to do with man receiving the witness of the Son as the Giver of Eternal Life.

3. As the witness of Jesus is true in every respect, such portrays that God is true to His Word.

(34) "FOR HE WHOM GOD HAS SENT

SPEAKS THE WORDS OF GOD: FOR GOD GIVES NOT THE SPIRIT BY MEASURE UNTO HIM."

The composition is:

1. Paul tells us that Christ *"redeemed us from the curse of the Law, having become a curse for us"* (Gal. 3:13).

2. He bore our curse, which is but another way of saying Substitution.

3. Paul is not saying, as some have thought, that God's Righteousness is shown in the fact that sin is forgiven, but that it is shown in the way in which sin is forgiven, i.e., by the Cross.

THE ONE WHOM GOD HAS SENT

The phrase, *"For He Whom God has sent speaks the Words of God,"* refers primarily to Jesus Who always spoke the Mind of God, which is the Word of God.

However, it has a secondary meaning in that all who are truly sent by God, *"Apostles, Prophets, Evangelists, Pastors, and Teachers,"* without fail, speak the Word of God, that is, if they are to please God (Eph. 4:11).

The problem with pulpits in America, or anywhere else in the world, for that matter, is the lack of *"thus saith the Lord!"* The Preacher is to hear from God and then deliver the Message which he has received from the Lord.

The tragedy is, most do not even seek God anymore. Consequently, what they deliver is not of God, but rather of man, and neither heals, nor delivers, nor saves anyone.

THE SPIRIT NOT BY MEASURE

The phrase, *"For God gives not the Spirit by measure unto Him,"* refers to the fact that all others, while having the Holy Spirit, did so by *"measure,"* which was not so with Jesus. We speak of the Prophets of old, etc., even the very greatest of them, whomever they may have been. That which the Holy Spirit would do within Jesus' Life and Ministry had no human or earthly limitations. Anything that the Father told the Son to do, such as raising the dead, cleansing lepers, calming storms, changing water to wine, etc., could be done without difficulty.

Jesus performed no Miracles as Deity, but

NOTES

always as a Man filled with the Holy Spirit. As God, He needed nothing. As a Man, although perfect, He still needed the Help of the Spirit. Even though we have previously alluded to the following, due to its vast significance, we will briefly deal with it again.

THE HOLY SPIRIT

The Ministry of Jesus began only after He was filled with the Holy Spirit. In fact, there was no Ministry whatsoever until this grand occasion (Mat. 3:16-17).

As well, there can be no true Ministry for Christ in any capacity without the Holy Spirit carrying it out through Spirit-filled Believers (Acts 1:4-5).

This means that those who do not believe in the Baptism with the Holy Spirit with the evidence of speaking with other Tongues do precious little, if anything, for God (Acts 2:4).

Jesus was Perfect, with absolutely no blemish on His Character, Life, or Nature, yet He needed the Holy Spirit. If He needed to be baptized with the Spirit, where does that leave us who always fall woefully short? The answer is obvious: we desperately need the Working and Operation of the Holy Spirit within our lives and Ministries.

There was a visible Manifestation when Jesus was baptized with the Holy Spirit (Lk. 3:22). The present manifestation is *"speaking with other Tongues, as the Spirit gives utterance"* (Acts 2:4).

It is true that Jesus did not speak in Tongues because the Holy Spirit in this capacity was not yet given (Jn. 7:39). However, He did say concerning the Church, *"In My Name . . . they shall speak with new Tongues"* (Mk. 16:17).

Immediately after being baptized with the Holy Spirit, Jesus was *"driven into the wilderness"* by the Spirit (Mk. 1:12-13). This tells us that we learn more from adversity, as painful as it may be, than we do Blessings.

Consequently, part of the Function of the Holy Spirit within our lives is to help us overcome Satan (Rom. 8:1-11).

The Anointing was then upon Jesus to *"preach the Gospel . . . heal the brokenhearted, preach Deliverance to the captives, recovering of sight to the blind, to set at liberty them who are bruised, and to preach the acceptable Year of the Lord"* (Lk. 4:18-19).

Once again, if Jesus needed the Holy Spirit to this extent, where does that leave the rest of us?

(35) "THE FATHER LOVES THE SON, AND HAS GIVEN ALL THINGS INTO HIS HAND."

The synopsis is:

1. The phrase, *"The Father loves the Son,"* signifies that the entirety of the foundation of God's Dealings with man is based on *"Love."* Consequently, it is not based on force.

2. As such, Christianity is not spread by the use of the sword, but rather by the Love of God, which inculcates itself in the hearts and lives of those who are Called by God, who then transmit this Love to others.

3. *"And has given all things into His Hand,"* refers to the great Plan of Redemption and it being carried out by the Lord Jesus Christ, which He did at the Cross.

4. These Passages proclaim the Father and the Son so close as to be indivisible. Consequently, the idea that one can get to God except through Jesus Christ is fallacy (Jn. 14:6)!

5. That means the Muslims do not reach God, despite their praying five times a day. All Salvation is committed unto the Son, and, as such, He Alone is the Door to the Father (Jn. 10:7).

(36) "HE WHO BELIEVES ON THE SON HAS EVERLASTING LIFE: AND HE WHO BELIEVES NOT THE SON SHALL NOT SEE LIFE; BUT THE WRATH OF GOD ABIDES ON HIM."

The construction is:

1. The phrase, *"He who believes on the Son has Everlasting Life,"* proclaims to one and all the simple Plan of Salvation.

2. The consequences of all this for man were eternal. Whoever believes on that Saviour, and that Saviour Alone, obtains the Life that is everlasting.

3. *"And He who believes not the Son shall not see life,"* refers to *"believing"* as far more than mere mental acceptance, but rather obedience as well! The *"Life"* here addressed is the *"Life of God,"* which is imparted to all true Believers.

NOTES

4. *"But the Wrath of God abides on Him,"* refers to a Wrath that is never-ending.

5. Thus, John the Baptist preached the Gospel. He told men of the Love of God and of the Wrath of God. He pointed to the Blood of Christ for their sins or the Lake of Fire in their sins (Mat. 3:7, 10, 12; Jn. 1:29). As well, Jesus said that John's Testimony was true (Jn. 5:32). John declared that simple trust in that Saviour made absolute eternal felicity.

6. John's Doctrine, therefore, conflicts with the theory that there neither was, nor is, anything between God and sinners which needed to be removed by the Death of Christ. Sin was between God and man and could be removed only by the Death of Christ on Calvary.

7. There are two Greek words for *"wrath,"* one signifying temporary wrath and the other, permanent wrath. The latter is the word used here.

8. This *"wrath"* can only be assuaged by one accepting Jesus as one's personal Saviour. Otherwise, it leads to eternal darkness and the Lake of Fire (Rev. 20:15).

"'Twas grace that taught my heart to fear,
"And grace my fears relieved;
"How precious did that grace appear
"The hour I first believed."

CHAPTER 4

(1) "WHEN THEREFORE THE LORD KNEW HOW THE PHARISEES HAD HEARD THAT JESUS MADE AND BAPTIZED MORE DISCIPLES THAN JOHN."

The structure is:

1. The phrase, *"When therefore the Lord knew,"* speaks of Christ the Man. While He never ceased to be God, He never performed one Miracle or did anything as God but always as a Man filled with the Spirit. While He laid aside the expression of His Deity, He never for a moment lost the possession of His Deity. Consequently, He *"knew"* this when told by the Spirit and not before.

2. *"How the Pharisees had heard that Jesus made and baptized more Disciples*

than John," speaks of the beginning of the Ministry of our Lord. After John was taken home to Glory, there is no record that Jesus continued the baptizing process.

3. Jehovah and Jesus were not two Persons, but One. The first title, Lord, i.e., Jehovah, reveals His Absolute Deity; the second, His Perfect Humanity — the only Perfect Man Who ever lived.

4. The Pharisees had always been opposed to John. They did not subscribe to his Baptism of Repentance, and neither did they heed his Message. Due to the great crowds, they were limited, at least at the outset, as to exactly what they could do to stop him. However, when the opportunity presented itself, they would then take full advantage. The opportunity came because of Herod's anger regarding John's statement concerning Herod's incestuous marriage.

5. The Pharisees not only never lifted a finger to help John at this time, but it seems that Herod's persecution of John was assisted by *"this offspring of vipers."*

6. However, the shutting up of John, at least when it did come, in no way ameliorated the situation. The crowds that had flocked to John now flocked to Jesus, even swelling to several times their previous size.

(2) "(THOUGH JESUS HIMSELF BAPTIZED NOT, BUT HIS DISCIPLES.)"

The exposition is:

1. Jesus performed no Baptisms Himself. His Disciples attended to that duty.

2. As stated, His Baptism was the same as that of John, a *"Baptism of Repentance,"* which greatly authenticated John's Ministry and, as well, this new rite of Water Baptism.

3. Actually, it would not have been proper for Jesus to have Personally performed this ritual inasmuch as the Saviour, Who would bring the reality of Salvation, would not engage in the symbolism of that great Gift, even as important as the symbolism was.

(3) "HE LEFT JUDAEA, AND DEPARTED AGAIN INTO GALILEE."

The exegesis is:

1. The order of events seems to be as follows:

After Jesus was baptized by John in the river Jordan, He then went into the wilderness to be tempted of Satan for 40 days and nights. With that concluded, He then chose several Disciples (Jn. 1:35-51). It seems that Andrew, John the Beloved, and possibly Peter were chosen in Judaea near the Baptismal site. Philip and Nathanael were chosen shortly after, either while still in Judaea or just entering Galilee (Jn. 1:43-46).

2. Upon His First Excursion into His Home District of Galilee after the beginning of His Ministry, He performed His First Miracle at Cana of Galilee. During this time, He probably chose more of His Disciples but not yet all Twelve. Actually, some of them would receive a second Call (Mat. 4:18-22).

3. Jesus then went to Jerusalem where He cleansed the Temple the first time and had the discussion with Nicodemus. After that, His Disciples began to baptize Converts in water, which seemed to have taken place in Judaea. This is what brought on the efforts of the religious leaders attempting to drive a wedge between Jesus and John. Upon hearing this information, Jesus went back into Galilee where the religious leaders were not apt to follow, at least at this particular time. Actually, there is not much evidence that Jesus continued with the Baptismal services.

(4) "AND HE MUST NEEDS GO THROUGH SAMARIA."

The overview is:

1. The Cross shows us that God is Just at the same time as it shows Him justifying believing sinners.

2. This must mean that God's Justice is vindicated in the way sin is dealt with.

3. This seems another way of saying that Christ bore the penalty of man's sin.

THE ISRAEL OF JESUS' DAY

The Israel of Jesus' Day was somewhat divided into some seven sections. They were:

1. Idumea, which was to the extreme south toward Egypt.

2. To the north of Idumea was Judaea, which included Jerusalem.

3. To the north of Judaea was Samaria.

4. To the north of Samaria was Galilee where Christ carried out most of His Ministry.

5. Northeast of Galilee was Paneas.

6. South of Paneas on the eastern side of

the Jordan River was Decapolis, the place of the 10 cities.

7. South of Decapolis was Perea, which extended to the Dead Sea.

THE SAMARITANS

The Jews did not consider the Samaritans to be true Israelites, but rather a mixture of Gentiles and Jews, which was unacceptable. Consequently, there was a tremendous animosity between these people, with the greater amount seeming to be on the part of the Jews.

The origin of the Samaritans came about after the defeat of the northern kingdom of Israel by the Assyrians (II Ki., Chpt. 17). This took place about 700 years before Christ.

With these Gentiles taking many Jews captive at that time, and with many Jews having fled after this defeat, the Assyrians populated the area with people from Babylon and other places (II Ki. 17:24). These gradually intermixed with the Jews, who were already there, and others who later came back, and were called *"Samaritans."*

About 332 B.C., the governor of Samaria under the Persians went over, it is stated, to the side of Alexander the Great, who gave him permission to build a Temple on Mount Gerizim like the one built by Ezra in Jerusalem.

He built it for his son-in-law and made him High Priest. The Samaritans then established rival worship to Jerusalem and accepted the Pentateuch as their Bible.

The great controversy between the Jews and Samaritans, who the Jews considered to be half breeds, was whether to worship on Gerizim or Moriah where the Jewish Temple stood in Jerusalem.

As stated, the rivalry was great, with most Jews so despising the Samaritans that when traveling between Judaea and Galilee, they would take the eastern route on the other side of the Jordan, even though it extended the journey some two days. However, as stated, Jesus ministered to the Samaritans, treating them the same as the Jews. Consequently, He would go through this area at this time because it was the Will of His Heavenly Father. As such, one of the greatest Conversions ever would be brought about.

NOTES

The idea is that the woman of this story could not come to Jesus, but Jesus came to her. The striking similarity exists with all.

We could not go to the Lord, but He came to us, with our situation as desperate as this dear lady at Jacob's well.

(5) "THEN COMES HE TO A CITY OF SAMARIA, WHICH IS CALLED SYCHAR, NEAR TO THE PARCEL OF GROUND THAT JACOB GAVE TO HIS SON JOSEPH."

The overview is:

1. The phrase, *"Then comes He to a city of Samaria, which is called Sychar,"* is said by some to refer to the ancient city of Shechem, while others claim it is a different town altogether. Irrespective, it was near Jacob's well.

2. *"Near to the parcel of ground that Jacob gave to his son Joseph,"* proclaims, as is obvious, this spot having a long Bible history.

3. The Patriarch Jacob purchased this area from the children of Hamor. For this piece of land, he paid *"an hundred pieces of money,"* however much that would be (Gen. 33:19).

4. Genesis 48:17-22 records Jacob giving this portion *"to his son Joseph."*

5. In Joshua 24:32, we find the bones of Joseph were deposited there, even at his request (Gen. 50:25-26).

6. This was done because, when dying, Joseph knew that God would surely redeem Israel out of Egypt. He knew the Promise that God had made to Abraham, to Isaac, and to his father Jacob concerning this land of Canaan. Here his people would grow into a great Nation and would ultimately bring the Messiah into the world.

7. Even though he had lived many years in Egypt, even as its viceroy, his heart was still in the Promised Land. There his Faith did reside, and now the very One in Whom his Faith was held sits on the very well dug by his father Jacob so long, long before. Jesus was the Author and Finisher of that Faith.

(6) "NOW JACOB'S WELL WAS THERE. JESUS THEREFORE, BEING WEARIED WITH HIS JOURNEY, SAT THUS ON THE WELL: AND IT WAS ABOUT THE SIXTH HOUR."

The diagram is:

1. The meaning of bearing sin is made clear by a number of Old Testament Passages

where the context shows that the bearing of the penalty is meant.

2. Christ's Bearing of our sin then means that He bore our penalty.

3. Substitution lies behind the statement in I Timothy 2:6 that Christ gave Himself *"a ransom for all."*

JACOB'S WELL

The phrase, *"Now Jacob's well was there,"* proclaims this historic site being preserved, even as it is unto this day, some 2,000 years after Jesus, and nearly 4,000 years after Jacob.

I have had the privilege of visiting this spot personally, which, with its valleys and hills, is one of the most beautiful in Israel. Inasmuch as wells are not easily moved, it is without question that this is the exact spot where Jesus ministered to the woman of Samaria.

JESUS WEARY?

The phrase, *"Jesus therefore, being wearied with His Journey, sat thus on the well,"* proclaims His Humanity. Hence, John impresses upon us the full humanity, the definite, human existence of Jesus, even though He was *"the Only Begotten Son of the Father,"* and He was *"the Word made flesh"* (Jn. 1:14).

The Gospel of John alone records His Presence and Miracle at Cana. His Travel-worn Sympathy with our weakness, His Making Clay with spittle and, consequently, bringing about the Miracle of Healing of the man born blind, His Weeping over the grave of a friend, His Thirst upon the Cross, the Blood that issued from His Wounded Side, and the obvious physical reality of His Risen Body thus furnishes the Church with the grounds on which the Apostle maintained His Divine Humanity.

"And it was about the sixth hour," has been argued as to its correct computation, which I think was noon.

(7) "THERE COMES A WOMAN OF SAMARIA TO DRAW WATER: JESUS SAID UNTO HER, GIVE ME TO DRINK."

The form is:

1. *"There comes a woman of Samaria to draw water,"* would prove to be the greatest moment of her life.

2. The phrase, *"Jesus said unto her, Give Me to drink,"* presents a startling moment for this woman inasmuch as most Jews, as she knew Jesus to be, would not even speak to a Samaritan, much less ask a favor.

3. Thus opens the scene at Jacob's well, which will prove to be one of the most amazing in human history. The dread Judge of both the quick and the dead and one of the vilest of sinners are met together. However, He is there not to condemn her but to seek and to save her.

4. The Mighty God, the Everlasting Father, and the Prince of Peace was sitting weary by a well and thirsty but had no means even to quench His Thirst. He, as Man, was dependent on an outcast woman for a little water. Rejected by Israel, His Grace and Love now poured out their fullness upon an impure Samaritan — for love is pained unless enabled to act.

5. The floodgates of Grace lifted themselves up to bless the misery which love pitied. Man's heart, withered with self-righteousness, cannot understand this. Thus sinners respond to the Grace which Pharisees proudly refuse, for Grace flows in the deep channels dug by the misery of sin (Williams).[1]

(8) "(FOR HIS DISCIPLES WERE GONE AWAY UNTO THE CITY TO BUY MEAT.)"

The order is:

1. It was probably noon, which would have been the case if reckoned by Jewish time. Their time began for the day at 6 a.m. So, the *"sixth hour"* would have been noon.

2. Even though most of the Disciples had gone into the city to purchase food, some expositors feel that John the Beloved, in fact, had remained behind with Jesus.

3. It was John's custom not to mention himself in relating these experiences even though he was present. The detail to which he outlined this extremely interesting episode gives credence to the thought that he was present.

(9) "THEN SAID THE WOMAN OF SAMARIA UNTO HIM, HOW IS IT THAT YOU, BEING A JEW, ASKS DRINK OF ME, WHICH AM A WOMAN OF SAMARIA?

FOR THE JEWS HAVE NO DEALINGS WITH THE SAMARITANS."

The pattern is:

1. It was at the Cross where Christ dealt fully with man's sin.

2. Paul saw in the Cross not only the Way of Salvation but also the Way of Deliverance from the bondages of sin.

3. Men are enslaved by sin, but in Christ, men are free (Rom. 6:14, 17, 22; 7:14).

THE WOMAN OF SAMARIA

The phrase, *"Then said the woman of Samaria unto Him,"* proclaims these two isolated hearts meeting — His, isolated by Holiness, for He was separate from sinners; hers, by sin, for she was separate from society. This encounter of Holiness and sinfulness resulted in the Salvation of the sinner, for Jesus is *"the Saviour."*

Jesus, as well, was the pattern Soul-winner. With Divine skill, He led this defiled woman by five steps into the Kingdom of God. These steps were:

1. Contact (Jn 4:7).
2. Interest (Jn. 4:10).
3. Conscience (Jn. 4:16).
4. Holiness (Jn. 4:24).
5. Revelation (Jn. 4:26).

He disarmed suspicion, opposition, and hostility and won sympathy, confidence, and Faith by asking for a drink of water. This was the point of contact. It touched her nature as a woman — for it was the appeal of need — and to that appeal, a woman's nature responds.

WOMAN

The tender word, *"Woman,"* occurs 13 times in this incident. The number, *"Thirteen,"* is a happy one for Believers. At the thirteenth circuit, the walls of Jericho fell down, and in the *"thirteenth year,"* Abraham won his great victory.

The question, *"How is that You, being a Jew, asks drink of me, which am a woman of Samaria?"* proclaims that she knew He was a Jew by His Speech, Dress, and Appearance, which were different from the Samaritans.

She was perplexed that He would address her at all, much less ask of her a favor!

NOTES

"For the Jews have no dealings with the Samaritans," referred to hospitality, for ordinary buying and selling were carried on.

While it was true that most *"Jews"* felt this way, Jesus did not entertain such animosity at all.

Racism, bias, and prejudice characterize the whole of humanity, at least those who do not know God. It is ugly and without merit and can be cured only by Christ. He cured it by example and, above all, by the Power of the changed heart, which He Alone can do. That's the reason Paul said, *"There is neither Jew nor Greek* (Gentile), *there is neither bond nor free, there is neither male nor female: for you are all one in Christ Jesus"* (Gal. 3:28).

(10) "JESUS ANSWERED AND SAID UNTO HER, IF YOU KNEW THE GIFT OF GOD, AND WHO IT IS WHO SAYS TO YOU, GIVE ME TO DRINK; YOU WOULD HAVE ASKED OF HIM, AND HE WOULD HAVE GIVEN YOU LIVING WATER."

The composition is:

1. Men are under the Wrath of God on account of their unrighteousness (Rom. 1:18), but Christ delivers from unrighteousness.

2. Believers are *"justified by His Blood"* and, thus, will *"be saved by Him from the Wrath of God"* (Rom. 5:9).

3. All who rely on works of the law are under its curse (Gal. 3:10).

THE GIFT OF GOD

The phrase, *"Jesus answered and said unto her,"* proclaims Jesus arousing interest in her heart, which should be the object of every Preacher.

"If you knew the Gift of God," proclaims Jesus as that Gift and the Salvation He Alone affords.

The tragedy is, she did not know the Gift or anything about the Gift. She had some rudimentary knowledge of God, but it was only fragmentary, as is that of most of the world. She knew nothing of His Great Plan of Salvation for the human family in the sending of His Only Son to redeem mankind.

"People are destroyed for lack of knowledge" (Hos. 4:6).

On the other side of the coin, it is our responsibility as Believers to take the

Message of the Gift of God to the entirety of the world. God's Way is to anoint Preachers of the Gospel to take the Word. The Holy Spirit through Paul asks, *"How shall they hear without a Preacher?"*

He then asks, *"And how shall they preach, except they be sent?"* (Rom. 10:14-15).

TAKING THE GOSPEL TO THE WORLD

That which the Holy Spirit said through Paul refers to the fact that not only must there be Preachers who are touched by God to take the Message, but, as well, those who remain behind must support them. For those whom God calls, He also calls an appropriate number to support them prayerfully and financially. Presently, we have two problems:

First of all, there aren't many who are truly Called of God to take the Message; and secondly, the few who are truly called, most of the time, get very little support.

Sadly, this is not something new, as it has always plagued the Work of God.

When Paul was in prison in Rome, he had difficulty in finding someone who would go to Philippi. He said, *"For I have no man like-minded, who will naturally care for your state."*

He then said, *"For all seek their own, not the things which are Jesus Christ's"* (Phil. 2:20-21).

Concerning finances, he said, *"Now you Philippians know also, that in the beginning of the Gospel, when I departed from Macedonia, no Church communicated with me as concerning giving and receiving, but you only"* (Phil. 4:15).

Verse 10 also tells us that even the Philippians had stopped for a period of time, leaving the Apostle in very short supply.

So, it is not a new problem. The tragedy is, one day all of us will stand at the Judgment Seat of Christ. We will all answer for our life lived in Christ respecting our Work for Him. Then, a lot of things we thought very important here will have no significance there. As well, we will find that the things which were so very important, and which had eternal consequences, too often, we were faithless of those.

LIVING WATER

The phrase, *"And Who it is Who says to you, Give Me to drink,"* proclaims her so close to Eternal Life, but yet, so far!

The phrase, *"You would have asked of Him, and He would have given You Living Water,"* proclaims Him asking her for water to slake the physical thirst while, in turn, He would give her *"Living Water,"* which would forever slake her Spiritual thirst.

The phrase, *"Living Water,"* expresses Salvation apart from religious ceremony, which characterizes so much of the world. In fact, Salvation is not in a church, ceremony, ritual, ordinance, or even that which is labeled a *"Sacrament,"* but only in Jesus. But yet, in most places, it has been reduced to formality, ceremony, creed, culture, ritual, etc. Multiple hundreds of millions wallow in religion all their lives, even as the Samaritans, and never really know God because they do not know His Son, the Lord Jesus Christ. He Alone is the Way to the Father (Jn., Chpt. 10).

As well, as here described by none other than the Lord Himself, to obtain this *"Living Water,"* all one has to do is *"ask,"* and it is his for the asking.

If it is so simple, why is it so hard?

ATTEMPTING TO EARN SALVATION

Millions attempt to earn it but fail, as fail they must. Others attempt to merit it but find only an empty heart.

Sometime back, I witnessed over television a Buddhist monk who had completed a seven-year regimen of physical torture and privation. It was an extreme regimen, so severe, in fact, that only a few in history had succeeded in finishing this tortuous course. He was one of that few. Consequently, quite a number of reporters were there from Japan, as well as elsewhere around the world, to record this momentous occasion because they were of the Buddhist persuasion.

When he came in from his last jaunt and crossed the threshold, which marked the finish line, the television cameras began to whirl, with scores attempting to touch him because he was now pronounced, *"Holy."*

A few minutes later, they interviewed him

for the press. His answers were revealing.

When asked, *"How do you feel?"* he replied, *"I don't know!"*

"Do you feel holy?" they asked, because this regimen was supposed to make him a holy man out of its successful completion.

"I feel no different!" he said.

Then he added, *"I think I will begin another seven-year regimen!"*

He said that because there was no satisfaction, fulfillment, or anything, for that matter, that greeted him at the end of this tortuous seven-year trek.

And yet, most of the world, in one way or the other, attempts to find God, or to reach some particular status or place, by similar actions of one type or the other. They serve a god of their own making, and, as such, this god, of necessity, must be inferior to its Maker. And yet, they try to improve themselves by that which is less than they already are.

(11) "THE WOMAN SAID UNTO HIM, SIR, YOU HAVE NOTHING TO DRAW WITH, AND THE WELL IS DEEP: FROM WHERE DO YOU GET THIS LIVING WATER?"

The synopsis is:

1. Christ, thank God, has redeemed us from the curse of the Law (Gal. 3:13).

2. To men of antiquity, death was a grim antagonist against whom none might prevail. However, Paul sings a song of triumph in Christ, Who gives victory even over death (I Cor. 15:55-57).

3. It is abundantly plain and clear that Paul sees a mighty Deliverance in Christ and what Christ did for us at the Cross.

THE WELL IS DEEP

The phrase, *"The woman said unto Him, Sir, You have nothing to draw with, and the well is deep,"* presents her thinking in material terms. She doesn't quite know what He is talking about, and yet, she is suspicious that there is far more to this than material things, as her other questions portray.

In reality, He was the only One on the face of the Earth Who actually could draw from this Well. Others have claimed to do so, as the fake luminaries of the past and the present, but none ever have because none ever can!

NOTES

"The well is deep," she said, and of that she was right, far deeper than even she imagined! It was and is so deep, in fact, that only God has plumbed its depths and reveals it to us only through His Son, the Lord Jesus Christ. This is why Jesus *"needs go through Samaria."* He was searching for a lost soul who was evidently hungry for God and had not been satisfied, and, in fact, could not be satisfied by the false religion of her worship.

WHERE DO YOU GET THIS LIVING WATER?

Her question, *"From where do You get this Living Water?"* portrays her being drawn out Spiritually, at least, to a small degree. She is puzzled by His Statement, but yet, finds the phrase, *"Living Water,"* to be intriguing!

And yet, it is intriguing not merely as a matter of curiosity but more so toward the thirst of her soul. The phrase must have been the most beautiful she had ever heard and, likewise, has it been to millions.

Living Water! What a symbolism; what a description!

Even as I dictate these words, I sense the Presence of God. It is as if I am there with her, standing nearby, and yet, close enough to hear these glorious Words which came from the lips of the Master. Somehow I know they are for me as well as for her. That day, she would drink of that well, that Spiritual well, and she would find it to be exactly as He had said. Since that time, millions have come, I among them. It is just as satisfying now as it was then. This was to be the greatest day of her life, as the Day of Salvation is the greatest for all. She would meet Jesus, Who, in reality, is the *"Living Water,"* and she would never be the same again.

(12) "ARE YOU GREATER THAN OUR FATHER JACOB, WHO GAVE US THE WELL, AND DRANK THEREOF HIMSELF, AND HIS CHILDREN, AND HIS CATTLE?"

The construction is:

1. The question, *"Are You greater than our father Jacob, who gave us the well . . . ?"* proclaims to us several things, with her being closer to the truth than even she realized. In her question concerning Jacob, we observe the claims of the Samaritans to be a

descendant of Ephraim, son of Joseph, and actually of Jacob himself, who dug the well. By her use of the pronoun, *"Our,"* she lays claim to the Patriarchs, exactly as the Jews. They did not recognize her claim, but Jesus did, at least in a limited sort of way.

2. The conclusion of the question, *"And drank thereof himself, and his children, and his cattle?"* pulls her back to material and even carnal things, which characterized the Samaritans. Their worship of God was based on a false premise and, therefore, unacceptable, as Jesus will soon relate. So, as millions do, she tried to link the *"Living Water"* with this ancient well!

3. How many millions of Catholics attempt to link God with a statue, a candle, a person such as the Pope, etc.?

4. How many Protestants attempt to link God with a church building or a particular religious denomination when, in reality, there is no connection?

5. Yes! Jesus was greater than Jacob, far greater, in fact, even greater than the Temple or the Sabbath. He is greater than anything one could ever name.

(13) "JESUS ANSWERED AND SAID UNTO HER, WHOSOEVER DRINKS OF THIS WATER SHALL THIRST AGAIN."

The structure is:

1. The Atonement says many things. It incorporates Redemption, Reconciliation, Justification, Adoption, and Propitiation.

2. Paul, who was given the meaning of the New Covenant, which is the Cross, saw things in the Cross of Christ not seen by anyone else.

3. He always proclaimed Christ as having solved every problem and answered every question by His Atoning Work on Calvary's Cross.

THE METHOD OF THE LORD

The phrase, *"Jesus answered and said unto her,"* presents Him slowly leading her to the meaning of His Great Spiritual Truth.

As with Nicodemus, so it was with the Samaritan. The Lord hastened to raise the question of sin in the conscience. Nicodemus was highly moral and this Samaritan grossly immoral, yet, there was no difference between them — both were sinners needing cleansing and Salvation.

That would come as a shock to most people in the world, and even to most Christians, but it happens to be true.

But yet, how different was the Lord's Method with each of them, and we continue to speak of Nicodemus and this Samaritan woman. The moralist was at once met with the abrupt words, *"You must be born again,"* but to the sinner He says, *"Whosoever drinks of the water that I shall give him shall never thirst."*

The phrase, *"Whosoever drinks of this water shall thirst again,"* presents one of the simplest, and yet, at the same time, one of the most profound statements ever uttered.

While Jesus certainly was speaking of the water from Jacob's well, He was also speaking of all other efforts to slake the Spiritual thirst in the soul by means other than Himself.

Men attempt to slake that thirst with money, power, prestige, education, culture, accomplishments, achievements, and a host of other things, all to no avail! As someone has said, *"The soul of man is so big that only God can fill it up!"*

(14) "BUT WHOSOEVER DRINKS OF THE WATER THAT I SHALL GIVE HIM SHALL NEVER THIRST; BUT THE WATER THAT I SHALL GIVE HIM SHALL BE IN HIM A WELL OF WATER SPRINGING UP INTO EVERLASTING LIFE."

The exposition is:

1. In the writing of Hebrews, Paul proclaims the fact that Christ is our Great High Priest.

2. On the Cross, Christ has dealt fully with man's sin. It is all atoned, at least for those who will believe (Jn. 3:16).

3. In fact, in the writings of John, there is the thought of Christ as the Special Revelation of the Father. He is One sent by the Father, and all that He does must be interpreted in the light of this fact.

THIRST

This statement as given by Jesus is so freighted, so weighty, and so all-encompassing that its potential could never be exhausted. The following is but a few of the great Truths it contains:

BUT

The conjunction, *"But,"* links the hope of this Promise to the hopelessness of the previous statement. It is such a short distance but has the length of eternity.

The skeptic may ask, *"If Christ satisfies to such an extent, why is it that virtually the entirety of the world does not accept Him?"* The answer is simple!

Men do not want to give up their sins, and they are deceived into believing that by coming to Christ, they will lose their pleasure and gain nothing. They do not realize that they will lose nothing but gain everything!

WHOSOEVER

All are lost; therefore, all can be Saved. None are excluded. When Jesus died on Calvary, He died for all of mankind for all time.

The hellish doctrine proposed by some of a *"limited Atonement,"* which means that Jesus died only for a few, which is an attempt to explain their erroneous concept of Predestination, is, in fact, hellish indeed!

Jesus died for every single human being who has ever lived, who is alive now, and who shall live in the future. *"Whosoever"* means exactly what it says.

DRINK

This means that there is a part for man to play. God does not give Salvation to those who refuse to receive. The *"receiving"* is the *"drinking."*

Holding a glass of water before someone will never slake his thirst. Irrespective as to how clear and cold it may be, he must drink of it. The Psalmist said, *"O taste and see that the LORD is good"* (Ps. 34:8).

THE WATER A SYMBOLISM

"Of the water": here Jesus uses *"water"* as a symbolism for Salvation, and an apt symbolism it is! Jesus has called it, *"Living Water!"*

THE GIFT

"That I shall give him": Jesus Alone is the Purveyor of this *"Living Water!"*

As well, it is *"given free of charge,"* and as the Prophet said, *"Without money and without price"* (Isa. 55:1).

NOTES

In fact, if one tries to merit, earn, or purchase this *"Living Water,"* one automatically forfeits its possession. However, if one comes to Christ, knowing that he deserves nothing good, throwing himself on God's Mercy and Grace, and trusting in Jesus to save, he will be given Eternal Life because Salvation is a *"Gift."*

SHALL NEVER THIRST

This is an unconditional guarantee. It means the searching is over, and the Pearl of Great Price has been found, but yet, given free of charge. In fact, there is nothing else in the world, irrespective of its content, which can satisfy or slake the thirst of the human heart. Only that which Jesus gives satisfies; consequently, it is priceless!

LIVING WATER THAT IS WITHIN

"But the water that I shall give him shall be in him": this speaks of the difference in man's efforts and God's Remedy.

Men attempt to assuage the problems by external means, which are the only means he has; consequently, he tries to rehabilitate, which is impossible!

Why?

Cancer cannot heal cancer, and weakness cannot cure weakness. Sin cannot cleanse from sin, and death cannot save from death, with but one exception. I speak of the Death of the Lord Jesus Christ, the Lord of Glory, Who provided the Perfect Sacrifice, that in His Death, we might find Life, even as He is Life.

The Lord begins with the heart, consequently, *"in Him!"*

EVERLASTING LIFE

"A well of water springing up into Everlasting Life": this speaks of a continuous fountain. In effect, in a spiritual sense, Jesus is saying, *"I do not give a single 'drink of water,' but I cause a spring, a perennial fountain, a river of Divine pleasure to issue and flow from that inward satisfaction which follows a reception of My Gift; and it is so abundant that it is enough for everlasting needs. The water that I give becomes a fountain, and the fountain swells into a river, and the river expands into and loses itself in the great ocean of eternity."*

However, we are never to conclude that once the Divine Life is given, it becomes consciously a self-dependent force within the soul. This would not be justified by all the analogy of the Divine working in humanity, which, though abundant and satisfying, never repudiates its Divine Source, the Lord Jesus Christ, but continually proclaims Him.

In effect, Jesus is saying that this fullness of the Gift of God transcends all the needs of this life and is enough for eternity and more!

Hallelujah!

The great problem with the world, and which characterizes the whole of humanity, is that this Creation of God, called mankind, attempts to find fulfillment in their work, in their husband or wife, with money, or whatever, for that matter! It never works, as it cannot work.

FULFILLMENT?

That is the reason that many marriages dissolve. The husband attempts to make his wife fulfill all his needs, and many wives attempt to make their husbands fulfill all their needs.

As always, one demands more of the other than could ever be given; consequently, the marriage breaks down.

As well, many people attempt to find fulfillment in religion; however, religion without Christ can never satisfy.

That is the reason Jesus spoke of *"thirsting again,"* as all do who attempt to fulfill themselves by means other than that which is provided by the Lord.

When one fully knows Jesus and makes Him the Lord of one's life, irrespective of where one is or what one does or doesn't have, one is automatically and instantly fulfilled in every way. While it is true that man does need bread for physical sustenance, still, he does not live by that alone, *"But by every Word that proceeds out of the Mouth of God"* (Mat. 4:4). Jesus can take the place of anything, but nothing can take the place of Jesus.

The world does not understand the elderly woman who lives alone with barely enough to keep body and soul together, and yet, exhibits a satisfaction and joy which are totally unexplainable to those who do not know Jesus. They brush it off as a poor individual who is simple-minded and, consequently, does not know how bad off she really is.

No! She, and millions like her, are not simple-minded. Actually, they have been *"transformed by the renewing of their minds, that they may now prove what is that good, and acceptable, and Perfect, Will of God"* (Rom. 12:2).

The truth is, those who ridicule her are the ones who are really simple-minded. In fact, the Holy Spirit refers to them as a *"fool"* (Ps. 14:1).

(15) "THE WOMAN SAID UNTO HIM, SIR, GIVE ME THIS WATER, THAT I THIRST NOT, NEITHER COME HERE TO DRAW."

The construction is:

1. The dividing line between the true Church and the apostate church is the Cross of Christ. In fact, this has always been the dividing line; however, it is, I believe, more pronounced now than ever.

2. The Cross of Christ is something that happened now some 2,000 years ago but has continuing positive results that will never be discontinued.

3. The Cross of Christ is the Means by which all things are given to us by the Lord, whatever they might be.

GIVE ME THIS WATER

The phrase, *"The woman said unto Him, Sir, give me this water,"* proclaims that she now has some understanding, although faint, of what Jesus is speaking. She senses that it is not literal water of which He speaks, but rather something else altogether. In that, she was right!

The words that Jesus gave unto her concerned *"Living Water,"* and that upon the reception of such Water, one would never *"thirst again."* As well, it would be perpetually in them, *"Springing up unto Everlasting Life."* Without a doubt, these words were accompanied by a strong and powerful Anointing of the Holy Spirit. Jesus had already stated that He was *"anointed to preach the Gospel to the poor"* (meek)

(Lk. 4:18). Consequently, she was greatly moved by this Anointing, with the Holy Spirit thrusting the meaning of these words deep into her heart. Of course, her understanding would have been shallow. Nevertheless, considering Who spoke these words concerning True Salvation, she probably had more knowledge then, even in a moment's time, than most others in Israel at that time.

THAT I THIRST NOT . . .

The phrase, *"That I thirst not,"* which was heavily anointed by the Holy Spirit, no doubt, caused her to see, although weakly, that this pertained to Spiritual thirst and had no relationship with literal water. As stated, her knowledge would have been scant. However, the Holy Spirit is able to reveal things very quickly, especially if the heart is open, as hers undoubtedly was.

A PERSONAL EXPERIENCE

Just the other day, while watching one of the network news programs, the commentator was addressing himself to the inner city gangs and the terrible difficulties of trying to reach these young men and women. They portrayed one young man who had just been shot in the neck and had miraculously survived. The ugly scar was very visible and portrayed the seriousness of his close brush with death.

As they questioned this young black man, possibly about 18 years old, his answers were far beyond his years. Briefly, he began to relate how he now looked at things totally different. You see, in this brush with death, he had given his heart and life to the Lord Jesus Christ, which is, in fact, the only answer to the inner city gangs, to the outer city depression, etc. Jesus Christ Alone can solve the problems of mankind and satisfy the hunger and the thirst of the human heart.

They then cut away to a shot of him praying, and the thing that amazed me was this:

Having no knowledge of his past but surmising that he probably had not had much Spiritual instruction in his life, having been raised in the inner city and having run with this gang for years, and knowing only immorality, drug-taking, violence, and bloodshed, I was pleasantly surprised as I heard him pray for a few moments.

He began to say, *"Lord, I come to You, not with my own good works or merit, but according to Your Grace and Love,"* or words to that effect! The point I wish to make is this:

In a very short period of time, the Holy Spirit had revealed to him that which most never learn in a lifetime. Irrespective of his background, which certainly was not conducive to the Ways of the Lord, the Spirit of God had portrayed to him what Salvation was all about, and what it meant to be truly Saved.

As stated, I was amazed at the Spiritual depth he exhibited in these few words I heard him pray. He was far ahead of most church members who have been raised in church all of their lives. The reason was, the Holy Spirit had brought about this miraculous change in this young man's life as he had accepted Jesus as his Lord and Saviour.

THE HOLY SPIRIT

The reason most church members have little knowledge of what I am speaking is because the Holy Spirit is not present in most churches simply because He is ignored, or else, downright denied. However, where the Holy Spirit has an opportunity, irrespective as to whom that person may be or what his background, in a moment's time, as Faith acts on the Word of God, Jesus Christ comes into the heart, with the Holy Spirit revealing Him to that person's soul. Actually, this is the Miracle of the New Birth; this is the reason it is not intellectual, philosophical, or psychological. It is Spiritual and, therefore, a Work carried out entirely by the Person and Office of the Holy Spirit. He Alone can reveal Jesus to the heart and life as He acts upon the Word of God.

So, the Conversion of this woman at Jacob's well is not nearly as strange as some would think, that is, if they know and understand the Moving and Operation of the Holy Spirit. In truth, all come the same way. The Spirit of God moves upon the spoken Word of God, and Jesus is made real to the heart.

All of a sudden, as Jesus speaks these

Words, the Holy Spirit takes them like an arrow straight to her heart. In a moment's time, He reveals to her the great need of her life and, as well, at least to a certain degree, what Jesus is actually saying.

The truth is, this woman had thirsted all her life. Her immorality had not slaked that thirst, and neither did her many husbands. As well, the religion of the Samaritans gave her no satisfaction at all. She was a thirsty woman, but not for that which this world gives, but that which only God can give.

RELIGION

The same can be said for every single person in the world who follows heathenistic religions, or even the part of Christianity which is apostate. In these religions, of whatever stripe, there is no satisfaction, no fulfillment, no development, and above all, no power to help them break the bondages of darkness and the terrible grip of sin. Only Jesus Christ can do that.

Actually, religion is that which is devised by man, which he claims will help him reach God or better himself in some way. It is not of God. Bible Christianity is not a religion, but rather a relationship with a Man, the Man Christ Jesus.

Some years ago, a woman questioned me rather sarcastically as to why didn't I cease my activities respecting the spreading of the Gospel to the world. She said, *"These people have their own religion, and they are happy with it. Leave them alone and quit trying to force your religion down their throats,"* or words to that effect.

The sadness of this is that this woman called herself a Christian. I'm afraid my answer to her was somewhat cryptic.

While it is true that these people do have their religions, it is also true that these religions are of the Devil and could never even think of slaking the thirst that's in the human heart. Actually, religion only makes it worse. There is only One Answer to their dilemma and, in fact, the dilemma of any and all, and that is Jesus.

No! I will never leave them alone because in doing so, such would consign them to a Devil's Hell forever and forever. That is the reason Jesus said, *"Go ye into all the world, and preach the Gospel to every creature"* (Mk. 16:15).

Actually, I seriously doubt that this woman who made this statement to me was Saved. I cannot understand how anyone could really and truly know Jesus Christ and be so ignorant in Spiritual things as to make the statement she did. Tragically, much of Christendom falls into the same category. Even though most do not express themselves as this poor deceived soul, still, by their actions of unconcern and apathy, they are saying the same thing that she said.

RELIGIOUS THINGS

The phrase, *"Neither come here to draw,"* proclaims that she knows He is not talking about literal water. In other words, it cannot be secured from this particular well, even though it once belonged to the great Patriarch, *"Jacob,"* or any other well, for that matter.

Regrettably, many in modern Christendom, that is, if they are to call themselves Christian, seem to not know nearly as much as this woman of so long ago. For instance, Catholicism is rife with religious things, whether real or imagined. Martin Luther said that one of the things that turned him off so terribly to Roman Catholicism, even though he had been a priest in that false religion, was the trip he took to Rome in order to visit the Vatican. He saw, he said, wagonload after wagonload of bones being brought to Rome, with someone claiming that these were the bones of particular Saints who had long since died, etc.

In Israel presently, a Catholic church or Greek Orthodox is built over most holy sites, or at least nearby. In other words, *"Jacob's well"* is big business and has always been; however, as the true Jacob's well brought no salvation then, neither does it bring any now. And yet, millions try to *"draw"* from these decrepit examples of the past but ever come up empty. When Jesus comes to the place, or any place, for that matter, then and then alone is Salvation procured. However, Jacob's well played no part. It just happened to be the place where this occurred.

(16) "JESUS SAID UNTO HER, GO, CALL YOUR HUSBAND, AND COME HERE."

The synopsis is:

1. Walking after the Spirit pertains to the Believer placing his or her Faith exclusively in Christ and the Cross (Rom. 8:2).

2. Religious men have always wanted revival without repentance, and above all, revival without the Cross, but such is not to be.

3. It is Christ and Him Crucified, or it is Hellfire. That is blunt, but it happens to be true!

SIN

The woman's sin is now to be dealt with, hence, Jesus telling her, *"Go, call your husband."*

A profession of Faith in Christ, which ignores the question of sin, the Holiness of God, the Spirituality of worship as distinct from sacerdotal ceremonies, the need of pardon, and the condition of trust in an Atoning and Revealed Saviour, is worthless.

The words, *"And come here,"* have a far greater meaning than geographical location or obedience to a particular request.

The idea behind the request, or demand, pertained to the impossibility of a mere human being resolving the terrible bondages of sin which plague the human family.

The world of psychology attempts to deal with these problems in many and varied ways. It attempts to shift blame and responsibility to sources other than the individual, such as things which happened to one as a child, etc. In some cases, psychology teaches that the thing is wrong only because the person thinks it is wrong. In other words, they must feel good about themselves, irrespective of what has been done, and then the guilt will go away, etc. This speaks of subjective truth, which, in reality, is no truth at all.

PSYCHOLOGY

There is no answer in psychology. It is a bankrupt system, which was conceived in the heart of unregenerate man. It proclaims a basic turning away from the God of the Bible and ridicules Jesus Christ as the Answer and Solution to the ills and problems of mankind. So, it is impossible for one to serve God, trust and depend on Him, and look to His Word for Leading and Guidance and, at the same time, trust the foolishness of man-derived psychology.

It is like evolution! One cannot believe in evolution and God at the same time. Some may claim they can, but they only do so out of ignorance, which results in no faith at all.

This woman could not go back and bring all her husbands to Jesus, or the terrible details of a sordid misused and misspent life. However, she could bring the sin to Jesus, and this is what He really desired of her. It must be dealt with, and now would be dealt with, but not in condemnation.

(17) "THE WOMAN ANSWERED AND SAID, I HAVE NO HUSBAND. JESUS SAID UNTO HER, YOU HAVE WELL SAID, I HAVE NO HUSBAND."

The exegesis is:

1. The phrase, *"The woman answered and said, I have no husband,"* presents a truth, but only partially so!

2. Undoubtedly, she suspected what was about to happen. Her life of misery, immorality, and reckless living was about to be revealed.

3. The Gospel always exposes sin. As a result, it glaringly portrays its horror and bondage. In doing so, it reveals to the heart of man exactly what he is, a sinner, lost and undone without God.

4. Men do not enjoy facing up to these realities. Actually, it is something they will not do unless forced by the Holy Spirit. Men love to blame others for their dilemma, even as Adam blamed God and Eve, and Eve blamed the serpent. The Gospel places the blame where it rightly belongs, squarely in the heart of the individual being dealt with.

5. This is why neither psychology nor any other philosophy of man can even begin to compare with that which is done by the Holy Spirit by the Word of God. Being human, even the best of us, whomever that may be, only sees the outward. The Lord sees the heart and judges accordingly!

6. The phrase, *"Jesus said unto her, You have well said, I have no husband,"* bores to the very heart of her problem. It speaks to her domestic and spiritual life and points out her problem and the solution.

7. Every problem has a solution. However, to all matters pertaining to behavior, irrespective as to direction, the solution is Spiritual, and Spiritual alone, i.e., Jesus and the Word of God. To address it in any other manner is doomed to failure even at the outset.

8. In this brief exchange, Jesus will tell her the problem, the cause, and the solution. As it was for her, so it is with us, for this exchange was meant for us as well!

(18) "FOR YOU HAVE HAD FIVE HUSBANDS; AND HE WHOM YOU NOW HAVE IS NOT YOUR HUSBAND: IN THAT SAID YOU TRULY."

The pattern is:

1. In the Ninth Chapter of Leviticus, we have fire coming out from the Lord, Who dwelt between the Mercy Seat and the Cherubim in the Holy of Holies, and consuming the sacrifice on the Brazen Altar.

2. Now, the same fire comes from the Lord from the same place, but rather kills two of the Priests, Nadab and Abihu, sons of Aaron. The first fire was Glory; the second was Judgment, although the same fire.

3. They died because of *"strange fire"* being offered unto the Lord as it regards being placed on the Golden Altar, which sat immediately in front of the Veil. The fire was supposed to come from the Brazen Altar, which was a type of the Cross, but instead, came from another ignition. This is the sin of the modern church, *"Strange fire."*

FIVE HUSBANDS

The phrase, *"For you have had five husbands,"* must have come as a shock to her, especially considering that she knew He did not know her. Incidentally, He knew this by the *"Word of Knowledge"* (I Cor. 12:8).

In this Revelation, one can feel the misery and heartache that must have resulted in a lifestyle which would bring about such aberration.

While it may be true that one or two of these former husbands had died, the implication is that such had not happened and, if so, had no bearing whatsoever on what brought this about.

Such activity proclaims a Spiritual *"thirst"* which is not satisfied and, in fact, cannot be satisfied by these means. And yet, the world continues to clamor after another wife, another husband, more money, a different place to live, etc., ad nauseam.

However, in this answer given to her by Jesus, we find the cause, which is far greater than her personally.

It is ironic that she had had *"five husbands"* and, as well, that this was the exact number of gods that had characterized the Samaritan religion from its inception.

When the northern kingdom called Israel (sometimes called Ephraim or Samaria) was taken by Assyria, the area was left almost without population. Tens of thousands of Jews had been killed, with tens of thousands taken captive, and others fleeing to surrounding countries. As a result, the land had few inhabitants.

In view of this, and as we have previously stated, Sennacherib, king of Assyria, sent people from Nineveh and other places to inhabit the area formerly known as Israel. They brought with them their gods, which were five in number, and set up worship to them in the land. This greatly influenced coming generations, of which Jesus particularly speaks. These gods are as follows:

FIVE GODS

1. The god Nergal: this was a well-known Assyrian deity. He is called, *"The god of battles"* and *"The god of the chase,"* the last being his principle title. He was the patron of hunting and was supposed to represent the deified hero and hunter, Nimrod. His symbol was a man-lion, or human-headed lion with eagle's wings.

2. The god Ashima: this was the god of Hamath, a deity worshipped under the figure of a goat without wool.

The goat is found among the sacred animals of the Babylonian monuments. Ashima corresponds with the Egyptian Mendez, the Greek Pan, and the Phoenician Esmun.

3. The gods Nibhaz and Tartak: these two gods were of the Avites, with both being similar and thought to be in the form of a man with a head of a dog or in the form of an ass.

4. The god Adrammelech: this was a god of the Sepharvites and was supposedly

identical with Molech.

5. The god Anammelech: this was also a god of the Sepharvites and was supposed to be in the form of a horse. Human sacrifices were offered to it as well!

SAMARITANS

The people of Samaria, as this region came to be known, with its people hence called *"Samaritans,"* worshipped all these gods in their own way, in all high places, and in their own cities. They feared Jehovah but served other gods (II Ki. 17:32-33), that is, they were afraid of Jehovah but not enough to serve Him or keep His Laws.

At a point in time, the Samaritans drifted partially toward the true worship of Jehovah and ultimately forsook these idol gods. However, Judah still would have nothing at all to do with them.

In 332 B.C., they built a temple to Jehovah on Mount Gerizim. As stated, they laid aside their idols and accepted the Pentateuch as their religious Text Book and began to attempt to observe the Law of Moses.

However, they rejected all the other Books of the Bible, which, in Jesus' Day, consisted of the entire Old Testament.

Nevertheless, recognizing a part of the Bible is not enough, which Jesus will exclaim momentarily.

The *"five husbands"* had taken their terrible toll!

NOT YOUR HUSBAND

The phrase, *"And he whom you now have is not your husband: in that said you truly,"* proclaims two things as well.

First of all, the man she was now living with was not her husband. This proclaims that she had thrown away all convention, with her life becoming more and more sordid, even by the day. This tells us that no pretense is left, with her basically exclaiming, *"What's the use!"*

Secondly, this false worship in which the Samaritans were presently engaged was no more of God than the idols of the past had been. Spiritually speaking, the Samaritans had no *"husband,"* i.e., True God!

So, her problem paralleled the entirety of Samaria. It also parallels the entirety of the human family basically for all time.

Most presently worship false gods, or else, have a corrupt form of Christianity exactly as the Samaritans had a corrupt form of the Law of Moses. Presently, I speak of Catholicism, Mormonism, and even many in so-called, old-line churches, who have substituted a works religion or man-devised variety of some nature. Despite all the religious activity, most do not actually know Jesus Christ as their Lord and Saviour.

(19) "THE WOMAN SAID UNTO HIM, SIR, I PERCEIVE THAT YOU ARE A PROPHET."

The diagram is:

1. The only way that the Believer can understand the Grace of God and have Grace flowing uninterrupted in his heart and life is to understand the Cross.

2. As the Cross and the Word are synonymous, one could, as well, say that the Cross and Grace are synonymous.

3. The Grace of God is merely the Goodness of God extended to undeserving Believers.

A PROPHET?

The phrase, *"Sir, I perceive that You are a Prophet,"* had to do with the beliefs of the Samaritans and their interpretations of Who the Messiah would be.

Although the Samaritans accepted the Books of Moses (Genesis, Exodus, Leviticus, Numbers, and Deuteronomy), they, as stated, did not accept the Historical, Wisdom, or Prophetic Books of the balance of the Old Testament.

They derived their interpretation of the Messiah from Deuteronomy 18:15, *"The LORD your God will raise up unto you a Prophet from the midst of you, of your brethren, like unto me; unto Him you shall hearken."*

While this Passage definitely was referring to the Messiah, Who would be Jesus Christ, the Samaritans were misinterpreting the Promise.

THE MESSIAH

The Samaritans did not understand the Incarnation, and they erroneously believed that the Messiah would be a Samaritan, i.e., *"from the midst of you."*

The Jews, as all know, were looking for a Messiah, as well, but had built up an exaggerated and carnal view of just Who He would be and what He would do. Consequently, both were wrong!

Israel was looking for a *"king,"* but the wrong type of king, while the Samaritans were looking for a *"Prophet,"* who would be a mere man, although charismatic, etc.

Not believing the Historical Books, the Samaritans did not understand that the Messiah would actually be David's Son. Not believing Isaiah, they did not believe He would be *"Virgin Born,"* and, in effect, *"The Son of God."*

So, their thinking, as the thinking of most in this world, was skewed simply because of a lack of believing the Word and a false interpretation of what little they did know and believe.

So, when this woman addressed Jesus as a *"Prophet,"* she thought in her heart that He just might be the long-awaited Messiah. And yet, He was a Jew, which was glaringly obvious, which confused her somewhat inasmuch as she believed that the Messiah would be a Samaritan.

(20) "OUR FATHERS WORSHIPPED IN THIS MOUNTAIN; AND YOU SAY, THAT IN JERUSALEM IS THE PLACE WHERE MEN OUGHT TO WORSHIP."

The overview is:

1. Most Christians function in law simply because they do not understand the Cross of Christ.

2. The only place Christians can be is in either *"law"* or *"Grace."* If they don't understand the Cross, they will automatically be in law, whether they realize it or not.

3. Unfortunately, all who are in law, and of any stripe, are under its curse (Gal. 3:10).

THE FATHERS

The phrase, *"Our fathers worshipped in this mountain,"* speaks of Mount Gerizim. It is about 50 miles north of Jerusalem.

As stated, rival worship in Jerusalem had been set up on this mountain, with the temple built in 332 B.C.

The *"father,"* of which she speaks, no doubt, goes back to Abraham, Isaac, and Jacob, who worshipped and labored at Shechem, which was nearby. This of which she speaks took place about 1,000 years ago.

As well, she used the word, *"Our,"* probably claiming they were the *"fathers"* of both the Jews and Samaritans, which was wrong. The Patriarchs were not the fathers of the Samaritans but only the Jews. (Abraham was also the father of the Arabs.)

JERUSALEM

The phrase, *"And You say, that in Jerusalem is the place where men ought to worship,"* pertains to her believing that Jesus fit the profile of the great Prophet Who would come as Moses had predicted, but she was perplexed because He was a Jew and worshipped in Jerusalem.

The Samaritans claimed Gerizim and the Jews Moriah as the place where Abraham offered his typical sacrifice. They both regarded the worship celebrated in each shrine — the daily Offerings, the annual Offerings (the Passover especially) — as giving worthiness to all the prayers and praises which they might be induced to offer in all places where they might sojourn.

All of this was very important, not a matter of mere semantics, because the worship was the sacrificial worship where sins such as hers could alone be cleansed, and where her conscience could be set free for calm and continuous communion with God.

However, she knew that her life had not been changed by the worship in which she had previously been engaged, and now she sensed that Jesus was about to give her what she had craved all along, Salvation from sin and true communion with God. However, as stated, she was confused because He did not match up to her beliefs.

How so much like the world and, at the same time, how so much unlike the world.

The similarity is in the woman needing help but looking for it in the wrong place; however, the similarity ends with her accepting Jesus while the world will not.

(21) "JESUS SAID UNTO HER, WOMAN, BELIEVE ME, THE HOUR COMES, WHEN YOU SHALL NEITHER IN THIS MOUNTAIN, NOR YET AT JERUSALEM, WORSHIP THE FATHER."

The exegesis is:

1. By not understanding the Cross regarding our Sanctification, unfortunately, the modern church jumps from one fad to the other.

2. When Believers have problems and they go to their Pastor, most of the time, they are given one of two answers, both which are useless. *"You've got to try harder,"* or *"You need psychological counseling."*

3. The Cross of Christ alone is the answer for man's dilemma.

BELIEVE ME

The phrase, *"Jesus said unto her, Woman, believe Me,"* presents an expression, which says several things.

He was asking her to believe Him, and He was answering her question that He is that *"Prophet,"* fulfilling Moses' Prophecies, but, in reality, much more. He is Deity, i.e., *"God, manifest in the flesh."*

In effect, He was saying that He held the answer to her dilemma, and rather than believing the arguing factions among the Samaritans and Jews, she was rather to *"believe Him!"* What a lesson for us presently!

Arguments over religion rage constantly, bringing hundreds of millions into its maw, exactly as it did in the day of Jesus. However, the one criterion, the one foundation, and the one principle which must be heeded is the Lord Jesus Christ. When one stands before God, whatever his church, religious denomination, preacher, etc., said will matter little. It's what God has said, hence, Jesus saying, *"Believe Me!"*

THAT WHICH IS SOON TO COME

The phrase, *"The hour comes, when you shall neither in this mountain, nor yet at Jerusalem, worship the Father,"* proclaims an unparalleled Truth.

Jesus was saying that the time was near and, actually, would be completed very shortly, when He would die on Calvary and be raised from the dead. The Day of Pentecost would signal the new form of worship.

In truth, all of the Temple worship, sacrifices, and Feast Days were about to draw to a close. All of these were Types of Jesus Christ and would have served their purpose upon His Coming and carrying out that to which they had pointed. So, the argument as to where men should worship would be moot very shortly anyway.

Actually, Jerusalem is the correct place, even as Jesus will shortly say, but it, too, is about to be brought to a close, having fulfilled its purpose.

Also, by Jesus using the title, *"Father,"* He proclaims that the coming worship will be far more intimate than the previous. God will be looked at in an entirely different light because a relationship will have been established by Believers, and because of what Jesus would do at Calvary and the Resurrection.

What must this woman have thought when Jesus used the title, *"Father,"* so readily, implying a relationship of previously unknown proportions?

The very way He used the word implied that such a relationship could never be brought about by sacrifices, Feast Days, ceremonies and rituals. This was a nearness to God that she had never known, heard of, or experienced. As well, He was intimating that all could have this relationship! How her heart must have thrilled at this.

(22) "YOU WORSHIP YOU KNOW NOT WHAT: WE KNOW WHAT WE WORSHIP: FOR SALVATION IS OF THE JEWS."

The exposition is:

1. In the 1970s, the *"self-esteem theory"* was promoted, claiming that if a Believer, or anyone, for that matter, had a problem, it was because of a low self-esteem.

2. They were then to find a way to increase the esteem of themselves.

3. The truth is, the problem with man is *"self,"* whether it be *"low self"* or *"high self."* Either way, it's a problem. The only answer for self is that it be placed into Christ, which it can be at the Cross, and only at the Cross (Lk. 9:23-24).

YOU WORSHIP YOU KNOW NOT WHAT

The phrase, *"You worship you know not what,"* tells her, in no uncertain terms, exactly what was right and wrong. Her Samaritan style of worship was wrong. It was that which God would not accept and, in fact, could not accept, irrespective as to how much they used His Name.

How this should be a lesson to all! To be frank, the Samaritan way of worship was far closer to Scriptural Truth than Catholicism, but yet, unacceptable. The same can be said for many Protestant churches and denominations. They really don't know what they worship.

Years ago, I happened to be in the presence of a very successful businessman in Houston, Texas. I asked him where he went to church.

He told me he was *"Episcopalian!"* He then added, *"I am in charge of the worship at our church."*

I asked him what that meant.

He then exclaimed that he was not sure if he understood what it meant himself. He related how he would collect the *"holy water,"* which was used in wedding ceremonies, keep it till the next Sunday, and then he would walk up and down the aisle, sprinkling it on individuals sitting nearby.

He then added how he had brought in *"folk singers,"* who sat on the Altar and sang folk songs. How that related to worship, I have not yet understood.

In truth, he had no idea what the true worship of God actually was. The man was not even saved, and neither was the pastor of his church. In truth, it is doubtful that anyone in that church truly was saved. No gospel was preached there; consequently, the Holy Spirit had no opportunity to function in any capacity. To be frank, the Holy Spirit was not in the proceedings whatsoever, as He was not in the proceedings of the Samaritans, etc. Sadly, He was not in the proceedings of the Jews, as well, as they had long since left the true worship of God, with the Temple rituals having deteriorated into mere formality.

THE PLAIN TALK OF JESUS

I realize that Jesus would be thought of as uncouth, or even argumentative, by many today by flatly stating that the Samaritan way was wrong. Such would be somewhat destructive to unity, they would say!

However, if the soul of man is important, then the lie he believes must be addressed.

To call it any other way than what it is is an affront to God and a terrible disservice to the individual in question.

In preaching the Gospel for many years and having seen literally hundreds of thousands brought to a Saving Knowledge of Jesus Christ, and I exaggerate not, I have found that while preaching the Truth may at times anger, it, as well, saves. Proverbially speaking, to beat around the bush says nothing. If one is to notice, the Lord plainly called things exactly as they were. There was no doubt as to what He was saying, even though it may have offended some.

It is the same with the presentation of the Gospel presently. If it's wrong, one must say it is wrong. If it's a doctrine that is causing people to be lost because it is a lie, even as the Samaritan doctrines, they must be addressed accordingly.

THE JUST SHALL LIVE BY FAITH

It is incumbent upon every Preacher of the Gospel to tell the Catholics that the church cannot save and, in effect, *"The just shall live by Faith."* They must be told that praying to the Virgin Mary is wrong and, actually, blasphemy against God. They must be told that confessing to a priest is unscriptural and that, in reality, when doing so, their sins are unforgiven.

As well, they must be told that there is no such thing as a *"priest"* in the New Covenant, and that the establishment of a priesthood is, as well, an abomination in the Eyes of God.

Protestants must be told, even as the Catholics, that their church cannot save them, and neither can Ordinances such as *"Water Baptism," "The Lord's Supper,"* etc.

Also, they must be told that denying the Baptism with the Holy Spirit with the evidence of speaking with other Tongues will, in effect, deny a great portion of the Word of God, which will leave them powerless and, for the most part, spiritually blind.

Finally, the Pentecostals must be told that they must return to the Holy Spirit, from Whom most have departed, and *"do the first works; or else I will come unto you quickly, and will remove your candlestick out of his place, except you repent"* (Rev. 2:5).

While preaching in this manner will not gain one many friends and will be the occasion of much opposition, as well, it will cause many to truly find Jesus as their Saviour and to get right with God.

So, the Preacher of the Gospel has a choice! He can compromise the Gospel and do nothing for God, or else, he can preach exactly as Jesus. This will win many souls but, at the same time, will incur great opposition and even persecution.

Regrettably, most opt for the former while rejecting the latter.

WE KNOW WHAT WE WORSHIP

The phrase, *"We know what we worship,"* proclaims unequivocally that there is a right way of worship. As well, I might quickly add that there is only one right way and not several. While all the spokes on a wheel may well lead to the hub, all ways do not lead to God. There is only One Way, and that One Way is Jesus, and Him Alone! We might even better say, *"It's Who He is, and What He has done."* He is God, and at the Cross, He redeemed mankind, at least all who will believe.

All worship must be in accordance with the Word of God, and, if so, it will truly have the Moving and Operation of the Holy Spirit.

The man of whom I spoke a few paragraphs ago had no idea what he was worshipping. He called it *"worship of God,"* but it was anything but that. Regrettably, such will be very similar in most churches this Sunday morning.

SALVATION IS OF THE JEWS

The phrase, *"For Salvation is of the Jews,"* means that it was not of the Samaritans, or anyone else, for that matter.

Irrespective of Israel's present backslidden condition and her departure from the True God, despite the continuing of the religious ceremonies and rituals, still, that which had been given to this world by God had come through the Jewish people.

It was to Abraham that God first spoke and gave the Promise concerning the people who would come from his loins, and from among those people, *"The Messiah,"* Who would redeem mankind (Gen. 12:1-3).

To Abraham and Sarah was born Isaac, through whom the Seed would come, the Lord Jesus Christ.

From Isaac came Jacob, from whom came the 12 sons who headed up the Twelve Tribes of Israel.

To these people, the Jews, were given the Prophets and the Word of God, i.e., the Bible. As well, ultimately, through them, the Tribe of Judah, the House of David, and the Virgin Mary, came the Messiah, not for the Jews only, but for the whole world (Jn. 3:16).

Consequently, the world owes an incredible debt to the Jews, but has mostly paid that debt with hatred, murder, vengeance, and the threat of annihilation. Actually, they would have long since been annihilated were it not for the Hand of God.

THE JEWS

While it is true that Israel has forfeited her position by her rejection of her own Messiah, still, the Prophets have proclaimed that Israel will ultimately be restored, which actually began in 1948, with Israel finally once again becoming a Nation after nearly 2,000 years. The full Restoration will not come until the darkened days of the Great Tribulation are past, even as Jesus said (Mat. 24:21). However, they will come, and Israel will finally accept her Messiah and will be restored to her proper place and position, even as the Promises were given to the Patriarchs and Prophets of old (Ezek., Chpts. 38-48; Zech., Chpts. 13-14; Rev., Chpt. 19).

In fact, much of the progress in this world, such as technological advancement and the rapid progress of medicine, as well as other scientific achievements, has been brought about by those of Jewish descent.

Some years ago, I had the occasion to be a part of the program in which Prime Minister Rabin was the principle speaker. This was shortly before he became Prime Minister.

He said, *"How many Jonas Salks or Albert Einsteins died in the Holocaust?"*

The point was well taken.

Yes, Salvation is of the Jews, *"Even though the world little knows it, and which* the Jews will not admit because of their rejection of Jesus Christ."

(23) "BUT THE HOUR COMES, AND NOW IS, WHEN THE TRUE WORSHIPPERS SHALL WORSHIP THE FATHER IN SPIRIT AND IN TRUTH: FOR THE FATHER SEEKS SUCH TO WORSHIP HIM."

The structure is:

1. Regarding the Old Testament, a man might say, *"Can I not offer a sacrifice in one place as well as another?"* The answer is, *"Life belongs to God, and His Claim thereto must be recognized in the place where He has appointed — before the Tabernacle of the Lord."*

2. That was the only meeting place between God and man. To offer elsewhere proved that the heart did not want God.

3. The moral of this is plain. There is one place where God has appointed to meet the sinner, and that is the Cross — the antitype of the Brazen Altar. To reject this meeting place is to bring down Judgment on oneself — it is to trample underfoot the just Claims of God and to arrogate to oneself a right to life, which all have forfeited.

THE HOUR COMES AND NOW IS

The phrase, *"But the hour comes, and now is,"* actually says the same as Verse 21, but with added emphasis respecting the time. Jesus was now here, and the entirety of things was about to change.

Every single Prophecy of the Old Testament, the sacrifices, along with the Feast Days, as well as what the Tabernacle and Temple stood for, all pointed to one Person, the Lord Jesus Christ. He was and is the Fulfillment of all these things, and He did so for the purpose of opening up the Way that the Holy Spirit could come down and dwell in the hearts and lives of Believers in a manner which could not be done previously.

When Jesus died on Calvary, thereby, satisfying the claims of Heavenly Justice and defeating Satan, as well (Col. 2:14-15), His Resurrection would afford a place and position with the Father for Believers heretofore unknown. Consequently, it would be the greatest pivot point in history, with Believers then becoming *"an habitation of God through the Spirit"* (Eph. 2:22).

It is amazing that Jesus would tell these things to a poor Samaritan woman, who had been immoral, to say the least, but would not reveal such to the religious hierarchy of Israel. It has not changed presently.

Those who accept God's Way, which is the Way of the Cross, which is the only Way of Righteousness, will, in turn, receive God's Revelation. Those who do not accept it, even those professing greatly, have nothing revealed unto them.

TRUE WORSHIP

The short phrase, *"When the true worshippers. . . ,"* tells us that there is much worship, but with most, it is false. Actually, the *"true and the false"* will be outlined graphically in the next phrase.

The phrase, *"Shall worship the Father in spirit and in Truth,"* refers to the spirit of man, but the Spirit of God, as well, and in the Truth of God's Word. The Story of the Bible is the Story of Jesus Christ and Him Crucified. We must understand that all things pertaining to God are made possible by the Cross, and only by the Cross. If one doesn't understand the Cross of Christ relative not only to Salvation but, as well, to Sanctification, in other words, how we live for God on a daily basis, such a person cannot truly and actually worship God, at least as they should.

All true worship of God has always been in this capacity. Due to the Holy Spirit not being able to take up abode in the hearts and lives of men because of sins not being taken away but only covered, this means that before Calvary, worship was far more ritualistic, pertaining to the sacrifices, Feast Days, etc.

Since the Cross, meaning that all sin was atoned, past, present, and future, at least for those who will believe (Jn. 3:16), now one can truly worship the Lord in spirit and in Truth.

Even though the word, *"Spirit,"* as used here by Jesus, pertains to the spirit of man, the Holy Spirit also is the very Person of the Godhead Who makes it possible for the Believer to truly worship God. We were given an example of this in the Tabernacle and Temple.

THE TABERNACLE

Even though all the items of furniture in the Tabernacle pertained to Jesus, the oil in the Golden Lampstand, as is obvious, pertained to the Holy Spirit. The Priests were commanded by the Lord to trim the wicks twice a day and to replenish the oil so that the flame would burn clearly and brightly. Without that Light, which actually typified Christ but was fueled by the Holy Spirit, the Priests could not see in order to carry out the duties required of them.

While there were narrow windows in the Temple, which emitted some light into the Holy Place (I Ki. 6:4; 7:4), within itself, such was woefully inadequate without the Light provided by the Golden Lampstand. There were no windows at all in the Tabernacle, so without the Golden Lampstand, those in the Tabernacle could see nothing. In other words, in that confine, it was pitch black save for the Light.

One might say that without the Baptism with the Holy Spirit, the modern Believer has some Light regarding worship, but not nearly enough. In fact, without the Holy Spirit, there really isn't any true worship of God carried forth.

If one is to notice, the services conducted by preachers who do not believe in the Baptism with the Holy Spirit with the evidence of speaking with other Tongues, are far more formal and stereotyped. In other words, they are all the same. As such, there is very little, if any, true worship. Most of the people who attend these churches think that by merely showing up and listening to the preaching, etc., they are worshipping; however, that is woefully incorrect.

When the Golden Lampstand began to burn, i.e., the oil of the Holy Spirit, a far greater amount of Light was given to the Holy Place. It also shone into the Holy of Holies, making it possible for the Priests to properly eat the Bread of the Face, which typified Jesus. As well, it enabled the Priests to put the coals of fire on the Altar of Worship, with Incense poured thereon, filling the Holy Place with a Divine fragrance.

THE SPIRIT-FILLED LIFE

So, only those who are truly Spirit-filled know how to worship God!

However, being truly Spirit-filled means far more than merely speaking in Tongues once in awhile. The true Spirit-filled life is that which makes Jesus supreme in one's heart and life, which the Holy Spirit will always do if given proper opportunity. This can only come about through prayer and the study of the Word of God. Regrettably, most who claim to be Spirit-filled are little characterized by these twin privileges; consequently, there is not much true worship.

When the Believer is baptized with the Holy Spirit, irrespective as to his or her form of background, certain characteristics will begin to come to the fore. There will be in him, even as Jesus said in Verse 14, *"A well of water springing up into Everlasting Life,"* actually referring to a gushing forth which never stops. This is the reason for the constant praises on the lips of true Spirit-filled Believers. Such has nothing to do with whether they are in church but is actually a part of their spiritual and mental makeup. Praises to the Lord become commonplace, irrespective as to where the person may be. Of course, most is carried on very quietly, even in one's subconscious much of the time, but it still constitutes Praise and Worship.

LIFT UP HOLY HANDS

As well, there is a constant uplifting of hands in public services as Jesus is extolled (I Tim. 2:8), which is a result of the Moving of the Holy Spirit and not the cause. In other words, many Pentecostals and Charismatics attempt to instigate a Moving of the Holy Spirit by these physical actions, but to no avail! The manner in which Believers express themselves, and which is Biblical, is always a result of the Moving and Operation of the Holy Spirit in one's heart and, as stated, not the cause.

The Holy Spirit is a Person, and He must be treated as One. As well, His business is to always glorify Christ, which will always be done according to the *"Truth"* of the Word of God.

If men seek to worship the Lord only in their spirit and devoid of *"Truth,"* i.e., the Word of God, excesses will always follow, with priorities becoming confused and spiritual anemia being the result.

THE SEEKING FATHER

The phrase, *"For the Father seeks such to worship Him,"* means that by the word, *"Seeks,"* such are not easily found.

As it is today, so it was then. The sinner tried by a proposed religious discussion about churches to put aside the matter of her shameful life. However, Jesus gently and courteously explained to her that the true Way of Salvation had been revealed to the Jews, even though it was little heeded, and that the true place of worship was the heart, not either Gerizim or Jerusalem, for God is Spirit and Truth. Worship, therefore, must be Spiritual and must be in subjection to the Word of God.

• The Holy Spirit seeks pupils (Jn. 16:13-15).
• The Father seeks holy worshippers (Jn. 4:23).
• The Son seeks sinners (Lk. 19:10).

Many in the church have concluded that God seeks holy worship. He does not! He seeks holy worshippers! There is a vast difference.

CEREMONIES?

All types of sacerdotal ceremonies are instituted in the Catholic church, as well as many Protestant churches, thinking that the beauty of such arrangements, which incorporate beautiful altars, candles, and vestments, constitutes holy worship. However, as stated, God is not looking for *"holy worship,"* but rather *"holy worshippers."*

In fact, there were many ceremonies in Judaism, such as the seven great Feasts conducted each year, which representative males from each household were obligated to attend. These Feasts were conducted in Jerusalem.

The Jewish Sabbath, which was Saturday, was not really a day of worship but actually a day of rest.

However, these ceremonies within themselves were only meant to aid the Believer in his worship of God, and actually constituted no worship whatsoever within themselves if they were not understood and engaged properly. In fact, and sadly so, Israel, by the time of Jesus, had, for the most part, ceased to worship God in reality, but mostly had degenerated to mere formality. This was so much the case that these great Feasts originally ordained by God had now degenerated until they were referred to by the Holy Spirit as *"a Feast of the Jews"* (Jn. 5:1).

Man degraded them so that they became mere formalities. So, what was meant to enhance worship was subverted to mean worship, which, in reality, could only come from the heart.

One worships God through praise, which should involve constant participation. Sometimes it may be vocal, and sometimes, even most of the time, it will be silent, but yet, coming from the heart.

WHY DOES GOD DEMAND WORSHIP?

As a creature, we owe worship to our Creator, Who is God. In that God seeks worshippers, it is not to satisfy ego, as it would be with man. It is that which man rightly owes God for many and varied reasons. He made us, keeps us, and sustains us. As such, worship shows gratitude and thanksgiving (Ps. 150:6).

As well, considering the price that Jesus paid at Calvary, which secured our Redemption, at least for those who will believe, I think it should be obvious that we should thank Him for that on a constant basis. In fact, the ransom paid at Calvary's Cross by our Lord is of such magnitude, such moment, and such eternal consequences that the price paid should be an occasion for constant praise and worship coming from our hearts. Without the Cross, we wouldn't be saved. Without the Cross, we would not have the Holy Spirit. Without the Cross, there would be no fellowship and communion with God. Without the Cross, we would still be in our sins. Without the Cross, there is no way that our names could be written in the Lamb's Book of Life. The Cross of Christ is the Means, and the only Means, by which all of these good things are given to us by the Lord. As stated, this should be the occasion for constant praise and constant thanksgiving.

PROPER RELATIONSHIP GUARANTEES WORSHIP OF GOD

There are millions of professing Christians who little worship God, if at all. The reason is, they have no relationship with Christ and actually aren't even saved. Most of these have accepted Christian philosophy, but without Christ. As such, they are Christian in name only.

Such people do not worship God, for who can worship philosophy? People worship the Lord because they have a relationship with Him. Christianity is really a Person, and that Person is Christ Jesus.

So, if one is truly Saved, one has Christ within one's heart, and, consequently, worship is an automatic response. One might say the following:

Praise is what we do while worship is what we are. This means that everything of our lives, the spiritual, the secular, the domestic, the material, etc., all should be a peon of praise to God on a constant basis.

It's not that we vocally praise Him all the time, but that subconsciously, we definitely do praise Him constantly. Personally, I worship the Lord in Tongues over and over again during daily life and living. If you stood right next to me, you would never hear me, but in my subconscious, I am praising Him in Tongues. To be sure, our praising the Lord does us a hundred times more good than it does Him. He doesn't need our praises, but we definitely do need to praise Him.

THE HOLY SPIRIT AND WORSHIP

Even though we have already addressed this, it behooves us to once again emphasize the significance played by the Holy Spirit in this all-important aspect of the Believer's relationship. Without the Baptism with the Holy Spirit (Acts 2:4), it is doubtful that any Believer can truly worship the Lord as he should. It is the Spirit Who gives the Power, Direction, and Leading (Jn. 16:12-15).

In the many years of seeing multiple thousands baptized with the Holy Spirit, I have noticed that irrespective of an individual's religious background, if any at all, and even though personalities definitely differ, still, there is a sameness, in a sense, about the worship of God respecting Spirit-filled people. As stated, it doesn't matter if their background is Catholic, Baptist, or Pentecostal; Spirit-led worship has characteristics which are identical.

Praise becomes spontaneous instead of scripted. As well, it comes from the heart because that's where the Holy Spirit resides. In other words, it is far more than mere formality.

So, I think true worship of God cannot be properly carried out without the Baptism with the Holy Spirit.

Without the Holy Spirit, much of the modern church world thinks that merely attending church constitutes worship. It does not! To be frank, church attendance and activities in many places have deteriorated exactly as the Jewish Feasts of old. As these Gifts of God degenerated into mere *"Feasts of the Jews,"* likewise, church, in many cases, has deteriorated in many circles to no more than an organization of man.

(24) "GOD IS A SPIRIT: AND THEY WHO WORSHIP HIM MUST WORSHIP HIM IN SPIRIT AND IN TRUTH."

The construction is:

1. The Cross of Christ is the focal point of the entirety of the Bible.

2. Everything either looks forward to the Cross (the Old Testament), or everything looks backward to the Cross (the New Testament).

3. In Old Testament times, if individuals insisted on offering up sacrifices in any place other than the Tabernacle or the Temple, the Scripture is clear, *"That man shall be cut off from among his people."* This meant that the man would lose his soul.

4. This means that if the Cross is ignored, abrogated, or denied, *"That soul will be cut off from the People of God."*

GOD IS A SPIRIT

The phrase, *"God is a Spirit,"* simply means that *"God is a Spirit Being."* In other words, He is not the sun, moon, stars, or an image of wood, stone, or metal. As well, He is not an animal or a man. He is not the air, wind, universal mind, the force, love, or some impersonal quality.

He is a Person with a personal spirit body, a personal soul, and a personal spirit like that of Angels and like that of man, except His Body is of spirit substance instead of flesh and bones (Jn. 13:8; Heb. 1:3). He has a personal spirit body (Dan. 7:9-14; 10:5-19); shape (Jn. 5:37); form (Phil. 2:5-7); and image and likeness of a man (Gen. 1:26; 9:6; Ezek. 1:26-28; I Cor. 11:7; James 3:9).

He has bodily parts such as back parts (Ex. 33:23), heart (Gen. 6:6; 8:21), hands and fingers (Ps. 8:3-6; Heb. 1:10; Rev. 5:1-7), mouth (Num. 12:8), lips and tongue (Isa. 30:27), feet (Ex. 24:10; Ezek. 1:27), eyes (Ps. 11:4; 18:24; 33:18), ears (Ps. 18:6), hair, head, face, arms (Dan. 7:9-14; 10:5-19; Rev. 5:1-7; 22:4-6), and loins (Ezek. 1:26-28; 8:1-4).

BODILY PRESENCE

He has bodily presence (Gen. 3:8; 18:1-22) and goes from place to place in a spirit body like all other persons, but yet, with the speed of thought (Gen. 3:8; 11:5; 18:1-5, 22, 33; 19:24; 32:24-32; 35:13; Dan. 7:9-14; Zech. 14:5; Titus 2:13).

He has a voice (Ps. 29; Rev. 10:3-4); breath (Gen. 2:7); and countenance (Ps. 11:7).

He wears clothes (Dan. 7:9-14; 10:5-19); eats (Gen. 18:1-8; Ex. 24:11); rests (Gen. 2:1-4; Heb. 4:4); dwells in a mansion and in a city located on a material Planet called Heaven (Jn. 14:1-3; Heb. 11:10-16; 13:14; Rev., Chpt. 21); sits on a Throne (Isa., Chpt. 6; Dan. 7:9-14; Rev. 4:1-5; 22:3-6); walks (Gen. 3:8; 18:1-8, 22, 33); and rides (Ps. 18:10; 68:17; 104:3; Ezek., Chpt. 1).

As well, the Lord has a personal soul with feelings of grief (Gen. 6:6); anger (I Ki. 11:9); Repentance (Gen. 6:6); jealousy (Ex. 20:5); hate (Prov. 6:16); love (Jn. 3:16); pity (Ps. 103:13); fellowship (I Jn. 1:1-7); pleasure and delight (Ps. 147:10); and other soul passions like other beings (Gal. 5:22-23).

AN ANTHROPOMORPHISM?

Some claim that these descriptions of God are mere anthropomorphisms, which means that the Holy Spirit gives these Attributes of God in human terms, or else, man would not understand anything about God. Personally, I do not believe that. If the Holy Spirit is giving something about the Lord that's not true, in other words, if the Holy Spirit says that He has hands, feet, etc., and He really doesn't, that constitutes a lie. The Holy Spirit does not lie.

It is true that figures of speech are used respecting hands or feet, etc., such as *"He had His Hand in that,"* while not really referring to the physical hand, but meaning that one is involved with whatever it is that's being discussed. However, it's obvious whenever the Holy Spirit is using figures of speech regarding mankind or the Lord.

I believe the Bible teaches, as we've already proven, I think, from the Scriptures, that God has a Spirit Body. Exactly what a Spirit Body is, I cannot say. Does it have intestines, lungs, etc.? Once again, I do not know, and I do not think anyone else does either. This I do know: the Spirit Body is not flesh, even though it does have some resemblance to flesh.

Some people think that God is some Spirit that floats around in space, which cannot be seen, heard, or felt. The Bible does not teach such. As stated, it teaches that God is a Person and has a Spirit Body.

WORSHIPPING HIM IN SPIRIT AND IN TRUTH

The phrase, *"And they who worship Him must worship Him in spirit and in truth,"* constitutes the second time this statement is given, and with Divine Purpose by the Holy Spirit. When something is repeated, it is done so for emphasis.

Several things are said here:

• If the worship is not in spirit (man's spirit moved upon by the Holy Spirit) and in Truth, which refers to the Word of God, it is worship that God will not accept and, in fact, cannot accept.

On this very day, tens of millions of Muslims will pray several times a day, going through their outward circumstances and motions. It is not in spirit and in Truth and, consequently, is not accepted by God. Tragically, the same would pertain, in one form or the other, to many, if not most, Christians.

• The word, *"Must,"* tells us that this is not one of several ways accepted by God but, in fact, is the only Way.

• The Holy Spirit will always abide by the Word, and that's the reason the Believer cannot properly worship the Lord except by the Revelation of the Holy Spirit.

(25) "THE WOMAN SAID UNTO HIM, I KNOW THAT MESSIAH COMES, WHO IS CALLED CHRIST: WHEN HE COMES, HE WILL TELL US ALL THINGS."

The synopsis is:

1. The phrase, *"The woman said unto Him,"* proclaims the tender word, *"Woman,"* occurring some 16 times in this incident. She was speaking to the One, actually the only One, Who could satisfy the longing of her soul. How privileged she was, and how privileged we are to be able to talk to Him as we do in prayer.

2. The phrase, *"I know that Messiah comes, Who is called Christ,"* proclaims that the Samaritans were also looking for a Messiah who would come as promised in Deuteronomy 18:15. So, it seems that she, as well as possibly many other Samaritans, had adopted the word, *"Messiah,"* which, in effect, was a Hebrew word, and was common among the Jews. Of course, there was no Messiah promised to the Samaritans, or anyone else, for that matter, other than the Jews, and that Messiah was Jesus. However, Israel did not know or recognize Him!

3. In similarities at the present time, as the Samaritans and Jews of old, the modern Muslims, along with the Jews, are looking for a Messiah as well! However, as there was no such thing as a Samaritan Messiah, likewise, there is no such thing as a Muslim Messiah.

4. The phrase, *"When He is come, He will tell us all things,"* constituted Truth, but not in the way this woman suspected. However, her statement, even though unscriptural and improper, nevertheless contained a hunger and thirst for Righteousness.

5. In this statement, one senses a weariness with religion and a longing for someone to set the record straight. In other words, her heart cried out for more than mere ceremonies, in which she had been busily engaged for so long. She realized that these ceremonies in the Samaritan religion had not changed her wasted, misused, and misspent life. Her five marriages and present situation loudly proclaimed this.

6. So, Jesus ignored her continued error and reached down into her heart, and did something so remarkable that it absolutely defies description! The next Verse tells us what.

(26) "JESUS SAID UNTO HER, I WHO SPEAK UNTO YOU AM HE."

The construction is:

1. If the preacher is not preaching the Cross, in reality, he is not preaching the Gospel (I Cor. 1:17).

2. The Power of the Gospel is in the Cross (I Cor. 1:18).

3. It is the Holy Spirit Who exhibits the Power, but He is able to do so because of what Jesus did at the Cross (Rom. 8:2).

THE REVELATION

It is nothing short of amazing that Jesus little revealed Himself to Nicodemus, except in a veiled way, but plainly and clearly revealed Himself to this woman, and a Samaritan at that!

The woman now arrives at the point:

A Redeemer is promised; everything will depend upon Him; *"He will tell us all things"*; and He will be the Saviour. Jesus clearly and plainly said unto her, *"I am He!"* She was saved in and by that Revelation (Mat. 11:27), for intelligence in Divine things comes by conscience and Revelation and not by intellect.

Thus, the Holy Spirit, as the Living Water, quickens the moral man (Nicodemus), yet unsaved, and indwells the Believer (the Samaritan). The water that flows from the Smitten Rock becomes, when drunk, an internal Well perpetually springing up and a life that is everlasting.

THE SELF-RIGHTEOUS?

Such was the life into which Nicodemus ultimately entered, along with the Samaritan, who instantly entered. Merit in the one case did not admit into that life, and demerit did not exclude from it.

The idea that Jesus would plainly and clearly reveal Himself to a woman, and a Samaritan at that, and one so grossly immoral, is not understood at all by the self-righteous, but yet, is the undergirding strength of Salvation.

To be qualified for Grace is to be unqualified and know it. One has to admit he is lost before he can be Saved. The self-righteous cannot do, but one such as the Samaritan can easily do. Hence, Jesus would later say, *"I thank You, O Father, Lord of Heaven and Earth, because You have hid these things from the wise and the prudent, and have revealed them unto babes."*

He then said, *"Even so, Father: for so it seemed good in Your Sight"* (Mat. 11:25-26).

The self-righteous always mistake Grace for a condoning of sin; therefore, they show no Grace and, thereby, receive no Grace. Consequently, Jesus said of them, *"The publicans and the harlots go into the Kingdom of God before you."*

He then said, *"For John came unto you in the way of righteousness, and you believed him not: but the publicans and the harlots believed Him: and you, when you had seen it, repented not afterward, that you might believe Him"* (Mat. 21:31-32).

(27) "AND UPON THIS CAME HIS DISCIPLES, AND MARVELLED THAT HE TALKED WITH THE WOMAN: YET NO MAN SAID, WHAT DO YOU SEEK? OR, WHY DO YOU TALK WITH HER?"

The structure is:

1. As we have said over and over, and we continue to say, the Cross of Christ is the focal point of the entirety of the Bible.

2. There is one place where God has appointed to meet the sinner, and that is the Cross.

3. Some claim that after Conversion, there is no more problem with sin. If that is the case, the Holy Spirit through Paul wasted a lot of space dealing with the Church about the problem of sin. In fact, he mentioned sin, actually, the sin nature, some 17 times in the Sixth Chapter of Romans alone.

4. Yes, sin is the problem!

THE DISCIPLES

The phrase, *"And upon this came His Disciples,"* refers to their coming back from the town where they had gone to purchase food. However, as stated, the possibility definitely exists that John the Beloved, who gave this account, stayed behind and witnessed the entire episode, hence, the remarkable attention to details.

The phrase, *"And marveled that He talked with the woman,"* may seem strange to most presently; however, there were no dealings normally between Jews and Samaritans. Even above that, Jewish rabbis did not converse with women in public or instruct them in the Law. No rabbi would even converse with his wife, sister, or daughter in public or in the street. Of course, these were rulings laid down by men and not by God.

Actually, this is one of the reasons that the Pharisees and ruling hierarchy of Israel hated Jesus so very much. He completely ignored their man-made rules and conducted the Will of the Father as if none of these rules existed.

PREJUDICE

The question, *"Yet no man said, What do You seek? or, Why do You talk with her?"* means that they kept their astonishment at Jesus' Actions to themselves.

Actually, one of the Miracles of the Lord's Ministry was to break down the wretched, rabbinical prejudice against the spiritual capacities of women and the oriental folly which supposed that she contaminated their sanctity. Jesus lifted women to their true position, by the side of man. Actually, women were His Most Faithful Disciples.

They ministered unto Him of their substance. They shared His Miraculous Healing Power, Feeding, and Teaching. They anointed His Feet; they wept over His Agony; they followed Him to the Cross; and, they were early at the Sepulcher. They greeted Him as the Risen Lord. They also received the Baptism with the Holy Spirit. Actually, in Christ, there is neither male nor female. Both are one in Him, and that means equal in everything.

Even as I write these words, the world is looking, or at least should be, with astonishment at the ridiculous demands made by the Muslims regarding women. Whenever going out, they must be covered from head to toe, preferably in black. They must not work at any outside job and must be subservient to man. In fact, in the Muslim religion, wherever it has its way, if a woman is raped by a man, and I said, *"Raped,"* she is killed, with nothing said to the man whatsoever. That's the kind of religion that the leaders of our nation seem to be embracing, thereby, closing their eyes to the true nature of that religion. God help us!

I would hope that the western world understands that the freedom enjoyed by women in western societies was paid for by the Lord Jesus Christ, and I speak of the Cross. He lifted woman from the position of condemnation and burden and restored to her that which religion had taken away. As we have attempted to properly elucidate, the Ministry of Christ gave ample proof of that.

(28) "THE WOMAN THEN LEFT HER WATERPOT, AND WENT HER WAY INTO THE CITY, AND SAID TO THE MEN."

The exposition is:

1. The action of the woman in leaving her waterpot and becoming an unconscious preacher demonstrates the death of self and the occupation of her heart with Jesus and His Grace and Goodness. So overwhelming was her consciousness of His Person and His Action that it, in a sense, annihilated the consciousness of her own sinfulness. Due to her acceptance of Christ, for that's what she did, Christ Himself filled all her world.

2. So, a woman became the first Preacher of the Gospel to the Gentile nations. So effective was her preaching, so to speak, that it resulted in a harvest of souls. She became a vessel to receive and then to minister the Gift of Life.

3. The phrase, *"The woman then left her waterpot,"* refers to her forgetting the object of her visit to the well because she had indeed been given, and had received, the *"Living Water."* This is a perfect example of how Christ affects one who accepts Him. Everything else is forgotten, or at least is placed in a very subservient position, as it should be!

4. *"And went her way into the city, and said to the men,"* refers to the fact that she went directly to the leaders of the particular Samaritan religion.

NOTES

(29) "COME, SEE A MAN, WHO TOLD ME ALL THINGS THAT EVER I DID: IS NOT THIS THE CHRIST?"

The exegesis is:

1. The Blood was an extremely important part of the Sacrifice of Christ because it represented and was, in fact, His Life being poured out.

2. In Old Testament times, if a person insisted on offering sacrifices some place other than the Tabernacle or the Temple, at least after the Temple was built, he would lose his soul, that is, if he remained in this stubbornness and self-will.

3. Considering that one could lose his eternal soul by such a position, it should tell us today that if one ignores the Cross, one will also lose his soul.

CHRISTIANITY

The word, *"Come,"* is the greatest evidence of all of everyone's Salvation. They hungrily desire to bring others to Jesus. Why?

Salvation, as afforded and given by Christ, is a peculiar thing in that its glory is not obvious until one has accepted Christ. When this happens, and I refer to one who is Born-Again, suddenly, the Glory appears, and the first desire is that others know as well.

The full phrase, *"Come, see a Man, Who told me all things that ever I did,"* is once again the epitome of Bible Christianity.

Christianity is not a philosophy and neither is it a religion. As stated, it is really *"a Man,"* the Man, *"Christ Jesus."* In fact, Jesus Christ is the New Covenant, and the Cross of Christ is the Meaning of the New Covenant.

All the things that Jesus said to this woman that day, we aren't told; however, He told her enough that she was thoroughly convinced as to Who and What He actually was. This is what makes Christianity so different from the religions of the world.

Such religions have to do with the externals only because it is impossible for them to do otherwise; consequently, they never address the real problem, only the symptoms.

As we have stated many times, Christianity is not a philosophy, even though many have tried to make it into such. It is a relationship, pure and simple, and with a Man, the Man *"Christ Jesus."* Also, Jesus Christ is God, the Creator of all things. As such, He is able to know all things and to do all things.

THE TESTIMONY

The Lord not only tells one what one has done but, also, can cure one for and from what one has done.

In other words, Jesus knows the problem, and He is the cure, in fact, the only cure.

For Jesus to relate to this woman only what she had done would have been of little consequence, as magnificent as it would have been. As well, He had to give her the Living Water, which healed the malignancy of her actions. Love must act, or it's not love.

The question, *"Is not this the Christ?"* presents a very clever way of expressing herself.

Her question presupposes that her fellow Samaritans, as stated, were looking for a Messiah. Evidently, such was the topic of many conversations and seems to have been the reigning subject at this time.

How was it possible for these men, who were obviously leaders in the Samaritan religion, to be so swayed so quickly by this woman's Testimony, especially considering who she was?

Who she was and what she was may have been the very reason they did heed her words. Evidently, there was a marked and obvious change in her, which could be readily observed in her spirit, and which made them extremely curious.

(30) "THEN THEY WENT OUT OF THE CITY, AND CAME UNTO HIM."

The overview is:

1. Verse 4 said, *"And He must needs go through Samaria,"* and now we know why.

2. The Holy Spirit knew there were hungry hearts in this place and would respond accordingly.

3. I wonder how many hungry hearts there are in the world at this time, but yet, there is no one to bring them the Gospel.

(31) "IN THE MEAN WHILE HIS DISCIPLES PRAYED HIM, SAYING, MASTER, EAT."

The diagram is:

1. Evidently, when the Disciples arrived, Jesus was finishing His Conversation with the woman, with her leaving shortly to go into the town in order to spread the Good News.

2. As stated, the Disciples were perplexed at Jesus' Dealing with her but, evidently, even more so when He seemed to express no appetite for the food which had been procured.

3. Their urging Him to eat was out of concern for His Health. They had come a ways and had a ways to go, and they knew that Jesus needed strength for the journey.

(32) "BUT HE SAID UNTO THEM, I HAVE MEAT TO EAT THAT YOU KNOW NOT OF."

The form is:

1. Every animal sacrifice in the Old Testament offered to Jehovah was a Type of the Cross of Christ.

2. If anyone attempts to reach God except through Christ and His shed Blood, all access will be barred by the Holy Spirit (Eph. 2:13-18).

3. This means that there is no salvation outside of Christ and Him Crucified and our Faith in that Finished Work (I Cor. 1:23).

SPIRITUAL REALITIES

This statement given by Christ has relationship to His Answer to Satan, *"Man shall not live by bread alone, but by every Word that proceeds out of the Mouth of God"* (Mat. 4:4).

The insensibility of the Disciples to Spiritual realities is again evidenced in Verses 31 through 38. His *"Meat"* and His *"Harvest"* were the Samaritans, who, at the moment, were leaving the city and coming to Him and, as well, believing on Him.

The huge crowd that pressed along the road from the city to the well was a glad harvest of souls to the Lord's Heart, which was saddened by the unbelief and rejection of Israel.

Let me try to more fully explain this Text. In countless crusades around the world, I have seen this very thing happen, even in this same fashion.

Oftentimes, the problems, of whatever variety, seemed to be multitudinous. As such, the care and concern weighed heavily, just as the securing of food did respecting the Disciples.

Then the Lord would move in a particular Service in a mighty way, with lives being changed and souls Saved. All of a sudden, everything would come into focus. The problems would vanish, or else, seem to retreat into insignificance. The Lord had moved with His Anointing; consequently, Spiritual Meat was furnished by the Holy Spirit, which provided a satisfaction and joy otherwise unobtainable.

Why did the Disciples not know of this Spiritual Meat?

THE HOLY SPIRIT

They did not know because the Holy Spirit had not yet been given, even as John would later say (Jn. 7:39), but which would be remedied on the Day of Pentecost. Then, they would truly *"know"* of *"this meat."*

Once again, I emphasize the fact that without the Holy Spirit, nothing will be done for the Lord. While one certainly is Saved by the Blood of Jesus, which is a result of evidencing Faith in Christ and, within itself, is of the Spirit, all work done for the Lord is done through and by the Person and Agency of the Holy Spirit. Even though it is done in the Name of Jesus and according to the Word of God, still, it is the Holy Spirit Who carries out such.

So, this means that the religious denominations who deny the Acts 2:4 experience, especially since the proliferation of the outpouring of the Holy Spirit in the last few years, will accomplish precious little, if anything, for the Lord. While there may be much activity, that's all it is. It is because their efforts are man-instituted, man-directed, and man-led. As a result, there may be much religious machinery, but there is precious little, if any, true Spiritual results.

I might quickly add that this not only goes for those who deny the Holy Spirit but for those, as well, who claim to be Pentecostal but, in reality, have forsaken the Holy Spirit for the wisdom of this world.

(33) "THEREFORE SAID THE DISCIPLES ONE TO ANOTHER, HAS ANY MAN BROUGHT HIM OUGHT TO EAT?"

The order is:

1. This question as asked by the Disciples proclaims, as well, the spiritual insensibility of much of the modern church. At this stage, and for the reasons given, they could only think in carnal terms whereas Jesus spoke almost exclusively in Spiritual terms.

2. No! No one had brought Him any physical food to eat, but He definitely had been brought by the Holy Spirit a meal of Spiritual Food.

3. This one question by the Disciples, *"Has any man brought Him ought to eat?"* presents the dividing line for most Believers.

4. Do we think carnally or Spiritually?

5. Are we looking to the Lord or to men to supply the need?

6. If we're looking to men, our frame of reference will be as the Disciples. If we're looking to God, it will be that of Jesus.

(34) "JESUS SAID UNTO THEM, MY MEAT IS TO DO THE WILL OF HIM WHO SENT ME, AND TO FINISH HIS WORK."

The pattern is:

1. Any other proposed means of reaching God except through the Cross is condemned by God, in fact, is cursed by God (Gal. 1:6-9).

2. When we realize that the Cross is presently all but ignored among the church world, the matter becomes frightfully fearful.

3. One of Satan's greatest stratagems is to have the preacher preach the Truth and then to subtly slip in the error. He is very successful!

THE WILL OF GOD

The phrase, *"Jesus said unto them,"* even though brief, constitutes the whole duty of man (Eccl. 12:13-14).

Several things are said here:

• Even though physical bread definitely is necessary, it is the Spiritual *"Meat"* which really counts. Tragically, this is reversed, even in the lives of most Believers. Too much attention is paid to the physical bread and not nearly enough to the Spiritual Bread.

• The Will of God is the single most important thing in the world. There is a definite Will for the entirety of the world, and there is a definite Will for each individual Believer. Nothing is happenchance with God! He has a definite place, purpose, and position for every single Believer.

• If the Believer claims that he does not

know what that *"Will"* is, then this shows an extremely improper relationship. In other words, if one has any relationship at all, God's Will for one's life will become obviously clear.

• Not only must we know that Will, but, as well, we must *"do that Will."* Knowing it and doing it are two different things altogether. So, every effort must be made to carry out the Purpose of God in our lives.

• Here is another principle of life. The true sustenance of life is to do God's Will and to accomplish what we are here for. Even in the natural realm, nothing stimulates, keeps alive, or maintains courage more than seeing success in the mission one is dedicated to bring about.

• When the Lord saves us, He then *"sends us."* To be sure, we are sent with a definite mission and purpose. As such an ambassador, we must carry out the Purpose of Him Who has sent us. Sadly, many, if not most, Christians are not *"sent"*; they merely went.

When He sends us, we have then the Power and Authority to use His Name (Mk. 16:15-20).

• The phrase, *"And to finish His Work,"* is the idea!

• Anything the Lord wants us to do, which constitutes His Will, he will give us a love for that thing, which means that nothing else will satisfy. The idea of God calling us to do something that's extremely distasteful, which experiences pain every time it is accomplished, is not the Lord.

A PERSONAL EXPERIENCE

Just yesterday, as I dictate these notes, I was looking in one of our Commentaries, which was written in July, 2011. In the statement made, I mentioned that our network (SonLife Broadcasting Network) was then going into 1 million homes here in the U.S. Now, just one year later (July, 2012), we are going into some 65 million homes in America alone, 24 hours a day, seven days a week. As well, we are going into some 17 million homes around the clock in the United Kingdom. Also, in just a few days, we will sign the contracts to go into some 17 million homes in Germany, some 2 million in Spain, and some 2 million in France. That is besides the satellite coverage in Central and South America and other parts of the world. This can be construed as none other than a Miracle. How so much we give the Lord the praise and the glory.

In 2010, the Lord spoke to my heart in prayer and told me that He was about to open this door wide. To be sure, it's a door that He has opened, which means that no man can shut it.

WHAT IS THE REASON FOR THIS NETWORK?

The reason is to proclaim the Message of the Cross. In fact, the *"Message of the Cross"* is what the Holy Spirit is presently saying to the churches. It's the Message that began the Church, which we refer to as the Early Church. Over a span of time, actually, several centuries, the Early Church lost its way, morphing into what is now known as the Catholic church. Then, the world entered the Dark Ages.

In the early 1500s, the world witnessed the Reformation, which took Believers back to Justification by Faith and not by works.

This was followed by the great Holiness moves in America and England in the 1700s and the 1800s. Probably one could say that the Methodist church was the leader in this. I might quickly add, the Methodist church then was altogether different than the Methodist church now.

Then, at the turn of the Twentieth Century, the great Pentecostal move shook the world. Sadly and regrettably, it is waning to a great degree at the present time.

But now, the Holy Spirit is bringing everything full circle. As the Cross of Christ was the Message of the Early Church, led by the Apostle Paul, the Holy Spirit is likewise bringing back the same Message to the Church presently. Back to the Cross! Back to the Cross! Back to the Cross!

(35) "SAY NOT YOU, THERE ARE YET FOUR MONTHS, AND THEN COMES HARVEST? BEHOLD, I SAY UNTO YOU, LIFT UP YOUR EYES, AND LOOK ON THE FIELDS; FOR THEY ARE WHITE ALREADY TO HARVEST."

The pattern is:

1. Atonement is always in the Blood,

and only in the Blood (Heb. 9:22).

2. As well, it is not the Blood and something else. It is only the Blood.

3. Of course, we are speaking of the shed Blood of Jesus Christ on the Cross of Calvary, with all the sacrifices of the Old Testament but a symbol of that which was to come and now has come (Rev. 12:11).

THE HARVEST

The question, *"Say not you, There are yet four months, and then comes harvest?"* refers to the three harvests of Israel. They were:

1. The barley harvest was first, coming in April.

2. Some 50 days later, sometime during the first part of June, was the wheat harvest.

3. Correspondingly, about four months later in October was the fruit harvest. Perhaps this harvest, at least in the natural, is that to which Jesus referred.

In the natural, it was time for the wheat harvest; consequently, this should have been attended to with all diligence before making plans for the coming fruit harvest some four months later.

In the spiritual sense, in which Jesus was actually speaking, He was telling His Disciples, and all who would follow thereafter, something very important.

They had Dispensations on their minds, which pertained to the coming Restoration of Israel, when they should have been attending to the matters at hand, which was the Salvation of souls.

The harvest is now!

LOOK ON THE FIELDS

The phrase, *"Behold, I say unto you, Lift up your eyes, and look on the fields,"* simply means that we don't have to go very far to see the need.

It also tells us, in no uncertain terms, exactly what priority should be. I speak of the Salvation of souls.

In this, Jesus tells us exactly what His Meat is; it is the Word of God.

So, what is that Will?

While it definitely is in different capacities for different Believers, still, the end result and priority must be the bringing of souls to Christ. If this is not priority, then we really are not doing the Will of God. To be sure, we should carefully consider that statement. In fact, it is impossible to read these Texts and not come to the conclusion I have just given.

Something is wrong with the church when it gets very excited about peripheral matters and shows little or no interest at all in the Salvation of souls. I cannot conceive of anything being more displeasing to the Lord than that.

THE PRIORITIES OF THIS MINISTRY

That priority is as follows:
- The Salvation of souls.
- Getting Believers baptized with the Holy Spirit if they have not already been filled.
- Seeing people healed and delivered by the Power of God.
- Seeing that every person in this world, at least those to whom we have the privilege to reach, has the opportunity of accepting Christ, whether they do or not.
- To preach the Message of the Cross to the Saints that they may grow in Grace and the Knowledge of the Lord. That is our priority because it is God's Priority. If anyone will take the trouble to look in the Book of Acts, which gives a description of the Early Church as outlined and directed by the Holy Spirit, they will see that it is the priority there as well!

WHITE ALREADY TO HARVEST

The phrase, *"For they are white already to harvest,"* is very special to me personally.

On July 1, 1985, which was a Monday morning, at about 8 a.m. or before, the Lord gave me a Vision of the harvest. It is as follows and has played a great part in charting the course for my life and Ministry:

At that particular time, every morning I would drive to a particular place about a mile from our home, a place, incidentally, which afforded privacy. There I would sit in the car and study the Word for a period of time. After that, I would proceed to walk down a roadbed, praying as I went, with this particular activity taking approximately an hour.

That July morning, after I had been praying a very short period of time, probably no more than five or 10 minutes, the Spirit of God came upon me in an extremely heavy way. Actually, it was so intense that I could little stand upright, which produced a sort of travail, accompanied by weeping. All of a sudden, the scene where I was completely changed.

As the Vision spread out before me, it seemed that the entirety of the landscape in every direction was one huge cotton field. As well, there were no leaves on the stalks, but rather each stalk was heavily laden with cotton ready to be harvested. In fact, it was the largest crop production I had ever seen, with everything in every direction looking like a wall of white.

What was so startling about that vast area that stretched over the horizon in every direction was that there were almost none gathering the harvest. I saw two or three mechanical cotton pickers working in the distance, the number of which was woefully inadequate for this huge task.

THE STORM

I then looked to my left up into the heavens and, behold, the most vicious, wicked storm I had ever seen was bearing down upon this huge harvest. The jagged forks of lightning were cutting swaths through the sky. I knew they were accompanied by violent winds, which would completely destroy this harvest if it weren't gathered quickly.

The Lord then began to speak to me, saying the following:

"I want you to place the telecast in every city in the world that will open the door to you. I have given you this Commission to help gather the harvest."

He then said, *"I will delay the storm for a period of time until the task can be completed."* He then added, *"Do not fail Me because there is no one else to carry forth the task. I have called others for localities, but I have called this Ministry for the entirety of the world."*

When the Vision ended, my immediate thoughts concerned the manner in which the Vision was given, portraying the harvest by a field of cotton. Such is almost always portrayed by the symbolism of wheat. However, in a very short period of time, these Words of Jesus came unto me, *"Lift up your eyes, and look on the fields; for they are white already to harvest."*

I immediately set out to try to fulfill the task, but events made it impossible for me to do what I felt that I had to do. During those intervening 20 years, I felt I had failed the Lord, and it broke my heart in a thousand pieces; however, there was nothing I could do.

THE COMMISSION

Then, at about the midpoint of 2011, or a little later, the Lord brought all of this back to me. He spoke the following to my heart.

"Don't you know that when I gave you the Commission in 1985 to place the television programming in every city in the world that would allow such to be, I knew what would happen in the future? And I want you to know at the present that the Commission still holds. You are to put the programming in every city in the world that will accept it."

I cannot even begin to relate how I felt when the Lord spoke those words. Of course, I knew that the Lord knows all things, past, present, and future. However, the situation with me personally had been so cataclysmic that, in my mind, I did not see the Lord renewing the Commission; however, He most definitely has.

WORLD EVANGELISM

As previously stated, in the past year, we have experienced the fastest growth with television that has ever been, and we give the Lord all the praise and all the glory. It is for the purpose of preaching the Message of the Cross. As Paul said, and by God's Help and Grace, I trust I will be able to say, as well, *"I was not disobedient to the Heavenly Vision."*

LIFT UP YOUR EYES AND LOOK ON THE FIELDS

Every Believer is responsible for taking the grandest Story ever told to the entirety of the world. Never before has it been so possible to reach hundreds of millions of people with the Gospel of Jesus Christ as it is presently. Please understand, even though the technology is available, the preacher, whomever he may be, has to have the right Message. That Message is, *"Jesus Christ and Him Crucified"* (I Cor. 1:23).

As God has called me for world Evangelism and has given us the tools to do it, and above all, the Message, still, He has called you, as well, to do the sending. I am reminded constantly by the Holy Spirit that I should remind all those who are blessed by this Ministry that they have been called as well. They are not just onlookers, but are rather a part of what God is doing in these last of the last days. How honored and blessed we are to have a part in this great Work. We must equip ourselves readily so. In other words, we must be very careful to obey the Lord in every respect.

(36) "AND HE WHO REAPS RECEIVES WAGES, AND GATHERS FRUIT UNTO LIFE ETERNAL: THAT BOTH HE WHO SOWS AND HE WHO REAPS MAY REJOICE TOGETHER."

The synopsis is:

1. The phrase, *"And he who reaps receives wages,"* speaks of the Believer, in fact, every Believer, who must enter into this *"sowing and reaping."*

2. If one is to notice, Jesus does not speak of Himself as the *"Reaper"* or *"Sower,"* but rather as *"the Lord of the Harvest"* (Mat. 9:37-38).

3. Actually, this is what we have been saying all the time. Jesus calls Preachers, but they cannot be sent unless there are senders (Rom. 10:14-15). So, the obligation of the Believer is to sow the seed of the Gospel and to reap its harvest respecting souls.

4. Of what type of *"wages"* does Jesus speak? He speaks of eternal souls and their being brought to Him.

5. The phrase, *"And gathers fruit unto life eternal,"* proclaims what that *"fruit"* actually is, i.e., the Salvation of souls. The *"life eternal"* speaks of that which the souls have gained and was made possible by the *"sowers and reapers."* In other words, every single person who helps bring a soul to the Lord, in whatever capacity, has the satisfaction of knowing that this is an effort which will reap eternal results. Every other investment has only a limited return for a limited period of time, but not so with eternal souls brought to Jesus. These will bring forth fruit forever and will be marked to the credit of the sowers and reapers. What an investment!

6. The phrase, *"That both he who sows and he who reaps may rejoice together,"* has to do with what Paul said, *"Now he who plants* (sows) *and he who waters* (reaps) *are one."* However, he had previously stated, *"But* (it is) *God* (as Lord of the Harvest) *Who gives the increase"* (I Cor. 3:7-8).

7. This speaks of all who play their parts and do so without failure.

(37) "AND HEREIN IS THAT SAYING TRUE, ONE SOWS, AND ANOTHER REAPS."

The exposition is:

1. This proclaims that God has a special Ministry for each individual.

2. However, that Ministry must fit into the Plan of God and, in fact, will if it is truly of God.

3. What does the reader think that the Lord's Response would be to anyone who seeks to hinder the *"sowers"* and *"reapers"*?

(38) "I SENT YOU TO REAP THAT WHEREON YOU BESTOWED NO LABOUR: OTHER MEN LABOURED, AND YOU HAVE ENTERED INTO THEIR LABOURS."

The structure is:

1. The phrase, *"I sent you to reap that whereon you bestowed no labour,"* actually says in the Hebrew, *"I proposed to send...."*

2. In this Scripture, Jesus is explaining to His Disciples, and all others, for that matter, that whatever is done for the Cause of Christ is brought to fruition as a result of much labor on the part of many different people, many unaware of the input of others. Actually, such can even span the centuries.

3. When an Evangelist preaches a revival with many people being Saved, one can be sure that others have entered into intercession for this Move of God, which may have begun many years before. So, in reality, and as stated, it is God Who actually gives the increase.

4. The phrase, *"Other men laboured, and you have entered into their labours,"* proclaims a truth that we must never forget.

5. Jesus was so sure of the success of this

mission that all is here contemplated as an accomplished fact. This is the language of Faith, and it is peculiar to the Bible.

(39) "AND MANY OF THE SAMARITANS OF THAT CITY BELIEVED ON HIM FOR THE SAYING OF THE WOMAN, WHICH TESTIFIED, HE TOLD ME ALL THAT EVER I DID."

The exegesis is:

1. The phrase, *"And many of the Samaritans of that city believed on Him for the saying of the woman, who testified,"* presents this as a unique instance in the Gospels of a true Moving of the Holy Spirit, produced by preaching apart from Miracles.

2. The Preachers were the Samaritan woman and the Messiah. Her Ministry was the more remarkable because, apparently, she was not ordained. In other words, she went without being sent. She was a volunteer Preacher.

3. The Holy Spirit often ordains, equips, and sends forth without outward appointment. So, her action was a beautiful instance of the Energy of the Spirit in making men and women witnesses for the Cause of Christ.

4. *"He told me all that ever I did,"* in no way expresses a mere fault finding session, but He, as well, gave her something, *"Living Water,"* i.e., Salvation.

5. While Jesus did expose her sin, as the Gospel always does, it was not done in a negative, condemnatory fashion, but rather to deliver her from that sin. He then gave her Eternal Life.

(40) "SO WHEN THE SAMARITANS WERE COME UNTO HIM, THEY BESOUGHT HIM THAT HE WOULD TARRY WITH THEM: AND HE ABODE THERE TWO DAYS."

The overview is:

1. The phrase, *"So when the Samaritans were come unto Him,"* bespoke hearts ready to receive from God. As stated, this group, no doubt, included some, if not most, of the religious leaders of that region. Due to the glorious change for the better of this woman, even an instant change, they had been so convinced that they had to see for themselves.

2. *"They besought Him that He would

NOTES

tarry with them,"* was a request that was not denied, in fact, a request that will never be denied.

3. This is a beautiful moment in the Ministry of the Master because much of the time, He was rejected, or at most, tolerated by the religious powers. Actually, the hostility on the part of the Jews, which had already begun, would continue to increase from this point forward until it came to a head at white-hot pitch. How different it could have been, and how different it would have been, if they had only believed Him.

4. *"And He abode there two days,"* presents Him doing what the Pharisees would not do, but, of course, their hearts were ruled by hate while His was ruled by love.

5. This one thing is sure: this *"two days"* was the greatest time that these people had ever experienced, or would ever experience.

(41) "AND MANY MORE BELIEVED BECAUSE OF HIS OWN WORD."

The diagram is:

1. This refers to the second group back in the city who heard Christ teach and preach during these two days and *"believed"* as well!

2. It could have easily numbered into the hundreds or perhaps even several thousands.

3. The next Verse tells us what they *"believed."*

(42) "AND SAID UNTO THE WOMAN, NOW WE BELIEVE, NOT BECAUSE OF YOUR SAYING: FOR WE HAVE HEARD HIM OURSELVES, AND KNOW THAT THIS IS INDEED THE CHRIST, THE SAVIOUR OF THE WORLD."

The exposition is:

1. The phrase, *"And said unto the woman, Now we believe, not because of your saying,"* should have been translated, *"Not only because of your saying,"* because her saying was the Testimony which originally brought them to Christ.

2. *"For we have heard Him ourselves, and know that this is indeed the Christ, the Saviour of the world,"* proclaims one of the most profound statements ever made, which occurs only one other time in the Bible (I Jn. 4:14). It fell from the lips of Samaritans.

3. These Samaritans recognized in Jesus not only the Anointed of Israel but, as well,

the Saviour of all mankind, i.e., *"the world."* And so He is!

4. Regrettably, toward the end of His Ministry, there were some Samaritans who would not receive Him (Lk. 9:51-56).

(43) "NOW AFTER TWO DAYS HE DEPARTED THENCE, AND WENT INTO GALILEE."

The form is:

1. Even though He left after two days, He left some very happy people, with the woman who had been at the well certainly not being the least.

2. *"Galilee"* was the site of the majority of His Ministry. Actually, He made His Headquarters in Capernaum. Most of His Disciples came from Galilee. As well, even though there was definitely some opposition, there was some acceptance also.

3. The Native Country of Jesus was Judaea, as He was of the Tribe of Judah. Also, He was born in Beth-lehem of Judaea.

4. Nevertheless, His Adopted Country was Galilee because Judaea rejected Him.

(44) "FOR JESUS HIMSELF TESTIFIED, THAT A PROPHET HAS NO HONOUR IN HIS OWN COUNTRY."

The order is:

1. The phrase, *"For Jesus Himself testified,"* presents the rule, which almost all the time is brought about.

2. *"That a Prophet has no honour in His Own Country,"* speaks of Judaea, as Jesus was the Son of David. He would later extend this statement to say, *"And among his own kin, and in his own house"* (Mat. 13:57; Mk. 6:4).

3. If such was true of Jesus, and it definitely was, then such is true of His Followers.

(45) "THEN WHEN HE WAS COME INTO GALILEE, THE GALILAEANS RECEIVED HIM, HAVING SEEN ALL THE THINGS THAT HE DID AT JERUSALEM AT THE FEAST: FOR THEY ALSO WENT UNTO THE FEAST."

The pattern is:

1. The phrase, *"Then when He was come into Galilee, the Galilaeans received Him,"* proclaims some of these people believing because, at the Feast, some had witnessed the great Miracles He performed. No doubt, when they returned home, He was the topic of every conversation, with the news spreading like proverbial wildfire.

2. Faith based on outward observances is, at best, feeble. However, as feeble as their Faith might have been, He, obedient to His Father's Will, acted in Grace and Power whenever He met with Faith, however poor.

3. The feeble Faith of these people is contrasted here with the richer Faith of the Samaritans, who believed upon Him without, it seems, any demonstration of miraculous action.

4. Such was the condition of Israel — little Faith and no joy. However, in these first two *"signs,"* He had brought back the boy from the very mouth of death, which we will momentarily see, and, as well, had filled the house of Cana with joy by turning the water into wine. All of this is symbolic of His Future Action in regards to Israel when, at the point of extinction, she will finally accept Christ and then will experience great joy (Zech., Chpt. 14; Rev., Chpt. 19).

5. *"Having seen all the things that He did at Jerusalem at the Feast: for they also went unto the Feast,"* proclaims undeniable proof of His Messiahship. Not only did the Galileans see all the things He did, but so did all of Israel as well! Even though it is not proper to base one's Faith solely upon outward externals, to which we have already alluded, still, the Miracles were undeniable and, consequently, left Israel totally without excuse.

(46) "SO JESUS CAME AGAIN INTO CANA OF GALILEE, WHERE HE MADE THE WATER WINE. AND THERE WAS A CERTAIN NOBLEMAN, WHOSE SON WAS SICK AT CAPERNAUM."

The composition is:

1. An acceptance of the Cross is an acceptance in totality of the Lord Jesus Christ.

2. It is a way of life, a total consecration, and a total dedication.

3. It draws the line regarding worldliness, regarding false doctrine, and regarding apostasy of any shape.

THE NOBLEMAN

The phrase, *"So Jesus came again into Cana of Galilee, where He made the water wine,"* no doubt, proclaims no small stir among the people, due to this Miracle He had performed sometime earlier.

"And there was a certain nobleman, whose son was sick at Capernaum," pertains to one who was an officer of Herod Antipas, tetrarch of Galilee.

As here made evident, the sickness of this nobleman's son proclaims the dread result of the Fall as being incumbent upon all, whether rich or poor, great or small! Consequently, the nobleman, who had probably very little religious leanings, needed Jesus exactly as Nicodemus, one of the most religious men in Israel, as well as the Samaritan woman, whose life had been wasted and misused.

The need in each heart is the same and is not changed at all by outward station, place, or position. The need is Jesus! Sadly, the world does not understand this, and neither does much of the church.

There are probably few churches in which Nicodemus, as well as the nobleman, would not have been overly welcomed. Both were influential and rich.

Conversely, because of her sordid past, there are precious few Churches who would want the Samaritan woman. And yet, Jesus did as much for her as the others!

THE NEED!

It is the business of the Church to see exactly as God sees. However, that can be done only if one has an excellent knowledge of God's Word and a proper relationship with Christ. In fact, I doubt very seriously that any Believer can see as they should see without a proper understanding of the Cross. Someone has said, *"The ground is level at the foot of the Cross,"* meaning that all, whether rich or poor, are in need.

If one looks closely, one will find that these people responded to Jesus because of an acute need within their lives or families. The woman at the well was desperate for reality, having found out the hard way that there is no lasting satisfaction in sin.

As well, even as the world could not satisfy her heart, likewise, religion could not satisfy the heart of Nicodemus.

Then, there was the desperation of the nobleman brought about by the acute illness of his son. Someone has said that man's extremity is God's Opportunity! And so it is.

What was it that brought you, dear reader, to Christ?

Quite possibly, the malady of any one of these three was and is your malady as well!

(47) "WHEN HE HEARD THAT JESUS WAS COME OUT OF JUDAEA INTO GALILEE, HE WENT UNTO HIM, AND BESOUGHT HIM THAT HE WOULD COME DOWN, AND HEAL HIS SON: FOR HE WAS AT THE POINT OF DEATH."

The pattern is:

1. The phrase, *"When he heard that Jesus was come out of Judaea into Galilee, he went unto Him,"* probably means that the news had spread to Capernaum that Jesus was back in Galilee, even at Cana, only about 20 miles distance. So, the man would hurry there to find Jesus!

2. *"And besought Him that He would come down, and heal his son,"* contains buried within the Text the faint idea that due to his place and position in the political structure of Galilee, he had the right to request such, or that Jesus would be impressed by who he was, an officer in Herod's court. While it is certain that desperation, no doubt, played the greater part in this request, due to the fact that his son was dying, still, he was accustomed to having men obey him, hence, feeling free to ask Jesus to walk some 20 miles to Capernaum.

3. While we do not desire to make too much of this, still, it must be said that Jesus never responds to one's station in life, whether rich or poor! He responds to need and Faith only.

4. *"For he was at the point of death,"* highlights the desperation, which is obvious.

(48) "THEN SAID JESUS UNTO HIM, EXCEPT YOU SEE SIGNS AND WONDERS, YOU WILL NOT BELIEVE."

The composition is:

1. The phrase, *"Then said Jesus unto him,"* proclaims the beginning of an answer that seemed somewhat brusque, even similar to that addressed to Nicodemus (Jn. 3:3).

2. *"Except you see signs and wonders, you will not believe,"* proclaims Jesus knowing this man's heart and its unbelief, so He

would draw him out.

3. Every statement made by our Lord, at least to the sick, sin-sore, and afflicted, was always designed to bring the person to the position to where the need could be met.

4. There are three types of people in the world relative to Christ:

• Those who believe even though they have not seen, which constitutes the highest form of Faith (Jn. 20:29).

• Those who must have a tangible, outward sign, such as the Miracles of which Jesus spoke.

• Those who will not believe even though confronted with Signs and Wonders. Such is called *"an evil heart of unbelief"* (Heb. 3:12).

5. The nobleman fell into the middle category. However, Jesus would pull him up higher, at least where Faith was concerned, as He ever seeks to do with any and all.

(49) "THE NOBLEMAN SAID UNTO HIM, SIR, COME DOWN OR ELSE MY CHILD WILL DIE."

The synopsis is:

1. Jesus would not heed his request to go to Capernaum but would give him the life of his child, which was that for which he came.

2. In the request, *"Sir, come down or else my child will die,"* we find that the man had come to the place that he knew Jesus was the Only Answer. No doubt, the doctors have long since been called in, but to no avail! So, his Only Hope was Christ, as Christ is the Only Hope for all of humanity.

3. One can feel the pathos in this man's plea, with this mild rebuke preparing him for what Jesus was about to say. While he still insisted that the Lord come to Capernaum, the emphasis had now been shifted from that to the need of his son. His Faith was now about to be tested!

(50) "JESUS SAID UNTO HIM, GO YOUR WAY; YOUR SON LIVES. AND THE MAN BELIEVED THE WORD THAT JESUS HAD SPOKEN UNTO HIM, AND HE WENT HIS WAY."

The composition is:

1. The Cross is not something that one can add to their present belief system. A proper understanding of the Cross of Christ is a complete and total belief system of its own.

NOTES

2. In fact, the Cross of Christ will not in any way tolerate any additions or deletions.

3. A proper understanding of the Cross of Christ gives one a proper understanding of the Word of God.

THE WORD WILL SUFFICE

The phrase, *"Jesus said unto him, Go your way; your son lives,"* presents a startling statement, and one which must have taken this man by surprise. In effect, Jesus was telling him that He did not have to be there Personally for this Miracle to be brought about, but that His Word would suffice.

I wonder what went on in this man's mind when he heard Jesus make this statement concerning his son.

He was a man who was accustomed to being obeyed, but now he realized that Jesus was not going to accompany him to Capernaum. But yet, he had a six word statement from Christ, which promised exactly that for which he had come. Would he continue to press for the Personal Presence of Jesus by the side of his dying son, or would he accept Jesus' Statement at face value?

The lesson here taught is valuable indeed! To be frank, and that which Jesus is portraying, the whole of humanity has but the Word of God on which to base their Faith. However, that is not only enough, but it is more than enough!

As the song says, *"Jesus said it, I believe it, and it's so!"*

FAITH IN ACTION

The phrase, *"And the man believed the Word that Jesus had spoken unto him, and he went his way,"* proclaims Faith in action. He *"believed,"* and that's exactly what the Lord wanted him to do. Consequently, it was a lesson not only for this man but also for Jesus' Disciples, and all others, for that matter.

As he speedily walked, or else, rode a horse or chariot in order to go home, he must have done so with great diligence.

What were his thoughts along the way? Did he berate himself for not insisting even stronger that Jesus Personally accompany him? He only had His Word, but I think the following Text portrays the fact that, as he went, his Faith strengthened instead of weakened.

As well, when Jesus gave him this promise, I have every confidence that the Presence of the Lord was exceptional and could be sensed by all. Consequently, it was not a mere Promise, but rather the *"Eternal Logos!"*

LOGOS

As said in commentary on the First Chapter of this Gospel, the New Testament writers never used the term, *"Logos,"* to denote *"reason"* or *"an expression of thought,"* as it is normally used, but always to denote *"speech," "utterance,"* or *"word."* In other words, while men *"reasoned,"* Jesus *"knows."* As well, while men express a *"thought,"* Jesus proclaims the exact *"Word,"* hence, the Eternal Logos.

God's Word is so intertwined with Him that it is indivisible and cannot be changed or looked at apart from Himself. Consequently, John would write, *"In the beginning was the Word, and the Word was with God, and the Word was God"* (Jn. 1:1).

As well, that's one of the reasons that Abraham said to the rich man in Hell, concerning his request that one be sent from the dead in order to speak to his unsaved relatives, *"If they hear not Moses and the Prophets, neither will they be persuaded, though one rose from the dead"* (Lk. 16:29-31).

In other words, the Word of God, whether spoken by Jesus or His Servants, is inviolable.

(51) "AND AS HE WAS NOW GOING DOWN, HIS SERVANTS MET HIM, AND TOLD HIM, SAYING, YOUR SON LIVES."

The pattern is:

1. The phrase, *"And as he was now going down,"* refers to the trip home, as is obvious. While the words, *"Going down,"* have to do with altitude, they also have to do with Spirituality. The way up is down!

2. This man had come to Jesus, it seems, with some thought of his own importance but left a different man. The phrase, *"His servants met him,"* proclaims a beautiful story.

3. No doubt, the servants had sat by the boy's bedside for some days now, slowly watching him weaken until he was at the point of death. All of a sudden, they saw a miraculous change. I wonder what their thoughts were.

4. The fever instantly broke! It was totally gone, with the boy made completely whole!

5. One can well imagine the joy that must have filled that home, with several servants leaving immediately to go find their master in order to give him the good news.

6. The phrase, *"And told him, saying, Your son lives,"* is charged with drama!

7. Quite possibly, he could see his servants coming to meet him even before they were in talking distance. What thoughts must have crossed his mind?

8. However, when they got close enough that he could see their faces, he knew the news was good. Beautifully and strangely enough, the servants used the exact same words concerning the boy's Healing that Jesus had used, *"Your son lives."* Never had a greater word fallen on this man's ear than the words of that moment.

"O happy day, O happy day."

(52) "THEN ENQUIRED HE OF THEM THE HOUR WHEN HE BEGAN TO AMEND. AND THEY SAID UNTO HIM, YESTERDAY AT THE SEVENTH HOUR THE FEVER LEFT HIM."

The order is:

1. The phrase, *"Then enquired he of them the hour when he began to amend,"* portrays him putting the times together when Jesus had spoken the Word and when the boy was healed.

2. *"And they said unto him, Yesterday at the seventh hour the fever left him,"* probably refers to 7 p.m. the day before.

3. There is some evidence that John, as well as government officials, as this man was, used the computation of the Romans in computing time, which is actually the same manner it is computed presently. Nevertheless, some believe he was using the Jewish reckoning, which would have made it 1 p.m. the day before.

4. However, it seems to me that if it had been 1 p.m., the man would have instantly started for home because of certainly being anxious to see the results of Jesus' Words. However, inasmuch as he spent the night, either in Cana or somewhere along the road,

it seems that the Roman accounting for time was used by John, which would have made it 7 p.m. the day before.

(53) "SO THE FATHER KNEW THAT IT WAS AT THE SAME HOUR, IN THE WHICH JESUS SAID UNTO HIM, YOUR SON LIVES: AND HIMSELF BELIEVED, AND HIS WHOLE HOUSE."

The pattern is:

1. The Story of the Cross is the Story of the Bible, as the Story of the Bible is the Story of the Cross. They are one and the same.

2. To the degree that one misunderstands the Cross, ignores the Cross, or repudiates the Cross, to that degree will they misinterpret the Word of God.

3. In fact, an improper understanding of the Cross is the major cause of all false doctrine.

DEFECTIVE FAITH?

The phrase, *"So the father knew that it was at the same hour, in the which Jesus said unto him, Your son lives,"* points to two possibilities.

The man was either not certain that it would be as Jesus said and now was greatly encouraged over the verification, not only of the Healing, but at the exact time it was carried out, or else, he believed fully and was overjoyed to see his Faith rewarded to this degree.

I think one can say that every single Believer in the world has defective Faith, at least to some degree. However, as should be overly obvious, Jesus was ever seeking to increase Faith in the hearts and lives of those with whom He dealt, and doing it in several different ways. The only ones in whom He found no response of Faith at all were the Pharisees and the religious leaders of Israel; consequently, they received nothing from the Lord. However, to all others, irrespective as to whom they may have been, a certain degree of Faith was present, which always increased because of contact with Jesus. Faith comes by hearing the Word, and Jesus was and is the Living Word (Jn. 1:7; Rom. 10:17).

ONLY BELIEVE

The phrase, *"And himself believed, and his whole house,"* speaks of all becoming Converts to Christ.

So, his son was not only healed and, thereby, spared from death, but, as well, the greater Gift of Salvation was given to all. What a blessed day this turned out to be, and all because of Jesus!

One can well surmise that the news quickly spread to every relative and friend concerning the tremendous Miracle of Healing which had taken place. It is easy to understand that people flocked to the home of this nobleman to see the young man and to hear the story as to exactly how Jesus healed him. I can see the father exclaiming to all who would listen, and all did, that He merely said, *"Go your way, your son lives!"*

He would then have told how he could hardly wait to get home and how the servants met him on the way, and they were shouting, no doubt, to the top of their lungs, *"Your son lives!"*

And then, I see the light as it literally shone on his face as he compared the time that the boy was healed and the time when Jesus had spoken the word, with him, no doubt, exclaiming, *"He was healed the moment He spoke the Word!"*

> *"Hail! Your Once Despised Jesus!*
> *"Hail! Your Galilean King!*
> *"You did suffer to release us;*
> *"You did free Salvation bring,*
> *"Hail! Your Agonizing Saviour,*
> *"Bearer of our sin and shame!*
> *"By Your Merits we find favour;*
> *"Life is given through Your Name."*

(54) "THIS IS AGAIN THE SECOND MIRACLE THAT JESUS DID, WHEN HE WAS COME OUT OF JUDAEA INTO GALILEE."

The order is:

1. The phrase, *"This is again the second Miracle that Jesus did,"* was speaking only of Galilee. Actually, he had performed quite a number of Miracles in the last few days in Jerusalem (Jn. 2:23).

2. So, the first Miracle he performed in Galilee was the changing of the water to wine. The second, under similar conditions, was the healing of a dying child by His Word.

3. *"When He was come out of Judaea into Galilee,"* proclaims that everywhere He

went, Miracles followed, plus the changing of lives, with the entirety of each community greatly bettered.

4. Were it not for Jesus, the home of the nobleman would now be grieving because of a recent funeral instead of being happy and joyous. Instead of the son laughing, talking, and providing an atmosphere of love in the home, he would now be a cold corpse in a tomb.

5. Jesus changes everything, and all for the better! He never leaves a place worse than He found it, but rather takes the person and the place to sublime heights of joy and peace.

6. Such was Jesus then, and such is Jesus now!

"Sing the wondrous Love of Jesus,
"Sing His Mercy and His Grace;
"In the mansions bright and blessed,
"He'll prepare for us a place."

"While we walk the pilgrim pathway,
"Clouds will overspread the sky,
"But when travelling days are over,
"Not a shadow, not a sigh."

"Let us then be true and faithful,
"Trusting, serving everyday;
"Just one glimpse of Him in Glory,
"Will the toils of life repay."

"Onward to the prize before us!
"Soon His beauty we'll behold;
"Soon the pearly gates will open,
"We shall tread the streets of gold."

CHAPTER 5

(1) "AFTER THIS THERE WAS A FEAST OF THE JEWS; AND JESUS WENT UP TO JERUSALEM."

The diagram is:

1. The Cross cuts all religious ties. Dependence on churches, ordinances, sacraments, rules and regulations, and denominations is out.

2. A proper understanding of the Cross of Christ is a proper understanding of Christ.

3. In fact, one cannot really trust and serve Christ as one should without properly understanding and embracing the Cross.

A FEAST OF THE JEWS

Some think that the phrase, *"After this there was a Feast of the Jews,"* speaks of the Passover. If that is correct, Jesus would have been a little over a year into His public Ministry; however, there is no actual proof as to which Feast it was.

If one is to notice, the Jews had so degraded these God-ordained Feasts until they were now described by the Holy Spirit not as *"Feasts of the Lord,"* but rather *"Feasts of the Jews."*

Within themselves, even when properly kept, they had no power to give life but only pointed to the One Who could, namely Christ. Inasmuch as He has now come, the impotency of these ceremonies to give life is here contrasted with Him Who is the Life. Men cling to forms and festivals all the more strongly when lacking the life that they symbolized under the First Covenant of Works, and use these forms to fight against Him of Whom these works witnessed.

Man's heart is incurably religious and, thereby, incurably evil!

JERUSALEM

The phrase, *"And Jesus went up to Jerusalem,"* speaks of the express purpose of keeping this *"Feast."* This is the second one He attended, at least after He began His public Ministry, that is recorded (Jn. 2:13-23).

Three times a year, representative males from every household were to keep these Feasts as directed according to the Law of Moses.

Three were conducted in April, *"Passover, Unleavened Bread, and Firstfruits."* This was the time of the barley harvest, to which these Feasts were connected.

• In the first part of June, some 50 days after the Passover, was the *"Feast of Pentecost."* This was the time of the wheat harvest.

• In October were the Feasts of *"Trumpets, Atonement, and Tabernacles."* This was the time of the fruit harvest.

FORMALITY

So, in attending three times during the

course of a year, all the Feasts could be honored with all the resultant Blessings. However, for long periods of time, Israel would ignore the Feasts and even the sacrifices, with Temple duties stopping altogether. Of course, these times pointed to acute spiritual declension, as should be obvious!

While Israel scrupulously kept these at this time, still, as said, they had deteriorated into mere formality, with their true purpose mostly lost.

Sadly, *"The Lord's Supper"* and *"Water Baptism"* have fallen into the same category in many Christian circles. These things, as the Feasts and sacrifices of old, become an end unto themselves, which, of course, abrogates their true purpose.

Everything must point to Jesus; however, their Messiah had now come, but they were so enamored with their religion that they did not recognize or know Him. As stated, it is the same presently.

In many circles, church has lost its true meaning and purpose, which is to learn the Word and to worship God. Many think, by associating with or attending particular churches, that, within itself, constitutes Salvation. Hence, all that it truly means is lost!

(2) "NOW THERE IS AT JERUSALEM BY THE SHEEP MARKET A POOL, WHICH IS CALLED IN THE HEBREW TONGUE BETHESDA, HAVING FIVE PORCHES."

The overview is:

1. The phrase, *"Now there is at Jerusalem by the sheep market a pool,"* should have been translated, *"By the sheep gate,"* because there is nothing in the Greek for the word *"market."*

2. This gate is now known as St. Stephen's Gate.

3. So, this pool would have been in that vicinity. It is thought that the waters of the pool were charged with iron and carbonic acid, along with other types of gases, which, in fact, did have some healing properties. But yet, at certain times, as we shall see, Divine intervention brought about miraculous Healings.

4. The phrase, *"Which is called in the Hebrew tongue Bethesda, having five porches,"* actually means, *"House of Grace and Mercy."* In other words, it was somewhat like a public infirmary, especially considering the curative properties of the water, and then, as stated, the Divine intervention.

5. The *"five porches"* seem to have protected the people from inclement weather as there seems to have always been a large crowd present.

(3) "IN THESE LAY A GREAT MULTITUDE OF IMPOTENT FOLK, OF BLIND, HALT, WITHERED, WAITING FOR THE MOVING OF THE WATER."

The form is:

1. The phrase, *"In these lay a great multitude of impotent folk, of blind, halt, withered,"* proclaims a perfect description of humanity.

2. Due to the Fall, man is *"impotent,"* i.e., *"helpless,"* at least to save himself.

3. As well, he is Spiritually *"blind,"* and that is the reason he cannot be reached for Christ through the intellect. Only the Holy Spirit can reveal Christ to the blind soul, and He does so on the authority of the Word of God. The word *"halt"* means that the mobility of the individual is seriously curtailed. Such is man.

4. *"Withered"* refers to paralysis and, in effect, *"spiritual paralysis."*

5. *"Waiting for the moving of the water,"* primarily speaks of the times when the pool was visited by an Angel, which brought Healing, at least to the first one in the water after the miraculous event.

(4) "FOR AN ANGEL WENT DOWN AT A CERTAIN SEASON INTO THE POOL, AND TROUBLED THE WATER: WHOSOEVER THEN FIRST AFTER THE TROUBLING OF THE WATER STEPPED IN WAS MADE WHOLE OF WHATSOEVER DISEASE HE HAD."

The order is:

1. A proper understanding of the Cross is a proper understanding of Christ.

2. In fact, one cannot really trust and serve Christ as one ought to without properly understanding and embracing the Cross.

3. To not understand the Cross of Christ puts one in the place and position of serving *"another Jesus"* (II Cor. 11:4).

AN ANGEL

The phrase, *"For an Angel went down at a certain season into the pool, and troubled the water,"* is not given by John as folklore, but rather as a fact.

Respecting Angels, the Bible is replete with the Ministry of these created beings, whose mission is to carry out that which is required by the Lord. I speak of righteous Angels, not those who rebelled with Lucifer.

Even though there is much information in both Testaments concerning Angels, at best, we are only given a glimpse into the Spirit world, trapped as we are in the material Universe. However, what we are shown is compelling evidence that there is a spiritual Universe that exists alongside the Universe we know through our senses. The Angels and other spiritual beings are real, and our God is the Ultimate Ruler of the invisible as well as of the visible.

The New Testament assumes all that the Old Testament teaches about Angels and goes on to add fresh information.

The New Testament word, *"Angelos,"* also means, *"Messenger."* It is used some 175 times; however, most of the activity of Angels in the New Testament concentrated around the Birth of Christ (Mat., Chpts. 1-2; Lk., Chpts. 1-2), and will again be prominent at Jesus' Return and the Judgment to take place then (I Thess., Chpt. 1; Bk. of Rev.).

EVIL ANGELS

There is evidence that approximately one-third of the angelic host threw in their lot, so to speak, with Lucifer when he led his revolution against God in the dateless past (Rev. 12:4).

Whenever God originally created the Angels, He created them, one might say, without number. There are more than likely billions of Angels. All Angels are of the same age, meaning they were all created by God at the same time and were created fully mature. This means that there has never been such a thing as a baby Angel. These are spirit beings with spirit bodies, meaning they can appear or disappear at will. They have phenomenal Power, given to them by God.

The revolution led by Satan in the dateless past must have been powerful indeed! Considering that one-third of the Angels threw in their lot with him, it tells us just how powerful that it really was.

Concerning evil Angels, Paul said this:

"For we wrestle not against flesh and blood, but against principalities, against powers, against the rulers of the darkness of this world, against spiritual wickedness in high places" (Eph. 6:12).

RANK AND DESIGNATIONS

The Greek scholars define the following in the realm of spiritual darkness respecting rank and designations:

• PRINCIPALITIES: these are the most powerful Angels functioning under Satan, helping him rule the kingdom of darkness.

• POWERS: these are also powerful fallen Angels, but not as powerful as the Principalities. In other words, they answer to the Principalities.

• RULERS OF THE DARKNESS OF THIS WORLD: these are, as well, fallen Angels, and powerful, to say the least, but they answer to the Powers as the Powers answer to the Principalities.

• SPIRITUAL WICKEDNESS IN HIGH PLACES: these are demon spirits under the control of the fallen Angels and Satan himself.

Human beings very seldom, if ever, have any contact with fallen Angels, but rather with demon spirits. A fallen Angel, or any kind of Angel, cannot possess a human being. Only demon spirits can do that. However, as Paul relates to us, in this *"warfare"* in which we as Believers are engaged, it includes fallen Angels, which give instructions to the demon spirits, etc. The *"wrestling,"* which we do as Believers, is not directly with these fallen Angels but against the demon spirits which they organize. In other words, fallen Angels are in charge of everything that's done, under Lucifer himself.

WHERE DO DEMON SPIRITS COME FROM?

God is the Creator of all things; however, there are certain things which were originally created by God but morphed, one might say, into that which they are presently. Demon spirits fall into that category.

It is believed that these beings were a particular race created by God, who served Lucifer on this Planet called Earth. This was before the revolution led by Lucifer. In fact, during that time and for a period of time, Lucifer served the Lord in Righteousness and Holiness. When Lucifer led his rebellion against God, this race of beings under him on Earth rebelled with him, and these demon spirits without spirit bodies are the result. In fact, in the Ninth Chapter of Revelation, we see beings that are totally strange to our thinking, which are the very epitome of evil. Once again, these are beings that threw in their lot with Lucifer, and the results are what is described in the Ninth Chapter of Revelation. Demon spirits have no body, spirit, physical, or otherwise, and, thereby, seek a body to inhabit, whether humans or animals.

THE PRESENT ROLE OF ANGELS

As we have already stated, the New Testament associates Angels closely with the First and Second Comings of Jesus. In the meanwhile, they are *"all ministering spirits, sent to serve those who will inherit Salvation"* (Heb. 1:14).

As well, Angels seem to have a special Ministry in relation to children (Mat. 18:10). An Angel was instrumental in releasing Peter from prison (Acts, Chpt. 12) and in preparing the way for the Conversion of Cornelius (Acts, Chpts. 10-11).

Angels in the unseen world are all under Jesus, *"Who is the Head over every power and authority"* (Col. 2:10). Jesus, not Angels, however, is always to be the focus of our Faith. He is the One in Whom we find fulfillment (Col. 3:1-4).

THE SUPERIORITY OF JESUS TO ANGELS

Jesus Christ the Man, but yet, the Son of God, ranks far above the Angels by virtue of His Nature (Phil. 2:6; Heb. 1:4-14). In the Incarnation, Jesus took on human nature. In the Resurrection, Jesus the God-Man took His Place as Lord, being set in authority over angelic beings of every rank and title (Eph. 1:20-22; Phil. 2:9-11; Col. 2:10-11).

NOTES

The superiority of Jesus to Angels is developed in the First Chapter of Hebrews. This Book was written to converted, Jewish Believers who were steeped in Old Testament lore and needed to be reminded that Jesus and the New Covenant He inaugurated were superior to the system that existed under the Old (Mosaic) Covenant.

COMPARING JESUS WITH ANGELS

The writer of Hebrews begins by comparing Jesus with Angels because the Angels were viewed by the First Century Jews as mediators of Revelation and as higher beings who deserved great respect. Paul launched his argument, and I believe Paul wrote Hebrews, by affirming Jesus as *"the Radiance of God's Glory and the exact Representation of His Being"* (Heb. 1:3), that is, as God Himself. The new Revelation is given, not by Angels, but by the God of the Angels!

The Superiority of Jesus, even in His Incarnation, is demonstrated by the following facts:

• God calls Jesus *"Son"* — a title not shared with Angels (Heb. 1:5).

• The Angels offer the Son worship (Heb. 1:6).

• Whereas Angels are referred to as servants, Jesus is given a Throne and a Kingdom (Heb. 1:7-8).

• The Angels were witnesses to the Creation, but Jesus both shaped and will outlast all of Creation (Job 38:7; Prov., Chpt. 8; Heb. 1:10-12).

• Jesus is now seated at the Father's Right Hand, whereas Angels are serving redeemed human beings (Heb. 1:13-14).

Since Jesus, as the Son of God, is so vastly superior to the Angels, who were communicators of the Old Covenant (Heb. 2:2), it is clear that the New Covenant must be vastly superior to the Old. The Jewish Convert can thus rest secure in his Christian Faith.

ANGELS AND HUMAN BEINGS

It is clear from the Word of God that Angels are presently superior to human beings in many ways. As direct Creations of God, these beings have unlimited lifetimes and unusual powers. Yet, the writer to the

Hebrews points out in awed tones that, *"It is not to Angels that He (God) has subjected the world to come"* (Heb. 2:5).

Jesus chose to share our humanity so that He might free us from the grip of sin. *"Surely it is not Angels He helps,"* Paul says in wonder, *"but Abraham's descendants"* (Heb. 2:16). Alive now in Jesus, we will be brought to Glory and lifted far above the Angels.

Angels, then, are not only God's Ministers, assigned to serve the heirs of Salvation, they are also eager witnesses to all that God is doing in this world (Lk. 15:10; I Cor. 11:10; I Tim. 3:16). Ultimately, human beings will be called on to judge the Angels (fallen Angels) (I Cor. 6:3).

GOD'S CONCERN

What we glimpse about Angels is intriguing and stimulates speculation, but the thrust of the Old Testament and New Testament is clear. Human beings, not Angels, are the focus of God's Concern. In return, God invites us to fix our thoughts and our Faith on Jesus, not on Angels.

We can trust Jesus as Lord to supervise the unseen Universe(s) for His Good Purposes and for our benefit. We can concentrate our efforts on coming to better know and love the One Who truly is Lord of all, *"The Lord Jesus Christ."*

THE TROUBLING OF THE WATER

The phrase, *"Whosoever then first after the troubling of the water stepped in was made whole of whatsoever disease he had,"* once again, is spoken not as folklore but as fact.

The scene portrayed here pretty well describes the modern church. Without Jesus, little, if anything, is done! With Jesus, everything is done, even to the Deliverance of the hardest cases. Tragically, too many churches continue to look back at something that may have happened in the distant past, with some faint but distant hope that it might happen presently. However, Jesus is here now and stands ready to do great and mighty things for those who will believe Him. He is the Saviour, Healer, Overcomer, and Coming King. He is everything!

The phrase of Verse 4 constituted, as should be obvious, a tremendous number of helpless people praying it would happen again, and that they may be first! Into this scene, Jesus came.

Earthly princes, upon entering a city, resort to the houses of the great and rich, but the feet of the Prince of princes immediately turn to the abode of misery and suffering, the fruits of sin.

(5) "AND A CERTAIN MAN WAS THERE, WHICH HAD AN INFIRMITY THIRTY AND EIGHT YEARS."

The pattern is:

1. No matter how zealous we might be, we are unable to overcome sin within our own strength and ability.

2. Sin can be overcome only by the Believer placing his or her Faith exclusively in Christ and the Cross, and maintaining it exclusively in Christ and the Cross, which then gives the Holy Spirit latitude to work (Rom. 8:2).

3. Jesus Christ atoned for all sin at the Cross, past, present, and future, at least for all who will believe (Jn. 3:16).

WHAT THE LAW COULD NOT DO

The healing of the impotent man contrasts the quickening Power of Christ with the powerlessness of the Law. It demanded strength on the part of the sinner in order to obtain the life it promised. However, man is without strength (Rom. 5:6), so, what the Law could not do because of the weakness of that upon which and through which it was to act, i.e., the carnal nature of man, Christ was sent by God effected, for He brought with Him the Power to accomplish that which Grace willed.

A single word from Christ sufficed. Strength was given, and the fact was demonstrated by the man carrying his bed.

LOVE

No doubt, love selected this man as being the most miserable, needy, and helpless in all that sad company, and wisdom chose him as a vessel of instruction to the Nation. As Israel, because of her sin, was helplessly shut up in the desert for eight and 30 years, so was this man for a similar period imprisoned because of his sin. As he vainly sought life in the pool of Bethesda because of being impotent, so Israel vainly sought life in the Law. In both cases, strength was required on the part of the person who sought what was promised through the disposition and ordination of Angels (Acts 7:53; Gal. 3:19).

God had not left Himself altogether without Testimony to His Love for His People under that Dispensation. An evidence of Blessing still remains.

An Angel imparted Healing to the pool from time to time, but strength was needed to profit by this angelic Ministry, and this man was without strength.

(6) "WHEN JESUS SAW HIM LIE, AND KNEW THAT HE HAD BEEN NOW A LONG TIME IN THAT CASE, HE SAID UNTO HIM, WILL YOU BE MADE WHOLE?"

The order is:

1. When the Christian begins to fight sin, and he does so by any means other than Faith in the Cross, he will lose that fight every single time. I'm referring, of course, to trying to overcome things in his life.

2. There is actually only one fight in which we are supposed to engage — it is the good fight of Faith (I Tim. 6:12).

3. Our Faith is to ever be in the Cross of Christ, for that is where all victory resides.

A PICTURE OF HUMANITY

The phrase, *"When Jesus saw him lie,"* presents a picture of present Israel but, as well, of all humanity.

Everything Jesus did was not only for the person or persons in question but, as well, was meant to portray a far wider lesson. As stated, this lesson pertained to Israel but, as well, portrays a picture of the human family.

In this man's helplessness, he could not go to Jesus, hence, Jesus came to him. The same is so for the world!

There was no way that man could reach God. Due to man's sinful condition, that door was closed. Therefore, Jesus came down to man.

"And knew that he had been now a long time in that case," portrays not only this man's condition but the condition of Israel as well. Actually, it speaks of all humanity.

What case is it that applies to the world?

NOTES

It is the case of spiritual hopelessness, which also affects the physical, mental, and domestical; however, most of mankind does not realize what *"that case"* actually is! While they may admit somewhat to man being a spiritual being, it is only in passing, and then with an erroneous concept.

Man's condition is terminal unless there is an intervention, as here, by Jesus.

GOD-CONSCIOUSNESS AND SELF-CONSCIOUSNESS

When man fell in the Garden of Eden, he fell from the lofty position of total God-consciousness down to the far, far lower level of total self-consciousness. Consequently, he is cut off from Spiritual Life, in fact, dead in trespasses and sins, for there is no spiritual life in man apart from God. As stated, he has been a long time *"in that case"* (Eph. 2:1-2).

WILL YOU BE MADE WHOLE?

Beyond a doubt, the question, *"He said unto him, Will you be made whole?"* must be the greatest question of all time!

As stated, man is not *"whole"* and, in fact, cannot be *"whole"* without Jesus. This is where the great contention is.

Even if man admits that he is not *"whole,"* he thinks that whatever his problem is can be assuaged through his own machinations. Hence, he thinks education, money, a better environment, or a host of other things is the answer. It is very difficult for him to admit that Jesus Alone is the Answer.

And yet, as Jesus asked this question so long ago, He continues to ask it even unto this hour with, in fact, some few replying in the affirmative and receiving the Eternal Life which only He can provide. Make no mistake about it, He Alone, as the Divine Intrusion, can set the record straight.

Due to spiritual blindness, it is somewhat understandable that the world rejects the Appeal of Jesus, but it is downright frightening whenever one considers that the church is, at least for the most part, rejecting Him as well! Instead of the Miracle-working Power of Christ, the church too often opts for humanistic methods, which may appear to be religious and, in fact, may be, but are not Scriptural.

SECULAR AND CHRISTIAN HUMANISM

Most Christians are familiar with the term, *"Secular humanism."* This basically means that man is the center of the Universe — and there is no God; consequently, seeking after God is unnecessary. Man can solve his own problems and bring about a utopian paradise — hence, the term *"secular,"* which means *"earthly"* or *"worldly."* Humanism, of course, refers to the human race.

In the denominational Christian world, Christian humanism has become the dominant philosophy.

Dave Hunt and T.A. McMahon, in their book, *"The Seduction of Christianity,"* said that such will not appear as a frontal assault or overt suppression of our religious beliefs. Instead, it will come as the latest fashionable philosophy, promising to make us happier, healthier, better educated — and even more spiritual.

The denominational world has already pretty much abandoned the Moving and Operation of the Holy Spirit as their Source for solving the problems of mankind. Instead, they look toward the *"fashionable philosophies,"* such as positive thinking, the healing of the memories, possibility thinking, self-help philosophies, and psychology. The total rejection of the Force and Power of the Holy Spirit has almost overwhelmed our religious institution.

However, most Pentecostal denominations are in no position to look with pious self-righteousness on their denominational brethren. Pentecostals, in fact, are so riddled with a *"departure from the Faith"* that we should point only at ourselves. In fact, all Pentecostal denominations in America and Canada have totally and completely embraced humanistic psychology as the answer to the aberrations of man. Please let it be understood, one cannot embrace psychology and the Cross at the same time. Either one cancels out the other.

THE GREED MESSAGE

For the most part, the Pentecostal and Charismatic denominations and fellowships have been riddled with the psychological message and the greed message. For sure, as it regards the greed message, anything that can promise instant riches to anyone will have great drawing appeal. However, the truth is, these messages do not draw attention to Christ, do not develop Spiritual Growth in the hearts and lives of Believers, and do not give victory over the world, the flesh, and the Devil, which can only be brought about by the Cross. In fact, as it regards the Charismatic world, for the most part, the Cross of Christ is ridiculed and referred to as the *"worst defeat in human history."* It is also referred to as *"past miseries."* This particular so-called Gospel is a mishmash of self-help programs, coupled with a form of Christian Science. In other words, it is not Biblical and is not of God. Anything that belittles the Cross of Christ has belittled the Gospel.

As a result, gullible people who follow this philosophy will not grow wealthy, either spiritually or financially. Actually, they will probably be separated from what little money they actually have.

On the other hand, there are those who accept the Message promoting Faith in God's Word, actually with their Faith anchored in the Cross of Christ, who believe God to meet every need according to His Riches in Glory. Their eventual goal is to become Christlike. These people alone will be the only ones who ultimately receive material Blessings — if that really matters.

THE WORD OF GOD

According to the Word of God, the Christian perspective should always place Christ at the center. Man is on the outside striving to move inward towards God. At least, that is the ideal! God is eternally at the epicenter, and everything must revolve around Him.

However, when this is distorted, man propels himself toward the center, and Christ is pushed to the periphery, if given any place at all. While remaining in the picture, God no longer retains His Proper Place in respect to man.

CHRISTIAN PSYCHOLOGY IS AN EXCELLENT CASE IN POINT

It is mostly since World War II that

psychology has infiltrated almost all seminaries in the land. Prior to this, a few theological schools offered counseling courses based on psychology. However, by the 1950s, almost all did, and over eighty percent were offering additional psychology courses.

In his book, *"Psychology as Religion, the Cult of Self-Worship,"* Paul Vitz, a psychology professor at New York University said:

"Psychology as a religion exists ... in great strength throughout the United States ... (it) is deeply anti-Christian ... (yet) is extensively supported by schools, universities, and social programs financed by taxes collected from Christians ... "

He then went on to say:

"But for the first time, the destructive logic of this secular humanism is beginning to be understood."[1]

Carl Rogers has stated that psychotherapy is the fastest growing area in the social sciences.[2] And now psychology has obtained the status of a neo-messiah whose scientific pretensions are relieving consciences of obedience to God.

Martin L. Gross had this to say in *"The Psychological Society"*:

"Psychology sits at the very center of contemporary society as an international colossus whose ranks number in the hundreds of thousands, and even millions ...

"It's experimental animals are an obliging, even grateful human race. We live in a civilization in which, as never before, man is preoccupied with self ...

"As the Protestant ethic has weakened in Western society, the confused citizen has turned to the only alternative he knows: the psychological expert who claims there is a new scientific standard of behavior to replace fading traditions ...

"Mouthing the holy name of science, the psychological expert claims to know all. This new truth is fed to us continuously from birth to the grave."[3]

THE CHURCH

With so many preachers now majoring in psychology, and almost all Christian Bible colleges and universities offering such, this pseudoscience has infiltrated the church in a wholesale manner.

NOTES

Pastors and other so-called spiritual leaders have accepted the claim that such is scientific and, therefore, *"neutral."* It is not neutral however. Psychology and psychotherapy are based on evolution, atheism, and secular humanism. They are actually a religion within themselves. In other words, Christianity and modern-day psychology are irreconcilable religious systems. This impossible melding of *"Christian psychology"* creates an unequal yoke that brings into the church the seductive influence of secular psychology. As we mentioned a moment ago, and we concur totally with him, Martin L. Gross stated that man is preoccupied with self. In fact, one writer stated, *"Whereas baseball used to be the American pastime, now it is self-improvement."*

Sometime ago, I saw a prominent television preacher make the statement, *"The way to glorify God is to glorify self. We must love ourselves."*

What did Jesus say?

"If any man will come after Me, let him deny himself (deny self), *and take up his cross, and follow Me.*

"For whosoever will save his life shall lose it: and whosoever will lose his life for My Sake shall find it" (Mat. 16:24-25).

Sad to say, as this so-called television preacher made this statement, he was surrounded by applauding Pentecostal preachers. God help us!

FALSE PROPHETS

When we think of false prophets presently, we normally think of the strange and the bizarre; however, this is not what we are warned of in Scripture.

The Bible describes these individuals as disguised in sheep's clothing. In other words, they *"look like the real thing and sound like the real thing."* They all say the right words — seeming plausible, palatable, and pleasant. However, Jesus said that inwardly they are *"ravening wolves"* (Mat. 7:15-23).

It is sadder still when one realizes that most Pentecostals and Charismatics, who boast of believing all of the Word of God, or at least they once did, seem to be the most deceived and deluded of all. There seems to be little, if any, Spirit of Discernment left.

On a Pentecostal program (Pentecostal?) not long ago, a particular *"spiritual teacher"* demeaned the Power of God and upheld humanism by telling the people, *"Whatever god you start with is satisfactory — be it the Muslim god, the Hindu god, the Buddhist god, or the Christian God. It's a good start, and you can build from there."*

He was speaking of people being rehabilitated respecting alcohol. Incidentally, the word, *"Rehabilitate,"* is not even in the Bible.

Someone stood in the audience and mentioned the Power of God to deliver the oppressed. The teacher admitted this was possible but said it was highly unlikely.

Then, the host of this Pentecostal program turned, held up this teacher's book, and recommended it to those viewing the program.

My answer is, *"And if the blind lead the blind, both shall fall into the ditch"* (Mat. 15:14).

UNITY AND CONFORMITY

The gospel of the hour is, *"Do not offend."* Everyone is accepted for *"what he is."* Every message is judged by *"take the good in it and leave the rest alone."* This is a prescription for disaster.

The victorious, overcoming Christian life is little mentioned anymore, especially considering that psychological therapy has become the throughway to modern spiritual results. Consequently, the *"Altar"* is ignored and even ridiculed, especially considering that it is a place on which one must *"die."*

Very few modern preachers speak presently of *"dying to the flesh."* How can they when, all the time, they are promoting the flesh?

However, through all the sham, falseness, and fads, if one listens carefully, one can hear the voice of the Illimitable Son of God, *"Will you be made whole?"*

When all else fails, and fail it must, Jesus Christ and Him Crucified is the Only Answer. As it was then, so it is now!

WHAT DOES IT MEAN TO BE WHOLE?

The Greek word that Jesus uses here is *"hugies"* and has reference basically to the sick being made well or *"whole."* The man was sick and had been so for many years and desperately needed healing. However, that which this episode represented pertained also to the spiritual and, consequently, spoke of a spiritual wholeness.

Actually, this represents the contention between God and man. Man knows he is not *"whole,"* but disagrees with his Creator as to what it will take to remedy the situation. He thinks, as stated, that money, entertainment, wealth, education, achievement, place, position, etc., will make him *"whole!"* Consequently, he pursues these things, even though the acquiring of such does not bring wholeness, of which the examples are abundant. Jesus said, *"For a man's life consists not in the abundance of the things which he possesses"* (Lk. 12:15).

SUCCESS?

Common terms used concerning what the world calls success, and respecting almost any walk of life, is, *"He made it!"*, *"She is a success!"*, etc.

Of course, one may ask the question, *"Made what?"* or, *"Success at what?"*

The truth is, there are far more suicides among those who have *"made it"* than the same number of their counterparts who do not reach those rarified heights.

Man's real problem is not a lack of things, education, or a hundred and one other things that could be named.

Along with being a physical and mental being, man is also a spiritual being. It is this part of man, the spiritual, which is unsatisfied. The spiritual pertains to God his Creator, which Satan or things can never satisfy. Consequently, the only way that man can be *"whole"* is to return to union with his Creator. However, due to the manner in which man fell, there was no way that man could return to God, at least according to his own efforts and ability. Consequently, all of the initiative had to be and has to be on God's Part.

THE FALL

However, the Fall was so severe and its results so final that even though God could decree worlds into existence, i.e., by the Words of His Mouth, He could not decree Salvation into existence, at least and be true to

His Nature. He had to literally become Man, which is called the *"Incarnation,"* in order that this great thing could be accomplished.

In the Garden of Eden, the price for disobedience was spiritual death, i.e., *"separation from God,"* which resulted in the death of all else as well! So, the price for life, the making of man whole again, was death, as well, but the Death of a Perfect Sacrifice.

Man could not provide that sacrifice because man was fallen and, thereby, what he presented to God was unacceptable. Neither could Angels provide this sacrifice because they were of another Creation. So, only in man, albeit a Perfect Man, could the claims of Heavenly Justice be satisfied. Therefore, God's Son became that Man (Jn. 3:16) and, thereby, did for man what man could not do for himself. He became our Substitute, and upon identification with Him, the Perfection that Jesus was and is, as well as the *"Wholeness"* He purchased, can now be given to all who believe (Jn. 3:3, 16). Identification with Him is brought about by Faith because this is the only way it can be brought about.

So, only God can make one whole, and He does so, without exception, upon the merit of His Son, the Lord Jesus Christ, and what Christ did for us at the Cross. That's the reason the Holy Spirit through the Apostle would say, *"How shall we escape, if we neglect so great Salvation?"* (Heb. 2:3).

THE CROSS OF CHRIST

The only answer to man's dilemma, and I emphasize the *"only,"* is the Cross of Christ. Jesus Christ is the Source of all things that man receives from God. In other words, man cannot reach God and can have no correspondence with God unless he goes through Jesus Christ and what He did for us at the Cross (Jn. 14:6).

It is the Cross of Christ, however, that makes everything possible. There, the Lord Jesus Christ atoned for all sin, past, present, and future, at least for all who will believe (Jn. 3:16). Sin provides the legal means for Satan to hold man captive, but with all sin removed, he has no more legal means to hold anyone captive. If he does so, and, regrettably, he does so for all of those who are unredeemed, it is because they will not accept what Jesus Christ has done.

When it comes to Believers, if the Believer looks to anything other than Christ and the Cross, he also will find bondage as a result, which means the sin nature is ruling him in some way. Let me say it again:

The Cross of Christ is the Means and the only Means by which the Lord gives good things to His Children. When the Believer's Faith is placed exclusively in Christ and the Cross, this gives the Holy Spirit the latitude to work within our hearts and lives to bring about what is necessary, which He Alone can do.

The Believer must understand that what we are facing in the spirit world is so far beyond our capabilities that we cannot hope to overcome by any method other than by God's Method.

WHAT IS GOD'S METHOD OF VICTORY?

His Method and His Only Method is the Cross of Christ. That is where Satan, all fallen Angels, and all demon spirits were totally and completely defeated (Col. 2:14-15). That's the reason that Satan hates the Cross with a passion. He doesn't really care what man does or how religious he becomes, just so he doesn't look to Christ and the Cross. Regrettably, the modern church, and that goes for all stripes, is looking everywhere except the Cross. God help us!

Please note the following diagram that possibly may be of help as it regards living a victorious life.

• Jesus Christ is the Source: this means that everything we receive from God must go through the Lord Jesus Christ (Jn. 1:1-3; 14:6; Col. 2:10).

• Jesus Christ is the Source while the Cross is the Means by which every good thing is given to us. Were it not for the Cross, God could not even look at man, much less have fellowship with Him. It is the Cross of Christ which has made and which does make everything possible (Rom. 6:1-14; Col. 2:10-15).

• With Jesus as the Source and the Cross as the Means, this means that the Cross of Christ must ever be the Object of our Faith. This is critically important. If we place faith in anything else except the Cross of Christ, we have violated God's Prescribed Order of Victory (I Cor. 1:17, 18, 21, 23; 2:2; Gal. 6:14; Col. 2:10-15).

• With our Lord as the Source and the Cross as the Means and the Cross of Christ as the Object of our Faith, then the Holy Spirit, Who works exclusively within the parameters, so to speak, of the Finished Work of Christ, will begin to work mightily on our behalf, making us what we ought to be (Rom. 8:1-11; Eph. 2:13-18). The Cross of Christ is God's Way, and His Only Way, because no other way is needed.

When it comes to Salvation, man cannot provide anything that contributes toward his Salvation. It is altogether Faith in Christ and what He did for us at the Cross. It's called, *"Justification by Faith."*

As well, as it regards the Believer who has sinned, likewise, he can contribute nothing toward his forgiveness, only accepting what the Lord has already furnished, once again, through the Cross. This is man's greatest problem, whether the unredeemed or the redeemed. He keeps trying to submit that which he thinks will guarantee Salvation or Grace, which God can never accept.

God can accept Jesus Christ and what He did for us at the Cross, and that alone. We accept that, and we are Saved. If it is rejected, then we are eternally lost. Regrettably and sadly, the modern church is filling the land with ways other than Christ and the Cross.

(7) "THE IMPOTENT MAN ANSWERED HIM, SIR, I HAVE NO MAN, WHEN THE WATER IS TROUBLED, TO PUT ME INTO THE POOL: BUT WHILE I AM COMING, ANOTHER STEPS DOWN BEFORE ME."

The diagram is:

1. Satan will do everything within his power to move our Faith to something else other than the Cross.

2. If he is successful in this, we will find that we are fighting the wrong fight, a fight we cannot win.

3. The reason is simple: it's because Jesus has already fought this fight and won it completely (Col. 2:14-15).

THE IMPOTENT MAN

The phrase, *"The impotent man answered Him,"* represents this man having no idea Who Jesus was or Who asked him this all-important question. In fact, Christ's Appearance little spoke of Who He actually was. He had no regal bearing in the sense of ostentatious display, as was the custom of those of importance, or at least those who thought they were important. In other words, Jesus had no runners going before Him, telling the people Who He was. Actually, Jesus was a Peasant; consequently, His Dress, as well as the dress of His Disciples who surrounded Him, was according to such station. In fact, if Jesus had been accompanied by a display of pomp and ceremony, man would have been easily impressed and would have accepted Him far more readily, but for all the wrong reasons. However, if such had been the case, it would only have exacerbated man's real problem of pride rather than meeting his true need. Consequently, the manner in which Jesus came, *"No beauty that we should desire Him"* (Isa. 53:2), was the manner in which He had to come so that man could be redeemed. To cater to man's pride, which ostentatious display would do, would have been the very opposite of what man needed.

If one is to notice, the world is greatly impressed by pomp, ceremony, riches, fame, and popularity. All else is relegated to a secondary position, if any position at all! This is because of man's pride, which actually speaks of the manner of his fall in the Garden of Eden and his desire to play god or be God. Regrettably, all too often, the church falls into this same trap — impressed by gaudy display.

So, if this man, in fact, had looked up when Jesus spoke to him, which he probably did not, he would not have seen One of regal display, at least the type recognized by the world, but rather One Who was totally different than the world had ever known.

To be sure, the regal display was there, and in a manner that was absolutely impossible for the world to duplicate. However, it was registered in Humility and Love, which the world did not recognize, or at least did not understand, and which, to be sure, the backslidden church of that day understood not at all.

THE IMPOTENCY OF MAN

The phrase, *"Sir, I have no man, when the water is troubled, to put me into the pool,"* tells us several things:

• There is a resignation in the man's answer, especially considering the many years of impotence, in which he despairs of ever finding help.

In fact, much of the world is in this same condition — no more hope remains. In other words, *"Having no hope, and without God in the world"* (Eph. 2:12). Actually, this is the awfulness of a life without God. No hope!

• The phrase, *"I have no man,"* proclaims his dependence on man, which has brought nothing but disappointment, and, in fact, can bring nothing but disappointment.

Regrettably, the world looks to *"man"* instead of God, and that is the reason for their sore disappointment. Without God, man has no love for his fellowman. He only desires to better himself and is readily willing to do so at the expense of others, hence, the war, privation, and want in the world.

However, it is sadder still when much of the church, even that which claims to know and understand the Power of God, in fact, no longer looks to Him but to *"man!"*

The world of humanistic psychology is a perfect case in point. Most in the church are not taught to look to the Lord, but rather to this broken reed. It is the same as Israel looking to Egypt in her waning days instead of asking the Lord for help. Despite the prophesying of Jeremiah, they ignored Jehovah, Who was only yards away in the Temple. Even at the expense of great treasure, they resorted to Egypt, which, in fact, could give them no help whatsoever.

How the mighty have fallen!

So, if we look to man, we will get the help that man provides. However, if we look to God, we will get the help that He provides, which is magnificent indeed, even as represented here.

• When the man addressed Jesus as *"Sir,"* he did so because he had no idea whatsoever that Jesus was the Messiah, i.e., the Son of God.

However, because of the Love and Humility resident in Jesus, these offenses never bothered Him, but rather He pressed in closer in order that He may heal this man.

THE TRAP

The phrase, *"But while I am coming, another steps down before me,"* proclaims the fact that in the last 38 years, the Angel had visited this place several times, with, it seems, some being healed, but due to his impotence, this man was not so fortunate.

As we have already stated, this man's condition was a type of Israel attempting to find life in the Law. However, in both cases, strength was required on the part of the person who sought what was promised, which guaranteed failure, as man has no spiritual strength within himself.

The greatest danger of all in the Church is for Believers to take that which points to Christ and attempt to make it an end within itself. The Church points to Christ, but the Church can save no one. Likewise, even as we have previously stated, the Lord's Supper and Water Baptism point to Christ but, within themselves, contain no salvation. They point to the One Who does, but many have mistaken these ordinances for Salvation.

In the Law, all pointed to Jesus, but Israel vainly attempted to make Salvation out of the Law.

I bear down on this point, even at the risk of repetition, simply because this problem is acute. As Israel fell into this trap, so does the modern church!

All who look to the Church, or even its sacred ordinances, will find themselves exactly as this impotent man beside the pool of Bethesda, imprisoned in a continued helplessness.

(8) "JESUS SAID UNTO HIM, RISE, TAKE UP YOUR BED, AND WALK."

The overview is:

1. In the words of Paul, anything other than the Cross of Christ is nothing more than *"profane and vain babblings, and oppositions of science falsely so called"* (I Tim. 6:20).

2. Then he said, *"Which some professing have erred concerning the Faith"* (I Tim. 6:20-21).

3. If we err, it is always *"concerning the

Faith." In other words, it's the wrong object of faith.

THE WORDS OF JESUS

There is no evidence that Jesus touched this man or did anything other than speak to him. However, what He said to him was totally different than anything anyone had ever spoken in his presence. As well, the Power of the Holy Spirit grandly accompanied these Words of Christ. So, the One Who said, *"Let there be light,"* now spoke Healing into existence. As His Word dispelled the darkness of so long ago, it now dispelled the sickness of the present moment (Gen. 1:3).

WHAT DID JESUS SAY TO HIM?

Even though Jesus was God and never ceased to be God, still, He never performed one single Miracle as God, but always as a Man filled and controlled by the Holy Spirit. The one great difference with Christ and other men was that He was Absolutely Sinless. He never sinned, not even one time, in word, thought, or deed; consequently the Holy Spirit had a Perfect Domicile, so to speak, in which to work. That cannot be said by any other man. Even in the best of us, there is so much that grieves the Holy Spirit, that even wounds the Holy Spirit, so to speak, which hinders Him from being what He wants to be and doing what He wants to do within our lives.

Now, as it regards this poor man, what did Jesus say to him?

RISE

This is what the Lord always does. He picks up fallen man. To be sure, there was no way within his own power that this man could rise from his bed of affliction. However, when Jesus spoke the word, *"Rise,"* the Power of God went all through this man's body, and what had been heretofore helpless, now was infused with strength, in other words, *"Divine strength."*

In a sense, this is a perfect example of the Salvation experience. Man, at least within himself, has no power to lift himself up Spiritually. However, when Jesus comes into the heart and life, Power is infused into the believing sinner, and he is lifted up to where he has not been before.

TAKE UP YOUR BED

This bed, which had once been his prison, instead, now becomes his prisoner. In other words, the prisoner takes over the prison.

This speaks not only of the *"dead"* in the physical sense but, also, in the spiritual sense, referring to bondages of darkness, which hold men in their iron grip, with no way to be free. I speak of alcohol, drugs, hate, prejudice, racism, religion, gambling, immorality, etc. However, once Jesus comes in, the jailer (Satan) and the prison (hate, alcohol, etc.) are taken prisoner. The former prisoner goes free and now becomes the jailer, so to speak.

WALK

For the first time in the believing sinner's life, he is now truly free. Consequently, he is able now to chart his own course, which is after Christ, whereas, heretofore, the course was charted for him — and a course of slavery it was! Please understand the following:

For every single person that's ever been delivered from the bondages of sin, be it alcohol, drugs, hate, immorality, nicotine, gambling, prejudice, jealousy, uncontrollable temper, etc., it was all done by the Lord Jesus Christ. Buddha has never set one captive free. Muhammad has never set one captive free. In fact, no religion has ever set anyone free but only increased the servitude. It is Jesus Christ alone Who sets the captive free, and Who can set the captive free.

Men try to deal with these bondages through psychology, education, money, and religion, all to no avail. It is Jesus Christ alone Who can do what needs to be done.

DECEPTION

Many would ask the question, if what I have just stated is true, that Jesus Christ has set free untold millions and is still doing so this very hour, *"Why is it that it's difficult to get men to trust Him?"*

It is difficult because of deception. Men are deceived. They are deceived into believing that up is down and down is up, black is white and white is black, etc.

Generally, it takes the person to be pushed against the wall, so to speak, or to be down for the count before that person will finally cry out to God. Even then, all too often, he wants to cry to Him in his own way, which, most of the time, is through and by error. However, if men will go to the Lord in humble, broken contrition, the Lord is always guaranteed to answer. The Scripture plainly says:

"But to this man will I look, even to him who is poor and of a contrite spirit, and trembles at My Word" (Isa. 66:2).

(9) "AND IMMEDIATELY THE MAN WAS MADE WHOLE, AND TOOK UP HIS BED, AND WALKED: AND ON THE SAME DAY WAS THE SABBATH."

The diagram is:

1. When Paul used the term, *"The Faith,"* or even the term, *"Faith,"* always and without exception, he was speaking of Christ and what Christ has done for us at the Cross, and our Faith in that Finished Work.

2. Every human being in the world has faith, but it's not faith that God will recognize. He recognizes Faith only in the context of Jesus Christ and the Cross being the Object of that Faith, which, in reality, is Faith in the Word.

3. The faith of most Christians is misplaced in that it's not anchored in Christ and the Cross.

THE MAN WAS MADE WHOLE

The phrase, *"And immediately the man was made whole,"* proclaims, in the spiritual sense, the immediate result of Salvation. As the man's Healing was *"immediate,"* likewise, upon Faith in Christ, Salvation is immediate as well! The Lord does not save people by stages. True Conversion is always instant.

Some make much out of the act of Faith, which the man had to exert in order to obey Christ. They picture him with no strength, timidly attempting to do what Christ told him to do, and finally, with success. However, that is not the way it happened.

The moment that Jesus said, *"Rise, take up your bed, and walk,"* Divine strength flooded the weakened and even dead muscles of this man's body, which had kept him from walking previously. While it certainly

NOTES

did take some Faith, it was Faith that came easily because Jesus' Word produced a Power in this man's body. It was to such an extent that it would probably have been harder for him to remain immobile than to obey Christ respecting him doing something he had not done in 38 years — walk.

FAITH

Faith is always the ingredient that is required. However, in the last few years, too much emphasis has been placed on Faith and not enough on the Power of Jesus Christ.

Many have made Faith a law unto itself. While that may be true concerning the world and the Faith it has in its own efforts, it is not true concerning Christ.

Christ is the One Who energizes Faith in the believing sinner, and He does so by His Spoken Word. As stated, while Faith is always required, it is not really the laboring process that many make it out to be simply because of the Power of Christ.

When Jesus spoke to that man, he did not have to make some herculean effort of Faith to obey, but rather so much Divine energy flooded his heretofore sick body that it would have been almost impossible for him not to have obeyed.

We sin when we make so much out of Faith that we reduce Christ. If one's eyes are on Jesus, and one properly hears His Words, *"Faith comes ... "* (Rom. 10:17).

THE PRISONER IS NOW FREE

The phrase, *"And took up his bed,"* proclaims this man doing such in obedience to Christ, which instantly became of no difficulty, whereas it had once been impossible. Thus is the difference instantly made by Christ. That which had once been impossible is now an insignificant, simple task.

The words, *"And walked,"* must have created some type of sensation. However, it is clear that Jesus left immediately after this man's miraculous Healing, without the man even knowing Who Jesus actually was. There is a reason for that, which will become very clear momentarily.

THE SABBATH

The phrase, *"And on the same day was the*

Sabbath," proclaims the greatest Sabbath this man had ever known, a *"Sabbath"* of rest and relief, which this noted day was meant by God to serve as an example.

What follows proves that the Lord presented this sign of His Messiahship to the Nation intentionally on the Sabbath that they might learn that He Himself was the True Sabbath in which God rested.

God's Creation Sabbath was wrecked by sin, and how could Love rest in misery? To test man's obedience and to awaken him to a consciousness of his impotency to profit by a rest, the enjoyment of which demanded strength on the part of man, the Sabbath was given as a token of the Covenant between Israel and Jehovah.

However, man's disobedience destroyed it again. That Sabbath was the close of the First Creation. The Christian Sabbath, so to speak — the Resurrection Day — opened the New Creation. The Christian rests not in the First Creation but in the Second and, therefore, observes the first day of the week because it is God's Redemption Rest (Heb., Chpt. 4). With Christ being that Sabbath, it is a rest that cannot be disturbed.

However, God is never defeated, and so, the great Sabbath Day of 1,000 years will be the seventh day of the First Creation, upon whose fourth day the Son of Righteousness first appeared (Gen. 1:14-18), in Whom, also, that future seventh day is secured.

(10) "THE JEWS THEREFORE SAID UNTO HIM WHO WAS CURED, IT IS THE SABBATH DAY: IT IS NOT LAWFUL FOR YOU TO CARRY YOUR BED."

The exposition is:

1. The Grace of God is simply the Goodness of God extended to undeserving Believers.

2. Grace is superintended by the Holy Spirit and is made available to us in unlimited quantities, due to what Christ did at the Cross.

3. God has always been a God of Grace. However, due to the fact that the blood of bulls and goats could not take away sins, He was limited at that time as to what could be done. Since the Cross, which atoned for all sin, which animal blood could not do, Grace can be extended in an unlimited quantity.

NOTES

THE JEWS

The phrase, *"The Jews therefore said unto him who was cured,"* proclaims, as we shall see, not joy over his Healing and Deliverance, but rather the opposite, as religion always does.

Religion has no concern whatsoever over Deliverance or the forgiveness of sin by God, but rather its rules and regulations.

In fact, the Rabbinic interpretations of the Sabbatic Law concerning the bearing of burdens were so intricate and detailed that the entire majesty of Law, as originally given by God, had been totally abrogated.

Of course, the question must be asked, *"Did Jesus break the Law of Moses by telling this man to take up his bed and walk, considering it was the Sabbath Day?"*

By all means, the answer is, *"No"*! In fact, Jesus obeyed the true Mosaic Law in every capacity. He was actually the Only One Who did keep the Law. However, He did break the man-made laws which had been added to the original Law of Moses, or rather He ignored them. Of course, this infuriated the religious hierarchy, as we shall see!

RELIGIOUS HIERARCHY

The problem that prevailed then prevails now. In the world of religion, and religion it is, great efforts will be made to force compliance with man-made rules and regulations, which are not the Word of God. The criterion always is the Word. It alone must chart the course and set the direction. Anything that abrogates the Word of God, even as the myriad of Jewish laws of old, must be ignored exactly as Christ ignored them.

As well, if any preacher or person acquiesces in any way to man-made religious rules and regulations, which, by their very origin, do not comply with the Word of God, that person or preacher has compromised his place in Christ.

Such does not mean that one is lost. However, it does mean that one is weakened by such improper obedience, which definitely can cause one to ultimately lose his way completely, that is, if the compromise continues, as compromise is intended to do. Ultimately, to compromise in one point is to compromise in all!

The only cure is Repentance, which will demand a return to the Word of God and, thereby, God's Ways, and a determination to please God and not man.

I believe that the time is coming, if it has not already arrived, that it will be virtually impossible for any person, that is, if he truly wants to obey God, to associate himself with any type of institutionalized religion. This speaks of denominations and denominationalism.

RULES

However, it is not institutionalized religion or denominations within themselves which are wrong, inasmuch as these are but lifeless vehicles, but rather the spirit of darkness which works in the children of disobedience. As such, this spirit is just as prominent in non-institutionalized religion as it is its opposite.

Men love to make rules, and religious men love to most of all. As well, they love to force people to obey those rules. So, to do the right thing, which constitutes obedience to the Word of God, will always carry a price tag. The trouble is, many desire the obedience without the price tag. Such is not to be!

So, the Jews had absolutely no regard or concern that the man was *"cured,"* but only that one of their little petty rules had been broken.

The phrase, *"It is the Sabbath Day,"* proclaims the fact that these religious leaders had made the Sabbath Day a law within itself.

In other words, they lost sight altogether as to What and Whom the Sabbath pointed. The Sabbath was meant to serve as a Symbol of Jesus Christ, Who would bring Spiritual rest to the believing sinner who placed his trust in Him. While it had other connotations as it pertained to Israel, its true meaning always pointed to the One Who its symbolism represented, the Lord Jesus Christ. He Alone is the True Sabbath.

Actually, that's what He was speaking of when He said, *"Come unto Me, all who labor and are heavy laden, and I will give you rest"* (Mat. 11:28).

NOTES

THE JEWISH SABBATH AND THE PRESENT DAY

It is unfortunate that some have attempted to pull the old Jewish Sabbath over into the present day, attempting to force it to fit into the New Covenant. The Book of Acts proclaims it no longer being observed by Christians because the True Sabbath, of which the old Jewish Sabbath was but a symbol, had come.

Not only was the old Jewish Sabbath done away with, but, as well, the sacrifices, Feast Days, etc. Even the Temple has been done away with, along with all of its appointments, such as the Brazen Altar, the Brazen Laver, the Table of Shewbread, the Golden Lampstand, and the Altar of Incense. It would also include the Ark of the Covenant and the Mercy Seat.

All of these things pointed to Christ. They were merely symbols and even though, as stated, very significant in their time because of to Whom they pointed, once Jesus came, the symbolism was no longer needed, as should be obvious.

These things were types, which provided a way for man to reach God, and more importantly, for God to reach man. They were never meant to be a means of Salvation within themselves; however, the Jews had attempted to make them so. By the time of Jesus, these beautiful symbolisms, as originally given by God, had lost most all of their meaning. Instead of Blessings, they had now become *"grievous burdens"* (Lk. 11:46).

The phrase, *"It is not lawful for you to carry your bed,"* pointed only to man's laws and not God's Laws.

Actually, this man carrying his bed on the Sabbath was one of the greatest examples that could ever be of the Victory, Healing, Freedom, and Deliverance offered by Jesus Christ, which the Sabbath actually proclaimed and portrayed.

Under the New Covenant, accepting Christ and making Him the Saviour of one's soul and the Lord of one's life translates into keeping the Sabbath. The Sabbath was a day and time of rest. It was meant to portray the *"rest"* that one would find in Christ and, thank God, can now be found.

(11) "HE ANSWERED THEM, HE WHO MADE ME WHOLE, THE SAME SAID UNTO ME, TAKE UP YOUR BED, AND WALK."

The overview is:

1. If one will keep his Faith placed in Christ and the Cross, he will ultimately find the victory promised by the Lord (Rom. 6:14).

2. Please understand that victory over the world, the flesh, and the Devil can be found in no place except Christ and the Cross.

3. As there was only one place of sacrifice in the Old Testament, and rightly so, there is only one place of victory under the New Covenant, the Cross, and rightly so.

TO BE WHOLE

The phrase, *"He answered them, He Who made me whole,"* proclaims the man using Jesus as his Authority, which is what he should have done.

The idea is that if Jesus had the Power to make him *"whole,"* which He did, and which He used regarding the sickness of this man, He, as well, should be obeyed. Actually, this is the idea of the entirety of this controversy.

Religious men demand that they be obeyed. However, neither they nor their rules can make anyone *"whole,"* so why should they be obeyed, especially considering that they are demanding that which is not Scriptural?

Conversely, the Lord demands obedience, and He has the right to demand such because He Alone is the Author of Salvation and needs no help from man.

However, as stated, what is presented here has soaked the Earth with blood. Religious man demands obedience, and God demands obedience. It is not possible to obey both.

By the Third Century, much of the Early Church had begun to apostatize, with man inserting his ways, thereby, abrogating God's Ways. As such, the Catholic church slowly came into being, and with its coming strength, it demanded obedience of all, even upon pain of death. Consequently, multiple tens of thousands chose to die rather than obey man, which, at the same time, meant to disobey God.

Jesus addressed this subject when He said, *"And fear not them which kill the body, but are not able to kill the soul: but rather fear Him* (God) *which is able to destroy both soul and body in Hell"* (Mat. 10:28).

Regrettably, this demand for spiritual control did not stop with the Catholic church but is quite prominent in Protestant circles as well. In other words, you do what I say do, or else, I will destroy you. Even though such would be denied, still, the denial in no way abrogates that which is true.

TAKE UP YOUR BED AND WALK

The phrase, *"The Same said unto me, Take up your bed, and walk,"* proclaims this command being eagerly obeyed because it also meant the Healing and Salvation of this cripple.

So, if one wanted Healing and Salvation, one must obey the Lord. If he wanted to remain sick and dying and spiritually lost, then he could obey man.

Likewise, much of the modern church ignores Repentance, which is God's Command, and demands obedience to their man-made rules, which, in effect, can deliver no one. The battle rages today, even as then!

(12) "THEN ANSWERED THEY HIM, WHAT MAN IS THAT WHICH SAID UNTO YOU, TAKE UP YOUR BED, AND WALK?"

The exegesis is:

1. There is no doubt that the religious leaders knew Who it was Who made this man to walk. What they desired was to use this man as an example in portraying Christ as a *"Lawbreaker."* They saw this Healing, especially on the Sabbath Day, as a threat to their place and position. Actually, religion always sees anything that is of God as a threat, as it rightly is.

2. Their opposition to Jesus would be so acute that, as we shall see, they wanted to kill Him, and ultimately did!

3. Consequently, the battle has ever raged between the true Church, i.e., *"Jesus Christ,"* and the apostate church, i.e., religion, i.e., Satan.

4. They asked what man it was who had done this thing. In reality, there is only One Man Who could do such a thing, and that is Jesus.

5. Why is it that they did not know and realize that One Who had the Power to do

such as this was, at the same time, the Son of God?

6. The act of healing itself should have been enough to have told them Who Jesus was, and, in fact, it was. However, they really did not have a sincere heart after God. Consequently, even though speaking of God constantly, in truth, they had no desire for anything that was of God. Their business was to protect their own religion and not that which was of the Lord.

7. As I have related elsewhere in these Volumes, for quite sometime, I erroneously thought that if the religious leaders of the denomination with which I was formerly associated would only come to the services and see the Power of God in operation, they would not feel about us as they did. However, I finally had to come to the conclusion that it was really the Power of God which they actually opposed. In other words, they did not want the Spirit of God, hence, their opposition to me and to all who truly know the Lord.

(13) "AND HE WHO WAS HEALED KNEW NOT WHO IT WAS: FOR JESUS HAD CONVEYED HIMSELF AWAY, A MULTITUDE BEING IN THAT PLACE."

The synopsis is:

1. The phrase, *"And he who was healed did not know who it was,"* means that almost immediately after the Healing Power of God had flowed through this man's body, Jesus left, so as not to create a scene. Consequently, the man did not really know Who it was Who actually healed him.

2. This was, it seems, the early part of Jesus' Ministry. Consequently, He was not as well known at this time, at least in Jerusalem, as He would be in the coming months.

3. *"For Jesus had conveyed Himself away, a multitude being in that place,"* proclaims He left because He knew the hatred of the leaders and the results of His Breaking their man-made laws. This is perhaps the reason He did not stay to heal others. He simply did not want to endanger Himself needlessly at this place and at this time. That time would come a little later, which it did!

(14) "AFTERWARD JESUS FINDS HIM IN THE TEMPLE, AND SAID UNTO HIM, BEHOLD, YOU ARE MADE WHOLE: SIN NO MORE, LEST A WORSE THING COME UNTO YOU."

The diagram is:

1. The phrase, *"Afterward Jesus found him in the Temple,"* proclaims Jesus seeking him out for a purpose.

2. The man was quite possibly going to the Temple to give thanks unto the Lord for what had just happened to him. It was truly a grand and glorious day in his life. However, it was about to become even grander. He was to meet Jesus, Who would now give him Eternal Life.

3. *"And said unto him, Behold, you are made whole,"* refers to the Salvation experience and not only physical Healing.

4. *"Sin no more, lest a worse thing come unto you,"* tells us one of two things, or both:

a. His sickness of 38 years had been brought upon him by sin.

Even though original sin is the cause of all sickness and disease, still, it does not mean that all sickness is necessarily the cause of immediate sin. And yet, much sickness is caused by immediate sin, such as nicotine, alcohol, drugs, or disobedience to God in any fashion.

b. Or else, the Lord was telling the man that if he did continue in sin, thereby, forgetting God, Who had given him this great Healing and Salvation, worse would come to him, which would mean the loss of his very soul.

5. In fact, Israel's 38 years in the desert was the fruit of sin. And yet, they sinned more by crucifying the Lord of Glory, and a worse punishment has come upon them.

(15) "THE MAN DEPARTED, AND TOLD THE JEWS THAT IT WAS JESUS, WHICH HAD MADE HIM WHOLE."

The overview is:

1. Some have claimed that it was gross ingratitude on the part of this man to go and tell the Jews that it was Jesus Who had made him whole. Some have even referred to him as a *"loveless being!"*

2. While such may definitely be true, there is nothing in the Scripture which proclaims such. There is no record that Jesus told him to say nothing, and the man, not knowing the animosity of the religious

leaders against Jesus, would have seen no wrong in telling them that it was Jesus Who had made him whole.

3. John only records the situation, with no implication being offered. Consequently, we have little reason to blame the man.

(16) "AND THEREFORE DID THE JEWS PERSECUTE JESUS, AND SOUGHT TO KILL HIM, BECAUSE HE HAD DONE THESE THINGS ON THE SABBATH DAY."

The exegesis is:

1. Since the Cross, which has opened the door, God can dispense Grace in an unlimited quantity.

2. That's the reason He told Paul that irrespective of the problems, *"My Grace is sufficient for you: for My Strength is made perfect in weakness"* (II Cor. 12:9). Believers, within ourselves, are no match for the Devil. We must learn that, sometimes the hard way. However, Jesus Christ has totally defeated Satan and all his cohorts of darkness. This victory is ours by our Faith being placed completely in Christ and the Cross, which then gives the Holy Spirit latitude to work within our lives.

HATRED OF CHRIST

The phrase, *"And therefore did the Jews persecute Jesus,"* proclaims the religious hierarchy and, no doubt, the Pharisees, confronting Jesus about healing the man on the Sabbath. They evidently spoke great words of anger and hatred against Him.

So, that which had been in their hearts all along now vented itself as to who and what they really were. From this point, they will seek to speak against Him at every opportunity, especially among themselves.

In this nation of America, which is supposed to be Christian, at least after a fashion, there is more hatred among the powers that be against Christ even than it is Muhammad, etc.

Why?

It's because Jesus Christ is real. He is the Son of God. He is the Saviour of man, the only Saviour, and is such by dying on the Cross and being raised from the dead. Muhammad and others suchlike are of their father the Devil, just as are many of the powers that be in this nation.

TO KILL JESUS

"And sought to kill Him," proclaims that which the Holy Spirit knew was in their hearts. They hated Him; consequently, they desired strongly to kill Him, which they ultimately did!

In fact, this type of opposition to the true Gospel of Jesus Christ has soaked the Earth with more blood than possibly anything else. It began with Cain as he killed Abel. Likewise, it fills the hearts of many, if not hundreds of millions, presently.

The only reason that modern religious leaders, at least for the most part, do not engage in actual murder is because the law of the land prevents such. This type of evil is the greatest evil of all! And yet, hundreds of thousands of Believers, if not millions, support with their money, time, and effort that which is overtly of Satan, thinking all the time that they are supporting the Work of God. Actually, this is true of many, if not most, religious denominations, as well as thousands of independent churches, etc.

At this stage, the question must be asked, *"Can the people support these religious leaders who sought to kill Jesus and be of God, or can the people support both the religious leaders and Jesus at the same time?"*

The answer is emphatically, *"No!"*

However, it must be understood that most of the religious offices of that time were filled by Rome, or at least with their tacit approval. Consequently, the people had little, if any, choice in the matter.

SUPPORT?

However, the record shows that most of the people did support these individuals who hated Christ, and, thereby, it stands to reason that they did not support Jesus. We know this from the small number who actually followed Him, even as the next Chapter portrays.

While the crowds were great and the accolades at that time of great capacity, still, it was more for the Healings, the Miracles, and even the Bread miraculously supplied than anything else. In other words, most of the people desired Jesus for What He could do instead of Who He actually was.

So, it was not popular then to follow Christ as it is not popular now. Actually, it soon came to the place that anyone who followed Jesus was threatened with excommunication from the synagogue, or actually experienced this humiliating spectacle, as was carried out on the Apostles (Acts, Chpt. 5).

THE SABBATH DAY

The phrase, *"Because He had done these things on the Sabbath Day,"* presented His Great Crime. In other words, as stated, he had broken one of their little petty rules. What He did was definitely not against the Law of God but against the made-up laws of these Jews.

These people had no desire for God or His True Way. Religion had become a business to them, and they were rewarded amply for their time and trouble. Consequently, they wanted nothing to hinder their occupation, which is the way all religion operates.

Inasmuch as it is man-directed and man-led, it cannot leave the defense to God because religion is not of God. Consequently, it must be defended, and is defended even to the point of violence.

What did Jesus actually do?

He healed a man on the Sabbath Day.

How was that wrong?

It was not wrong. There was nothing in the Law of Moses that forbade such but, in fact, everything that encouraged such. During the time of Christ, the Jews had so corrupted the Law by adding to it and changing its meaning that it no longer even resembled what it actually once was.

For instance, during that time, a woman could not even comb her hair on the Sabbath Day simply because there may be a speck of dust in her hair, and if the dust was moved by the brush, this would be conceived as plowing. It is true that the Law of Moses did forbid plowing ground on the Sabbath, as should be obvious, but moving a speck of dust? Come now!

As well, a person on the Sabbath was not even allowed to drag a chair across the floor because, once again, there may be dust on the floor, and it would be moved and, thereby, construed as plowing.

NOTES

Men love religion, and they love to make rules, and they love to force other people to keep those rules.

Jesus totally ignored all of these man-made rules and healed the man, which He did often on the Sabbath Day. However, these religious leaders did not care anything at all about this man. They could not care less about his sickness and what healing would mean to him. Please believe me, it has not changed from then until now. Most so-called religious leaders could not care less about people going to Hell; they only want to make sure that their little rules are kept. So, it hasn't changed from then until now. The only difference is, the law of the land will not allow religious leaders to carry out what is actually in their hearts, which is murder.

(17) "BUT JESUS ANSWERED THEM, MY FATHER WORKS HITHERTO, AND I WORK."

The exposition is:

1. The phrase, *"But Jesus answered them,"* proclaims that this was a face-to-face confrontation. Actually, almost all of the things that Jesus said about the hypocrisy of the Pharisees and religious leaders of Israel were face-to-face confrontations. He said little, if anything, behind their backs that He did not say to their faces. Actually, this would have been extremely upsetting to them, considering that almost always great crowds of people were in attendance and overheard the exchange of remarks.

2. That He would challenge their authority and, in effect, completely ignore it had the tendency, as should be obvious, of throwing extra fuel on the fire.

3. *"My Father worked* (works) *hitherto, and I work,"* proclaims a relationship that the Pharisees denied was possible.

4. Williams said:

"For it declares that neither He nor the Father could find their Sabbath in the midst of the sad fruits of sin (Mal. 2:17). Theirs was a Love incessant in its activities toward fallen and disobedient man, and therefore was He found at the Pool of Bethesda."[4]

5. By Jesus using the word, *"Works,"* concerning His Father and Himself, He was, in effect, saying, among other things, that

both worked on the Sabbath as well as other days, upholding the Universe and directing its infinite mechanism, as well as working in all providence, watching over and caring for all Creation of dependent creatures.

6. So, Christ healing this man on the Sabbath was a continuation of these duties.

7. Consequently, by making this simple statement, Jesus completely abrogated the foolishness of the petty rules made by these religious leaders. However, His Statement would not only not abate their anger, but would actually give them greater grist for their mill, as we shall see.

(18) "THEREFORE THE JEWS SOUGHT THE MORE TO KILL HIM, BECAUSE HE NOT ONLY HAD BROKEN THE SABBATH, BUT SAID ALSO THAT GOD WAS HIS FATHER, MAKING HIMSELF EQUAL WITH GOD."

The structure is:

1. There is only one way the Believer can walk in perpetual victory, and that is by placing one's Faith exclusively in Christ and what He did for us at the Cross.

2. While the Bible does not teach sinless perfection, it most definitely does teach that sin is not to have dominion over us (Rom. 6:14).

3. Dominion is a strong word, meaning *"to lord over."* This is the power of Satan. The only Power stronger than that is the Power of God. It is made available to us through Who Jesus is and What Jesus did, namely the Cross.

GOD MANIFEST IN THE FLESH

The phrase, *"Therefore the Jews sought the more to kill Him,"* means that He not only did not seek any type of accommodations with these hypocrites, but rather reinforced His Position to such an extent that no one had absolutely any doubt as to what He was saying or doing.

"Because He not only had broken the Sabbath," which He actually did not, proclaims, as stated, their first charge against Him.

"But said also that God was His Father, making Himself equal with God," was a charge not disclaimed by Jesus because He did make Himself equal with God, and rightly so!

On the contrary, in Words of lofty solemnity, He affirmed it. He claimed absolute equality with God the Father; He declared that He did the same things and in the same manner; and He willed as the Father willed.

He asserted the Personal distinctions in the Godhead, their Unity of nature and Oneness of interest and action, as well as Essence of being. He claimed that He Himself was God, for He raised the dead, even as we shall see in Verse 21 of this Chapter, and imparted life to whomsoever He willed. He said that all Judgment and administration rested in His Hands, and that all men should worship Him as God.

He announced that He gave Eternal Life to whomever believed on Him as sent by God, as seen in Verse 24, and that the eternal destiny of all men should be decided by Him (Jn. 5:28-29). That being the case, if they would not receive Him as Light-giver, they would be rejected by Him as Doom-utterer.

DEITY

Of course, the proclamations of Jesus concerning Who He was proclaimed in no uncertain terms His Messiahship. Concerning the statements given in the balance of this Chapter, there was absolutely no doubt as to what He was saying, with every evidence that the religious leaders and Pharisees understood Him perfectly.

So, it was not a lack of understanding respecting Who He was, but a flat-out denial of His Claims, which ultimately destroyed the Jewish Nation.

Actually, His Action of claiming Deity for Himself was not uncommon in the First Century. The Roman emperors claimed to be divine and required their subjects to worship them. Other officials (Herod, for example) deified themselves; consequently, the Herodians actually claimed Herod as the Messiah.

However, because of the great number claiming deity, the secular historians of the First Century took little notice of Jesus of Nazareth. Therefore, other than Josephus, little was said concerning His Place and Position because of the reasons stated.

JESUS OF NAZARETH

As we have stated, it was a common

practice in the Roman world to deify rulers. However, Jesus of Nazareth must have been something more than a mere man, and His Followers must have been convinced of that fact, for they willingly suffered a horrible martyrdom for their Testimony of His Deity. Thousands upon thousands of people do not go to a violent death for something they know to be a fraud. There is only one way one can explain the willing acceptance of Jesus of Nazareth as Saviour by a sin-loving pagan, who accepted with Him what he formerly hated, namely Righteousness. By acceptance, he forsook the sin he loved, knowing that by so doing, he would become liable to capital punishment for his act. That explanation is on the basis of a supernatural working in his heart, providing for the willing acceptance of what he formerly hated, Righteousness.

Jesus of Nazareth, therefore, stands as history's outstanding enigma unless He is accorded the place which the Bible gives Him, Very God of Very God. One cannot explain Him without this fact of His Deity. One can dismiss Him with an, *"I do not believe that,"* but that does not solve the problem or block Him from the pages of history. He stands there, astride the world of mankind, a Unique Individual, God and Man in One Person.

FAKE LUMINARIES

Muhammad never claimed deity for himself. He called himself a prophet. While Islam claims over 1 billion followers, one cannot use this to argue that this religion is of Divine origin. When one examines the sources of its growth, one discovers that they were all natural.

This religion of Islam was first spread by force of arms.

The religion of Islam requires no regeneration. Its worship consists of external rites. The conscience is not touched. The person is allowed to go on in his sin, just as long as he observes certain outward rules. Man is incurably religious. Actually, he demands the exercises of religion, which Islam satisfies.

The chief reason for the outstanding success of Islam is that it is a religion that gives people what they want, their sin, and which caters to their evil natures. However, as stated, with all of this, Muhammad never claimed deity for himself.

BUDDHISM

Likewise, the founder of Buddhism, Gautama, an Indian Prince who lived about 550 B.C., instigated this religion. He had become dissatisfied with the gross sensuality of the Hinduism surrounding him, and withdrew from the world to mystical contemplation in an endeavor to escape from the pain and sorrow of life.

He formulated eight ways of deliverance:

1. Right belief — belief in the doctrines he taught.
2. Right feelings — namely, absence of all feelings toward anyone and anything.
3. Right speech — not to lie so as to be found out.
4. Right actions — negative rules of restraint of one's passions.
5. Right means of livelihood — getting one's living by means of begging.
6. Right endeavor — mental labor only.
7. Right memory — thought about Buddha's doctrines.
8. Right meditation — putting one's mind in a trance in order to communicate with Buddha, or the annihilation of thought.

Instead of this being a way of Salvation, as is obvious, it is only a degrading and pessimistic laziness. The success of Buddhism is found in the fact that it presented a way of escape from the cares of life through the opium of annihilation of all desire.

However, as with Muhammad, its founder, Gautama, never claimed deity for himself.

CONFUCIANISM

As well, Confucius, the founder of the system of belief that bears his name, never claimed deity. Confucius saw the breakdown of morality in China and started out to counteract it by gathering together, studying, and teaching the wisdom of the past to all who would listen to him.

The enormous success of his ethical system is seen in the fact that the Confucian Classics were the basis of all instruction of the young in the schools of China. In addition to that, all preferment in government positions was dependent upon a knowledge of the teachings of Confucius. However, this Chinese sage never claimed deity for himself.

Of course, as already stated, scores of others did claim deity, but not the founders of the major religions of the world.

ONLY JESUS

Jesus of Nazareth stands alone among all the founders of the great religions in asserting that He was God and in accepting the worship of individuals.

When Jesus faced Satan in the 40 days and 40 nights of fasting and testing, He was put to the test and solicited to do evil by the Devil. Exhausted, emaciated, and famished, He was the target of the final assault by Satan, who says in his first temptation, *"In view of the fact that You are the Son of God by nature, command that these stones become loaves of bread"* (Mat. 4:3).

There was no *"if you be"* in the Devil's theology. It was not an unfulfilled, future, hypothetical condition with him. It was not that Satan was not sure whether Jesus of Nazareth was the Son of God. The Greek has the conditional particle of a fulfilled condition. In other words, the Devil knew that Jesus of Nazareth was the Son of God by nature.

That is, he subscribed to the doctrine which teaches that Jesus is Very God of Very God, proceeding by eternal generation from God the Father. As well, Jesus of Nazareth did not deny that fact. He is the only Person Who ever lived a sinless life on Earth, against Whom no one has ever successfully pointed an accusing finger, and would have acted a monstrous lie if He was not God. He accepted the title because the title rightly belonged to Him because He rightly was and is God.

THE JEWS AND JESUS

In this very Passage in John 5:18, the Jews who opposed Jesus were the Jewish religious leaders, who were well educated and learned in the Old Testament Scriptures. They had heard that Jesus claimed that God was *"His"* Father.

However, in our understanding the Text

NOTES

as it is given in the English translation, the pronoun *"His"* does not bring out the full force of the Greek. Actually, the word in the Greek is *"idios,"* which means *"one's own private, unique individual possession."* That is, Jesus claimed to own God as His Father in a way different from the way in which Believers have God as our Father.

His relationship to God as His Son was different, uniquely different, from that relationship sustained by every other person who claims sonship.

These astute theologians saw clearly that in making this claim, Jesus was making Himself equal with God, and any person equal with God must be God.

THE DIFFERENCE IN BELIEVERS AND HIMSELF

On another occasion, Jesus differentiated between the sonship of Believers and that of Himself. He said to Mary, *"Go to My Brethren, and say to them, I ascend unto My Father, and your Father, and to My God, and your God"* (Jn. 20:17).

In other words, even though He stated that God was the Father of all Believers, still, He was not, as He was to Jesus, the Father's Only Son.

As theologians, these Jewish religious leaders were well acquainted with the implications of Jesus' Words. They rejected Him and His Claims because of sin in their lives and by reason of their entrenched ecclesiasticism, which would allow no interference with its position. It would be well to remember that the Testimony to the effect that Jesus claimed Deity for Himself did not come from His Followers but from the ranks of the opposition.

The opposition of the Jewish theologians put Jesus on the defensive, and He found it necessary time and again to assert His Deity.

He said on another occasion, *"Your father Abraham rejoiced to see My Day: and he saw it, and was glad."*

Then the Jews said to Him, *"You are not yet fifty years old, and have You seen Abraham?"*

Jesus said to them, *"Verily, verily, I say to you, Before Abraham came into existence, I am"* (Jn. 8:56-58).

ETERNAL EXISTENCE

Jesus used the verb which speaks of coming into existence when speaking of Abraham, but when alluding to Himself, He used the verb of being, and in this instance, in such a way that it is clear that He is speaking of eternal existence.

The Jews understood it to do so, for the record continues, *"Then they took up stones to cast at Him."* Jesus here reminded His Jewish Heroes of the time when Moses asked Jehovah of the Old Testament what answer he should give Israel when they asked him the Name of God Who sent him, and God's answer was, *"I AM THAT I AM"* (Ex. 3:14).

Consequently, Jesus claimed to be the *"I AM THAT I AM"* of the Old Testament, the God of the Jews, the self-existent One.

JESUS STANDS ALONE

Thus, Jesus of Nazareth stands alone among all the founders of the great religions of the world in claiming Deity for Himself. Unless we accept His Claim as true, He becomes the greatest enigma of history.

There He stands — Jesus of Nazareth, astride the ages, a figure in history with Whom one must reckon. He cannot be ignored by any thinking person. He is either accepted or rejected.

Paul, in his address to the Athenian Greeks, spoke of Jesus of Nazareth as the Man Whom God will use to judge the world. Here are his words:

"He has appointed a day, in the which He will judge the world in Righteousness by that Man Whom He has ordained; whereof He has given assurance unto all men, in that He has raised Him from the dead" (Acts 17:31).

Jesus of Nazareth offers to become the Saviour of any and all who will believe Him as such. However, rejected as Saviour, He then becomes the Judge when that great time does come about.

So, one must accept Jesus as Who He said He was, *"Very God of Very God,"* or brand Him as the greatest imposter of all the ages. One cannot have it both ways. He either is or isn't! If He is, the course is clear. If He isn't, then His Appalling Claims are the most preposterous in all of history, paling into insignificance all fake luminaries. So, one had better consider this very, very carefully!

The truth is, Jesus is exactly Who and What He said He was and is. He is God, and as such, the truth is absolutely incontrovertible.

(The notes on the Deity of Christ were derived from the teaching of Greek scholar, Kenneth Wuest.)[5]

(19) "THEN ANSWERED JESUS AND SAID UNTO THEM, VERILY, VERILY, I SAY UNTO YOU, THE SON CAN DO NOTHING OF HIMSELF, BUT WHAT HE SEES THE FATHER DO: FOR WHAT THINGS SOEVER HE DOES, THESE ALSO DO THE SON LIKEWISE."

The exegesis is:

1. Unless one preaches the Cross, then one is preaching another Jesus (II Cor. 11:4).

2. This *"other Jesus"* might look good, might sound good, and might seem good to the carnal mind, but if it's not *"Jesus Christ and Him Crucified,"* then it's not the Jesus of the Bible (I Cor. 1:23; 2:2).

3. The entirety of the Old Testament proclaims Christ and the Cross. In fact, that is the emphasis of the entirety of the Bible.

IN POWER AND WORKS

The phrase, *"Then answered Jesus and said unto them,"* proclaims Him not only claiming equality with God in nature, as He did in Verse 17, but, as well, in Power and Works.

"Verily, verily, I say unto you, The Son can do nothing of Himself," proclaims the Humanity of Christ, with Him freely giving up the expression of His Deity while never losing its possession.

There are not two Gods, but One God manifested in the flesh; for there could not be two Beings both Supreme and both Omnipotent as it regards the Incarnation. This means that Jesus Christ, while never ceasing to be God, never functioned as God in His Earthly Sojourn. Every Miracle He performed was done by the Power of the Holy Spirit and was the Will of the Father. In fact, Jesus did nothing apart from the Father, either in action or in teaching (Jn. 14:10).

THE FATHER

"But what He sees the Father do," proclaims His Total Subservience to the Father, but yet, even though lacking expression by choice, never lacking possession. We speak of Deity and equality with the Father, which He expressed by the proclamation of His Unique Relationship with the Father in Verse 17.

WHAT HE SEES THE FATHER DO

"For what things soever He does, these also do the Son likewise," proclaims, as stated, His Subservience to the Father, for the very purpose of setting an example of humility and dependence, which the human family seriously lacked.

His Incarnation was all done for man, even sinful man, and not for Himself. He came as the Second Man and, therefore, the Last Adam in order to purchase back by His Perfect Obedience that which the first Adam ingloriously lost by disobedience.

Actually, even though these statements are very brief as given by Christ, they lay the foundation for all that man is to be and can be in Christ. It is defined actually in *"obedience or disobedience."* It is that simple!

As stated, this is the area where Satan attacked Jesus so vehemently. Satan desired that Jesus step out of the Will of God and use His Great Power to provide for Himself, which, on the surface, seemed to be logical and even desirable. However, it was not logical or desirable in that the Will of the Father would have been abrogated. He sought only to do the Will of God, which He must do in order that He would serve as the Perfect Example, which He did!

We are to follow suit in earnestly seeking and desiring that Perfect Will, and God's Will only! As the *"Son did likewise,"* the Believer is to likewise follow.

(20) "FOR THE FATHER LOVES THE SON, AND SHOWS HIM ALL THINGS THAT HIMSELF DOES: AND HE WILL SHOW HIM GREATER WORKS THAN THESE, THAT YOU MAY MARVEL."

The form is:

1. The phrase, *"For the Father loves the Son,"* proclaims several great Truths:

a. The obedience of the Son is based on the love the Father has for the Son. Consequently, He knows that all things asked of Him will be that which is right.

b. Anything that is not based on *"love,"* of necessity, must be based on works, which are unacceptable to God. Whereas works can show approval, that is, if the works are satisfactorily done, by their very nature, they cannot show love.

2. So, in this Passage, the Lord is telling us that He now deals with us in Love and Grace, which demands only Faith, whereas Law demanded performance, in which man always failed. However, this Covenant of Love cannot fail because it is guaranteed in Jesus Alone as both God and Man.

3. *"And shows Him all things that He does Himself,"* plainly says that everything Jesus is doing, even the healing of the cripple on the Sabbath, is that which the Father has shown Him to do. Consequently, He has not done these things on His Own but on the stipulation of His Father. As a result, when these religious leaders criticized Him, they were actually criticizing the very One Whom they pretended to serve, the Jehovah of the Old Testament.

So, if these men were looking for ammunition regarding their accusations, Jesus has given them more than enough.

"And He will show Him greater works than these, that you may marvel," has to do with Verses 28 and 29, which speak of the coming Resurrection.

In other words, if they marveled at what He was presently doing, then they would truly have something in which to marvel at the time of the coming Resurrection.

(21) "FOR AS THE FATHER RAISES UP THE DEAD, AND QUICKENS THEM; EVEN SO THE SON QUICKENS WHOM HE WILL."

The pattern is:

1. The Holy Spirit works exclusively by and through the Cross of Christ (Rom. 8:2).

2. To have His Help, our Faith must be exclusively in Christ and the Cross (I Cor. 1:18; Rom. 8:2).

3. The Cross of Christ is the only harbor, the only place of safety (I Cor. 1:17).

THE RESURRECTION

As Jesus claimed equality with God in nature and relationship (Jn. 5:17), and equality with God in Power and Works (Jn. 5:19-20), likewise, He now claimed equality with God in Resurrection Power.

The phrase, *"For as the Father raises up the dead, and quickens* (makes alive) *them,"* proclaims as a fact the Truth of the coming Resurrection of Life.

The Sadducees, the party which basically controlled the High Priesthood of Israel at that time, did not believe in a coming Resurrection, whereas the Pharisees, who were now contesting Christ and His Claims, did believe in a Resurrection. However, His Answer would infuriate them even further.

JESUS AND RESURRECTION POWER

The phrase, *"Even so the Son quickens* (makes alive) *whom He will,"* claimed, as the Father, Resurrection Power. So, Jesus was telling the Pharisees that the Doctrine of the Resurrection, in which they professed to believe, was actually embodied totally within Himself. However, He left them without recourse.

By using the word, *"Quickens,"* as it was used, He made the claim that every single person He healed, which included the man healed on the Sabbath, proclaimed the actual use of this Resurrection Power. In other words, the same Power that healed these individuals would also raise the dead. Actually, it is Resurrection Power in the heart and life of the Believer, all made possible by the Cross and our Faith in that Finished Work, that gives us the wherewithal to overcome the world (Rom. 8:11). So, one might say, and be absolutely correct, that the same Power that raised Jesus from the dead is that which gives us victory over the world, the flesh, and the Devil.

So, the Pharisees and religious leaders stood speechless because they could not refute what He was saying due to the obvious healing of the man who had been a cripple for 38 years.

As well, the word, *"Quickens,"* as used here, refers not only to physical Healing but, as well, and as stated, to spiritual and moral healing also!

It actually means that as the Lord will *"make alive"* the Sainted dead bodies at the Resurrection, reunited in a Glorified State with the soul and spirit, He, likewise, *"makes alive"* the Spiritual Life of man, who is dead in trespasses and sins.

So, if His Detractors were flabbergasted at His Previous Statements, they must have been even more appalled by this one.

A NATIONALISTIC SALVATION?

The Jews had come to believe in a nationalistic salvation. In other words, if one was born a Jew and, therefore, a Child of Abraham, he was a good Jew, which meant the keeping of all the myriad man-made laws, and this constituted Salvation. In this short, simple statement, Jesus completely refuted this error by actually claiming that He is the Saviour, and is Alone the Saviour.

As well, and even more succinctly, the phrase, *"Whom He will,"* portrays the truth that Salvation is not of him who wills (in the sense of willing Salvation by works, etc.), but of God Who shows Mercy.

The persons whom the Son wills to save are those in Verse 24 who believe the Father's Testimony concerning Jesus. At once, because they simply believe apart from works, these become possessors of a life that is eternal, and are assured that they shall never come into Judgment.

(22) "FOR THE FATHER JUDGES NO MAN, BUT HAS COMMITTED ALL JUDGMENT UNTO THE SON."

The structure is:

1. The phrase, *"For the Father judges no man,"* proclaims to these antagonists the very opposite of that which they were claiming.

They were claiming to serve God and carrying out His Will in opposing Jesus, Whom they branded as a fraud.

"But has committed all Judgment unto the Son," in effect, has Jesus saying, *"You answer to Me!"*

2. As we have previously stated, these men were theologians, that is, they claimed to be expert in the Scriptures. As such, they understood perfectly what He was saying. With Him making claims of such

magnitude, if He was not what He said He was, His Claims had to be the most preposterous in history.

3. He not only claimed Deity, but He also claimed all the attributes of Deity, which they understood and attributed only to Jehovah. As well, His Explanations and Statements were so involved and so detailed that it was literally impossible for one to have such knowledge and to say such things without being Who He claimed to be.

4. The conclusion of this Chapter, which concludes this face-down, so to speak, does not give their response, if any. More than likely, they were so nonplussed at what they had heard that it left them speechless. As well, and as stated, in effect, He was saying that His Healings and Performance of Miracles were proof positive of His Claims. So, as the Healings and Miracles were irrefutable, such made His Claims irrefutable as well!

5. As we have stated, Jesus Christ is the Saviour of mankind; however, if men refuse Him as Saviour, they will face Him as Judge.

As such, it will not then be with Grace, because Grace has been refused, but by Law, with its penalty being exacted in totality. It's called, *"The Great White Throne Judgment"* (Rev. 20:11-15).

The curse of the broken Law is death, but Jesus took that curse upon Himself. However, if His Payment for our sins is rejected, the penalty of the curse must be exacted (Gal. 3:13).

(23) "THAT ALL MEN SHOULD HONOUR THE SON, EVEN AS THEY HONOUR THE FATHER. HE WHO HONOURS NOT THE SON HONOURS NOT THE FATHER WHICH HAS SENT HIM."

The diagram is:

1. The phrase, *"That all men should honour the Son, even as they honour the Father,"* claims equality with God regarding honor (Heb. 2:7-9).

Actually, this statement by Christ proclaims the intersection of all humanity. Much of the world believes there is a God, but there the agreement ends.

2. Concerning Jesus Christ, His Very Name arouses either love or hate, but rarely indifference. While the Jews rejected His Claims, likewise, most of the balance of the world does as well.

All Muslims reject Him, numbering somewhat over a billion people; likewise, the Shintoists, Hindus, Buddhists, Mormons, Judaizers, Confucianists, and humanists. To be frank, with the deification of Mary, the Catholics must be construed as following suit.

BOTH OR NONE

"He who honours not the Son honours not the Father which has sent Him," proclaims in no uncertain terms that if the Son is dishonored, the Father is dishonored as well! So, this means that the Muslims are not really praying to God when they dishonor the Son, which they do. It, as well, tells us that the Catholics are dishonoring the Father when they dishonor Jesus by pushing Him aside in favor of Mary, which is totally unscriptural.

While the Catholics and many others claim that they honor Jesus, in truth, it is a type of honor which God will not accept. He must be honored in the manner in *"which God has sent Him,"* i.e., the Saviour and Redeemer of all mankind.

He who refuses to worship Jesus as God, as well, refuses to worship God.

(24) "VERILY, VERILY, I SAY UNTO YOU, HE WHO HEARS MY WORD, AND BELIEVES ON HIM WHO SENT ME, HAS EVERLASTING LIFE, AND SHALL NOT COME INTO CONDEMNATION; BUT IS PASSED FROM DEATH UNTO LIFE."

The overview is:

1. If the Cross of Christ is repudiated, then the Jesus we are serving will not be the Jesus of the Bible but a Jesus of our own making (II Cor. 11:4).

2. To be sure, if that be the case, it is a Jesus that God will never recognize.

3. There is only one answer for the world, and that is the Cross. Jesus said:

"And I, if I be lifted up from the Earth, will draw all men unto Me."

"This He said, signifying what death He should die" (Jn. 12:32-33).

THE WORDS OF CHRIST

The phrase, *"Verily, verily, I say unto you,"* proclaims the high ground of authority on which Jesus stands. This is an authority which proceeds from the Father and has been given unto the Son.

In effect, it says that this authority cannot be yielded to the religious hierarchy of Israel, who actually demanded such, or to anyone else, for that matter, be it person, government, or philosophy. His Word constitutes the First Word and the Last Word (Jn. 1:1-3).

In a sense, every God-Called man or woman falls into the same category. While the younger Preacher in the local church surely must submit himself to the principle Pastor of that congregation (I Pet. 5:5), no other submission is allowed. As well, if the senior pastor is unscriptural in policy or decision, this would negate any submission by the younger, as well, because the Word of God is always the final authority because it is the written form of the Living Word, the Lord Jesus Christ (Jn. 1:1). However, should such be the case, the younger Preacher must still recognize the fact that this particular local church is not his but continues under the authority of the senior pastor, right or wrong. As such, at least in most cases, the younger Pastor should quietly resign, leaving the matter up to the Lord as the Head of the Church, and seek the Will of God regarding Ministry elsewhere.

HEARING THE WORD

The phrase, *"He who hears My Word,"* proclaims Jesus Christ, as stated, as the Living Word, which, in effect, is the same as the Written Word. So, Jesus not only claimed Deity respecting these Pharisees and most religious leaders but, as well, claimed that all of the Old Testament, which they claimed to follow but actually did not, was, in truth, His Very Own Word.

So, He was telling them that not only is the Bible His Word, but, as well, all of these added rules and regulations devised out of their own wicked hearts were not His Word and in no way could be honored. In effect, He declared war on their false way by laying down the gauntlet of truth. Consequently, they were now faced with a dilemma.

They must accept Him as the Messiah or kill Him!

NOTES

FAITH IN THE FATHER

The phrase, *"And believes on Him Who sent Me,"* turns the tables on these religious leaders, telling them, in essence, that if they did not believe in Him, they, as well, did not believe in the Father, Whom they so grandly claimed to believe.

"Has Everlasting Life," says several things:
- The Believer in Christ has Eternal Life, which means Life without end.
- He has this Eternal Life the moment he believes Christ.
- This Eternal Life comes from the Father through Jesus.
- It cannot be obtained any other way. In fact, every single effort pertaining to other directions is automatically condemned, with the individuals concluded as *"thieves and robbers"* (Jn. 10:1).

NO CONDEMNATION

"And shall not come into condemnation," refers to Judgment.

Judgment being completed does not require repetition. The idea is this:

Jesus suffered the condemnation and Judgment that we should have suffered. He did so on Calvary's Cross, taking the punishment that should have come to us. He did so fully and completely, actually, even being *"smitten of God,"* which was the blow we should have received (Isa. 53:4).

Upon Faith in what Jesus did at Calvary and the Resurrection, Judgment for the Believer's sins can never come upon the Believer because Jesus has already taken that Judgment in our place. Once again, it is the Doctrine of Substitution and Identification. He became my Substitute and I identify with Him; consequently, I am allowed to go free.

PASSED FROM DEATH UNTO LIFE

"But is passed from death unto Life," proclaims the Born-Again experience.

The type of *"death"* spoken of here refers to spiritual death or separation from God, which is brought about by man's sinful and wicked condition. Upon Faith in Christ, the believing sinner is imparted the Divine Nature, which infuses *"Life"* into him, which he heretofore had not possessed. In fact, the sinner is dead in trespasses and sins, but upon Faith in God, he passes from that death to *"Life."*

This is what makes Christianity so superior to any religion or philosophy in the world. All other things merely deal with externals, which, if anything at all, merely treat the symptoms, etc. Conversely, Christ changes the heart of man, which, in reality, is the seat of all problems. He does it by this Miracle Work of Redemption, which first sanctifies the individual (makes one clean) and then justifies him, which is a legal work, thereby, declaring the person righteous. As we have repeatedly stated, all of this is done upon simple Faith in Christ (I Cor. 6:11).

The *"passing from death unto Life"* is not a process over a period of time but is actually done instantaneously upon Faith exercised in Christ by the believing sinner (Jn. 3:16).

(25) "VERILY, VERILY, I SAY UNTO YOU, THE HOUR IS COMING, AND NOW IS, WHEN THE DEAD SHALL HEAR THE VOICE OF THE SON OF GOD: AND THEY WHO HEAR SHALL LIVE."

The overview is:

1. The phrase, *"Verily, verily, I say unto you,"* once again signifies a statement of the highest authority and proclaims Jesus as that Authority.

2. *"The hour is coming, and now is, when the dead shall hear the Voice of the Son of God,"* actually has a threefold meaning:

a. It refers to those who are spiritually dead, but who hear the *"Voice of the Son of God,"* demanding Repentance, with the offer of Eternal Life. They hear it and receive it. Such has transformed the lives of untold millions.

b. As well, all those who were then in Paradise, which included all Believers from the very dawn of time unto the time of the Cross, would hear the Voice of Christ and would be delivered from that place.

c. In addition, it refers to the coming Resurrection (Jn. 5:28-29), where those who are in Christ will be raised incorruptible because they have passed from death to Life.

3. The phrase, *"And they who hear shall live,"* actually means that all Believers definitely will *"hear"* because they are Believers.

(26) "FOR AS THE FATHER HAS LIFE IN HIMSELF; SO HAS HE GIVEN TO THE SON TO HAVE LIFE IN HIMSELF."

The exegesis is:

1. The phrase, *"For as the Father has Life in Himself,"* refers to God as the Eternal Fountain of Life, the Source Ultimate. As well, it speaks of something that always has been and always shall be.

2. *"So has He given to the Son to have Life in Himself,"* probably would have been better translated, *"So has He given to the Son of God to have Life in Himself."* As such, this declares more fully than any other Passage in the New Testament the lofty and unique character of the Sonship which He claimed. This has to do with the Incarnation, God becoming Man. As God, He always had that Life, but now as Man, He also is the Source of Life.

3. Jesus is saying that He is not merely a participator in this *"Life,"* but, in fact, is the Source of Life and, in truth, the Ultimate Source, exactly as the Father.

4. The idea is that even though Jesus emptied Himself respecting the Incarnation (God becoming Man), He still continued to be both the Son of God and Son of Man. As such, the Father, even in Jesus' Lessened Incarnate State, endowed Him with all functions of both. He did not lose the infinite fullness of Life-giving Power or the fullness of being the Ultimate Source of Life.

5. As such, He *"quickens* (makes alive) *whom He will,"* having Life in Himself (Jn. 5:21).

(27) "AND HAS GIVEN HIM AUTHORITY TO EXECUTE JUDGMENT ALSO, BECAUSE HE IS THE SON OF MAN."

The exposition is:

1. Christ does not deal with us on the basis of good or evil on our part.

2. In the first place, we do not have any good that He will recognize. Secondly, if He rejected us because of evil, He would accept no one.

3. He deals with us strictly on the basis of Faith in Christ and what Christ has done for us at the Cross (Rom. 5:1-2; 6:1-14; Eph. 2:8-9, 13-18; Gal. 5:6).

AUTHORITY

The phrase, *"And has given Him Authority to execute Judgment also,"* refers to the following:

• As the Son of God, He saves and imparts Life.

• As Son of Man, He exercises and executes Judgment. He does this on the basis of the price He paid, or would pay, on Calvary's Cross.

This has to do with all Judgment, whether the coming *"Judgment Seat of Christ,"* which pertains to Believers only (Rom. 14:10), or the *"Great White Throne Judgment,"* which will take place at the conclusion of the Kingdom Age (Rev. 20:11-15).

"Because He is the Son of Man," refers to Christ, as stated, paying the price on Calvary's Cross, and by the merit of such, He will also be the *"Judge."*

In effect, Jesus is telling the religious leaders of Israel, as well as all others, that this One Whom they think is merely a Peasant, is, in reality, the Son of God even though He is also the Son of Man. As well, irrespective of what they think of Him, they will accept Him as Saviour or face Him as Judge.

Jesus would face these same men again at His Trial, and in their questioning of Him, He said, *"Hereafter shall the Son of Man sit on the Right Hand of the Power of God"* (Lk. 22:69).

In effect, He was saying, *"Here you are judging Me, but in a coming day, at the Great White Throne Judgment, I will judge you!"*

RIVALRY?

We must be careful in this inference that we avoid all suspicion of schism or rivalry between the Father and the Son. The Son is not more merciful than the Father, for the Father of the Old Testament pities His Children and knows their frame (Ps. 103:13-14), and the Father of Jesus Christ loves the world and counts the very hairs of our heads.

To be sure, the Son will not exercise this Judgment with less regard to the claims of eternal justice than the Father; His Knowledge of humanity is, by the nature of the case, a guarantee of such application of the Justice of God to the case of every individual.

The fact of it is the ground that He Who knows what is in man should be the Judge of man.

By personal experience of man's temptations and frailties; by knowing every aggravation of our sins, every extenuation of our failures, every aggravation of our weakness; by gazing through human eyes with human consciousness upon our mysterious destiny, He is Competent to judge; whereas by being Son of God as well as Son of Man, He is entrusted with Power to execute the Judgment of the eternal. The principle involved is based upon perfect justice (Reynolds).[6]

While the Father can do such through Omnipotence (all-power) and Omniscience (all-knowing, past, present, and future), He cannot, as Christ, do such through experience, hence, the Incarnation and the granting of these privileges to Christ by the Heavenly Father.

(28) "MARVEL NOT AT THIS: FOR THE HOUR IS COMING, IN THE WHICH ALL WHO ARE IN THE GRAVES SHALL HEAR HIS VOICE."

The construction is:

1. In our statements made, it is not meant to imply that the Christian can exercise Faith and continue in evil. In Paul's words, *"God forbid."* The Lord doesn't save us in sin, but rather *"from sin"* (Rom. 6:13-14).

2. The Way of Faith, and we are speaking of Faith in Christ and His Sacrificial Offering of Himself, is the Way to Victory, and the only Way.

3. John wondrously said, *"This is the victory that overcomes the world, even our Faith"* (I Jn. 5:4).

MARVEL!

The phrase, *"Marvel,"* means that the religious leaders of Israel were marveling greatly at the things they were hearing, which seems to have left them speechless.

As one reads these statements, one must come to the conclusion, as we have stated, that no mere mortal could have made such statements. Such would have been impossible! The details given regarding knowledge of the Father and the authority delegated to the Son, as well as that which the Son is delegated to do, could have come from the lips of none other than the Son of God. Man, at his brightest and most intellectual, could not have even remotely made such statements with any degree of comprehension. However, when one hears these words as they come from Jesus, one knows that He knows exactly what He is saying and understands perfectly what it all means. Such astounding statements are made, respecting Eternal Life and the Resurrection, that no man, irrespective of his bravado, would have dared say such or would have known to have said such, even if so desired.

THE MOST COMPLEX SUBJECTS

There is no way that these religious leaders could misunderstand what was being said, and neither could they honestly ascribe such to an imposter or deceiver. The strict Spiritual Intelligence is so far beyond mortal comprehension that it defies description. As well, the most complex subjects, in fact, the most complex of all, are reduced to amazing simplicity, which, within itself, is absolutely beyond the pale of mere human endeavor.

"For the hour is coming, in the which all who are in the graves shall hear His Voice," speaks, as the next Verse portrays, of all people, both righteous and unrighteous. Consequently, we are speaking of Power of such magnitude that it is beyond human comprehension. So, if these religious leaders of Israel were nonplussed over Jesus making Himself equal with the Father (Jn. 5:18), His Explanation of what all of that means, as the balance of the Chapter portrays, as we have stated several times, must have left them absolutely beyond words.

(29) "AND SHALL COME FORTH; THEY WHO HAVE DONE GOOD, UNTO THE RESURRECTION OF LIFE; AND THEY WHO HAVE DONE EVIL, UNTO THE RESURRECTION OF DAMNATION."

TWO RESURRECTIONS

The phrase, *"And shall come forth,"* portrays both Resurrections, as we shall see, and according to *"His Voice!"*

"They who have done good, unto the Resurrection of Life," pertains to the First Resurrection, or as commonly referred, *"The Rapture"* (I Thess. 4:16-17).

This pertains to every Believer who has ever lived from the time of Abel to the conclusion of the coming Great Tribulation. It is the time when the soul and spirit of the righteous dead will be reunited with the body, but in Glorified Form.

"And they who have done evil, unto the Resurrection of Damnation," pertains to all who are unbelievers, covering the same span of time just mentioned, plus the time of the coming Kingdom Age.

This Last Resurrection will take place approximately a thousand years (the time of the Kingdom Age) after the First Resurrection of Life (Dan. 12:2; Rev., Chpt. 20).

THE EMPHASIS OF THE EARLY CHURCH REGARDING THE RESURRECTION

The most startling characteristic of the first Christian preaching is its emphasis on the Resurrection. The first Preachers were sure that Christ had risen, and sure, in consequence, that Believers would, in due course, rise also.

This set them apart from all the other teachers of the ancient world. There are Resurrections elsewhere, but none of them are like that of Christ. They are mostly mythological tales connected with the change of the season and the annual miracle of spring, etc.

The Gospels tell of an individual Who truly died but overcame death by rising from the dead. That Person is Christ. If it is true that Christ's Resurrection bears no resemblance to anything in paganism, it is also true that the attitude of Believers to their own Resurrection, of which Jesus' Resurrection is an example, is radically different from anything in the heathen world. Nothing is more characteristic of even the best thought of the day than its hopelessness in the face of death. Clearly, the Resurrection is one of the cardinal Doctrines of the Christian Faith.

THE CHRISTIAN RESURRECTION

The Christian idea of Resurrection is to be distinguished from both Greek and Jewish ideas. The Greeks thought of the body as a hindrance to true life, and they looked for the time when the soul would be free from its shackles. They conceived of life after death in terms of the immortality of the soul, but they firmly rejected all ideas of Resurrection (the mockery of Paul's preaching in Acts 17:32).

The Jews were firmly persuaded of the values of the body and thought these would not be lost. Thus, they looked for the body to be raised, but they thought it would be exactly the same body.

The Christians thought of the body as being raised but also transformed so as to be a suitable vehicle for the very different life of the age to come, which would be without end (I Cor. 15:42). Consequently, the Christian teaching is thus distinctive in that it was given by the Holy Spirit to Paul.

THE RESURRECTION OF BELIEVERS

Not only did Jesus rise from the dead, but one day, all men, too, will rise. Jesus refuted the skepticism of the Sadducees on the point with an interesting argument from Scripture (Mat. 22:31-32). The general New Testament position is that the Resurrection of Christ carries with it the Resurrection of all Believers.

Jesus said, *"I am the Resurrection, and the Life: he who believes in Me, though he were dead, yet shall he live"* (Jn. 11:25). This speaks of the coming Resurrection.

Several times He spoke of raising Believers up at the last day (Jn. 6:39-40, 44, 54).

The Sadducees were grieved because the Apostles were *"proclaiming in Jesus the Resurrection from the dead"* (Acts 4:2). Paul tells us that *"As by a man came death, by a Man came also the Resurrection of the dead. For as in Adam all die, even so in Christ shall all be made alive"* (I Cor. 15:21-22; I Thess. 4:14).

Likewise Peter says, *"We have been born anew to a living hope through the Resurrection of Jesus Christ from the dead"* (I Pet. 1:3). It is plain enough that the New Testament writers did not think of Christ's Resurrection as an isolated phenomenon. It was a great Divine Act and one fraught with consequences for men.

Because God raised Christ, He set His Seal on the Atoning Work wrought out on the Cross. In fact, due to the fact that the wages of sin is death, if there had been even one sin left unatoned, Christ could not have been raised from the dead. His being raised from the dead proved beyond the shadow of a doubt that He atoned for all sin.

He demonstrated His Divine Power in the face of sin and death and, at the same time, His Will to save men. Thus, the Resurrection of Believers follows immediately from that of their Saviour. So characteristic of them is the Resurrection that Jesus could speak of them as *"Sons of God, being Sons of the Resurrection"* (Lk. 20:36).

RESURRECTION OF LIFE AND RESURRECTION OF DAMNATION

To which we have already briefly alluded, this does not mean that all who rise, rise to a Blessing. Jesus speaks of two Resurrections, as are outlined in this Twenty-ninth Verse. They are:

1. The Resurrection of Life.
2. The Resurrection of Damnation.

The plain New Testament teaching is that all will rise, but with the Resurrection of Damnation taking place about a thousand years after the Resurrection of Life, when every Believer will then be raised.

The plain New Testament teaching is that all will rise, but that those who have rejected Christ will find the Resurrection a serious matter indeed. For Believers, the fact that their Resurrection is connected with that of the Lord transforms the situation. In the light of the Atoning Work of Christ at Calvary, for Believers, we face Resurrection with calmness and joy (I Thess. 4:13-18).

THE NATURE OF THE RESURRECTED BODY

Of the nature of the Resurrected Body, Scripture says little. Paul can speak of it as *"a Spiritual Body"* (I Cor. 15:44), which appears to mean a body that meets the needs of the Holy Spirit. In fact, whereas the life of the flesh is now in the blood, then it will be in the Holy Spirit. In other words, there is no indication that the Glorified Body, and that's what it will be at the Resurrection, will contain any blood (Lk. 24:39). Yes, it will contain flesh and bones but, no, there will be no blood!

Paul expressly differentiates the Glorified Body from the physical body, which we now have. The *"body"* which we will have will answer to the needs of the Holy Spirit in some respect different from that which we now know. The Glorified Body will have the qualities of incorruptibility, meaning that it will not grow old, and meaning, as well, that it will last forever. It will also have the qualities of Glory and Power (I Cor. 15:42). Our Lord has taught us that there will be no marriage after the Resurrection and, thus, no sexual function (Mk. 12:25).

WE SHALL BE LIKE HIM

Perhaps we can gain some help by thinking of the Resurrection Body of Christ, for John tells us that *"we shall be like Him"* (I Jn. 3:2), and Paul says that *"our lowly body"* is to be *"like His Glorious Body"* (Phil. 3:21).

Our Lord's risen Body appears to have been, in some sense, like the natural body and, in another sense, that which is different. Thus, on some occasions, He was recognized immediately after His Resurrection (Mat. 28:9; Jn. 20:19), but, on other occasions, He was not instantly recognized (notably the walk to Emmaus, Lk. 24:16; Jn., Chpt. 21). He appeared suddenly in the midst of the Disciples, who were gathered with the door shut (Jn. 20:19), while contrariwise, He disappeared from the sight of the two at Emmaus (Lk. 24:31). He spoke of having *"flesh and bones"* (Lk. 24:39), but, as stated, He said nothing about blood.

On occasion, He ate food with His Glorified Body (Lk. 24:41-43), though we cannot hold that physical food is a necessity for life beyond death. In fact, there are indications that it isn't (I Cor. 6:13). It would seem that the Risen Lord could conform to the limitations of this physical life, or otherwise. In other words, it's whatever He chose to do, and this may indicate that when we rise, we shall have a similar Power.

THE DOCTRINAL IMPLICATIONS OF THE RESURRECTION

The Christological significance of the Resurrection is considerable. The fact that Jesus prophesied that He would rise from the dead on the third day has important implications for His Person. One who would do this is greater than the sons of men, as should be obvious. Paul clearly regards the Resurrection of Christ as of cardinal importance, even as he should. *"If Christ has not been raised,"* he says, *"then our preaching is in vain, and your Faith is in vain ... if Christ has not been raised, your Faith is futile and you are still in your sins"* (I Cor. 15:14, 17).

The point is that Christianity is a Gospel. It is Good News about how God sent His Son to be our Saviour, which He accomplished by going to the Cross. While the Resurrection was of tremendous significance, as should be overly obvious, still, Redemption was completed at the Cross, i.e., *"it is finished"* (Jn. 19:30). One might say that the Resurrection ratified that which was done at Calvary. In fact, if even one sin had not been atoned, whether past, present, or future, Jesus could not have risen from the dead. The Scripture plainly says, *"The wages of sin is death"* (Rom. 6:23). Due to the fact that He most definitely was raised from the dead, this means that every sin was atoned, which means that Redemption was complete at Calvary.

However, to look at the other side, if Christ did not really rise from the dead, then we have no assurance that our Salvation has been accomplished. Thus, the reality of the Resurrection of Christ is of deep significance, as should be obvious.

The Resurrection of Believers is also of supreme significance. Paul's view is that if the dead do not rise, and we speak of Believers, we may, as well, adopt the idea, *"Let us eat and drink; for tomorrow we die"* (I Cor. 15:32). Believers are not men for whom this life is all. Our hope lies elsewhere (I Cor. 15:19). This gives us perspective and makes for depth in living.

RAISED FOR OUR JUSTIFICATION

The Resurrection of Christ is connected

with our Salvation, as again ought to be obvious. Paul says, *"Jesus our Lord was put to death for our trespasses* (the Cross) *and raised for our Justification* (His Resurrection — Rom. 8:33)" (Rom. 4:25). But yet, due to the fact that He definitely atoned for all sin, there was no question about His Resurrection.

Some claim that Jesus had to fight demons and Satan himself to come from the dead; however, there is nothing in the Word of God that substantiates such thinking. At the Cross, every principality and power was defeated (Col. 2:14-15). In fact, to be sure, after He died, which means all sin was atoned, neither Satan, fallen Angels, nor demon spirits wanted anything to do with Him. When He went down into Paradise to set those captives free, He met no opposition from Satan whatsoever because Satan was then a defeated foe. In other words, Jesus did not go down into the heart of the Earth during the time of His Death as a victim, but He went as a Conqueror. And yet, we must always understand this Salvation is not something that takes place apart from the Resurrection of Christ. In a sense, they are two parts of one act. However, at the same time, we must always understand that it is the Cross which effects Redemption, and, as stated, Resurrection ratified that great event.

THE POWER OF HIS RESURRECTION

Paul speaks of his desire to know Christ *"and the Power of His Resurrection"* (Phil. 3:10), and he exhorts the Colossians, *"If then you have been raised with Christ, seek the things that are above ... "* (Col. 3:1).

However, that which Paul is speaking of is the *"Newness of Life"* that all Believers have in Christ. We died with Him, we were buried with Him, and we were raised with Him in Newness of Life (Rom. 6:3-5).

The Resurrection of Christ signaled many things for the Believer. Possibly, one could say that the principle factor of the Resurrection has to do with our coming Resurrection when we shall put off this vile body and take on a Glorified Body. But yet, the Resurrection of Christ plays a great part in our everyday life and living, as we've already briefly dealt with. Every Believer has Resurrection Power within our life and living. It means that the same Power that raised Jesus from the dead (Rom. 8:11) also is with us that we may overcome the powers of darkness and live the life that we ought to live. In other words, this Resurrection Power is meant to work in our hearts and lives on a continuous basis, with the culminating effect being the Resurrection when the Trump of God sounds (I Thess. 4:13-18).

Actually, the two words, *"Rapture"* and *"Resurrection,"* mean the same thing. It is just two words for the same event. So, when some say that they don't believe there is such a thing as a Rapture, ask them if they believe in the coming Resurrection. In fact, for a person to be Saved, he has to believe in the coming Resurrection. That being the case, he believes in the Rapture. While we may argue as to the timing of this event, there is no argument as it regards the fact of this event.

(30) "I CAN OF MINE OWN SELF DO NOTHING: AS I HEAR, I JUDGE: AND MY JUDGMENT IS JUST; BECAUSE I SEEK NOT MINE OWN WILL, BUT THE WILL OF THE FATHER WHO HAS SENT ME."

The diagram is:

1. Faith in the Cross creates humility. Faith in ourselves or other things creates self-righteousness.

2. Sadly, most that is preached behind modern pulpits is *"another Gospel,"* which means that the Cross of Christ is ignored (II Cor. 11:4).

3. There is only one Gospel, and that is the Gospel of *"Jesus Christ and Him Crucified"* (I Cor. 1:23).

THE HUMANITY OF CHRIST

The phrase, *"I can of My Own Self do nothing: as I hear, I judge,"* proclaims the Humanity of Christ, but in the realm of perfect humanity, which cannot even be comprehended by the natural mind.

The Judgment He pronounced was that of which He heard in His Ear by the Father (Isa. 50:4).

Consequently, the Judgments that Jesus pronounced on the Scribes and Pharisees, as well as others, including Jerusalem and the world, for that matter, are Revelations of the Father's Mind. As such, they are Judgments that are just, which means they are absolutely free from any selfhood, from any reflex influence, or reaction from men to Himself.

MY JUDGMENT IS JUST

The phrase, *"And My Judgment is just,"* speaks of the perfection of such Judgment simply because the Incarnation is perfect. In a sense, it means that the Manhood of Jesus has not obliterated the Divinity, nor has the Godhead absorbed the Manhood.

"Because I seek not My Own Will, but the Will of the Father Who has sent Me," proclaims the fact that the human consciousness of the Son becomes the basis for the Father's Judgment, which is uttered absolutely and finally through human lips.

What we are attempting to say is that the type of Judgment of which Jesus speaks could not be rendered by the Father in such a manner through any of the Prophets of old, but only through the Lips of the Son of God. The Consciousness of Christ is unique. Neither legend nor imagination, to say nothing of history, has ever transcended it.

This can be done because of the entire conformity of His Will and Himself to the Divine Will. No other human being could ever remotely boast of such total and complete consecration. As stated, it is unique in history.

(31) "IF I BEAR WITNESS OF MYSELF, MY WITNESS IS NOT TRUE."

The overview is:

1. *"Spiritual adultery"* is one placing one's Faith in something, actually, anything other than the Cross of Christ (Rom. 7:1-4).

2. The modern church has not only left the Cross, which is spiritual adultery, but, as well, it is also practicing idolatry. Religion and all of its many forms have become the idol of the modern church.

3. To sin in ignorance portrays a condition of the heart that's not quite right with God. In other words, the *"flesh"* is attempting to take the place of Christ and the Cross.

THE TRUTH

If one reads John 8:14, it would seem as though there is a gross contradiction in that Verse and Verse 31; however, that is not the case.

In John 8:14, Jesus is simply making the claim, and rightly so, that He is telling the Truth concerning the things He has said and done. Anyone would say the same thing, providing they were telling the truth, as Christ certainly was.

However, in John 5:31, even though basically saying the same words, Jesus is speaking of something else entirely.

He has just given a dissertation concerning His Relationship with the Father, Who He is, and that which He is sent to do.

In respect to these claims He has just made, the Law of Moses states that a single witness is not enough, but rather *"at the mouth of two witnesses, or at the mouth of three witnesses, shall the matter be established"* (Deut. 19:15).

So, Jesus is saying, in effect, *"If I Alone bear witness of Myself, My Witness Alone will not stand up in court, without collaboration."*

FOUR WITNESSES

Jesus then proceeded to give four witnesses to what He was saying as verification in the following Verses:

1. John the Baptist
2. The Personal Works of Christ
3. The Father
4. The Scriptures

All that He was saying and doing was fully corroborated by these Witnesses, which the Pharisees and religious leaders of Israel could not deny. In other words, He was saying, *"I am legal, and you know I am legal,"* i.e., *"legal according to the Word of God."*

Whether He made this statement because they were contesting the things He had said, or that He anticipated what they would say, is not clear. However, either way, one can be certain that they would demand proof as to His claims, which He would now provide.

(32) "THERE IS ANOTHER WHO BEARS WITNESS OF ME; AND I KNOW THAT THE WITNESS WHICH HE WITNESSES OF ME IS TRUE."

The exegesis is:

1. The phrase, *"There is another who bears witness of Me,"* speaks of John the Baptist.

2. However, some claim that this was not John, but rather the Father, because Jesus would not receive a Testimony from man. While that part is true, still, Jesus used John as a witness because he was a witness, but He simply did not count him in the mix. Other than John, He would give three more witnesses, satisfying the demands of the Law.

3. *"And I know that the witness which he witnesses of Me is true,"* proclaims that while Jesus knew it to be true, the Pharisees and religious leaders would not accept the witness of John.

(33) "YOU SENT UNTO JOHN, AND HE BEAR WITNESS UNTO THE TRUTH."

The exposition is:

1. The phrase, *"You sent unto John,"* refers to the happenings of John 1:19-27.

2. *"And he did bear witness unto the truth,"* proclaims these things that John told them when they asked if he was the Messiah.

3. He said, *"I am the voice of one crying in the wilderness, Make straight the Way of the Lord, as said the Prophet Isaiah."*

4. He then said, in effect, *"I am not the Messiah, He it is, Who coming after me is preferred before me, Whose shoe's Latchet I am not worthy to unloose"* (Jn. 1:23, 27).

(34) "BUT I RECEIVE NOT TESTIMONY FROM MAN: BUT THESE THINGS I SAY, THAT YOU MIGHT BE SAVED."

The structure is:

1. The phrase, *"But I receive not Testimony from man,"* in effect, says, *"Even though John's Testimony is true, I will not use a Testimony from any man."*

2. In other words, the Testimony that Jesus was about to give is so ironclad as to be irrefutable, at least if one wants to be honest.

3. *"But these things I say, that you might be Saved,"* simply verifies John's Testimony and, as well, his Message demanding Repentance on the part of Israel.

4. In other words, Jesus was telling these men that not only were they in error, but, in fact, they were unsaved, and unless they did exactly what John said, which was to repent, they would be eternally lost! One

NOTES

can well imagine how that was received!

(35) "HE WAS A BURNING AND A SHINING LIGHT: AND YOU WERE WILLING FOR A SEASON TO REJOICE IN HIS LIGHT."

The construction is:

1. The phrase, *"He was a burning and a shining light,"* meant exactly that, but he was not *"The Light."* That *"Light"* was Jesus, and Jesus Alone!

2. *"And you were willing for a season to rejoice in his light,"* refers to John being the first Prophet in the past approximately 400 years, actually since Malachi.

3. In this respect, the Pharisees and religious leaders of Israel were willing for a brief period to listen to him, but when they saw that the major thrust of his Ministry was to introduce Jesus as the Son of God and Lamb of God, they turned away.

(36) "BUT I HAVE GREATER WITNESS THAN THAT OF JOHN: FOR THE WORKS WHICH THE FATHER HAS GIVEN ME TO FINISH, THE SAME WORKS THAT I DO, BEAR WITNESS OF ME, THAT THE FATHER HAS SENT ME."

The synopsis is:

1. The phrase, *"But I have greater witness than that of John,"* does not in any way demean the witness of John, for if the religious leaders had accepted it, they would have admitted the Divine Authority of One Who was *"Mightier"* than John. Respecting John, the record shows that Jesus made a similar appeal to the conscience of his critics on a later occasion (Mat. 21:25). However, the witness He would now give was even greater.

2. *"For the works which the Father has given Me to finish, the same works that I do,"* had to do with His Miracles, the Words of Life that He preached, which, as well, imparted Life, along with what He would do at Calvary and the Resurrection.

3. If one is to notice, even the worst haters of Christ did not question His Miracles. It was obvious that they were authentic, and it was obvious as to the Power it took to bring about these miraculous things.

4. As well, when He spoke, even His harshest Critics said, *"Never man spoke like this Man"* (Jn. 7:46).

5. Even though these critics may have denied the veracity of Calvary, there was no way they could deny the Power of the Resurrection, that is, if they would be honest with themselves.

6. So, the *"works"* were abundant and were obvious proof as a witness as to Who He said He was.

7. *"Bear witness of Me, that the Father has sent Me,"* proclaims that only the Power of God could bring about such miraculous works and results.

8. The Miracles of Jesus, as Miracles, were not, within themselves, conclusive of His Claim to Deity. However, the manner in which He performed them and the nature of them, as predicted in the Scriptures, were, in fact, conclusive. No Prophet or Apostle ever said, or could say, with power and majesty, referring to the leper, *"I will; be thou clean,"* and the leper instantly become clean!

(37) "AND THE FATHER HIMSELF, WHICH HAS SENT ME, HAS BORNE WITNESS OF ME. YOU HAVE NEITHER HEARD HIS VOICE AT ANY TIME, NOR SEEN HIS SHAPE."

The composition is:

1. The phrase, *"And the Father Himself, Who has sent Me, has borne witness of Me,"* has reference to the Miracles Jesus performed, which the Father gave Him Power to do.

2. As God became Man, i.e., *"Jesus Christ,"* which He had to do in order to redeem man, He voluntarily stripped Himself of all the attributes of Deity, even though He never ceased to be Deity (Phil. 2:5-8).

3. In this capacity, He had to have the Power of the Holy Spirit (Lk. 4:18) in order to perform these Miracles, which was granted Him by the Father.

4. Nicodemus, who was a member of the Sanhedrin, said, *"We know that You are a Teacher come from God: for no man can do these Miracles that You do, except God be with Him"* (Jn. 3:2).

5. *"You have neither heard His Voice at any time, nor seen His Shape,"* proclaimed only those Jews who were standing there that day before Jesus. In fact, in times past, many heard His Voice at Sinai (Deut. 5:22-33), and others even at the Water Baptism

NOTES

of Jesus (Mat. 3:17; 17:5). As well, men in other ages had seen His Bodily Form (Gen. 18:1-8; 32:24-30; Ex. 24:9-11; Josh. 5:13-15; Judg. 6:11-23; 13:3-23; I Chron. 21:16; Job 42:5; Isa., Chpt. 6; Ezek. 1:26-28; Dan. 7:9-14; 10:5-6; Amos 9:1; Acts 7:56-59; Rev., Chpts. 4-5).

6. Actually, this very statement made by Jesus in this Verse proves that God has a Voice and a Bodily Shape.

7. In essence, Jesus is saying that these Jews to whom He was speaking believed that God existed, even though they had never heard His Voice or seen His Shape. Therefore, why would they not believe the One sent by the Father, especially considering that He was doing the Father's Will, which the Miracles and Deliverances proved?

(38) "AND YOU HAVE NOT HIS WORD ABIDING IN YOU: FOR WHOM HE HAS SENT, HIM YOU BELIEVE NOT."

The composition is:

1. The phrase, *"And you have not His Word abiding in you,"* is a strong statement and must have rankled these critics greatly.

2. This tells us that if one truly has the Lord, one will have God's Word abiding in one's heart. The two are indivisible, Salvation and a hunger for the Word.

3. *"For Whom He has sent, Him you believe not,"* basically says the following:

Never having seen God or heard His Voice and not having His Word abiding in them, the Pharisees were incompetent to judge whether Jesus was or was not equal with God. As well, their rejection of Jesus demonstrated not only ignorance of God but, in fact, hostility to Him.

(39) "SEARCH THE SCRIPTURES; FOR IN THEM YOU THINK YOU HAVE ETERNAL LIFE: AND THEY ARE THEY WHICH TESTIFY OF ME."

The pattern is:

1. Everything the Believer receives from God is made possible by the Cross and the Cross alone.

2. It was there, the Cross, where Jesus atoned for all sin, past, present, and future, at least for all who will believe (Jn. 3:16).

3. The Faith of the Believer is to make the Finished Work of Christ its Object, and its only Object.

SEARCH THE SCRIPTURES

The phrase, *"Search the Scriptures,"* proclaims an imperative command and not a mere suggestion.

Actually, every Believer should search the Scriptures constantly in respect to everything pertaining to Life and Godliness (II Pet. 1:3-4). There is not a single life problem but which the solution is found in the Word of God.

THE MESSAGE OF THE BIBLE

The Bible has played, and continues to play, by far, the most notable part in the history of civilization. Many languages have been reduced to writing for the first time in order that the Bible, in whole or in part, might be translated unto them in written form. This is but a minor sample of the civilizing mission of the Bible in the world.

This civilizing mission is the direct effect of the central Message of the Bible. It may be thought surprising that one should speak of a central Message in a collection of writings which reflect the history of civilization in the Near East over several thousands of years. However, a central Message there is, and it is the recognition of this that has led to the common treatment of the Bible as a Book and not simply a collection of Books.

ITS CENTRAL MESSAGE

The Bible's central Message is the Story of *"Jesus Christ and Him Crucified,"* and throughout both Testaments, three strands, one might say, in this unfolding Story can be distinguished. They are:

1. The Bringer of Salvation, Who is the Lord Jesus Christ.

2. The Way of Salvation, which is the Cross, always the Cross, and only the Cross.

3. The heirs of Salvation, which pertains to every Believer.

This could be reworded in terms of the Covenant idea by saying that the central Message of the Bible is God's Covenant with men, and that the strands or parts are the Mediator of the Covenant, the basis of the Covenant, and the Covenant people.

God Himself is the Saviour of His People; it is He Who confirms His Covenant Mercy with them. The Bringer of Salvation, the Mediator of the Covenant, is Jesus Christ, the Son of God, in effect, Who is the New Covenant. In other words, the Person of Jesus Christ is the New Covenant. The meaning of that Covenant is the Cross of Christ, the meaning of which was given to the Apostle Paul (Gal., Chpt. 1).

The Way of Salvation, which is the basis of the Covenant, is God's Grace calling forth from His People a response of Faith and Obedience. In effect, the only thing that man can furnish to God which God can accept is *"a willing mind and an obedient heart."* The heirs of Salvation, the Covenant people, are the Israel of God, the Church of the Living God, constituting the Body of Christ, which is made up of all Born-Again people.

Now, when we say, *"The Israel of God,"* we aren't promoting a replacement theology. In other words, the Church has not taken the place of Israel. While it serves, one might say, as a stopgap measure, Israel will ultimately be brought back to its rightful place in the great Plan of God, which will take place at the Second Coming.

The continuity of the Covenant people from the Old Testament to the New Testament is obscured for the reader of the common English Bible because *"Church"* is an exclusively New Testament word, with the reader thinking of it as something which began in the New Testament.

However, the Greek word, *"Ekklesia,"* which means, *"Called out from,"* and stands for *"Church,"* was also used to denote Israel as the Assembly of *"Yahweh,"* i.e., Jehovah.

CHURCH

To be sure, it has a new and fuller meaning in the New Testament. Nevertheless, this *"Church,"* or *"called out ones,"* referred to Israel of old exactly as it does presently of the Church.

Humanity has always been saved in just one way, and that is by looking to Jesus and what He did at the Cross, of which the Sacrificial system of the Old Testament was a type or shadow of that great event. The sacrifices of old, even though they could not save, pointed to One Who was coming, Who could save. It was Faith in that

One, even though His Name as Jesus was not then known, which actually saved all before Calvary. In other words, men were saved then by looking forward to Calvary while men are saved now by looking back to Calvary. Irrespective, it has always been Jesus, *"For there is none other name under Heaven given among men, whereby we must be Saved"* (Acts 4:12).

The Message of the Bible is God's Message to man, communicated *"in many and various ways"* (Heb. 1:1) and finally incarnated in Christ. Thus, *"the Authority of the Holy Scripture, for which it ought to be believed and obeyed, depends not upon the Testimony of any man or Church, but wholly upon God, Who is Truth Himself, the Author thereof; and therefore it is to be received, because it is the Word of God."*

The phrase, *"For in them* (the Scriptures) *you think you have Eternal Life,"* in the English translation, does not come out quite like it was originally said. In essence, Jesus is saying, *"You claim to believe the Scriptures, so believe what they say about Me."*

UNBELIEF

In fact, the religious leaders of Jesus' Day did not believe the Scriptures, even as Jesus said in Verse 38. Over the last 200 or 300 years, the Pharisees had added over 600 oral laws to the original Law of Moses. Actually, some of them claimed that the oral laws, which were rules and regulations made up by men with no Scriptural validity, should take precedence over the original Scriptures. So, by the time Jesus came, the Word of God had been so skewed and compromised that the people little knew anymore what it actually said. Considering that copies of the Scrolls of what we refer to now as various Books of the Bible were somewhat expensive, it would not have been very easy for most common people to have obtained such. So, most were at the mercy of the Scribes who taught in the synagogues, who, most of the time, gave twisted versions and interpretations of the Scriptures. Satan had done his work well in working from the inside, twisting and distorting the Scriptures, which, more than anything else, set the stage for the negative spiritual posture in which Israel found herself at the time of Christ.

As we have stated, by Jesus completely ignoring these man-devised laws, He infuriated the Pharisees and ruling hierarchy of Israel.

THE WORD OF GOD TESTIFIES OF JESUS

The phrase, *"And they are they* (the Scriptures) *which testify of Me,"* presented evidence in concrete black and white of the Veracity of Christ.

The very first Promise concerning the Coming Redeemer was made by the Lord to Satan in the Garden of Eden immediately after the fall of Adam and Eve. He said, *"And I will put enmity between you and the woman, and between your seed and her Seed; it shall bruise your head, and you shall bruise His heel"* (Gen. 3:15).

The *"Seed"* spoken of here by the Lord pertained to Jesus Christ, Who would fulfill this prediction. Thereafter, every single happening and prediction in the Word of God pointed either directly or indirectly to Christ (Jn. 1:1-3).

Both the Tabernacle and Temple, along with all its sacred items of furniture, were symbols of Christ.

As well, all the sacrifices pointed directly to Christ, with constant Promises continuing to be given down through the centuries as to this coming Redeemer. Actually, the proof was so abundant that only one who was totally deceived by his own evil heart could fail to see the portrayal of Jesus in the Old Testament.

The histories, the experiences, the ceremonials, the dynasties, the offices, the songs and prayers, and the predicted and typical sorrows there depicted were all conscious and unconscious Prophecies of Himself.

So, in the giving of these *"witnesses,"* Jesus answered every argument of the Pharisees and religious leaders.

Tragically, the world continues to follow suit, believing myths about Christ, or not believing at all, refusing to see what the Scriptures actually say. Then again, most do not believe the Scriptures.

(40) "AND YOU WILL NOT COME TO

ME, THAT YOU MIGHT HAVE LIFE."

The pattern is:

1. Someone has said that Verse 40 is the saddest statement ever made!

2. Tragically, not only would Israel not come to Him, but, as well, most of the world for all time falls into the same category.

3. Not only does this Passage proclaim the stubborn unbelief of the Jews and all others, but it also proclaims that Jesus Alone is the Giver of Eternal Life. As we have stated, Jesus is not only the Giver of this priceless possession but, as well, the Actual Source. In other words, Life originates in Him.

4. This means that Eternal Life cannot be derived from Muhammad, Confucius, Buddha, Joseph Smith, or anyone or anything else for that matter! In fact, all who attempt to find *"Life"* in these false sources will not only be lacking, but will be consigned to eternal Hell, as blunt as that may seem (Jn. 3:16; Rev. 20:11-15).

(41) "I RECEIVE NOT HONOUR FROM MEN."

The order is:

1. Why did Jesus make this statement? Quite possibly, the religious leaders had intimated that despite the Miracles performed, and the irrefutable proof given (proof which they could not deny or refute), He did not have their approval. However, whether that happened or not, Jesus plainly told them that the claims He made and the proof he gave were in no way meant to curry favor with these people simply because it was not honor from men that He was seeking, but rather to do the Will of the Father. Actually, this very thing had happened on His First Trip to Jerusalem when He began to perform Miracles.

2. At that time, the people attempted to give Him honor, but He would not accept it simply because their motives were not right. As we have already stated, they were singing His Praises for altogether the wrong reasons. They wanted Him to deliver them from Rome and thought to use His Power to bring this about. Consequently, He rejected their praise and accolades (Jn. 2:23-25).

3. The sad truth is that this one thing, the attempt to receive honor from men, has probably been the greatest hindrance to the Gospel of all of Satan's tactics. This is what compromises many, if not most, Ministries. Too many preachers relish the praise of men. Consequently, they do things to please men which are contrary to the Word of God. To be frank, it is virtually impossible, at least in the capacity of which we speak, to receive *"honor"* from both God and men. If one satisfies men, one cannot satisfy God. Regrettably, if one satisfies God, one cannot satisfy men (Gal. 1:10).

(42) "BUT I KNOW YOU, THAT YOU HAVE NOT THE LOVE OF GOD IN YOU."

The form is:

1. When the Believer's Faith is exclusively in Christ and the Cross, the Holy Spirit, Who works exclusively within the framework of the Finished Work of Christ, will then greatly help the Believer (Rom. 8:2). Every effort of man to live for God outside of the realm of Grace is shot down before it begins (I Cor. 1:17).

2. Paul, in essence, said that if any man can be righteous by any other way than trust in Christ and what He did at the Cross, then Jesus died unnecessarily (Gal. 2:21).

THE LOVE OF GOD

The phrase of Verse 42, *"But I know you,"* is meant as an indictment.

"That you have not the Love of God in you," in effect, says they do not have God. If a man truly has God, he will, at the same time, have the *"Love of God."*

The New Testament makes it all too clear that human beings do not naturally love God. Their natural condition is that they are *"alienated* (from God) *and enemies* (of God) *in their minds"* (Col. 1:21).

A humanity that lays dead in sin can only follow the desires and thoughts of the sinful nature (Eph. 2:1-3). Human beings in themselves are without hope and without God in the world; only Christ's Blood can bring Life and, with it, a personal love relationship with the Lord (Eph. 2:12-13).

The New Testament shows us that the first response to God, which marks the Passage from death to Life, is Faith. Once a person establishes a personal relationship with the Lord through trust, Love can exist, and Love will grow.

John emphasizes this aspect of Faith's Life in his writings. Jesus confronted the Pharisees with evidence that they had left the path marked out by Abraham. Abraham believed God and responded to Him.

If the Pharisees had had a relationship with God, they would have responded as Abraham did. *"If God were your Father, you would love Me,"* Jesus explained (Jn. 8:42; I Jn. 5:1).

Love for God is a response closely linked with Faith. It is created by an awareness of what God has done for us in Christ. Actually, it is impossible for one to love God apart from Christ. As John says, *"We love Him, because He first loved us"* (I Jn. 4:19).

(43) "I AM COME IN MY FATHER'S NAME, AND YOU RECEIVE ME NOT: IF ANOTHER SHALL COME IN HIS OWN NAME, HIM YOU WILL RECEIVE."

The pattern is:

1. To try to live for God by any means other than the Cross insults Christ.

2. It is an insult because it ignores what He has done for us, without which, we could not even be saved.

3. For us to think we can, in essence, calls God a liar. Paul said:

"I do not frustrate the Grace of God: for if Righteousness come by the Law, then Christ is dead in vain" (Gal. 2:21).

MY FATHER'S NAME

The phrase, *"I am come in My Father's Name, and you receive Me not,"* proclaims that the real reason they did not receive Him is because they did not know the Father, despite their claims.

The religious world in Jesus' Day listened eagerly for some echo of the Trumpet-peals of Sinai. It desired a king greater than Solomon, a Prophet more terrible than Elijah.

When Jesus came with the real Glory-robes of the Love of God and with the Majesty of the Name of the Lord, there was widespread disappointment and cruel rejection of His Commission.

THE ANTICHRIST

"If another shall come in his own name, him you will receive," actually speaks of the coming Antichrist, as well as all other false messiahs.

The Antichrist will better suit the unredeemed heart of man, which seeks honor from man.

However, inasmuch as they missed the greatest Blessing that could ever come upon any people by their rejection of Christ, likewise, they will be cursed just as readily by their acceptance of the false Christ.

Immediately after the Rapture of the Church, the Antichrist will make his debut in respect to the fulfillment of Bible Prophecy (II Thess. 2:6-8). However, he will, no doubt, be tremendously active sometime before this, which will make it possible for him to begin this great foray into darkness.

At his striking debut, Israel will think surely that he is the long-awaited Messiah. Placing implicit trust in his promises, Israel will sign a seven-year contract with him, which will guarantee their borders and their protection (Dan. 9:27).

He will be empowered by Satan as no other man ever has been, and wayward Israel will respond to this satanic influence, which is so cleverly disguised. In other words, if one will not accept the Lord, he will automatically be deceived and accept that which looks like God but really isn't! Actually, much of humanity follows that train presently and, in fact, always has.

So, the word, *"Another,"* refers not only to all the false Christs who have come and gone, but primarily, of the coming Antichrist.

(44) "HOW CAN YOU BELIEVE, WHICH RECEIVE HONOUR ONE OF ANOTHER, AND SEEK NOT THE HONOUR THAT COMES FROM GOD ONLY?"

The form is:

1. The beginning of the question, *"How can you believe, which receive honour one of another ... ?"* proclaims that God does not minister to the pride of man or modify truth so as to please it and feed it. As well, these statements reveal the total moral wreckage of fallen man's will and nature.

2. This portrays to us the reason for the condition of the modern church. Despite its claims, the far greater majority simply do not believe the Word of God. Here we are

told that the basic reason for such unbelief is the efforts of men to please other men.

3. The basic structure of most religious denominations presently is that it is ruled by a religious hierarchy, which has no Biblical reality but, in fact, the very opposite. As such, many of its preachers, and even laymen, seek to please this hierarchy, even at the expense of the Word of God. Actually, most laymen follow suit, seeking to adhere to the party line, irrespective as to how unscriptural it may be. All of it is to seek honor of men.

4. However, when such happens, unbelief is the result, as here noted, with the church then casting about for false saviours, such as the field of psychology, etc.

5. The conclusion of the question, *"And seek not the honour that comes from God only?"* proclaims such as building Faith, which is the opposite of unbelief, but, at the same time, will incur the wrath of man.

6. Once again, please allow us to state that one cannot have both honor from God and man. One or the other has to go!

(45) "DO NOT THINK THAT I WILL ACCUSE YOU TO THE FATHER: THERE IS ONE WHO ACCUSES YOU, EVEN MOSES, IN WHOM YE TRUST."

The pattern is:

1. The phrase, *"Do not think that I will accuse you to the Father,"* actually means that they are already accused.

2. *"There is one who accuses you, even Moses, in whom you trust,"* points to the Scriptures.

3. These religious leaders claimed to obey the Law of Moses and held up this claim as an example. However, Jesus tells them, in effect, that they were not obeying the Law of Moses, and they were only using that Prophet as a front for their hypocrisy. He is actually saying that Moses will condemn them in the Judgment.

(46) "FOR HAD YOU BELIEVED MOSES, YOU WOULD HAVE BELIEVED ME: FOR HE WROTE OF ME."

The construction is:

1. The phrase, *"For had you believed in Moses, you would have believed Me,"* puts the ball squarely in their court.

2. He is simply telling them that despite their claims, they really did not believe the Bible and did not, as stated, keep the Law. If they did, they would believe Christ.

3. *"For he wrote of Me,"* is found in Genesis 3:15; 12:3; 17:18; 49:10; Deuteronomy 18:15-18; Lk. 24:27, 44, to name a few.

(47) "BUT IF YE BELIEVE NOT HIS WRITINGS, HOW SHALL YOU BELIEVE MY WORDS?"

The synopsis is:

1. The beginning of the question, *"But if you believe not his writings ... ?"* plainly and bluntly tells them to their faces that despite their claims to the contrary, they were, in fact, unbelievers. All of the religious machinery was but a show! At heart, they did not believe the Bible any more than the heathen.

What an indictment!

2. The conclusion of the question, *"How shall you believe My Words?"* proclaims the Unity of Christ and the Scriptures. Their statements and His Words agree in concord and equality and of necessity, for He is the Author of the Bible.

3. In this exchange, the thought presents itself that if men are truly of God, they will know that which is of God. If they are not, as the Jews of old, they will not know!

4. As well, if one is truly of God, one will not oppose that which is of God. People who claim to be of God but oppose that which is truly of the Lord are placed in the same posture as when Jesus spoke of someone that was attempting to cast out demons by the power of the Devil. If Satan did that, he would destroy his kingdom.

5. Likewise, God's Kingdom would be totally destroyed if that which is truly of Him opposes that which is truly of Him. Such cannot be!

The truth is, if one opposes that which is truly of God, one has placed oneself on the side of Satan exactly as the Jews did in their opposition to Jesus. They destroyed them, as all such activity will destroy.

"When my lifework is ended,
"And I cross the swelling tide,
"When the bright and glorious morn-
ing I shall see;
"I shall know my Redeemer when I
reach the other side,

"And His Smile will be the first to welcome me."

"Oh, the soul-thrilling rapture,
"When I view His Blessed Face,
"And the luster of His Kindly Beaming Eye;
"How my full heart will praise Him for the Mercy, Love, and Grace,
"That prepared for me a mansion in the sky."

"Oh, the dear ones in Glory,
"How they beckon me to come,
"And our parting at the river I recall;
"To the sweet vales of Eden they will sing my welcome home,
"But I long to meet my Saviour first of all."

"Through the gates to the city,
"In a robe of spotless white,
"He will lead me where no tears will ever fall;
"In the glad song of ages I shall mingle with delight;
"But I long to meet my Savior first of all."

CHAPTER 6

(1) "AFTER THESE THINGS JESUS WENT OVER THE SEA OF GALILEE, WHICH IS THE SEA OF TIBERIAS."

The diagram is:

1. There is nothing that one can personally do to make oneself righteous. Such can only be given by God, and He does so on Faith evidenced in Christ and what Christ did for us at the Cross.

2. There is nothing one can personally do to obtain victory over sin. Once again, sin was dealt with at the Cross. So, it demands that our Faith be exclusively in Christ and what Christ did for us at the Cross. Then and only then can we have victory.

3. In fact, the only thing standing between mankind and eternal Hell is the Cross of Christ (I Cor. 2:2).

JERUSALEM

The phrase, *"After these things Jesus went over the Sea of Galilee,"* refers to the recent trip to Jerusalem where the tremendous exchange took place between Jesus and the religious leaders of Israel. Actually, this was His Second Visit to Jerusalem, which was probably the Feast of Pentecost, or else, Tabernacles. At any rate, there is no record that Jesus entered Jerusalem except at the time of the Feasts. He would do this in obedience to the Law of Moses, but, otherwise, His Presence there was scarce.

The spirit of darkness, which characterizes all religion, was abundant in Jerusalem, hence, his lack of welcome, with outright hostility directed toward Him.

Jesus was probably now in Capernaum where He had made His Headquarters, which He now leaves, going across the corner of the lake, as Luke accounts it, to a place called *"Bethsaida."* If, in fact, this was the place, it was situated on the northeastern shore of the Sea of Galilee, actually, only a short distance from Capernaum.

THE SEA OF GALILEE

The phrase, *"Which is the Sea of Tiberias,"* means that the Sea of Galilee was referred to by several names, *"Chinnereth"* (Num. 34:11), *"Chinneroth"* (Josh. 12:3), *"Lake of Gennesaret"* (Lk. 5:1), as well as the *"Sea of Tiberias."*

During that time, the shores of this lake were the sight of one town after the other, where much of Christ's Ministry was carried out. In His Time, they formed a flourishing and almost continuous belt of settlements around the lake and communicated and traded across it with each other.

Today, only Tiberias remains as a town. There is no record that Jesus ever visited this place. It was built by Herod Antipas and called after the name of Tiberius Caesar. From the time of Antipas to that of Agrippa, it was the chief town of the area, at least as far as Herod was concerned.

After the destruction of Jerusalem, it became for centuries the site of a celebrated school of Hebrew learning and one of the sacred cities of the Jews.

(2) "AND A GREAT MULTITUDE FOLLOWED HIM, BECAUSE THEY SAW HIS MIRACLES WHICH HE DID ON

THEM WHO WERE DISEASED."

The order is:

1. If anything other than the Cross is looked at by Believers, such comes up to the Lord as self-righteousness, which God cannot tolerate.

2. Everything about the Christian experience must center on Christ and the Cross.

3. Christ must never be separated from the Cross, referring there to what He did, inasmuch as that was the very reason that He came to this world.

FOLLOWING JESUS

The phrase, *"And a great multitude followed Him,"* was now getting to be the norm. How many this particular *"multitude"* was is not known; however, there were at least 5,000 men besides the women and children.

"Because they saw His Miracles which He did on them who were diseased," presents the reason for the great crowds. No doubt, the sick were being brought in from all over the region, with Him healing every type of disease and affliction. None were turned away, irrespective of whom they were or what they had done. There was a reason for this.

Jesus came as the Bearer of Grace, which demanded that all be healed who came to Him.

Without a doubt, this was to date the greatest moment in the history of the Earth. God had come down in the form of Man to live with man and, above all, to redeem man. Along the way, he would display His Power to such an extent as the world had never known in all of its history, and by far.

THE MIRACLES

It is impossible for us to comprehend or realize the magnitude of these Miracles and what must have happened at these meetings. To think of blinded eyes instantly being opened, with lepers instantly cleansed, and all manner of diseases instantly healed, must have brought a joy unparalleled in the history of humanity. Jesus was the Topic of every conversation, the last thought before going to sleep at night, and the first thought upon awakening.

Those who had recently been healed were, no doubt, spreading the Good News to others far away that they too could be instantly and gloriously healed and delivered.

And yet, as grand as that was, it was but a foretaste of what is coming on that grand day when Jesus comes back to this Earth to rule and reign for 1,000 years, and then forever. What was then local, in that coming glad day, will be worldwide. His Mighty Healing Power will be so grand that, in fact, there will be no more sick people on the face of Planet Earth. Man is unable to grasp this fully. It is beyond comprehension to think of a day where there will not be a single hungry stomach or even one sick body on the face of the Earth, and neither will a weapon of war be lifted up against one's fellowman. However, it will happen just exactly as the Prophets have foretold (Isa. 9:6-7; 11:3-10).

(3) "AND JESUS WENT UP INTO A MOUNTAIN, AND THERE HE SAT WITH HIS DISCIPLES."

The overview is:

1. The phrase, *"And Jesus went up into a mountain,"* seems to express a desire for solitude. However, such was not to be found, at least not now!

2. *"And there He sat with His Disciples,"* contemplates a time of teaching and instruction. However, that was to be limited as well!

3. How privileged these Disciples were to have the Lord of Glory Personally teaching them.

(4) "AND THE PASSOVER, A FEAST OF THE JEWS, WAS NEAR."

The exegesis is:

1. Corresponding with the Passover mentioned in John 2:13, it seems that Jesus' Ministry has now passed the milestone of its first year.

2. However, as little effort is made to chronologically list these happenings, it could well have been the second Passover and, therefore, the completion of the second year of His Ministry. Whichever it was, there is little record that Jesus attended this Feast due to the animosity directed against Him by the Jews (Jn. 7:1).

3. All the Feasts were very special, but, quite possibly, the *"Passover"* was the most special of all. The Disciples hardly knew it, but Jesus, of course, was very well aware that He actually was the Passover, to Whom all the others had pointed for nearly the last 1,500 years.

(5) "WHEN JESUS THEN LIFTED UP HIS EYES, AND SAW A GREAT COMPANY COME UNTO HIM, HE SAID UNTO PHILIP, WHERE SHALL WE BUY BREAD, THAT THESE MAY EAT?"

The synopsis is:

1. The phrase, *"When Jesus then lifted up His Eyes, and saw a great company come unto Him,"* represented this great multitude that had followed Him.

2. Who can blame them! To be in His Presence, no sacrifice was too great or no effort to toilsome.

3. According to Matthew, Mark, and Luke, the question, *"He said unto Philip, Where shall we buy bread, that these may eat?"* has been preceded by a period of time given over to teaching and healing.

4. According to Matthew, it was growing late and concern was registered for the welfare of the people regarding food, etc. Now commences this great Miracle, which is recorded by all four Evangelists.

5. Inasmuch as the Holy Spirit devoted this much attention to this one happening, we should certainly seek to understand the lesson being taught, other than the obvious.

6. In reality, the lesson is powerful, referring to Jesus as the Giver of the True Bread of Life, and how He Alone can satisfy the longing of the human heart.

7. In effect, every Miracle performed by Jesus not only addressed itself to the need at hand but, as well, was meant to portray a lesson of far greater magnitude, pertaining in some way to all of humanity. This Miracle would certainly be an apt description of Christ as the Supplier of every need and, more importantly, the Giver of Eternal Life.

8. Even though He posed this type of question to Philip concerning the purchase of bread, Jesus had no intention whatsoever of purchasing anything. The next Verse gives us His Intended Direction.

(6) "AND THIS HE SAID TO PROVE HIM: FOR HE HIMSELF KNEW WHAT HE WOULD DO."

The construction is:

1. Without the Cross, man could not be set free.

2. Without the Cross, there is no salvation, no baptism with the Holy Spirit, no grace, no peace, no hope, and no power. Without the Cross, there is nothing!

3. With the Cross, we can have everything because the Cross has made it possible.

PROVING THE BELIEVER

The phrase, *"And this He said to prove Him,"* has the idea in the Greek of testing or examining him.

While God has every right to *"test"* or *"prove"* His People, human beings have no right whatsoever to test God (Deut. 6:16), unless specifically invited by the Lord to do so, as He did in Malachi 3:10. This concerns the giving of our substance to His Work and His subsequent Blessings upon us. Because God is totally trustworthy, demanding truth of His Power or Presence constitutes an insult, demonstrating a failure to walk by Faith, with the one exception mentioned (Mat. 4:5-7).

The word *"test"* in the Hebrew is *"sarap"* and refers to the process by which gold or silver is refined. This process is used to illustrate God's Purification of His People, usually through Judgment (Jer. 6:27-30; Ezek. 22:18-22).

Another Hebrew word for test or prove is *"vahan,"* which deals specifically in the spiritual realm, with a focus on some quality, such as integrity. It has the sense of an examination designed to prove the existence of the quality sought and is actually what Jesus was doing with Philip.

TESTING EVERY MAN'S WORK

Paul mentioned the *"fire that would test every man's work"* in I Corinthians 3:13. It is not intended to display our failures but, instead, to eliminate the worthless in order to leave that which is beautiful and pure, uncluttered and untainted. Then it can be properly displayed.

Jesus singled out Philip simply because Philip needed teaching in this particular area of trust and confidence. Actually, all the Disciples were in need of such.

When problems arose, they were too quick to resort to carnal solutions instead of taking the thing to Jesus. That seems strange, considering that He was constantly performing Miracles of every description.

However, the human heart, even in the best of us, is so prone to look to carnal means that God is sought only as a matter of last resort. Little by little, Jesus was bringing them to a place where they would look first to Him, which He fully intended.

As to Philip and the other Disciples, this was meant to be a lesson for all Believers for all ages. Every single problem which arises, irrespective of how seemingly insignificant or, on the other hand, how large, should immediately be taken to the Lord. This is His Desire for our lives. Such shows trust, Faith, confidence and dependence on Him, which the Holy Spirit is building within us.

Most of the time, as stated, we first resort to human efforts, and when those are fully exhausted, with the situation improved not at all, only then do we resort to the Lord. However, even though the Lord will oftentimes answer in these circumstances, still, such direction is not the Will of God at all, thereby, hindering our Faith instead of doing otherwise.

SPIRITUAL GROWTH

The ideal, and the place to which the Holy Spirit is striving to bring us, is that we think of every single thing in Spiritual terms. The Lord wants total involvement in our lives but will only do such if freely given the opportunity. Any and all things are to be taken immediately to the Lord in prayer, seeking His Guidance, Strength, and Help. If this is done, soon we will begin to think as He does, consequently, ordering everything according to His Word. Then He is truly guiding our lives, with amazing results, which are sure to follow.

However, we must also remember that even though the Lord definitely will bless us in all things, instead, it is *"Spiritual Growth"* that is the far more important and the basic area in which the Holy Spirit works. The Kingdom of God, which pertains to the Will of God in all things, must be sought first, and all the other things we are promised will be added.

THE LORD KNOWS WHAT TO DO

The phrase, *"For He Himself knew what He would do,"* presents this as an example of all things. In other words, the Lord always knows exactly what He will do, which presents us with a certain direction and obligation. It is as follows:

• We should understand this in the light exactly as Jesus has spoken the Words. The Lord has the solution for every single problem, and we should understand that.

• We should, as well, understand that He wants to be directly involved in every facet of our lives and, therefore, desires to apply His Wonderful and Miraculous Solution to any and all problems we may have.

• We should immediately go to Him respecting all difficulties, problems, or desires.

• We should avidly seek His Will in the matter, realizing that He knows what to do, with us giving Him latitude in our lives to do what He desires. If the answer is not forthcoming soon, we should continue to seek His Face until we know His Mind. If time is of the essence, we should breathe a prayer to Him, asking for immediate Help and Guidance, and trust Him to give such immediately.

• Once this becomes a habit, we will find it the most exciting, glorious, and wonderful way to live that any human being could ever have. It is God's Way, with Him desiring that it be our way as well!

(7) "PHILIP ANSWERED HIM, TWO HUNDRED PENNYWORTH OF BREAD IS NOT SUFFICIENT FOR THEM, THAT EVERY ONE OF THEM MAY TAKE A LITTLE."

The composition is:

1. The phrase, *"Philip answered him,"* proclaims his carnal thinking, which too often characterizes us as well. As we shall see, it was not the proper answer and showed little trust in Jesus.

2. *"Two hundred pennyworth,"* in 2012 dollars, would have been worth about $40,000.

3. *"Two hundred pennyworth of bread is not sufficient for them, that every one of them may take a little,"* proclaims Philip already computing in his mind the normal way to meet such a need. He was visualizing the amount of money it would take and, still, with the needs scarcely being met.

4. As well, Matthew records that the Disciples had already told Jesus that probably

they should *"send the multitude away, that they may go into the villages, and buy themselves victuals"* (Mat. 14:15).

5. As we see, all of their solutions were carnal and, thereby, of extreme difficulty. As stated, this is our manner too often as well!

(8) "ONE OF HIS DISCIPLES, ANDREW, SIMON PETER'S BROTHER, SAID UNTO HIM."

The exposition is:

1. Now enters Andrew! What was he thinking? While he had no solution, still, as we shall see, he came closer to truth and, therefore, the answer to the situation than the others.

2. As someone has ventured, Andrew seems to have had this trait of finding things and bringing them to Jesus.

3. He first brought his brother, Simon Peter, to Jesus (Jn. 1:40-41). Now, he finds the boy with a small amount of bread and fish.

4. The moral of this is that even though Andrew had not even remotely climbed to the rarified heights of Faith, which Jesus would now reveal, still, he had included Jesus in the mix, with a foundation being laid on which the Miracle could be produced.

5. As is obvious, the solutions ventured by the others did not include Jesus at all!

(9) "THERE IS A LAD HERE, WHICH HAS FIVE BARLEY LOAVES, AND TWO SMALL FISHES: BUT WHAT ARE THEY AMONG SO MANY?"

The form is:

1. The phrase, *"There is a lad here, which has five barley loaves, and two small fishes,"* presents that which, within itself, is of no consequence, as should be obvious.

2. Who was this boy?

Some expositors have suggested that he was employed by the Disciples for the purpose of bearing their food, especially considering that they were in a somewhat secluded place. Actually, from the way Matthew, Mark, and Luke address this boy, it seems that very well could have been the case. And yet, *"five loaves and two fish"* would hardly seem sufficient to feed 13 men unless he had started out with much more, and this was all that was left.

3. The question, *"But what are they among so many?"* presents that which was certainly true in normal circumstances. Once again, Andrew, along with the others, was thinking in natural and not Spiritual terms.

4. Every single thing the Believer thinks should be thought of in the realm of the miraculous. Of course, this is not an appeal for foolhardiness, but it is an appeal to think of every situation and to look at every situation in the Light of what God can do.

5. If one looks at the *"five loaves and two fish"* only in the sense of what they actually are, one will see nothing of consequence. However, if one looks at such in the Light of what God can do, everything takes on a brand new perspective. This is at least a part of what I believe Jesus is teaching His Disciples.

(10) "AND JESUS SAID, MAKE THE MEN SIT DOWN. NOW THERE WAS MUCH GRASS IN THE PLACE. SO THE MEN SAT DOWN, IN NUMBER ABOUT FIVE THOUSAND."

The overview is:

1. Without the Cross of Christ, there is nothing!

2. With the Cross of Christ, we can have everything because the Cross has made it possible.

3. The Cross of Christ, referring to what Jesus there did, thereby, opens the door, so to speak, for everything.

JESUS CHRIST IS THE ANSWER

The phrase, *"And Jesus said,"* now presents that which alone is of consequence.

Some of the Disciples said that the people should be sent away.

Philip said that a staggering amount of money would be needed to feed this multitude.

Andrew said that there was a boy there with a little bread and fish, but, in essence, what good could that do?

Only when Jesus spoke was the miraculous solution found. Actually, when the question concerning the need of the great multitude regarding food was first broached, Jesus was warning Philip to first look to Him for the solution. Sadly, neither Philip nor any of the others, for that matter, arose to the occasion at that time, but the lesson was not lost on them.

As with them, we so seldom learn the Things of God easily or quickly. Even as I dictate these words, weeping fills my heart when I realize the terrible pain I have had to bear, all because I did not fully trust Him. I did not give the right answer the first time either, and I doubt that many others have as well! In fact, I have given the wrong answer to the Master so many times, but yet, He did not lose patience. He continued to work with me, as He does with all, until at long last, I have begun to finally see some things, which I feel I should have seen so long ago. How so much we want to chide the Disciples for their spiritual dullness, but yet, most of us probably did not learn even as quickly as they did. Maybe we are really chiding ourselves because we see ourselves in them.

AN ORDERLY PROCESSION

Regarding the phrase, *"Make the men sit down,"* Mark added, *"By hundreds, and by fifties"* (Mk. 6:40).

As all of these people, which, no doubt, included the women and children, were being told what to do in this respect, I wonder what was in their minds. At the moment, they little realized they were to be a part of and participants in one of the greatest Miracles ever performed by Jesus.

Some have said that these different groups all represented different nations of the world, with the *"bread"* representing the Word of God and the *"fishes"* representing the souls who would come to Christ.

If that is the case, and it very well could be, we should grasp the Truth that all received an equal amount of bread and fish, which, of course, would be the Will of God concerning the nations of the world. Regrettably, that has little been the case. Some received much, with others receiving almost none at all! That is surely tragic when one considers that many of the nations of the world can now be reached with the Gospel by television in a very short period of time.

ABOUT FIVE THOUSAND MEN

The phrase, *"Now there was much grass in the place,"* coincides with Verse 4 as it spoke of the coming Passover that took place in the first part of April, which, for the hemisphere above the equator, is spring.

"So the men sat down, in number about five thousand," probably totaled altogether about 10,000 to 15,000, counting women and children as well.

Five is the number of God's Grace, which would coincide perfectly with what Jesus intended for this episode and its manner presented, to represent the nations of the world receiving the Gospel.

Jesus had five parts to His Name, Isaiah 9:6; suffered five wounds at Calvary, the whip, thorns, nails, spear, and beard plucked; five types of sacrifices were offered, Leviticus 1:5; there were five posts in front of the Tabernacle, with the Ministry being a fivefold Calling, Ephesians 4:11.

Also, the words *"sat down,"* concerning the people, represent a Gospel without works, but rather accepted by Faith (Eph. 2:8-9).

(11) "AND JESUS TOOK THE LOAVES; AND WHEN HE HAD GIVEN THANKS, HE DISTRIBUTED TO THE DISCIPLES, AND THE DISCIPLES TO THEM WHO WERE SET DOWN; AND LIKEWISE OF THE FISH AS MUCH AS THEY WOULD."

The composition is:

1. Worldly wisdom doesn't recognize the Cross of Christ at all.

2. It doesn't believe in the Cross of Christ at all and, thereby, counts it as nothing.

3. In the thinking of worldly wisdom, the Death of Christ on the Cross was just an unfortunate end to the life of this Great Moral Philosopher, they say!

GIVING THANKS

The phrase, *"And Jesus took the loaves; and when He had given thanks,"* represented the beginning of this Miracle. As the song says, *"Little is much, if God is in it."*

The type of *"loaves"* mentioned here were *"barley loaves,"* which were the coarsest and, therefore, the most humble type of food.

As well, men look at the Gospel and consider it to be of little consequence. Diverse from Jesus, that would be true; however, in His Hands and coming from Him, it contains life-giving properties, i.e., Eternal Life. As well, these loaves were *"five"* in number and speak, as stated, of Grace.

DISTRIBUTION

The phrase, *"He distributed to the Disciples,"* proclaims the ones He had called, who would serve as distributors.

This is the same as the empowered Gospel coming from Jesus, Who is the *"Living Word!"* The Preacher of the Gospel is to seek the Face of God until he is given the *"Bread."* He can then say, *"Thus says the Lord!"* If the God-Called Preacher is to do anything for the Lord, he is to receive directly from the Lord, which will then guarantee a Word for the individuals in need.

"And the Disciples to them who were set down," portrays not only the feeding of the multitude that day but, as well, could be a symbol of the giving of the Gospel, as stated, to the nations of the world.

The phrase, *"And likewise of the fish as much as they would,"* is said to have begun with only two fish. However, adding the five loaves and two fish together, the total is seven, God's Number of Perfection, which characterizes the True Gospel of Jesus Christ. It alone will solve the problems of humanity. It alone will slake the thirst of the human heart. Everything else falls short because it originates with man. The Gospel, originating with God, is, consequently, perfect. As such, it brings about a perfect work in one's life.

As well, this entire episode speaks of the *"Lord's Supper,"* which represents Christ giving Himself for mankind. He actually is the Bread of Life.

(12) "WHEN THEY WERE FILLED, HE SAID UNTO HIS DISCIPLES, GATHER UP THE FRAGMENTS THAT REMAIN, THAT NOTHING BE LOST."

The pattern is:

1. Christ was and is God manifested in the flesh (Isa. 7:14).

2. At the outset, it should be understood that every single thing that Christ did and all that He was and is are significant beyond compare.

3. So, to minimize anything He did presents itself as Spiritual and Scriptural ignorance of the highest order.

THEY WERE FILLED

The phrase, *"When they were filled,"* represents the Gospel Alone, and more perfectly, Jesus Alone, Who can satisfy the hunger of the human heart. Actually, the Gospel and Jesus are indivisible, with Him being the Living Word. Everything else, irrespective as to how intellectual it might seem to be, leaves one empty.

"He said unto His Disciples, Gather up the fragments that remain, that nothing be lost," was not speaking of the crumbs on the ground, but rather that which was left over after feeding the great host. This shows us that the Gospel is enough for the Salvation of the entirety of the world. Actually, it is impossible to exhaust its potential.

The only way this Miracle can be explained, that is, if any Miracle can be explained, is that the moment Jesus began to break the loaves, as Matthew, Mark, and Luke stated, but John did not mention, the multiplication process automatically began.

THE MIRACLE

Even though it is not stated, quite possibly, Jesus told the Disciples to each get a basket, or else, they did so on their own, with Jesus breaking the five loaves and putting a fragment or two in each basket. From that moment, it seems that it began to multiply and continued to do so just as fast as the people reached into the baskets and helped themselves. The same would have happened with the two fish.

Quite possibly, Jesus placed one fish in one basket and the other fish in another. However, the moment this was done, they, as well, began to multiply, with these two Disciples giving of the fish, which had miraculously appeared, to their fellow Disciples. As fast as the people took the fish, it, too, continued to multiply.

Evidently, the people were reaching into the baskets and helping themselves to the bread and fish, with none being restrained as to the amount they took, but with the baskets not being emptied but continuing to be replenished. In other words, the entirety of the world could have fed from these baskets without any basket being depleted. Such is the Power of God, and such is the Gospel.

The words, *"that nothing be lost,"* refer to the Gospel that must be given to the world and does no good if it is not given. The sadness is that most True Gospel is "lost," either not given, or else, not used at all, with "another gospel" being used, which will help no one but will rather hurt (II Cor. 11:4).

(13) "THEREFORE THEY GATHERED THEM TOGETHER, AND FILLED TWELVE BASKETS WITH THE FRAGMENTS OF THE FIVE BARLEY LOAVES, WHICH REMAINED OVER AND ABOVE UNTO THEM WHO HAD EATEN."

The composition is:

1. While everything Jesus did was of vast significance, still, the major theme of His Life and Ministry was the Cross.

2. Actually, the prediction came forth immediately after the Fall that Satan would be defeated by God becoming Man and going to the Cross (Gen. 3:15).

3. The Word of God teaches us that the Cross of Christ was planned even before the foundation of the world (I Pet. 1:18-20).

THE LEFTOVER FRAGMENTS

The phrase, *"Therefore they gathered them together, and filled twelve baskets with the fragments of the five barley loaves,"* implies that each Disciple had a basket. It also implies that maybe bread had been piled up in several places for individuals to help themselves, with now the leftovers or fragments gathered up. The fragments filled, as stated, 12 baskets, which meant that they ended this scenario by having far more than when they had begun. Such is the Way of the Lord!

As well, the number *"12"* speaks of God's Perfect Government.

"Which remained over and above unto them who had eaten," presents a Law known only to God, of which man has no understanding.

How can one begin with five loaves and two fish, feed 15,000 to 20,000 people, giving them as much as they desired, and then finish up with 12 basketfuls of leftovers?

This is what makes living for Jesus light years ahead of any other religions in the world. There is Miracle-working Power attached to Christ, which becomes a part of the Jesus experience.

THE BREAD OF LIFE

Of course, all of this was meant to represent Jesus as the Bread of Life and how He is more than enough. It also speaks to our everyday living and the miraculous way He provides. At least, this is the way it should be!

Regrettably, much of the modern church has so diluted the Gospel, compromising its Power, until it is little more in some circles than a mere philosophy. Of course, that is what Satan desires! However, let it ever be known that as Jesus was then, Jesus is now! Any other type of Jesus preached is not the Jesus of the Gospel (II Cor. 11:4).

Most of the church spends all of its time telling what God will not do instead of what He will do! Men do this because they have no faith. Despite their claims, they simply do not believe the Bible.

It should be noticed that no fish was mentioned respecting the fragments. That is proper, and for the following reason:

As stated, the *"bread"* represents Jesus, with that left over representing that He is more than enough. However, the *"fish"* represents souls which are Saved as a result of the Gospel, and which the *"type"* would demand that nothing be left over.

(14) "THEN THOSE MEN, WHEN THEY HAD SEEN THE MIRACLE THAT JESUS DID, SAID, THIS IS OF A TRUTH THAT PROPHET WHO SHOULD COME INTO THE WORLD."

The synopsis is:

1. Jesus Christ is the New Covenant. This means that He doesn't merely have the New Covenant but, in effect, is the New Covenant.

2. It was to Paul that the meaning of the New Covenant was given, which, in effect, is the meaning of the Cross.

3. In Paul's preaching, he said, *"I determined not to know anything among you, save Jesus Christ, and Him Crucified"* (I Cor. 2:2).

THE BAROMETER OF FAITH?

The phrase, *"Then those men, when they had seen the Miracle that Jesus did, said,"* presents a picture of Israel desiring to use

Jesus for their own purposes instead of realizing the true Purpose for which He came. Such is the modern church!

Much of the modern church is presently using the Gospel, i.e., Jesus, attempting to get rich. Actually, it is a very popular gospel. As someone said, *"I have been poor and I have been rich, rich is better!"*

However, this false gospel, and false it is, projects the make of one's suit and the model of one's car as a barometer of one's Faith. Even though in this genre, Jesus is talked about much, and what they label as the Gospel is presented constantly, still, it is, in fact, *"another gospel,"* which means the True Gospel of Jesus Christ has been grossly perverted (II Cor. 11:4).

The end of this *"greed message"* is financial success, or rather its intended goal. Actually, its devotees not only do not receive anything from the Lord, at least according to this gospel, but are rather relieved of what little they do have, with mostly the preachers getting rich. However, due to the greed that is resident in most hearts, for every dropout, there are several others to take their place.

It is an ironic twist that some preachers claim they can make people rich while the Holy Spirit is attempting to make people holy.

THE WORD OF GOD

What does the Bible have to say about this particular gospel?

Paul said, and I quote from THE EXPOSITOR'S STUDY BIBLE:

"But Godliness with contentment *(content with what we have, which means we are thankful to God for what we have, and I speak of the material sense)* **is great gain** *(true gain).*

"For we brought nothing into *this* world, *and it is* certain we can carry nothing out. *(This speaks of worldly possessions. The only thing a person can keep is their Faith, that is, if it's true Faith, which refers to Faith in Christ and the Cross.)*

"And having food and raiment let us be therewith content. *(The Lord can never bless grasping greed.)*

"But they who will be rich fall into temptation and a snare, and *into* many foolish **and hurtful lusts** *(speaks of the sacrifice of principle),* **which drown men in destruction and perdition.** *(This refers to the wreck and ruin of the mind and body, but more particularly to the awful ruin of the eternal soul.)*

"For the love of money is the root of all evil *(there is no conceivable evil that can happen to the sons and daughters of men, which may not spring from covetousness — the love of gold and wealth):* **which while some coveted after, they have erred from the Faith** *(speaking of Believers who have lost sight of the True Faith, which is the Cross, and have ventured into a false faith, trying to use it to garner much money),* **and pierced themselves through with many sorrows** *(the end result of turning in that direction; let all understand that the Word of God is true, and what it says will happen, will happen!)"* **(I Tim. 6:6-10).**

Then Paul said, *"But you, O man of God, flee these things"* (I Tim. 6:11).

The phrase, *"This is of a truth that Prophet Who should come into the world,"* refers to Deuteronomy 18:15. As the people in Jerusalem of John 2:23-25, these recognize Jesus as the Messiah, but for all the wrong reasons, as we shall see!

(15) "WHEN JESUS THEREFORE PERCEIVED THAT THEY WOULD COME AND TAKE HIM BY FORCE, TO MAKE HIM A KING, HE DEPARTED AGAIN INTO A MOUNTAIN HIMSELF ALONE."

The diagram is:

1. There is only one answer for sin, and that's the Cross.

2. God doesn't have 50 ways, 20 ways, or two ways, just one — the Cross of Christ.

3. The Holy Spirit through Paul wrote and said:

"But this Man (Christ Jesus), *after He had offered One Sacrifice for sins forever* (the Lord Jesus Christ), *sat down on the Right Hand of God"* (Heb. 10:12).

A KING

The phrase, *"When Jesus therefore perceived that they would come and take Him by force, to make Him a King,"* represented the type of king which Israel did not need.

As stated, they wanted to make Him *"King,"* not of their hearts and lives, but of their selfish ambitions. In fact, He was a *"King,"* actually, the *"King of kings."* However, to have done what they wanted would not have solved their real problem, which was sin, but only cause it to be exacerbated.

They wanted Jesus as King in order that His Power could be used to overthrow Rome, thereby, making them the premier Nation in the world once again. While it was true that they needed Deliverance, it was a type of Deliverance they did not want, which was Deliverance from their sins. For Jesus to have done such a thing would have made them far worse tyrants even than their Roman conquerors. In fact, they were not interested in the Will of God, only their own selfish wills. Such is most of the modern church!

KING OF KINGS AND LORD OF LORDS

One day Jesus will come back and will reign *"King of kings and Lord of lords"* (Rev., Chpt. 19); however, this will happen only after Israel has been broken, which she would not do at His First Advent.

On the other hand, with too many modern Preachers, if God uses us a little bit, we very quickly allow the people to make us king, and in so doing, reap all the bitter fruit. Not many have the fortitude and courage to run away as Jesus did!

The phrase, *"He departed again into a mountain Himself Alone,"* refers to Him having already sent the Disciples away, actually commanding that they get into a ship without Him and go back to the other side.

Then He ascended the mountain and from thence silently watched His Disciples, i.e., the believing Remnant of Israel, passing through the dark, stormy night of their present affliction, and then, the worst one even yet to come. Then He will quickly descend to their rescue, bringing them to the land of their future millennial rest (Zech., Chpts. 12-14; Rev., Chpt. 19).

(16) "AND WHEN EVENING WAS NOW COME, HIS DISCIPLES WENT DOWN UNTO THE SEA."

The pattern is:

1. The phrase, *"And when evening was now come,"* refers to night drawing on.

NOTES

It had been quite a day, with a Miracle of unprecedented proportions being performed by Jesus.

2. Actually, so much was done on this particular day and held such vast significance that it would be quite sometime before the Apostles fully understood all that Jesus said and did. As we have stated, it must be remembered that everything He did not only addressed itself to the issue at hand but, as well, portrayed a tremendously valuable lesson applicable for all people for all time.

3. *"His Disciples went down unto the sea,"* presents them doing so according to instructions from Jesus. Actually, the Disciples had not wanted to leave without Him, for He would stay behind for awhile and, thus, they had to be sternly commanded to obey (Mat. 14:22).

(17) "AND ENTERED INTO A SHIP, AND WENT OVER THE SEA TOWARD CAPERNAUM. AND IT WAS NOW DARK, AND JESUS WAS NOT COME TO THEM."

The order is:

1. The phrase, *"And entered* (the Disciples) *into a ship, and went over the sea toward Capernaum,"* represented only a short distance, probably no more than a couple of miles or maybe a little more.

2. As we have stated, all they had to do was cut across the northwestern corner of the lake, actually remaining near the shore, in order to reach their destination of Capernaum.

3. *"And it was now dark, and Jesus was not come to them,"* as written by John, is meant to set the stage for that which will now appear.

(18) "AND THE SEA AROSE BY REASON OF A GREAT WIND THAT BLEW."

The diagram is:

1. The Sacrifice of Christ will suffice forever, meaning that there will never be the need for another sacrifice or more sacrifices.

2. All of this means that His Work is *"a Finished Work,"* which has the Scripture saying of Him, *"He is sat down on the Right Hand of God"* (Heb. 10:12).

3. Regrettably and sadly, the modern church is, for all practical purposes, Cross illiterate.

THE GREAT WIND

The Scripture does not say that it was a storm, but that the wind was adverse and evidently blowing from the northwest, pushing them out into the middle of the lake, which seems to have been the case. Consequently, we must assume that Jesus purposely sent them into these adverse conditions. As He proved Philip, as well, He will now prove all of the Disciples.

While all of us want Blessings from the Lord, and rightly so, the truth is that we learn very little from Blessings. Most of what we learn is from adversity. Admittedly, it is an expensive lesson, but it seems that man is so constituted that if blessed to any degree at all, he oftentimes is pulled away from the Lord instead of near Him.

If it is to be carefully studied, it seems that all the Bible Greats were forced to trod this path of affliction. As stated, this is certainly not something we want or desire, but yet, that which seems to be necessary for our Spiritual Growth.

Upon the advent of Blessings, too often we tend to think it was our consecration or Faith which brought such about; consequently, we tend to become more and more lifted up within ourselves. On the contrary, adversity causes men to pray and search their hearts. It shows us how inadequate we actually are and teaches us trust and dependence upon Christ, or at least that is what it is designed to do.

FAITH

The Faith of the Disciples had been centered up in Jesus' Personal Presence. Even then, it seemed to be weak, as brought out by their proposed solutions regarding the feeding of the people.

However, they were now to be taught another lesson in Faith, which would tell them that Jesus is watching, irrespective of His Personal Presence. This, no doubt, would prove to be one of the most valuable lessons ever.

It is contradictory to much of the modern gospel to think that Jesus will purposely send His Chosen Disciples into the midst of adverse circumstances, but He did! He continues to do so, as well, for all the obvious reasons.

(19) "SO WHEN THEY HAD ROWED ABOUT FIVE AND TWENTY OR THIRTY FURLONGS, THEY SEE JESUS WALKING ON THE SEA, AND DRAWING NEAR UNTO THE SHIP: AND THEY WERE AFRAID."

The diagram is:

1. There is no salvation outside of the Cross.
2. There is no baptism with the Holy Spirit outside of the Cross.
3. There is no victorious living outside of the Cross.
4. The answer to the ills of man is conclusively the Cross of Christ.

THE FOURTH WATCH OF THE NIGHT

The phrase, *"So when they had rowed about five and twenty or thirty furlongs,"* represents approximately four miles and portrays them being pushed out into the middle of the lake, as stated. As well, Mark said that Jesus *"saw them toiling in rowing."* Matthew said that it was *"in the fourth watch of the night,"* which meant it was between 3 a.m. and 6 a.m. (Mat. 14:25). So, they had been in these adverse straits almost all night long, trying their best to get to their desired destination, but rather being pushed the other way. As is obvious, Jesus was observing all the time, exactly as He observes us in our struggles.

Among other things, the lesson was meant to teach them to trust and believe Him in any and every circumstance, but was also meant to teach that without Him, no progress can be made.

FEAR

"They see Jesus walking on the sea, and drawing near unto the ship: and they were afraid," presents another Miracle of astounding proportions.

In their exhaustion and fear, and, no doubt, greatly perplexed because they could not seem to do what Jesus had told them to do, which was go back to Capernaum, their mental, physical, and spiritual situation had speedily deteriorated. This, as well, is a perfect lesson for all of us.

Many have the erroneous idea that if God tells one to do something, all is smooth sailing thereafter; however, most of the time, that is the opposite of the truth. As should be obvious, Satan seeks to hinder in every way possible, even with the Lord allowing him certain latitude, as here. Consequently, due to circumstances at times, it seems difficult, or even impossible, to carry out and finish the task to which we have been appointed. Even at times, as here, it seems as if the Lord is not with us because if He were, why would the wind be contrary, even causing us to go in the opposite direction of that appointed? As well, our greatest efforts, as the Disciples, cannot assuage the situation. Instead of being in Capernaum where they were supposed to be, which was normally a His journey of only an hour or so, they found themselves further away than when they began, despite all their efforts.

JESUS

In the midst of this perplexing situation, all of a sudden, they saw Jesus. It happened instantaneously, but in a strange manner. He was walking on the sea and, as well, the fading darkness of night, mingling with the coming light of morning, caused them to doubt what they were seeing. Matthew said they thought it was a *"spirit,"* which meant a *"phantom"* (Mat. 14:26). As well, His walking toward the ship, suddenly appearing out of nowhere, and, above all, walking on top of the water, resulted in fear, and no wonder!

It should be obvious that fear was already a factor in their situation. Most of these men had been raised on the Sea of Galilee and knew how quickly storms could arise. Even now, especially considering the adverse wind which seemed to be blowing at near gale force, they probably feared somewhat even for their lives.

(20) "BUT HE SAID UNTO THEM, IT IS I; BE NOT AFRAID."

The overview is:

1. The literal translation is, *"I am; be not afraid."* In effect, He was telling them that He was the *"I am"* of the Old Testament, i.e., *"Jehovah!"*

2. This Glorious Name, *"I am,"* was first made known to Israel as it was given to

NOTES

Moses (Ex. 3:14), to Abraham, then to Isaac, and finally to Jacob. The Lord revealed Himself as *"El-Shaddai,"* that is, *"God, the Almighty,"* for that was the Revelation they needed.

3. However, to Israel, enslaved and helpless, a further Revelation was necessary, and the Glorious Name *"I am"* was given to her as a blank check so that she could write after these two words whatever her need demanded.

4. For example, she needed a Deliverer, and, at once, she had the answer, *"I am the Deliverer."* She needed a Comforter and again came the response, *"I am the Comforter."* She needed all kinds of provision — needs immeasurably beyond human skill to meet — and, at once, her Faithful God said, *"I am the Provider."*

5. Actually, Moses was commanded to tell the Children of Israel that this Almighty God, Jehovah, was the God of Abraham, the God of Isaac, and the God of Jacob, and that is His Name forever and His Memorial to all generations. He changes not. He is the same yesterday, today, and forever. His Name is Jesus, and that is God's Greatest Name! (Ex. 3:15-22).

So, Jesus was saying to His Disciples, and to all other Believers, as well, and for all time, *"I am all you need in any and every circumstance, irrespective of its nature or power."*

6. John does not mention the situation with Peter walking on the water (Mat. 14:28-31) because John is presenting Jesus as *"God,"* while Matthew presented Him as *"King."*

(21) "THEN THEY WILLINGLY RECEIVED HIM INTO THE SHIP: AND IMMEDIATELY THE SHIP WAS AT THE LAND WHERE THEY WENT."

The exegesis is:

1. Due to the fact of the modern church ignoring the Cross, it means that almost all of the present ministry is dysfunctional.

2. Actually, the only spiritual disqualification regarding preachers is the failure of the preacher to *"preach the Cross"* (Col. 2:14-15).

3. It doesn't matter how many denominations with which the preacher is associated, how many famous preachers he has for his

"covering," or how he is applauded by the church or the world, if he doesn't preach the Cross, as far as the Holy Spirit is concerned, he is disqualified (I Cor. 1:23).

RECEIVING JESUS

The phrase, *"Then they willingly received Him into the ship,"* leaves much unsaid, as we have already stated.

Having been raised on this lake, most of these men were well acquainted with storms or adverse wind conditions. However, as should be obvious, this scenario, which had lasted all night long, seemed to have an eerie feel about all that had happened. In other words, there were spiritual forces at work here, powerful spiritual forces!

How Satan played into these happenings, if at all, we are not told. However, I think it is obvious that Jesus pretty well orchestrated the entirety of the happenings in order to teach several lessons.

THE SHIP OF LIFE

Without Jesus in the ship of life, it is pretty much at the mercy of the elements, as here proposed. As well, all of man's abilities, as those of the Disciples, even though greatly familiar with the variances of the lake, are insufficient for the task. Even if man manages to work out the economic situation, which, incidentally, most of the world does not do, he is left with the spiritual variances of which he cannot cope. So, without Jesus, he is left at the mercy of whatever adverse condition happens to prevail. Hence, much of the world goes to bed hungry each night. Worse than that, most, being helpless, have to suffer the hardships of man's inhumanity to their fellow man. So, without Jesus in the boat, it pretty much drifts from one difficulty to the other.

IMMEDIATELY

The phrase, *"And immediately the ship was at the land where they went,"* speaks of a distance of nearly four miles and means exactly what it says.

By the Power of God, that which multiplied the loaves and fishes now propels this ship to the shore instantly without effort.

As is obvious, this tells us that with Jesus in the boat, that which could not be done with an expended effort all night, and with the situation even growing worse, could be done now in a moment's time.

The wind or waves had no bearing whatsoever upon Christ. Actually, all things, irrespective as to what they may be, are subservient to Him.

It is a shame that much of the church world does not believe in Miracles or a Miracle-working Christ. Actually, they have pretty much accepted little more than a philosophy of Christianity, which is basically little better than the eastern cult religions of the world, because it denies Christ. Jesus is the Centerpiece of all things. Without Him, all the grand directions of Christianity cannot be achieved, as noble as the effort may be.

Jesus is not a one hour on Sunday morning experience, but rather a 24-hour a day, seven days a week lifestyle, which is the grandest, most rewarding, most fulfilling, and, actually, the most powerful life there could ever be. While He can take the place of anything, nothing can take the place of Him.

Along with being a physical and a mental being, man is also a spiritual being, which can only be satisfied by Christ. He Alone is the True Bread of Life, which the Miracle of this Chapter is meant to portray.

(22) "THE DAY FOLLOWING, WHEN THE PEOPLE WHICH STOOD ON THE OTHER SIDE OF THE SEA SAW THAT THERE WAS NONE OTHER BOAT THERE, SAVE THAT ONE WHEREINTO HIS DISCIPLES WERE ENTERED, AND THAT JESUS WENT NOT WITH HIS DISCIPLES INTO THE BOAT, BUT THAT HIS DISCIPLES WERE GONE AWAY ALONE."

The overview is:

1. The phrase, *"The day following, when the people which stood on the other side of the sea saw that there was none other boat there, save that one whereinto His Disciples were entered,"* speaks of boats from Capernaum, as there were boats there from Tiberias, as the next Verse proclaims.

2. The idea seems to be that after enjoying the Miracle bread furnished by Christ, a great number of the people spent the

night in the area, probably making a bed wherever they could, as best as they could. However, this little minor hardship was nothing in comparison to what they had received from Christ.

3. *"And that Jesus went not with His Disciples into the boat, but that His Disciples were gone away alone,"* simply refers to the fact that at least some of them had witnessed the boat leaving in a late hour the day before, but not with Jesus.

4. There is some indication that they may have searched for Jesus, thinking He would be nearby, but with no success.

(23) "(HOWBEIT THERE CAME OTHER BOATS FROM TIBERIAS NEAR UNTO THE PLACE WHERE THEY DID EAT BREAD, AFTER THAT THE LORD HAD GIVEN THANKS.)"

The exegesis is:

1. This plainly says, as is obvious, that there were other boats present in this place close to Bethsaida, but it seemed to have been known that they were from Tiberias and not from Capernaum.

2. Consequently, and possibly upon inquiring, they were told by the owners that they had not taken Jesus to Capernaum, or anywhere else, for that matter.

3. So, the people were left wondering how that He came to Capernaum since He didn't come in another boat. They had no idea that He had walked on the water to go to the boat which contained His Disciples, and that when that was done, the boat was instantly at Capernaum.

(24) "WHEN THE PEOPLE THEREFORE SAW THAT JESUS WAS NOT THERE, NEITHER HIS DISCIPLES, THEY ALSO TOOK SHIPPING, AND CAME TO CAPERNAUM, SEEKING FOR JESUS."

The exposition is:

1. The phrase, *"When the people therefore saw that Jesus was not there, neither His Disciples,"* seems to imply, as stated, that the people had searched for Jesus, knowing that He had not gone with the Disciples when they left the night before.

2. *"They also took shipping, and came to Capernaum,"* implies that some of them possibly hired some of the boats from Tiberias.

NOTES

3. *"Seeking for Jesus,"* regrettably, portrays people seeking not to be saved from their sins, but to be filled with bread, etc.

4. To be frank, and sadly so, much of the Pentecostal and Charismatic church world presently follows accordingly. Being Pentecostal, I feel I can speak with some authority.

5. Many are little interested anymore in the true things of the Spirit, i.e., Deliverance from sin, victory over the flesh, drawing closer to Jesus, or for that matter, seeing souls Saved and baptized with the Holy Spirit, but rather in the modern phenomenon labeled as *"prosperity seminars,"* etc. People are little interested in the things of the Spirit, irrespective of what label it goes under.

6. As is here portrayed, to seek Jesus is not enough. The question must be asked, *"For what and why are we seeking Him?"*

7. The truth is, the far greater majority of the church, at least those who claim to believe the Bible, are seeking for that which is wrong, to say the least!

(25) "AND WHEN THEY HAD FOUND HIM ON THE OTHER SIDE OF THE SEA, THEY SAID UNTO HIM, RABBI, WHEN DID YOU COME HERE?"

The structure is:

1. The phrase, *"And when they had found Him on the other side of the sea,"* proclaims Him now being in Capernaum.

2. The question, *"They said unto Him, Rabbi, from when did You come here?"* presents Jesus little answering their question, for His Mission was a moral rather than an intellectual or material one.

3. They had seen the Disciples leave alone in the only boat, at least, that was going to Capernaum, and they were puzzled as to how that He had reached the other side before them.

(26) "JESUS ANSWERED THEM AND SAID, VERILY, VERILY, I SAY UNTO YOU, YOU SEEK ME, NOT BECAUSE YOU SAW THE MIRACLES, BUT BECAUSE YOU DID EAT OF THE LOAVES, AND WERE FILLED."

The construction is:

1. The Cross of Christ is something that happened now nearly 2,000 years ago, and

has continuing positive results, which will never be discontinued.

2. The only spiritual disqualification regarding preachers is the failure of the preacher to *"preach the Cross"* (I Cor. 1:17, 18, 23; 2:2).

3. If a preacher places the emphasis of his message elsewhere other than the Cross, he is spiritually disqualified.

JESUS ANSWERED THEM

The phrase, *"Jesus answered them and said,"* began a Message that was so startling in concept, so grating to the carnal mind, and so impossible to the unspiritual, that most of the great crowds would now filter away. This was in spite of the greatest Miracles the world had ever known and the greatest Words of Life ever spoken. In other words, most were there for all the wrong reasons, as most are presently!

"Verily, verily, I say unto you, You seek Me, not because you saw the Miracles," would have probably been better translated, *"You seek Me, not because you properly understood the Miracles...."*

In fact, they did not properly understand the Miracles at all, but more than that, their misunderstanding was brought about, not by mere lack of knowledge, but rather a false understanding of their needs and the true Mission of Christ. In no way did they see themselves as sinners needing a Redeemer, for, after all, at least in their minds, they were God's Chosen People! They saw only what He could do and how it could be used by them.

Once again, how so much this parallels much of the modern gospel, *"the greed message."*

The phrase, *"But because you did eat of the loaves, and were filled,"* reads perfectly their true motives.

They were interested in what Jesus could do for them in the material, political, and intellectual sense, not at all in the Spiritual.

They did not get beyond the superficial phenomenon, not understanding whatsoever what the Miracles actually meant. All they knew was that they had eaten of miraculously-supplied bread and *"were filled!"* In other words, they did not see beyond their stomachs.

THE GREED MESSAGE

At this present time, despite what else is said, how many conventions and seminars are being conducted all over the world for the express purpose of telling people how to get rich, all by what they claim Jesus wants them to be?

Some foolishly claim that Joseph *"invested"* the gold given to Jesus by the Wise Men when He was a little Child, and that when He began His Public Ministry at 30 years of age, He was worth many millions of dollars, etc. Consequently, they say this is what He wants us to be as well!

Never mind that there is not a whiff of Scriptural support for such stupidity, the greedy hearts of men readily respond because most want to be rich. As well, when most can suppose such under the guise of *"Faith in God,"* it becomes extremely palatable and draws to its message many devotees.

Of course, it is not true, at least in the way that is being presented in those circles. The Power of God is not expended on us to merely fill our stomachs but, most of all, and primarily, to deliver us from sin and draw us nearer to Christ.

Incidentally, the only ones who get rich in this scenario are a few preachers. The people get nothing.

(27) "LABOUR NOT FOR THE MEAT WHICH PERISHES, BUT FOR THAT MEAT WHICH ENDURES UNTO EVERLASTING LIFE, WHICH THE SON OF MAN SHALL GIVE UNTO YOU: FOR HIM HAS GOD THE FATHER SEALED."

The synopsis is:

1. It doesn't matter how many denominations with which the preacher is associated, how many famous preachers he has for his *"covering,"* or how he is applauded by the church or the world, if he doesn't preach the Cross, as far as the Holy Spirit is concerned, he is disqualified.

2. Paul said that if we preach Jesus without the Cross, we are actually promoting *"another Jesus,"* meaning it's not the Jesus of the Bible (II Cor. 11:4).

3. If we are preaching *"another Jesus,"*

pure and simple, that is *"another gospel"* (Gal. 1:6-9).

LABOUR NOT FOR THE MEAT WHICH PERISHES

The phrase, *"Labour not for the meat which perishes,"* hits squarely the modern *"greed gospel,"* which was really the spirit of Israel at the time of Christ. Consequently, this approach by Satan is not new. Sometimes he packages his wares a little differently but underneath, it is the same lie!

The word *"labor"* in the Greek is *"ergazomai"* and means *"to perform manual work."*

Jesus is not speaking of earning one's Salvation, for that has nothing to do with works and is by Faith. He is speaking of great effort that we should put forth to obtain the Things of God.

For example, thousands of people had walked around the northwestern rim of the lake in order to hear Jesus. This was work. As well, they went all day without food before such was miraculously supplied by Christ that late afternoon. To be sure, none of this *"labor"* earned them anything with God, as it never earns any of us anything either! However, it does proclaim the effort made, of which Jesus is particularly speaking, that can put us in a position to where we can receive things from the Lord.

Sadly, this was not the case with this great crowd that particular time because they placed a wrongful value on what they actually did receive. In other words, their *"labor"* was for nothing!

Many give large sums of money for the sole purpose of becoming wealthy because some preacher has told them that this is what they should do, and even promised gigantic rewards for certain amounts, etc.

While God certainly does bless people, and abundantly so, for their giving, this is not the chief end of the Gospel but, actually, only a part, and relative to most other important Spiritual things, a very small part.

THE MEAT THAT ENDURES UNTO EVERLASTING LIFE

The phrase, *"But for that meat which endures unto Everlasting Life,"* speaks of our *"labor"* being expended on that which is the Will of God. Once again, such has nothing to do with earning one's Salvation.

If one truly serves the Lord as one should, there is much effort required in this activity, actually, full time effort. Such can certainly be described as *"labor."*

Attending Church several times a week, giving to the Work of God, studying the Word, and attending meetings where the Word is correctly preached and proclaimed, all constitute labor, as should be obvious. So, the idea is that this labor, although it earns us nothing with God, is required, that is, if we want to be all we can be in the Lord. Living for Jesus is a full time job. Actually, it requires full time attention as well. However, it is so rewarding in drawing nearer to Him that we really do not look at it as *"labor,"* but, if so, it is a *"labor of love."*

FRUITLESS EXERCISES

The idea is that we not waste this effort on fruitless exercises, exactly as these people in Israel were doing during the time of Christ, but rather toward that which has an eternal consequence respecting *"Everlasting Life."* As well, this applies to laymen exactly as it does to Preachers of the Gospel, albeit in its own way. I'll give an example from my own life, even though it would certainly differ from that of the laity, but not in spirit.

I generally get to the office each morning at approximately 6 a.m. Immediately upon arriving, I go to the Lord in prayer and, for a few minutes, ask His Blessings and Help for the day. I will then work on these Commentaries or other material until about 6:40 a.m., when I leave for the television studio for the live program, *"THE MESSAGE OF THE CROSS."* This program lasts one hour and 15 minutes, not counting the preparation.

After that, I come back to the office and start work again on the Commentaries or other material, with our effort being to attempt to produce material by the Help of the Holy Spirit that will help the Believer in his or her walk with the Lord.

To be sure, I'm only touching the high spots, but the point is, this is *"labor,"* exactly as Jesus said, even though it earns me nothing with the Lord. However, the study of the Word and prayer do definitely draw me nearer to Him in the capacity of consecration and dedication, as it does all Believers.

MEAT WHICH PERISHES

The idea is that all of this *"labor"* must be for the *"meat which endures unto Everlasting Life,"* instead of that which *"perishes!"* Every Believer, consequently, must take spiritual stock according to what Jesus has said.

Because of this very thing, many Believers, while their souls will be Saved, will lose all their reward (I Cor. 3:15) because they *"labor for the meat which perishes."*

However, many, as the Jews of Jesus' Day, will lose their souls, to which this Passage actually points. Still, much of the world labors in the realm of religion, in which there is no life. Whatever we do, we must labor correctly, which can only be in Him.

THE SON OF MAN

The phrase, *"Which the Son of Man shall give unto you,"* is used in this fashion instead of *"Son of God"* for a particular reason.

While Jesus was Very God, He did not walk this Earth and pay the price for man's Redemption as God, but rather as a *"Man,"* i.e., the Incarnation, the Last Adam, even though God was in Him, reconciling the world unto Himself. The only way that man could be redeemed was by another man. However, all men, as a result of Adam's fall, are born in sin and, therefore, could not pay the price demanded by Heavenly Justice. So, God became Man, doing for man what the first Adam failed to do. Through His Perfect Life and, above all, His Perfect Sacrifice of Himself on the Tree, He purchased man's Redemption.

Consequently, inasmuch as Jesus is the One Who has paid the price, He Alone can give Eternal Life, for He Alone is the Ultimate Source.

THE SEAL

The phrase, *"For Him has God the Father sealed,"* refers to the One and the Only One Who can and, in fact, has filled this role. He has been accredited by the Father as Worthy and Confident to discharge such duties, and to render this which the Father has planned, in effect, having the key to this boundless treasure, this Eternal Blessing.

As is obvious, as we have stated, men must labor to receive so great a Gift. However, it will still prove to be a Gift, even if they put forth their most strenuous energy to receive it, simply because it cannot be purchased or earned in this fashion. So, our labor is in order to provide to the Lord a *"willing mind and an obedient heart."* That's all that man can honestly do. If we think about it a moment, we will realize, as simple as that is, *"a willing mind and an obedient heart"* is not at all easy to do.

(28) "THEN SAID THEY UNTO HIM, WHAT SHALL WE DO, THAT WE MIGHT WORK THE WORKS OF GOD?"

The form is:

1. The question of the Twenty-eighth Verse, as posed by the people to Jesus, tells us that they still did not understand what He was saying because of preconceived, erroneous beliefs.

2. In truth, most of them were not even saved. However, due to their great religious activity and, especially, because they were Jews and, therefore, sons and daughters of Abraham, they thought such constituted Salvation. They wanted to do the Works of God when, in reality, they did not even know God, despite the fact that they talked about Him constantly.

3. Of all the bondages in the world, religious bondage is the worst of all. While all sin carries deception with it, religion carries the most deception of all. While the Publicans and harlots were definitely deceived by their sin, as all such are, still, they are much easier to reach for Christ than the religious zealot who does not know Christ. Jesus said so! (Mat. 21:31).

(29) "JESUS ANSWERED AND SAID UNTO THEM, THIS IS THE WORK OF GOD, THAT YOU BELIEVE ON HIM WHOM HE HAS SENT."

The order is:

1. Under Grace, the rules, one might say, are far more stringent than they ever were under the Law, as they should be.

2. The Law demanded but gave no power for the person to accomplish the demand.

3. It's simply the Goodness of God extended to undeserving people.

4. Grace, totally different than the Law because of what Jesus did at Calvary, will provide the necessary Power for the Commandments of the Lord to be obeyed.

THIS IS THE WORK OF GOD

The phrase, *"Jesus answered and said unto them,"* proclaimed the greatest Word they had have ever heard, but yet, they would not heed!

"This is the Work of God, that you believe on Him Whom He has sent," tells us several things.

• He was telling them that their Salvation rested in Faith instead of works. They must *"believe on Him,"* i.e., Christ.

It offends the self-righteous to tell them that without Faith, it is impossible to please God (Heb. 11:6), and that, therefore, the great Work that God requires is Faith in His Beloved Son Whom He sent. Otherwise, works, however pious, are *"dead works."*

• He was steering them to Salvation because, as stated, most of them were not saved. They were religious, and they carried forth many works in that capacity, but the truth is, they really did not know the Lord.

To believe on Jesus meant to declare Him as the Messiah and the Saviour of mankind, as foretold by the Prophets. Of course, to do this would incur the wrath of the religious leaders of Israel, which it did, as is obvious in the Gospels and the Book of Acts.

• Believing, not works, and more specifically, to *"believe on Him,"* is the key.

The opposite of believing, of course, is *"unbelief."* This is the sin which characterizes humanity. The Jews of that day did not believe that Jesus was the Son of God and, therefore, the Saviour of the world, and neither does most of humanity presently.

UNBELIEF

To *"reprove the world of sin"* was the very first thing carried out by the Holy Spirit when He came on the Day of Pentecost and, in fact, ever since (Jn. 16:8). The *"sin"* of which He speaks is the sin of not believing on Jesus and what He did for us at the Cross (Jn. 16:9). So, whenever the Holy Spirit convicts the soul as a result of the preached Word of God, the first thing He does is to direct the individual to the Crucified, Risen Jesus.

Jesus is held up as the Saviour, the Redeemer, and the Answer to man's dilemma. In truth, man is not sure of that and must have it nailed down by the Holy Spirit when seized by Conviction. If that is not addressed and settled first, the individual cannot be saved. To be sure, the very moment the sinner believes, wherever the person may be, he is instantly *"Born-Again."*

(30) "THEY SAID THEREFORE UNTO HIM, WHAT SIGN DO YOU THEN SHOW, THAT WE MAY SEE, AND BELIEVE YOU? WHAT DO YOU WORK?"

1. The word *"Atonement,"* as used in the Old Testament, means *"to cover"* or *"a making at one."*

2. The need for Atonement is brought about by three things:
• The universality of sin.
• The seriousness of sin.
• Man's inability to deal with sin.

WHAT SIGN DO YOU SHOW US?

The beginning of the question, *"They said therefore unto Him, What sign do you then show . . ."* presents these people ignoring what Jesus has just said concerning *"believing on Him"* and, at once, demanding a *"sign."*

This is strange considering that they had just witnessed the greatest sign that any group of human beings had ever seen in all the history of mankind, Jesus feeding 10,000 people or more with five loaves of bread and two fish. And yet, they asked for a sign.

One must marvel at the patience of Christ. Above that, how it must have hurt Him to have witnessed the spiritual stubbornness and pride of these people.

THAT WE MAY SEE AND BELIEVE

The conclusion of the question, *"That we may see, and believe You?"* proclaims them completely ignoring His Statement concerning *"believing on Him,"* instead, demanding something they could *"see!"*

If one refuses to believe the Word of God, one will have to have bigger and grander signs in order to keep on believing. Regrettably, too much of Christendom falls into this category. As a result, they flit from place to place and church to church, ever looking for a new phenomenon. When they find it, they also find with it, much of the time, Scriptural error, which they are too shallow to know. They momentarily become greatly enamored but then quickly tire, seeking something else which titillates the flesh. There is not only no spiritual growth in such, but rather such activity portrays tremendous spiritual immaturity.

The question, *"What do You work?"* actually portrays insult gone to seed.

As stated, He was continually performing Miracles, so astounding, in fact, that they beggared description, with these very people recently having eaten of the Miracle bread, but now they demanded some type of sign! In fact, nothing could be done that would have pleased them simply because their motivation was wrong, their direction was wrong, and they had no true faith, which characterizes much of the modern church.

(31) "OUR FATHERS DID EAT MANNA IN THE DESERT; AS IT IS WRITTEN, HE GAVE THEM BREAD FROM HEAVEN TO EAT."

The order is:

1. These stubborn unbelievers now quoted a Scripture to Jesus, which they improperly understood, forgetting the great sign He had given them the previous day and the Miracles He had just wrought (Mat. 14:14). They replied that Moses had accredited himself as sent from God by giving Israel the Manna, as stated in Psalms 78:24, and that he had fed upwards of several millions of people for some 40 years.

2. The rabbis taught that the former redeemer, Moses, caused Manna to descend from Heaven for them, and that the latter Redeemer, the Messiah, would perform a similar Miracle. So, this was what they were bringing to the Attention of Jesus.

3. They seemed to not understand that the entirety of Psalm 78 proclaims an indictment against Israel's unbelief at the time of Moses, with her children doing exactly the same in the time of Christ.

(32) "THEN JESUS SAID UNTO THEM, VERILY, VERILY, I SAY UNTO YOU, MOSES GAVE YOU NOT THAT BREAD FROM HEAVEN; BUT MY FATHER GIVES YOU THE TRUE BREAD FROM HEAVEN."

The synopsis is:

1. The phrase, *"Then Jesus said unto them,"* proclaims the continued statement by Christ respecting Him as the One sent from God, Israel's Messiah. However, despite incontrovertible proof, they would not believe!

2. *"Verily, verily, I say unto you, Moses gave you not that bread from Heaven,"* tells us several things:

a. Whereas these unbelievers were quoting some particular rabbis, who had obviously twisted the Word of God, Jesus spoke the Word with authority, referring to no one but the clearly Written Word of God. In other words, by using this phrase, He was proclaiming His present Statements as the Word of God, which would match up exactly with the Written Word.

b. He set them straight in that the Psalm in no way gives credit to Moses for sending the bread from Heaven, but it was rather sent from the Heavenly Father.

c. So, their error tells us that once men get their eyes off the Word of God, they almost always make gods out of men. They had elevated Moses to a place of God-like qualities, which many do today with certain preachers.

3. Actually, this problem did not die with the Jews of Jesus' Day but was rampant in the Corinthian Church, even as Paul addressed himself (I Cor. 1:10-13).

4. *"But My Father gives you the True Bread from Heaven,"* proclaims the Father as being the Giver of the Bread during the time of Moses and, also, the Giver of the *"True Bread,"* i.e., Jesus Christ. Regrettably, much of the world will not accept this *"True Bread!"*

(33) "FOR THE BREAD OF GOD IS HE WHICH COMES DOWN FROM HEAVEN, AND GIVES LIFE UNTO THE WORLD."

The pattern is:

1. Verse 33 proclaims the Plan of Redemption for all of mankind.

2. The Bread of God is Jesus Christ. The implication is that as physical bread is to be eaten and gives life to the physical body, likewise, Jesus must be experienced in the same manner.

3. When one accepts Christ as one's Saviour, the results are far more than the embracing of a philosophy, as it is with all other things. One literally becomes a part of the Body of Christ, with Him becoming a part of the sinner by virtue of imputed Righteousness. Consequently, the statement *"Bread of God"* is meant to convey the impression that not only does the Believer enter into life by eating of this Bread but, as well, sustains himself ever after in the same manner. It is such a *"oneness"* that Paul used the phrase, *"Baptized into Jesus Christ"* (Rom. 6:3).

4. Jesus came *"down from Heaven."* Consequently, Salvation is all of God and none of man. In fact, without God taking the initiative, there was no way for man to reach God. Because of man's sin, he was locked off from any contact with the Father and bereft of Eternal Life in any measure. Actually, he incurred spiritual death at the Fall, *"separation from God!"*

5. So, the Lord instituted the Plan of Redemption, which was brought about *"before the foundation of the world"* (I Pet. 1:18-20).

6. He Alone, this *"Bread of God,"* is above to *"give Life unto the world."* Outside of Christ, there is no *"life,"* with the world dead in trespasses and sins.

7. Also, this Life is a *"Gift,"* which cannot be earned or merited simply because it is not possible for man to do so. In other words, the debt was so large, even if an individual could think of it in such terms, still, it was impossible for man to pay. However, Jesus, thankfully, paid it all at Calvary's Cross.

(34) "THEN SAID THEY UNTO HIM, LORD, EVERMORE GIVE US THIS BREAD."

The composition is:

1. The statements made by Jesus previous to this request were enough for them to know what He was speaking about. Still, because of unbelief, they really did not properly understand, and thought He was still speaking of some kind of physical bread that imparts some type of Miracle life, etc.

2. As well, we shall see that they wanted this *"bread,"* but they did not want Jesus. To accept that the Bread and Jesus are One and the same, they would not do. The world has continued to follow in the same train.

3. It wants *"Eternal Life"* and *"Living Water,"* but it refuses to admit that this and Jesus are One and the Same! Consequently, they continue to try without Jesus, which is impossible! This is the reason for all the man-devised religions in the world, as well as each individual's homemade religion or personal way of salvation.

4. When asked the all-important question concerning Christ and Eternal Life, most in the world will respond by saying, *"I believe. . . ,"* while then proceeding with some homegrown remedy and ignoring the Bible.

(35) "AND JESUS SAID UNTO THEM, I AM THE BREAD OF LIFE: HE WHO COMES TO ME SHALL NEVER HUNGER; AND HE WHO BELIEVES ON ME SHALL NEVER THIRST."

The synopsis is:

1. The universality of sin is addressed in the phrase, and others similar, *"There is no man who does not sin"* (I Ki. 8:46).

2. The seriousness of sin is seen in Passages which show God's Aversion to it (Hab. 1:13).

3. Man, within himself, cannot deal with the situation. He is not able to keep his sin hidden (Num. 32:23), and he cannot cleanse himself of it (Prov. 20:9).

I AM THE BREAD OF LIFE

The phrase, *"And Jesus said unto them, I am the Bread of Life,"* proclaims Him dropping all disguise and gathering up into one burning Word all the previous teaching, which they might have fathomed, but did not.

The Lord also referred to Himself saying, *"I am the Light of the world"* (Jn. 8:12), *"I am the Good Shepherd"* (Jn. 10:14), *"I am the Resurrection and the Life"* (Jn. 11:25), and *"I am the True Vine"* (Jn. 15:1).

SHALL NEVER HUNGER

*"He who comes to Me shall never

hunger," pertains to Spiritual hunger.

There is a *"hunger"* in the heart of man which cannot be satisfied by other things. Man was originally created in the Image of God. As such, he is a spiritual being and definitely not the product of mindless evolution. However, in his fallen state, he has cut himself off from God, Who Alone can satisfy this hunger.

God made a way for man to approach Him through the sacrifices of clean animals of old, which, within themselves, could not perform the task. However, through Faith in Who and What they represented, namely Christ, this hunger can be satisfied. Regrettably, only a few take advantage of this great Gift of God.

SHALL NEVER THIRST

The phrase, *"And he who believes on Me shall never thirst,"* falls into the same category as the *"hunger."*

Man has a natural desire for food and water. He is so created that these are necessities, that is, if he is to remain alive.

In the spiritual sense, it is the same, but that man is spiritually dead, i.e., *"separated from God."* Consequently, he does not function properly in any capacity, be it spiritual, physical, or mental. This is the reason for all the wars and man's inhumanity to man.

Since the Fall in the Garden of Eden, men have dealt with this problem in many and varied ways, all without success. He has tried to address it with money, education, politics, government, etc., as well as various philosophies, such as humanistic psychology. All have failed, as all must fail!

Jesus is now telling these people, and all the world, for that matter, that He, as the Son of Man and, as well, the Son of God, has come down to this world as the *"Bread of Life"* to make man whole again. Only He can do so! He is not one of several solutions but, in fact, the Only Solution!

If one is to notice, Jesus used the Words, *"Come to Me,"* respecting the satisfaction of Spiritual hunger, while He used the Word, *"Believe on Me,"* respecting the satisfying of Spiritual thirst. Consequently, these are the two requirements for Salvation: one must *"Come to Christ,"* and one must *"Believe on Christ."*

Both *"hunger and thirst"* have to do with something that is perpetual, in other words, ongoing; consequently, food and water have to be imbibed on a regular basis. In other words, no food that one eats or water that one drinks, at least in the physical sense, will suffice for always.

However, Jesus proclaims that upon receiving Him as one's Saviour, the Spiritual *"hunger and thirst"* are forever ended, with never a recurrence.

(36) "BUT I SAID UNTO YOU, THAT YOU ALSO HAVE SEEN ME, AND BELIEVE NOT."

The diagram is:

1. If man has to depend upon himself to be Saved, he will never be saved.

2. If the Son of God came to Earth to save men, then men were sinners and their plight serious indeed.

3. God and man, then, are hopelessly estranged by man's sin, and there is no way back from man's side. However, God provides the Way. That Way is Jesus Christ and Him Crucified.

YOU HAVE SEEN ME
AND BELIEVE NOT

The phrase, *"But I said unto you,"* refers back to John 5:40, *"And you will not come to Me, that you might have life."*

"That you also have seen Me, and believe not," in effect, means they rejected what they saw.

Why?

It was not for lack of evidence pertaining to His Claims, for that was abundant on every hand. Actually, He fulfilled the Scriptures, which they professed to believe.

If each had been asked, the answers would, no doubt, have been many and varied; however, the real reason then, as now, is *"deception."*

Adam and Eve fell in the Garden through deception. In other words, they believed a lie. As a result, this characteristic has followed man from then to now. He remains deceived, and it is much easier for him to believe a lie than it is the truth.

Some would argue that inasmuch as

man is in this state, and he is basically there through no fault personally of his own, then he should not be held accountable.

MAN IS FALLEN

While it is true that man's fallen condition is not his personal fault, still, the truth remains that because of Adam's sin, he is fallen. A person may have a contagious disease through no fault of his own, but that does not make the disease any less contagious.

And yet, God, at a tremendous price, has made a way for man to be lifted out of this quagmire of deception and lies. That Way is Jesus!

As well, man cannot avoid responsibility as he would like to do, because he has the power of choice or free moral agency. As such, he has the capacity to reason and to form a conclusion. Admittedly, that is all he can do, which, within itself, effects no Salvation! However, that is all God requires of man, even as Jesus has stated here. God only requires man to *"come"* and *"believe."* Everything else is furnished freely by the Lord.

WHY DO SOME COME AND BELIEVE, AND MOST DO NOT?

First of all, God does not predestine anyone to be Saved or lost. If, in fact, His Dealings with man are weighed in the balances respecting pros and cons, it would have to be concluded that it weighs in favor of man being Saved. The Scripture says, *"God is not willing that any should perish, but that all should come to Repentance"* (II Pet. 3:9). On top of that, as stated, God has made a way through Jesus Christ for man to come.

As well, it is not that, at his birth, man has a propensity toward one or the other, believing Christ or rejecting Christ. The Scripture says, *"He fashions their hearts alike,"* meaning that all begin on an equal basis, at least respecting this all-important principle (Ps. 33:15).

In the matter of *"choice,"* which all men have, Satan pulls heavily upon the individual, attempting to keep him in his deception, in which he is mostly successful. However, the Holy Spirit also moves mightily upon the individual's heart, at least when the Word of God is proclaimed. He overrides the powers of darkness and helps man to see himself as he truly is and Jesus Christ as the Saviour of the world. It would seem that under this type of powerful onslaught, man would readily and eagerly accept (Jn. 16:7-11). However, man easily seems to be able to throw off even the powerful probing of the Holy Spirit. So, the answer rests with man's choice (Rev. 22:17). He makes a conscious decision to accept or reject for his own purposes and reasons, be they ever so right or wrong.

(37) "ALL WHO THE FATHER GIVES ME SHALL COME TO ME; AND HIM WHO COMES TO ME I WILL IN NO WISE CAST OUT."

The construction is:

1. The sacrifices of old point us to certain truths concerning Atonement.

2. The lamb must always be unblemished, which indicates the necessity for perfection.

3. The victories cost something, for Atonement is not cheap, and sin is never to be taken lightly.

THOSE WHOM THE FATHER GIVES TO CHRIST

The phrase, *"All who the Father gives Me shall come to Me,"* refers to all, whomever they may be, whether Israelites, Gentiles, Pharisees, scoffers, harlots, or even the very castaways of the Devil.

God draws sinners to Christ by a spiritual operation consonant to their moral nature and enlightening their rational conviction, and He effects this through the Scriptures as written by the Prophets.

Jesus based all His Teaching, especially His *"hard sayings,"* upon the Bible. It externally illuminates, and the Holy Spirit internally reveals. All, thus enlightened and Divinely drawn, come, without fail, to Christ and cannot possibly perish.

The Scripture teaches plainly from Genesis through Revelation the overwhelming principle of *"Whosoever will"* (Mat. 11:28-30; Rev. 22:17).

PREDESTINATION?

This, within itself, negates the erroneous

conception of predestination, which teaches that some are born to be Saved and some to be lost. However, having said that and knowing that God is Omniscient, meaning that He knows all things, past, present, and future, being creatures, it is impossible for us to fully comprehend what omniscience actually is. We can surmise, but having perfect knowledge of all things and for all time is beyond mortal comprehension.

Predestination is a Scriptural Doctrine; however, it is the plan that is always predestined and not who will be in that plan. Who will be in it is *"whosoever will."*

Some have contended that God purposely limits His Knowledge respecting the Salvation of eternal souls so as not to infringe upon their free moral agency. However, to believe such limits God, which we must not do. We must believe that God, even though knowing all things, is still able to deal with all on a fair and just basis, irrespective that He knows all things. In this area of foreknowledge, which is beyond our comprehension, there is one thing we do know. To understand it, we cannot! To accept it, we must!

When one reaches the portals of Glory, as I heard a dear preacher friend say many years ago, one will see inscribed over the entrance, *"Whosoever will let him come!"* As stated, that is the heart and sinew of the Gospel (Rev. 22:17).

But yet, when one walks through that portal and then looks back, he will find inscribed on the inside, *"He has chosen us in Him before the foundation of the world"* (Eph. 1:4).

ACCEPTANCE

The phrase, *"And him who comes to Me I will in no wise cast out,"* proclaims to all a Promise of unparalleled proportions. No, no one ever has to fear that upon coming to Him, he will be turned away. We have His Promise that such will never be.

Admission is not the working of some impersonal law, as some have made it out to be, and as we have stated regarding an erroneous concept of predestination, etc., but rather the *"individual response"* to Him Who has come down to give Life.

As far as man is concerned, it turns on his voluntary coming and on his willingness to be fed with Heavenly Food, i.e., Christ. This process of genuinely coming to Christ constitutes the ones given to the Son by the Father.

Satan makes many people believe that they have done so bad that Jesus will not accept them. Of course, he knows how to build his case step-by-step, as he is a master of accusation and condemnation. So, regrettably, many have died eternally lost because they believed a lie.

The truth is, Jesus will accept anyone who comes to Him, irrespective as to what he has done, and I mean whatever it may have been. If the person cries to the Lord, we have His Promise that he or she will not be turned away. Thank God, untold millions have believed that Promise and have eternally reaped its unfathomable rewards.

(38) "FOR I CAME DOWN FROM HEAVEN, NOT TO DO MY OWN WILL, BUT THE WILL OF HIM WHO SENT ME."

The synopsis is:

1. The phrase, *"For I came down from Heaven,"* proclaims God becoming Man, thereby, the *"Incarnation."*

2. *"Not to do My Own Will, but the Will of Him Who sent Me,"* proclaims the reason that He came.

3. So, He is telling the Jews that Jehovah, Whom they claim to know and serve, is the very One Who has sent Him, and that everything He is doing is exactly that which He has been instructed to do by the Father. Consequently, His Statements, Ministry, and Lifestyle completely shattered the false presentation of God as given the people by these so-called religious leaders.

4. As well, respecting man's obedience to God, Jesus set the stage by example by seeking only God's Will.

5. Also, it shows that the problem with the world is that the will of man is totally contrary to the Will of God, hence, all the sorrow, heartache, sickness, suffering, war, and death. Ultimately, the *"Will of God"* over the entirety of the world will be brought about, which will end the suffering and sorrow that has characterized man's existence from the very beginning (Mat. 6:10).

(39) "AND THIS IS THE FATHER'S WILL WHICH HAS SENT ME, THAT OF ALL WHICH HE HAS GIVEN ME I SHOULD LOSE NOTHING, BUT SHOULD RAISE IT UP AGAIN AT THE LAST DAY."

The structure is:

1. The New Testament takes the line that the sacrifices of old were not the root cause of the putting away of sins.

2. Redemption was obtained, even from the transgressions under the First Covenant, only by the Death of Christ, symbolized by the sacrifices (Heb. 9:15).

3. The Cross is absolutely essential to the New Testament and, indeed, to the whole Bible. All before leads up to it, and all after looks back to it.

THE FATHER'S WILL

The phrase, *"And this is the Father's Will Who has sent Me,"* proclaims that which will ultimately mean the destruction of the Jewish Nation.

In effect, the religious leaders of Israel were making claims that the Ministry of Jesus had little future. They considered Him to be outside the religious community and, therefore, some type of maverick. However, the words He will now relate to them will be startling, to say the least, and will pronounce the very opposite of what they are faking.

As well, His Statement will serve as a Foundation for all Believers for all time.

NONE WHO COME TO HIM WILL BE LOST

The phrase, *"That of all which He has given Me I should lose nothing,"* states several things:

• Rather than His Ministry being of no consequence, it was, in fact, the very opposite, actually, the only Ministry recognized by God. In effect, He was saying that despite what they said, all who come to Him will be Saved, and that He guarantees!

At the same time, He is saying that those who do not come to Him will be eternally lost, which, as stated, means the destruction of the State of Israel, because they would not accept Him.

• This statement by Christ does not mean, as some teach, that once a person is Saved, it is impossible for him to be lost. Man's free moral agency is never violated, irrespective of whether he is Saint or sinner.

The idea is that the Father has given Jesus, His Son, total Power, not only to save but, as well, to serve as the Resurrection and the Life, guaranteeing that the dead will be raised. None will be lost!

• Coupled with Matthew 16:18, this, in essence, speaks of the New Testament Church. To be sure, under the Old Covenant, Israel will definitely be included in the Resurrection just as those in the New Covenant, at least, those who died in the Faith believing. However, the great Doctrines, such as the Resurrection, etc., were only in shadow under the Old Covenant while they flower into full bloom under the New.

The phrase, *"But shall raise it up again at the last day,"* speaks of the Resurrection of the Righteous, which will take place at the Rapture (I Thess. 4:13-18), and not the unrighteous dead, who will be raised 1,000 years later (Rev., Chpt. 20).

(40) "AND THIS IS THE WILL OF HIM WHO SENT ME, THAT EVERY ONE WHICH SEES THE SON, AND BELIEVES ON HIM, MAY HAVE EVERLASTING LIFE: AND I WILL RAISE HIM UP AT THE LAST DAY."

The exposition is:

1. All must agree that according to the Bible, the Atonement proceeds from the Love of God. That should be obvious!

2. It is not something wrung from a stern and unwilling Father, perfectly just but perfectly inflexible, by a loving Son.

3. The Atonement shows us the Love of the Father just as it does the Love of the Son.

THE WILL OF GOD

The phrase, *"And this is the Will of Him Who sent Me,"* speaks of that which the Father desires.

He willed the Salvation of them all, at least all who believed in Jesus, and revealed a way of life that the simplest could understand. Whoever, notwithstanding his moral condition, looked upon Jesus and believed upon Him immediately received a life that was everlasting and was given a pledge — which carried with it absolute assurance

— of Resurrection into eternal felicity at the last day.

Just as shipwrecked men looking at a lifeboat entrust themselves to it for salvation and are surely brought to land, so guilty sinners looking upon the Lord Jesus and committing themselves by Faith to Him enter into a position of safety, and are made certain of being brought to the Resurrection Shore.

BELIEVING ON JESUS

The phrase, *"That every one who sees the Son, and believes on Him,"* proclaims the human side of Salvation with the first phrase the Divine side. The one, it is in the words, *"All whom the Father gives"*; the other, in the words, *"Believes on Him."* Consequently, the door is opened wide so that all may come, and the fact is stated that the Divine purpose in Redemption cannot be defeated.

EVERLASTING LIFE

The phrase, *"May have everlasting life,"* is a Promise of such magnitude that there is nothing to equal it in the human equation. To be sure, no one would make such a Promise, at least if he were in his right mind, unless able to carry it forth. Only God could do such a thing, so Jesus, once again, proclaims that which only Deity could proclaim.

The phrase, *"And I will raise him up at the last day,"* is stated for the second time.

In the Old Testament, the Resurrection was briefly mentioned at times, but not so boldly, even remotely so, as these statements made by Christ.

The idea is not so much to prove the Doctrine of the Resurrection as to prove its Power and Authority, Who is Jesus. In other words, He not only has the Power to resurrect the dead, which, within itself, is staggering, to say the least, but, in fact, is the *"Resurrection and the Life."*

Again, he makes statements which no mortal would ever think of making. As well, He ties the same Power that it would take to raise the dead to the healing of the sick and the performing of Miracles. So, His claims are absolutely undeniable!

(41) "THE JEWS THEN MURMURED AT HIM, BECAUSE HE SAID, I AM THE BREAD WHICH CAME DOWN FROM HEAVEN."

The exegesis is:

1. The phrase, *"The Jews then murmured at Him,"* actually means they were muttering one to another.

2. The word *"murmured"* has a very strong negative connotation and is used to denote very rebellious feelings against God (Ex. 16:7-9; Num. 11:1; 14:27) (Reynolds).[1] More than anything else, the sin of *"murmuring"* by Israel in the wilderness aroused the Anger of God. It showed gross unbelief in God. Sadly, this generation to whom Jesus ministered fared no better!

3. *"Because He said, I am the Bread which came down from Heaven,"* presents them now understanding perfectly what He has said. Reynolds said:

"The Jews did not misunderstand His meaning. They understood it perfectly, and rebelled against it."[2]

4. The Holy Spirit through John, to a far greater degree than the other three Gospels, proclaims in glaring detail the absolute proof presented by Jesus Christ in every direction, concerning Who and What He was. He satisfied every Scriptural, Spiritual, and physical demand as to the Authenticity of Himself as the Messiah, God manifested in the flesh. These people did not rebel against a lack of proof, but rather against a mountain of truth. They did it willfully, deliberately, and caustically! They simply refused to believe despite the overwhelming evidence. It has not changed.

5. Hatred of the True Gospel, which alone can set men free, is not only rampant in the world presently but, as well, in the church. Most of the modern church is a product of the flesh and, as a consequence, will always persecute that which is of the Spirit (Gal. 5:11).

(42) "AND THEY SAID, IS NOT THIS JESUS, THE SON OF JOSEPH, WHOSE FATHER AND MOTHER WE KNOW? HOW IS IT THEN THAT HE SAYS, I CAME DOWN FROM HEAVEN?"

The overview is:

1. The Death of Christ was no accident. It was rooted in a compelling Divine necessity.

2. In the Book of Hebrews, we read that it was *"by the Grace of God"* that Christ

tasted death for us all (Heb. 2:9). Jesus Christ came specifically to die for our sins (Jn. 1:1, 14, 29).

WHO IS JESUS?

The question, *"And they said, Is not this Jesus, the son of Joseph, whose father and mother we know?"* represents that they well understood His Terminology concerning His Claims of being the Son of God and that Jehovah was His Father. He had made it crystal clear, and they understood accordingly! However, they simply did not believe Him!

As well, we are not to take from this that Joseph was still alive, even though he may well have been. They are simply saying that they knew and have known the parents of Jesus, or at least those they thought to be.

Had they known Isaiah 7:14, they would have understood the manner of His Birth. As well, had they known Isaiah 9:1-2, they would have known that it had been prophesied that the home of Jesus would be Galilee. Had they known Isaiah 61:1, they would have known the type of Ministry the Messiah was to have, which Jesus fulfilled in totality. They were not people of the Word, even though they claimed to be. Consequently, they did not know Him because they did not know what the Word said about Him.

THE INCARNATION

The question, *"How is it then that He says, I came down from Heaven?"* presents them understanding perfectly what He said about Himself and from Whom He came. They did not understand the Incarnation or the necessity of such in order to redeem mankind. Actually, they did not even really think they needed Redemption.

Israel was looking for her Messiah at this time and felt that the Bible (Old Testament) clearly proclaimed such, which it did! However, they did not rightly divide the Word of Truth

They definitely expected a descendant of David to appear, knowing that the Messiah must be in David's lineage (II Sam., Chpt. 7). Also, when this expected Deliverer would appear, God's Hidden Plans and Purposes were to be unveiled.

NOTES

DEITY

Their vision of the Messiah was that God's Anointed would redeem Israel, rule as King over the restored kingdom, and answer all of mankind's questions about God's Plans and Purposes. In other words, they were looking for a Victorious Messiah instead of a Suffering Messiah, which Isaiah, Chapter 53, described. They even had a vague idea that He would be the Very Son of the Blessed One.

However, for Him to have the type of Oneness with the Father, which, in effect, made Him Deity, was beyond their thinking and that which they did not believe.

Israel's problem was basically the problem of all mankind. As Israel wanted a Messiah on her terms, the world wants God on its terms. Israel wanted Salvation, but it was a type of Salvation which would not have helped them, i.e., deliverance from Rome. As well, the world wants Salvation, but the type it wants is not the type that God gives and, actually, if they had it, it would only tend to exacerbate their problem instead of serve as a solution.

Men must accept Christ on His Terms and not on theirs. Most of the world does not desire to do this!

(43) *"JESUS THEREFORE ANSWERED AND SAID UNTO THEM, MURMUR NOT AMONG YOURSELVES."*

The diagram is:

1. The answer, as given by Jesus, shows that He understood exactly what they were saying, whether He actually heard them in the physical sense or not.

2. Their *"murmuring"* showed their disapproval and rejection.

3. At this present time, these people who rejected Him are now in Hell and will be there forever and forever.

(44) *"NO MAN CAN COME TO ME, EXCEPT THE FATHER WHICH HAS SENT ME DRAW HIM: AND I WILL RAISE HIM UP AT THE LAST DAY."*

The overview is:

1. The Cross of Christ will never be understood unless it is seen that thereon the Saviour was dealing with the sins of all mankind.

2. In doing this, He fulfilled all that the old sacrifices had foreshadowed. Peter spoke of *"the Precious Blood of Christ, like that of a Lamb without blemish or spot"* (I Pet. 1:19).

THE FATHER DRAWS SINNERS TO JESUS

The phrase, *"No man can come to Me, except the Father Who has sent Me draw him,"* presents a tremendous Doctrine, which opens up the manner of God's Love as it is manifested in His Son and our Redeemer.

The idea is that all initiative toward Salvation is on the Part of God toward the sinner and not from the sinner himself. Without this *"drawing of the Father,"* no individual will come to God, or even have any desire to come to God. Such is called *"total depravity."*

It means that man, who is totally devoid of any spirituality whatsoever and is *"dead in trespasses and sins,"* does not and, in fact, cannot, at least within himself, have any heart toward God (Eph. 2:1-3).

Some may deny that, claiming that they had thought about God many times before their Conversion, even with some interest or desire.

That is, no doubt, true. However, such came about because, in some manner, they heard the Word of God, and, irrespective as to how limited that hearing was, the Holy Spirit then began to act upon that which was heard, which caused an impulse toward the Lord. However, it did not initiate with the individual, but rather with the Lord. This is the reason that preaching of the Word of God is so very important. It must be preached over television, radio, the Internet, through literature, in churches, and, in fact, any way possible. The Father does not *"draw"* unless He has something to draw upon, which is always the Word.

THE WHOLE WORLD

As well, Jesus is not saying here that the Father only draws some while not drawing others at all, as some have attempted to claim. The emphasis is on the impossibility of man coming to God without the Father drawing him.

NOTES

We know that Jesus came for the whole world (Jn. 3:16). So, if God loved the entirety of the world enough to send His Only Begotten Son, then, of necessity, the Door of Salvation, Who is Christ, must be open to all, which it is (Rev. 22:17).

This *"drawing"* is always done by the Holy Spirit as He is sent by the Father, Who always acts on the Word of God. As one preacher said, *"As to the kind of drawing, it is not violent so as to compel men by external force, but, still, it is a powerful influence which makes men willing who formerly were unwilling."*

The phrase, *"And I will raise him up at the last day"* once again portrays the great Doctrine of the Resurrection, and for the third time in this Chapter alone!

(45) "IT IS WRITTEN IN THE PROPHETS, AND THEY SHALL BE ALL TAUGHT OF GOD. EVERY MAN THEREFORE WHO HAS HEARD, AND HAS LEARNED OF THE FATHER, COMES UNTO ME."

The overview is:

1. The phrase, *"It is written in the Prophets, And they shall be all taught of God,"* is found in Isaiah 54:13. This Passage has one meaning but with two directions:

a. It means that everyone who comes to the Lord does so because they are given the Word of God, which teaches them, and is acted on by the Holy Spirit.

b. It has reference to the day that is coming when this shall be fulfilled in totality, which will be in the coming Kingdom Age. The Word of God shall spread across the entirety of the world at that time and in every heart, with converted Jews and Glorified Saints serving as teachers and aided by the Holy Spirit.

2. The phrase, *"Every man therefore who has heard, and has learned of the Father, comes unto Me,"* presents the manner in which they come and which, without Jesus, they cannot come.

3. This is what Paul was speaking of when he asked, *"How shall they believe in Him of Whom they have not heard? and how shall they hear without a preacher?"* (Rom. 10:14).

(46) "NOT THAT ANY MAN HAS SEEN THE FATHER, SAVE HE WHICH IS OF

GOD, HE HAS SEEN THE FATHER."

The form is:

1. The phrase, *"Not that any man has seen the Father,"* refers to fully comprehending or understanding the Father. The word *"seen,"* as used here, in the Greek is *"horao,"* and means *"to fully comprehend and understand with the mind; to see truth fully."*

2. *"Save He Who is of God, He has seen the Father,"* speaks of Jesus. He Alone fully understands and comprehends the Father. So, all that is learned about God must be learned through Jesus Christ. Of course, the Word of God is a part of that which Jesus does and is, with all being illuminated by the Holy Spirit.

3. If one wants to know what the Father is like, one need only look at Jesus, Who is a Perfect Replica of the Father in every way.

4. As well, Jesus was telling the Jews that despite all of their talk about God, they really knew nothing about Him. In reality, had they known God, they would have known Jesus. In contrast to their ignorance concerning these things, He proclaimed His Total Knowledge and Full Comprehension.

(47) "VERILY, VERILY, I SAY UNTO YOU, HE WHO BELIEVES ON ME HAS EVERLASTING LIFE."

The order is:

1. Several things are said in this Verse. They are:

2. Jesus offers *"Everlasting Life"* to all, even these rebellious Jews. It is an unparalleled offer!

3. Death is the nemesis of man and is the result of sin, i.e., original sin. Man dreams of somehow putting this monster in abeyance. However, it has already been done! Jesus is the Source of this *"Everlasting Life."*

4. As well, it does not mean *"mere existence,"* but rather, *"more Abundant Life"* (Jn. 10:10).

5. The way to receive this Life is to *"believe on Jesus."* This expresses an initial act, but it also speaks of a continued process. In other words, one believes and must continue to believe.

Believe what?

6. One must believe that Jesus is the Saviour and that He will save all who come to Him (Jn. 3:16).

NOTES

7. The word *"has"* means that this *"Everlasting Life"* is obtained immediately upon *"believing."* It is not something the Believer shall have but something the Believer presently has.

8. However, the full results of this *"Everlasting Life"* have not yet been realized. Speaking of our present situation, Paul called it *"the earnest of our inheritance,"* meaning the *"pledge or down-payment"* (Eph. 1:14).

(48) "I AM THAT BREAD OF LIFE."

The pattern is:

1. By using the words *"I am,"* Jesus plainly identified Himself as the Jehovah of the Old Testament (Ex. 3:14).

2. Jesus was Jehovah, Very God of Very God, even then while He was Very Man. As Man, He did not have the expression of Deity, but He definitely had the *"possession of Deity."* In other words, He was just as much God then as He was when He dwelt *"in the Light which no man could approach unto"* (I Tim. 6:16).

3. Jesus likened Himself as *"Bread,"* and more perfectly, *"The Bread of Life."*

4. Why did He use bread as a symbolism? As men eat natural bread to sustain the physical body, Jesus, as the Spiritual Bread, sustains the spiritual man, that is, if imbibed regularly. The symbolism is intended to express the idea that as physical bread is to be eaten constantly, likewise, the Believer is to feed on Jesus constantly.

5. In the remaining Verses of this Chapter, Jesus tells us how this can be done.

(49) "YOUR FATHERS DID EAT MANNA IN THE WILDERNESS, AND ARE DEAD."

The composition is:

1. Now Jesus goes back to the very words of the Jews in Verse 31.

2. The Manna which God gave in the wilderness was a Type of Christ. It was meant to portray Christ, which it did! However, *"types"* had no life within themselves and, therefore, could not effect Salvation. Hence, the writer of Hebrews is saying that the *"blood of bulls and goats could not take away sins."* One might quickly add that neither could the Brazen Altar on which the sacrifices were laid, or any of the other holy instruments, etc.

3. However, believing in Whom the Manna represented and to Whom the sacrifices pointed could save one. So, Jesus was telling these Jews that the One to Whom the Manna pointed is now here.

4. He then went on to say that the ones who partook of the Manna, even though from God, died because there were no life-giving properties in this symbolism. Of course, Jesus, by His Life, Death, and Resurrection, ratified what the sacrifices could not give within themselves, but to what they pointed — Salvation.

5. The Jews were trying to cling to the symbolism while refusing the reality. Many do the same thing presently!

6. Millions think the church saves or that Salvation is in the ordinances, such as the *"Lord's Supper"* or *"Water Baptism."* No! All of this, at best, is symbolism and is meant only to point to Jesus.

(50) "THIS IS THE BREAD WHICH COMES DOWN FROM HEAVEN, THAT A MAN MAY EAT THEREOF, AND NOT DIE."

The synopsis is:

1. The phrase, *"This is the Bread which comes down from Heaven,"* quite possibly was said with Jesus pointing to Himself. In essence, He would have been speaking of His Physical Body, which was to be given in Sacrifice for the purchase of lost humanity.

2. *"That a man may eat thereof, and not die,"* speaks of the spiritual and means that man is restored to union with God when, previously, he had been alienated, which meant dead to the Things of the Lord.

3. However, the day is coming, to which Jesus has already alluded several times, that those in the graves (Righteous) will hear His Voice and live!

4. This speaks of God giving the soul and the spirit, which, in the meantime, have been in Heaven, a Glorified Body, which, in essence, will complete the Salvation process.

5. Believers are now sanctified and justified but not yet glorified. This will take place at the Resurrection (Rapture) (I Thess. 4:13-18). At this time, every rudiment of death concerning the Believer, both spiritual and physical, will be forever defeated.

(51) "I AM THE LIVING BREAD WHICH CAME DOWN FROM HEAVEN: IF ANY MAN EAT OF THIS BREAD, HE SHALL LIVE FOREVER: AND THE BREAD THAT I WILL GIVE IS MY FLESH, WHICH I WILL GIVE FOR THE LIFE OF THE WORLD."

The exposition is:

1. The Death of Christ on the Cross was no accident. It was rooted in a compelling Divine necessity.

2. This we see also in our Lord's Prayer in Gethsemane that the Will of the Father be done (Mat. 26:42).

3. Similarly, in Hebrews, we read that it was *"by the Grace of God"* that Christ tasted death for us all (Heb. 2:9).

LIVING BREAD

The phrase, *"I am the Living Bread which came down from Heaven,"* now proclaims Jesus presenting Himself as God (I am), while in the previous Verse, He presented Himself as Man. So, He is the God-Man, Jesus Christ.

"If any man eat of this Bread, he shall live forever," says the same thing as in the previous Verse but in a different way. In the previous Verse, He said, *"and not die,"* whereas now He says, *"shall live forever."* The latter adds to the former.

Merely not dying, while grand within itself, does not speak to the entirety of that which Jesus does in the heart and life of the Believer. To *"live,"* as expressed here by Jesus, is the type of life which springs directly from Jesus as the Ultimate Source, providing a fulfillment of which man cannot presently comprehend. As well, it will be *"forever."* As stated, such is the dream of man but is unobtainable except through Christ.

THE HOLY FLESH OF CHRIST

The phrase, *"And the Bread that I will give is My Flesh, which I will give for the life of the world,"* points to two things:

1. It speaks of the Incarnation, His Body being given as a Sacrifice to atone for the sins of man.

2. The doing of this had to be done in the *"flesh,"* albeit sinless flesh. As such, it was the only such example in the world, in fact, ever had been, since the fall of man. Adam's fall, which spoke for all of humanity because all were in his loins, was brought about in

the flesh even though he was sinless up to that point. Consequently, until the Fall, the flesh of Adam was perfect.

As a result of the Virgin Birth, Jesus was not born with original sin as all others had been after Adam. As such, His *"Flesh"* was perfect and remained that way because He never sinned. In the flesh, He would take the punishment due mankind, thereby, loading upon Himself the sin of the world. Even though He had kept the Law perfectly and, consequently, had not incurred its curse, still, He would take the penalty of the curse on our behalf. He became a *"Sin-Offering!"*

Inasmuch as His Flesh was perfect, God could accept it as a Perfect Sacrifice, with it, thereby, atoning for the sin of man. When this was done, the claims of Heavenly Justice were satisfied. As well, the iron grip of sin was broken, with Satan having no more claim or right over Redeemed Humanity, who, by Faith, were in Christ when He died, was buried, and was resurrected (Rom. 6:3-5).

Such becomes even more astounding when we realize that Jesus did all of this for a world that hated Him, which presents to us a love that is incomprehensible to mere mortals.

(52) "THE JEWS THEREFORE STROVE AMONG THEMSELVES, SAYING, HOW CAN THIS MAN GIVE US HIS FLESH TO EAT?"

The exegesis is:

1. The phrase, *"The Jews therefore strove among themselves,"* presents the inevitable results of unbelief.

2. The question, *"Saying, How can this Man give us His Flesh to eat?"* presents them thinking in the physical while He was speaking in the spiritual.

3. Despite all their claims on God and their boasts of being God's Chosen People, in reality, they did not know God and, consequently, could not think in spiritual terms any more than their modern counterparts.

4. In spite of all of his intellectual loftiness, unredeemed man cannot think as God thinks, despite so-called education and self-improvement. For all that, he thinks little above the level of an animal.

(53) "THEN JESUS SAID UNTO THEM, VERILY, VERILY, I SAY UNTO YOU, EXCEPT YOU EAT THE FLESH OF THE SON OF MAN, AND DRINK HIS BLOOD, YOU HAVE NO LIFE IN YOU."

The exegesis is:

1. In dying on Calvary, Jesus fulfilled all that the old sacrifices had foreshadowed.

2. It is agreed by most Bible students that Christ's Death was vicarious, i.e., *"substitutionary."*

In one sense, Christ died *"for sin,"* and in another sense, He died *"for us."*

3. We must understand, as well, that the Death of Christ was and is Representative. He was our Representative as He hung on the Cross.

EATING THE FLESH AND DRINKING THE BLOOD

The phrase, *"Then Jesus said unto them, Verily, verily, I say unto you,"* presents the Lord's Reply to their thought of it being impossible to eat His Flesh. Instead of softening or modifying this seemingly harsh Doctrine, He instead intensified it by declaring it indispensable to Salvation.

"Except you eat the Flesh of the Son of Man, and drink His Blood, you have no life in you," presents the demand that caused *"many of His Disciples to go back, and walk no more with Him"* (Jn. 6:66). It does the same presently!

A comparison of Verses 47 and 48 with Verses 53 and 54 shows that believing on Christ is the same thing as eating and drinking Him, which refers to believing what He did for us at the Cross. Actually, such figurative speech was quite familiar to the Jews at that time, as is shown by the Talmud.

As well, even though many, especially the Catholic church, have attempted to read the Eucharist into this, it is without Scriptural success.

For the first four Centuries, all that was done was to apply the argument of this Passage in order to express the importance of communicating sacramentally. However, this led the Romanist writers to go further and, ultimately, to regard the participation in the sacramental body and blood as essential to Life Eternal.

The Bishop of Rome in A.D. 402 was the first to interpolate from this Passage,

"Except you receive the Eucharist, you have no life in you," consequently, instituting the Catholic Mass.

ONLY THE CROSS OF CHRIST

In truth, this whole Passage has no relation to the Lord's Supper and its corruption — the Mass. The Lord's Message in the synagogue in Capernaum, for that is where He was, could not possibly have meant that because His Audience would not have understood Him if He had spoken of what men call the Eucharist, i.e., *"the Lord's Supper."*

As we shall see, Jesus will explain that His Words were Spiritual and living and not fleshly and material. He added that as He lived by the Father, so He who ate His Flesh lived by Him. Consequently, the sense in which the Believer partakes and lives upon Christ is similar to that existing between Christ and the Father. In that type of *"eating,"* there cannot possibly be any material food.

As stated, by Jesus using these terms of *"eating His Flesh, and drinking His Blood,"* He was speaking of the Cross and what would there be accomplished. The person's Faith in Christ makes it possible for the believing sinner to die with Him, be buried with Him, and be raised with Him in Newness of Life (Rom. 6:3-5). To be sure, it is a Spiritual thing which happens to the believing sinner upon coming to Christ. In effect, we become so much a part of Christ that we eat His Flesh and drink His Blood, referring to the fact that this is what saved us.

Death, therefore, at least the Death that Jesus died, is the Believer's life. He Who knew no sin put away by death the sin that death brought in. He, as the Sin-Offering, becomes the Meal-Offering upon which the Believer feeds, exactly as the Jews of old in their eating the Meal-Offering, which was a type of what Jesus was speaking of.

EXPATIATION

Expatiation (to put an end to) being complete and infinite, the enjoyment of Christ as the Meal-Offering is assured. With the only disturbing factor between the soul and God, i.e., sin, being infinitely and eternally removed, nothing remains but a Feast. That Feast sustains, as the Meal-Offering, the Life received through the Sin-Offering. However, it is impossible to know and enjoy Christ as the Bread of Life in the Meal-Offering until He is believed upon as the Atoning Saviour in the Sin-Offering, giving His Priceless Life in expatiation of man's sin. (The Meal-Offering was a Thanksgiving-Offering.)

Had Jesus not so died, He must have abode alone, for a Meal-Offering without a Blood-Offering would have been a Cain offering. However, Faith in His Death being established, a Risen and Living Saviour can be feasted upon.

A dead Christ does not exist and, therefore, transubstantiation, as taught by the Catholics, and consubstantiation, as taught by Episcopalians, are human follies.

(Transubstantiation, as taught by the Catholics, claims that the bread and wine turn into the literal Flesh and Blood of Jesus Christ when consumed. Consubstantiation, as taught by the Episcopalians, claims that it does so in Spirit, but not literally, with both claiming Salvation in the partaking of the ingredients.)

The Meal-Offering, as given in Leviticus, Chapter 2, prefigured Christ's spotless Humanity. The flour, not merely ground corn, but flour, revealed Him as Perfect and ready for God's Service. All of this means that there was nothing in Him that was coarse or rough, in other words, He was Without Spot and Without Blemish.

The fineness of the flour predicted that in Him there should be no unevenness or roughness. The flour was to be mingled with oil and oil poured upon it. Such was the Man, Christ Jesus.

He was born of the Holy Spirit and afterwards, anointed by the Holy Spirit (Lk. 4:17-19).

Aaron and his sons ate the Meal-Offering, which was the only offering that was not a blood sacrifice. All the frankincense was burnt, together with a portion of the flour and oil, for a sweet savor unto the Lord.

The highest Christian energy (which the sons of Aaron represented) may partially apprehend the perfection and beauty of Christ's Life as a Man, but the frankincense of that Life was for God. Jesus, as a

Man, said, did, thought, felt, and desired everything to the Glory of God. God Alone could understand, value, and enjoy such frankincense.

NO FERMENTATION

As well, there was neither leaven nor honey, but there was salt in the Meal-Offering. Honey causes fermentation. There was neither error nor corruption in Jesus, but in Him was very visible the salt of the incorruptible, preservative, and faithful Word of God.

The Meal-Offering was to be eaten in a Holy Place, and only by the male children of the High Priest, which was symbolic of those who serve Jesus Christ, our Great High Priest.

These Laws clothed with dignity the Meal-Offering. They taught the necessity of holiness of heart and conduct, and that energy of Spiritual intelligence is needed to feed upon Christ as the Bread from Heaven.

So, these statements as made by Christ concerning the *"eating of His Flesh, and the drinking of His Blood,"* even though somewhat startling to the unknowing Gentile, should not have seemed strange at all to the Jewish listeners of Christ. They should have understood instantly that He was speaking of the *"Meal-Offering,"* which was a type, and grandly so, of those who would partake of Christ. Once again, the only reason these things sounded strange to their ears is because they simply did not know the Word of God. Everything Jesus said was ensconced in the Old Testament and was properly explained. They were supposed to be the people of the Law and, consequently, to understand these things. Sadly, they did not understand!

(54) "WHOSO EATS MY FLESH, AND DRINKS MY BLOOD, HAS ETERNAL LIFE; AND I WILL RAISE HIM UP AT THE LAST DAY."

The synopsis is:

1. The phrase, *"Whoso eats My Flesh, and drinks My Blood, has Eternal Life,"* can be explained, as well, in this fashion:

"Eating His Flesh" was a figure of speech, speaking of the Sacrifice He would offer at Calvary, made up of His Own Body, i.e.,

NOTES

"My Flesh." His Body was given as a Perfect Sacrifice because it was Perfect and, consequently, that which God could accept, and did accept! When one partakes of that by Faith, at that moment, God gives the Believer Eternal Life on the basis of what Christ did for us (Acts 3:16; 4:12; 15:9; Rom. 3:24-25; 5:1-11; 10:9-10; Gal. 2:16-20; 3:1-26; Eph. 2:8-9; I Pet. 1:5-13; Col. 2:10-15; Rom. 6:1-14).

2. The *"Drinking of His Blood,"* again, is a figure of speech, which speaks of one placing his trust in the Blood shed by Jesus at Calvary's Cross, which washed away the sin of man, at least for those who will believe. Upon Faith in that great Act, God grants to the Believer the benefits thereof of a life that is sanctified, justified, and, ultimately, will be glorified (I Cor. 6:9-11).

3. *"And I will raise him up at the last day,"* constitutes the fourth time this is spoken by Jesus. Consequently, the Believer has a fourfold assurance, which speaks of a complete assurance that is undeniable.

(55) "FOR MY FLESH IS MEAT INDEED, AND MY BLOOD IS DRINK INDEED."

The diagram is:

1. The idea is that Christ's Flesh and Blood stand in the same relation to the true life of man that food and drink do to the physical life on Earth.

2. Some may object to Jesus using the two phrases, *"My Flesh"* and *"My Blood,"* as metaphors, which are obviously physical, to describe a very Spiritual experience. However, the union with Christ that one obtains upon Salvation can best be described in the exact manner that Jesus used. Our Salvation was not purchased, as Peter said, *" ... with corruptible things, as silver and gold, from your vain conversation* (lifestyle) *received by tradition from your fathers;*

"But with the Precious Blood of Christ, as of a Lamb without blemish and without spot" (I Pet. 1:18-19).

Incidentally, Peter speaking of *"vain conversation* (vain lifestyle) *received by tradition from your fathers,"* spoke of all the man-made laws added to the original Law of Moses, which could save no one.

Actually, the Jews in Jesus' Day considered they were saved by these very laws and, therefore, rejected what Jesus said must be, *"the eating of His Flesh, and the drinking of His Blood,"* and, therefore, were eternally lost.

(56) "HE WHO EATS MY FLESH, AND DRINKS MY BLOOD, DWELLS IN ME, AND I IN HIM."

The pattern is:

1. The shrinking of Christ in Gethsemane shortly before His Crucifixion was because He Who knew no sin was made to be sin, which is something no member of the Godhead had ever done before.

2. This did not mean that He sinned, for He never sinned, but it did mean that He took the penalty for sin by becoming the Sin-Offering.

3. In His Death, He took our place, and His Holy Soul shrank from this identification with sinners, as should be obvious.

DWELLING IN THE LORD

The phrase, *"He who eats My Flesh, and drinks My Blood,"* presents Jesus using this phrase again, which, by now, must have become very offensive to these rebellious Jews.

"Dwells in me, and I in him," presents the Oneness of Christ and the Believer, which can only be brought about by this method.

The Greek verb is in the present tense, consequently, implying the continuous appropriation of the Divine Sustenance (Reynolds).[3]

This short Verse concerning the Believer dwelling in Christ and Christ dwelling in the Believer guarantees unparalleled victory.

Inasmuch as Jesus was Virgin Born and, therefore, without original sin, upon Faith in Him, God allots this untainted Birth to the Believer as well.

Likewise, Jesus lived and walked for 33 and one-half years without sin, the perfection of which is, as well, given to the Believer upon Faith.

THE CROSS

As Jesus hung on the Cross and died, likewise, the Believer died in Him, which is actually why Jesus died because it was not for Himself. When He was buried, we were buried with Him, which means that as God accepted His Death as payment for sin, in Him, my sin was paid in full, and the old Jimmy Swaggart was buried with Christ (Rom. 6:3-6).

When Jesus walked out of the Tomb in Newness of Life, I, by Faith, walked out in Him. As a result, every single Victory He won, and He won them all, becomes my victory. Consequently, I do not have to overcome the world, the flesh, or the Devil through some effort of struggle on my part, but simply rest in the fact that Jesus has already overcome the Evil One, and, consequently, I am an overcomer.

If the Believer ever attempts to struggle against sin or to overcome sin in any manner other than what Jesus has provided and finished, no matter how holy or Spiritual, it does despite to the Spirit of Grace. Such presents an insult to the Integrity of God and a denial that Jesus finished the Work at Calvary.

OVERCOMING SIN

While no right-thinking Believer would dare do such a thing, still, all of us, at one time or the other, have been guilty of attempting to overcome sin or attacks by Satan in the spiritual realm by efforts of our own, such as prayer, fasting, the quoting of Scripture, etc. Inasmuch as these things are good, and even holy and correct in their own manner, we do not think of doing such as wrong. However, even though the doing of those things helps us greatly in other ways, they cannot help us to overcome sin simply because nothing is needed for such an effort inasmuch as it has already been done. The Lord demands that we not fight the war all over again which He has already won. He, as well, demands that we not fight Satan again, who He has already defeated.

While it is true that we do fight, still, it is a *"good fight of Faith"* and not efforts of our own. The Believer must understand that we are engaged in spiritual warfare. Paul called it *"war"* (II Cor. 10:3-5). So, inasmuch as it is war, this means that it is not a simple matter. Even though we do things right, with our Faith placed in that which is correct, namely Christ and Him Crucified, still, that doesn't mean that Satan is going to fold his tent and run, so to speak. Please understand, as Believers, with our Faith properly placed, the Holy Spirit will then help us. Considering that the Holy Spirit is God and can do anything, if we do not flag in our Faith, to be sure, the Holy Spirit will win this conflict, which means that we win the conflict as well.

THE SIN NATURE

Many Believers, and that includes all of us at one time or the other, attempt to overcome sin by our own efforts, which never works and results in failure. This, in turn, inflames the sin nature (Rom. 7:21). Then, sin dominates us, irrespective of how much we love God and are striving to do His Will.

The Believer is to always *"reckon himself to be dead indeed unto sin, and alive unto God through Jesus Christ our Lord"* (Rom. 6:11).

Regarding the person who is *"dead to sin"* and understands that he is made that way by what Christ did at Calvary and the Resurrection, and that he was in Him when these things were done, sin has no more hold on that person. Satan may probe and tempt, but, ultimately, he is doomed to failure, as long as the Believer refuses to fight him, simply because there is no need to do so. Jesus has already fought him and won. We are to simply *"rest"* in the Victory of our Lord, which, incidentally, is eternal (Mat. 11:28-30).

(57) "AS THE LIVING FATHER HAS SENT ME, AND I LIVE BY THE FATHER: SO HE WHO EATS ME, EVEN HE SHALL LIVE BY ME."

The overview is:

1. Paul tells us that Christ has *"redeemed us from the curse of the Law, having become a curse for us"* (Gal. 3:13).

2. He bore our curse, which is but another way of saying *"substitution."*

3. Regarding what Christ did at the Cross, Atonement is not a matter of passing over sin as it had been done before the Cross. In the Cross, sin was totally addressed with the sin debt totally and completely paid (Rom. 3:25).

THE LIFE-GIVING FATHER

The phrase, *"As the Living Father has sent Me,"* speaks of the Father as He is spoken of nowhere else in Scripture — *"Living Father."* It means *"Life-giving Father."*

The phrase, *"And I live by the Father,"* speaks of the Incarnation. As God, Jesus was Himself the Source of Life; however, as Man, He had to derive Life from the Father, which He did!

"So he who eats Me, even he shall live by Me," proclaims the Truth that as Jesus did not live an independent life apart from the Father, so the Believer does not and, in fact, cannot, live an independent life apart from Christ.

Once more He uses the words *"eats Me,"* which alone can properly explain the union of the Believer with Christ. This is true only of Christianity, i.e., accepting Christ.

The religions of the world, being mere philosophies, boast of no such union with its devotees simply because it is not possible to *"eat"* a philosophy, etc. Consequently, there is no life-changing experience in these man-devised systems of ethics.

LIVING BY CHRIST

With Christianity, i.e., Christ, Faith registered in Him produces a changed life, even a more Abundant Life, because everything Jesus purchased, respecting His Perfect Life, Death on Calvary, Burial and Resurrection, actually becomes the property of the Believer. Jesus did all of this for us, and if proper Faith is registered in Him, in effect, it is the same as us being in Him when all of these things were done. He, as the Representative Man, did for us what we could not do for ourselves.

Consequently, when He speaks of *"living by Me,"* He is speaking of our everyday walk, in other words, the life we live upon this Earth.

As I said in commentary on the last Verse, we do not have to do all over again these things that Jesus has already done for us. Even risking being overly repetitive, please understand that the Believer does not have to be an overcomer in the sense of doing something himself, but simply by trusting Christ, Who is an Overcomer. Upon Faith in Him and what He did for us at the Cross, we automatically are overcomers. Likewise, we do not have to defeat the Devil, as he has already been defeated by Jesus. We just accept Christ's Victory and walk therein. If Satan can maneuver the Believer into fighting Him or contesting Him in any manner, the Believer is sure to lose.

CHRISTIANITY IS REST

Christianity is not a struggle with sin or, at least, is not supposed to be. As Paul said, we are *"dead to sin"* simply because Christ has already overcome sin and broken its grip. Let me say it again:

Christianity is not a struggle, fight, or warfare, at least in this particular capacity. It is a *"rest,"* hence, Jesus saying, *"Come unto Me, and I will give you rest!"* (Mat. 11:28-30).

Yes, there is *"warfare"* involved, and struggle, as well, in other areas, such as the work we carry out for Christ, etc. As well, there is a struggle and warfare in our Faith, which Paul calls a *"good fight"* (I Tim. 6:12). However, living a victorious life, which Jesus is really speaking of by the Words, *"Live by Me,"* is a victory we do not have to win, labor for, struggle for, or earn, but simply accept. Jesus has already won the Victory, and He did it for us, not for Himself. As such, I have no struggle with sin in my daily walk with Christ simply because Christ has done it, and it is a Finished Work. I *"rest"* in Him!

THE CHRISTIAN EXPERIENCE

Admittedly, I have not known this Truth all of my Christian experience, which caused me great problems, and I suspect is true, at least to some extent, with every Believer. To be sure, it was this way with Paul, as we find out in Romans, Chapter 7. If we do not properly understand what we are in Christ, this Christian life will be a continuous struggle, which it is not meant to be.

As a sinner, I trusted in Christ for Salvation without any effort on my part. By the simple act of believing Him, He granted me Eternal Life. As a Believer, I am to continue to trust Him in the same manner. As a sinner, I could do nothing to earn my Salvation, and as a Believer, I do not have to do anything to earn my victory. As Jesus paid the price for my Redemption, He also paid the price for my victorious walk. And yet, many, if not most, of the Christian world do not see the things we have just said but continue to struggle, attempting to win a victory over sin that has already been won.

I'm sure the reader understands that we are speaking of the Believer who wants to walk clean and true before the Lord, and not someone seeking to continue in sin.

Let us say, as well, *"Yes, there is warfare, and there is struggle in the sense of our Faith."* In fact, that struggle will remain until we die or the trump sounds. Sometimes, even often, this warfare can become very intense. The matter is always about Faith, and it must be Faith in the correct Object, which is the Cross of Christ (Rom. 6:1-14; Col. 2:10-15). Our Faith and the correct Object, which is the Cross, will ever be contested by Satan, and mightily so. This warfare will not end but, as stated, will last until we die or the Lord comes. However, this we can win, as well, and must win, and we do so by keeping our Faith exclusively in Christ and the Cross.

(58) "THIS IS THAT BREAD WHICH CAME DOWN FROM HEAVEN: NOT AS YOUR FATHERS DID EAT MANNA, AND ARE DEAD: HE WHO EATS OF THIS BREAD SHALL LIVE FOR EVER."

The overview is:

1. The Cross shows that God is just at the same time as it shows Him justifying Believers.

2. This means that God's Justice is vindicated in the way sin was dealt with, which was at the Cross.

3. This is another way of saying that Christ bore the penalty of man's sin (Heb. 9:28; I Pet. 2:24).

4. To say that Christ bore our sin is at the same time saying that He bore the penalty for our sin.

THE BREAD FROM HEAVEN

The phrase, *"This is that Bread which came down from Heaven,"* once again points to Himself and extols the outsized superiority over the Law, etc.

"Not as your fathers did eat Manna, and are dead," merely makes the comparison between that bread, which was only a symbol, to the True Bread, which was to come, and now has come.

The Jews had made Salvation, or had attempted to do so, out of the Law of Moses; consequently, it was perverted, distorted, abused, and twisted. In other words, its true intent and purpose, as originally given by God, had been all but completely lost.

So, Jesus told them that if they thought that Salvation was in the Law, whether the eating of *"Manna,"* offering of sacrifices, or minutely keeping all the ceremonies and rituals, they would die lost, as everyone who thought such died lost, i.e., *"are dead."* There was no Salvation in the Law, and neither was it meant to be.

THREE PURPOSES OF THE LAW

The Law of Moses was actually given for three purposes:

1. The Law was given that man may have a pattern for living. There were all types of laws in the world, but all were man-devised and, therefore, grossly unfair and of little help to anyone.

The Law of Moses, which was actually from God, addressed itself to every facet of life, telling man what was right and what was wrong.

2. The Law was given to show man how inadequate he was and that, within his own strength, he had no power to keep the Law, no matter how hard he tried. Considering that not one single person ever kept the Law, even Moses, one is made to realize the weakness of man's terrible fallen condition.

3. Realizing this, man was to look to the One to Whom the Law pointed, namely Jesus Christ. Man was meant to realize his inadequacy and, therefore, to throw himself on the Mercy and Grace of God, trusting in the coming Redeemer, Who had been promised from the very beginning.

Now the Redeemer had come, but Israel did not want Him. They would rather continue trying to find life in the Law, when it had no life, and was never meant to have life. So, Jesus plainly told them that if their trust was in the Law to save, they would die in their sins.

HE WHO EATS THIS BREAD SHALL LIVE FOREVER

The phrase, *"He who eats of this Bread shall live forever,"* proclaims Himself as the contrast and, actually, the One to Whom the Law pointed. He Alone, as the True Bread of Life, could give Eternal Life, but one had to *"eat of this Bread"* in order to have this Life. This meant to accept Him for Who He was and What He would do, which spoke of Calvary and the Resurrection.

Regrettably, too many in the modern church continue as the Jews of old. They accept Christianity as a philosophy while rejecting Christ. However, Christianity as a philosophy is of no greater consequence than Islam, Buddhism, etc. Jesus is the Life, the Power, and the Strength of Christianity. In other words, He is Christianity, which means, as we have constantly stated, that it is not a religion but a relationship.

Millions today attempt to keep the *"Golden Rule"* without knowing Christ and without *"eating of this Bread!"* They are what is referred to as *"moralists."*

In other words, they devise a set of rules from Christianity while ignoring Christ or paying Him lip service only.

Their situation, and they number into the millions, is the same as the Jews of old; they will die in their sins. Ethics or law-keeping never saved anyone, only Faith in what Christ did at the Cross. If the Cross is pulled away from Christ, this means the person is worshipping *"another Jesus,"* which presents *"another gospel,"* and does so by *"another spirit"* (II Cor. 11:4).

(59) "THESE THINGS SAID HE IN THE SYNAGOGUE, AS HE TAUGHT IN CAPERNAUM."

The overview is:

1. This was a Message that no one had ever heard preached in this synagogue before. As well, there is evidence that He would not preach it there again.

2. In the first place, they did not want this type of preaching, and secondly, our Lord's Earthly Ministry was quickly coming to a close.

3. To be sure, there are thousands of churches where the Word of God has never been preached and will never be preached. Regrettably, if it was preached, as in the synagogue at Capernaum and most other synagogues in Israel at that time, the people

would not receive it, as they did not receive it that day upon hearing Jesus.

4. So, the Son of God was teaching in the synagogue at Capernaum, but the people did not want what He taught. Consequently, they would not accept what He taught, and would not accept Him either!

(60) "MANY THEREFORE OF HIS DISCIPLES, WHEN THEY HAD HEARD THIS, SAID, THIS IS AN HARD SAYING; WHO CAN HEAR IT?"

The exegesis is:

1. Substitution lies behind the statement in I Timothy 2:6 that Christ gave Himself a *"ransom for all."*

2. It actually means *"Substitute-ransom."*

3. Thayer defined it as *"what is given in exchange for another as the price of his redemption."*[4] It is impossible to empty the word *"ransom"* of *"substitutionary associations."*

DISCIPLES

The phrase, *"Many therefore of His Disciples,"* spoke of those other than the Twelve.

The word *"Disciples"* in the Greek is *"mathetes"* and means *"one who is not only a pupil, but an adherent."* In other words, they are imitators of their teacher, in this case, Christ. Even though God Alone knew their hearts, still, I think one would have to say that these individuals were Believers, i.e., *"Saved."* However, they come under the heading of those of whom Jesus spoke in the Parable of the Sower, who *"heard the Word, and anon with joy received it; yet has he not root in himself, but endures for a while: for when tribulation or persecution arises because of the Word, by and by* (immediately) *he is offended"* (Mat. 13:20-21).

I think it is obvious that these Disciples were offended because of the *"Word"* spoken by Jesus. So, this refutes the unscriptural doctrine of Unconditional Eternal Security.

A HARD SAYING?

The question, *"When they had heard this, said, This is an hard saying; who can hear it?"* proclaims them muttering one to the other.

The *"eating His Flesh"* and *"drinking His Blood,"* to which He constantly referred, was greatly offensive to them.

Did they understand properly what He was saying?

No, they did not because unbelief will not allow one to properly understand. However, they understood enough to know that He was speaking of His Death, and especially the manner in which He would die, which they would not accept.

Concerning this, Westcott said, *"They were unwilling to accept the bloody death of their Messiah, or to entrust themselves to a Divine Personality Whose most distinctive act would be His Sacrifice of Himself. This was the gross and terrible offense which made the Cross a stumblingblock to the Jews"*[5] (Mat. 16:21; I Cor. 1:23; Gal. 5:11).

Is what Jesus said a hard saying?

In truth, it is! It is hard because man does not want to believe that he is so sinful, wicked, and corrupt that it would take such an act, constituting such a price, in order to effect his Redemption.

MAN ADMITTING WHAT HE IS

As well, if man finally admits that he does need help in order to be Saved, which he is loath to do, the simple act of having Faith in what Jesus did at Calvary and the Resurrection is an offense to him simply because he is not allowed to contribute something himself, which he thinks he can surely do.

Finally, this Suffering Messiah, hanging on a Cross and being placed in a Tomb, is not the kind of Messiah that Israel or the world desires. A Triumphant Messiah, splendid in regal attire and lifting Israel to sublime heights, is more what they had in mind!

Even though Jesus did not have regal bearing because He was a Peasant and, as a result, *"there was no beauty that He would be desired,"* still, His Miracles were abundant and so powerful that they attracted a large following. However, that which He is saying now was so offensive to them that even the Miracles could not keep their loyalty.

THE WORD

This tells us that if men will not believe the Word but follow only after Miracles, etc., sooner or later, their attention and devotion will flag.

Incidentally, their continuing to refer to the Manna in the wilderness, which they considered to be the right *"sign,"* better fits the type of Messiah they wanted. Even though Jesus had fed the thousands with five loaves and two fish, they did not even remotely consider that as great a Miracle as the Manna. The Manna fell early every morning and was an ever present supply for them.

It doesn't matter that their forefathers in the wilderness had murmured and complained about the Manna, saying, *"There is nothing at all, besides this Manna, before our eyes."*

Then Moses wrote, concerning this murmuring, *"And the anger of the LORD was kindled greatly"* (Num. 11:6, 10).

Concerning the archeological excavations of Capernaum in the early part of the Nineteenth Century, the remains of an ancient synagogue were uncovered. It is said that on turning over a large block of stone, they found a pot of Manna engraved on its face.

The one giving account of this incident said, *"This very symbol may have been before the eyes of those who heard the Lord's Words that day in Capernaum as He gave this very Message."*

So, the fathers were not satisfied with the Manna that the Lord gave from Heaven, and neither were their children satisfied with the True Bread which came down from Heaven, the Lord Jesus Christ.

(61) "WHEN JESUS KNEW IN HIMSELF THAT HIS DISCIPLES MURMURED AT IT, HE SAID UNTO THEM, DOES THIS OFFEND YOU?"

The pattern is:

1. Paul saw in the Cross the way of Deliverance and, in fact, the only way of Deliverance.

2. Man does not need treatment. He needs Deliverance.

3. Men are naturally enslaved by sin but, in Christ, can be made free.

MURMURING

The phrase, *"When Jesus knew in Himself that His Disciples murmured at it,"* as stated, proclaims Disciples other than the original Twelve.

NOTES

There is a twofold meaning respecting Jesus knowing the negative response to His Message:

1. The murmuring of the crowd was, no doubt, evident and was very easy to discern. Signs of rebellion at what He was saying were very obvious.

2. However, in conjunction with the obvious, the Holy Spirit told Him of the depths of their rebellion. In other words, He was able to look down into their hearts and see the blackness.

AN OFFENSE

The question, *"He said unto them, Does this offend you?"* could well be asked of the whole world and, in fact, is!

We Preachers desire to preach a message that will fill the house, but this Message preached by Jesus emptied the place. Actually, the True Gospel will always have that type of effect.

In 1982, the Lord spoke to my heart and said, *"If you preach what I tell you to preach, your own will turn against you, and you could lose everything."* He was speaking of a worldwide Ministry, the Bible College, the Church, as well as the telecast, which covered a great part of the world.

Whether I did what He told me to do as well as it could have been done, the Lord will have to be the Judge. However, I did my best, and what He said came to pass exactly as it had been spoken to me.

The church world, especially the Pentecostal and Charismatic varieties, objected strongly to my stand against humanistic psychology. They also objected strongly to my stand against Catholicism. I could say the same for the so-called Christian rock music. Also, my emphasis on the Holy Spirit greatly offended them.

This is in spite of tens of thousands of people being Saved, with entire nations being touched with the Gospel. They objected so strongly that when they found something in my own spiritual warfare that pointed to failure, they were quick to seize it and to use every means at their disposal to destroy me. No, I do not blame them or anyone else for my own failures. That is mine and mine alone. However, the position they took had little to do with that, with that being only an excuse. It was the Message I preached which they despised.

THE OFFENCE OF THE CROSS

Now, along with those things mentioned, it is the Message of the Cross which offends much of the church world. Actually, the Message of the Cross is an offense and, in fact, has always been, and continues to be so today (Gal. 5:11).

Men want a watered-down Gospel which caters to their self-esteem and self-importance. Above all, they do not want any Conviction of sin. Consequently, they search out churches, which have excellent social programs, and where the Holy Spirit is not present, and, therefore, they are not convicted. Then, their consciences are appeased in their religiosity, not realizing how deceived they actually are.

There are very few Preachers of the Gospel who earnestly seek the Lord that His Presence would fill their hearts and lives, who, upon hearing from God, arise from the altar of self-abnegation proclaiming, *"Thus saith the Lord."* Even though such Preachers get people Saved and Believers baptized with the Holy Spirit, with lives miraculously changed, their Message is not popular and, in fact, has never been popular. If the world sings the praises of the preacher, or even the church sings the praises of the preacher, he simply is not preaching the Gospel!

(62) "WHAT AND IF YOU SHALL SEE THE SON OF MAN ASCEND UP WHERE HE WAS BEFORE?"

The order is:

1. In effect, Jesus is saying that if His Death is to be a stumblingblock to them, how much more would be His Resurrection?

2. However, would not that prove the reality and value of His Death and, as well, the depth of their unbelief?

3. He had been speaking of Himself coming down from Heaven as the Bread of Life, and now He speaks of going back to Heaven!

4. Even though Jesus constantly referred to Himself as *"the Son of Man,"* speaking of His Humanity, yet, He, as well, refers time and again to His existence before the world was, thereby, proclaiming His Deity.

(63) "IT IS THE SPIRIT WHO QUICKENS; THE FLESH PROFITS NOTHING: THE WORDS THAT I SPEAK UNTO YOU, THEY ARE SPIRIT, AND THEY ARE LIFE."

The form is:

1. Paul told us again and again that the *"flesh"* is our enemy as a Christian.

2. The *"flesh"* pertains to our personal ability, education, willpower, talent, ability, etc., in other words, that which is indicative to a human being.

3. We simply cannot live for God by that means because the flesh is woefully inadequate (Rom. 8:10).

IT IS THE HOLY SPIRIT WHO MAKES ALIVE

The phrase, *"It is the Spirit Who quickens,"* proclaims the very heart of the Gospel of Jesus Christ and what makes it so potent.

The reason they did not understand His Words concerning *"the eating of His Flesh, and the drinking of His Blood,"* is because they did not have the Holy Spirit. While, in fact, many of these *"Disciples"* may very well have been Saved, as the Text seems to bear out, unbelief filled their hearts respecting this part of Jesus' Message, which negated the Moving and Operation of the Holy Spirit. This ultimately resulted in many of them being eternally lost.

As well, there is, no doubt, a great percentage of Christians at present, even those who are Spirit-filled, who have allowed unbelief to fill their hearts and lives. As a result, many of them will ultimately be eternally lost or, at least, severely stunted in the spiritual sense.

The Holy Spirit can only work in an atmosphere of Faith. As well, He always, and without exception, functions on the promise and foundation of the Word of God. So, if the Word is faithfully sought with every determination to obey, the Holy Spirit will work in the heart and life of the Believer, irrespective of other types of spiritual weakness, etc.

THE MESSAGE OF THE CROSS

That which Jesus was giving to the people at that time was actually *"the Message of the Cross."* True enough, it was in veiled form, but, still, that's what it was. Man has never wanted to admit that his life is so messed up, so to speak, so awry, and so perverted that it would take God becoming Man, thereby, coming down to this world in order to die on a Cross, that is, if man was to be redeemed. In fact, it has always been the Cross. Upon the fall of Adam and Eve in the Garden and their being driven out and not allowed to return, the Lord still told them, and all who followed thereafter, that they could have forgiveness of sins and communion with Him. This would be by the means of the Sacrificial system, the death of an innocent victim, a lamb. It has always been the Cross, of which the sacrifices of the Old Testament were a type.

The Message of the Cross is the Story of the Bible. One could say, *"Jesus Christ and Him Crucified"* (I Cor. 1:23). As well, the Holy Spirit works exclusively on the premise of the Cross. In fact, only the Spirit of God can quicken the Word of God to one's heart and life. He attends every single thing that is done for God in the world. Without Him, nothing will be accomplished, at least for the Lord. That is the reason the Preacher, along with the Saints, must be full of the Holy Spirit. It is on this ground alone that God's Word, in every capacity, can be carried out.

The intellect does not quicken, and neither do talents, ability, nor education. It is only the Holy Spirit Who makes alive.

Sadly, grouping both Catholic and Protestant churches together, most, in fact, have never had the Moving and Operation of the Holy Spirit in any capacity. They are loaded with religious machinery, but despite that, there is nothing done for the Lord Jesus Christ. Despite the heavy covering of religion, no lives are changed, no sick bodies are healed, and no bondages are broken. For all practical purposes, even though His Name is mentioned, Jesus is not there. Wherever the Holy Spirit is, Jesus will be paramount, and not the Virgin Mary, etc.

THE HOLY SPIRIT

It is very sad that many of the giant Pentecostal denominations, having begun in the fires of revival and the Moving of the Holy Spirit, have, at present, few earmarks of His Presence. Secular means are employed and carried out, all under the guise of the Spirit, but which, in actuality, have originated with man.

That is the reason much of the modern church little knows what is right and wrong anymore. The Holy Spirit is not there to lead them because He is not wanted. Consequently, the church refers people with problems to humanistic psychology and directs their young people to so-called Christian rock music, under the guise of reaching young people for Christ. The truth is, they are not reaching anyone for anything except the powers of darkness.

As well, many in the modern church flit from one fad and phenomenon to the other, labeling almost everything as being *"a Moving of the Spirit,"* even though it is blatantly unscriptural.

Despite the noise, racket, activity, religious machinery, bloated numbers, $10 million church buildings, conferred degrees, greed, and political messages, the truth is, the modern church has never been so lacking in the true Moving and Operation of the Holy Spirit, at least since the Reformation.

PRAISING GOD TO WHOM THEY NO LONGER PRAY

If the Holy Spirit is present and prevalent, souls will be Saved and not bloated, hyped figures thrown out, with few, if any, of these *"conversions"* being found the next day. People will truly be healed of their afflictions, not merely some type of confession principle claiming such, where there is no proof or reality. Believers will be baptized with the Holy Spirit with the evidence of speaking with other Tongues, of which there is precious little interest at present. Lives will be gloriously changed by the Power of God and not merely referred to some group counseling sessions.

The modern Pentecostal church, which cannot even really legitimately be called Pentecostal anymore, has learned to praise a God to Whom they no longer pray. Get-rich-quick seminars are the rage at present, all under the guise of Bible Faith, with little mention anymore of Righteousness and Holiness. Likewise, politics has entered the church, with much of its resources and energies going to elect some public official, claiming this will solve the problems of America, etc. Giant auditoriums are packed to capacity, with tens of thousands of young people screaming their approval of rock shows under the guise of Gospel, when the only real reason is to make money.

THE BOOK OF ACTS

One will look in vain in the Book of Acts for such foolishness. As well, this account must be our criterion, for it is the Holy Spirit Who orchestrated its contents.

Sadly, one Pentecostal leader (Pentecostal?) suggested the other day that the Book of Acts should no longer serve as the guideline for the church, inasmuch as we have learned to be much more efficient presently. To be blunt, that is stupidity gone to seed!

The True Gospel of Jesus Christ is a Miracle Gospel in every respect simply because the Holy Spirit is the Superintendent of mighty things. To have less than Him is to have nothing. To have Him is to have everything because He always leads one to the Word and to Jesus. That is His Business, and He does it well.

THE FLESH

The phrase, *"The flesh profits nothing,"* in effect, says, *"If you could literally eat My Flesh and drink My Blood, it would not save your souls."*

What is the flesh?

As previously stated, the *"flesh"* is that which is indicative to human beings. It speaks of our personal talents, ability, motivation, education, desires, willpower, etc. While these things, within themselves, aren't wrong, the idea is, and blatantly so, that one cannot live for God by that means. We can only live for God by the Moving and Operation of the Holy Spirit.

If men concentrate on these things named, they may be said to *"set their minds on the things of the flesh"* (Rom. 8:5), and to set the mind on the flesh *"is death"* (Rom. 8:6). This is explained as *"enmity against God"* (Rom. 8:7).

The man whose horizon is limited by the flesh is by that very fact opposed to God. He lives *"according to the flesh"* (Rom. 8:13), and this is the flesh that *"lusts against the Spirit"* (Gal. 5:17). Actually, for a dreadful list of the *"works of the flesh,"* see Galatians 5:19-21.

If we try to live for the Lord by the means of the flesh, which I should think is by now overly obvious, we will fail every single time.

WALKING AFTER THE FLESH AND WALKING AFTER THE SPIRIT

Paul said:

"There is therefore now no condemnation to them ... who walk not after the flesh but after the Spirit" (Rom. 8:1).

So, how does one walk after the Spirit, i.e., *"Holy Spirit"*?

One must understand how the Holy Spirit works. So, how does He work within our lives?

The Holy Spirit works exclusively within the parameters, so to speak, of the Finished Work of Christ (Rom. 8:1-11). It is what Jesus did at the Cross that gives the Holy Spirit the legal means to do all that He does. He doesn't require very much of us, but He does demand that our Faith be exclusively in Christ and the Cross, and be maintained exclusively in Christ and the Cross. With our Faith firmly fixed and maintained, then the Holy Spirit can work within our lives, doing what He Alone can do.

Of course, as all know and understand, the Holy Spirit is God. That means that He is Almighty and can do anything. He can do anything, He knows all things, and He is everywhere. To be sure, without His Leading, Guidance, Empowerment, and Ability, all evidenced on our behalf, we simply cannot live for God as we should. The spirit world of darkness is far too great for us to overcome such by our own means and methods. It cannot be done. The Holy Spirit Alone can carry out this task, and He can do so because of what Jesus did at the Cross (Rom. 8:1-11).

WHAT DID JESUS DO AT THE CROSS?

He atoned for all sin, past, present, and future, at least for all who will believe (Jn.

3:16). Sin is the legal means that Satan has to hold man captive. With those legal means removed, this satisfied the claims of Heavenly Justice, with God declaring the debt as fully and completely paid. The legal means were removed by the price that Jesus paid by the giving of His Own Precious Blood, in essence, giving His Life. Sin is the problem, and the only answer to sin is the Cross of Christ. I want that statement to be looked at very carefully.

Humanistic psychology contains no answer whatsoever, and education, as in the realm of the world, holds no solutions whatsoever. There is only one answer and one solution, and that is the Cross of Christ. That's why Paul said:

"I determined to know nothing among you, save Jesus Christ, and Him Crucified" (I Cor. 2:2).

For instance, if a Believer attempts to overcome sin by a regimen of so much prayer each day, fasting so many days, or confessing certain Scriptures, this constitutes that which is wholly Scriptural being used for the wrong purpose. While these things are of tremendous value and consequence in their own right and should be engaged constantly by Believers, still, if they are used for the purpose of overcoming sin, the Lord marks them down as *"flesh,"* which will achieve no results.

Why?

Even though these efforts are Scriptural and commendable, to use them in this fashion constitutes *"law"* and, consequently, cannot achieve its desired purpose simply because that purpose has already been achieved in Christ.

Paul said, *"I find then a Law, that, when I would do good* (try to overcome sin by any method other than what Christ did for us at the Cross), *evil is present with me"* (Rom. 7:21).

RELIGIOUS FLESH

Paul is saying that if he tries to overcome sin in any manner, except by reckoning himself already as an overcomer through what Christ did, and standing on that, there is a *"law"* that demands that he fail, thereby, finding *"evil present with him,"* i.e., will find himself sinning despite all of his efforts to not do so!

So, the *"flesh"* is a very subtle thing. We understand it readily when it pertains to works of the flesh, such as *"adultery, witchcraft, hatred, fornication,"* etc., but we find ourselves being deceived very easily when it comes to *"religious flesh."*

THE WORD OF GOD

Jesus said, *"The Words that I speak unto you, they are Spirit, and they are Life,"* tells us two things:

1. Jesus' *"Words"* constitute the Bible. We ought to understand that between its covers, every single problem of life and godliness is addressed (II Pet. 1:3-4). If it's not Scriptural, it is of the *"flesh"* and will bring only destruction, even if it is religious.

2. The manner in which His *"Words"* are *"Spirit"* is that the Holy Spirit energizes that which He has said and makes these *"Words"* real to our hearts and lives.

The *"Word"* without the Holy Spirit energizing it, even if it is preached and believed correctly, will bring no life. It is only the Word of God energized by the Holy Spirit which affords *"Life."* As well, the Believer must have Faith in order for this complement to be realized. We must believe the Word, and then the Spirit of God will do His Great Office Work of energizing *"Life"* within us, either in the Born-Again experience, if Salvation is needed, or in our daily walk in this world as Believers. Unbelief stops the Spirit of God because He will not function in such a climate. Faith in God and His Word is the ingredient in which the Spirit works.

(64) "BUT THERE ARE SOME OF YOU WHO BELIEVE NOT. FOR JESUS KNEW FROM THE BEGINNING WHO THEY WERE WHO BELIEVED NOT, AND WHO SHOULD BETRAY HIM."

The pattern is:

1. The phrase, *"But there are some of you who believe not,"* proclaims exactly what I have just said relative to Faith. They did not believe the Word. Consequently, there was no ground on which the Holy Spirit could work. Therefore, there was no life.

2. *"For Jesus knew from the beginning

who they were who believed not, and who should betray Him," does not mean from the beginning of time or even in the beginning of their unbelief. It is speaking primarily of the beginning of Jesus' Public Ministry.

3. No doubt, the Spirit of God told Him things, but, as well, the *"unbelief"* registered in these people would have been quite obvious to Jesus. Unbelief shows itself in many and varied ways. The response to the Word of God is not as it should be. Often there is very little joy or jubilance. When others are greatly rejoicing over the things the Lord is doing, the one registering unbelief, if rejoicing at all, only does so in a perfunctory manner.

4. When Jesus spoke of *"betrayal,"* He was speaking of Judas, as should be obvious. Consequently, we are given the cause of this man's betrayal, which is *"unbelief."*

5. While there is every likelihood that he believed that Jesus was indeed the Messiah, he felt, as it seems to be obvious, that Jesus was not using His Power in the manner he (Judas) thought desirable. Quite possibly, he was chagrined when Jesus would not allow Himself to be made King as the people desired after the feeding of the thousands with the five loaves and two fish (Jn. 6:14-15).

6. If the truth be known and Jesus were here now in the flesh, most would take the same position as the Jews and Judas of old. While they might believe that He is truly the Messiah, most would not agree as to the manner of His Deity. Men strongly desire to use God for their nefarious ends but little desire to do His Will. The criterion for Faith, at least true Faith, is always *"Not my will, but Your Will be done"* (Lk. 22:42).

(65) "AND HE SAID, THEREFORE SAID I UNTO YOU, THAT NO MAN CAN COME UNTO ME, EXCEPT IT WERE GIVEN UNTO HIM OF MY FATHER."

The construction is:

1. The phrase, *"And He said, Therefore said I unto you,"* refers back to Verse 37.

2. *"That no man can come unto Me, except it were given unto him of My Father,"* does not refer to predestination as some teach. What it does say is this:

3. God will give no one to His Son Jesus Christ except one come by Faith, and that

NOTES

means Faith properly placed and believing in What and Who Jesus really is. If one believes, the Holy Spirit will energize such Faith, even as weak as it may possibly be, with the Father giving that person to Christ for attendant Salvation and all that it means.

4. The Scripture plainly says, *"For God so loved the world, that He gave His Only Begotten Son, that whosoever believes in Him should not perish, but have Everlasting Life"* (Jn. 3:16).

5. The teaching which claims that God purposely gives some Faith while not giving it to others is erroneous. The Lord does not tamper with the individual's free moral agency. It is still, as stated, *"whosoever will!"* The Spirit of that Truth runs all the way from Genesis through the Book of Revelation and actually closes in that context (Rev. 22:17).

6. Now, the question may be asked, *"Did God originally give Judas to Jesus as one of the Twelve?"*

7. One has to assume that He did, or else, Jesus was outside the Will of God when He selected Him, which we know is incorrect. Every evidence is that Judas, at the outset, truly believed. However, for whatever reasons, Judas, little by little, ceased to believe and, thereby, betrayed Christ and lost his soul.

The entire episode of this Sixth Chapter of John proclaims the Cross of Christ. Judas simply did not want the Cross. He wanted a Messiah, but he wanted one that would deliver Israel from Rome, and not one that would deliver Israel from sin. So, the Cross was too much for him.

8. Peter said, *"That he may take part of this Ministry and Apostleship, from which Judas by transgression fell, that he might go to his own place"* (Acts 1:25).

Before one can *"fall,"* one must first be in such a position from which to fall. The ungodly do not fall because they are already fallen.

9. As well, God did not give Judas to Jesus in order that he might fulfill Prophecy respecting the betrayal (Zech. 11:12). Prophecy is merely foreknowledge and not predestination.

10. What Judas did was not the Will or Desire of God but Judas' own choice. The

Scripture plainly says that *"God is not willing that any should perish, but that all should come to Repentance"* (II Pet. 3:9).

(66) "FROM THAT TIME MANY OF HIS DISCIPLES WENT BACK, AND WALKED NO MORE WITH HIM."

The structure is:

1. It is hard to conceive that men would do such a thing, considering the great Power of God which accompanied Christ, but they did!

2. Reynolds said, *"Those who a few hours before were ready to call Him their Messianic King, were now entirely disenchanted."*

He then went on to say, *"The claims of Christ were so profoundly different from what they anticipated, that they now refused to accept Him at all!"*[6]

3. In truth, the Power of God, which is an undeniable proof of the Presence of God and, therefore, the Will of God, should be enough to convince anyone. However, it seldom is.

4. Considering my own Ministry, the Holy Spirit, at times, moves with great convicting Power, which is obvious to all, and which brings many to Christ, but, still, most will not believe that God is with me.

Why?

5. It is the same now as then. The Testimony of the Word, and, therefore, the Moving and Operation of the Holy Spirit, are not enough, at least in the thinking of these unbelievers. They always demand something else, which is something man-devised and man-directed. In other words, they leave the Word of God and miss what God has for them exactly as these Jews of old missed the greatest moment in human history.

6. It must always be remembered that the Word of God, along with the Spirit of God, not only attracts men but, as well, tests men.

7. The Doctrine that said they were sinners and needed a Saviour, and that Saviour was Jesus, and that Salvation would come by means of the Cross, *"eating His Flesh and drinking His Blood,"* finally alienated them. It still alienates multitudes, for it humiliates man's pride and annihilates his self-importance and self-righteousness.

(67) "THEN SAID JESUS UNTO THE TWELVE, WILL YOU ALSO GO AWAY?"

The pattern is:

1. The defection of these former Disciples must have deeply pained the Lord's Heart, for He turned to the Twelve, now first mentioned in this Gospel of John, with the pathetic words, throbbing with love's anxieties, *"Will you also go away?"*

2. If it were not possible for such to happen, as those who believe Unconditional Eternal Security teach, then the question, as asked by Jesus, made no sense.

3. The truth is that anyone can come, and anyone can leave, that is, if they so desire. As we have previously said, the True Gospel of Jesus Christ will not only attract but, as well, will drive others away, in fact, most!

4. Sometime ago, I heard a newscast respecting several of the giant megachurches in America (churches with 2,000 or more in attendance). Of course, the things I am about to say certainly would not include all churches of this size, but definitely will include some, in fact, those they sought to interview.

5. Upon asking the reason for their success, one pastor said, *"We give the people what they want!"*

He then went on to say, *"We have many social programs, and we never sing any of the old songs about the Blood, the Crucifixion, etc., although,"* he said, *"Some of those songs are beautiful."*

6. In fact, this church was such in name only. It had nothing to do with God, did not have the Holy Spirit, and, consequently, was no more than some type of religious social program. Regrettably, the far greater majority of the churches in America and Canada, and in the world, for that matter, fall into the same category. The preachers have long since departed from God, that is, if they ever knew Him, which most probably never did.

7. With sadness, one must come to the conclusion that most, in fact, *"have gone away,"* or else, are in the process of doing so, exactly as those Disciples of long ago.

(68) "THEN SIMON PETER ANSWERED HIM, LORD, TO WHOM SHALL WE GO? YOU HAVE THE WORDS OF ETERNAL LIFE."

The pattern is:

1. The question, *"Then Simon Peter answered Him, Lord, to whom shall we go?"* presents this Apostle confessing Who Jesus is for the second time, but in more emphatic language.

2. The phrase, *"You have the Words of Eternal Life,"* must have been like a balm of medicine to the saddened and wounded Heart of our Lord.

3. While Peter had his faults, he also had Faith.

(69) "AND WE BELIEVE AND ARE SURE THAT YOU ARE THAT CHRIST, THE SON OF THE LIVING GOD."

The overview is:

1. The phrase, *"And we believe and are sure,"* means that there are times when Faith is tried by speculative difficulties, and its foundation seems to become a swaying platform.

2. At such times, it is felt that to turn away from the Lord Jesus is to face darkness, desolation, and death. So, recoiling from this, the heart falls back on *"we have believed and have proved by experience,"* and a recovery of Faith and an unspeakable relief is then enjoyed.

3. *"That You are the Christ, the Son of the Living God,"* means, *"We have believed, and have got to know — have learned by experience — that You are the Messiah, the Son of the Living God."*

(70) "JESUS ANSWERED THEM, HAVE NOT I CHOSEN YOU TWELVE, AND ONE OF YOU IS A DEVIL?"

The diagram is:

1. The beginning of the question, *"Jesus answered them, Have not I chosen you Twelve. . . ?"* proclaims far more than random selection, but rather specific direction as given to Him by the Father. In fact, Jesus prayed all night long, seeking the Will of the Father respecting the choice of these men (Lk. 6:12-16). The truth is, Jesus chose Judas, and Judas, as well, at first, chose Christ. However, Judas' choice was turned by unbelief, as it has with millions.

2. The conclusion of the question, *"And one of you is a devil?"* does not mean that Judas had always been this way, but he became this way when he freely chose to go in selfish directions when he then became a tool of the Devil.

3. It is morally inconceivable that Jesus, in His Divine Foreknowledge, and according to the Will of the Father, chose Judas to special reprobation, knowing him then to be devilish in his nature, so that he might have his character demoralized by this close contact with Christ's Holiness and, thus, be trained for the damnation of the traitor's sin and doom.

Actually, Jesus brought him nearer to Himself and gave him fresh opportunity of acquiring a correct knowledge of the Kingdom and its methods. By these warnings, the Lord was giving him chance after chance of escaping from this coming doom but, sadly and regrettably, all to no avail.

4. This tells us that *"environment," "participation,"* and *"association,"* all of which Judas had, do not bring success in the Lord. Such can only come by Faith.

(71) "HE SPOKE OF JUDAS ISCARIOT THE SON OF SIMON: FOR HE IT WAS WHO SHOULD BETRAY HIM, BEING ONE OF THE TWELVE."

The overview is:

1. The phrase, *"He spoke of Judas Iscariot the son of Simon,"* means that he was a *"man of Kerioth,"* a place in Judah (Josh. 15:25). As far as is known, he was the only one of the Twelve who came from Judah, the Tribe of Jesus.

2. *"For he it was who should betray Him, being one of the Twelve,"* is said like this by the Holy Spirit for purpose and reason.

3. In the history of man and of all the great things which have happened, to have had the privilege of being chosen as one of the *"Twelve"* was a privilege indeed! Actually, because of its association with Jesus, nothing could be superior to that Calling and position. So, Judas had the opportunity of all opportunities and the privilege of all privileges!

4. Jesus mentioning and using the stern statement, *"One of you is a devil,"* meant that the seed of rebellion was already beginning to germinate in Judas' heart. What form it took, we do not know. However, even though great efforts would be made by Christ to pull this man back from the brink,

the slide from here on was ever downward.

5. Today, he burns in Hell, and will be there forever and forever, when he could have had his name inscribed on the Twelve foundations of the wall of the New Jerusalem (Rev. 21:14).

6. However, such speaks of almost the entirety of the world. All could live with Jesus in this New Jerusalem, enjoying Eternal Life, and as someone has said, *"The bliss the Blood-washed know,"* but instead, will live in eternity without end, with Judas who forsook the Lord.

"Come ye sinners, lost and hopeless,
"Jesus' Blood can make you free.
"For He saved the worst among you,
"When He saved a wretch like me."

"And I know, yes, I know;
"Jesus' Blood can make the vilest sinner clean.
"And I know, yes, I know,
"Jesus' Blood can make the vilest sinner clean."

CHAPTER 7

(1) "AFTER THESE THINGS JESUS WALKED IN GALILEE: FOR HE WOULD NOT WALK IN JEWRY, BECAUSE THE JEWS SOUGHT TO KILL HIM."

The construction is:

1. The phrase, *"After these things Jesus walked in Galilee,"* covers a span of approximately six months, from the Passover to the Feast of Tabernacles.

2. During this time, many glorious and wonderful things happened, which are recorded by Matthew, Mark, and Luke, but are omitted by John.

3. *"For He would not walk in Jewry, because the Jews sought to kill Him,"* spoke of Jerusalem and Judaea. These were the religious leaders of the Nation and are to be distinguished from the multitude of the people. Consequently, Jesus remained in Galilee and seemingly did not attend the Feast of Pentecost, which is held 50 days after the Passover (sometime in the latter part of May).

NOTES

4. This was now approximately six months before the Crucifixion of Christ, with the hatred and animosity against Him rising to a fever pitch among the religious leaders.

5. Men who are in error respecting the Bible are seldom content with verbally opposing the Truth, but rather feel they must silence the voice altogether, and will use any tactic to do so. This pertains to Satan's most fertile field, the field of religion, which he defends the most. In fact, many, if not most, of the wars in history have had religious overtones. It is the same presently!

6. It is ironic, to say the least, that these are the very people who claimed to be the *"Chosen of God,"* and, now, they were plotting to kill the Lord of Glory. Deception is an awful thing. It makes people believe they know God when, in reality, they do not!

(2) "NOW THE JEWS' FEAST OF TABERNACLES WAS AT HAND."

The diagram is:

1. At the Cross, Christ dealt fully with man's sin.

2. In the writings of John, there is the thought of Christ as the Special Revelation of the Father. He is the One sent by the Father, and all that He does must be interpreted in the light of this fact.

3. So, John saw Christ as winning a conflict against the darkness and as defeating the Evil One, which He did at the Cross.

THE FEAST OF TABERNACLES

This Feast was conducted in October, along with the Feast of Trumpets and the Feast of Atonement, which immediately preceded the Feast of Tabernacles. The Passover came at the beginning of the barley harvest, and the Feast of Tabernacles came at the end of the harvest, in this case, the Fruit Harvest.

The designation, *"Feast of Booths"* (Tabernacles), comes from the requirement that everyone born an Israelite live in booths made of boughs of trees and branches of palm trees for the seven days of the Feast (Lev. 23:42).

Sacrifices were offered on the seven days, beginning with 13 bullocks and other animals on the first day, and diminishing by one bullock each day until on the seventh day, seven bullocks were offered. On the eighth day, there was a solemn assembly when one bullock, one ram, and seven lambs were offered (Num. 29:36). This is the last day, *"That Great Day of the Feast,"* alluded to in John 7:37.

As a Feast, Divinely instituted, it was never forgotten. It was observed in the time of Solomon (II Chron. 8:13), Hezekiah (Deut. 16:16; II Chron. 31:3), and after the Exile (Ezra 3:4; Zech. 14:16, 18-19).

REDEMPTION

The Feast of Tabernacles had a historical reference to the Exodus from Egypt and reminded the Jews of their wandering and dwelling in booths in the wilderness, hence, their being required to spend this time in booths made of branches, etc. (Lev. 23:43).

Spiritually, it pointed to the truth that Israel's life rested upon Redemption, which, in its ultimate meaning, is the forgiveness of sin and is typified by Israel's Deliverance from Egypt.

As the prior Chapter presents Jesus as the True Fulfillment of the Passover, when He would shed His Blood and lay down His Life to deliver man from death, likewise, Jesus is the True Feast of Tabernacles to Whom that Feast pointed. It represented man resting in Christ and enjoying the Salvation presented to him freely upon Faith.

If one is to notice, there is no mention of the Feast of Pentecost in this scenario, with the reader being brought directly from the Passover to the Feast of Tabernacles. The reason is that the Gift of the Holy Spirit provides a continuous Pentecost for those who find Life in Christ and are privileged to be baptized with the Holy Spirit.

(3) "HIS BRETHREN THEREFORE SAID UNTO HIM, DEPART HENCE, AND GO INTO JUDAEA, THAT YOUR DISCIPLES ALSO MAY SEE THE WORKS THAT YOU DO."

The overview is:

1. The phrase, *"His brethren therefore said unto Him,"* proclaims one of the saddest moments in history. It is inconceivable that Jesus' Half-brothers did not believe in Him, as the Scripture will momentarily declare. We must quickly add that these were not cousins, as the Catholic church loves to proclaim, but those who shared the same mother, Mary.

2. *"Depart hence, and go into Judaea, that Your Disciples also may see the works that You do,"* is actually a proclamation of sarcasm.

3. By the use of the words, *"Your Disciples,"* they were saying that they (His Brothers) were not His Disciples and wanted all to know that they had no association with His Group.

4. As well, the manner in which they used the word *"works,"* describing His Miracles, was not an outright denial, because such could not be denied, but was used in a light, flippant sense. How such could be spoken of in this manner is beyond comprehension! However, the Lord's Family, sunk in unbelief, understood none of these things and, thereby, rejected Him, at least at the first.

(4) "FOR THERE IS NO MAN WHO DOES ANY THING IN SECRET, AND HE HIMSELF SEEKS TO BE KNOWN OPENLY. IF YOU DO THESE THINGS, SHOW YOURSELF TO THE WORLD."

The composition is:

1. The phrase, *"For there is no man who does any thing in secret, and he himself seeks to be known openly,"* proclaims several things:

a. There is no doubt that they knew full well of the tremendous animosity of the religious leaders against Jesus. So, they could not help but know that He would be greatly risking His Life if He went there at this time. The evidence is, so it seems, that they really did not care.

b. They were not thinking in Spiritual terms at all, but rather in a carnal sense. They did not realize that Jesus did what He was told to do by His Heavenly Father.

c. If He really was Who He said He was, God manifest in the flesh, let Him proclaim this in Jerusalem where it really mattered.

2. *"If You do these things, show Yourself to the world,"* is very similar to the temptations offered by Satan in the wilderness (Mat. 4:1-11).

(5) "FOR NEITHER DID HIS BRETHREN BELIEVE IN HIM."

The construction is:

1. Had Jesus' Mother, Brothers, and Sisters come as moral lepers for cleansing from their sins, they would have learned Who and What He was.

2. Knowledge of Spiritual realities only reaches the soul through a sin-convicted heart, and not through a religious intellect.

(6) "THEN JESUS SAID UNTO THEM, MY TIME IS NOT YET COME: BUT YOUR TIME IS ALWAYS READY."

The form is:

1. The phrase, *"Then Jesus said unto them, My time is not yet come,"* has a two-fold meaning:

a. Jesus was speaking of the time of His Crucifixion, which would take place in about six months. They did not understand this, not even His Closest Disciples. Their problem was an improper evaluation of their true need, which was Salvation from sin. They did not see themselves in that role at all. Consequently, if they wanted Jesus at all, it was on their terms, which meant they would use Him to overthrow Rome and make Israel great once again. They did not have the slightest idea how jaded, corrupt, and even evil this position actually was.

b. It spoke, as well, of the *"time"* when He will truly come to this Earth as King of kings and Lord of lords and will then rule the world in Righteousness.

2. *"But your time is always ready,"* tells us several things:

a. His Statement meant that their ideas were akin to the world and, hence, the Devil.

b. The ideas, as then held by Israel and subscribed to by His Brethren, were not of God, albeit very religious.

c. This tells us that most of the thinking of most of the church world, for all time, has actually been opposed to God and, in reality, is the Work of Satan. As it held true then, it holds true now.

3. When the church errs from the Word of God, which it mostly does, its ideas and directions become man-devised and, consequently, man-directed. As such, it cannot be of God.

(7) "THE WORLD CANNOT HATE YOU; BUT ME IT HATES, BECAUSE I TESTIFY OF IT, THAT THE WORKS THEREOF ARE EVIL."

The order is:

1. The Epistle to the Hebrews interprets the ritual of the Day of Atonement as a type of the Atoning Work of Christ, emphasizing the perfection of the latter in contrast with the inadequacy of the former (Heb., Chpts. 9-10).

2. Jesus Himself is termed our *"Great High Priest,"* and the Blood shed on Calvary is seen as typified in the blood of bulls and goats offered in sacrifice.

3. Unlike the Old Testament Priesthood, the sinless Christ did not have to make sacrifice for any sins of His Own, for He was Sinless.

THE SYSTEM OF THIS WORLD

The phrase, *"The world cannot hate you,"* refers to the idea that their thinking, albeit religious, came from the same spirit as the thinking of the world, which was Satan.

The *"world,"* as here used by John, does not refer to the Planet, as such, but rather to its system. It speaks of *"humanity unregenerate, humanity without Grace and apart from God."*

Consequently, if the preacher is praised by the world, that is a sure sign that he is not preaching the Gospel of Jesus Christ. The more popular the church is to the world, the greater its departure from the Faith.

THE HATRED AGAINST CHRIST

The phrase, *"But Me it hates,"* refers not only to Jesus but to all who truly follow Him.

The world lies in the grip of Satan, and most of its subjects, being unregenerate, do the work of Satan. These are the children of darkness and this group is comprised of almost all the people.

Conversely, there are a few in the world who have accepted Jesus Christ as their Saviour, and, as such, they are the Children of Light. Consequently, there is a continuing animosity between the darkness and the Light, which is unavoidable. Of course, the less Light in one's life, the less opposition by the darkness, as would be obvious.

EVIL WORKS

The phrase, *"Because I testify of it, that the works thereof are evil,"* will always constitute the marks of a true Preacher of the Gospel.

It is amazing that many Pentecostal and Charismatic preachers seem to fall over themselves, attempting to give accolades to the Pope, even going so far as to call him a, *"Godly man,"* etc.

The truth is, he is not only not godly but, in fact, most ungodly.

For instance, going back to Pope John Paul, he claimed to have seen a Vision of Mary many years ago, who told him he would one day occupy the position of Pope.

Did he truly have a Vision of Mary?

No!

This was a demon spirit, referred to as a *"familiar spirit,"* that appeared to this man. Consequently, under his administration, the paganistic worship of Mary greatly exacerbated.

Not long before he died, he made the ridiculous statement that evolution is scientific and, therefore correct, which completely negates the Biblical Truth of Creation. Of course, the whole Catholic system is of the world, i.e., *"Satan,"* and, as such, it is applauded by the world.

It should be noted that Jesus was not speaking of the normal vices of the world here, which are obvious, but the religious systems of the world. These religious systems, even Judaism, hate Him because *"their works are evil."* Even though these *"works"* would pertain to many things, by and large, they pertain to anything in the religious sense, which is not Scriptural. To be sure, when these *"works"* are pointed out, such preaching will not gain the plaudits of religious man.

(8) "GO YE UP UNTO THIS FEAST: I GO NOT UP YET UNTO THIS FEAST; FOR MY TIME IS NOT YET FULL COME."

The form is:

1. The phrase, *"Go ye up unto this Feast,"* contains the idea that most of those who would participate in this *"Feast of Tabernacles"* hardly knew or understood what its true meaning and purpose actually was. Hence, it was now a *"Feast of the Jews"* instead of a *"Feast of the Lord,"* as originally given.

2. Such is true of most of those who claim to be Believers in that they little understand God or His Word. They are more involved in the social aspect of the church than anything else.

3. *"I go not up yet unto this Feast; for My Time is not yet full come,"* really means that His Time for fulfilling what the *"Feast of Tabernacles"* actually represented had not yet come. In fact, it represented the Millennial Glory, which will be enjoyed by all Saints, especially Israel.

4. There is much more to what Jesus was saying than appears on the surface. He had offered Israel the Kingdom at the beginning of His Ministry, saying, *"Repent: for the Kingdom of Heaven is at hand,"* but the offer was rejected (Mat. 4:17).

5. As such, this, which the Feast of Tabernacles represented, could not be fulfilled and brought to pass. In reality, Jesus is the Feast of Tabernacles exactly as He is the Passover, along with all the other Feast Days, Sabbaths, and sacrifices, etc.

6. However, inasmuch as He was not accepted, the realization of fulfillment could not come to Israel at that time, even though it does come to the hearts and lives of Believers, whomever and wherever they may be. Of course, until Israel comes back into Covenant, which will be at the Second Coming, and after much suffering, the totality of fulfillment cannot come to pass and be realized even for Believers. This will take place, as stated, at the Second Coming.

(9) "WHEN HE HAD SAID THESE WORDS UNTO THEM, HE ABODE STILL IN GALILEE."

The form is:

1. Knowing the animosity against Him of the religious leaders in Jerusalem, Jesus was evidently told by His Heavenly Father to keep a low profile, at least at this time.

2. So, *"He abode still in Galilee."*

3. This was probably only three or four days before He would then go to Jerusalem.

(10) "BUT WHEN HIS BRETHREN WERE GONE UP, THEN WENT HE ALSO UP UNTO THE FEAST, NOT OPENLY,

BUT AS IT WERE IN SECRET."

The construction is:

1. Almost every Christian would quickly and readily exclaim their devotion to the Cross of Christ.

2. However, most Christians little understand what they are actually saying.

3. In fact, about all that most Christians know about the Cross is, *"Jesus died for me."* While that is certainly true and of utmost significance, still, most Christians don't actually know what that really means.

THE BROTHERS OF CHRIST

The phrase, *"But when His Brethren were gone up, then went He also up unto the Feast,"* in some way insinuates that Jesus did not want to travel with His Brethren at this time, considering their hostility, even though His Other Reasons for delay were far weightier. It would not have been a pleasant journey, as it wasn't in any case.

However, let it quickly be said that at least two of His Brothers, James and Jude, became stalwarts of the Faith and contributed two Epistles to the New Testament. So, our God is a Great and Merciful God. The manner of their Repentance is not recorded; but this we do know: these two, and, quite possibly, all of His Brothers and Sisters, found their way to His Feet. However, I think it can be said that it took Calvary for them to properly know Who He actually was.

It is said that neither James, who became the head of the Church in Jerusalem, nor Jude would refer to themselves as *"Apostles,"* but rather as a *"Servant ... of the Lord Jesus Christ,"* simply because of their opposition to Him during His Earthly Ministry. So, the world that hated Jesus came to hate James and Jude as well!

ANIMOSITY AGAINST CHRIST

The phrase, *"Not openly, but as it were in secret,"* proclaims such being done for particular reasons.

The time was drawing ever closer for His Ultimate Confrontation with the religious leaders in Jerusalem. However, it must not come about until the appointed time, which would be about six months later. Actually, every evidence is that when He left Galilee at this time, He would not return until after the Resurrection.

To be sure, there was animosity against Him in Galilee, but it was somewhat of another variety and not nearly as vehement. Jerusalem was another matter altogether! It was the religious seat of the Nation and, without a doubt, harbored the greatest concentration of demon spirits in the entirety of the Nation.

In all my years of evangelistic work, preaching all over the world, I have never sensed the powers of darkness anywhere to the degree that I have in some particular cities or areas where denominational headquarters of particular churches are located. One would think it would be the very opposite; however, most religious denominations are operated by men and not God. While that certainly would not be true of all, it is true, I think, of most.

As such, this actually means that Satan is more or less guiding the thing! When a religious denomination is guided by its constitution and bylaws instead of the Bible, that means it is no longer led by the Holy Spirit, but rather by men, i.e., *"Satan."*

I remind the reader that it was the church that crucified Christ. Sadder still, they crucified the Lord in the Name of the Lord! What an irony!

(11) "THEN THE JEWS SOUGHT HIM AT THE FEAST, AND SAID, WHERE IS HE?"

The overview is:

1. The *"Jews"* mentioned here spoke of the religious hierarchy of Israel.

2. To be sure, they were not seeking Him for the right reasons but because they hated Him!

3. Luther said that their malice was so great that they *"forbore to name Him."* Actually, these rulers or the Pharisees never called Him by Name but only addressed Him as, *"Teacher,"* or *"Rabbi!"*

(12) "AND THERE WAS MUCH MURMURING AMONG THE PEOPLE CONCERNING HIM: FOR SOME SAID, HE IS A GOOD MAN: OTHERS SAID, NO; BUT HE DECEIVES THE PEOPLE."

The exegesis is:

1. In the lives of most Christians, the

Cross is relegated solely to the initial Born-Again experience.

2. One cannot merely tack the Cross onto whatever it is that one is presently believing.

3. The Cross of Christ must be the Foundation of all Doctrine, which means that it's not merely another doctrine (I Pet. 1:18-20).

MURMURING

The phrase, *"And there was much murmuring among the people concerning Him,"* pertained to both negative and positive remarks. Actually, this was one of the reasons Jesus delayed His Arrival at the Feast. By now, He was the talk of all people, and in many and varied ways. Also, it seems that it had been approximately one and one-half years since His last Visit to Jerusalem. In that period of time, He had performed hundreds, if not thousands, of Miracles, with even the dead being raised. So, as we shall see, the lines were being drawn, with sides being taken.

A GOOD MAN!

"For some said, He is a Good Man," was proclaimed because of His Miracles of healing the sick and casting out demons. But yet, even these did not venture, at least at this stage, to proclaim Him as Messiah, which He really was.

"Others said, No; but He deceives the people," were, no doubt, those who were attempting to curry favor with the religious hierarchy of Israel, whom they knew were in opposition to Christ. Consequently, in this one Verse of Scripture, one can pretty well see the disposition of the church. Some have their eyes on Jesus while others have their eyes on religious leaders, who, for the most part, feel threatened by Christ. Of course, they would not admit to such, but when the Word of God is subtly, or not so subtly, set aside, the position becomes clear.

Jesus Christ is the Head of the Church. As such, all must be subservient to Him. However, His Position as *"Head"* has been pretty much abrogated by men, themselves desiring to be the head. This was the problem then, and it is the problem now!

They accused Him of *"deceiving the people,"* but they never ventured as to how this was being done.

In fact, He was deceiving no one. There was deception alright, but it was on the part of the religious leaders of Israel. They were the ones deceiving the people!

(13) "HOWBEIT NO MAN SPOKE OPENLY OF HIM FOR FEAR OF THE JEWS."

The synopsis is:

1. When one has a proper understanding of the Cross, one will then have a proper understanding of the Word of God.

2. To turn it around, one cannot have a proper understanding of the Word of God unless one has a proper understanding of the Cross.

3. The first Promise of Redemption that came out of the Mouth of God after the Fall pertained to the Cross (Gen. 3:15).

TO SPEAK FAVORABLY OF JESUS

Verse 13 means to speak favorably of Jesus! They feared these religious authorities, who would have come down on them with a heavy hand had they been overheard, at least to any degree, for saying anything positive about our Lord. How sad!

Regrettably, this spirit did not die with the religious hierarchy of Israel. Actually, it has little changed, if at all! Most preachers are afraid to say what they really believe, that is, if they believe something that is contrary to the powers that be. Such is a compromise and as it destroyed Israel of old, it will ultimately destroy all others who follow suit. Man fear, especially religious man fear, hurts the Testimony and Work of God perhaps more than anything else.

The Word of God must be the criterion for all that we say and do. If what denominational heads say match up with the Word of God, fine and well! If it does not, the Man of God must stand upon the Word and not give ground, even in the slightest. It is so easy to give a little here and a little there, which constitutes a *"little leaven."* However, the *"little leaven"* will ultimately leaven the whole lump!

Anything anyone asks me to do, I will gladly do, that is, if it's Scriptural. If it is not, I cannot do such, irrespective of the demand or its origin.

A PERSONAL EXPERIENCE

Sometime ago, we were in a particular foreign country for a series of meetings. We were scheduled for a particular city for which others had made the arrangements without my involvement, and they had actually secured the cooperation of the Pastors.

The chairman of the meeting pastored one of the largest Pentecostal Churches in the city. The meeting was not of long duration, only two nights; however, God moved in those two nights as I have seldom seen Him move. Scores, possibly even hundreds, responded to the Altar calls.

About a year or so later, I found out what had transpired in that meeting. The Pastor who agreed to be the chairman was a member of one of the large Pentecostal denominations in that country. As well, I did not know him and had actually never met him.

When he agreed to be chairman, I am told that the leaders of that particular denomination were not happy at all concerning his decision. However, I am told that he said the following to them, or words to this effect:

"Gentlemen, the position you are taking is Scripturally wrong, and I will not abide by such. I believe the Lord has told me to serve as the chairman of this Crusade, and that is what I am going to do. If you feel like you cannot accept that, my resignation from this denomination will be forthcoming immediately."

I am told that they backed down and said nothing more.

RIGHT OR WRONG

Most preachers would have taken the position that this was only one meeting, and they should not jeopardize their ministries for such. However, what they fail to realize is, it is not the meeting that is in question but their obedience to the Word of God. Actually, we are tested in this capacity every day. Do we adhere to the Word, in other words, do that which we know to be right, or, out of man fear, do we look the other way?

Regrettably, the type of Pastor of whom I spoke in the illustration just given is few and far between. Not many will take such a stand. They put the responsibility on others or give whatever excuse that comes to mind.

As someone has said, there are a thousand excuses one may give in order to do wrong, or to do nothing, while there is only one reason to do right, and that is because it is right!

(14) "NOW ABOUT THE MIDST OF THE FEAST JESUS WENT UP INTO THE TEMPLE, AND TAUGHT."

The exposition is:

1. It is said that rabbinical law required all to be there the first day for the performance of many of the rites. However, as they were mostly of human invention, the Lord might have thought it improper to attend.

2. One could well imagine the stir that rippled through the hundreds, or even thousands, gathered in the Temple compound as Jesus made His entrance. As they began to gather around Him, He began to *"teach."*

3. How privileged these people were to sit under His Teaching, in fact, the greatest teaching of the Word of God by far that had ever been uttered. How so much the Words were alive! How so much the Spirit of God accompanied all that He said! How so clear it was, that which He spoke unto them.

4. Most of the rabbis and scribes spoke in ways to purposely confuse the people but, in reality, did so because they had little knowledge, if any at all, of the subject at hand. So, to hear Jesus was such a departure from that to which they had been so accustomed. Many of the people, for the first time in their lives, were truly hearing the Word of God. How refreshing it was! How wonderful it was!

(15) "AND THE JEWS MARVELED, SAYING, HOW KNOWS THIS MAN LETTERS, HAVING NEVER LEARNED?"

The diagram is:

1. The Bible begins with the Cross (Gen. 3:15) and ends with the Cross (Rev. 22:3).

2. The Cross alone, typified by the use of the title *"lamb,"* is what has lifted the curse.

3. To take the Cross out of Christianity leaves nothing but a vapid philosophy.

THEY MARVELLED

The phrase, *"And the Jews marveled,"* spoke of the ruling and learned class, in other words, the men of power and weight in Jerusalem, who heard His Teaching.

Despite their opposition to Him, the immediate effect of His Message was great astonishment. In spite of themselves, they were moved by what He said and how He said it.

The question, *"Saying, How knows this Man letters, having never learned?"* spoke of the great theological schools in Jerusalem.

This is a valuable Testimony against ancient and modern assertions that Christ's Knowledge was derived from human sources. The Sermon on the Mount is, as well, a fatal blow to that theory.

The mystery of His Training as a Man in the village of Nazareth is one of the evidences given to the world that there was an unknown element in His Consciousness. However, the Psalmist explained His Great Wisdom. He said:

THE WORD OF THE LORD

"Oh how I love Your Law! It is my mediation all the day.

"You through Your Commandments have made me wiser than my enemies: for they are ever with me.

"I have more understanding than all my teachers: for Your Testimonies are my meditation.

"I understand more than the ancients, because I keep Your Precepts.

"I have refrained my feet from every evil way, that I might keep Your Word.

"I have not departed from Your Judgments: for You have taught me" (Ps. 119:97-102).

THE SECRET

The secret was His Perfect Life, Perfect Devotion to God the Father, and the Holy Spirit teaching Him!

Raised in Nazareth, actually, as a Peasant, He, no doubt, spent countless hours in prayer and meditation, as well as study of the Sacred Scrolls. His Bible would have been the Old Testament, which He learned by the Flow and Moving of the Holy Spirit, and devotion to its Text.

The Bible was then written in longhand on Scrolls, which consisted mostly of animal skins sown together; consequently, the Scroll of Isaiah would have been quite large, etc. As well, these were not inexpensive, as should be obvious! But yet, Jesus probably had a Scroll for each Book in the Old Testament.

It was, no doubt, quite common, especially on the Sabbath when no labor was allowed, to see Him, Scroll in hand, walking up one of the nearby hills, where He would have a time of prayer and meditation before His Heavenly Father. I personally think that every moment not given over to His Work as a carpenter and other required duties was given over to prayer, meditation, and study of the Word.

(16) "JESUS ANSWERED THEM, AND SAID, MY DOCTRINE IS NOT MINE, BUT HIS WHO SENT ME."

The overview is:

1. The phrase, *"Jesus answered them,"* no doubt, means that He overheard their remarks.

2. *"And said, My Doctrine is not Mine, but His Who sent Me,"* presents a far greater claim than even any of the Prophets of old.

3. They gave their pronouncements with a *"Thus Saith the LORD,"* but Jesus said that His Thoughts were God's Thoughts, and His Ways were God's Ways. His Teachings were not His Own but altogether those of Him Who sent Him.

4. In effect, He was saying, *"I am not a self-taught Man, as though out of the depths of My Own Independent Human Consciousness; I span such."*

5. As well, His Statement says, in effect, *"If you have sat at the feet of those who taught you, I too, am a Representative of another."* It introduces the absolute Source of all His Teachings as from the *"One Who sent Me."*

6. There is no hint that He was putting down their schools, but only that the Source of His Message was not man, but rather God. As such, it was irrefutable!

(17) "IF ANY MAN WILL DO HIS WILL, HE SHALL KNOW OF THE DOCTRINE, WHETHER IT BE OF GOD, OR WHETHER I SPEAK OF MYSELF."

The exegesis is:

1. The phrase, *"If any man will do His Will,"* could be said, *"Is willing to do His Will."*

What is the Will of God?

2. The Will of God is the Word of God. It is to be the rule of all conduct and the solution for all problems, at least that which pertains to *"life and godliness"* (II Pet. 1:3-4).

3. The criterion for all things is, or should be, *"Is it Scriptural?"*

4. *"He shall know of the Doctrine, whether it be of God, or whether I speak of Myself,"* in effect, puts the ball in their court.

5. He was saying, *"If you truly know God and are striving to do His Will, you will instantly recognize My Words as Truth, thereby, knowing them to be from God."*

6. Jesus claimed the Authority of the Father for everything He did. The religious leaders of Israel claimed the same, but in a very indirect way.

7. They were claiming that their man-made rules and regulations were from God, while Jesus anchored everything He said in the Scriptures. The validity of His Claims was immediately obvious, that is, if one truly knew the Word of God. Regrettably, even though these men were the religious men of Israel, they simply did not know the Word. As a result, they based everything they did on their own man-devised commandments, which they called, *"Oral laws."*

8. Regrettably, the practice did not cease with the Pharisees but continues to plague the church to this very hour.

(18) "HE WHO SPEAKS OF HIMSELF SEEKS HIS OWN GLORY: BUT HE WHO SEEKS HIS GLORY WHO SENT HIM, THE SAME IS TRUE, AND NO UNRIGHTEOUSNESS IS IN HIM."

The structure is:

1. While we definitely are *"complete in Him,"* because all perfection is in Him, still, even though that is our *"standing"* in Christ, it is hardly our *"state."*

2. As human beings, we are so feeble and faltering within ourselves, so full of failure and infirmity, and so prone to err and stumble that we could not stand for a moment were it not that *"He ever lives to make intercession for us"* (Heb. 7:25-26).

TO THE GLORY OF GOD

The phrase, *"He who speaks of himself seeks his own glory,"* refers to those who speak words of man's origin, whether of themselves or others.

In fact, these Jewish theologians continuously based their statements on *"Rabbi so and so said this,"* or *"Rabbi so and so said that!"* They almost never referred to the Scripture; consequently, the Words of Jesus were extremely telling upon them.

"But He who seeks His Glory Who sent Him, the same is true, and no unrighteousness is in Him," speaks of Himself but, as well, of all who would claim to be Preachers of the Gospel.

Jesus' Words proceeded a step further and recognized the fact that the Glory of God, and not His Own Glory, was the sole end of His Teaching. As well, He stated that the direct Command from Him Who sent Him formed the substance of His Doctrine, however it might clash with the preconceived ideas or dominant prejudices of the religious hierarchy.

SEEKING THE GLORY OF GOD

Inasmuch as He set the example, all men are to follow that example by *"seeking the Glory of God,"* and not their own glory. To be frank, the sentence is short, as uttered by Christ, but extremely telling on the motives of all.

Why are we doing what we are doing?

Our first answer must be that God has called us to do this which we do. The second answer must be that we do it for His Glory!

All else is untrue and reeks of self-righteousness.

In Jesus' Day, religion was big business. Actually, it was the business of Israel. It was profitable in the monetary sense, at least to the ruling hierarchy. It controlled the people, which was second only to the economics of the effort. As well, it was structured so as to handsomely reward in every way the ruling clique.

Consequently, they hated Christ because they saw Him as a threat to the entirety of their structure, which it was, as such always is.

As well, religion could probably be said to be the biggest business in the world at the present time. It is easy to think of Microsoft, IBM, Apple, or Boeing as such; however, these are mere child's play in comparison to the religion business. As well, Satan has not changed his tactics from then until now. Once again, the factors of money and control are always the overriding concern of most religious denominations. If that is threatened in any way, the same animosity that was prevalent in Jesus' Day is present now as well! Also, as they played the game then with bloody intent, determined to protect their own and meaning to do whatever it took to do that, likewise, such continues to this hour.

(19) "DID NOT MOSES GIVE YOU THE LAW, AND YET NONE OF YOU KEEP THE LAW? WHY DO YOU GO ABOUT TO KILL ME?"

The structure is:

1. The question, *"Did not Moses give you the Law, and yet none of you keep the Law?"* proclaims a tremendous indictment because it pertained to all.

2. The fact that these religious leaders had not kept the Law, nor had any man, for that matter, was not, within itself, the strength of this statement. The idea is that they claimed before one and all that they did keep the Law, and Jesus, in effect, and to their faces, was calling them liars.

3. The question, *"Why do you go about to kill Me?"* was, within itself, an indictment against their claims of Law-keeping inasmuch as the Law forbade murder. However, their great sin was not only in their invalid claims of keeping the Law but even more so in twisting it to conform to their perversions. In fact, they would claim that they were legal and just regarding the Law in crucifying Christ! The irony was, they killed the Lord in the Name of the Lord. So, their sin was twofold.

4. In fact, Jesus was the only One Who kept the Law of Moses in its entirety.

5. If one is to notice, the Statements of Jesus, as directed to these men, contain no diplomacy and pull no punches. The situation was this: if the raw, naked, unvarnished Truth did not stop them, then nothing would! When He said these things, they were, no doubt, given with a mighty Anointing of the Holy Spirit, which caused their impact to be phenomenal, to say the least! Still, it seemed to have had no positive effect on them.

(20) "THE PEOPLE ANSWERED AND SAID, YOU HAVE A DEMON: WHO GOES ABOUT TO KILL YOU?"

The synopsis is:

1. The phrase, *"The people answered and said, You have a demon,"* pertained to the great crowd which had gathered, not the religious leaders.

2. The question, *"Who goes about to kill You?"* means that these people, who were probably residents of other cities, were ignorant of the plots of the Pharisees, so they were astonished at His Announcement.

3. This, that One Who taught so wonderfully should imagine what they deemed a moral impossibility and dark delusion, was an outburst of insolent and ignorant amazement on their part.

4. As well, how unspiritual were the hearts of these people who, standing in the very Presence of the Son of God, would dare to speak to Him in this fashion!

(21) "JESUS ANSWERED AND SAID UNTO THEM, I HAVE DONE ONE WORK, AND YOU ALL MARVEL."

The exegesis is:

1. The *"one work"* of which He spoke concerned the healing of the man on the Sabbath, which was done about one and one-half years previously.

2. He had no respect for their man-made rules, and neither did He have any respect for them, as is obvious from His Blunt Statements made to their faces. Of course, this one Miracle of which He spoke was only one of the many, possibly hundreds or even thousands. So, these religious leaders were in a dilemma.

3. They must either submit to Him, for He was not One to be ignored, or they must kill Him as a blasphemer.

4. They had accused Him of breaking the Sabbath by healing this man on that particular day, and even encouraging him to take up his bed and walk. Consequently, they were aghast at this bold breaking of their man-devised laws, which, incidentally, were not God's Laws. Now, as then, religious men are never satisfied with the Bible. They must always add to or subtract from, whatever the case may be.

(22) "MOSES THEREFORE GAVE UNTO YOU CIRCUMCISION; (NOT BECAUSE IT IS OF MOSES, BUT OF THE FATHERS;) AND YOU ON THE SABBATH DAY CIRCUMCISE A MAN."

The order is:

1. The phrase, *"Moses therefore gave unto you Circumcision,"* means that the Lord told Moses to include circumcision in the Law.

2. *"Not because it is of Moses, but of the father's,"* means that it actually had its beginning with Abraham. Moses mentioned it only in Exodus 12:44-48 and Leviticus 12:3, but the Law concerning it, as stated, was given to Abraham (Gen. 17:9-14).

3. *"And you on the Sabbath Day circumcise a man,"* presents Jesus pointing out that if circumcision, which physically benefits a man in a minor degree, was lawful on the Sabbath Day, how much more lawful is an action which benefited his entire being, both physical and spiritual?

4. Here is a seeming conflict between two Laws, the Law of the Sabbath and the Law demanding circumcision on the eighth day, as it did of all little boy babies. Circumcision had priority, for it was of Abraham and handed down by Moses.

(23) "IF A MAN ON THE SABBATH DAY RECEIVE CIRCUMCISION, THAT THE LAW OF MOSES SHOULD NOT BE BROKEN; ARE YOU ANGRY AT ME, BECAUSE I HAVE MADE A MAN EVERY WHIT WHOLE ON THE SABBATH DAY?"

The form is:

1. A true confession is not a bad confession.

2. The truth is, we are perfect and complete in Christ.

3. On the negative side, our *"state"* is not up to our *"standing,"* which the Holy Spirit ever seeks to remedy.

CIRCUMCISION

The beginning of the question, *"If a man on the Sabbath Day receive Circumcision, that the Law of Moses should not be broken,"* simply means that *"circumcision"* was the removal by surgical means of what was regarded as a cause and sign of physical impurity. It was also the seal of the Covenant made with the family of Abraham that his Seed should be the heir of the world, and that in that Seed, all the nations of the Earth should be blessed. We are also to understand that the principle of the higher law always succeeds that of the lower law.

The conclusion of the question, *"Are you angry at Me, because I have made a man every whit whole on the Sabbath Day?"* has simple reference to the fact that the man being made whole on the Sabbath Day actually proclaimed a fulfillment of both the Law of Circumcision and the Law of the Sabbath. This meant that Jesus, Who was actually the fulfillment of these Laws and to Whom they originally pointed, had done the very thing these Laws symbolized but could not perform.

As *"circumcision"* pointed to separation and, therefore, the Covenant, Jesus had gloriously fulfilled the symbolism by separating this man from his sinful present and past by healing him and giving him Salvation, which now made him truly a part of the Covenant.

THE REST

This man now had Salvation, which had been provided by Jesus, Who Alone could provide such. He would now truly enter into His Sabbath, *"rest,"* because he had entered into Christ, of Whom the Sabbath was but a symbol.

To these Jews, the Law had become all in all, in other words, Salvation within itself. Consequently, they lost all understanding of what its true purpose was, which it did very effectively — portraying what was sin and man's inability to obey it. As a result, the sacrifices, along with the Sabbaths and Feast Days, had been given in order that Atonement could be made for man's sins. All pointed to Christ, Who was to come! In other words, there never was any salvation in the Law, and neither was there meant to be. It was a stopgap measure given by God in order to show man how weak he really is and, thereby, to seek the Salvation which only the Saviour could afford.

However, as stated, the Jews had abrogated all of that, devising their own man-induced salvation out of the Law, which could never be recognized by God. As such, they would greatly oppose the Very One Who the Law represented and Who had actually given the Law.

(24) "JUDGE NOT ACCORDING TO THE APPEARANCE, BUT JUDGE RIGHTEOUS JUDGMENT."

The composition is:

1. Back up to Verse 21, Jesus completely disregarded their question of Verse 20 and continued to speak to the Judeans, recalling the Miracle of John 5:1, which still offended them. He pointed out that if circumcision, which physically benefits a man in a minor degree, was lawful on the Sabbath Day (which it was), how much more lawful was an action which benefited his entire being. So, He demanded of them righteous Judgment and not prejudiced and objective injustice.

2. *"Judge not according to the appearance,"* in effect, says, *"If you think you have not violated the Sabbath in circumcision, then how can you think I broke the Sabbath when I healed one of you who had been helpless for 38 years?"*

3. *"If you will view My act in the same light as your own, then you will not class Me as a criminal. The Covenant of Healing (Ex. 15:26) should be obeyed as much as the Covenant of Circumcision (Gen. 17:9-14)."*

4. *"Sickness in your midst proves you have broken God's Covenant just as much as a foreskin would prove you have broken it. If you admit that circumcision is necessary, then why do you not admit that it is necessary for a man to be cured on that day?"*

5. The phrase, *"But judge righteous Judgment,"* in effect, says that Judgment must be rendered according to the whole Word of God and not merely by taking a part and perverting it to one's own satisfaction.

(25) "THEN SAID SOME OF THEM OF JERUSALEM, IS NOT THIS HE, WHOM THEY SEEK TO KILL?"

The exegesis is:

1. The phrase, *"Then said some of them of Jerusalem,"* concerned natives of that city and not those who had come in from other parts of Israel for the Feast.

2. The question, *"Is not this He, Whom they seek to kill?"* means that the plot to kill Jesus by the religious authorities was not a complete secret, at least to those in Jerusalem.

3. By now, the animosity was becoming widespread and known by many! As well, it was not mere rumor, which had been enlarged by repeated telling, but was actually the truth. They wanted to kill Him!

(26) "BUT, LO, HE SPEAKS BOLDLY, AND THEY SAY NOTHING UNTO HIM. DO THE RULERS KNOW INDEED THAT THIS IS THE VERY CHRIST?"

The synopsis is:

1. The phrase, *"But, Lo, He speaks boldly, and they say nothing unto Him,"* tells us two things:

a. Even though their animosity was great, and they were truly trying to kill Him, still, He tempered His Message not at all, continuing to speak *"boldly"* to the crowd.

Actually, the Truth cannot be altered, compromised, or hidden. The very nature of what it is demands that it be proclaimed without reservation.

The word *"boldly"* should characterize all Preachers and, in effect, all Believers! Even though all of us should use wisdom, still, at all times, we should *"be ready always to give an answer to every man who asks you a reason of the hope that is in you with meekness and fear"* (I Pet. 3:15).

b. The rulers said nothing to Him at this time simply because of the massive crowds listening to Him, with some of these people having been healed of the worst types of diseases. In other words, they were fearful that if they did not take Him in a subtle way, many of the people could turn on them. Consequently, they said nothing at this time.

2. However, in the very near future, they would become so desperate to stop Him that they would eagerly grasp at the opportunity, which afforded itself by the betrayal of Judas.

3. The question, *"Do the rulers know indeed that this is the Very Christ?"* proclaims how widespread and how detailed was the idea of the Coming Christ.

4. The idea of the question is that the *"rulers"* should stop Jesus from ministering,

especially considering the things He was saying. As is obvious, this group, whoever they were, was antagonistic toward Christ.

(27) "HOWBEIT WE KNOW THIS MAN WHENCE HE IS: BUT WHEN CHRIST COMES, NO MAN KNOWS WHENCE HE IS."

The composition is:

1. The phrase, *"Howbeit we know this Man whence He is,"* is said in a negative sense. They were meaning that they knew His Parentage, the place of His early Life, His Father, Mother, Brothers and Sisters (Mat. 13:55-58). They gave Him no credence and no respect but met His Statements and Claims with sarcasm.

2. In other words, they were saying, *"Does this Peasant really think that we would for a moment consider Him to be the Messiah?"*

3. *"But when Christ comes, no man knows whence He is,"* proclaims a common error of that time concerning the Messiah.

4. The rabbis taught that when the Messiah would be born, He would hide Himself, in that when He appeared, no man would know from where He had come. They had a proverb, *"Three things come unexpectedly: a thing found by chance, the sting of a scorpion, and the Messiah."* Of course, all of this was unscriptural!

5. They also taught another error, which was probably taken from Daniel 7:13 and Malachi 3:1. The error was that the Messiah would make a sudden descent on the Temple — a dazzling appearance of His Messianic Enthronement, coming in the clouds of Heaven — and that none would *"declare His Generation"* (Isa. 53:8).

6. Believing this error, they looked at Jesus, Who had not made any dazzling appearance, and, thereby, showed their contempt for His Claims.

7. When men leave the Word of God, there is nowhere to go but into error. The error will not correct itself but only compound itself, with the individual getting further and further off base.

8. They did not know the Word of God, which caused them to take isolated Scriptures out of context. The reason they did not know it was because they did not know the Lord. They were following their own selfish, carnal, ungodly pursuits and, despite constantly talking about God, were, in reality, bitterly opposed to His Word.

9. As we have stated, religion was a business to these people, and as such, they interpreted the Word of God wrongly in order to seek their own desires and evil hearts. Sadly, millions follow in their train!

(28) "THEN CRIED JESUS IN THE TEMPLE AS HE TAUGHT, SAYING, YOU BOTH KNOW ME, AND YOU KNOW WHENCE I AM: AND I AM NOT COME OF MYSELF, BUT HE WHO SENT ME IS TRUE, WHOM YOU KNOW NOT."

The order is:

1. The phrase, *"Then cried Jesus in the Temple as He taught, saying, You both know Me, and you know whence I am,"* in effect, says, *"You think you know Me and where I come from, but you actually do not."*

2. Their traditions and selfish interpretation of particular Scriptures had blinded them until they did not really recognize the Lord, although looking directly at Him. The cause was actually unbelief.

3. The same malady affects many in the modern church. Many, if not most Believers, do not know what is of God or what is not of God simply because of unbelief, which stems from an improper interpretation of the Word of God. In other words, they do not know the Word at all and, consequently, accept without question what some preacher says simply because he appeals to their self-will, etc.

4. Others do actually study the Word of God, but only to make it conform to their beliefs instead of having their beliefs formed by it, which is the Intention of the Holy Spirit.

5. *"And I am not come of Myself,"* means that His Ministry and Life were not a farce, as these unbelievers intimate, but rather that He was sent by the Father and, in a sense, that no Prophet of old, or anyone else, for that matter, has been sent. He is in total union with the Father, a union, in fact, that is so close as to be indivisible. As such, He says only what the Father tells Him to say, and, in effect, it is the same as the Father saying these things.

6. *"But He Who sent Me is True,"* in

effect, says, *"You know Me as Jesus of Nazareth; and yet, you do not know Me, for you do not know Him Who sent Me; but I am from Him, and He did send Me."*

7. *"Whom you know not,"* plainly tells them that they do not know God, despite all their claims and great display of religion. Tragically, *"Whom you know not,"* would have to be applied to most today who call themselves *"Believers."*

8. If one is to remember, Jesus spoke of the Way being narrow and straight and said, *"Few there be who find it"* (Mat. 7:14).

(29) "BUT I KNOW HIM: FOR I AM FROM HIM, AND HE HAS SENT ME."

The construction is:

1. The phrase, *"But I know Him,"* has a far greater reference than mere recognition. As stated, the union between Christ and His Father was of such magnitude that they were of the same essence. As such, He did not merely know Him, but rather was a part of Him and He of Christ. By contrast, these unbelievers knew nothing!

2. *"For I am from Him, and He has sent Me,"* means that His Great Knowledge is derived from a perfect union, and has reference to the fact that He is from the Father in a unique way and position that no Prophet or Angel ever was.

3. As well, Jesus was not just One of many who were sent, but rather sent in a unique way in which no other has been sent. So, their dealings with Him were, in effect, their dealings with the Father. As such, it would either spell Life or death for them, according to their acceptance or rejection.

(30) "THEN THEY SOUGHT TO TAKE HIM: BUT NO MAN LAID HANDS ON HIM, BECAUSE HIS HOUR WAS NOT YET COME."

The synopsis is:

1. The phrase, *"Then they sought to take Him,"* means that because of the things He was saying, they became so incensed, so angry, and so empowered by Satan that they would have taken him then and there but for the many people overhearing this exchange who believed on Him (Jn. 7:31).

2. *"But no man laid hands on Him, because His hour was not yet come,"* means that the Holy Spirit orchestrated these

NOTES

events accordingly because it was not yet the time that Jesus should be crucified. When that time came, and it would about six months later, the Holy Spirit would allow certain things to happen in order for such to be brought to pass.

3. Did Jesus know at this time when that *"hour"* would be?

4. I have no doubt that He did, even from the beginning of His Public Ministry when the Holy Spirit came upon Him.

(31) "AND MANY OF THE PEOPLE BELIEVED ON HIM, AND SAID, WHEN CHRIST COMES, WILL HE DO MORE MIRACLES THAN THESE WHICH THIS MAN HAS DONE?"

The composition is:

1. The phrase, *"And many of the people believed on Him,"* did not refer at all to the religious authorities but, instead, to the crowds gathered for the Feast of Tabernacles. They had come from all over Israel, and even other parts of the Roman Empire. These were not swayed by the religious leaders or the sarcasm of others, who sought to *"toady"* to these reprobates. They saw things as they were and believed accordingly!

2. The question, *"And said, When Christ comes, will He do more Miracles than these which this Man has done?"* proclaims that the evidence of the Power of God in delivering people was obvious to all, and now aroused an excitement in the people. Consequently, the religious leaders were now on the horns of a dilemma.

3. If they sought now to take Him by force, the hundreds, if not thousands, of people in Jerusalem may have come to His Defense, which would have aroused the ire of Rome, and could have jeopardized their religious positions.

4. However, if they did nothing, it seemed as if His Popularity was gaining almost by the hour, and soon His Position might be unassailable.

(32) "THE PHARISEES HEARD THAT THE PEOPLE MURMURED SUCH THINGS CONCERNING HIM; AND THE PHARISEES AND THE CHIEF PRIESTS SENT OFFICERS TO TAKE HIM."

The overview is:

1. The phrase, *"The Pharisees heard that the people murmured such things concerning Him,"* constituted a different group than the rulers, but yet, equally opposed to Him. In fact, the Pharisees and rulers were often greatly opposed to each other but now joined forces against a common foe, in this case, Christ.

2. This time, some of the *"murmuring"* was in His Favor, whereas, previously, it had been negative (Jn. 7:12).

3. *"And the Pharisees and the Chief Priests sent officers to take Him,"* proclaims these two groups, as stated, joining forces against Him.

4. Evidently, the Pharisees, who had been sprinkled among the crowd, overheard some of the people speaking in a positive way of Christ, and even speaking of Him as the Messiah. They quickly informed the rulers of this, who seemed to make a hasty effort to take Christ then and there, but without success. What happened, as we shall see, will prove to be very interesting.

5. The *"Chief Priests"* here mentioned included the High Priest, but probably ex-High Priests, as well, and even possibly the heads of the 24 courses of Priests. At any rate, almost the entirety of the ruling clique of Israel was opposed to Him, and the opposition was enough to kill Him if the opportunity presented itself.

(33) "THEN SAID JESUS UNTO THEM, YET A LITTLE WHILE AM I WITH YOU, AND THEN I GO UNTO HIM WHO SENT ME."

The exegesis is:

1. In effect, Jesus was saying that in about six months, which would actually be at the next Passover, He would become the Passover Lamb for all men. Then, He would go back to God Who had sent Him.

2. The Father is the One Who has sent Him.

3. So, when they rebelled against Christ, they rebelled, as well, against God the Father.

(34) "YOU SHALL SEEK ME, AND SHALL NOT FIND ME: AND WHERE I AM, THERE YOU CANNOT COME."

The pattern is:

1. The phrase, *"You shall seek Me, and shall not find Me,"* refers to the time when they would desperately need Him. It would be about 37 years in the future, when Titus would destroy their city and the very Temple in which they now stand.

2. The Nation as a whole was blinded. They crucified their King, the Lord of Glory, and they brought uttermost extinction on themselves as a Nation.

3. *"And where I am, there you cannot come,"* actually means they can come now, but because of their unbelief and rebellion, they would not do so.

4. Consequently, at that time, the door would be shut simply because *"you have not known the day of your visitation"* (Lk. 19:44).

(35) "THEN SAID THE JEWS AMONG THEMSELVES, WHERE WILL HE GO, THAT WE SHALL NOT FIND HIM? WILL HE GO UNTO THE DISPERSED AMONG THE GENTILES, AND TEACH THE GENTILES?"

The composition is:

1. The Holy Spirit is given to us in order that He may root out all sin within our lives.

2. Actually, there are two distinct aspects to the Christian experience on which the Holy Spirit constantly works. Those two aspects are *"self"* and *"sin."*

3. When Jesus died on the Cross, He died not only to save us from sin but, as well, from self.

WHERE WILL HE GO?

The question, *"Then said the Jews among themselves, Where will He go, that we shall not find Him?"* presents minds which are darkened by unbelief and sin. Therefore, they were putting ironic and confusing meanings into His Words in order to pour an air of contempt over His Reply.

The question, *"Will He go unto the dispersed among the Gentiles, and teach the Gentiles?"* refers to Jews who lived in foreign countries among the Gentiles and, actually, the Gentiles themselves. Consequently, their question constituted the utter scorn of the Jewish mind for a pseudo-Messiah, Who, failing with His Own People and here in the courts of the Lord's House, would instead turn to the Gentiles. However, even though they meant it as the insult of all insults, still, they were far closer to the truth than they ever would dare realize.

GENTILES

The irony of history is seen in the fact that the very words of these Jews of Israel are recorded in Greek by a Jew then presiding over a Christian Church in a Gentile city, which was made up mostly of Gentiles.

Long before John reported this exchange between Christ and these Pharisees, etc., he himself had taken up his seat in Ephesus. In all the great cities of the empire, it was avowed on both sides that *"in Christ Jesus there was neither Jew nor Greek."* Actually, Jesus came for the entirety of the world, but because the Promises were first given to the Jews, they would have the privilege of being offered the *"Kingdom of Heaven"* first of all. Regrettably, they refused and destroyed themselves in the process. As a result, the Church came into being, which was an outgrowth of the Covenant between God and Israel, and has touched the entirety of the world, saying that all who will may come (Rev. 22:17).

However, even though Israel then rejected Christ and, as stated, brought upon themselves sure and swift destruction, still, they will finally accept Him Whom they have rejected, but only after great sorrow (Ezek., Chpts. 38-39; Zech., Chpt. 12; Mat., Chpt. 24).

(36) "WHAT MANNER OF SAYING IS THIS THAT HE SAID, YOU SHALL SEEK ME, AND SHALL NOT FIND ME: AND WHERE I AM, THERE YOU CANNOT COME?"

The overview is:

1. It is not possible to conquer self by personal strength.

2. A denial of *"self"* simply means that we are not to depend on self at all but, actually, on the Lord exclusively.

3. When Jesus spoke of *"denying oneself,"* He was referring to the Believer who must not trust self and must not depend on self but entirely on Christ.

UNBELIEF

The question, *"What manner of saying is this that He said, You shall seek Me, and shall not find Me?"* is asked in sarcasm. Because of their unbelief, they ridiculed His Words, not realizing they were sealing their own doom, as well as that of the Nation.

By the very tenor of its construction, the conclusion of the question, *"And where I am, there you cannot come?"* proclaims the Spiritual meaning to be completely lost on them.

That which He was warning so sternly, they said in jest. They had no idea that the One standing before them was really the Lord of Glory, their Messiah, the Maker of all things! Because of their terrible unbelief, they could not realize that without Him, they could not be saved but were doomed to spend eternity without God, even in everlasting fire.

THE HORROR OF ALL HORRORS

To be sure, if these people continued in their unbelief, upon their deaths a short time later, they would go to a place from which He had attempted to save them. It certainly seems that they did continue in unbelief, refusing to accept Him as the Saviour of the world. This last 2,000 years, they have relived this scene over and over multiple thousands of times. They can see His Face and hear His Words, but now, it is too late! As well, they have the sickening realization that one day, they will stand before Him at the Great White Throne Judgment (Rev. 20:11-15). As He now desired to be their Saviour, but they refused, He will then be their Judge.

The sentence will not be to their liking, however, but rather the horror of all horrors. They will live forever in the Lake of Fire, when they could have had Eternal Life, with it actually being free for the asking. They were so close, but yet, so very far away.

Sadly and regrettably, almost the entirety of the world follows in their train, with the Name of Jesus, if mentioned at all, said in the form of a vulgarity or obscenity! However, the One Whom they like to dismiss, they will one day stand before.

(37) "IN THE LAST DAY, THAT GREAT DAY OF THE FEAST, JESUS STOOD AND CRIED, SAYING, IF ANY MAN THIRST, LET HIM COME UNTO ME, AND DRINK."

The exegesis is:

1. Taking up the Cross daily and following Jesus means that we look exclusively to Christ and what He did for us at the Cross (Lk. 9:23).

2. Taking up the Cross daily doesn't refer to suffering, as most Christians think.

3. It actually means the opposite, taking up its benefits, which Jesus afforded us by what He did at Calvary.

THE GREAT DAY OF THE FEAST

The phrase, *"In the last day, that great day of the Feast,"* spoke of the eighth day of the *"Feast of Tabernacles."* It was great for several reasons:

It was a day of great assembly and offering of sacrifices for Israel. The first seven days, they professed to offer sacrifices for other nations (Lev. 23:34-36).

On this day, a Priest drew water from the pool of Siloam in a Golden Vessel and brought it to the Temple. At the time of the morning sacrifice, while it was on the Altar, he poured this water, mingled with wine, upon it, with the people all the while singing with great joy, *"Oh, give thanks unto the Lord."*

At this time, the Priests compassed the Altar seven times before the sacrifices were kindled, and the songs accompanying the ceremony of this day were called *"The Great Hosanna."*

As the Priest bearing the Golden Vessel approached the Altar, it would have been quite a sight to behold. If the measurements of the Great Altar were the same as that which the Lord had given to David respecting Solomon's Temple, it would have been 30 feet wide, 30 feet long, and 15 feet high (II Chron. 4:1). An earthen ramp would have led to the top in order for the Priests to attend to their sacrificial duties.

While the people sang that day, the Priest bearing the Golden Vessel would have ascended the ramp, finally standing above the Great Altar, holding high the Golden Vessel filled with water mixed with wine.

THE CROSS

As he stood there for a few moments, he, no doubt, looked around at the massive number of people which filled the Temple courts, even over to the Mount of Olives facing the Temple on the east.

As the Priest held the Vessel aloft, he would have waited for the great number of singers to finish *"the Great Hosanna."* When the last note died away and silence gripped the vast throng, slowly, he would have turned the Vessel upward, with the water mixed with wine falling onto the blazing coals of fire upon the Great Altar. Whether he fully understood what all of this meant is anyone's guess! However, the meaning now is clear.

The Brazen Altar was a type of Calvary and the Judgment that Jesus would suffer with the Wrath of God being poured out upon Him instead of upon the believing sinner. The fire typified that Judgment, while the sacrifices typified Jesus. The Altar was a type of the Cross.

The water mixed with wine poured out upon the blazing Altar was a type of the Holy Spirit, Who could now come into the hearts and lives of believing men and women as a result of what Jesus did at Calvary for humanity.

Before Calvary, this was not possible because the blood of bulls and goats could not take away sins but only cover them. Consequently, the debt was left owing and, as a result, continued to be held against the believing sinner.

However, when Jesus came and paid the price at Calvary, the sins were not merely covered, but taken away; consequently, nothing was left owing against the Believer. All of that which had been done in Type since the Fall in the Garden of Eden had now becoming a reality.

IF ANY MAN THIRST, LET HIM COME UNTO ME AND DRINK

The phrase, *"Jesus stood and cried, saying,"* probably took place from a vantage point somewhere near the Great Altar, and commenced immediately after the singing had died down and the water began to pour upon the fire of the sacrifice.

The phrase, *"If any man thirst, let him come unto Me, and drink,"* presents the greatest Invitation ever given to mortal man.

When the great throng was gradually silenced as the singing died down, and some could see and hear the water pouring upon the coals of fire, the Voice of Jesus rent the air and in clear tones, He cried out the Invitation of the ages. When He spoke, I have no doubt that the Spirit of God powerfully accompanied that moment, which literally picked up this host of people in its appeal, with a force and power, yet attended by gentleness, such as they had never known before. What must that have been like?

In a moment's time, thousands of faces were, no doubt, wet with tears. For a few moments, hearts beat faster! The actual One Who fulfilled the *"Feast of Tabernacles"* and, in reality, was the *"Feast of Tabernacles,"* was in their very midst. As well, as John the Baptist had prophesied, He was also the Baptizer with the Holy Spirit. Of all the moments of Jesus' Earthly Ministry, this had to be the most electrifying and the most impressive to date. That which had been practiced for nearly 1,600 years and pointed to the One Who was to come, was now about to be fulfilled, at least in a spiritual sense, if not in the physical and material.

Several things are said here, which, within themselves, constitute the most important Invitation ever given:

JESUS STOOD AND CRIED

This Invitation was given with bombast and power, and was meant for all to hear. As well, it was given by none other than the Lord of Glory Himself; heretofore, it had been by the Patriarchs and Prophets. Now, He said it Himself, and powerfully so.

IF ANY MAN

This speaks of any and all, Jew and Gentile, irrespective of color, nationality, or race. This means that none can be excluded, for if one is excluded, then all must be excluded. It speaks to the rich, the poor, the great, and the small! It speaks to the young, to the old, to the male, and to the female! It speaks of the sick, and it speaks to the healthy! It speaks to the child, and it speaks to the adult! It speaks to the most wicked of sinners and to the most moral of humanity! As stated, it speaks to all.

THIRST

This thirst of which Jesus spoke is from the spiritual part of man and cannot be slaked or satisfied in any other way or manner, other than Jesus. It is deep-seated, unending, and cannot be slaked by money, education, power, prestige, accomplished place, or position. It is truly a *"thirst."*

LET HIM

This means that nothing is to hinder the seeking soul. As the Holy Spirit deals with his heart, nothing must stand in his way as he comes to Christ. Regrettably, Satan has been very successful in the world of religion to hinder those who would desire to come. He mostly uses the church to do so. How tragic that is! How awful that is! And yet, as Israel of old, so it is in the modern church!

COME UNTO ME

As obvious, this speaks of Jesus. He Alone is the Answer and can slake the thirst. No other can, be he Muhammad, Buddha, Confucius, or any other fake luminary. Jesus Alone redeemed man, so it is to Jesus that one must come. To bypass Him in any fashion is to bypass Salvation. To attempt to worship God without Him is to effect no worship at all, for it is a worship that God will not accept. In other words, no man comes to the Father but by Jesus, and that means in any capacity (Jn. 14:6).

AND DRINK

This takes Salvation out of the philosophical and places it in the realm of the personal, with One Person, the Lord Jesus Christ, dealing with another person, the believing sinner. To *"drink"* is to believe!

(38) "HE WHO BELIEVES ON ME, AS THE SCRIPTURE HAS SAID, OUT OF HIS BELLY SHALL FLOW RIVERS OF LIVING WATER."

The composition is:

1. Many Preachers preach the Cross as it regards Salvation but go no further. Thank God for that, but to stop there is to miss God's Prescribed Order of Life and Living.

2. The Cross plays every bit as much into our Sanctification as it does our Salvation.

3. This information was given by the Lord Jesus Christ to the Apostle Paul, with him giving it to us in his 14 Epistles.

BELIEVING

We now continue with the Statement given by Christ at the Feast of Tabernacles.

He said, *"He who believes on Me"*: such presents the requirements of the sinner in order to receive Salvation.

Believe what?

One must believe that Jesus Christ is the Son of God, Who came down to this Earth in the form of Man, and paid the price at Calvary's Cross for man's Redemption. One must believe that accepting Him as one's Saviour provides Salvation, and that it cannot be earned but is a Free Gift.

In truth, the sinner may little understand the things just said, but if simple Faith is offered, the Lord will provide the balance, with Salvation freely given and guaranteed.

AS THE SCRIPTURE HAS SAID

The phrase, *"As the Scripture has said,"* proclaims the foundation of Salvation as being ensconced in the Scripture, which actually is what the Scripture is all about. The Story of the Bible is the Story of *"Jesus Christ and Him Crucified,"* which is the Story of the Redemption of man. Everything that Jesus said and did had already been forecast in the Word of God. As well, all of that pictured, predicted, and proclaimed in the Old Testament, such as the sacrifices, Tabernacle, and Temple, along with all the furnishings, as well as the Feast Days, even encompassing the Sabbath, all spoke of Jesus and the Plan of Redemption.

RIVERS OF LIVING WATER

The phrase, *"Out of his belly* (innermost being) *shall flow rivers of Living Water,"* speaks of Jesus directly and only of Believers indirectly. Christ is the Eternal and Inexhaustible Source of all Spiritual Blessings (Isa. 13:3; 55:1; 58:11; Ezek. 47:1; Joel 3:18; Zech. 13:1; 14:8).

The contrast here is between the lifeless water, quickly exhausted, which a mortal Priest carried in a Golden Vessel, and the Life-giving Water flowing in eternal and inexhaustible fullness from out of the Divine and human affections of the Great High Priest. The lesson to be learned is that ceremonies, however magnificent, venerable, and Scriptural in their own right, can never satisfy the deep thirst of the soul. That thirst can only be satisfied by personal union with the Lord Jesus, which is done by Faith. He is the Smitten Rock Who, in Resurrection Power, sends forth a stream of life to dying men and to a thirsty world.

(39) "(BUT THIS SPOKE HE OF THE SPIRIT, WHICH THEY WHO BELIEVE ON HIM SHOULD RECEIVE: FOR THE HOLY SPIRIT WAS NOT YET GIVEN; BECAUSE THAT JESUS WAS NOT YET GLORIFIED.)"

The exegesis is:

1. Everything that Jesus here said is, without exception, all made possible by the Cross of Christ.

2. The Cross of Christ was formulated in the Mind of the Godhead from before the foundation of the world (I Pet. 1:18-20).

3. This means that the Cross of Christ is the oldest Biblical Doctrine. It also means that every Bible Doctrine, irrespective as to what it is, all and without exception, is made possible by the Cross.

4. In addition, it means that all false doctrine begins with an erroneous interpretation of the Cross, an ignoring the Cross, or an outright denial of the Cross.

THE HOLY SPIRIT

The Scripture plainly says concerning the Words of our Lord, *"But this spoke He of the Spirit."* This tells us several things as it regards the Person of the Holy Spirit and the Baptism with the Holy Spirit. Without the Holy Spirit, very little is going to be done for the Lord. It should be obvious as to its significance when we consider that Jesus is the Son of the Living God, in effect, God manifest in the flesh, the One Who was and is Perfect. But yet, He did not begin His Ministry until He was first baptized with the Holy Spirit (Mat. 3:16-17). The question comes back to look us right in the face, *"If Christ needed the Holy Spirit, where in the world does that leave us?"*

While Jesus was God and never lost that

possession, still, He never functioned as God but always as a Man filled with the Holy Spirit.

THEY WHO BELIEVE ON HIM SHOULD RECEIVE

Jesus is the Baptizer with the Holy Spirit. John the Baptist said:

"**I indeed baptize you with water unto Repentance** *(Water Baptism was an outward act of an inward work already carried out)*: **but He** *(Christ)* **Who comes after me is mightier than I, Whose Shoes I am not worthy to bear: He shall baptize you with the Holy Spirit, and *with* fire** *(to burn out the sinful dross [Acts 2:2-4])*:

"**Whose fan *is* in His Hand** *(the ancient method for winnowing grain)*, **and He will thoroughly purge His Floor** *('purging it, that it may bring forth more fruit' [Jn. 15:2])*, **and gather His Wheat into the garner** *(the end product as developed by the Spirit)*; **but He will burn up the chaff with unquenchable fire** *(the wheat is symbolic of the Work of the Spirit, while the chaff is symbolic of the work of the flesh)*" **(Mat. 3:11-12).**

THE SACRIFICE OF CHRIST

While the Holy Spirit was with Believers before the Cross (Jn. 14:16), He was not then in Believers (Jn. 14:17). There was a reason for that.

Before the Cross, the Holy Spirit could not come into the heart and life of a Believer to dwell permanently simply because animal blood was woefully insufficient to take away the sin debt. That awaited the Sacrifice of Christ. The moment that Jesus paid that price, which He did at Calvary's Cross, it meant that the sin debt was forever paid, at least for all who would believe. This means that the Holy Spirit now comes into the heart and life of every person at Conversion and does so to abide permanently (Jn. 14:16).

However, there is a vast difference in being *"born of the Spirit"* than being *"baptized with the Spirit."* While being born of the Spirit takes place automatically at Conversion, which means the Holy Spirit comes into such a heart and life, still, that is not the Baptism with the Spirit.

According to the Word of God, everyone who is baptized with the Spirit speaks with other Tongues as the Spirit of God gives the utterance (Acts, Chpts. 2, 8, 9, 10, 19). In fact, ninety-nine percent of everything done for the Lord around the world in the last 100 years has been done by Believers who have been baptized with the Holy Spirit. I'll say again what we have previously said, *"If Jesus had to have the Baptism with the Spirit before He could begin His Ministry, it stands to reason that we should follow suit."*

FOR THE HOLY SPIRIT WAS NOT YET GIVEN

At the time that Jesus was at the Feast of Tabernacles and made the great statement saying, *"Come unto Me and drink,"* the Holy Spirit had not yet come in the new dimension. To be sure, when John wrote this, He most definitely had come.

The reason that the Holy Spirit could not come in the dimension that He does now was simply because animal blood was woefully insufficient to take away the terrible sin debt brought upon all of humanity as a result of the fall of Adam. However, when Jesus died on the Cross, thereby, satisfying the debt, in other words, paying the Ransom, which God readily accepted as payment in full, this meant that for all who believe, they are Born-Again. The Holy Spirit can then come into such a heart and life to abide forever. It was all predicated on the Cross.

In fact, before the Cross, when Believers died, and we speak of all Old Testament Saints, none were taken to Heaven, but rather were taken down into Paradise. Actually, they were captives of Satan there; however, he could not in any way hurt them, but, still, they were his captives. That's what Paul was talking about when he said that Jesus *"ascended up on high, He led captivity captive"* (Eph. 4:8).

This means that when Jesus, after His Death at the Cross of Calvary, went down into the heart of the Earth, He went down there as a Conqueror and not a victim. He took all of those Saints in Paradise, who were in the heart of the Earth, and led them out, and they then went to Heaven. Now (since the Cross), when a Saint dies, his soul and spirit immediately go to Heaven to be with the Lord Jesus Christ. It is all made possible by the Cross.

JESUS GLORIFIED

The phrase, *"Because that Jesus was not yet glorified,"* once again, refers to the Feast of Tabernacles, which was conducted about six months before the Crucifixion of our Lord. Jesus was not *"Glorified"* until the Cross was a fact.

Being *"Glorified"* has to do with the Glorified Body given to Christ at His Resurrection. It is the same Body that we will have when the Trump sounds (I Cor. 15:53). John said, *"We shall be like Him"* (I Jn. 3:2).

(40) "MANY OF THE PEOPLE THEREFORE, WHEN THEY HEARD THIS SAYING, SAID, OF A TRUTH THIS IS THE PROPHET."

The pattern is:

1. The phrase, *"Many of the people therefore, when they heard this saying,"* represents the massive crowd that had gathered on the Temple mount for the ceremonies on the last day of the Feast of Tabernacles. As we have stated, I know there was a mighty Moving of the Holy Spirit when Jesus uttered this Great Invitation, which, no doubt, greatly moved many. Never in all the nearly 1,600 years of the keeping of this Feast had they experienced what had taken place this day. The shame of it all is that they did not really know who was in their very midst.

2. *"Said, Of a truth this is the Prophet,"* probably referred to Deuteronomy 18:15.

3. If one is to notice, the Messiah was referred to by the Jews by several different names. It seems that very few of them, if any, had learned to combine all the features of the Prophet, Priest, and King into one and the same, which the Messiah would actually be. As well, He was the *"Branch of the Lord,"* the *"Lamb of God,"* and the *"Prince of Peace."* Due to a lack of proper understanding of the Scriptures and the mixing of tradition with what little of the Word of God they actually knew, their understanding was basically flawed concerning this all-important event.

NOTES

(41) "OTHERS SAID, THIS IS THE CHRIST. BUT SOME SAID, SHALL CHRIST COME OUT OF GALILEE?"

The pattern is:

1. The phrase, *"Others said, This is the Christ,"* yet gives Him another Name that means *"the Anointed,"* which alone, at least in this fashion, spoke of the Messiah.

2. The question, *"But some said, Shall Christ come out of Galilee?"* proclaims that they did not Scripturally connect Galilee with the Messiah. They were overlooking the remarkable prediction in Isaiah 9:1 where Galilee is spoken of as the scene of extraordinary illumination, which plainly and obviously proclaims this area as the Abode of the Messiah.

3. Once again, they had a smattering of knowledge of the Word, which showed little attendant diligence to this, the single most important thing in the world. Is it any different now?

4. A great percentage of professing Believers know far more about sports figures, Wall Street, or scores of other things than they do about the Word of God. How tragic that is! How so much is this Scriptural ignorance the cause of so many problems!

(42) "HAS NOT THE SCRIPTURE SAID, THAT CHRIST COMES OF THE SEED OF DAVID, AND OUT OF THE TOWN OF BETHLEHEM, WHERE DAVID WAS?"

The structure is:

1. The beginning of the question, *"Has not the Scripture said. . . ?"* presents the appeal of the people to the Bible as a valuable Testimony to the authority of Scripture as the infallible judge.

2. However, as we shall see, while they did resort to Scripture, they also resorted to the religious leaders who had no regard or concern for Scripture, except how they could twist it to their own purposes (Jn. 7:48). Consequently, the problem that prevailed then prevails now and actually proves to be the greatest area of contention. Are we going to accept the Word of God or the word of men?

3. The continuing of the question, *"That Christ comes of the Seed of David. . . ?"* was correct (II Sam., Chpt. 7; Isa. 11:1, 10; Jer. 23:5; Mic. 5:1-2).

4. The conclusion of the question, *"And out of the town of Bethlehem, where David was?"* again proves to be correct (Mic. 5:1-2). However, it seems that they somewhat misunderstood Micah's prediction, thinking that the Messiah would make this little village His Home. However, Micah did not say that but only that this *"Ruler in Israel"* would come out of Bethlehem. Of course, Jesus fulfilled that when He was born in that small village.

(43) "SO THERE WAS A DIVISION AMONG THE PEOPLE BECAUSE OF HIM."

The pattern is:

1. The *"division"* was caused by a lack of understanding of the Scriptures, plus a desire on the part of some to win the approval of the religious leaders (Jn. 7:48). That same problem persists presently!

2. This *"division"* here outlined was caused, as is obvious, by some who believed that Jesus was indeed the Messiah of Israel, while others did not. This type of division has always been and will continue to be, at least until the Coming of the Lord. This is the reason for all the many different religious denominations and particular types of ministries. It was pandemic in Paul's day (I Cor., Chpt. 1), and, regrettably, the situation has not improved.

3. One of the favorite expressions of the unity crowd is, *"He is causing division in the Body of Christ!"* Actually, the accusation is correct.

4. If error is presented and believed, it must be confronted. Jude said, *"That you should earnestly contend for the Faith which was once delivered unto the Saints"* (Jude, Vs. 3).

5. Of course, certain types of division are wrong, as should be obvious. However, to point out error and at the same time proclaim Truth, which definitely will cause division, is not wrong, but rather right.

(44) "AND SOME OF THEM WOULD HAVE TAKEN HIM; BUT NO MAN LAID HANDS ON HIM."

The composition is:

1. The truth is, the far greater majority of the modern church doesn't have the foggiest idea as to how to live a successful Christian life.

2. Many may think they do! Others may claim they do! While some precious few do know, the truth is, almost all don't know.

3. Unless the Believer understands the Cross of Christ, the understanding of which Paul gave to us in his 14 Epistles, the fact is, such a Believer simply does not know how to live for God.

RELIGION AT WORK

What means the Holy Spirit used to stop those who would then and there have arrested Christ is not known; however, they were stopped!

In this scenario, one is observing religion at work. It always opposes the true Purpose of God simply because it is man-devised and, therefore, man-led. While it talks about God, it does not know God. While it covers itself in all types of religious accoutrements, it, in fact, knows no salvation. It will protect its interests at all costs.

That which is truly of God is left in the Hands of God simply because Jesus is the True Head of the True Church and can protect His Own.

Religion will always try to stop the voice of Truth and will use any means at its disposal to do so, including murder.

Actually, at this very hour, if some of the religions of the world had their way, they would force their beliefs on all, or else, make them suffer the consequences. Regrettably, much of that which is called *"Christianity"* falls into this category.

Were there no laws of the land to stop them, and if they had the power to do it, they would shut up every church not of their liking and stop every Preacher who did not mouth their party line. If the law allowed it, they would use imprisonment, murder, and wholesale killings, all in the Name of the Lord.

The reasons are obvious. These people do not know God and have no relationship with Jesus Christ, despite their frequent conversations about Him, etc. They are as Israel of old, whose very business was religion, and in the process, made all types of spiritual claims but, in reality, knew God not at all!

Incidentally, religion is that which is totally man-devised and claims to better one in some way or to reach God. It is not of God because it is solely of man.

A PERSONAL EXPERIENCE

Way back in 1970, when we first went on radio with the *"Campmeeting Hour,"* which was a 15 minute daily program, Monday through Friday, every effort was made by certain religious organizations to get the program taken off the air. They told lies, concocted schemes, and spared no expense in carrying out their evil designs, but they were not successful because the Lord had opened the door, and no man could close it. However, I emphasize, it was not for lack of trying that they failed.

Sadly, the denomination with which we were formerly associated did the same thing respecting our television program. They seemed to feel that they had a mandate from God to get the program removed from many or all stations on which it was being aired, irrespective of the fact that we were no longer a part of that denomination, etc. Actually, if such had been done in the secular world, it would have been looked at as unlawful, which, in fact, it was, with the perpetrators suffering dire consequences.

If we had desired to resort to the courts, I have no doubt that we could have prevailed, at least if the court were honest. However, I did not feel it was right for a Believer to do such, so we turned to the Lord exclusively, asking Him to protect our interests. Even though we did suffer great loss at the hands of these people, still, the Lord has grandly and gloriously protected that which is His. We continue to trust Him unto this hour, and by His Grace, will continue to do so.

(45) "THEN CAME THE OFFICERS TO THE CHIEF PRIESTS AND PHARISEES; AND THEY SAID UNTO THEM, WHY HAVE YOU NOT BROUGHT HIM?"

The pattern is:

1. The phrase, *"Then came the officers to the Chief Priests and Pharisees,"* refers back to Verse 32.

2. They had evidently heard the Great Invitation, as given by Jesus, because, even though they had been sent to arrest Him, they were so moved by what He had said that they became very fearful of laying hands on Him in any negative way. Who these *"officers"* were, we do not know, of course. However, this we do know: they were far closer to God than the religious leaders of Israel.

3. The question, *"And they said unto them, Why have you not brought Him?"* means they had firmly intended that He be arrested.

(46) "THE OFFICERS ANSWERED, NEVER MAN SPOKE LIKE THIS MAN."

The composition is:

1. Three things come out of this episode. They are as follows:

a. That which Jesus said regarding the Great Invitation was of such magnitude, such power, and such moment that anyone, at least if he were honest, would be forced to take into consideration this great Promise. It was the longing of the human heart to have this *"Living Water,"* which would be perpetual and eternal.

b. That which was said also proclaimed the Identity of the Speaker. Only God could make such a statement, which should be obvious to all.

c. When Jesus uttered this Word, as stated, the Holy Spirit so powerfully anointed what was said that it had a profound effect on all the people there, whether negative or positive. If the heart, as these officers, was somewhat tender toward the Lord, the effect would be positive. Otherwise, it would be the opposite!

2. In all of their years of hearing all types of lectures, sermons, and Bible studies, this which Jesus said was so markedly different, so refreshing, and so filled with life that it caused all others to pale into insignificance.

3. So, once again, the proof becomes absolutely undeniable as to Who and What He really is!

(47) "THEN ANSWERED THEM THE PHARISEES, ARE YOU ALSO DECEIVED?"

The overview is:

1. The phrase, *"Then answered them the Pharisees,"* seems to indicate that this group was the leading spirit in this assault upon Jesus. They considered themselves the guardians of the orthodoxy of Israel. In the haughty pride of this order, they were piqued and angry.

2. Strangely enough, the Pharisees considered themselves fundamentalists, in other words, those who believed all of the Bible and strictly adhered to its Teachings.

3. The question, *"Are you also deceived?"* even though directed at these officers, was, in reality, their problem. The Pharisees were deceived, and this deception would destroy them and ultimately destroy their Nation.

(48) "HAVE ANY OF THE RULERS OR OF THE PHARISEES BELIEVED ON HIM?"

The diagram is:

1. The only way the Believer can properly address *"self"* is to look to the Cross.

2. In fact, the only real description there ever was of humility is the Cross of Christ.

3. Every Believer has a twofold problem: *"sin and self."* Jesus answered both at the Cross.

THE PHARISEES

The question of Verse 48 is asked by the Pharisees of these officers.

In fact, some few of the Pharisees, such as Nicodemus, who was standing nearby overhearing the conversation, had believed on Jesus (Jn. 3:1-2). He was not only a Pharisee but, as well, was a *"ruler,"* being a member of the Jewish Sanhedrin, the highest ruling body in Israel. Actually, Joseph of Arimathea fell into the same category (Mat. 27:57).

However, most Believers do not chart their own course according to the Word of God, but rather follow religious leaders and church denominations. The proud question of this Verse, in effect, sets the church above the Scriptures. Let it ever be known that anytime the Word of God is compromised in this fashion, the seed of destruction has already begun.

The greatest favor that any Preacher or layman, for that matter, could ever do for the denomination with which he is affiliated is to always place the Word of God as the criterion for all things. If the denomination demands something that is not Scriptural, the Word of God must be obeyed at all costs. If enough would do this, it would help the denomination to set its house in order. Even if it did not do such, and the individual was expelled, far better to suffer that indignity than to receive the plaudits of men for obeying an unscriptural position. The Believer must never equate the church with the Scripture, as many presently do.

THE TRUE CHURCH

Religious denominations, even those which are truly attempting to do the Work of God according to the Word of God, are still man-devised institutions. That means that there is nothing spiritual or Scriptural about the organization as such. It also means that belonging to such accords no one special Spiritual status, and neither does leaving one diminish one in Spiritual stature. As long as men understand that, then it's not wrong to be a part of a religious denomination, joining efforts in like Faith and purpose to take the Gospel to the world. However, the moment that Spiritual significance is attached to its man-devised offices or association with its membership, then such becomes unscriptural and should be avoided. The point I am about to make will be strong, but I believe it to be true.

Even though the true Church, which is anchored in the Word of God, is of tremendous Blessing to the world because it lifts up Christ, the false or apostate church, which makes up the far greater majority, has caused more people to die eternally lost than all the vices of the world put together.

So, the Church as a human instrument must never be set above the Scriptures!

(49) "BUT THIS PEOPLE WHO KNOW NOT THE LAW ARE CURSED."

The synopsis is:

1. According to Williams, this Verse could be translated, *"But this ignorant rabble, unlearned in the Law, are a cursed set."* He went on to say, *"Carnal religion makes people use very rude language when angered by conflict with true spiritual Salvation."*[1]

2. Of course, the Pharisees were speaking of those who spoke favorably of Jesus. The truth is, the Pharisees did not know or keep the Law of Moses. Anyway, neither knowing the Law nor keeping it saves the soul. The Law only condemned and made guilty (Rom. 3:9-23; 7:7-25; I Jn. 3:4).

3. Reynolds says that the manner in which the phrase, *"This people,"* was used

was a most contemptuous expression, equivalent to *"the scum of the Earth."*[2]

4. Actually, they showed nothing but contempt for the masses of the people, considering themselves to be of the Spiritual elite, keepers of the Law of Moses, and, consequently, endued with special culture and knowledge. The truth was that they were *"wretched, and miserable, and poor, and blind, and naked"* (Rev. 3:17).

5. Religion does not really care for people because people are not their purpose. Their purpose is money and control. The people are just necessary instruments to be used to further the ends and purposes of the religious elite.

6. One of the things that angered the Pharisees, among all the other things about Jesus that angered them, was His Kindness toward the masses. He spoke to them with dignity and respect, treating them with deference, and ministering to even the most humble of those who came before Him. This showed up the Pharisees, which should be obvious! So, now they would vent their spleen, so to speak, at this *"unwashed, unlearned rabble,"* as they referred to them.

(50) "NICODEMUS SAID UNTO THEM, (HE WHO CAME TO JESUS BY NIGHT, BEING ONE OF THEM.)"

The synopsis is:

1. The phrase, *"Nicodemus said unto them,"* presents this vaunted member of the Sanhedrin, who, incidentally, greatly outranked the Pharisees, now speaking up for Jesus.

2. *"He who came to Jesus by night, being one of them,"* refers back some two and one-half to three years earlier.

3. This intervening period of time must have been one of great consternation for Nicodemus. He still had not broken completely with his present association in order to follow Jesus. So, the battle raged within his soul, as it has raged in the souls of untold millions.

4. Actually, it would take Calvary before Nicodemus would completely make this break. But yet, it was Calvary that sealed this great Truth for all of us!

(51) "DOES OUR LAW JUDGE ANY MAN, BEFORE IT HEAR HIM, AND KNOW WHAT HE DOES?"

The order is:

1. Feeble and timid as was the plea of Nicodemus, yet it was precious to the Lord, and so, it is here honorably recorded by the Holy Spirit.

2. The truth is, they were breaking the Law of Moses themselves, while all the time loudly trumpeting their keeping it. Actually, the rules for the Judgment of a Prophet were stringent, and no attempt had been made to put these prophetic claims to the test (Deut. 18:19-22). Consequently, they ran off upon an utterly false tact.

3. The Law plainly said that they were not to receive a false report. *"Hear the causes between your brethren, and judge righteously between every man and his brother"* (Deut. 1:16).

4. The truth is, Jesus is the Only One Who ever kept the Law, while all else, even Moses, failed, and especially these Pharisees, who were the biggest Law-breakers of all!

(52) "THEY ANSWERED AND SAID UNTO HIM, ARE YOU ALSO OF GALILEE? SEARCH, AND LOOK: FOR OUT OF GALILEE ARISES NO PROPHET."

The form is:

1. Their desire to accuse Jesus so overwhelmed them and clouded their judgment that they failed to check out the facts. Jesus was born in Bethlehem, not Galilee.

2. As well, they seemed to have forgotten the Messianic Prophecy of Isaiah 9:2, which spotlighted Galilee.

3. Also, had they searched the Scriptures, or even had a rudimentary knowledge of them, they would have found that Jonah, Hosea, Elijah, Elisha, and others were from the northern kingdom and not from Judaea. Consequently, their Scriptural ignorance was just as bad as their spiritual poverty.

(53) "AND EVERY MAN WENT UNTO HIS OWN HOUSE."

The form is:

1. Even though these men had houses to which they could retire, Jesus actually had no place to lay His Head. So, the next Verse says that He *"went unto the Mount of Olives."*

2. Most probably, the Disciples were with Him, but, as should be obvious, the

accommodations, of necessity, must have been very Spartan. During His Public Ministry, even though He visited Jerusalem a number of times, there is no record that He spent a single, solitary night in the city, other than the night He was arrested.

3. This city, which had been chosen by Him at the very beginning (II Chron. 6:6), was now so filled with religious demons that He found it very uncomfortable. Regrettably, this characterizes all religions of the world and even much of that which calls itself *"Christianity."*

"When all my labors and trials are o'er,
"And I am safe on that beautiful shore,
"Just to be near the dear Lord I adore,
"Will through the ages be glory for me."

"When by the gift of His Infinite Grace,
"I am accorded in Heaven a place,
"Just to be there and to look on His Face,
"Will through the ages be glory for me."

"Friends will be there I have loved long ago;
"Joy like a river around me will flow;
"Yet, just a smile from my Saviour, I know,
"Will through the ages be glory for me."

CHAPTER 8

(1) "JESUS WENT UNTO THE MOUNT OF OLIVES."

The exposition is:

1. For those who have not been to Jerusalem, the *"Mount of Olives"* lies east of the city. The brook Kidron runs at its base, between it and Mount Moriah, on which sat the Temple. Consequently, the Temple facing east was facing the Mount of Olives.

2. The Mount actually has a small range of four summits, with the highest being about 2,500 feet.

3. It is said to have been thickly wooded in Jesus' Day and rich in the olives, which occasioned its name.

4. It is claimed that several of the olive trees still standing were there during the Time of Christ. I have personally looked upon these trees, and they do look extremely ancient as they, no doubt, are. However, it is also claimed that all of the trees, of whatever variety, were cut down during the siege of Jerusalem by Titus. At any rate, the ground is holy, for Christ unquestionably walked there, and as stated here, spent a number of nights on its slopes.

5. Sadly enough, Solomon built high places on this mount to the idol gods Chemosh and Molech for his heathen wives, which was probably the reason one summit was dubbed the Mount of Offense.

6. It is to this place that Jesus will return, and we speak of the Second Coming, with the mountain then parting in two as He stands on it (Zech. 14:4).

(2) "AND EARLY IN THE MORNING HE CAME AGAIN INTO THE TEMPLE, AND ALL THE PEOPLE CAME UNTO HIM; AND HE SAT DOWN, AND TAUGHT THEM."

The order is:

1. *"Saving our life,"* as spoken in Luke 9:24, refers to us trying to do this thing by our own strength, which means that we are going to lose.

2. *"Losing our life for the sake of Christ,"* refers to placing our life and living entirely into Christ. When we do that, we *"shall save it."*

A PARTICULAR MORNING

The phrase, *"And early in the morning He came again into the Temple,"* speaks of daybreak.

As stated, Jesus had spent the night under the stars on Mount Olivet and evidently arose somewhat before daylight and very soon made His Way to the Temple. This is the day after the Feast of Tabernacles had concluded. No doubt, many thousands of people were still in the city, with many of them planning to leave that day or later.

"And all the people came unto Him," gives us no clue as to exactly how many were there but, no doubt, hundreds, if not more. It is even possible that many who

lived elsewhere in Israel, plus in Jerusalem, had come to the Temple that early morning hour with the very hope that Jesus would be there. If that were the case, which it, no doubt, was with some, they would not be disappointed. This day, they would be privileged to be a part of, and behold with their eyes, the greatest exhibition of Grace that possibly the world had ever known to date.

TEACHING THE MULTITUDES

The phrase, *"And He sat down, and taught them,"* proclaims Him revealing Himself as the *"Word of God,"* the *"Light of the World,"* and the *"Eternal Life."* As well, this Chapter, plus those following, will record His Rejection in all these relationships.

To have the privilege of hearing Him teach would result in no less than that said by the officers, *"Never man spoke like this Man,"* that is, if one has an honest heart. No doubt, hundreds pushed in close so as not to miss a single word. As well, the Spirit of God gently moved upon each and every heart, at least those who would allow Him to do so. As such, one would have heard a stifled sob here and there. With others, the tears would have rolled unchecked as they heard the Word in a fashion as never before, and anointed by the Holy Spirit as they had never experienced. Whatever duties the people had, which may have seemed so urgent a little bit before, now were completely forgotten, as the hearer became lost in what Jesus was saying.

This could well be a symbol, a preview, and a striking moment, if you will, of that which will take place on a grander scale in the coming Kingdom Age. As the Redeemed Saints on that coming Glad Day gather around Him, His Words will be such as our minds cannot presently comprehend. For then, as John later said, *"We shall see Him as He is"* (I Jn. 3:2).

(3) "AND THE SCRIBES AND PHARISEES BROUGHT UNTO HIM A WOMAN TAKEN IN ADULTERY; AND WHEN THEY HAD SET HER IN THE MIDST."

The synopsis is:

1. This scenario would prove to be one of the greatest occasions of the Grace of God ever evidenced.

NOTES

2. The Law said that this young lady should be stoned, but yet, Jesus did not advocate such. How could He do that and not break the Law?

3. He did it for her the same as He has done it for all of us, by going to the Cross in our place and paying the price we should have paid but could not pay.

THE WOMAN TAKEN IN ADULTERY

The phrase, *"And the Scribes and Pharisees brought unto Him a woman taken in adultery,"* actually means in the Greek that she was *"dragged by main force."*

There is little or no indication that the Sanhedrin had any part in this particular action of the *"Scribes and Pharisees."* More than likely, they would have considered this act as beneath their place and position. While they hated Christ and would do anything they could to stop His Ministry, which they ultimately did a few months later, still, a public scene such as this was not what they desired.

However, the Pharisees, having been defeated regarding their accusations of Jesus healing a man on the Sabbath Day, now brought forth this woman in the hope of confounding Jesus. If He condemned her, He was not a Saviour — the Law did that — and if He let her go, He despised and disallowed the Law. So, as far as they were concerned, whatever He did, whether forgiving her or stoning her, would lessen Him in the eyes of the people.

However, how foolish it is of man to try and be clever when dealing with God.

Another thought that must be addressed is about all that organized religion can do, and this was organized religion, is to stop the Message of Christ from getting to the people. This is what happened at this time. They interrupted Jesus while He was teaching the people, something they would liked to have done all the time if such had been possible. The following statement is strong, but I believe it to be true:

HINDERING THE WORK OF GOD

If all the major religious denominations in Christendom were properly analyzed, I think it would be obvious that most are doing far more to hinder the spread of the Gospel than they are the opposite. In other words, most of them are being used by Satan exactly as these Pharisees of old!

Without exception, all of the Work of God that is being done is done as the Lord calls an individual, whether man or woman, for a particular task, and anoints him with the Holy Spirit. This should be obvious, at least to those who know their Bibles. He does not call denominations to do anything. If one would carefully read his Bible, one would see that God deals with individuals, not organizations, etc.

Ideally, the organization or denomination should aid and help the person to carry out the Call of God on his or her life. To be sure, some have done that in the past, and some few continue to do so at present. However, for the most part, which is Satan's business, they seek to hinder that Call and do so in many ways.

In the denomination with which I was formerly associated, it has deteriorated Spiritually to such an extent that those who claim to have a Call of God on their lives, respecting the taking of the Gospel to the world, are treated in a very cavalier fashion, at least regarding their Call.

These prospective Missionaries are given batteries of psychological tests, and if those tests are not passed, the person is automatically rejected. As well, the place or country to which the would-be Missionary claims that the Holy Spirit desires to send him is, many times, altogether ignored. If he passes the psychological tests, the individual is sent to where a committee desires that he or she go. There may be some few exceptions, but not many!

THE HOLY SPIRIT

Without going into detail at all, I think it should be obvious from the few things said that the Holy Spirit has little say in anything that is done in this type of atmosphere. It has become a business, with the things of the world, such as psychology, becoming the criteria. In fact, God has no part in such activities.

As a result, very few true Men and Women of God are being sent to the foreign field by these denominations, but rather amateur sociologists and psychologists. As I have said, most of all they are doing, with some few exceptions, is to hinder the True Gospel of Jesus Christ. Regrettably, the hundreds of thousands of people who attend these particular churches have no knowledge of the things I have said, consequently, continuing to funnel money into these efforts, thinking all the time that they are helping to take the Gospel to the world. However, for the most part, their money is not only wasted, but it actually goes to help and aid the work of Satan. Please believe me, anything that is not instigated by the Holy Spirit and, therefore, guided, led, directed, and ordered, performs no Work for God whatsoever. If it's not of God, then it must be of the Evil One, irrespective of how religious it may be.

In traveling all over the world, preaching Crusades in many of the largest cities, and airing television in scores of countries, even translated into various languages, I have seen, and continue to see, literally hundreds of thousands of people brought to a Saving Knowledge of Jesus Christ. Basically, that type of *"fruit"* is the proof! Consequently, I do know what I am talking about.

THE WOMAN

The phrase, *"And when they had set her in the midst,"* proclaims the results of self-righteousness, i.e., religion.

Public humiliation is of such pain and shock that there is very little way that words can properly describe it. Someone has said that it is somewhat akin to having the skin flailed from the body and exposing all the nerve ends. To be sure, that description is not an exaggeration.

Sometime back, overhearing a secular television talk show host comment on this very thing, he said, *"Most never survive such an ordeal."*

He went on to say, *"They either kill themselves, or retreat into drugs or alcohol, or at the very least, withdraw from society."* In other words, without God, it is almost impossible for one to survive such a thing to which this woman is now being exposed.

So, it is with great pity that we look at

this woman, this poor creature, standing in the *"midst"* of the great crowd. At that moment, I am sure that death would have been sweet, and I am also sure that she fully expected to die.

The phrase, *"Taken in adultery,"* meant that her guilt was undeniable; however, why did they not bring forward the equally guilty man? The Law commanded that both should be stoned.

(4) "THEY SAY UNTO HIM, MASTER, THIS WOMAN WAS TAKEN IN ADULTERY, IN THE VERY ACT."

The form is:

1. The Cross of Christ was the answer at the very beginning for man's dilemma, and it is the answer now, and the only answer.

2. The only Way to God is through Jesus Christ (Jn. 14:6), and the only Way to Christ is through the Cross (Lk. 9:23).

3. The problem with the modern church is that it has substituted for *"Jesus Christ and Him Crucified,"* a Crossless Christ!

ADULTERY

The phrase, *"They say unto Him, Master,"* was not meant at all as a term of endearment, as we would think of such now. They were merely referring to Him as a *"Teacher"* or *"Rabbi,"* which the word *"Master"* meant!

The phrase, *"This woman was taken in adultery, in the very act,"* makes one wonder exactly how such a thing could be brought about. In other words, how could they catch her in the act without some type of collaboration in this matter as it regards the man?

Even though the act of these religious leaders is repulsive, to say the least, one, as well, must not ignore the terrible sin of *"adultery."* It is not only a sin against God but against the institution of marriage, as well as a violation of the human body, which is supposed to be a Temple of the Holy Spirit. So, this sin is dark and destructive and has a greater negative consequence than many other sins. In view of that, did these religious leaders have the right to do what they were doing?

What role should the Church play in such situations?

NOTES

RESTORATION

Actually, the New Testament is very clear on this situation, and that alone is what matters.

If a Believer falls into such sin, He must repent and turn from such (I Cor. 5:4-5; I Jn. 1:9).

If the person does repent, the Church is to forgive him (or her) and *"confirm your love toward him"* (II Cor. 2:6-8).

If the individual will not repent and, therefore, cease such activity, fellowship is to be withdrawn (I Cor. 5:13).

Some claim that probation is needed even though there is Repentance, with punishment continuing for a particular period of time, etc. However, those types of laws are made up by men. They are not in the Bible and, consequently, are unscriptural. Upon sincere Repentance, the individual is to be restored to full fellowship immediately (Gal. 6:1).

The entirety of the Church must understand and consider that all must be very careful when judging another. None are without sin of some nature, consequently, continuing to come short of the Glory of God. To take a harsh, unyielding, and unbending stand is opposed by the entirety of the tenor of the Word of God, and for obvious reasons.

MERCY

It is not difficult to tell if a person is sincere and if he truly has repented. Such earmarks become quickly obvious. As a stubborn, intractable, and unyielding spirit is very quickly obvious, likewise, so is a broken and contrite spirit. As well, if one is to err, one should err on the side of Mercy rather than otherwise (Mat. 7:1-2).

If one is to be Biblical, such judgment and action must remain in the local Church where the action of failure took place. This is the criterion of the New Testament and should not be ignored. Consequently, it is not proper for anyone outside of the local Church to engage in any type of judgment or decisions respecting that local body, and for all the obvious reasons (II Cor. 2:6-11).

While it is true that Paul, and even the Word of God, gave advise regarding such matters, which the local Church wants to obey, still, this was done because Paul had planted many, if not all, of these Churches. As well, there were very few guidelines at that time, with the Lord giving such to Paul, which we now have as the Word of God. There is no authority given in the New Testament higher than that of the local Church. Consequently, it is improper and unscriptural for denominational heads to usurp authority over the local Church in these matters. While such should feel free to give counsel and advice when asked, that's as far as it should go.

ELDERS OF THE LOCAL CHURCH

If a person is in a place of leadership, as often happens, each case would have to be decided by the Elders of the local Church in question, respecting the situations involved in that case. Respecting Restoration, there is no hard and fast rule regarding exactly what is to be done in any and all situations of this nature. However, whatever decision is made, the leaders in the local Church should seek the Face of the Lord respecting wisdom and direction, ever remembering that the Lord Alone is the Head of the Church. In such situations, the Holy Spirit will guide and lead into all Truth (Jn. 16:13-15).

In all of this, it should be obvious that sin can never be treated lightly. If it is allowed to remain unchecked, with a lack of repentance, ultimately, the whole will be *"leavened,"* i.e., totally corrupted. It is the Business of the Holy Spirit to convict of sin and help the Believer live above sin. Regrettably, all Believers have had to go before the Lord time and again seeking His Mercy and Forgiveness. Still, the Lord saves from sin, not in sin!

AS WE ARE JUDGING OURSELVES

Having said that, the truth is, failures remain! As such, and as far as is humanly possible, those who are Spiritual (Gal. 6:1) are to deal with Mercy and Grace with those who have failed, never forgetting that this is the manner in which God has dealt with us. Actually, the tenor of the Scriptures respecting such situations is that when we pass judgment, as sometimes we are forced to do, we must do so as if we are judging ourselves (Mat. 7:1-2; I Cor. 5:12; II Cor. 2:7-9; Gal. 6:1).

To be sure, the greater the Leading of the Holy Spirit, the greater the Mercy and Grace, while at the same time, never condoning sin. However, the less of the Holy Spirit and the more of religious self-righteousness, the less Mercy and Grace will be shown, as is obvious among these Pharisees in this Eighth Chapter of John.

THE WORD OF GOD

What I have given about this matter is, I think, the Word of God. To add to or take away from the Word invites disaster. Sooner or later, such will destroy the perpetrators.

Many years ago, a Message was preached, of which some part was passed down to this generation. Three things, especially, were stated, which bear repeating. Even though I have given them elsewhere in these Volumes, I think it would be proper to do so again here:

1. When we hear something negative about a fellow Believer, we must remember that we are hearing gossip, and, as such, we may be hearing only half-truth or no truth at all. It should be treated accordingly!

2. If we think we truly know the details, still, we should remember that we have little knowledge concerning the spiritual warfare involved. As such, we should judge accordingly, *"considering ourselves, lest we also be tempted"* (Gal. 6:1).

3. If we were faced with the same situation, would we have done any better or even as well?

(5) "NOW MOSES IN THE LAW COMMANDED US, THAT SUCH SHOULD BE STONED: BUT WHAT DO YOU SAY?"

The diagram is:

1. The Lord can bear with ignorance and infirmity (spiritual weakness), but He cannot sanction neglect or disobedience.

2. The Cross of Christ was the answer at the very beginning for man's dilemma, and it is the answer now (Gen. 3:15; Col. 2:14-15).

3. The Cross of Christ is the Means, and the only Means, by which the Grace of God comes to us.

THE LAW OF MOSES

The phrase, *"Now Moses in the Law commanded us, that such should be stoned,"* was true for both the man and the woman (Lev. 20:10).

Many may object to the Law of Moses, calling it cruel and harsh; however, it is not so but, in reality, the very opposite. Some of the following points may help clarify the issue:

RIGHT AND WRONG

The Law of Moses did what law is supposed to do, proclaim what is right and what is wrong. Inasmuch as this was the Law of God, it was absolutely perfect in its quality and perfect in its fairness. In truth, as should be obvious, it far eclipsed all human law that was in the world at that time. It showed man his responsibility to God and his responsibility to his fellowman. It was a system that told man how to live, which placed Israel in a greatly advantageous position relative to the other nations in the world, at least when they tried to adhere to the Law.

PENALTY

There was a penalty attached to the Law, as all law must have. Law without penalty is really no law at all! As well, it was God Who set the penalty, which meant that it was just, and, as such, it was totally impartial and fair to all.

To note, capital punishment could not be carried out on an individual, although guilty, unless there were two or more witnesses to the act. So, the truth is, there were very few executions in Old Testament times.

NO SALVATION IN THE LAW

There was no Salvation in the Law, as there is no Salvation in any type of law. The very nature of law precludes such.

However, the Lord provided the sacrifices of particular clean animals that a man could offer, which would atone for his breaking the Law, whereby, Mercy would be extended. To be sure, the blood of bulls and goats could not take away sins, but it could cover it, thereby, shielding it from the eyes of a Thrice-Holy God, which would suffice until the Ultimate Sacrifice of God's Son was brought about.

DAVID

In truth, as stated, one reads of very few people in the Old Testament being stoned or executed in any manner, even for the worst of sins, such as murder, adultery, incest, etc., which all carried the death penalty. In fact, David, one of the greatest Men of God who ever lived, committed the two terrible sins of adultery and murder, which carried the death penalty. So, how did he escape from being stoned to death?

Many may argue that he was the king, and, as such, he was exempt in one way or the other; however, the Law exempted no one! In fact, if possible, he was held more responsible even than others.

David plainly stated in his prayer of Repentance, *"For You desire not sacrifice; else would I give it: You delight not in Burnt Offering"* (Ps. 51:16).

Actually, he was saying, and rightly so, that there was no animal sacrifice appointed by God which could atone for these sins of adultery and murder. So, how did he escape penalty?

THE PRECIOUS BLOOD OF JESUS CHRIST

David looked beyond the sacrifices to Whom and What they represented, namely, the Lord Jesus Christ. To do this, he had to go all the way back to the Deliverance of the Children of Israel from Egypt, which typified the cleansing experience of all and the blood which was applied to the doorpost. This blood, which came from a slain lamb, and which typified the Blood of Jesus Christ that would be shed in the future, was that which brought Israel to Salvation and, no doubt, many adulterers and murderers as well! Hence, Moses wrote, *"And the blood shall be to you for a token upon the houses where you are: and when I see the blood, I will pass over you, and the plague* (death) *shall not be upon you to destroy you"* (Ex. 12:13).

That is the reason David said, *"Purge me with hyssop, and I shall be clean: wash me, and I shall be whiter than snow"* (Ps. 51:7).

The *"hyssop"* was a grass-like substance

which grew abundantly, and which was used by the Israelites to dip down into the blood and apply it to the doorposts. It was a type of the Human Body of Jesus, which would be given in Sacrifice, that is, when He came.

That is the way that David escaped the death penalty, and all others who fell into this category, for that matter.

It remains the same presently!

BUT WHAT DO YOU SAY?

Concerning its answer to the question, *"But what do You say?"* it is the only answer that really matters. It is what Jesus says that counts and not Pharisees, Scribes, or anyone else, for that matter!

In effect, what was He going to do?

Even though the Pharisees did not know such, Jesus was actually the One Who originally gave the Law. As well, He was the Only One Who kept the Law in its totality. Many others tried, but all failed!

So, if the Law of Moses said that this woman should be stoned, and it did, He was obligated to adhere to the strict letter of the Law. The Word of God demanded such, with Righteousness demanding such as well! In fact, if He did not hold to the strict letter of the Law in all respects, the entire fabric and system of Justice, along with Righteousness, would completely break down. So, what was at stake was of far greater significance than the mere trap or scheme these reprobates had concocted.

If He let the woman go without the price being paid for her sin, then the entirety of humanity had nothing on which to stand and would ultimately be destroyed.

On the other hand, if He stoned her to death, as the Law demanded, He would have been accused by the Romans of usurping authority and would, as well, have portrayed the very opposite of the Love, Mercy, Grace, and Compassion for which He was noted so strongly.

As well, the audience of hundreds, who were observing that day, knew full well that this Law had not been previously applied literally, and that the Sanhedrin had not enforced it. They also knew that if they had endeavored to do so, Roman power would have stepped in with a strong hand. So, it must have been obvious to the people of the hypocrisy of the Pharisees.

Nevertheless, none of that had any bearing on what Jesus would do. His Actions were not based on what Rome did or thought or on what the Pharisees would or would not do. His Actions were based on the Word of God.

(6) "THIS THEY SAID, TEMPTING HIM, THAT THEY MIGHT HAVE TO ACCUSE HIM. BUT JESUS STOOPED DOWN, AND WITH HIS FINGER WROTE ON THE GROUND, AS THOUGH HE HEARD THEM NOT."

The overview is:

1. Jesus must never be separated from the Cross as it regards its benefits.

2. Through the Cross, He opened up the way to the Holy of Holies that whosoever will may come (Rev. 22:17).

3. Without the Cross, man would never have been able to bridge that great gulf. However, the Cross bridged it, which means that Jesus became our Sin-Offering.

THE TEMPTING OF THE PHARISEES

The phrase, *"This they said, tempting Him, that they might have to accuse Him,"* was, as stated, a very clever trap!

According to the Greek text, there is every evidence that these hypocrites stood there with stones in their hands, waiting for His Answer. Had He said, *"Yes,"* they were ready to stone the woman then and there and, subsequently, to throw the responsibility of such violation of Roman jurisdiction upon the Lord Jesus as its instigator.

On the other hand, if He said, *"No,"* they would accuse Him of deliberately ignoring and repudiating the authority of the Law of Moses.

This was their plan, and this poor woman caught in this terrible situation, even though guilty, was made their pawn. Actually, to use people is all religion can do!

JESUS WROTE ON THE GROUND

The phrase, *"But Jesus stooped down, and with His Finger wrote on the ground, as though He heard them not,"* actually meant that He wrote in the dust on the stone, for the Temple Court was paved.

This recalled His Action (Ex. 31:18) in stooping down from Heaven to Mount Sinai and writing with His Finger upon the stone tablets of the Law.

Once more, Almighty God, now manifested in the Flesh, stooped earthwards and, once more, that Finger wrote upon stone, but now, not that which condemned to death, but that which was ordained to life.

His Action in writing on the ground should have opened their eyes as to Who He was. He did not excuse or deny the woman's guilt or the fact that the Law justly doomed her to death.

WHAT DID JESUS WRITE?

Had the Holy Spirit wanted us to know, it would have been recorded. Had it been necessary for our spiritual enlightenment, it would have been given.

During Jesus' Earthly Ministry, there is no record that He wrote anything which was meant to be recorded. There was a reason for that.

All of the Word of God, beginning with Genesis through the Book of Revelation, was given to men to write and, accordingly, inspired by the Holy Spirit, meaning there is no contradiction or error (II Pet. 1:21). There were three exceptions to that:

1. He wrote on the stone tablets at Sinai in the giving of the Law (Ex., Chpt. 31).

2. He wrote on the wall in the palace at Babylon a Message of Judgment, which was interpreted by Daniel (Dan., Chpt. 5).

3. He wrote in the dust on the paving in the Temple at Jerusalem.

The first writing had to do with the Law and pertained to the disposition of the world. The second had to do with Judgment, which, of necessity, must follow law. The third spoke of Grace, which would assuage the necessary Judgment, at least for those who would believe.

(7) "SO WHEN THEY CONTINUED ASKING HIM, HE LIFTED UP HIMSELF, AND SAID UNTO THEM, HE WHO IS WITHOUT SIN AMONG YOU, LET HIM FIRST CAST A STONE AT HER."

The exegesis is:

1. Seiss said, *"Everywhere, even in our holiest moods and most sacred doings, there*

NOTES

still flashes out the stern and humiliating accusation — 'O man, you are a sinner!'"

2. Seiss continued, *"All your goodness is but abomination apart from Christ!"*

3. And finally, *"Your only hope is in Him Whose Body was broken and Whose Blood was shed for the remission of sins!"*[1]

HE WHO IS WITHOUT SIN AMONG YOU . . .

The phrase, *"So when they continued asking Him,"* means they pressed the issue, demanding an answer as to what He would say respecting the Law of Moses and its application.

"He lifted up Himself, and said unto them," means that He stood upright. The great crowd was listening intently, and this group of hypocrites was about to hear something they had not anticipated.

"He who is without sin among you, let him first cast a stone at her," now turned the tables from her, and Him, for that matter, onto the accusers.

The word *"without sin"* in the Greek is *"anamartetos"* and means *"sinless!"* Some have claimed that He said, *"He who is without this sin among you."* However, while it did include that, that seems not to be the direct thrust of His Statement.

If one is to notice, His Statement to them in no way condoned sin, and neither did He mean that only the sinless, of which there were none, could pronounce a verdict upon the guilty, as must be done in some cases.

However, due to the fact that none are sinless and that all have had to plead for the Mercy of God, His Statement or Challenge absolutely forbids Believers (we speak in a moral sense) of taking part in any type of execution of punishment. God reserves such solely for Himself (Rom. 12:19).

PUNISHMENT?

As well, James said, and I paraphrase, *"There is One Lawgiver* (God), *Who is able to save and to destroy: who do you think you are, thinking you are morally qualified to judge another?"* (James 4:12).

This means that no church, religious denomination, pastor, or fellow Believer has any Scriptural right to exert punishment in any form on a fellow Believer. As stated, that is reserved solely for God.

While upon refusal to repent, the Church or individual may withdraw fellowship or even quit praying for the impenitent one, still, that is the limit of one's liberty for such (I Cor. 5:5, 13).

If one thinks one is worthy to administer punishment to a fellow Believer, one should again read the Challenge of Jesus to the Pharisees.

When put before them in this manner, these hypocrites did have enough Grace to silently slink away, while their modern counterparts do not even come up to that standard, which, as obvious, is abysmally low.

(8) "AND AGAIN HE STOOPED DOWN, AND WROTE ON THE GROUND."

The form is:

1. This tells us that the Lord wrote twice on the stones at His Feet. He wrote twice at Sinai as well! One tablet related to God; the other to man as to obedience and responsibility.

2. Some have suggested that He may have written on the first stone, *"God sent not His Son into the world to condemn the world, but that the world through Him might be Saved."*

3. On the second stone, He might have written the words, *"He who believes on the Son has Everlasting Life, and comes not into condemnation."*

However, that is only speculation.

(9) "AND THEY WHICH HEARD IT, BEING CONVICTED BY THEIR OWN CONSCIENCE, WENT OUT ONE BY ONE, BEGINNING AT THE ELDEST, EVEN UNTO THE LAST: AND JESUS WAS LEFT ALONE, AND THE WOMAN STANDING IN THE MIDST."

The order is:

1. The songwriter said:
"Sit, forever viewing,
"Mercy streaming in His Blood."

2. The Sacrificial Atoning Death of our Lord in the shedding of His Life's Blood underlies everything else. It is this and this alone.

3. The shed Blood of Jesus Christ is the beginning, the middle, and the end of all human Sanctification.

CONVICTION

The phrase, *"And they who heard it, being convicted by their own conscience,"* tells us that their position was so spiritually and morally untenable that even though they would not heed the Scripture, their own consciences convicted them because they knew they were sinners. In a moment's time, the Holy Spirit must have brought to their minds, which acted upon their conscience, their terrible moral unworthiness, which instantly became glaringly obvious to them. This was so much so that they must have imagined that this great crowd standing there observing these events saw right through them, down into the very recesses of their souls. In other words, they became spiritually and morally naked before God and man, and had reduced themselves to that state by their own actions.

Men are so prone to say, *"But he (or she) is guilty!"* Quite often, that is true, even as here. However, due to our own unworthiness and especially considering the Grace and Mercy of God extended to us, every verdict and word must be rendered accordingly! To do anything less is to instantly convict ourselves.

DROPPED THE STONES

The phrase, *"Went out one by one, beginning at the eldest, even unto the last,"* portrays them, one by one, dropping the stones held in their hands and quietly retiring away from this Awful Presence.

When we compare ourselves with others, quite possibly, we may hypocritically find something to boast about. However, when standing before Him, the Perfection of Perfection and the Purity of Purity, then our pitiful self-righteousness fades like fog under a hot morning sun.

"And Jesus was left alone," proclaims this glaring Truth because He Alone is without sin.

The multitudes who had gathered around Him were still waiting for His Words and had closely observed the proceedings; however, they had wisely not thrown themselves into the place of judgment as had the Pharisees.

So, the Pharisees turned away from Him

Who had convicted them. They could not stay in the merciless beams of that Light and try to hide their guilt and shame. How much wiser it would have been for them, like the woman, to have remained in that Light and to have confessed their sin, and they also would have heard the gracious words, *"Neither do I condemn you."*

THE WOMAN

The phrase, *"And the woman standing in the midst,"* probably presented her continuing to cower in shame and mortal fear. Even though this had begun as the worst day of her life, it would turn out to be the greatest day, for she would find Jesus. Here accusers thought they were bringing her to her death or, at the least, to horrifying shame and humiliation, never realizing that they were bringing her to forgiveness of all sin and the obtaining of Eternal Life.

Augustine said, *"These two, 'Misery and Pity,' face one another, and in the presence of a multitude of Disciples and their listeners, Misery waits for Pity to speak — for perfect Holiness and perfect Mercy to do its will. For there is One seated there Who is without sin."*

(10) "WHEN JESUS HAD LIFTED UP HIMSELF, AND SAW NONE BUT THE WOMAN, HE SAID UNTO HER, WOMAN, WHERE ARE THOSE YOUR ACCUSERS? HAS NO MAN CONDEMNED YOU?"

The form is:

1. The phrase, *"When Jesus had lifted up Himself,"* refers to Him once again standing.

2. The first time, He had stood before His and her accusers, for when we accuse the one who comes to Him, we accuse Him. However, under that withering look of Perfection, they had wilted away.

3. Now, He stood again, but His Words would be different. To self-righteous accusation, they were one thing, while to contrition and Repentance, they were quite another!

4. The phrase, *"And saw none but the woman, He said unto her,"* simply means that her accusers were gone, while the great multitude continued to observe the proceedings.

5. The question, *"Woman, where are those your accusers?"* simply means that

NOTES

none are qualified to *"accuse."*

6. By all means, this lesson should not be lost upon the Church. The obviousness of its Truth is so glaring in its simplicity that even a child need not misunderstand. But yet, the accusers abound!

7. Do they not know and understand the judgment they are pronouncing upon themselves?

8. The question, *"Has no man condemned you?"* was addressed to the church of that day and to this day as well.

9. As we have stated, the Believer must properly understand who he is, which means that he was a lost sinner before Jesus saved him, and within himself, there was no way he could be Saved. But yet, God loved him supremely and upon simple Faith, gave him His Great Salvation.

10. After coming to the Lord, the Believer has had to resort to Him countless times, asking for Mercy and Grace, relative to faults, failures, and sins committed. The Lord has always been Gracious, Longsuffering, Patient, Kind, and Forgiving.

11. Realizing that, the Believer condemns not at all and is quick to forgive.

12. As someone has said, if a Believer is loath to forgive, and to forgive quickly, that just may be a sign that he is only a professing Believer and, in fact, does not truly know the Lord and, consequently, has not experienced forgiveness himself.

(11) "SHE SAID, NO MAN, LORD. AND JESUS SAID UNTO HER, NEITHER DO I CONDEMN YOU: GO, AND SIN NO MORE."

The exposition is:

1. If one has a proper view of the Cross, then one will have a proper view of sin.

2. The idea is, *"What He is, I am, but all because of the Cross."*

3. However, despite what I am in Christ, I must recognize the fact that the sin nature is ever present with me (Rom. 6:1-14).

NEITHER DO I CONDEMN YOU

The phrase, *"She said, No man, Lord,"* proclaims the fact, by her calling Him *"Lord,"* that she had made Him her Salvation. As well, He Who read her heart knew that she believed upon Him. How could she do otherwise, considering His Mercy? Why would anyone even want to do otherwise, considering His Mercy?

"And Jesus said unto her, Neither do I condemn you: go, and sin no more," records the sweetest words she had ever heard in all of her life. In effect, her life was given back to her, as is beautifully obvious.

Why would He not *"condemn,"* especially considering that she was unquestionably guilty and that He had every right to do so?

His Mission to the world was not to condemn simply because it was not necessary. Man was already condemned, with a load of guilt that spoke its awful sentence on a continual basis. At any rate, Jesus came to save!

Let the reader understand that as His Message was such then, it remains the same presently. All who come to Him will experience the same Grace, Love, and Mercy.

Actually, in this Fourth Gospel, there are three sinful women brought into the Presence of Jesus.

1. For the first (Jn., Chpt. 4), the Message was, *"No reprobation."*

2. For the second (Jn., Chpt. 8), *"No condemnation."*

3. For the third (Jn. 20:17), *"No separation."*

MERCY AND GRACE

However, as the reader studies this beautiful example of Mercy and Grace, still, the fact of the Law continues to loom above us. By obligation, those guilty of such a sin, as we have stated, were condemned to death. So, how did Jesus satisfy the Law, which He was obligated to keep, in a fashion never before done by others, especially considering that the guilt of this woman was not in doubt?

Jesus did satisfy the obligations of the Law for this woman and all others. He took her place on the Cross, as for all. He satisfied the demands of the Law that death be visited for this awful sin. He suffered its penalty in totality in order that she and all who believe in His Gracious and Glorious Name, and what He did that day at Calvary, might be Saved. Truly, it is the Grandest Story ever told.

There is no debt left owing for the guilty sinner because it was gloriously and wondrously paid at Calvary's Cross. Heaven's Courts were satisfied.

However, it did not stop there. Jesus, as well, gave us Eternal Life, which speaks of the Eternal Bread of Life, namely Jesus, on Whom we can feast and live forever.

"Neither do I condemn you,
"Precious words Divine.
"Fallen from the lips of Mercy,
"Like the sweetest chimes,
"Neither do I condemn you,
"Sing them o'er and o'er,
"Neither do I condemn you,
"Go and sin no more!"

(12) "THEN SPOKE JESUS AGAIN UNTO THEM, SAYING, I AM THE LIGHT OF THE WORLD: HE WHO FOLLOWS ME SHALL NOT WALK IN DARKNESS, BUT SHALL HAVE THE LIGHT OF LIFE."

The form is:

1. We are no longer our own. We are bought with a price.

2. Find the holiest man or woman on Earth and through that individual, in one day, and sometimes even one hour, enough evil thoughts and evil passions arise in that heart to doom that soul forever and forever, but for the Precious Blood of Jesus Christ.

3. To the Believer who will not admit his personal frailty, faults, and failures, deception has become the rule (I Jn. 1:8).

THE LIGHT OF THE WORLD

The phrase, *"Then spoke Jesus again unto them, saying, I am the Light of the world,"* is, of course, true in the literal sense but, as well, spoke to the Jewish mind of that time.

The Jews added a ninth day to the Feast of Tabernacles on which they lighted a lamp, putting it in the chest instead of the Sacred Books to illustrate Proverbs 6:23 and Psalms 119:105.

Consequently, most of the multitude that day would have understood perfectly what He was saying.

However, on a much broader scale, actually covering the entirety of the Earth for all time, He is the Light of the world because He is the Source of its Light.

Again, Jesus spoke that day, claiming to be the Light not only of Israel, but of the entirety of the world. As such, all may come because He came for all!

WHAT DID HE MEAN BY LIGHT?

It refers to the right way that things should be done respecting the spiritual, physical, and material. The nations of the world, which recognize Christ in some semblance, have experienced tremendous Blessings even though Christ is followed only from afar, with only a small part of His *"Light"* being heeded. In essence, Jesus and the Bible are One and the same (Jn. 1:1). As such, the Bible is to serve as the Standard of Righteousness for all mankind.

Whenever the courts of this land, or any land, for that matter, deviate from the Word of God concerning the Standard for Righteousness, gross inequality and abuse are always the result. For instance, when the Supreme Court of the United States made abortion legal, they violated the Word of God. This has soaked this nation in blood by the killing of untold millions of unborn babies. To be sure, that blood will ultimately be required at the hands of this nation.

As well, the other Standards of Righteousness given in the Bible, such as marriage only between a man and a woman, are being stricken down and ignored, such as the condemnation of homosexuality, adultery, fornication, etc.

SIN

However, when such things are done, sin and evil do not remain static. In other words, the slide downward commences and grows faster by the moment. Now, the government, as stated, is being pressured to recognize so-called homosexual marriages, which are an abomination in the Eyes of God. As well, it is being demanded that society recognize the terrible sin of homosexuality as merely an alternate lifestyle. On television sitcoms, etc., adultery and fornication are held up as the normal thing in which all indulge. As a result, especially to the children, the nation is sowing to the wind and will certainly reap a whirlwind. If one sows to corruption, which is exactly what this country is doing, one will reap corruption, and of that, one can be sure. That is the Law of God. To be sure, man's laws may change, but not God's!

The Word of God not only tells men what not to do, it also shows them what to do! When it is followed even partially, great Blessings result. That has been the Source of America's freedom and prosperity, not our type of government, great universities, etc. To be sure, it was the Standard of the Word of God which guaranteed the type of government we presently have and is, consequently, the Source of all Blessings.

THE WORD OF GOD

Also, it must be understood that it is impossible to follow the Word of God, consequently, reaping its Blessings and benefits, without accepting Jesus Christ as the Lord of Glory, the Saviour of mankind, and the Son of God. In other words, Jesus is the *"I am"* of the Old Testament and, therefore, the One to Whom men will ultimately answer.

The Life in which this *"Light"* resides is the recipient of all that is good and, thereby, the Source of all Blessing. As well, let it be understood that there is no other *"light!"* Jesus Alone has this distinction.

A PERSONAL EXPERIENCE

Sometime back, I had the privilege of speaking to one of the fraternities at Yale University. That night, the room was packed, the largest crowd, I was told, they had ever had.

They had assigned to me the subject they desired that I address, which I did.

As I stood there that night speaking to these young men and women, I knew that to be in this university, and especially this particular fraternity, they had had to be far above average respecting intellect, etc. I also knew that the possibility definitely existed that future leaders of this nation were sitting before me that night.

As I began to deal with the subject at hand, the Spirit of the Lord began to move upon me to address spiritual problems, such as the hunger of the human heart, which can never be satisfied with drugs, alcohol, etc. As I began to speak in that vein, a hush fell over that group and, immediately, they began to be convicted as I attempted to hold up Jesus that night as the Light of the world.

When it ended, I asked them to bow their heads as I prayed for them. Faces were wet with tears and even after the meeting was over, young men and young ladies were constantly coming after me, asking that I pray for them.

It was so very obvious! Even though they were privileged to be in one of the greatest universities in the world, with most of them coming from very affluent homes, still, the hunger and thirst of their souls were not being satisfied and, in fact, could not be satisfied with these things, but only by Christ.

After the meeting, they gave me a brief tour of this prestigious university. As I was taken into the law library, reputed to be one of the greatest in the world, I looked at the thousands of volumes which graced its shelves. I knew that these volumes contained facts and many things which were true. However, I also knew that the single copy of the Bible in that library was the only Book there, and anywhere in the world, for that matter, which, in fact, is Truth. In other words, the Bible doesn't merely contain Truth; it is Truth (Jn. 1:1-2).

THE LIGHT OF LIFE

The phrase, *"He who follows Me shall not walk in darkness, but shall have the Light of Life,"* in effect, says that all who do not follow Jesus do walk in darkness. That is a blunt statement, but there is no other conclusion to which one can arrive.

The *"Light of Life"* is found only in Jesus because He is God.

In our brief studies in the past of the various religions of the world, I have made mention of the fact that of all the founders of these religions, such as Islam, Buddhism, Confucianism, etc., although claiming enlightenment, none of these religion founders claimed to be God. Of course, many people in the world have claimed to be God, but not the founders of these religions. Jesus is the only One Who made this claim.

As well, if one properly examines these claims, as we have briefly done in commentary of this very Gospel of John, one must come to the conclusion that it would be impossible for a mere human being to make such claims as Jesus did, even if he desired to do so. One can look into the great writings of history that were generated by the most brilliant of men, and one will not find anything that even remotely comes close to the statements by Jesus concerning His Deity. If men refuse to believe concerning Him Alone being the *"Light of Life,"* then it is done so out of spiritual stubbornness because the evidence is overwhelmingly obvious.

DARKNESS

Actually, the reason for such opposition to the Claims of Christ is because of the powers of darkness. Satan does not contest what people believe respecting error but will contest greatly any type of belief in Christ, hence, the terrible unbelief respecting His Person and Mission.

The reason for all the sorrow, war, heartache, privation, sickness, and suffering in the world today is because almost all the world *"walks in darkness,"* i.e., follows the direction of Satan who *"steals, kills, and destroys"* (Jn. 10:10). As we have repeatedly stated, every semblance of freedom and prosperity in the world has come about because of the few who know Jesus Christ, and who walk in His *"Light of Life."*

(13) "THE PHARISEES THEREFORE SAID UNTO HIM, YOU BEAR RECORD OF YOURSELF; YOUR RECORD IS NOT TRUE."

The pattern is:

1. The phrase, *"The Pharisees therefore said unto Him,"* proclaims the church of that day denying Him and answering Him in unbelief. It is sad, but much of the modern church world follows in that train by denying Jesus Christ.

2. He is denied by refusing Him His Rightful Place and Position as Head of the Church. Denominational heads too often usurp authority over Christ in this respect. I do not judge their motives or intent respecting this, but I do know that by the sheer direction of their constitution and bylaws, many treat Christ as if He is a Passive Head instead of an Active Head. Please believe me; He is not only active, but very active!

3. When this position is abrogated, as with the Pharisees of old, the Lord will little serve in a diminished capacity but will simply leave.

4. *"You bear record of Yourself; Your Record is not true,"* brings up the same argument used in John, Chapter 5. There, He properly gave four witnesses, *"John, His Own Works, The Father, and the Scriptures."* He will now answer their accusation again but will not go into nearly the detail as before.

(14) "JESUS ANSWERED AND SAID UNTO THEM, THOUGH I BEAR RECORD OF MYSELF, YET MY RECORD IS TRUE: FOR I KNOW FROM WHERE I CAME, AND WHERE I GO; BUT YOU CANNOT TELL FROM WHERE I COME, AND WHERE I GO."

The diagram is:

1. Christ and His Glory cannot at all manifest Himself unless we go through the Cross.

2. The only way to the Holy of Holies is through the Blood of Christ.

3. Atonement means Reconciliation. Its ultimate conclusion is the Reconciliation of God and man through the Sacrificial Death of Jesus Christ.

THE RECORD

The phrase, *"Jesus answered and said unto them, Though I bear record of Myself, yet My Record is true,"* now proclaims the Lord's Reply to be a double one.

While it was true that the Law demanded a double Testimony, still, the command had no application to Him because of His Origin and His Destination, and because of their lack of ability to recognize Who He was. However, in condescension to their ignorance, as we shall see, He added that He had a Second Witness, the Father.

As He now neared the end of His Ministry, He no longer placated the Pharisees as He did in John, Chapter 5, but rather used Himself as a Witness. This He did not do in John, Chapter 5, but He was certainly entitled to have done so.

Of course, they would not accept Him as His Own Witness as they would not accept anything He did. So, there was nothing He could have done to appease their accusations. Sadly, they were blind to the Truth. Sadder still, it was a willful blindness.

"For I know from where I came, and where I go," proclaims His Deity. This was the gist of the argument. They did not want to recognize Him as the Son of God, the Jehovah of the Old Testament. They possibly may have grudgingly conceded to the fact that He was merely a Prophet. However, when He proclaimed Himself as God manifest in the flesh, this they vehemently denied.

UNBELIEF

"But you cannot tell from where I come, and where I go," is freighted with meaning respecting their unbelief.

First of all, they could not tell from where He had come or where He was going relative to Heaven and the Throne of God simply because of unbelief. It was not because of lack of proof because they had a mountain of evidence, but because they refused to believe. Actually, no amount of evidence would have convinced these unbelievers.

Secondly, that He would have to die to redeem them from sin, they would not accept at all simply because they did not even believe that they needed Redemption. So, they did not know from where He had come, from what He had come, or to where He would go. They registered a vote of no confidence respecting the entirety of His Being and Purpose.

(15) "YOU JUDGE AFTER THE FLESH; I JUDGE NO MAN."

The overview is:

1. The phrase, *"You judge after the flesh,"* has reference to His Incarnation. He was so Totally Man, and even a Peasant at that, that in seeing the Appearance of His Flesh, which had *"no beauty that they might desire Him,"* they absolutely refused to accept His Deity.

2. They did not understand that God had to become Man in order to redeem man, despite the fact that Isaiah had prophesied such, which should have been clear to them (Isa. 7:14). However, they did as so many others, judging Him according to their own prejudice and not by the Scriptures, which should have been the criterion.

3. The phrase, *"I judge no man,"* simply means that He did not come to judge, but rather to save.

4. Even though they paid no heed to His Words, *"I judge no man,"* passing it off with a wave of the hand, still, had He judged them then and there, they would not have at all enjoyed the results. However, that is reserved for a later day, which will come about at the Great White Throne Judgment (Rev. 20:11-15).

(16) "AND YET IF I JUDGE, MY JUDGMENT IS TRUE: FOR I AM NOT ALONE, BUT I AND THE FATHER WHO SENT ME."

The exegesis is:

1. The phrase, *"And yet if I judge, My Judgment is true,"* simply means that His Previous Statement of *"judging no man"* is not in any way meant to abrogate His Position as the Ultimate Judge of all men, but simply that this was not His Mission at present!

2. *"For I am not alone, but I and the Father Who sent Me,"* places an entirely different perspective on the Claims of Christ. In effect, He was saying that the Judgment rendered, if, in fact, was now rendered, did not rest on mere human consciousness, but rather on the infallible decisions of Him *"Who gave Me My Commission,"* i.e., *"the Heavenly Father."*

3. It would seem that the Pharisees would have registered some type of fear respecting these statements, especially considering that they were not hollow words but were backed up by the Miracle-working Power of Jesus in healing the sick and even raising the dead! However, their unbelief was so ingrained that, in reality, they had closed minds, which no amount of proof could have penetrated.

4. Unbelief is a terrible thing, springing from an evil heart, and always aided and abetted by Satan and his works of darkness. It would result in the loss of their souls as well as the destruction of their Nation. Unbelief is always destructive in one form or the other simply because it cuts off all that God can do for an individual. Consequently, such people are left to the strategy of Satan, which is always to *"steal, kill, and destroy."*

(17) "IT IS ALSO WRITTEN IN YOUR LAW, THAT THE TESTIMONY OF TWO MEN IS TRUE."

The exposition is:

NOTES

1. Jesus used the pronoun, *"Your,"* in the phrase, *"It is also written in your Law."* It was said in this manner because the Pharisees were constantly referring to the Law of Moses as the basis for their spiritual position.

2. So, with Jesus using this word, it was done both as an appeal to them and with a touch of sarcasm as well! The truth was, they really did not know their Law even though they claimed it constantly.

3. The phrase, *"That the Testimony of two men is true,"* is derived from Deuteronomy 17:6 and 19:15.

4. Jesus was merely saying that upon the common principles of jurisprudence, as laid down in the Law of Moses, He was willing to rest His Claim.

(18) "I AM ONE WHO BEARS WITNESS OF MYSELF, AND THE FATHER WHO SENT ME BEARS WITNESS OF ME."

The structure is:

1. The phrase, *"I am One Who bears witness of Myself,"* reflects His Own Divine Self-consciousness. The fact that the Pharisees would in no way accept Him using Himself as a Witness in no way abrogated the veracity of His Position. The idea seems to be that He would now say things exactly as they were, in other words, revealing all the Truth. Previously, as stated, He had not used Himself as a Witness in the exchange in John, Chapter 5, which was approximately 18 months before. However, it now seems as if He had ceased appealing to them, consequently, laying out the Truth without garnishment whatsoever.

2. *"And the Father Who sent Me bears witness of Me,"* proclaims such being done in several ways.

3. The Miracles that God sent Him to perform were a constant witness that was unmistakable and irrefutable respecting His Claims (Jn. 5:32, 36; 11:42; 14:11; Acts 10:38).

4. As well, His Virgin Birth, which had been prophesied by Isaiah, was *"another witness"* (Isa. 7:14). Of course, they could have denied such and, no doubt, did, but they could not refute the Prophecy as given by Isaiah.

5. That He was the *"Son of David"* was another *"Witness,"* with His Genealogy

going all the way back to David through Solomon on His Foster Father's side, and through Nathan, another son of David, through His Mother Mary.

(19) "THEN SAID THEY UNTO HIM, WHERE IS YOUR FATHER? JESUS ANSWERED, YOU NEITHER KNOW ME, NOR MY FATHER: IF YOU HAD KNOWN ME, YOU SHOULD HAVE KNOWN MY FATHER ALSO."

The construction is:

1. The question, *"Then said they unto Him, Where is Your Father?"* is really asked in acute sarcasm! They did not ask, *"Who or What is He?"* but rather, *"Where is He?"*

2. The phrase, *"Jesus answered, You neither know Me, nor My Father,"* presents a declarative statement, which leaves no room for misunderstanding. Bluntly, He told them that they were without God and, consequently, without hope!

3. *"If you had known Me, you should have known My Father also,"* presents another utterance, implying the most intimate relation between Himself and the Father.

4. In effect, Jesus was grandly saying that if they knew the Father, they would know Him. They did not know Jesus, at least Who He was, because they did not know the Father even though they talked of Him constantly!

5. Millions do the same thing presently. They are members of churches, very religious, and speak of God constantly but, in fact, do not know Him! The simple fact is, one cannot know God unless one knows Jesus Christ. Christ is not an option but, in truth, the Only Way to the Father (Jn. 14:6).

(20) "THESE WORDS SPOKE JESUS IN THE TREASURY, AS HE TAUGHT IN THE TEMPLE: AND NO MAN LAID HANDS ON HIM; FOR HIS HOUR WAS NOT YET COME."

The synopsis is:

1. The phrase, *"These words spoke Jesus in the treasury, as He taught in the Temple,"* proclaims that in this place, the *"treasury"* where He was preaching, stood two colossal Golden Lampstands on which hung a multitude of lamps. These were lit during the Feast of Tabernacles and around them, the people danced with great rejoicing.

NOTES

2. However, just as the water in the Golden Bowl carried by the High Priest in John 7:37 could give no life to the soul, so these Golden Lamps could give no light to the heart. As He had proclaimed Himself as the *"Water of Life"* at that time, He now proclaimed Himself as the *"Light of Life,"* relative to these Lamps.

3. *"And no man laid hands on Him; for His Hour was not yet come,"* is the same as John 7:44, and tells us that no one had any power over Him in any capacity save only that which was given them by the Father.

4. This phrase shows us how bitterly the ecclesiastical authorities resented His Statements. As well, as should be obvious, this was no isolated occurrence. They hated Him with such passion that the only thing that stopped them from doing Him bodily harm was the Power of God.

(21) "THEN SAID JESUS AGAIN UNTO THEM, I GO MY WAY, AND YOU SHALL SEEK ME, AND SHALL DIE IN YOUR SINS: WHERE I GO, YOU CANNOT COME."

The composition is:

1. The Cross was not an incident or an accident.

2. Jesus came to this world not only to live but, as well, to die.

3. Furthermore, He specifically came to die on a Cross.

THE MESSIAH

The phrase, *"Then said Jesus again unto them, I go My Way, and you shall seek Me,"* refers to the fact that they had rejected Him, the True Messiah, and would, consequently, continue to look for a Messiah but, obviously, in vain! In fact, they continue to do so unto this very hour.

Sometime back, while in Israel, one of their government leaders told me, *"That is the Messiah,"* concerning the crops which grew abundantly in Israeli soil! Tragically, as always, error only compounds itself.

Regrettably, this fruitless *"seeking"* will ultimately lead them to the Antichrist, whom they will think to surely be the Messiah. This will be the second worst mistake they ever make, the first being their rejection of Jesus Christ!

DYING IN ONE'S SINS

The phrase, *"And shall die in your sins,"* represents a statement of sobering effect because it covers such a span of time, resulting in a loss of most every Jew since that particular time, now nearly 2,000 years ago. So, when Jesus uttered these words, little did His listeners realize the portent of His Statement. To say it was awful, and imagining the worst, could not even begin to touch the reality of the horror of what their unbelief was to bring upon them.

Many Jews presently strongly resent these implications, claiming that they had nothing to do with something that happened nearly 2,000 years ago. While that is true, still, the rejection, and even hatred, of Christ by most modern Jews is little less, if any at all, than their fathers of so long ago.

YOU CANNOT COME

The phrase, *"Where I go, you cannot come,"* presents His Departure to the Father by a blood-stained pathway, by violent death, which was unspeakably perplexing to even His Most Intimate Friends.

While all of Israel was looking for the Messiah at that particular time, the type for which they were looking was of their own making and not according to Scripture. A Suffering Messiah, which the Scripture plainly foretold that Jesus would be, in no way figured into their plans simply because the thing which He would suffer, death on Calvary for the sins of man, they in no way felt they needed.

The kind of Messiah they wanted, who would lift them above the Roman yoke if granted, would have only exacerbated their already bloated idea of themselves and their self-righteousness.

In their minds, they were the Children of Abraham, consequently, the only people on Earth to whom the Word of God had been given and, therefore, the Chosen Ones. On top of that, they were very religious; consequently, the idea that they needed someone to redeem them was totally foreign to their way of thinking.

They were looking for a Messiah who would make his entrance in glorious splendor, not only dazzling Israel but the entirety of the world, and especially Rome. Instead, they were confronted by this Peasant, Who was the very opposite of all they sought and desired, irrespective of the many Miracles He performed.

THE LORD OF WHO?

Is the Christ which Israel demanded so much different than the One demanded by most today?

Many want a Lord Who will make them rich! Others want a Lord Who is there when they need Him, which is only in an emergency; otherwise, they do not desire Him interfering in their lives in any way. Others want a Lord Who is, in reality, the church with all its ceremonies and rituals, One, incidentally, Who they can meet once a week and leave in the same place an hour later.

Others want a Christ Who will save them but, at the same time, allow them to continue in their sin. Others want a Christ Who will save them, but they have no desire for the Holy Spirit Whom He presents!

Millions, even in Pentecostal and Charismatic circles, want Him as Saviour, but they do not want Him as Deliverer. They will seek that from the psychologists, who are far more popular at this time.

As well, many want Him as a Miracle Worker but have little desire for His Presentation of Holiness and Righteousness!

So, the situation is little different today than then!

(22) "THEN SAID THE JEWS, WILL HE KILL HIMSELF? BECAUSE HE SAID, WHERE I GO, YOU CANNOT COME."

The synopsis is:

1. The question, *"Then said the Jews, Will He kill Himself?"* spoke of suicide!

2. Reynolds said, *"This query was one of harsh mockery, and can hardly be exaggerated regarding malign intent."*[2]

3. *"Because He said, Where I go, you cannot come,"* portrays that inasmuch as He was determining the time of His Departure, they thus reasoned that He had to be speaking of suicide.

4. Other than the sarcasm, the absolute spiritual dullness of these people who were, in reality, the spiritual leaders of Israel, is

appalling, to say the least. In essence, they were making jokes of the Atoning Work that He would carry out for the Redemption of mankind. Nothing could be more ungodly, satanic, or beastly!

5. That there was nothing left for them but total destruction, which was carried out some 37 years later, quickly becomes very obvious as to the reason.

(23) "AND HE SAID UNTO THEM, YOU ARE FROM BENEATH; I AM FROM ABOVE: YOU ARE OF THIS WORLD; I AM NOT OF THIS WORLD."

The composition is:

1. The Cross was a necessity because Jesus had to atone for all sin, even the most hideous of sins.

2. The price for that Redemption was high. In fact, it was so high that no man could pay the price.

3. To redeem fallen man, a Perfect Life would have to be given, and that Life was that of our Lord.

YOU ARE FROM BENEATH

The phrase, *"And He said unto them, You are from beneath,"* does not necessarily speak of Hell, but rather of this Earth. However, they are both one and the same, with one exception.

As these Jews stood now, their demeanor, efforts, motives, and spirit were of Satan, therefore, in opposition to all that is of God. But yet, if they would humble themselves before Christ, thereby, accepting Him as Saviour, they could still be Saved. However, even that door was closed with many of them because they blasphemed the Holy Spirit (Mat. 12:24-32).

I AM NOT OF THIS WORLD

The phrase, *"I am from above,"* spoke of Heaven.

So, He was saying to them that irrespective of what they thought, He was not a mere Peasant Who lived in Nazareth, but rather had His Origin in Heaven itself.

"You are of this world; I am not of this world," in effect, says that they were lost without God. So, they were really no different than the Rome they hated, both being of the same spirit, i.e., *"the spirit of this world."* Actually, they were worse! Paganistic corruption, which characterized Rome, was what it was, and was obvious. By comparison, religious corruption is much worse simply because in its self-righteousness, which characterized Israel, it feels justified in doing anything because it does so in the Name of the Lord when, actually, it is being guided by Satan.

Even though Jesus was now in the world, He was not of the world, meaning that He did the Will of His Heavenly Father exclusively. He was guided not at all by the worldly system.

THE CHURCH

The church being in the world is actually, at least at this time, where the Lord desires it to be. However, if the world gets in the church, then the church loses its effectiveness.

It is like a ship on the ocean. As long as that vessel is in the water, it can perform a great service for its owners, etc. However, if the water gets in the ship, disaster looms.

Likewise, while in this world, the Believer is to abide by the laws of the land, at least if they do not violate the Word of God, doing all within his power to serve as *"Salt"* and *"Light,"* consequently, making the world a better place to live. However, in actuality, he is a citizen of Heaven, with the Bible as his compass and Jesus Christ as his King.

(24) "I SAID THEREFORE UNTO YOU, THAT YOU SHALL DIE IN YOUR SINS: FOR IF YOU BELIEVE NOT THAT I AM HE, YOU SHALL DIE IN YOUR SINS."

The composition is:

1. No person can be saved except by trusting Christ and what Christ has done for us at the Cross.

2. The *"Sin-Offering"* of the Old Testament was *"most holy"* because it symbolized Christ taking the guilt of the sinner and making it His Own.

3. The *"Burnt-Offering"* symbolized the Perfection of Christ and Him giving that Perfection to the sinner.

THE CLAIMS OF CHRIST

The phrase, *"I said therefore unto you,"* presents Jesus making almost all of these statements concerning His Deity while in the Temple in Jerusalem. Even though things similar were said while in Galilee, still, the full brunt of His Claims was made to the religious leaders of Israel. Consequently, He did absolutely nothing behind their backs, but rather to their faces, leaving absolutely no doubt as to His Intention and Meaning. So, their accusations against Him, claiming that He was fomenting sedition in secret, were absolutely baseless.

"You shall die in your sins," was blunt but to the point and left no room for doubt. To be sure, this type of preaching arouses great animosity and hatred on the part of those whom it affects. I suspect that Jesus, if ministering presently, would be vilified greatly for His supposed crudeness and lack of respect for other people's religions. However, His Purpose was not popularity, but rather the presentation of the Word, which addressed itself to their souls, and which they rejected.

THE CENTRAL FOCUS OF DIVINE REVELATION

The phrase, *"For if you believe not that I am He, you shall die in your sins,"* states in no uncertain terms the reason for their spiritual depravity.

Three times in this Chapter, the Lord represents the Object of Faith, the central focus of the Divine Revelation, to be, *"I am."* This, in effect, says that He is the Jehovah of the Old Testament.

Some theologians have said that the *"I am"* of these Passages cannot be regarded as equivalent to the *"I am that I am"* of Exodus or to the incommunicable Name of the Eternal One. However, I beg to disagree!

He is, or He isn't! Here, He plainly says that He is, i.e., *"I am."*

As well, the entire Foundation of Salvation rests in Him, with Faith in Him as its requirement.

So, the Jews, as well as all Gentiles, must believe that He is Very God as well as Very Man. In addition, all must believe that as Man, He died for lost humanity, paid the price for man's Redemption, and rose from the dead.

Unnumbered millions believe in Jesus as a Prophet, Miracle Worker, or some such like luminary; however, such effects no Salvation!

(25) "THEN SAID THEY UNTO HIM, WHO ARE YOU? AND JESUS SAID UNTO THEM, EVEN THE SAME THAT I SAID UNTO YOU FROM THE BEGINNING."

The composition is:

1. The question, *"Then said they unto Him, Who are You?"* in effect, says, *"Who are You to deal out threatenings to us like this?"*

2. So, once again, they threw it into His Face that He was but a Peasant, consequently, not on their level and, therefore, inferior to them. In fact, they were greatly offended at Him in every capacity.

3. He had not come up through their ranks. He was not a graduate of their schools or a student of their teachers. On top of that, He did not ask permission for all the things He did and completely ignored their ruling authority as if it did not exist.

4. None of this was done by Jesus with malice but simply because their system was no longer of God. Above that, He did only what His Heavenly Father told Him to do. As it should be obvious, He did not come to this world to obey man, but God.

5. Even though all kindness and deference must be shown to our fellow laborers in the Lord, still, that requirement holds true for all Believers as well. We must obey God!

6. Actually, the only thing that one Believer owes to another Believer, irrespective of whom it may be, is *"love"* (Rom. 13:8).

7. *"And Jesus said unto them, Even the same that I said unto you from the beginning,"* goes back to John 8:12, *"I am the Light of the world."* Consequently, in that Light, He judged them, and His Judgment was infallible, for everything He said was Divine because it was from God.

(26) "I HAVE MANY THINGS TO SAY AND TO JUDGE OF YOU: BUT HE WHO SENT ME IS TRUE; AND I SPEAK TO THE WORLD THOSE THINGS WHICH I HAVE HEARD OF HIM."

The order is:

1. The phrase, *"I have many things to say and to judge of you,"* is a statement of exceptional power, whether the hearers felt so or not!

2. Jesus was saying that they will be judged, as well as all, according to their reaction to what He was saying. Consequently, they could dismiss His Words as inconsequential, but the bitter consequences will be reaped nonetheless!

3. That which He was saying is recorded in the four Gospels and primarily has to do with Who and What He is. Every statement is primarily to establish this fact, to which we have alluded, that He is the *"I am"* of the Old Testament and, therefore, *"Jehovah!"* Unequivocally, He establishes this Truth! Unequivocally, men will be judged by their reaction to that Truth!

4. The phrase, *"But He Who sent Me is True,"* means that, consequently, His Statements are true as well. So, men are dealing not only with what is said but, as well, with the One Who said it. This presents an entirely different picture.

5. All who do not heed these words will one day stand at the Great White Throne Judgment where Jesus will then be the Judge, as He is now the Saviour. So, in essence, His Statement is, *"Face Me now, or face Me then!"*

6. The phrase, *"And I speak to the world those things which I have heard of Him,"* says several things:

a. The things He said were from God and, consequently, absolutely infallible. It is the Word of God.

b. That which He said was for the entirety of the *"world,"* and not just for Israel. So, all must answer!

c. It is the business of the Preacher of the Gospel, and the entirety of the church, for that matter, to see to it that these Words spoken by Jesus reach the entirety of the world. Nothing is more important!

(27) "THEY UNDERSTOOD NOT THAT HE SPOKE TO THEM OF THE FATHER."

The form is:

1. Their lack of understanding was for a reason. As plainly as He spoke to them and as clearly as He delineated His Position, absolutely no doubt was left as to the Identity of His Reference.

2. The One they professed to serve is the One of Whom He spoke. They did not correlate the two simply because they did not know either One. If one truly knows God, one will truly know what is of God! Sadly, the modern church little knows what is of God simply because not many truly know God, despite their professions.

3. It is impossible to oppose that which is truly of God and, at the same time, be of God. And yet, this is a spiritual and Scriptural yardstick which must be employed if the Truth be followed.

4. As an example, men could not oppose David and, at the same time, follow the Lord. Likewise, Israel could not oppose Jeremiah and, at the same time, be of God. The same is very obvious with Christ. Israel claimed to be of God, and loudly so, but they opposed God's Son, which meant that they really did not know God. As they did not know Who the Son was, likewise, they did not know Who the Father was!

(28) "THEN SAID JESUS UNTO THEM, WHEN YOU HAVE LIFTED UP THE SON OF MAN, THEN SHALL YOU KNOW THAT I AM HE, AND THAT I DO NOTHING OF MYSELF; BUT AS MY FATHER HAS TAUGHT ME, I SPEAK THESE THINGS."

The pattern is:

1. Man's solutions never work because he can only deal with externals, and that not very well, while Christ deals with the heart.

2. In the old Levitical Law, it took five great Offerings to properly portray the one Sacrifice of Christ.

3. In the Book of Leviticus in the Old Testament, we find that *"sacrifice is the basis of worship."*

THEN YOU SHALL KNOW

The phrase, *"Then said Jesus unto them, When you have lifted up the Son of Man, then shall you know that I am He,"* actually refers to the time when they will look upon Him Whom they have pierced (Zech. 12:10). They will then get to know that He is indeed Jehovah. Here is an amazing statement: a naked Man hanging upon a Cross demonstrated God manifest in the flesh and proved Christ's Claim to be Jehovah! The triumphant Word on the Cross, *"Finished,"* disclosed His Godhead.

"And that I do nothing of Myself," proclaims perfect obedience to the Father and

sets the example for the Church, at least as it ought to be.

"But as My Father has taught Me, I speak these things," presents an interesting statement.

THE SON OF MAN

Not only is He *"the Son"* and *"the Son of God,"* but, as well, He is also *"the Son of Man."* He had come down from Heaven and was before them as a Man among men — One Jesus. He had taken upon Himself the form of a slave, the fashion of man.

The Manifestation of the Divine should be perfectly realized in the human, though a fundamental Truth lying at the heart of all Revelation is, nevertheless, not the alphabet of Divine teaching. It is actually far above that, even the very highest and most concrete of all Truths.

In effect, Jesus was saying three things:

1. As we have stated, He presented Himself as the *"Son of Man,"* Who would give Himself on the Cross, thereby, redeeming humanity. In other words, He was presenting the Incarnation, which they had ridiculed by speaking of Him as a Peasant.

2. He was not a product of their schools, or of any man, for that matter; consequently, this was at least a part of the reason for their great animosity.

Men love to control other men, and religious men love to control other men most of all! In fact, denominational heads demand that preachers answer to them and them alone, insinuating, or stating plainly, that they speak for God. Such is not so and, in fact, never has been!

3. Jesus was taught clearly and plainly the Word of God by His Father and, as well, all that He would say in His Role as *"Son of Man."* As a result, His Wisdom was incomparable! The Father not only taught Him but, as well, told Him what to say and when to say it.

(29) "AND HE WHO SENT ME IS WITH ME: THE FATHER HAS NOT LEFT ME ALONE; FOR I DO ALWAYS THOSE THINGS THAT PLEASE HIM."

The diagram is:

1. Acceptable worship to God must be based on a Sacrifice acceptable to Him.

NOTES

2. Man is guilty and unclean. As such, he needs a Sacrifice to remove his guilt and to cleanse him from his defilements.

3. The Sacrifice alone fits man for the Holy Presence of God.

HE WHO HAS SENT ME

The phrase, *"And He Who sent Me is with Me,"* actually speaks of a union that is beyond comprehension to mere mortals. Jesus and the Father were indivisible.

"The Father has not left Me alone," is a direct warning not only to the Jews of that day but, as well, to all the world and for all time.

The argument with the world is not with God as such, but rather with Jesus Christ. However, Jesus here says that the rejection of One is the rejection of Both! As well, the true acceptance of One is the acceptance of Both!

"For I do always those things that please Him," proclaims in the words of Reynolds that this self-consciousness of Christ is the loftiest and most entirely unique phenomenon recorded in history.[3] This absolute confidence, with reference to His Whole Course, which, incidentally, no other human being could even remotely think to proclaim, lifts our Lord to a pinnacle of the loftiest elevation.

Jesus declared Himself absolutely free from sin, even in thought or deed, and to have left undone nothing that seemed good to the Father.

Some men have done some things some of the time that pleased God, but no man, other than Christ, has always, without fail, done all things that *"please Him."*

(30) "AS HE SPOKE THESE WORDS, MANY BELIEVED ON HIM."

The diagram is:

1. Even though they did believe on Him when they heard His Words because of the undeniable proof of what He was saying, still, their *"believing"* or Faith was misplaced and, as we shall see, unacceptable!

2. Millions follow this path, *"Believing on Him,"* but for all the wrong reasons.

3. Many believed on Him as the expected Messiah Who would restore the Davidic throne.

4. Such a Faith, being carnal and ignoring the facts of the Fall, of sin and of its eternal Judgment, was worthless. The Lord, at once, as the Light of the world, unmasked it by telling these professed Believers that they were morally bond slaves of sin and, consequently, children of the Devil, even though in the physical sense, children of Abraham.

(31) "THEN SAID JESUS TO THOSE JEWS WHICH BELIEVED ON HIM, IF YOU CONTINUE IN MY WORD, THEN ARE YOU MY DISCIPLES INDEED."

The overview is:

1. As the Cross, through the sacrifices, formed the basis of all worship in Old Testament times, it has not changed one iota as it regards the present. 2. Sacrifice, i.e., *"the Cross,"* still forms the basis of all worship.

3. If we do not come to God through the Blood of the Lamb, Who is Jesus Christ, the Holy Spirit will take special care to block all access (Eph. 2:13-18).

ALL THE TRUTH

The phrase, *"Then said Jesus to those Jews which believed on Him,"* now presents a part of the Message upon which their Faith will falter. Thus resides millions!

Most preachers, in order to hold a crowd, will not present all the Truth as Jesus did here, but instead, will stop short. Consequently, the church is filled with people who claim to be Believers but, in reality, have never been Born-Again.

It is very easy for one to believe certain things about Christ and, consequently, to call oneself a *"Believer!"* Such faith is only a partial faith and is unacceptable to God.

While the Lord does many things for all Believers, the primary function of Christ and, actually, the very reason for which He came to this world, was to save men from sin. Faith in Him for this great Miracle of Redemption imputes to man Righteousness and Holiness. If that ever ceases to be the central theme of our Salvation, then it is faith that God will not honor.

As someone has said, *"If man's problem had been money, God would have sent a banker. If man's problem had been physical sickness, God would have sent a doctor. If man's problem had been mechanical, God would have sent an engineer. If man's problem had been ignorance, God would have sent a teacher."*

However, man's problem was and is sin, and God sent a Saviour!

CONTINUING IN THE WORD OF GOD

The phrase, *"If you continue in My Word, then are you My Disciples indeed,"* simply means that one has to believe all the Word and not just part. To *"continue in the Word,"* one has to hear all the Word and then believe it.

Millions today believe in Jesus as a *"Good Man,"* but not the Son of God. Even though, in a sense, these people are Believers, still, they are not saved, and for the obvious reasons.

Others believe in Jesus as the Saviour but not as the Baptizer with the Holy Spirit. As such, even though Saved, they do miss out on so very much that God has for them in the Salvation process, which can only be attained as one is baptized with the Holy Spirit.

Is the Lord saying that unless one receives all of Him, one has none of Him?

I think He is!

LIGHT

However, that would mean that one is walking in all the Light he has, but not that he understands all things about that Light. In truth, all Believers at some point have embraced error in one fashion or the other in their experience with Christ. As such, they did not have all of Christ, or rather all that He could do in their lives, but such was not by design but because of lack of maturity.

However, whenever further Light is given to the Believer, and he refuses to walk in that Light, it is impossible for him to advance in Christ or even remain static. As a result, he begins to go backward, which is actually what Israel did and was ultimately lost.

In that sense, I firmly believe that Catholics who truly give their hearts and lives to Jesus Christ will then have to leave the Catholic church. I believe they will actually desire to do so because the Light they now have has exposed the darkness. So, it becomes impossible for them to remain in that false doctrine.

The idea of *"continuing in the Word"* is to *"continue with Jesus."*

(32) "AND YOU SHALL KNOW THE TRUTH, AND THE TRUTH SHALL MAKE YOU FREE."

The overview is:

1. This one Scripture is the secret of all Abundant Life in Christ. It is the secret of victory over sin and of living an overcoming Christian Life.

2. The phrase, *"And you shall know the Truth,"* actually means to know Jesus, for He is Truth. As well, when one *"knows"* that Truth, one continues in that Truth, for how could one not do so?

3. *"And the Truth shall make you free,"* means exactly what it says. However, it is only the Truth that one knows which will make one free. To not know the Truth does not lessen the veracity and Power of the Truth, but, at the same time, that Power and veracity cannot be effective in one's life if one is not aware of it.

4. Free from what?

5. As we shall see in the following Verses, it means freedom from sin! However, if that is truly understood, that can, as well, bring freedom from sickness, freedom from poverty, and freedom from self. Actually, it is the fourfold freedom from *"sin, sickness, poverty, and self."*

6. This is all gained exclusively through the Cross. That's the reason Jesus said that we must take up the Cross daily (Lk. 9:23). God's Prescribed Order of Life and Living is for the Believer to place his or her Faith exclusively in Christ and what Christ did for us at the Cross. This being done, the Holy Spirit, Who works exclusively within the parameters, so to speak, of the Finished Work of Christ, will work mightily on our behalf. That's the only way that the Believer is going to have victory over the world, the flesh, and the Devil. This is God's Way, and His only Way (Rom. 6:1-14; 8:1-11; Col. 2:10-15).

(33) "THEY ANSWERED HIM, WE BE ABRAHAM'S SEED, AND WERE NEVER IN BONDAGE TO ANY MAN: WHY DO YOU SAY, YOU SHALL BE MADE FREE?"

The overview is:

NOTES

1. Christ's Sacrifice being perfect gives a perfected conscience and, therefore, a peace that nothing can destroy.

2. The Cross is not a mere doctrine, but rather the Foundation of all Doctrine (I Pet. 1:18-20).

3. I am positive that Jesus considered that His Death on the Cross, with all of its implications, must be looked at as far more than a mere doctrine.

BONDAGE?

The phrase, *"They answered Him, We be Abraham's seed, and were never in bondage to any man,"* proclaims an ironic statement inasmuch as they had been in bondage to the Egyptians, the Assyrians, the Babylonians, the Persians, the Greeks, and they were even at that moment in bondage to the Romans.

From their statement, we see that the Jews believed in a nationalistic Salvation. In other words, being born a Jew and, consequently, of the Seed of Abraham, in their minds, made them God's Chosen and, as a result, right with God. As is obvious, they referred to themselves not at all on an individual basis, but as a collective part of the Work of God on Earth, consequently, seldom thinking of themselves as personally needing Redemption.

Actually, the same spirit that characterized these people characterizes many, if not most, church members presently. When confronted personally, most fall back on their religious works and, above all, their association with and participation in particular religious denominations. In their minds, this equates to Salvation when, in reality, it equates nothing.

A PERSONAL EXPERIENCE

I remember receiving a letter sometime ago, which would be typical of many thousands we have received, from a lady who had been a member of a quite prominent Baptist church for many years. Unfortunately, this can be the case in any denomination. She stated that she was so versed in Baptist Doctrine that she taught doctrine classes and was looked upon as one of the stalwarts of that particular church.

She went on to relate as to how she was watching the telecast one Sunday morning as the Spirit of God began to deal with her. She stated, or words to that effect, *"Brother Swaggart, all of a sudden, I realized that while I was very religious, I was not actually saved. I had equated all my religious works with Salvation and was, therefore, deceived."*

She then said, *"That morning, I asked Jesus to come into my heart, and in a few minutes' time, I knew what it was to truly be Saved. And then, I realized, as Jesus replaced religion in my heart, just how lost I had actually been."*

Unfortunately, that is the state of most who call themselves Christians, but sadly, with most of them never coming to the true realization of Salvation.

RELIGIOUS BONDAGE

In truth, these people facing Jesus were very much in *"bondage,"* actually, the greatest and most debilitating bondage of all, *"religious bondage."* It is far easier to see one delivered from alcohol, drugs, etc., than it is from this great deception of Satan, i.e., *"religious bondage."*

These Jews looked with disdain at the Gentiles and their paganistic worship, never really realizing that their spiritual condition was no better. Likewise, millions of Christians look at the religion of Islam, Buddhism, etc., easily recognizing these terrible bondages of false lights, but never realizing that they are in the same boat.

The bondage of which Jesus spoke was that of sin, to which these would not admit, and to which most will not admit! Once again, that is the foundational reason that Jesus came: to set men free from sin.

FREE!

The question, *"Why do You say, you shall be made free?"* proclaims them not seeing or admitting their true spiritual condition, which Jesus would now readily address.

Jesus had spoken a Truth, which was a puzzle to these people, because they simply believed that they already possessed the Truth. They had the Law of Moses and were people of the Patriarchs and Prophets.

NOTES

So, in their minds, they were not only possessors of such but, as well, depositaries of Truth. In other words, they were the very ones to whom God had given this great Truth, and they alone were its guardians.

They did not realize that they had made a god out of their religion and had long since perverted and twisted the Word of God until very little of its origin remained. So, the idea that Jesus would speak to them of *"Truth,"* implying that they did not know such, was an insult to them of the highest order, as it is to their modern religious counterparts! In their minds, they had the *"Truth"* and were *"free!"*

(34) *"JESUS ANSWERED THEM, VERILY, VERILY, I SAY UNTO YOU, WHOSOEVER COMMITS SIN IS THE SERVANT OF SIN."*

The form is:

1. Under the old Law, it was the Sacrificial System which God explained first of all to Moses (Lev. 1:2).

2. By doing this, he was telling us that the Sacrifice of Christ must always be preeminent.

3. In all the religions of the world, with the exception of Christianity, there is no teaching on the subject of forgiveness. That is because there is no atonement. Without the Cross, there can be no forgiveness.

SIN

The phrase, *"Jesus answered them, Verily, verily, I say unto you,"* proclaims a pointed statement to these Jews, and to all others, and for all time, for that matter.

As well, His Words were with Power and constituted the Word of God because He was saying what His Father told Him to say. The idea is that they knew beyond the shadow of a doubt that He was talking directly to them and was not speaking of Gentiles.

"Whosoever commits sin is the servant of sin," was taken up by Paul, and from these very words, *"Do you not know, that to whom you yield yourselves servants to obey, his servants you are to whom you obey; whether of sin unto death, or of obedience unto Righteousness?"* (Rom. 6:16).

Jesus was telling these people that they

were sinners and, therefore, *"servants of sin,"* and, consequently, not *"free!"*

The notion of personal transgression producing a bondage, fettering the soul and the will, and separating it from the glorious liberty of true Sonship in Christ, lay outside of their notion of Discipleship. They were not requiring Deliverance from sin or its bondage. What they wanted was the full realization of the national hope, respecting Israel's prominence once again, which would necessitate deliverance from Rome.

THE SERVANT OF SIN

The idea is this and must not be taken lightly:

Every single unbeliever in the world, irrespective as to how religious he may be (believing in the wrong thing), is a *"servant of sin."* As well, as Paul also addressed in Romans, Chapter 6, even Believers can come under the bondage of sin once again, with it ruling in their lives (Rom. 6:12), if they do not properly understand that their victory is in Christ and His Cross instead of our own efforts.

So, what Jesus is here saying is powerful indeed inasmuch as this is the problem of humanity. Jesus came to this Earth in order to satisfy the claims of Heavenly Justice against man for the terrible sin debt. As well, He came to break the grip of sin in the human heart and life, which comes about by Faith in what Christ did at Calvary. Sadly, there are many, if not millions, of true Believers who truly love the Lord and are striving to please Him, but have a misconception of what Christ truly did for them. Despite all of their efforts, they are, in fact, *"servants of sin."* To be honest, we fool ourselves if we think this is not true. And yet, in a moment's time, with any Believer, if he can truly understand what Jesus has purchased for him and what He truly did, and will have Faith in this, he will immediately be set free from this *"weight, and the sin which does so easily beset us"* (Heb. 12:1).

GOD'S PRESCRIBED ORDER OF VICTORY

To be as brief as is possible, please note the following very carefully. I believe that it describes God's Way of Life and Living and is easy to understand.

- Jesus Christ is the Source of all things that we receive from God (Jn. 1:1, 14, 29; 14:6; Col. 2:13-18).
- While Jesus is the Source, the Cross of Christ is the Means, and the only Means, by which all of these wonderful things are given to us (Rom. 6:1-14; I Cor. 1:17, 18, 21, 23).
- While Jesus is the Source and the Cross is the Means, this tells us that the Cross of Christ must ever be the Object of our Faith. This is critically important (I Cor. 2:2; Gal. 6:14).
- With Jesus as the Source and the Cross as the Means and the Cross of Christ ever being the Object of our Faith, the Holy Spirit, Who works exclusively within the parameters, so to speak, of the Finished Work of Christ, will then work mightily on our behalf (Rom. 8:1-11; Eph. 2:13-18).

Without the Aid and Help of the Holy Spirit, there is no way the Believer can walk in victory over the world, the flesh and the Devil. We must have the Help of the Holy Spirit. Please remember, it is the Cross of Christ which has given and does give the Holy Spirit the legal means to do all that He does with us (Rom. 8:2). So, He doesn't demand much of us, but He most definitely does demand one thing, and that is that the Cross of Christ ever be the Object of our Faith (Rom. 6:14; Gal. 6:14; Col. 2:14-15).

THE PRACTICING OF SIN

One must notice that Jesus used the word *"whosoever,"* meaning that irrespective of who the person is, if he practices sin, he will quickly become a *"servant of sin."*

The relation between sin as a principle and sins as acts of the will is a great New Testament Revelation (Rom., Chpt. 7). Sins as acts of the will pertains to a Believer who is being overcome by Satan, with Satan literally overriding the will of the Believer because of him not properly understanding his rightful place in Christ. The personal committing of sin augments the force of the corrupt tendency (the sin nature), which leads to and facilitates fresh transgressions. Every compliance with evil forges a new fetter and imposes it on the will of the transgressor (Rom. 7:15).

Many Believers are taken aback at the idea that Satan can force his will upon a Believer, actually overriding the Believer's will and forcing him to do something he does not want to do. This is all because the Believer is addressing the sin question and Satan's efforts in a wrong way. Actually, that Satan can override a Believer's will is a frightening thing, but he can, even as Paul said!

ROMANS, CHAPTER SEVEN

Many erroneously claim that Romans, Chapter 7, is an account of Paul's life before Conversion; however, that is totally incorrect. The language that Paul uses in Romans 7:15 is not the language of an unbeliever. Unbelievers do not hate sin; they, in fact, love sin! They hate its effects but not its commission. Only a true Believer hates sin!

Too often, Believers attempt to overcome Satan and sin in a wrong way; consequently, their lives become a constant struggle, which is anything but the *"rest"* promised by Christ (Mat. 11:28-30).

Even though we have previously addressed this, and while this account will be repetitive, still, due to the extremely serious nature of this matter, I would ask the reader to please allow me some repetitive latitude.

The Believer does not have to do anything to overcome sin and, in fact, can do nothing to overcome sin, even by prayer, fasting, the memorizing of certain Scriptures, etc. All of these things are extremely important and will greatly advance the individual in Christ and draw him closer to the Lord. Still, these efforts, as holy and righteous as they may be in their own way, if carried on in this manner, constitutes *"works"* and will not and, in fact, cannot bring victory over sin. The reason is simple!

A FINISHED WORK

The Believer should constantly do these things we've just mentioned, which constitutes Christian disciplines. However, if we do them in the capacity of which I have stated, whether we realize it or not, it is saying that Christ did not finish the Task at Calvary, and something else needs to be done or added

NOTES

to His Finished Work. Consequently, this is something God will not and, in fact, cannot honor. The answer is this:

We are to totally trust what Christ did at the Cross. We must understand that He did it solely for us and that we were and are, in fact, in Him by Faith (Rom. 6:3-6), and that He completed the task. He broke the grip of sin within our lives in that Satan now has no more hold on us. We should believe and understand that and *"rest"* in it. When we have Faith in that, the overcoming sin will fall away, and the person will begin to walk in victory. That means the sin will dissipate, even though it may be sins which some have fought so hard and so long and made no headway, but rather have regressed.

FAITH

By simply having Faith in what Christ did, and the fact that we were in Him (by Faith), thereby, trusting that completely, this makes us dead to sin. We are no longer a *"servant of sin,"* but rather victorious in Christ over every sin (Rom. 6:11). While the Bible does not teach sinless perfection, it most definitely does teach that sin is not to have dominion over us (Rom. 6:14).

Most of the church world thinks only of unbelievers as *"servants of sin."* However, Believers can and do fall into the same category simply because of not fully knowing or understanding their rightful place and position in Christ. Once again, it is *"knowing the Truth, and the Truth makes us free."* However, it is error in believing that all Christians have all the Truth. They do not! In truth, I think one could say, without any fear of exaggeration or contradiction, that no Believer, no matter how mature he is in the Lord, has total understanding of all the Truth given to us by God. Even Paul said, *"Not us though I had already attained, either were already perfect: but I follow after, if that I may apprehend that for which also I am apprehended of Christ Jesus"* (Phil. 3:12).

(35) "AND THE SERVANT ABIDES NOT IN THE HOUSE FOR EVER: BUT THE SON ABIDES EVER."

The diagram is:

1. The phrase, *"And the servant abides*

not in the house for ever," presents a simple truth, and if we think of it in the terms of simplicity, it will be understood.

2. A *"servant,"* in this case, a *"servant of sin,"* if continuing in that respect, has no relationship with the Father, or at least will lose that relationship if the practice of sin is continued, and will ultimately be cast out. The word *"servant"* in the Greek here is *"doulos"* and means *"slave."* As should be obvious, slaves have no rights.

3. *"But the Son abides ever,"* means that Sonship is the only principle on which continuance in the house (the House of God's Salvation) can be secured.

4. If one is trusting Christ completely, one will reap the great rewards and victories that Sonship provides and will have victory over sin, which is the only way such can be attained.

5. No, this does not mean that a Believer who fails, and even fails many times, not having victory in some area, will be cast out. He will not be cast out as long as that person continues to trust Christ, asking Him to forgive, cleanse, and wash him, so to speak (I Jn. 1:9). However, if one thinks he can deliberately live a sinning life, in other words, the continuous practicing of sin, and still, at the same time, continue in Salvation, Jesus here plainly says that such cannot be.

(36) "IF THE SON THEREFORE SHALL MAKE YOU FREE, YOU SHALL BE FREE INDEED."

The diagram is:

1. The *"Son"* here refers to the Incarnation of Christ. It was in His Perfect Human Body that He effected our Salvation by offering it as a Perfect Sacrifice before God.

2. What He did in His Incarnate Form at Calvary was not for Himself but for sinners.

3. By trusting and believing in what He did at Calvary and understanding that by Faith, we died, were buried, and rose with Him, we are made free from sin. This is the way God looks at us. The sin debt is paid and, consequently, Satan has no more grip on the Believer. This is the cardinal Truth of the Plan of God for the human family.

4. As well, only *"the Son,"* the Lord Jesus Christ, can set the sinner free.

NOTES

5. In effect, Jesus is here urging the necessity of the New Birth — for how could children of the Devil be Children of the Kingdom? He taught that that birth takes place when Faith is reposed in Him as the Saviour from the doom of sin, from the defilement of sin, and from the dominion of sin.

6. Such was the Faith of the adulteress in John, Chapter 11, but not of *"the Believers"* in John 8:30-31, as is proven in John 8:45-46.

7. These professors began by accepting His Claim as Messiah (Jn. 8:30) and ended by taking up stones to murder Him in rejection of His Claim as Jehovah (Jn. 8:58-59). Had they continued in the path of Faith on which they momentarily entered, He would have led them, as He led others into the Faith that saves. Then, they would have become His Real Disciples, for they would have gotten experimentally to know Him, Who is the Truth. He would have freed them from the dominion of sin, as from its doom and defilement. Further, He would have made them sons in the Father's House, to which we have just alluded.

8. Here, therefore, are contrasted Salvation and Sonship in the Kingdom of God, with slavery and sonship in the kingdom of Satan.

(37) "I KNOW THAT YOU ARE ABRAHAM'S SEED; BUT YOU SEEK TO KILL ME, BECAUSE MY WORD HAS NO PLACE IN YOU."

The pattern is:

1. There is no place for sin except the Cross of Christ.

2. There, Jesus atoned for all sin, past, present, and future, at least for all who will believe (Jn. 3:16).

3. While the Bible does not teach sinless perfection, it definitely does teach that sin is not to have dominion over us (Rom. 6:14).

ABRAHAM'S SEED?

The phrase, *"I know that you are Abraham's Seed,"* tells us much.

In effect, Jesus was saying that being *"Abraham's Seed"* by physical birth contained no Salvation. It was only in the *"Son"* and Faith in what He would do at Calvary which would give one Salvation and, consequently, freedom from sin.

"But you seek to kill Me," which was an obvious fact, completely negated their spiritual claims. While they were children of Abraham in the flesh, they were not children of God! If they were true Children of God, they would not have murder in their hearts.

CHILDREN OF GOD?

The sad truth is that millions presently are children of particular religious denominations or churches, but not children of God! The fruit of their lives, which is sin, is obvious. As well, these *"children"* seldom repent or ask the Lord for forgiveness of sin (I Jn. 1:9). As the Jews of old, they are locked up in their self-righteousness and, consequently, cannot even see themselves as they really are. The Jews were calling themselves, *"God's Chosen,"* while, at the same time, plotting and planning to kill God's Son. What an irony! And yet, is it any different now?

Millions claim to be Believers and, thereby, *"Children of God,"* while, all the time, opposing that which is of God. Jesus plainly exposes this hypocrisy!

THE WORD OF GOD

The phrase, *"Because My Word has no place in you,"* signifies the reason for their murderous hearts, despite their claims. They did not believe or adhere to the Word of God. Whenever men veer from the Word, there is nothing but error that remains. We must abide by the Word at all times and must be sure that we do so, even at any and all costs. As Jesus says here, nothing is more important!

At this particular time in Jesus' Ministry, which was about six months before His Crucifixion, He was welcome in precious few synagogues in Israel. Could one say that those who did not want Him were of God? The answer to that is obvious!

When religious men obey other religious men other than God, i.e., *"His Word,"* plainly and simply, they are not following the Lord.

(38) "I SPEAK THAT WHICH I HAVE SEEN WITH MY FATHER: AND YOU DO THAT WHICH YOU HAVE SEEN WITH YOUR FATHER."

The pattern is:

1. The animal used for a sacrifice in Old Testament times had to be without blemish. It represented Christ.

2. As one advances in the Divine Light, He becomes conscious that those sins which he has committed are but branches from a root or streams from a fountain. Moreover, that sin in his nature is that fountain — that root.

3. This leads to a far deeper exercise, which can only be met by a deeper insight into the Work of the Cross.

JESUS CHRIST

The phrase, *"I speak that which I have seen with My Father,"* in effect, says, *"If you want to know God and be right with God, you have to deal with Me."* That was the gist of His Statements and, of course, what infuriated the Jews.

As it was then, so it is now. Millions want to know God and be right with God, but they want to bypass Jesus. This is not to be done because such cannot be done!

The word *"seen"* has reference to the fact that not only did Jesus hear God's Words to Him, but, as well, He had *"seen"* the Father, had dwelt with Him, and was actually a Member of the Godhead. So, His Place and Position were of far greater import than merely hearing from the Lord and delivering what He had heard, as the Prophets. He, in fact, is God and has seen everything of which He speaks.

SATAN IS YOUR FATHER

The phrase, *"You do that which you have seen with your father,"* now proclaims, in no uncertain terms, that despite all the claims of these Jews concerning God, in reality, they were of the Devil, who was their father. What an indictment!

The reader must see this, hear this, and literally feel this! They were the most religious people on the face of the Earth, talked about God constantly, and continually claimed to keep His Commandments. However, despite all their religious activity, actually, they did not know God at all but were tools and instruments, even children of the Devil.

Even though my repetition may become laborious, much of the modern church world falls into the same category, despite its claims! One is either of God or of Satan, for there is no other position to occupy. As well, if one is of God, he will not fight that which is of God.

If one is truly of God, God's Word will abide in Him, and the fruit of that Word will be obvious.

If not, the fruit of Satan's works will become clear also! This speaks primarily of opposition to all that which is of God. While it certainly does refer to sins of the flesh, that, however, is not the main thrust in these Passages. The main thrust pertains to one's attitude, spirit, motives, and, actually, where one truly stands, referring to the Word of God. If that thrust is not on God's Word, it is on Satan's word, and, thereby, it makes that person a child of the Devil. Once again, we are speaking of the world of religion and not the world's system per se.

ONE OF TWO CAMPS

As well, this statement by Christ tells us that the entirety of the world is in one of two camps. There is no in-between! God is either the individual's Father, or else, Satan is the individual's father. As should be obvious, one cannot be both at the same time!

However, the true Believer can get off track at times because of self-will, or many reasons. For instance, when a particular Samaritan village would not receive Christ, James and John said, *"Lord, will You that we command fire to come down from Heaven, and consume them, even as Elijah did?"*

"But He turned, and rebuked them, and said, You know not what manner of spirit you are of" (Lk. 9:54-55). The *"spirit"* of which He spoke was actually the spirit of Satan. So, at that moment, these two Disciples, even though loving the Lord greatly, were functioning in the wrong spirit, which was actually of Satan, and can characterize any Believer. Zeal without knowledge and failure to rightly divide the Word of Truth can cause well-meaning men to greatly err.

THE SPIRIT OF SATAN

Functioning in the spirit of Satan, which is greatly detrimental if continued, will cause great problems for the individual, and if not corrected, can cause the loss of the soul. Still, at the outset, it does not mean that the person, although greatly erring, is of Satan. That is the reason the Believer must stay humble before the Lord, accordingly having a spirit which can be easily corrected.

However, these Jews were not momentarily veering off course but had actually never been on course, or if they had, they had left it completely. Theirs was not a momentary deviation from Truth but was, in fact, the total wrong direction, i.e., of Satan.

(39) "THEY ANSWERED AND SAID UNTO HIM, ABRAHAM IS OUR FATHER. JESUS SAID UNTO THEM, IF YOU WERE ABRAHAM'S CHILDREN, YOU WOULD DO THE WORKS OF ABRAHAM."

The form is:

1. The phrase, *"They answered and said unto Him, Abraham is our father,"* was true according to the flesh, hence, *"Abraham's seed"* (Jn. 8:37), but not true spiritually.

2. To be one's seed simply speaks of the flesh, which means little or nothing regarding spiritual things. However, for Abraham to truly be one's father in the moral and spiritual sense, the *"seed"* would have to be morally and spiritually like him as well!

3. *"Jesus said unto them, If you were Abraham's children, you would do the works of Abraham,"* which meant that Abraham loved God, had Faith in God, and longingly looked for God's Son, Who would ultimately come. These Pharisees did the very opposite, so they were children of Abraham in name only.

(40) "BUT NOW YOU SEEK TO KILL ME, A MAN WHO HAS TOLD YOU THE TRUTH, WHICH I HAVE HEARD OF GOD: THIS DID NOT ABRAHAM."

The diagram is:

1. The phrase, *"But now you seek to kill Me,"* as well, should have signaled to them greatly as to Who He was simply because the true intent of their hearts, which only God could know, was open and obvious to Him. However, nothing He did, no matter how

miraculous, seemed to faze them. Their unbelief had locked them in a darkness, which they would not allow the Light of God to penetrate.

2. *"A Man Who has told you the Truth,"* presents the first and only time that Jesus referred to Himself in this fashion, *"A Man!"* He did so to mark the contrast between Him and the *"man-slayer"* of John 8:44. *"Murderer"* is man-slayer in the Greek text. Jesus is a Man-saver, hence, the occupation of His Followers. Satan is a man-slayer, hence, the occupation of his children.

3. *"Which I have heard of God,"* presents the highest representation of the very conception of a Divine Commission and a Divine Message.

4. They were seeking to stamp out a Divine Fire, to drown a Heavenly Voice, and to refuse and trample upon a Sacred Messenger.

5. *"This did not Abraham,"* proclaims that they might be Abraham's *"seed,"* but not his children, and, in this sense, he could not be their *"father."*

6. By contrast, the manifestations of God to Abraham were so readily accepted by that Prophet that his Faith is a Proverb, and his greatest name is *"friend of God."*

(41) "YOU DO THE DEEDS OF YOUR FATHER. THEN SAID THEY TO HIM, WE BE NOT BORN OF FORNICATION; WE HAVE ONE FATHER, EVEN GOD."

The overview is:

1. The phrase, *"You do the deeds of your father,"* should have been attached to the previous Verse.

2. Jesus is plainly saying that they were doing the deeds not of Abraham, but rather the Devil, which was obvious to all who truly followed the Lord.

3. *"Then said they to Him,"* presents them loudly and rudely interrupting His Statements, incensed by His Accusation.

4. *"We be not born of fornication,"* was a reference to the false worship and idolatry which so often characterized Israel of old, and was regarded by God as *"spiritual fornication and spiritual adultery."*

5. However, by their loud claim of not being *"born of fornication,"* at the same time, they may have been accusing Jesus

NOTES

of having been thusly born.

6. It is quite possible that they had heard the story of the Angel Gabriel visiting Mary, telling her that the Holy Spirit would overshadow her, with her becoming pregnant with Jesus, even before her marriage to Joseph. Of course, they would not have believed this at all, calling it a fabrication.

7. Actually, the monstrous lie would later be told, and may well have originated during the Ministry of Christ, that Mary was made pregnant by a drunken Roman soldier, with that man being the Father of Jesus. The lie went on that Joseph had married her out of pity! In truth, there is no limit to the vulgar, obscene, and wicked lies perpetrated by these people. They continue unto this hour, concerning the Person of our Lord and Saviour Jesus Christ. As should be obvious, evil has no stopping place.

8. The phrase, *"We have one Father, even God,"* is the proud claim made still by those who are morally the children of Satan. However, the test of true sonship is the attitude of the heart toward Jesus. If He is loved and His Book obeyed, then is true sonship manifest.

(42) "JESUS SAID UNTO THEM, IF GOD WERE YOUR FATHER, YOU WOULD LOVE ME: FOR I PROCEEDED FORTH AND CAME FROM GOD; NEITHER CAME I OF MYSELF, BUT HE SENT ME."

The exegesis is:

1. The phrase, *"Jesus said unto them, If God were your Father, you would love Me,"* proclaims, as we have said, that Jesus is Alone the yardstick. He is the *"tried Stone, a precious Corner Stone, a sure Foundation."* He is *"the Line and the Plummet"* (Isa. 28:16-17).

2. This means that God is not the Father of Muslims because they have rejected Jesus for Muhammad!

3. This means that God is not the Father of the Catholics because they have rejected Jesus for Mary!

4. This means that God is not the Father of the Mormons because they have rejected Jesus for Joseph Smith!

5. This means that God is not the Father of many who call themselves *"Christians"* because they have traded Jesus for their

particular religious denomination, church, or doctrine!

6. *"For I proceeded forth and came from God,"* means that He Alone has done this, with no other able to say such a thing.

7. *"Neither came I of Myself, but He sent Me,"* in effect, places the entirety of the Godhead in unison, respecting the Redemption of mankind, concerning that which Jesus would do.

8. The idea is that His Coming is the result of a carefully crafted plan, which *"was foreordained before the foundation of the world, but was manifest in these last times for you"* (I Pet. 1:20).

9. So, the rebellion of the Jews against Christ was a rebellion against all that God had done, was doing, and would do, respecting the single most important thing, man's Redemption.

10. Jesus coming as He did was exactly what God ordained. His being born of a Virgin was an absolute necessity. As well, His living as a Peasant was a necessity also! The way He conducted Himself, His Type of Ministry, and the Message He brought were orchestrated down to the most minute detail, all of which the Pharisees and religious leaders rejected.

(43) "WHY DO YOU NOT UNDERSTAND MY SPEECH? EVEN BECAUSE YOU CANNOT HEAR MY WORD."

The synopsis is:

1. The question, *"Why do you not understand My Speech?"* is explained in the next phrase.

2. *"Even because you cannot hear My Word,"* proclaims the fact that to understand the subject taught is to understand the words by which it is taught, otherwise, they are unintelligible.

3. His *"Word,"* i.e., that which He taught, is Truth; His *"Speech"* — the words used in preaching it. The one was the subject; the other the form. So, they could not understand the Words because they did not intuitively believe and accept the Revelation made in and by the Words. A man who is destitute by birth of musical sense listening to a lecture on music would find the words unintelligible.

4. In fact, Jesus was speaking very clearly and plainly, with absolutely no doubt as to what He was saying. So, He asked the reason they could not understand Him, not because He did not know, but because He did know, and gave the answer.

5. To understand the Bible, i.e., what Jesus is saying, there must first be Faith. Regrettably, there is not much faith in the world respecting God and His Word. As such, it has no meaning, clarity, understanding, intelligence, or direction for the hearer. That is one reason that Jesus continued to say, *"He who has ears to hear, let him hear"* (Mat. 11:15).

6. As well, Faith is not a commodity which is arbitrarily withheld or conversely given by God upon the hearing of the Word. The will of man is never tampered with respecting undue pressure either way. While Satan definitely does hinder the sinner, still, the Lord will not allow him undue latitude. As well, the Lord deals with a person but will not force the issue.

7. So, self-will is actually the dominant force in these situations, and is made so by the Lord. The Jews were spiritually dumb by their own free choice! Had they so desired, they could have accepted and believed the Lord, and what He was saying would have become overly obvious. In fact, some did, such as Nicodemus and Joseph of Arimathea, concerning the rulers in Israel.

(44) "YOU ARE OF YOUR FATHER THE DEVIL, AND THE LUSTS OF YOUR FATHER YOU WILL DO. HE WAS A MURDERER FROM THE BEGINNING, AND ABODE NOT IN THE TRUTH, BECAUSE THERE IS NO TRUTH IN HIM. WHEN HE SPEAKS A LIE, HE SPEAKS OF HIS OWN: FOR HE IS A LIAR, AND THE FATHER OF IT."

The exposition is:

1. Before the foundation of the world, God through foreknowledge knew He would create man, and man would fall.

2. It was determined by the Godhead that man would be redeemed by God becoming man and going to a Cross (I Pet. 1:18-20).

3. So, the Cross was the Destination of Christ. This means it was not an accident, an incident, an execution, or an assassination. It was a Sacrifice.

YOUR FATHER THE DEVIL

The phrase, *"You are of your father the Devil, and the lusts of your father you will do,"* presents the Lord repudiating in terrible language the spiritual claims made by these Jews respecting their association with Jehovah.

The *"lusts"* of the Devil are falsehood, murder, lying, and slaughter. As well, he is a slanderer and an accuser. His children will likewise have these traits, which they proved so openly in murdering Jesus.

This one statement by Christ explains man's inhumanity to man, as well as sickness, suffering, war, crime, stealing, killing, and destroying, which characterize the world.

I watched, as did millions of Americans sometime ago, while the heads of the large tobacco companies in America held up their hands and swore that they did not know that nicotine was addictive.

Yes, they knew, and unequivocally so! I do not know how much they care concerning the nearly one-half million each year who die from nicotine-related illnesses, but this I do know, they love money more than they care about the suffering, etc.

EVIL

Sometime back, *"Newsweek Magazine"* carried an article respecting *"evil,"* which was its cover story, and if there was such a thing, where did it come from? Of course, modern psychology denies evil, claiming that all men are good but do bad things because of the fault of someone else, etc.

Yes, there is such a thing as evil! It originates with Satan but finds fertile ground in Satan's children, which consists of all who do not truly know Jesus Christ as their Saviour. While some may be worse than others, still, the *"lusts"* of Satan are present in all unbelievers.

A LYING MURDERER

The phrase, *"He was a murderer from the beginning,"* refers to what He did, bringing forth death, which fastened itself to the entirety of the human family. Consequently, from that moment until now, the Earth has been filled with death and dying.

NOTES

The phrase, *"And abode not in the Truth,"* means that he actually was in Truth for a time until he rebelled against God. That is when he *"abode not"* or rebelled against Truth (Ezek. 28:11-17; Isa. 14:12-14). This was before Adam's day, for he came into Adam's Eden (Gen., Chpt. 3).

The phrase, *"Because there is no truth in him,"* has reference to the fact that he, at the time of his rebellion, declared himself as God and, therefore, the embodiment of truth. He is still telling them that lie unto this moment, with billions having believed it, reaping its eternal results of damnation.

"When he speaks a lie, he speaks of his own," means that instead of being the embodiment of Truth, as he claims, which only God is, instead, he is the embodiment of the *"lie."* *"His own"* means that he is the originator of the lie, *"For he is a liar, and the father of it."*

This is the problem with the world in that it builds on a *"lie,"* functions on a *"lie,"* and practices the *"lie."* From it has spawned evolution, psychology, witchcraft, war, atheism, agnosticism, communism, etc., as well as all the religions of the world. The only Truth in the world is that which comes from the Word of God. Anything without that (the Bible) has as its foundation the *"lie!"*

TRUTH

In effect, all law in the world, at least if it has a semblance of Truth, is more or less built on the Ten Commandments. The less they serve as a foundation, the less freedom, justice, and prosperity! The closer to the Truth, the more of these great qualities!

As I have explained elsewhere in these Volumes, there is a philosophy called *"subjective truth,"* which means that truth is subject to circumstances, individuals, or whatever one wants to say it is. In other words, what is truth for you, they say, may not be truth for me. In fact, subjective truth is a *"lie!"*

"Objective Truth" is that which is based on the Word of God and changes not. It is the same for all, and for all time. If any society attempts to build on *"subjective truth,"* it will ultimately self-destruct.

Whenever the Supreme Court of the United States bases its rulings on other than the Foundation of the Word of God, that is *"subjective truth,"* and will result in gross unfairness for some members of society. I speak of the rulings on abortion, etc.

The world has a choice: it can follow the *"Truth"* or the *"lie!"* However, it is actually impossible for Satan's children, who, in fact, make up the far greater majority of the population, to follow anything other than the *"lie."* So, that means that true Believers in the Lord Jesus Christ and His Power to save are the only ones who can follow Truth and, consequently, are the *"Salt"* (preservative) and *"Light"* (illumination) in the world.

Of course, the world does not recognize such and tends to persecute and even hate that which is the very source of its prosperity, because a lie cannot recognize the Truth.

As well, in this Verse, Jesus asserts the personality of Satan, the archenemy of God, and the originator of all evil. This tells of the impurity and malignity of his nature; consequently, Satan's *"lusts"* his children will willingly do because of possessing the same nature as their father. That is the reason the sinner has to be *"Born-Again"* in order to come from the *"lie"* to the *"Truth,"* i.e., the Lord Jesus Christ.

(45) "AND BECAUSE I TELL YOU THE TRUTH, YOU BELIEVE ME NOT."

The structure is:

1. In brief, *"Truth"* is Jesus Christ and what He did at Calvary for lost humanity.

2. All of this means that Truth is not a philosophy, but rather a Person, the Lord Jesus Christ (Jn. 14:6).

3. Outside of Christ, there is no truth.

LIARS

If Jesus had spoken lies to these religious bigots, they would have greedily received them. That is the reason people have a tendency to believe psychics or to follow some guru even though they are plainly deceiving them and only after their money. It is because a liar eagerly believes a lie.

That is the reason, among other things, the news media will ridicule people for giving money to God's Work, calling the Preacher a crook and the giver a chump, while they say nothing at all derogatory about the gambling business. Millions of poor people, who can hardly afford to put food on the table, will spend their hard-earned money for lottery tickets. They have about one chance in several millions of winning anything. This, in fact, is the cruelest form of taxation there is; however, the media says not a derogatory word.

Why?

It is because they are all liars, the media, the gambling interests, and the poor people who fall for this lie, thinking they are going to win something.

TRUTH

Jesus told them the *"Truth,"* but they would not believe Him because a liar cannot believe the Truth.

In this Verse, the *"I"* is emphatic, meaning that Jesus is Truth and, therefore, what He is saying is Truth.

The *"You"* is emphatic, as well, but in the opposite direction. While those who know Truth can easily recognize the lie, liars are locked in their prison of darkness and cannot recognize Truth.

There is a tragic force almost unparalleled about this charge of their not believing the Truth, implying the most willful estrangement from God, a rejection of known Truth because it is Truth, a love of darkness because it is darkness, a moral tragedy, which is the embodiment of evil.

This is the reason that it is literally impossible for an unbeliever to come to Faith on his own. There is no way within his own ability that he can climb out of this prison of darkness and the *"lie"* which encases him like a cocoon.

The only opportunity of Salvation that the unbeliever has is that he hears the Word of God in some fashion, and the Holy Spirit moves upon that Word, which is Truth, and, thereby, places the sinner under conviction. Even then, most, even with the Help of the Holy Spirit, find it easier to remain in the lie, believing it rather than Truth. However, a few, by the Help, Moving, and Operation of the Holy Spirit upon the Word of God, make the decision to come to Christ. When they do, the *"lie"* is overcome instantly by *"Truth,"* and the individual is *"Born-Again."*

RELIGION

That is one of the reasons it is impossible to reach men for God through intellectual preaching, or with talent, entertainment, or ability. Such has no power to break through the lie. It takes the Truth of the Word of God, empowered by the Holy Spirit, for the prison of the lie to be opened and the Truth to enter.

There is another direction in this scenario, which is the most dangerous of all, and which has caused more people to be lost than anything else. I speak of Satan's greatest lie, that of religion! In fact, the Holy Spirit has a much greater success rate addressing those who follow the lie of *"lust of the flesh,"* rather than the religious world, which engages in *"the pride of life."* The latter are far harder to reach because the religious lie is Satan's greatest weapon. Actually, it has *"murdered"* the far greater majority of the population of every generation.

Hasn't the one who dies while locked in religious bondage, i.e., the lie, actually been murdered by Satan and his children?

(46) "WHICH OF YOU CONVINCES ME OF SIN? AND IF I SAY THE TRUTH, WHY DO YOU NOT BELIEVE ME?"

The form is:

1. Jesus, offering up Himself as a Sacrifice on the Cross, paid the sin debt that man owed, which, incidentally, man could not pay.

2. When Jesus gave Himself in Sacrifice, He atoned for all sin, past, present, and future, at least for all who will believe (Jn. 3:16).

3. When this was done, Satan and all of his cohorts of darkness were totally and completely defeated (Col. 2:14-15).

JESUS CHRIST AND SIN

The question, *"Which of you convinces Me of sin?"* means that inasmuch as it was not possible to lay a charge of sin or a wrongdoing of any nature against Jesus, on that basis alone, they should believe what He was saying.

Not only was this a basis for believing in Him, as well, it was so because He was Absolutely Perfect in every sense.

NOTES

From Moses to Paul, and all others of the saintliest men and women who have ever lived, all have been aware of their weaknesses, flaws, and moral bankruptcy, at least within themselves. In fact, the saintlier they are, the more that is obvious; consequently, Job could say when confronted by the Most High, *"I am vile"* (Job 40:4). Isaiah would say when he saw Jesus, *"Woe is me! for I am undone; because I am a man of unclean lips, and I dwell in the midst of a people of unclean lips"* (Isa. 6:5). Peter would say, *"Depart from me; for I am a sinful man, O Lord"* (Lk. 5:8).

The Standard of Jesus is not only higher than that of any other but is perfect. He is absolutely without need of Repentance, is presently above the power of temptation, and beyond the range of conviction.

ETERNAL TRUTH

Consequently, to His Challenge as thrown out before them, they stood forever covered with the shame of their own incompetence to convict Him of any type of sin or moral turpitude. If they could not do so to His Face, let them at least show a tiny bit of class and keep their mouths shut ever after. They could not convict him of sin or moral turpitude even while they were rejecting Him. This would have been the time, especially considering that a great crowd was overhearing the exchange, which would have greatly furthered their cause.

The question, *"And if I say the Truth, why do you not believe Me?"* means that inasmuch as they could not bring a charge of sin against Him, they must assume that He stands in Eternal Truth, is the Absolute Truth of all things, that He cannot, from His Moral Purity, deceive or misinform them, and that His Testimony to Himself is final, sufficient, and trustworthy. As such, what reason could they give for not believing Him?

He could convict them of sin (Jn. 8:9), and though He challenged them, they could not convict Him.

(47) "HE WHO IS OF GOD HEARS GOD'S WORDS: YOU THEREFORE HEAR THEM NOT, BECAUSE YOU ARE NOT OF GOD."

The pattern is:

1. Sin is the means by which Satan holds man captive, but with all sin atoned, Satan's legal right is ended (Col. 2:10-15).

2. Therefore, if any man is captive to Satan, and most are, this means that they aren't taking advantage of what Jesus did at the Cross (I Cor. 1:18).

3. Sadly and regrettably, because most Christians do not understand the Cross of Christ relative to Sanctification, they too are in bondage.

THE WORD OF GOD

The phrase, *"He who is of God hears God's Words,"* could be said in this fashion: *"The closer to God one is, the more he hears and abides by the Word of God."* Conversely, that would also mean that the further away one is from the Lord, the less the Word plays a part in one's life.

Actually, nearness to God is tied inextricably to the Word of God and its application to one's life.

The phrase, *"You therefore hear them not, because you are not of God,"* presents the reason they are not of God.

Jesus here ties His Words, the things He has been saying in this exchange, with the Old Testament to flesh out the New Covenant. His Words include all else that He said, that which was ultimately given to us in the Gospels, and that which He would give to the Apostle Paul and others.

Actually, everything that Jesus is saying here is given somewhere in the Old Testament, whether by direct statement or in shadows or symbols. If the Believer does not properly understand the Old Testament, even as those Pharisees of old, one cannot have a proper understanding of Jesus either. Everything in the Old Testament, in one way or the other, pointed to Him. Consequently, we learn from the Golden Lampstands in the Tabernacle and Temple that Jesus is the Light of the world exactly as He has said here. We also learn from the Manna that He is the Bread of Life. As someone has said, *"The Old Testament is the New Testament concealed, while the New Testament is the Old Testament revealed."*

When religious denominations tend to lose their way, if one had the opportunity to properly investigate, one would see that every single time it is because of subtracting from the Word of God or adding to the Word of God. Little by little, other things become the criteria compared to the Word.

It is the same in the immediate Believer's life. The Word must be the criterion for all that we do as Christians.

THE TWISTING AND PERVERTING OF THE SCRIPTURES

As one notices, the Pharisees claimed all the things of which we are saying, but were bluntly told here by Jesus that despite all of their claims and talk about the Word of God, in truth, they did not know the Word at all! Had they properly known it and allowed it to be the guiding force in their lives, they would have instantly and without question recognized Jesus as to Who He was and What He was. Actually, it was their additions to the Law of Moses and their twisting and perverting the True Scriptures which destroyed them, and will destroy all others as well!

Let the reader understand: when one stands before God, one will be judged strictly by the Word of God and not by what Priests or Preachers said, or anyone else, for that matter. Many at the Judgment Seat of Christ will attempt to shift the blame of their wrongdoing to their denomination or others. At that time, they will claim that this is what their denomination, pastor, or priest taught and, considering they were religious leaders, it was automatically assumed that they were right. However, I remind the reader that during the time of Christ, the whole of Israel could either hear Him or the religious leaders. Those who listened to Him were eternally Saved while those who listened to the others were eternally lost!

The Believer should know the Word of God for himself for many reasons; however, to know if what he is hearing is the Truth is certainly not the least of those reasons.

Tragically, most do not know the Word of God and make little effort to remedy the situation.

(48) "THEN ANSWERED THE JEWS, AND SAID UNTO HIM, SAY WE NOT WELL THAT YOU ARE A SAMARITAN,

AND HAVE A DEMON?"

The order is:

1. Jesus became sin only in the sense of becoming the Sin-Offering (Isa. 53:10).

2. If it is to be noticed, Paul didn't say, *"For He has made Him to be a sinner for us,"* but rather, *"To be sin for us."*

3. To be a sinner, one has to sin, and Jesus did not sin in any capacity. However, He did become a Sin-Offering.

ISRAEL'S RESPONSE TO CHRIST

The phrase, *"Then answered the Jews,"* records an outburst of scorn and insult in answer to the charge leveled by Jesus that they, the leaders of Israel, were *"not of God."*

If one is to notice, they could not refute His Statements or charge Him with sin, so they attacked Him Personally, which is by and large the tactic of those who cannot refute what is being said.

The phrase, *"Say we not well that You are a Samaritan,"* coupled with the last phrase, presents the greatest insult that they could level at anyone. In their minds, this meant that He was a heretic, a schismatic, an idolater, and a man self-excommunicated with whom no man should fellowship.

The Jews hated the Samaritans, whom they considered to be half-breeds, idol-worshippers, etc. Considering that they had come to believe that being born a Jew was the equivalent to Salvation, it becomes easier to understand their thinking respecting the Samaritans, who were only part Jew, if at all!

In truth, even as Jesus said in John 4:22, the Samaritans were totally wrong respecting their way of worship and claims on Salvation. However, such did not warrant the strident animosity, and even hatred, leveled against them by their Jewish neighbors. Actually, Jesus ministered to these people quite a number of times, showing no favoritism or partiality.

So, they were saying to Him that His Doctrine was as the Samaritans, false, corrupt, and, in effect, a lie.

BLASPHEMY

The conclusion of the question, *"And has a demon?"* was not meant to imply that He may or may not have such, but that their original contention of Him performing His Miracles by the power of Satan, and even being demon possessed, was valid!

So, their belief in Him, as recorded in John 8:30, had now turned to blasphemy, which means, glaringly so, that they, as millions, did not *"continue in His Word"* (Jn. 8:31).

To attribute to Satan that which is actually of God is just as bad as attributing to God that which is actually of Satan. All of this is done because of not knowing the Word of God.

A PERSONAL EXPERIENCE

A short time ago, an Assemblies of God Missionary, who had been away from the States for several years, returned on furlough and began to itinerate in quite a number of Assembly of God churches.

He made the statement in the presence of my sister-in-law, who attended an Assemblies of God Church where he was conducting a service, or else, it was related to her, *"I am shocked at what I am seeing in our churches!"*

He related how he had observed people in some of these churches writhing on the floor, barking like dogs, roaring like lions, or engaging in uncontrollable fits of laughter and claiming that these things were of the Spirit of God.

He was aghast, and rightly so, at the lack of proper discernment and the quickness to label things as of the Spirit, which had no Scriptural validity!

These things were being done because the people did not know the Word of God, or else, they did know it but refused to make it the criterion for what was happening, which is even worse! Too many in the modern Pentecostal and Charismatic churches are attempting to find Scriptural validity for their actions, which is the very opposite of Truth. Our actions must conform to the Word of God, not the opposite of trying to force some Scripture out of context into giving credence to one's foolishness.

(49) "JESUS ANSWERED, I HAVE NOT A DEMON; BUT I HONOUR MY FATHER, AND YOU DO DISHONOUR ME."

The overview is:

1. Our Salvation is 100 percent in Christ and what he did for us at the Cross.

2. He paid the price by shedding His Life's Blood, which paid the debt we could not pay (Eph. 2:13-18).

3. That payment, His Shed Blood, was accepted by God the Father as payment in full.

4. All that is required for a person to be Saved is to accept what Jesus has done for us at the Cross and to believe it with all of our hearts.

SELF-RIGHTEOUSNESS

The phrase, *"Jesus answered, I have not a demon,"* presents a simple denial, with Him taking no notice of the charge, *"You are a Samaritan."*

What dark, ignoble deed had He done which could have occasioned such a charge of Him being demon possessed? In fact, He had done nothing but good in healing the sick, casting out demons, and giving Words of Life. In truth, He was the Only Perfect, Pure, Infallible, Untainted, Unspoiled, Absolutely Free from Sin Person Who had ever lived. So, that of which they accused Him was in actuality the very opposite of what He truly was and is.

Self-righteousness will always accuse imputed Righteousness. The idea of an individual receiving perfect Holiness and Righteousness simply by believing God cannot at all be abided by self-righteousness. This was the problem of the Jews then and, in fact, has always been the problem, even unto this hour.

INSTANT RIGHTEOUSNESS

As an example, very few in the modern church believe that a proper yielding and Repentance before the Lord will give one instant Righteousness (Righteousness imputed freely by Christ upon simple Faith in Him). Most of the time, they feel that they must add something to the already Finished Work of Christ. For instance, many feel that such an individual, whomever he may be, must be placed on some type of probation, which, in reality, is a type of penance. Of course, doing such does despite to the Spirit of Grace and actually repudiates the Finished Work of Christ. Such constitutes Jesus plus, which, in reality, eliminates Jesus and His Work altogether!

So, those who were full of the Devil accused the One Who was Absolutely Perfect and Absolutely Pure.

Jesus did not address the Samaritan accusation because the charge was foolish. In other words, He would not dignify it with an answer. He answered the second because of the seriousness of its nature and because it was an affront to the Father as well!

The phrase, *"But I honour My Father, and you do dishonour Me,"* in effect, says that by dishonoring Him, they were dishonoring the Father, as well, whom they claimed to serve.

How does the Believer honor the Father?

We honor Him by believing His Word and acting on its Promises! Anything less is dishonor.

(50) "AND I SEEK NOT MY OWN GLORY: THERE IS ONE WHO SEEKS AND JUDGES."

The exegesis is:

1. The phrase, *"And I seek not My Own Glory,"* in effect, states that Jesus did not come to this Earth for *"Glory,"* but rather to redeem mankind. He was actually seeking the Glory of the Father, which should be an example to all of us.

2. Had He sought Personal Glory, He certainly would not have come as a Peasant or died such an ignoble death, which was humiliation of the highest order. However, He did seek the Glory of the Father, which these things, self-abnegation, would bring about.

3. The phrase, *"There is One Who seeks and judges,"* actually means that God sought Glory for Jesus and judged Him worthy of Glory.

4. So, if we seek God's Glory, denying ourselves, He, in turn, will seek our glory (Rom. 8:17).

(51) "VERILY, VERILY, I SAY UNTO YOU, IF A MAN KEEP MY SAYING, HE SHALL NEVER SEE DEATH."

The exposition is:

1. The phrase, *"Verily, verily, I say unto you,"* denotes, as should be obvious, a very

important statement, which actually sums up all that has been said previously.

2. *"If a man keep My Saying, he shall never see death,"* means he shall not see spiritual or eternal death, which refers to separation from God.

3. This is the strongest statement of this Glorious Truth and is here appropriately found, for He was here presenting Himself as the *"Eternal Life."*

4. Actually, Jesus lifted the words *"life"* and *"death"* to a far higher connotation than previously understood. He was introducing death here as a moral state and not an event in the physical existence.

5. Life speaks of the *"Born-Again"* experience, which abrogates spiritual death, and makes the person a *"New Creature"* in Christ Jesus, which, as well, places *"Life"* on a far higher plane than mere existence.

(52) "THEN SAID THE JEWS UNTO HIM, NOW WE KNOW THAT YOU HAVE A DEMON. ABRAHAM IS DEAD, AND THE PROPHETS; AND YOU SAY, IF A MAN KEEP MY SAYING, HE SHALL NEVER TASTE OF DEATH."

The structure is:

1. The sacrifices under the Old Covenant, to be sure, were no church picnic. This terrible place, however, was the very heart and center, the seat, of true Holiness.

2. Later, Calvary would afford no pleasant scene either. That Hill would offer the most hideous, horrible spectacle that Heaven and Earth would ever see.

3. In fact, the scene of Calvary would be so horrible that even God the Father would not look upon it.

THE ACCUSATION OF THE JEWS AGAINST JESUS

The phrase, *"Then said the Jews unto Him, Now we know that You have a demon,"* proclaims them continuing the accusation but, even above that, the denying of Him Who Alone could give Life! Even though they did not, at this time, realize such, they had just signed their death warrant. They would accordingly die lost without God, and then, horror of horrors, would burn in Hell forever and forever (Rev. 21:8).

I take no delight at all in saying these things, as Jesus took no delight in the response of the Jews. However, the truth must be understood that to reject Christ is not only to reject Life but, as well, is to consign oneself to eternal Hellfire. Jesus is not One of several ways of Salvation but, in reality, the Only Way of Salvation (Jn. 14:6).

If one does not desire Jesus, one does not have the privilege of turning to another, for there is no other. Jesus is the One Who satisfied the claims of Heavenly Justice, paid the sin debt, and broke the grip of sin in the human heart and life. Consequently, as no one else has done that and, in fact, cannot do that, He Who paid the price is the One, and the only One, to Whom man may look.

DEATH?

"Abraham is dead, and the Prophets," portrayed their total lack of understanding of what He had said. While these were dead physically, they were very much alive Spiritually and, actually, at that very moment, with all the other Saints in Paradise, awaiting Deliverance by the Lord Jesus Christ.

"And You say, If a man keep My Saying, he shall never taste of death," presents a corruption or perversion of what Jesus actually said! He said, *"Shall never see death,"* which is not the same thing.

By inserting the word *"taste"* in place of the word *"see,"* they had reduced His Statement from the spiritual to the physical. As stated, Jesus was speaking of the second or eternal death, which means eternal separation from God. All Believers, with the exception of two, Enoch and Elijah, have *"tasted"* of death, which even includes our Lord. As well, these two just mentioned will come back as the two witnesses in the latter half of the coming Great Tribulation, and after their Ministry is finished, will die as all other men (Rev. 11:3-12). However, they will be resurrected almost immediately. As well, Jesus has taken the terrible fear and sting out of death.

These statements, as given by these Pharisees, portray a perfect example of the carnal man misunderstanding the Word of God and the religious man who perverts its meaning.

To be frank, *"The natural man receives*

not the things of the Spirit of God: for they are foolishness unto him: neither can he know them, because they are spiritually discerned" (I Cor. 2:14).

When the sinner comes to Christ as the Word is preached to him, it is not so much because he understands that Word, but because the Holy Spirit has used the Word to convict him of *"Sin, Righteousness, and Judgment"* (Jn. 16:8-11).

(53) "ARE YOU GREATER THAN OUR FATHER ABRAHAM, WHICH IS DEAD? AND THE PROPHETS ARE DEAD: AFTER WHOM DO YOU MAKE YOURSELF?"

The pattern is:

1. All sin is against God.
2. Sin is an insult to God, a willful, flagrant, disavowal of His Word, which is the highest insult to the Creator.
3. Inasmuch as all sin is committed against Him, it is before Him that we must come in order to have sin forgiven and cleansed.

ARE YOU GREATER THAN ABRAHAM?

The question, *"Are You greater than our father Abraham, who is dead?"* is a question that must be answered in the affirmative.

"And the Prophets are dead," falls into the same category as the question concerning Abraham.

Jesus would answer these questions in such plain terms that they did not have to guess what He had said, which greatly incensed them, as we shall see.

The question, *"After whom do You make Yourself?"* is an incorrect and, therefore, improper question. He did not make Himself anything, neither were His Words boastful concerning His Deity and what that meant. To have said less would have been a denial, which He could not do.

This last question, as asked by these religious leaders, pretty well sums up the spirit and attitude of most religious leaders.

The idea is that they were supposed to be the ones who did all the doing respecting spiritual things in Israel. No one was to do anything unless their hands were laid upon him. All had to have their permission and, at the same time, only say what they were told to say by these religious leaders.

NOTES

GOD WORKS THROUGH INDIVIDUALS

Therefore, all such attitude and spirit, which continues unto this very hour, will always strongly oppose all who are truly sent from God. Almost always, they claim the individual, as these did Jesus, as anointing himself. They pretty well deny that God actually calls someone, thereby, giving him a commission. Of course, that is really the only way God works.

He never works through committees, boards, church denominations, constitutions and bylaws, etc. Neither does He work by proxy, nor does He ask permission.

In fact, the Work of God is not a democracy and never has been! The Will of God is not voted on, and neither does it seek popular approval. To tell the truth, it seldom has much approval by anyone!

A PERSONAL EXPERIENCE

Some years ago, I had a religious leader in the denomination with which I was associated at that time, incidentally, a man I did not know, to write me and ask the following questions:

"Why are you on radio and television? Who gave you permission to do so?"

At first, I was somewhat taken aback because his questions were so utterly foolish.

He was insinuating that the only preachers who could be on radio and television were those who were appointed by the leadership of that denomination.

It is difficult to understand how a man, who is supposed to know and understand the Word of God, and who, in fact, is a religious leader, could have no more Scriptural knowledge than that.

I wrote him back, stating words to this effect:

"My Brother, I did not have permission from anyone, neither did I seek such. I am doing what God has told me to do, and will continue to do my best to carry out that which I believe is His Calling for my life."

We were to see literally hundreds of thousands of souls brought to Christ as a result of doing what He called us to do, but which would not have been done if this man, and scores of others like him, had had their way.

A DISAGREEMENT?

If there had been a disagreement between this brother and me, or had there been some type of problem, I might have understood his questions. However, nothing like that had happened. In fact, as I stated, I didn't even personally know him.

Regarding this denomination and scores of others similar, the idea was, and is, that no one is to do anything for the Lord unless the permission of these people is sought and given, which is completely unscriptural.

While some few things may fall under that category, the Call of God on one's life definitely does not fall into such thinking. It is God Who calls the person, and it is God Who gives the Message. Accordingly, it is God to Whom one must look for Leading, Guidance, and Direction. To seek permission from some poor man to carry out the plainly-revealed Will of God for one's life is an insult to God.

To this man's credit, whom I have just mentioned, and whom I never really did get to know, he completely changed, I was told, after he left that unscriptural office he was occupying. He said to a friend of mine shortly before he died, *"While I was in that religious office, there was a spirit that controlled me, and some of the things I did, I look back now and see how ungodly they actually were."* I am told that, at that time, he also had some very gracious and kind things to say about me and our Ministry.

How so much I thank the Lord for what this dear brother came to be, but how so much hindrance he and others like him are to the Kingdom of God simply because of their unscriptural positions.

(54) "JESUS ANSWERED, IF I HONOUR MYSELF, MY HONOUR IS NOTHING: IT IS MY FATHER WHO HONOURS ME; OF WHOM YOU SAY, THAT HE IS YOUR GOD."

The synopsis is:

1. The phrase, *"Jesus answered, If I honour Myself, My Honour is nothing,"* is used here to address Himself to their question or accusation, *"After whom do You make yourself?"*

2. *"It is My Father Who honours Me,"* should have given them room for pause.

NOTES

He repeatedly linked Himself to the Father in every conceivable way. Therefore, He was telling them that their rejection of Him was a rejection of God, but nothing seemed to faze them.

3. *"Of Whom you say, that He is your God,"* is given by Jesus and validates their claim.

4. The idea is that they were claiming great allegiance to God and, therefore, great service for Him.

(55) "YET YOU HAVE NOT KNOWN HIM; BUT I KNOW HIM: AND IF I SHOULD SAY, I KNOW HIM NOT, I SHALL BE A LIAR LIKE UNTO YOU: BUT I KNOW HIM, AND KEEP HIS SAYING."

The overview is:

1. The phrase, *"Yet you have not known Him,"* was blunt and spoke exactly the truth.

2. He was not only saying that they did not know God presently, but they had never known Him, which was quite an accusation.

3. The truth is that most who claim a profession of Faith at present, in fact, have never known the Lord. Their claim to Faith pertains to some things they do or do not do! In other words, it is a righteousness by works pure and simple, exactly as these Pharisees of old, which God can never accept. I suspect that if one knew the truth, the number of people truly Born-Again is shockingly small (Mat. 7:13-14).

4. *"But I know Him,"* is used unequivocally! In fact, even though all true Believers *"know the Lord,"* still, none know Him as does Jesus. Of course, that should be obvious!

5. The idea is that if we are going to know God, we will have to know Him through Jesus Christ and no other way because there is no other way. God is revealed to Believers only through Christ.

6. *"And if I should say, I know Him not, I shall be a liar like unto you,"* presents the severity of Jesus, Who pulled no punches.

7. Reynolds said, *"No cowardly modesty is possible to Him. He knows, and must speak. He cannot, dare not, be silent, or allow these bitter enemies, with their ready malice and perverse and continuous misinterpretation of His Words, to be ignorant, either of the ground of His self-consciousness or His penetration of their flimsy excuses."*[4]

8. *"But I know Him, and keep His Saying,"* is in contrast to these religious leaders, which Jesus maintains, and rightly so, even in the face of the most bitter adversity. Actually, He would not allow this Divine Consciousness to be taken from Him, even by the shame and agony of the Cross.

(56) "YOUR FATHER ABRAHAM REJOICED TO SEE MY DAY: AND HE SAW IT, AND WAS GLAD."

The form is:

1. The phrase, *"Your father Abraham rejoiced to see My Day,"* means that he rejoiced exceedingly. *"And he saw it, and was glad,"* means the following:

a. God was going to use Abraham to help bring forth His Great Plan for the entirety of the world. To be selected accordingly was an honor and distinction unparalleled in human history!

b. He understood fully that this Plan called for God to become Man and, accordingly, be born into this world, and to redeem mankind. By Faith, and in his spirit, he saw that coming day, as well as all that it meant, even to what type of Ministry Jesus would have. Above all, he saw what He would do and upon understanding that, he *"rejoiced exceedingly!"*

c. He saw this Redeemer coming through his own lineage, which included the Miracle child Isaac, with, ultimately, *"All families of the Earth being blessed"* (Gen. 12:3).

2. In this, he believed what the Lord told him, and the Scripture says, *"He* (the Lord) *counted it to him for Righteousness"* (Gen. 15:6).

3. The joy that was produced in Abraham, even exceeding joy, was that which always accompanies true Salvation, that is, if it is properly understood. This is the *"more Abundant Life"* spoken of by Jesus (Jn. 10:10).

4. So, we learn from this statement by Christ that some of the Prophets and Patriarchs of old, at least Abraham and, no doubt, David, Isaiah, etc., fully understood the coming Incarnation. It was not a mystery to them, and it brought great joy to their hearts.

5. Therefore, Jesus was saying to the religious leaders of Israel that there was no reason they should not know Him, especially considering that Abraham knew this some 2,000 years before.

(57) "THEN SAID THE JEWS UNTO HIM, YOU ARE NOT YET FIFTY YEARS OLD, AND HAVE YOU SEEN ABRAHAM?"

The construction is:

1. The phrase, *"Then said the Jews unto Him, You are not yet fifty years old,"* refers to the fact that, at that time, the Jews believed that a man did not reach full maturity, regarding wisdom and the intellect, until 50 years old. Other than that, it had no mysterious meaning, as some have tended to imply.

2. The question, *"And have You seen Abraham?"* proclaims the Jews once more misinterpreting His Words and, consequently, putting a physical or materialistic tone to what He had said.

3. There is a possibility that they did not understand what He was saying but that they did not believe Him. Consequently, they answered sarcastically!

(58) "JESUS SAID UNTO THEM, VERILY, VERILY, I SAY UNTO YOU, BEFORE ABRAHAM WAS, I AM."

The structure is:

1. Jesus now unequivocally made the supreme declaration that He is Jehovah. In essence, He said, *"Before Abraham was brought into being, I was eternally existent."*

2. He then said, *"Abraham 'was' but 'I am'"* — not that He came into existence before Abraham did, but that He never came into being at any time because He had always existed.

3. What an amazing Revelation! A man despised, rejected, poor, ill-treated, and hated was God Himself! He was there, come down from Heaven, and standing in their midst. It was an amazing fact for those who loved Him and for those who hated Him.

4. He was there as a Saviour. As such, He was both hidden and manifested — hidden as to His Glory, manifested as to His Person.

5. This *"I am,"* as all the others, is basically the same as the *"I am that I am"* of Exodus 3:14.

(59) "THEN TOOK THEY UP STONES TO CAST AT HIM: BUT JESUS HID HIMSELF, AND WENT OUT OF THE TEMPLE, GOING THROUGH THE MIDST

OF THEM, AND SO PASSED BY."

The synopsis is:

1. The phrase, *"Then took they up stones to cast at Him,"* presents the second of three occasions when His Life would be thus threatened, each time, because He claimed to be God (Jn. 5:18; 8:59; 10:31).

2. *"But Jesus hid Himself,"* probably refers to them rushing to the Court of the Gentiles in order to pick up stones to cast at Him, but upon arriving back, they did not find Him there, at least not immediately.

3. *"And went out of the Temple, going through the midst of them, and so passed by,"* probably means that when their anger had cooled somewhat, He slowly walked through them and went on His Way.

4. Thus was the response of the religious leaders of Israel to their Messiah! In about six months, they would have the opportunity to take Him into custody, and then, the full darkness of their hearts would become obvious. They then would do all the things to Him that they had desired to do all along. Such is religion!

5. To be sure, it has changed not at all, and would continue in that vein presently were it not for the laws of the land. It only lacks opportunity, with no lack of desire at all!

"O, do not let the Word depart,
"And close your eyes against the Light,
"Poor sinner, harden not your heart,
"Be Saved, O, tonight."

───■───

CHAPTER 9

(1) "AND AS JESUS PASSED BY, HE SAW A MAN WHICH WAS BLIND FROM HIS BIRTH."

The form is:

1. Blind from birth typifies spiritually the condition of the unredeemed. They are born spiritually blind.

2. Only the Power of God can open the eyes of such a one.

3. This is what Jesus was talking about when He said, *"The Spirit of the Lord is upon Me, because He has anointed Me … to recover sight to the blind"* (Lk. 4:18).

NOTES

JESUS PASSED BY

The phrase, *"And as Jesus passed by,"* records another instance of that which Christ did, not only greatly benefiting the one for whom the Miracle was performed but, as well, serving as a statement for the whole of humanity for all time, in this case, Jesus as the Light of the world.

John, Chapter 8, introduced the Light, while John, Chapter 9, proclaims the eyes miraculously opened by Christ, which made it possible for these formerly blinded eyes to now see the Light.

We will see in this Chapter exactly how impossible it is for the spiritual and moral eyes of man to be opened, other than by a Revelation of Christ to the soul and, consequently, a demonstration of God's Power. Therefore, in this, we see the twin necessities of Salvation — *"Revelation and Power."*

HE SAW A MAN WHO WAS BLIND FROM HIS BIRTH

The phrase, *"He saw a man who was blind from his birth,"* proclaims the only instance of such a Healing being recorded — the healing of one born blind.

The Light that justified the adulteress and exposed and confounded her accusers in John, Chapter 8, now enlightened the blind man and put to shame his haters. Having brought these lost sheep into the fold (Jn., Chpt. 10), that same Light revealed their safety and the Grace and Truth of their Shepherd. So, Grace saved them, and Truth enlightened them.

This woman and this man symbolize Israel as a church adulteress and as a Nation blind. However, He Who is Israel's Light and Salvation will reveal Himself to her ultimately and will say, *"Neither do I condemn you."*

As this man of our study was blind from birth, so was Israel morally, and so are all men, but Jesus gave him sight. He produced in him that which he had not known previously. He was in darkness but now became Light in the Lord because he was enlightened by the Lord. That inward Light was not his by natural birth but entered into him physically and morally on contact with Him Who is the Light of the world.

As Jesus observed the blind man, there he sat, the very type of the race which says, *"We see,"* but which, to Christ's Eye, was proclaiming its utter helplessness and blindness, not asking even to be illumined, and revealing the fundamental injury done to the very race and nature of man. He called for all the Healing Power that He had been sent into the world to dispense.

MORALLY AND SPIRITUALLY BLIND

The world without Christ is morally and spiritually blind but, tragically, does not even realize it. As well, this absolute liability, brought about by the Fall, affects every strata of society in every capacity.

It should be noted that it is impossible to *"show"* a blind man anything simply because he is helpless to see. Therefore, this bit of wisdom tells us that it is absolutely impossible to reach the sinner through the intellect. Consequently, the myriad of preachers, which actually constitutes most, continuing to try in this fashion, come up empty, at least where Conversion is concerned.

Just last night as I watched a particular preacher over television for a few minutes, much of what he preached was correct. However, he was absolutely devoid of the Spirit of God and, in fact, did not even believe in the Moving and Operation of the Holy Spirit, at least not as the Bible proclaims. Consequently, he was appealing to the intellect, whether he realized it or not, which presents an impossibility of reaching an individual for Christ.

TRUTH

Many preachers erroneously think that the Truth alone is sufficient. However, the Power of Christ, which flowed from the Holy Spirit, was of absolute necessity in order that the Truth be understood and received. Sadly, even then, most continue to reject Christ. However, those who are brought to Him can only be brought as the Power of the Holy Spirit illuminates the Truth to the person's soul. Then, by the Power of God, Salvation is effected.

Paul said, *"For our Gospel came not unto you in word* (Truth) *only, but also in Power, and in the Holy Spirit"* (I Thess. 1:5).

This is the reason so few people are truly Saved! First of all, most preachers do not even believe the Truth of the Word of God; consequently, there is nothing they can say that will help anyone. Secondly, most of the few who do know the Truth and strive to preach it have no Moving or Operation of the Holy Spirit within their lives and Ministries. Consequently, precious little, if anything, is actually effected for the Cause of Christ.

The Knowledge and Presentation of the Truth, with the Anointing and Power of the Holy Spirit acting upon that Truth, is that alone which will bring men to Jesus. There are a few Preachers of this category but not many, even as there never have been many.

THE HOLY SPIRIT

That is the reason Jesus *"Commanded them that they should not depart from Jerusalem, but wait for the Promise of the Father"* (Acts 1:4).

As a result of the lack of the Truth and it coupled with the Holy Spirit, churches are filled with people who really have not been *"Born-Again,"* but only indoctrinated in some philosophical, spiritual quest. In other words, it is no more than a mental, intellectual acceptance of the philosophy of Christianity but, actually, without Christ.

(2) "AND HIS DISCIPLES ASKED HIM, SAYING, MASTER, WHO DID SIN, THIS MAN, OR HIS PARENTS, THAT HE WAS BORN BLIND?"

The order is:

1. All sin is directed against God.
2. Sin is a disobedience of the Word of God.
3. There is only one solution for sin, and that is the Cross of Christ.

MASTER, WHO DID SIN ... ?

The phrase, *"And His Disciples asked Him, saying,"* presents to us a question which has been asked since the dawn of time, concerning the cause of tragedy, affliction, poverty, sickness, disaster, etc.

The question, *"Master, who did sin, this man, or his parents, that he was born blind?"* gives us some clue into the thinking of Israel at that time.

Many believed, as evidenced by the question of the Disciples, that every peculiar disaster pointed to some special or particular sin. Actually, they seem not to have learned much from the Book of Job, which repudiates this thinking.

Some Jews believed that pious souls were reincarnated as a reward, not punishment, and that the wicked were put into eternal prisons to be tormented forever (Josephus, Ant. Book XVIII, and War, Book II).

As well, some Asiatics and some Jews believed that souls came back into bodies as a penalty for sins committed in a preexistent state. Controversies raged, as stated, over whether some physical infirmity was the result of one's sins or sins by the parents, as evidenced here by the Disciples. They even held that marks on the body caused by birth defects proved sin in the soul.

As another example, Hindus, in their religion, identify the sins of a previous life with afflictions of the present. For example, headaches, they say, are for irreverence to parents; epilepsy for poisoning someone; pain in the eyes for coveting another man's wife; blindness for murder of one's mother; etc.

THE FALL

The truth is, all of these things, adversity, sickness, affliction, tragedy, etc., came about as a result of the fall of man in the Garden of Eden (Rom. 8:10). Due to that Fall, Satan has become the *"god of this world."* As a result, he and his children, which number all who do not make Christ their Saviour, do his work, which is *"stealing, killing, and destroying"* (II Cor. 4:4; Jn. 10:10).

As a result of the Fall, sin became the dominating factor in the Earth, which, in its more simplistic meaning, simply refers to disobedience to God, which is done by disobeying His Word. As a result of the wrongness of these actions, destructive results are the fruit.

THE DEFINITION OF SIN

The most characteristic feature of sin in all its aspects is that it is directed against God (Ps. 51:4; Rom. 8:7). Any conception of sin, which does not have at the forefront

NOTES

the contradiction which it offers to God, is a deviation from the Biblical representation.

The common notion that sin is mere selfishness betrays a false assessment of its nature and gravity. Essentially, sin is directed against God, and this perspective alone accounts for the diversity of its form and activities. It is a violation of that which God's Glory demands and is, therefore, in its essence, rebellion against God.

THE ORIGIN OF SIN

We do know that sin was present in the Universe before the fall of Adam and Eve (Gen. 3:1; Jn. 8:44; II Pet. 2:4; I Jn. 3:8; Jude 6). The Bible, however, does not deal directly with the origin of evil in the Universe, being concerned rather with sin and its origin in human life (I Tim. 2:14; James 1:13). The real thrust of the demonic temptation in the account of the Fall in Genesis, Chapter 3, lies in its subtle suggestion of man's aspiring to equality with his Maker (*" … you will be like God … "* Gen. 3:5). Satan's attack was directed against the integrity, veracity, and loving possession of God, and consistent in an enticement to wicked and blasphemous rebellion against man's proper Lord, His Creator.

In this act, man snatched at equality with God (Phil. 2:6), attempted to assert his independence of God, and, hence, to call into question the very nature and ordering of existence whereby he lived as a creature in utter dependence upon the Grace and Provision of His Creator.

MAN'S PRETENTION TO BE GOD

Niebuhr said, *"Man's sin lies in his pretension to be God."*[1] In this act, man further blasphemously withheld the worship and adoring love, which is ever his proper response to God's Majesty and Grace, and, instead, paid homage to the enemy of God and to his own foul ambitions.

Thus, the origin of sin according to Genesis, Chapter 3, ought not to be sought so much in an overt action (Gen. 2:17; 3:6), but in an inward, God-denying aspiration, of which the act of disobedience was the immediate expression.

As to the problem of how Adam and Eve

could have been subject to temptation had they not previously known sin, Scripture does not enter into extended discussion. However, we do know that they had the power of choice inasmuch as they were created in this manner. For God as Creator to derive from His Choice Creation what He desired, it necessitated the ability to choose good or evil. This had to be a part of man's spiritual, physical, and mental creation.

The ultimate origin of evil is part of the *"mystery of lawlessness"* (II Thess. 2:7). However, an arguable reason for Scripture's relative silence is that a *"rational explanation"* of the origin of sin would have the inevitable result of directing attention away from the primary concern of the Bible, the confession of one's personal guilt.

THE CONSEQUENCES OF SIN

The sin of Adam and Eve was not an isolated event. The consequences for them, for posterity, and for the world are immediately apparent and have taken their deadly toll ever since.

Sin is the cause of all of man's inhumanity to his fellowman, all war, crime, selfishness, etc.

Let's look at some of the consequences of sin.

MAN'S ATTITUDE TO GOD

The changed attitude to God on the part of Adam indicates the revolution that took place in their minds. They *"hid themselves from the presence of the LORD God"* (Gen. 3:8). Made for the Presence and Fellowship of God, Adam and Eve now dreaded encounter with Him (Jn. 3:20). Shame and fear were now the dominant emotions (Gen. 2:25; 3:7, 10), indicating the disruption that had taken place.

GOD'S ATTITUDE TO MAN

Not only was there a change in man's attitude to God but, also, in God's Attitude to man. Reproof, condemnation, curse, and expulsion from the Garden are all indicative of this. Sin is one-sided, but its consequences are not. Sin necessarily elicits God's Wrath and Displeasure because it is the contradiction of what God is like.

NOTES

For God to be complacent toward sin is an impossibility since it would be for God to cease to take Himself seriously. He cannot deny Himself.

CONSEQUENCES FOR THE HUMAN RACE

The unfolding history of man furnishes a catalog of vices (Gen. 4:8, 19, 23; 6:2-3, 5).

The sequel of abounding iniquity results in the virtual destruction of mankind (Gen. 6:7, 13; 7:21-24). The Fall had an abiding effect not only upon Adam and Eve, but upon all who descended from them, which includes all. There is racial solidarity in sin and evil.

CONSEQUENCES FOR CREATION

The effects of the Fall extend to the physical cosmos. *"Cursed is the ground because of you"* (Gen. 3:17; Rom. 8:20). Man is the crown of Creation, made in God's Image, and, therefore, God's Vice-regent (Gen. 1:26).

The catastrophe of man's fall brought the catastrophe of curse upon that over which he was given dominion. Sin was an event in the realm of the human spirit, but it has its repercussions in the whole of Creation.

THE APPEARANCE OF DEATH

Death is the epitome of sin's penalty. This was the warning attached to the prohibition of Eden (Gen. 2:17), and it is the direct expression of God's Curse upon man, the sinner (Gen. 3:19).

Death in the phenomenal realm consists in the separation of the integral elements of man's being. This disillusion exemplifies the principle of death, mainly separation, and it comes to its most extreme expression in separation from God. This was actually the type of death of which God spoke and which brings every other type of death, etc. (Gen. 3:23). Because of sin, death is infested with a fear and terror for man (Lk. 12:5; Heb. 2:15).

THE IMPUTATION OF SIN

The first sin of Adam had unique significance for the whole human race (Rom. 5:12, 14-19; I Cor. 15:22). Here, there is sustained emphasis upon the one trespass of the one man as that by which sin, condemnation, and death came upon all mankind.

The sin is identified as *"the transgression of Adam," "the trespass of the one," "one trespass,"* and *"the disobedience of the one."* Consequently, there can be no doubt that the first trespass of Adam is intended.

Hence, the clause, *"Because all men sinned,"* in Romans 5:12, refers to the sin of all in the sin of Adam. It cannot refer to the actual sins of all men, far less to the hereditary depravity with which all are afflicted, for in Romans 5:12, the clause in question clearly says why *"death spread to all men."* In the succeeding Verses, the *"one man's trespass"* (Rom. 5:17) is stated to be the reason for the universal reign of death.

If the same sin were not intended, Paul would be affirming two different things with reference to the same subject in the same context. The only explanation of the two forms of statement is that all sinned in the sin of Adam. The same inference is to be drawn from I Corinthians 15:22, *"In Adam all die."* If all die in Adam, it is because all sin was in Adam.

THE PARTICIPATION OF ALL IN ADAM'S SIN

The diagram is:

1. According to Scripture, the kind of solidarity with Adam, which explains the participation of all in Adam's sin, is the kind of solidarity which Christ sustains to those united to Him.

2. The parallel in Romans 5:12-19; I Cor. 15:22, 45-49, between Adam and Christ, indicates the same type of relationship in both cases. We have no need to suppose anything more ultimate in the case of Adam and the race than we find in the case of Christ and His People. In the latter (Jesus), it is Representative Headship, and this is all that is necessary to ground the solidarity of all in the sin of Adam. To say that the sin of Adam is imputed to all is but to say that all were involved in his sin by reason of his representative headship. This is all that is necessary to ground the solidarity of all in the sin of Adam. To say that the sin of Adam is imputed to all is but to say that all were involved in his sin by reason of his representative headship.

The manner in which man participated in Adam's original sin is the manner in which Adam was created. In essence, due to his ability of procreation, all human beings were in Adam's loins. Consequently, when he brought children into the world, they were afflicted with his malady, as all succeeding births, with the exception of the Birth of Christ, Who was Virgin Born.

It was God's original Intention that man would bring sons and daughters of God into the world (Lk. 3:38; Gen. 5:1). However, due to the Fall, Adam was able only to bring sons and daughters into the world, *"In his own likeness, after his image,"* instead of the Image of God (Gen. 5:3).

As well, the parallel between Adam as the first man, who brought death, and Christ as the Last Adam, Who brought Life, shows that the accomplishment of Salvation in Christ is based on the same operating principle as that by which we have become sinners and the heirs of death. In other words, as in Adam all die, in Christ all can live, that is, upon Faith in Christ.

THE HISTORY OF MANKIND

As a result of Adam's sin and Jesus' Victory over sin and Restoration of Life, mankind is placed in one of two positions — the position of sin, condemnation, and death, or the other position of Righteousness and Justification found only in Christ.

The former arises from man's union with Adam, the latter from man's union with Christ. These are the two orbits within which we live and move. God's Government of men is directed in terms of these relationships. If we do not reckon with Adam, we are, thereby, excluded from a proper understanding of Christ. All who die, die in Adam; all who are made alive are made alive in Christ, and Christ Alone!

THE DEPRAVITY OF MAN

Sin never consists merely in a voluntary act of transgression. Every disobedience to God proceeds from something that is more deep-seated than the sin itself. A sinful act is the expression of a sinful heart (Mk. 7:20-23; Prov. 4:23; 23:7). Sin must always include, therefore, the perversity of the heart, mind, disposition, and will.

This was true, as we have addressed, in the case of the first sin, and it applies to all sin. For the imputation to be to the entirety of the human family, the sin of Adam must, therefore, carry with it involvement in all that sin is and does.

The depravity which sin entails, and with which all men come into the world, is for this reason a direct implication of our solidarity or union with Adam and his sin. We come to be as individuals by natural generation and, as individuals, we never exist apart from the sin of Adam reckoned as ours. Therefore, the Psalmist wrote, *"Behold, I was brought forth in iniquity, and in sin did my mother conceive me"* (Ps. 51:5), and our Lord said, *"That which is born of the flesh is flesh"* (Jn. 3:6).

THE WITNESS OF SCRIPTURE

The witness of Scripture to the totality of this depravity is explicit. Genesis 6:5 and Genesis 8:21 provide a closed case. The latter reference makes it clear that this indictment was not restricted to the period before the Judgment of the Flood. There is no evading the force of this Testimony from the early pages of Divine Revelation, and later assessments are to the same effect (Jer. 17:9-10; Rom. 3:10-18).

From whatever angle man is viewed, there is the absence of that which is well-pleasing to God. Considered more positively, all have turned aside from God's Way and become corrupted. In Romans 8:5-7, Paul refers to the mind of the flesh, and flesh, when used ethically, as here, means human nature directed and governed by sin (Jn. 3:6).

AND WHAT IS THE FLESH?

The flesh is the part of us that is indicative to man, in other words, what man can do regarding his education, motivation, ability, talents, etc. The Holy Spirit through the great Apostle Paul told us in about every way possible that while these things just mentioned are not necessarily sin or wrong, the truth is, due to the Fall (Rom. 8:10), man is left, within himself, incapable of doing what needs to be done to live for God. We must have the Help of the Holy Spirit on a constant basis.

HOW DOES THE HOLY SPIRIT WORK?

The Holy Spirit, Who is God and Who can do anything, works within a set pattern from which He will not deviate. He works entirely within the means and the parameters, so to speak, of the Finished Work of Christ, in other words, what Jesus did at the Cross. The Work that Christ carried out at the Cross was a legal work, meaning that a debt was owed by man to God, which man could not pay, but which God paid for us, in the giving of His Only Son. He satisfied the Righteousness of God by giving Himself as a Sacrifice on the Cross of Calvary. While Jesus Christ, one might say, is the Source of all Blessings, it is the Cross of Christ which provides the Means by which all of these good things are given unto us.

When the Believer places his or her Faith exclusively in the Cross, and maintains it exclusively in the Cross, which shuts out all works, then everything that the Lord has becomes ours. Again I state, *"It is the Cross of Christ which makes it all possible."* When we speak of the Cross, I'm sure the reader understands that we aren't speaking of the wooden beam on which Jesus died, but rather what our Lord there accomplished in the giving of Himself as a Sacrifice, in the shedding of His Life's Blood, which atoned for all sin, past, present, and future, at least for all who will believe (Jn. 3:16).

When the Believer places his or her faith in something other than Christ and the Cross, no matter how good the other thing may be in its own right, this, in the Eyes of God, constitutes spiritual adultery. In other words, by trusting in something other than Christ and the Cross, the Believer is being unfaithful to the Lord. Everything that we need is found in Christ and what He did for us at the Cross.

ANOTHER JESUS, ANOTHER SPIRIT, ANOTHER GOSPEL

When we try to worship the Lord outside of the Cross, or when we try to function outside of the Cross, we are left with *"another Jesus,"* which incorporates *"another spirit,"* which plays out to *"another Gospel,"* which God can never recognize (II Cor. 11:4). Sadly and regrettably, that's where most of the modern church is, worshipping *"another Jesus."* Let me say it again:

The Lord will accept no worship and will function on our behalf not at all outside of the Cross of Christ. It is what Jesus did at the Cross that makes everything possible. The Cross opened the door simply because what Jesus there did addressed the terrible sin problem in totality. Please understand, when the church comes up with means and ways of eliminating sin other than the Cross of Christ, such is the sure road of defeat and destruction. There is no salvation outside of the Cross, no baptism with the Holy Spirit outside of the Cross, no victory outside of the Cross, and no healing outside of the Cross. In fact, there is nothing outside of the Cross. The Cross is the means, as stated, by which all of these wonderful things are given to us by the Grace of God. Fasting is definitely Scriptural and will bless the Believer. However, when the Believer says that he can overcome sin by fasting so many days, if his faith is in such an effort to overcome sin, it is an effort that God can never bless. That's the problem with the modern church. What few people are trying to depend on the Lord have their faith anchored in that which is not correct. Satan doesn't care how much faith we have in whatever, just as long as it's not in Christ and the Cross.

HOSTILITY TO GOD

Anything we do outside of the Cross, which is labeled by the Lord as *"the flesh,"* presents itself as being hostile to God. Paul said:

"Because the carnal mind *is* enmity against God *(once again, this refers to attempting to live for God by means other than the Cross, which places one 'against God')***: for it is not subject to the Law of God, neither indeed can be** *(in its simplest form means that what is being done, whatever it may be, is not in God's Prescribed Order, which is the Cross)***" (Rom. 8:7).**

No stronger condemnatory Judgment could be arrived at, for it means that the thinking of the natural man is conditioned and governed by enmity (hostility) directed against God, whether the individual realizes or not. Nothing less than a Judgment of total depravity is the clear implication of these Passages, i.e., there is no area or aspect of human life which is absorbed from the somber effects of man's fallen condition. Hence, there is no area which might serve as a possible ground for man's justification of himself in the Face of God and His Law.

THE CONSCIENCE

Depravity, however, is not registered in actual transgression to an equal extent in all. In other words, some men are more evil than others, as should be obvious.

There are multiple restraining factors. God does not give over all men to uncleanness, to a base mind, and to improper conduct (Rom. 1:24, 28).

Total depravity (total, that is, in the sense that it touches everything) is not incompatible with the exercise of the natural virtues and the promotion of civil righteousness. This means that there is still some trace of the Image of God left in fallen man. It expresses itself in their *"conscience"* and the *"work of the Law written upon their hearts,"* so that in measure and at points they do, at times, fulfill some of its requirements. In fact, without that, the world would have been destroyed a long time ago (Rom. 2:14).

Actually, this is what threw the Jews. They did keep some points of the Law at some particular times, as all men do, even the most unregenerate. In this keeping of some of the Laws, Israel felt this made her righteous, exactly as most of the world. However, God can only accept perfection (the keeping of all His Laws), to which man cannot hope to attain, except through the Representative Man, the Lord Jesus Christ.

The Doctrine of Depravity, however, means that these works, though formerly in accord with what God commands, are not good and well-pleasing to God in terms of the full and ultimate criteria by which His Judgment is determined.

The criteria of love to God as the animating motive, the Law of God as the directing principle, and the Glory of God as the controlling purpose is that which God demands, and which man cannot hope to attain, at least within himself (Mat. 6:2, 5, 16; Mk. 7:6-7; Rom. 8:7; 13:4; I Cor. 2:14; 10:31; 13:3; Titus 1:15; 3:5; Heb. 11:4, 6).

THE INABILITY OF MAN

Concerning the inability of man, Paul tells us the reason. He said: **"And if Christ be** in you *(He is in you through the Power and Person of the Spirit [Gal. 2:20])*, **the body *is* dead because of sin** *(means that the physical body has been rendered helpless because of the Fall; consequently, the Believer trying to overcome by willpower presents a fruitless task)*; **but the Spirit *is* Life because of Righteousness** *(only the Holy Spirit can make us what we ought to be, which means we cannot do it ourselves; once again, He performs all that He does within the confines of the Finished Work of Christ, which gives Him the legal means to do all that He does)*" **(Rom. 8:10).**

All of this means that inability is concerned with the incapacity arising from the nature of depravity. If depravity is total, affecting every aspect and area of man's being, then inability, pertaining to what is good and well-pleasing to God, is likewise incumbent upon man respecting his own efforts.

We are not able to change our character, at least within ourselves, or act differently from it. In the matter of understanding, the natural man cannot know the things of the Spirit of God because they are spiritually discerned (I Cor. 2:14). In other words, there is nothing in him in his unconverted state that can respond favorably to God, at least on his own.

In respect of obedience to the Law of God, he is not only not subject to the Law of God but, in fact, cannot be, simply because, as stated, it is impossible for him to do so (Rom. 8:7). They who are in the flesh (one's own ability) cannot please God (Rom. 8:8). A corrupt tree cannot bring forth good fruit (Mat. 7:18).

Paul also said concerning the total depravity of man:

"And you *has He* quickened *(made alive)*, **who were dead in trespasses and sins** *(total depravity due to the Fall and original sin)*; **"Wherein in time past you walked according to the course of this world** *(refers to the fact that the unredeemed order their behavior and regulate their lives within this sphere of trespasses and sins)*, **according to the prince of the power of the air** *(pertains to the fact that Satan heads up the system of this world)*, **the spirit that now works in the children of disobedience** *(the spirit of Satan, which fills all unbelievers, thereby working disobedience)*:

"Among whom *(the children of disobedience)* **also we all had our conversation** *(manner of life)* **in times past in the lusts of our flesh** *(evil cravings)*, **fulfilling the desires of the flesh and of the mind** *(the minds of the unredeemed are the laboratory of perverted thoughts, impressions, imaginations, etc.)*; **and were by nature the children of wrath, even as others** *(God's Wrath is unalterably opposed to sin, and the only solution to sin is the Cross of Christ)*" **(Eph. 2:1-3).**

Going back to Verse 1, Paul said that before Conversion, *"We were dead in trespasses and sins."* I remind the reader, *"dead"* is *"dead."* That means we were not just a little bit off course or depraved some of the time, but rather totally and completely all the time, at least until we gave our hearts to the Lord.

The impossibility of man righting himself is here undeniable. It is our Lord Who affirms that even Faith in Him is impossible apart from this Gift and Drawing of the Father (Jn. 6:44, 65).

This witness on God's Part is to the same effect of His Insistence that apart from one's physical birth and Spiritual Birth, the latter of which is of the Holy Spirit, no one can have intelligent appreciation of or entrance into the Kingdom of God (Jn. 1:13; 3:3, 5, 8; I Jn. 2:29; 3:9; 4:7; 5:1, 4, 18).

THE NECESSITY OF REGENERATION

The necessity of so radical and momentous a transformation and re-creation as *"Regeneration"* is proof of the whole witness of Scripture to the bondage of sin and the hopelessness of our sinful condition. In other words, Salvation is all of God and none whatsoever of man. It originates in totality with God. The moment that man attempts to add something or take something from the great Plan of God, it is instantly neutralized.

The bondage that captures man implies that it is a moral and spiritual impossibility for the natural man to receive the things of the Spirit, to love God and to do what is well-pleasing to Him, or to believe in Christ to the Salvation of his soul, without the Aid and Help of the Holy Spirit upon the Word of God, ministered in some capacity to him.

It is this enslavement which is the premise of the Gospel, and the Glory of the Gospel lies precisely in the fact that it provides release from the bondage and slavery of sin, all through the Cross. It is the Gospel of Grace and Power for the helpless, once again, all made possible by the Cross of Christ.

THE TERRIBLE LIABILITY OF SIN

Since sin is against God, He cannot be complacent toward it or indifferent with respect to it. He reacts, as should be obvious, inevitably against it. This reaction is specifically His Wrath. The frequency with which Scripture mentions the Wrath of God compels us to take account of its reality and meaning.

In the Old Testament, these expressions are found in Exodus 4:14; 32:12; Numbers 11:10; 22:22; Deuteronomy 29:23; Joshua 7:1; Job 42:7; Psalms 21:9; Isaiah 10:5; Jeremiah 7:20; Ezekiel 7:19; Hosea 5:10; Nahum 1:6; and Zephaniah 2:2.

In the New Testament, these references, to name a few, are found in John 3:36; Romans 1:18; 2:5, 8; 3:5; 5:9; 9:22; Ephesians 2:3; 5:6; I Thessalonians 1:10; Hebrews 3:11; and Revelation 6:17.

THE REALITY OF THE WRATH OF GOD

The Wrath of God is, therefore, a reality, and the language and teaching of the Scripture are calculated to impress upon us the severity by which it is characterized. There are three observations which particularly require mentioning:

1. The Wrath of God against sin must not be interpreted in terms of the fitful passion so commonly associated with anger in us. God's Wrath is rather the deliberate, resolute displeasure which the contradiction of His Holiness demands.

2. It is not to be construed as vindictiveness but as Holy indignation. Nothing of the nature of malice attaches to it. It is not malignant hatred but rather Righteous detestation.

3. We must not reduce the Wrath of God to His Will to merely punish. Wrath is a positive outgoing of dissatisfaction — as sure as that which is pleasing to God involves complacency. We must not eliminate from God what we term emotion. The Wrath of God finds its parallel in the human heart, exemplified in a perfect manner in Jesus (Mk. 3:5; 10:14).

The epitome of sin's liability is, therefore, the Holy Wrath of God. Since sin is never impersonal but exists in and is committed by persons, the Wrath of God consists in the displeasure to which we are subjected. In other words, we are the objects.

The penal afflictions that we suffer are the expressions of God's Wrath. The sense of guilt and torment of conscience are the reflections of our consciousness of the Displeasure of God. The essence of final perdition will consist in the infliction of God's Indignation, which pertains to eternal Hell, that is, if the sinner does not make peace with God. Such can only be done by accepting Jesus Christ as one's Saviour (Isa. 30:33; 66:24; Dan. 12:2; Mk. 9:43, 45; 47).

THE CONQUEST OF SIN BY JESUS CHRIST

Despite the somberness of the theme of sin, the Bible never completely loses a note of hope and optimism when dealing with sin. The heart of the Bible in its witness to God's Mighty Offensive against sin in His Historical Purpose of Redemption centered in Jesus Christ, the Last Adam, the Second Man, God's Eternal Son, and the Saviour of sinners.

Through the whole Work of Christ, His Miraculous Birth, His Life of Perfect Obedience, supremely His Death on the Cross and Resurrection from the Dead, His Ascension to the Right Hand of the Father, His Reign in history and His Glorious Return, sin has been overcome.

Its rebellious, usurping authority has been vanquished, its absurd claims exposed, its foul machinations unmasked and overthrown, the baleful effects of the Fall in Adam counteracted and undone, and God's Honor vindicated, His Holiness Satisfied, and His Glory extended. Hallelujah! While everything Christ did was of utmost significance, still, it was at the Cross, and the Cross alone, where sin was vanquished, its power broken, its guilt terminated, and its awful eternal results made void.

Paul said, **"Who** *(meaning Christ)* **needs not daily** *(refers to the daily sacrifices offered by the Priests under the old Jewish economy)***, as those High Priests, to offer up sacrifice, first for his own sins, and then for the people's** *(refers to the work of the Jewish High Priest on the Great Day of Atonement, which specified their unworthiness; Christ did not have to function accordingly)*: **for this He did once, when He offered up Himself.** *(This refers to His Death on the Cross, which atoned for all sin — past, present, and future, making no further sacrifices necessary)*" **(Heb. 7:27).**

The great Apostle also said, **"So Christ was once offered to bear the sins of many** *(the Cross was God's Answer to sin and, in fact, the only answer)*; **and unto them who look for Him shall He appear the second time without sin unto Salvation.** *(This refers to the Second Coming. 'Without sin' refers to the fact that the Second Coming will not be to atone for sin, for that was already carried out at the Cross at His First Advent. The Second Coming will bring all the results of Salvation to this world, which refers to all that He did at the Cross. We now only have the 'Firstfruits' [Rom. 8:23])*" **(Heb. 9:28).**

In Christ and the Cross, God has conquered sin. Such are the great glad tidings of the Bible. This conquest is demonstrated in the People of God, who, by Faith in Christ and His Finished Work, are already delivered from the guilt and Judgment of sin, and are already experiencing, to a degree, the conquest of sin's power through our union with Christ. This process will be culminated shortly with the Rapture of the Church. The Saints will then be glorified, with sin banished from God's good Creation, and at the end of the Kingdom Age, a New Heaven and New Earth will be brought into being, in which Righteousness will dwell (Gen. 3:15; Isa. 52:13; 53:12; Jer. 31:31-34; Mat. 1:21; Mk. 2:5; 10:45; Lk. 2:11; Jn. 1:29; 3:16; Acts 2:38; 13:38; I Cor. 15:3, 22; Eph. 1:3-14; 2:1-10; Col. 2:11-15; Heb. 8:1; 10:25; I Pet. 1:18-21; II Pet. 3:11-13; I Jn. 1:6; 2:2; Rev. 20:7-14; 21:22; 22:5).

(The Bibliography on the subject of sin was derived partially from *"The Christian Doctrine of Sin,"* 1877; J. Orr, *"Sin as a Problem of Today"* 1910; F. R. Tenant, *"The Concept of Sin,"* 1912; C. Ryder Smith, *"The Bible Doctrine of Sin,"* 1953; E. Brunner, *"Man in Revolt,"* 1939; R. Niebuhr, *"The Nature and Destiny of Man,"* 1941 and 1943; J. Murray, *"The Imputation of Adam's Sin,"* 1959; G. C. Berkouwer, *"Sin,"* 1971.)

(3) "JESUS ANSWERED, NEITHER HAS THIS MAN SINNED, NOR HIS PARENTS: BUT THAT THE WORKS OF GOD SHOULD BE MADE MANIFEST IN HIM."

The overview is:

1. The phrase, *"Jesus answered, Neither has this man sinned, nor his parents,"* does not mean that our Lord asserts in these words that these people are sinless, but rather severs the supposed link between their conduct and the specific affliction before them.

2. In fact, this man and his parents, as all, were and are sinners!

3. The phrase, *"But that the Works of God should be made manifest in Him,"* simply means that Jesus did not come to the Earth to condemn men for their fallen condition because, in fact, they were already condemned, but that He should set man free by the Power of God.

4. Tragically and sadly, the far greater majority of the church, especially considering its foray into humanistic psychology, basically only points a finger at symptoms. Jesus is telling us that such is not to be the mission of the Church, but rather to preach Deliverance and Healing to the world, irrespective of its condition.

5. The *"Works of God"* are found in the Words of Jesus:

a. *"The Spirit of the Lord is upon Me."*

b. *"Because He has anointed Me to preach the Gospel* (this Good News) *to the poor."*

c. *"He has sent Me to heal the brokenhearted."*

d. *"To preach Deliverance to the captives."*

e. *"And recovering of sight to the blind."*

f. *"To set at liberty them who are bruised."*

g. *"To preach the acceptable Year of the Lord"* (Lk. 4:18-19).

6. In this, the Love, Wisdom, and Power of God are manifested toward man.

7. This, and this alone, is to be the mission of the Church. In this, Jesus said, *"The gates of Hell shall not prevail against it"* (Mat. 16:18).

8. While some few truly do carry out these *"Works of God,"* for the most part, most of the church is engaged in other things, such as political involvement, psychological referrals, seeker sensitive efforts, and the perversion of the Gospel to acquire so-called riches.

(4) "I MUST WORK THE WORKS OF HIM WHO SENT ME, WHILE IT IS DAY: THE NIGHT COMES, WHEN NO MAN CAN WORK."

1. The phrase, *"I must work the Works of Him Who sent Me,"* refers not only to Christ but all Believers as well.

2. Jesus further said, *"Teaching them to observe all things whatsoever I have commanded you: and, lo, I am with you always, even unto the end of the world* (age)*"* (Mat. 28:20).

3. Luke wrote, *"Of all that Jesus began both to do and teach,"* implying its continuance by His Followers for all time (Acts 1:1).

4. These *"Works"* concern that which we have mentioned and incorporate every single Believer in one way or the other.

5. God calls some few to preach and teach His Word, while He calls others to support them financially and prayerfully. As Paul outlined in Romans 10:14-15, both are equally important.

6. The phrase, *"The night comes, when no man can work,"* refers to the end of this life's span for every Believer, ever how long that may be. The *"night"* speaks of death.

NOTES

7. Irrespective, it is the responsibility of every Believer to find his place in Christ respecting the task assigned to him, whatever it may be, with it being faithfully discharged. Regrettably, most Believers tend to think that living for God and serving Him consists of showing up on Sunday morning for an hour or so! Nothing could be further from the truth.

8. All are to do our part, and nothing is menial or insignificant in the Eyes of the Lord, Whose Eyes alone really matter.

(5) "AS LONG AS I AM IN THE WORLD, I AM THE LIGHT OF THE WORLD."

The exposition is:

1. The phrase, *"As long as I am in the world,"* referred to His Precise Work to do on Earth. Every particular of it was arranged for Him, with each action having its precise time and place, and all limited to a determined number of years, referring to His Ministry, which was about three and one-half years.

2. *"I am the Light of the world,"* proclaims Jesus as sublimely conscious of His Power to do for the moral world what the sun was doing for the physical world. He was the Occasion of its life, the Condition of its activity, the Means of its instruction, and the Source of its beauty, its joy, and its progress.

3. The fact that He is the Light leads Him to remind the Disciples that He is the True Source of Spiritual Eyesight as well as the condition of Spiritual Vision.

4. As well, these *"conditions of Spiritual Vision"* refer to the preaching of the Gospel of Jesus Christ under the Anointing of the Holy Spirit, which alone can penetrate spiritual darkness.

(6) "WHEN HE HAD THUS SPOKEN, HE SPAT ON THE GROUND, AND MADE CLAY OF THE SPITTLE, AND HE ANOINTED THE EYES OF THE BLIND MAN WITH THE CLAY."

The structure is:

1. The man who is not in Christ is still in his sins. There is no middle ground.

2. Mackintosh said:

"If there is a single hair's breadth between you and Christ, you are in an actual state of wrath and condemnation."

3. *"But, on the other hand, if you are in Him, then are you 'as He is' before God, and so accounted in the presence of Infinite Holiness. Such is the plain teaching of the Word of God."*[2]

JESUS AS THE LIGHT OF THE WORLD

The phrase, *"When He had thus spoken,"* presents Him, as stated, using the occasion of the man's physical blindness to portray Himself as the Light of the world. As we have mentioned previously, everything Jesus did was meant not only to meet the need of the individual(s) involved but, as well, on a far broader basis, to serve as an example or symbol of a much broader lesson.

LOWLY CLAY

"He spat on the ground, and made clay of the spittle," is meant to express to the eyes of men, morally blind, Christ in a Body of lowly clay, animated by Divine Breath. The clay symbolized His Humanity and the moisture of His Lips, the Life that animated it. In other words, this clay made of His Spittle was meant to portray His Incarnation, i.e., *"God becoming Man."*

THE ANOINTING

"And He anointed the eyes of the blind man with the clay," was meant to serve as a symbol of the Human Body of Christ serving as the Perfect Sacrifice for sin.

However, as we shall see, this Perfect Body, as symbolized by the *"clay,"* within itself could not effect Healing. As the clay did not bring sight to the blind man, the Miracles of Christ, and even His Virgin Birth and His Perfect Life, could not bring Spiritual Sight to the morally blind, although these Attributes of Christ were necessary and served their purpose respecting certain aspects of the Believer's Victory. It took the Cross of Christ to change man, in other words, to make the spiritually blind capable of seeing.

Just as the man saw nothing after the clay had been put upon his eyes, so men are blind to the Person and Work of Christ though He places Himself right before their very eyes.

NOTES

Their eyes become the more completely closed, as was the case with this man. Although the Hand that put the clay upon his eyes was there, he could not see it. Still, it is upon this action and presentation that the Holy Spirit operates. He makes Christ known as the Sent One from the Father, He Himself having been sent from both the Father and the Son.

(7) "AND SAID UNTO HIM, GO, WASH IN THE POOL OF SILOAM, (WHICH IS BY INTERPRETATION, SENT.) HE WENT HIS WAY THEREFORE, AND WASHED, AND CAME SEEING."

The construction is:

1. There is no such thing as a partial Justification. One is either justified totally and completely or not at all.

2. All of this means that all stand in one acceptance, in one Salvation, in one life, and in one Righteousness. As stated, there are no degrees in Justification.

3. The person who has just come to Christ, in other words, a babe in Christ, stands in the same Justification as the Saint of 50 years or more.

THE SHED BLOOD OF THE LORD JESUS CHRIST

The phrase, *"And said unto him, Go, wash in the pool of Siloam,"* is meant to symbolize the Shed Blood of Jesus Christ, which cleanses from all sin.

The *"clay,"* as stated, represented His Perfect Human Body, but until that Perfect Body was offered in Sacrifice to God, thereby, paying the price for man's sin, it was not possible for one to be saved. Man's lost condition could not be rectified by the Miracles of Christ or even the great Teaching and Preaching of Christ. As well, His Sinless Life, within itself, could not break sin's grip and Satan's hold. Only when He shed His Life's Blood could such a transformation become possible.

In fact, before the Cross, individuals were Saved by looking forward to that coming event as we are now Saved by looking backward to that completed event.

Even though this pool of Siloam was only a symbol, still, it portrayed the great lesson here taught beautifully and wondrously!

HE WASHED AND CAME SEEING

"Which is by interpretation, Sent," refers to the meaning of the word *"Siloam"* and, as well, refers to Jesus being sent from God for the Salvation of the world.

"He went his way therefore, and washed, and came seeing," refers to His Miracle Healing and, as well, to the Salvation of all who are washed in the Precious Shed Blood of the Lord Jesus Christ. Only then did he *"see"* as only then (after accepting Christ) can the washed and cleansed sinner now *"see."*

Going back to the literal Miracle, I wonder what was the reaction of this man who had been born blind and, all of a sudden, could now see. Being born in this condition, he had no reference as to how anything looked. He could have had a flower explained to him all day long, but without seeing such, there was no way he could properly understand what was being said. Such would be the case for all things.

However, the instant his eyes were opened, that must have been a moment that words could not even begin to express. One can well imagine him drinking in the sight of all that which he had touched all his life but had never seen!

THE LOST SOUL COMING TO CHRIST

How so much this epitomizes the lost soul, spiritually blind, but, all of a sudden, gloriously given Spiritual Sight by Jesus Christ. Instantly, because of the Miracle wonder of Redemption wrought by the Holy Spirit, the New Creation, made so by Jesus Christ, can *"see"* God and understand His Word.

How so much the illustration of the healing of this man born blind shoots down the moralist, who has accepted the philosophy of Christianity while rejecting Christ and the Cross. By these, Jesus is accepted as a *"Good Man,"* or even a *"Miracle-Worker,"* but not the Son of God, Who gave His Life at Calvary's Cross. They cannot conceive that man is so bad that it took this for man to be Saved. They imagine themselves to be made righteous by their own machinations of their flawed morality; however, it is that which God cannot accept! Without Christ and what He did at Calvary and the Resurrection, there is no Salvation!

> *"At the Cross, at the Cross,*
> *"Where I first saw the Light,*
> *"And the burden of my heart rolled away,*
> *"It was there by Faith, I received my sight,*
> *"And now I am happy all the day!"*

(8) "THE NEIGHBOURS THEREFORE, AND THEY WHICH BEFORE HAD SEEN HIM WHO WAS BLIND, SAID, IS NOT THIS HE WHO SAT AND BEGGED?"

The synopsis is:

1. While there may be various degrees in the knowledge of the fullness and extent of Justification, and even various degrees in the ability to exhibit its power upon the heart and life, still, we must never confuse that knowledge with the degree of Justification.

2. Let us say it again: there are no degrees in Justification. Everyone truly justified is 100 percent truly justified.

3. This is what makes the gospel of *"works"* so deadly. One's Justification is judged by the amount of works or the validity of works. While Justification will bring about good works, good works will never bring about Justification. Justification comes solely by Faith in Christ and what Christ has done for us at the Cross.

THE MIRACULOUS CHANGE

The phrase, *"The neighbours therefore, and they which before had seen him who was blind, said,"* proclaims those who had known him and now see a miraculous change.

When one is blind, especially having been born in this condition, it causes particular contortions on the face and countenance. As well, when this situation is changed instantly, as happened to this man, the appearance of the person will be dramatically changed. Incidentally, this had never happened in history and probably hasn't happened since, unless Jesus had healed others of which there is no record, which could well be the case. So, the neighbors were not certain if this was the same man, and yet, they thought it was.

IS THIS NOT THE BEGGAR?

The question, *"Is not this he who sat and begged?"* presents the status to which he had been reduced but from which he had been lifted by none other than the Christ of Glory.

As I have already mentioned, it would literally be impossible for anyone to fully understand what happened to this man. As I dictate these words, my mind goes not so much to the moment in question, but to the years that followed, even after Jesus had ascended back to Glory. Of course, we have no way of knowing what turn his life took. However, I can well imagine that countless times, he told his story as to exactly what Jesus did for him.

He would have related it in detail, savoring each moment, and especially the moment that his eyes miraculously opened. I can see him as he would try to explain that moment and then be unable to proceed further, with his voice choking and his eyes filled with tears. He was unique among humans, the only one in history, at least that is recorded, who had been born blind but had been miraculously and instantly healed by the Son of the Living God. This I do know, in the ages to come, I want to personally ask him to relate his story one more time, which I am certain he will be glad to do!

This one thing is sure, he is no longer a *"beggar,"* but rather with the One Who touched him on that glad day so many years ago and, consequently, changed his life forever.

(9) "SOME SAID, THIS IS HE: OTHERS SAID, HE IS LIKE HIM: BUT HE SAID, I AM HE."

The composition is:

1. The phrase, *"Some said, This is he: others said, He is like him,"* presents them seemingly conversing among themselves as to the man's true identity.

2. No doubt, they had seen him countless times sitting in a particular place begging alms, and now were quite taken aback at his change of appearance, as well as change of attitude and spirit. However, the greatest change was yet to come, for in a matter of hours, he would make Jesus His Lord and Saviour!

3. *"But he said, I am he,"* immediately tells us something about this man that seems to make him somewhat different than many others. There is a courage and a strength that now comes to the fore, which had been locked away because of the horrible darkness in which he lived.

4. How many others are like that?

Because of this terrible disability, he was reduced to the lowest possible station in life. Consequently, that which was golden was covered by the darkness!

Isn't that the same with all men, spiritually speaking?

5. At this moment, millions toil and live on an endless treadmill, with only a tiny part of their potential actually realized. If they could only know Jesus, blatant potential could be unleashed with startling and beautiful things happening. However, it is only in Christ!

6. The record will show that this man, formerly blind, wanted everyone to know who he was, and above all, who had performed this great Miracle for him.

(10) "THEREFORE SAID THEY UNTO HIM, HOW WERE YOUR EYES OPENED?"

The pattern is:

1. The phrase, *"Therefore said they unto him,"* was in response to his unequivocal admittance as to who he was.

2. The question, *"How were your eyes opened?"* is the logical thing to ask, especially considering that they probably knew that he had been born in this condition. Consequently, the Miracle was of such outstanding proportions as to beggar description! As stated, there had never been anything in history which approximated this happening.

3. Medical science could not do this thing then or now! Even more importantly, what was said physically can, as well, be said spiritually, which Jesus meant to symbolize by this Miracle.

4. Does the reader fully understand that every single thing that is truly good which has been brought about in a person's life has been brought about by Jesus Christ? Every drunkard truly made sober, every harlot truly made holy, every bondage truly broken,

and every life truly changed has been done so by Jesus Christ and Jesus Alone. This means that all the other luminaries, fake, incidentally, such as Muhammad, Joseph Smith, Confucius, etc., have never changed one heart or life for the better, but only for the worse.

5. Jesus Christ stands Alone because He Alone is God!

(11) "HE ANSWERED AND SAID, A MAN WHO IS CALLED JESUS MADE CLAY, AND ANOINTED MY EYES, AND SAID UNTO ME, GO TO THE POOL OF SILOAM, AND WASH: AND I WENT AND WASHED, AND I RECEIVED SIGHT."

The order is:

1. The phrase, *"He answered and said,"* presents the first time he would give his Testimony, no doubt, followed by hundreds or even thousands of times.

2. *"A Man Who is called Jesus made clay, and anointed my eyes, and said unto me, Go to the pool of Siloam, and wash,"* proclaims this former blind man repeating almost exactly what Jesus had told him to do. No wonder!

3. As well, he in no way blanched in the slightest regarding Who had wrought this great Miracle. However, at the moment, he seemed to know very little as to Who Jesus actually was, but one can tell from the way he pronounced His Name, that he did so with reverence and awe!

4. Reynolds said, *"He began, where all Disciples must, with the Man, i.e., 'A Man called Jesus.'"*[3]

5. What he was saying was all he could say. The Miracle was unexplainable apart from Jesus. Clay does not heal blindness, and neither does the water of Siloam. So, there must be a higher, a loftier, and a much grander explanation, and so it was!

6. *"And I went and washed, and I received sight,"* should have been translated, according to Meyer, *"And I looked up."*[4]

7. The idea seems to be that he knelt by the edge of the pool of Siloam and washed the clay from his eyes. He then turned those sightless orbs toward the heavens, and all of a sudden, it happened. The first thing he saw was the sky, which, within itself, told him that this Great Gift had come from above (James 1:17), for Jesus came from Heaven. Then, the color and sight of all his surroundings seemed to fill his two eyes, which, in effect, were two Miracles.

8. Once again, please allow me to exclaim as to what his joy must have been at that moment. There is no way that words could even begin to express this rapture.

"Oh, the joy of sins forgiv'n,
"Oh, the bliss the Blood-washed know,
"Oh, the Peace akin to Heav'n,
"Where the Healing Waters flow."

(12) "THEN SAID THEY UNTO HIM, WHERE IS HE? HE SAID, I KNOW NOT."

The form is:

1. The question, *"Then said they unto him, Where is He?"* seems to be asked with some sarcasm.

2. If, in fact, it was, one must wonder at such an attitude in the face of one of the greatest Miracles the world has ever known. But yet, the heart of man is so desperately wicked that there is absolutely no limit to his depravity.

3. The phrase, *"He said, I know not,"* seems to be said with the thought in mind that even though he did not then know, he was determined to find out, and rightly so!

(13) "THEY BROUGHT TO THE PHARISEES HIM WHO AFORETIME WAS BLIND."

The diagram is:

1. Why did these people, whomever they were, bring this man to the Pharisees?

2. The Pharisees were the generally accredited religious guides of the people.

3. It is said that in Jerusalem, there existed two minor councils or synagogue courts, of 23 assessors each, corresponding with similar courts in other Jewish cities. These two courts stood in relation to the Sanhedrin, and they possessed the authority or power to excommunicate those whom they so desired from the synagogues in Israel. Even though, in taking the former blind man to the Pharisees, the people may not have had these courts in mind, every evidence is that one of these courts ultimately became involved.

4. At this time, this beggar, occupying the very lowest station of life, would have

probably had little knowledge of the terrible animosity against Jesus held by the Pharisees and ruling hierarchy of Israel. When he was asked how his eyes were opened, and he said, *"A Man Who is called Jesus made clay . . ."* it implies that he was not so very well acquainted with Jesus, if at all! So, allowing himself to be taken to the Pharisees was in no way meant to cause problems for Jesus, but was rather done, it seems, out of ignorance of the situation.

(14) "AND IT WAS THE SABBATH DAY WHEN JESUS MADE THE CLAY, AND OPENED HIS EYES."

The overview is:

1. In the gospel of *"works,"* one's Justification is judged by the amount of works or the validity of works.

2. As stated, while good works will always follow proper Justification, good works will never cause Justification.

3. The church, at times, seems to believe in two Justifications — one for the sinner and one for the Saint. While many accept the sinner coming to Christ being Saved instantly and, thereby, instantly justified, when it comes to the Saint, far too often, the church attempts to mix works with Faith, which God can never accept.

THE SABBATH DAY

Whether this Miracle and the confrontation happened on the same day, which was a *"Sabbath,"* is not clear. It is not actually known if these courts sat on the Sabbath or not! It is quite possible that this confrontation with the Pharisees took place the day after the Sabbath. Irrespective, there was very little lapse of time between the Miracle and that which followed.

The idea, as expressed in this Fourteenth Verse, is that the Pharisees were claiming that Jesus broke the Sabbath when He *"made clay, and opened his eyes, and sent the man to the pool of Siloam in order to be healed."*

The myriad of man-made laws, which had been added to the Law of Moses by the Pharisees and Scribes over the last 200 or 300 years, were basically ignored by Jesus, which constantly caused the religious leaders to accuse Him. For instance, one law stated that while wine could, by way of remedy, be applied to the eyelid on the ground that it might be treated as washing, it was sinful to apply it to the inside of the eye.

As well, another man-made law stated that it was positively forbidden to apply saliva to the eyelid because this would be the application of a remedy. Actually, all medicinal appliances, unless in cases of danger to life or limb, were likewise forbidden to be used on the Sabbath. In fact, there were a little over 600 of these types of man-devised laws added to the Law of Moses. As stated, Jesus ignored these things as though they did not exist.

THESE HYPOCRITES

As far as these hypocrites were concerned, nothing good was to be done on the Sabbath, except for material gain. For instance, one could take an animal out of a ditch which had fallen therein but could not save a man from death, Hell, and the grave. Such utter senselessness in religion exists even to this day in many respects! Is it any wonder that sensible men reject outward forms, rituals, and teachings that have no practical and beneficial value at all!

The great sin of modern religious denominations is the making of laws, rules, and regulations, which have no validity in Scripture, or else, are diametrically opposed to Scripture. As the sin of the ancient Pharisees, so the sin of their modern counterparts!

When men deviate from the Word of God, which alone must be the Standard of Righteousness, then they fall to the far lower level of religion. This makes their brand of *"Christianity"* little different than Buddhism, Hinduism, etc., at least respecting faithfulness to the Word.

In looking at the history of religious denominations, one will find that many of them began right and were correspondingly blessed by the Lord. However, little by little, it seems that man's ways more and more intruded, with God's Ways, i.e., His Word, less and less heeded! At this stage, denominational heads refer to their constitution and bylaws instead of the Bible. The downward slide then accelerates, which destroys these organizations spiritually, even though they may remain viable in an economic and religious sense. However, as Israel of old, they are no longer viable with God.

(15) "THEN AGAIN THE PHARISEES ALSO ASKED HIM HOW HE HAD RECEIVED HIS SIGHT. HE SAID UNTO THEM, HE PUT CLAY UPON MY EYES, AND I WASHED, AND DO SEE."

The overview is:

1. For anyone to present any type of works before God as an Atonement for sin insults Christ to the highest degree.

2. Such action actually says that what Christ did at the Cross was not enough, and so we have to add something to that Work that is supposed to be finished.

3. We should, as well, understand that there is no such thing as progress in Justification. The Believer is fully justified or not justified at all. As well, he is no more justified today than he was yesterday, etc.

THE PHARISEES

The phrase, *"Then again the Pharisees also asked him how he had received his sight,"* begins the interrogation. As is glaringly obvious, they had no regard or concern whatsoever that this man had experienced one of the greatest Miracles ever recorded in human history. They were concerned only about their petty rules and regulations. However, it was more than that!

They strongly resented the Anointing of the Holy Spirit upon Jesus, which they did not have, but which they were forced to recognize, even though they claimed it was of Satan! As well, they were extremely jealous of the tremendous crowds that flocked to His Side and the fact that He had the ear of the people. Religion cannot stand such a thing, looking at all such activity, even from the Son of God, as a threat. So, they were attempting to find infractions to the Law with which they could charge Him, hence, this nit-picking.

Let it be clearly understood that all religion, even that which is ensconced in Christianity, has no regard whatsoever for the Work of God but only in protecting its own interest, whatever they surmise that may be. Let me give you an example:

NOTES

A PERSONAL EXPERIENCE

In the summer of 1995, I was invited by the Pastor of a large Pentecostal Church in Pachuca, Mexico, to come to that city for an area-wide Crusade. Actually, this brother's Church is the headquarters of the largest Pentecostal organization in the Country of Mexico. They flew to Laredo, Texas, where we were in a meeting, to extend this invitation.

I had not previously known these brethren, and told them that I would make it a matter of prayer, which I did!

In turn, they invited Donnie down for a series of meetings, which were conducted in the first part of December of that year. Donnie had tremendous meetings, with quite a number of people being Saved. In turn, they extended another invitation to us, which we felt led of the Lord to accept. The dates were set for the summer of 1996. It was to be conducted in a new bullring just built in that city of approximately 1 million population.

The meeting was an outstanding success, with the crowds beginning at about 4,000 and closing on the last night with about 8,000. Well over a thousand people each night responded to the Altar Calls. Of course, how many of those people actually gave their hearts to the Lord, only the Lord could ascertain. However, there were powerful Moves of the Holy Spirit, which resulted in sweeping Conviction over the congregation each night with a tremendous response.

Immediately before the meeting began, the general superintendant of the Assemblies of God in Mexico wrote the general superintendent of the organization in question, strongly urging him to cancel the Crusade, and warning him that the news media would be very derogatory because of me personally, along with other charges, etc.

WHY?

It should be understood that the Assemblies of God had nothing to do with this meeting and actually had only one small church in that city, if my information is correct. Thankfully, these admonitions were ignored, and the meeting went ahead as planned, with many people being Saved, as stated!

However, the question must be asked as to why the Assemblies of God would go to all of this trouble, trying to stop the meeting, when it did not involve them whatsoever, and neither did it pertain to their preachers or churches in any manner. In fact, had they been successful, the thousands of people who responded to the Altar Calls, with many of them being Saved, simply would not have had the opportunity. In other words, people who are now Saved by the Precious Blood of Jesus Christ would not now be Saved, and if continuing in that condition, would be lost forever. Why would they try to stop such a meeting? Was I preaching some strange doctrine? The answer is, *"No!"* Neither did they claim that I was preaching a false doctrine. Was I attacking them in any way? The answer again is, *"No!"*

The only answer that can be given falls into the same category as the Pharisees at the Time of Christ.

Why did the Pharisees oppose Christ? The principle is the same, with the reason being the same in all similar cases, whether then or now. As the Lord was no longer the Head of the Church at the time of Christ, at least that which came under the auspices of organized religion, neither is He the Head in many, if not all, modern religious denominations. Many take umbrage at my statement, but it is true! Any Move of God, as in the time of Christ, is a threat to religion. Consequently, they deal with that threat by opposing it in every way, while all the time claiming to be of God, exactly as Israel of old.

THE WICKEDNESS OF RELIGION

It is a very subtle thing! Before Jesus exposed Pharisaism for what it really was, most of the people in Israel thought of these religious leaders as godly people. After all, they had impeccable reputations over Israel, and were, as stated, the spiritual guides of the people.

As well, many think of modern religious denominations in the same manner because of certain religious practices carried out. However, even though most modern Christians do not have enough spiritual discernment or enough knowledge of the Word of God to properly evaluate these situations, even as Israel of so long ago, still, in no way does that change the wickedness of religion.

Incidentally, religion is that which is totally devised by man, which claims to reach God or to better oneself in some way. It is not of God and, in fact, cannot be of God. It is impossible to oppose the true Work of God and, at the same time, be of God. The truth is, the Word of God has no place in such people, whether then or now (Jn. 8:37). So, the words of Jesus are apropos now as then, *"He who is of God hears God's Words: you therefore hear them not, because you are not of God"* (Jn. 8:47).

"He said unto them, He put clay upon my eyes, and I washed, and do see," is the answer given, with this man beginning to suspect that some charge was being trumped up against Jesus. Therefore, he shrewdly omitted the *"saliva,"* the *"making"* of the clay, and what Jesus told him to do, as well as the place where he had been sent to wash. These were the things the Pharisees claimed were the breaking of the Law of Moses.

(16) "THEREFORE SAID SOME OF THE PHARISEES, THIS MAN IS NOT OF GOD, BECAUSE HE KEEPS NOT THE SABBATH DAY. OTHERS SAID, HOW CAN A MAN WHO IS A SINNER DO SUCH MIRACLES? AND THERE WAS A DIVISION AMONG THEM."

The diagram is:

1. Any soul who is *"in Christ Jesus"* is as completely justified as if he were before the Throne.

2. Such a person is *"complete in Christ,"* in fact, he is *"as Christ"* (Col. 2:10).

3. While there may be, and certainly should be, progress in the knowledge of Justification, there can be no progress in Justification in self. As stated, there is no such thing as a partial Justification. One is either totally justified or not justified at all.

PETTY RULES WHICH HAVE NO SCRIPTURAL FOUNDATION

The phrase, *"Therefore said some of the*

Pharisees, This Man is not of God, because He keeps not the Sabbath Day," as it is given in the Greek, is especially contemptuous. The words, *"This Man,"* in the Greek are thrown emphatically to the end of the sentence, which greatly insults Christ.

The True Word of God is the Salvation of souls, the changing of lives, the breaking of satanic bondages, the Healing of sick bodies, and Believers being baptized with the Holy Spirit. However, the Work of God to these Pharisees was the keeping of petty rules which had no Scriptural basis or foundation.

This does not pertain to the major religions of the world, which have never had any knowledge of God. It pertains to those who have once known God, even as the Pharisees of old, but have gradually inserted their own man-devised rulings into the Word of God, with it gradually being shoved aside altogether. That is the manner of apostasy and pretty well characterizes the modern-day church. It is very subtle in its approach; consequently, it deceives many!

The question, *"Others said, How can a man who is a sinner do such Miracles?"* presents a dilemma for the Pharisees.

The truth is, a *"sinner"* could not do such Miracles! Jesus told us how the true and false could be judged. He said:

"Beware of false prophets (or false teachers, false religious leaders, etc.), *which come to you in sheep's clothing, but inwardly they are ravening wolves."*

He then said, *"You shall know them by their fruits"* (Mat. 7:15-16).

WHAT WAS THE FRUIT OF THE MINISTRY OF JESUS?

It was exactly what we've already said, souls being Saved, lives being changed, Miracles being performed, and the Word of God being given to the people.

What was the fruit of the Pharisees?

It was none of the above! Their *"fruit"* was making more and more petty rules and opposing the true Work of God.

The modern Believer should take Jesus' Words to heart. What kind of fruit does a ministry or church have?

Unfortunately, many Believers believe whatever they are told. They never really check the fruit or question ridiculous claims. A short time back, I overheard a so-called television personality, whose name would be recognized by all, say, *"Tens of millions of people have been saved through this Ministry!"* speaking of his Ministry. It was not a slip of the tongue; it was a contrived statement. He then went on to say that they were going to see a *"hundred million Saved"* respecting some program they were launching.

Tens of millions of people represent large numbers, as should be obvious.

The truth is that very few people have truly been won to the Lord by this alleged ministry, which, in effect, is no ministry at all, at least if the Word of God is to be the criterion. Sadly, most modern Believers are very poor fruit inspectors.

The phrase, *"And there was a division among them,"* proclaims that which always occurs.

Every Believer must make a decision as to whether they are going to follow the Bible, i.e., Christ, or follow man. To be sure, it will not be easy to follow the Lord inasmuch as opposition will arise, and, as well, it will never be popular. To follow Jesus in His day meant to be excommunicated from the synagogue, while to follow Christ presently will mean to be excommunicated from many so-called churches!

(17) "THEY SAY UNTO THE BLIND MAN AGAIN, WHAT DO YOU SAY OF HIM, WHO HAS OPENED YOUR EYES? HE SAID, HE IS A PROPHET."

The overview is:

1. The question, *"They say unto the blind man again, What do you say of Him, Who has opened your eyes?"* portrays in its spirit the idea, as presented by the Pharisees, that this Miracle may have been performed by Jesus through the agency of demon spirits. They could not deny the veracity of the Miracle because it was obvious to all. So, now they must try to discredit its obvious statement.

2. It is remarkable at the lengths to which unbelieving man will go to resist the Lord, especially unbelieving religious man! The evidence of the truth as to Who Christ

actually was is overwhelming and is no less today. But yet, most deny Christ in one way or the other, even those who call themselves *"Christians!"*

3. The phrase, *"He said, He is a Prophet,"* proclaims something about this man which must inculcate itself in all who would name the Name of Christ.

4. Not having seen Jesus as of yet, only having obeyed Him, which resulted in his great Miracle, he had but scant knowledge of Christ. However, what knowledge he had was undeniable. He called Jesus a *"Prophet"* because that was the highest title he could now apply. As well, and yet extremely important, he did not really care what the Pharisees thought, whose antagonism toward Jesus was now very obvious.

5. He knew their religious authority and to get crossways of them, especially in regard to Jesus, was dangerous indeed! However, he had just experienced one of the greatest Miracles in history. As such, he was not about to curry favor with anyone opposed to Jesus, irrespective of the results. This is the attitude and spirit which must incorporate itself in all who come to Christ.

6. It does not matter what others think, what the world says, or even what religious authorities think. Christ must be confessed before all (Mat. 10:32)!

(18) "BUT THE JEWS DID NOT BELIEVE CONCERNING HIM, THAT HE HAD BEEN BLIND, AND RECEIVED HIS SIGHT, UNTIL THEY CALLED THE PARENTS OF HIM WHO HAD RECEIVED HIS SIGHT."

The exegesis is:

1. We should understand that the manner in which we look at Justification is the manner in which we look at Christ.

2. He either paid it all, or He didn't!

3. The Cross was either enough, or it wasn't! In fact, as one views the Cross, one will view Justification.

UNBELIEF

The phrase, *"But the Jews did not believe concerning him, that he had been blind, and received his sight,"* presents the Pharisees doing what all must ultimately do upon denying Christ. They now denied what had been done, claiming they needed more proof.

The world is filled with skeptics claiming that God does not perform Miracles, or that such may have happened long in the past but no longer occurs presently. However, as the Pharisees of old, only blind prejudice takes such a view. Regrettably, this view of doubt and unbelief is more ensconced in the church than anywhere else!

Many religious denominations spend far more time proclaiming what they claim God will not do, rather than what He will do! They specialize in doubt and unbelief.

In fact, many religious denominations do not believe that Jesus presently answers prayer, reveals Himself to His People, heals the sick, or performs Miracles. They do not believe that Jesus baptizes with the Holy Spirit with the evidence of speaking with other Tongues, and neither do they believe in the Gifts of the Spirit, claiming they passed away with the Apostles. Many, if not most, do not even believe the Bible is the Word of God, claiming that much of it is myth and fable! To attend those churches, whatever the name on the door may be, is tantamount to consigning one's soul to Satan himself. Jesus said of this crowd then and now, *"Woe unto you, Scribes and Pharisees, hypocrites! for you compass sea and land to make one proselyte, and when he is made, you make him twofold more the child of Hell than yourselves"* (Mat. 23:15).

Consequently, it is extremely important where the individual attends church, as should be obvious.

SPIRITUAL LEADERSHIP!

It is almost impossible, as should be obvious, for one to rise above one's spiritual leadership. The characteristic of what is taught behind the pulpit always manifests itself in those who sit in the pew. So, it is much better to gather with a group of people who truly love the Lord, even though despised by the world, than to associate oneself with the fashionable, popular churches, which have the plaudits of the world.

The phrase, *"Until they called the parents of him who had received his sight,"* presents something totally ridiculous in that they would not accept a Miracle that Jesus had performed, or even the word of the former blind man, as to identity. In their self-righteousness, they must verify these claims; consequently, they called his parents.

This is the same spirit, which characterizes many in the modern church, who will not accept true Bible Repentance, but must levy several years of punishment as well! When people leave the Word of God, the only place left to go is the absurd!

(19) "AND THEY ASKED THEM, SAYING, IS THIS YOUR SON, WHO YOU SAY WAS BORN BLIND? HOW THEN DOES HE NOW SEE?"

The exegesis is:

1. The question, "*And they asked them, saying, Is this your son, who you say was born blind?*" implies that they somewhat even doubted the Testimony of the parents.

2. The further question, "*How then does he now see?*" suggests their skepticism. However, the evidence is literally undeniable.

3. Even though the man's countenance was totally changed by this Miracle, which would alter his appearance somewhat, still, he was known of too many people for anyone to suspect a hoax, as should be overly obvious.

4. To be sure, these Pharisees knew beyond a shadow of a doubt that this Miracle had transpired and that Jesus was the One Who had done this great thing. So, it was not really proof for what they were looking. They were trying to find someway to discredit this Miracle and would use any means to do so. Such is religion!

(20) "HIS PARENTS ANSWERED THEM AND SAID, WE KNOW THAT THIS IS OUR SON, AND THAT HE WAS BORN BLIND."

The overview is:

1. The parents verified the fact of this man being their son, and they also verified the fact that he was "*born blind,*" which proclaimed this as one of the greatest Miracles ever.

2. Of course, any Miracle performed by Christ is great. Still, due to the great amount of information given, especially concerning the opposition by the Pharisees,

NOTES

we learn from this how the apostate church will always oppose that which is truly of God.

3. Along with the man being a type of the sinner born in spiritual blindness, this other picture presents itself as well. The greatest hindrance to the Word of God on Earth is that which purports to be of God but really is not. We have a perfect example of this in this scenario outlined by the Holy Spirit through John the Beloved.

(21) "BUT BY WHAT MEANS HE NOW SEES, WE KNOW NOT; OR WHO HAS OPENED HIS EYES, WE KNOW NOT: HE IS OF AGE; ASK HIM: HE SHALL SPEAK FOR HIMSELF."

The exegesis is:

1. The phrase, "*But by what means he now sees, we know not,*" is true in that they only knew what their son had told them. He had stumbled forth as usual on the morning of that Sabbath and had returned home in transports of joy, no doubt, relating in full flower what had happened to him. However, due to his Miracle taking place a short time after Jesus had spoken to him, he really had not personally seen Jesus. It seems, as well, that he had little knowledge of Who Christ actually was. So, about all he could tell his parents was what Jesus had told him to do and how it had resulted in this great Miracle.

2. "*Or who has opened his eyes, we know not,*" does not quite present all the truth. Surely they knew it was Jesus, but experiencing the obvious animosity of these Jews against Jesus, they would not confess Christ.

3. They represent the majority of those in the modern church who will not stand up for that which is of God because they fear the heavy hand of religious authorities. If the party line is not followed in totality, they could well be put out of their church, as many have!

4. It is my belief that we are now entering into the age of apostasy and that organized religion, of whatever stripe, is going to become more and more antagonistic toward the True Gospel of Jesus Christ while, all the time, trumpeting their claim to Righteousness. Religion is a sick business, which finds its perfect example in these Pharisees and religious leaders of

Israel, who would ultimately kill the Lord in the Name of the Lord!

5. *"He is of age; ask him: he shall speak for himself,"* actually presents them distancing themselves from the Miracle and, in a sense, from their own son.

(22) "THESE WORDS SPOKE HIS PARENTS, BECAUSE THEY FEARED THE JEWS: FOR THE JEWS HAD AGREED ALREADY, THAT IF ANY MAN DID CONFESS THAT HE WAS CHRIST, HE SHOULD BE PUT OUT OF THE SYNAGOGUE."

The exposition is:

1. Everything is based upon the Divine Protection of the Work of Christ on the Cross.

2. It was never a question of what the worshipper was. That was understood. It was always what the Sacrifice was.

3. That's what makes Faith so important. Christ has done it, and we cannot do it. However, our Faith in Him grants us all that He has done.

MAN FEAR

The phrase, *"These words spoke his parents, because they feared the Jews,"* proclaims the man fear which Jesus had earlier addressed, *"And fear not them which kill the body, but are not able to kill the soul: but rather fear Him which is able to destroy both soul and body in Hell"* (Mat. 10:28).

The idea is that the threats of men, even of our lives, must not be allowed by the Believer to cause denial of Christ or His Word in any way. As well, most of the time, the opposition will come from religion and not from the world.

EXCOMMUNICATION

The phrase, *"For the Jews had agreed already, that if any man did confess that He* (Jesus) *was Christ* (Messiah), *he should be put out of the synagogue,"* proclaims stern measures indeed! The heavy hand of organized religion was now coming down upon all those who follow Christ. It was but a portent of all which would follow thereafter, resulting in severe persecution down through the ages, with many paying with their lives.

NOTES

There were three types of excommunication practiced at that time:

1. The first, which was the mildest, would exclude the individual from all religious privileges for seven or 30 days, according to the dignity of the authority by whom it was pronounced. This meant that the individual so punished could not enter the synagogue for that period of time, cutting off all worship of God, at least in that capacity. As well, all educational privileges for children, in other words, the schooling of that time, was carried on in the synagogues. Actually, it was the center of all religious, cultural, and even economic strength of most in Israel.

Expulsion could also include the ceasing of everything associated with the synagogue in whatever capacity for the given period of time.

2. The second type of excommunication, more severe than the first, was accompanied by the blast of a trumpet and terrible curses, which deprived the sufferer of all kinds of social intercourse. The individual was avoided as a leper: if he died, he was buried without a funeral or mourning. This lasted for several months or even for several years.

3. The third and final excommunication was the worst of all and could last for life. What type of excommunication Followers of Christ were threatened with, we are not told, but considering their animosity, it is positive that they were speaking of the second kind and possibly the third.

However, it was far better to be thrown out of the synagogue and be with Jesus than to stay in the thing and not have Him.

Is it possible to do both, have Him and remain in such an antagonistic atmosphere towards Him?

EXAMPLES!

I think not! For example, immediately after the Day of Pentecost when the Holy Spirit fell, thousands began to be put out of the synagogue in Jerusalem, which caused tremendous hardship among the people. However, the Scripture said, *"Neither was there any among them who lacked: for as many as were possessors of lands or houses sold them, and brought the prices of the things that were sold,*

"And laid them down at the Apostles' feet: and distribution was made unto every man according as he had need" (Acts 4:34-35).

This need was brought about because when excommunicated, many lost their employment and were even evicted from their homes, that is, if they were paying rent, etc., and not allowed other accommodations.

Actually, this continued until Jerusalem was destroyed in A.D. 70, inasmuch as people were continuing to be Saved. This is why Paul was receiving offerings, as outlined in II Corinthians, Chapters 8 and 9, which was about 27 years after the notable Day of Pentecost.

If one is to truly follow Christ, one must absent himself from that which is opposed to Christ, even though it may be ever so religious. This is where the Believer must know the Word of God enough that he will know what is of God or not. The Word of God is always the criterion and must never be compromised in any fashion.

(23) "THEREFORE SAID HIS PARENTS, HE IS OF AGE; ASK HIM."

The pattern is:

1. The Holy Spirit brings this out twice as to the position taken by the parents in that they were adamant in refusing to accept any responsibility whatsoever for the opinions of their son about his Healer.

2. They knew it was Jesus Who had opened the eyes of their son but were very reluctant to say so.

3. To be sure, they did not better themselves by the position they took.

(24) "THEN AGAIN CALLED THEY THE MAN WHO WAS BLIND, AND SAID UNTO HIM, GIVE GOD THE PRAISE: WE KNOW THAT THIS MAN IS A SINNER."

The form is:

1. The phrase, *"Then again called they the man who was blind, and said unto him, Give God the praise,"* implies that they wanted the man to repudiate Jesus.

2. The statement about giving God praise was the words used in making an oath. To give God praise was the equivalent of swearing to tell the truth (Josh. 7:19).

3. *"We know that this Man is a sinner,"* is strange indeed considering that Jesus had openly challenged them to prove that He had committed any type of sin, error, or falsehood (Jn. 8:46). Of course, they could not do such a thing because such did not exist.

4. After putting the former blind man under oath, so to speak, they now sought to force him to say that Jesus was a sinner. However, we will find that they made no headway in this effort.

(25) "HE ANSWERED AND SAID, WHETHER HE BE A SINNER OR NO, I KNOW NOT: ONE THING I KNOW, THAT, WHEREAS I WAS BLIND, NOW I SEE."

The order is:

1. The phrase, *"He answered and said, Whether He be a sinner or no, I know not,"* was used by the man Ironically. In other words, even though in the translation it seems to leave doubt, in the original Greek text, there is no hint of such. In effect, he was saying, *"You assert it, but the facts of my experience are altogether of a different kind."*

2. The phrase, *"One thing I know, that, whereas I was blind, now I see,"* pulls the attention back to the great Miracle which had been performed by Jesus. They had an argument while he had an experience!

3. It is amazing at the Spiritual Insight this man had, considering that he had been a beggar much of, if not all, of his life. His Spiritual Knowledge far surpassed that of the religious leaders of Israel. As well, he was determined to not diminish Jesus in any way, and no wonder!

4. To think of what Jesus had just done for him is so astounding that it beggars description. He had lived in a constant night of darkness. Born this way, his lot in life was to beg alms.

The song says:

"Like a blind man who walked in the darkness,
"I had longed, I had searched for the light,
"Then I met the Master,
"Now I walk no more in the night."

"And all things were changed when He found me,
"A new day broke through all around me,
"For I met the Master,
"Now I belong to Him."

(26) "THEN SAID THEY TO HIM AGAIN, WHAT DID HE TO YOU? HOW OPENED HE YOUR EYES?"

The pattern is:

1. The question, *"Then said they to him again, What did He to you?"* represents the third time they have asked him how he was healed.

2. The question, *"How opened He your eyes?"* is asked for the purpose of hopefully soliciting some type of answer with which Jesus could be charged with heresy, working in league with Satan, etc. Perhaps they desired to hopefully get him to say something he had not previously said, which would substantiate their charge that Jesus had broken the Sabbath, or so they claimed.

3. When one looks at these people, especially in the face of such overwhelming evidence regarding Christ, it is no wonder as to why the Lord allowed the terrible Judgment of A.D. 70 to be brought on them, with over 1 million slaughtered by Titus, the Roman General, and, for all practical purposes, their Nation coming to a catastrophic end! It is not surprising that the Lord carried out this Judgment, but that He did not do so sooner!

(27) "HE ANSWERED THEM, I HAVE TOLD YOU ALREADY, AND YOU DID NOT HEAR: WHEREFORE WOULD YE HEAR IT AGAIN? WILL YE ALSO BE HIS DISCIPLES?"

The exposition is:

1. The phrase, *"He answered them, I have told you already, and you did not hear,"* presents a courage that few in Israel had at that time.

2. In effect, he was saying, *"I have already told you what happened, and furthermore, the evidence is undeniable! You will not hear or believe because you have no interest in the truth."*

3. The question, *"Wherefore would you hear it again?"* actually asks, *"What is the point of telling you again?"*

4. The question, *"Will you also be His Disciples?"* is asked in sarcasm because he knew for anyone to even remotely suggest that these Pharisees desired to be the Disciples of Jesus would be to them the highest insult! So, he actually asked this last

NOTES

question in order to goad them. He was so animated at this point, and ready, not withstanding the threat of the great excommunication hanging over him, to announce his own Discipleship to any extent and at any risk.

5. When one reads the answers as given by this former blind man, one is reading that which must characterize every Believer who names the Name of Christ. Jesus must be confessed before men, and in terms that leave absolutely no doubt as to one's place and position. One must be prepared to suffer the consequences, but far better to suffer those consequences than the alternative.

6. Even though I have stated the following repeatedly, inasmuch as the situation is so serious, actually involving the very souls of men, one should look at this scenario as it applies to all true Followers of Christ as opposed to organized religion.

7. The same Satan who energized the Pharisees of old continues to do so with the modern variety. It is not possible to oppose that which is of Christ and not, as well, oppose Christ! Also, it is not possible to be neutral in this area. One cannot placate the Pharisee spirit and, at the same time, please Christ.

8. When I speak of organized religion, I am not speaking of religious denominations only, but rather a spirit, which characterizes many so-called independent churches as well.

(28) "THEN THEY REVILED HIM, AND SAID, YOU ARE HIS DISCIPLE; BUT WE ARE MOSES' DISCIPLES."

The composition is:

1. We should understand that the manner in which we look at Justification is the manner in which we look at Christ.

2. He either paid it all, or He didn't! The Cross was either enough, or it wasn't!

3. In fact, as one views the Cross, one views Justification. The two are inseparable.

THE RELIGIOUS LEADERS REVILED THE FORMER BLIND MAN

The phrase, *"Then they reviled him,"* in the Greek text is *"loidoreo"* and means *"to vilify, to rail at, and to abuse by words."*

What had he done to justify their actions?

Of course, he had done nothing except take a stand for Christ. These hypocrites would have much rather seen this man live out the rest of his days in that horrible night of blindness than to be healed by Christ. Sadly and regrettably, I face the same spirit, as do others, when religious heads attempt to stop our meetings, in effect, saying that they would rather see people die eternally lost and go to Hell than be Saved in one of our Crusades.

A PERSONAL EXPERIENCE

When we went on television in Russia, which the Lord used in a miraculous way, at the outset, we were looking for an interpreter. It had to be someone who knew the Russian language firsthand and who, at the same time, knew the Lord. We found such a brother who was pastoring a Church and who actually had been Saved through our telecast. He was a Russian but was now living in the States. We asked him to translate for us. He gladly consented to do so, but, a couple of days later, he called us saying that he could not serve as the translator. When asked why, he said that the organization with which he was associated would not allow him to do so.

Jim Woolsey called the head of that organization and asked why that he could not serve as the Russian voice, considering he was Russian, etc.

The man adamantly refused, claiming that they would never allow him to do that. Jim made the statement that many people would be Saved as a result of the programming, and if they didn't hear the Gospel, Jim continued, they would die and go to Hell. The man's answer was startling!

He said, *"I would rather see them die and go to Hell before we will let our man serve as the voice of your program."*

I realize it's almost impossible to believe that somebody who calls himself a Christian, much less a preacher, would say such a thing. However, that is the face of religion. That's the same spirit that crucified Christ. Unfortunately, it is alive and well presently.

Incidentally, the Lord gave us another voice, who did an excellent job.

I might quickly add, we received over a million letters from Russians, telling us how they'd given their hearts to Christ as a result of the television programming in that great country. How we give the Lord all the praise and glory for such.

THE LORD JESUS CHRIST

Of course, even as the Pharisees of old claimed that Jesus was not really the Son of God but actually of the Devil, their children do the same! Their modern counterparts justify themselves by claiming that I am not of God and that these people are not really being saved.

How could they claim such?

As Christ would not obey the silly man-made laws devised by the Pharisees, neither do I pay attention to rules made up by men, which have no foundation in the Word of God. Just as the Pharisees grew exceedingly angry, doing everything within their power to stop Christ, so do those who follow in their train.

No, I am not likening myself to Christ by any means, but I do claim Him as my Lord and Saviour and, as well, the One Who called me to preach His Gospel. As such, I follow Him, at least to the best of my ability. As such, I also understand that I will suffer the same opposition, even as all others who truly follow Christ.

As well, I also know that most of the opposition will come from the church of this day exactly as it came from the church of Jesus' Day. So, please allow me to say one more thing:

AN HONOR

It was an honor, at least in the Eyes of God, for this former blind man to be excommunicated from the church of that time, and I personally consider it an honor to serve and walk in the same capacity presently!

The phrase, *"And said, You are His Disciple,"* for a change, presents them telling the truth.

Whatever it was the man meant in his answer to them, the Jews took it as proof of his virtual confession of Discipleship to Jesus.

The phrase, *"But we are Moses' Disciples,"* now sees them reverting back to form, which was the *"lie."* Despite their claims, they were not Moses' Disciples. Had they truly been such, they would have known Jesus and readily accepted Him as Lord and Master. Had Moses been alive at this moment, they would have opposed him just as readily as they opposed Christ because Moses was of Christ.

(29) "WE KNOW THAT GOD SPOKE UNTO MOSES: AS FOR THIS FELLOW, WE KNOW NOT FROM WHENCE HE IS."

The pattern is:

1. It was never a question of what the worshipper was. That was understood. It was always what the Sacrifice was.

2. That's what makes Faith so important. Christ has done it, and we cannot do it, but our Faith in Him grants us all that He has done.

3. In other words, when we claim Christ and do so by Faith, God no longer looks at us but looks at Him.

MOSES

The phrase, *"We know that God spoke unto Moses,"* proclaims them now once again seeking that which was true; however, they did not at all obey what God spoke to Moses. Claiming to be something, and actually being that, are two different things altogether.

Millions presently talk glibly about the Bible and claim to know its Author; however, to any true Manifestation of the Holy Spirit, they are vehemently opposed. Like the Pharisees of old, they only claim to believe that which is in the past by believing nothing that pertains to the present. The next phrase tells us why:

THIS FELLOW?

The phrase, *"As for this Fellow, we know not from where He is,"* as is obvious, speaks of Jesus.

The Appearance of Jesus Christ always proves what people actually do believe, despite their loud profession. The Moving and Operation of the Holy Spirit presently places the church in the same position as it did then. Even though 2,000 years removed, the scenario is identical! Due to its significance, please allow me to say it again:

It was easy for the Pharisees to speak glowingly of something that happened 1,500 years before. However, when Jesus appeared, His Very Presence showed exactly what was really in their hearts, which was not what they claimed.

Even though He is not here in the physical sense presently as He was those days of long ago, still, He is just as much here now as then, or even more so. I speak of all that the Holy Spirit presently does, which is actually at the behest of Christ, and is the same as Christ being Personally present (Mat. 3:11; Jn. 16:7-15).

BLESSED CONSISTENCY!

It is somewhat remarkable that in John 7:27, they had been very explicit in declaring, *"We know from where He is,"* while now they claim the very opposite! Blessed consistency!

The Pharisees never called Jesus by Name, but rather by an appellative such as *"Teacher,"* etc., or else, with a contemptuous expression, such as used here by the word *"this."* The word *"fellow"* was inserted by the translators and was not in the original Text.

When the Bible student reads the four Gospels, it becomes very obvious as to the evil and wickedness of the Pharisees and Scribes. However, it was not obvious to all of the people of that day inasmuch as most of these religious leaders were looked at with very high regard and, as stated, as having excellent reputations. It took the Light of Christ to fully expose them for what they really were, and even then, it was not so readily discernable to many.

Despite the great number of Miracles performed by Christ, even to the raising of the dead, the last year of Jesus' Public Ministry saw the crowds somewhat smaller than previously. The reason was obvious!

The religious community was now coming out in the open with their opposition to Christ, even threatening Followers with excommunication from the synagogue. As a result, most would openly take their stand with the Pharisees, or else, attempt to remain neutral, even as the parents of this former blind man. In comparison to the whole, precious few actually stepped out publically for Christ, at least at this time.

(30) "THE MAN ANSWERED AND SAID UNTO THEM, WHY HEREIN IS A MARVELLOUS THING, THAT YE KNOW NOT FROM WHENCE HE IS, AND YET HE HAS OPENED MINE EYES."

The pattern is:

1. The phrase, *"The man answered and said unto them, Why herein is a marvellous thing,"* proclaims an undeniable truth, which the former blind man was about to spring upon these hypocrites.

2. *"That you know not from where He is, and yet He has opened my eyes,"* in effect, says, *"Even you ought to know, only God can open blinded eyes!"*

3. In the face of undeniable proof, how could these Pharisees and Scribes continue this charade?

(31) "NOW WE KNOW THAT GOD HEARS NOT SINNERS: BUT IF ANY MAN BE A WORSHIPPER OF GOD, AND DOES HIS WILL, HIM HE HEARS."

The form is:

1. The phrase, *"Now we know that God hears not sinners,"* in effect, says, *"We know God does not listen to the cry of sinners, when as sinners, they ask from the ground of their sin, to secure their own central purpose."* However, when the sinner turns from his sins to the Lord, his cry for Mercy is then in harmony with the Will of God and will correspondingly be answered!

2. In one sense, every prayer is the prayer of sinful men, but it is the Divine Life working within them that offers inseparable prayer. However, as stated, the prayer of the sinner as such is not heard, exactly as the former blind man said.

3. The phrase, *"But if any man be a worshipper of God, and does His Will, him He hears,"* proclaims the deepest truth of the Divine Revelation about the conditions of acceptable prayer. These conditions are:

a. *"Be a worshipper of God"*: this speaks of Praise and thanksgiving offered to the Lord constantly on the part of the seeker, knowing that God is the Giver of all good things. As such, He is to be correspondingly worshipped.

b. *"And does His Will"*: this simply means to obey the Word of God. This is basically what Paul was speaking about when he said, *"And we know that all things work together for good to them who love God, to them who are the called according to His Purpose"* (Rom. 8:28).

3. In turn, John the Beloved, who wrote this account, would later say, *"And this is the confidence that we have in Him, that, if we ask anything according to His Will, He hears us"* (I Jn. 5:14).

(32) "SINCE THE WORLD BEGAN WAS IT NOT HEARD THAT ANY MAN OPENED THE EYES OF ONE WHO WAS BORN BLIND."

The form is:

1. If the Lord looks at us at all, It is at our Faith.

2. When Jesus died on the Cross, He not only covered our sin but, in reality, took it away.

3. Jesus, at the Cross, dealt with the very cause of sin, which is Satan.

A MIRACLE OF UNPRECEDENTED PROPORTIONS

The phrase, *"Since the world began,"* even though coming from the lips of a beggar who had formerly been blind, stands correct. There is no record of any cure of blindness in the Old Testament. As well, even though Jesus did heal blindness on other occasions, this is the only account of one being healed who was *"born blind!"*

Not able to read, this man would have had to obtain all his information concerning the Lord by hearing it from others. How many would want to take such time with a blind beggar is anyone's guess. Be that as it may, his conversation with these religious leaders shows he had an excellent knowledge of the Lord and a heart toward God.

Born and living in this midnight of darkness, he had undoubtedly queried those, who would spare him a few minutes, concerning the Miracles of the Bible, which indicates that he was looking for some example that God would perform such a Miracle. Perhaps he did not voice this to others. Perhaps, even within his own heart, he may have wondered if he was asking too much, considering there was no record that God had ever done such a thing.

FAITH

However, this very example should be a Testimony to all that God will always honor true Faith, irrespective of its seeming impossibility. It makes no difference that He has never done such before, at least that is recorded. If true Faith is evident, He will always respond!

I know that Satan must have done all within his power to discourage this man. He was but a beggar, and the general consensus in Israel at that time was that such people were cursed by God, or else, they would not be in that state. So, it is doubtful that he would have received much encouragement from anyone.

As well, considering that he had no concrete example in the Bible of God doing such a thing, he had to reach out into unchartered territory.

BUT, ISN'T THAT WHERE FAITH ALWAYS TAKES US?

I believe that this man's Faith in God was the very reason that Jesus was drawn to him. We know that Jesus did nothing but what His Father told Him to do; therefore, the Holy Spirit led Christ to this man, at least in part, because of his Faith.

It did not matter that all of Israel said that such was impossible! In the theology of that day, such people were write-offs. In other words, they did not count and were even looked at as outside the Covenant.

However, irrespective of what Israel thought, or anyone, for that matter, it was what God thought that counted

Never forget this, the stands may jeer or the stands may cheer, but it is the man in the striped suit who calls the game.

WAS THERE EVER A MIRACLE OF THIS SORT?

The phrase, *"Was it not heard that any man opened the eyes of one who was born blind,"* not only portrays the magnitude of the Miracle which had transpired but, as well, addresses itself to another question.

Even though it is not overtly mentioned here, the Pharisees and Scribes had previously claimed that Jesus did what He did by the power of Satan (Mat. 12:24-32). So, in answer to that veiled charge, the former blind man was asking, in essence, why Satan had not done such before. Of course, the whole idea of such thinking is ludicrous, to say the least, and only shows the ridiculous length to which unbelief will go to keep from admitting what is really the truth.

(33) "IF THIS MAN WERE NOT OF GOD, HE COULD DO NOTHING."

The exegesis is:

1. And now, with one final thrust, the man sealed the argument.

2. This astounding, miraculous act of Healing was proof to anyone that Jesus is of God and not of Satan.

3. Thus, the Jews were compelled for a few moments to hear from one known as a street beggar words of teaching along the finest lines of a deep experience.

(34) "THEY ANSWERED AND SAID UNTO HIM, YOU WERE ALTOGETHER BORN IN SINS, AND DO YOU TEACH US? AND THEY CAST HIM OUT."

The synopsis is:

1. Calvary satisfied the Honor, the Justice, and the Character of God, which nothing else could do.

2. The price was so high that only God could pay it, which He did at the Cross.

3. The Cross of Christ is the Means, and the only Means, by which God can deal with sinful man.

WARPED, TWISTED THINKING

The phrase, *"They answered and said unto him, You were altogether born in sins,"* reinforces the idea that they believed he was cursed by God, hence, his station in life.

In view of this, the Israel of that day would have made little effort to help anyone of this nature because, in their thinking, this is what one deserved, being under the curse of God. Consequently, to offer help would be going against God, at least in their warped, twisted thinking.

The situation has little changed! Most of the modern church arrives at similar ridiculous conclusions. Because some unsaved religious head has made some unscriptural decree, they reason that if kindness is shown, such will be against God.

However, as Israel of old was not following the Lord, but rather ungodly religious men, their modern counterparts do the same.

THE FORMER BLIND MAN WAS TEACHING ISRAEL

The question, *"And do you teach us?"* presents them unable to answer his Scriptural charge, so they had no other weapon to use but invectiveness and persecution.

In truth, he was teaching them simply because his knowledge of God was of far greater dimension than theirs. Actually, they had no true knowledge of God despite the fact that they were the religious leaders of Israel. Paul would later say, *"And base things of the world, and things which are despised, has God chosen, yes, and things which are not, to bring to naught things that are."*

He then said, *"That no flesh should glory in His Presence"* (I Cor. 1:28-29). Consequently, God honors Faith only, irrespective if it is in the heart of a beggar, while He dishonors religious pomp and pride!

Concerning the charge that this beggar was teaching them, it should be remembered that anytime anyone strays from the Word of God, irrespective as to whom it may be, he needs to be taught, whether he accepts it or not!

THE RELIGIOUS LEADERS EXCOMMUNICATE THE FORMER BLIND MAN

The phrase, *"And they cast him out,"* means that they excommunicated him from the synagogue. However, it should be quickly noted that while they cast him out, Jesus took him in, as we shall see. The portrayal of this contrast is not by accident but purposely designed by the Holy Spirit.

That to which I have already alluded, I must say again: the time is coming, if it has not already arrived, that if one is to truly live for God, one is going to have to come out of institutionalized religion. That is not to say that the organization is wrong, but that such has been organized by man and not by God.

To turn it around, if one is associated with organized religion and he refuses to compromise the Word of God, he will ultimately be *"cast out!"*

Whenever religious denominations make rules which have no Scriptural foundation or principle, such must not be obeyed and, in fact, must be disobeyed exactly as Jesus ignored the silly rules of the Pharisees. To cater to such, even though secretly disagreeing, is compromise and, therefore, sinful and wicked in the Eyes of God.

(35) *"JESUS HEARD THAT THEY HAD CAST HIM OUT; AND WHEN HE HAD FOUND HIM, HE SAID UNTO HIM, DO YOU BELIEVE ON THE SON OF GOD?"*

The exposition is:

1. As convicted sinners, we gaze on the Cross of our Lord Jesus Christ and behold therein that which meets all of our needs.

2. But then, as kings and priests, we can look at the Cross in another light even as the grand consummation of Christ's Holy Purpose to carry out, even unto death, the Will of the Father.

3. The Cross alone can give and does give perfect peace to the conscience.

JESUS

The phrase, *"Jesus heard that they had cast him out,"* means that someone evidently told Him. It was not something that the Holy Spirit directly revealed to Him. Once again, this proclaims the Perfect Humanity of the Son of God, that He *"was made flesh,"* and had *"come in the flesh,"* though He was *"from God."*

JESUS FOUND HIM

The phrase, *"And when He had found him,"* presents a beautiful Action of the Lord as the Good Shepherd seeking out the lost sheep in the wilderness and not resting till He found him.

It is sad that this man, who had aforetime never looked on a human face, had, after his Healing until now, seen only angry faces and averted glances. Even his cowardly parents would have hesitated to receive him into their poor abode; however, this was about to change!

DO YOU BELIEVE?

The question, *"He said unto him, Do you*

believe on the Son of God?" asks, and at the same time, says so much!

In effect, Jesus was introducing Himself as the Messiah of Israel. Even above that, He was repudiating the wrong notion held then by Israel as to Who and What exactly the Messiah would be!

There is no doubt, at least in my mind, that this beggar was fully acquainted with Israel's erroneous notions, so Jesus would dispel this error by proclaiming the Messiah as not merely a Mighty Man but, actually, the *"Son of God."*

The pronoun *"you,"* as Jesus used it, is emphatic, which means to emphasize, in this case, this man and his Faith.

The man had declared that his Healer was *"from God,"* that He was *"a Prophet,"* One Who *"did God's Will,"* and Whom *"God hears,"* even when he asks for apparently impossible things. So, now the Lord would take him to the highest of Spiritual heights, as his Faith was expanded beyond those former horizons, with Jesus as the Son of God revealed to him.

Let it ever be known that Faith ever expands and ever reaches out to new horizons. Let it also be known that there is no limit as to what Faith in God can see and bring about!

WHAT DOES IT MEAN TO BELIEVE ON THE SON OF GOD?

Let us first see what it does not mean.

It does not refer to mere mental assent, for millions believe that Jesus is the Son of God in that context, and are not saved. To be frank, even Satan and all demons believe such (James 2:19).

To truly believe on Him, at least as He speaks here, is to follow Him unreservedly, to the exclusion of all else, taking on oneself the Nature and Character of that which is believed, namely Christ. According to this type of Faith, the Holy Spirit will perform the work of making one Christlike. Actually, all the sinner can do is believe, but that is all the sinner needs to do!

In truth, it is the same for one who has already come to Faith. To truly believe Christ for our continued walk demands that one desire His Will, and His Will only! It is impossible to truly believe God, as should be obvious, without wanting and desiring His Perfect Will.

Many claim all types of things from God, automatically assuming they always know God's Will in the matter, when, in reality, they often do not. Consequently, such action is not real faith, but rather presumption.

John said, *"And this is the confidence that we have in Him, that, if we ask anything according to His Will, He hears us:"*

He concluded by saying, *"And if we know that He hears us, whatsoever we ask, we know that we have the petitions that we desired of Him"* (I Jn. 5:14-15).

(36) "HE ANSWERED AND SAID, WHO IS HE, LORD, THAT I MIGHT BELIEVE ON HIM?"

The structure is:

1. This question as asked was done so with the idea that he already suspected that Jesus was speaking of Himself!

2. There is a particular emphasis on the *"Who,"* which points to that fact. In essence, he now knew Who and What Jesus was! As well, he was ready at that very moment to *"believe on Him."*

3. Jesus must always be the Object of our Faith. The Scripture says, *"Looking unto Jesus the Author and Finisher of our Faith"* (Heb. 12:2).

4. This means that the Object of our Faith is not to be Healing, money, victory, etc., but Jesus. In truth, He is the Giver of all these things. However, the only way they can be received is by looking at the Giver instead of the gift, as we are so prone to do.

5. I am persuaded that this is why Faith breaks down so often. We allow the object to be transferred from the Giver to other things. When this happens, our faith becomes centered on ourselves instead of Christ.

6. In truth, believing the Lord for various things we need is no different than when we came to Jesus for Salvation. As we were to believe on Him then, we are to continue to believe on Him for whatever we need. The Object of Faith must always be Him.

(37) "AND JESUS SAID UNTO HIM, YOU HAVE BOTH SEEN HIM, AND IT IS HE WHO TALKS WITH YOU."

The structure is:

1. The phrase, *"And Jesus said unto him, You have both seen Him,"* means that whereas Jesus had been to him the *"Light of the world,"* He now would become to him the *"Bread of Life."*

2. *"And it is He Who talks with you,"* proclaims the greatest Revelation that could ever be given to any person at any time!

3. It is beautiful as to the manner and to whom Jesus manifested Himself as the Son of God, the Messiah of Israel. He did so plainly to the woman at the well, even though she was a moral wreck (Jn. 4:26), even as He did here to this beggar, who had just been excommunicated from the synagogue.

4. Why would He reveal Himself in this fashion to these while refusing to do so to the religious leaders of Israel?

5. It all hinges on Faith. The Lord will little reveal Himself to doubt and unbelief, which characterized the religious leaders at that time. He seeks Faith, and where it is found, the most glorious Revelation is the result.

(38) *"AND HE SAID, LORD, I BELIEVE. AND HE WORSHIPPED HIM."*

The synopsis is:

1. Any sinner can definitely be Saved if he identifies with Christ on the Cross.

2. In fact, that is the only way in which a person can be Saved (Rom. 6:3-5; Jn. 3:16; Eph. 2:8-9; Col. 2:10-15).

LORD, I BELIEVE

The phrase, *"And he said, Lord, I believe,"* constitutes the most wonderful words that could ever be spoken by any human being. It is that simple, that wonderful, and that beautiful!

What did he believe?

He believed that Jesus was and is *"The Son of God,"* the Saviour of mankind, the Redeemer of the world, and the Messiah of Israel.

Why did the Lord make Faith the basis of Salvation?

There was no other way it could be done. If God had demanded payment on the part of the sinner, the debt was so astronomically high that no one could ever hope to pay. Hence, Peter would say, *"You were not redeemed with corruptible things, as silver and gold … but with the Precious Blood of Christ, as of a Lamb without blemish and without spot"* (I Pet. 1:18-19).

Besides that, the type of payment that God demanded, which was a perfect life, even as Peter has just said, could not in any way be provided by man. So, God would have to do for man what man could not do for himself. God would become Man, take upon Himself a human body, and then do all the things required, beginning with the Virgin Birth. The perfection demanded by God was such that man could not even comprehend much less carry out.

ADAM

When Adam fell in the Garden of Eden, the whole of humanity for all time fell with him because all, in essence, were in his loins. He was the representative man; therefore, when he sinned, he did so not only pertaining to himself, but to all others as well. That is what is referred to as *"original sin,"* and into which all are born. In other words, man comes from a diseased stock, which means he is doomed before he even begins.

So, the Virgin Birth would bypass original sin and not violate the type. Adam and Eve originally had God as their Father, and so did Jesus (Lk. 3:38).

As well, Jesus walked perfectly sinless all the days of His Life and then died as the Sin-Offering, the Perfect Sacrifice, which God could and would accept. As well, He rose from the dead, thereby, defeating death and throwing off the chains which have shackled humanity from the beginning. Now, death and Satan have no hold on the believing sinner, for its deadly grip has been broken, and, above all, the terrible sin debt which man owed God has been paid.

The Wrath of God abides on sin, as it must, inasmuch as sin is the destroyer of God's Choice Creation (Rom. 1:18). As such, it abides on man who is the sinner.

THE LORD OF THE COVENANT

However, because of the Sacrifice offered by Christ at Calvary, the Wrath of God has been appeased. What rightly should have been poured out on us, because we were the sinners, in fact, was poured out on Christ, Who became our Substitute.

Simple Faith in what He did grants to the believing sinner all that He purchased and gained at Calvary and the Resurrection, which the first Adam lost. Hence, when the man said, *"Lord, I believe,"* immediately, Eternal Life was given unto him, as it is to all who follow in his train (Jn. 3:16).

If it is to be noticed, he referred to Jesus as *"Lord,"* which, in effect, meant, *"Lord of the Covenant."*

In the Garden of Eden, God had promised a Redeemer, and now the Promise was kept! Jesus is the Redeemer (Gen. 3:15)!

WORSHIP

The phrase, *"And he worshipped Him,"* refers to him doing so not only for the great Miracle of Healing that Jesus had given unto him, but even more so for the Great Salvation now afforded and received.

As well, one must note that though this man was an Israelite, and as such, a part of the Covenant people, in fact, until now, he was not saved. Actually, most people in Israel were not saved, despite being very religious. In fact, most people in churches presently are not saved. They are religious, even as Israel of old, but they have really never trusted Christ as their Saviour.

A PERSONAL EXPERIENCE

Sometime back over our daily radio program, several Preachers were on the panel, and we were discussing the Baptism with the Holy Spirit. One of our Ministers related how he came into the Pentecostal experience. He mentioned the churches in which he was brought up, which, incidentally, were not Pentecostal.

He went on to relate how that the study of the Bible in that atmosphere primarily amounted to approaching it as one does any text book in which one desires to learn its contents. There was absolutely no Moving or Operation of the Holy Spirit, Who Alone can give one understanding of the Word of God. It was all done strictly as if they were addressing a problem in algebra or another suchlike subject. Actually, he went on to say that the entirety of their Christian experience mostly consisted of an intellectual, professional attachment.

Whereas only the Lord knows the hearts of people, and final Judgment, of course, would have to be His, still, it is very doubtful that many of these people truly knew the Lord. Basically, they had accepted the philosophy of Christianity without having any type of experience with Christ as Saviour, even though claiming such. Actually, it would probably be shocking if one knew just how few people really are Saved, despite all of the profession.

(39) "AND JESUS SAID, FOR JUDGMENT I AM COME INTO THIS WORLD, THAT THEY WHICH SEE NOT MIGHT SEE; AND THAT THEY WHICH SEE MIGHT BE MADE BLIND."

The structure is:

1. The Burnt Offering of old signified how horrible and how deep a thing sin is. Sin is not merely exterior; it is interior as well. It is not just outward; it is inward. It is a disease, one might say, of our vitals. It affects every single part of the human being.

2. There is only one answer for sin, only one, and that is the Cross of Christ.

3. In fact, the only thing standing between Hell and mankind is the Cross of Christ. We should think about that!

JUDGMENT

The phrase, *"And Jesus said, For Judgment I am come into this world,"* proclaims a foundational Truth.

He did not come, at least at this time, to execute Judgment, but with a view to bring about a judicial decision on the moral condition of mankind. In other words, Jesus is the Touchstone of humanity. What men think of Christ is the question which decides in every age their moral condition before God.

Of course, understanding this, all other rules of measurement concerning morality construed by man, be they religious or otherwise, will not in any way stand the acid test.

This *"Judgment"* is always based on a Spiritual Foundation, which is the Word of God (Jesus is the Living Word), and always falls out into one of two directions:

1. *"That they which see not might see"*:

the idea incorporates those who have no opportunity to see, but even more so, it pertains to those who know they have no spiritual intelligence. Actually, this may not be obvious until the Gospel is presented unto them, but, at that time, they realize their spiritual and moral bankruptcy, thereby, accepting Christ. However, this number is very small in comparison with that which is to follow.

2. *"And that they which see might be made blind"*: this actually can be translated, *"They which think they see, but in reality do not, and with the presentation of the Gospel, refuse to accept it, thinking they have no need of such."* This incorporates almost all of the world for all time!

RELIGION

Most of the world claims religion of some sort, which, in its deception, makes them think they have no need of anything else.

Others, while not a part of any formal religion, still, have devised their own religion in one way or the other and, thereby, see no need for Christ.

Light rejected is Light withdrawn! Consequently, if a person walks in all the Light he has, more Light will be given in which he must walk. Otherwise, he will lose what little Light he already has.

A perfect case in point is the Baptism with the Holy Spirit.

LIGHT

Before the Light on the Holy Spirit was made known to a great degree, many Believers were greatly used of God, although not being baptized with the Spirit. They did not have the Light on the subject, but they did walk in all the Light they had.

However, since the great Latter Rain Outpouring, which actually began at approximately the turn of the Twentieth Century, and has increased in intensity until this moment, the Lord expects all to walk in that Light (Joel 2:23). Some few have, but regrettably, most have not, actually rejecting it in no uncertain terms.

As a result, they have become, and are becoming, more and more blind spiritually, with what little Light they have being taken away.

NOTES

In other words, preachers and people who reject the Holy Spirit, at least according to Acts 2:4, are by and large totally ineffective respecting the Work of God. While there may be much religious activity, just as with Israel of old, still, little or nothing is really accomplished for Christ.

As well, even those who claim to accept the Holy Spirit according to Acts 2:4, if they forsake His Leading and Direction, they too will suffer the loss of the Light, which is presently happening to many, even entire Pentecostal denominations.

The Thirty-ninth Verse, as given by Christ, should be read very carefully and understood as to exactly what is being said. Its significance, as should be obvious, is of extreme weight!

(40) "AND SOME OF THE PHARISEES WHICH WERE WITH HIM HEARD THESE WORDS, AND SAID UNTO HIM, ARE WE BLIND ALSO?"

The composition is:

1. The phrase, *"And some of the Pharisees which were with Him heard these words,"* means they were privy to the Salvation of the former blind man and to the things said.

2. The question, *"And said unto Him, Are we blind also?"* seems to have been asked in sarcasm. No other commentators, whose words I have read, say such, but it seems to me that the following Verse proclaims that the Pharisees in no way saw themselves as being spiritually *"blind."* They actually claimed the very opposite, and to a great degree!

3. They did not believe anything Jesus said, so why would they believe Him presently?

(41) "JESUS SAID UNTO THEM, IF YE WERE BLIND, YE SHOULD HAVE NO SIN: BUT NOW YOU SAY, WE SEE; THEREFORE YOUR SIN REMAINS."

The synopsis is:

1. When Faith and trust are placed in Christ and what He did at the Cross, every sin is atoned, and nothing is left, in other words, *"My sins are gone."*

2. The Work of Christ on the Cross was a *"Finished Work"* (Heb. 1:3). This means that nothing remains to be done.

3. As the Burnt Offering of the Old

Testament typified Christ in death, the *"Meat Offering"* typified Him in *"Life."*

BLIND

The phrase, *"Jesus said unto them, If you were blind, you should have no sin,"* does not mean that because of having no Light that they would not be sinners. All men are sinners (Rom. 3:9-18).

Jesus is saying that if they admitted they were spiritually blind, which they were, then this particular sin of rejecting the Light would not be attributed to them

This is somewhat of that which He was speaking when He said, *"That the publicans and the harlots go into the Kingdom of God before you.*

"For John came unto you in the way of Righteousness, and you believed him not: but the publicans and the harlots believed him: and you, when you had seen it, repented not afterward, that you might believe him" (Mat. 21:31-32).

The phrase, *"But now you say, We see; therefore your sin remains,"* in effect, proclaims these religious leaders saying that they already had the Light and, therefore, did not need the Light as presented by Jesus, which, in their thinking, was false. Therefore, they were guilty of the terrible sin of refusing the True Light, which meant the Light they did have would be taken away, with them being left totally *"blind"* in the spiritual sense. This is exactly what happened!

THE JEWS

Their Nation was destroyed in A.D. 70, with the Jews being scattered all over the world where they wandered from nation to nation for about 1,900 years. Even though they now are a Nation once again, they are still spiritually blind, fulfilling exactly what Jesus said.

In fact, many, if not most, Jews would probably fall into the category of being atheistic or, at least, agnostic. Even those who claim to believe in God do so in a twisted sort of way, which could only be the case concerning their rejection of the True Light, the Lord Jesus Christ.

As we have already stated, this dictum, as stated by Jesus, applies to everyone, not only the Jews, hence, many modern religious denominations! Actually, the same can be said for each individual.

For those who have truly once known God and turned their backs on Him, Jesus said, *"No man, having put his hand to the plough, and looks back, is fit for the Kingdom of God"* (Lk. 9:62).

This does not mean that the backslider cannot be Saved! It does mean that if one remains in the position of going backwards, i.e., not walking in the Light, he or she can and will be eternally lost.

"A charge to keep I have,
"A God to glorify,
"A never-dying soul to save,
"And fit it for the sky."

"Help me to watch and pray,
"And on Your Grace rely,
"Assured You'll my trust this day,
"Nor shall I ever die."

CHAPTER 10

(1) "VERILY, VERILY, I SAY UNTO YOU, HE WHO ENTERS NOT BY THE DOOR INTO THE SHEEPFOLD, BUT CLIMBS UP SOME OTHER WAY, THE SAME IS A THIEF AND A ROBBER."

The diagram is:

1. The phrase, *"Verily, verily, I say unto you,"* was said emphatically, and was meant to be emphatic! Coming from Christ, it expressed complete authority. In other words, that which He was saying was the Word of God in contrast to what these false shepherds were saying, which constituted that of their own devising.

2. Having appeared to the blind man's joy, the Lord proceeded to confound and put to shame those who cast him out by declaring them to be spiritually blind and willfully sinful. He also declared them to be false shepherds, thieves, robbers, and hirelings.

3. At the same time, He deepened the man's joy, and that of the woman (Jn. 8:2-11), by telling them that they were sheep of the true fold. He stated that He was the

Good Shepherd, giving His Life for them, and that He endowed them with Eternal Life. He added that they should never perish, irrespective as to what the Pharisees said, and that nothing and no one could pluck them out of His Hand, least of all, the Pharisees.

4. The phrase, *"He who enters not by the Door into the sheepfold,"* proclaims to us that there is a *"Door,"* and, in fact, only one *"Door!"*

5. In contrast to these false shepherds, He was the Good Shepherd. He came in by the Door into the sheepfold, and He was Himself, at the same time, the *"Door for the sheep."*

6. The sheepfold was the Abrahamic Covenant, which, in effect, included all, both Jew and Gentile (Gen. 12:1-3).

7. The phrase, *"But climbs up some other way, the same is a thief and a robber,"* refers to using a *"way"* other than Christ and Him Crucified. He Alone is the Door, as He shall say, with all other ways false and all other false shepherds labeled as *"thieves and robbers!"*

8. This means that those who proclaim Mary as the way are thieves and robbers! The same goes for Joseph Smith, Buddha, Confucius, Muhammad, and any other fake luminary.

9. We must also remember that this *"Door"* is a *"bloody Door."* Some 3,500 years ago when the Children of Israel were delivered from Egypt, their safety was in the blood that was placed on the lintel above the door and on the two side posts, which, in a sense, were parts of the door. Now, it is the Cross of Christ.

(2) "BUT HE WHO ENTERS IN BY THE DOOR IS THE SHEPHERD OF THE SHEEP."

The synopsis is:

1. The True Shepherd came in by the Door. That is, He submitted to all the conditions ordained by Him Who built the sheepfold.

2. These conditions were given through Moses, accordingly, He was born of a woman under the Law, was circumcised, and fulfilled all that the Law demanded of the Messiah and all that was predicted concerning Him. He was Jehovah's Perfect Servant, living by every Word that proceeded out of the Mouth of God, continually doing those things that pleased Him.

3. Actually, it was only the True Shepherd of the sheep Who knew the *"Door."*

4. Even though He submitted to the Law in all points, still, the actual *"Door"* was Faith. Consequently, *"The life which I now live in the flesh I live by the Faith of the Son of God, Who loved me, and gave Himself for me"* (Gal. 2:20).

(3) "TO HIM THE PORTER OPENS; AND THE SHEEP HEAR HIS VOICE: AND HE CALLS HIS OWN SHEEP BY NAME, AND LEADS THEM OUT."

The structure is:

1. The phrase, *"To Him the porter opens,"* means that the Law, the Doorkeeper, immediately admitted Him because He had perfectly kept the Law, and actually was the only One Who had done such a thing. The *"Porter"* did not open to any of the religious leaders of Israel because, despite their claims, none of them had ever kept the law. So, they sought to build their own *"sheepfold,"* which the Lord would not and, in fact, could not recognize.

2. *"And the Sheep hear His Voice,"* means that True Sheep hear the Voice of the True Shepherd. The Pharisees, Scribes, and Priests did not hear His Voice, at least for the most part, because they were not His Sheep.

3. *"And He calls His Own Sheep by name,"* was a custom then of shepherds and their sheep. They gave them names, with the sheep responding to the name as it was called.

4. As well, this speaks of relationship, which Salvation automatically brings.

5. By contrast, religion has no such relationship. Actually, it has no interest in people individually, only as it can force these people by fear or intimidation to do what is demanded of them. Consequently, religion rules by control and demands money through fear.

6. The phrase, *"And leads them out,"* has to do once again with relationship and speaks of the finding of suitable pasture.

As well, if one is to notice, He speaks of

these sheep being *"His Own,"* because they are. Consequently, He is Owner as well as Shepherd of the sheep and, therefore, has a double love for them, so to speak.

(4) "AND WHEN HE PUTS FORTH HIS OWN SHEEP, HE GOES BEFORE THEM, AND THE SHEEP FOLLOW HIM: FOR THEY KNOW HIS VOICE."

The composition is:

1. The phrase, *"And when He puts forth His Own Sheep, He goes before them,"* means that He has Personally inspected the pasture and every part of the place where they will be. In other words, exactly as it says, *"He goes before them."*

2. This means that for every hardship, test and trial, or difficulty which He requires that we go through, He has been there before us and knows exactly the extent of what will be. Actually, for one to properly understand this Tenth Chapter of John, one should, as well, read Psalm 23.

3. *"And the Sheep follow Him,"* proclaims trust, dependence, confidence, and love. That is what John was also speaking of when he mentioned that *"perfect love casts out fear"* (I Jn. 4:18).

4. If the *"Sheep"* properly love, the Sheep will also properly trust, and there will be no fear as they properly follow.

5. The phrase, *"For they know His Voice,"* speaks again of relationship, which means His sheep will always follow His Voice.

6. Out from under the condemnation of the Law, He led His Sheep — He Himself going before them to Calvary. The Sheep followed Him, for their safety depended on knowing the One Voice, which was Life to them.

7. Further, He was the Door for the Sheep. He was their Authority for going and their Means for entering in. The sheepfold, which had been to them a prison because of the Law, He turned into a refuge, for He perfectly kept the Law. His Obedience was granted unto us upon our Faith in Him. So, now, the Sheep go in for safety and go out for pasture.

8. As well, the word for *"know"* in the Greek means *"to know intuitively"* — which means to know by Spiritual birth and not by religious education.

NOTES

(5) "AND A STRANGER WILL THEY NOT FOLLOW, BUT WILL FLEE FROM HIM: FOR THEY KNOW NOT THE VOICE OF STRANGERS."

The exegesis is:

1. Mackintosh said:

"The Lord Jesus Christ was the only Perfect Man Who ever trod this Earth."

2. *"He was all Perfect — Perfect in thought, Perfect in word, Perfect in action."*

3. *"In Him every moral quality met in Divine and, therefore, Perfect proportion. No one feature was out of kilter. In Him were exquisitely blended a majesty which overawed, and a gentleness which gave perfect ease in His Presence."*[1]

THE STRANGER

The phrase, *"And a stranger will they not follow,"* coupled with the knowledge of *"His Voice,"* is a strong statement indeed!

The *"stranger"* here mentioned refers to *"thieves and robbers,"* i.e., *"false prophets"* (Mat. 7:15-20).

Does this mean a true Believer cannot be deceived?

Does it mean a true Believer will not fall for false doctrine?

I believe it means exactly that!

There are preachers who do, in fact, preach some sound doctrine but have ulterior motives. In other words, they are out to fleece the sheep.

Because of the sound doctrine, some true Believers may follow such briefly; however, very shortly, the false direction will become obvious. The telltale signs will begin to quickly show! As well, no true Believers, who truly follow the Voice of the Lord, will be swayed by flattery, etc. They will quickly see through such hypocrisy. Actually, the moment flattery begins, one can pretty well rest assured that the fleecing has already begun.

THAT WHICH IS NOT SCRIPTURAL

As well, no true Believer will follow an unscriptural message. Knowing the Word of God, the Believer will very quickly be able to spot the error, even though cleverly disguised.

However, that of which we have spoken concerns mature, developed, Word-filled Believers who have a close relationship with the Lord. But yet, we all know that new Converts, or even those relatively new, will not have such knowledge, hence, becoming easy prey for a very cleverly disguised message, etc.

This is where the under-Shepherd comes in, the one appointed as a Shepherd under Christ, who is mature, etc. Moses, about to die, said to the Lord, *"May the LORD, the God of the spirits of all mankind, appoint a man over this community to go out and come in before them, one who will lead them out and bring them in, so the LORD's People will not be Sheep without a Shepherd"* (Num. 27:16-17).

Consequently, Jesus, the Sheep Shepherd, told a restored Peter, *"Feed My Lambs," "Take care of My Sheep,"* and *"Feed My Sheep"* (Jn. 21:15-17).

Paul said to the Ephesian Elders (Pastors), *"Keep watch over yourselves and all the flock of which the Holy Spirit has made you overseers"* (Acts 20:28), and Peter spoke to other Elders, charging them, *"Be Shepherds of God's Flock that is under your care, serving as overseers"* (I Pet. 5:2).

In each Passage, the Shepherd's attitude of loving concern for the Sheep is emphasized. Special note should be taken of Peter's words because he guards us against overextending the image. He says that Shepherds are to be *"eager to serve,"* not lording it over those entrusted to them, but being examples to the flock (I Pet. 5:2-3).

It is extremely disconcerting to watch Sheep as they begin to follow the voice of a *"stranger,"* despite all the under-Shepherd can do to keep them in the fold. Such happens because of self-will, which is a lack of having the Will of God.

FLEEING FROM FALSE SHEPHERDS

The phrase, *"But will flee from him,"* speaks of that which must be done respecting false shepherds, i.e., *"false prophets."*

The lure of a false prophet is always tantalizing and is designed to pull in the unwary. However, the moment the true Sheep begins to notice that which is not Scriptural, there should be no tarrying; he must quickly flee. When I speak of things not being Scriptural, I am speaking of that which pertains to false doctrine or ulterior motives. This speaks of the false shepherd having no regard for the welfare of the Sheep, but rather for his own welfare. As stated, the true Sheep must quickly flee!

STRANGERS

The phrase, *"For they know not the voice of strangers,"* actually means that the moment they detect the *"strange voice,"* they must *"flee."*

The word *"flee"* is used as encouraging haste because of the allurement of cleverly designed deception. Deception actually has a spirit, which, in a sense, blinds the victim to Truth. The moment it is detected, it must be instantly rejected!

What is a strange voice?

• It is a voice which is not according to the Word of God. The Bible is always the criterion for everything. Everything must be judged according to *"thus saith the Lord!"*

• It is one with ulterior motives, irrespective as to what is preached, be it true or otherwise. As stated, many preachers do not have a Shepherd's heart, but rather are *"wolves in sheep's clothing"* (Mat. 7:15).

• It is a voice of *"envy and strife"* (Phil. 1:15). These preachers are not led by the Lord at all. Rather, they have their own agenda, promoting some particular doctrine or merely desiring to oppose someone, or they are after money. Whatever they preach stirs up strife, fomenting a contentious spirit in the listeners.

(6) "THIS PARABLE SPOKE JESUS UNTO THEM: BUT THEY UNDERSTOOD NOT WHAT THINGS THEY WERE WHICH HE SPOKE UNTO THEM."

The pattern is:

1. In the Incarnation, God becoming Man, Jesus laid aside the expression of His Deity while, at the same time, retaining possession of His Deity.

2. In other words, even though He definitely is God, He functioned as a man.

3. As well, He performed no Miracles as God but always as a Man filled with the Holy Spirit (Acts 10:38).

PARABLE

The phrase, *"This Parable spoke Jesus unto them,"* does not really refer to Parables, as the word is normally used, but in the Greek, it is *"paroimia,"* meaning, *"Proverb or extended saying."*

The pronoun, *"Them,"* proclaims Jesus speaking directly to and of the Pharisees, who were not true shepherds, but rather *"thieves and robbers."*

In respect to these religious leaders, they were confident of their own position and gloried in their influence over men. Actually, they felt that Jesus was greatly undermining their influence over people, and this they strongly resented. This battle rages even unto this hour and, in fact, has always raged.

Jesus is to be the Head of the Church, not men! This is at least one of the reasons that religious denominations generally become a great hindrance to the Work of God, even though some of them may have had a Scriptural beginning. The denominational structure, by its own nature, has a tendency to do this. Administrative positions in church denominations are not generally occupied by spiritual men. Those who have a true Call of God on their lives are carrying out the functions of that Call and have little interest in any type of hierarchical administration. As someone has said, *"Those who can, do, and those who cannot, administrate."*

RELIGIOUS HIERARCHY

However, herein is the problem. Gradually, the constitution and bylaws of a denomination begin to take authority over the Bible, with the Word of God gradually being pushed aside. When things happen, the Bible is little consulted, if at all, but rather these rules of men.

Religious hierarchy is brought about for the express purpose of ruling the Church. Incidentally, religious hierarchy is not found in the Book of Acts whatsoever. It is greatly wicked because it usurps authority over the Headship of Christ as the Chief Shepherd of the Church, even as the Pharisees of old. It becomes man-led, man-devised, man-operated, and man-inspired, and as a result, it ceases to be a Work of God on Earth, but rather a work of man.

So, the gist of Jesus' Statements, respecting Him being the *"Door"* and the *"Chief Shepherd,"* is that He Alone can occupy these positions, and men must follow either Him or others. It is not possible to follow both at the same time. True *"Apostles, Prophets, Evangelists, Pastors, and Teachers,"* will always present Jesus as the True Head, consequently lifting Him up, and not particular denominations, etc. (Eph. 4:11-12).

JESUS AND THE RELIGIOUS STRUCTURE

When the Bible student presently reads the four Gospels, it becomes quickly obvious as to the opposing sides, that of Jesus and the religious structure which greatly opposed Him. However, during the time of His Ministry, that distinction was not so obvious. As we have previously stated, the Pharisees and Scribes were thought of by the people, at least for the most part, as their spiritual guides. In fact, they held, at least as a whole, excellent reputations over Israel. So, only those who were truly Spiritual, of which there were few, actually understood what was taking place, quickly seeing the reason for the great animosity of these religious leaders against Jesus. In fact, if Jesus had not possessed the great Miracle-working Power of God, which saw all manner of Healings and Miracles brought about, even to the raising of the dead, He would have been given little notice at all, so engrained was this religious structure.

Due to the heavy covering of religion which spread over the people like a canopy, they were grossly deceived. The truth is, these religious leaders did not know God, were not carrying out His Work, were deceivers of the people, and, in fact, even though terribly blunt, were leading them straight to Hell. Consequently, I have said that in order to say this:

THE SITUATION HAS LITTLE CHANGED

This situation has little changed presently and, in fact, has always existed in this manner. The Early Church, as recorded in the Book of Acts, was Spirit-led and

Spirit-directed because it was Spirit-originated. As such, it touched the world of that day. However, even then, efforts were made to usurp authority over Christ as the Head of the Church. Paul fought these interlopers constantly.

Tragically, after the death of the Apostles and those who knew them, apostasy slowly set in until the church gradually became what is now known as the *"Catholic church!"* As should be obvious, the Catholic church did not begin on the Day of Pentecost, and Peter was not the first Pope. He was not Pope at all!

The first Pope was not appointed until the mid 300s. He was Pope Damasus, who had been the Bishop of Rome.

The Protestant Reformation brought about a Move of God which ultimately broke the stranglehold of the Catholic church. Regrettably, even the Reformation began to apostatize after a period of time.

In the Nineteenth Century, the great Holiness Movement sprang up, which saw a Move of God across America and other parts of the world. However, it soon went the way of legalism, with the great Pentecostal Move being ushered in at the turn of the Twentieth Century. Regrettably, it, as well, at least for the most part, has long since begun to apostatize until it is only a shell, Spiritually speaking, of what it once was.

The point of all this is that if men look to churches, most will be eternally lost. One must always look to Jesus as the Head of the Church, which will ensure Salvation. While the Church is definitely important, it must be understood in the context that the true Church of Jesus Christ has nothing to do with religious denominations and, in fact, never has!

FAMILY WORSHIP CENTER MEDIA CHURCH

In about 2005, if I remember the year correctly, Frances and I felt led of the Lord to begin what we came to call *"FAMILY WORSHIP CENTER MEDIA CHURCH."* We were being bombarded with emails and letters from people telling us that they could not find a church in their area that preached, taught, and believed in the Cross of Christ. So, from that day, and especially this year, we have had thousands to join FAMILY WORSHIP CENTER MEDIA CHURCH. The only requirement is to be Born-Again.

We urge the people to come to at least one of the Campmeetings each year, if it is possible to do so. It's not mandatory, as ought to be obvious. As well, we encourage these people to tell others about Jimmy Swaggart Ministries. We encourage the people to pay their tithes to the Ministry because this is where they are getting fed, but that's not mandatory.

Many of these people invite friends and neighbors to worship with them as they join with us over SONLIFE BROADCASTING NETWORK at the Service times at FAMILY WORSHIP CENTER.

Some of these people live all the way around the world. So, we encourage them, if they so desire, to tape the services, whether Sunday morning, Sunday night, Wednesday night Bible Study, or the Campmeeting Services. We feel this is a viable Scriptural alternative. It is far better, as should be overly obvious, to receive sound doctrine rather than that which is not Scriptural. Anyone who attends a church that is promoting false doctrine will be greatly hindered by his attending such a church.

In reality, Church can be said to be that which is preached and taught from behind the pulpit. While there are many other things that are attached to Church, still, it is the Word of God that really makes Church what the Church ought to be. Every person around the world who is truly Born-Again is a member of the Body of Christ, which is Church, whatever name it goes under. In other words, when an individual is Born-Again, at that moment, wherever he is and whomever he is, his name is written down in the Lamb's Book of Life, and he is a part of the Body of Christ.

THE RELIGIOUS LEADERS OF ISRAEL

The phrase, *"But they understood not what things they were which He spoke unto them,"* is strange indeed, considering that they were the religious leaders of Israel.

The former blind man had heard His Voice, obeyed, found healing, and advanced step-by-step from a bare knowledge of *"a Man called Jesus"* to a confession of Him as One empowered by God, to a belief that He was a *"Prophet,"* and finally, to a ready acknowledgement that He was indeed the Son of God. However, the Pharisees were conscious of nothing He said or of Who He was. Consequently, they could make nothing of His Words.

If one knew at present the Mind of the Holy Spirit regarding the condition of the modern church, it is doubtful that it would be that much different from the Pharisees of Jesus' Day. Jesus is as shut out of most modern churches presently as He was of most synagogues of His Time.

THE CROSS OF CHRIST AND THE MODERN CHURCH

Due to the fact of not understanding the Cross of Christ relative to Sanctification, virtually all, even those who are truly Saved and who love God supremely, are dominated by the sin nature in some way, which is certainly not the Will of God.

Sometime back, the Devil came very close to making me believe a certain thing that was to prove very wrong. At the first, I did not know it was Satan. He began to subtly suggest to me that there may be a few people who need the Message of the Cross, but for the most part, most Christians are getting along well. I was to find out differently.

It was a Sunday night, and Donnie was preaching. He wasn't preaching on the Deliverance of the Children of Israel from Egyptian bondage. However, in the course of his Message, he happened to mention the Deliverance of the Children of Israel. It was the account of Moses through Aaron telling Pharaoh, *"Let My people go."*

The moment Donnie said that, the Spirit of God covered me like a glove. I began to weep as the Lord began to speak to my heart. He told me that His People, and we speak of this present time, are in the same condition as the Children of Israel were in Egypt. They were slaves to Pharaoh, and most Christians today, by not understanding the Cross of Christ, are being dominated by sin in some way, i.e., *"the sin nature,"* which means, if the truth be known, *"O wretched man that I am."* The answer for sin, and the only answer for sin, is the Cross of Christ. Unfortunately, the Cross has been so little preached the last several decades that for all practical purposes, the modern church is Cross illiterate. This means they don't know the answer to the problems that face humanity. That answer is the Cross of Christ.

(7) "THEN SAID JESUS UNTO THEM AGAIN, VERILY, VERILY, I SAY UNTO YOU, I AM THE DOOR OF THE SHEEP."

The form is:

1. We must ever understand that Christ never took our fallen nature into union with Himself.

2. He was not a product of the Fall, as all other human beings are, as a result of the fall of Adam in the Garden of Eden.

3. In fact, Jesus did not have a sin nature. Actually, that was the reason for the Virgin Birth. Had He been born by normal procreation, He would have been born as all other babies, in original sin, which would have translated into a fallen nature. However, to escape that fallen nature, He was born of the Virgin Mary.

I AM THE DOOR OF THE SHEEP

The phrase, *"Then said Jesus unto them again,"* proclaims Him now speaking very plainly, explaining exactly what He has said in order that all would understand perfectly.

Between Verses 6 and 7, there could have been a pause, during which time the Pharisees uttered their disapproval of what Christ had said, even though they little understood its meaning. In other words, they opposed whatever He said, irrespective as to what it was.

"Verily, verily, I say unto you," is pointed directly towards the Pharisees but, as well, applies to the entirety of the world and for all time.

However, it should be understood and not forgotten that Jesus is, more than all, directing His Words toward the world of religion. He wants there to be absolutely no misunderstanding as to what He is saying, and that any abrogation of His Declaration is a forfeiture of Salvation.

The phrase, *"I am the Door of the Sheep,"* proclaims an emphatic statement. In other words, *"I am,"* exclusive of all others!

As well, this tells us there is only *"One Door,"* and that *"Door"* is Christ.

THE HEAD OF EACH MEMBER INDIVIDUALLY

Also, it tells us that not only is He the One Door to *"the fold"* but, as well, of each individual Sheep in his individual capacity. So, He is not only the Corporate Head of the Church, but the Head of each member individually.

This means that if any member of this Body of Christ allows a preacher or priest to demand of them something unscriptural, with it being obeyed, such could result in the loss of one's soul. Everything must be subject to Christ and His Word. To do otherwise is to abrogate the Position of Christ as Head of the Church, and each member particularly.

Regrettably, multiple tens of millions have been eternally lost because they did this very thing. They allowed a preacher or priest to serve as their chief shepherd instead of Christ.

This does not mean that the Callings of *"Apostles, Prophets, Evangelists, Pastors, and Teachers,"* are to be ignored. Quite the contrary! These Callings are given *"the perfecting of the Saints, for the work of the Ministry, for the edifying of the Body of Christ"* (Eph. 4:11-12).

It does mean that these are to never take the place of Christ as the True Head of the Church. Above all, it means that no denominational heads are to take His Place.

All are to function properly in their rightful place. If so done, it will perfect a healthy, mature Body.

(8) "ALL WHO EVER CAME BEFORE ME ARE THIEVES AND ROBBERS: BUT THE SHEEP DID NOT HEAR THEM."

The construction is:

1. It has been argued for ages as to whether Jesus could have sinned. Yes, He could have sinned. To be the *"Last Adam,"* He had to have that freedom. However, He did not sin, not even one time, in word, thought, or deed.

2. While Christ never unites with us in our fallen nature, we, in fact, do unite with Him in His Divine Nature (II Pet. 1:4).

3. And yet, as our Substitute, He died *"for us."* As our Representative Man, He died *"as us."*

THIEVES AND ROBBERS

The phrase, *"All who ever came before Me are thieves and robbers,"* pertains to any and all before Christ, or after, who claim to have a way of Salvation without Christ.

It pointedly pertained to all the Scribes and Pharisees who, before Christ and after Him, attempted to devise their own salvation by means of the Law of Moses, along with their glosses. They were *"thieves and robbers!"* Tragically, many fall into the same category presently.

It also pertained to all the ridiculous heathen assertions, such as reincarnation, or any type of supposed salvation outside of Christ.

This means that Gautama, who founded Buddhism, is a *"thief and robber,"* as well as Muhammad, Confucius, Joseph Smith, and all other fake luminaries!

WHY DID JESUS USE THE APPELLATIVE "THIEVES AND ROBBERS"?

There is nothing worse than a false way of Salvation. For people to think they are Saved, having been seduced by false teachers of whatever stripe or variety, is deception of the highest order. To be sure, and sadly, almost the entirety of the world for all time falls into this category.

Consequently, the purveyors of this false salvation, deceiving themselves, set about to steal what true opportunity of Salvation that one may have and, thereby, rob them of any chance of Eternal Life.

The phrase, *"But the sheep did not hear them,"* pertains to those who truly know the Lord in all ages and, thereby, are not seduced by these *"thieves and robbers!"*

Why?

They truly know the Voice of the *"Good Shepherd"*; consequently, *"they know not the voice of strangers"* (Vss. 4-5).

This is a beautiful and wonderful security, but it pertains to only those who are truly His Sheep.

Primarily, Jesus was speaking of those who lived before He came. Consequently, the idea is that if He kept them then, and He did, how much greater is His Keeping Power since He has now come and defeated Satan and all his minions of darkness! Previously, all the Sheep had was a Promise; however, the Promise was enough! Under the New Covenant, all Believers are privileged to enjoy the Finished Work of Christ. Consequently, one need not fear.

(9) "I AM THE DOOR: BY ME IF ANY MAN ENTER IN, HE SHALL BE SAVED, AND SHALL GO IN AND OUT, AND FIND PASTURE."

The exposition is:

1. Jesus is God and always will be God. However, due to the Incarnation, He now functions as a Man and, in fact, will forever function as a Man (Zech. 12:10; 13:6).

2. The purpose for Jesus becoming Man (the Incarnation) was that He may serve as the *"Last Adam"* (I Cor. 15:45).

3. He had to do what the first Adam did not do, which was to completely obey God.

I AM THE DOOR

The phrase, *"I am the Door,"* presents an emphatic statement.

The church is not the door to Eternal Life as the Roman Catholic priests teach, but Christ is the Door to all that God has for us. How simple is Salvation! He promises Eternal Life to all who base their claim for entrance upon Him Alone.

The phrase, *"By Me if any man enter in, he shall be Saved,"* says several things:

• Jesus is the Saviour, and there is none else!

• Any and all may enter in, irrespective as to whom they may be. There is no such thing as some being predestined to be lost while others are predestined to be Saved. The invitation is open to all (Rev. 22:17).

• The moment the believing sinner enters in, he is then Saved. As well, the statement is empathic! In other words, it is all inclusive, meaning that the guarantee is given by Jesus Himself.

PASTURE

"And shall go in and out, and find pasture," denotes the free use of an abode by one who is at home in the house (Deut. 28:6; 31:2; Acts 1:21). Above all, it speaks of freedom!

Living outside of the Saving Grace of Jesus Christ, the only other alternative is for one to be a slave of Satan and sin. Consequently, the only freedom that such a one has is the freedom to do what Satan and sin demand. Otherwise, there is no freedom in Satan.

In Jesus, one's freedom is absolute. The unbeliever erroneously thinks there are many things that the Christian cannot do. He misunderstands!

With the entirety of the nature of the Believer being changed, it is not that he cannot, but that he does not desire those sinful things anymore. He has something far better to take their place.

The truth is that the spiritual part of man craves that which is spiritual, and which Satan tries to satisfy with things, which is impossible. However, the moment the believing sinner comes to Christ, his spiritual thirst is slaked, actually providing that which he has craved all along. At that time, other things lose their attraction.

When one comes to Christ, one does not enter a prison as Satan makes many believe, but is rather released from a prison. Isaiah said, *"To open the blind eyes* (spiritually blind), *to bring out the prisoners from the prison, and them who sit in darkness out of the prison house"* (Isa. 42:7).

(10) "THE THIEF COMES NOT, BUT FOR TO STEAL, AND TO KILL, AND TO DESTROY: I AM COME THAT THEY MIGHT HAVE LIFE, AND THAT THEY MIGHT HAVE IT MORE ABUNDANTLY."

The synopsis is:

1. The Holy Spirit can function in us only because our Faith is in a Perfect Christ.

2. More particularly, it is the Cross of Christ that gives the Holy Spirit the legal means to do all that He does.

3. Our Faith in Christ and what He did for us at the Cross gives us His Perfection, which makes it possible for the Holy Spirit to work with us as He does.

THE THIEF

The phrase, *"The thief comes not, but for to steal, and to kill, and to destroy,"* speaks indirectly of Satan, which would be obvious, but directly, it speaks of his emissaries who peddle a false way of Salvation. At the moment, Jesus was speaking of the Pharisees and Scribes, but, as well, it incorporates all who fall into this category. The sadness is, for everyone truly Called of the Lord who points to Jesus as the Only Way, there are thousands of *"thieves!"*

As well, irrespective of what *"thieves"* may promise, the end result will always be, and without exception, *"theft, murder, and destruction."*

MORE ABUNDANT LIFE

The phrase, *"I am come that they might have life, and that they might have it more abundantly,"* presents one of the grandest of our Lord's Claims. He gives from overflowing stores (Titus 3:6).

The Source of this *"Life"* is Christ. All others who promise such but, of course, cannot deliver, are as He said, *"Thieves and robbers."*

Of what type of life does He speak?

It is not mere existence. It is the entire cause, purpose, and reason for living. It is the privilege of serving God, for which man was originally made and which, as stated, sets him free. It is actually Jesus Himself. There is no life apart from Christ.

This is the reason that a person can have this overflowing *"Abundant Life,"* actually, *"more Abundant Life,"* even though he may have little of this world's goods or even physical health. All the things which Satan promises are exterior, which can never satisfy, because it never deals with the true need of man because Satan cannot deal with the true need of man.

That which Jesus gives is that which He places in the heart, which actually emanates from Him, all made possible by the Cross. This *"Life"* is a constant flow in overflowing amounts, which one can never exhaust.

Of all the religions in the world, despite all their claims, none even remotely promises anything similar to Christ.

Islam promises no satisfaction of heart whatsoever, only that one will gain an exotic, passionate, sensual paradise upon death, which is heavily weighted in favor of men, with women being no more than servants.

MORE THIEVES AND ROBBERS

Buddhism holds out the hope of some type of nirvana, which is a place or state of oblivion of care, fame, or external reality. However, it is only a goal hoped for but, so far, unattainable!

Confucianism only promises a particular code of ethics but changes not at all the heart and passions of an individual.

Shintoism is a cultic devotion to supposed deities of natural forces and veneration of the Emperor of Japan as a descendant of the sun goddess. As should be obvious, this, as well, has no effect on the natural disposition of an individual. Consequently, it changes nothing!

Jesus Alone changes hearts and lives of individuals, which only He can do, simply because He Alone is God. As well, the fruit of what He does, respecting changed lives, is evident and obvious all over the world.

So, why is it that the far greater majority opts for things other than Christ?

Deception is the reason that *"thieves and robbers"* are successful in their efforts to damn the souls of men. As stated many times, the propensity of deception came about as a result of the Fall in the Garden of Eden. In other words, man finds it much easier to believe a lie than to believe the Truth!

(11) "I AM THE GOOD SHEPHERD: THE GOOD SHEPHERD GIVES HIS LIFE FOR THE SHEEP."

The overview is:

1. The phrase, *"I am the Good Shepherd,"* speaks of Jesus dying for the Sheep.

2. As the Good Shepherd dies for the Sheep, the Great Shepherd lives for the Sheep (Heb. 13:20), and the Chief Shepherd comes for the Sheep (I Pet. 5:4).

3. Here, Jesus calls Himself *"Good,"* while in Matthew 19:17, He said to the rich young ruler, *"Why do you call Me good? there is none good but One, that is, God."*

In the account as given by Matthew, Jesus was not saying that He was not good but that God only was good. Jesus is God!

4. As well, the type of *"good"* of which the rich young ruler was speaking was really self-righteousness, which God never classifies as *"good."*

5. The phrase, *"The Good Shepherd gives His Life for the Sheep,"* proclaims the exact opposite of what Israel thought her Messiah would be. Jesus came as the Suffering Messiah while they were looking for the Conquering Messiah.

6. To be sure, He definitely was and is a Conqueror, but not in the way they had surmised. They wanted Him to conquer Rome while He came to conquer the world, the flesh, and the Devil. This He did, and grandly so! However, He would have to suffer, actually laying down His Life in order for this to be done, and it was all for you and me.

As well, He calls on all who follow Him, and I mean all, to likewise *"give our lives"* for His Cause. Of course, in doing that, He gives us a far greater Life, exactly as He said in the latter portion of the Tenth Verse.

7. There are two types of shepherds in the world, which He places in contrast, the *"Good Shepherd"* and the *"hireling."*

(12) "BUT HE WHO IS AN HIRELING, AND NOT THE SHEPHERD, WHOSE OWN THE SHEEP ARE NOT, SEES THE WOLF COMING, AND LEAVES THE SHEEP, AND FLEES: AND THE WOLF CATCHES THEM, AND SCATTERS THE SHEEP."

The order is:

1. Christ and Him Crucified must always be the Foundation of our Faith (I Cor. 1:23).

2. The greatest Promise that God made, and of which the Meat-Offering was a Type, was that He would send a Redeemer into the world to lift man out of this darkness.

3. This One sent would be the Perfect One, actually, God's Only Son (Jn. 3:16).

THE HIRELING

The phrase, *"But he who is an hireling, and not the shepherd,"* presents the one who poses as a shepherd but really is not.

What is an *"hireling?"*

The word *"hireling"* in the Greek is *"misthotos"* and means *"one who has no real interest in his duty,"* and, as well, *"is unfaithful in the discharge of it."* It also speaks of one *"whose motives are other than that of the Lord's."*

The phrase, *"Whose own the sheep are not,"* in its broader state refers to the individual who is not of the Lord. In other words, if a person is of the Lord, consequently attempting to truly carry out the Will of God, he will do nothing to harm the Sheep in any fashion.

Using Family Worship Center as an example, I have seen quite a number of preachers come and go throughout the history of this Church. Some of them had motives in mind which were not of God. Their interest in the Sheep was not that which was right.

Some did all they could to draw people after them in order to start another church. However, all such churches are doomed spiritually from their beginning. They are begun by *"hirelings,"* and, as such, it is something the Lord can never bless.

THE WOLF

The phrase, *"Sees the wolf coming, and leaves the sheep, and flees,"* presents an obvious conclusion.

When an individual is leading the Sheep for the sake of money or other erroneous purposes, if difficulties arise, which they do sooner or later, the *"hireling"* will always flee. His purpose is not to protect the Sheep but to fleece the Sheep.

"And the wolf catches them, and scatters the sheep," as well presents the obvious conclusion.

Once again, referring to our own Church, I have seen many Sheep pulled aside by *"hirelings,"* with the end result always being that of which Jesus said. Actually, it can be no other way!

Most of the time, the Sheep who follow the *"hireling"* are destroyed at some point. In other words, they cease to exist for the Lord in any capacity.

Also, even those who remain with the hireling experience no spiritual growth but actually the reverse.

That the *"wolves"* will come is a given. The true Shepherd, however, will protect from such while the *"hireling"* will leave the Sheep at the mercy of the *"wolf,"* i.e., Satan.

Jesus lamented the fact that the Israel of His Day was, *"As sheep having no shepherd,"* therefore, *"They fainted, and were scattered abroad"* (Mat. 9:36).

RELIGIOUS WOLVES

In this statement, Jesus was not only referring to the Sheep but also to the Scribes and Pharisees, who were supposed to be the shepherds of the people, but were rather the opposite.

As well, *"wolves"* come in various shapes and sizes but are always religious wolves. They propose to have the Truth, but do not, or they may really have the Truth, but impure motives. As a result, their *"truth"* ceases to be Truth. A *"hireling"* may very well lead Sheep to proper pasture and water; however, at the first sign of danger, he flees. Many people (sheep) are fooled because the pasture and the water are ample; however, they reckon without the enemy, who sooner or later comes.

Even though the examples of *"hirelings"* are almost unending, please allow me to name a few:

HIRELINGS

The evangelist tells the assembled congregation that the Lord has told him that if they will come forward and give $1,000, their homes will be paid for by the end of the year (or some such time), irrespective of how much is presently owed!

A preacher sends out a letter telling the people that the Lord has told him that all who respond will get a hundredfold return.

Another preacher looks into a television camera and says that the Lord has told him that all who call in the next 10 minutes (or whatever period of time) will receive tenfold, etc., in return.

Another preacher writes and says that the Lord has spoken to him directly about the person receiving the letter when, in fact, that same letter has gone to thousands of people.

Actually, as stated, the varieties of schemes are almost unending. Not all deal with money but with other situations, such as place, position, etc.

At any rate, it is exploitation and, consequently, is not of God. Tragically and sadly, too many Sheep fall for such schemes and are always weakened spiritually, some greatly so!

Actually, anytime Sheep are led by *"hirelings,"* they will never be developed but always exploited.

(13) *"THE HIRELING FLEES, BECAUSE HE IS AN HIRELING, AND CARES NOT FOR THE SHEEP."*

The exegesis is:

1. The phrase, *"The hireling flees, because he is an hireling,"* portrays the end result. The *"hireling"* is not there for the sheep, but rather for himself, in whatever capacity.

2. *"And cares not for the sheep,"* means he has never cared for the sheep but always had something else in mind.

3. As I have said repeatedly, religion uses people. It wants money, and it wants control while, at the same time, it has little concern for the spiritual welfare of the people. Actually, it is my personal feeling that the hierarchy of religious denominations, for the most part, falls into that category. There are exceptions, but not many. How do I know that?

4. There is no such thing as a hierarchy in the New Testament Church, so that means that such is unscriptural. Consequently, spiritual men do not occupy such positions, only those who are *"hirelings."* As such, they are interested in preserving the denomination and their positions, with the spiritual welfare of the people too often relegated to second place, if any place at all! Actually, this was the position of Israel in Jesus' Day.

(14) *"I AM THE GOOD SHEPHERD, AND KNOW MY SHEEP, AND AM KNOWN OF MINE."*

The synopsis is:

1. Three things are said in this Verse:

a. *"I am the Good Shepherd"*: in effect, Jesus was saying that He is the Chief Shepherd, with all other Shepherds called by Him serving as under-Shepherds.

This means that the various religions of the world headed up by such as Muhammad, Joseph Smith, the Pope, Confucius, etc., are not shepherds at all, but rather *"hirelings,"* and of the worst sort.

It also means that no particular church or religious denomination is a Shepherd. It is Jesus and Jesus Alone Who is the *"Good Shepherd!"*

b. *"And know My sheep"*: the word *"know"* in the Greek is *"ginosko"* and means *"to be approved,"* in this case, by the Lord. In other words, the Lord approves those who are His because they have trusted Him for Salvation. However, the relationship implied may involve *"remedial chastisement,"* for God takes such action regarding those He loves (Heb. 12:6-8).

c. *"And am known of Mine"*: such knowledge is obtained, not by mere activity, but by Operation of the Holy Spirit consequent upon acceptance of Christ and the desire to be led by the Spirit (Rom. 8:1-2).

2. As well, this knowledge of the Sheep, in respect to the Shepherd, has no limitations. It is impossible to exhaust knowledge concerning Jesus. As well, He will give us as much knowledge of Him as we desire, hence, Paul saying, *"That I may know Him ..."* (Phil. 3:10).

(15) "AS THE FATHER KNOWS ME, EVEN SO KNOW I THE FATHER: AND I LAY DOWN MY LIFE FOR THE SHEEP."

The order is:

1. The phrase, *"As the Father knows Me, even so know I the Father,"* has Jesus proclaiming equality of knowledge with the Father, which is an assertion of Deity. In effect, Jesus was claiming Omniscience exactly as God, for He is God!

2. *"And I lay down My Life for the Sheep,"* spoke of His Coming Crucifixion.

3. Over and over, the Lord has impressed upon me all that was done at Calvary, of which we only know in part, but more particularly, that it was done totally and completely for us. God did not need us and actually needs nothing. Therefore, what was done respecting Calvary is beyond our comprehension.

4. As well, the laying down of His Life not only assured our Salvation, at least upon Faith in Him, but, as well, guarantees a life of victory thereafter. However, the Faith exhibited must be ongoing respecting victory, even as Salvation.

(16) "AND OTHER SHEEP I HAVE, WHICH ARE NOT OF THIS FOLD: THEM ALSO I MUST BRING, AND THEY SHALL HEAR MY VOICE; AND THERE SHALL BE ONE FOLD, AND ONE SHEPHERD."

The structure is:

1. The Believer should ever be directed to the Cross, which is the Foundation Doctrine of all Doctrine (I Pet. 1:18-20).

2. In fact, all false doctrine begins with an improper interpretation of the Cross.

3. The Resurrection was a foregone conclusion in that Jesus atoned for all sin at the Cross. Had one sin been left unatoned, Jesus could not have been raised from the dead (Rom. 6:23).

THE GENTILE CHURCH

The phrase, *"And other Sheep I have, which are not of this fold,"* speaks of the Gentile Church.

It was always God's Plan that the entirety of the world would hear and know the Gospel (Jn. 3:16). Actually, this was to be one of the purposes of the Nation of Israel, to take the Gospel to the Gentiles. However, due to their self-righteousness, they became so sectarian that they pretty much shut everyone out except themselves, and then, tragically, found themselves shut out as well!

One must always understand that the Plan of God will never be defeated. While the Will of God is seldom carried out, at least in this Dispensation, ultimately, the Plan of God always is. To those who set themselves in opposition to that Plan, whatever it might be, will ultimately, as Israel of old, find themselves broken. Jesus said, *"The Kingdom of God shall be taken from you, and given to a nation bringing forth the fruits thereof.*

"And whosoever shall fall on this stone shall be broken: but on whomsoever it shall fall, it will grind him to powder" (Mat. 21:43-44).

The phrase, *"Them also I must bring, and they shall hear My Voice,"* proclaims that the Gentile Church will be built, which it was, because it responded to His Voice.

ONE FOLD AND ONE SHEPHERD

In effect, the Church was supposed to be both Gentile and Jewish; however, even though it began totally Jewish, it soon came to be virtually Gentile. While there are, of course, some few Jews in the Church, the number is insignificant by comparison to the whole.

The phrase, *"And there shall be one fold, and One Shepherd,"* actually makes the same statement I have just made. However, good Greek authorities state that it should have been translated, *"And there shall be one flock, and One Shepherd."*

This has a greater meaning even than the Church, with it ultimately speaking of the entirety of the world. Of course, I speak of the coming Kingdom Age when Jesus will rule Personally from Jerusalem, and then, in reality, there will be only one Church, that of the Lord Jesus Christ. This will commence at the Second Coming.

The Lord said through Isaiah, *"It shall come, that I will gather all nations and tongues; and they shall come, and see My Glory"* (Isa. 66:18).

When the Lord used the words *"other Sheep,"* He was thinking of you and me.

(17) "THEREFORE DOES MY FATHER LOVE ME, BECAUSE I LAY DOWN MY LIFE, THAT I MIGHT TAKE IT AGAIN."

The diagram is:

1. The phrase, *"Therefore does My Father love Me,"* proclaims what Christ was to do and held a special value in God's Heart.

2. His laying down His Life and His taking it again was, in itself, pleasing to the Father, apart altogether from its value for the Sheep.

3. Man cannot furnish motives in order to attract God's Love. The Divine Son Alone can do so, for His Death was a manifestation of the reality of God's Love for the sinner and a vindication of this Justice of God's Judgment upon sin.

4. *"Because I lay down My Life, that I might take it again,"* has been judged by some skeptics as suicide. However, His Life was His Own as Creator, and He had the Power of taking it again, and He was conscious of that Power.

5. By contrast, a Preacher's life is not his own. He can destroy it, as some do by suicide, but he cannot resume it. Christ's Death was wholly voluntary. He did not die

NOTES

from physical weakness, as some assert. This was proven by His Loud Cry just before He died, which physical weakness would not have allowed (Mat. 27:50).

6. The entirety of the idea of the Incarnation was to purposely *"lay down His Life,"* which, of course, addresses the Cross. In order that man be redeemed, His Perfect Life in the form of His Shed Blood had to be poured out, along with His Unblemished Body offered in Sacrifice as a Sin-Offering. However, as that was an absolute necessity, likewise, the Resurrection, *"That I might take it again."*

7. His Death at Calvary and His Burial guaranteed man's Redemption, at least upon Faith, which meant that the old man of sin was destroyed. This guaranteed the victorious New Life in Jesus. As well, His Resurrection guaranteed two things:

a. First of all, His Resurrection guaranteed our Resurrection into a New Life, referring to walking in victory.

b. Secondly, His Resurrection guaranteed our coming Resurrection when we will have a Glorified Body (Rom. 6:3-6).

(18) "NO MAN TAKES IT FROM ME, BUT I LAY IT DOWN OF MYSELF. I HAVE POWER TO LAY IT DOWN, AND I HAVE POWER TO TAKE IT AGAIN. THIS COMMANDMENT HAVE I RECEIVED OF MY FATHER."

The composition is:

1. The price that God demanded was high, so high, in fact, that it beggars description. However, we have no argument, seeing that He paid the price Himself.

2. Only the Spotless Lamb of God could pay the price, and the Meat-Offering of the Levitical system proclaimed the Purity of Christ, in fact, a Perfect Purity.

3. The unredeemed man thinks that his *"good"* will save him, which it won't! Regrettably, the redeemed man often tries to live for God by the means of his so-called goodness. Neither will suffice!

THE LIFE OF CHRIST WAS NOT TAKEN BY ANY MAN

The phrase, *"No man takes it from Me, but I lay it down of Myself,"* tells us several things.

Due to the fact that Jesus was not born of natural procreation and, therefore, had no sin nature, in effect, had He so chosen, He would have lived forever in that state. This was what God originally intended for man.

In other words, had Adam and Eve not sinned, they would still be alive today and, in effect, forever.

Jesus, as the Last Adam, in effect, the Perfect Adam, did not die as one thinks of death. Actually, His Death was totally unlike anyone else who has ever died. He literally breathed out His Life, willing His Own Death, which was ordained by the Holy Spirit (Heb. 9:14).

At His Death, He said, *"Father, into Your Hands I commend My Spirit"* (Lk. 23:46).

He probably then said, *"It is finished: and He bowed His Head, and gave up the ghost"* (Jn. 19:30).

As there had never been a life like His, likewise, there had never been a death as His!

POWER

The phrase, *"I have Power to lay it down, and I have Power to take it again,"* proclaims that which He did, He did voluntarily. He did not step out of the path of obedience, for He died as commanded. Thus Love, Obedience, and Dependence shine as golden rays from His Cross.

As stated, this *"Power"* not only had to do with the disposition of His Life but, as well, its protection from any and all.

"This Commandment have I received of My Father," pertains to several things:

• It pertained to the Incarnation, God becoming Man, which was for the very purpose of voluntarily laying down His Life and then taking it up again.

• The end result was the Redemption of mankind, for which He came, at least for all who will believe (Jn. 3:16).

• He was given full latitude by the Father in that He could do so or not do so. In effect, the *"Commandment"* had to be in this fashion, or else, it could not be accepted by the Father. His Death had to be voluntary, not forced by God, man, or evil spirits.

This is why He said in the Garden of Gethsemane, *"Father, if You be willing, remove this cup from Me: nevertheless not My Will, but Yours, be done"* (Lk. 22:42).

(19) *"THERE WAS A DIVISION THEREFORE AGAIN AMONG THE JEWS FOR THESE SAYINGS."*

The composition is:

1. This tells us of the fact of the Division, while the cause of the Division lay with the religious leadership of Israel. This is the sadness of it all, then and now.

2. Whomever the people think resides in a position of spiritual leadership will mostly be followed, right or wrong. Regrettably, now, as then, most do not know their Bibles well enough to make a Scriptural judgment. They simply follow the crowd.

3. Actually, and sadly so, the far greater majority of the time, even as in Jesus' Day, those who the majority of the people look to as religious leadership are mostly wrong. Uncounted millions have died eternally lost because they followed such leadership, even as many Jews followed the religious hierarchy of that day and time.

(20) *"AND MANY OF THEM SAID, HE HAS A DEMON, AND IS INSANE; WHY DO YOU HEAR HIM?"*

The overview is:

1. The phrase, *"And many of them said, He has a demon,"* proclaims the policy of the Pharisees and Scribes, who claimed that Jesus cast out demons by the power of Satan. Consequently, some of the people believed the same thing. However, the Pharisees who charged Jesus in this manner blasphemed the Holy Spirit and sealed their doom (Mat. 12:24-32).

2. *"And is insane,"* proclaims some of the people claiming this. For what reason?

3. The question, *"Why do you hear Him?"* shows the Pharisees seeking to dissuade the people from paying any attention to such discourses Jesus had just delivered. This was the Church of that day!

4. Just today, I answered a letter from a lady who had been watching our telecast and had come under great Conviction by the Holy Spirit. In other words, she wanted to be Saved but had not yet yielded.

She mentioned that she had spoken to a lady, a fellow employee, who was a member of the same denomination with which I had been formerly associated. She had told her that she was watching our telecast, but the woman strongly encouraged her not to do so anymore.

Why would she do that, especially considering that this woman claimed to be Saved and baptized with the Holy Spirit?

In effect, it seems that the woman would rather this lady die eternally lost than be Saved under our Ministry. She was saying the same thing as the Pharisees of old, *"Why do you hear Him?"*

What are we doing that is so bad that this woman should not watch the telecast?

5. We are seeking God day and night in order that the Holy Spirit may move through us that people, exactly as this dear lady, may be Saved. As well, we preach the same Gospel that we always have, which has seen hundreds of thousands come to a Saving Knowledge of Jesus Christ.

6. This poor lady believed the things that she said simply because those who call themselves spiritual leaders told her to do so. It was the same in Jesus' Day.

7. In the case of Jesus, Perfect Righteousness incurred the wrath of self-righteousness. Likewise, imputed Righteousness incurs the same wrath!

(21) "OTHERS SAID, THESE ARE NOT THE WORDS OF HIM WHO HAS A DEMON. CAN A DEMON OPEN THE EYES OF THE BLIND?"

The exegesis is:

1. The phrase, *"Others said, These are not the words of Him Who has a demon,"* as it was obvious to some, should have been obvious to all. To listen for a few moments to the things Jesus was saying quickly disputed the idea that He was of Satan, at least if one sought to be honest. Please allow me another indulgence.

If anyone would listen to our network, SonLife Broadcasting Network, only for a few minutes, he, too, would have to come to the conclusion that *"these are not the words of him who has a demon."*

2. With Jesus, it was not really a difficult decision to make. It only took a little common sense and some spiritual honesty, which, sadly, was lacking in most of the church of Jesus' Day.

NOTES

3. The question, *"Can a demon open the eyes of the blind?"* as it is asked, must have, *"No,"* as an answer.

4. While it is true that Satan and some demon spirits can perform miracles (Ex. 7:10-12; 8:7, 18-19; Mat. 24:24; II Thess. 2:8-12; Rev., Chpt. 13, 19:20), still, such miracles will never be in this fashion, which were done strictly in the manner of love. Demons do not heal diseases in this fashion or pour light on sightless eyes. Consequently, the Goodness of the Lord triumphs over the vile insinuations of the Pharisees.

5. If the people had only looked at the fruit of Jesus' Ministry instead of listening to what the religious leaders said, it would have been obvious as to Who and What He was.

6. That should be the criterion at present as well (Mat. 7:15-20).

(22) "AND IT WAS AT JERUSALEM THE FEAST OF THE DEDICATION, AND IT WAS WINTER."

The synopsis is:

1. This *"Feast of the Dedication"* was appointed by Judas Maccabaeus to commemorate the purification of the Temple after it had been defiled by Antiochus Epiphanies, who offered a sow (a hog) on the Altar and polluted the Temple by sprinkling its broth all around. This took place on the 25th of Chisleu (December), 164 B.C., and would have corresponded with our December 19th. Thus John mentioned five feasts Christ attended (Jn. 2:13; 5:1; 7:2, 10; 10:22; 12:1; 13:1). This feast was not one of the Feasts ordained in the Law of Moses, hence, was not Biblical.

2. More than anything else, this particular feast heightened the enthusiasm of the people for deliverance from the Roman yoke. Actually, the Jews would probably have eagerly accepted Jesus as Messiah if He had been ready to take up the role of a political leader.

3. While He definitely was the Messiah and, consequently, the Fulfillment of all the Prophecies, He was not the Christ of the Jewish expectation.

(23) "AND JESUS WALKED IN THE TEMPLE IN SOLOMON'S PORCH."

The pattern is:

1. The eastern side of the Temple Court

was called, *"Solomon's porch,"* and was built by him and left standing when Nebuchadnezzar took the city.

2. It was of grand design and was over 800 feet long. Some say that the porch was built later but on the substructure of Solomon's Temple.

3. This porch was where the Apostles afterward adopted as a preaching platform for some of their most explicit assertions of the Gospel (Acts 3:11; 5:12).

(24) "THEN CAME THE JEWS ROUND ABOUT HIM, AND SAID UNTO HIM, HOW LONG DO YOU MAKE US TO DOUBT? IF YOU ARE THE CHRIST, TELL US PLAINLY."

The diagram is:

1. The question, *"Then came the Jews round about Him,"* portrays them doing such in a threatening manner, demanding an immediate answer.

2. *"And said unto Him, How long do You make us to doubt?"* was asked improperly. Jesus was not the One Who made them to doubt, but rather their own unbelief.

3. The phrase, *"If You are the Christ, tell us plainly,"* presents another farce.

4. Actually, He had told them in every conceivable way possible and, above all, had fulfilled the Scriptures in totality.

5. What He said or did not say, as should be obvious, was of extreme significance. However, the Word of God was to be the criterion. In truth, they were in great trouble presently simply because they were listening to men and not the Word of God.

(25) "JESUS ANSWERED THEM, I TOLD YOU, AND YOU BELIEVED NOT: THE WORKS THAT I DO IN MY FATHER'S NAME, THEY BEAR WITNESS OF ME."

The order is:

1. The phrase, *"Jesus answered them,"* in so many words, proclaimed the correct answer, but it was not the type of answer they were seeking. In effect, Jesus directed them once again to the Word.

2. *"I told you, and you believed not,"* refers to their expectations of a type of Messiah, the role which Jesus would not fill. As stated, had he taken a political role, the possibility is high that they would have accepted Him. However, such was impossible for Him to do simply because their problem was not political but spiritual, and would require His Death on Calvary in order to redeem humanity. But they *"believed not"* and remained unredeemed!

3. The phrase, *"The Works that I do in My Father's Name, they bear witness of Me,"* presents a threefold guarantee as to Who He was:

a. The *"Works"* themselves were miraculous and could only be done by God.

b. They were done in the *"Father's Name,"* which would not have been possible had Jesus been of Satan. Therefore, when they were ridiculing Him, they were ridiculing Jehovah as well!

c. The *"witness"* was Scriptural and, therefore, pointed Israel to the Bible (Isa. 61:1).

(26) "BUT YOU BELIEVE NOT, BECAUSE YOU ARE NOT OF MY SHEEP, AS I SAID UNTO YOU."

The form is:

1. Why were they not His Sheep?
2. Were they predestined thusly?
3. No! They were not His Sheep because they did not desire to be His Sheep. The decision was theirs and was reached because of unbelief.
4. Actually, Israel was God's Elect (Isa. 45:4), but election does not necessarily mean Salvation. The term simply means *"chosen."* Any person or group of persons selected or chosen of God for any particular purpose is the Elect of God. However, many, as with Israel, even though elected, choose to go in the opposite direction of God and are, thereby, lost exactly as Israel was in Jesus' Day.
5. There are no direct statements of God choosing to save certain individuals contrary to their own will, as some teach. God never violates the free moral agency of any man. He will deal with people, address them, speak to them, and even move greatly upon them, but He will never force one to accept Christ and live for God. That must be their own free choice.

(27) "MY SHEEP HEAR MY VOICE, AND I KNOW THEM, AND THEY FOLLOW ME."

The overview is:

1. The phrase, *"My sheep hear My*

Voice," means that Christ is the Leader of the Church, and not men. Sadly, much, if not most, of the modern church listens to the voice of man rather than that of Christ. While the Believer certainly should glean all that is possible from those whom God has truly called (Eph. 4:11-12), still, the Believer is to know the Word of God well enough that he will know if what is taught is right or wrong. Multiple millions at present are in Hell simply because they listened to other voices.

2. The Believer must walk close enough to the Lord that he not only hears His Voice but, as well, knows it is from the Lord and understands what is being said.

3. *"And I know them,"* refers, as would be obvious, to perfect and absolute knowledge, even on an individual basis. Even though God does address Himself corporately to the Church, His Greater Dealings, by far, are with the individual. It is the same as a shepherd knowing each sheep by name, and actually having a relationship with each individual sheep. Of course, a human shepherd can take this only so far while such is unlimited with the Lord.

4. He knows us in the sense of wanting to have fellowship with us and wanting to be totally and completely involved in every aspect of our lives. However, His Involvement will never be forced but always must be freely invited by the Believer.

5. The phrase, *"And they follow Me,"* once again proclaims that which true Sheep will do.

6. In essence, the Lord was saying that the people of Israel could follow Him or their religious leaders. They could not follow both! That problem is no less pronounced presently.

7. The truth is, most of the modern church follows denominations, men, doctrines, etc. Only a few truly follow Christ.

8. Once again, this does not mean that it is improper to belong to religious denominations, etc. It does mean that we are to understand that these things are merely tools to help us in our walk with the Lord, or rather is what they are supposed to be. When they become more than that, which they are in many, if not most, cases, then the person is no longer following Christ but rather man.

(28) "AND I GIVE UNTO THEM ETERNAL LIFE; AND THEY SHALL NEVER PERISH, NEITHER SHALL ANY MAN PLUCK THEM OUT OF MY HAND."

The form is:

1. It is Faith in Christ and the Cross that got us in and Faith in Christ and the Cross that keeps us in.

2. If we accept Jesus and ignore the Cross, we are left with *"another Jesus,"* meaning that it's not Biblical (II Cor. 11:4).

3. The Cross of Christ is the Means by which the Lord gives us all things. In other words, the price that Jesus paid at the Cross makes it all possible.

ETERNAL LIFE

The phrase, *"And I give unto them Eternal Life,"* carries with it a Promise which cannot be matched elsewhere under any circumstance.

"Eternal Life" refers to the Life of Christ being imparted unto the believing sinner as that individual has Faith in Christ. To be sure, it has far more to do than mere physical life, but it actually speaks to the soul and the spirit of man.

Due to the Fall in the Garden of Eden, the death sentence was passed upon all humanity in that man was then separated from God, Who Alone is the Giver of Life. If that separation continues, man will be eternally lost, which actually means to exist in the Lake of Fire forever and forever (Rev. 20:11-15).

Upon acceptance of Christ, Eternal Life is instantly granted, which speaks of a regained union with God. As such, the Believer will live with God forever instead of Satan. Consequently, man has a choice: he can refuse God, throw in his lot with Satan, and reap the eternal results which will be Satan's due. Or else, man can accept Christ and reap those eternal results, which are Life Everlasting, which means to live with the Lord forever.

NEVER PERISH

The phrase, *"And they shall never perish,"* simply means that they never need fear that God will change His Mind respecting their Salvation, or that the results of Salvation will be taken away. It is forever!

The phrase, *"Neither shall any man pluck them out of My Hand,"* refers to any and all outside forces because the Power of God is ever present to guarantee the fulfillment of the Promise.

However, while it is certainly true that no outside force can do this, still, there is no protection here guaranteed against oneself. In other words, if one so stupidly chooses to do so, he can take himself out of God's Hands inasmuch as God never violates a person's free moral agency.

From this one Verse of Scripture, much error has been propagated, with it largely being the basis of the unscriptural doctrine of Unconditional Eternal Security. Let us look at that.

THE ERROR OF UNCONDITIONAL ETERNAL SECURITY

Let me state that we most definitely do believe in eternal security; however, we do not believe in unconditional eternal security. In fact, the entirety of the great Book of Hebrews was written, at least in part, to address this very subject.

Because of discouragement, family opposition, persecution, or any number of things, some of the Jews who had accepted Christ were going back into Judaism, which referred to Temple worship, or at least were seriously considering doing so. Paul addressed this. Please read carefully what he said, as well as our notes, with the notes coming from THE EXPOSITOR'S STUDY BIBLE.

Please remember that Paul was addressing Jews who have definitely accepted Christ as their Saviour and their Lord, which means they were Born-Again. Some of them were denying their Faith, going back into Judaism. I'm going to relate quite a bit of information which he gave, even more than I normally would. However, I think it is imperative that I do so in order that this most important subject would be properly addressed.

THE WORDS OF THE APOSTLE PAUL, i.e., THE WORD OF GOD

"Of Whom we have many things to say *(refers to Christ)*, **and hard to be uttered** *(his difficulty was in adapting the interpretation to the capacity of his readers)*, **seeing you are dull of hearing.** *(These Jewish Christians were slow and sluggish regarding their understanding of the teaching of New Testament Truth. This made it difficult to teach them.)*

"**For when for the time you ought to be teachers** *(refers to the fact that they had been saved long enough to be mature in the Word by now)*, **you have need that one teach you again which** *be* **the first principles of the Oracles of God** *(pertains to the Old Testament and what it really meant, instead of the way it was being erroneously taken by these Christian Jews)*; **and are become such as have need of milk, and not of strong meat** *(refers to their lack of maturity)*.

"**For every one who uses milk** *(doesn't refer to one who has just been saved, but rather to those who have been saved for quite some time, and should have advanced in the Word of the Lord)* *is* **unskillful in the Word of Righteousness** *(refers to the benefits of the Cross, from which Righteousness is derived)*: **for he is a babe.** *(This refers to the individual who does not understand or know all the benefits of what Jesus did at the Cross.)*

LEAVING THE PRINCIPLES OF THE DOCTRINE OF CHRIST

"**But strong meat belongs to them who are of full age** *(refers to those mature in the Lord)*, *even* **those who by reason of use have their senses exercised to discern both good and evil.** *(Such a person is walking after the Spirit. This refers to placing one's Faith in the Cross and not after the flesh, the flesh refers to depending on other things [Rom. 8:1-2, 11])*" **(Heb. 5:11-14).**

"**Therefore leaving the Principles of the Doctrine of Christ** *(speaks of the 'first principles,' which refers to the Old Testament; Christ is the Centerpiece of the entirety of the Bible)*, **let us go on unto perfection** *(speaks of the New Testament Sacrifice, the Lord Jesus, and the Testament He inaugurated with His Work on the Cross)*; **not laying again the Foundation of Repentance**

from dead works *(refers to these Jewish Christians going back to the Old Sacrificial System, etc.)*, **and of Faith toward God** *(refers to Faith toward God in the realm of the Old Testament Way, which God will not accept now inasmuch as Jesus has fulfilled the Old Testament Law)*,

"**Of the Doctrine of Baptisms** *(should have been translated, 'the Doctrine of Washings'; this concerned the many 'washings' contained in the Old Testament Sacrificial System)*, **and of laying on of hands** *(goes back to the Levitical Offerings of the Old Testament; when the person brought the animal for Sacrifice, he had to lay his hands on the head of the innocent victim, confessing his sins, thereby transferring them to the innocent animal which would be slain [Lev. 16:21])*, **and of Resurrection of the dead** *(refers to Resurrection as taught in the Old Testament; there, this Doctrine was very incomplete, even as all Doctrine in the Old Testament was incomplete; the true meaning could not be given until after the Cross and the Resurrection of Christ, which the Lord gave to Paul [I Cor., Chpt. 15])*, **and of Eternal Judgment.** *(In the Old Testament, the Lord was looked at more so as a Judge than anything else. Since the Cross, He is looked at more as the Saviour.)*

"**And this will we do** *(in other words, if we don't do this [refers to going on to the perfection of Christ], the results will be disastrous)*, **if God permit.** *(This refers to the fact that all dependence must be in Christ and the Cross. God will not allow any other type of Faith)*" **(Heb. 6:1-3).**

LACK OF FAITH IN CHRIST AND THE CROSS

"**For *it is* impossible for those who were once enlightened** *(refers to those who have accepted the Light of the Gospel, which means accepting Christ and His great Sacrifice)*, **and have tasted of the Heavenly Gift** *(pertains to Christ and what He did at the Cross)*, **and were made partakers of the Holy Spirit** *(which takes place when a person comes to Christ)*,

"**And have tasted the good Word of God** *(is not language that is used of an impenitent sinner, as some claim; the unsaved have no relish whatsoever for the Truth of God, and see no beauty in it)*, **and the powers of the world to come** *(refers to the Work of the Holy Spirit within hearts and lives, which the unsaved cannot have or know)*,

"**If they shall fall away** *(should have been translated, 'and having fallen away')*, **to renew them again unto Repentance** *('again' states they had once repented, but have now turned their backs on Christ)*; **seeing they crucify to themselves the Son of God afresh** *(means they no longer believe what Christ did at the Cross, actually concluding Him to be an imposter; the only way any person can truly repent is to place his Faith in Christ and the Cross; if that is denied, there is no Repentance)*, **and put *Him* to an open shame** *(means to hold Christ up to public ridicule; Paul wrote this Epistle because some Christian Jews were going back into Judaism, or seriously contemplating doing so)*" **(Heb. 6:4-6).**

THE REJECTION OF CHRIST

"**For the earth which drinks in the rain that comes oft upon it** *(presents the Apostle using natural things to represent spiritual realities, which is common throughout Scripture)*, **and brings forth herbs** *(presents the natural result of ground that is properly cultivated and receives rain; there will be a harvest)* **meet for them by whom it is dressed** *(received by individuals who do the cultivating of the land, etc.)*, **receives Blessing from God** *(presents the inevitable result of proper Faith)*:

"**But that which bears thorns and briers *is* rejected** *(this speaks of Believers who have turned their backs on Christ and the Cross, and now bring forth no proper fruit, but rather 'thorns and briars')*, **and *is* nigh unto cursing** *(refers to judgment)*; **whose end *is* to be burned.** *(This refers to the simple fact that if a person who was once a Believer remains in that state, he will lose his soul.)*

"**But, Beloved** *(presents the fact that these Christian Jews were not only the object of God's love, but also of Paul's care and concern)*, **we are persuaded better things of you** *(he is speaking specifically to those who were seriously contemplating* turning their backs on Christ), **and things that accompany Salvation** *(the Blessings which will come if the Believer properly anchors his Faith in Christ and the Cross),* **though we thus speak.** *(The Apostle is not speaking from guesswork, but from many years of experience)"* **(Heb. 6:7-9).**

Paul also addressed the same subject in the Tenth Chapter of Hebrews.

THE CONSEQUENCES OF REJECTING CHRIST AND THE CROSS

The Apostle continues to say:

"For if we sin willfully *(the 'willful sin' is the transference of Faith from Christ and Him Crucified to other things)* **after that we have received the knowledge of the Truth** *(speaks of the Bible way of Salvation and Victory, which is 'Jesus Christ and Him Crucified' [I Cor. 2:2]),* **there remains no more Sacrifice for sins** *(if the Cross of Christ is rejected, there is no other Sacrifice or way God will accept),*

"But a certain fearful looking for of judgment and fiery indignation *(refers to God's Anger because of men rejecting Jesus Christ and the Cross),* **which shall devour the adversaries.** *(It is hellfire, which will ultimately come to all who reject Christ and the Cross.)*

"He who despised Moses' Law died without mercy under two or three witnesses *(there had to be these many witnesses to a capital crime before the death sentence could be carried out, according to the Old Testament Law of Moses [Deut. 17:2-7]):*

TRODDING UNDERFOOT THE SON OF GOD

"Of how much sorer punishment, suppose ye, shall he be thought worthy, who has trodden under foot the Son of God *(proclaims the reason for the 'sorer punishment'),* **and has counted the Blood of the Covenant, wherewith he was Sanctified, an unholy thing** *(refers to a person who has been saved, but is now expressing unbelief toward that which originally saved him),* **and has done despite unto the Spirit of Grace?** *(When the Cross is rejected, the Holy Spirit is insulted.)*

"For we know Him Who has said, Vengeance *belongs* **unto Me, I will recompense, says the Lord** *(is meant to imply that every single thing is going to be judged by the Lord, Who Alone is the Righteous Judge).* **And again, The Lord shall Judge His people** *(chastise His People [Deut. 32:35-36]).*

"It is a fearful thing to fall into the hands of the Living God. *(This refers to those who have once known the Lord, but now express no Faith in the Cross)"* **(Heb. 10:26-31).**

UNDENIABLE

These Passages that we have just quoted from the Sixth and Tenth Chapters of Hebrews leave no room for doubt. They proclaim, even dogmatically so, that these Jews, who had accepted Christ, and now, because of discouragement, opposition, persecution, etc., were turning their backs on Christ, disavowing Him, and going back into Temple worship. The Scripture emphatically states that if they continued in this direction, despite the fact of once having been truly Born-Again, they would be eternally lost. In truth, these Believers become unbelievers, as should be obvious.

THE ONE INGREDIENT IS FAITH

It is certainly true that no sin will keep a Believer out of Heaven, even as destructive, as debilitating, and as hurtful as sin is. Don't misunderstand:

Sin is an awful thing. It will definitely hurt the Believer, will exact its toll, and if continued, will harden the heart. However, as far as sin itself is concerned, as bad as it is, it will not cause one to lose one's soul. It if did, to be frank, there would be no Believer who would make Heaven his home.

This is the reason that Jesus Christ serves as our Intercessor, and does so on a continuing unending basis. Concerning this, Paul also said:

"But this Man *(the Lord Jesus Christ),* **because He continues ever** *(proclaims the Priesthood of Christ as Eternal, while death was inevitable as it regarded the Aaronic Priests),* **has an unchangeable Priesthood.** *(This not only refers to that which is Eternal, but to that which will not change* *as far as its principle is concerned as well. The reason is the Finished Work of the Cross is an 'Everlasting Covenant' [Heb. 13:20].)*

INTERCESSION

"Wherefore He *(the Lord Jesus Christ)* **is able also to save them to the uttermost** *(proclaims the fact that Christ Alone has made the only true Atonement for sin; He did this at the Cross)* **who come unto God by Him** *(proclaims the only manner in which man can come to God)***, seeing He ever lives to make intercession for them.** *(His very Presence by the Right Hand of the Father guarantees such, with nothing else having to be done [Heb. 1:3])"* **(Heb. 7:24-25).**

Christ is our Intercessor, Who intercedes on our behalf, and does so constantly as it regards sin, which all of us need on a continuing basis. As one Preacher said, and rightly so, *"We couldn't do without the Intercession of Christ for even one single day, not even an hour."* How right he is!

Now, let's look at what got us into Salvation, which is Faith in Christ and what He did for us at the Cross, and what can cause us to lose that Salvation, which is faith that's no longer in Christ and what He did for us at the Cross.

If a Believer ceases to believe, which, sadly and regrettably, many have, even as Paul said in Hebrews, Chapters 6 and 10, *"There remains no more Sacrifice for sins, but a certain fearful looking for of judgment and fiery indignation"* (Heb. 10:26-27). Faith got us in (Rom. 5:1-2; Eph. 2:8-9), and a lack of faith can throw us out.

WHAT KIND OF FAITH?

It was to Paul that the meaning of the New Covenant was given, the meaning of which is the Cross. When Paul speaks of Faith, always and without exception, he is speaking of Faith in Christ and what Christ did for us at the Cross (Gal. 2:16, 20). One does not get Saved by works or by merit, even as Paul also graphically explains in Romans, Chapters 4 and 5. We are saved strictly by Faith, but it must be Faith in Christ and what Christ did for us at the Cross, or else, it's faith that God will not recognize (Rom. 6:3-5).

NOTES

UNDENIABLE EVIDENCE

Greek scholar Kenneth Wuest, whom, incidentally, I respected very much, who is now with the Lord, was, as well, a staunch proponent of the *"Unconditional Eternal Security"* doctrine.

He recognized that the statements given in Hebrews, Chapters 6 and 10, are undeniable as it regards the *"falling away"* (Heb. 6:6). In other words, the Scripture is so emphatic in these Passages that a Believer can fall away by losing Faith, which many have done, that this great Greek scholar could not deny this obvious Truth and said so. So, how did he reconcile these Passages as it regards his doctrine of *"Unconditional Eternal Security"*?

His answer was, and I quote him verbatim, *"It could only be committed in the First Century and by a Jew, or a Gentile proselyte to Judaism, and for the reason that conditions since A.D. 70 have been such as to make impossible the committing of that sin."* He went on to say, *"The Temple at Jerusalem was destroyed on that date. There is no Jewish Sacrifices to leave nor to return to. This was apostasy, a most serious sin"* (Wuest's Word Studies from the Greek New Testament — Golden Nuggets, pages 21-22).

NOT A PROPER EXEGESIS OF SCRIPTURE

As I have stated, I held, and continue to hold, this brother and his work in high regard. However, to try to set aside these Jews in Paul's day, who were going back into Judaism, as a special case or as *"one of a kind,"* meaning that it could *"never be repeated,"* is not a proper exegesis of Scripture, to say the least. The truth is, it didn't really matter who these people were, Jews or Gentiles. If they lost faith, meaning to lose faith in Christ and what He did for us at the Cross, whether they went back to Temple worship or to something else, the results were the same.

If they continued in that vein, which was a vein of faithlessness, it was impossible *"to renew them again unto Repentance; seeing they crucify to themselves the Son of God afresh, and put Him to an open shame"* (Heb. 6:6), irrespective if they lived 2,000 years ago or whether they were Jew or Gentile.

At the same time, if any of these individuals would turn back to the Lord, most definitely, He would forgive and cleanse them and take them back. However, if they continued in that erroneous path, and if anyone does the same presently (a renouncing of Christ even after one has first known Christ), such guarantees that one will be lost.

IMPOSSIBLE?

The retort to that statement is that if a person is truly Saved, it is impossible for him to disavow Faith in Christ. My answer is: that's not what Paul said in Hebrews, Chapter 6 (Heb. 6:4-6) and Chapter 10 (Heb. 10:26-29).

FREE MORAL AGENCY

When a person comes to Christ, he does so through his free moral agency. While the Holy Spirit will deal with him, talk to him, speak to him, and move upon him, still, He will not force any person to give his heart to Christ. It is *"whosoever will"* (Rev. 22:17).

Once the person has come to Christ, likewise, the Lord still doesn't force his will, as should be overly obvious. If a Believer sets his heart and mind to do something wrong, while the Lord will warn him, He will not force him to turn back. Likewise, if any person who has known the Lord and, without a doubt, ceases to believe in Christ, he will definitely lose his soul. To cease to believe in Christ is to cease to believe in what He did for us at the Cross, which is that which got us in, which is Faith. Considering that it is no longer present, such a person, if remaining in that state, will lose his soul. In other words, the Believer has reverted to being an unbeliever.

There are many other Passages in the Word of God to which one can investigate as it regards the subject of *"Unconditional Eternal Security."* However, the two Passages we have given from Hebrews, Chapters 6 and 10, are, we think, sufficient.

ETERNAL SECURITY

As long as a person maintains Faith in Christ, which got him in, irrespective of his ups and downs regarding his consecration, such a person is Saved and will not lose his Salvation.

I'm afraid that many Believers simply do not understand the fact of *"Justification by Faith."* Many Christians are still functioning from a Justification by works syndrome, which God will never recognize. Such, instead of leading to Righteousness, rather leads to self-righteousness. It's very easy to pronounce others as lost while conveniently overlooking our own situation. Let us state it again:

Justification means to be declared not guilty by God due to one's Faith in Christ and the Cross, and one's Faith in Christ and the Cross only. It cannot be forfeited, in fact, will not be forfeited, unless faith is lost. As long as Faith remains, the Justification is secure. As someone has well said, *"It's not easy to turn off the Lights that God has hung up in one's soul since infancy."*

When we look at all of this, it is no wonder that Paul devoted two full Chapters on the subject of Justification by Faith in the great Book of Romans (Chpts. 4-5). He is at pains to declare the impossibility of gaining such Justification by works or merit. It simply cannot be done. He said:

"For what says the Scripture? Abraham believed God, and it was counted unto Him for Righteousness (Gen. 15:6)" (Rom. 4:3).

THE CROSS OF CHRIST

The only thing that stands between mankind and eternal Hell is the Cross of the Lord Jesus Christ. This we must never forget. Unfortunately, it seems that millions of Christians have forgotten this great Truth. They keep trying to place their church, a particular pet doctrine, their religious denomination, or their good works between themselves and eternity. It is a fruitless task. In fact, the entirety of the Gospel can be boiled down, so to speak, to the one simple phrase, *"Jesus Christ and Him Crucified"* (Rom. 6:1-14; I Cor. 1:17, 18, 23; 2:2; Col. 2:10-15).

THE GOSPEL AND THE CROSS OF CHRIST

In the First Chapter of John, we are given the Story of the Gospel in very simple terms. John said, and I continue to quote from THE EXPOSITOR'S STUDY BIBLE:

"**In the beginning** *(does not infer that Christ as God had a beginning, because as God He had no beginning, but rather refers to the time of Creation [Gen. 1:1])* **was the Word** *(the Holy Spirit through John describes Jesus as 'the Eternal Logos')*, **and the Word was with God** *('was in relationship with God,' and expresses the idea of the Trinity)*, **and the Word was God** *(meaning that He did not cease to be God during the Incarnation; He 'was' and 'is' God from eternity past to eternity future)*.

"**The same was in the beginning with God** *(this very Person was in eternity with God; there's only one God, but manifested in three Persons — God the Father, God the Son, God the Holy Spirit)*.

"**All things were made by Him** *(all things came into being through Him; it refers to every item of Creation one by one, rather than all things regarded in totality)*; **and without Him was not any thing made that was made** *(nothing, not even one single thing, was made independently of His cooperation and volition)*.

"**In Him was Life** *(presents Jesus, the Eternal Logos, as the first cause)*; **and the Life was the Light of men** *(He Alone is the Life Source of Light; if one doesn't know Christ, one is in darkness)*.

THE LIGHT

"**And the Light shines in darkness** *(speaks of the Incarnation of Christ, and His Coming into this world; His 'Light,' because it is derived from His Life, drives out 'darkness')*; **and the darkness comprehended it not** *(should have been translated, 'apprehended it not'; it means that Satan, even though he tried with all his might, could not stop 'the Light'; today it shines all over the world, and one day soon, there will be nothing left but that 'Light')*" **(Jn. 1:1-5).**

So, we are told in Verse 1 of this Passage that Jesus Christ is the *"Word,"* meaning that the entirety of the Bible points to Him, reveals Him, and proclaims Him.

Now we are told what that Word did. John continued to say:

THE WORD WAS MADE FLESH

"**And the Word was made flesh** *(refers to the Incarnation, 'God becoming Man')*, **and dwelt among us** *(refers to Jesus, although Perfect, not holding Himself aloft from all others, but rather lived as all men, even a peasant)*, **(and we beheld His Glory, the Glory as of the Only Begotten of the Father,)** *(speaks of His Deity, although hidden from the eyes of the merely curious; while Christ laid aside the expression of His Deity, He never lost the possession of His Deity, not even for a moment)* **full of Grace and Truth** *(His Deity)*" **(Jn. 1:14).**

Now we are told that Jesus, the Eternal Word, became flesh.

Why did He become flesh, i.e., a human being?

THE CROSS

John tells us by quoting John the Baptist. The great Prophet said, when introducing Christ, **"Behold the Lamb of God** *(proclaims Jesus as the Sacrifice for sin, in fact, the Sin-Offering, Whom all the multiple millions of offered lambs had represented)*, **which takes away the sin of the world** *(animal blood could only cover sin, it could not take it away; but Jesus offering Himself as the Perfect Sacrifice took away the sin of the world; He not only cleansed acts of sin, but, as well, addressed the root cause [Col. 2:14-15])*" **(Jn. 1:29).**

We see from these Passages that God became flesh and did so for the purpose of going to the Cross.

This is the reason that Faith in Christ and the Cross is an absolute necessity. Continuing this further and to show how absolutely significant all of this is, please note the following:

THE FOUNDATION OF THE GOSPEL

God becoming Man, i.e., the Incarnation and the Cross of Christ, were not an afterthought. In other words, this was not something that was suddenly worked up because of the Fall in the Garden of Eden. Listen to Simon Peter:

"**Forasmuch as you know that you were not redeemed with corruptible things,** *as* **silver and gold** *(presents the fact that the most precious commodities [silver and gold] could not redeem fallen man)*, **from your vain conversation** *(vain lifestyle)* **received by tradition from your fathers** *(speaks of original sin that is passed on from father to child at conception)*;

"**But with the Precious Blood of Christ** *(presents the payment, which proclaims the poured out Life of Christ on behalf of sinners)*, **as of a Lamb without blemish and without spot** *(speaks of the lambs offered as substitutes in the Old Jewish economy; the Death of Christ was not an execution or assassination, but rather a Sacrifice; the Offering of Himself presented a Perfect Sacrifice, for He was Perfect in every respect [Ex. 12:5])*:

"**Who verily was foreordained before the foundation of the world** *(refers to the fact that God, in His Omniscience, knew He would create man, man would fall, and man would be redeemed by Christ going to the Cross; this was all done before the Universe was created; this means the Cross of Christ is the Foundation Doctrine of all Doctrine, referring to the fact that all Doctrine must be built upon that Foundation, or else it is specious)*, **but was manifest in these last times for you** *(refers to the invisible God Who, in the Person of the Son, was made visible to human eyesight by assuming a human body and human limitations)*" **(I Pet. 1:18-20).**

A PROPER UNDERSTANDING

The Cross of Christ is the only thing standing between mankind and eternal Hell. The very reason that God became Man was to offer Himself as a Perfect Sacrifice on the Cross. The Cross of Christ is the Foundation Doctrine of the Gospel, meaning that every single Doctrine in the Bible must be built squarely on the Foundation of the Cross, or else, it will be specious. Once we begin to understand all of this, we see how important the Cross of Christ actually is. That's why

NOTES

we must have Faith in Christ and the Cross, and Christ and the Cross alone.

That and that alone guarantees Eternal Life. Failure to act accordingly will guarantee that one will be eternally lost.

Regrettably and sadly, even catastrophically, the modern church, at least in the last few decades, has preached the Cross so little that the modern church hardly knows anymore where it has been, where it is, or where it is going.

THE BAPTIST PREACHER

One Baptist Preacher wrote me the other day, saying, and I paraphrase him, *"Brother Swaggart, your Message on the Cross is so very much needed presently."* He went on to say, *"To understand how far the modern church has fallen from a true Scriptural position, one only has to consider that some 20 years ago, your Message on the Cross of Christ would not have seemed out of the ordinary, but now it does."*

Sadly, he is right! The Message of the Cross was once the Message, as it always must be the Message. Regrettably, it is no longer the Message, having been replaced with more modern utensils but, regrettably, with that which will not save and will not deliver.

Back to our original subject, as long as one maintains Faith in Christ and the Cross, and we speak of a heartfelt Faith and not merely a mental affirmation, such a person cannot be lost. However, if any person, even one who has been truly Saved, ceases to express Faith in Christ and what He did for us at the Cross, actually counting such as an unworthy thing, such a person, even though once Saved, if continuing on that path, will revert from a Believer to an unbeliever. If he remains there, he will be eternally lost. The moment that God labels such a person as *"lost"* instead of *"Saved"* is at His Discretion and not ours. He Alone is the Saviour, and, therefore, He Alone can be the Judge. No mortal is qualified to stand in such a place. James said:

"**There is one Lawgiver, Who is able to save and to destroy** *(presents God as the only One Who can fill this position)*: **who are you who judges another?** *(The Greek* *actually says, 'but you — who are you?' In other words, 'who do you think you are?')"* **(James 4:12).**

THE DISPENSATION OF GRACE

Many Believers, including preachers, have a wrong concept of Grace; consequently, they come up with wrong conclusions, hence, the doctrine of *"Unconditional Eternal Security."*

This is the Dispensation of Grace in which we now live, and has been ever since the Cross, a time frame now of approximately 2,000 years.

Many erroneously think that because we are living in the Dispensation of Grace, Grace is automatic, and automatic irrespective as to what anyone might do. That is totally incorrect!

While this is, as stated, most definitely the Dispensation of Grace, that doesn't mean that it is an automatic process. There is no license to sin, no license for failure, and no license to live an ungodly life provided for in Grace. The idea that one can live like the Devil and make Heaven his eternal home simply because this is the Dispensation of Grace is facetious indeed! Listen to Paul, and I'll quote from THE EXPOSITOR'S STUDY BIBLE, both Scripture and notes:

WORKS OF THE FLESH

"Now the works of the flesh are manifest, which are these *(if one attempts to function by means of Law of any nature, the 'works of the flesh' will be manifested in one's life)*; **adultery, fornication, uncleanness, lasciviousness,**

"Idolatry, witchcraft, hatred, variance, emulations, wrath, strife, seditions, heresies,

"Envyings, murders, drunkenness, revellings, and such like *(if one is walking after the flesh [Rom. 8:1], one or more of these sins will manifest themselves in one's life; the only way, and I mean the only way, one can walk in perpetual victory is to understand that everything we receive from God comes to us by means of the Cross; consequently, the Cross must ever be the Object of our Faith; this being the case, the Holy Spirit, Who works exclusively within the confines of the Sacrifice of Christ, will*

NOTES

exert His mighty Power on our behalf, which will enable us to live a Holy life): **of the which I tell you before, as I have also told you in time past** *(refers to the fact that the Apostle was not afraid to name specific sins)*, **that they which do such things shall not inherit the Kingdom of God.** *(This tells us in no uncertain terms that if our Faith is not everlastingly in Christ and the Cross, we simply won't make it. God doesn't have two ways of Salvation and Victory, only one, and that is 'Jesus Christ and Him Crucified')"* **(Gal. 5:19-21).**

PAUL IS WRITING TO BELIEVERS

Now, I remind the reader that Paul was writing to Believers and when he said, *"That they who do such things shall not inherit the Kingdom of God,"* he was not speaking to the unredeemed but to those who had been Saved and were, in fact, now Saved. He was plainly telling them and us that if we try to live for God outside of His Prescribed Order, which is Christ and the Cross, and Christ and the Cross exclusively, works of the flesh are going to manifest themselves. If it remains that way, *"We shall not inherit the Kingdom of God."* That's about as plain as it can get. That completely refutes the unscriptural doctrine of *"Unconditional Eternal Security."*

The idea is, the Grace of God doesn't cover our erroneous directions, our rebellion against God and His Word, or the charting of our own course, which means we have rejected the Ways of the Lord.

WHAT ARE THE WAYS OF THE LORD?

Paul said, *"We preach Christ Crucified"* (I Cor. 1:23).

The following diagram, although brief, I think will help you to understand what the Ways of the Lord actually are. If you can understand what we will give you and will believe it, you will have a basic understanding of the New Covenant.

• Jesus Christ is the Source of all things we receive from God (Jn. 1:1-2, 12, 29; 14:6, 20; Col. 2:10-15).

• While Jesus is the Source, the Cross of Christ is the Means, and the only Means, by which all of these good things are given to us. It is the Cross which makes the Grace of God available to us (Rom. 6:1-14; I Cor. 1:17, 18, 23; 2:2).

• With Jesus being the Source and the Cross being the Means, then we must understand that the Cross of Christ must be the Object of our Faith, and that alone. In fact, the Story of the entirety of the Bible is *"Jesus Christ and Him Crucified."* So, when one has his Faith anchored squarely in Christ and the Cross, that is the same as having it anchored squarely in the Word. In fact, the Cross of Christ and the Word, one might say, are synonymous (Rom., Chpts. 6-8; Col. 2:14-15).

• With Christ as the Source and the Cross as the Means, and the Cross as the Object of our Faith, then the Holy Spirit, Who works exclusively within the parameters of the Finished Work of Christ, i.e., *"the Cross,"* will then work mightily on our behalf. What Christ did at the Cross was a legal work, which makes it possible now for the Holy Spirit to abide permanently in the hearts and lives of Believers, which He does. In other words, the Cross of Christ is what makes the New Covenant (Rom. 8:1-11; Eph. 2:14-18).

The truth is, one cannot successfully live for God without subscribing to His Prescribed Order. One can be Saved without understanding this, but one cannot successfully live for the Lord, which means to walk in victory over the world, the flesh, and the Devil.

No, we are not teaching or preaching sinless perfection because the Bible does not teach such; however, it does teach that sin is not to have dominion over us (Rom. 6:14).

WHAT IS GOD'S PRESCRIBED ORDER?

As we have already stated any number of times, His Prescribed Order is *"the Cross of Christ."* Again, Paul said:

"But God forbid that I should glory (boast), **save in the Cross of our Lord Jesus Christ** *(what the opponents of Paul sought to escape at the price of insincerity is the Apostle's only basis of exultation)*, **by Whom the world is crucified unto me, and I unto the world.** *(The only way we can overcome the world, and I mean the only way, is by placing our Faith exclusively in the Cross of Christ and keeping it there)"* **(Gal. 6:14).**

Let me take you back to the great Book of Exodus and look for a moment at the Old Economy of God, which pointed explicitly toward the New. Sometimes we learn as much from the types and shadows as we do from the reality.

THE LORD JESUS CHRIST

The Lord said to Moses, and I continue to use THE EXPOSITOR'S STUDY BIBLE:

"And you shall put the Mercy Seat above upon the Ark; and in the Ark you shall put the Testimony *(Ten Commandments)* **that I shall give you.**

"And there I will meet with you, and I will commune with you from above the Mercy Seat, from between the two Cherubims which are upon the Ark of the Testimony, of all things which I will give you in Commandment unto the Children of Israel. *(It is only above the Blood-stained Mercy Seat that God will meet with sinful human beings, because that's the only place that He can meet with sinful human beings, and not malign His Righteousness and Holiness. Concerning this, Mackintosh says:*

"'Thus it is that the soul of the believing sinner finds peace. He sees that God's Righteousness and His Justification rest upon precisely the same basis, namely Christ's accomplished Work. When man, under the powerful action of the Truth of God, takes his place as a sinner, God can, in the exercise of Grace, take His place as a Saviour, and then every question is settled, for the Cross having answered all the claims of Divine Justice, Mercy's copious streams can flow unhindered. When a Righteous God and a ruined sinner meet on a Blood-sprinkled platform, all is settled forever — settled in such a way as perfectly glorifies God, and eternally saves the sinner')" **(Ex. 25:21-22).**

God's Way has never changed. It has been the same since Adam's fall even unto this hour, and will never change. That Way is the Sacrifice of Christ.

If the Believer is to walk in victory, he can only do so by expressing his Faith totally and completely in Christ and the Cross and not allow it to be moved. This will then give the Holy Spirit latitude and liberty to work in his life. Due to the fact that the Holy Spirit is God, victory can be ours in totality.

FRUSTRATING THE GRACE OF GOD

Paul said:

"**I am Crucified with Christ** *(as the Foundation of all Victory; Paul, here, takes us back to Rom. 6:3-5)*: **nevertheless I live** *(have new life)*; **yet not I** *(not by my own strength and ability)*, **but Christ lives in me** *(by virtue of me dying with Him on the Cross, and being raised with Him in Newness of Life)*: **and the life which I now live in the flesh** *(my daily walk before God)* **I live by the Faith of the Son of God** *(the Cross is ever the Object of my Faith)*, **Who loved me, and gave Himself for me** *(which is the only way that I could be Saved.)*

"**I do not frustrate the Grace of God** *(if we make anything other than the Cross of Christ the Object of our Faith, we frustrate the Grace of God, which means we stop its action, and the Holy Spirit will no longer help us)*: **for if Righteousness** *come* **by the Law** *(any type of Law)*, **then Christ is dead in vain.** *(If I can successfully live for the Lord by any means other than Faith in Christ and the Cross, then the Death of Christ was a waste)*" **(Gal. 2:20-21).**

In our notes from THE EXPOSITOR'S STUDY BIBLE, I think we have adequately explained what frustrating the Grace of God actually means. Regrettably, most of the modern church is living in a state of frustrated Grace. In other words, the Grace of God cannot function properly in one's life unless the Believer understands the means of Grace.

WHAT IS THE MEANS OF GRACE?

It is the Cross of Christ which makes Grace possible. The truth is, God had just as much Grace 3,000 years ago as He does presently. God cannot change. However, due to the fact that the blood of bulls and goats could not take away sins, which means that the sin debt continued to hang over the head of every person, God was limited as to what He could do as it regarded Grace.

NOTES

The Sacrificial system before the Cross was all that was had. While it was the best that could be had then, still, it would run a poor second to the actual Work of the Cross. That's the reason that Grace now can be much more abundant.

Since the Cross, Grace, one might say, is unlimited because the Cross paid it all. In other words, it opened up the way. That's why we say that Christ is the Source and the Cross is the Means.

If the Believer will maintain his Faith in Christ and the Cross, whatever else happens, the Grace of God will continue to come to him in an uninterrupted flow. This provides the greatest life and living that man could ever know, hence, Jesus saying that He would give us *"life, and give it to us more abundantly"* (Jn. 10:10). That He has done, and that He does do.

To digress for a moment, the Believer is secure in Christ, at least as long as he remains in Christ. The free moral agency of a person is never tampered with by God. The free moral agency got us in, as far as we are concerned, and it keeps us in. However, if one wants out, and so foolishly demands, which means he ceases to believe in Christ and what He did for us at the Cross, he can get out. Thank God, not many opt for that disastrous course. And yet, my heart bleeds for the few who do.

(29) "MY FATHER, WHICH GAVE THEM TO ME, IS GREATER THAN ALL; AND NO MAN IS ABLE TO PLUCK THEM OUT OF MY FATHER'S HAND."

The diagram is:

1. The phrase, *"My Father, which gave them to Me, is greater than all,"* proclaims the Power of God, which is able to keep any and all. When one serves God, he has at his disposal Almighty Power, which is *"greater than all!"*

2. *"And no man is able to pluck them out of My Father's Hand,"* is, as should be noticed, slightly different than the similar quote from the previous Verse.

3. In that Verse, He said *"My Hand,"* whereas in this Verse, He says *"My Father's Hand."*

4. The idea is, *"My Hand"* and *"My Father's Hand"* are one Hand.

5. Once again we emphasize that the Believer is protected against any and all outside dangers but is not protected from himself. As we have laboriously stated, if one so desires, one, by his own volition, can take himself out of the *"Father's Hand."* The Lord will not force anyone to stay who wants to go. However, I want to make it abundantly clear that under no circumstances do I want out. In Christ is Life, and without Him, there is no life.

(30) "I AND MY FATHER ARE ONE."

The overview is:

1. The words *"are One"* in the Greek text are actually *"We are One"* and, consequently, plural.

2. The word *"One"* is neuter singular and actually means *"One in unity"* (Jn. 17:11, 21-23), not One in person or individuality (Dan. 7:9-14; Acts 7:55; Rom. 8:34; I Cor. 8:6; 11:3; Eph. 1:20-23; 4:1-6; I Tim. 2:5; Heb. 1:3; 8:1; 12:2; I Pet. 3:22; I Jn. 5:7; Rev. 5:1-7).

3. *"We are One,"* as it is in the Greek, affirms distinction of Persons and *"One"* unity of nature and purpose. Thus, these simple words destroy the teaching of those who deny the distinction of Persons in the Godhead, of those who question the Deity of Christ, and of those who oppose verbal inspiration.

4. In these Passages, the Lord declares that He can bestow Eternal Life and Blessedness upon those who stand in close living relation with Himself, and between whom and Himself there is mutual recognition and the interchanges of Love and Truth, which come about by Faith.

5. He bases the claim on the fact that the Father's Hands are behind His, and that the Father's Eternal Power and Godhead sustain His Mediatorial Functions and, more than all of that, the Father's Personality and His Own Personality are merged in one essence and entity.

6. If He merely meant to imply moral and spiritual union with the Father, as some claim, or completeness of Revelation of the Divine mind, why should the utterance have provoked such fierce resentment, as the next Verse proclaims?

No, Jesus was claiming equality with the Father and, therefore, Deity.

(31) "THEN THE JEWS TOOK UP STONES AGAIN TO STONE HIM."

The form is:

1. Their anger was raised to fever pitch because they understood perfectly that Jesus was claiming equality with God and, in essence, that He is God.

2. As well, His Claims portrayed Himself as Messiah in a far greater Revelation than the supposed Messiah of the Jews.

3. Some thought that the Messiah would be a reincarnation of one of the great Prophets of the past, such as Isaiah, Jeremiah, etc. Others felt He would be a man of powerful political persuasion, dazzling the people with revelations of grandeur. Above all, He would rescue them from the Roman yoke. However, Jesus completely debunked these man-devised theories, which had no Scriptural foundation. In fact, the great Prophet Isaiah said the very opposite (Isa., Chpt. 53).

4. The idea in their minds that this Peasant from Nazareth could be the Messiah was ludicrous, to say the least, but especially the fact that He claimed Deity and, in fact, Oneness with the Father was preposterous to these unbelievers. In fact, His referring to God as *"My Father,"* as well, proclaimed a relationship with Jehovah on a par completely unknown in the past.

5. Despite His Miracles, even to the place of raising the dead, and the gracious words which proceeded out of His Mouth, their response was *"to stone Him."* To be sure, the word *"again"* tells us that this was not their first attempt.

6. Thus was the answer of *"God's chosen People"* to *"God's chosen Gift,"* the Lord Jesus Christ! It is still basically the same answer today!

(32) "JESUS ANSWERED THEM, MANY GOOD WORKS HAVE I SHOWED YOU FROM MY FATHER; FOR WHICH OF THOSE WORKS DO YOU STONE ME?"

The exegesis is:

1. The unredeemed man thinks that his *"good"* will save him. It won't!

2. Regrettably, the redeemed man often tries to live for God by the means of his so-called good.

3. Let it be understood that this particular *"good,"* whether in the unredeemed or the Redeemed, cannot be accepted at all by God (Rom. 7:18).

JESUS ANSWERED THEM

The phrase, *"Jesus answered them,"* represents a plausibility that is unanswerable on their part, but the truth is, they would not have believed Him irrespective of what was said or done. He had given them enough proof to satisfy a thousand courts, but their minds and hearts were closed to Him and would never be opened. Sadly and regretably, they would die in this blindness, as uncounted millions have down through the ages, and will be in Hell forever and forever.

Man fell in the Garden of Eden by believing a lie; consequently, he continues to believe a lie very easily, while it is very difficult for him to believe the Truth.

GOOD WORKS

"Many good works have I showed you from My Father," speaks of healing the sick, casting out demons, cleansing lepers, raising the dead, feeding multitudes, and bringing forth the Truth, works, incidentally, never performed in the annals of human history.

As well, once again He claimed that everything He was doing was that which He had been given instructions by the Father to do. So, when they rebelled against Him, He was telling them that they were rebelling against God.

That rebellion, to be sure, was to be costly, the most costly in history. They were to lose their place and their Nation, and, worse still, many generations would lose their souls.

TO STONE JESUS

The question, *"For which of those works do you stone Me?"* is a good question indeed!

Would they stone Him for cleansing lepers? Would they stone Him for raising the dead?

At the present, as always, men resist Christ, but why?

Do they resist Him because He changes lives for the better — the untold better? Do they resist Him because He heals the sick?

NOTES

Do they resist Him because He gives hope where there is no hope?

No! They resist Him for the most sinister of reasons. As the Jews of old, they will not admit that He is God. A Prophet, maybe! A Great Teacher, maybe! A Good Man, maybe! But not God!

If He is God, then He is the One to Whom they must answer. So, they would rather deny His Deity and use flimsy excuses to do so.

The unbelief of mankind is truly something which makes one marvel, especially considering the insurmountable proof!

(33) "THE JEWS ANSWERED HIM, SAYING, FOR A GOOD WORK WE DO NOT STONE YOU; BUT FOR BLASPHEMY; AND BECAUSE THAT YOU, BEING A MAN, MAKE YOURSELF GOD."

The exposition is:

1. The only truly good that is within us, at least that which God will recognize, is that which comes exclusively by and through Christ.

2. All of this means that all goodness that proceeds from our flesh is rejected by God.

3. Paul uses the word *"flesh"* in the sense of our own efforts, strength, motivation, education, ability, power, etc. Within themselves, these things aren't wrong, but to try to live for God by the means of the *"flesh"* guarantees certain defeat.

WHO IS JESUS CHRIST?

The phrase, *"The Jews answered Him,"* represented the worst answer they ever gave. As well, every single individual in the world must answer! What kind of answers are being given concerning the claims of Jesus?

Jesus Christ is the Eternal Logos, the Living Word, the Son of the Living God; Jesus Christ is God!

He was and is Very God and was and is Very Man. This means that He wasn't part God and part Man but totally God and totally Man.

THE EXPRESSION OF HIS DEITY

When God became Man, not for a moment did He lose the possession of His Deity, rather retaining it completely. However, He did lose the expression of that Deity, which

He willfully laid aside, the evidence of which is that such expression will be lost forever. On another side of the Incarnation, God becoming Man, He is greater today than ever before.

Jesus Christ is the Creator of all things (Jn. 1:1-3); however, He is also the Saviour. So, coupled with Creator, He is now the Saviour, which is greater than ever. One cannot improve upon Perfection, but one can add to Perfection, which has been done in the case of Christ.

THE SELF-EMPTYING OF CHRIST

Paul wrote, and I quote from THE EXPOSITOR'S STUDY BIBLE:

"**Let this mind be in you** *(refers to the self-emptying of Christ)*, **which was also in Christ Jesus** *(portrays Christ as the supreme example)*:

"**Who, being in the form of God** *(refers to Deity, which Christ always was)*, **thought it not robbery to be equal with God** *(equality with God refers here to our Lord's co-participation with the other members of the Trinity in the expression of the Divine Essence)*:

"**But made Himself of no reputation** *(instead of asserting His Rights to the expression of the Essence of Deity, our Lord waived His Rights to that expression)*, **and took upon Him the form of a servant** *(a bondslave)*, **and was made in the likeness of men** *(presents the Lord entering into a new state of Being when He became Man; but Him becoming Man did not exclude His Position of Deity; while in becoming Man, He laid aside the 'expression' of Deity, He never lost 'possession' of Deity)*:

HUMILITY

"**And being found in fashion as a man** *(denotes Christ in men's eyes)*, **He humbled Himself** *(He was brought low, but willingly)*, **and became obedient unto death** *(does not mean He became obedient to death; He was always the Master of Death; rather, He subjected Himself to death)*, **even the death of the Cross.** *(This presents the character of His Death as one of disgrace and degradation, which was necessary for men to be redeemed. This type of death alone would pay the terrible sin debt, and do so in totality.)*

"**Wherefore God also has highly exalted Him** *(to a place of supreme Majesty; Jesus has always been Creator, but now He is Saviour as well)*, **and given Him a Name which is above every name** *(actually says, 'The Name,' referring to a specific Name and Title; that Name, as Verse 11 proclaims, is 'Lord')*:

"**That at the Name of Jesus every knee should bow** *(in the sphere of the Name, which refers to all it entails; all of this is a result of the Cross, the price paid there, and the Redemption consequently afforded)*, **of *things* in Heaven, and *things* in earth, and *things* under the earth** *(all Creation will render homage, whether animate or inanimate)*;

"**And *that* every tongue should confess that Jesus Christ *is* Lord** *(proclaims 'Lord' as the 'Name' of Verse 9; it means 'Master' of all, which again has been made possible by the Cross)*, **to the Glory of God the Father.** *(The acknowledgement of the Glory of Christ is the acknowledgement of the Glory of the Father)*" **(Phil. 2:5-11).**

THE MINISTRY WORKS OF CHRIST

Even though God, and never ceasing to be God, our Lord performed no Miracles by virtue of His Deity when on this Earth, but rather totally and completely by and through the Power and the Person of the Holy Spirit. The Scripture plainly says:

"**How God anointed Jesus of Nazareth with the Holy Spirit and with Power** *(as a Man, Christ needed the Holy Spirit, as we certainly do as well! in fact, everything He did was by the Power of the Spirit)*: **Who went about doing good** *(everything He did was good)*, **and healing all who were oppressed of the Devil** *(only Christ could do this, and Believers can do such only as Christ empowers them by the Spirit)*; **for God was with Him** *(God is with us only as we are 'with Him')*" **(Acts 10:38).**

As God, Jesus needed no anointing to do anything, but as a Man, He did need that Anointing.

SUBSTITUTION AND IDENTIFICATION

Jesus Christ came to this world as the Substitute Man. In other words, as He was the True Israel, He, likewise, is the True Man. He did for us what we could not do for ourselves. Paul labeled him as *"the Last Adam,"* and *"the Second Man"* (I Cor. 15:45-47).

As our Substitute, Jesus died *"for us."* As our Representative Man, He died *"as us."*

As our Substitute Man, He kept the Law perfectly in every respect, not violating its precepts either in word, thought, or deed. He did it all on our behalf, actually, as our Representative Man.

Not only did He keep the Law in every respect, but, as well, He satisfied the demands of the broken Law by going to the Cross as a Perfect Sacrifice. He there satisfied the demands of a thrice-Holy God by the offering up of Himself, which completely paid the price. Our identification with Him, which simply means that we evidence Faith in Him and what He did for us at the Cross, guarantees us Eternal Life (Rom. 6:23).

That's what makes Jesus Christ stand out in the annals of human history. While He was Man, Very Man, at the same time, He was God, Very God!

WHAT JESUS DID AT THE CROSS

While Jesus was our Substitute in all things and, actually, as stated, *"The Substitute Man,"* still, it was His Work at the Cross of Calvary which provided victory. Everything He did was absolutely necessary as it regards Redemption. However, all that He was and all that He did, and I speak of His Perfect Conception, His Perfect Birth, His Perfect Life, His Perfect Ministry, His Perfect Healings and Miracles, His Perfect Doctrine, etc., would have had no meaning had He not gone to the Cross. It was at the Cross where it all came together where the Great Redemption Plan was made complete.

Some claim that it was the Resurrection that made it complete; however, that is incorrect. The Resurrection was not a part of the Atoning process, but rather a ratification of the Atoning process. In that, it was of extreme significance, as should be obvious. The truth is, if there had been one single sin unatoned, Jesus would not, in fact, could not, have risen from the dead. The Scripture plainly says, *"The wages of sin is death"* (Rom. 6:23).

The fact that Jesus was raised from the dead proves that He atoned for all sin, that the great price of Redemption was paid at Calvary, and that the Work there was finished in totality.

SIN AND BONDAGE

It is sin that gives Satan the legal right to hold man captive. With all sin atoned, which was done at the Cross, Satan's legal right to hold man captive was forever removed, at least for those who will believe (Jn. 3:16). This means that not a single person in the world need remain a slave to bondage of any nature. It was all settled at the Cross, and totally at the Cross.

So, that being the case, why is it that most of the world is still in bondage?

They are in bondage simply because they will not avail themselves of the opportunity given to them, which refers to accepting the Lord and making Him the Saviour of the soul and the Lord of their lives. The door is wide open, and all who will may come and take of the Water of Life freely (Rev. 22:17).

THEY WOULD STONE JESUS

The phrase, *"Saying, For a good work we stone You not,"* at the same time, meant that the Jews had no regard for His *"Good Works"* and, in reality, would have stopped them had they the power. They were given no consideration at all!

In the past years, I have had any number of derogatory articles written in newspapers, magazines, etc., about my person, but not one single time do I recall that it was mentioned that we built 176 schools in Third World countries, plus provided literally millions of meals for deprived children. Neither were the some 76 mobile medical units mentioned, which gave free medical care, and even dental care in some places, plus medicine, etc., all free of charge.

Why were not these things mentioned, considering their magnitude?

The answer lies in the fact that we did them in the Name of the Lord, and the same spirit which opposed Jesus, opposed us, and will continue to oppose all who Name the Name of Christ.

We have even had the news media to deny that these things were being done, even when the proof was obvious for all to see.

The phrase, *"But for blasphemy,"* was the accusation of these unbelievers, but they were not true. In fact, they were the blasphemers and not Christ.

The phrase, *"And because that You, being a Man, make Yourself God,"* proclaims our Lord declaring His Deity.

It was true that He was Man, the Man, Christ Jesus, and, as well, God; however, He did not make Himself God, for He always was God (Jn. 1:1-3). Perhaps the better translation would have been, *"Represented Yourself as God,"* which was true!

(34) "JESUS ANSWERED THEM, IS IT NOT WRITTEN IN YOUR LAW, I SAID, YOU ARE GODS?"

The form is:

1. The beginning of the question, *"Jesus answered them, Is it not written in your Law ...,"* presents the Lord taking up one illustration from among many in Holy Scripture, that the union between man and God lay at the heart of their Law, i.e., the Law of Moses.

2. By Jesus using the word *"your,"* He was not implying that the Law was not His. Actually, there is not a shadow of disrespect cast on the Law by the pronoun, but it was used in such a sense that His Hearers might identify with it.

3. The conclusion of the question, *"I said, You are gods?"* is taken from Psalms 82:6. The word *"Law,"* at times, as here, was sometimes used in all the Sacred Writings.

4. Jesus used this Scripture in this fashion because Judaism had widened the chasm between God and man, and He came to fill up that chasm. As Reynolds said, *"Even more so, to show the Divine and human in living, indissoluble union."*[2]

5. The argument of Verses 10:32-38 is a double one based on the Scriptures and the Miracles. If the Scriptures labeled as *"gods"* these magistrates appointed by the Word of God and Prophets energized by the Word of God, and it did — persons to whom the Word of God merely *"came"* — must not He Whom the Father had set apart for a special purpose and sent into the world, and Who executed the benevolent Works of the Father, must not He be the Son of God in a unique sense, so that He was in the Father and the Father was in Him!

6. To the magistrates (judges), for that's actually what the word *"gods,"* as used here, meant, and Prophets, *"The Word of the Lord came,"* and that was true of even the greatest Prophets. However, this formula is never used in connection with Jesus, for He was the Word of God in all its infinitude.

7. Further, His Works of benevolence prove His Claim, for how could a demon do good works, and how could God accredit by them the person and doctrines of a blasphemer? His Miracles were Good Works, i.e., works of benevolence, and the Scriptures approved His Teachings. Therefore, the chiefs of the Hebrew church were bound to accept Him as Messiah.

8. However, they willfully refused to do so, and being themselves evil and, therefore, hating goodness, they twice attempted to murder Him.

(35) "IF HE CALLED THEM GODS, UNTO WHOM THE WORD OF GOD CAME, AND THE SCRIPTURE CANNOT BE BROKEN."

The order is:

1. The phrase, *"If He called them gods, unto whom the Word of God came,"* refers to several things:

a. All to whom the Word of God comes are in a favored position, as would be obvious.

b. The word *"gods,"* as used in this sentence regarding *"magistrates and judges,"* at least for their ancient Jewish Law, would apply to Preachers and teachers of the Bible presently. We are to be careful to interpret it correctly.

c. The Bible is to be the criterion for all things.

2. The phrase, *"And the Scripture cannot be broken,"* proclaims to one and all the standard to which our Lord held the Scripture.

3. His Words proclaimed the Inspiration and infallibility of the Bible. Inasmuch as it is the Word of God, it is perfect, without error, and its predictions will come to pass exactly as it proclaims. As I have said many times, the Bible is the only Revealed Truth in the world and, in fact, ever has been. Other works may contain things which are true, but that is far different than *"Truth."*

4. However, the modern church, as Israel of old, is by and large forsaking the Bible, or else, wrongly dividing its Truth.

(36) "DO YOU SAY OF HIM, WHOM THE FATHER HAS SANCTIFIED, AND SENT INTO THE WORLD, YOU BLASPHEME; BECAUSE I SAID, I AM THE SON OF GOD?"

The overview is:

1. Man, even redeemed man, from his own strength and ability, cannot originate anything that is good.

2. This is because of the Fall.

3. Whatever it is that God chooses to use, it always originates with God and never with man.

I AM THE SON OF GOD

The beginning of the question, *"Do you say of Him, Whom the Father has sanctified, and sent into the world, You blaspheme …?"* simply means that Jesus was sent by the Father for a specific purpose. That purpose was the Redemption of mankind. By the phraseology He used, He was informing them of the seriousness of their charge. They were accusing God and His Purpose and Plan of Redemption.

The conclusion of the question, *"Because I said, I am the Son of God?"* presents Him presenting Himself in a far greater dignity than even they had aspired that the Messiah would be. He was plainly saying, *"I am the Son of God!"*

As such, He was telling them that their accusations against Him of blasphemy were not directed at a mere man as they assumed, but rather God, which puts an entirely different complexion on the matter.

While they thought the Messiah would be a special kind of person, in no way did they consider Him to be the *"Son of God,"* as Jesus here proclaimed. So, this entire scenario had been taken to rarified heights. To say something negative about a mere man, although he be exceptionally holy, is one thing, but to say something negative about God is quite something else altogether! In this is an intended warning, which they should have heeded. However, they were so blinded in their deception that they heeded nothing but blundered on until they ultimately sealed their doom.

In these actions, the terrible destruction by Titus of Jerusalem in A.D. 70 was brought about.

(37) "IF I DO NOT THE WORKS OF MY FATHER, BELIEVE ME NOT."

The form is:

1. While the Believer may suffer because of sins, the sins of others or his own, there is no such thing as a Believer suffering for his sins. We refer to such suffering as being an Atonement.

2. To even think such, in effect, says that what Christ did at the Cross was not enough, and we, therefore, have to add to His Atonement by our suffering for sin as well.

3. To think such, the Believer might as well go to a Cross and attempt to hang himself on that wooden beam, which, of course, is ridiculous!

THE MIRACLES

Jesus was telling these Pharisees to judge Him on the basis of the Miracles He has performed and, in effect, telling them that everything He did was commanded Him by God.

He was saying that if He was speaking words only, that would be one thing. However, considering that He was backing up these words and claims with the most astounding Miracles the world has ever known by far, a thousand times over, such should be proof enough as to what He was saying and Who He was.

Jews of Jesus' Day, even the most esteemed religious leaders, were so mixed up in their theology, brought about by acute self-righteousness, that they little understood what the Word said regarding God's Plan of Redemption and the manner in which He would carry it out.

They did not understand Jesus calling

God His Own Unique Personal Father. They did not even believe that the Messiah would be Deity but merely, as stated, a reincarnated Prophet of old or a charismatic individual.

The idea of God becoming Man was foreign to them even though Isaiah had plainly prophesied such (Isa. 7:14; Chpt. 53).

WORKS OF THE FATHER

Had they known the Bible, they would have known what the *"Works of the Father"* actually were. Those *"Works"* were spiritual and not political. In other words, Jesus came to set captives free from sin and all its results. That, of course, is spiritual.

However, the Jews had a political Messiah in mind, which a correct interpretation of the Word of God would have debunked.

As to which we have already alluded, it was impossible for them to correctly understand the Word because of their acute self-righteousness. The same malady holds true presently and, in fact, always has regarding the Word of God. If the message is not *"Jesus Christ and Him Crucified,"* then such a message will always, and without exception, lead to self-righteousness. This means a self-righteous church cannot understand the Bible because it reads it not in the light of its true Revelation, but rather with effort to force it into a conformity of self-will.

As well, the modern church should understand that it is supposed to carry out the *"Works of the Father,"* and not its own agenda. That agenda presently, at least for the most part, is political, exactly as Israel of old, instead of spiritual. It is not the primary business of the church to elect particular individuals to high political office, but rather to proclaim the Gospel of Jesus Christ, which will set captives free.

At the present, Satan has carefully maneuvered the Body of Christ into a grossly unscriptural position. Two strong television networks, which purport to be Christian, are the spearheads of this false direction.

One is wholly political, claiming that the world will be *"Christianized"* by political means, which appeals to the pride of the Body of Christ.

The other specializes in gross false doctrine, which, coupled with corruption, effectively destroys the true purpose of what the Church ought to be. Hundreds of millions of dollars go into these efforts, which are not only wasted, but actually are helping to build and sustain the kingdom of darkness.

HIRELINGS

This is primarily brought about because the church, as a whole, has rejected that which is truly Called of God and accepted *"hirelings"* instead.

As well, this effort of Satan is far more than a mere sidetrack, but rather a part of the last day plan of spiritual apostasy in which the church has already entered. From now on, this apostasy will deepen and, as well, will be extremely deceptive. In other words, many will think it is the True Way of God.

At any time, the Rapture will take place, with all true Believers taken out, with the apostasy then becoming total.

In essence, Jesus was telling the Pharisees that if He had violated the Word of God in any manner or failed to fulfill the Prophecies regarding the Messiah, then they should not believe Him. However, even as the next Verse states, if, in fact, these things were done, which they were, then they had no choice but to believe Him or suffer the consequences.

(38) "BUT IF I DO, THOUGH YOU BELIEVE NOT ME, BELIEVE THE WORKS: THAT YOU MAY KNOW, AND BELIEVE, THAT THE FATHER IS IN ME, AND I IN HIM."

The overview is:

1. The Catholic church teaches penance, which, in effect, is an attempt to atone for sin, which is a gross insult to Christ.

2. Penance is an act of self-abasement or punishment of some kind, which is supposed to pay for sin.

3. But yet, most in the Protestant world, while not quite so blatant, actually do the same thing.

BELIEVE THE WORKS

The phrase, *"But if I do,"* refers to the carrying out of these Mighty Works. Actually, what is being referred to is that these Works are of such magnitude that it would be impossible for such to be done other than by the Power of God. Therefore, the doing of these Works guaranteed the identity of the Performer.

"Though you believe not Me, believe the Works," actually says that they were without excuse.

There was no reason they should not have believed Jesus, especially considering the things He said and the Power with which He spoke. Joined with that were the Miracles, even to the raising of the dead.

To which we have already alluded, the *"Fruits"* were there and are actually to be the criterion for any and all Ministries, and for all time (Mat. 7:15-20).

BIBLICAL PROOF

The tragedy is that the Biblical criterion for what they were seeking was not acceptable. That Jesus could be accepted, the Sanhedrin must place their seal of approval upon Him, which they would not. Of course, the rupture was far deeper than that, with gross unbelief fuelled by self-righteousness being the actual culprit.

At present, the religious community carries the same earmarks. The Biblical Fruit of the Ministry is little accepted anymore. To be frank, it is probably detrimental as far as most religious leadership is concerned. So, modern Sanhedrins accept Jesus no more presently than they did 2,000 years ago. It is the same spirit on both counts. Other earmarks are similar as well!

As that segment of the church was completely destroyed about 37 years later, likewise will its modern variety be destroyed at the Second Coming.

The phrase, *"That you may know, and believe, that the Father is in Me, and I in Him,"* further explains Verse 30, *"I and My Father are One."*

Actually, Jesus enlarged this Phrase in Verse 38 by saying a little later, *"At that day you shall know that I am in My Father, and you in Me, and I in you"* (Jn. 14:20). So, this union of Jesus and the Father is enlarged to include all Believers.

This is a union which can only be brought about by the Holy Spirit.

(39) "THEREFORE THEY SOUGHT AGAIN TO TAKE HIM: BUT HE ESCAPED OUT OF THEIR HAND."

The diagram is:

1. This was the seventh attempt to kill Jesus.

2. If one is to notice, the true Work of God is totally different than anything else in the world. Men may disagree politically, socially, economically, or philosophically, and those disagreements at times may become heated. However, nothing can approach the animosity or even hatred which accompanies those who are religious but without knowing Jesus. Regrettably, that makes up the far greater majority, hence, the cause of much of the bloodshed in this world.

3. The phrase, *"Therefore they sought again to take Him,"* speaks of their efforts, but without success.

4. *"But He escaped out of their hand,"* probably refers to Him once again merely walking through their midst and going His Way.

5. Reynolds said, *"His escape was facilitated by the strange moral power He could exert to render their physical assaults upon Him in vain. They stretched out their hands which dropped harmlessly at their side, verifying the solemn statement of Verse 18."*[3]

6. Some have erroneously concluded from this Passage, and similar others, the heresy of Docetism, a belief that claimed Christ only seemed to have a human body and only seemed to suffer and die on the Cross.

7. No! Jesus was Fully Human as well as being Fully God. However, not one time did He use His Powers of Deity but only the Power of the Holy Spirit, which is available to all Believers, at least to a certain extent.

(40) "AND WENT AWAY AGAIN BEYOND JORDAN INTO THE PLACE WHERE JOHN AT FIRST BAPTIZED; AND THERE HE ABODE."

The overview is:

1. The phrase, *"And went away again beyond Jordan,"* probably referred to the Jericho area.

2. This was the latter part of December, and He would be crucified at the next

Passover, which was in April. Consequently, He had about three and one-half months of Ministry remaining.

3. *"Into the place where John at first baptized; and there He abode,"* does not give us any exact time frame.

4. The record seems to indicate that He spent a period of time there, then went back into Galilee, and then returned to Jerusalem for the Passover in April, i.e., the Crucifixion (Lk. 17:11).

5. It is believed that the Jericho area of the Jordan River (not Jericho itself) is where Jesus was baptized by John. There, Andrew and Peter and probably John, Philip, and Bartholomew were drawn to Him.

6. It seems that John the Beloved, who wrote this account, had a fond memory of this place, as would be understandable. This was where he, along with others, had first heard Jesus.

(41) "AND MANY RESORTED UNTO HIM, AND SAID, JOHN DID NO MIRACLE: BUT ALL THINGS THAT JOHN SPOKE OF THIS MAN WERE TRUE."

The structure is:

1. The phrase, *"And many resorted unto Him,"* seems to indicate that they did so in the right way. The attitude and spirit of these people were entirely different than that of Jerusalem. Jerusalem was the center of religion and, consequently, the gathering area of many religious spirits, no doubt. Jesus could no longer remain in the area, but His Rejection there would be the Blessing of this area of Jordan. There He would minister, with many brought to a Saving Knowledge of the Grace of God.

2. The phrase, *"And said, John did no miracle: but all things that John spoke of this Man were true,"* proclaims, in a sense, that Jesus ended His Ministry basically where it had begun. While He did other things after this, even travelling to Galilee, as stated, still, this seems to be the last place where He abode any length of time.

3. The people here had a fond memory of John the Baptist, remembering many things which he had said, especially about the coming Messiah.

4. In this wilderness beyond Jordan, those who had been baptized of John came to Jesus and believed upon Him. John had said that Jesus was *"mightier"* than he — that He was the Son of God, the *"Baptizer with the Holy Spirit and with Fire"* and *"the Lamb of God, Who takes away the sin of the world"* (Lk. 3:16; Jn. 1:29). All of these things seem to have been well remembered in their minds.

5. No doubt, having heard much about Jesus since He was there slightly over three years earlier, they eagerly accepted Him and allowed Him gloriously and wondrously to be the Saviour of their souls.

(42) "AND MANY BELIEVED ON HIM THERE."

The pattern is:

1. These recognized the fact of sin and the need of pardon, which, no doubt, evidenced a true Faith, and which was, therefore, different from the carnal faith of John 2:23 and John 8:30.

2. Whereas the religious leaders of Jerusalem would not believe on Him and, therefore, died lost, these were quick to do what the others would not do. They *"believed on Him"* and received that which such Faith always brings, Salvation of the soul and Peace with God.

3. Thank God that I, along with millions of others, have, as well, *"believed on Him!"*

"I've reached the land of corn and wine,
"And all its riches freely mine;
"Here shines undimmed one blissful day,
"For all my night has passed away."

"My Saviour comes and walks with me,
"And sweet communion here have we;
"He gently leads me by His Hand,
"For this is Heaven's border land."

"A sweet perfume upon breeze is borne,
"From ever vernal trees,
"And flowers, that never fading grow,
"Where streams of life forever flow."

"The zephyrs seem to float to me,
"Sweet sounds of Heaven's melody,
"As Angels with the white-robed throng,
"Join in the sweet Redemption song."

CHAPTER 11

(1) "NOW A CERTAIN MAN WAS SICK, NAMED LAZARUS, OF BETHANY, THE TOWN OF MARY AND HER SISTER MARTHA."

The overview is:

1. The Cross is the symbol of our union with Christ (II Cor. 5:14).

2. If the Believer doesn't understand the Cross relative to Sanctification, he is a target for Satan (I Cor. 1:17).

3. The greatest hindrance to Faith in Christ and what He did for us at the Cross is *"works"* (Eph. 2:8-9).

LAZARUS

The phrase, *"Now a certain man was sick, named Lazarus,"* does not proclaim the same Lazarus of Luke, Chapter 16, who had died some time before now.

This Lazarus was the brother of the two sisters, Mary and Martha. All that we know of him is given in Chapters 11 and 12 of this Book. And yet, one of the greatest Miracles ever recorded in the annals of human history was performed on Lazarus. He was raised from the dead even after four days of being in the tomb. John, no doubt, was an eyewitness of these events, and in his usual style, goes into detail respecting this momentous happening.

Strangely enough, despite the great Miracle here recorded, not a single word of Lazarus is recorded. Nothing is told us either about his experiences during *"those four days"* when he was in the tomb, actually, in Paradise, and no revelation is made concerning the conditions of life in the Paradise of that time.

BETHANY

The phrase, *"Of Bethany, the town of Mary and her sister Martha,"* speaks of this small village, which was about two miles from Jerusalem, situated on the eastern slope of the Mount of Olives. When in Jerusalem, the account seems to imply that Jesus often resorted to this little village at night, even to the home, at times, of this brother and his two sisters.

There is some indication that they may have been people of means, due to the fact that Mary anointed Jesus with a very costly ointment. Because of their hospitality to Jesus, they were privileged to experience three things:

1. To sit at His Feet and hear Words of Life, unparalleled in human history.

2. Lazarus would be raised from the dead.

3. To anoint the Feet of Jesus.

Such is the wonder of anyone who is privileged to have Jesus as his Lord. The things He will do, in every capacity, literally defy description. If that is not the case, such can only point to an extremely tepid relationship and total lack of consecration.

However, the sadness is that the majority of those who claim to follow Christ little take advantage of Who He actually is and what He actually can do! To describe such a loss, one cannot! To be sure, as He did wondrous things for this family, He will do for any and all who will dare to believe Him.

I think if any one word could explain the *"why"* and *"how"* of these things, that word would be *"relationship."* This trio had an excellent relationship with Jesus, which anyone can have if he so desires. *"Who is He,"* which can only be learned by relationship, is the key to *"What He does."*

(2) "(IT WAS THAT MARY WHICH ANOINTED THE LORD WITH OINTMENT, AND WIPED HIS FEET WITH HER HAIR, WHOSE BROTHER LAZARUS WAS SICK.)"

The construction is:

1. The phrase, *"It was that Mary which anointed the Lord with ointment,"* is the manner in which John identified Mary and, as well, proclaimed the significance of this act. The *"anointing"* took place very shortly before the Crucifixion and after the event of Lazarus being raised from the dead.

2. *"And wiped His Feet with her hair,"* proclaims her, I think, anointing this portion of His Body because she believed that One Who could raise her brother from the dead could, as well, overcome death Himself and walk out of that tomb, which He did! This one thing is sure: this Mary was not at the tomb on that glorious morning of His

Resurrection. I think she knew He would not be there.

3. The phrase, *"Whose brother Lazarus was sick,"* tells us the following:

a. Even though great Blessings came to this house as a result of the association with Jesus, still, this did not mean that they were immune from the trials and vicissitudes of life, even as this sickness proclaims.

b. The error that proclaims that upon a proper confession of Faith, one can avoid all unpleasant circumstances is error indeed!

c. *"Many are the afflictions of the righteous: but the LORD,"* as here stated, *"delivers him out of them all"* (Ps. 34:19).

(3) "THEREFORE HIS SISTERS SENT UNTO HIM, SAYING, LORD, BEHOLD, HE WHOM YOU LOVE IS SICK."

The form is:

1. The phrase, *"Therefore his sisters sent unto Him,"* presents that which has been done countless times since.

2. At all times, but especially in times of crisis, we send for *"Him,"* the only One, in fact, Who can really help, for He has the Power of Life and Death in His Hands.

3. *"Saying, Lord, behold, he whom You love is sick,"* refers to something more than just a mere malady, but rather a life-threatening affliction, which, in fact, did take his life, at least at the time.

4. The word *"love,"* as used here, has to do with relationship. The implication is that Jesus and Lazarus, as well as the sisters, were very close friends. And yet, from the study of this relationship, we know that this friendship with Jesus was different, as it had to be, than it would be with other men and women. The best way for it to be explained would probably be in the realm of the shepherd and the sheep.

5. I do not personally feel that anyone was buddy, buddy with Jesus. It certainly was not that He was aloof, for He was not. The idea has to do more with the Sheep than the Shepherd. All who were close to Jesus immediately found, as the Text suggests, that even though a great nearness and friendliness were possible, no doubt, more so than any other person, still, there was something about Him that placed Him in an altogether different position than other human beings. His demeanor inspired worship rather than comradeship.

(4) "WHEN JESUS HEARD THAT, HE SAID, THIS SICKNESS IS NOT UNTO DEATH, BUT FOR THE GLORY OF GOD, THAT THE SON OF GOD MIGHT BE GLORIFIED THEREBY."

The pattern is:

1. To properly understand Faith, at least that which is given to us in the Word of God, we must understand the *"Object of Faith."*

2. The *"Object of Faith"* must be *"Jesus Christ and Him Crucified,"* i.e., *the Cross."*

3. The Lord will recognize no faith other than that which is centered in Christ and the Cross (I Cor. 1:17).

THIS SICKNESS IS NOT UNTO DEATH

The phrase, *"When Jesus heard that, He said,"* presents the messenger, having been sent by the sisters, now arriving and giving Jesus the message.

At this time, Jesus was *"beyond Jordan, at the place where John had first baptized,"* a distance of approximately 25 to 30 miles (Jn. 10:40).

The Text seems to imply that Jesus was not aware of the situation until informed by the messenger, but immediately, it seems, the Holy Spirit gave Him instructions respecting what should be done.

The phrase, *"This sickness is not unto death,"* seems to be contradicted by the facts. However, the Greek Text actually proclaims Jesus saying, *"He shall not fall a prey to death,"* which is the way it should have been translated.

"But for the Glory of God, that the Son of God might be glorified thereby," gives us in the word *"glorified"* a greater insight into what was happening.

GLORIFIED

The word *"glorified"* in the Greek Text, as it is used elsewhere, means *"Sacrifice on behalf of."* So, here the very suffering of Lazarus and of the sisters, and the tears of Jesus over the grave, are part of the Sacrificial Ministry of which the Glory of God, as it pertains to the Son of God, may be advanced (Reynolds).[1]

This tells us that even though the Lord does not receive glory from sickness, He definitely does receive glory from the healing of sickness. The same could be said for sin, in which sickness actually has its original roots.

Of course, God receives no glory out of any type of sin, but He does receive glory in delivering people from sin.

In no way can God be blamed for the maladies and depravity of the human race, for He is neither the author nor instigator of such, but rather Satan himself is. In other words, sin, sickness, poverty, ignorance, and death are all *"the works of the Devil"* (I Jn. 3:8). Jesus came to destroy those evil works!

As well, as is the case with the Miracles of Jesus, a far broader picture is presented here.

The impotent man (Jn., Chpt. 5), the blind man (Jn., Chpt. 9), and Lazarus picture Israel as morally impotent, blind, and dead. Of these three demonstrations of Christ's Deity, the last was the greatest.

The sick may be healed, but there is no remedy for death. Death convicts man as being a sinner and conducts him to Judgment, for, because of sin, it is appointed unto man once to die and after this the Judgment (Heb. 9:27).

SACRIFICIAL MINISTRY

So, Jesus waited for sin to do its utmost to the body of Lazarus and then went to manifest His Divine Glory in raising him to life, although already corrupt from being dead four days.

Such is His Present Action in respect to Israel. The Nation, spiritually speaking, is dead. However, the Lord loves it, even as the sister suggested in Verse 3, and at the Second Coming, He will raise the Nation unto millennial life (Hos. 6:2).

Also, in a sense, this demonstration, as here recorded, represents not only Israel but every individual who has ever lived. The Born Again experience is the Spiritual application of Resurrection. The sinner is raised from the death of sin to the Life of God, a Work only Jesus could bring about by His Death and Resurrection.

Even though we have already touched on the subject, due to its weight, please allow me the privilege of addressing myself to the *"Sacrificial Ministry"* in which every Believer, in some sense, must be engaged. As we have stated, the cause of these things, in whatever capacity that may be, is not to be laid at the Feet of the Lord. Nevertheless, He is glorified in overcoming sin, sickness, and death. Therefore, in one way or the other, all Believers are to be a part of *"Sacrificial Ministry,"* that is, if they allow the Lord to handle the situation, whatever it may be. Regrettably, many, if not most, Believers resort to other means, which effect little or no help, and rob Christ of the Glory which He could derive from effecting Deliverance.

A PERSONAL EXPERIENCE

If I remember correctly, it was in November, 1991. At that time, there seemed to be no hope whatsoever for this Ministry. The confidence of the people, which an Evangelist must have in order to carry out that which God has called him to do, had been shattered. In truth, in every way one could look, the situation was virtually impossible. In other words, it could not be salvaged by human means.

I blame no one but myself for any and all failure. However, at the same time, these situations are never as simple as many make them out to be.

It is very easy to criticize David for what happened in his life, Abraham respecting his lying about Sarah, or the failure of Simon Peter, but until you have been engaged in the type of spiritual warfare which they encountered, it would be far the better to hold judgment to yourself.

The occasion of what happened took place on a Sunday morning as we were having Service at Family Worship Center.

The song service was in progress, and we were all standing and worshipping. Of course, my heart was broken in a thousand pieces. There was so much I didn't understand, and, as well, self-recrimination can become a weight impossible to bear.

All of a sudden, the Spirit of God came all over me, and I began to weep. Then, these very Words of Jesus strongly came into my heart:

"This sickness is not unto death, but for

the Glory of God, that the Son of God might be glorified thereby" (Jn. 11:4).

Even though I had read this Text many, many times, I had not read it lately, and it had not even been on my mind. I am saying that it was not the product of wishful thinking. Beyond the shadow of a doubt, especially considering the manner in which it was given, I know it was from the Lord.

As I have stated, the Lord receives no glory out of sin or failure of any nature; however, He does receive great glory out of victory over sin and failure.

This I believe He has done, and to an even greater degree, such will be in the near future.

In this sense, even as Lazarus of old and so many millions of others, the Lord can and, in fact, has made this a *"Sacrificial Ministry."*

LOOK WHAT THE LORD HAS DONE

At the time of this writing (September, 2012), THE SONLIFE BROADCASTING NETWORK is, as far as we know, the fastest growing network in the world. In two years' time, we are in some 60 million homes in America alone, 24 hours a day, seven days a week. Counting Europe, Asia, Africa, the Middle East, plus Mexico, Central and South America, and even the Far East, we are going into well over 130 million homes, 24 hours a day, seven days a week. As well, THE EXPOSITOR'S STUDY BIBLE is one of the best selling Study Bibles ever. All I can say is, *"Look what the Lord has done, and is doing, with the future yet to be even greater."* How we give Him all the Praise and all the Glory.

As well, we are anticipating the greatest harvest of souls that the world has ever seen, or the Church, for that matter. I believe it's going to be the last great Move before the coming Great Tribulation, and I believe the potential is there for millions to be swept into the Kingdom of God. The Lord has told me that this Ministry (Jimmy Swaggart Ministries) is going to play a great part in this great Move of God. Again, look what the Lord has done. ...

(5) "NOW JESUS LOVED MARTHA, AND HER SISTER, AND LAZARUS."

NOTES

The form is:

1. Normally, the man would be placed first. However, *"Martha"* is placed first here because, in all probability, she was head of the household.

2. The manner in which this was stated, especially the way the word *"loved"* was used, tells us that this was the result of a long acquaintance.

3. Actually, of all the families in Israel at that time, it seems that Jesus may have spent more time at this home than any other. What a Blessing it was to have the Holy Spirit say of these three how much they were loved by Jesus. No greater honor could be bestowed on anyone than to have such forever inscribed in the Word of God.

(6) "WHEN HE HAD HEARD THEREFORE THAT HE WAS SICK, HE ABODE TWO DAYS STILL IN THE SAME PLACE WHERE HE WAS."

The exegesis is:

1. The phrase, *"When He had heard therefore that he was sick,"* seems to indicate that a messenger was sent before Lazarus died. Consequently, when the message was delivered, Lazarus had already died, probably expiring a short time after the messenger had left. However, there was no way that he could be apprehended in order that the correct message be given to Jesus. Nevertheless, the Holy Spirit would reveal to our Lord that Lazarus had died.

2. *"He abode two days still in the same place where He was,"* proclaims that He did so on instructions from the Holy Spirit.

3. Evidently, it took a day for the messenger to arrive to where Jesus was located. Jesus then waited two more days, with the journey to the home of Lazarus taking another day, making four in all, even as the Scripture said (Jn. 11:17).

(7) "THEN AFTER THAT SAID HE TO HIS DISCIPLES, LET US GO INTO JUDAEA AGAIN."

The synopsis is:

1. If it is to be noticed, all of Paul's life and living was predicated on the fact that he was *"crucified with Christ"* (Gal. 2:20).

2. It is all in Christ and what He did at the Cross, and our Faith in that Finished

Work, which gives the Holy Spirit the latitude to bring about good things.

3. Otherwise, it is *"works"* which God can never accept.

THE GLORY OF GOD

The Action of Jesus in waiting seemed to contradict His Profession of affection. His Statement that the sickness was not unto death, or rather that *"Lazarus would not fall prey to death,"* seems to be a contradiction by death actually occurring. However, Resurrection would solve this difficulty.

The purpose of the sickness was not to demonstrate the power of sin and death, as it normally would, but to furnish an occasion for the Glory of God, i.e., a Manifestation of His Glorious Power in Resurrection, that the Son of God might be glorified thereby, i.e., through it.

EVERYTHING THAT JESUS DID

The phrase, *"Then after that said He to His Disciples,"* portrays to us the exact Timing of the Holy Spirit. Everything Jesus did was according to instructions given Him by the Spirit of God. He was totally led and directed by the Spirit, which should be an example to us.

For example, He prayed all night long before the choosing of His Disciples, portraying to us the absolute necessity of a very strong prayer life (Lk. 6:12-13).

If Jesus, as the Son of God, had to seek the Face of the Father to such an extent in order to find the direct Will of God, how much more is it incumbent upon us to do the same! Tragically, most Christians, even preachers, pray little at all. This is the reason so much is done that is not of God, simply being that He has not been sought for Leading and Guidance. The results of such actions are always detrimental to the true Work of God.

The phrase, *"Let us go into Judaea again,"* was for the purpose of raising Lazarus from the dead.

Reynolds said:

"The use of the word 'again' points forcibly back to the last visit, when He told both friends and foes that the Good Shepherd would snatch His sheep from the jaws of death, even though He laid down His Own

NOTES

Life in the doing of it."[2]

(8) *"HIS DISCIPLES SAID UNTO HIM, MASTER, THE JEWS OF LATE SOUGHT TO STONE YOU; AND YOU ARE GOING THERE AGAIN?"*

The exegesis is:

1. The phrase, *"His Disciples said unto Him,"* presents a true and sincere concern for His Welfare.

2. The word *"Master"* is actually the word *"Rabbi"* and is frequently used by John as the term of respect applied to both the Baptist and our Lord. This title, incidentally, was one of extraordinary dignity as it was then used by the Jews.

3. The question, *"The Jews of late sought to stone You; and You are going there again?"* refers to His last Visit to Jerusalem and the account as given in Verse 31 of the previous Chapter. As stated, His Disciples had great concern for Him.

4. How different this language is from that of His Own Brothers (Jn. 7:3-5)!

(9) *"JESUS ANSWERED, ARE THERE NOT TWELVE HOURS IN THE DAY? IF ANY MAN WALK IN THE DAY, HE STUMBLES NOT, BECAUSE HE SEES THE LIGHT OF THIS WORLD."*

The exegesis is:

1. The question, *"Jesus answered, Are there not twelve hours in the day?"* proclaims the Lord balancing the length of the days, which were about 14 hours at their longest during the summer and about 10 hours at their shortest in the winter, at least in His Part of the world. He was using this terminology as an analogy.

2. The phrase, *"If any man walk in the day, he stumbles not, because he sees the light of this world,"* refers to the sun shining on the world according to the rotation of the Earth and consequently providing light. Most work was done during the day at that time because there was very little artificial light, only candles or torches.

3. The idea of the statement pertains to the Believer understanding that the only *"Light"* is from the Holy Spirit, regarding direction, guidance, leading, and opportunity. All else is darkness. So, inasmuch as most work is done during the day respecting natural light, the Believer must look at the

Holy Spirit as the Giver of *"Light,"* and that all must be done in that *"Light."*

4. The reason that much of the church world *"stumbles"* so much is because it does not have the *"Light"* of the Spirit for instruction and guidance. Incidentally, such instruction and guidance will never vary from the Word of God.

5. Jesus was telling His Disciples two things:

a. Despite the animosity of the Jews against Him, He was going back into Judaea because the Holy Spirit had given Him Instructions to do so. As stated, He likened it as *"Light."*

b. The absolute necessity of all Believers being led by the Spirit is portrayed in this statement as well.

(10) "BUT IF A MAN WALK IN THE NIGHT, HE STUMBLES, BECAUSE THERE IS NO LIGHT IN HIM."

The exposition is:

1. The Lord Jesus suffered for Righteousness during His Life. He suffered for sin in His Death.

2. Jesus underwent a suffering on the Cross when He suffered for sin, our sins, incidentally, and certainly not His Own, which no human being will ever be able to fully comprehend.

3. When it came to suffering for sin, Jesus did so on the Cross that we might not have to suffer for it. He endured the Wrath of God that we might not have to endure it.

WALKING IN THE NIGHT

The phrase, *"But if a man walk in the night, he stumbles,"* uses a natural expression to express a Spiritual Truth.

All Believers must have the Leading and Guidance of the Holy Spirit in all that we do, which can only be brought about by a strong prayer life and a constant study of the Word of God. Above all, our Faith must be anchored solely in Christ and what He did for us at the Cross. Sadly, these traits are in short supply in the lives of most Believers.

In the fall of 1991, the Lord instructed me to conduct two prayer meetings a day (minus Saturday morning and Service times). This we did, which has been the greatest thing that has ever happened to me personally.

However, I have noticed that most modern Believers, even those who claim to be Pentecostal and are supposed to know and understand the value of prayer, in truth, little understand it at all.

I had some few to mention, and, no doubt, many others who thought such, *"Nothing is happening in these prayer meetings,"* thinking that their purpose was for Prophecies, prayer for the sick, etc. While those things definitely may happen at times, that is not the purpose of prayer meetings.

THE PURPOSE OF SEEKING GOD

We were there to seek God, not necessarily to minister to each other, even though, as stated, those things at times would most definitely happen. However, most modern Believers, even Pentecostals and Charismatics, who ought to know better, have totally forgotten, that is, if they ever knew, what true prayer is all about. Prayer is simply meant to be times of us speaking to the Lord and, more importantly, the Lord speaking to us. These are the times that the Spirit of God gives enlightenment. As well, and I think I can say without exaggeration, He does so most of the time through the Word of God. However, as stated, irrespective of His Manner, it will never contradict the Word. If so, it is not the Spirit of God but another spirit entirely.

Incidentally, we kept up these prayer meetings for over 10 years, and I still do so, twice a day, on a personal basis.

NO LIGHT IN HIM

The phrase, *"Because there is no Light in him,"* destroys the doctrine of the *"Inner Light,"* as claimed by man in natural birth. In truth, man within himself has no light. He is totally estranged from God, Who is the Source of all Light, because He is Light. As such, man *"stumbles"* respecting any and everything he does, irrespective of what direction it takes.

I have always maintained, and continue to do so, that every single freedom in this world, as well as all prosperity, has come about as a result of the *"Light"* of the Gospel of Jesus Christ.

Sometime back, a billionaire from Texas

gave several millions of dollars to Yale University in order that they may establish a *"chair"* respecting *"western civilization."* In other words, what was western civilization, and how did it come about?

After several years, the benefactor called Yale, asking what had happened to this particular study course. I was told that the president of Yale said to him, *"We do not know how to address ourselves to such a subject."*

They were exactly right; they did not have a clue!

The idea that the greatest freedoms and prosperity the world has ever known has come about because of the *"Light"* of the Gospel of Jesus Christ, which has resulted in *"western civilization,"* is lost completely upon these professors of education. It is lost upon them because they have no *"Light."* However, those who have this *"Light"* know!

Tragically, almost all of the world *"walks in the night,"* and consequently *"stumbles,"* because they have had no opportunity to have this *"Light,"* or else, it has been presented, and they have rejected it.

Consequently, these Words, as given by Jesus, proclaim the Source of all intelligence, understanding, and knowledge, at least about things as they really are.

(11) "THESE THINGS SAID HE: AND AFTER THAT HE SAID UNTO THEM, OUR FRIEND LAZARUS SLEEPS; BUT I GO, THAT I MAY AWAKE HIM OUT OF SLEEP."

The overview is:

1. When the Scripture speaks of our having fellowship with the Sufferings of Christ, it refers simply to His Sufferings for Righteousness — His Sufferings at the hand of man.

2. When it came to suffering for sin, He did so on the Cross that we might not have to suffer for it.

3. The infinite fullness of the Atoning Sacrifice of Christ needed many Offerings, namely five, to show forth, even faintly, its plentitude.

THE INSTRUCTIONS OF THE HOLY SPIRIT

The phrase, *"These things said He,"* refers to the fact that the Disciples did not quite understand why Jesus wanted to go back into Judaea, especially considering that the animosity there was so great against Him that His Very Life would be in danger. As well, if He was going to return, why would He wait two whole days before leaving?

The Truth given in John 11:9-10 proclaims that Jesus did what He did because that is what the Holy Spirit had instructed Him to do. As stated, this is to be the criterion for all Saints — to be led by the Spirit of God in all things.

"And after that He said unto them, Our friend Lazarus sleeps," presents further information given to Him by the Holy Spirit in that Lazarus had died.

SOUL SLEEP?

It is interesting that Jesus used the word *"sleeps"* respecting death. Actually, the Holy Spirit uses the term frequently concerning other Saints regarding death (Acts 7:60; I Cor. 11:30; 15:18-20; I Thess. 4:13-17). Jesus also used this term respecting the death of Jairus' daughter (Mat. 9:24; Mk. 5:39; Lk. 8:52).

Some have derived a false doctrine from this statement by Christ, and others similar, claiming that when the Believer dies, his spirit, soul, and body sleep until the Resurrection. It is called, *"Soul sleep."* However, this is totally incorrect.

In the Greek Text, we know that the object of this metaphor is to suggest that as the sleeper does not cease to exist while his body sleeps, so the dead person continues to exist despite his absence from the region in which those who remain can communicate with Him. As well, as sleep is known to be temporary, so the death of the body will be found to be temporary also.

In other words, it is only the body of the Believer that sleeps, and not the soul and the spirit, which immediately go to be with Christ. Actually, the soul and spirit of Lazarus went down into Paradise at this time because Jesus had not yet been glorified.

THE STATE OF THE DECEASED BELIEVER

Since that state in which the Believer, absent from the body, is at home with the Lord, Paul described this state in Philippians 1:23 as being *"far, far better."* Of course, he was speaking of the state of the deceased Believer and not for the loved ones left on Earth, and even for the Work of God, for that matter. That is why Paul also said, respecting his continuing to live instead of going to be with the Lord, *"Nevertheless to abide in the flesh is more needful for you"* (Phil. 1:24).

The phrase, *"But I go, that I may awake him out of sleep,"* refers to the fact that the Holy Spirit had told Jesus to raise this man from the dead.

That which He would do respecting Lazarus was an *"earnest"* of what He will do in the coming Resurrection when all the Sainted Dead will be raised (I Thess. 4:16-17).

The Greek word for *"earnest"* is *"arrabon"* and means *"a pledge or first-payment."* In other words, the raising of Lazarus from the dead was *"a"* Resurrection but not *"the"* Resurrection.

(12) "THEN SAID HIS DISCIPLES, LORD, IF HE SLEEP, HE SHALL DO WELL."

The composition is:

1. Their answer proclaims that they did not know what Jesus was saying.

2. If one is to notice, the understanding of the Disciples concerning spiritual things was woefully inadequate at this time even though they definitely were Saved men. The reason for this spiritual dullness was the absence of the Holy Spirit, at least as He would come on, and then after, the Day of Pentecost, even unto this time. The difference in these men after Pentecost, in every way, is astounding to say the least! That is remarkable considering that they were walking shoulder to shoulder with Jesus for some three and one-half years. However, the infilling of the Holy Spirit, as it would be given on the Day of Pentecost, because Jesus had been Glorified (His Death and Resurrection), would prove in a sense to be even greater, at least regarding their Spiritual Growth, than their personal walk with Jesus.

3. That is why Jesus said, *"It is expedient for you that I go away: for if I go not away, the Comforter* (Helper) *will not come unto you; but if I depart, I will send Him unto you"* (Jn. 16:7). Of course, Jesus was speaking of the coming of the Holy Spirit, which would be in a new dimension.

4. How could this be better for the Disciples even than Jesus' Personal Presence with them?

5. The answer is found even in the question. Jesus was only with them, while the Holy Spirit would literally be in them and, consequently, able to give them the Power and capabilities of understanding the Things of God. Also, Jesus, in His Physical Body, could only be in one place at a time while the Holy Spirit can be in all, at all times, and everywhere, simply because the Holy Spirit is God.

6. If one looks at this scenario, one can easily see the difference in Spirit-filled Believers and those who are not Spirit-filled. Sadly, the far greater majority of Spirit-filled Believers little allow the Holy Spirit to have proper latitude within their lives, therefore, greatly hindering what He desires to do within them.

(13) "HOWBEIT JESUS SPOKE OF HIS DEATH: BUT THEY THOUGHT THAT HE HAD SPOKEN OF TAKING OF REST IN SLEEP."

The exegesis is:

1. The phrase, *"Howbeit Jesus spoke of His Death,"* portrays John, who wrote this account, as outlining in detail the exact moment of this particular time. He did not hide the fact of their spiritual dullness.

2. *"But they thought that He had spoken of taking of rest in sleep,"* proclaims them putting a carnal interpretation on His Statements.

3. I wonder how many of us presently tend to misread that which the Holy Spirit gives unto us.

4. Paul said, *"That the God of our Lord Jesus Christ, the Father of Glory, may give unto you the Spirit* (Holy Spirit) *of Wisdom and Revelation in the knowledge of Him."*

5. He then said, *"The eyes of your understanding being enlightened; that you may know ... "* (Eph. 1:17-18).

(14) "THEN SAID JESUS UNTO THEM PLAINLY, LAZARUS IS DEAD."

The synopsis is:

1. No! There is no contradiction with Verse 4, where Jesus said, *"This sickness*

is not unto death." As we have stated, the actual meaning and the way it should have been translated was that Lazarus *"shall not fall prey to death,"* at least at this time.

2. While, in fact, death would attempt to claim him, Jesus would nullify the efforts of the grim reaper, showing that His Power to give Life, as He has been constantly stating, also means the Power to overcome death.

3. In other words, the two go hand in hand. To have the Power to give Life is, at the same time, to have Power to overcome death.

(15) "AND I AM GLAD FOR YOUR SAKES THAT I WAS NOT THERE, TO THE INTENT YOU MAY BELIEVE; NEVERTHELESS LET US GO UNTO HIM."

The composition is:

1. The phrase, *"And I am glad for your sakes that I was not there,"* portrays the fact that if Jesus had been there, Lazarus would not have died. Jesus would have healed him. However, a greater Miracle would now be performed in the raising of Lazarus from the dead, which was what Jesus meant.

2. Actually, there is no record of anyone dying in the Presence of the Prince of Life. Also, there is some indication that He broke up every funeral in which He came in contact. Augustine, who lived a little over 300 years after Christ, stated that our Lord raised many from the dead, even other than the accounts given in the Gospels.

3. The phrase, *"To the intent you may believe,"* has reference to the fact that the Holy Spirit instructed Jesus to perform this Miracle for a variety of reasons, among them, to teach the Disciples the fact of the coming Resurrection.

4. To be sure, Jesus had raised others from the dead but none who had been dead four days as Lazarus, signifying what the coming Resurrection will be like.

5. As we have repeatedly stated, everything Jesus did was not only for the sake of the person or persons involved but, as well, to proclaim a much grander lesson.

6. Also, everything Jesus did was designed to increase the Faith of His Followers. It continues in this vein presently.

7. The Lord designs every happening and every act to be a lesson in Faith. Even our failures, which He certainly does not orchestrate or cause, are meant to serve as an instructor in this all-important aspect of our Christian experience.

8. As well, every attack by Satan against the Believer, irrespective of the nature of that attack, whether it be physical, domestic, financial, or spiritual, is designed by the Evil One for one purpose, and one purpose alone, the weakening, or even the destruction, of our Faith. Actually, the only fight in which the Believer is to engage is *"the good fight of Faith"* (I Tim. 6:12).

9. The phrase, *"Nevertheless let us go unto him,"* has a double meaning:

a. All Believers will ultimately go the way of death, even as Lazarus, except those who are alive at the time of the Rapture (I Thess. 4:17).

b. All Believers will experience a Resurrection, whether dead or alive, even as Lazarus, with one glaring difference. That difference is that the Saints at that time will put on a Glorified Body, and, in fact, Lazarus will then be one of those that falls into this category, even among the untold millions.

(16) "THEN SAID THOMAS, WHICH IS CALLED DIDYMUS, UNTO HIS FELLOW-DISCIPLES, LET US ALSO GO, THAT WE MAY DIE WITH HIM."

The diagram is:

1. The phrase, *"Then said Thomas, who is called Didymus, unto his fellow-Disciples,"* speaks of John mentioning this Disciple, of which he will say more after the Resurrection of Christ.

2. Thomas is perhaps branded unfairly as a doubter, etc. However, if one closely analyzes his statements, a far different portrayal begins to appear. While he did have a problem being convinced, the record portrays, I think, that once he was convinced, his Faith flowered. It is said that he ministered greatly in Parthia and India in his future Ministry and there suffered martyrdom.

3. Incidentally, Thomas was the very first one to give the Title of God to Jesus, other than the Prophets in predicting these events.

4. This happened after the Resurrection of Jesus with him exclaiming after observing the print of the nails, *"My Lord, and my God!"* (Jn. 20:26-28).

5. The phrase, *"Let us also go, that we may die with Him,"* tells us several things:

a. Thomas realized the tremendous animosity of the Jews against Jesus. By this time, he was not in doubt as to their hatred or the reason for that hatred.

b. This shows that the body of the Disciples was being more and more blended into a unity.

c. In seeing the danger to the Lord, with the spirit of self-surrender, he was ready to share His Fate.

d. By this statement, it seems that Thomas had pretty much given up hope of a Messianic Kingdom, which the Disciples had thought Jesus would introduce immediately.

As a footnote, tradition has associated Thomas with Jude, the Lord's Half-brother, the writer of the short Epistle which bears his name.

(17) "THEN WHEN JESUS CAME, HE FOUND THAT HE HAD LAIN IN THE GRAVE FOUR DAYS ALREADY."

The overview is:

1. The phrase, *"Then when Jesus came,"* proclaims to the carnal mind that He was too late. However, irrespective of the time, Jesus is never late. He has the Power to rectify the situation, irrespective of the degree of difficulty.

2. *"He found that he had lain in the grave four days already,"* implies that upon inquiry, Jesus was given this information.

3. Some of the Jews taught that the spirit of the deceased wandered about the sepulcher for three days, called, *"Days of weeping."* It did so, they said, seeking an opportunity to return to the body. On the fourth day, decomposition sets in.

4. So, there was no doubt about the death of Lazarus, especially considering that he had been in the tomb four days already.

(18) "NOW BETHANY WAS NEAR UNTO JERUSALEM, ABOUT FIFTEEN FURLONGS OFF."

The exegesis is:

1. Bethany was then about a mile and a half or two miles from Jerusalem but, now, is actually a part of the city.

2. When in Jerusalem, Jesus often resorted to Bethany to spend the night.

NOTES

3. This means that Christ only spent one night in Jerusalem before His Death, and that was the time of His Trial.

(19) "AND MANY OF THE JEWS CAME TO MARTHA AND MARY, TO COMFORT THEM CONCERNING THEIR BROTHER."

The order is:

1. The fact that many Jews should have taken the trouble to walk nearly two miles to comfort the bereaved sisters shows that the family at Bethany could well have been one of some wealth, position, and importance.

2. At any rate, all of this activity portrays the fact that no one could question the death of Lazarus.

3. There was no way anyone could question his being raised from the dead. One can be certain that the detractors of Christ would do anything they could to deny His Miracles, even claiming the person was not actually dead, etc. However, there was absolutely no way this could be done with Lazarus.

(20) "THEN MARTHA, AS SOON AS SHE HEARD THAT JESUS WAS COMING, WENT AND MET HIM: BUT MARY SAT STILL IN THE HOUSE."

The synopsis is:

1. When it came to suffering for sin, Jesus did so on the Cross that we might not have to suffer for it.

2. He endured the Wrath of God that we might not have to endure it.

3. On the Cross, He was the *"Sin-Offering"* and the *"Trespass-Offering."*

MARTHA

The phrase, *"Then Martha, as soon as she heard that Jesus was coming, went and met Him,"* implies that Jesus, upon coming close to Bethany, stopped short of coming into the town and, above all, of going to the house of the two sisters. Knowing the tremendous animosity against Him, He did not desire to attract any undue disturbance, especially at this time. Evidently, He had sent someone to their home to inform them that He had arrived with information as to where He was. Martha immediately went to meet Him.

It is inconceivable that the anger and hostility of the religious leaders against Jesus had become so acute that it was dangerous for the two sisters to even be seen in the Presence of their and our Lord. However, that was the state of affairs at that time.

A PERSONAL EXPERIENCE

Regrettably, on a personal basis, I am very well aware of this spirit. I have had preachers of a particular denomination stand outside the auditoriums where we were conducting Crusades in an attempt to note anyone who was a member of that particular denomination, be it preacher or otherwise, who was attending the meeting. As a consequence, these people would be heavily censored, whomever they were, and sometimes even asked to leave the church where they had attended for many years or even all of their lives.

Why? I guess the question should be asked, *"What were we doing that would be of such harm to these people?"*

We were doing nothing but preaching the Gospel, and I might say by the Grace of God, which was heavily anointed by the Holy Spirit and resulted in many people being Saved and many lives being changed.

The situation became very bad in one city where we were to conduct a Crusade (1990). Many of the pastors of that particular denomination were threatening their people so severely, at least if the members came to the meetings, that even one of the area newspapers printed an article asking the question, *"Is this not America? Cannot people attend church where they like?"*

To be sure, the same spirit which opposed Christ of that day so long ago is the same spirit that opposed us, and continues to do so. It is satanic, as should be obvious! At the same time, even as in Jesus' Day, very few people would stand up to those apostate religious leaders by doing what is right and Scriptural.

Most laymen take the position now as then, that there must be something very badly wrong with the person, or else, the religious leaders would not take such a stand of opposition. As well, most do not desire to be forced to leave a particular church where they have attended for many years, and where they have many friends. So, most fall into line with these leaders exactly as they did during the Time of Christ.

SHEEP HAVING NO SHEPHERD

Of course, such attitude and position always brings spiritual declension because the Spirit of God can never sanction such attitudes. In the case of Christ, it meant the destruction of Israel simply because most people would not buck the system. It is the same presently and, in fact, always has been. That is why it was said of Jesus concerning Israel, *"He was moved with compassion on them, because they fainted, and were scattered abroad, as sheep having no shepherd"* (Mat. 9:36).

Oh yes! Israel had scores of religious leaders who called themselves shepherds but, in reality, were *"hirelings."*

THE MORE IT WILL BE OPPOSED

To be frank, Satan's greatest efforts against the Work of God do not come from the world's system, but rather that which calls itself *"church."* The more of Christ that something is, the more it will be opposed. This is the reason it is absolutely imperative that each and every Believer know and understand the Word of God for themselves. As well, they must be prepared to obey what it says and be willing to pay whatever price is demanded. That may seem stringent, but all must understand that we are speaking of the souls of men. In other words, there is far more at stake than meets the eye. The very soul of each individual is hanging in the balance.

As we have previously stated, during the time of Christ, the Pharisees had impeccable reputations over Israel. They were looked at as the spiritual guides of the people and, in fact, were extremely religious, but yet, totally lost! As a result, it would have been very difficult to persuade the majority in Israel that these men were murderers at heart. However, that is exactly what they were, as is now grossly obvious. The same is true presently!

MURDEROUS INTENT IN THEIR HEARTS

Most Christians think and believe that all who call themselves religious leaders, in whatever capacity, be they denominational heads or otherwise, are, in fact, godly people. While that certainly is true of some few, it is definitely not true of most. Most have the same murderous intent in their hearts as the Pharisees of old. The only reason they do not carry out these intents is simply because the law of the land prohibits such. I realize that most would think that I am extreme in my statements, but I am not extreme at all!

The truth is, while there are some few good Churches with godly Pastors who truly love the Lord and are attempting to preach the Gospel without compromise, the far greater majority are in the opposite camp, despite their claims, and are actually furthering the cause of Satan.

The reader may weary of me constantly mentioning these things, but one must understand that I do so only because this is what is borne out in the Scriptures and represents Satan's greatest efforts to destroy the Work of God. As we have repeatedly stated, he does a thousand times more damage from within than he does from without. Consequently, every Believer must take serious inventory as to where he or she attends church and what is taught and preached from behind the pulpit. They must forget about particular denominational names, irrespective if their family has attended a particular church for several generations. Those things do not count!

The only thing that counts is the Gospel that is preached behind the pulpit, and the laymen in the pew knowing enough about the Word of God to properly ascertain the Scripturality of what is being preached. Multiple hundreds of millions are in Hell right now simply because they failed to do what I am saying, blindly following so-called religious leaders unto spiritual oblivion.

The phrase, *"But Mary sat still in the house,"* seems to proclaim this done with purpose because friends of the family were constantly coming by to pay their respects, and someone had to be there to receive them.

(21) "THEN SAID MARTHA UNTO JESUS, LORD, IF YOU HAD BEEN HERE, MY BROTHER HAD NOT DIED."

The structure is:

NOTES

1. The phrase, *"Then said Martha unto Jesus,"* refers, as is obvious, to her finding Jesus, wherever He had been waiting.

2. *"Lord, if You had been here, my brother had not died,"* places Martha in the position of limiting Jesus. It does not seem that she thought of Jesus as being able to raise the dead, or else, she reasoned in her mind that inasmuch as her brother had been dead for four days, such a Miracle could not be.

3. Surely she had knowledge of Jesus having raised others from the dead, but it does not seem to enter her mind that He would do such for her brother. Perhaps the fact of her brother having been in the grave for four days already proved an insurmountable object for her to overcome. However, before we criticize her, we need to look at ourselves.

(22) "BUT I KNOW, THAT EVEN NOW, WHATSOEVER YOU WILL ASK OF GOD, GOD WILL GIVE IT TO YOU."

The form is:

1. Martha's terminology shows that she had not risen to the highest light on the Lord's Mysterious Relation to the Father. She spoke of Him and to Him as of a strangely-gifted human friend, but to the full understanding of Who Jesus was exactly, it was not completely clear to her. However, she would learn from this exchange things about Jesus she had not previously known.

2. Due to His Humanity, in other words, being totally human (while never ceasing to be God), it seems that such was so overwhelming that all, even His Most Ardent Followers, had difficulty in understanding that He was also Deity, in other words, the Jehovah of the Old Testament.

3. Considering the human equation, and on top of that, adding that He was but a Peasant, not at all of the aristocracy of Israel, it greatly exacerbated the difficulty.

4. On the other hand, His Miracles were so astounding that it was impossible for such to be done, other than by the Power of God. As well, more than one time, He explained fully Who He was and exactly what His Mission entailed. However, due to the fact that His Humanity was so overwhelming, it was, it seems, very difficult to see past that.

5. Even though Martha used the word *"whatsoever"* regarding what Jesus would ask of the Father, still, it seems she limited such in her own mind.

(23) *"JESUS SAID UNTO HER, YOUR BROTHER SHALL RISE AGAIN."*

The form is:

1. Very plainly, Jesus told her what was about to happen, but in her doubt, she misunderstood.

2. Before we criticize her, we need to look at ourselves. Would we have done any better?

3. She was about to see, plus all others present that day, the greatest Miracle performed by Christ, the raising of a man from the dead who had been in the tomb for some four days.

(24) *"MARTHA SAID UNTO HIM, I KNOW THAT HE SHALL RISE AGAIN IN THE RESURRECTION AT THE LAST DAY."*

The pattern is:

1. The phrase, *"Martha said unto Him,"* proclaims her answer regarding the Resurrection and her understanding of this great Doctrine to be far in advance of most in Israel.

2. *"I know that he shall rise again in the Resurrection at the last day,"* portrays that which she had probably learned at the Feet of Jesus, for He had said much about the Resurrection (Dan. 12:2, 13; Jn. 6:39-40, 44, 54; 12:48).

3. Still, what Jesus was about to do now was beyond her thinking.

(25) *"JESUS SAID UNTO HER, I AM THE RESURRECTION, AND THE LIFE: HE WHO BELIEVES IN ME, THOUGH HE WERE DEAD, YET SHALL HE LIVE."*

1. Were there no sin nature, there would have been no need for the Peace-Offering or the Trespass-Offering of the Mosaic Law.

2. The more closely we view these Offerings, the more fully do we see the necessity of the five Offerings of the Levitical Order in order that Christ be properly portrayed, as it regards His Finished Work.

3. The Peace Offering portrayed communion with God and, we might quickly add, communion restored. It was the only Offering in which the offerer could partake, which signified that peace had now been restored.

NOTES

I AM THE RESURRECTION AND THE LIFE

The phrase, *"Jesus said unto her, I am the Resurrection, and the Life,"* puts an entirely different perspective on this Doctrine.

In other words, Jesus was saying to Martha, *"Martha, look at Me. You are looking at the Resurrection and the Life."* This means that Jesus was not merely a Teacher of this Doctrine, or even a part of such, but, in reality, the actual *"Resurrection"* because He is the *"Life."*

This also means that Jesus does not merely contain Salvation but, in fact, is *"Salvation!"* He does not merely contain *"Life"* but, in fact, is *"Life!"* He does not merely know the *"Word"* but, in fact, is the *"Word"* (Jn. 1:1-2).

This places Him in an entirely different perspective than anything or anyone else. Others show the way, while He is the *"Way!"* Others have *"truth,"* while He is *"Truth"* (Jn. 14:6). Others have *"love,"* while He is *"Love"* (I Jn. 4:8).

This means that He is the Reservoir of all these things. He is the *"Resurrection and the Life"* simply because He has overcome death and paid the price for man's Redemption. These things He did in His Perfect Humanity. However, these resident forces within Him, and the ultimate Power to carry them out, pertained to His Deity. So, we have the joining of the two, His Humanity and His Deity, so closely intertwined that He has only one personality and one nature.

BELIEVE ON ME

The phrase, *"He who believes in Me, though he were dead, yet shall he live,"* says two things:

1. It speaks of the Spiritual Life that is imparted to the believing sinner, which brings him from spiritual death to Spiritual Life. When man fell in the Garden of Eden, he died spiritually, which means separation from God, Who is the Life Source. Consequently, unregenerate man is *"dead in trespasses and sins"* (Eph. 2:1). Upon Faith in Christ, Saving Grace is imparted to the believing sinner. He is then restored to God,

now having *"Life,"* and is no more *"dead,"* i.e., *"separated from God."*

2. The statement pertains to the coming Resurrection of the dead (those in Christ). This is the moment that the soul and the spirit are reunited with a New Glorified Body, which can never again suffer physical death, sickness, etc. This is what is referred to as the *"Out* (out from the old way) *Resurrection from the dead,"* when the Sainted Dead will be resurrected from among the wicked dead, who will not be resurrected until a thousand years later (I Cor. 15:51-57; I Thess. 4:16-17; Rev. 20:5-6).

(26) "AND WHOSOEVER LIVES AND BELIEVES IN ME SHALL NEVER DIE. DO YOU BELIEVE THIS?"

The diagram is:

1. As it regarded the Levitical Law of the Old Testament, there was none of the Offerings in which the Communion of the worshipper so fully unfolded as in the *"Peace-Offering."*

2. In the *"Burnt-Offering,"* it is Christ offering Himself to God, in other words, giving His Best.

3. In the *"Meat-Offering,"* we have Christ's Perfect Humanity.

4. Then, passing on to the *"Sin-Offering,"* we learn that sin, in its root, is fully met.

5. In the *"Trespass-Offering,"* there is a full answer to the actual sins (Mackintosh)[3].

SHALL NEVER DIE

The phrase, *"And whosoever lives and believes in Me shall never die,"* in effect, says, *"Whoever believes in Me in this life will live eternally"* (Jn. 6:27). This is, without a doubt, one of the greatest promises found in the entirety of the Word of God.

The key is *"believing,"* and more perfectly, believing in Jesus.

What does that mean?

In its most simplistic form, it means that the sinner must believe that Jesus Christ is God, and that He came down to this world, took upon Himself a human body, and offered it up on Calvary's Cross as a Sin-Offering in order to pay man's terrible sin debt. The sinner must believe that this Sacrifice of Christ paid it all, and that whosoever believes in Him and what He did for us at the Cross will have Eternal Life imparted unto him.

To be sure, the believing sinner may only have a partial grasp of the few things I have said, but God looks far more at the heart than He does the actual words expressed, or even our total understanding or the lack thereof (I Sam. 16:7).

Of course, many other things are a part of Salvation, such as the Resurrection, which the Believer will ultimately come to know.

DO YOU BELIEVE THIS?

The question, *"Do you believe this?"* states the condition.

Martha believed that Jesus could heal the sick and that there would be a future Resurrection, but these facts were valueless in the presence of death. However, Jesus was there, and He was not only the Resurrection but also the Life.

Lazarus being dead, life had to come first, which it did. Christ, by His Death, abolished sin, death, judgment, and all that belonged to the Life that man had lost, respecting the Fall in the Garden of Eden. In other words, Jesus died that we might have Life and that we might live.

Jesus at Calvary went under all the power of the enemy in all its totality and came up from it in the Power of a New Life in Resurrection, which was done exclusively for sinners.

In respect to that Life He purchased at Calvary and the Resurrection, He becomes Life to the Redeemed, for He communicates it to them.

As a result of this impartation, the Believer is in a wholly new state, with the old life and all the wrath attached to it being behind him forever.

All of this Power of Resurrection and of Life is lodged in the Person of Christ, and the Resurrection of Lazarus demonstrated that fact. Jesus would raise Himself from the dead (Jn. 2:19), and God, as well, would raise Him from the dead (Acts 3:15). Hence, He raised Lazarus, for He is God. However, this Resurrection was exercised in obedience to, and dependence on, the Father.

Resurrection is the end of death and, consequently, death has no more to do with the Redeemed. It has done all it can do. It is finished! The Redeemed live in the imparted Life that put an end to it. For us, the old life and its death and judgment no longer exist.

(27) "SHE SAID UNTO HIM, YES, LORD: I BELIEVE THAT YOU ARE THE CHRIST, THE SON OF GOD, WHICH SHOULD COME INTO THE WORLD."

The overview is:

1. The phrase, *"She said unto Him, Yes, Lord,"* proclaims her affirmation of Faith, which now took her to a Spiritual height to which she had not known previously. So, this of which Satan attempted to do, the killing of Lazarus, would instead serve as a greater opportunity that *"The Son of God might be glorified thereby."*

2. To be frank, most of the great Spiritual victories are won at times when it seems like there is great defeat.

3. *"I believe that You are the Christ, the Son of God,"* proclaims her belief in the Lord in a different light than she had known Him previously.

4. Whatever she had once known now comes into full flower. He is no longer merely a Man with extraordinary power. He is *"Christ,"* i.e., *"The Anointed,"* i.e., *"The Messiah,"* *"The Hope of Israel,"* and *"The Hope of the World."*

5. As well, she now knew that He is *"The Son of God"* and not merely one of the Prophets of old, as some believed the Messiah was to be.

6. She now believed that Jesus is God!

7. *"Who should come into the world,"* refers to Jesus being the Fulfillment of the Prophecies (Gen. 3:15; 12:3; 22:14; 49:10; Isa. 7:14; Chpt. 53).

(28) "AND WHEN SHE HAD SO SAID, SHE WENT HER WAY, AND CALLED MARY HER SISTER SECRETLY, SAYING, THE MASTER IS COME, AND CALLS FOR YOU."

The order is:

1. The phrase, *"And when she had so said, she went her way,"* undoubtedly portrays a springing well of hope and joy that must have filled her heart. A few minutes before, all was darkness, but now, all is Light. From the statements given by Jesus,

NOTES

I believe that she now knew that He was going to raise Lazarus from the dead.

2. To be frank, no one has ever left the Presence of Jesus without being blessed in such a way that it defies all description, that is, if he believes on Him. While it may not be as dramatic as it was with Lazarus being raised from the dead, still, this encounter has been even greater with untold millions, who have come to a Saving Knowledge of Jesus Christ. Their *"way"* is made immeasurably easier by this glorious and wonderful encounter.

3. *"And called Mary her sister secretly,"* proclaims Martha making her way to the side of Mary, even while many others were, no doubt, in the house at that time. How much she secretly revealed to her sister at that time concerning what Jesus had said, we cannot now know. However, I do believe that when Mary looked at Martha's face, she knew that something wonderful had happened.

4. *"Saying, The Master is come, and calls for you,"* has to be one of the most beautiful statements found in the entirety of the Word of God.

5. Jesus had evidently requested Mary to be present so she could witness the Resurrection of her brother. Jesus waited for her to come before proceeding to the tomb.

(29) "AS SOON AS SHE HEARD THAT, SHE AROSE QUICKLY, AND CAME UNTO HIM."

The form is:

1. The phrase, *"As soon as she heard that,"* proclaims the greatest Message that she, or anyone, for that matter, could ever hear. As stated, it is not known exactly what Martha related to Mary, but there is an excellent possibility that she told her all, especially on the short journey to where Jesus was outside the small town.

2. *"She arose quickly, and came unto Him,"* proclaims that she did such with a great spirit of anticipation.

3. What would Jesus do?

4. Whatever it was, it would be wonderful. Could it be that He would really raise her brother from the dead?

(30) "NOW JESUS WAS NOT YET COME INTO THE TOWN, BUT WAS IN THAT PLACE WHERE MARTHA MET HIM."

The diagram is:

1. The phrase, *"Now Jesus was not yet come into the town,"* was all carried out in this manner, no doubt, so as not to arouse the religious authorities, etc.

2. *"But was in that place where Martha met Him,"* was probably a very short distance from the home of the sisters.

3. Whatever they imagined, I hardly think that it was possible for them to grasp the fact that Jesus was actually going to raise their brother from the dead. They anticipated something great, but I'm not sure that they could go that far in their anticipation.

(31) "THE JEWS THEN WHICH WERE WITH HER IN THE HOUSE, AND COMFORTED HER, WHEN THEY SAW MARY, THAT SHE ROSE UP HASTILY AND WENT OUT, FOLLOWED HER, SAYING, SHE GOES UNTO THE GRAVE TO WEEP THERE."

The overview is:

1. The phrase, *"The Jews then who were with her in the house, and comforted her,"* seems to be a different set than those mentioned in Verse 19. Actually, this was the custom, with some coming to weep and mourn, etc.

2. *"When they saw Mary, that she rose up hastily and went out, followed her,"* presents them observing what had happened respecting the coming of Martha and Mary leaving with her, but with no knowledge as to what had transpired between them.

3. *"Saying, She goes unto the grave to weep there,"* was their assumption. Little did they know or realize what was about to happen, actually not even knowing that Jesus had come.

(32) "THEN WHEN MARY WAS COME WHERE JESUS WAS, AND SAW HIM, SHE FELL DOWN AT HIS FEET, SAYING UNTO HIM, LORD, IF YOU HAD BEEN HERE, MY BROTHER HAD NOT DIED."

The exegesis is:

1. The phrase, *"Then when Mary was come where Jesus was, and saw Him, she fell down at His Feet,"* represents, in a sense, her anticipation.

2. *"Saying unto Him, Lord, if You had been here, my brother had not died,"* is word for word what her sister had said a short time earlier.

3. Even though her words seemed to indicate that she was not expecting the Resurrection of her brother, still, I think that was not the case. As stated, it is almost positive that her sister related to her what Jesus had said concerning Lazarus being raised from the dead. However, in view of the preponderance of this situation, I am sure that both Mary and Martha did not want to be shown as assuming more than they should.

4. In human history, such had never been done, the raising of one who had been dead for four days. As well, it was very difficult for one to even think of the actual happening of such an event. So, I think we should not jump to the conclusion that Mary was registering unbelief. I think it was not so much unbelief as it was the difficulty of coming to *"belief,"* or of Faith, as the record, I think, will show.

(33) "WHEN JESUS THEREFORE SAW HER WEEPING, AND THE JEWS ALSO WEEPING WHICH CAME WITH HER, HE GROANED IN THE SPIRIT, AND WAS TROUBLED."

The exegesis is:

1. The phrase, *"When Jesus therefore saw her weeping, and the Jews also weeping which came with her,"* proclaims these mourners following her to the Side of Jesus.

2. He did not seem to mind their presence or their going with Him and the sisters to the tomb.

3. *"He groaned in the Spirit, and was troubled,"* portrays His Response to death and all that Satan had done to humanity.

4. The Greek word for *"groaned"* is *"embrimaomai"* and means *"to be very angry, and moved with indignation."*

5. What He was moved against here was, no doubt, the satanic powers that had Lazarus in their grip, which was death (Heb. 2:14-15).

6. At this moment, Reynolds said, *"Jesus saw the long procession of all mourners from the first to the last, all the agony, all the hopelessness which sin had brought into the world, in thousands of millions of instances. There flashed upon His Spirit all*

the terrible moral consequences of which death was the ghastly symbol."[4]

7. In a short time, He would take upon Himself the sins of man and would, as well, take upon Himself man's death.

8. The words, *"In the Spirit,"* refer to the Holy Spirit and present the entirety of the Godhead in opposition to the terrible results of the Fall, for both Jesus and the Holy Spirit were sent by the Father and came from the Father.

(34) "AND SAID, WHERE HAVE YOU LAID HIM? THEY SAID UNTO HIM, LORD, COME AND SEE."

The exposition is:

1. The question, *"And said, Where have you laid him?"* presents the beginning of this momentous occasion.

2. The skeptic, completely misunderstanding the Person of Christ, would scoff at Jesus not knowing the location of the tomb. However, they fail to understand that while Jesus was God and, in fact, never ceased to be God, He did lay aside voluntarily the expression of His Deity while never losing the possession of His Deity.

3. Consequently, all that He did was done as a Man empowered by the Holy Spirit. So, the Holy Spirit told Him some things, and other things were not related to Him. In that case, He found out things as all other men come to information.

4. *"They said unto Him, Lord, come and see,"* proclaims the Jews, who followed Mary, answering Him. In other words, they would lead Him to the tomb!

(35) "JESUS WEPT"

The structure is:

1. Reynolds said, *"This is the shortest Verse, but one of the most suggestive in the entirety of Scripture."*[5]

2. Some claim that Jesus was weeping for sorrow regarding Lazarus. However, this is not true, for He would raise Lazarus from the dead in a matter of minutes.

3. His Weeping was caused by His Fellow-feeling with human misery in all of its forms then imaged before Him in the grave of Lazarus.

4. Other than the Person of Jesus, mankind or the world has never been viewed as they were originally made. Both man

NOTES

and the world are under a curse because of the Fall in the Garden of Eden, which has brought untold misery and heartache. This will only be assuaged when Jesus comes back to reign supremely, which He will do at the Second Coming. Then the world will know peace and prosperity as it has not known previously.

5. However, until then, the tears that Jesus shed were but symbolic of an ocean of tears shed by all of humanity.

(36) "THEN SAID THE JEWS, BEHOLD HOW HE LOVED HIM!"

The construction is:

1. They were right in that Jesus did love Lazarus very much and, in fact, the entirety of the world, for that matter.

2. However, His Tears had to do with a far greater degree of misery than was evident here.

3. In fact, God is Love!

(37) "AND SOME OF THEM SAID, COULD NOT THIS MAN, WHICH OPENED THE EYES OF THE BLIND, HAVE CAUSED THAT EVEN THIS MAN SHOULD NOT HAVE DIED?"

The synopsis is:

1. The beginning of the question, *"And some of them said, Could not this Man, Who opened the eyes of the blind ... ?"* suggests in the original Greek that the cure of the blind man by Jesus, which had created so great a commotion, was, according to these people, only a delusion.

2. It is difficult to believe that they had not heard of the raising of the daughter of Jairus or the widow's son of Nain, for behold, all of what He did was spread far and wide. However, it seems that the dreaded virus of unbelief had wreaked its terrible toll on these, who seemed to have been somewhat different than those of Verse 36.

3. The conclusion of the question, *"Have caused that even this man should not have died?"* as stated, seems to be said with some sarcasm!

4. The hearts of men, especially religious men, are evil beyond compare. No hatred was manifested toward Jesus by those who made little or no claim of religion, even though they were obviously wicked. It remained for the religious crowd to express

their hatred, which they would do in a very bloody way in a very short time.

5. While all unsaved people are greatly deceived, still, religious deception is the worst of all! It not only conjures up its own Salvation but, as well, bitterly opposes that which is truly of God — and that is the greatest hurt of all.

(38) "JESUS THEREFORE AGAIN GROANING IN HIMSELF COMES TO THE GRAVE. IT WAS A CAVE, AND A STONE LAY UPON IT."

The synopsis is:

1. In both the *"Peace-Offering"* and the *"Trespass-Offering"* of the Old Testament, we learn of the presence of the sin nature in the heart and life of the Believer.

2. However, we find out, even more fully in the Peace-Offering, that even though the sin nature dwells in us, it is not to rule in us (Rom. 6:12).

3. Were there no sin nature, there would have been no need for the Peace-Offering or the Trespass-Offering.

GROANING IN HIMSELF

The phrase, *"Jesus therefore again groaning in Himself comes to the grave,"* seems to portray once again the Lord being seized by this terrible sorrow, which resulted in what seems to be overwhelming indignation.

If there is anything which symbolizes all the pain and hurt resulting from the fall of man, the *"grave"* or *"tomb"* is that example. Death in all of its forms is a result of the Fall. In death is sickness and in sickness is the germ of man's inability to save himself. Despite all the vaunted medical technology, sickness is just as rampant at present as it ever was.

We must realize that God created man to live forever and that, in actuality, the physical body is so wondrously made that medical science is not sure why the organs age and ultimately die. They tell us that the human body somewhat rejuvenates itself every seven years, and that there is no reason the organs, such as the heart, lungs, etc., should not last forever.

THE SOURCE OF DEATH

Romans 6:23 says, *"The wages of sin is death,"* consequently giving us the Source.

The Bible, respecting both the Old and New Testaments, traces the entry of sin into the world back to Adam. Looking at the Fall, Paul explained that *"Just as sin entered the world through one man* (Adam), *and death through sin, and in this way, death came to all men, because* (in Adam) *all sinned"* (Rom. 5:12).

Adam's sin was not his alone. He sinned for the entirety of the human race. The death that struck him, and was expressed not only physically but in every relationship, has been passed on to every succeeding generation. Paul stated that even before Moses, those who did not sin by breaking a particular Commandment (Rom. 5:14) still found themselves in the grip of death. Death then is not *"natural."* It is not rooted in the nature of the Universe; it is not simply an expression of the way things are.

Death is unnatural, brought on mankind by a shadowing event that shook the material Universe (Rom. 8:19-22), and so warped human nature as to affect the experience of every person ever born.

Death is the direct result of original sin. The fact of death testifies to the overwhelming importance of a personal, obedient relationship with God, the Creator of the Heavens and the Earth, which anyone can have through the Lord Jesus Christ, if they so desire.

THE NATURE OF DEATH

"Death" is a very complex term as outlined in the New Testament. One aspect of death is the biological end of life. Human beings sense their own uniqueness. They feel intuitively that somehow they are too significant to be simply snuffed out. This sense of death's wrongness, as well as the mystery of the unknown, arouses fear of death, and Satan uses this fear to enslave human beings (Heb. 2:15).

In ancient times, the Greeks saw death as the end. One might turn inevitable death into an achievement by dying gloriously, but most then believed that existence ended at the close of every lifespan.

However, a segment of society sought comfort in philosophy. Of these, some said that since death is natural, each person rightly journeys toward it.

Some consoled themselves with the idea that people continue to live on in their children. On the other hand, some argued that death was a welcome end to human struggles and pains in the uncaring Universe. Plato advanced the notion that personality, being moral and immaterial, must continue after the death of the body. However, those who lived in the world of the First Century held no common belief about immortality, and the notion of Resurrection was completely foreign to them.

In the Greek culture, death conveyed the idea that the dead had become mere matter. Whatever it was that had made the corpse or person and animated the body was gone. The person had reached that final state, their destiny, or so they said, as decreed for all people.

WHAT THE BIBLE SAYS!

The Bible teaches us that death is not simply a biological phenomenon. Death is also a theological phenomenon, with impact in the spiritual as well as the physical realm. As for the physically dead, God is well able to raise them (Acts 26:8). Mankind's problem and God's great Challenge have to do with the grim darkness of a living death (spiritual death) that to some extent shrouds human existence for time as well as for eternity.

In the nature of death, we find that man's sinful nature is not responsive to God and is filled with corrupt cravings, desires, and thoughts. Actually, human society itself is so twisted that it reflects Satan rather than God.

Other Passages in the Bible view death as an active principle (Rom. 8:2), affecting man's outlook and warping his natural passions (Rom. 8:5-8). Just as human beings are helpless in the grip of biological death, they are likewise powerless in the grasp of their inner moral corruption.

DEATH AS A DESCRIPTION

Death is also descriptive of man's relationship with God. Ephesians, Chapter 2, affirms that we *"who were dead in trespasses and sins, were at that time* (before Conversion) *by nature objects of wrath"* (Eph. 2:1-3).

Those who are dead in trespasses and sins, which is what led to physical death to begin with, are helpless and lie under the righteous Judgment of God. What is more, spiritual death is a state of actual antagonism toward God.

Paul shows that God has revealed Himself to all human beings (Rom. 1:18-20), but what reaction did He get? *"Although they knew God, they neither glorified Him as God nor gave thanks to Him"* (Rom. 1:21). Spiritual death is therefore marked not only by rejection of God, but by actual antagonism, turning human beings against the only possible source of Deliverance from sin.

Without God, man is carried inevitably into a religious and moral cesspool (Rom. 1:21-32). Spiritual death, as a state of enmity with God, isolates human beings from a personal relationship with Him and subjects them to Divine Judgment.

An individual who remains in this state of death (dead in trespasses and sins, speaking of spiritual death) throughout his or her biological lifetime stands in eternal peril. *"Man is destined to die* (physically) *once,"* Hebrews 9:27 says, *"And after that to face Judgment."*

The Book of Revelation graphically portrays the result of that Judgment. According to Revelation 20:14, it is endless existence in *"the Lake of Fire,"* and this is *"the Second Death."*

DEATH AND BELIEVERS

The Bible views man as a whole being. The biological (physical) and spiritual are linked. Thus, even though Jesus has dealt with death in fact and in principle at Calvary, physical death maintains its foothold in the Believer's personality. Only biological transformation or Resurrection will cleanse the body from every taint of sin and complete man's release from the realm of death.

This leads to a danger to the Believer. Biological death has its claim on Christians as well as on the lost. In Romans, Chapter 7, Paul links sin and death with law and shared his struggle to do what the Law commanded.

He discovered that the principles of sin and death were so deeply rooted in his personality that he was unable to experience the Righteousness that the Law of Moses portrayed.

However, Paul learned, as he told us in Romans 8:1, that the Believer is released from condemnation and need not fear the second death. However, even the Believer must be rescued daily *"from this body of death,"* which actually is sin (Rom. 7:24).

JESUS

Paul found the answer in Jesus, Who introduces within us a Power that will even *"give life to our mortal bodies through God's Spirit, Who lives in us"* (Rom. 8:11).

However, this is done in a certain way, and that way is according to the following:

• Jesus Christ is the Source of all things we receive from God (Jn. 1:1-3, 14, 29; Col. 2:10-15).

• With Jesus as the Source, the Cross is then the Means by which all of these wonderful things are given to us. In other words, it is the Cross, which settled the sin debt, that makes everything possible (Rom. 6:1-14; Col. 2:10-15).

• With our Lord as the Source and the Cross as the Means, the Cross of Christ must ever be the Object of our Faith. This is critical, for it is God's Way, and His Only Way (I Cor. 1:17, 18, 23; 2:2).

• With Jesus as the Source and the Cross as the Means, and the Cross being the Object of our Faith, then the Holy Spirit, Who works exclusively within the parameters, so to speak, of the Finished Work of Christ, will then work mightily on our behalf (Rom. 8:1-11; Eph. 2:13-18).

What we have just given in brief presents God's Way, and He only has one Way. To bring it down to the bottom line, it is the Cross of Christ.

Death then is a biological concept that is applied theologically to graphically convey the true state of humankind. The death that grips mankind is moral and physical and, of course, spiritual. Death warps and twists man out of the pattern of original Creation.

Every human potential is distorted; every capacity — for joy, for relationships, for harmony with God, for true goodness — is tragically misshapen.

Because each ugly twist and turn gives expression to sin, man — intended to reflect God's Image and Likeness — falls instead under God's Condemnation. The striking and terrible image of death is designed to communicate how desperately we need God and how hopeless we are without Him.

It is as foolish to expect one who is spiritually dead to win God's Favor by his works as it would be to expect a corpse to rise from his coffin and walk.

THE DEATH OF JESUS

The Bible views Jesus' Death not as a tragedy or injustice, even though it was definitely an injustice, but as a mighty Act of God. His Death has a significance parallel only to the Fall. Adam's sin gave death its chilling grip on the race: Jesus' Death for sin conquered death and breathed life into humanity again.

As Romans 4:25 puts it, *"He was delivered over to death for our sins and was raised to life for our Justification."*

Christ's substitutionary Death breaks the power of death in all its aspects. We are reconciled to God *"through the death of His Son"* (Rom. 5:10). We are even released from death's crippling impact on our present experience as Believers.

"By sending His Own Son in the likeness of sinful man to be a Sin-Offering (God), *condemned sin in sinful man, in order that the righteous requirements of the Law might be fully met in us"* (Rom. 8:3-4).

Through Jesus, Believers experience a transition from spiritual death to Spiritual Life. Paul told the Colossians, God *"has reconciled you by Christ's physical Body through death to present you holy in His Sight"* (Col. 1:22).

Ultimately, the complete meaning of this release will be known, for redeemed humanity will never experience death after their Resurrection.

In view of the varied and terrible meanings that Scripture ascribes to death, it would be wrong to think of Jesus' Death as a mere biological event. When the Bible teaches that Jesus suffered death and tasted death (Heb. 2:9), a full experience of all that death involves is implied. That this extends even to the awful separation from God that rends the heart of the godly is revealed in Jesus' Cry from the Cross: *"My God, My God, why have You forsaken Me?"* (Mat. 27:46).

KEY BIBLE PASSAGES RELATING TO DEATH

• Romans 5:12-21: two events dominate human history. Each event is summed up in a man. In Adam, death by sin was introduced into the race. In Christ, death was defeated and life restored.

• Romans 6:1-10: the Believer is so completely identified with Jesus and in such a perfect union through Faith that the death of Jesus is, in fact, the Believer's own death. As well, the Resurrection of Jesus is the Believer's Restoration to Life.

• Romans 7:7-25: The principle of death is still active within the Believer. Death, with its companions, sin and the law, can still make the Christian's life ineffective and unproductive.

• Romans 8:1-11: the Holy Spirit, present in the Believer, breaks the grip of sin and quickens even mortal bodies. We can live a righteous and fulfilling life through the Spirit. Life — that full experience of human potential and intimate relationship with God — becomes possible for the Believer.

• I Corinthians 15:12-57: the grip of death on the human personality will be broken when Believers experience Resurrection. Then, when the mortal is clothed with immortality, it will at last be true that *"death has been swallowed up in victory."*

• Ephesians 2:1-10: the impact that death has on the personality is shown in Paul's picture of the cravings, desires, and thoughts of those who are corrupted by sin.

• Hebrews 2:9-16: Jesus took on Himself human nature (but not the sin nature) so that by His Death He might release mankind from death's power and lift Believers to that Glory God has always intended for humanity.

VICTORY OVER DEATH

The Scripture faces death as it faces all reality. However, its interest is in life, and death is treated more or less incidentally as that from which men are Saved. Christ took upon Himself our nature, *"That through death He might destroy him who had the power of death, that is, the Devil"* (Heb. 2:14).

The Devil's power is always regarded as subject to God's Overruling (Job 2:6; Lk. 12:5). He is no absolute disposer of death. Nevertheless, death, the negation of life, is his (Satan's) proper sphere.

Christ came to put an end to death. It was through death, as we have stated, that He defeated Satan. It was through death that He put away our sin. *"The death He died, He died to sin, once for all"* (Rom. 6:10).

Apart from Christ, death is the supreme enemy, the symbol of our alienation from God, and the ultimate horror. However, Christ has used death to deliver men from death. He died that men may live. It is significant that the New Testament can speak of Believers as *"sleeping"* rather than as *"dying"* (I Thess. 4:14).

Jesus bore the full horror of death. Therefore, for those who are *"in Christ,"* death has been transformed so that it is no more than sleep.

The extent of the victory over death that Christ won is indicated by His Resurrection. *"Christ being raised from the dead will never die again; death no longer has dominion over him* (the Believer)*"* (Rom. 6:9). The Resurrection is the great triumphant event, and the whole of the New Testament notes victory originated here.

Christ is *"The Prince of Life"* (Acts 3:15), *"Lord both of the dead and the living"* (Rom. 14:9), *"The Word of Life"* (I Jn. 1:1). His Victory over death is complete.

His Victory is made available to His People. Death's ultimate destruction is certain (I Cor. 15:26; Rev. 21:4).

As well, this Second Death, which refers to being cast into Eternal Hell, has no power over the Believer (Rev. 2:11; 20:6). In keeping with this, the New Testament understands Eternal Life not only as the immortality of the soul but, as well, in terms of the Resurrection of the body. Nothing could more graphically illustrate the finality and the completeness of the defeat of death.

A GLORIOUS PRESENT AND A GLORIOUS FUTURE

Not only is there a glorious future for the Child of God, but there is, as well, a glorious present! The Believer has already passed out of death and into Life (Jn. 5:24; I Jn. 3:14). He is *"free from the Law of Sin and Death"* (Rom. 8:2). Death cannot separate him from God (Rom. 8:38).

Jesus said, *"If anyone keeps My Word, he will never see death"* (Jn. 8:51). Such words do not deny the reality of biological death. Rather, they point us to the Truth that the Death of Jesus means that the Believer has passed altogether out of the state which is death. He is brought into a new state, which is aptly characterized as *"Life."*

He will, in due course, pass through the gateway we refer to as physical death, that is, if the Rapture doesn't take place first (I Thess. 4:13-18). However, the sting has already been pulled. The Death of Jesus means victory over death for His Followers.

(Bibliography: C. S. Lewis, Miracles, 1947; J. Pelican, The Shape of Death, 1962; Lawrence Richards, Expository Dictionary of Bible Words; K. Rahner, On the Theology of Death, 1961).

THE STONE

The phrase, *"It was a cave, and a stone lay upon it,"* presents the striking end of all men, for it is *"appointed unto men once to die."*

Even though the appointments may vary all the way from a simple clapboard box to an expensive mausoleum, the remains are the same.

Somebody asked the question about a particular rich man who had died, *"How much did he leave?"*

The answer is revealing. *"He left it all,"* the man said!

So it is, irrespective of the poverty or plenty, nothing can be taken with the deceased except his or her Faith in God.

(39) "JESUS SAID, TAKE YE AWAY THE STONE. MARTHA, THE SISTER OF HIM WHO WAS DEAD, SAID UNTO HIM, LORD, BY THIS TIME HE STINKS: FOR HE HAS BEEN DEAD FOUR DAYS."

NOTES

The overview is:

1. The phrase, *"Jesus said, You take away the stone,"* presents one of the most poignant moments in human history.

2. As someone has said, the Believer can *"throw stones"* or *"roll away the stone."* In fact, the entirety of Christianity is on one side or the other. It is throwing stones or removing stones.

On which side are you?

3. *"Martha, the sister of him who was dead, said unto Him, Lord, by this time he stinks,"* presents what now seems to be a vacillation on the part of Martha.

4. Had she really believed that Jesus was going to raise Lazarus from the dead even as He had said?

5. Did she properly understand His Explanation of Himself as the *"Resurrection and the Life"*?

6. Or, was it that her Faith began to wane and weaken when she stood before the cold reality of this tomb?

7. The idea seems to be that she had originally believed, but now the magnitude of what Jesus had stated descended upon her. Not only was her brother dead, but corruption had already set in on the body.

8. The phrase, *"For he has been dead four days,"* seems to express the idea that irrespective of what Jesus had said, her Faith simply could not reach to these outer limits.

9. I seriously doubt if any of us would have done any better!

(40) "JESUS SAID UNTO HER, SAID I NOT UNTO YOU, THAT, IF YOU WOULD BELIEVE, YOU SHOULD SEE THE GLORY OF GOD?"

The form is:

1. The beginning of the question, *"Jesus said unto her, Said I not unto you …?"* presents Him reminding her of what He had said that He would do.

2. Corruption, whether physical or moral, is no obstacle to Him Who is the Resurrection and the Life.

3. The continuing of the question, *"That, if you would believe …?"* does not mean that her Faith, or the lack of it, had any bearing whatsoever on what Jesus would do. It merely referred to the fact that if she had enough Faith to stand there and observe,

she would see this great Miracle.

4. As well, this tells me that Martha had believed when Jesus said what He would do respecting the Resurrection of her brother. It seems that she took this Faith and His Promise with great joy to her sister. However, now, the cold reality of death, even to the condition of the corpse, is staring her in the face.

5. Lest we criticize her too severely, we need to remind ourselves of the times we have allowed circumstances to weaken or even rob us of Faith. As well, I must remind the reader that whatever the circumstances were that caused us difficulties, they were insignificant to this which faced Martha and her sister Mary. Thankfully, the Lord does not require perfect Faith, only perfect obedience. How many times have we obeyed, even as Martha would do here, in allowing the rolling away of the stone when, actually, we have little capacity left to believe?

6. The conclusion of the question, *"You should see the Glory of God?"* presents Jesus proving to Faith that He could and would destroy the power of death, rob him of its sting, swallow up the grave in Victory, and proclaim the everlasting curse of this mysterious flesh of ours to be a vanquished foe.

7. The *"Glory of God"* refers to God's Glorious Power manifested in Resurrection.

(41) "THEN THEY TOOK AWAY THE STONE FROM THE PLACE WHERE THE DEAD WAS LAID. AND JESUS LIFTED UP HIS EYES, AND SAID, FATHER, I THANK YOU THAT YOU HAVE HEARD ME."

The pattern is:

1. The phrase, *"Then they took away the stone from the place where the dead was laid,"* portrays several evidently removing this huge slab from the tomb.

2. At this point, it was very simple for the onlookers to see the body of Lazarus lying on the shelf provided for the corpse, wrapped in its mummy-like burial shroud. This was done to hold the spices next to the body, which would tend to lessen the odor of the corruption.

3. *"And Jesus lifted up His Eyes, and said, Father, I thank You that You have heard Me,"* proclaims this as a thanksgiving for that which had already been prayed and heard.

4. Evidently, the Holy Spirit had already informed Christ of what was here to be done, which probably was revealed some three days before. It seems that Jesus had sought His Heavenly Father after this information was imparted unto Him as to exactly what steps He was to take in carrying out this Miracle.

(42) "AND I KNEW THAT YOU HEAR ME ALWAYS: BUT BECAUSE OF THE PEOPLE WHICH STAND BY I SAID IT, THAT THEY MAY BELIEVE THAT YOU HAVE SENT ME."

The overview is:

1. When we speak of Faith, we must always understand that it's Faith in Christ and His Cross.

2. The Cross must never be divorced from Christ or Christ from the Cross (I Cor. 1:23).

3. No, by that, we're not meaning that Christ is still on the Cross. In fact, He is presently in Heaven, seated by the Right Hand of the Father (Heb. 1:3). As well, all true Believers are seated with Him, spiritually speaking (Eph. 2:6).

GOD THE FATHER AND GOD THE SON

The phrase, *"And I knew that You hear Me always,"* presents a powerful statement:

• This that Jesus said speaks of relationship. It was not a prayer of petition, but rather thanksgiving, as we have already stated.

The relationship between Christ and His Father was meant, among other things, to serve as an example for all Believers.

What type of relationship do you have as a believer with your Heavenly Father?

Incidentally, if you want to know what the Father looks like, just look at Jesus in the four Gospels. There you will see a Perfect Copy of the Father.

I do not mean to imply that any Believer can have the exact type of relationship that Jesus had with the Father. However, I am greatly persuaded that such a relationship can be grandly improved in the hearts and lives of all Believers, that is, if we diligently seek for it to be improved. To be sure, such improvement can only come about with a proper prayer life and a proper regimen of the study of the Word of God. It is not that these things earn us anything before God, for they do not. It simply means that it is impossible to have proper communion and fellowship without prayer and a proper understanding of the Word.

THE WILL OF GOD

• Because of this relationship, every single thing that Jesus asked of the Father was instantly granted. Jesus said that the Father heard Him *"always."* John also said, *"If we ask anything according to His Will, He hears us:"*

He then said, *"And if we know that He hears us, whatsoever we ask, we know that we have the petitions that we desired of Him"* (I Jn. 5:14-15).

• If our relationship is as it ought to be with the Lord, we will never ask anything that is not of His Will. Actually, the primary concern of a true relationship is not that the Lord answers our prayers, but that, above all, the Will of God be done.

So, Faith that does nothing but claim answers, with little concern for the Will of God, is, in truth, no faith at all!

THAT THEY MAY BELIEVE

The phrase, *"But because of the people which stand by I said it, that they may believe that You have sent Me,"* is uttered in this fashion for several reasons:

• Jesus wanted the people to understand the link between Him and the Father. He was praying to the Father and now the dead would be raised. Above all, this should lay to rest the idea that He was performing these Miracles by the Power of Satan, as the religious leaders had claimed.

• If this conclusion was drawn, which it had to be if a person was honest, then the people had to also admit that God had sent Him and that He truly was the Messiah.

• Even though He did not refuse praise Himself, and rightly so, still, He desired the people to praise the Father instead of Him, at least in this setting.

Actually, at the early part of His Ministry, He had refused to accept the praise of the people simply because their motivation was improper (Jn. 2:23-25).

NOTES

That which He now did would cause some to *"believe on Him"* (Jn. 11:45).

(43) *"AND WHEN HE THUS HAD SPOKEN, HE CRIED WITH A LOUD VOICE, LAZARUS, COME FORTH."*

The overview is:

1. The phrase, *"And when He thus had spoken,"* proclaims the conclusion of His Prayer.

2. Jesus seldom prayed long prayers in public but in privacy, at least one time, prayed all night long (Lk. 6:12).

3. *"He cried with a loud voice,"* has been explained in many and varied ways as to the reason for the loudness. However, I think this statement is probably closer to the exact reason. He spoke loud enough that all standing could hear the command and see that even the dead were subject to Him.

4. The phrase, *"Lazarus, come forth,"* constitutes a command by the Creator of the ages.

5. Someone has suggested that Jesus called the name of Lazarus in order that only he would come forth. The implication is that inasmuch as Jesus is the Lord of Glory, the Resurrection and the Life, He had to be specific, considering He was addressing the dead, or all the Sainted Dead would have come forth. That is, no doubt, true!

6. Speaking of the Resurrection, Paul said, *"For the Lord Himself shall descend from Heaven with a shout,"* which could well be the Words, *"Come Forth"* (I Thess. 4:16). We do know that whatever that shout will be, it will cause all the Sainted Dead to *"rise first!"*

(44) *"AND HE WHO WAS DEAD CAME FORTH, BOUND HAND AND FOOT WITH GRAVECLOTHES: AND HIS FACE WAS BOUND ABOUT WITH A NAPKIN. JESUS SAID UNTO THEM, LOOSE HIM, AND LET HIM GO."*

The construction is:

1. To properly understand Faith, at least that which is given to us in the Word of God, we must understand the correct *"Object of Faith."*

2. In truth, every human being in the world, whether they realize it or not, has faith. However, only a tiny few have the right kind of Faith, which refers to the correct

Object of Faith, which is *"Jesus Christ and Him Crucified"* (I Cor. 1:17-18, 21, 23; 2:2).

3. So, the non-spiritual kind, and even the religious kind, which is not anchored in Christ and Him Crucified, is not recognized by God.

LAZARUS CAME FORTH

The phrase, *"And he who was dead came forth,"* had to be, due to the circumstances, the greatest Miracle performed by Christ and, consequently, the greatest in human history.

What must have been the reaction of the people as they saw Lazarus rise up from the place where they had laid him and then walk out of that tomb? How could one describe such a scene? What did the two sisters think?

"Bound hand and foot with graveclothes," has been the cause of some discussion.

Some claim that the burial wrappings had been wound tightly about him, which would have made it impossible to walk, therefore, constituting another Miracle when he *"came forth."* However, that seems to be unlikely.

Most likely, his legs were bound separately, which would have made it difficult to walk, but not impossible, hence, the latter Command of Christ.

"And his face was bound about with a napkin," concerns a cloth which had been tied over his face, but which he had probably partially removed.

"Jesus said unto them, Loose him, and let him go," refers, as is obvious, to this burial shroud being taken off his body.

As well, it refers, I think, to the idea that his legs were wrapped separately, etc.

PARADISE

Lazarus was called up from Paradise where he had been for the past four days. One can only surmise what happened when the Voice of Jesus rang out in that place concerning Lazarus.

However, I think that during the three and one-half years of Jesus' Public Ministry, Paradise had become quite accustomed to hearing that Voice in one way or the other. As I have stated, even though the Gospels only give us the account of three people being raised from the dead by Christ, no doubt, He raised many more as well!

Actually, from this moment, it would only be about two months until the whole of Paradise would be emptied. All of the Sainted Dead, who had been placed there and even held captive by Satan, would be liberated by Jesus Christ and taken to Heaven itself. This included all of the Old Testament Greats, along with John the Baptist and others (Mat. 27:52-53; Eph. 4:8-10).

Before Jesus died on Calvary, thereby, satisfying the claims of Heavenly Justice and, as well, destroying the power of Satan and death, all the Sainted Dead went to Paradise, which was separated from the burning side of Hell only by a great gulf (Lk. 16:19-31).

While these people were definitely Saved by Faith in Christ exactly as all are Saved, still, their sins were not taken away, but only covered, because the blood of bulls and goats could never take away sins (Heb. 10:4).

However, when Jesus came and paid the price at Calvary, then Satan had no more claim because sins were taken away and were no longer held against anyone who expressed Faith in Christ (Jn. 1:29). Consequently, Satan had to let them go. Now, every Believer who dies instantly goes to be with the Lord Jesus Christ in Heaven, all because of the Cross (Phil. 1:23).

(45) *"THEN MANY OF THE JEWS WHICH CAME TO MARY, AND HAD SEEN THE THINGS WHICH JESUS DID, BELIEVED ON HIM."*

The overview is:

1. The phrase, *"Then many of the Jews which came to Mary,"* probably refers back to Verse 20 when Mary remained in the house to accept the condolences of those who came to pay their respects while her sister Martha went to meet Jesus.

2. *"And had seen the things which Jesus did, believed on Him,"* should certainly have garnered this response.

3. However, Jesus would later say, *"Blessed are they who have not seen, and yet have believed"* (Jn. 20:29).

(46) *"BUT SOME OF THEM WENT THEIR WAYS TO THE PHARISEES, AND*

TOLD THEM WHAT THINGS JESUS HAD DONE."

The form is:

1. The phrase, *"But some of them went their ways to the Pharisees,"* proclaims something extremely hard to believe. How is it that individuals could observe the type of Miracle just witnessed and still oppose Christ?

2. Christ's Miracles and Words produced a twofold effect and made a frequent division among the Jews, thus bringing to light who were and who were not His True Disciples. The same fact excited Faith in some and roused animosity in others. The Great Sign has been dividing men into hostile camps ever since.

3. *"And told them what things Jesus had done,"* constitutes such being done not with joy, but with skepticism and sarcasm. Consequently, they were rejecting God with cold calculation and in the face of incontrovertible proof. One must remember, this was the church of Jesus' Day!

(47) "THEN GATHERED THE CHIEF PRIESTS AND THE PHARISEES A COUNCIL, AND SAID, WHAT DO WE? FOR THIS MAN DOES MANY MIRACLES."

The pattern is:

1. The phrase, *"Then gathered the Chief Priests and the Pharisees a Council,"* does not represent a formal meeting of the great Council but a lesser convening, with probably some of the members not present. If a formal meeting of the entirety of the Sanhedrin (for that is what it was) had been called, it would have said *"the Council."*

2. The Council at this time had lost its actual power of inflicting capital punishment and was merely a court of appeals from lower courts in the province, framed after the same model.

3. Pharisees and Sadducees were alike to be found in their number. The family of Annas, his sons and his son-in-law, Caiaphas, were all Sadducees and embraced the priestly part of the Assembly. They were deadly enemies of Christ throughout.

4. The question, *"And said, What do we?"* presents both the Pharisees and Sadducees joining in their denunciation of Jesus, even though they were normally bitter enemies between themselves.

5. When Jesus denounced ritualism, literalism, and tradition and laid emphasis on moral Law, to some extent, He was approved by the Sadducees. However, when He cleansed the Temple of the priestly bazaar, which was owned mostly by Sadducees, He was then somewhat approved by the Pharisees.

6. Nevertheless, their hatred of Him was far more pronounced than their hatred for each other. Therefore, they joined forces against Him, laying their personal animosities aside.

7. The phrase, *"For this Man does many Miracles,"* presents them not at all denying the Miracles, but actually admitting to their veracity.

8. Consequently, their sin was against Light and, in fact, the Greatest *"Light"* that the world had ever known. Therefore, the Judgment would be severe indeed!

(48) "IF WE LET HIM THUS ALONE, ALL MEN WILL BELIEVE ON HIM: AND THE ROMANS SHALL COME AND TAKE AWAY BOTH OUR PLACE AND NATION."

The exegesis is:

1. The phrase, *"If we let Him thus alone, all men will believe on Him,"* presents their reasoning.

2. Due to the Miracles, many people believed on Jesus, and the religious leadership saw itself losing control. Religion, as we have repeatedly stated, operates on the two principles of money and control. If either one or both are threatened, it will take any steps to protect itself, even to the murder of Christ, as recorded here.

3. *"And the Romans shall come and take away both our place and Nation,"* portrays a complete misunderstanding of Who Jesus was and What was His Mission.

4. Even though Israel was a province of the Roman Empire, still, the religious hierarchy was invested with great powers. In Jesus, they saw their positions threatened because they were political appointees themselves.

5. Their fears were groundless! However, in their darkened, twisted, distorted minds, they did not and, in fact, could not see Him as He actually was but, as stated, only as a threat!

(49) "AND ONE OF THEM, NAMED CAIAPHAS, BEING THE HIGH PRIEST THAT SAME YEAR, SAID UNTO THEM, YOU KNOW NOTHING AT ALL."

The synopsis is:

1. The phrase, *"And one of them, named Caiaphas, being the High Priest that same year,"* presents the political spectrum of this high religious office.

2. In the Law of Moses, the Priests were in office for life, but here, it was an annual term, as the phrase, *"That same year,"* specifies. Actually, the Romans and Herod chose whom they pleased for this office. Therefore, as stated, it had long since ceased to be spiritual, but was rather totally political. According to Josephus, the man's name was *"Joseph Caiaphas."*

3. It is sad, but most denominational hierarchies presently fall, at least in principle, into the same political spectrum. Most are elected by popular ballot, which makes them little different than their contemporaries of nearly 2,000 years ago, at least according to the way it is presently handled in most cases.

4. While it is certainly possible for the Lord to have His Way and to work therein, respecting popular balloting, still, if it once becomes political, the Holy Spirit, I think, quickly absents Himself.

5. By political, we refer to efforts of self-promotion, which automatically takes the decision out of the Hands of the Holy Spirit. As well, I speak of men attributing Spiritual Authority to these man-devised offices, which is usually the case. While it is possible for godly men to occupy such offices, it is rare because of the very structure which they occupy.

6. Caiaphas' first words of, *"You know nothing at all,"* presents him as brusque, rough, and imperious, which Josephus said was the manner of the man. It presents him taking even a harder stand than his contemporaries, i.e., *"You do not understand the dangers we face."*

(50) "NOR CONSIDER THAT IT IS EXPEDIENT FOR US, THAT ONE MAN SHOULD DIE FOR THE PEOPLE, AND THAT THE WHOLE NATION PERISH NOT."

The synopsis is:

NOTES

1. The Death of Jesus, proposed and commanded by the High Priest, was resolved upon that fearful moment, for the raising of Lazarus had brought their malignity to a head.

2. At that time, the Jews believed that the High Priest, when speaking officially, was inspired. Of course, that was no more true than the Catholics believing that when the Pope speaks in such an official manner, he is inspired!

3. In the warped thinking of this High Priest, he believed that the Death of Jesus would spare the Nation when, in reality, it had the very opposite effect.

4. Had they accepted Jesus, at the same time, they would have had the Protection of God against the Romans, and anyone else, for that matter, as evidenced in the Power of Jesus to raise the dead, etc. So, when they killed Him, they destroyed the very Power that was actually their protection, but of which they were too spiritually insensitive to know.

5. When they rejected Christ, they rejected their only Saviour and protection, and opened themselves to total destruction, which they experienced. As stated, their thinking was 180 degrees wrong, as is all thinking which opposes Christ.

(51) "AND THIS SPOKE HE NOT OF HIMSELF: BUT BEING HIGH PRIEST THAT YEAR, HE PROPHESIED THAT JESUS SHOULD DIE FOR THAT NATION."

The construction is:

1. The phrase, *"And this spoke he not of himself,"* actually means that their condemning Jesus to death, even though evil and wicked, for which they would pay dearly, would be used of God for the Redemption of mankind. However, in no way does this absolve these religious leaders of their culpability. At times, God even uses the Devil, in fact, quite often, but that doesn't mean the Devil is right in any shape, form, or fashion.

2. *"But being High Priest that year, he prophesied that Jesus should die for that Nation,"* once again fell out to that which was ordained by God, but which in no way absolved these individuals of blame.

3. As well, in no way does it mean that

God predestined Caiaphas and the Sanhedrin to do this thing, for He did not. This was their own choice which came from their own wicked, ungodly hearts. While through foreknowledge, God saw that it would happen as was prophesied in Isaiah, Chapter 53, in no way does it mean that He tampered with their free moral agency.

(52) "AND NOT FOR THAT NATION ONLY, BUT THAT ALSO HE SHOULD GATHER TOGETHER IN ONE THE CHILDREN OF GOD WHO WERE SCATTERED ABROAD."

The order is:

1. The phrase, *"And not for that Nation only,"* refers to the fact that when Jesus died, He died for the entirety of the world and not for Israel only!

2. *"But that also He should gather together in one the Children of God who were scattered abroad,"* refers to the *"Church"* being the result of the Crucifixion, Resurrection, and outpouring of the Holy Spirit on the Day of Pentecost, thereby, joining both Jews and Gentiles.

3. Once again I emphasize that by John using the phrase *"He prophesied,"* it in no way means that the Holy Spirit used this ungodly man in the manner of which we normally think of Prophecy, but that which Caiaphas said or did actually turned out in that manner.

(53) "THEN FROM THAT DAY FORTH THEY TOOK COUNSEL TOGETHER FOR TO PUT HIM TO DEATH."

The synopsis is:

1. If men reject Christ, the next step is to kill Him, i.e., repudiate Him for Who and What He is.

2. In the last year, they had begun excommunicating His Followers, and now, after this evil Council, they will set about to destroy Him. Actually, even though they realized it not at all, their *"Counsel"* would actually totally destroy them!

(54) "JESUS THEREFORE WALKED NO MORE OPENLY AMONG THE JEWS; BUT WENT THENCE UNTO A COUNTRY NEAR TO THE WILDERNESS, INTO A CITY CALLED EPHRAIM, AND THERE CONTINUED WITH HIS DISCIPLES."

The exposition is:

NOTES

1. The phrase, *"Jesus therefore walked no more openly among the Jews,"* concerns the time the Sanhedrin made its final decision to destroy Him. The raising of Lazarus was the last of three great Miracles, which brought this to a climax:

a. Healing the impotent man on the Sabbath (Jn. 5:1-16).

b. Healing the blind man on the Sabbath (Jn. 9:16, 22, 34).

c. Raising Lazarus from the dead (Jn. 11:46-54).

2. It is inconceivable that the Son of God, the Lord of Glory, and the Creator of all things could not even minister among His Own people. They were so ungodly that they did not even know Who He was!

3. I wonder how many in the modern church actually know Who Jesus really is.

4. To many, He is merely a historical figure, with little or no present involvement in their lives. To others, He was a Great Prophet but not the Son of God. To several hundreds of millions of Catholics, He is merely the Son of Mary. However, to those who truly know Him, He is Saviour, Healer, Baptizer with the Holy Spirit, Deliverer, and Coming King!

5. *"But went thence unto a country near to the wilderness, into a city called Ephraim,"* seems to represent a place in connection with Bethel (II Chron. 13:19). It was probably about 15 miles north of the Jerusalem of that day.

6. The phrase, *"And there continued with His Disciples,"* does not really tell us how long.

7. We know that during this time, an approximate two months to the coming Passover, He would also spend some time in Samaria and Galilee (Lk. 17:11).

(55) "AND THE JEWS' PASSOVER WAS NIGH AT HAND: AND MANY WENT OUT OF THE COUNTRY UP TO JERUSALEM BEFORE THE PASSOVER, TO PURIFY THEMSELVES."

The diagram is:

1. The phrase, *"And the Jews' Passover was nigh at hand,"* represents the greatest Passover of all, which had continued for nearly 1,600 years. It had begun in Egypt and represented the shed Blood of the

Lamb, which symbolized Jesus.

2. Consequently, He would fulfill the type at this time by dying on Calvary. And yet, none of the religious leaders would know or understand What or Who was in their midst.

3. *"And many went out of the country up to Jerusalem before the Passover, to purify themselves,"* pertained to going through Levitical ceremonial cleansing from touching the dead and other unclean things (Num. 9:6-10).

(56) "THEN SOUGHT THEY FOR JESUS, AND SPOKE AMONG THEMSELVES, AS THEY STOOD IN THE TEMPLE, WHAT THINK YE, THAT HE WILL NOT COME TO THE FEAST?"

The overview is:

1. The phrase, *"Then sought they for Jesus,"* seems to present the authorities seeking Him in order that He be arrested.

2. The question, *"And spoke among themselves, as they stood in the Temple, What do you think, that He will not come to the Feast?"* seemingly presents them in somewhat of a dilemma.

3. Almost any and every place, He was surrounded by hundreds, if not thousands, of people seeking to hear Him or to be healed by Him. Consequently, they would not find their task of arresting Him so easy, at least after this fashion. However, Satan would supply Judas for them, who would solve their problem.

(57) "NOW BOTH THE CHIEF PRIESTS AND THE PHARISEES HAD GIVEN A COMMANDMENT, THAT, IF ANY MAN KNEW WHERE HE WERE, HE SHOULD SHOW IT, THAT THEY MIGHT TAKE HIM."

The structure is:

1. The phrase, *"Now both the Chief Priests and the Pharisees had given a commandment,"* presents them openly opposing Jesus at this time. They were going to push this thing to a showdown. They had determined that He must be stopped at all costs. However, as we have repeatedly said, they were signing their own death warrants.

2. *"That, if any man knew where He was, he should show it, that they might take Him,"* presents the commandment but gives

NOTES

no method as to how such could be done.

3. The wording of the statement seems to imply that they were concerned first of all about locating Him, and then they would attempt to formulate a plan regarding His Arrest. As stated, Judas would solve their problem.

4. As well, they felt that they had to humiliate Him as much as possible, with every attempt being made to destroy His Influence among the people. However, this was not to be an easy task.

5. They had only two charges they could bring against Him, and even those were fragmented. He had healed on the Sabbath, but Scripturally, they would have great difficulty in making a charge of Sabbath-breaking stick! As well, they had understood Him to say that He was God, which they considered a capital offense, with death as the punishment. However, this charge, as well, would be very hard to prove, as He had rebutted them by quoting Psalms 82:6.

6. So, to humiliate Him before the massive throngs which filled Jerusalem at this time, with many, if not most, friendly toward Him, they would find impossible to do. Consequently, they would have to carry out the foul deed at night when the people were asleep.

"Some day the silver chord will break,
"And I no more as now shall sing;
"But oh! the joy when I shall wake,
"Within the Palace of the King!"

"Some day my earthly house will fall,
"I cannot tell how soon 'twill be,
"But this I know, my All-in-all,
"Has now a place in Heaven for me."

"Some day, when fades the golden sun,
"Beneath the rosy tinted west,
"My Blessed Lord will say, 'Well done!'
"And I shall enter into my rest."

"Some day, till then I'll watch and wait,
"My lamp all trimmed and burning bright,
"That when my Saviour opens the gate,
"My soul to Him may take its flight."

CHAPTER 12

(1) "THEN JESUS SIX DAYS BEFORE THE PASSOVER CAME TO BETHANY, WHERE LAZARUS WAS WHICH HAD BEEN DEAD, WHOM HE RAISED FROM THE DEAD."

The exegesis is:

1. The only thing standing between mankind and eternal Hell is the Cross of Christ.

2. Jesus came to this world, in effect, God becoming Man, for many reasons. However, the main reason of all was to go to the Cross where there, the price would be paid for man's Redemption.

3. The only solution for sin, and I mean the only solution, is the Cross of Christ. There is no other!

THE LAST DAYS OF OUR LORD

The phrase, *"Then Jesus six days before the Passover came to Bethany,"* represents the closing days of His Ministry and Work. This, which had been planned from before the foundation of the world (I Pet. 1:19-20), was now about to be brought to pass.

It is ironic! Rome ruled the world of that day and boasted itself of its knowledge respecting its far-flung empire. However, the greatest event in the history of mankind was about to be carried out, but Rome had absolutely no knowledge whatsoever of this event, the greatest of all! Sadder still, the church of that day, i.e., Israel, did not know either, or else, some of them did know but refused to believe. In fact, only a handful of people had any knowledge of this event, and even their knowledge was fragmentary.

Such portrays the utter depravity of the human family. Man is created a triune being composed of spirit, soul, and body. The physical body relates to the world while the soul relates to self. The spirit relates to God, or at least it does if it is regenerated by the Power of the Holy Spirit. To make it a little easier to understand, one could say that the body is world-conscious while the soul is self-conscious, and the spirit is God-conscious, or at least it is supposed to be.

NOTES

This tells us that during Jesus' Day, precious few people were conscious of God and His Ways, or they would have known Who Jesus was and for what He had come. Regrettably, even the few who knew Him, as stated, only had a very fragmentary knowledge of Him. This shows that their God-consciousness was very weak.

Thankfully, it is some better at present due to the Holy Spirit being poured out for nearly 2,000 years, and especially in this last century.

LAZARUS

The phrase, *"Where Lazarus was who had been dead, whom He raised from the dead,"* proclaims Jesus going to where He was welcome.

He was not welcome in the Temple even though it was His House, so, in a short time, His Presence there would be looked at as an intrusion, as it is in most churches presently. Likewise, He was not welcome where the High Priest was carrying out his duties, even though the High Priest was supposed to be a Type of Christ, exactly as He is not welcome in the lives and ministries of most modern preachers and priests. So, that of which we witness here is somewhat similar to what would be witnessed now were Jesus to appear.

The Holy Spirit here proclaims the notable Miracle of the raising of Lazarus from the dead for several reasons:

• Lazarus is a type of all Believers who have died in Christ and will be raised at the Resurrection.

• Speaking in a spiritual sense, he is a symbol of one who had been dead in trespasses and sins but has been *"raised from the dead,"* i.e., *"Born- Again."*

• Not only was he raised from the dead, but the sickness which had brought on the death to start with had been totally healed. This symbolizes the washing of sins by the Blood of Jesus, sins which caused spiritual death in all men to begin with.

(2) "THERE THEY MADE HIM A SUPPER; AND MARTHA SERVED: BUT LAZARUS WAS ONE OF THEM WHO SAT AT THE TABLE WITH HIM."

The exposition is:

1. If the preacher is not preaching the Cross, whatever it is he is preaching, it's not the Gospel.

2. The Cross of Christ is the Foundation of every single Biblical Doctrine.

3. If it is to be noticed, if one doesn't understand the Cross, not only for Salvation but, as well, for Sanctification, he has little understanding of coming prophetic events as well!

THE SUPPER

The phrase, *"There they made Him a supper,"* does not tell us exactly where it was, but it was probably in the house of Simon the leper (Mat. 26:6; Mk. 14:3).

Some have suggested that Simon was the husband of Martha, which may well have been, but the Scripture gives no proof. As well, some contend that there were two anointings at this time, one in the house of Simon and the other in the house of Lazarus. However, there is no proof of that, and I think there was only one anointing.

As well, even though Jesus did come to Bethany six days before the Passover, as outlined in Verse 1, that does not mean that the supper was then made. Actually, the mention of *"two days"* by both Matthew and Mark does not, within itself, necessitate that the supper took place at that time either. Without violating Scripture, the supper could have taken place any time during the six days Jesus was in Bethany before the Passover.

MARTHA

The phrase, *"And Martha served,"* seems to have been her manner (Lk. 10:38-42); however, she would have served Jesus and the others at this time with a far greater joy than any time previously. The reason was that not only Lazarus her brother had been raised from the dead, but even more so, she, along with the others, saw Jesus in an entirely different light than before. They now knew Him as *"the Resurrection and the Life!"*

The phrase, *"But Lazarus was one of them who sat at the table with Him,"* in effect, I think, tells us that there were more at the table even than Mary and Jesus'

NOTES

Disciples. As stated, I believe Simon the leper was at the table as well.

If, in fact, Simon was there at that table, there would be seated two transcendent proofs of the Power of Jesus to save.

1. Simon the leper was Saved from the semblance of death, which leprosy represented and which represented sin, but was cleansed by Christ.

2. The Resurrection of Lazarus, possibly the greatest Miracle ever performed, was a Salvation from the reality of death, which only the Lord could carry out.

(3) "THEN TOOK MARY A POUND OF OINTMENT OF SPIKENARD, VERY COSTLY, AND ANOINTED THE FEET OF JESUS, AND WIPED HIS FEET WITH HER HAIR: AND THE HOUSE WAS FILLED WITH THE ODOUR OF THE OINTMENT."

The construction is:

1. The Word of the Cross, which is God's Way, and humanistic psychology, which is man's way, cannot coexist.

2. Either one cancels out the other.

3. The idea that one can embrace humanistic psychology and, at the same time, embrace the Cross of Christ presents a double-minded man. Such will never receive anything from the Lord.

THE OINTMENT

The phrase, *"Then took Mary a pound of ointment of spikenard, very costly,"* is very difficult to translate into the proper worth respecting the money of our day. However, according to what Judas said that it might be worth (300 pence), it would probably translate into a year's wages at modern minimum wage, which would be approximately $15,000.

Some have even suggested, but without proof, that this *"alabaster box,"* as recorded by Matthew, could have been brought out of Egypt some 1,600 years earlier, thereby, being in the family all of this time. If, in fact, this could possibly be true, then the phrase, *"Very costly,"* becomes even more apropos.

THE ANOINTING

The phrase, *"And anointed the Feet of Jesus,"* is specified particularly by John, while Matthew and Mark mentioned that

Mary anointed His Head (Mat. 26:7; Mk. 14:3). Jesus simply used the term, *"She is come aforehand to anoint My Body to the burying"* (Mk. 14:8). There is no contradiction, as we shall see!

"And wiped His Feet with her hair," gives us the reason, I think, that John the Beloved only spoke of anointing His Feet.

Harmonious with the purpose of this Gospel in setting forth the Deity of the Lord Jesus, only the anointing of His Feet is recorded.

By the performing of this act, Mary of Bethany proclaimed that Jesus had a value transcending all else. Thus, the Faith that regards Him and knows His Love, which passes knowledge, is a sweet odor, and it fills all the house.

Man misjudged her, as we shall see; Jesus vindicated her and understood her. That was all she wanted.

She unconsciously erected to herself an eternal monument as lasting as the Gospel, and linked with it. Thus, the facts of His Earthly History constitute the substance of the Gospel: His Prediction of the enduring remembrance of Mary's action demonstrates His Judicial Supremacy in the government of the world.

At His Feet, she probably learned that on the third day, He would rise again, and so, the spikenard she had prepared for His Dead Body, she now poured *"beforehand"* on His Living Body.

It was a Testimony to His Resurrection, and she knew she would have no other opportunity. Incidentally, Mary was not found at the empty Sepulchre. She was too Spiritually intelligent to be there.

THE RESURRECTION

By Mary anointing His Feet and wiping them with her hair, she testified to His Coming Resurrection, which she seems to be the only one who believed this great Truth. While Jesus would be carried into the Tomb, He would walk out under His Own Power, hence, the emphasis on His Feet.

As well, by the emphasizing of the anointing of His Feet, John testified to His Humility, while Matthew and Mark, speaking only of the anointing of His Head, testified to His Supremacy. I think one could say without fear of contradiction that such is unique in Christ, *"Humility joined with Supremacy."*

As most Bible students know, John portrayed Jesus as *"God,"* while Matthew portrayed Him as *"King,"* Mark as *"Servant,"* and Luke as *"Man."*

How wonderful that the Holy Spirit links humility with Deity when the thoughts of men would be otherwise.

THE ODOUR OF THE OINTMENT

The phrase, *"And the house was filled with the odour of the ointment,"* speaks of the preciousness of Jesus to His Father and should speak accordingly to the world, as well, but seldom does.

To the Church, and we speak of the true Church, His True Body, *"Your Name is as ointment poured forth"* (Song of Sol. 1:3). As the *"ointment"* was poured forth, so was His Life.

The type of *"ointment"* used by Mary contained *"spikenard,"* which was an herb related to valerian. It was imported from North India and was, as the Scripture said, *"Very costly."* Likewise, as stated, such typified the Preciousness of the Life of Christ.

The type of ointment used by Mary was almost exclusively a perfume, while the type spoken of in the Song of Solomon mostly had a soothing, healing effect. So, we learn from this that His Name is not only symbolic of great Power but, as well, is a healing medicine. This is the type made of olive oil and used by shepherds to soothe the bruised foreheads of sheep having scraped themselves in foraging for food.

In our everyday walk before God, we become bruised and need the Healing Ointment, which only His Name can provide. Consequently, when a person has been with Jesus, the *"odour of the ointment"* fills the house, i.e., the heart and life of the Believer.

As that which Mary's act symbolizes, wherever Jesus is found, this wonderful fragrance, so to speak, fills the place.

(4) "THEN SAID ONE OF HIS DISCIPLES, JUDAS ISCARIOT, SIMON'S SON, WHICH SHOULD BETRAY HIM."

The exegesis is:

1. To punish someone for sin impugns the Righteousness of Christ. Jesus has already paid the price at Calvary's Cross, making further punishment unnecessary and, in fact, unscriptural.

2. The Message of the Cross is the dividing line between the true Church and the apostate church, even as it always has been.

3. Every sacrifice offered in Old Testament times was, and was meant to be, a type, a symbol, if you will, of the coming Crucifixion of Christ.

JUDAS ISCARIOT

The phrase, *"Then said one of His Disciples, Judas Iscariot, Simon's son,"* was not Simon the leper in whose house this supper was prepared, as should be obvious.

Judas is spoken of accordingly in order to distinguish him from the other Disciple named Judas, who was also called Lebbaeus or Thaddaeus (Lk. 6:16; Mat. 10:3).

"Who should betray Him," was written by John about 50 years after the actual happening of the event.

Unfortunately, Judas was not the only one who has betrayed Christ. Actually, every preacher who fails to preach the Word of God, but rather proclaims *"another gospel,"* is betraying Christ. Likewise, every Believer who does not follow Him with all of their hearts, in some way, betrays Him. While it may not be as serious as that of Judas, still, it is betrayal.

The word *"betray"* in the Greek is *"paradidomi"* and means *"to deliver over treacherously by way of betrayal to an enemy."* Consequently, when preachers do not preach the Word, they are delivering over to Satan the True Word, i.e., *"Christ,"* and doing so treacherously. They have betrayed their Calling and their Christ.

(5) "WHY WAS NOT THIS OINTMENT SOLD FOR THREE HUNDRED PENCE, AND GIVEN TO THE POOR?"

The synopsis is:

1. The word *"Atonement"* is used only one time in the New Testament and actually should have been translated *"reconciliation"* (Rom. 5:11).

2. The word *"Atonement"* means *"to cover, to make at one."*

3. Inasmuch as the blood of bulls and goats could not take away sins, the best that could be done was to cover the sins, which was done. Under the New Covenant, the sin is taken away. That's the reason that the word *"Atonement"* is not used in the New Testament. It does not efficiently describe Redemption.

THE MASK OF REVERENCE FOR ANOTHER VIRTUE

Reynolds said, *"Sinful motive often hides itself under the mask of reverence for another virtue."*[1]

In fact, what should be the priority of the Church?

While to help the unfortunate, in whatever capacity, is definitely a part of Christianity, even as is borne out in the Book of Acts and elsewhere, still, that is not priority for the Church.

The business of the Church, actually, the main business, and the priority must always be the spread of the Gospel of Jesus Christ (Mk. 16:15). There are several reasons for that, which should be obvious:

• The Salvation of the soul is the single most important thing there could ever be. Even though the *"poor"* are definitely in need of many things, still, a person can be right with God although poor. However, an individual cannot be right with God if he does not hear the Gospel and have an opportunity to accept Jesus.

• It is true that the world, at least at this present time, will always have its complement of the *"poor."* Still, when the Gospel is presented to the poor and it is accepted, a way out of poverty is always given. In other words, the old adage is apropos that if you give a man a bushel of corn, you will have provided food for him for several meals. However, if you teach a man how to plant corn and cultivate it, you have shown him a way out of hunger. The Gospel of Jesus Christ does exactly that! It proclaims to any and all, along with the great Plan of Salvation, the way even to economic prosperity.

• The moment the person comes into the Family of God, irrespective of his economic poverty, the Blessings of God automatically begin to come to him, thereby, lifting him out of this state of privation and want.

Actually, Jesus told us to *"take no thought"* regarding these things (Mat. 6:25-34). Once an individual enters into Salvation, he then comes under the care, guidance, leading, protection, and blessing of God, hence, Jesus saying, *"But seek you first the Kingdom of God, and His Righteousness; and all these things shall be added unto you"* (Mat. 6:33).

A PERSONAL EXPERIENCE

In the 1980s, we were conducting citywide Crusades in some of the largest stadiums in the world in various countries. The crowds were enormous, up to 100,000 people per night.

The Lord specifically told me to preach *"Jesus"* to these people. He told me to proclaim in no uncertain terms that Jesus was their Answer, not government, not America, not anyone or anything else, for that matter. The reason is obvious.

Once the person accepts Jesus, he has entered into the Kingdom of God, and if he will believe God, great and glorious things are always brought unto him. As well, it covers every facet of one's life, be it domestic, physical, economic, or spiritual.

So, Judas, by this act, was casting an aspersion upon Christ, Who Alone could alleviate the problems of the poor, or anyone else, for that matter. While Judas seemed to have been the ringleader in this dissension, Matthew stated that some, if not all, of the other Disciples chimed in with their protests as well (Mat. 26:8). Of course, Judas, as the next Verse portrays, had little, if any, regard for the poor. And yet, this tells us how that once such negativism and skepticism is presented, it can easily be picked up, even by good people such as the other Disciples.

(6) "THIS HE SAID, NOT THAT HE CARED FOR THE POOR; BUT BECAUSE HE WAS A THIEF, AND HAD THE BAG, AND BEAR WHAT WAS PUT THEREIN."

The construction is:

1. While good works will always follow proper Justification, good works will never cause Justification.

2. Once justified, one is never unjustified, at least as long as one continues to believe in Christ.

3. This means that the Christian who sins does not lose his Justification, as awful as sin is.

JUDAS WAS A THIEF

The phrase, *"This he said, not that he cared for the poor,"* means that this was not his real reason.

"But because he was a thief, and had the bag, and bear what was put therein," proclaims the fact that he desired that this expensive ointment be sold and the money placed in the common treasury, with him as the dispenser of such. Then he would have the opportunity to steal at least a part, if not all, of the proceeds.

Several questions arise out of this:

• How long had he been stealing? Of course, that is anyone's guess. However, it probably had begun only a short time before when he came to the realization that Jesus was not going to set up an earthly kingdom. With that door of advancement closing, the next step was to pilfer the funds, which, evidently, he began doing.

Even though I believe the Scripture plainly proclaims that Judas was right with God at the beginning, self-will slowly but surely began to gain the upper hand. Now, his service for Christ was in the realm of, *"What's in it for me?"* Regrettably, the modern greed gospel fosters the same attitude and spirit in its followers.

• Why was Judas appointed to serve as the treasurer? As stated, I think the record is clear that Judas was not a thief at the beginning, but he only became such after a period of time. Inasmuch as Jesus allowed it, one has to conclude that his appointment was the Will of God. He, no doubt, showed great diligence at the beginning and probably served in an admirable way in this capacity.

LARGE SUMS OF MONEY

During the first two years of Jesus' Ministry, especially considering the tremendous number of people being healed, and considering the size of the crowds, there were probably great sums of money given to the Lord respecting gratitude on the part of those who had experienced His Miracle-Working Touch. Considering that He had not too much short of 100 people traveling with Him much of the time, the care and upkeep of such a group would have required quite large sums, as should be obvious.

• Did Jesus know when the stealing began on the part of Judas? He undoubtedly did! Saying nothing of the situation does not speak of ignorance, but rather Grace. I think the Scripture is replete with every effort being made by Christ, attempting to turn this man from the awful course on which he had placed himself.

Actually, there are thousands of people presently in high positions in the realm of the Gospel who are, in one way or the other, doing the same as Judas. For long periods of time, the Lord will show Mercy and Grace, but His Seeming Silence does not indicate ignorance and certainly not approval. As stated, it only portrays His Love and Grace. Ultimately, that is, if no repentance is forthcoming, their end will be the same as Judas, at least as far as the loss of their souls is concerned.

(7) "THEN SAID JESUS, LET HER ALONE: AGAINST THE DAY OF MY BURYING HAS SHE KEPT THIS."

The pattern is:

1. There is no such thing as partial Justification. One is either totally justified or not justified at all.

2. If sin is committed, the Believer is to confess it before the Lord, Who has promised *"to forgive us our sins, and to cleanse us from all unrighteousness"* (I Jn. 1:9). However, as bad as sin is, as stated, the Christian doesn't lose his Justification at this time.

3. If sin is committed, there is only one way that it can be forgiven, washed, and cleansed, and that is by continued Faith in Christ and what He has done for us at the Cross.

PRIDE AND HUMILITY

The phrase, *"Then said Jesus, Let her alone,"* is proclaimed in this manner for two reasons:

1. Jesus placed His Seal of Approval on that which she was doing and in effect,

NOTES

demanded that any activity against this act be stopped.

2. Her act also proclaimed that she knew and understood that He was soon to die, even though none of the Disciples seemed to have any comprehension, despite all the things Jesus had said about this very event. In effect, it seems her Spiritual intelligence far exceeded anyone else at that particular time.

The phrase, *"Against the day of My Burying has she kept this,"* seems to indicate that Mary had had this expensive *"nard"* in her possession for quite some time. Perhaps she had had many opportunities to sell it for a considerable sum, but for whatever the reason, had not done so. Now, she knew why she had kept this expensive perfume. It was for the Burial of Christ, the single most important thing in human history.

Why was it that Mary seemed to have a far greater understanding of the Mission of Christ, even than His Chosen Disciples?

I personally think it goes back to self-will. As someone has said, *"Pride has its own agenda while humility has the Agenda of Christ."*

MARY BELIEVED

The Disciples pictured Jesus as a Conquering Messiah, Who would overthrow Rome and make Israel once again the premier Nation in the world. Of course, they would be His Chief Lieutenants, occupying positions of power and honor in this Kingdom. However, that was not the Mission of Christ even though the Disciples kept trying to force the issue.

Mary evidently saw the situation as it actually was. While her understanding at this time would have probably been limited, still, she believed what Jesus said about His Death and Resurrection. None of the others did!

As well, this act of Mary anointing the Head and Feet of Jesus with this expensive ointment, even with its wonderful fragrance filling the house, portrays to us what God thought of the Sacrificial Offering of His Only Son. It was to be a beautiful and wonderful thing in the Sight of God, even though it would be at such price, simply because it would redeem with love, mankind, God's Greatest Creation. This is evident even in the sacrifices of old.

It was said of Noah's sacrifice after the flood, *"And the LORD smelled a sweet savor"* (Gen. 8:21).

Concerning the Peace-Offering as outlined in the Book of Exodus, it says, *"And you shall burn the whole ram upon the Altar: it is a Burnt Offering unto the LORD: it is a sweet savour"* (Ex. 29:18). Actually, the entirety of the Pentateuch is filled with this statement, *"A sweet savour unto the LORD,"* speaking of sacrifice (Lev. 1:9; 2:2, 9, 12; 3:5; Num. 15:3, 7, 10, 14, etc.). All of this represented the Offering up of Christ at Calvary.

(8) *"FOR THE POOR ALWAYS YOU HAVE WITH YOU; BUT ME YOU HAVE NOT ALWAYS."*

The form is:

1. At times, the church seems to believe in two Justifications — one for the sinner and another for the Saint.

2. In other words, they understand and accept the sinner coming to Christ, being Saved, and, thereby, instantly justified. However, when it comes to the Saint, far too often, the church attempts to mix works with Faith.

3. As previously stated, once justified, which takes place at the Born-Again experience, one is never unjustified, at least as long as one continues to believe in Christ.

THE POOR

The phrase, *"For the poor always you have with you,"* presents that which is regrettable but true! Sadly, it will remain this way until the Second Coming of the Lord. At that time, all poverty will be forever erased, along with every other malady that besets the human family.

The phrase, *"But Me you have not always,"* refers to Jesus being present at that time in the flesh. While He is with us now and, in fact, always has been, at least in the hearts and lives of Believers, such is carried out through the Person, Ministry, and Agency of the Holy Spirit.

It is very sad that this thing which was so dear to the Heart of God, the Offering up of His Son for the Redemption of humanity, was understood not at all by even His Choice Disciples, with them construing this *"anointing"* as a waste.

I have to wonder if the True Plan and Purpose of God is too often presently treated accordingly!

(9) *"MUCH PEOPLE OF THE JEWS THEREFORE KNEW THAT HE WAS THERE: AND THEY CAME NOT FOR JESUS' SAKE ONLY, BUT THAT THEY MIGHT SEE LAZARUS ALSO, WHOM HE HAD RAISED FROM THE DEAD."*

The pattern is:

1. The Gospel of *"works"* is deadly.

2. The Gospel of works is the greatest enemy to *"Faith."*

3. This is not to say that works aren't important, for they are. However, works are a result of proper Faith and never the cause of proper Faith.

RAISED FROM THE DEAD

The phrase, *"Much people of the Jews therefore knew that He was there,"* indicates, as is obvious, a large number.

The news concerning the raising of Lazarus from the dead had, no doubt, spread like wildfire over the entirety of Jerusalem and surrounding areas. The one's who witnessed and even observed this, without a doubt, the greatest Miracle in human history, probably became celebrities themselves.

The phrase, *"And they came not for Jesus' Sake only, but that they might see Lazarus also, whom He had raised from the dead,"* presents, as should be obvious, the occasion for unparalleled curiosity. There could well have been thousands, and, no doubt, were, coming to see both Jesus and Lazarus.

There probably were many and varied questions that people had concerning death, which they desired to ask Lazarus. And yet, the Scripture is silent on this subject.

(10) *"BUT THE CHIEF PRIESTS CONSULTED THAT THEY MIGHT PUT LAZARUS ALSO TO DEATH."*

The structure is:

1. We should, as well, understand that there is no such thing as progress in Justification.

2. The Believer is no more justified today than he was yesterday, nor will he be more justified tomorrow than he is today.

3. Any soul who is *"in Christ Jesus"* is as completely justified as if he were before the Throne. He is *"complete in Christ."*

THE CHIEF PRIESTS

It had been about two months since Jesus had performed this greatest of Miracles and, by now, the excitement had reached a fever pitch as the news had spread like wildfire. One would think that such a happening would have struck fear into the hearts of these religious leaders, but it seemed to have the very opposite effect. Unbelief fueled by self will is a strange thing. It cannot see because it does not desire to see. It cannot hear because it does not desire to hear. It cannot know because it doesn't want to know. In other words, it is a willful blindness, a willful deafness, and a willful ignorance, spiritually speaking!

The word *"death,"* as it is used here, in the Greek is *"apokteino"* and means *"to kill one violently."* In other words, they were not speaking of a judicial execution, but rather how they could hire some brigand to murder Lazarus in cold blood.

They saw him as a constant Testimony to the Miracle-Working Power of Jesus Christ, actually, the greatest Testimony of all! So, their evil plot to kill Christ would broaden in order to include Lazarus.

Inasmuch as there seems to be no record of such happening, quite possibly, the news quickly surfaced concerning their plot, therefore, making it more dangerous to carry out the act than to leave him alone.

When one is given a glimpse of the black hearts of these religious leaders, one then understands the judicial Judgment that followed, with the only unanswered question being as to why it was not done sooner!

(11) "BECAUSE THAT BY REASON OF HIM MANY OF THE JEWS WENT AWAY, AND BELIEVED ON JESUS."

The pattern is:

1. We should understand that the manner in which we look at Justification is the manner in which we look at Christ.

2. He either paid it all, or He didn't!

NOTES

3. The Cross of Christ was either enough, or it wasn't!

MANY BELIEVED ON JESUS

No doubt, the many Converts to Christ, due to the Miracle of Lazarus, is what helped spur the Triumphal Entry which now would take place.

Also, the manner in which the Text is given proclaims that not only did these people believe on Jesus, but at the same time, they were repudiating the religious leaders. In fact, it is impossible for one to be done without the other. One cannot be in sympathy with Christ and, at the same time, remain in league with the evil of this religious hierarchy. One or the other must go!

(12) "ON THE NEXT DAY MUCH PEOPLE WHO WERE COME TO THE FEAST, WHEN THEY HEARD THAT JESUS WAS COMING TO JERUSALEM."

The order is:

1. It was never a question of what the worshipper was. That was understood. It was always what the Sacrifice was.

2. That's what makes Faith so important. Christ has done it, and we cannot do it.

3. Our Faith in Him grants us all that He has done.

MANY PEOPLE

The phrase, *"On the next day much people who were come to the Feast,"* speaks of the Passover. Actually, three Feasts were kept at this particular time: *"The Feast of Unleavened Bread,"* which typified the Spotless, Pure, Life and Body of Christ, which would be offered in Sacrifice; *"The Feast of Passover,"* which typified Christ being offered up at Calvary; and *"The Feast of Firstfruits,"* which portrayed His Resurrection.

These *"people"* would have included many from all over Israel, as well as the entirety of the Roman Empire. Josephus said that over 1 million people would swell Jerusalem at this particular time. Probably one could say with very little fear of contradiction that most every single person in the city was aware of this notable Miracle by Jesus, especially considering that He had been the topic of most every conversation for the past three and one-half years.

WHEN THE PEOPLE HEARD...

The phrase, *"When they heard that Jesus was coming to Jerusalem,"* spoke of Him leaving the home of Lazarus, Mary, and Martha, and Martha in Bethany, and coming into the city proper. Bethany being situated on the east slope of the Mount of Olivet, Jesus would have crossed the mountain, coming in through the eastern gate of the city.

This undoubtedly was a scene unlike anything else which had happened in the three and one-half years of Jesus' Public Ministry. Thousands of people, hearing that He was at the home of Lazarus, had, no doubt, encamped near or in Jerusalem to serve as an escort for Him as He came into the city. It would have been a scene of unparalleled joy.

(13) "TOOK BRANCHES OF PALM TREES, AND WENT FORTH TO MEET HIM, AND CRIED, HOSANNA: BLESSED IS THE KING OF ISRAEL WHO COMES IN THE NAME OF THE LORD."

The exegesis is:

1. Paul told us to *"Examine yourselves, whether you be in the Faith"* (II Cor. 13:5).

2. The Faith, in simple terms, is *"Jesus Christ and Him Crucified."*

3. If the Lord looks at us at all, it is at our Faith.

THE KING OF ISRAEL

The phrase, *"Took branches of palm trees, and went forth to meet Him,"* presents them waving these palm branches, as was the custom, in token of the approach of a Conqueror.

"And cried, Hosanna," in the Hebrew means *"saved we pray."* According to the expositor, the word seems to have become an utterance of praise rather than a prayer.

Palm branches were used at the *"Feast of Tabernacles,"* with the *"last day of the Feast"* actually called, *"The Great Hosanna."*

The phrase, *"Blessed is the King of Israel Who comes in the Name of the Lord,"* is taken from Psalms 118:25-26.

Even though each of the Evangelists uses slightly different wording, all are based on these two Verses from Psalm 118. Without a doubt, some were shouting exactly that which John, as well as Matthew, Mark, and Luke, recorded (Mat. 21:9; Mk. 11:9-10; Lk. 19:38). Such does not show a contradiction or discrepancy but, actually, is a verification of that which happened exactly as recorded. If each account were identical, especially coming from a vast group of people such as this, such would show that the Text had been doctored.

THE NAME OF THE LORD

The waving of the palm branches, even though it was not the Feast of Tabernacles, proclaims that the people actually thought it was the beginning of the Kingdom Age, which this Feast represented. Consequently, Jesus was hailed by the people as King of Israel, the Head of the coming Kingdom of their father David, with them giving Glory to God.

The Name of the Lord is the Manifestation and compendium of all the Perfections of the Lord. For centuries, the gracious hope had rung forth in the sacred liturgy, and now the people saw that this hope was on the point of realization.

However, the religious leadership of Israel did not see it that way at all. While the people were at that moment proclaiming Jesus as King, they were plotting His Death!

What would it have taken for the religious leaders to have accepted Him?

The answer, of course, is very complex. However, to use an oversimplification, one might say that His Heart would have to have been as wicked as their hearts. His Perfect Righteousness was a constant rebuke to their total unrighteousness. It ate right through their thin veneer of religion, totally exposing their hypocrisy, and consequently showing them up for what they really were — hirelings, wolves in sheep's clothing.

(14) "AND JESUS, WHEN HE HAD FOUND A YOUNG ASS, SAT THEREON; AS IT IS WRITTEN."

The overview is:

1. Sin is the cause of all the problems and trouble in this world, and sin is a form of insanity! (Rom., Chpt. 3).

2. There are degrees of sinful insanity. For instance, some sins are worse than others.

3. As an example, the Muslims do what

they do, which is to steal, kill, and destroy, because they are blinded by spiritual insanity and conduct themselves accordingly.

THE ENTRANCE OF CHRIST

The phrase, *"And Jesus, when He had found a young ass, sat thereon,"* actually presents an animal that had never before been ridden.

Matthew tells us that the foal was accompanied by its mother, and both animals satisfied the prediction of Zechariah, Chapter 9, and of Isaiah 62:11.

It is even quite probable that Jesus rode upon both animals — at first, upon the mother, and then, upon the colt.

Despite what had been said, Jesus' Disciples, as well as the people, thought that on entering His Royal City, He would at once establish His Kingdom. However, by the Parable of the Pounds, the Lord had taught them that that day was yet far distant (Lk. 19:11-27).

The phrase, *"As it is written,"* proclaims the event having been foretold by the Prophet Zechariah a little over 500 years earlier (Zech. 9:9).

(15) "FEAR NOT, DAUGHTER OF SION: BEHOLD, THE KING COMES, SITTING ON AN ASS'S COLT."

The synopsis is:

1. Everyone who doesn't know the Lord lives in spiritual darkness.

2. The only answer to that darkness is Jesus Christ, Who is the Light of the world.

3. To have that Light, Christ must be accepted as one's Saviour, which can only be brought about by what He did at the Cross.

DAUGHTER OF ZION

The phrase, *"Fear not, daughter of Sion,"* is said a little differently than that given by Zechariah, *"Rejoice greatly, O daughter of Zion"* (Zech. 9:9). The idea seems to be according to the following:

While this method of presentation, the riding on a donkey, had been used by notables many years before, Alexander the Great had changed all of this. Upon his rise to power, he adopted the white war horse as the symbol of the conquering victor. Consequently, from that time about 200 years before Christ, this symbol prevailed and was adopted by Rome.

Therefore, Jesus choosing the ancient method, which projected humility, spoke to the entirety of Israel, and Rome, as well, that His Intentions were peaceful. In other words, His Vast Power, the greatest ever manifested in a Human Being, would not be used to overthrow Rome or any other worldly empire, at least at this time. It would be used instead to overthrow the greatest enemies of all, Satan, sin, and death. So, the charge leveled against Jesus by the religious leaders, accusing Him of fomenting insurrection against Rome, held no validity whatsoever.

THE SECOND COMING

However, when He comes the Second Time, He will, in fact, be riding a glorious white charger, i.e., war horse, as He leads the Armies of Heaven. This will take place during the Battle of Armageddon (Rev. 19:11-21).

So, at this time, neither Rome nor the religious leaders of Israel had anything to *"fear,"* hence, the *"fear not."*

The phrase, *"Behold, the King comes, sitting on an ass's colt,"* presents His Humility, even as Zechariah had prophesied, *"Just, and having Salvation; lowly, and riding upon an ass, and upon a colt the foal of an ass"* (Zech. 9:9).

This was a definite prediction by Zechariah that the Messiah would be the King of the Jews, i.e., *"Israel."* However, we must quickly add, a King rejected!

The religious leaders at Jesus' Trial said that they had no king but Caesar, and, to be sure, Caesar has proven to be a hard taskmaster (Jn. 19:15).

(16) "THESE THINGS UNDERSTOOD NOT HIS DISCIPLES AT THE FIRST: BUT WHEN JESUS WAS GLORIFIED, THEN REMEMBERED THEY THAT THESE THINGS WERE WRITTEN OF HIM, AND THAT THEY HAD DONE THESE THINGS UNTO HIM."

The exegesis is:

1. The Jews were never taught that the killing or offering of the animal in sacrifice was an Atonement in itself.

2. They knew that it was a foreshadowing

and educating of the world for the appreciation of the one Atonement, which was to come in Christ.

3. Under the Atonement of the Old Testament, the sins were only covered, not taken away.

HIS DISCIPLES

The phrase, *"These things understood not His Disciples at the first,"* refers to His Disciples being a part of this great celebration, but yet, not knowing or realizing that they were fulfilling Prophecy.

This proclaims that their knowledge of the Word was somewhat weak at that time. Actually, that very reason caused them to misunderstand His Mission at the beginning. However, the Day of Pentecost would rectify that, with them then becoming great scholars of the Word (Acts 6:4).

"But when Jesus was glorified," refers to the Glorified Body of Jesus after His Resurrection. It had such a magnificence about it that He could appear and disappear at will, with material objects proving no obstacles whatsoever. It also signified that the great task of the Redemption of mankind, which had been afforded at Calvary, had been completed. As well, the Resurrection ratified that great Victory, with the Glorified Body of Jesus being a tangible, observable proof of what had been done.

"Then remembered they that these things were written of Him," speaks of the time after the Day of Pentecost when they were baptized with the Holy Spirit, with the Spirit bringing all of these things into focus.

"And that they had done these things unto Him," simply means that they had been a part of the fulfilling of these Prophecies, even though, at the time, they were not aware of such being done.

(17) "THE PEOPLE THEREFORE WHO WAS WITH HIM WHEN HE CALLED LAZARUS OUT OF HIS GRAVE, AND RAISED HIM FROM THE DEAD, BEAR RECORD."

The structure is:

1. Justice demands that what a man sows, that shall he reap.

2. Man sows sin and reaps the necessary results.

3. Man cannot be pardoned and restored on his own merits, for he has none.

THE PROOF OF THE RAISING OF LAZARUS

The phrase, *"The people therefore who was with Him when He called Lazarus out of his grave,"* proclaims those who were standing there that day and seeing and hearing all that was done. They were eyewitnesses, and they heard every word spoken. In other words, the phrase, *"Lazarus, come forth,"* would never be forgotten by them to their dying day, and no wonder!

The phrase, *"And raised him from the dead,"* proclaims them seeing and hearing the Command that brought Lazarus out of the tomb, no longer a corpse, but rather filled with life. It was unlike anything anyone in history had ever seen, witnessed, or experienced.

The short phrase, *"Bear record,"* means they had been giving this Testimony of what they had seen and heard from the moment it happened, with, no doubt, ready ears to listen.

As well, it also seems to indicate that these eyewitnesses of this great Miracle were going in and out with the thousands of Galilean pilgrims and others, and were uttering their Testimony on all sides.

In other words, they were exclaiming with great joy, while they pointed to Jesus, saying, *"He is the One Who raised Lazarus from the dead! I was there, and I saw it happen!"*

No doubt, while this was happening, scores of others who had been healed by Jesus in months past were, as well, giving their Testimony, which only caused the exclamation of joy to increase to a fever pitch.

This was the Son of God, but the religious leaders of Israel would not recognize Him as such.

(18) "FOR THIS CAUSE THE PEOPLE ALSO MET HIM, FOR THAT THEY HEARD THAT HE HAD DONE THIS MIRACLE."

The overview is:

1. Under the Old Covenant, Atonement meant that the sins were covered and the sinner as well.

2. In reality, one cannot separate the sinner from the sin or the sin from the sinner.

3. Now, under the New Covenant, because of the Cross, our sins are not covered but, in reality, are taken away (Jn. 1:29).

THIS MIRACLE

The phrase, *"For this cause the people also met Him,"* proclaims the raising of Lazarus as the catalyst which instigated the Triumphal Entry.

The phrase, *"For that they heard that He had done this Miracle,"* proclaims scores of them hearing it from the eyewitnesses themselves. I think the evidence is clear, considering that Lazarus had been dead for four days, that this was the greatest Miracle performed by Christ. In the minds of the people, they saw in this which was done that if He could do this, He could do anything. In that, they were correct!

There will come a day when multiple millions, who will come from every generation, will repeat this scene on a grand scale, of which this was but a symbol. No soul has ever been helped in any capacity, be it spiritual, physical, or mental, but that Jesus was the cause, whether directly or indirectly. As such, the Praises, and rightly so, will fill the Earth, fulfilling that predicted by David of so long ago, *"Let everything that has breath praise the LORD. Praise you the LORD"* (Ps. 150:6).

(19) "THE PHARISEES THEREFORE SAID AMONG THEMSELVES, PERCEIVE YE HOW YOU PREVAIL NOTHING? BEHOLD, THE WORLD IS GONE AFTER HIM."

The exegesis is:

1. When any person accepts Christ, he is entering into a whole different order of life and being.

2. It is the Divine Order: the order which operates in the Spiritual Life and, for that matter, in Heaven itself.

3. We might think of this heavenly system of governance as the *"Economy of Grace."*

THE PHARISEES

The phrase, *"The Pharisees therefore said among themselves,"* presents the very opposite of what was happening on the road that lead from Bethany to Jerusalem. The religious leaders of Israel had no positive regard for this Miracle whatsoever and, in fact, would have killed Lazarus if a way had been open to them. Such was the leadership of the church then, and I am afraid it has little changed unto the present. While there are certainly some few godly men in capacities of leadership around the world, regrettably, that number is in short supply. Sad to say, most fit the order of the Pharisees!

The question, *"Perceive ye how you prevail nothing?"* actually presents a cry of rage.

The Pharisees were frantic when they saw the multitudes leaving them and following Jesus. Something had to be done, but caution had to be exercised lest the people turn on them and destroy them.

At this moment, their anger was at themselves because they had resorted to half measures, and now vowed to do whatever it took in their murderous designs to stop Jesus.

This public entrance, associated with the supreme Miracle of the raising of Lazarus, compelled priests and people to a decision. While the people were praising Him, the priests decided to crucify Him. However, they could have *"prevailed nothing"* had He not voluntarily surrendered Himself.

POWER!

These men were so deceived that they seemed not to understand that He, had He so desired, could have turned this Power on them. Anyone who could raise the dead could do anything! But yet, they would bull their way through, perhaps thinking that they could so fabricate the charges that Rome would come in on their side. In so doing, they, no doubt, felt that surely He could not defeat the entirety of the garrisons here stationed that belonged to imperial Rome. Little did they know or realize that had such been the Father's Will, even in the Words of Jesus as He spoke to Peter, *"Do you think that I cannot now pray to My Father, and He shall presently give Me more than twelve legions of Angels?"* (Mat. 26:53).

They could only do to Jesus what He allowed them to do; consequently, they would completely destroy themselves and their Nation.

"Behold, the world is gone after Him," is their response to the Triumphant Entry.

As stated, they would now set about in

earnest to destroy Him. In their minds, it was either Him or them! Despite the Miracles, they would not admit Who He really is.

It was their time, the moment they could have changed the world, but they threw it away and condemned mankind to nearly 2,000 more years of war, suffering, sickness, and pain. As well, they would consign themselves to spiritual oblivion! Never in history has there been such a moment, and never was so much lost.

And yet, even as John would later write concerning the Second Coming of Christ, this moment will repeat itself but, this time, and wondrously so, with far different results. Then, on that coming day, they will accept Him, the very One Whom they rejected upon His First Advent.

Then, the world will truly go after Him, and rightly so, even as it should have done all along.

(20) "AND THERE WERE CERTAIN GREEKS AMONG THEM WHO CAME UP TO WORSHIP AT THE FEAST."

The structure is:

1. Man is estranged from God. Innocent blood, the Blood of Christ, cures this estrangement.

2. It makes God and the sinner *"at one"* again.

3. When John uttered the words, *"Lamb of God"* (Jn. 1:29), every Jew standing nearby understood exactly what he was talking about.

THE GREEKS

The phrase, *"And there were certain Greeks among them,"* pertained to a large group of Gentiles.

"Who came up to worship at the Feast," does not present something out of the ordinary, for there were always a number of Gentiles who worshipped and served the God of Abraham, Isaac, and Jacob.

It is not known for certain if they were proselytes to the Jewish Faith, but there is some indication they were. It had always been the Will of God for Gentiles to be included, hence, a special section reserved for them at the Temple called, *"The Court of the Gentiles."* Regrettably, this was the area where the Chief Priests, who were mostly Sadducees, had set up their stalls to exchange money, to sell doves, etc. (Mat. 21:12). Consequently, it quickly becomes obvious that the religious leadership of Israel had little concern about the Gentiles and their knowing the Lord. Actually, Gentiles, such as these *"Greeks,"* were more or less tolerated rather than encouraged. Still, it seems a goodly number of Gentiles always came to worship, despite the obvious insults.

I wonder how many modern churches fall into the same category, with only a certain class of people welcome! I think it should be obvious that such is an abomination in the Eyes of God.

(21) "THE SAME CAME THEREFORE TO PHILIP, WHICH WAS OF BETHSAIDA OF GALILEE, AND DESIRED HIM, SAYING, SIR, WE WOULD SEE JESUS."

The form is:

1. Only what Jesus did at the Cross in giving Himself as a Sacrifice, thereby, shedding His Life's Blood, can take away sin.

2. This means that the only answer for sin is the Cross of Christ.

3. There is no other answer because there need be no other answer.

WE WOULD SEE JESUS . . .

The phrase, *"The same came therefore to Philip,"* represents one of the Twelve Apostles (Mat. 10:3; Mk. 3:18; Lk. 6:14; Acts 1:13). He is, as well, the brother of Nathaniel (Jn. 1:45-50).

"Who was of Bethsaida of Galilee," could mean, as some expositors think, that these Greeks were citizens of one of the Greek cities of the Decapolis, which were east of the Jordan River.

Bethsaida of Galilee bordered this district and could well have meant that Philip was familiar with these people, but that is only speculation.

The phrase, *"And desired him, saying, Sir, we would see Jesus,"* was probably prompted by the tremendous Reception of Jesus by the people at the Triumphant Entry. They were ready to plead with Him to go among them and to offer His Message to the Gentiles!

At the Birth of the Messiah, the Persians came from the east saying, *"Where is He?"* (Mat. 2:2), and at the Death of the Messiah, the Greeks came from the west saying, *"We would see Jesus."* In the ancient world, the Persians and the Greeks were the most intellectual — the former were famous for religion and astronomy; the latter for philosophy and art.

(22) "PHILIP COMES AND TELLS ANDREW: AND AGAIN ANDREW AND PHILIP TELL JESUS."

The form is:

1. The Lamb, God's Lamb, would actually separate the sin from the sinner (Jn. 1:29).

2. Jesus would not only atone — in other words, satisfy the Wrath of God — but He would make the person a brand-new creature (II Cor. 5:17).

3. He would refer to such a person as being *"Born-Again"* (Jn. 3:3).

PHILIP AND ANDREW

The phrase, *"Philip comes and tells Andrew,"* presents these two men as being very close. Actually, when Jesus performed the Miracle of the loaves and the fishes, Philip and Andrew were very visible in this scenario as John records the incident (Jn. 6:1-8).

Andrew was one of, if not the earliest, of the Disciples and brought his own brother, Simon Peter, to Jesus (Jn. 1:40-42). He is mentioned as in close association with Peter, James, and John as partners with them in the fishing trade on the Lake of Galilee (Mk. 1:16, 29; 3:18). Philip was called by Christ the very next day after Andrew and Peter, and some believe that John was included at this time, as well, although unmentioned.

There is some hint that after the first Call to become Followers of Christ, Andrew and John clung to Him and went with Him to Jerusalem, and then they returned with Jesus through Samaria, after which occurred the second Call of the brothers, Simon and James.

There are some who think that this incident occurred after Jesus had claimed Psalm 110 as an Oracle which described His own divine Claims and His universal Victory as the Lord and Son of David and Royal Warrior-Priest (Mat. 22:41-46). If, in fact, this chronology is correct, Philip may have felt this moment to be a most critical one in history. The idea is that the Jews would not accept Christ as the Messiah, but, quite possibly, the Gentiles would, especially considering that these Greeks desired to see Jesus.

More than likely, this happened immediately after Jesus had cleansed the Temple, which John does not mention (Lk. 19:45-48), and which infuriated the religious leadership of Israel.

EVERYTHING SHOULD BE TAKEN TO JESUS

The phrase, *"And again Andrew and Philip tell Jesus,"* may present more, much more, than just the passing on of information. As stated, they probably saw a glimmer of hope in this situation. However, they were misreading and misunderstanding the Mission of Christ, that is, if, in fact, they truly had these thoughts in mind regarding Jesus going over to the Gentiles.

There is an aside to this drama that should not be lost upon the Bible student. Everything should be taken to Jesus exactly as Andrew and Philip did here.

Jesus Himself is the Just and Reasonable Source of all enlightenment. He is the Highest Expression of man and his destiny. He is also the Perfect Manifestation of the Father, the only Mediator between God and man, and One with both, as should be obvious.

It is through Jesus that we know what and Who God Is and What God would have us to think and to be, and to learn what man may become. We take to Him the puzzles of our logic, the accusations of our conscience, and the burdens of our heart.

Inasmuch as Jesus had cleansed the Temple that week and declared it to be a *"House of prayer for all nations,"* such must have deeply stirred the souls of Greeks and, as well, stirred the imagination of these Disciples, as we have attempted to portray.

It is so sad when the majority of the modern church little thinks of consulting the Lord during times of crisis, but rather looks toward psychologists, who, at best, are merely feeble men and women.

(23) "AND JESUS ANSWERED THEM, SAYING, THE HOUR IS COME, THAT THE SON OF MAN SHOULD BE GLORIFIED."

The form is:

1. Christ, foreshadowed by the Burnt-Offering, is not for the sinner's conscience but for the Heart of God.

2. Of all the Old Testament sacrifices, the whole Burnt-Offering was the foundation offering, so to speak, of the five presentation offerings.

3. While each sacrifice played its part and served its purpose, it was the whole Burnt-Offering that made everything possible simply because it satisfied the Wrath of God.

THE HOUR IS COME

The phrase, *"And Jesus answered them, saying, The hour is come,"* proclaims a twofold meaning:

1. The idea that *"the hour is come,"* was a foretaste of the Glory and Kingdom promised to Him by the Father. He came as King to Zion, His Own received Him with shouts of Hosanna (the people, not the religious leaders), and the Gentiles, represented by these Greeks, pressed forward to do Him homage.

However, the formula, *"Is come,"* was prophetic as well as illustrative, for, in Prophecy, the present tense is frequently used to emphasize certainty. So, the sentence may read, *"The hour shall come,"* and that which was then happening foreshadowed its certain arrival. The Messiah will be King in Zion, and the Gentiles shall flock together to His Name, which speaks of the Second Coming.

2. It spoke of Calvary and the Resurrection, with Calvary not at all seeming to be any part of Glory. However, it definitely did pertain to His Glory because, at this horrid place, Jesus defeated Satan, Sin, Death, and Hell. As well, He did it not as God but as a mere man, in effect, the Last Adam.

The Resurrection ratified that great Victory and brought upon Jesus the Glory that this Victory had won. If there had been no Resurrection, Calvary would have been in vain, as should be obvious! However, there was no thought or hint that the Resurrection would not take place. In fact, had Jesus failed to atone for even one sin, the Resurrection could not have taken place. Due to the fact that He atoned for all sin, past, present, and future, at least for all who will believe, the Resurrection was a given, so to speak (Jn. 3:16).

GLORIFIED

As well, this is the *"hour"* that had been planned before the foundation of the world and was now coming to pass (I Pet. 1:18-20). It was to be the greatest *"hour"* in human history and, in fact, was of such magnitude that sacrificial ceremonies will be carried out forever, even in the eternal future, in order that men not forget what Jesus did for humanity at that *"hour"* (Ezek. 46:11-15).

The phrase, *"That the Son of Man should be Glorified,"* in effect, guarantees the Resurrection.

If it is to be noticed, Jesus used the appellative, *"Son of Man,"* of Himself, rather than *"Son of God."*

What was to be done could only be done by a Man, hence, the Incarnation, God becoming Man. The Highest Man is now about to assume His Supreme Glory, to go forth as the Mighty Man to defeat the powers of darkness in totality and, ultimately, to rule in the world of men, which He shall.

THE SON OF MAN

After Calvary and the Resurrection, the Son of Man would ascend to His Eternal Throne where He would be clothed with all authority of Judgment and Mercy in Heaven and Earth.

Actually, the Glorification of the Son of Man is one of the high main themes of the Gospel, and its Justification is to be found in the fact that the Son of Man is indeed the Logos (Eternal Word) made flesh. He is the Lamb slain and, as well, is to be lifted up, which He was on the Cross. As the True Shepherd, He lay down His Life that He might take it again.

In effect, His Passion was so inextricably interwoven with His Glory that the former became verily the prelude of His Victory and supreme Exaltation. His Death, which Satan thought was His Defeat, was but His Glory, especially regarding what it accomplished.

Also, the approach of the Gentiles suggested the universal belief in Him which would follow upon His Passion and Resurrection, and He now *"foretells that the hour of His Glorification was already come."*

(24) "VERILY, VERILY, I SAY UNTO YOU, EXCEPT A CORN OF WHEAT FALL INTO THE GROUND AND DIE, IT ABIDETH ALONE: BUT IF IT DIE, IT BRINGS FORTH MUCH FRUIT."

The overview is:

1. The great Book of Leviticus in the Old Testament is at least one of the most important works in the entirety of the Word of God.

2. It goes into detail in explaining what Christ has done for us as it regards the Sacrifice of Himself on the Cross of Calvary.

3. It does so by portraying and even detailing the Sacrificial system of the Levitical Law.

THE CORN OF WHEAT

The phrase, *"Verily, Verily, I say unto you,"* presents a profound statement. Considering that to which it referred, the Death of Christ, it is the most profound in human history. As well, the pronoun, *"You,"* is emphatic toward the Disciples, that their idea of circumventing His Death was a violation of the Word of God and a hindrance to the very purpose and reason for which He came.

The phrase, *"Except a corn of wheat fall into the ground and die, it abideth alone,"* in effect, says that His Atoning Death was a preliminary necessity. Not one single person could be delivered from the doom of death if Christ had not atoned for sin by His Death, for the wages of sin is death. The corn of wheat must die, otherwise, He would abide alone, i.e., *"Would deliver no one from death."*

"But if it die, it brings forth much fruit," proclaims the very purpose for His Death, which would bring forth Life.

That which Jesus did in totality, including His Virgin Birth, Perfect Sinless Life, and Death and Resurrection, all were done, not at all for Himself, but rather for man. He must take upon Himself the curse of the Law, which was Death, in order that we, who were lawbreakers, would not suffer its penalty. God demanded a Perfect Sacrifice, which was the perfect, sinless, unspoiled, unsullied, and uncorrupted Body of the Lord Jesus Christ. It was not possible for man to provide such a sacrifice because man was corrupted and spoiled, consequently, that which God could not accept.

THE CROSS

So, when Jesus died on Calvary, in effect, having Faith in what He did, to all who believe Him, we died with Him (Rom. 6:3-5). Consequently, the demands of Heavenly Justice were satisfied in that the price was paid by the pouring out of His Precious Blood from His Perfect Body, which, in effect, is the pouring out of His Life, for *"the life of the flesh is in the blood"* (Lev. 17:11).

This which Jesus did broke the grip of sin that Satan had on humanity, with, as well, Satan having no more claim on the believing sinner. Consequently, the Evil One is defeated! It is truly the Greatest Story ever told!

As well, this example set by Christ is to serve as the death of self-will for the Believer, with *"self"* hidden in Christ. This is what Jesus meant by the Believer taking up the Cross daily to follow Him (Lk. 9:23).

This is the reason that Calvary is to ever be the theme in the life and daily walk of the Believer. It not only represents the price paid for our Salvation but, as well, victory in our daily walk in this present world. Consequently, Calvary and what it did and represented is as much a part of our present life as it was when we were Saved. That is the reason Paul said, *"For I determined not to know anything among you, save Jesus Christ, and Him Crucified"* (I Cor. 2:2).

He also said, *"But God forbid that I should glory, save in the Cross of our Lord Jesus Christ, by Whom the world is crucified unto me, and I unto the world"* (Gal. 6:14).

John said, *"And this is the victory that overcomes the world, even our Faith"* (I Jn. 5:4).

However, Faith in what?

FAITH

It is Faith in what Jesus did for us at Calvary, even as Paul stated in Galatians 6:14.

So, when our so-called faith friends claim that Calvary has no significance in the Faith walk of the Believer, claiming that such was necessary only for Salvation, if that, they completely misunderstand what Calvary was all about. While the very basis of their message is faith, which is good, still, they err when the end result of that faith is not really the Word of God as they claim but, actually, themselves. The Object of Faith is to always be Jesus Christ, with Calvary as the Means of bringing about all of this which we desire, not only in Salvation but, as stated, in our continued daily walk before the Lord (Heb. 12:2).

(25) "HE WHO LOVES HIS LIFE SHALL LOSE IT; AND HE WHO HATES HIS LIFE IN THIS WORLD SHALL KEEP IT UNTO LIFE ETERNAL."

The construction is:

1. Calvary tells us just how horrible that sin was and is.
2. It tells us that sin is not merely exterior; it is interior.
3. It is not just outward; it is inward. It is a disease, one might say, of our vitals. It affects every single part of the human being.

LOVING ONE'S LIFE

The phrase, *"He who loves his life shall lose it,"* hits at the very heart of man's problem, be he Believer or unbeliever. It could be paraphrased, *"He who loves self shall not see fulfillment."*

Of course, the far greater majority of the world will not serve Christ because of unbelief. However, there are many who do know that He is the Son of God and the Saviour of man but refuse to serve Him because of self-will. Many Believers realize only a tiny part of their full Spiritual potential simply because of self-will. *"Self"* is the culprit!

The entirety of the idea of this statement as given by Christ is that the individual desire the Will of God in his life at all cost.

Many Believers have the erroneous idea that if they consecrate fully to the Lord, He will demand something of them that they strongly do not desire to do. That is basely incorrect.

If the Lord truly calls someone to a particular place or position, as He often does, at the same time, He will give him a love for that place and that work as nothing else. As well, if he does not carry out that which God has called him to do, he will find nothing but dissatisfaction in what he is presently doing.

The way to a troubled life, which brings confusion, lack of fulfillment, and an absence of peace of mind, is to be out of the Will of God, in other words, putting self ahead of Christ.

HATING ONE'S LIFE

The phrase, *"And he who hates his life in this world shall keep it unto Life Eternal,"* simply means that one prefer one's life and will less, far less, than the Will of God.

Whenever the person does not do this, as the first phrase proclaims, one is actually saying that he knows more about life than God and that he can chart his course far better than his Creator. Such is gross facetiousness, to say the least!

The idea is that we give our lives over to Christ in totality, reserving nothing for our own whims and personal satisfaction, but wholly desiring the Perfect and Sweet Will of God.

A PERSONAL EXPERIENCE

Frances and I began evangelistic work in 1956. About two years later, Donnie was ready for school. From the first grade through the sixth, Frances taught him in what is referred to now as *"homeschooling."* We used the Calvert School Course, which was the very best on the market at that time, but required four to six hours of instruction each and every day. To say the least, such was very difficult for Frances, especially considering that during all of this time, she did not miss a single night in Service. I tried to help as best I could, but I'm afraid that my efforts were woefully inadequate.

After completing the sixth grade, which I think was as far as the Calvert School Course went at that time, we enrolled Donnie in public schools. Most all of our meetings lasted anywhere from four to six weeks in length, and he would change schools at the end of each meeting. Actually, Donnie attended some 32 schools, if I remember correctly, in nearly as many states. However, when he reached the ninth grade, Frances stayed home with him in Baton Rouge while he finished high school.

DIFFICULT!

During this time when we were changing Donnie from school to school, it was very difficult for him, to say the least. Some parents think it is a tragedy if a child has to change schools one time. Considering that he was changing six to eight times a year, one can imagine the difficulties involved.

It is during this time that I want to call the reader's attention, which occasioned something that I think illustrates the point of the statement as given by Christ.

Both of us were very tired, and I am certain that Donnie felt the same way, even though he really did not know anything else except the changing of schools constantly.

The Lord had called me to be an Evangelist, and when He called me, He called Frances, as well, to help me carry out this which the Lord had directed us to do. In other words, her Call was just as real as mine.

At that time, if I remember correctly, Donnie was in the eighth grade, and, as stated, we were changing him from school to school. All three of us were very weary and tired of living out of a suitcase, with our home being a motel room or a room in the church, which, most of the time, was woefully inadequate.

A DECISION

We were in Revival in a small church in Alabama. God was blessing mightily, with the small auditorium being packed to capacity each and every night, with many people being Saved and baptized with the Holy Spirit. But yet, I longed, as I know Frances did, to just simply have some place we could call home and not have to travel constantly. Above all, we wanted a home so that Donnie could enroll in one school and stay there.

My dad then pastored a small Church

NOTES

in Baton Rouge, Louisiana, and mention was made of me coming and pastoring this Church, etc. To be honest, everything in me wanted to do this, for the obvious reasons. The consternation and prayer about this situation went on, I suppose, for several weeks; however, it was at this meeting in Alabama that the Lord gave me direction.

I had gone out to the Pastor's office that morning to seek the Lord for the Service that night. As I began to pray, the taking of the Church in Baton Rouge began to weigh heavily upon my heart. As I have stated, it was very attractive to the flesh, and that part of me strongly desired that particular direction.

However, as I began to pray, the Spirit of God began to move mightily upon me and I began to tell the Lord, *"I am asking You for Your Perfect Will in this matter."* I remember stating that distinctly.

THE WILL OF GOD

In those days, and, I suppose, still is, there was a teaching called, *"The permissive Will of God,"* and I remember saying to Him, *"Lord, if such a thing exists, that is not what I desire. I do not want any permissive will, but only Your Perfect Will in this matter."* Then, the Lord spoke to my heart.

He said, *"You have asked Me for My Perfect Will. I called you as a child to be an Evangelist, and I have not lifted that Call."*

That was it! But yet, I knew I had the answer. It was God's Will that we continue doing exactly as He had called us, irrespective of the difficulties involved.

RADIO, TELEVISION, AND CITYWIDE CRUSADES

At that time, which was 1966, if I remember correctly, I had no idea at all that in 1969, the Lord would put us on radio. The program would vastly expand to some 600 stations daily, and then, just a little later, we would go on television. Those things were not even a glimmer at that moment, but, of course, the Lord knew exactly what the future held.

In 1966, I could not look ahead and see that the Lord would use us in a Move of God, which would see hundreds of thousands, and

I exaggerate not, swept into the Kingdom and touch a great part of this world through television. However, I am convinced that if I had not done exactly what the Lord wanted at that time, in effect, placing God's Will ahead of self, these things would have never happened. How I thank the Lord that I prayed that kind of prayer, desiring the Perfect Will of God, rather than a prayer of self-will. An untold number of souls, I believe, are now in the Kingdom of God because of that moment of consecration. Yes, at times, the Lord does ask some things of us that seem to be very difficult and, in fact, are. That cannot be denied; however, whatever He asks of us, He will always make it up a thousand times over. Of that, one can be assured.

It wasn't easy for Abraham and Sarah to leave their home in Ur of the Chaldees where they had every comfort then known to man. In fact, they would live the rest of their lives in a tent, but if they had not obeyed, we would have never heard of Abraham. As it was, even though at times it was difficult, this man touched the world for all time.

(26) "IF ANY MAN SERVE ME, LET HIM FOLLOW ME; AND WHERE I AM, THERE SHALL ALSO MY SERVANT BE: IF ANY MAN SERVE ME, HIM WILL MY FATHER HONOUR."

The form is:

1. We as Believers are *"nothing at all,"* but in Christ, we are purged worshippers.

2. In a sense, this means that we do not stand in the Sanctuary, so to speak, as a guilty sinner but as a worshipping Priest, clothed in *"garments of glory and beauty."*

3. In fact, to be occupied with guilt in the Presence of God is not humility as it regards myself, but unbelief as it regards the Sacrifice.

FOLLOWING JESUS

The phrase, *"If any man serve Me, let him follow Me,"* means that to properly serve the Lord, we must also follow the Lord. Actually, this is the place and source of great contention.

Satan attempts to get Believers to follow other than Christ, whether it is other Christians, preachers, church denomination, etc. While all of these things are meant to play a positive role in our lives, ideally, they are supposed to help us follow Christ more perfectly. All too often, others demand allegiance that is due only Christ. That allegiance to Christ must never be abrogated. However, in too many hearts and lives, it is abrogated.

Many blindly follow their church denominations irrespective of the direction it is leading. They do so for many and varied reasons.

Perhaps that is what their families have been for generations past, or they take the position that they, as laymen, are not responsible for the weightier matters, and, consequently, they leave it up to others, blindly doing what they are told. Such has led untold millions, to be blunt, to an eternal Hell and continues to do so unto this moment.

First and foremost and always paramount in one's life is for the Believer to follow Jesus. As well, Jesus will never lead the Believer astray from the Word of God, with the Word always serving as our criterion.

To be sure, this relationship is to be of such magnitude that the Believer will always know the direction the Lord is leading.

It is tragic that some of the leadership of major Pentecostal denominations, which once greatly encouraged the personal following of our Lord, now frown upon such. They claim that they, the religious leadership, will hear from the Lord and then inform the underlings as to what they should do. This is the spirit that controls Catholicism and, actually, the same spirit which ultimately destroyed the Early Church.

The Lord, as the Good Shepherd, individually leads each person with each one to individually follow.

A PERSONAL EXPERIENCE

Some three weeks ago as I dictate these notes, a dear lady sat across the table from Frances and me and others and spoke of the Call of God upon her life. The denomination with which she was associated was demanding that she do a certain thing and go to a certain place.

She stated to us, and me in particular, *"That is not what God has called me to do!"* She then said, *"What should I do, Brother*

Swaggart?" My answer to her was the same as it would be to any and all. *"You must follow the Leading of the Holy Spirit and not men."*

With the breakfast ending, we all stood up to go our different ways, and I felt led of the Lord to have us pray at that time respecting this situation, which we did.

As I began to pray, the Spirit of God began to move, powerfully so, I might quickly add!

The lady in question sat down, lay her head on the table, and began to literally sob as the Spirit of God began to move upon her.

I did not ask her what she was going to do because that was really not my place. However, I do know that the Lord spoke to her at that moment, and the peace that now became evident upon her face was obvious to all.

If she did what she felt the Lord was telling her to do, it was going to mean great contention with the denomination in question, with her probably being forced to leave this with which she had been associated all of her life.

This is a very traumatic thing for many; however, we must always understand that Satan will use every method at his disposal to get us to follow men instead of Jesus. Actually, the far greater number of efforts he makes is in the religious realm. So, the person has to stay close to God, guaranteeing an excellent relationship, in order that he always listen to the Lord instead of men.

ULTIMATELY TO CHRIST

The following should be remembered: the Lord does not want us to lean on the arm of even a good man. While such advice and counsel may be desirable and beneficial in certain situations, still, the Lord wants, and even demands, that we look ultimately to Him.

The phrase, *"And where I am, there shall also My Servant be,"* actually means to be *"crucified together"* and *"Glorified together"* (Gal. 2:20; Rom. 8:17).

The phrase, *"If any man serve Me, him will My Father honour,"* presents a glorious picture.

For the Father to honor a poor child of dust seems almost more than we can grasp.

However, the *"honor"* here spoken is reserved only for those who follow Jesus and not other things or other people.

Please allow me to say it again. I love my brothers and sisters in the Lord. I often seek their counsel and advice, and deeply appreciate their fellowship in this manner and take it very seriously. However, in the final alternative, I must be led exclusively by the Holy Spirit as He helps us to follow Christ.

(27) *"NOW IS MY SOUL TROUBLED; AND WHAT SHALL I SAY? FATHER, SAVE ME FROM THIS HOUR: BUT FOR THIS CAUSE CAME I UNTO THIS HOUR."*

The pattern is:

1. Paul vehemently came against any doctrine that impugned the Cross in any way. So should we!

2. That's the reason we presently take such a stand against the so-called Word of Faith doctrine, which, in reality, is no faith at all simply because it demeans the Cross.

3. Once again we state, *"The Cross of Christ is the Means, and the only Means, by which we receive everything from God."*

FOR THIS CAUSE

For Jesus, so pure and perfect, to have to take upon Himself the sin of man, in effect, becoming a Sin-Offering, was so repugnant that it is impossible for us to fully comprehend what it all meant. At that time, of necessity, He would be separated from the Father.

The question, *"And what shall I say? Father, save Me from this hour,"* could be translated, *"Should I pray to the Father that He save Me from this hour?"*

The phrase, *"But for this cause came I unto this hour,"* could be translated, *"No, for this cause came I unto this hour."*

Even though He would face this agony, still, the horror that death had for Jesus disproves the assertion that His Death was that which all men must suffer. That is incorrect in that multitudes, whether martyrs or skeptics, have faced death and suffered it under cruel torments without flinching and often with sacred or profane songs or statements.

However, Christ shrank from it because it was an Atoning Death beneath the Wrath of God, and so, in it, there was an element of horror impossible for man to comprehend or understand.

In other words, the Death of our Lord was totally unlike any other death that has ever been in that His Life was not really taken from Him but, actually, freely given up, i.e., *"breathed out."* As well, it was for a specific purpose, which was to satisfy the demands of Heavenly Justice in that the sin debt be paid. This, in turn, broke the grip of that monster upon humanity (at least for all who will believe), and left Satan with no acceptable accusation against man or claim upon man, once again, for all who believe (Jn. 3:16).

(28) "FATHER, GLORIFY YOUR NAME. THEN CAME THERE A VOICE FROM HEAVEN, SAYING, I HAVE BOTH GLORIFIED IT, AND WILL GLORIFY IT AGAIN.

(29) THE PEOPLE THEREFORE, WHO STOOD BY, AND HEARD IT, SAID THAT IT THUNDERED: OTHERS SAID, AN ANGEL SPOKE TO HIM."

The pattern is:

1. As is obvious, Paul came against any doctrine that impugned the Cross in any way.

2. He did this because the Cross of Christ is the Means, and the only Means, by which we receive from God.

3. What Jesus did at the Cross makes everything possible.

GLORIFYING THE NAME OF THE HEAVENLY FATHER

The phrase, *"Father, glorify Your Name,"* proclaims that which Jesus always sought to do, to *"glorify"* the Name of His Heavenly Father. That must be our ambition as well!

Our business is to glorify God and not ourselves. In effect, that is what Jesus was talking about when He spoke of the Believer *"loving his life and losing it,"* versus preferring the Lord over one's own desires and, thereby, gaining *"Life Eternal."*

The phrase, *"Then came there a Voice from Heaven, saying, I have both glorified it, and will glorify it again,"* refers, at least at this time, to the Resurrection of Lazarus and then glorifying it again at the Resurrection of Christ.

THE VOICE FROM HEAVEN

The phrase, *"The people therefore, who stood by, and heard it, said that it thundered,"* does not mean that it was unintelligible, but that the Voice sounded with such Power that it was like thunder.

The phrase, *"Others said, An Angel spoke to Him,"* proclaims the fact that they did hear what was said and did understand it, at least the words, even though they did not understand the meaning.

(30) "JESUS ANSWERED AND SAID, THIS VOICE CAME NOT BECAUSE OF ME, BUT FOR YOUR SAKES."

The form is:

1. No Believer ever matures beyond the Cross!

2. The whole of the Christian life is simply learning what it means to live by Grace through Faith alone in Christ Alone.

3. That, of course, is what the Protestant Reformation was and is all about.

FOR YOUR SAKE

Actually, every single thing Jesus did, along with that of His Heavenly Father, as recorded here, was for the sake of man.

The phrase, *"Jesus answered and said, This Voice came not because of Me,"* proclaims in no uncertain terms that Jesus was not in doubt as to Who and What He was.

The phrase, *"But for your sakes,"* refers to God making this statement and in an audible voice that all who were there might hear and know.

There is every evidence that He was now in the Temple, no doubt, surrounded by hundreds of individuals, all hearing the Voice of God. However, men very easily explain away that which is the Lord, claiming, at least in this case, that it was *"thunder"* or even an *"Angel."* In fact, this Verse proves that the *"Voice"* was intelligible.

When one properly ascertains the lengths to which God went in order to prove Himself to these unbelievers, who claimed to be Believers, one quickly sees the Love, Grace, Mercy, and Efforts of the Lord in operation on their behalf and even on our behalf. Man could not go to such lengths and, actually, would not even if he could. So, Israel's subsequent destruction and scattering all over the world was done only after every effort had been exhausted to bring them to their spiritual senses. However, it seems that they responded in no favorable way, as many even today!

(31) "NOW IS THE JUDGMENT OF THIS WORLD: NOW SHALL THE PRINCE OF THIS WORLD BE CAST OUT."

The pattern is:

1. To forget the Grace of God in Christ, which comes to us by the Means of the Cross, is foolish indeed!

2. Some of the Galatians were doing just that. So, the Holy Spirit through Paul addressed them as, *"You foolish Galatians!"*

3. He said to them, *"Who has bewitched you ... before your very eyes Jesus Christ was clearly portrayed as crucified"* (Gal. 3:1).

THE JUDGMENT OF THIS WORLD

The phrase, *"Now is the Judgment of this world,"* pertains to that which Jesus would do at Calvary.

The Greek word for *"Judgment"* is *"krisis"* and means *"a turning-point."* In other words, from the time of Calvary, Truth in a greater way than ever would be in the world, and would ultimately result in greater freedoms and prosperity than man had ever known previously.

However, this does not mean that the world will be Christianized, with all false religions ultimately falling into line. Actually, this will not happen until Jesus comes back in Glory, which Revelation, Chapter 19, proclaims. However, it does refer to the world being bettered to such a degree as it had never known before.

As well, the *"Judgment"* centered up in Jesus, with Him suffering the Wrath of God instead of us. Had the world suffered such, it would have been completely destroyed.

THE PRINCE OF THIS WORLD CAST OUT

The phrase, *"Now shall the prince of this world be cast out,"* actually means that through Calvary, Satan would lose his grip of sin on believing sinners, with the result being that sin and death are defeated.

Satan is the *"prince of this world"* and, as such, has held humanity in an iron grip of slavery. As stated, Jesus broke that grip by His Sacrificial Atoning Death at Calvary; however, the full results will not be seen in totality until the Second Coming of the Lord.

This means that much of the authority that Satan now expresses is, in fact, a pseudo authority. In other words, through ignorance or wrong teaching, Believers do not evidence the Power and Authority over Satan that is freely given to us by Christ, which allows him latitude that he should not have.

Satan, sin, and death were defeated at Calvary's Cross. Sin was the legal means that Satan had to hold man captive. With that legal means removed, which Jesus did by atoning for all sin, past, present, and future, at least for all who will Believe, this means that man can live free from sin. No, we are not teaching sinless perfection, for the Bible does not teach such. However, it most definitely does teach that *"sin, i.e., 'the sin nature,' shall not have dominion over us"* (Rom. 6:14). It is the *"dominion"* of which we speak. To be sure, dominion is a strong word. It means that Satan is lording it over the Believer, forcing that Believer into a course of action or a state of being to which the person does not desire to go. It's not a very pleasant way to live.

The answer to this dilemma, and thank God there is an answer, is the Cross of Christ, and the Cross of Christ Alone! This means that the Believer is to place his or her Faith exclusively in Christ and what Christ did for us at the Cross, realizing that all Victory was won at the Cross. When this is done, then the Holy Spirit, Who works exclusively within the parameters, so to speak, of the Finished Work of Christ, will then work mightily on our behalf. However, if the Believer has his or her faith in something other than Christ and the Cross, the Holy Spirit constitutes such as *"spiritual adultery"* (Rom. 7:1-4). Thank God, even under those circumstances, the Holy Spirit does not leave; however, due to misplaced faith, He is greatly limited in what He can do for us. Sadly and regrettably, this is where most Believers are. Their Faith is in something other than Christ and the Cross, and it doesn't really matter what it is. If it's not Christ and the Cross, it's Faith that God will not honor (Rom. 6:1-14; 8:1-11; I Cor. 1:17, 18, 23; 2:2; Gal. 6:14; Col. 2:10-15).

THE FOUNDATION

The only answer for sin is the Cross of Christ (Col. 2:14-15; Heb. 7:27; I Cor. 1:17-18). That's the reason that Paul said: *"For I determined not to know anything among you, save Jesus Christ, and Him Crucified"* (I Cor. 2:2).

The Cross of Christ is the *"Wisdom of God"* (I Cor. 2:6-8). In fact, the Cross was the greatest and the highest expression of the Wisdom of God known to man.

God's Wisdom leads sinful men to the great Sacrifice of history, the offering up of Jesus on the Cross of Calvary, which paid the terrible sin debt of man, at least for all who will believe. In fact, the Cross is the very first Doctrine, of which we are made aware, which took place in the Mind of God from before the foundation of the world (I Pet. 1:18-20; I Cor. 2:7). This means that every single Bible Doctrine is built squarely on the Foundation of the Cross. In fact, any doctrine that is not built squarely on the Foundation of the Cross is spurious, meaning that it is wrong. That's where all false doctrine begins, a lack of understanding respecting the Cross of Christ, an ignoring of the Cross of Christ, or an outright denial of the Cross of Christ.

What is the alternative to the Cross of Jesus Christ? The only alternative is to fall back once again upon our own resources, which guarantees failure. In fact, if the Cross of Christ is wrong, then we have no other resource. What resources do I personally have? What strength do I personally have? What merit do I personally have? What do I have to offer a Holy and Just God? Nothing! So, if I am to be Saved, if anyone is to be Saved, it must be by Faith in Christ and what He did for us at the Cross, and Faith in the Cross of Christ alone. In fact, if the preacher is not preaching the Cross, whatever he is preaching may be about the Gospel, but it's not the Gospel (I Cor. 1:17).

(32) "AND I, IF I BE LIFTED UP FROM THE EARTH, WILL DRAW ALL MEN UNTO ME."

The construction is:

1. Let us ask it again, *"What is the alternative to the Cross of Jesus Christ?"*

2. The only alternative is to fall back once again upon our own resources, which we will find to be very inadequate.

3. When one takes one's eyes off the Cross of Christ, one is left with nothing.

THE DEATH OF CHRIST AT CALVARY

The phrase, *"And I, if I be lifted up from the Earth,"* refers to Jesus' Death at Calvary. He was *"lifted up"* on the Cross.

"Will draw all men unto Me," refers to the Salvation of all who come to Him, believing what He did and trusting in its Atoning work.

The Cross made it possible for men to come to Christ; otherwise, there was and is no access. So, if the preacher is not preaching the Cross, he has then closed the door to Salvation.

Had Jesus not died on the Cross, none would have been saved. However, because He did die the Atoning Death on the Cross, all kinds of men were drawn to Him and are being drawn to Him. As a result of the Cross, they can be Saved.

In effect, this is the same thing Jesus told Nicodemus when He spoke of the Son of Man being lifted up even as the serpent was lifted up in the wilderness (Jn. 3:14).

(33) "THIS HE SAID, SIGNIFYING WHAT DEATH HE SHOULD DIE."

The overview is:

1. The only way one can be justified is by putting his Faith in Christ and what He did for us at the Cross.

2. The believing sinner may understand precious little of what I've just stated, but if he reaches out to the Lord, he will be Saved.

3. Justification is not by good works, merit, or effort. It is only by Faith in Christ and His Atoning Work at the Cross of Calvary.

THE CROSS OF CHRIST

In the words of Verse 33, we learn that the attraction of the Cross of Christ will prove to be the mightiest and most sovereign motive ever brought to bear on the human will. When wielded by the Holy Spirit as a Revelation of the matchless Love of God, it will involve the most sweeping judicial sentence that can be pronounced upon the world and its prince.

If the Cross of Christ is removed from Christianity, we have nothing left but a vapid philosophy. Sadly and regrettably, it has already been removed from most churches, meaning that there is nothing left by which man can be Saved.

(34) "THE PEOPLE ANSWERED HIM, WE HAVE HEARD OUT OF THE LAW THAT CHRIST ABIDES FOREVER: AND HOW DO YOU SAY, THE SON OF MAN MUST BE LIFTED UP? WHO IS THIS SON OF MAN?"

The order is:

1. Turning from the Cross means to turn from the only way of coming to God and the only way to having fellowship with God.

2. It is foolish to exchange the free Grace of God for the bondage of your own works.

3. Whenever individuals claim that Grace is only a license to sin, always and without exception, such comes from a heart of self-righteousness.

THE WORD OF GOD

The phrase, *"The people answered Him,"* proclaims an answer that is unsatisfactory. Actually, it was an answer of unbelief!

The record is clear that the people simply did not know the Word of God. While this was mostly the fault of their leaders, still, each will answer individually, as all will answer individually.

Isaiah, along with Jeremiah, Ezekiel, and all the minor Prophets, for that matter, spoke of the coming Kingdom Age, which the people, at this time, had in mind and thought the Messiah would now fulfill. Still, Isaiah, Chapter 53, plainly proclaimed Who and What the Messiah would be, i.e., a Suffering Messiah. So, there was no excuse for their misinterpretation, as there is no excuse presently.

THE LAW?

"We have heard out of the Law that Christ abides forever," refers to several Passages out of the Old Testament being taken out of context. They could have been referring to Psalms 89:29; 110:4; Isaiah 9:6-7; Daniel 7:14, plus many others of similar content. As stated, they were looking for a Victorious Conqueror and not a Suffering Saviour!

NOTES

The question, *"And how do You say, The Son of Man must be lifted up?"* presents these people attempting to excuse their unwillingness to obey a moral appeal to the conscience by raising some Bible difficulty.

Jesus had said that He was the Messiah and that He was about to be crucified. His hearers objected to that statement, claiming otherwise.

The question, *"Who is this Son of Man?"* is a question that Jesus would not answer. As the Thirty-seventh Verse proclaims, they had enough proof, even a thousand times over, to know Who and What He was. Their state of unbelief was their own choice and in the face of irrefutable proof!

The truth is, He could have pointed to Himself and plainly said, *"I am the Son of Man,"* exactly as He did the Samaritan woman, but still, they would not have believed Him.

(35) "THEN JESUS SAID UNTO THEM, YET A LITTLE WHILE IS THE LIGHT WITH YOU. WALK WHILE YOU HAVE THE LIGHT, LEST DARKNESS COME UPON YOU: FOR HE WHO WALKS IN DARKNESS KNOWS NOT WHERE HE GOES."

The pattern is:

1. Man is not justified by his attempts to obey the Law. Rather, a man is Just in the sight of God by the work of another: the Lord Jesus Christ.

2. That is why Paul was absolutely dumbfounded that the churches in Galatia and elsewhere were deserting the Gospel of the Cross in favor of Law.

3. We see how shocked he was by looking at the introduction to the Epistle to the Galatians.

THE LIGHT

The phrase, *"Then Jesus said unto them, Yet a little while is the Light with you,"* is a warning to these people that He is the Light, that their day was nearly gone, and that the eternal darkness was coming.

"Walk while you have the Light, lest darkness come upon you," presents a choice!

He was saying, in effect, that He is the Light, and there is no other light. If they rejected Him, which they did and which most do, there was nothing left but *"darkness!"* To be sure, it has *"come upon"* untold millions.

WALKING IN DARKNESS

"For he who walks in darkness knows not where he goes," proclaims the majority of the world at present and, in fact, since the beginning of time.

When the Light of the world is spurned and a godless evolution made to supply its place, humanity and the world have no goal set before them. There is no end at which they aim — no mind or will to guide the progress of mankind. Such is this present world!

Even America, which is supposed to be Christian, in fact, is not Christian and has, for all practical purposes, turned its back on God. As such, it wanders aimlessly, not understanding where it has been, where it is, or where it is going because, without God, there is no direction, no light, no anchor, and no purpose — in other words, no moral compass.

Our public schools attempt to project education without values, and if values are raised, they are generally those not of the Bible. This generation by and large is a valueless generation simply because it is an MTV generation. This music television presentation, which has guided this generation, at least for the most part, has ridiculed all values of the Word of God, projecting their own, which, in effect, presents no values at all. As such, this is an aimless, even perverted generation.

THE CHURCH

What was to blame in Jesus' Day, and what is to blame presently?

When one understands that these people who were denying Christ, in fact, were members in good standing of the church of that present time, we have to understand that the blame must be laid at the doorstep of the religious leaders of Israel. The problem is the same presently.

The modern church world is faced with the problem of unbelieving Believers (an oxymoron). In other words, as their counterparts of so long ago, they simply do not believe the Bible. Some claim to while all the time explaining it away, or else, denying it outright.

NOTES

This is the major reason for the church, almost as a whole, accepting the psychological way. Despite what they say, they simply do not believe the Bible.

They do not believe that what Jesus Christ did at the Cross answers the ills, the aberrations, the sins, and the perversions of man. It must be understood that when one embraces humanistic psychology, one has denied the Cross. When one accepts the Cross, he has denied humanistic psychology. Either one cancels out the other. You cannot have both.

There is no way that anyone who claims to be knowledgeable in the Word of God cannot, in fact, fail to see the glaring contradiction between the Word of God and modern psychology. One is the Bible Way, and the other is the psychological way, with the former being the Word of God and the latter being the word of man.

They either claim to know the Word of God but really do not, which I suspect is the case to a great extent, or else, flatly disbelieve what it says, as proved by their actions. One cannot have it both ways.

When one follows the Bible, one *"walks in Light."* When one follows anything other than the Bible, one *"walks in darkness."*

(36) "WHILE YOU HAVE THE LIGHT, BELIEVE IN THE LIGHT, THAT YOU MAY BE THE CHILDREN OF LIGHT. THESE THINGS SPOKE JESUS, AND DEPARTED, AND DID HIDE HIMSELF FROM THEM."

The overview is:

1. The Law of Moses was not given to reform people and to make them good. The Law came to crush all self hopes and to drive one out of oneself, thereby, into Christ.

2. It is foolish to accept Law when the purpose of the Law was to crush all hopes of being accepted by God on those terms.

3. In fact, there is no salvation in the Law, only condemnation. The simple reason is, man cannot keep the Law. Salvation is in Christ Alone!

BELIEVE IN THE LIGHT

The phrase, *"While you have Light, believe in the Light, that you may be the Children of Light,"* tells us two things:

1. Jesus was and is the Light, and other

than Him, there is no light.

2. The Light will not remain forever and, at some point, will be withdrawn. It will be withdrawn quicker if rejected.

"These things spoke Jesus, and departed, and did hide Himself from them," is believed by some that it should have followed Verse 50.

Actually, when one places the Forty-fourth Verse in the position of following the first phrase of Verse 36, it fits perfectly.

At any rate, irrespective of that being the case or not, the discourse in the Temple presents the Last Public Word of Jesus. It was in part accepted by some of His Hearers, as we see from Verse 42, even though they seemed to little follow up on that which they knew to be right.

It must be understood, if the Word of God is rejected, ultimately, the Lord will hide Himself, fulfilling Proverbs 1:24-30.

"Because I have called, and you refused; I have stretched out My Hand, and no man regarded;

"But you have set at nought all My Counsel, and would none of My Reproof:

"I also will laugh at your calamity; I will mock when your fear comes;

"When your fear comes as desolation, and your destruction comes as a whirlwind; when distress and anguish comes upon you.

"Then shall they call upon Me, but I will not answer; they shall seek Me early, but they shall not find Me:

"For that they hated knowledge, and did not choose the fear of the LORD:

"They would none of My Counsel: they despised all My Reproof."

(37) "BUT THOUGH HE HAD DONE SO MANY MIRACLES BEFORE THEM, YET THEY BELIEVED NOT ON HIM."

The order is:

1. It is foolish to exchange what is free for the relentless demands of the Law.

2. The Gospel of Grace says: God gives and gives! The Law says: you must do and do!

3. Law demands. It never quits, but it always wants more. It is foolish to exchange the Good News of Heaven for the bad news of my own strength.

THE HOLY SPIRIT

In Verses 37 through 50, the Holy Spirit reviews and summarizes the Ministry of Christ when on Earth. He first records His Miracles (Jn. 12:37); then the dignity of His Person (Jn. 12:38-46); and lastly, His Teaching (Jn. 12:47-50).

"But though He had done so many Miracles before them," seems to be proclaimed with a sigh by the Holy Spirit. One Miracle would have been enough, but there was a plethora of Miracles, which presented undeniable proof.

There were signs in Heaven, Earth, and Sea; startling Miracles on human nature, and even on dead men. However, such did not compel Faith.

The phrase, *"Yet they believed not on Him,"* reveals their spiritual condition, but no reproach is cast upon the method which the Lord took to reveal His Divine Mission.

Consequently, if people will not Believe the Word of God, they will little believe Miracles either!

In this, the Holy Spirit is telling us that Love, Truth, and Power were united in seeking their Salvation, and yet, He had to hide Himself from them! Such is the heart of man!

(38) "THAT THE SAYING OF ISAIAH THE PROPHET MIGHT BE FULFILLED, WHICH HE SPOKE, LORD, WHO HAS BELIEVED OUR REPORT? AND TO WHOM HAS THE ARM OF THE LORD BEEN REVEALED"?

The form is:

1. Look at all the wonderful things that God has done for you in your Christian life. Did those things come to you because of your effort?

2. Did those things come to you because of your merit?

3. Did those things come to you because you obeyed the Law perfectly?

ISAIAH THE PROPHET

As we have repeatedly stated, the phrase, *"That the saying of Isaiah the Prophet might be fulfilled, which he spoke,"* refers to the Fifty-third Chapter of the Book of Isaiah. Who and What Jesus would be and how He would be treated were given in such simple, glaring detail that there was no excuse for anyone to remain in ignorance.

The question, *"Lord, who has believed our report?"* does not mean that no one believed, for some few did, but does mean that the far greater majority did not!

To be sure, it was a *"report"* beautifully and wondrously devised and presented but refused!

The question, *"And to whom has the Arm of the Lord been revealed?"* speaks of the Messiah as that appendage. He was revealed to Israel!

(39) "THEREFORE THEY COULD NOT BELIEVE, BECAUSE THAT ISAIAH SAID AGAIN."

The construction is:

1. The Believer must begin his Christian life, and continue his Christian life, by trusting in the Cross of Christ and looking to Him Alone.

2. When Paul questioned the Galatians because they were beginning to go into Law, he asked, *"Who has bewitched you?"*

3. The Apostle was using a term that means *"the evil eye."* Who has put the hex on you that you would believe this lie?

UNBELIEF

The phrase, *"Therefore, they could not believe,"* means that Israel willfully shut their eyes to the Message and the Miracles. The word *"therefore"* proves that the unbelief of Verse 38 was willful and, accordingly, by a just Judgment, a judicial blindness darkened their hearts unto the present hour.

The Passage definitely does not mean that God predestined them to be thus, but that they willfully placed themselves in a position of unbelief. In this position, they *"could not believe."*

The idea is that an individual makes a willful choice on his part to not believe something from then on. If one is to notice, irrespective of the evidence otherwise, all he can venture forth is skepticism, sarcasm, and a negative attitude. Such was Israel!

The phrase, *"Because that Isaiah said again,"* refers to the reason for their unbelief.

(40) "HE HAS BLINDED THEIR EYES, AND HARDENED THEIR HEART; THAT THEY SHOULD NOT SEE WITH THEIR EYES, NOR UNDERSTAND WITH THEIR HEART, AND BE CONVERTED, AND I SHOULD HEAL THEM."

The overview is:

1. If the Believer thinks he can begin the Christian life with the Cross and then somehow leave the Cross and go in other directions, it will lead to despair every time.

2. Many see Christ as an accuser. He isn't! He is the Saviour.

3. One must understand, *"Christ is pro me!"* He is for me. He is not against me!

4. God receives me through my Reconciler, my Redeemer, my Saviour, my Master, and my Lord.

BLINDED EYES AND HARDENED HEARTS

The phrase, *"He has blinded their eyes, and hardened their heart,"* means that God has set in motion the *"Law of Unbelief."* In effect, it is the *"Law of Sowing and Reaping."* Sin is punished by its natural consequences: unbelief is punished by insusceptibility to clearest evidence; prejudice by blindness; rejection of Divine Love by inability to see it at its best. These things are brought about by the Laws of God. It is God's Way of acting with all moral agents.

As these Laws are given in the spiritual sense, likewise are natural laws given by God.

Understanding the law of gravity, a sensible person does not blame God for the failure of an individual to use the common sense that God has given him by stepping off the roof of a five story building, thinking he can fly. He can disbelieve the law of gravity all he desires, but the moment he steps out into space, that very law in which he claims not to believe will take effect, and he is going to fall.

So, the only way that it can be said that God is responsible for men falling or the unbelief of Israel is that He made the laws which go into effect when certain things are done.

SEE, HEAR, AND UNDERSTAND

The phrase, *"That they should not see with their eyes, nor understand with their heart, and be converted, and I should heal them,"* simply means they willfully refused to believe, and due to that fact, God has willed a judicial blindness and hardness accordingly.

The Holy Spirit causes this statement by Isaiah to be quoted seven times in the New Testament (Mat. 13:14-15; Mk. 4:12; Lk. 8:10; Jn. 12:39-40; Acts 28:26-27; Rom. 11:8).

With the Holy Spirit repeating this, we should understand that unbelief, without fail, will bring about spiritual blindness and hardness of heart.

If one refuses Light, there remains no other avenue for one to travel. The end result is always darkness.

Is it possible for one to turn around after starting on this road of unbelief?

Of course, God is the only One Who knows the heart of an individual and can judge accordingly; however, this one thing is certain, unbelief must give way to Faith or the person cannot be saved. The deeper one goes into unbelief, the more difficult it is for one to turn around.

And yet, the Scripture plainly tells us that if anyone comes to the Lord, irrespective of his spiritual condition, the Lord will never turn that person away. Of course, we are speaking of those who are sincere (Jn. 6:37).

PREDESTINATION?

From this Verse and others similar, men have devised an unscriptural understanding of predestination. They claim that these people, and all like them, have no choice in the matter, for God has done this thing to them and, with Him being Almighty, there is nothing that can be done!

However, even a cursory investigation of the Text shows otherwise. Everything was done to reach these people but with no success. Were it predestined that they be lost, why would the Lord work against His Own Purposes, making every effort to save them?

The proposed idea that He does such in order that they may not be able to say they lacked opportunity is silly, to say the least. God does not play games. To perform all these Miracles and plead with these individuals to accept and walk in the Light, knowing that it was impossible for them to do such because it had been predestined, places God in the position of carrying out a charade. Even a superficial knowledge of the Word of God debunks such foolishness!

No! Their decision was theirs alone.

NOTES

They were not coerced by God into refusing Christ, but rather every effort was made, short of forcing them to do so, to get them to accept Christ.

Their unbelief was their own choice and, therefore, they reaped its results.

Isaiah used the word *"healed,"* implying a spiritual sickness which requires a spiritual healing. It speaks of being made *"whole."*

So, in that very word *"heal,"* at least as it is used by the Prophet, is the idea that if one will only believe a little, the Lord will act upon that and, if given any opportunity at all, will bring the person to total spiritual wholeness. So, it is possible for God to bring one back, that is, if one will only believe, even though having sunk to the uttermost, because our Lord saves to the *"uttermost"* (Heb. 7:25).

(41) "THESE THINGS SAID ISAIAH, WHEN HE SAW HIS GLORY, AND SPOKE OF HIM."

The exegesis is:

1. Salvation by works? Without exception, such always leads to despair.

2. The Believer must keep his gaze fixed on Christ Crucified.

3. Christ was set forth as a Propitiation to satisfy the Anger of God in order that we might be accepted freely through the Blood of the Lord Jesus Christ.

THE JEHOVAH OF THE OLD TESTAMENT WAS JESUS

In Verse 41, John proclaims that the Vision Isaiah had of the Lord (Isa. 6:1-2) was actually of the pre-Incarnate Christ. So, we are here told that the Jehovah of the Old Testament was Jesus.

In the Vision, he saw *"His Glory,"* which was not obvious in His Appearance as the Incarnate Christ. However, that was in appearance only, for His Miracles and Message spoke preponderantly of His Deity, but it was still unrecognized by the religious leadership of Israel. However, their unbelief in no way made Him any less than what He really was, *"God manifest in the flesh"* (Isa. 7:14).

(42) "NEVERTHELESS AMONG THE CHIEF RULERS ALSO MANY BELIEVED ON HIM; BUT BECAUSE OF THE

PHARISEES THEY DID NOT CONFESS HIM, LEST THEY BE PUT OUT OF THE SYNAGOGUE."

The diagram is:

1. Why did it have to be Christ Crucified?

2. It was because a perfect substitute was needed in order to reconcile man to God.

3. Fear is dispelled in no other way but by the Cross of Christ.

MAN FEAR

The phrase, *"Nevertheless among the Chief Rulers also many believed on Him,"* does not relate exactly who they were, with the exception of Nicodemus and Joseph of Arimathea.

The others, and even these two, it seems, were at first ashamed and afraid to confess their Faith; however, the two mentioned did identify themselves with Him as He died on Calvary.

The phrase, *"But because of the Pharisees they did not confess Him, lest they be put out of the synagogue,"* proclaims not only their excuses but the excuses of many millions the world over.

In fact, Nicodemus and Joseph of Arimathea were Pharisees themselves, as well as being members of the Sanhedrin. Also, it is probably true that other Pharisees accepted Christ, but only a few.

At first glance, this seems strange, especially considering that the Pharisees claimed to be fundamentalists, in other words, to believe all of the Bible. They were the religious guides of Israel but were bitterly opposed to Christ.

I have noticed it in my own Ministry. Many who claim to be fundamentalists are very difficult to reach with the deeper Things of God because, as the Pharisees of old, they think they already have everything and, consequently, need nothing! That is the very reason that the far greater majority of them have rejected the Baptism with the Holy Spirit.

Conversely, modernists know they do not have anything, at least the things promised in the Word of God; consequently, it is easier to reach them than even their extremely religious counterparts.

To accept Christ then meant to be put out of organized religion, i.e., *"the synagogue."*

It is fastly coming to that very same place at the present!

(43) "FOR THEY LOVED THE PRAISE OF MEN MORE THAN THE PRAISE OF GOD."

The structure is:

1. The Infinite Son of God became Man, and he hung upon a Cross and was cursed so that you might not be cursed but be free from the curse.

2. How foolish then to try to walk in the labyrinth of works of self-righteousness, of my own merit.

3. The Gospel is not insight for living. The Gospel is not tips for living. The Gospel of Christ Crucified is for sinners.

THE PRAISE OF MEN

The phrase, *"For they loved the praise of men,"* speaks of religious men.

"More than the Praise of God," means they counted Him as less than these *"men."*

The word *"praise"* in the Greek, at least in the manner in which it is used here, means *"glory."* So, it means that the Glory of God Himself in His awful Holiness was of less interest than the glory of the Sanhedrin and the approval of the world. This *"glory"* is nearer, more obvious, and has more to do with tangible and sensuous advantages than the Divine approval.

This one Passage tells us two things:

1. It tells us why sinful men do not come to God even though they believe that Jesus is the Lord of Glory and the Saviour of the world. They fear what their fellowman will say.

2. It tells us why religious people do not receive God's Best. They count the approval of men as worth more than the Approval of God, even though they know and realize the truth of what they lack.

These particular religious leaders in Jesus' Day knew that He was the Messiah. They had become convinced in their own hearts that He was the One promised by the Prophets. His Miracles were undeniable, as well as the things He said. Without a doubt, He was the Fulfillment of the Prophecies.

THE PRICE TAG

But yet, to accept Him publicly, which

He had already stated must be done, had a price tag attached, which they felt was more than they could pay. He had publicly stated that if one accepted Him, one must publicly confess Him before men. If one did not, one could not be said to be a true Follower of Christ (Mat. 10:32; Lk. 12:8).

To publicly confess Christ, they would be summarily dismissed from their place and position. On top of that, they would be excommunicated from the synagogue, meaning that they would be placed outside the boundaries of all organized religion in Israel.

Also, the possibility definitely existed that their economic situation would immediately be drastically changed. In addition, they would lose all their friends and become the laughing stock of the other religious leaders of Israel. As well, their families would be held up to ridicule, and their world as they had come to know it would simply cease to exist.

Most felt that the price was too high, so they simply said and did nothing.

However, the truth of the matter was that the price was far higher in the other direction. They lost their souls, which was the grandest possession of all.

Let these Passages ever be a warning to all that one cannot have the praise of men and of God at the same time. It simply cannot be. If religious men and the world's system embrace the preacher of the gospel, it is a sure sign that he has compromised that which he is commissioned to deliver. If he truly preaches the Gospel without fear, compromise, or favor, he will, without exception, incur the wrath not only of the system of this world but of the religious system as well!

(44) "JESUS CRIED AND SAID, HE WHO BELIEVES ON ME, BELIEVES NOT ON ME, BUT ON HIM WHO SENT ME."

The synopsis is:

1. The Gospel is really an ugly Portrait of a Crucified Jew with blood, dirt, filth, pain, gore, and flies. It is the Son of God bearing your sin, no matter what that sin has been.

2. It is not a pretty picture, and it was never meant to be a pretty picture, but in that Cross is Life.

3. God's Answer to sin and to sinners is the Cross of Christ. Rejecting that, there is no other means of Salvation.

BELIEVING CHRIST

The phrase, *"Jesus cried and said, He who believes on Me,"* proclaims the absolute necessity of believing on Christ as God manifest in the flesh and, therefore, the Saviour of mankind. Jesus is not just one of the Prophets or one of the good men of history, but He is unalterably, unequivocally, and undeniably the God of Heaven come down among men. One must believe that in order to be Saved.

"Believes not on Me, but on Him Who sent Me," in effect, says, *"Believes not just on Me, but on Him Who sent Me."*

It is not possible to have the Son without the Father, as it is impossible to have the Father without the Son. To accept One is to accept the Other, and to refuse to accept either is to refuse to accept both. Consequently, the Muslims are not truly praying to God, whom they call *"Allah,"* simply because they refuse to recognize that Jesus is God's Son, and only through Him can the Father be reached.

(45) "AND HE WHO SEES ME SEES HIM WHO SENT ME."

The composition is:

1. The Gospel of Jesus Christ is never based upon your feelings!

2. The Gospel is not something that is based upon your changing moods.

3. The Gospel does not depend upon your whims or your changing emotions. We're Saved on account of Christ through Faith.

BY FAITH

The phrase, *"And he who sees Me,"* had to be done by Faith because Christ in His Human Form offered no expression of Deity. As stated, He was but a Peasant even though performing Miracles and proclaiming the Word of God as no man ever had. So, one had to have Faith in order to *"see Him"* as He truly was and is.

The phrase, *"Sees Him Who sent Me,"* presents a pinnacle which can only be reached if one sees Jesus properly.

When He is seen according to the Word of God, then one instantly begins to see the Father.

The Incarnation of Christ is the sticking point of most of mankind.

Man is loath to believe that he is a sinner in desperate need of a Saviour. He seems to realize that something is wrong, but he thinks that the maladjustment is minor and can be corrected with proper education, therapy, counseling, etc.

When he finally arrives at the spiritual place to where he admits he is hopelessly lost, he is very close to Salvation. The admittance of being lost is, at the same time, admitting the need of a Saviour, and that Jesus Christ is that Saviour, and that Saviour Alone!

DIRE CIRCUMSTANCES

To come to this place, man oftentimes has to come to dire circumstances, whether domestic, physical, economic, or spiritual. Until then, he thinks of himself as invincible, impregnable, and untouchable.

One of the major problems with man, which presents a large part of Satan's grand scheme, is that, in his unconverted state, he cannot understand God or anything about Him or His Word. These things are a total blank to the unconverted mind. Consequently, whatever he says about God, God's Word, the Holy Spirit, or the Lord Jesus Christ has no resemblance whatsoever to the Truth. These things are spiritually discerned, and he has absolutely no spirituality whatsoever in this unconverted state to discern anything (I Cor. 2:14).

Consequently, the Word of God must be presented to Him, with the Holy Spirit using the Word to reveal his lost condition and need for Christ.

Speaking of the lost is one thing while speaking of the religious lost is something else altogether! It is difficult to reach them, even as Israel of old, because they think they have the Light, not realizing that what they actually have is error and, consequently, *"darkness."* Jesus said, *"If therefore the light* (false light) *that is in you be darkness, how great is that darkness!"* (Mat. 6:23).

Inasmuch as they are in *"darkness,"* it is very difficult for them to *"see"* anything, hence, Israel's state!

(46) "I AM COME A LIGHT INTO THE WORLD, THAT WHOSOEVER BELIEVES ON ME SHOULD NOT ABIDE IN DARKNESS."

The diagram is:

1. The Gospel is not based upon our moral condition but is based on His Moral Condition.

2. Believe it or not, Christ died for our failures as well!

3. It is not my worth but the Worth of Christ that saves me.

JESUS IS THE LIGHT

The phrase, *"I am come a Light into the world,"* reveals His Purpose as Verses 41, 44, and 45 reveal the dignity of His Person as God. As we have stated, when Isaiah in a Vision saw Jehovah sitting upon a Throne, high and lifted up, He saw Him Who would be revealed in time as Jesus of Nazareth. Jesus Himself said that whoever believed upon Him, believed upon God, whoever saw Him, saw God, and that He was the Light and, therefore, God.

Jesus as the *"Light"* reveals all understanding, all purifying, and all gracious influence which are shed on human affairs, nature, or destiny. All are the result of the Divine Life which, under every Dispensation, has wrought great things in humanity. As stated, all of this is in Jesus and Jesus Alone!

As a perfect example, one can look at the nations of the world presently which, in some semblance, recognize Jesus or recognize Him not at all. Those which recognize Him, at least in some fashion, are the bearers of Light, prosperity, freedom, and, actually, the nations which set the standard for the world. To be sure, and regrettably, even these proclaim Jesus only partially so by allowing freedom of religion, etc.

NO LIGHT

However, I must quickly add that nations of the world where Catholicism is predominant are not in any sense proclaimers of Jesus Christ. In these countries, Mary is the standard of righteousness, which is grossly unscriptural and, therefore, no righteousness at all.

The nations of the world, which little

proclaim Jesus, offer to the world little prosperity, freedom, or advancement.

Of course, one could look at Japan and hold up their prosperity as an example, even though Jesus Christ plays no part in their affairs or worship, with that nation being Shintoist or Buddhist. While that may be true, still, their prosperity is owed primarily to America, which, at least to some extent, does champion the Lord Jesus Christ.

One can say without any fear of Biblical contradiction that every iota of progress made in the world through the many centuries, be it in the realm of technology, freedom, prosperity, or proper government, all can be traced back to Jesus Christ, the Light of the world.

NOT ABIDE IN DARKNESS

The phrase, *"That whosoever believes on Me should not abide in darkness,"* proclaims exactly that which I have just stated.

In Christ Alone is the *"Light,"* and without Him, there is nothing left but *"darkness."*

Naturally, Jesus is speaking here of spiritual darkness; however, with spiritual darkness comes social darkness, economic darkness, technological darkness, and political darkness.

Again I wish to emphasize the point that Jesus did not say, *"Whosoever believes on Mary or some dead Saint,"* etc., but on Him Personally! As well, there is no hint whatsoever in the Word of God of Mary being the gate or door to Jesus. Such teaching is actually of darkness and only foments more darkness.

There is not a true Believer who reads these words but that he or she can look back at their lives before Christ, and now that they are in the Light, the darkness of those bygone days is now so obvious. However, until one truly has the *"Light,"* i.e., the Lord Jesus Christ, one has no idea of the magnitude of his darkness. One can only gauge or measure such darkness by the present Light which he now has. That is the reason the unbeliever scoffs at these statements. He does not know or realize the degree of his spiritual blindness.

(47) "AND IF ANY MAN HEAR MY WORDS, AND BELIEVE NOT, I JUDGE HIM NOT: FOR I CAME NOT TO JUDGE THE WORLD, BUT TO SAVE THE WORLD."

The structure is:

1. As you live life with your best intentions, you are going to fail! Go to the Cross and receive bravely that which the Cross offers you, which is victory.

2. There are only two ways in the world: they are the religion of law and the Gospel of Grace.

3. In Grace alone, which streams from the Cross, there is victory.

JESUS CAME NOT TO JUDGE

The phrase, *"And if any man hear My Words, and believe not, I judge him not,"* means that He is not now pronouncing sentence. He has come as Saviour. Were that not true, the world would have been destroyed at His First Coming simply because only a precious few then truly believed Him. Actually, the same could be said for any generation.

Consequently, men scoff at God and blaspheme His Name, but because they do not suffer immediate ill effects, they claim there is no God, etc.

Oh yes, there is a God, and He is just as involved in the affairs of men as the Bible proclaims; however, He is here now to save and not condemn.

The phrase, *"For I came not to judge the world, but to save the world,"* proclaims His Present Mission, which has lasted now for nearly 2,000 years.

However, in the future, in the near future at that, Jesus Christ will judge this world, which will be in the time of the coming Great Tribulation. At that time, the Scripture says, *"The great day of His Wrath is come; and who shall be able to stand?"* (Rev. 6:17).

SAVIOUR TODAY, JUDGE TOMORROW

As well, the Lord will judge the entirety of mankind who has ever lived, at least those who are unbelievers, at the Great White Throne Judgment (Rev. 20:11-15). This Judgment will take place at the end of the one thousand year Millennial Reign of Christ called, *"The Kingdom Age."*

So, do not mistake His Lack of Judgment now, at least in the totality in which it will come in the future, as a condoning of evil or a lack of power.

The type of Judgment of which Jesus here speaks, which pertains to His Personal Judgment, is not to be confused with the Judgment which comes because of the Law of Sowing and Reaping, at least sowing that which is evil, etc. In fact, that Judgment came upon Israel in A.D. 70 when Titus completely destroyed Jerusalem and the Nation of Israel as a whole. That type of Judgment is also constantly at work in the world, in individuals, and in entire nations.

Please understand, while Jesus Christ is the Saviour of man today, He will be the Judge tomorrow. One thing is certain, in one way or the other, every human being is going to face Jesus Christ.

(48) "HE WHO REJECTS ME, AND RECEIVES NOT MY WORDS, HAS ONE WHO JUDGES HIM: THE WORD THAT I HAVE SPOKEN, THE SAME SHALL JUDGE HIM IN THE LAST DAY."

The exegesis is:

1. The Good News of the Gospel declares that you must get rid of the idea that you can do anything to be accepted by God!

2. It is one-hundred percent Christ. It is zero concerning what you do.

3. It is all of Grace from first to last.

THE WORDS OF GOD

The phrase, *"He who rejects Me, and receives not My Words, has One Who judges,"* presents a Truth that the church, and the entirety of the world, for that matter, desperately needs to hear and understand. As is here plainly stated, the criteria are Jesus Christ and the Word of God.

The phrase, *"The Word that I have spoken, the same shall judge him in the last day,"* speaks of the *"Judgment Seat of Christ"* for Believers and the *"Great White Throne Judgment"* for unbelievers.

The former will take place immediately before the Second Coming of the Lord and, of course, after the Rapture. Sins will not here be judged, for that was already done at Calvary. The *"works"* of the Believer will here be judged as to one's motives, actions, and reasons. While no one's soul will be lost, rewards then will definitely be lost because of wrong motives, etc.

The Word of God will be the criterion for this Judgment of one's works.

As well, the Word of God will be the criterion for the Great White Throne Judgment. In fact, no one at that Judgment will be saved, but all will be lost. Consequently, it's purpose will not be to ascertain one's Salvation, for there will be no one who has Salvation, but rather the reason for their being lost, i.e., the rejection of Jesus Christ and the Word of God. As well, every single sin and action of each will stand on the record and will be undeniable.

AN AWFUL UTTERANCE

One writer said, *"There is no more awful utterance than this Statement made by Jesus concerning each and every person being judged according to His Word."*

This means that no one will be able to hold up his church, doctrine, or even another person as the standard of Judgment. Hundreds of millions of people have died eternally lost because they did not know the Word of God for themselves, but blindly followed some church, preacher, etc. In fact, hundreds of thousands of preachers and priests encourage people to follow them exclusively, irrespective of what is demanded. They claim that if they are wrong, they will be responsible and not the one who is following.

Nothing could be more untrue! In all cases, the Word of God will be the criterion and not someone or something else. In other words, no one will be able to say in that day, *"But Lord, he said so, and inasmuch as he was a spiritual leader, I thought he could be trusted!"* In fact, some few can be trusted; however, it is incumbent upon each and every Believer to know the Word of God for themselves. To blindly follow someone or a church denomination is spiritual ignorance of the highest order and has caused untold millions to be cast into Hell!

Actually, such blind following is the foundation of the entirety of the Roman Catholic church. In this church, the Bible is not the criterion, but rather the teachings of the church, which changes constantly, and which the far greater majority of the time contradicts the Word of God. However, hundreds of millions follow this gross error, and hundreds of millions are lost.

THE RIGHT WAY AND THE WRONG WAY

As well, even in many Protestant churches, the people are strongly encouraged at times to do what the preacher says do, irrespective of its Scriptural veracity or the lack thereof. In fact, the Pentecostal denomination with which I was once formerly associated has come to the place that some of its leaders tell their preachers that what they say must be obeyed, whether it is Scriptural or not! Some have plainly stated that the Scripturality of the demand is not the business of the preacher but of the leader. *"And if it is wrong,"* they say, *"it will be our responsibility alone."*

Nothing could be more wrong or more unscriptural, and, to be sure, any preacher or person who would yield to such stupidity is not only bringing great harm to his Ministry but, as well, is putting his very soul in danger.

The preacher I quoted above who spoke of the terrible significance of this Statement by Christ was right in what he said. Men will answer personally according to the Word, but most do not know or understand that. Most people look for an excuse to divest themselves of responsibility. They want to put the blame on others. Consequently, to have others making spiritual decisions for them, especially those who have high sounding religious titles, places an aura of legitimacy on their actions. As well, it is much easier to simply follow someone blindly, rather than digging into the Word of God to see what it actually says.

Also, people have a tendency to gravitate toward those who tell them what they want to hear. Many are afraid that if they seriously study the Word of God, they will have to change some of their ways or beliefs. Consequently, it is much easier to simply find someone with whom they agree, and, in most cases, who condones their wrongdoing, etc., with that person, at least in the Believer's mind, taking the responsibility.

(49) "FOR I HAVE NOT SPOKEN OF MYSELF; BUT THE FATHER WHICH SENT ME, HE GAVE ME A COMMANDMENT, WHAT I SHOULD SAY, AND WHAT I SHOULD SPEAK."

The exegesis is:

1. The question is: *"Is the Cross of Christ staked at the core of your being?"*

2. When Jesus and His Work at the Cross are marginalized, it creates a vacuum.

3. The Cross of Christ is the Means, and the only Means, by which all of the good things come to us from God.

THE FATHER WHO SENT ME

The phrase, *"For I have not spoken of Myself,"* means that His Words are not simply His Own, but rather from the Father, i.e., in effect, the entirety of the Godhead.

The phrase, *"But the Father Who sent Me,"* presents His Claims in the Light of something far greater than Himself Alone. He was sent by the Father for a distinct Purpose and Mission. Consequently, the reaction to Him by Israel, or anyone for that matter, is a reaction to the entirety of the Bible and the Divine Trinity. In other words, when one deals with Jesus, he is dealing with the Entirety of the Godhead and, as well, one cannot deal with the Godhead unless he deals with Jesus.

The phrase, *"He gave me a Commandment, what I should say, and what I should speak,"* in effect says, *"In rejecting Me and My Words, men reject and insult the Father. His Word that they dare to renounce is as solemn and unalterable as the Word spoken on Sinai. They not only reject Me, but they count themselves unworthy of Eternal Life. They not only spurn Law, but, as well, they spurn Love."*

(50) "AND I KNOW THAT HIS COMMANDMENT IS LIFE EVERLASTING: WHATSOEVER I SPEAK THEREFORE, EVEN AS THE FATHER SAID UNTO ME, SO I SPEAK."

The construction is:

1. The fact that the fire was to never go out on the Brazen Altar of old proclaims the fact that the Cross Alone is the answer to the sins of mankind.

2. Furthermore, it proclaims that it will ever be the answer.

3. The fact that it was to never go out also proclaims the absolute necessity that we understand that the Cross is the Foundation of our Faith. It is not a mere Doctrine, but rather the Foundation of all Doctrine.

LIFE EVERLASTING

The phrase, *"And I know that His Commandment is Life Everlasting,"* says that in His Words is Life Everlasting and, as well, says that Life Everlasting is found in the words of no one else. This completely shoots down every religion, belief, or faith in the entirety of the world that is not based squarely on the Word of God.

The phrase, *"Whatsoever I speak therefore, even as the Father said unto Me, so I speak,"* means that His Doctrine, its Substance, and the very words used in its proclamation are all of Divine Origin.

Thus, He here destroys the theory that He was only a Jew of His Day, teaching what He had learned from His Human Teachers.

In effect, He says that what He has spoken is not from Himself. His Constant Claim was that what He taught, even His Very Words were from the Father. If, therefore, He erred, God erred!

So, the Gospel which He preached from the Father was Life Everlasting if received and eternal Judgment if rejected.

"More about Jesus would I know,
"More of His Grace to others show;
"More of His Saving Fullness see,
"More of His Love Who died for me."

CHAPTER 13

(1) "NOW BEFORE THE FEAST OF THE PASSOVER, WHEN JESUS KNEW THAT HIS HOUR WAS COME THAT HE SHOULD DEPART OUT OF THIS WORLD UNTO THE FATHER, HAVING LOVED HIS OWN WHICH WERE IN THE WORLD, HE LOVED THEM UNTO THE END."

The exposition is:

1. Religious men have always wanted revival without repentance and, above all, revival without the Cross, but such is not to be.

2. Let all understand, God has no other way, no other path, and no other solution — only the Cross.

3. When Believers look to the Cross, God gets the glory, but when they look to other things, man gets the glory.

THE FEAST OF THE PASSOVER

The phrase, *"Now before the Feast of the Passover,"* refers to the preparation day of the Passover, which would have been the fourteenth of the month, our Tuesday sunset to Wednesday sunset, the day of the Crucifixion.

Incidentally, Jesus was not crucified on a Friday as is commonly believed, but rather a Wednesday. He stayed three full days and nights in the Tomb. He was raised from the dead probably very shortly after the sun had set on Saturday evening.

The way that the Jews reckoned time then was by sunset. At that time, a new day began. Presently, we reckon time for a new day to begin at midnight.

This Passover was very special, actually, the most special one of all the last nearly 1,600 years, in that He would fulfill the type. He would literally become the Sin-Offering, i.e., actually *"the Lamb of God."*

HIS HOUR

The phrase, *"When Jesus knew that His Hour was come,"* refers to the Crucifixion, which was the purpose for which He came. In order to redeem man, this was an absolute necessity. There was no other way! It would actually constitute the greatest *"hour"* in human history before or since. There, and we speak of Calvary, every sin would be atoned, past, present, and future, at least for all who would believe (Jn. 3:16). As well, the grip of sin, so to speak, would be broken, along with Satan and all principalities and powers defeated (Col. 2:14-15).

THE RESURRECTION AND THE ASCENSION

The phrase, *"That He should depart out of this world unto the Father,"* refers to the Resurrection and the Ascension.

Because of what He did at Calvary, upon death, the Believer instantly goes to be with the Heavenly Father. Therefore, Jesus made and paved the way, so to speak.

Before Calvary, Believers were taken down into Paradise where they were actually held captive by Satan. However, when Jesus paid the price at Calvary, He went down into Paradise and *"led captivity captive."* That strange phrase means that all of those people in Paradise were held captive by Satan. He could not hurt them, but because the blood of bulls and goats could not take away sins, they were still under his domain. However, when Jesus died on the Cross, which atoned for all sin, Satan now had no more claim on anyone, and we speak of all who were in Paradise and all on Earth who had trusted Him. He made all of those in Paradise His Captives, with them being immediately transported to Glory. Now, when Believers die, their soul and their spirit instantly go to be with the Lord (Eph. 4:8-10; Phil. 1:23-24).

LOVE

The phrase, *"Having loved His Own which were in the world, He loved them unto the end,"* presents not so much an expression of time as of degree. He loved them to the uttermost, to any extent and to any depth, even to becoming a Slave and washing their feet, and the next day suffering the shameful death of a slave.

Such is His Love for the Church: His Body. I do not think that any of us quite understand the Love of God as we should. To be frank, I think it is impossible for a human being to fully comprehend God's Love and, as well, His Love extended to us.

(2) "AND SUPPER BEING ENDED, THE DEVIL HAVING NOW PUT INTO THE HEART OF JUDAS ISCARIOT, SIMON'S SON, TO BETRAY HIM."

1. Our Faith is ever to be in Christ and what He did at the Cross.

2. The Story of the Bible, all the way from Genesis 1:1 through Revelation 22:21, is *"Jesus Christ and Him Crucified."*

3. Every sacrifice offered in Old Testament times was a Picture, a Portrayal, and a Symbol of Christ and what He would do for us at the Cross.

NOTES

JUDAS ISCARIOT

The phrase, *"And supper being ended,"* actually refers to the *"preparation"* for the supper being ended and not the supper itself. Actually, it was just beginning.

In effect, this was the time in which our Lord terminated the Old Testament Dispensation and introduced the New.

"The Devil having now put into the heart of Judas Iscariot," means that a short time before, Satan did this thing.

Satan suggested the betrayal to the heart of Judas, and with this suggestion being entertained, he then took possession of him (Vs. 27).

Even though the idea came from the Devil, still, the purpose of the Devil was not irrevocable. Judas could have then thrown it off, and most certainly could have when Jesus appealed to him (Vs. 26). In other words, it was not predestined that Judas do this thing. The act and the choice were his even though spurred by the Evil One.

Some claim that Judas was evil from the very beginning, in other words, from the very moment that Jesus chose him. That is not correct. Our Lord prayed all night long, seeking the Father's Will as it regarded who would be the chosen Twelve. The Father would not have picked one that was of the Devil.

As well, Jesus gave His Twelve Disciples, which included Judas, *"power against unclean spirits, to cast them out, and to heal all manner of sickness and all manner of disease"* (Mat. 10:1). To give someone power to cast out unclean spirits who was of the Devil himself would have posed Satan working against himself, which Jesus plainly said would not happen (Mat. 12:26).

No! At a point in time, which was actually Judas rejecting the Message of the Cross, even as we have already stated, was when he began to turn (Jn. 6:71). It seems that with this Message as delivered by Christ, the Message of the Cross, rebellion began in Judas' heart.

The Cross of Christ is the only thing standing between man and eternal Hell. That rejected, there is no more avenue of escape.

Looking at the modern church, the Holy Spirit, even through this Ministry (Jimmy Swaggart Ministries), is beginning to proclaim the Message of the Cross all over the world. Please understand, if it is rejected, the end result will be the loss of the soul for the majority, even as Judas. When men reject the Cross, and I especially speak of the church, they have rejected the only means of Salvation. I might quickly add this:

It is impossible for Believers to accept humanistic psychology and still retain that which the Cross of Christ affords. One or the other must go. Either one cancels out the other. Regrettably, as stated, the modern church, for the most part, has embraced humanistic psychology. In other words, they have opted for man's way, thereby, rejecting God's Way.

THE BETRAYAL

The phrase, *"Simon's son, to betray Him,"* speaks of betraying Christ to the religious leaders of Israel. In other words, as sordid, sick, and sinful as the vices are, it was not the thieves, the drunks, etc., who crucified Christ, but rather the church. The ironic thing about it is, they crucified the Lord in the Name of the Lord. What a travesty!

Only God knows what was in the mind of Judas at this time. However, the possibility does suggest itself that he thought Jesus would use His Great Power in order to overthrow the efforts of this ungodly High Priest. In his thinking, that is, if these were his thoughts, Jesus would then be forced to take over the rulership of Israel and use His Great Power, which would then catapult the Nation to greatness. However, he completely misread Christ, even as did the other Disciples, concerning His Purpose and Mission.

The Cross was always the Purpose and Mission of Christ. That's why He came. Man's problem, including Israel, was sin, and the only solution for sin is *"Jesus Christ and Him Crucified."*

As well, whatever these thoughts were in the hearts of the other Disciples, it seems that none went so deep as that of Judas. If Jesus would not take the initiative in this direction, then Judas would!

Of course, what we say is mere speculation. But yet, the evidence somewhat leads in that direction. This is self-will run riot, which, in effect, plays God, and is actually the same sin committed by Adam and Eve in the Garden of Eden. They wanted, as well, to play God, going in a direction forbidden by the Lord. Let me say it again:

The only solution for man's problem is the Cross of Christ. There is no other, as there need be no other. As we've already stated the following in this Volume, still, because of the tremendous significance of what we are attempting to say, please allow the following repetition:

• Jesus Christ is the Source of all things we receive from God (Jn. 1:1-3, 14, 29; Col. 2:10-15).

• With Jesus Christ as the Source, the Cross of Christ is the Means, and the only Means, by which all of these good things are given to us (Rom. 6:1-14; Gal., Chpt. 5; 6:14; Col. 2:14-15).

• With our Lord as the Source and the Cross as the Means, the Object of Faith must be the Cross of Christ, and the Cross of Christ alone. Of course, the reader understands that we aren't speaking of the wooden beam on which Jesus died, but rather the price He there paid and the Victory He there accomplished. Faith in anything else constitutes *"spiritual adultery"* (I Cor. 1:17, 18, 21, 23; 2:2; Rom. 7:1-4).

• With our Lord as the Source, the Cross as the Means, and the Cross as the Object of our Faith, and the Cross alone as the Object of our Faith, then the Holy Spirit, Who works exclusively within the parameters, so to speak, of the Finished Work of Christ, will then grandly and gloriously help us to live this life we ought to live. It is the Cross of Christ which gave and gives the Holy Spirit the legal right and the legal means to do all that He does. There, all sin was atoned, which opened the door for the Spirit of God to do great things for the Believer, even to live within our hearts and lives forever. This is God's Way, and it is the only Way of life and living. It is the Message of the Cross (Rom. 8:1-11; Eph. 2:13-18).

(3) "JESUS KNOWING THAT THE FATHER HAD GIVEN ALL THINGS INTO

HIS HANDS, AND THAT HE WAS COME FROM GOD, AND WENT TO GOD."

The construction is:

1. God has no respect for any proposed way of Salvation other than *"Jesus Christ and Him Crucified."*

2. If sin in someway is dominating the Child of God, this means that the Believer is not properly availing himself of the great Victory purchased by Christ at the Cross.

3. Considering the price that He there paid, it is a travesty of the highest sort for us not to avail ourselves of all that for which He has paid.

THE DEITY OF CHRIST

The phrase, *"Jesus knowing that the Father had given all things into His Hands,"* portrays two things in His Heart as He girded Himself (Vs. 4):

1. His Conscious Deity.
2. The heartless conduct of Judas.

But neither the Glory of the Divine relationship, which had given all things into the Hands of Christ, nor the anguish of a treachery that delivered Him into sinner's hands, chilled the love which bound His Heart to the Disciples, or caused it to forget their needs, or their sorrows (Williams)[1].

The phrase, *"And that He was come from God, and went to God,"* was not something that Christ came to know, but He knew all these things about Himself all along.

As to the exact time He knew this is not known, but it seems from His Statement in Luke 2:42-49 that He did know such by the time He was 12 years old.

Paul, in his Epistle to the Philippians (2:6-8), had adequately grasped the same thought long before John penned this Gospel (II Cor. 8:9).

(4) "HE ROSE FROM SUPPER, AND LAID ASIDE HIS GARMENTS; AND TOOK A TOWEL, AND GIRDED HIMSELF."

The construction is:

1. The Cross came up before God as the Holiest Work of the Saviour, eclipsing any and everything else which He had done, as important as all the other things may have been.

2. That's the reason that Paul said, *"But God forbid that I should glory* (boast), *save in the Cross of our Lord Jesus Christ, by Whom the world is crucified unto me, and I unto the world"* (Gal. 6:14).

3. The fact that the fire on the Altar of old was to never go out proclaims the fact that the Cross alone is the answer to the sins of mankind and, furthermore, that it will ever be the answer, and the only answer.

THE SUPPER

The phrase, *"He rose from supper,"* means He rose from the table when the preparation had been completed and not after the supper had been eaten. What He would do, the washing of their feet, was His Answer to their argument about who would be *"the greatest among them"* (Lk. 22:24).

During the early time of His Ministry, He had rebuked this kind of spirit by setting a little child in their midst and stating that they had to become as little children and not seek to lord it over each other (Mat. 18:1-10).

Some time had gone by now, but they had not yet learned their lesson, it seems! Our Lord must rid from among them this passion for worldly honor and dignity, which would have wrecked the foundation of the Church after His Death.

LAID ASIDE HIS GARMENTS

The phrase, *"And laid aside His Garments,"* refers to the removing of His Outer Robe. It, as well, refers to His Incarnation. At that time, He laid aside the expression of Deity while never losing its possession. Paul said, *"But made Himself of no reputation, and took upon Him the form of a servant, and was made in the likeness of men"* (Phil. 2:7).

AND TOOK A TOWEL

The phrase, *"And took a towel,"* refers to the action of the lowliest slave or servant in the household. As well, the *"towel"* represents the servant spirit possessed by Christ.

Nothing is more amazing than the fact of God assuming manhood in order to serve man. Man could only be Saved through the self-humiliation of Christ.

AND GIRDED HIMSELF

The phrase, *"And girded Himself,"* speaks of wrapping Himself in the towel. Such He did, as well, in the Human Body provided for Him by the Father (Heb. 10:5).

As we have previously indicated, Jesus was completely Human, so much so, in fact, that the prideful Pharisees could not see His Deity. This was necessary for two reasons:

1. It was imperative that He have a Human Body in order that it could be offered in Sacrifice, which it was. God cannot die! Therefore, He had to take upon Himself Human Form, which, in fact, constituted the Only Perfect Human Being Who ever lived.

2. He was a Peasant even though of the royal lineage of David through Solomon. This was in the Plan of God as well!

The problem with the human family was pride. Therefore, He would be the very opposite of this malady, which is humility, i.e., *"meek and lowly in heart"* (Mat. 11:28-30).

(5) "AFTER THAT HE POURED WATER INTO A BASIN, AND BEGAN TO WASH THE DISCIPLES' FEET, AND TO WIPE THEM WITH THE TOWEL WHEREWITH HE WAS GIRDED."

The diagram is:

1. The truth is, there is less preaching of the Cross presently than there has been at any time, I believe, since the Reformation.

2. This means that the church presently, sad to say, is in worse spiritual condition than it has been at any time since the Reformation.

3. The Holy Spirit is given less and less place because the preaching of the Cross has been given less and less place.

THE SERVANT PRINCIPLE

The phrase, *"After that He poured water into a basin,"* proclaims His Ministry and Life as a Servant and, consequently, an example to the Church.

The crowning trump of unsaved man is to be served by others. The more who serve him (or her), the greater the individual is in the eyes of the world; however, with Christ, it is the opposite! Greatness resides in the person according to the number of people he serves and the manner in which the serving is done.

How so obvious it then becomes as to the way of the world and the Way of the Lord; one is served while the other serves. The first breeds pride while the latter breeds humility. Here, more than all, is the definition of true Christianity.

WASHING THE FEET OF THE DISCIPLES

The phrase, *"And began to wash the Disciples' feet,"* was done even though He was about to leave them and resume the Glory which He had with the Father before the world was. So, He would fit them to walk with Him in the life of communion. To walk those courts, they needed cleansed feet, i.e., a cleansed spiritual walk. This is walking after the Spirit.

However, the teaching of the *"Servant Principle,"* which His Entire Incarnation portrayed, was epitomized, most of all, as John portrayed it by this example.

Williams said, *"The Lord's lowly action in washing as a slave the feet of the Disciples, Judas included, was performed however in the consciousness of His essential Deity, and because of His Godhead, which more than all portrayed that great Truth."*[2]

The basin and the water in it figure the Bible and its contents.

As Jesus began to wash their feet, He is washing His People's Feet still with the washing of water by the Word. Its teaching, applied by the Spirit to the heart and conscience, instructs the Believer as to all that defiles, and by separating him from it, cleanses him.

Williams further said, *"In Luke 12:37 Jesus promises that He will in the Glory act as a Servant to those who love Him. There He will minister Heaven's highest joys to the satisfying of His people's deepest happiness."*[3]

THE TOWEL

The phrase, *"And to wipe them with the towel wherewith He was girded,"* adequately presents Jesus as a Servant but, more than all, portrays the Love of God as it probably could be portrayed in no other way.

The greatest Manifestation of God was in the Revelation of the exceeding limits and the infinite depth which Love could compass.

On this occasion, the highest conception

of His Divine Personality, Origin, and Destiny was blended with the deepest descent of the Lord's Entire Humanity to the level of weakness, pollution, and sin, even though He, of course, never sinned.

John did not record the *"Transfiguration,"* even though he was there. However, there were other moments, as well, in the Life and Ministry of Christ which produced a tremendously profound impression upon him, and in which he veritably saw the Glory of the Only Begotten of God in His Master's Form. This, without a doubt, is one of those occasions!

Too often, too many Believers are seeking royal robes when the suitable garment, as provided by Christ and that is more Christlike than anything else, is the *"towel."* However, it is not the *"towel"* as a symbol but the *"towel"* in use.

(6) "THEN COMETH HE TO SIMON PETER: AND PETER SAID UNTO HIM, LORD, DO YOU WASH MY FEET?"

The composition is:

1. All of the symbols, ceremonies, and rituals of the Old Covenant were Types of Christ.

2. When Christ came, He fulfilled them all, hence, we have presently a *"better Covenant"* based on *"better Promises"* (Heb. 8:6).

3. All the lambs offered under the Old Covenant were to be without blemish because they typified Christ.

SIMON PETER

The phrase, *"Then came He to Simon Peter,"* seems to indicate that it was Peter whom He first approached.

The Holy Spirit with purpose uses both names for Peter. The name, *"Simon,"* means, *"Hearing,"* while *"Peter"* means, *"A piece of a rock."* Consequently, Peter would ultimately become the *"rock,"* which his name portrays, if he would only *"hear"* and *"do"* the Word of God, which he did!

The question, *"And Peter said unto Him, Lord, do You wash my feet?"* was not asked out of stubbornness or self-will, but rather of embarrassment that the Lord of Glory would perform such a menial task, and he would be the beneficiary! At the moment, he did not understand the purpose or the reason, but very soon, he would!

Williams said, *"The flesh cannot understand spiritual realities. It is either too backward (Vs. 6), or too forward (Vs. 9), or too courageous (Vs. 37), or too cowardly (Vs. 38). It is incapable of ever being right: And it is impossible of improvement. Hence it must 'die.'"*[4]

(7) "JESUS ANSWERED AND SAID UNTO HIM, WHAT I DO YOU KNOW NOT NOW; BUT YOU SHALL KNOW HEREAFTER."

The order is:

1. At Calvary, our Lord took away our sin by taking away the debt. He paid the price, and with the price being paid there, there is no more debt and no more sin.

2. The blood of bulls and goats under the Old Covenant couldn't take away sins, so this means that the debt was not actually paid at that time.

3. The word *"Atonement,"* as used quite frequently under the Old Covenant, is used almost not at all in the New. Why? The word *"Atonement"* actually means *"to cover."* The Blood of Jesus Christ did not merely cover our sin, but rather took it away. That being the case, the word *"Atonement,"* regarding the New Covenant, would not really suffice (Jn. 1:29).

HEREAFTER

The phrase, *"Jesus answered and said unto him,"* presents an answer which, no doubt, caused Peter to think upon or contemplate the rest of his life.

"What I do you know not now; but you shall know hereafter," no doubt, referred to the coming of the Holy Spirit on the Day of Pentecost, Who filled the hearts and lives of the waiting Believers, Peter included.

The marked change in the Disciples after this momentous occasion (the coming of the Holy Spirit) is so obvious, and for the better, we must quickly add, that there is no comparison regarding before and after. Without a doubt, the Holy Spirit illuminated to the Disciples, and all others, for that matter, all the things that Jesus did portraying the deep Spiritual meaning in obvious clarity. Peter would not learn the lesson at the moment, but he would shortly, with his life of humility becoming a Testimony to the Power of the Person of Christ.

I know it can be said at present that the Entrance of the Holy Spirit into the heart and life of the Believer is of more value even than the Personal Presence of Christ when He walked the Earth. One could also say that God the Father and God the Son are with the Believer through the Person and Agency of the Holy Spirit to a far greater degree than He was with individuals when He was Personally present on Earth.

(8) "PETER SAID UNTO HIM, YOU SHALL NEVER WASH MY FEET. JESUS ANSWERED HIM, IF I WASH YOU NOT, YOU HAVE NO PART WITH ME."

The form is:

1. Any message referred to, other than the Message of the Cross, is labeled by the Holy Spirit as *"the great whore"* (Rev. 17:1).

2. When we think about such, it becomes an apt description.

3. The Cross of Christ is the only Way. There is no other as there need be no other.

THE WASHING OF THE FEET

The phrase, *"Peter said unto Him, You shall never wash my feet,"* actually says, *"Not while eternity lasts."*

Calvin said, and rightly so, *"With God obedience is better than worship."*[5]

The phrase, *"Jesus answered him, If I wash you not, you have no part with Me,"* presents the Lord replying in such a way that goes far beyond the symbolic washing, presenting a moral significance which He had not mentioned before, and with reason.

Jesus' Statement speaks to the constant cleansing needed regarding our everyday walk before Christ, which the washing of the feet, at least in part, represented.

Aaron's sons at their first consecration as Priests had been washed completely. That washing was not repeated because it spoke of one's Salvation.

However, for this heavenly life of communion and service, they needed cleansed feet, which they obtained by washing in the Brazen Laver every time they entered the Tabernacle.

Consequently, this tells us that while coming to Christ is one thing, continuing with Christ is something else altogether.

REPEATED INSPECTION BY THE WORD, WHICH ALSO CLEANSES

If Jesus is to be fully understood, He is telling us in His Statement to Peter that the Believer must have repeated inspection by the Word, which also cleanses, of which the Brazen Laver of the Old Covenant was a type. If it is not done, the terminology is clear and simple in that the Believer can ultimately lose his way, being rejected because of spiritual pollution.

Consequently, along with the teaching of the *"Servant Principle,"* as illustrated here, we learn of our continued need of perpetual spiritual washings of our spiritual feet in our daily walk before Christ in this world.

Now we understand more fully why the Priests had to wash their feet and their hands in the Brazen Laver every time they entered the Holy Place. Becoming defiled by occupational use, the hands and feet required continuous cleansing. That which was a type is no less incumbent upon the modern Believer presently, which is carried out by our occupation with the Word of God and the Moving of the Holy Spirit toward our consecration.

(9) "SIMON PETER SAID UNTO HIM, LORD, NOT MY FEET ONLY, BUT ALSO MY HANDS AND MY HEAD."

The pattern is:

1. The Precious shed Blood of Jesus Christ cleanses from all sin (I Jn. 1:7).

2. While the feet of the Believer, symbolically speaking, need constant washing because of our walk in this polluted world, the hands, symbolically speaking, do not need to be washed because that speaks of *"doing,"* which has already been done by Christ.

3. The foot washing lesson, as given by Christ, is extremely valuable, which makes it incumbent upon the Believer to understand what is being said and done.

PETERS REPLY

The phrase, *"Simon Peter said unto Him,"* presents, as usual, Peter going beyond the Lord.

Chrysostom says, *"In his deprecation he was vehement, and his yielding more* vehement, but both came from his love."[6]

Reynolds says, *"But even here we see the same eagerness in Peter to dictate the course to be pursued."*[7]

The phrase, *"Lord, not my feet only, but also my hands and my head,"* rightly proclaims his obedience but also shows his ignorance of the lesson being presented by Christ. However, he would learn this lesson well after the Advent of the Holy Spirit!

(10) "JESUS SAID TO HIM, HE WHO IS WASHED NEEDS NOT SAVE TO WASH HIS FEET, BUT IS CLEAN EVERY WHIT: AND YOU ARE CLEAN, BUT NOT ALL."

The structure is:

1. God's Way is the Cross of Christ. There is no other because no other is needed.

2. Satan doesn't too much care where we place our faith as Believers, just so it isn't the Cross.

3. It was at the Cross that Satan and all his cohorts of darkness were defeated. Hence, he hates the Cross, as should be obvious.

THE WASHING

The phrase, *"Jesus said to him, He who is washed needs not save to wash his feet,"* could have been translated, *"He who is washed completely needs afterward only that his feet be washed."*

As stated, the lesson which Jesus graphically teaches pertains to that which deals with our everyday walk before Christ. That's the reason that our Lord said we must take up the Cross daily (Lk. 9:23). It's almost as though we start all over again each and every morning with our Faith placed in the Cross of Christ. We must make certain that it is there placed. It is so easy for the Believer's faith to be moved to something else. The *"something else"* is always very religious, which deceives us. So, we must make sure that our Faith is properly placed.

Please understand that it's not so much what we do, but rather what we believe. If we believe correctly, then we're going to do correctly. If we try to do correctly without believing correctly, we will fail every single time.

IS CLEAN EVERY WHIT

The phrase, *"But is clean every whit,"* refers to Salvation and pertains to the Precious Blood of Jesus that cleanses from all sin (Heb., Chpts. 9-10). That one infinite Sacrifice needs no repetition. So, he who is *"bathed"* in that bath needs repeated washings only concerning that which pertains to his everyday walk before God. In other words, our Salvation does not come and go. This means that when the Believer sins, he doesn't have to get Saved all over again. He has only to go to Christ, confess his sin, and forgiveness and cleansing are instantly enjoined (I Jn. 1:9).

ONE HERE IS NOT CLEAN

The phrase, *"And you are clean, but not all,"* refers to all the Disciples being Saved, with one exception, who was Judas. At this time, he had already yielded to Satan and forfeited what he had had in previous days with Christ.

As Peter graphically learned this lesson as taught by Jesus and, as well, by the Holy Spirit, such possibly accounts for some of his intensely interesting expressions.

In I Peter 5:5, he enjoins Christians to *"tie on humility like a dress fastened with knots"* and, also, for his insight into the true meaning of Water Baptism as being not the putting away of the filth of the flesh, but the answer of a good conscience toward God.

(11) "FOR HE KNEW WHO SHOULD BETRAY HIM; THEREFORE SAID HE, YOU ARE NOT ALL CLEAN."

The diagram is:

1. While the Believer can be Saved without having an understanding of the Cross respecting Sanctification, he cannot live a victorious life.

2. The only way that we can obtain victory over the world, the flesh, and the Devil is by placing our Faith constantly in Christ and what He did for us at the Cross.

3. As the Cross was so necessary for Salvation, likewise, it is necessary for Sanctification.

BETRAYAL

The phrase, *"For He knew who should betray Him,"* portrays Him knowing this quite some time earlier.

"Therefore said He, You are not all clean," presents Jesus making another appeal to Judas.

At any time, this man could have turned around, and he would have been instantly forgiven, for the Lord has never turned one away who came to Him in sincerity and honesty (Jn. 6:37).

(12) "SO AFTER HE HAD WASHED THEIR FEET, AND HAD TAKEN HIS GARMENTS, AND WAS SET DOWN AGAIN, HE SAID UNTO THEM, DO YOU KNOW WHAT I HAVE DONE TO YOU?"

The composition is:

1. As Salvation separates men and women from the world, the Baptism with the Holy Spirit separates them from cold, dead, and dry religious formalism.

2. The Cross of Christ is the dividing line between the true Church and the apostate church. In fact, it has always been that way.

3. To proclaim Jesus without the Cross presents, in fact, *"Another Jesus"* (II Cor. 11:4).

DO YOU KNOW WHAT I HAVE DONE TO YOU?

Verse 12 presents the Master as having finished this example and now no longer in the posture of a slave but of their Teacher and Lord.

The question, *"He said unto them, Do you know what I have done to you?"* proclaims that they must consider the meaning of it all.

Reynolds said, *"There was no affectation (pretense) of humility about it. The purpose of the Lord was distinctly practical and ethical."*

Even though at that time they did not fully understand at all concerning the things He had done, still, when He ceased His Manifestation in the likeness of sinful flesh and was set down on the Right Hand of God, He sent His Spirit to teach them all things, which the Spirit did, and which they wondrously learned.

As John the Beloved wrote these words, it is very clear that he understood perfectly that which Jesus had proclaimed, showing the veracity of the Spirit's Work.

(13) "YE CALL ME MASTER AND LORD: AND YOU SAY WELL; FOR SO I AM."

NOTES

The pattern is:

1. The Holy Spirit and the Cross of Christ, the latter of which provides the legal means for the Divine Spirit to do His Work, are so closely intertwined that they, for all practical purposes, are one (Rev. 5:6; Rom. 8:2).

2. In fact, the Holy Spirit cannot be properly preached and lived without the Cross.

3. The Cross cannot be properly preached and lived without the Holy Spirit.

MASTER AND LORD

The phrase, *"You call Me Master and Lord,"* presents a double title which was not given except to the most accredited teachers. The title, *"Master,"* meant, *"Rabbi."*

The title, *"Lord,"* as used here by Jesus, has a higher and loftier meaning than normally used in the New Testament. The word, as used here, has Old Testament associations, which spoke of the Lord as *"Covenant God."*

The idea is that His Purpose did not become clear to the Disciples until after His Resurrection and, more particularly, after the Advent of the Holy Spirit on the Day of Pentecost. Then the Revelation of His Deity became far more pronounced.

The full significance of this Association of Jesus with God under the one appellation, *"Lord,"* is seen when it is remembered that these men belonged to the only monotheistic (One God) class of people in the world. To associate with the Creator, one known to be a creature, however exalted, though taught erroneously by pagan philosophers, was quite impossible to a Jew. Actually, this is what incensed the religious leaders of Israel in that Jesus constantly referred to Himself as One with the Father, in essence, claiming Deity.

THE TRINITY

While they were right, extensively so, that there was only *"One God,"* they were wrong in failing to understand that He could and, in fact, was manifested in Three Persons, *"God the Father, God the Son, and God the Holy Spirit."*

It is not recorded that in the days of His Flesh any of His Disciples either addressed the Lord or spoke of Him by His Personal Name of Jesus. They called Him, *"Lord"* or *"Master,"* as is here recorded.

However, their use of the title, *"Lord,"* especially in the earlier days of His Ministry, was used in the lower meaning, referring to *"Owner"* or *"Sir."* As time went on, however, and they witnessed His Mighty Power in the performing of Miracles of every description, gradually, they began to use the title, *"Lord,"* in the higher sense. This spoke, as stated, of Him as *"Covenant God,"* as used in the Old Testament. In other words, they recognized that while He was a Man, He was far more than a Man. In fact, He was Deity.

The phrase, *"And you say well; for so I am,"* proclaims Jesus placing His Seal of Approval on their higher use of the title, *"Lord,"* referring to Himself. As well, He was telling them that even though He has washed their feet, in no way does this diminish His Position as the Lord God of Glory.

By this, He explained to them that they, as well, would not be diminished by such activity (the Servant Principle, evidenced by the foot washing episode), but rather exalted.

What a beautiful lesson!

(14) "IF I THEN, YOUR LORD AND MASTER, HAVE WASHED YOUR FEET; YOU ALSO OUGHT TO WASH ONE ANOTHER'S FEET."

The form is:

1. The substitution of something else that is totally opposed to God's Word, or to substitute something other than the Cross, was first evidenced by Cain (Gen., Chpt. 4).

2. The Cross is God's Way, of which the Old Testament sacrifices were symbols.

3. The Lord's Way for Salvation is the Cross. His Way for Sanctification is the Cross.

LORD AND MASTER

The phrase, *"If I then, your Lord and Master, have washed your feet,"* speaks of and proclaims the example set.

"You also ought to wash one another's feet," is not meant to be taken literally but is to serve as an example of the Servant Principle.

True Bible students have, for the most part, looked below the mere form to the real substance of the Lord's Teaching, and only thus can we appreciate it adequately.

The service demanded is the self-forgetting ministry of love, which places the interests of self behind and below those of others. Nothing is more theoretically easy and acceptable than this principle, but nothing is more difficult of accomplishment.

(15) "FOR I HAVE GIVEN YOU AN EXAMPLE, THAT YOU SHOULD DO AS I HAVE DONE TO YOU."

The order is:

1. To satisfy the broken Law, God demanded that a perfect life be given, which is the reason that God became Man.

2. God cannot die, and if justice was to be completely satisfied, a perfect life had to be offered up. Since no human being could qualify, the Lord would have to pay the price Himself.

3. Death was demanded but not the death of just anyone. It had to be One Who was Perfect, meaning that it had to be Christ.

THE EXAMPLE

The phrase, *"For I have given you an example,"* is meant to be exactly that.

He had set before His Disciples a parallel and an example, a symbolic type of the service they were to render to one another. It was not meant to establish a custom or exact ordinance. Otherwise, we miss the lesson here taught.

"That you should do as I have done to you," can be compared to *"This do in remembrance of Me,"* concerning the Lord's Supper (Lk. 22:19).

Regrettably, the professing church misinterprets the one Command and neglects the other. It should be recognized that both Commands are spiritual and not material, are both equally imperative, and that both were to be imitated. He *"washed"* and He *"gave."* They were to *"remember Him"* in order to imitate Him.

They were to serve others and to die for others (I Jn. 3:16). All here is Spiritual and heavenly, for where He enters, symbols disappear.

Millions, misunderstanding the symbolism of the Lord's Supper, partake of this beautiful example, never fully understanding it's meaning and, thereby, rendering it useless as a mere ceremony. Thus, they eat and drink damnation unto themselves.

Likewise, many engage in literal *"foot washings,"* while forgetting what it actually represents, reducing it, as well, to ceremony.

Had it been the mere ceremony Jesus desired that one remember and practice, He would not have made the statement, *"What I do you know not now; but you shall know hereafter"* (Vs. 7). Were it mere ceremony, they would have instantly known what He was doing.

The true meaning would be revealed by the Holy Spirit, which it was and is.

(16) "VERILY, VERILY, I SAY UNTO YOU, THE SERVANT IS NOT GREATER THAN HIS LORD; NEITHER HE WHO IS SENT GREATER THAN HE WHO SENDS HIM."

The diagram is:

1. Due to Adam's fall, all are born in original sin.

2. The only thing that could deal with original sin was and is the Cross of Christ.

3. We must understand that the Cross was not an incident, not an assassination, and not an accident. It was a Sacrifice.

THE SERVANT

The phrase, *"Verily, Verily, I say unto you, The servant is not greater than his Lord,"* simply means that if Jesus, Who is Lord, has set the example, we then should follow.

Actually, this must hold true in every facet of our lives and experiences. This speaks of our prayer life. If Jesus had a consistent prayer life, which He certainly did, then we should do so as well. If He used the Word of God as His Constant Foundation for all that He did, then the Word of God must be our Foundation, as well, for He is the Example.

If He set the example for the Servant Principle, and He certainly did, then He means for us to follow. However, understand: He is the *"Example,"* and not others!

The phrase, *"Neither He who is sent greater than He Who sends him,"* presents a simple truth, but yet, one we seem to have to learn over and over.

The idea is that if Jesus, Who is *"Greater"* than us, and He most definitely is, had to do these things, then we, who are so much less than He, most definitely must follow in His Steps, at least as far as is possible.

A perfect example is the Holy Spirit. Jesus was Perfect, Pure, Unsullied, and, in fact, was and is the Son of God. But yet, He needed the Holy Spirit to carry forth His Work.

The idea is that if He had to have the Holy Spirit, how much more do we, who are imperfect, weak, and constantly coming short of the Glory of God, need the Holy Spirit. As stated, He has set the Example, and it is incumbent upon us to follow that Example.

(17) "IF YE KNOW THESE THINGS, HAPPY ARE YOU IF YOU DO THEM.

(18) I SPEAK NOT OF YOU ALL: I KNOW WHOM I HAVE CHOSEN: BUT THAT THE SCRIPTURE MAY BE FULFILLED, HE WHO EATS BREAD WITH ME HAS LIFTED UP HIS HEEL AGAINST ME."

The exegesis is:

1. The term, *"Justification by Faith,"* simply means that I am fully justified by exhibiting Faith in Christ and what Christ has done for me in the Sacrifice of Himself on the Cross.

2. The word *"justify"* means *"to prove or show to be just, right, or reasonable."*

3. Christ was the *"Last Adam,"* Who came to this world to do what the first Adam did not do, which was to render a perfect obedience to God and to undo what the first Adam did do.

CHOSEN

The statement made by Christ, *"If you know these things, happy are you if you do them,"* presents Reynolds saying, *"Knowing and doing are often perilously divorced"*[8] (Mat. 7:21; Lk. 6:46; 12:47; James 1:25). How right he is!

The phrase, *"I speak not of you all,"* in a sense, changes completely the tone of the conversation. It will be another attempt to bring Judas back from the crumbling edge but, sadly, without success!

"I know whom I have chosen," goes back to the time at the beginning of the Ministry of Christ when He sought His Heavenly Father all night long for the Will of God concerning whom these all-important Twelve would be (Lk. 6:12-16).

What does He mean by the word *"chosen?"*

He did not choose Judas as a wicked man, or that he should become such! To accuse the Heavenly Father of telling Jesus to choose someone of such present wickedness runs counter to everything taught in the Word of God.

Having said that, should we ask the question, *"Does God use evil?"*

DOES GOD USE EVIL?

To answer that question, the word *"use"* would have to be defined.

In the sense of the Holy Spirit doing His Work within hearts and lives, the Lord emphatically does not and, in fact, cannot use evil in any form. That should be obvious; however, He definitely does use the results and circumstances of evil oftentimes. Events, situations, happenings, and occurrences, often caused by that which is evil, at times, are used by the Lord in order to shape events. That should be obvious as well! (I Ki. 22:19-23).

Having said that, we must quickly add that the Lord did not choose Judas in order that he might betray Him, as many teach. He chose a man who had potential, even as all the other Disciples. As well, there is every evidence, as we have previously stated, that Judas loved the Lord at that time.

He had the same struggles, trials, and tests as all the other Disciples. The same questions were in his mind as the others; however, he never repented of his error, as did the others, but instead, pushed it to its ultimate darkness. The fault was his and his alone.

THE FULFILLING OF THE SCRIPTURES

The phrase, *"But that the Scripture may be fulfilled, He who eats bread with Me has lifted up his heel against Me,"* is taken from Psalms 41:9.

As well, He was saying, *"I am the Person spoken of in that Psalm."*

However, He was not saying that God gives Prophecy through the Prophets and then, at the appointed time, forces someone to fulfill what has been said many years before.

NOTES

He was saying that God, in His Omniscience in knowing everything, past, present, and future, looks down through time and through foreknowledge, tells the Prophets what is going to happen, with them then giving the Prophetic Utterance. In that context, Jesus was saying, *"That the Scripture may (will) be fulfilled."* In other words, what God has said will happen, will happen!

We have dealt with the subject repeatedly and do not desire to belabor the point, but considering its significance, allow me to say again: God does not predestine anyone to go to Heaven or Hell. That is always the choice of the individual.

However, He does predestine certain things, but never that which tampers with the free moral agency of man. Every Scriptural evidence is that such is always held sacrosanct by God.

(19) "NOW I TELL YOU BEFORE IT COME, THAT, WHEN IT IS COME TO PASS, YOU MAY BELIEVE THAT I AM HE."

The overview is:

1. The Cross of Christ was planned from before the foundation of the world (I Pet. 1:18-20).

2. So, if any man belittles the Cross, demeans the Cross, or ignores the Cross, let him understand that he is demeaning the very Plan of God and, without that Plan, which is the Cross, no one can be saved.

3. When Jesus died and shed His Life's Blood, which means that His Life was poured out, His Shed Blood atoned for all sin, past, present, and future, at least for all who will believe (Jn. 3:16).

BELIEVING

The phrase, *"Now I tell you before it come,"* proclaims Him knowing exactly what was going to happen, at least according to what the Scripture has foretold.

Naturally, He knew the Word of God as no one else ever has because He was and is the Living Word and, accordingly, knew each Passage that pertained to Him.

In studying the four Gospels, one constantly sees the erroneous direction taken by the Disciples, which was contrary to the Word of God. Of course, the normal response to such action, as we have stated repeatedly, is: had they known the Bible as they should, they would have had a far greater grasp of Who Jesus was, and What was His Mission.

As well, before we criticize them too much, we should look at ourselves. Are we doing any better than they? Are we doing as good?

We must remember that the Disciples didn't have the Holy Spirit as we now have Him. That would come on the Day of Pentecost, but all of these things were taking place before the Day of Pentecost, which is obvious.

From the Day of Pentecost forward, these men were so different as to be almost incomparable. It is almost like they changed instantly from incompetence to mighty men, which they actually did!

The phrase, *"That, when it is come to pass, you may believe that I am He,"* once again, as stated, proclaims Himself as being the One spoken of in Psalms 41:9.

(20) "VERILY, VERILY, I SAY UNTO YOU, HE WHO RECEIVES WHOMSOEVER I SEND RECEIVES ME; AND HE WHO RECEIVES ME RECEIVES HIM WHO SENT ME."

The overview is:

1. After He died, Jesus went down into the Paradise side of Hell, as well, the prison side of Hell. There is no Scriptural record whatsoever that He went to the burning side of Hell.

2. Jesus preached to the spirits in prison, which were fallen Angels who were locked up because of some monstrous sin that they committed, which was probably the cohabitation with women. As well, Jesus delivered all of the Saints who were in Paradise. These things are all that the Bible says that He did during that three days and nights.

3. There is no record in the Word of God that Jesus died spiritually, as some claim. He died physically, which, within itself, paid the price for man's Redemption.

RECEIVING

The phrase, *"Verily, Verily, I say unto you, He who receives whomsoever I send receives Me,"* in effect, says that however they might be hated and betrayed, like the Master, their mission was Divine.

If that is true, and it certainly is, then whosoever refuses to receive the one sent by the Lord, at the same time, refuses the Lord, as is obvious.

This is a solemn statement and should be read and heeded carefully. To lay one's hand on one sent by the Lord, or even to reject his Message, does not stop with the messenger but extends to Christ and even to the Heavenly Father.

The phrase, *"And He who receives Me receives Him Who sent Me,"* proclaims, as stated, the acceptance or rejection as reaching all the way to the Throne of God.

I marvel as great numbers in the modern Body of Christ think nothing of speaking ill of those who are definitely Called of God and that which is of God. They do so, I greatly suspect, because their leaders do such before them.

Not everyone who goes is sent by the Lord. However, those who are truly Called and sent by Him, as should be obvious, are held by Him as very important as to their person and their Message. Actually, those who serve in this capacity are the same as an ambassador from a particular country. The leaders of the country to whom the ambassador is sent may not appreciate him, but there is a certain protocol that is followed simply because they know and realize that he represents a nation. If, in fact, he represents a powerful nation, even greater care is taken.

To be sure, nothing is higher than the Throne of God. As such, Ambassadors sent from that Throne must be understood as to Whom they represent.

(21) "WHEN JESUS HAD THUS SAID, HE WAS TROUBLED IN SPIRIT, AND TESTIFIED, AND SAID, VERILY, VERILY, I SAY UNTO YOU, THAT ONE OF YOU SHALL BETRAY ME."

The pattern is:

1. The Way of the Lord is the Way of the Cross.

2. Without the Cross, there is no salvation and no sanctification.

3. That's the reason that Paul said, *"For the preaching of the Cross is to them who*

perish foolishness; but to we who are Saved it is the Power of God" (I Cor. 1:18).

TROUBLED IN SPIRIT

The phrase, *"When Jesus had thus said, He was troubled in spirit,"* proclaims a strong expression used of the Sorrows of Christ. This was from deep down in His Nature.

The distress penetrated from *"Body"* to *"Soul"* and then to His Inmost *"Spirit."* The Lord was terribly perturbed, not merely by approaching agony, aggravated by treachery and desertion, but by the contrast between His Love and the issue between an Apostle and His Doom.

If, in fact, Judas had been predestined to do such a thing, such sorrow would not have gripped Jesus.

The phrase, *"And testified, and said, Verily, Verily, I say unto you, that one of you shall betray Me,"* now proclaims Jesus saying plainly that which He had previously hinted (Vs. 18).

(22) "THEN THE DISCIPLES LOOKED ONE ON ANOTHER, DOUBTING OF WHOM HE SPOKE.

(23) NOW THERE WAS LEANING ON JESUS' BOSOM ONE OF HIS DISCIPLES, WHOM JESUS LOVED."

The order is:

1. When Jesus, while on the Cross, said, *"It is finished"* (Jn. 19:30), *"Father, into Your Hands I commend My Spirit,"* at that moment, the price was fully paid, and Redemption was complete (Lk. 23:46).

2. Jesus was put on the Cross at 9 a.m., which had been the time of the morning sacrifice for some 1,600 years. He died at 3 p.m., the time of the evening sacrifice, totally fulfilling the Biblical types.

3. At noon, while Jesus was on the Cross, the Scripture says, *"There was darkness over all the land until the ninth hour,"* which refers to 3 p.m. (Mat. 27:45). During those three hours when darkness covered the land, Christ was bearing the sin penalty of the human race.

ASTONISHMENT

The astonishment created by what Jesus had just said registered on the Disciples, even in their outward expressions. Judas was not suspected, showing that his actions of the past had not been that of treachery. This, as well, refutes the contention that he had been wicked from the beginning.

The phrase, *"Now there was leaning on Jesus' Bosom one of His Disciples,"* presents the manner in which they then reclined when dining. Meals were then much more formal than now.

Now, it seems that, basically, eating is just a time to satisfy hunger. Then, such was a time of fellowship and communion as well!

The phrase, *"Whom Jesus loved,"* pertains to John the Beloved who wrote this Gospel.

(24) "SIMON PETER THEREFORE BECKONED TO HIM, THAT HE SHOULD ASK WHO IT SHOULD BE OF WHOM HE SPOKE."

The order is:

1. To demean or ignore the Cross of Christ is to ignore the Plan of God for the human race.

2. We must understand that God has no other plan than the Cross.

3. If we preach Jesus or think of Jesus without the Cross, then the one we are worshipping is *"another Jesus"* (II Cor. 11:4).

SIMON PETER

The phrase, *"Simon Peter therefore beckoned to him,"* seems to imply that he was located down the table or across the table from Jesus and, as someone said, far enough off to beckon but near enough to speak.

Whatever side John was on, some have claimed that Peter was on the other side of Jesus; however, the language does not seem to imply such.

Due to the things stated, there is great evidence, according to Matthew 26:23, that Judas was immediately on the other side of Jesus. This one thing is certain: he was close enough to dip his hand in the same dish as Jesus, which necessitated him being very close.

If that is the case, and it certainly seems to be, this was another effort by Jesus to bring this man to his senses. In eastern culture, all who were seated next to the host, Who, in this case, was Jesus, were placed there purposely because of acquaintance, friendship, and devotion. This coincides perfectly with the statement of the Psalmist, *"Yes, my own familiar friend, in whom I trusted, which did eat of my bread, has lifted up his heel against me"* (Ps. 41:9).

The phrase, *"That he should ask who it should be of whom He spoke,"* refers to Peter sitting far enough away from Jesus that he could not whisper to Him Personally so that others would not hear, so he would ask John to do so for him.

(25) "HE THEN LYING ON JESUS' BREAST SAID UNTO HIM, LORD, WHO IS IT?"

The construction is:

1. By no stretch of the imagination is the Cross a hidden symbol in the Word of God, but is rather the glaring centerpiece of its proclamation.
2. It is that way all the way from Genesis 1:1 through Revelation 22:21.
3. It takes an acute deception to miss this glaring fact.

FELLOWSHIP

The phrase, *"He then lying on Jesus' Breast said unto Him,"* proclaims the manner, as we have previously stated, in which they then dined.

The familiarity here mentioned was not a part of the custom of that day but was simply an exhibition of John's love for Jesus.

They did not then sit at tables as we do presently, but rather somewhat sat or reclined on cushions on the floor in order to partake of the meal. The tables were very low, as should be obvious.

This custom evolved over the centuries out of the hospitality then shown, the type of dress they wore, and the lack of the type of furniture we are accustomed to presently.

There is a Spiritual insight here respecting John leaning on the Breast of Jesus, which we should address ourselves to briefly. It concerns the nearness of one's relationship with Christ. I think it proclaims, at least after a fashion, that one can have as near a relationship as one desires:

THE CALL

The Scripture says that Jesus *"appointed other seventy also, and sent them two and two before His Face into every city and place, where He Himself would come"* (Lk. 10:1).

This represents the Call of God upon the hearts and lives of all Believers. In other words, Salvation contains within it a Call, which is to be answered and carried out with faithfulness. It represents every single Child of God.

POWER

"And when He had called unto Him His Twelve Disciples, He gave them power against unclean spirits, to cast them out, and to heal all manner of sickness and all manner of disease" (Mat. 10:1).

As should be obvious, this Call has a somewhat deeper significance than the Call extended to the Seventy. It proposes a nearer relationship with Christ.

RELATIONSHIP

"And it came to pass about an eight days after these sayings, He took Peter and John and James, and went up into a mountain to pray" (Lk. 9:28).

It should be understood from this account that Jesus took Peter, James, and John into a closer relationship with Himself, even than the remainder of the Twelve. He not only did this at the Transfiguration but, as well, when He raised the daughter of Jairus from the dead (Lk. 8:51), and also in the Garden of Gethsemane, a short time before His Arrest (Mat. 26:37).

Why this closer relationship with these three, we are not told! However, knowing that the Lord is no respecter of persons, the only explanation is that these three had a greater hunger and thirst in their hearts and lives for Jesus than even the remainder of the Twelve.

A COVETED POSITION

The fourth occasion is the subject of our present Text, John *"lying on Jesus' Breast,"* at the Last Supper. This presents him as being close enough to the Heart of Jesus that he had at least some insight into His Feelings. It also presented him in a position so close to Jesus that others, even such as Peter, asked him to speak to the Master concerning certain things. This coveted position can be obtained by anyone, be it Preacher or otherwise.

This speaks of a relationship which knows the Heart of God, and which is the nearest and dearest of all.

These are the people who are the backbone of any local Church, providing it is privileged to have any of this nature at all! In a general sense, it also speaks of those who are the strength of the Church all around the world. I think I can say without fear of contradiction that this is the place (the Bosom of Jesus) where the Holy Spirit is attempting to take us all. Regrettably, few attain this coveted position, and I am concerned that those who do are not only reviled by the world, but by much of the Church as well!

SPIRITUAL INSIGHT

This we do know: John was given by Jesus spiritual insight to a degree that He gave no other. I speak not only of the writing of this Gospel but, as well, the three short Epistles and, more particularly, the Book of Revelation, which presents a portrayal of the Spirit world that was given to no other man or woman. This is the reason the Holy Spirit allowed John to speak of himself as the one *"whom Jesus loved"* (Jn. 13:23).

This place of the nearest relationship to Christ, to which few attain, is one of such magnitude, as should be obvious, that it is difficult to properly explain. Perhaps this is exactly of what Paul spoke when he said, *"That I may know Him"* (Phil. 3:10).

LORD, WHO IS IT?

The question asked by John, *"Lord, who is it?"* speaking of Judas, once again proclaims none of the Disciples having any idea whatsoever of the action about to be taken by Judas. In other words, as I have said several times, if this spirit had been in Judas all along, it would have been easily detected by the others. They did not detect such because it had not previously been there, coming only at this time, with the seed being planted by Satan shortly before!

(26) "JESUS ANSWERED, HE IT IS, TO WHOM I SHALL GIVE A SOP, WHEN I HAVE DIPPED IT. AND WHEN HE HAD DIPPED THE SOP, HE GAVE IT TO JUDAS ISCARIOT, THE SON OF SIMON."

The structure is:

1. All Salvation is found in the Cross of Christ.

2. All Sanctification is found in the Cross of Christ.

3. All relationship is found in the Cross of Christ!

IDENTIFICATION

The phrase, *"Jesus answered, He it is, to whom I shall give a sop, when I have dipped it,"* spoke of the unleavened bread taken in the Hands of Jesus and dipped into the sauce made of grape juice and fruit. It is mentioned in Ruth 2:14.

The phrase, *"And when He had dipped the sop, He gave it to Judas Iscariot, the son of Simon,"* which, in its normal sense, was a mark of honor for the guest who received it.

The Lord had appealed to the conscience of Judas in Verse 21. Now, He appealed to his heart, but it was too hard to respond.

Judas took the sop, which probably means, as stated, that he was sitting right next to Jesus.

If one is to notice, the name of Judas, the name of his father, and the name of the place cursed by being his birth place, are once again introduced at length (Jn. 6:71).

(27) "AND AFTER THE SOP SATAN ENTERED INTO HIM. THEN SAID JESUS UNTO HIM, THAT YOU DO, DO QUICKLY."

The synopsis is:

1. Everything pertaining to Redemption is based one hundred percent on the Foundation of *"Jesus Christ and Him Crucified"* (I Cor. 1:17-18, 21, 23; Gal. 6:14; Eph. 2:13-18; Jn. 3:16).

2. Considering presently that the Cross is little preached in modern churches, where does that leave the church?

3. There is only one answer for sin, just one, and it is the Cross of Christ.

SATAN

The phrase, *"And after the sop Satan entered into him,"* represents a moment unequalled in history respecting the spurning of the Call and Love of God.

As stated, when Jesus gave Judas this

morsel of bread, with it representing honor, at that moment, Judas had before him Eternal Life or eternal death. It was his decision to make, as it is the decision of all!

This is the only time that the name *"Satan"* is mentioned in this fourth Gospel and carries with it a tremendous lesson.

The battleground, as is obvious, was the heart of Judas. Both Jesus and Satan appealed to his heart. As stated, the decision was his!

The appeal that was made by Jesus, as I trust we have explained, was freighted with love, tenderness, grace, and petition. Jesus had given him an honored place at the table, even possibly by His very own Side. He had given him the *"sop,"* which spoke of honor, friendship, love, and covenant. In other words, Jesus was pleading with him not to break the Covenant, which is what the entirety of this meal actually represented, the establishing of the New Covenant.

Satan, as well, appealed to Judas, as is obvious. However, what could he say to Judas which would be more enticing than that which Jesus had said and done?

In this question hangs all the reasons that men accept Jesus or Satan. The contest is glaringly obvious before all. It is the battleground of the soul.

SELF-WILL

The only answer that could be given, which I think applies to all, is that self-will intermeshed with the lying promises of Satan. If one's will is not lost completely in Christ, it will always provide a fertile field for Satan's evil designs. When people want and desire something other than what God wants them to have, or they purposely set their own course that is not the one laid out for them by the Holy Spirit, they will always go in the direction of Satan. They may heap great religious phraseology and claimed consecration over this erroneous direction, but the end result will always be the same, which is wreckage. To be straightforward, no Believer can overcome this problem without the Cross of Christ being the centerpiece of his or her consecration. In fact, anything that we are in the Lord, anything that we do for the Lord, and any relationship with Him, the Cross of Christ is always the centerpiece of the effort. That being lost, as it is in most spiritual circles, self-will takes over. In fact, this is exactly what happened to Judas. The Cross of Christ did not appeal to him. He heard what Jesus said as is recorded in the Sixth Chapter of this great Book. That Chapter closes with the Words of Christ, *"Have I not chosen you Twelve, and one of you is a demon? He spoke of Judas Iscariot the son of Simon: for he it was who should betray Him, being one of the Twelve"* (Jn. 6:70-71).

Looking at other things, whatever it was that Judas wanted, it had its roots in the same thing that caused the Fall in the Garden of Eden. The early pair did not take God at His Word but determined to put their own spin on His Direction. The results were catastrophic with them, as it was with Judas and all who have followed in that train.

At that moment when Jesus gave him the *"sop,"* Judas had to make a decision. It was something he had been contemplating for months. In effect, he must make it now because Jesus was demanding an answer, as was Satan. Tragically and horribly so, he made the decision for Satan, i.e., *"self-will!"*

At that moment, *"Satan entered into him,"* i.e., began to control him.

THE END OF THE APPEAL

The phrase, *"Then said Jesus unto him, That you do, do quickly,"* presents our Lord now giving him up as well! It would truly be better for him that he had never been born.

The vehement effort, which the traitor must have made to resist all gracious influences, opened the way for the powers of Hell and darkness to take possession of him. He actually strengthened himself to do evil, for to sin against Love is to accept hate. To sin against Light is to accept darkness. To sin against Jesus is to accept Satan, for it is one or the other!

I wonder how many people there are whom the Lord has dealt with repeatedly, yet they have spurned all pleadings of the Holy Spirit. If the Lord lets them go, as He did Judas, and He will at some point, then the die is cast, and the ultimate loss of that soul is all but certain!

The reader must understand that if a

person wants sin and iniquity, in other words, he desires rebellion against God, the Lord will ultimately remove all restraining influence from that person. This happens not only with individuals but even churches, at least as a whole, along with entire religious denominations. Even nations can go the same way!

This does not mean that a person cannot be Saved thereafter, at least if he will turn to the Lord, for He will never turn anyone away who truly comes to Him. However, the deeper into Satan's control that one sinks, the harder it is for that person to come back. As stated, precious few make it back after sinking to this level.

The very Words of Jesus, *"That you do, do quickly,"* proclaim that this thing had come to Judas in stages.

AN EARTHLY KINGDOM

As we have stated, it, no doubt, began with Judas, as the other Disciples, pushing hard for this earthly kingdom to commence. The idea of Jesus dying on Calvary did not at all fit into these plans. So, all hardly heard Jesus speaking these particular words and, at one point, saw Peter rebuking Him, with Jesus, in turn, strongly rebuking Peter (Mat. 16:21-25). Then, at some given time, Judas began to steal from the treasury of the group. How this came about is anyone's guess! Possibly, the first time, he intended to replace the money, but that never happened. Thereafter, it became easier to pilfer the funds, with the slide downward increasing.

An individual turning one's back upon God is never done immediately, I think one can say. It is always done in stages. If the Spirit of God is not allowed to move on that soul, which He certainly will attempt to do, the slide downward will continue. That is the reason Church services are so important with the Spirit of God moving. At these times, the Holy Spirit speaks strongly to individuals who are on the wrong road and, in fact, losing their way with God. If the admonitions are heeded, the downward slide can be instantly stopped, with the person pulled back to his First Love. If not heeded, it will become more difficult the next time for the Spirit of God to touch the heart because with each rejection, the heart becomes harder!

THE HOLY SPIRIT

It is sadder still when one realizes that the Spirit of God is not allowed to move in the manner of Conviction in many, if not most, churches. Actually, almost the entire so-called *"faith movement"* does not even believe in this of which we speak. In other words, many of them label the convicting Power of the Holy Spirit as condemnation, thereby, missing the entirety of a great part of the office work of the Third Person of the Godhead (Jn. 16:8-11). Blessed are the people who have the privilege of attending a Church where the Holy Spirit is allowed to function in His rightful Capacity!

(28) "NOW NO MAN AT THE TABLE KNEW FOR WHAT INTENT HE SPOKE THIS UNTO HIM."

The exegesis is:

1. If Judgment is held back, it is only done so by the preaching of the Cross (I Cor. 1:17).

2. God has no respect for any proposed way of Salvation other than *"Jesus Christ and Him Crucified."*

3. Religious men have always wanted revival without repentance, and above all, revival without the Cross, but such is not to be.

LACK OF DISCERNMENT

The evidence is that the other Disciples heard what Jesus said as He addressed Judas, but it seems that none knew, not at all, what was really happening!

Once again, I want to emphasize the fact that these men, at this time, were not baptized with the Holy Spirit, which, in fact, would come shortly. Consequently, their Spiritual discernment was extremely weak, as it is with all people who, even though Saved, are not Spirit-baptized. Thankfully, the Day of Pentecost would remedy this (Acts 2:4).

Exactly as we observed, the spiritual dullness, as it then registered in the Disciples, and for the reason we have spoken, so follows entire religious denominations that do not believe in the Baptism with the Holy Spirit with the evidence of speaking with other Tongues (Acts 2:4). The following statement may be strong, but I know it to be true:

People who are not Spirit-filled can little be Spirit-led. Considering that every single thing done in this world by the Lord is done through the Person and Agency of the Holy Spirit, this leaves such people as doing all they do through the agency of the flesh, which is death (Rom. 8:6-8).

This is the reason that the serious Bible student recognizes the Holy Spirit urging with haste that all Believers be filled, and quickly so! (Acts 1:4; 8:14-15; 19:1-6).

(29) "FOR SOME OF THEM THOUGHT, BECAUSE JUDAS HAD THE BAG, THAT JESUS HAD SAID UNTO HIM, BUY THOSE THINGS THAT WE HAVE NEED OF AGAINST THE FEAST; OR, THAT HE SHOULD GIVE SOMETHING TO THE POOR."

The synopsis is:

1. The Cross of Christ is the dividing line between the true Church and the apostate church. In fact, it has always been that way, beginning with Genesis, Chapter 4.

2. The only thing standing between the Church and apostasy is the Cross.

3. If the church embraces humanistic psychology, which it has, it, at the same time, has denied the Cross. Either one cancels out the other.

A LACK OF UNDERSTANDING

The phrase, *"For some of them thought, because Judas had the bag,"* refers to the fact of Judas being the treasurer of the group, as previously stated.

"That Jesus had said unto him, Buy those things that we have need of against the Feast," pertained to the balance of this time, which was some seven days. Actually, they had just eaten the Passover. (They partook of this Feast a day early inasmuch as Jesus would be crucified on the actual day of the Passover, which was the following day.)

Actually, at this time, there were three Feasts celebrated: *"The Feast of Unleavened Bread,"* which typified the Perfect Life of Christ; *"The Feast of Passover,"* which portrayed the Cross; and *"The Feast of Firstfruits,"* which pertained to the Resurrection.

NOTES

From the way the phrase, *"Or, that he should give something to the poor,"* is said, it seems to be something they did quite regularly.

(30) "HE THEN HAVING RECEIVED THE SOP WENT IMMEDIATELY OUT: AND IT WAS NIGHT."

The synopsis is:

1. The Gospel of Jesus Christ is the Message of the Cross (I Cor. 1:17).

2. Every Blessing of the Lord that comes to us is all made possible by the Cross.

3. The Cross of Christ is the Means by which everything is done.

AND IT WAS NIGHT

The phrase, *"He then having received the sop went immediately out,"* from all accounts, and especially Luke 22:14-23, tells us that the supper was now finished. As well, I think the account is clear that Judas was not present when Jesus gave His Discourse as given in the next four Chapters, which immediately followed the supper.

The phrase, *"And it was night,"* portrays such in more ways than one!

Dark as was the night upon Judas' head, there was a blacker night in his heart. All was darkness in his soul.

Doubtless, he expected and believed that the Lord would deliver Himself as usual; however, good can never come out of sin!

(31) "THEREFORE, WHEN HE WAS GONE OUT, JESUS SAID, NOW IS THE SON OF MAN GLORIFIED, AND GOD IS GLORIFIED IN HIM."

The construction is:

1. The Holy Spirit works entirely within the parameters of the Finished Work of Christ (Rom. 8:2).

2. The Holy Spirit will not work outside of those parameters.

3. In other words, it is the Cross which gives the Holy Spirit the legal means to do all that He does. That's the reason it is called a *"law"* (Rom. 8:2).

NOW IS THE SON OF MAN GLORIFIED

The phrase, *"Therefore, when he had gone out,"* is said with finality and refers to the fact that Jesus could not give His Discourse, which now follows, to the Disciples until the traitor had left.

The Lord would now begin His Farewell to the Disciples by leading them as *"little children"* into direct communication with the Father. Among so many other things, He was about to tell them that even though He would leave them, He would come back.

The phrase, *"Jesus said, Now is the Son of Man Glorified, and God is Glorified in Him,"* refers to Christ glorifying God in death and God glorifying Jesus in Resurrection (Rom. 6:3-5).

God dealt with Job in discipline, but with Christ, in justice; for He, on the Cross, became the Sin Offering, and there made a glorious exhibition of the attributes of God in justice, majesty, truth, and love. All were vindicated and thus was God glorified.

THE CROSS

At Calvary, infinite wrath against sin and infinite love toward the sinner were demonstrated. God was dishonored in the first man, Adam, but infinitely glorified in the Second and, thereby, the Last, the Lord Jesus Christ. Straightway, He glorified Him in raising Him from the dead.

At this stage of Jesus' Life and Ministry, we are entering the Holy of Holies. We have indeed come through the Courts of the Temple, we have left the Courts of the Gentiles, of the women, of the Priests behind us, and have been waiting in the Holy Place of Sacrifice and Incense and Ablution; now we follow our Great High Priest to the Veil over the Holiest of all, and He prepares us to listen to the Intercession that He makes before the unveiled Majesty of the Father's Love (Olshausen)[9].

Jesus will now give His Disciples a higher Revelation of the nature of His Own Person and of those relations between *"The Son"* and *"The Father,"* which are imaged and shadowed forth in those between *"The Son of Man"* and *"God,"* which they could more readily understand.

(32) "IF GOD BE GLORIFIED IN HIM, GOD SHALL ALSO GLORIFY HIM IN HIMSELF, AND SHALL STRAIGHTWAY GLORIFY HIM."

The exegesis is:

NOTES

1. In the last few years, we've heard a lot about *"covering."* What exactly does it mean?

2. It means that certain preachers claim they serve as a *"covering"* for other preachers, or that denominations serve as a *"covering"* for those who are associated.

3. While such statements sound good to the flesh, they are totally unscriptural. In fact, such thinking is so unscriptural that it is an insult to Christ. No human being can serve as a covering for anyone, not even himself.

GLORIFIED

The phrase, *"If God be Glorified in Him,"* refers to the Perfect Obedience of Jesus Christ as the *"Last Adam!"*

This obedience included the Cross, where the terrible sin debt of man was paid by the pouring out of Jesus' Own Blood, which satisfied all Heavenly Justice and, as well, broke the grip of sin on the human family, at least for those who will believe. In that, God was vindicated and thus *"Glorified!"*

The words, *"Glory"* or *"Glorify,"* mean, *"To make glorious by bestowing honor, praise, and admiration."* It also means, *"To elevate to celestial glory on which to shed radiance and splendor."* As well, it speaks of *"beauty, power, magnificence, wonder, brilliance, and manifestation."*

In the case of God, for Him to be *"Glorified,"* it would refer to a beauty and magnificence so absolutely grand that it far surpasses anything imagined by a human being. However, the greatest glorification of all, as it refers to God, is the fact of Jesus on the Cross of Calvary paying the price for lost humanity, thereby, making real that great reality of Redemption.

Inasmuch as the Cross was a great Victory for God in that His Plan of ridding the world and the Universe of all sin and rebellion, it is now much closer to fulfillment.

GLORIFY HIM

The phrase, *"God shall also Glorify Him in Himself,"* refers to God in turn glorifying Jesus.

The Son of Man on the Cross was glorified in a much more admirable way than

He will be by the Millennial Glories attaching to that title; for on the Cross, as the Son of Man, He perfectly displayed all the Moral Glory of God.

He was there tested to the uttermost as to His Ability to sustain that Glory, but He fully succeeded in so doing. When made sin, or rather a Sin-Offering, He sacrificed Himself in order to fully glorify God. Thus, He established the Foundations of the New Heavens and the New Earth, which was all done as a result of the Cross. Thereby, He satisfied all the claims of Righteousness and of violated law against man, making it possible for Him to throw wide all the doors to men that they may enter into the Kingdom of Heaven.

STRAIGHTWAY

The phrase, *"And shall straightway Glorify Him,"* refers to God doing this immediately in the Resurrection of Christ from the dead.

Jesus was not only *"Glorified"* when He came out of the Tomb, He continued to be *"Glorified,"* and will actually continue thusly forever. The word *"straightway"* means *"immediately"* or *"forthwith."*

We learn from this Statement by Christ exactly the value that God the Father placed on that which Jesus did at Calvary. Were one to use every adjective or superlative in attempting to describe this Glorious Victory won at that place of infamy, the Cross, one would still fall woefully short.

As well, whoever it might be who more fully understands what that great Victory at Calvary meant to the human family, still, that person has not scratched the surface. The magnitude of Calvary is incomprehensible! The reason is that it speaks of so many things.

First of all, Calvary was the greatest exhibition of Love that humanity has ever known. Actually, it is a Love so profound that, once again, it is beyond the comprehension of even the most Spiritual Believer.

As well, the Power here evidenced was, once again, greater than the imagination can conceive. One of the reasons is that it was a different type of Power than had ever been exhibited. It broke the terrible grip of sin and death upon the human family but in a way that Power had never before been exhibited. It brought life out of death, and, more particularly, by death, life was gained. What made it even more striking is that Satan did not recognize this Power. He rather looked at it as weakness instead! (II Cor. 13:4). Therefore, it destroyed him! Regrettably, there are many in the modern church who do not recognize the Power of Calvary, rather looking at it as a weakness. God forbid!

VICTORY

The Victory won was of such a magnitude that it will last forever. The Cross is something that took place now nearly 2,000 years ago but has eternal benefits, benefits which will never be curtailed or stopped. Once again, this is a type of Victory of which man can little conceive. Mighty empires have risen, but, ultimately, they fall. By contrast, this Victory won by Christ will never fall!

These Passages tell us that while God is *"Glorified"* by many things, such as answered prayer, Healing, Miracles, and many other things, He, according to these Passages, is *"Glorified"* greater than all concerning the price paid by our Lord at Calvary's Cross. In other words, the Sacrificial Atoning Work of Christ at Calvary glorified God to a greater degree than anything else that had ever been done or ever will be done.

(33) "LITTLE CHILDREN, YET A LITTLE WHILE I AM WITH YOU. YOU SHALL SEEK ME: AND AS I SAID UNTO THE JEWS, WHERE I GO, YOU CANNOT COME; SO NOW I SAY TO YOU."

The construction is:

1. For any person to claim that another man or woman, or even a religious denomination, is his covering is, at the same time, saying that Christ is not sufficient.

2. Paul emphatically states: *"For there is one God, and one Mediator between God and men, the Man Christ Jesus"* (I Tim. 2:5).

3. Do we realize how much of an insult it is to Christ when we claim that somebody else is our covering? The only covering that man can furnish is a covering of *"fig leaves,"* i.e., *"Adam and Eve after the Fall."*

SPIRITUAL IMMATURITY

By using the words, *"Little children,"* as Jesus addressed the Disciples, and all others at that time, for that matter, He was speaking of spiritual immaturity. Of course, this would be rectified greatly on the Day of Pentecost. Also, He spoke those words by Faith in that they would become humble and selfless, exactly as He had taught them. To be sure, even as this very Chapter portrays, such did not come easily.

He would only be with them for about another 44 days before the Ascension.

He was with them that particular day, then remained in the Tomb three full days and nights, and was then with them 40 days after the Resurrection.

The phrase, *"You shall seek Me,"* simply had reference to the fact that He would be gone.

The Disciples still had it in their minds that He was going to institute the Kingdom now, continuing even to believe such after the Resurrection (Acts 1:6-7). So, the idea that He was going to leave was not in their thinking.

"And as I said unto the Jews, Where I go, you cannot come," is said differently than that spoken to His Disciples. Ultimately, His Disciples would not only seek but follow and find. However, when it came to the *"Jews"* of whom He spoke, they would not be able to go where He was simply because they did not know God and, in fact, would die eternally lost.

The phrase, *"So now I say to you,"* presents an entirely different statement than that given to the faithless Jews.

(34) "A NEW COMMANDMENT I GIVE UNTO YOU, THAT YOU LOVE ONE ANOTHER; AS I HAVE LOVED YOU, THAT YOU ALSO LOVE ONE ANOTHER."

The order is:

1. Concerning covering, no human being can serve as a *"covering"* for anyone, and to think otherwise shows a complete ignorance of the Word of God (Isa. 30:1).

2. Anytime we go astray, which means to leave the Word of God for directions of our own making, in some way, it is because of an improper interpretation of the Cross.

3. This particular sin of man-made coverings is worse than most sins because it strikes at the very heart of the Plan of Redemption respecting Christ as the Mediator, and the only Mediator.

A NEW COMMANDMENT

The phrase, *"A new Commandment I give unto you, That you love one another,"* is beyond the Old Commandment in Leviticus 19:18, *"You shall love your neighbour as yourself."*

The phrase, *"As I have loved you, that you also love one another,"* proclaims the ingredients of this New Commandment.

In the Leviticus 19:18 Commandment, which embraces the whole Law, self-love is assumed and is made the standard for the love of one's neighbor.

On the other hand, the *"Love"* of which Jesus here spoke is based on a new principle altogether. It is measured by a higher standard and has a greater depth than the measurement of self-love.

Christ's Love to His Disciples was self-abandoning, self-sacrificing Love, which went far beyond self-love.

In effect, He was saying, *"I have loved each of you unto death; in loving one another, you are loving Me; you are loving an object of My Tender Love."*

What makes this so remarkable is that the entirety of the New Covenant has as its Foundation this *"New Commandment"* of this new kind of Love.

(35) "BY THIS SHALL ALL MEN KNOW THAT YOU ARE MY DISCIPLES, IF YOU HAVE LOVE ONE TO ANOTHER."

The structure is:

1. Jesus Christ is our Substitute because He Alone could be our Substitute.

2. We are to identify with Him in every capacity, especially His Death, Burial, and Resurrection (Rom. 6:3-5).

3. In this manner alone are we *"in Christ"* (Jn. 14:20).

THE NEW COVENANT

The phrase, *"By this shall all men know that you are My Disciples,"* not only proclaims this *"Love"* as the Foundation of the New Covenant but, as well, proclaims it as the basis for recognition that one is truly in the New Covenant.

Reynolds said: *"But this in its fullness, and as sustained by this motive, or inspired by this pattern, and lifted to this standard, is new to the human race; and it is the power which has revolutionized thought, society, and life."*[10]

He went on to say, *"So long as this great power prevailed, the Church made astounding progress; when the so-called Disciples of Christ began to hate and kill one another, the progress was arrested."*[11]

As well, the inference as here given by our Lord is that if we have all the things, such as power, greatness, etc., but do not have this *"Love,"* then none of the other is of any consequence. No doubt, Paul had this statement by Christ in mind when he said, *"Though I speak with the tongues of men and of Angels, and have not charity* (love), *I am become as sounding brass, or a tinkling cymbal"* (I Cor. 13:1).

The phrase, *"If you have love one to another,"* in effect, says, *"You have been ambitious, envious, and at strife for supremacy. This cannot be. You must love as I love. By this, others shall know you to be Christians."*

THE GOD KIND OF LOVE

This type of *"love"* (Agape) is the God-kind of Love and is impossible for anyone to have without accepting Christ as one's Saviour. At this time, such Love is instilled in one's heart, but cooperation with the Holy Spirit thereafter alone guarantees its maturity.

If one could properly explain such, the type of Love of which Jesus spoke, as should be obvious, goes far beyond that of which one would normally think. It is very easy to love someone who loves in return, but something else again to love someone who not only does not love in return, but would actually do you harm, even great harm. But yet, Jesus died for people who hated Him and in no way loved Him!

It is very easy to love someone who has been official and helpful, but not so easy at all to love someone who is of the opposite conduct. But yet, Jesus loved those, even His Own Disciples, who, most of the time, were at cross purposes with Him. In other words, they were in no way beneficial, but rather the opposite; however, He saw people not so much as they were but what they could be in Him. We should *"see"* accordingly!

When one is popular, it is very difficult to know what truly is Love, or rather that which is self-seeking.

When one is down and absolutely defenseless, and others can say or do any harmful thing to that person they desire without any fear of reprimand, but rather approval, then one finds out very quickly who truly has the God kind of Love!

(36) "SIMON PETER SAID UNTO HIM, LORD, WHERE ARE YOU GOING? JESUS ANSWERED HIM, WHERE I GO, YOU CANNOT FOLLOW ME NOW; BUT YOU SHALL FOLLOW ME AFTERWARDS."

The form is:

1. When we accepted Christ, we were *"baptized into His Death."* This does not refer to Water Baptism, but rather to the Crucifixion of Christ.

2. In fact, it has nothing to do with Water Baptism.

3. In the Mind of God, when we accepted Christ, we died with Him, were buried with Him, and rose with Him (Rom. 6:3-5).

SIMON PETER

The question, *"Simon Peter said unto Him, Lord, where are You going?"* proclaims, as stated, that the Disciples had no idea what Jesus was saying regarding His Departure.

The phrase, *"Jesus answered him, Where I go, you cannot follow Me now; but you shall follow Me afterwards,"* proclaims several things:

• His Statement proclaims the Ascension, which would follow in about 44 days.

• He would go back to the Throne of God in Heaven.

• The Disciples would not follow Him at this particular time but would remain here as the nucleus of the Early Church, and would be used mightily of the Lord. In reality, this is at least one of the most important reasons for their being chosen in this capacity.

• He assured them that where He was

going, they would later follow, which they did! Actually, James, the brother of John, was the first to be taken, with John being the last.

(37) "PETER SAID UNTO HIM, LORD, WHY CANNOT I FOLLOW YOU NOW? I WILL LAY DOWN MY LIFE FOR YOUR SAKE."

The form is:

1. Virtually the entirety of the Word of God is the Story of *"Jesus Christ and Him Crucified"* (Jn. 1:1, 14, 29).

2. It basically centers up in how the Believer is to live for God. That is at least one of the reasons that the unredeemed cannot understand it.

3. While no Chapter in the Bible is more important than any other, still, there are some Chapters that bring everything to a head. The Sixth Chapter of Romans falls into that capacity. It just might be the most important Chapter in the entirety of the Word of God.

WAS PETER SINCERE?

The question, *"Peter said unto Him, Lord, why cannot I follow You now?"* proclaims a total misunderstanding on Peter's part. As stated, the immaturity of the Disciples was so obvious at this time, but would change after the Day of Pentecost.

The phrase, *"I will lay down my life for Your Sake,"* is probably the basis for the great Truth spoken by the Apostle Paul, that it is possible to die a martyr's death and yet to be without true love (I Cor. 13:1-3).

As the record shows, Peter did not really know what he was saying. Reynolds said: *"Peter thought himself ready to die for His Lord, before His Lord had died for him."*[12]

Did Peter really mean what he said?

I believe he did! However, being sincere about something is one thing while having enough strength to carry it forth is something else entirely. Lest we berate the fisherman too soundly, perhaps we should look at ourselves first!

(38) "JESUS ANSWERED HIM, WILL YOU LAY DOWN YOUR LIFE FOR MY SAKE? VERILY, VERILY, I SAY UNTO YOU, THE ROOSTER SHALL NOT CROW, TILL YOU HAVE DENIED ME THRICE."

NOTES

The pattern is:

1. Jesus Christ is the Source of all things we receive from God (Jn. 1:1, 14, 29; Col. 2:10-15).

2. The Cross of Christ is the Means by which all of these things are given to us (Rom. 6:1-14; Col. 2:14-15; Gal. 6:14).

3. With the Cross being the Means, the Cross must be the Object of our Faith at all times. When we say, *"The Cross,"* we aren't speaking of the wooden beam on which Jesus died, but rather what He there accomplished in His Death (I Cor. 1:17, 18, 21, 23; 2:2).

4. With Christ as the Source, the Cross as the Means, and the Cross as the Object of our Faith, then the Holy Spirit, Who works entirely within the parameters of the Finished Work of Christ, will grandly help us to live the life we ought to live. Otherwise, He won't (Rom. 8:1-11; Eph. 2:13-18).

DENIAL

The question, *"Jesus answered him, Will you lay down your life for My Sake?"* is not really asked expecting an answer because the answer was already known.

"Verily, verily, I say unto you, The rooster shall not crow, till you have denied Me thrice," proclaims a coming terrible moment in the life of Peter, and that which was the very opposite of what he was claiming.

This answer, as given by Jesus, completely refutes the idea that education is the solution to man's problems. While God certainly does not place any premium on ignorance, still, the impartation of knowledge, even though extremely helpful, cannot provide the strength needed to do that which is right. If education were the answer, then Peter would not have failed. Surely, with this type of knowledge given to him by Jesus concerning his near future, he could ward against the coming storm. However, as we know, it was not sufficient.

INSUFFICIENT RESOLVE?

To argue that Peter's problem was insufficient resolve is to ignore the plain facts, which spoke otherwise.

Men think they can educate the problem of racism out of bigots. Others feel that if criminals had the proper instruction, this would solve their particular problem.

However, I remind the reader that if that were the case, prisons would have no educated people in their confines. The truth is, prisons are filled with lawyers, doctors, educators, and, in fact, very intelligent people. So, what went wrong?

Without a moral change within one's heart and life, which comes about only by accepting Christ as one's Saviour, one will do little or no better than did Peter.

As well, even Believers as Peter are not immune at all to failure, as should here be obvious. In fact, if the Believer doesn't have his faith anchored solidly in Christ and the Cross, and maintained solidly in Christ and the Cross, such a Believer is going to be ruled by the sin nature, which means he's living a life of constant failure. This is not very pleasant, but it happens to be the truth as it regards most Christians of this particular age. The reason is: while the church has at least some understanding respecting the Cross regarding Salvation, it has none at all regarding the Cross and Sanctification.

Then, to make a bad matter worse, Peter would not deny Christ once but three times! It would be done that very night, even before the crowing of the rooster at dawn.

The song writer said:

"My stubborn will at last has yielded;
"I would be Yours and Yours Alone;

"And this the prayer my lips are bringing,
"Lord, let in me Your Will be done."

CHAPTER 14

(1) "LET NOT YOUR HEART BE TROUBLED: YOU BELIEVE IN GOD, BELIEVE ALSO IN ME."

The construction is:

1. Everything we receive from God comes from Christ as the Source and the Cross as the Means.

2. Faith in the Cross claims the supremacy of the Saviour and the helplessness of the Believer.

3. Any Christian who thinks he has outgrown the Cross has just invited disaster for himself.

A TROUBLED HEART?

The phrase, *"Let not your heart be troubled,"* is said by Christ immediately after predicting Peter's shameful denial.

As well, He had just related to them that He was leaving shortly. Of course, they did not understand at all, at least at that time, what His Statement meant. Nevertheless, from His Admonition to them concerning their troubled hearts, it is obvious that it brought great consternation.

They were facing far more difficulties than they could even begin to imagine. Despite Him telling them repeatedly that He would die and be raised from the dead, they could not bring themselves to believe these words. Surely, He would use His great Power to turn aside such a horrible thing. As well, they, no doubt, thought, *"What good would His Dying do relative to the great good He is now accomplishing by healing the sick and casting out demons?"*

Being steeped in the traditions of Israel and knowing that the Prophets of old had spoken volumes concerning the coming Kingdom Age, surely, this was it, or so they reasoned!

It is strange, but it seems that they did not know or understand exactly what the sacrifices meant! In the Jewish mind, they had become an end unto themselves, forgetting that God had ordained that they point to a coming Redeemer. Actually, the whole framework of the Mosaic Law had lost its meaning through subtractions and additions, especially additions! So, the Messiah, as predicted in Isaiah, Chapter 53, was foreign to their thinking. That Jesus would die on Calvary, bearing the sin penalty of the world, was not understood at all, despite Isaiah saying, *"He was cut off out of the land of the living: for the transgression of My People was He stricken"* (Isa. 53:8).

THE CROSS

Yes, the absolute good that Jesus would accomplish by dying on Calvary would so far eclipse His Personal Ministry of healing the sick, etc., that there was no comparison. The word *"good"* is woefully inadequate to even begin to explain such a benefit. However, neither the Disciples at that time, nor anyone else for that matter, could even remotely see or understand such a thing.

Due to what He had just said about leaving, all they knew and realized, at least at that moment, was that they were facing an uncertain or even perilous future. So, He would respond to that fear by telling them that they should not be troubled.

As well, this word was not spoken only to the Disciples of that day but, actually, to all who follow Christ for all time. If we truly follow Him, trusting in His Word, seeking to walk as cleanly before Him as is possible, and allowing the Holy Spirit to have His Way within our lives, many may be the afflictions, but they need not trouble us. Now, He tells us why!

FAITH IN CHRIST

The phrase, *"You believe in God, believe also in Me,"* simply means to have Faith in God and, as well, in Christ. This is His highest and most complete Revelation of Himself as God.

He claimed from the Disciples, and all His Followers for that matter, and for all time, the same kind of sentiment, as by right of Creation and Infinite Perfection, that God Almighty had demanded from them.

He is telling them and us to repose in the same trust and confidence in His Forgiving Love and Almighty Power and Care as we repose in God. As stated, this is His Greatest Commanding Claim to equality with God!

As well, what balm this must have been to Peter's troubled heart at daybreak on the next day when, weeping bitterly, he lay broken-hearted in the depths.

To be sure, the Master's Own Heart was *"troubled"* (Jn. 13:21). However, He put His own Trouble aside and told them not to be troubled, for He would never cease to care for them, and though He must leave them, He would be busy preparing mansions for them.

(2) "IN MY FATHER'S HOUSE ARE MANY MANSIONS: IF IT WERE NOT SO, I WOULD HAVE TOLD YOU. I GO TO PREPARE A PLACE FOR YOU."

The form is:

1. There is an insanity to sin, which only the Cross can cure.

2. That's the reason for all the wars, man's inhumanity to man, criminal activity, etc.

3. There is only one solution for sin, only one, and that is, as stated, the Cross of Christ. Humanistic psychology is helpless before this evil power.

MANSIONS

The phrase, *"In My Father's House are many mansions,"* proclaims Heaven as a large place. It is a place so large, actually, that its possibilities transcend one's imagination and exceed our comprehension.

The idea is that there would be room for every single Believer. We know that all Believers will ultimately live on this Earth with Jesus, and I speak of the coming Kingdom Age. Still, it seems that each will also have a *"mansion"* in Heaven, which, at the conclusion of the Kingdom Age, will be transferred from Planet Heaven to Planet Earth. John said:

"And I John saw the Holy City, New Jerusalem, coming down from God out of Heaven, prepared as a Bride adorned for her husband.

"And I heard a great Voice out of Heaven saying, Behold, the Tabernacle of God is with men, and He will dwell with them, and they shall be His People, and God Himself shall be with them, and be their God" (Rev. 21:2-3).

The manner in which Jesus used the term *"Father's House"* proclaims that His Father is now their Father also! As a result, the *"Father's House"* is now their *"House."*

The word *"mansion"* means *"abiding place"* and is translated also *"abode"* in Verse 23.

The phrase, *"If it were not so, I would have told you,"* has reference to the fact that He is speaking from firsthand knowledge. He has been there and is going back.

Even though His Statements are grand, so grand, in fact, that they are difficult to believe, still, they are true!

PREPARATION

The phrase, *"I go to prepare a place for you,"* refers to Him Personally superintending this extra building project in Heaven, especially considering the fantastic number who, through the centuries, would come to Christ.

So, that awaiting the Believer at the end of this life is amazing, to say the least! What a wonderful Promise! This means that every Saint of God who has gone on is now living in one of these mansions. No wonder Paul said: *"For I am in a strait betwixt two, having a desire to depart, and be with Christ, which is far better"* (Phil. 1:23).

(3) "AND IF I GO AND PREPARE A PLACE FOR YOU, I WILL COME AGAIN, AND RECEIVE YOU UNTO MYSELF; THAT WHERE I AM, THERE YOU MAY BE ALSO."

The exegesis is:

1. While the Cross can be spoken of as a Doctrine, it must be understood that it is the Foundational Truth from which all supplemental Doctrine springs.

2. I'm sure that Jesus addressed what He had done on the Cross as more than a mere Doctrine among Doctrines.

3. If one properly understands the Cross, then one has a working knowledge of the Bible.

THERE YOU MAY BE

The phrase, *"And if I go and prepare a place for you, I will come again, and receive you unto Myself,"* proclaims the first mention of the Rapture of the Church (I Thess. 4:13-18). At this time, He will receive unto Himself all the dead and living in Christ, who will come back to Earth with Him at the Second Coming (Zech. 14:5; Jude, Vs. 14; Rev. 19:11-21).

"That where I am, there you may be also," refers to Heaven, where the Saints of God will go at the Resurrection.

Without a doubt, the Apostle Paul took these Passages to Jesus for deeper explanation when confronted by the Thessalonians concerning those among them who had died. As a result, the Lord gave Paul the expanded teaching given to us in I Thessalonians 4:13-18.

(4) "AND WHERE I GO YOU KNOW, AND THE WAY YOU KNOW.

(5) "THOMAS SAID UNTO HIM, LORD, WE KNOW NOT WHERE YOU GO; AND HOW CAN WE KNOW THE WAY?"

The form is:

1. To not understand the Cross means that, in some way, the individual has a perverted view of the Word of God.

2. In fact, the Story of the Cross is, in effect, the Story of the Bible.

3. This is so closely intertwined that we can say, as well, that the Story of the Bible is the Story of the Cross.

WHERE I GO

The phrase, *"And where I go you know,"* refers to the fact that the Lord has just told them, and they are to believe Him concerning His Father's House.

"And the Way you know," actually spoke of Himself, for Jesus is the *"Way,"* which He will say forthwith (Vs. 6).

"Thomas said unto Him, Lord, we know not where You go," presents this Disciple striving after Truth and reality through intellectualism and not faith. Consequently, what he could not grasp was almost all things said by Jesus because of the manner in which he attempted to comprehend or understand.

Every single time, if faith is set aside and we attempt to grasp the great Truths of the Bible by the root of intellectualism only, we will, as Thomas, come up short. While these Truths certainly can be understood intellectually, and are supposed to be, still, they have to be first taken by Faith, or else, the door will remain closed.

This is why the Gospel is an offense to many! And yet, the explanation is simple.

If the Lord had made intellectualism the criterion for acceptance of the Gospel and the receiving of its many benefits, this would have left out a great percentage of the world's population. As well, it would have probably been almost impossible for even the most intelligent to fully grasp these things, even if they were the root, simply because everything God does is beyond the pale of human knowledge and, therefore, can only be spiritually discerned.

Nicodemus appealed to the Lord in the same manner regarding intellectualism. He desired to understand the *"Born-Again"* experience intellectually, which, in effect, Jesus said could not be done. In explaining this extremely complex subject, Jesus said, *"The wind blows where it lists, and you hear the sound thereof, but cannot tell from where it comes, and where it goes: so is everyone who is born of the Spirit"* (Jn. 3:8).

FAITH

Among other reasons, God has chosen the way of *"Faith"* simply because of Who He is and What He proposes. It is of such magnitude that it is simply beyond human capability, at least without the Help of the Holy Spirit. Consequently, the Gospel can only be accepted by Faith, as should be obvious! However, once it is received, to which we have already alluded, the Spirit of God also quickens the intellect in that it can be understood and comprehended, at least up to a point.

The Fall in the Garden of Eden has so incapacitated man spiritually that what intellect he does have, which has been seriously impaired, as well, is not capable of grasping spiritual things. He has to be *"Born-Again"* before he can come by such understanding, which can only be received by Faith.

But yet, Thomas loved Jesus supremely and would gradually learn the Faith walk.

As plainly as Jesus had spoken concerning His *"Father's House,"* Thomas should have known the place of which He spoke!

The question, *"And how can we know the way?"* will be answered immediately by Jesus.

Someone has said, *"There often seems in the language of skepticism much common sense, and in the dry light of science a straightforward honesty."* However, the answer, as will be given by Jesus, will once again steer Thomas, and all others for that matter, down the path of Faith. The Lord never really tries to prove Himself. While He will always answer honest inquiry, He will never respond to skepticism and doubt.

(6) "JESUS SAID UNTO HIM, I AM THE WAY, THE TRUTH, AND THE LIFE: NO MAN COMES UNTO THE FATHER, BUT BY ME."

The construction is:

1. The study of the Tabernacle and of the Sacrificial System of the Old Testament, all, and in totality, is a study of the Cross.

2. The only answer for sin, which is the problem, is the Cross of Christ.

3. That's the reason it is hopeless and helpless to try to address the problem of sin in any other way than the Cross.

THE WAY, THE TRUTH, AND THE LIFE

The phrase, *"Jesus said unto him, I am the Way, the Truth, and the Life,"* proclaims in no uncertain terms exactly Who and What Jesus is.

For instance, He does not merely show the *"Way"* but, in fact, is the *"Way!"*

As well, He does not merely contain *"Truth"* but, in fact, is *"Truth!"*

He does not merely have *"Life"* but, in fact, is *"Life!"*

"I am the Way": this tells us that not only is He the *"Way,"* but the *"Only Way,"* for the statement is emphatic.

The *"Way"* of which He speaks is the Way to the Father Himself, for that is the entire goal. From the Father, He came and to the Father, He was moving, not for His Own Sake only but, also, as King Messiah for all His Subjects.

He declares positively that this idea of God as Father, this approach to God for every man, is through Him — through what He is and What He is doing.

If one is to notice, man proposes all types of ways to God, even proposing that man himself become God! However, all these alleged ways are specious.

Prideful man bridles at the thought of there being only one way and, above all, that Jesus is that One Way. His skepticism arises out of the fact that he is not allowed to chart his own course.

THE TRUTH

Some have suggested that *"Truth"* and *"Life"* were added to throw greater light upon the *"Way"* to the Father.

While they, no doubt, do that, still, they

embody a Revelation of Christ all their own.

As being a personification of Truth, we learn that all of reality finds its focus in Christ. He Who created and sustains the Universe is also man's Redeemer and the goal toward which all history strains (Col. 1:15-23).

As a Believer, we can *"know the Truth"* simply by knowing Jesus and, thus, be set free by keeping Jesus' Words (Jn. 8:31-32).

TRUTH AS TRUE INTELLECTUALISM

Intellectualism is simply *"the capacity for rational or intelligent thought."* It is the power of knowing as distinguished from the power to feel and to will: the capacity for knowledge.

As such, even though Jesus Christ must be accepted by Faith, once that comes about, true intellectualism comes about as well. It is *"the full or real state of affairs,"* hence, Truth.

Jesus as Truth is the absolute sense of that which is real and complete as opposed to what is false and wanting (Mk. 5:33; Eph. 4:25). Bible Faith in particular is Truth (Gal. 2:5; Eph. 1:13). As we are stating, Jesus claimed that He was Truth Personified (Jn. 14:6; Eph. 4:21). As such, He mediates the Truth (Jn. 1:17), and the Holy Spirit leads men into it (Jn. 14:17; 16:13; I Jn. 4:6), so that Jesus' Followers know it (Jn. 8:32; II Jn., Vs. 1), do it (Jn. 3:21), abide in it (Jn. 8:44), and their New Birth as God's Children rests upon it (James 1:18).

This *"Truth"* is more than a credible formula; it is God's Active Word, which must be obeyed (Rom. 2:8; Gal. 5:7).

JESUS AS TRUTH

Truth carries the sense of something real as opposed to mere appearance or copy. Consequently, Jesus is thus a Minister of the True Tabernacle (Heb. 8:2) in contrast with the shadows of the Levitical ritual (Heb. 8:4).

In clear allusion to the words of institution of the Lord's Supper, Jesus declares that He is the True Bread (Jn. 6:32, 35) and the True Vine (Jn. 15:1), i.e., that He is the Eternal Reality symbolized by the Bread and Wine. In other words, everything pointed to Him as Truth.

NOTES

TRUTH IS NOT A PHILOSOPHY BUT A MAN

Of course, that Man is Jesus!

While there are many things which are true, that does not necessarily mean they are *"Truth!"* It is true that if one takes poison, one will die or at least get very ill. However, the poison, or the fact of the poison, is not *"Truth"* but merely something which is true. As well, two plus two equal four, but again, that is not *"Truth"* but merely something that is true.

Webster defines truth as *"Keeping close to fact."* However, that premise is so wrong, 180 degrees, in fact. It is so wrong that it provides no correct foundation whatsoever and, actually, would be what one might refer to as *"subjective truth."*

How can something be *"Truth"* if it is merely *"close"* to whatever standard is being used? No! Truth has nothing to do with facts, even though the facts may be true.

Subjective truth, which is actually no truth at all, refers to something which is interpreted solely on one's personal experience, in other words, as one believes something to be. The foundation of such error is the circumstances and happenings as they relate to the person in question.

As should be obvious, such so-called truth changes according to the whims of present circumstances. Regrettably, it is this type of truth on which America, and the entirety of the world for that matter, is basing its direction. I speak of the legislative and judicial systems of the nation. In fact, almost the whole of the population of the world falls into the same category.

Most people interpret Salvation according to their whims or fancy, with the Bible not at all serving as their foundation; consequently, they believe a lie! Such is subjective truth.

OBJECTIVE TRUTH VERSUS SUBJECTIVE TRUTH

Objective Truth is that which is based on a Standard which changes not, i.e., the Bible. What was Truth 5,000 years ago is Truth presently. In fact, it never changes simply because it does not need to change and, actually, if it did change, it would not be truth. Consequently, if a nation or a person builds the fabric of its society and existence on that which changes not, they have built and, in fact, are building on a Rock that cannot be moved by storms, circumstances, or difficulties (Mat. 7:24).

By contrast, subjective truth builds upon sand, and the houses always fall sooner or later (Mat. 7:27).

Subjective truth changes according to situations, etc., which, in reality, is no truth at all.

In this light, it is understandable as to why *"Truth"* could not be a philosophy: it is simply because philosophies change by their very nature. Truth must reside in a Person, but an unchangeable Person, Who Alone is Christ.

ALL TRUTH IS GOD'S TRUTH?

A short time ago, I happened to read a short article in the *"Pentecostal Evangel,"* the official publication of the Assemblies of God. It was written by a psychologist associated with that group, and he was touting the philosophy, *"All truth is God's Truth!"*

He was advocating that, in their studies of human behavior, some of the leading psychologists of the past (and present, I assume) had come upon great truths which could benefit society. He was advocating that irrespective as to who received these truths or how they came by them, they originated with God and were therefore valid.

Even though he did not say so, that is, if I remember correctly, I suppose he was basing his conclusion on the premise that many scientists, who make no profession of faith in Christ, have discovered certain laws, such as the Law of Gravity, etc., which we know originated with God, with their discovery proving to be a tremendous benefit to humanity. Inasmuch as that is true, and it is, such thinking concludes that *"truths"* discovered by so-called behavioral specialists originated with God and should be used for the betterment of humanity as well!

Actually, that would be true were the assumption correct concerning behavioral study; however, it just happens to not be true.

THE BIBLE

The Bible is not a textbook on mathematics, chemistry, physics, etc., even though all the laws governing these vast subjects originated with God. However, what little it does say on these vast subjects is absolute Truth.

The Bible does not deal with these things as its primary subject because man's problem is not engineering or science. Man's problem is behavior, which is caused by sin, and for which the Bible claims to hold all the answers. Actually, that is the very reason Jesus came to this world. He did not come to show men how to build airplanes, skyscrapers, etc. He did come to show men how to live, which has everything to do with one's behavior.

Psychology teaches the very opposite of the Word of God and contradicts itself constantly concerning the cause and the cure of man's behavioral problems. So, to claim that psychology is a valid science is done through ignorance of what true science really is, ignorance of the Word of God, or outright unbelief. There are no *"truths"* concerning man's behavior outside of the Word of God; therefore, it is not possible for Believers or unbelievers to discover such in that framework, for such does not exist.

To say or claim that such *"truths"* exist is, at the same time, saying that the Holy Spirit, in giving the Scripture to *"Holy Men of God,"* did not have all the knowledge concerning this all-important subject. In fact, one preacher with the denomination mentioned several paragraphs back actually said that modern man is facing problems not addressed in the Bible and, therefore, must have the help of psychology, along with the Bible, etc. To be blunt, that is a crock.

The Word of God plainly tells us that the Lord *"has given unto us all things that pertain unto life and godliness, through the knowledge of Him Who has called us to Glory and Virtue"* (II Pet. 1:3).

Now, if that is true, and it most definitely is, then psychology is a lie because it claims to have discovered *"truths"* not found in the Bible.

If the Bible is not true, then we should

abandon it altogether and follow after the teaching of Freud, Maslow, Rogers, etc. As well, if the Bible contains even one error, then it cannot be trusted at all.

ALL TRUTH CONCERNING BEHAVIOR IS FOUND IN THE BIBLE

The Truth is, the Bible is the Word of God and, as such, is without error and does contain every single *"Truth"* regarding human behavior. To add to it is blasphemy! To take from it is ignorance! When Jesus came to this world and died on the Cross, He addressed the behavior problem of man in totality. Nothing can be added to His Finished Work, and, in truth, nothing needs to be added. To do such, or rather attempt to do so, is an insult to the great price He paid that memorable day nearly 2,000 years ago.

No! The claim that *"All truth is God's Truth"* is invalid simply because there is no truth, which these proponents claim, outside of the Bible.

LIFE

"And the Life": the Word actually means *"the Life Eternal"* and means that Jesus is the Possessor, Author, Captain, Giver, and Prince of Life — the Life in the heart of believing man that can never die.

As *"Life"* is added last, such must be anchored in that which is *"Truth,"* for anything other than Truth is a lie and brings forth death.

Both *"Life"* and *"Truth"* must, of necessity, reside in *"The Way,"* Who is Jesus as well! As we have stated, Jesus is not a way-shower but, in truth, *"The Way!"*

The phrase, *"No man comes unto the Father, but by Me,"* presents Jesus as the *"Way"* to the Father, which is *"Truth"* and, as well, gives *"Life."*

This emphatic Statement made by Christ, and it is emphatic, plainly tells us that inasmuch as the Father cannot be reached other than by Him, the whole of Islam is satanic, for it claims to reach God through Muhammad.

The New Agers claim to reach God through self and, in fact, claim self to be God. The fallacy of that premise need not be dignified with an answer.

NOTES

The Jews claim to reach God through their various Mosaic rituals, which they do not seem to understand were only Types of Christ, i.e., to be used until He came. So, to deny Jesus is to deny God and, in fact, closes the door to any true spiritual activity.

JESUS, THE ONLY WAY TO THE FATHER

The reason that Jesus is the Only Way to the Father is because He is the One Who paid the price for man's Redemption. He hung on the Cross, not someone else! He faced sin, Satan, and death and won the Victory hence, *"Ten thousand times ten thousand, and thousands of thousands;*

"Saying with a loud voice, Worthy is the Lamb that was slain" (Rev. 5:11-12).

Consequently, He is *"Worthy,"* not only because of Who He is but, as well, because of What He has done!

So, when He said that He was the only Way to the Father, it was said for purpose and reason.

Please note the following:

• The only way to God is through Jesus Christ (Jn. 14:6).

• The only way to Jesus Christ is through the Cross (Lk. 14:27).

• The only way to the Cross is by a denial of self (Lk. 9:23).

(7) "IF YOU HAD KNOWN ME, YOU SHOULD HAVE KNOWN MY FATHER ALSO: AND FROM HENCEFORTH YOU KNOW HIM, AND HAVE SEEN HIM."

The structure is:

1. Neither humanistic psychology nor any other effort by man can address itself to the sin question.

2. It is the Cross and the Cross alone that answers this horrible malady of the human race.

3. There is no answer for sin but the Cross. If we try something else, we try in vain!

IF YOU KNOW ME, YOU KNOW THE FATHER

The phrase, *"If you had known Me, you should have known My Father also,"* means, *"If you had learned to know Me spiritually and experimentally, you should have gotten to know that I and the Father are One,"* i.e., *"One in essence and unity, not in number."*

Jesus is saying that to know Him is to know the Father. The key is found in the word *"know"* or *"known."*

The word *"known"* is used by Jesus twice but is actually two different words in the Greek Text.

When He said, *"If you had known Me,"* He was using the Greek word *"ginosko,"* which means *"to come to know,"* and to ultimately have complete understanding. In other words, it is a progressive knowledge which increases with time because of an earnest effort and sincere desire to get to know the person or object better.

The word *"known,"* as used by Jesus the second time, in the Greek is *"oida"* and means *"fullness of knowledge."* The idea is this:

KNOWING JESUS AND KNOWING THE FATHER

Most people do not know the Father because they do not know Jesus. They may know Him in a historical sense, or they may even know Him in the sense of Salvation, having accepted Him as Saviour. However, the type of knowledge of which Jesus speaks concerning Himself is that which comes from a sincere relationship with Him, which provides a true knowledge of Who He is and What He has done! This comes about only by Revelation from the Holy Spirit, which, of necessity, must be accompanied by a strong prayer life and total consecration to the Person and Purpose of Christ. Concerning this, being *"Born-Again"* is only the beginning. As well, there is no limit to the expansion of this type of knowledge, as evidenced by the Apostle Paul, who said, *"That I may know Him ..."* (Phil. 3:10).

As well, it is not possible for any Believer to fully know the Lord as one should unless he knows and understands the Cross of Christ. When I speak of understanding the Cross, I am speaking of understanding it not only as it regards Salvation but, as well, our Sanctification. It is absolutely imperative that the Believer understand the bedrock, the foundation, of the great Plan of Redemption, which centers up in the Cross. Perhaps the following will help the reader

NOTES

to understand the Cross a little better. Even though the same information is given elsewhere in this Volume, still, because of its great significance, please allow the repetition.

• Jesus Christ is the Source of all things we receive from God (Jn. 1:1-3, 14, 29; Col. 2:10-15).

• With Christ as the Source, we find that the Cross is the Means, and the only Means, by which all of these wonderful things are given to us (Rom. 6:1-14; I Cor. 1:17; Col. 2:10-15).

• With Christ as the Source and the Cross as the Means, and the only Means, it is imperative that the Object of our Faith be the Cross of Christ, and the Cross of Christ exclusively. Inasmuch as the Story of the Bible is *"Jesus Christ and Him Crucified,"* when one places one's Faith exclusively in Christ and the Cross, that is placing it strictly in the Word of God (I Cor. 1:18, 23; 2:2; Gal. 6:14).

• With Christ as the Source and the Cross as the Means, and the Cross as the Object of our Faith, then the Holy Spirit, Who works exclusively within the parameters, so to speak, of the Finished Work of Christ, will work mightily on our behalf. In fact, through the Cross is the way that the Holy Spirit works, and the only Way that He works (Rom. 8:1-11; Eph. 2:13-18).

THE PROGRESSIVE ORDER

Upon this knowledge of Jesus, which is far more than mental assent, but rather a Spirit Revelation based on the Word of God, which begins at Salvation, knowledge of the Father is then automatic, which opens up the entirety of the Word.

However, the progressive order here must be understood and maintained. One does not learn about the Father first and then get to know the Messiah, which is actually what Israel was attempting to do. The Muslims do the same thing, with most of the world following suit. It is impossible to have a knowledge of God in this capacity because Jesus, as the Door, is rejected or at least ignored.

Jesus must be accepted first as the Saviour of man and Revelation of the Father. Only on this basis will the Holy Spirit perform His Work of Revelation concerning the Father.

Actually, the word *"known"* as Jesus used it of the Father, speaks of Divine Revelation! Consequently, such cannot be learned through the five senses, as everything else is learned, but only by Revelation from the Holy Spirit. As we have repeatedly stated, Jesus is the Door to that Revelation, and Jesus Alone.

HENCEFORTH

The phrase, *"And from henceforth you know Him, and have seen Him,"* has reference, by the word *"henceforth,"* that previously, even His Nearest and Dearest only partially knew Him. I speak of His Chosen Disciples! Actually, even His own flesh and blood Brothers and Sisters (half-brothers and half-sisters) did not really know Him at all! They did not see the Father because they did not truly *"see Jesus."*

The reason He used the word *"henceforth"* is because in about 51 days, the Holy Spirit would come (the Day of Pentecost).

As glorious and wonderful was the Person of Jesus, and as mighty and powerful as were His Miracles, and even though He totally fulfilled all the Scriptures concerning Who the Messiah would be, still, without the Holy Spirit, it was not possible for anyone to really know Jesus. The reason is simple: one cannot truly know Him in the flesh. That is one of the reasons that He kept pointing Himself out to His Disciples, showing them how He was the Fulfillment of the Scriptures, and even asking them as to Who they thought He was (Mat. 16:21).

At that time, the Disciples were able to give a mental affirmation, which was based on true Faith, as to Who Jesus really was; however, it would take the Advent of the Holy Spirit to fully reveal Christ.

(8) *"PHILIP SAID UNTO HIM, LORD, SHOW US THE FATHER, AND IT SUFFICES US."*

The form is:

1. How is the modern church addressing its problems? Regrettably, it is looking to anything and everything except the Cross.

2. However, now the Holy Spirit is bringing the Message of the Cross into full view of the Church, to where it has absolutely no choice but to either reject it or accept it.

3. The Cross of Christ is the dividing line between the true Church and the apostate church.

SHOW US THE FATHER

The phrase, *"Philip said unto Him, Lord,"* presents him referring to Jesus as *"lord,"* but in the lower case. In other words, it was a title only of respect, such as *"sir"* or *"rabbi,"* and was not actually linked with Deity. Many were referred to as *"lord"* at that time!

However, Thomas was the first one of the Disciples, in fact, to link the title *"Lord"* to Deity (Jn. 20:28).

Even though the same title *"Lord"* continued to be used by the Apostles in the Epistles, after the Day of Pentecost, it took on a completely different meaning. In other words, it was not used of any person other than Jesus and meant *"Deity,"* even though the Greek meaning of the title *"Kurios"* remained the same.

To say it in another way, there is no record that *"Kurios"* (Lord) was ever again used by Believers in addressing any except God and the Lord Jesus (Acts 2:47; 4:29-30).

How soon and how completely the lower meaning of *"lord"*, as used as *"sir"* or *"teacher"*, had been superseded, as seen in Peter's declaration in his first Sermon after the Resurrection, *"God has made Him — Lord"* (Acts 2:36), and in the house of Cornelius, *"He is Lord of all,"* (Deut. 10:14; Mat. 11:25; Acts 10:36; 17:24). It continued to be used in this manner throughout the New Testament.

THE FATHER

The phrase, *"Show us the Father, and it suffices us,"* portrays that Philip, with his fellow disciples, had not yet learned the Sacred Truth that they had already had the opportunity of seeing in the Life of the God-Man, the Lord Jesus Christ, the most explicit Manifestation of the Father.

There was really no excuse for this question, as Jesus would momentarily imply. Actually, the key, as Jesus would say, is *"Believe!"* At the risk of being overly repetitious, the Day of Pentecost would rectify this.

As Philip, the whole world, at least for the most part, wants to see God, but the far greater majority reject the only manner and way to see Him, which is through the Lord Jesus Christ.

(9) "JESUS SAID UNTO HIM, HAVE I BEEN SO LONG WITH YOU, AND YET HAVE YOU NOT KNOWN ME, PHILIP? HE WHO HAS SEEN ME HAS SEEN THE FATHER; AND HOW DO YOU SAY THEN, SHOW US THE FATHER?"

The exegesis is:

1. It is the shed Blood of Christ on the Cross alone that effects our Salvation.

2. Don't we, then, see the veracity of the Cross of Christ?

3. Everything we receive from God, and I mean everything, comes through Jesus Christ by the Means of the Cross, all superintended by the Holy Spirit.

THE HEAVENLY FATHER CAN ONLY BE SEEN IN JESUS

The question asked by Philip was answered by Jesus.

Reynolds said, *"There is no right understanding of Jesus Christ until the Father is actually seen in Him."* He then said, *"He is not known in His Humanity until the Divine Personality flashes through Him on the eyes of Faith."*[1]

Actually, this is what Jesus had been telling His Disciples all along, hence, using such phrases as, *"He who sees Me sees Him Who sent Me,"* (Jn. 12:45), and *"I and my Father are One"* (Jn. 10:30), or *"If you had known Me, you should have known My Father also"* (Jn. 8:19).

As we have previously stated, Israel believed in One God and, in fact, were the only people on Earth at that time who had this Revelation, with other nations worshipping many gods, which, in fact, were no gods at all!

However, Israel did not understand, even though it was clear in Scripture, that while there was only One God, He was manifest in Three Persons, *"God the Father," "God the Son,"* and *"God the Holy Spirit"* (Gen. 19:24; Ps. 8:5-6; 16:8-10; 110:1, 5; Isa. 4:2; 10:16-17; 28:16; Dan. 7:9-14; Zech. 3:8-10; 6:12-13).

ERRONEOUS THINKING

As well, inasmuch as the Jews had so diluted the Word of God, they had a completely false interpretation respecting Who and What the Messiah would be. Some thought He would be a reincarnation of one of the Prophets of old, such as Jeremiah, etc., with some having ideas that He would be a very charismatic Person with great wisdom and ability. However, virtually none believed that He would be God manifest in the flesh, despite what Isaiah had said (Isa. 7:14).

So, this thinking that permeated Israel had, as well, taken its toll upon the Disciples, as is obvious!

It is very difficult to rid anyone of error in the religious sense. It has a force all its own because it is seated in the self-will of the individual. Consequently, it is in the self-interest of the person to believe such, or so they think, whatever type of error it may be. To be sure, only the Holy Spirit can reveal the Truth of the Word of God to anyone, which is done by the Power of God. For that to be done, the heart must be opened to God, as few are!

ONE CANNOT SEE THE FATHER UNTIL ONE HAS SEEN JESUS

The phrase, *"He Who has seen Me has seen the Father,"* presents the very embodiment of Who and What the Messiah would be. Although in the flesh, the Messiah was God and, at the same time, was the Manifestation of God, which refers to the Incarnation. Actually, that was the very idea of Who and What the Messiah would be.

Some have erroneously attempted to take this particular statement, plus others similar, and force God the Father and God the Son into being the same Person. However, the reference, as Jesus here uses such, has reference to One in Unity and Essence and not One in number. Even though Both are God, God the Father and God the Son are two different Persons altogether. And yet, by being One in Perfect Unity and Essence, to see Jesus is to see the Father. In truth, that should not be difficult to understand.

Actually, men constantly use such a statement concerning some natural fathers and sons, *"When you have seen one, you have seen the other!"* By using such a statement, they are not saying that both are the same person, but that the characteristics are so similar that to recognize one is to recognize the other.

If that is true about men, and it is, how totally true is it about God the Father and God the Son, considering that their Unity and Essence so far exceed that of mere men.

So, there is absolutely no reason to misunderstand what Jesus was saying, which should have been obvious to the Disciples, and would have been, at least to a degree, had their thinking not been confused by the error that plagued Israel at that time.

SHOW US THE FATHER?

The question, *"And how do you say then, Show us the Father?"* in effect, says the same thing I have just said.

If men want to know what God is like, they must look at Jesus, for He is the Personification of the Father. His Actions, Miracles, Direction, Persona, Attitude, Personality, and even His Very Essence are that of the Father. When one saw Jesus in action, one saw the Father. When one heard His Messages, one heard the Father. When one witnessed His Opposition to the religious hierarchy of that day, one was seeing the Opposition of the Father. When one saw the Salvation offered by the Son, one saw that offered by the Father. They are One and the Same!

That is the basic reason that most Catholics know little or nothing about the Father: because they attempt to go through Mary instead of Jesus. Such is impossible! The same can be said for Muslims respecting Muhammad. Even though I am being overly repetitious, due to the significance of this great Truth, one must proclaim such and continue to do so: that everything, irrespective as to what it might be in the spiritual sense, must go through and come from Jesus Christ.

(10) "DO YOU BELIEVE NOT THAT I AM IN THE FATHER, AND THE FATHER IN ME? THE WORDS THAT I SPEAK UNTO YOU I SPEAK NOT OF MYSELF: BUT THE FATHER WHO DWELLS IN ME, HE DOES THE WORKS."

The exegesis is:

1. What is the modern church doing about the Cross?

2. Sadly, it is looking to anything and everything except the Cross.

3. Any problem in most church organizations is automatically appealed to the psychologist.

DO YOU BELIEVE?

The question, *"Do you not believe that I am in the Father, and the Father in Me?"* carries within its statement the very ingredient of Salvation. The key is *"believing!"* It's not so much what one does as what one believes.

For those who wanted proof to buttress their Faith, the Lord had already given that proof. John the Baptist, who was born and raised for the specific purpose of introducing Christ, was proof. Jesus' Miracles were also proof, and the very fact of Him being in the world proved that the Father had sent Him. Also, the Scriptures are, no doubt, the greatest proof of all. In His Own Words, He said, *"They are they which testify of Me"* (Jn. 5:31-39).

However, proof to a doubting soul, irrespective of its veracity, will not be accepted. Therefore, as always, we come back to the ingredient of *"Faith!"* To be Saved, to know and understand, one must *"believe!"*

MY WORDS WHICH I SPEAK UNTO YOU

The phrase, *"The Words that I speak unto you I speak not of Myself,"* carries a weight all out of proportion to the actual statement itself.

In effect, Jesus is saying that the Words which are coming out of His Mouth are, in fact, those of the Heavenly Father. Consequently, if they are spurned, there remains no other way of Salvation. To refuse Jesus is to refuse God! So, the Jews were sealing their own doom by rejecting Him, as has most of the world ever since.

The phrase, *"But the Father Who dwells in Me, He does the works,"* tells us several things:

• As the *"Words"* were from the Father, likewise, the Miracles are from the Father.

• *"Dwells"* is from the Greek word *"meno"* and actually means *"abide,"* which should have been translated accordingly instead of *"dwells."*

This does not speak of a physical union, as certainly should be obvious, but rather a spiritual union. As the Father is in Christ, so Christ is also in the Father (Jn. 14:20). As well, Believers are in both the Father and the Son (Jn. 14:20; I Jn. 2:24; II Cor. 5:17). Also, the Holy Spirit is in Believers, and Believers are in the Holy Spirit (Rom. 8:9).

It means in union and essence with consecration to the same — one in mind, purpose, and life.

THE UNION OF CHRIST AND THE FATHER

However, having said that, one must reckon that the Union of Jesus and the Father is far greater than any other type of union. It is actually a union of essence that is incomprehensible to humans, hence, our understanding is only partial. Even though, as a Believer, I am in Christ, even as all Believers, still, such union is not perfect inasmuch as we are human. As well, Jesus is in the Believer, but that union is not perfect either, with the same adage holding true.

However, Jesus Christ, even in the Incarnate State, was Perfect in every respect; consequently, His Union and Essence with the Father was perfect also!

It is the same idea as God being the Father of both Jesus Christ and all Believers; however, He is not my Father in the same sense as He is with Jesus, His Only Begotten Son. While Believers are adopted into the Family of God, Jesus is the Family, with Him having a relationship with the Father that is impossible for any human being to have, except on a limited basis.

• As this example is here given concerning the manner in which the Message and the Miracles were carried out in the Life and Ministry of Christ, likewise, the same holds true for Believers. For any Work of God to be accomplished, the Holy Spirit, Who resides in Believers, must perform these works and even, in reality, preach the Gospel through the Believer. In fact, the Holy Spirit is the consummate Preacher. As Jesus set the example, so must it be in Believers.

In viewing the example of Christ, we are told what and how things are done for the Lord. For God to use an individual, that individual must be totally consecrated to the Purpose of God and not himself. There must be an absolute dependency, even as it was with Christ, as well as a constant and total relationship. Regrettably, such is not the case in most.

(11) "BELIEVE ME THAT I AM IN THE FATHER, AND THE FATHER IN ME: OR ELSE BELIEVE ME FOR THE VERY WORKS' SAKE."

The construction is:

1. The Holy Spirit is now bringing the Message of the Cross, even as Paul taught it, into full view of the church.

2. It has absolutely no choice but to either publicly reject it or accept it.

3. Sadly and regrettably, Biblical information bears out that the far greater majority will reject it (Rev. 3:14-22).

TO BELIEVE

The phrase, *"Believe Me that I am in the Father, and the Father in Me,"* once again places Faith as the vehicle and Jesus as the Object. He said, *"Believe Me!"*

The phrase, *"Or else believe Me for the very works' sake,"* presents a level which should be obvious to all, and includes present observation as well.

It should have been understood, and, in fact, was to some, that these Miracles could not have been performed by Jesus were He not from God and, in reality, God manifest in the flesh. They were of such astounding content in their operation that only stubborn unbelief could deny the Source of what was being done. In effect, Jesus was saying, *"If you want proof, the Miracles are proof enough and more!"*

BIBLE CHRISTIANITY

The same can be said for true Bible Christianity for all time. The proof remains and always shall. All the millions of people on this Earth, even at present, who have had their lives marvelously, gloriously, and even miraculously changed, have come about only through the Gospel of Jesus Christ. Islam cannot boast one single human being that has ever been delivered from anything. The same goes for Buddhism, Shintoism, humanism, Catholicism, or Hinduism.

Of the untold numbers of drug addicts instantly and wondrously set free, alcoholics delivered, broken homes put back together, broken hearts healed, and captives set free, all, and without exception, can be laid at the Feet of Jesus Christ. Not a single bondage has ever been broken through the auspices of Islam, Buddhism, Hinduism, humanism, etc. Actually, these religions are bondages within themselves. So, for the proof of the validity of true Bible Christianity, Christ is enough to convince anyone, at least if one is honest in his heart respecting such proof.

(12) "VERILY, VERILY, I SAY UNTO YOU, HE WHO BELIEVES ON ME, THE WORKS THAT I DO SHALL HE DO ALSO; AND GREATER WORKS THAN THESE SHALL HE DO; BECAUSE I GO UNTO MY FATHER."

The structure is:

1. The Cross of Christ has always been the dividing line between the true Church and the apostate church.

2. However, the Holy Spirit is making this Message, and all for which it stands, so prominent presently that it can no longer be ignored.

3. This means that a decision is going to have to be made by literally millions.

FAITH

The Faith of which Jesus here speaks says several things:

Faith is held up as the vehicle which must be entertained before these things can be understood and carried out. The following might provide some help as to the type of Faith of which Jesus speaks.

THE CORRECT OBJECT OF FAITH

There have probably been more books on faith written in the last several decades than the balance of the entire time of Christianity, which is nearly 2,000 years. Despite all of these books, the truth is, there is probably less true faith now than ever. Why?

The Object of Faith, which is so very, very important, is mostly not understood at all by most Christians.

If a Christian were asked as to the Object of his Faith, it would probably take him by surprise, little having heard such a question.

If he answered at all, he would probably say, *"I have Faith in the Bible," "I have Faith in the Lord,"* etc. While these certainly are correct statements, the old adage still holds, *"That which says too much, in effect, says nothing."*

Everyone, I suppose, who claims to be a true Christian will say that they have Faith in the Word of God and Faith in the Lord, as they most certainly should. However, to pinpoint the situation, the correct Object of Faith, in fact, the only Faith that God will recognize, is always and without exception *"Jesus Christ and Him Crucified."* Actually, this is the Story of the Bible (Rom. 6:1-14; 8:1-2, 11; I Cor. 1:17-18, 23; 2:2; Gal. 6:14; Eph. 2:13-18; Col. 2:10-15).

CHRIST IS THE SOURCE WHILE THE CROSS IS THE MEANS

What does that heading mean?

It simply means that Christ is the Source of all things that we receive from God, Him being the One Who has made everything possible. When we say, *"Everything,"* we mean, *"Everything."*

And yet, it is the Cross of Christ that is actually the Means of all of these good things being given unto us.

Every single thing we receive from the Lord, irrespective as to what it might be, comes from Christ as the Source and the Cross as the Means. The problem, however, is as follows:

While most would agree that everything comes from Christ as the Source, they have a problem, at least some do, with the Cross being the Means. However, Jesus plainly tells us that if we are to come after Him, we must deny ourselves and take up our Cross daily and follow Him (Lk. 9:23).

He then said that if we didn't do such, we could not be His Disciple (Lk. 14:27).

Jesus and Him Crucified is always to be the Object of one's Faith, hence, Him constantly referring to Himself as that Object! Hundreds of millions of people have Faith, in fact, everybody has Faith of some sort, but almost all in the wrong things.

THE APOSTLE PAUL

It was to Paul that the meaning of the New Covenant was given, the Meaning of which is the Cross of Christ. In fact, Jesus Personally is the New Covenant. That means He doesn't merely have the New Covenant or know the New Covenant but, in fact, is the New Covenant. As stated, He gave the meaning to the Apostle Paul, and let us say it again, which is the Cross of Christ. Of course, as I'm sure the reader knows, we aren't speaking of the wooden beam on which Jesus died, but rather what He there accomplished. In fact, so much was accomplished that I think it would be impossible for any human being to fully comprehend what was done at that particular time, now nearly 2,000 years ago.

THE CROSS OF CHRIST

• At the Cross, Jesus satisfied the claims of Heavenly Justice (Heb. 7:27).

• He paid the debt by the giving of Himself as a Perfect Sacrifice, which man owed but could not pay (Heb. 9:28).

• He removed the blight of original sin, which, as is obvious, began with Adam, meaning that it is no longer held against Believers (I Cor. 15:22).

• Sin was the legal means that Satan had to hold man captive. With that legal means removed, which it was removed at the Cross, Satan has no more right to hold anyone in bondage (Rom. 8:2).

• The Cross of Christ was formulated in the Mind of the Godhead from before the foundation of the world. God through foreknowledge knew that He would create this world and this Universe, and He would create man, and man would fall. It was therefore determined by the Godhead that man would be redeemed by God becoming Man and giving Himself as a Perfect Sacrifice on the Cross (I Pet. 1:18-20).

• In fact, the entire Story of the Bible is

NOTES

"Jesus Christ and Him Crucified." So, one cannot really understand the Bible as one should without understanding the Cross of Christ (I Cor. 1:23).

• Every single thing that anyone has ever received from God has all been made possible by the Cross of Christ. In Old Testament times, all the hundreds of millions of sacrifices of little lambs and other clean animals offered up were a Picture, a Symbol, a Type, if you will, of the coming Redeemer (I Cor. 1:17).

• The only thing standing between mankind and eternal Hell is the Cross of Christ (Jn. 3:16).

• The Cross of Christ opened up the way for man to come to the very Holy of Holies of God Almighty. It was the Cross that made it possible (Heb. 4:16).

• The Cross of Christ atoned for all sin, past, present, and future, at least for all who will believe (Jn. 3:16).

• Satan, every fallen Angel, and every demon spirit were totally and completely defeated at the Cross of Christ (Col. 2:14-15).

• As we have stated, if the object of one's faith is not Christ and the Cross, then whatever type of faith it is, it is that which God will not recognize (I Cor. 1:17; Gal. 6:14).

• It is the Cross of Christ that gives the Holy Spirit the legal means to do all that He does for us. In fact, the Cross is the Way the Holy Spirit works (Rom. 8:2).

• The Cross of Christ did away with the earthly priesthood, meaning that now Christ is the one Mediator between God and men (I Tim. 2:5).

• Every single thing that man receives from God, whatever it is, is all made possible by the Cross of Christ (I Cor. 2:2).

• The Message of the Cross is the Gospel. It does not merely contain the Gospel, it is the Gospel (I Cor. 1:17).

• The Word of the Cross is the Power of God (I Cor. 1:18).

• Every bondage of darkness was broken at the Cross of Christ, awaiting only Faith on the part of the needful person to receive its benefits (Heb. 9:28).

• The Cross of Christ has made it possible for all to come, both Jew and Gentile alike (Col. 3:11; Gal. 3:28).

• Before the Cross, the Holy Spirit was very limited as to what He could do with individuals. However, with Jesus offering Himself as a Perfect Sacrifice on the Cross, this paid the sin debt, making it possible for the Holy Spirit to now come into the heart and life of the Believer to live forever, which could not be done before the Cross (Jn. 14:16).

• Even in the Perfect Age to come, which will be without end, the Cross of Christ is alluded to some seven times by referring to Christ as the *"Lamb"* (Rev., Chpts. 21-22). It is done for purpose, telling us that all of these wonderful things, which will last forever and forever, all and without exception, are made possible by the Cross.

(13) "AND WHATSOEVER YOU SHALL ASK IN MY NAME, THAT WILL I DO, THAT THE FATHER MAY BE GLORIFIED IN THE SON."

The synopsis is:

1. As it regards the shed Blood of Jesus Christ, Seiss says, *"Approaching those admirable Courts (speaking of the Old Testament), our attention would have been attracted on all sides with marks of blood.*

2. *"Before the Altar, 'blood'; on the horns of the Altar, 'blood'; in the midst of the Altar, 'blood'; on its top, at its base, on its sides, 'blood'; and tracked along in the deepest interior of the Tabernacle, 'blood'!"*

3. Paul said that the preaching of Christ Crucified to the Jews was a stumblingblock and to the Greeks foolishness. However, to those of us who know what sin actually is and what is implied in Redemption from it, it will ever hail the announcement of the Cross where the Blood of Christ was shed as the most glad tidings that ever fell upon the ear of Earth.

THE AUTHORITY OF THE BELIEVER

In Verse 13, the Christian is given the power of attorney to use the Name of Jesus. What does that mean?

The following should be noted:

• Every Believer in the world has Authority; some more than others due to their Calling.

• That Authority is never used on human beings, but rather Satan, fallen Angels, and demon spirits, in other words, the evil spirits of the spirit world of darkness (Mk 16:17-18).

• Unfortunately, some have tried to turn the Authority of the Believer into the demands of the Believer over other Believers. The Lord never gives such latitude to anyone.

WHAT ARE THE QUALIFICATIONS FOR THE USE OF THE NAME OF JESUS?

First of all, the individual must be *"Born-Again."* As well, such a Believer must be baptized with the Holy Spirit with the evidence of speaking with other Tongues (Acts 2:4). Power comes with that infilling, and without that infilling, there is no power (Acts 1:8). In fact, Jesus told His Followers then and now that they were not to attempt to plant churches, conduct revival meetings, witness for Him, or do anything in His Name until they were first baptized with the Holy Spirit. That was not a suggestion, but rather a command (Acts 1:4).

On the set of *"A STUDY IN THE WORD,"* Gabriel asked me the other day, *"Papaw, is the Command that Jesus gave to His Followers to be baptized with the Holy Spirit before they did anything in His Name incumbent upon us today?"* The answer was immediate!

"Most definitely, Yes." The Command is general, meaning that it was not only for Believers then but, as well, for Believers now and, in fact, always has been and always will be.

THE CROSS OF CHRIST

Secondly, the Believer must, as we've already stated, have his or her Faith exclusively in Christ and the Cross, understanding that Jesus is the Source and the Cross is the Means. Why is this so necessary?

It is necessary because it was at the Cross where Satan, fallen Angels, and every demon spirit were totally and completely defeated (Col. 2:14-15). Remember that the Authority we now have in the use of the Name of Jesus is always over evil spirits and never over other human beings. It was at the Cross where the great Victory was won over these spirits of darkness. That's the reason we must have our Faith exclusively, absolutely, and totally in Christ and the Cross. In fact, the very Name of Jesus means *"Saviour,"* which is made possible by what He did at the Cross.

WHAT DOES THE NAME OF JESUS MEAN IN THE SPIRIT WORLD?

To be sure, it carries a Power that is far beyond the comprehension of mere mortals.

Jesus defeated every power of darkness at Calvary by His satisfying the claims of Heavenly Justice, paying sin's debt, and, thereby, loosing the grip of sin on the believing sinner. In other words, Satan's teeth were pulled and his authority over the human family destroyed.

By and large, whatever authority he presently has is, for the most part, a pseudo-authority, meaning that which he has usurped from Believers. Most of the things Satan does in the world are done simply because Believers do not exercise their Authority in the use of the Name of Jesus, which will curtail his activities, if not halt them entirely.

It was a terrible thing that happened in Connecticut with the murder of 20 little children plus several adults. In fact, things of this nature are happening all over the world constantly. The world does not know what to do with it, doesn't have an answer, has no solution, and, in fact, never will.

The solution lies with Believers, i.e., the Church.

The great question that was asked during this tragedy in Connecticut, and untold thousands of others similar all over the world, *"Why would God allow such a thing to happen?"*

Admittedly, God is Omnipotent, meaning all-powerful, and meaning that He can do anything. He is Omniscient, meaning that He knows all things, past, present, and future. Also, He is Omnipresent, meaning that He is everywhere at the same time.

Yes, God has the Power to do anything, so that being the case, why doesn't He stop all of these terrible things that we've just mentioned?

He presently doesn't do so simply because He has given His Word otherwise.

NOTES

In other words, the Lord gave to Adam, as stated, dominion over all things that he had created. Unfortunately, Adam forfeited that dominion to Satan. This is what the Holy Spirit said through David, and I quote from THE EXPOSITOR'S STUDY BIBLE, including the notes.

THE DOMINION GIVEN TO MAN

"What is man, that You are mindful of him? and the son of man, that You visit him? *(God became man and went to Calvary in order to redeem fallen humanity. The price that was paid for that Redemption proclaims to us the worth of man, which, in fact, is God's highest Creation.)*

"For you have made him a little lower than the Angels, and have crowned him with glory and honor *(the Hebrew word 'Elohim' here translated 'Angels' should have been translated 'God' or 'Godhead,' for that's what the word actually means; there is no place in the Old Testament where 'Elohim' means 'Angels'; this means that man was originally created higher than the Angels, and through Christ will be restored to that lofty position [Rom. 8:14-17])***.**

"You made him to have dominion over the works of Your Hands; You have put all things under His Feet *(in their fullness, these words given here are only true of the God-Man, Jesus Christ [Mat. 28:18]; Christ has been exalted to a place higher than Angels or any other being except the Father; redeemed man is to be raised up to that exalted position with Him [Eph. 2:6-7])***:**

"All sheep and oxen, yes, and the beasts of the field;

"The fowl of the air, and the fish of the sea, and whatsoever passes through the paths of the seas *(man was made to have dominion over all this)***.**

"O LORD our Lord, how excellent is Your Name in all the Earth! *(Christ is the Head of the Church, which is His Body; ultimately, that which is given by Promise will, upon the Resurrection of Life, be carried to its ultimate victorious conclusion)"* **(Ps. 8:4-9).**

As stated, this dominion given to man by God was forfeited to Satan by the fall of Adam.

This means that Satan is *"the god of this world"* (II Cor. 4:4). So, in effect, all of the sorrow, heartache, murder, mayhem, war, destruction, broken hearts, and wasted lives are caused by Satan and not God.

The only time that God will step in to change something, to begin something, or stop something is when His People begin to seek His Face, asking for His Help (Jn. 15:7). That's the reason that the Lord said to Solomon so long, long ago:

"If My People, who are called by My Name *(Believers)***, shall humble themselves** *(humility)***, and pray, and seek My Face** *(the prayer of Repentance)***, and turn from their wicked ways** *(which proclaims the manner of true Repentance)***; then will I hear from Heaven** *(but not otherwise)***, and will forgive their sin, and will heal their land** *(God's Prescription for spiritual sickness)*" **(II Chron. 7:14).**

However, if God's People do not do what the Lord here demands, the Lord will not and, in fact, cannot take the initiative. Yes, He has the power to do such and, in fact, can do anything, but He made that Covenant with Adam, and He will not go back on His Covenant.

THE END OF SATAN'S DOMINION IS NEAR

Now, some would ask as to why God doesn't do something about all of this?

He did do something. It's called *"the Cross."* Now, very soon, and I mean very soon, He is going to come back to this Earth and take dominion of it totally and completely, with Satan locked away in the bottomless pit, along with all fallen Angels and demon spirits (Rev., Chpt. 20).

However, the great reason that there is so much evil in the world is because the church does not exercise the Power and dominion that it can have. It is through the Cross of Christ, but, regrettably, the church quit preaching the Cross a long time ago. So, if we want to lay the blame as to what is happening in this world regarding sorrow and heartache, we will have to lay at least a great part of that blame at the feet of the church.

Now, don't misunderstand. Even if the Church was on fire for God, preaching the Cross, and doing exactly what it ought to do, due to the fact that Satan is the *"god of this world,"* there would still be heartache, pain, and suffering, but not nearly as much as it is otherwise.

WHY IS THE PREACHING OF THE CROSS SO IMPORTANT?

Paul said, *"The preaching of the Cross is to them who perish foolishness; but to we who are Saved, it is the Power of God"* (I Cor. 1:18).

How is the preaching of the Cross the Power of God?

There is really no power within itself in the wooden beam on which Jesus died. In fact, there was really no power in His Death. The Scripture says that *"He was crucified through weakness"* (II Cor. 13:4). Now, it must be understood that this was a contrived weakness. In other words, He had the Power to do whatever He would have wanted to do but purposely would not use it. Thank God, He didn't, for if He had, we would not be here today.

The Power is in the Holy Spirit. How is it in the Holy Spirit?

Before the Cross, the blood of bulls and goats could not take away sins, so the sin debt remained, which greatly hindered the Holy Spirit as to what He could do for individuals. However, when Jesus died on the Cross, this removed the sin debt, i.e., *"original sin,"* making it possible for the Holy Spirit to come into the heart and life of the Believer, there to abide forever (Jn. 14:16). Now, He could use His Power on our behalf in a greater way than ever. Formerly, before the Cross, the Holy Spirit was with the Believer. Now, He is in the Believer. That is a vast difference (Jn. 14:17). For that Power to be unleashed, the Believer must, without fail, have his or her Faith exclusively in Christ and the Cross, understanding that this is where Satan was totally and completely defeated.

As stated, if Believers knew and understood the Word of God and the Power of the Cross, many of the problems of this world could be addressed and eliminated. Of course, with the church in the condition that it's in presently, this opens the door for Satan to do even greater damage, which he most definitely is doing. It all goes back to, *"If My people who are called by My Name...."*

So, for most of the problems in this world, the fault is not in God; it's in Believers, believe it or not. We have Authority but only if we know how to use it. So, if the Church preaches the Cross, the place where Satan was defeated, this stops many of the efforts of the Evil One. However, if the church fails to preach the Cross, regrettably, this opens the door for Satan to *"steal, kill, and destroy"* (Jn. 10:10). Sadly, in the last 50 odd years, the church has more and more ceased to preach the Cross, rather depending on the uselessness of humanistic psychology.

(14) "IF YOU SHALL ASK ANYTHING IN MY NAME, I WILL DO IT."

The structure is:

1. To ask in His Name is to ask that which is in harmony with His Character and Will.

2. The Lord foresaw that this Promise would go hard with human reason, and that it would be much assailed by the Devil. Therefore, it is, in essence, stated the third time, with the first two times in Verses 12 and 13. In other words, He means what He says!

3. His being able to do anything proves His Deity, for only God could do such things.

ANYTHING?

Yes, anything! However, we must understand that the *"anything"* must be within the framework, as stated, of His Will. God will never allow His Word to be used against Himself. What do we mean by that?

If all Believers could do whatever it was they wanted and not what the Lord wants, there are so many immature Believers that the entire Plan of God would be wrecked by such efforts and direction. As stated, the Lord will not allow His Word to be used against Himself.

If it is to be noticed, most of the time, prayer is not answered quickly or easily. And yet, if whatever it is we are asking is not only in the Will of God but, as well, the Wisdom of God, ultimately, it will come. There are many things which constitute God's Will, but it's not His Wisdom. He knows that if we had such, it would hurt us instead of help us, so His Wisdom dictates the direction that things ought to go.

NOTES

It seems to be very hard for most Christians to turn over the direction of their lives to the Lord. It's hard for us to realize that the Lord is the Only One Who knows the way through the wilderness. The Believer should constantly pray that the Will of the Lord would be realized in his or her life. He should seek and desire that Will, and nothing else. That being our desire, the Lord will bring it to pass within our lives, which will provide the most wonderful, beautiful, and fulfilling life that one could ever begin to have (Jn. 10:10).

(15) "IF YOU LOVE ME, KEEP MY COMMANDMENTS."

The structure is:

1. The Lord has a way that the Believer can overcome the *"Law of Sin and Death."* It is by the *"Law of the Spirit of Life in Christ Jesus"* (Rom. 8:2).

2. The only Law in the world that is stronger than the *"Law of Sin and Death"* is the *"Law of the Spirit of Life in Christ Jesus."*

3. While there is much more to victory than that, still, if the Believer can come to understand the *"Law of the Spirit of Life in Christ Jesus,"* he is well on his way to more Abundant Life.

LOVE

The only way that we can properly love God and properly keep His Commandments is by placing our Faith exclusively in Christ and what He did for us at the Cross. That is the key to Righteousness, the key to overcoming Power, the key to live the life that we ought to live, and, I might quickly add, the only key.

If we truly love the Lord, we want to please Him. That being the case, how do we please Him?

Concerning one of the greatest Men of God who ever lived, Paul wrote, *"By Faith Enoch was translated that he should not see death; and was not found, because God had translated him: for before his translation he had this Testimony, that he pleased God"* (Heb. 11:5).

What was this Testimony that pleased God? The next Verse tells us.

"But without Faith it is impossible to please Him: for he who comes to God

must believe that He is, and that He is a Rewarder of them who diligently seek Him" (Heb. 11:6).

When we try to live any way other than God's Way, which is the Way of the Cross, such irritates our Heavenly Father, as ought to be obvious, because of the price that He paid for us and the suffering that He endured. It was a price, I might quickly add, that we will never fully understand the height and depth of such a Sacrifice. He doesn't ask much of us, but He does ask one thing, and that is that our Faith be exclusively in Christ and what Christ has done for us at the Cross (I Cor. 1:17, 18, 23; 2:2).

The reason for the Cross was the inability on our part to save ourselves. I don't care how strong we are, we are no match for the powers of darkness, at least within ourselves. So, the Lord paid the price on our behalf, a price so staggering that it beggars description. When we ignore that and, thereby, place our Faith in something else, can you imagine how that must irritate the Lord?

THE CROSS OF CHRIST AND THE LOVE OF GOD

The greatest exhibition of the Love of God was and is the Cross of Calvary. Our greatest exhibition of our love for Him is for us to simply evidence Faith exclusively in Christ and what He did for us at the Cross. Nothing pleases God any more than that.

I don't care how much we try to explain our love for God and God's Love for us. If we leave out the Cross, we have just lost the key to the entirety of that which we need. Sadly and regrettably, the modern church has lost that key, i.e., *"the Cross."*

COMMANDMENTS?

The question is not so much, *"What are the Commandments?"* but rather, *"How do we keep them, whatever they might be?"*

There is only one way they can be kept. That way is by the Believer placing his or her Faith exclusively in Christ and what Christ has done for us at the Cross, and maintaining his Faith exclusively in Christ and the Cross.

Upon reading these notes, some will, no doubt, think, *"Brother Swaggart, you claim the Cross of Christ as the answer for*

NOTES

everything." Now you are beginning to understand what we are saying. Yes, that's exactly what we are doing because that is the answer, and the only answer.

For whatever the need, for whatever the desire, and for whatever the Commandment, we are to look exclusively to Christ and the Cross and not at all to ourselves.

When many Christians read this, they will automatically stop and say, *"No, we've got to fast,"* or else, they will say, *"We've got to do this or that."* This is what sorely displeases the Lord. When will we learn that there's really nothing that we can do that will make any difference? It will only hurt. We must trust in what our Lord has already done, and I continue to speak of the Cross.

No, the question is not, *"Do we keep the Commandments?"* The question is, *"How do we keep the Commandments?"* That's where the great problem is!

The only way it can be done is by the Means of the Cross.

(16) "AND I WILL PRAY THE FATHER, AND HE SHALL GIVE YOU ANOTHER COMFORTER, THAT HE MAY ABIDE WITH YOU FOREVER."

The exegesis is:

1. Due to the Person and the Work of the Messiah, the Reverence was enjoined by the two Laws respecting the 'fat' and the 'blood.' They express excellency and efficiency.

2. *"This is My Beloved Son"* declared the one, and *"Peace through the Blood of His Cross,"* proclaimed the other (Col. 1:20).

3. The prohibition against the eating of blood was brought over into the New Covenant for the obvious reasons (Acts 15:19-20).

ANOTHER COMFORTER

The phrase, *"And I will pray the Father, and He shall give you another Comforter,"* refers to the Holy Spirit. The Greek word for *"Comforter"* is *"Parakletos"* and means *"One called to the side of another to help."*

The idea is that it is impossible for one to love the Lord as one should, or to keep His Commandments, without the Help of the Holy Spirit, which has been made possible by the Cross.

The word *"another"* refers to the fact that Jesus would no longer be with them in the physical sense and, consequently, would pray to the Father that another Person of the Divine Godhead would be sent to take His Place.

The word *"Parakletos"* is, as well, a legal word and refers to legal proceedings and criminal charges so that the word *"Advocate,"* which means *"pleader for us and in us,"* can be used of the Spirit as well. So, the Holy Spirit can be said to strengthen on the one hand and defend on the other.

Christ is, as well, an Advocate and pleads the Believer's cause with the Father against the accuser, Satan (Rom. 8:26; I Jn. 2:1; Rev. 12:10). The Holy Spirit as Advocate pleads the cause of the Believer against the world (Jn. 16:8) and pleads Christ's Cause with the Believer (Jn. 14:26; 15:26; 16:14).

THAT HE MAY ABIDE WITH YOU FOREVER

The phrase, *"That He may abide with you forever,"* means simply that the Holy Spirit will not come and go and, in fact, will not leave at all. Consequently, the Holy Spirit is, in a literal sense, the only Member of the Godhead presently in this world. While it is true that both Jesus and the Father are in the world through the Person and Agency of the Spirit, and being Deity, are Omnipresent, still, in a strict sense, only the Holy Spirit is Personally present as He resides in the hearts and lives of all Believers (I Cor. 3:16).

In truth, the Holy Spirit, even as the next Scripture proclaims, can have nothing to do with this sinful world except to *"reprove it of sin, and of Righteousness, and of Judgment"* (Jn. 16:8). He dwells in the Believer with the understanding that He, as Deity, is also everywhere, even as the Father and the Son.

Before Jesus died on Calvary, satisfying the claims of Heavenly Justice and paying sin's debt, the Holy Spirit, although able to help individuals as He did respecting Old Testament Saints, still could not come to dwell in Believers as He now does since the Day of Pentecost. That is the reason Jesus said concerning John the Baptist, *"But he who is least in the Kingdom of God is greater than he"* (Lk. 7:28).

NOTES

This was said respecting the New Covenant, which John the Baptist was not privileged to enjoy. Due to what Jesus did at Calvary and the Resurrection, the New Covenant is far better than the Old, hence, all in it having greater privileges, etc. It is not the person of whom Jesus speaks as being greater, but rather his place in the New Covenant, which is far better!

The word *"forever"* means exactly what it says. The Holy Spirit will not be taken out of the world at the Rapture as some claim, but will, in fact, be here forever. This includes the coming Tribulation, Millennium, and the Perfect Age to come as well (Zech. 12:10; Acts 2:16-21; Rev. 7:14; 12:17; 19:10).

(17) "EVEN THE SPIRIT OF TRUTH; WHOM THE WORLD CANNOT RECEIVE, BECAUSE IT SEES HIM NOT, NEITHER KNOWS HIM: BUT YOU KNOW HIM; FOR HE DWELLS WITH YOU, AND SHALL BE IN YOU."

The form is:

1. It is impossible for one to properly understand the New Testament unless one properly understands the Old Testament.

2. By all the rules and regulations given in the Old Testament, especially considering the Law, this tells us of the awfulness of sin.

3. When we are made to realize that Jesus has paid it all, in other words, satisfied every single rule and regulation, and did so by the Sacrificial Offering of Himself on the Cross, then we are made to realize the Greatness of Christ.

THE SPIRIT OF TRUTH

The phrase, *"Even the Spirit of Truth,"* actually means in the Greek Text, *"The Spirit of the Truth."*

Of all the Attributes of the Holy Spirit, Who is God, the greatest of all is *"Truth,"* which He superintends. Actually, He does far more than merely superintend this attribute but, in reality, as Christ, *"is Truth"* (I Jn. 5:6).

Even though Jesus is the Living Word, still, the Holy Spirit superintends the Bible in every respect, guaranteeing its veracity. Hence, it is error free, which characterizes it as the only such Writings or Book in the world (II Pet. 1:20-21).

Satan attempts to counterfeit that which is of the Lord, consequently, helping evil spirits to foment false doctrine, etc. As the Holy Spirit is Truth and proclaims Truth, likewise, evil spirits instigate error.

Inasmuch as the Holy Spirit is Truth, i.e., the Word of God, this means that one cannot properly understand the Word without His Aid.

Paul said, *"Now we have received, not the spirit of the world, but the Spirit which is of God; that we might know the things that are freely given to us of God."*

He then said, *"Which things also we speak, not in the words which man's wisdom teaches, but which the Holy Spirit teaches; comparing spiritual things with spiritual"* (I Cor. 2:12-14).

THE BAPTISM WITH THE HOLY SPIRIT

As well, I want to emphasize the fact that even though the Holy Spirit definitely comes into the Believer's heart at Salvation, which speaks of Regeneration, it is only when one has been baptized with the Holy Spirit according to Acts, Chapter 2, that the Spirit of God can fully lead the individual. I think this is the reason we see the urgency of Believers being Spirit-filled after Salvation, as outlined in the Book of Acts: 1:4; 8:14-15; 9:17; 10:44-46; 19:1-2.

The sadness is that entire segments of the Christian community, such as the Baptists, Methodists, Presbyterians, Nazarenes, Holiness, Lutherans, etc., only pay lip service to the Holy Spirit, with most denying the Acts 2:4 experience, and by and large ignoring His Function and Work in the life of the Believer. Sadder still, great parts of the Pentecostal community, which claim to be built on the very premise of the Pentecostal experience, have, for all practical purposes, abandoned the Moving and Operation of the Spirit of God.

In one of the major religious publications, an article was written concerning this very thing. It basically stated, regarding one Pentecostal denomination, that many Assemblies of God churches, in fact, are no different than Baptist churches, etc. The article seemed to imply that it was intended as a compliment; however, whatever they intended, such is no compliment!

It is the Holy Spirit Who makes the Church what it ought to be, and, of course, that pertains to His Involvement in the hearts and lives of Believers, for the Spirit of God does not dwell in buildings, organizations, etc.

WHOM THE WORLD CANNOT RECEIVE

The Holy Spirit can and does convict the sinner of his sin and need for Christ, which is a great part of His Office Work. However, He cannot come into the heart of the unbeliever until that person makes Christ his or her Saviour.

Before the Blood of Jesus cleanses from all sin, which can only come about respecting the Born-Again experience, the sinner remains a polluted being, which the Holy Spirit cannot tolerate.

Once the believing sinner makes Christ his Saviour, the Blood of Jesus instantly cleanses from all sin, with the Holy Spirit then able to effect the great work of Regeneration in the heart and life of that person. Actually, there is a three-step process which takes place at Conversion, as Paul outlines in I Corinthians 6:11. It is as follows:

• *"But you are washed"*: this speaks of being cleansed by the Blood of Jesus, which washes all sin away. This is done as the person exhibits Faith in Christ and what He did at Calvary. This cleansing is absolutely necessary and cannot be done without the shed Blood of Jesus being applied to the believing sinner by Faith (I Jn. 1:7).

• *"But you are sanctified"*: this speaks of the one now cleansed being *"set apart"* exclusively as belonging to Christ. The believing sinner has now changed masters.

• *"But you are justified"*: this is a legal work, which, in effect, declares the individual, *"Not guilty,"* on the basis of that person's Faith in Christ and what He did for us at the Cross. In other words, God declares him before any and all to now be a fit subject for the Kingdom of God.

This is all done as Paul said, *"In the Name of the Lord Jesus, and by the Spirit of our God."*

However, until these things are done, the Spirit of God cannot indwell the person.

THE WORLD DOESN'T SEE THE HOLY SPIRIT, NEITHER KNOWS HIM

The phrase, *"Because it sees Him not, neither knows Him,"* refers to the fact that only Born-Again Believers can understand the Holy Spirit and know Him.

While the Holy Spirit does convict the world of sin, Righteousness, and Judgment, still, the unbeliever does not know or understand at all this Work of the Spirit. He yields, at least those who do, to that which the Holy Spirit points, a recognition of his sin and his need of the Saviour. But still, he has no knowledge that the Holy Spirit is the One Who is doing these things.

In fact, if one will carefully notice, Old Testament Believers, while having some knowledge of the Holy Spirit, still, were very limited. It was not until Jesus died on Calvary, which then made it possible for the Holy Spirit to function in a new dimension, that Believers fully understood Who He was and What He was!

BUT YOU KNOW HIM

The phrase, *"But you know Him,"* would have been better translated, *"But you shall get to know Him."* This spoke of when, in a very short time, He would come in this new dimension of taking up abode in the hearts and lives of Believers.

The phrase, *"For He dwells with you, and shall be in you,"* proclaims in this short sentence the Occupation of the Spirit with Believers in both Covenants.

Before Jesus died on Calvary, the sins of Believers were not really taken away but only covered through the offering up of clean animals in sacrifice, which was but a symbol of the One to come, Jesus Christ. Consequently, due to these sins continuing to be against Believers, Satan had a legal claim upon them. Therefore, the Holy Spirit could not fully occupy the individuals under these circumstances even though they were fully Saved. He could dwell with them and help them in their efforts, which He did; however, as valuable as that was, it was a far cry from His Occupation within.

NOTES

After the sin debt was paid by Jesus at Calvary, all sins against Believers were taken away, with Satan now having no claim whatsoever on the Believer (Jn. 1:29).

As a result, and as previously stated, the Holy Spirit could now dwell in the Believer, and do so permanently. There is no comparison to the help afforded in this New Dispensation.

(18) *"I WILL NOT LEAVE YOU COMFORTLESS: I WILL COME TO YOU."*

The order is:

1. Intercession, as it pertains to Christ, is simply His Presence at the Throne of God, all on our behalf (Heb. 1:3).

2. This means that God has accepted Him, has accepted His Sacrifice of Himself, and has accepted its Finished Work.

3. As well, and we repeat, His very Presence before God guarantees Intercession on our behalf. This means that He doesn't have to do anything in this Intercession, with the Sacrifice of Himself having said and done it all.

I WILL NOT LEAVE YOU COMFORTLESS

Verse 18 refers to the Coming of the Holy Spirit in a brand new dimension on the Day of Pentecost.

The word *"comfortless"* in the Greek is *"orphanos"* and means *"orphans."* In other words, He will not leave them as orphans.

Disciples of a particular teacher were called his children, and upon his death, they were considered orphans. Christ called His Disciples *"Children,"* as well (Jn. 13:33), and now promises that He will not leave them orphans.

The phrase, *"I will come to you,"* has a two-fold meaning:

1. It speaks of coming to them in the Person and Agency of the Holy Spirit. Inasmuch as it was the Business of the Holy Spirit to glorify Christ (Jn. 16:14), in fact, the Disciples would learn even more about Jesus by the Revelation of the Holy Spirit than they had learned while He was with them in the flesh.

If one is to notice, not one time do you read in the Book of Acts where the Disciples grieved for the Lord even though He was no longer with them in the flesh. They did not do so because they now had the Holy Spirit, Who constantly made Christ real to them.

2. It has reference, although in an extended manner, to the Second Coming. At that time, Israel will accept Him, whereas they rejected Him the first time, hence, Jesus using the pronoun, *"You."*

(19) "YET A LITTLE WHILE, AND THE WORLD SEES ME NO MORE; BUT YOU SEE ME: BECAUSE I LIVE, YOU SHALL LIVE ALSO."

The construction is:

1. The Lord can bear with ignorance and infirmity (spiritual weakness), but He cannot sanction neglect or disobedience.

2. If the Word of God is disregarded, the Glory of God will not appear.

3. Let us say it again, *"The Lord can bear with ignorance and infirmity (spiritual weakness), but He cannot sanction neglect or disobedience."*

JESUS WAS ABOUT TO LEAVE

The phrase, *"Yet a little while, and the world sees Me no more,"* refers to His Crucifixion, after which, He would reveal Himself no more to the world, even during the 40 days after His Resurrection and before His Ascension. During this time, He did reveal Himself a number of times to His Disciples and other Followers.

In effect, Israel and the world had stated that they did not want to see Him anymore; consequently, their petition would be granted. However, when they expelled Him, they expelled the Only Hope for this world, thereby, submitting it to at least another 2,000 years of sorrow, war, sickness, pain, and death.

BECAUSE I LIVE, YOU SHALL LIVE ALSO

The short phrase, *"But you see Me,"* refers to the appearances He made to His Disciples after the Resurrection and, as well, the Revelation of His Person by the Holy Spirit.

As stated, at that time, they would *"see"* Jesus as they had never seen Him before! It is the Business of the Holy Spirit to reveal Jesus to the seeking soul. To be sure, this He does, and in a way absolutely unparalleled in the Old Testament.

"Because I live, you shall live also," refers to His Coming Resurrection.

In His Resurrection, He would defeat death, not only for Himself, but for all who would believe in His Name. In effect, His Resurrection guaranteed the Resurrection of all Believers at that coming Glad Day.

It also speaks of the quickening of the Holy Spirit in the life of the Believer, for no person can be said to be spiritually alive unless one has been Born-Again and indwelt by the Holy Spirit. He takes the life, which is in Christ, and imparts it to the Believer on a continuing basis. As a result, it is the grandest life in the world, unequalled by anything Satan may have to offer.

(20) "AT THAT DAY YOU SHALL KNOW THAT I AM IN MY FATHER, AND YOU IN ME, AND I IN YOU."

The form is:

1. The Cross of Christ was the answer at the very beginning for man's dilemma (Gen. 3:15, Chpt. 4).

2. It is the answer now and will always be the answer (Gal. 6:14).

3. The only way to God is through Jesus Christ, and the only way to Christ is through the Cross (Jn. 14:6; Jn. 1:1-2, 14, 29).

AT THAT DAY

The phrase, *"At that day,"* refers to the Day of Pentecost and thereafter, which speaks of the Holy Spirit indwelling the heart and life of the Believer. He is speaking of the time when the *"Comforter"* has come.

The phrase, *"You shall know,"* speaks of a particular kind of knowledge — a knowledge, in fact, that the world does not have and cannot have. This is what Paul was mentioning, as we have stated, when he said, *"Now we have received ... the Spirit which is of God; that we might know the things that are freely given to us of God"* (I Cor. 2:12).

The unsaved person is spiritually dead (Eph. 2:1-3). As such, there is no way one can understand or *"know"* anything about God while in that state.

Whenever the Gospel is preached, the Holy Spirit moves mightily upon the Word of God to the heart of the lost soul, which convicts one of sin, etc. At that moment, the sinner realizes his or her lost condition and need for Jesus Christ as Saviour. Sadly, even then, many resist, but thankfully, some accept. Incidentally, the Holy Spirit moves only upon the Word of God and nothing else!

THE DIVINE DEGREE

How is it that one can know that Jesus is in the Father, and we are in Him, and He is in us?

We are given the answer in the Sixth Chapter of Romans. Paul said, and I quote directly from THE EXPOSITOR'S STUDY BIBLE, including the notes:

"**What shall we say then?** *(This is meant to direct attention to Rom. 5:20.)* **Shall we continue in sin, that Grace may abound?** *(Just because Grace is greater than sin doesn't mean that the Believer has a license to sin.)*

"**God forbid** *(presents Paul's answer to the question, 'Away with the thought, let not such a thing occur').* **How shall we, who are dead to sin** *(dead to the sin nature),* **live any longer therein?** *(This portrays what the Believer is now in Christ.)*

THE DIVINE ENTANGLEMENT

"**Know you not, that so many of us as were baptized into Jesus Christ** *(plainly says that this Baptism is into Christ and not water [I Cor. 1:17; 12:13; Gal. 3:27; Eph. 4:5; Col. 2:11-13])* **were baptized into His Death?** *(When Christ died on the Cross, in the Mind of God, we died with Him; in other words, He became our Substitute, and our identification with Him in His Death gives us all the benefits for which He died; the idea is that He did it all for us!)*

"**Therefore we are buried with Him by baptism into death** *(not only did we die with Him, but we were buried with Him as well, which means that all the sin and transgression of the past were buried; when they put Him in the Tomb, they put all of our sins into that Tomb as well):* **that like as Christ was raised up from the dead by the Glory of the Father, even so we also should walk in newness of life** *(we died with Him, we were buried with Him, and His Resurrection was our Resurrection to a 'Newness of Life').*

NOTES

"**For if we have been planted together** *(with Christ)* **in the likeness of His Death** *(Paul proclaims the Cross as the instrument through which all Blessings come; consequently, the Cross must ever be the Object of our Faith, which gives the Holy Spirit latitude to work within our lives),* **we shall be also** *in the likeness* **of His Resurrection** *(we can have the 'likeness of His Resurrection,' i.e., 'live this Resurrection Life,' only as long as we understand the 'likeness of His Death,' which refers to the Cross as the Means by which all of this is done)*" (Rom. 6:1-5).

As stated, these Passages tell us how that Jesus is in the Father, and we are in Him, and He is in us — it is all by and through the Crucifixion of Christ. The moment the believing sinner evidences Faith in Christ, in the Mind of God, as previously stated, that person is literally placed in Christ, and then Christ is placed in the person, spiritually speaking. However, again I emphasize: it is all by and through the Cross of Christ.

AND YOU IN ME

By the ingredient of Faith, the Lord allows the believing sinner far more than cooperation or even alignment with, but rather identification with Christ, to such an extent that, from the moment of Conversion, the Father looks at us as being in Christ, which we are. Actually, this is what the entire Plan of Salvation is all about, all made possible by Who Christ is and What Christ did, and we speak of the Cross. Incidentally, it is all achieved by Faith.

THE NEW COVENANT

As well, this New Covenant cannot fail because Jesus acted as both God and Man, which He was, actually, "*the God-Man, Jesus Christ.*" So, this means that this Covenant is eternal. It cannot fail unless Christ fails, and Christ cannot fail.

When God the Father looks at us, He really sees the Lord Jesus Christ, Who is Perfection. Our Salvation is all in Christ. Our Life is all in Christ. That's the reason it is demanded that we have constant Faith in Christ as to Who He is, the Son of the Living God, actually, God manifest in the flesh, and What He did, which speaks entirely of the Cross of Christ, where Christ offered Himself as a Sin-Offering, Whose Sacrifice was accepted by the Father. It is all in Christ and what He has done to make all of this possible. We have a wonderful Salvation!

AND I IN YOU

The short phrase, *"And I in you,"* portrays our victorious everyday walk before God because Christ is living in us, in effect, living this life through us, which guarantees our success. Always remember the following: not only did Jesus die for the sins of the sinner, but He also died for the failures of the Saints. This is what Paul was speaking of when he said:

"I am crucified with Christ: nevertheless I live *(I am spiritually alive due to the Crucifixion and Resurrection of our Lord)*; **yet not I, but Christ lives in me** *(is effective in me, making it possible to have a 100 percent effective walk)*: **and the life which I now live in the flesh** *(my everyday walk before God)*, **I live by the Faith of the Son of God** *(the Faith provided by the Holy Spirit, anchored in the Word of God)*, **Who loved me** *(continues to love me despite occasional failures)*, **and gave Himself for me** *(gave Himself that I might not only be Saved, but have ultimate and total Victory within my life)*" **(Gal. 2:20).**

If it is to be noticed, this Twentieth Verse of the Second Chapter of Galatians begins with the Cross and ends with the Cross.

Consequently, we are not only *"in"* Christ at His Virgin Birth, His Perfect Life, and at Calvary and the Resurrection, but, as well, He is *"in"* us in order to guarantee that we receive all the benefits for which He bled, suffered, and died.

(21) "HE WHO HAS MY COMMANDMENTS, AND KEEPS THEM, HE IT IS WHO LOVES ME: AND HE WHO LOVES ME SHALL BE LOVED OF MY FATHER, AND I WILL LOVE HIM, AND WILL MANIFEST MYSELF TO HIM."

The form is:

1. The great sin of the church is ignoring the Word of God, changing the Word, adding to the Word, or taking from the Word.

2. How long will it take us to learn that God means what He says and says what He means?

3. For instance, the modern church has adopted humanistic psychology as the answer to the aberrations and perversions of man despite the fact that the Holy Spirit through Peter said: *"According as His Divine Power has given unto us all things that pertain unto life and godliness, through the knowledge of Him Who has called us to Glory and Virtue"* (II Pet. 1:3).

THE WORD OF GOD

The phrase, *"He who has My Commandments,"* points to the Word of God. As always, the *"Word"* is the criterion, not church denominations, other men, the law of the land, or even what we think, etc.

The phrase, *"And keeps them,"* is tied to the previous phrase, *"And I in you."* In other words, He does command that we keep His Commandments, but now, conditions are totally different than they were under the Old Economy of God. Now, Jesus lives in us and will actually keep the Commandments for us if we will only trust Him and believe. He does it through the Person, Ministry, Power, Agency, and the Glory of the Holy Spirit (Rom. 1:11). Consequently, there is no excuse for not keeping everything He has said. If we fail, we do so because we attempt to obey Him in our own efforts, which constitutes the flesh, and which God cannot bless or condone (Rom. 8:1).

LOVING THE LORD

The phrase, *"He it is who loves Me,"* in effect, says that if we do not keep His Commandments, especially considering that He does it for us through the Spirit, such portrays that we do not love Him. Consequently, irrespective of what one claims, it is only obedience which makes real our claims in the Eyes of God.

This does not mean sinless perfection because no Believer can claim such because the Bible does not teach such. However, it does mean that sin is not to have dominion over the individual and, therefore, the person is doing all within his power to obey the Lord, and will constantly strive to maintain this place of Victory provided to us by Christ.

WHAT COMMANDMENTS?

It can probably be easier said that we do whatever He wants us to do. The New Covenant has taken us out from under the rituals, ceremonies, Commandments, and formulas of the Old Covenant. In fact, the New Covenant, all in Christ and superintended by the Holy Spirit, takes us far greater into obedience than the Old Covenant ever could. The reason is simple: Jesus has paid the price at the Cross of Calvary, thereby, removing original sin, at least for those who believe. This gives the Holy Spirit latitude to abide permanently within our hearts and lives. Now, the Spirit leads us, not according to rules and regulations, but altogether through the direction that He wants us to go. We are to be so close to Him that a simple push is all that is needed.

I know my wife to such an extent that I can look at her face and tell when she wants something or doesn't want something. She really doesn't have to say anything. It is because of relationship. It is the same with the Holy Spirit.

When we get close enough to the Lord, it will be very easy to ascertain what He wants or doesn't want. Let me give you a personal example.

A PERSONAL EXAMPLE

Many years ago, actually, back in the early 1960s, in a couple of places where we were preaching Meetings, we had become very good friends with the Pastors and their wives, etc. Sometimes, after the Sunday night Church Service, we would go bowling. Now, there's nothing wrong with bowling, nothing wrong with rolling a wooden ball down a hardwood floor to strike some pins, etc. There's nothing sinister, ugly, vulgar, or ungodly about that.

Nevertheless, after a short period of time, the Holy Spirit spoke to my heart and told me that I was not to do that anymore. Now, why did He do that?

I really cannot answer that. That's part of living for God. Sometimes, He tells us what and why, but most of the time, He doesn't. Our business is simply to follow.

I've not been in a bowling alley from then until now and never expect to go into one again. However, I'm not getting up and preaching, telling people that it's a sin to go bowling. That which the Lord wants me to do may have nothing to do with you, and vice versa. He wants to lead us and guide us, and that's what He means by having His Commandments and keeping them. As stated, it is far more stringent than it was under the Old Covenant. It requires relationship, which can only be gained by the Believer placing his or her Faith exclusively in Christ and the Cross, and maintaining it exclusively in Christ and the Cross. This then gives the Holy Spirit the latitude and the Power to work within our hearts and lives. Of course, the Holy Spirit is God. He can do anything; however, He will never violate our free moral agency. He will suggest, move upon, speak to us, and deal with us, but He won't force us to do anything.

JESUS

The actual fact is, Jesus has already won the Victory over every single spiritual problem, moral weakness, and sin, which was done at Calvary. His Work is a Finished Work and requires no further effort on our part, with such effort actually being an insult to God. Such struggle, by its very definition, says that Jesus did not pay it all, and something else remains to be done. He did pay it all, and that means in every capacity!

Last of all, the victory is ours in totality, that is, if we will only take God at His Word. While we do struggle, it is a struggle of Faith to maintain the victory instead of attempting to gain the victory, which Jesus, as stated, has already done!

THE ANSWER IS THE CROSS OF CHRIST

When we say the answer is the Cross of Christ, we are speaking of every single thing we do for the Lord, He does for us, the direction that we take, the Power that we need, or whatever. It is the Cross and the Cross Alone where all Victory was won, which was done for you and me. That's the reason the Believer must, without fail, make the Cross of Christ the Object of your Faith. In fact, that's the only Faith that God will actually recognize.

As previously stated, actually several times:

• Jesus Christ is the Source of all things we receive from God (Jn. 1:1-3, 14, 29; Col. 2:10-15).

• Jesus is the Source, the Cross of Christ is the Means, and the only Means, by which all of these wonderful things are done for us and are given to us (Rom. 6:3-14; I Cor. 1:17; Gal. 6:14).

• With Christ as the Source and the Cross as the Means, the Object of our Faith must always be, without exception, Christ and the Cross. It is Who He is, the Son of the Living God, and What He did. It is the greatest Victory afforded humanity, which was accomplished at the Cross (I Cor. 1:18, 21, 23; 2:2; Gal., Chpt. 5; Col. 2:14-15).

• With Christ as the Source and the Cross as the Means, and the Cross of Christ ever the Object of Faith, with our understanding that everything we receive from God is made possible by the Cross, then the Holy Spirit, Who is God, and Who can do anything, will go to work within our hearts and lives, bringing our state up to our standing, which He Alone can do (Rom. 8:1-11). In a nutshell, in extremely abbreviated form, what I have just given you is the key to all victory.

IF WE LOVE CHRIST, THE FATHER WILL LOVE US

The phrase, *"And he who loves Me shall be loved of My Father,"* provides the criterion of approval by the Father. As well, the Love the Father has for the Believer is, in a sense, far more intense than that in which God is said to love the world (Jn. 3:16). The simple fact is, *"God the Father loves those supremely who love the Son."*

The phrase, *"And I will love him, and will manifest Myself to him,"* means far more than Jesus manifesting Himself in some minor way, but rather to fully disclose His Person, Nature, and Goodness to the Believer. As well, it speaks of every capacity and is a Manifestation which never stops.

Inasmuch as Jesus is *"Life,"* is the *"Resurrection,"* is the *"Manifestation of the Father,"* and is *"All in All,"* there is no limit to the Blessings and fulfillment. No wonder Jesus said, *"I am come that they might have life, and have it more abundantly"* (Jn. 10:10). All of this is done through the Person and Agency of the Holy Spirit, even as said in Verse 17, all made possible by the Cross.

(22) "JUDAS SAID UNTO HIM, NOT ISCARIOT, LORD, HOW IS IT THAT YOU WILL MANIFEST YOURSELF UNTO US, AND NOT UNTO THE WORLD?"

The form is:

1. Regrettably, the church has been pushed away from the True Foundation of the Cross.

2. It has been pushed away to such an extent that it hardly knows where it's been, where it is, or where it is going.

3. Sadly, I believe personally that the modern church is in worse spiritual condition presently than it has been since the Reformation.

THADDAEUS

The phrase, *"Judas said unto Him, not Iscariot,"* speaks of the Apostle also known as Lebbaeus or Thaddaeus (Mat. 10:3; Mk. 3:18). He was the brother of James the Less (Mk. 15:40), and other Apostles, and not to be confused with James, the half-brother of Jesus, or James, the brother of John. As well, as is obvious, he was not the traitor, even though having the same name.

LORD, HOW LONG?

The question, *"Lord, how is it that You will manifest Yourself unto us, and not unto the world?"* as posed by Thaddaeus, had implications of Israel being restored to her place of glory and grandeur.

The Apostle was somewhat confused, continuing to think that Jesus would ultimately use His Power to bring Israel to her rightful place. Of course, if this were to be done, it certainly would involve the world of that day and, more particularly, the Roman Empire, which then controlled Israel. So, he was wondering how Jesus could do all of this without the world being aware and, in fact, only manifesting Himself to His Close Followers.

The *"Manifestation"* of which Jesus spoke was not at all what Israel then desired. They wanted Him to manifest His Power on their behalf, that is, if they could maintain complete control. The religious leaders saw not at all their spiritual needs, but rather their political needs.

Jesus was speaking of a Spiritual Manifestation, which is man's true need, rather than a political manifestation, of which Thaddaeus spoke!

(23) "JESUS ANSWERED AND SAID UNTO HIM, IF A MAN LOVE ME, HE WILL KEEP MY WORDS: AND MY FATHER WILL LOVE HIM, AND WE WILL COME UNTO HIM, AND MAKE OUR ABODE WITH HIM."

The pattern is:

1. The Cross of Christ is actually the Foundation of all Doctrine as it regards the Word of God.

2. Any doctrine that is not based squarely on the Foundation of the Cross is spurious.

3. In fact, all false doctrine is brought about simply because of ignoring the Cross, misunderstanding the Cross, or outright denying the Cross.

THE ANSWER GIVEN BY CHRIST

The phrase, *"Jesus answered and said unto him,"* addresses the real need of man, which is Salvation from the curse of the Law and the terrible depraved state in which man now finds himself.

Religion is a terrible business in that it makes people believe things which are not true. Israel was immersed in religion at that time and because of such, strongly denied any need for God whatsoever. Consequently, what Jesus proposed was met with no enthusiasm, but rather hostility.

Man keeps thinking that if he can change governmental leaders, get rich, or secure a particular type of education, the problems will be solved. True enough, there are some governmental leaders who are much better than others, as should be obvious. However, despite man's quest in these areas, the problems remain!

What Jesus will give is the only answer to man's dilemma. Man must be changed, but it can only be done so from within, which can only be carried out by Deity.

Men address every problem from the externals because that's all that man can do. Actually, that is all the religions of the world can do. However, Christ, being God, can change men, and He does so from within, even as it must be.

LOVE FOR THE LORD

The phrase, *"If a man love Me, he will keep My Words,"* presents this of which Jesus spoke as based on Love, which is the exact opposite of what the Apostles were speaking, which was force.

They wanted Jesus to use His Power to force Rome and other people of the world to recognize Israel as the premier Nation. However, Jesus spoke of *"Love,"* and not on a national basis, but rather on an individual basis, which is the opposite of the world.

In the culture of the world, men seek to gain followers by exciting the masses. In fact, certain things can be done in this fashion; however, only external matters can be addressed, and that poorly!

By contrast, Salvation is a personal experience and deals with each individual with Love as its Foundation.

However, this is *"Love"* channeled in a particular direction, actually, toward Christ, and then extends to others. Consequently, this Kingdom is built on *"Love,"* and more particularly, on Christ as the Object of that Love because He is the One Who paid the price for man's Redemption.

If the Foundation is *"Love,"* and it is, the requirements are the keeping of His Words, which we have already discussed.

Man must have direction, and to be sure, Satan attempts to provide direction, but, of course, it is a false direction. Only the Lord provides the correct direction, and that is the Word of God. It is the single most important thing in the entirety of the world and always has been, which is meant to serve in every capacity in this regard. Men go astray because they leave the Word of God. The church goes astray because it leaves the Word of God. To be sure, such wrong direction will destroy a person, a church, and even the entirety of a nation, as America now is being destroyed.

THE LOVE OF GOD

The phrase, *"And My Father will love him,"* presents an entirely different activity of the Love of God than extended to sinners. It is here portrayed as the activity of a Father's Love for His Children, hence, the conscious enjoyment and Manifestation of that Love as dependent upon obedience. Naughty children are loved but are not caressed.

If the Spirit be grieved, the Divine Manifestations to the heart cease to be consciously enjoyed, communion is interrupted, and the Spirit has to deal with the conscience in Conviction rather than with the heart in Manifestation. Thus, communion and obedience are interrelated.

DWELLING WITH THE LORD

The phrase, *"And We will come unto him, and make Our Abode with him,"* tells us several things:

• Even though the Doctrine of the Trinity is not necessarily being taught in this Verse, still, the plural pronoun, such as *"We"* and *"Our,"* assert their unity at work in Omniscience, resulting in the abiding of Both the Father and the Son. Thus, we have two Persons of the Trinity mentioned here, with the Third mentioned in Verse 17.

• This phrase speaks, as well, of the Omnipresence of Christ. In the days of His Life on Earth, He was localized, as well as other human beings, and limited in knowledge and other powers. However, now that He has been Glorified as Deity, He is everywhere, hence, able to make His Abode with every Believer.

• The word *"abode"* here is the same as *"mansion"* in Verse 2. In effect, the Lord is saying that He will make a *"mansion,"* if you will, of the Believer (I Cor. 3:16).

There could be no greater honor, privilege, help, sustenance, or power than having Both the Father and the Son abiding within our hearts and lives, as well as the Holy Spirit (Vss. 16-17). Actually, the Abiding of the Father and the Son is through the Person and Agency of the Holy Spirit. The Unity of these Three is of such perfection that it is virtually impossible for the Believer to fully comprehend or understand the magnitude of what is spoken here. Irrespective, the Believer is the recipient of this Miraculous Presence.

(24) "HE WHO LOVES ME NOT KEEPS NOT MY SAYINGS: AND THE WORD WHICH YOU HEAR IS NOT MINE, BUT THE FATHER'S WHICH SENT ME."

The construction is:

1. The modern church has been pushed away from the true Foundation of the Cross to such an extent that it hardly knows where it's been, where it is, or where it is going.

2. Sadly, I believe the modern church is in worse spiritual condition than it has been since the Reformation.

3. The Word of the Cross (I Cor. 1:18) is the Gospel. It is not a part of the Gospel or some of the Gospel but, in actuality, is the Gospel.

LACK OF LOVE FOR GOD ALSO IGNORES HIS WORD

The phrase, *"He who loves Me not keeps not My Sayings,"* once again joins the two, but in a different manner.

As we have stated, love for Jesus is claimed by hundreds of millions. However, such is only an empty claim if His *"Sayings"* are ignored.

This means that Catholics do not really love Him if they ignore His Word, accepting rather the words of mere men, i.e., the church, which contradicts God's Word. To be frank, the same would go for any and all who call themselves Believers. In fact, the Protestant world has long since begun to follow suit in ignoring the Word of God.

For instance, millions of Baptists ignore what Jesus has said about the Holy Spirit, rather accepting the teaching of their *"church!"* I mention these because they explicitly claim to be fundamentalists, who claim to believe in and obey all of the Bible.

Sadly, many, if not most, Pentecostals fall into the same category, abandoning the Word of God for the Purpose Driven Life façade, the Seeker Sensitive debacle, humanistic psychology, etc.

Love involves obedience, and obedience involves love. Consequently, obedience is the great proof of love, and if love is absent, this means that obedience to the Word is absent as well. The two go together.

THE WORD OF GOD

The phrase, *"And the Word which you*

hear is not Mine, but the Father's Who sent Me," places the Statements of Christ on an entirely different level.

This means that what Jesus said and did was not self-originated, but was rather the Plan of God, originating with the Father; however, this speaks only of His Incarnation. In that lowered state, He proclaimed no expression of Deity even though He never lost the possession of Deity.

Before the Incarnation, all things done came from God, which included the Three Persons of the Trinity (Gen. 1:26; 3:22).

(25) "THESE THINGS HAVE I SPOKEN UNTO YOU, BEING YET PRESENT WITH YOU."

The construction is:

1. The phrase, *"These things have I spoken unto you,"* is said with the knowledge that the Disciples did not at that time understand what He spoke.

2. However, this would all change upon the Advent of the Holy Spirit, even as He declares in the next Verse.

3. *"Being yet present with you,"* tells us that His Time is short in this capacity. Actually, from this moment, He would be with them approximately 51 more days. He would then ascend back to the Father.

(26) "BUT THE COMFORTER, WHICH IS THE HOLY SPIRIT, WHOM THE FATHER WILL SEND IN MY NAME, HE SHALL TEACH YOU ALL THINGS, AND BRING ALL THINGS TO YOUR REMEMBRANCE, WHATSOEVER I HAVE SAID UNTO YOU."

The form is:

1. As few people in the world, I think I have been made to realize how necessary it is that we adhere strictly to the Word.

2. Even when we stray from the Word through ignorance, or do not know how to apply the Word because of ignorance, such ignorance cannot be overlooked by God and, to be sure, will reap its bitter fruit.

3. As it regards the great Message of the Cross, which is the Gospel (I Cor. 1:17), we must realize that it comes in two parts, so to speak: that for our Salvation and that for our Sanctification.

THE COMFORTER

The phrase, *"But the Comforter, Who is the Holy Spirit,"* proclaims the Third Person of the Godhead. As stated, He is a *"Parakletos,"* or, *"One called alongside to help."*

The Personality of the Holy Spirit appears in this farewell in the terms: *"teaching," "reminding," "testifying," "coming," "convincing," "guiding," "speaking," "hearing," "prophesying," "taking,"* and *"bringing."*

THE NAME OF JESUS

The phrase, *"Whom the Father will send in My Name,"* expresses authority and character.

For the Father to send the Holy Spirit in the *"Name of Jesus"* refers to the fact that Jesus Alone paid the price in removing the sin debt in order that the Holy Spirit could abide within the hearts and lives of Believers. It was the Blood of the Lord Jesus Christ which was shed in order to pay the price; consequently, the Holy Spirit, by rights, is sent in *"His Name!"*

THE TEACHER

"He shall teach you all things," proclaims the Holy Spirit as the Great Teacher of the Word of God, which is the only way one can learn the Word.

That does not mean that Believers are not in need of Bible teachers, but that the Holy Spirit will anoint the Believer to know if what he is being taught is Scriptural (I Jn. 2:27). It is actually the Holy Spirit Who uses *"Apostles, Prophets, Evangelists, Pastors, and Teachers"* (Eph. 4:11). So, even though men and women are used by God in the capacity of preaching and teaching, still, it is *"the Spirit of Truth,"* Who is the final authority, Who actually gave the world the Word of God and is responsible for its contents.

REMEMBRANCE

The phrase, *"And bring all things to your remembrance, whatsoever I have said unto you,"* refers to all of these things said by Jesus during His three and one half years of public Ministry.

As one reads the four Gospels, it becomes obvious that the Disciples understood very little of what Christ was saying. It seems His Parables, as well as His Teaching concerning

Himself and the Kingdom of God, were a mystery to them. However, after the Holy Spirit was sent, with His Abiding in the hearts and lives of Believers, which was all made possible by the Cross, it is also very obvious in the Book of Acts and the Epistles that the Disciples then understood perfectly what Jesus was saying. In short order, the Holy Spirit made real the Words of Christ to their hearts and lives.

In fact, immediately after receiving the Holy Spirit, Peter preached, as some have said, the inaugural Message of the Church, which took place on the Day of Pentecost. Even though his Message was delivered only minutes, or an hour or two at the most, after the infilling of the Holy Spirit, it becomes quickly obvious that Peter was a changed man. His knowledge and, more perfectly, his understanding of the Word of God, even in this short time, stands out to such an extent that it cannot be denied. All of this was and is the Work of the Holy Spirit.

THE HOLY SPIRIT IN THE BELIEVER

As Jesus stated, before Calvary, the Holy Spirit was with those in the Covenant but not in them (Jn. 14:17). As valuable as that was, however, it could not compare with Him being in a Believer, which takes place at Salvation. So, the point I am attempting to make concerns the great difference in the First Covenant and the Second Covenant. That difference is very obvious here.

As well, and which is also obvious, the fact that the Believer can also be baptized with the Holy Spirit with the evidence of speaking with other Tongues adds greatly to this of which He already does in the life of the Believer. In fact, being baptized with the Holy Spirit is such a given in the Book of Acts that it becomes very clear that this is the Intention, and greatly so, of the Spirit of God. There is a large segment of the Christian community which teaches that while it may have been valid for the Early Church, everything is received at Salvation, and the Baptism with the Holy Spirit according to Acts 2:4 is not valid presently. This is totally wrong! Such is not only unscriptural, but constitutes a tremendous denial of the Power of God that enables Believers to continue the great Move of the Early Church, which is intended by the Spirit of God. In fact, without the Baptism with the Holy Spirit with the evidence of speaking with other Tongues, precious little is going to actually be done for the Lord. There may be much activity, but it's all man generated, which means it's not generated by the Holy Spirit. The teaching that He is no longer needed short-changes that which Christ made possible at Calvary, denying the Believer so much of what Christ paid for with His Own Life.

(27) "PEACE I LEAVE WITH YOU, MY PEACE I GIVE UNTO YOU: NOT AS THE WORLD GIVES, GIVE I UNTO YOU. LET NOT YOUR HEART BE TROUBLED, NEITHER LET IT BE AFRAID."

The overview is:

1. If one doesn't understand God's Prescribed Order of Victory, which is the Cross of Christ, then no matter how hard one tries, one cannot live a victorious life.

2. As important as the Cross of Christ is for our Salvation, as important it is for our Sanctification.

3. The problem is sin, and the only answer for sin is the Cross of Christ.

PEACE

The phrase, *"Peace I leave with you, My Peace I give unto you,"* has to do with *"Sanctifying Peace!"*

There are two types of *"peace"* proclaimed in the Word of God.

1. *"Peace with God"*: this comes at Salvation as a result of the enmity being removed due to the sinner coming to terms with his Maker in accepting the provision of Christ paid for at Calvary (Eph. 2:14-17). In other words, every Believer has peace with God, which comes automatically with the Salvation experience. This means the condemnation is gone, and the guilt is gone because the person is at one with God.

2. *"The Peace of God"*: there is a vast difference in *"peace with God,"* which comes with Salvation, than *"the Peace of God,"* of which Jesus here speaks. Whereas every Believer has *"peace with God,"* most do not

have *"the Peace of God,"* even though Jesus here plainly tells us it is ours.

The way this *"Peace,"* which is Sanctifying Peace, comes to us is by the Believer placing his or her Faith exclusively in Christ and the Cross. The Cross is where all Victory was won, and it is where all Victory is won on our behalf as well. When one places one's Faith entirely in Christ and the Cross, that is total dependence on Christ. When we place our Faith in anything else, no matter how good or even scriptural the other thing might be, at least in its own right, there will be no Sanctifying Peace.

I am persuaded that this is the reason that so many Christians experience nervous disorders, emotional disturbances, and certain types of sicknesses. It is because of a lack of Sanctifying Peace.

Once again, the reader may say, *"Brother Swaggart, you seem to conclude that the Cross of Christ is the answer for everything."* One more time, I will state, *"Now you are beginning to hear what we are saying."* That is most definitely the truth. The Cross of Christ is the solution, the answer, and the only answer, for anything and everything that we receive from the Lord. It is the Means, and I speak of what Jesus there did, that makes it possible for the Holy Spirit to make real to us all of these things. Without the Believer's Faith exclusively in Christ and the Cross, the Fruit of the Spirit is seriously hindered. A proper prayer life is seriously hindered. Faith is seriously hindered. The reason is simple: whenever we place our Faith in something other than Christ and the Cross, it is misplaced Faith, which God can never recognize.

THE CROSS OF CHRIST AND SANCTIFYING PEACE

That's why Paul said, *"God forbid that I should glory* (boast), *in anything save the Cross of Christ, by which I was crucified to the world and the world unto me"* (Gal. 6:14). When our Faith is placed in anything except the Cross, then the boasting centers up on us. In other words, we get the glory, which we in no way deserve, as should be overly obvious. However, when we place our Faith exclusively in Christ and the Cross, then all the Glory goes to the Lord Jesus Christ, which it most definitely should because He and He Alone is the One Who paid the price.

So, this Peace given to the Saint of God by the Lord Jesus Christ is yours for the asking; however, it is predicated on our Faith being exclusively in Christ and the Cross.

NOT AS THE WORLD GIVES

The phrase, *"Not as the world gives, give I unto you,"* simply means that the *"Peace"* of which Jesus here speaks cannot be given by the world, is not understood by the world, and cannot be obtained from the world. I don't care how much money the person has, how much fame and glory the person may have, or what position he may occupy, there is no *"peace"* in any of this. Once again, allow me to state that this is the cause of much sickness, emotional disturbances, nervous disorders, etc. In other words, the opposite of this Peace is fear. If the Child of God is plagued by fear, it's simply because his Faith is misplaced.

Once the Believer's Faith is exclusively in the Cross, there is a peace that passes all understanding that fills one's heart and never leaves. It is the happiest life on the face of the Earth. The sadness is: most Believers do not understand the peace and do not enjoy the peace of which Jesus here speaks because they do not have the peace of which Jesus here speaks.

How do I know that?

I know it because the only way this peace can be obtained is by one's Faith in Christ and the Cross, and the modern church is not teaching that whatsoever. The modern church has opted almost entirely for humanistic psychology. When that is done, the Cross of Christ must go. Either one cancels out the other.

When I was a young man just beginning to preach, the Cross in Pentecostal churches, and even Baptist churches, etc., thankfully, was preached strongly. However, even then, the Cross of Christ was not understood respecting Sanctification. So, most Believers tried to live this life by placing their Faith in something other than Christ and the Cross. The truth was and still is: most modern Believers, and we speak of those who truly love God, simply do not know how to live for God. I realize that's a statement that would cause somebody to blink, but it happens to be true. Most Believers, even though they love Jesus and are trying their best to live the life they ought to live, still, simply do not know how to live for God. It is because they do not understand the Cross of Christ as it regards Sanctification. Yes, they understand the Cross for Salvation, but, no, they do not understand it for Sanctification!

NO FEAR

Jesus said, *"Let not your heart be troubled, neither let it be afraid,"* which proclaims, by its very structure, that this life, even for the Christian, and especially the Christian, is not trouble free. However, even though the Lord does not promise a trouble free existence, as some claim, He does promise *"peace"* in the midst of that trouble, whatever it might be.

The word *"afraid,"* as Jesus here used it, actually means *"terrified,"* which is the only time that word is used in this manner in the New Testament. So, this means that some problems will be of extremely severe nature.

Irrespective, the Lord is saying that our trust in Him must not waiver because He has promised to see us through and, as well, to give peace in the midst of whatever problem may arise.

David said, *"Many are the afflictions of the righteous: but the LORD delivers him out of them all"* (Ps. 34:19).

However, if the Believer doesn't have this *"Sanctifying Peace,"* such trouble will overcome such a one, which is, as stated, the cause of many nervous breakdowns, etc. In essence, the Lord said:

"Let not your heart be troubled, neither let it be terrified." We have One Who is watching over us, and doing so constantly. As I keep saying, *"He doesn't require much of us, but He does demand one thing"*:

He demands that our Faith be exclusively in Christ and the Cross. That's why Paul said to the Church at Corinth, and all others, as well, and for all time:

"I determined not to know anything among you, save Jesus Christ, and Him Crucified" (I Cor. 2:2).

Our Lord's Legacy of Peace was not only the peace for heart and conscience secured by the *"Blood of His Cross"* (Col. 1:20), but His Own Peace in which He lived when on Earth as a Man. There was a *"Peace"* in Him that the world could neither touch, nor reach, nor destroy. In that Peace, He Himself walked as a Man in fellowship with His Father. He wants us to have the same Peace. We can have it if we place our Faith exclusively in Christ and What He did for us at the Cross.

(28) "YOU HAVE HEARD HOW I SAID UNTO YOU, I GO AWAY, AND COME AGAIN UNTO YOU. IF YOU LOVED ME, YOU WOULD REJOICE, BECAUSE I SAID, I GO UNTO THE FATHER: FOR MY FATHER IS GREATER THAN I."

The overview is:

1. In the Revelation of the Cross of Christ given to this Evangelist, the very first thing the Lord showed me was the sin nature, what it is, and how it works. He took me to the Sixth Chapter of Romans. I was to understand later that this is the very first thing that was shown to the Apostle Paul as well.

2. A few days later in prayer, the Lord then showed me the solution to the sin nature, in fact, the only solution, which is the Cross of Christ. Once again, He took me to Romans 6:3-5.

3. Some weeks after that, He showed me how the Holy Spirit works in all of this in that He works entirely within the framework of the Finished Work of Christ. He doesn't demand much of us, but He does demand that our Faith be exclusively in Christ and the Cross (Rom. 8:2).

I GO AWAY, BUT I WILL COME AGAIN UNTO YOU

The phrase, *"You have heard how I said unto you, I go away, and come again unto you,"* represents that which would happen very shortly but, as well, will happen in the future. The latter speaks of the Second Coming.

As we have stated, the Jews at this time had an erroneous concept as to Who and What the Messiah would actually be.

However, of all the things they thought of Him, despite what the Word of God said, they did not understand Him, at least at this time, to be God manifest in the flesh. They should have but did not!

So, Him speaking of going away, even at the very height of His Powers, was incomprehensible to His Disciples. They wanted Israel liberated politically while Jesus came to liberate mankind spiritually, which is the answer to all problems. Consequently, Him speaking of being crucified and rising from the dead was totally beyond their comprehension.

They did not understand that in a matter of hours, He would totally fulfill and complete the Mission for which He came and then would go back to the Father. As well, at this time, they did not understand Him coming back through the Person and Agency of the Holy Spirit. Also, the Second Coming, which this, as well, carries in its full explanation, was not understandable either, at least at this time.

However, as we have repeatedly stated, the Advent of the Holy Spirit would solve these problems, fully explaining to them what Jesus spoke, with God's Plan perfectly outlined.

REJOICE?

The phrase, *"If you loved Me, you would rejoice, because I said, I go unto the Father,"* proclaims, in effect, that even though at present they did not understand His Statement, their *"love"* for Him placed their care in His Hands.

In His Wondrous Grace, He reckoned upon their affection for Him, and it was a precious thought to Him that they would rejoice in His Glory and Joy.

Actually, this Passage should speak to every Believer. There are many things the Lord requires that we go through, and He does not give us any explanation. He wants us to love Him enough that we will trust Him, and irrespective as to the direction, we know it is for our good, and He will see us through. It must always be remembered that everything God does is for the good and betterment of His Children and never for their hurt.

NOTES

MY FATHER IS GREATER THAN I

The phrase, *"For My Father is greater than I,"* speaks of the Incarnation.

In the Incarnation, God becoming Man, the Lord had to divest Himself of all expressions of Deity even though He never lost the possession of Deity. In this *"form of a servant and made in the likeness of men,"* He was of necessity less than His Father, which should be obvious.

And then, even beyond the Incarnation, there is a sense in which the Father is the Head of the Divine Trinity (Jn. 14:16; 16:23-26; I Cor. 11:3).

As well, I think this Passage, plus scores of others similar, plainly proclaim that Jesus is not the Father or the Holy Spirit, as some claim. Even though there is but One God, He is manifested in Three Persons as clearly outlined, God the Father, God the Son, and God the Holy Spirit.

(29) "AND NOW I HAVE TOLD YOU BEFORE IT COME TO PASS, THAT, WHEN IT IS COME TO PASS, YOU MIGHT BELIEVE."

The overview is:

1. When anyone rejects the Cross, he does not do so on theological grounds, but rather on moral grounds.

2. Theological grounds means that it's too difficult to understand.

3. In fact, the Message of the Cross is so simple and easy to understand that it can easily be understood by a child.

BELIEVING

The phrase, *"And now I have told you before it come to pass,"* refers to all of the things He would do, which pertained to the Crucifixion, the Resurrection, and the Ascension. As well, it spoke of Him sending back the Holy Spirit, Who, in effect, would take His Place.

"That, when it is come to pass, you might believe," has reference to the fact that the fulfillment would be very soon, actually, beginning the next day.

The word *"believe"* in the Greek, as it is here used, is *"Pisteuo"* and has its root in *"Pistis."* It means to *"have reliance upon, not mere credence."*

"Pistis" also means *"a conviction respecting God and His Word, and the Believer's relationship to Him."*

The Disciples had a problem from the very beginning believing what Christ told them respecting His Purpose and Mission. This was because of their error of misinterpreting the Word of God and actually succumbing to the wrong teaching of almost the entirety of Israel at that time. It is impossible for a person to believe error and truth about the same thing at the same time. So, to believe the perverted teaching of that time was to disbelieve Christ.

However, they would see all the things He had spoken come to pass, and then the Holy Spirit would make the picture complete.

(30) "HEREAFTER I WILL NOT TALK MUCH WITH YOU: FOR THE PRINCE OF THIS WORLD COMES, AND HAS NOTHING IN ME."

The structure is:

1. Men reject the Cross simply because of pride and self-will.

2. The Cross of Christ is an offense to the world and most of the church simply because it exposes all the wrong ways and directions.

3. Cain did not refuse to offer up a sacrifice but only that which God demanded.

THE PRINCE OF THIS WORLD

The phrase, *"Hereafter I will not talk much with you,"* could be translated, *"Hereafter I will not have much more time to talk with you."* Actually, He would only have this day before His Death and then 40 days after the Resurrection. However, in the 40 days and nights, it seems as if He was not with them continually, only making appearances at certain times. So, the time of instruction for the past three and one-half years was running out, with Him soon to ascend to the Father.

"For the Prince of this world comes," speaks of Satan.

By referring to Satan in this manner, Jesus proclaims the fact that Satan by and large rules and governs this present world.

At the Fall, Satan gained a pseudo sovereignty over man on the principle of possession and consent of a responsible agent or government by consent of the governed.

In other words, he gained this sovereignty from Adam and Eve by false claims, but, nevertheless, it was his.

It does not appear that Adam and Even initially knew and understood that their rebellion against God by disobedience would automatically allow Satan's rule and authority over them, and their offspring, as well, which, in fact, includes the entirety of the human family, even up to this moment.

THE CROSS

This is the basic reason Jesus came. At Calvary, He would destroy the power of Satan over the human family by breaking the grip of sin and atoning for all sin, past, present, and future, at least for all who would believe. All of this pertained to the stranglehold that Satan exercised over all of mankind. As such, he was the Prince of this world, hence, war, privation, want, sickness, sin, poverty, suffering, pain, death, and destruction.

What did Jesus mean by speaking of Satan as coming?

The Evil One was coming in order to kill Christ.

How did he think he could do this, considering that Jesus was not born of the seed of man and, therefore, did not have the penalty of death within or upon Him? In fact, He could not die unless He willingly would give up His Life, which He did.

As deceived as Satan's dupes are, so is Satan deceived himself! In other words, he is so deceived because of his rebellion against God that he actually believed he could kill Christ, even as he attempted to do when He was a Baby and several times since. He knows the Bible, but he does not believe the Bible, even as the world does not believe the Bible.

Even now, he still thinks he can pervert the Plan of God, with the coming Antichrist being his greatest effort of all.

When Jesus died, actually breathing out His Own Life, meaning that neither Satan nor man took it from him, still, in the Eyes of God, Satan was accounted as a murderer because this is what he desired even though he did not have the power to carry it out.

SATAN HAS NOTHING IN JESUS

God permitted Satan to defeat himself by causing him to kill (or attempt to do so) an innocent Victim over Whom he had no claim. When he inflicted death on Christ, even by the Consent of Christ, he forfeited all of his claims, rights, and pseudo authority. Even though he had this right over all others, he had no right regarding Jesus. Consequently, he lost the right to inflict death (spiritual death) on all others who became the Property of Christ by virtue of His Redemption for them.

The phrase, *"And has nothing in Me,"* gives credence to the statements we have just made. Satan had no hold over Jesus, no claim on Jesus, no sin in Jesus, and nothing of evil about Jesus. He was totally, wholly, completely, absolutely, and irrevocably above sin and Satan.

If the Prince of this world, i.e., Satan, could find nothing in his Rival, the Messiah, in which to appeal, why then should Jesus die, for death was in the power of Satan (Heb. 2:14)?

It was because the Father had commanded the Son to offer up Himself as a Sacrifice for sin for its expiation. By so dying, the Son manifested to the world His Love and Obedience to the Father, which, incidentally, removed Satan's claim on humanity, which was sin. Sin gives Satan a claim on human beings because of Adam's fall. However, with Jesus atoning for all sin, past, present, and future, at least for all who will believe, this removed Satan's legal means to hold anyone captive. So, if anyone is captive to the powers of darkness in any fashion, it is simply because he is not expressing the proper Faith in Christ and what He did for us at the Cross. Faith in Him and what He did gives us His Victory. In other words, we are changed from the position of lawbreaker to the position of law-keeper, all because of Christ and our Faith in Him and what He did for us at the Cross (Rom. 6:1-14; 8:1-11; I Cor. 1:17, 18, 21, 23; 2:2; Gal., Chpt. 5; 6:14; Col. 2:10-15).

(31) "BUT THAT THE WORLD MAY KNOW THAT I LOVE THE FATHER; AND AS THE FATHER GAVE ME COMMANDMENT, EVEN SO I DO. ARISE, LET US GO HENCE."

The order is:

1. Every sin was neutralized at the Cross, at least for all who will believe (Jn. 3:16).

2. This means that the only way that the human being can overcome sin is by his Faith being placed exclusively in Christ and the Cross (I Cor. 1:18).

3. The Lord can meet man only at the Cross (Gal. 6:14).

THE COMMANDMENT GIVEN TO CHRIST

The phrase, *"But that the world may know that I love the Father,"* presents Himself in the same mode that He demanded of His Disciples. He told them that if they really loved Him, they should keep His Commandments. Consequently, He loved the Father and would keep His (the Father's) Commandments.

"And as the Father gave Me Commandment, even so I do," proclaims His Perfect Example. We are to follow accordingly!

That which God demanded of His Son, which, of course, was the Cross, He will never demand of us. In fact, what He does demand is that we place our Faith exclusively in Christ and the Cross, and maintain it exclusively in Christ and the Cross. In short, that is His Commandment to us, by us, for us, and of us.

Regrettably, most Believers think of the Cross as something awful, something terrible. Whenever something bad happens, many Christians are prone to say, *"Well, that's his cross that he has to bear."*

The truth is, taking up the Cross daily (Lk. 9:23) presents the greatest Blessing that mankind could ever know. It is at the Cross that every Victory was won, and was won for you and for me. So, instead of the Cross of Christ being a matter of pain and suffering, while it was definitely such for Him, it is the very opposite for us. It is the secret of all Blessing, all Power, all overcoming strength, and all forgiveness of sin, in other words, every single good thing we receive from God is made possible by the Cross of Christ.

"Would you be free from the burden of sin?

"There's Power in the Blood, Power in
the Blood;
"Would you over evil a victory to win?
"There's wonderful Power in the
Blood."

"Would you be free from your passion
and pride?
"There's Power in the Blood, Power in
the Blood;
"Come for a cleansing to Calvary's tide;
"There's wonderful Power in the
Blood."

"Would you be whiter, much whiter
than snow?
"There's Power in the Blood, Power in
the Blood;
"Sin-stains are lost in its life-giving
flow;
"There's wonderful Power in the
Blood."

"Would you do service for Jesus your
King?
"There's Power in the Blood, Power in
the Blood;
"Would you live daily His Praises to
sing?
"There's wonderful Power in the
Blood."

CHAPTER 15

(1) "I AM THE TRUE VINE, AND MY FATHER IS THE HUSBANDMAN."

The overview is:

1. Old Testament Saints were saved by looking forward to the Cross while we are saved by looking backward to the Cross.

2. Whenever you trusted Christ as a believing sinner, you were *"baptized into His Death,"* *"buried with Him by baptism into death,"* and then *"raised with Him in Newness of Life"* (Rom. 6:3-5).

3. The word *"baptized"* as here used, has absolutely nothing to do with Water Baptism.

THE TRUE VINE

The phrase, *"I am the True Vine,"* is, as well, the same thing as saying that Jesus is the *"True Israel!"*

In fact, the *"Vine"* was the image of Israel. The Prophets and Psalms abound with this reference (Ps. 80:8-19; Isa. 5:1; Ezek. 19:10, etc.).

Reynolds said, *"The "I" of this Passage is not only that of the Eternal Logos, nor is it the mere humanity, nor is it simply the Divine-Human Personality, but the new existence, which by union with Him formed one personage with Him — the Believer being united to Him as He is to the Father."*[1]

The relationship of this Chapter to the prior one is very important. The Personal Glory of Christ as the True Priest is the theme of the previous Chapter, and His Personal Glory as the True Vine is the subject of this Chapter.

Israel had been elected by God as both Priest and Vine (Isa., Chpt. 5; Hos. 4:6) but lost both glories through disobedience. However, God had His True Priest and His True Vine in reserve in the Person of Christ.

Again, John, Chapter 14, concerns the Gift of the Holy Spirit to man, but Chapter 15, His Activities in man.

In Chapter 14, Believers as Priests live a life of fellowship with Christ in heavenly places. In Chapter 15, we live a life of Testimony and beneficence as Vine Branches in earthly places.

Chapter 14 is the Epistle to the Ephesians, so to speak; Chapter 15, the Epistle to the Philippians, so to speak.

Chapter 14 is the Indwelling of the Spirit in the Believer within the Veil; Chapter 15, the outward working of the Spirit in the Believer outside the camp.

THE HUSBANDMAN

The phrase, *"And My Father is the Husbandman,"* refers to God not simply as the Vinedresser but, also, the Owner of the land as well.

Even though all Judgment is committed unto the Son, still, the *"Father"* remains as the Head of the Divine Trinity. As such, even as this Chapter proclaims, He is not a passive Head, but rather extremely active. Once again, the harmony, essence, and unity with which the Three Personalities of the Godhead work is set before us. Actually, this Chapter is meant to portray the Believer being brought into the harmony and actually becoming one with the Godhead, at least in the sense of spiritual adoption (Rom. 8:15).

(2) "EVERY BRANCH IN ME THAT BEARS NOT FRUIT HE TAKES AWAY: AND EVERY BRANCH THAT BEARS FRUIT, HE PURGES IT, THAT IT MAY BRING FORTH MORE FRUIT."

The exegesis is:

1. One cannot have the Leading of the Holy Spirit, I believe, without being first baptized with the Holy Spirit.

2. We're speaking of being baptized with the Spirit according to Acts 2:4.

3. Being baptized with the Spirit does not save anyone or make anyone more Saved. That is not its purpose. Its purpose is to give us Power to help us carry out the Work of God.

THE BRANCH BEARS FRUIT OR ELSE IT WILL BE TAKEN AWAY

The phrase, *"Every branch in Me that bears not fruit He takes away,"* tells us several things.

He said these branches are *"in Me,"* which speaks of Salvation. Actually, every Believer is referred to by this illustration, or it is meaningless.

If the Believer is fruitful, he is purged to produce more fruit. If he is fruitless, he is taken away or removed from being part of the Vine. The Father does this, not man. No man is able to pluck one branch from God's Hands, but if we say that God cannot cut off any branch that is necessary, then we limit God and make the dead, fruitless, and useless branches to be more powerful than He is.

To take this position would be like saying to the Vinedresser that it would be unlawful to prune the Vine and remove any dead branches. No man can cut off any branch that is not actually in the Vine. It is absurd and contrary to the letter and spirit of this illustration to talk about branches that are cut off as merely professing to be branches.

If the idea here is only a professed union of the Vine and branches, then there could only be a professed cutting off and burning. So, the Passage would mean nothing because it says nothing to any purpose.

We are told in this Passage that there are two kinds of branches — unfruitful and fruitful. In the Greek structure of the sentence, great attention is called to this.

As well, we are told that it is possible to come into this organic relation with the True Vine, Who is Jesus Christ, to be in it (in Him) and to be part of it (part of Him), and to bring forth no fruit.

UNPRODUCTIVE!

Were it not for Verse 5, we might say that these branches were nations, customs, institutions, etc., but the context forbids it.

The relation to Him in this unproductive manner must therefore be one that is insufficient to secure life, fruit, or continuance.

This plainly tells us that there are Believers who have been truly Born-Again, baptized in water, and as a consequence, are *"in Him."* However, because of bringing forth no fruit, despite the fact of the continued efforts of the Father, the Son, and the Holy Spirit, they continue to be unproductive and, as such, will ultimately be *"taken away,"* i.e., *"cast into the fire and burned"* (Vs. 6).

Actually, this goes back to the Parable of the Sower (Mat. 13:18-23).

THE PURGED BRANCH

The phrase, *"And every branch that bears fruit, He purges it, that it may bring forth more fruit,"* proclaims the exact opposite of the first phrase.

He plainly tells us that the branch which bears fruit will be purged, which, in the Greek, means *"to cleanse, as in to make pure."*

One may wonder as to how fruit could be developed when there is uncleanness and impurities.

The truth is, there are no perfect Christians, but the Lord looks beyond the surface and, as well, the impurities, etc., *"searching the heart, trying the reins, even to give every man according to his ways, and according to the fruit of his doings"* (Jer. 17:10). The very fact that the branch is bearing fruit shows there is a hunger for God, even a hunger and thirst which are intensifying, desiring all that God has for the Believer.

However, once again, this does not mean perfection, and indeed cannot, at least as long as we live in this body of flesh.

However, many, if not the majority, in the church wrongly interpret purging, thinking it is destruction. As such, they write off such as being of no more consequence. What they do not seem to realize is that the *"purging"* is not because of a lack of fruit but the very opposite. There has been fruit, and wonderful fruit at that, but the Holy Spirit sees that there is a potential for much more. Consequently, the Father, Who is the Vinedresser, purges the branch in order that it may bring forth *"more fruit,"* which refers to greater quantity, but above all, greater quality.

WHAT IS THIS FRUIT?

• *"The Fruit of the Spirit"*: this speaks of the Character of God developed in the Believer by the Holy Spirit, consisting of *"love, joy, peace, longsuffering, gentleness, goodness, faithfulness, meekness, and temperance"* (Gal. 5:22). This is in contrast to the antagonistic *"works of the flesh."*

• *"Fruits of Righteousness"*: this is found in Philippians 1:11 and in Hebrews 12:11, and is described as *"Peaceable Fruit,"* which is the outward effect of Divine chastening.

• *"Fruits"*: this speaks of works or deeds, spoken of as fruit, and is the visible expression of Power working inwardly and invisibly, the character of the fruit being evidence of the character of the Power producing it (Mat. 7:16). As the visible expressions of hidden lusts are the works of the flesh, so the invisible Power of the Holy Spirit in those who are brought into living union with Christ produces the right kind of fruit.

• Souls won to Christ as the result of evangelistic effort is spoken of as *"Fruit"* (Jn. 4:36; Rom. 1:13; Phil. 1:22).

None of this can be brought about unless the Believer has his or her Faith properly placed, and we speak of Faith in Christ and the Cross. For anything that one does for the Lord, asks of the Lord, or desires that the Lord work through him, it is an absolute necessity that one's Faith be in the proper object, which is always and without exception, *"Christ and Him Crucified"* (I Cor. 1:17, 18, 23; 2:2).

(3) "NOW YOU ARE CLEAN THROUGH THE WORD WHICH I HAVE SPOKEN UNTO YOU."

The form is:

1. Let the reader understand that all the laws, rules, and regulations of the Mosaic Law place the emphasis totally and completely on the Crucifixion of Christ and very little on the Resurrection, Ascension, and Exaltation of Christ, as important as those things actually are.

2. However, I remind the reader that these latter things were a forgone conclusion once the price was paid at the Cross.

3. As it regarded the Mosaic Law, the laying on of hands by the Priests upon the head of the bullock for the Sin-Offering represented their sins being transferred to this innocent victim, typifying Christ taking our sins upon Himself.

THE PURGING

The cleansing effect of the purging is brought on by the Word of God; consequently, it is the criterion for all things pertaining to God. In other words, the *"Vinedresser"* does whatever is necessary to bring one's life in every respect in accordance with the *"Word."* The actual carrying out of this task is done by the Holy Spirit through Whom the *"Vinedresser"* works. This is partly what John the Baptist meant when he spoke of Jesus *"baptizing with the Holy Spirit, and with fire"* (Mat. 3:11-12). This is the refiner's fire, as spoken of by Malachi (Mal. 3:3).

The word *"clean"* in the Greek is *"Katharos"* and means *"to be free from impure admixture, without blemish, spotless, and blameless,"* which can only be brought about by the shed Blood of Jesus Christ, with the Believer making that the Object of his Faith.

JOB

Regrettably, this *"purging"* or *"cleansing"* does not come quickly, and seldom does it come easily. Job is a perfect example! Concerning this man, Williams said:

"Job's account in the Bible explains why good men are afflicted. It is in order to their Sanctification. Inasmuch as the Book

of Job is believed to be the first written, it is interesting that this difficult question should be taken up first and answered in the Bible."[2]

Williams went on to say, "*In the Book of Job, we learn the discovery of the worthlessness of self, which is the first step in the Christian experience. We also learn the worthfulness of Christ, which sadly seems to be the last step. This is expressed in the "Song of Solomon," but cannot be reached until "Job" has been first passed through.*"[3]

Williams continues, "*As should be obvious, Job does not symbolize an unconverted, but a converted man. It was necessary that one of God's Children should be chosen for this trial: for the subject of Job is not the conversion of the sinner, but the consecration of the Saint.*"[4]

It is evident that an unconverted man needs to be brought to an end of himself. However, that a man who feared God and was perfect in his efforts to please the Lord, and who hated evil, should also need this is not so clear. And yet, this is what Jesus meant when He spoke of one who was bearing fruit but should be purged that he bring forth more fruit.

HOW GOD WORKS

Let us continue with Williams, "*At times in the Book of Job we learn that God uses Satan, calamity, and sickness to be His instruments in creating character and making men partakers of His Holiness. Such were the instruments, but the Hand that used them was God's; and the facts of Job explain to Believers, who like Job are conscious of personal integrity as a result of their Salvation, yet why calamities, sorrows, and diseases at times are permitted to afflict them.*"[5]

Continuing to use Job as an example, "*We find that the effect of the Divine action upon Job was that he ultimately 'abhorred himself,' which the Holy Spirit was attempting to portray to him all along.*

"*This language shows us that he had previously thought well of himself. His Creed was orthodox, for he approached God through Sacrifice, and his conduct was faultless, for he was a just man and hated evil.*

"*But these sharp trials, and especially the anger which the unjust accusations of his friends stirred up in his heart, revealed to himself unknown depths of moral ugliness; and finally his being challenged to measure himself with God, made him conscious that in him, that is in his 'flesh' there dwelt no good thing.*"[6]

This is a deep and painful experience that all Believers have not reached, but which the purging process reveals.

"*His Word*" cleansed the Vine by removing the fruitless branch. The effect thereof of His Teaching was to remove Judas Iscariot and the untrue disciples who walked no more with Him. So, speaking to the Eleven, He could say, "*You are clean,*" i.e., purged branches.

(4) "ABIDE IN ME, AND I IN YOU. AS THE BRANCH CANNOT BEAR FRUIT OF ITSELF, EXCEPT IT ABIDE IN THE VINE; NO MORE CAN YOU, EXCEPT YOU ABIDE IN ME."

The pattern is:

1. Everything Christ did was done for us (Gal. 6:14).

2. Understanding that everything comes to us through the Cross, the great Sacrifice of Christ must ever be the Object of our Faith (I Cor. 1:17).

3. Faith is the key, but it's the correct Object of Faith that makes Faith in God what it ought to be. That correct Object is Christ and the Cross (Rom. 6:3-5).

ABIDE IN ME, AND I IN YOU

The phrase, "*Abide in Me, and I in you,*" tells us several things:

• We can abide in Christ only by the means of the Cross. When the believing sinner comes to Christ, in the Mind of God, we die with Christ, are buried with Christ, and are raised with Christ (Rom. 6:3-5).

Paul used the term, "*In Christ,*" or one of its derivatives, such as "*In Him,*" etc., some 170 times in his 14 Epistles, that is, if he wrote Hebrews, which I definitely believe he did.

This is all made possible by the Cross. Jesus Christ was and is our Substitute and our Representative Man.

Using the same terminology as Jesus,

the vital self proceeds from Christ Alone and not at all from our corrupted nature, which must be grafted into His Life and become a part of Him in order to have Life and maintain Life. As stated, this can only be done by the means of the Cross.

Many may seem to be a part of Christ, which, no doubt, numbers a large percentage of those who call themselves *"Christian,"* and even be sacramentally or outwardly united to Him, and yet, their end is fruitlessness and rottenness. This necessitates removal by fire, if it can be removed at all. Actually, this probably numbers a very high percentage of Christendom. Considering both Protestants and Catholics, nearly 2 billion people in the world refer to themselves as *"Christian."* And yet, Jesus said, *"And few there be who find it,"* speaking of Eternal Life (Mat. 7:14).

So, this means that hundreds of millions are in the church but not *"in Christ."* As well, it speaks of tremendous numbers of others who are truly *"in Christ,"* but will ultimately be removed for lack of fruit bearing. In other words, they forsake the Cross for something else.

THE PURPOSE

• As we have stated, the abiding in Him guarantees Him abiding in us; however, our abiding in Him is for a different purpose than Him in us.

We abide in Him in order to draw sustenance from Him because He Alone is the Life Source; however, He draws no life from us because He needs none. Besides that, all the life we truly have has already come from Him.

So, one might say that His Abiding in us is twofold:

1. He desires and, in fact, must bring about harmony and unity of the Believer with the Godhead.

2. He abides in us in order that He may live through us the godly, Holy life, which guarantees fruit bearing, that is, if we allow Him to have His Way (Gal. 2:20).

BEARING FRUIT?

The phrase, *"As the branch cannot bear fruit of itself, except it abide in the Vine,"* presents Jesus giving us a simple lesson on horticulture. He constantly applied everyday things that were common to all to His Teaching, which made it very simple to understand. This is but another example!

The phrase, *"No more can you, except you abide in Me,"* proclaims the requirement for fruit bearing.

Fruit is the evidence of vital union with Christ. It glorified the Father and manifested true Discipleship.

The life of the Believer as a Vine Branch is one of dependence and obedience, as Verses 4 and 7 proclaim.

As should be obvious, Christ, as the Life Source, provides everything the Believer needs. This means that properly abiding in Him fulfills every single need, want, and desire. Actually, as one reads these words, one is reading the cause, just to name one thing, of most of the divorces.

Husbands and wives demand more of their mates than they are able to provide. In other words, they are demanding that which only Christ can give. As such, the marriage finally comes apart. Actually, this applies to every facet and walk of life.

(5) "I AM THE VINE, YOU ARE THE BRANCHES: HE WHO ABIDES IN ME, AND I IN HIM, THE SAME BRINGS FORTH MUCH FRUIT: FOR WITHOUT ME YOU CAN DO NOTHING."

The form is:

1. As it regards his daily living, the Believer is to understand that every Blessing comes from the Lord and is made possible by the Cross.

2. Nothing must be added to that, and nothing must be removed from that. If we try to go beyond the Cross, we lose our way.

3. If one goes beyond the Cross, where does he go?

THE VINE AND THE BRANCHES

The phrase, *"I am the Vine, you are the branches,"* proclaims in simple terms the true order. The Holy Spirit does this for a purpose.

There is no other life-producing vine but Jesus, which excludes the fake luminaries of false religions and the philosophies of man. Jesus Alone stands as the Life Source, and anyone, especially one who calls himself a Believer, who would look at other directions has passed foolishness and gone into stupidity.

As well, we are *"branches,"* and as such, have no life or fruit without union with the Vine, i.e., Jesus.

Hundreds of millions have attempted to replace Jesus with the church or the Virgin Mary, and even though they may speak of Jesus very favorably, it becomes quickly obvious as to their priority. Consequently, they bear no fruit!

MUCH FRUIT

The phrase, *"He who abides in Me, and I in him, the same brings forth much fruit,"* speaks of that which the purging has accomplished.

First He speaks of *"Fruit"* (Vs. 2), and then, *"More Fruit"* (Vs. 2), and now, *"Much Fruit."*

The phrase, *"For without Me you can do nothing,"* proclaims that without the branch being securely in the Vine, no fruit will be developed because the branch has, within itself, no independent fruitfulness or stability. It is a shame that many religious leaders do not recognize this!

All the powers of the branch are derived from this Supernatural Source and, consequently, depend on Christ's Faithfulness to His Own Nature and Functions. To be sure, He abides faithful.

As should be obvious, these words are not addressed to unconverted men but to Disciples who have to learn their constant need of spiritual contact with their Invisible Lord. Let a Believer and an Apostle sever himself from Christ and live on his own past reputation, his supposed strength, on the clearness of his intellect, the vigor of his body, or the eminence of his position, but Jesus plainly and even abruptly says, *"He can and will do nothing!"*

WITHOUT ME YOU CAN DO NOTHING

It would seem to me that these very Words of Jesus are a slap in the face to those who call themselves Believers, but yet, have forsaken the Bible for the drivel of humanistic psychology.

NOTES

In effect, He is saying that irrespective as to how intelligent, brilliant, educated, or learned a person may be, and irrespective of the claims he may make concerning the behavior of man, in reality, these people have no answers, for without Jesus, they can do nothing.

As well, it is impossible to attempt to meld the two by attempting to draw sustenance from the beggarly elements of this world, which, in reality, have no sustenance, and Jesus at the same time. So, the practitioners of that called, *"Behavioral Science,"* which is no science at all, insult Christ by trying to mesh a lie with His Truth.

THE LIE OF PSYCHOLOGY

Psychology is a lie, and the problem with that lie is all the other lies used to buttress its false claims. Lies breed more lies!

It does not take much genius to figure out the ever-changing philosophy of psychology. The practitioners of this shamanism have no miracle or wonder medicines to prescribe for that which is referred to as *"psychological ills."* All they can do is sit and talk to someone and have someone talk to them. That is the beginning and the end of their prescription.

Common sense should tell a person, especially a Believer, that if behavioral problems could, in fact, be talked away, Jesus came all the way from Heaven and suffered the horrors of Calvary unnecessarily (Gal. 2:20-21).

The truth is, it is impossible to talk these problems out of a person. Only the Power of God can do such! As well, the sin problem, which is the cause of the behavioral problem, is not a mere mendacity or slight maladjustment, but rather a deep-seated power of such evil that even God, Who is Almighty, could not speak it out of man. That is quite a statement, especially when one realizes that God spoke the Restoration of the world into existence (Gen., Chpt. 1). However, having its roots in all that is wicked and destructive, this horrible problem of sin was and is so powerful and strong that God had to become Man and die on a horrible Cross in order that this terrible grip on the human family be broken. Thank God, it was broken at Calvary 2,000 years ago!

Of course, God could have accomplished all of this without the Cross but to do so would have gone against His Nature and Character, and that He will not do. So, the only legitimate step was the Cross.

Considering that, surely an intelligent response must understand that modern-day humanistic psychology (and it is totally humanistic) is but another effort of man to solve his behavioral problems, which has always failed in the past and continues to fail at the present. Jesus is the Solution, and Jesus Alone!

CODEPENDENCY FOR ALL

Around this lie of psychology has sprung up other philosophies which are equally debilitating. *"Codependency"* is but one of the recent.

Codependency probably sprang from alcoholics who were dependent on someone, such as a husband, wife, etc., in order that they may survive. In turn, the one who is helping the alcoholic actually becomes dependent on the one he or she is helping. This is so much so, in fact, that his or her entire life revolves around the dependent one; consequently, they become codependent.

Thousands of people are flocking to bookstores to read about *"codependency."* Most of them are women. They read books that describe the symptoms, join self-help groups, and seek therapy to find out if they are *"codependent."*

They enter an endless cycle in hopes of curing their newly-discovered *"disease,"* and they find they are not alone. In fact, there seems to be an epidemic of self-diagnosed, group-diagnosed, and therapist-diagnosed codependents. The list of symptoms is so long and the possibilities so wide that everyone in any kind of unsatisfactory relationship may conceivably be labeled, at least in psychological jargon, *"codependent."*

THE ADDICTION TREATMENT INDUSTRY

The Codependency/recovery movement is one of the newest and largest offshoots of the addiction treatment industry and the 12-Step program of Alcoholics Anonymous. Approximately 500,000 self-help meetings are held in this country every week. The fastest growing of these *"free confessional meetings"* is Codependents Anonymous. There are over 1,800 Codependents Anonymous groups in this country, as well as other self-help groups, such as Adult Children of Alcoholics (ACoA) and Al-Anon. There are also numerous workshops, conferences, treatment centers, and therapists. It must be admitted that the professionals are glad to have the business. One writer, who contends that *"the vicious cycle of codependency can only be stopped through intervention and professional care,"* declared in 1984: *"Happily, our profession is on the cutting edge of making codependency a national issue, both on the social level and on the health level."*

Indeed, the awareness level has reached new heights of popularity and expanded revenues — in other words, money! As the world goes, sadly and regrettably, so goes the church in this newest rage of psycho-heresy. Not to be outdone, many psychologists, psychiatrists, and treatment centers offer the same theories and therapies under the guise of being Biblical. Churches are joining ranks with 12-step addiction and codependency/recovery programs.

CODEPENDENCY: A PLAGUE UPON THE LAND

The estimated numbers of supposedly afflicted codependents range from tens of thousands to 40 million to 100 million and upwards to ninety six percent of the population. That last estimate is a bit high when one considers that most of the people who are labeled codependent are women. However, such numerical inconsistencies do not seem to bother the *"experts"* in the field.

John Bradshaw, a leading recovery guru, claims that *"codependency is a plague upon the land."* He dramatically adds, *"The Black Plague does not even compare to the ravages of our compulsions caused by codependency."*

Considering how many people are attempting to cope with unsatisfactory relationships and difficult situations, the potential market for self-help books and codependency/recovery treatment is astronomical. The list of books on codependency/recovery swells along with those dealing with addictions. They are popular bestsellers in Christian bookstores as well as in general bookstores. Evidently, something is there! Something is wrong! People are looking for answers. Suggested remedies and supposed cures lie hidden in the books. However, are these remedies the kind that Jesus offers? Are these so-called cures consistent with the Word of God?

SERIOUS PROBLEMS WITH PROBLEM SOLUTIONS

These many books show that people are attempting to address these problems. Some are suffering in relationships that have little or no resemblance to the kind of love demonstrated and taught in the Bible. Numerous others are entangled in their own destructive simple habits and in the life-dominating sins of those around them. Relationships that are supposed to reflect the love relationship of Christ and His Church may indeed more resemble a macabre dance of death.

Yes, there are serious problems! However, we question the diagnosis, answers, formulas, and systems that are being offered in the name of help, in the name of love, and even in the Name of Christ. Beneath many programs that purport to be Christian lurk ideas, philosophies, psychologies, and religious notions that are antithetical to Biblical Christianity.

Codependents/recovery books, groups, programs, and therapists attempt to rescue people from what they believe to be unhealthy relationships. They give so-called codependent strategies to empower self, build self-esteem, emotionally separate from others, and focus on one's own feelings, ideas, and desires.

THE WISDOM OF MAN AND THE WORSHIP OF FALSE GODS

Most systems of codependency and addiction recovery are based upon various psychological counseling theories and therapies and upon the religious and philosophical teachings of Alcoholics Anonymous (AA).

NOTES

In short, such programs are based upon the wisdom of man and the wisdom of false gods. There is actually no other way in which it can be said.

While the Bible may be used at times, it is not used in its fullness or proclaimed as solely sufficient for all matters of life and conduct (II Pet. 1:2-4). Instead, the Bible is placed in a subservient role to support popular psychological theories, therapies, and techniques, that is, if it is given any place at all. In other words, if any Scripture is used, it is made to seem that it supports the theory in question. Of course, anyone who has even the slightest knowledge of the proper manner of studying the Word of God knows that this is a blatant error. We must make our doctrines conform to the Word instead of attempting to force the Word into supporting our doctrines. In this world of so-called Christian psychology, God is repeatedly redefined according to the limited understanding of human beings.

Besides serious theological problems inherent in the codependents and addiction recovery movement, there are many questions about the effectiveness of such programs and about the high rate of recidivism.

Looking at the situation as it should be observed, there is no scientific reason to add the philosophies and psychologies of the recovery movement to the Principles and Promises in the Bible. In fact, there are strong theological reasons not to.

MINIMIZING THE PROBLEMS?

In voicing our concerns, we are not minimizing the problems being addressed. Instead, we believe the problems are even more serious than any of the propagators of popular programs and systems of so-called help realize. While such programs aim at helping a person solve certain problems and unsatisfactory patterns of living, we must remember that there are eternal consequences.

While the problem of *"codependency"* is real, some questions certainly should be asked respecting the programs devised to alleviate the situations, especially considering that the programs are changing constantly. This, within itself, says that they are not working.

Then, of course, the all-important test which these programs and self-help theories must pass is the Bible. If it does not pass muster in this category, plain and simple, it is of no benefit to anyone, anywhere, or anytime.

I believe the Bible holds all the answers relative to life and godliness. At least, that is what the Holy Spirit said through Simon Peter. He said, and I quote all the Text and notes from THE EXPOSITOR'S STUDY BIBLE:

"**Grace and Peace be multiplied unto you through the knowledge of God, and of Jesus our Lord** *(this is both Sanctifying Grace and Sanctifying Peace, all made available by the Cross)*,

"**According as His Divine Power has given unto us all things** *(the Lord with large-handed generosity has given us all things)* **that** *pertain* **unto life and godliness** *(pertains to the fact that the Lord Jesus has given us everything we need regarding life and living)*, **through the knowledge of Him Who has called us to Glory and Virtue** *(the 'knowledge' addressed here speaks of what Christ did at the Cross, which alone can provide 'Glory and Virtue')*:

THE DIVINE NATURE

"**Whereby are given unto us exceeding great and Precious Promises** *(pertains to the Word of God, which alone holds the answer to every life problem)*: **that by these** *(Promises)* **you might be partakers of the Divine Nature** *(the Divine Nature implanted in the inner being of the believing sinner becomes the source of our new life and actions; it comes to everyone at the moment of being 'Born-Again')*, **having escaped the corruption that is in the world through lust.** *(This presents the Salvation experience of the sinner, and the Sanctification experience of the Saint)*" **(II Pet. 1:2-4).**

So, we have a choice! We can believe the Bible, or we can believe the theories of men, which change almost daily. We cannot have it both ways.

THE MAIN CONCERN

The problem is that most Believers do not know the Bible well enough to know whether something is Scriptural or not. That is tragic when one considers that our eternal destiny rides on the pages of the Word of God. We are speaking of eternity here, and eternity is a long, long time.

If there is ignorance of the Word of God or rank unbelief, then the opinions of men will take precedence over the Word of God in explaining why people are the way they are and how they can change.

Authors of books on codependency/recovery base their ideas on unproven psychological theories and subjective observations, which are based on neither the rigors of scientific investigation nor the rigors of proper Bible study. The field of addiction and codependency treatment is filled with human opinions on the nature of man, how he is to live, and how he changes. Christian treatment centers (so-called), recovery programs, and books on addiction and codependency are also based on the same flimsy foundation of psychological opinion rather than on true science or the Bible.

Jesus came to give life and liberty to all who are in bondage. He said:

"The Spirit of the Lord is upon Me, because He has anointed Me to preach the Gospel to the poor; He has sent Me to heal the brokenhearted, to preach Deliverance to the captives, and recovering of sight to the blind, to set at liberty them who are bruised, to preach the acceptable Year of the Lord" (Lk. 4:18-19).

THE CROSS OF CHRIST ALONE IS THE ANSWER

Jesus preached the Gospel to those who were poor in spirit, who were cast down, who were discouraged, who had exhausted their means of coping with life, and who realized they were destitute.

He came *"to heal the brokenhearted,"* those whose dreams have turned to despair and whose love has been fused with pain and disappointment. He came to preach Deliverance to those in bondage to sin, to themselves, to other people, and to life-crippling habits. He came to give sight to those blinded by the wisdom of men and the enemy of their souls. Jesus came to set at liberty those who have been bruised by the world, the flesh, and the Devil.

Who is not included among those who are in desperate need of the Saviour? Indeed, all who find themselves caught in the wreckage of their lives and who are now turning to addiction and codependency/recovery programs need our Lord more than anything or anyone else.

Therefore, the question must be asked: *"If Jesus is truly the Answer to life's problems and, indeed, the very Source of Life, why are both non-Christians and Christians looking for answers elsewhere?"*

THE POWER OF THE CROSS

It is understandable as to why the unredeemed look to humanistic psychology. Not looking to the Lord, they have nowhere else to turn. However, the shame presents itself in the form of those who refer to themselves as Believers, preachers included, who, as well, turn to the foolishness of men as it relates to the problems of life. There are two basic reasons for this. They are:

1. *"Ignorance"*: most Christians have at least a modicum of knowledge as it regards the initial Salvation experience provided by the Cross of Christ. However, the only knowledge that most Christians have, and I am referring to virtually all, is the Cross of Christ as it pertains to Salvation. The words *"Jesus died for me"* are, without a doubt, the greatest statement ever made; however, that is where the knowledge of the Cross with most Believers begins and ends. Most have absolutely no idea whatsoever as to the part the Cross of Christ plays in our everyday life and living. They do not realize that their everyday joy, strength, overcoming power, and victory over the world, the flesh, and the Devil, in fact, anything of which one could think, all and without fail finds its answer in the Cross of Christ.

When Jesus died on the Cross, He atoned for all sin, past, present, and future, at least for all who will believe (Jn. 3:16). However, He also did something else. He broke the bondage of sin, which means He throttled its power. He broke the grip of sin on all who will believe, but it all comes through the Cross. This means that the Cross of Christ, and we are speaking of what Jesus there did, must always be the Object of our Faith. In fact, the entirety of the Story of the Bible is *"Jesus Christ and Him Crucified."*

THE OLD TESTAMENT

Of all the millions upon millions of sacrifices offered from the time of Adam and Eve to the time of Christ, a time frame of approximately 4,000 years, every one of these sacrifices represented the Lord Jesus Christ and what He would do at the Cross in order to redeem the fallen sons of Adam's lost race. That's why Paul said:

"Christ sent me not to baptize, but to preach the Gospel: not with wisdom of words, lest the Cross of Christ should be made of none effect" (I Cor. 1:17).

He then said, *"For the preaching of the Cross is to them who perish foolishness; but to we who are Saved it is the Power of God"* (I Cor. 1:18).

Actually, the word translated *"preaching"* in the Greek is *"Logos"* and should have been translated *"Word"* or *"Message,"* making it read, *"For the Word of the Cross is to them who perish foolishness, but to we who are Saved it is the Power of God."* That is what we are here attempting to give you, the Word of the Cross.

WHAT IS THE WORD OF THE CROSS?

In short, it is Salvation for every sinner who desires to be Saved and victory for every Child of God over the world, the flesh, and the Devil (Rom. 6:1-14; 8:1-11; I Cor. 1:17, 18, 23; 2:2; Gal. 6:14; Col. 2:10-15). The Child of God must understand this and must believe this, meaning that every single thing we need is found in the Cross of Christ.

UNBELIEF

2. *"Unbelief"*: whereas ignorance is a tremendous problem, the greatest problem of all, however, is *"unbelief."* In other words, most of Christendom simply doesn't believe that what Jesus did at the Cross answers not only the Salvation need but, also, the everyday need of life and living. Whatever they say, they just simply don't believe it. How do I know that?

I know it simply because they continue to turn to the rudiments of this world, which hold no answer whatsoever.

I think possibly that God hates unbelief more than anything else. Listen to what the Scripture says, and once again, I quote from THE EXPOSITOR'S STUDY BIBLE:

"Let us *(modern Believers)* therefore fear *(refers to the fact that Salvation can be lost if the Believer ceases to believe)*, lest, a Promise being left *us* of entering into His rest *(the Promise of Salvation)*, any of you should seem to come short of it. *(This proves it is possible for such to be done, which means the loss of the soul.)*

"For unto us was the Gospel Preached, as well as unto them *(there is only one Gospel, and that is 'Jesus Christ and Him Crucified')*: but the Word preached did not profit them *(if the Cross is abandoned as the Object of our Faith, Christ will profit no one anything [Gal. 5:2])*, not being mixed with Faith in them who heard it. *(The Israelites had Faith, but not in the right object. It must be Faith in Christ and the Cross, or it's not valid Faith)*" **(Heb. 4:1-2).**

The great Apostle then said, "Seeing therefore it remains that some must enter therein *(speaks of the New Covenant and the Church)*, and they to whom it was first preached entered not in because of unbelief *(proclaims from Verse 2 that the Israelites of Old had the same Gospel preached unto them as we do, but to no avail)*" **(Heb. 4:6).**

WHAT THE CHILD OF GOD IS FACING

One of the problems with Believers is that they do not understand what they are facing in the spirit world, which is so much stronger than we are, at least within ourselves. That's the reason that humanistic psychology is such a crock. There is nothing that man has that can overcome these powers of darkness which confront Believers everyday of our lives. Listen again to Paul:

He said: "For we wrestle not against flesh and blood *(our foes are not human; however, Satan constantly uses human beings to carry out his dirty work)*, but against principalities *(fallen Angels of the highest rank and order in Satan's kingdom)*, against powers *(more fallen Angels but who rank immediately below the 'Principalities')*, against the rulers of the darkness of this world *(again, fallen Angels who carry out the instructions of the 'Powers')*, against spiritual wickedness in high places. *(This refers to demon spirits)*" **(Eph. 6:12).**

Then Paul said:

"For though we walk in the flesh *(refers to the fact that we do not yet have Glorified Bodies)*, we do not war after the flesh *(after our own ability, but rather by the Power of the Spirit)*:

"(For the weapons of our warfare *are* not carnal *(carnal weapons consist of those which are man-devised)*, but mighty through God *(the Cross of Christ [I Cor. 1:18])* to the pulling down of strongholds;)

"Casting down imaginations *(philosophic strongholds; every effort man makes outside of the Cross of Christ)*, and every high thing that exalteth itself against the Knowledge of God *(all the pride of the human heart)*, and bringing into captivity every thought to the obedience of Christ *(can be done only by the Believer looking exclusively to the Cross, where all Victory is found; the Holy Spirit will then perform the task)*" **(II Cor. 10:3-5).**

Understanding what we are facing in the spirit world on a daily basis, we surely should realize that within ourselves, we cannot overcome these powers, and, at the same time, the smartest men in the world fall into the same category. In other words, the world holds no answers whatsoever to these things that we are addressing. However, there is an answer. That answer is the Cross of Christ through which the Holy Spirit works. Now, let's look at the Holy Spirit.

THE POWER OF THE HOLY SPIRIT

The Holy Spirit is God! That means that He is Almighty, All-knowing, and, in fact, is everywhere. He is, we might say, the Third Person of the Triune Godhead. Whereas we are no match for Satan and his cohorts of darkness, these cohorts of darkness are no match for the Holy Spirit.

However, most Believers simply do not know how the Holy Spirit works. If they think of Him at all, they sort of take Him for granted. While it is definitely true that the Holy Spirit is in the heart and life of every person who is truly Born-Again, that doesn't mean that He automatically does all the things that need to be done.

Then, there are millions who have been baptized with the Holy Spirit with the evidence of speaking with other Tongues, which should be the case with all Believers, and they somehow think that speaking with other Tongues will give them power over the powers of darkness. While speaking with Tongues is greatly beneficial to the Believer and should be engaged constantly, still, that is not the answer for the sin problem, and it is sin to which we address ourselves.

So, how do I get the Holy Spirit to work mightily within my heart and within my life, doing what only He can do?

We are to simply place our Faith exclusively in Christ and what He has done for us at the Cross (Rom. 8:1-11). In other words, the Holy Spirit works exclusively within the parameters, so to speak, of the Finished Work of Christ. What Jesus did at the Cross is what gives the Holy Spirit the legal means to do all that He does with us and for us. So, understanding that, our Faith must ever rest in Christ and the Cross. The Holy Spirit doesn't demand much of us, but He does demand one thing and on that He will not bend. He demands that our Faith be exclusively in Christ and what Christ has done for us at the Cross, and then He will work mightily on our behalf. Listen again to Paul:

"**For the Law** *(that which we are about to give is a Law of God, devised by the Godhead in eternity past [I Pet. 1:18-20]; this Law, in fact, is 'God's Prescribed Order of Victory')* **of the Spirit** *(Holy Spirit, i.e., 'the way the Spirit works')* **of Life** *(all life comes from Christ, but through the Holy Spirit [Jn. 16:13-14])* **in Christ Jesus** *(any time Paul uses this term or one of its derivatives, he is, without fail, referring to what Christ did at the Cross, which makes this 'life' possible)* **has made me free** *(given me total Victory)* **from the Law of Sin and Death** *(these are the two most powerful Laws in the Universe; the 'Law of the Spirit of Life in Christ Jesus' alone is stronger than the 'Law of Sin and Death'; this means that if the Believer attempts to live for God by any manner other than Faith in Christ and the Cross, he is doomed to failure)*" **(Rom. 8:2).**

NOTES

Once the Believer learns how the Holy Spirit works, then the Believer is on the road to victory.

This is the answer to life and living, and the only answer to life and living, simply because no other answer is needed. What Jesus did at the Cross answers every question, solves every problem, and meets every need because what He there did defeated every power of darkness in totality. Once again, read carefully the words of Paul:

PRINCIPALITIES AND POWERS

"**And you are complete in Him** *(the satisfaction of every spiritual want is found in Christ, made possible by the Cross)*, **which is the Head of all principality and power** *(His Headship extends not only over the Church, which voluntarily serves Him, but over all forces that are opposed to Him as well [Phil. 2:10-11])*:

"**In Whom also you are circumcised with the Circumcision made without hands** *(that which is brought about by the Cross [Rom. 6:3-5])*, **in putting off the body of the sins of the flesh by the Circumcision of Christ** *(refers to the old carnal nature that is defeated by the Believer placing his Faith totally in the Cross, which gives the Holy Spirit latitude to work)*:

"**Buried with Him in Baptism** *(does not refer to Water Baptism, but rather to the Believer Baptized into the death of Christ, which refers to the Crucifixion and Christ as our substitute [Rom. 6:3-4])*, **wherein also you are risen with *Him* through the Faith of the operation of God, Who has raised Him from the dead.** *(This does not refer to our future physical Resurrection, but to that spiritual Resurrection from a sinful state into Divine Life. We died with Him, we are buried with Him, and we rose with Him [Rom. 6:3-5], and herein lies the secret to all Spiritual Victory.)*

NAILING IT TO HIS CROSS

"**And you, being dead in your sins and the uncircumcision of your flesh** *(speaks of spiritual death [i.e., 'separation from God'], which sin does!)*, **has He quickened together with Him** *(refers to being made spiritually alive, which is done through* being 'Born-Again'), **having forgiven you all trespasses** *(the Cross made it possible for all manner of sins to be forgiven and taken away)*;

"**Blotting out the handwriting of Ordinances that was against us** *(pertains to the Law of Moses, which was God's Standard of Righteousness that man could not reach)*, **which was contrary to us** *(Law is against us, simply because we are unable to keep its precepts, no matter how hard we try)*, **and took it out of the way** *(refers to the penalty of the Law being removed)*, **nailing it to His Cross** *(the Law with its decrees was abolished in Christ's Death, as if Crucified with Him)*;

"***And*** **having spoiled principalities and powers** *(Satan and all of his henchmen were defeated at the Cross by Christ Atoning for all sin; sin was the legal right Satan had to hold man in captivity; with all sin atoned, he has no more legal right to hold anyone in bondage)*, **He** *(Christ)* **made a show of them openly** *(what Jesus did at the Cross was in the face of the whole universe)*, **triumphing over them in it.** *(The triumph is complete and it was all done for us, meaning we can walk in power and perpetual Victory due to the Cross)*" **(Col. 2:10-15).**

REASONS CHRISTIANS LOOK ELSEWHERE

Due to very little Gospel truly being preached from behind modern pulpits, and we speak of the Message of the Cross, many Christians have little understanding of what the Gospel of Jesus Christ actually is and what it entails. Rather than recognizing their need for a Saviour to save them from their own sins, they may have been looking for a Saviour Who would save them from their circumstances and/or Who would make life easy and pleasant. They may have misunderstood the need to die to self and thought that Jesus was there to make them feel better about themselves, build their self-esteem, and cater to their desires.

While Jesus most definitely meets every true need of the Believer, and while life in Him holds a marvelous new dimension of peace with God and the Hope of Eternal Life, all problems do not simply vanish. Jesus and what He did at the Cross being the answer to problems of living does not mean that He necessarily takes all the problems away instantly. He gives strength and purpose, and at times, He even uses problems to make a Believer more like Himself.

THOUGHTS OF GOD

There are Christians who expect God to be little more than a glorified bell-hop Who solves all problems and changes circumstances. When these things do not come to pass, they may think poorly of God and even begin to blame Him for allowing bad things to happen, etc.

They may resent God for letting them down. Those feelings come from a misunderstanding of the Character of God, the sinful condition of man, and the influence of *"the Prince of the power of the air"* on the circumstances of this world.

Rather than getting angry with God or doing what psychology says in *"forgiving Him,"* which some wrongfully teach, Christians who have an erroneous view of God need to have their vision restored by the Word of God and the Work of the Holy Spirit.

God is Holy, Pure, Righteous, and Full of Compassion and Mercy. He is Perfect in every respect. He has provided Salvation for the lost through the Death of His Only Begotten Son, and He fulfills all His Promises.

However, having said that, the real reason that most Christians turn to the psychological way instead of the Word of God is simply because they are encouraged to do so by their pastors, so-called religious leaders of their denomination, etc.

THE PSYCHOLOGICAL WAY OR THE SPIRITUAL WAY

Due to what is being preached behind many pulpits presently, which, I might quickly add, is the opposite of the Word of God, many Christians are turning to particular recovery programs because they have been fed the lie of psychological theories about the nature of man, and they believe them. To be sure, the encroachment of the psychological way into Christianity has been a subtle, gradual movement, which began in the world and moved into seminaries and pastoral counseling classes.

Catholics embraced it first of all simply because, as a matter of Biblical understanding, the Bible has little place in Catholic dogma and doctrine.

As an aside, I heard some news commentators over television the other day discussing the terrible problems in the Catholic priesthood as it regards child molestation. They talked about how many tens of billions of dollars this had cost the Catholic church, etc.

Then, one of the men stated, *"I don't understand."* he said, *"The Catholics have the best psychologists in the world. Why is it that they are not getting help from that source?"*

The truth is, most every one of these priests who fall into this terrible perversion of child molestation have, in fact, spent untold hours with Catholic psychologists, all to no avail. In other words, it simply doesn't work.

Regrettably, the liberal denominations, such as the Lutherans, Episcopalians, Methodists, etc., quickly followed. Then, the fundamentalists, such as the Baptists and the Holiness, jumped on board, etc. Now, the Pentecostal denominations, along with most of the Charismatics, have swallowed this bait hook, line, and sinker, as it is offered up by Satan.

UNBELIEF

The psychological way has its roots totally and completely in the wisdom of men and is, therefore, satanic. Due to so-called pastors and religious leaders either not believing the Bible or not properly understanding the Bible and falling for it, Christians have turned almost exclusively to this worldly way, which really offers no true help at all.

Because the entirety of the industrial world is, for the most part, totally psychologized, Christians have been led to believe that the psychological way is a true science (which it is not). Therefore, they believe it to be a legitimate tool which can be used to help people with emotional and behavioral problems.

NOTES

In this psychological way is the idea that Preachers of the Gospel are not adequate to address these needs, and, therefore, the petitioners must turn to *"professional help."*

As well, some who call themselves evangelical Christians have become psychologists, and they have worked hard to convince church leaders that psychological theories and therapists are necessary for helping Christians.

To be sure, it is disheartening to see conservative churches, denominations, and fellowships running after psychological theories and therapies and acting as if Jesus Christ is not enough, as if the Holy Spirit indwelling a Believer is impotent, or nearly so, and treating the Word of God as only useful for minor problems or theological questions, if any use at all.

TWO LIES

Instead of searching the Scriptures and warning their sheep, too many pastors believe two lies:

1. They (the preachers) can only deal with spiritual matters, which, in the overall aspect, has a very limited definition.

2. Only those who are professionally trained are equipped to deal with psychological matters (which virtually includes everything about understanding the nature of man and how to help him change, which is impossible).

As a result, the church is increasingly reflecting a society which is saturated with the kind of psychology that seeks to understand why people are the way they are and how they change. Consequently, psychological language has become a part of everyday language, and psychological solutions are accepted as life's solutions.

Concerning the co-dependency/recovery movement, Dr. Robert Coles says, *"You don't know whether to laugh or cry over some of this stuff."* He says this movement is a *"typical example of how anything packaged as psychology in this culture seems to have an all too gullible audience."*

The Assemblies of God is another case in point. Under their denominational policy, any preacher who has any type of problem must submit to psychological counseling and cannot be readmitted until signed off by a psychologist. In other words, they have completely abandoned the Bible Way in favor of the psychological way. Regrettably, many Believers, little knowing the Bible and, as well, knowing little of the psychological way, think that because such is advocated by the leaders of their denomination, it must be Scripturally valid. Sadly, the Church of God, the second largest Pentecostal group in the world, falls into the same category.

CONTRADICITONS AND DECEPTIONS

Many Christians do not realize that the psychological theories, therapies, and techniques used by these so-called Christian psychologists were created by non-Christians, many of whom have repudiated and opposed the Word of God and Christianity in general.

One Pastor said that even though the word *"psychology"* means in its purest form *"the study of the soul,"* psychology, in truth, *"cannot really study the soul."* He says:

"Outside the Word and the Spirit, there are no solutions to any of the problems of the human soul. Only God knows the soul, and only God can change it. Yet, the widely accepted ideas of modern psychology are theories originally developed mostly by atheists on the assumption that there is no God, and the individual alone has the power to change himself into a better person through certain techniques."

As a result, so-called Christian psychologists use the same theories, therapies, and techniques as secular psychological counselors and psychotherapists simply because there are no others. Many Christians mistakenly believe that such theories are scientific when, in fact, they are simply unproven, unscientific notions of men.

The part of psychology which deals with the nature of man, how he should live, and how he should change is filled with contradictions and deceptions simply because it ignores the Bible, which Alone holds these answers. Moreover, because those theories deal with the nonphysical aspects of the person, they intrude upon the very essence of Biblical Doctrines of man, including his fallen condition, Salvation, Sanctification, and relationship of love and obedience to God.

Christians who embrace the psychological opinions of the world have moved from absolute confidence in the Word of God for all matters of life and conduct to an expression of faith in the unproven, unscientific, psychological opinions of men.

THE GOSPEL OR TWELVE-STEPS?

What is the answer to the vast problems that are being addressed by the addiction and codependency/recovery movement? Is it the Good News of Jesus Christ, or is it some version of twelve-step recovery and/or psychological treatment programs? Well, of course, the answer is obvious. Even though some Christian psychologists attempt to make the Bible fit in some loose way with psychological theories, the truth is that Jesus Christ and His Way have been totally abandoned. It is impossible to have both! Either one cancels out the other. Furthermore, many who go under the guise of Christian do not even attempt anymore to wed the Bible with these theories. While they still claim it to be Biblical, they know in their hearts that the two are absolutely opposed to each other. Therefore, they have dropped all pretense, using only psychological methods, which they have been actually doing all along anyway. It is the case of a little leaven ultimately corrupting the whole, and that's exactly what has happened in the church.

The Biblical Answer, Jesus Christ and Him Crucified, is the only Answer that will suffice:

Paul said: *"For I am not ashamed of the Gospel of Christ: for it is the Power of God unto Salvation to everyone who believes; to the Jew first, and also to the Greek.*

"For therein is the Righteousness of God revealed from Faith to Faith: as it is written, The Just shall live by Faith" (Rom. 1:16-17).

Now, either the Gospel of Christ and the Power of God is the Answer, or else, it is not! I know it is the Answer because hundreds of millions have been gloriously and wondrously set free by Christ and what He did at Calvary, with not one single person to which anyone can truthfully point ever having been helped by the psychological way.

THE BIBLE WAY IN BRIEF

Even though we have already given the following in this Volume, and possibly will give it again, we do so because it's very important. The following is the Way the Holy Spirit works in solving behavioral problems, etc. Please read it carefully:

• Jesus Christ is the Source of all things we receive from God (Jn. 1:1-3, 14, 29; Col. 2:10-15).

• While Jesus Christ is the Source, the Cross of Christ is the Means, and the only Means, by which all of these good things are given to us (Rom. 6:1-14; I Cor. 1:17, 18, 23).

• While Jesus is the Source, and the Cross is the Means, the Object of our Faith must ever be Christ and the Cross (I Cor. 2:2; Col. 2:14-15; Gal., Chpt. 5).

• While our Lord is the Source, and the Cross is the Means, and the Cross must ever be the Object of our Faith, the Holy Spirit will then work mightily on our behalf. He Alone can do whatever it is that is needed (Rom. 8:1-11; Eph. 2:13-18).

It takes Power to solve the problems of man, and the Holy Spirit has that Power. However, the problem is most Christians do not know how the Holy Spirit works. We must ever understand that He works exclusively, and I mean exclusively, within the parameters, so to speak, of the Finished Work of Christ. It is the Cross which has given and does give the Holy Spirit the latitude to do all that He does within our hearts and lives. Paul said in conjunction with that:

"The Law of the Spirit of Life in Christ Jesus has made me free from the Law of Sin and Death" (Rom. 8:2).

JESUS CHRIST SETS PEOPLE FREE

He said: *"I am the Way, the Truth, and the Life: no man comes unto the Father, but by Me"* (Jn. 14:6). Twelve-step recovery programs and psychological treatment programs are based upon the wisdom of men. Most promise the ability to please and serve self and others, but they cannot please God because they are not of God (Rom. 8:8). The end result of psychological therapies does not lead a person to Christ, but rather bondage to self and even bondage to the *"Prince of this world."*

Satan is very subtle in this way as he leads men down the primrose path. For instance, some few people may truly be healed at some of the Catholic shrines such as Lourdes; however, their healing does not come from the Lord. It actually comes from Satan, who can easily remove something from a person, which he originally instigated in the first place. Millions being greatly deceived then think the whole thing is of God when, in reality, none of it is from the Lord.

The Believer must understand that if it is not Biblical, it is not and, in fact, cannot be Truth even though it may be true. Actually, many things are true, but they are not necessarily *"Truth."*

So, the few people who claim to be helped by the psychological recovery programs are, in reality, only led from one bondage to another and, as a result, are not truly helped at all, but rather hurt.

A NEW RELIGION?

Through the language of so-called addiction and recovery, Christians are being enticed into a totally different belief system based on psychological foundations.

One Preacher said, and rightly so, *"There may be no more serious threat to the life of the church today than the stampede to embrace the doctrines of secular psychology. They are a mass of human ideas that Satan has placed in the church as if they were powerful, life-changing Truths from God."*

The truth is, the attempt to wed the Bible with psychology is impossible. One cannot mix Truth with a lie or the real with the false. One concludes only with heresy, which today plagues the greater majority of the church.

In truth, if modern psychology can alleviate the problems of man, or even help in doing so, then Jesus wasted His Time coming from Heaven and dying on a cruel Cross. Man's problems are not surface; they are not minor; and they are not slight. Man is not slightly maladjusted; he is rather totally and completely a spiritual wreck. Romans, Chapter 3, tells us this. Man is not slightly off course; he is going completely in the wrong direction because of having believed a lie. Man's heart is evil, wicked, and ungodly. As such, it cannot be changed by external methods such as psychology. It can only be changed by the Power of God as it is in Jesus Christ and what He did at Calvary.

The Way of the Bible and the way of psychology are 180 degrees opposed to each other. As previously stated, either one cancels out the other.

EXTERNAL

Psychology teaches that man's problems are external, such as environment, abuse by others, etc., and that he is a victim. It teaches that man's answer is within himself.

The Bible teaches the very opposite, in that man has no answers within himself, only problems. One might quickly add, his problems are most severe, in fact, so severe that man, within himself, is helpless to change his situation. That problem is sin! It has to do with man's fall, with the whole world placed in the same category of lostness (Rom. 3:9-18).

To that problem, which is so severe that it cannot be changed by man, God sent His Son, the Lord Jesus Christ, Who died on Calvary in order that man may be set free (completely free) from the terrible results of the Fall. In fact, even as we have previously stated, the problem of sin in the heart of man is so bad that, even though God could speak Creation into existence (Gen., Chpt. 1), He could not speak man's Salvation into existence, at least and remain true to His Nature. Jesus had to come to this Earth and pay a terrible price, even the shedding of His Own Blood, in order to liberate man. Thankfully and beautifully, this is done by man's simple Faith and trust in Christ (Jn. 3:16; 14:6).

How it is that men who call themselves Saved and Spirit-filled cannot see this is beyond comprehension! The simple fact is, as we have previously stated, even though purporting to be religious leaders, they either do not know the Bible, or they do not believe the Bible.

Without a doubt, this psychological heresy is one of the signs of the times, that

NOTES

"some shall depart from the Faith, giving heed to seducing spirits, and doctrines of demons" (I Tim. 4:1). This is exactly what psychoheresy is, *"Seducing spirits, and doctrines of demons."*

The answer to man's sin, perversions, aberrations, etc., is the Cross of Christ, and the Cross of Christ alone. Man can believe that, act upon it, and be Saved and delivered, or he can ignore that and go ever deeper into more bondage.

(Most of the material on codependency and psychoheresy was derived from the book written by Martin and Deidre Bobgan, *"Twelve Steps To Destruction."*)

(6) "IF A MAN ABIDE NOT IN ME, HE IS CAST FORTH AS A BRANCH, AND IS WITHERED; AND MEN GATHER THEM, AND CAST THEM INTO THE FIRE, AND THEY ARE BURNED."

The construction is:

1. God accepts nothing from humanity except it comes by the way of the Cross.

2. This means that man can come to God only by the way of the Cross (I Cor. 2:2).

3. This means that if the church is not preaching the Cross, then whatever that particular church is doing is totally unacceptable to God (Phil. 3:17-19).

THE WITHERED BRANCH

The phrase, *"If a man abide not in Me, he is cast forth as a branch, and is withered,"* proclaims that life must be continually drawn from the Master by the Believer. If one looks in any other direction, as millions today are doing, even as we have just spoken concerning psychoheresy, the withering process begins immediately.

However, *"withering,"* by its natural definition, does not happen instantly; it is a gradual wasting away. Such happens to individuals, churches, and entire religious denominations. Through false doctrine, self-will, or unbelief, Believers begin to look elsewhere other than Christ. Unless pulled back by the convicting Power of the Holy Spirit, which He will do, and Repentance engaged, the ultimate end will be spiritual destruction.

The reader must understand that this Statement by Christ of the Believer abiding in Him is strong indeed! This can only be done by the Means of the Cross. We died with Him, were buried with Him, and raised with Him in Newness of Life (Rom. 6:3-5). That is the manner of the *"in Christ"* position. As stated, it can only come by the Means of the Cross — meaning that the Believer must have his Faith placed absolutely in the Cross of Christ, and it must be maintained absolutely in the Cross of Christ.

Abiding in Christ speaks of Christ providing all that is needed for the Believer in every capacity; consequently, one need not look elsewhere. If one does, and such is surely possible or Jesus would not have made this Statement, it is an insult to Christ of the highest order. It is a repudiation of all that He did at Calvary, in effect, saying that it was not enough. It is identical with Israel of old turning from Jehovah and looking toward idols.

TO ULTIMATELY DIE

To *"wither"* is to ultimately die! It is sad, but entire religious denominations, which at one time claimed to be fundamentalists and even Pentecostal, no longer can claim such and, in effect, are dying, if not already dead — dead while they live.

In this state, they may continue to produce great amounts of religious machinery, with the noise and racket fooling many people. However, if they abide not in the Vine, i.e., Jesus, they are producing absolutely nothing that is of God.

BURNED

The phrase, *"And men gather them, and cast them into the fire, and they are burned,"* can proclaim only one thing: that person is eternally lost despite having once been Saved.

Christ cannot abide in a withered branch which produces nothing. As well, the *"withering"* is not caused at all by something improper in the *"Vine"* because it is a Perfect Vine. Everything the branch needs, and much, much more, is in the Vine. So, if the branch withers and dies, it is sorely because of attempting to draw sustenance elsewhere, in fact, sustenance which does not exist.

NOTES

As should be obvious, this completely refutes the unscriptural doctrine of Unconditional Eternal Security.

If one is to notice, there are conditions for remaining in the *"Vine"* and are found in Verses 6, 10, 18 through 20, 22, and 24.

(7) "IF YOU ABIDE IN ME, AND MY WORDS ABIDE IN YOU, YOU SHALL ASK WHAT YOU WILL, AND IT SHALL BE DONE UNTO YOU."

The composition is:

1. The *"intercession"* made by Christ for us, which He does continually, is intercession for sin (Heb. 7:25-27).

2. Without the Intercession of Christ on our behalf on a constant basis, the best of us, whomever they might be, wouldn't last one hour.

3. His *"Intercession"* for us is not something that the Lord does. It's actually something He has already done.

ABIDING IN JESUS

The phrase, *"If you abide in Me, and My Words abide in you,"* proclaims the manner in which abiding in Him is made possible. It is adherence to the Word of God. Over and over, Jesus, as our Example, alludes to the Scripture concerning all He said and did. When the Word of God ceases to be the criterion, abiding in Him is no longer possible.

This is the reason the Believer should study the Word and should make it a lifelong project, setting aside a certain time each day for that purpose and giving it priority. However, many Believers know more about sports than they do the Word of God. They are far more knowledgeable concerning the stock market or particular interests than they are the Word. I wish that group was in the minority; however, I fear the opposite is rather the case!

As well, the Believer cannot really understand the Word as he or she should unless he understands the Cross of Christ. That is the key that unlocks the Word. So, what I'm actually saying is, *"If one doesn't understand the Cross of Christ as it regards our Sanctification, in other words, how we live for God on a daily basis, one will not understand the Word as a whole as one should."* It is absolutely imperative that the Cross of Christ, which is really the heart of the Gospel, be understood.

ASKING AND RECEIVING

The phrase, *"You shall ask what you will, and it shall be done unto you,"* proclaims several things:

• Such a Promise opens up to the Believer any and all possibilities. God answers prayer! Do most Christians believe that?

I would suspect that most all say they do; however, if they really did believe this of which Christ has said, they would pray much more. The truth is, most Christians pray little at all. Such mostly occasions unbelief! However, Satan, as well, fights prayer as nothing else because he knows what it will do.

• Such petitions are to be enjoined only upon the basis of the Word of God. The Word must be the foundation for what we ask. If the Word says that the Lord will heal, and it does say that, then we should ask the Lord for healing, etc.

However, as it regards healing, we must understand that the Lord has not promised in His Word that the physical body, given time, will not grow old and wear out. That's all because of the Fall. Thank God, that will be changed at the First Resurrection, but, in the meantime, we do suffer afflictions due to age. While prayer will alleviate some of that, it will not stop that process.

• The entire structure of the Promise demands that what is asked be in the Will of God. If one is close to the Lord and knows the Word of the Lord, one will not ask for things outside of the Will of God. Let us say it again, *"If one doesn't understand the Cross of Christ relative to our Sanctification, it is likely that one will not know or understand the Will of God either."*

Many Christians, motivated by some particular teaching they have heard, set their sights on things which have little Scriptural validity. For instance, some years ago, I encountered a lady who was spending all her energy and prayer asking the Lord that He would replace a tooth she had lost some years before.

Is the Lord able to do such a thing?

Of course, He is! However, we do not find Him doing very many of these types of things. To be frank, I have never heard of the Lord replacing a tooth, and for all the obvious reasons. As stated, that is about the same as a Believer asking the Lord to stop the aging process. He is able to do that, but there is nowhere in His Word that He has promised such a thing. Actually, it tells us the very opposite.

Paul said, *"For we know that if our earthly house of this tabernacle* (our physical body) *were dissolved"* (II Cor. 5:1), meaning that it is gradually being dissolved, irrespective as to how close to God we are or how much Faith we have. The reason is simple!

WE ARE NOT IN THE KINGDOM AGE YET

When that time comes, we will have experienced the Resurrection and will have a new, Glorified Body. At that time, there will be no more aging, sickness, or dying.

So, for the dear lady to pray for something which is opposed to the natural process is pretty much a waste of time. Some may argue that a baby born to Abraham and Sarah when he was 100 and she was 90 was opposed to the natural process. That is correct; however, the Promise was given to them by God long before the baby was born. As well, God can interrupt His Natural Order anytime He desires, but that does not mean that we can do so on our own.

Anything that is not the Will of God, at the same time, is not the Word of God. It is impossible to have one without the other. So, to take Verse 7, or many others similar, and attempt to believe for foolish things violates the Will of God, which nullifies the Word of God.

(8) "HEREIN IS MY FATHER GLORIFIED, THAT YOU BEAR MUCH FRUIT; SO SHALL YOU BE MY DISCIPLES."

The composition is:

1. Self-examination, according to the measuring rod of the Cross, is here demanded (II Cor. 13:5).

2. The single most important thing in the world is at stake, your eternal soul.

3. Deception is Satan's greatest weapon, and this means that the human race is plagued with deception.

BEARING MUCH FRUIT

The phrase, *"Herein is My Father Glorified, that you bear much fruit,"* presents fruit-bearing, as well, as a condition of answered prayer. This is very important and something that should be studied very carefully.

Fruit is the exhibition in Christian conduct of the Spirit and example of the Lord Jesus Christ so that from the conduct of the Disciple, the world may learn what the Master was like. His Spirit in the Believer produces the Fruit of the Spirit (Gal. 5:22-23).

As well, the open door to prayer, as outlined in Verse 7, is, for the most part, intended to be a petition that we seek, yearn, and ask that we should bear much fruit. This prayer will always be heard, with the Promise that it will be answered, and such will glorify the Father.

THE DISCIPLES OF THE LORD

Reynolds says, *"In the fruitfulness of the Vine is the Glory of the Husbandman."*[7]

The phrase, *"So shall you be My Disciples,"* in effect, says, *"If you are truly My Disciples, you will bear much fruit."*

So, we have before us the simple black and white statement, which should be easily understood by all, that there are only two kinds of Believers:

1. Believers who do not bear fruit ultimately lose their way with Christ, therefore, becoming unbelievers. At some point in time, even after the Holy Spirit has labored incessantly to bring such a person to the desired place but to no avail, that person is cut off. That means he loses his soul!

The idea is, that which got us into Salvation, which is Faith in Christ and what He did for us at the Cross, is what keeps us in Salvation. If such Faith is lost, the individual then becomes an unbeliever.

2. Believers who bring forth fruit are always purged in order that they will bring forth more fruit, and then finally, *"much fruit."* These glorify the Father and are true Disciples.

Reynolds says: *"Discipleship is a very large word, never altogether realized. Just as Faith leads to Faith, and Love to Love, and Light to Light, so does Discipleship to Discipleship."*[8]

A Disciple is a pupil but is also an adherent; hence, he is spoken of as an Imitator of his Teacher, in this case, Christ.

(9) *"AS THE FATHER HAS LOVED ME, SO HAVE I LOVED YOU: CONTINUE YE IN MY LOVE."*

The composition is:

1. God's Greatest Glory is His Creation of man. However, due to the Fall, man has turned after the ways of unrighteousness, thereby, turning the Glory of God into shame.

2. Other than the few hours Adam lived righteously before the Fall, the only True Man Who has ever truly lived is the Lord Jesus Christ.

3. Unredeemed man loves vanity, which stems from pride. This, within itself, is the foundation sin of the human race (Prov. 6:16-17; I Jn. 2:16).

LOVE

The phrase, *"As the Father has loved Me, so have I loved you,"* proclaims the type and kind of love expressed and shown to us by Jesus. Consequently, we are speaking of love that is absolutely beyond the comprehension of mere man.

The phrase, *"You must continue in My Love,"* actually gives us the reason that unproductive branches are broken off and burned. For the Believer to be shown the type of love of which Jesus here speaks, and for that love to be repudiated and, in effect, blasphemed, portrays the magnitude of such rebellion. It is love betrayed!

What does it really mean to continue in His Love?

If one is to notice, He said, *"You must continue in My Love,"* not, *"You must continue to love Me."* The Believer is to continue in the enjoyment of Jesus' Love, which is measured by the Father's Love to Him.

Jesus' Enjoyment of the Father's Love resulted from His Life of Dependence and Obedience as a Man on Earth in the path of service.

If we enjoy that love as we should, we will, even as the next Verse says, *"Keep His Commandments."*

(10) "IF YOU KEEP MY COMMANDMENTS, YOU SHALL ABIDE IN MY LOVE; EVEN AS I HAVE KEPT MY FATHER'S COMMANDMENTS, AND ABIDE IN HIS LOVE."

The pattern is:

1. The first Miracle that Jesus performed in His Earthly Ministry was the changing of water to wine in the little village of Cana of Galilee.

2. Incidentally, this was not an intoxicating beverage, but rather grape juice.

3. The Greek word used here for wine is *"Oinos,"* which means either fermented or unfermented wine. This was the unfermented variety.

COMMANDMENTS

The phrase, *"If you keep My Commandments, you shall abide in My Love,"* proclaims in no uncertain terms the criterion.

As we have already stated, inasmuch as He lives in us and, as such, will live through us, that is, if we will allow Him to do so, there is no excuse for our not keeping His Commandments. In effect, He does it for us, and Faith in Him doing such is honored by God as if we had actually performed the task ourselves (Gal. 2:20).

WHAT COMMANDMENTS?

The *"Commandments,"* of which Jesus here speaks, simply refer to God's Word. We are to keep the Word, which we can do only by placing our Faith exclusively in Christ and what Christ has done for us at the Cross. That being done, the Holy Spirit, Who works exclusively within the parameters, so to speak, of the Finished Work of Christ, will work mightily on our behalf.

It is the Cross of Christ that gave and gives the legal right to the Holy Spirit to do all that He does for and with us. He doesn't demand much of us, but He does demand that the Cross of Christ ever be the Object of our Faith.

We must understand that we cannot live this life within ourselves; we cannot keep these Commandments within ourselves; and we cannot obey the Lord within ourselves. We must have the Help, the Power, the Agency, and the Ministry of the Holy Spirit. To be sure, He will work with us, for us, and within us if we will only give Him the opportunity. We give Him the opportunity by our Faith — but it must be Faith in Christ and the Cross, and that exclusively.

(11) "THESE THINGS HAVE I SPOKEN UNTO YOU, THAT MY JOY MIGHT REMAIN IN YOU, AND THAT YOUR JOY MIGHT BE FULL."

The form is:

1. The entrance into the human family is by natural birth and into the Divine Family by Spiritual Birth.

2. As it is impossible to enter the human family except by birth, so it is likewise impossible to enter the Divine Family.

3. How could a look to the Saviour on Calvary's Tree effect a New Birth? Both are impossible to the fallen intelligence of sinful man.

JOY

The phrase, *"These things have I spoken unto you, that My Joy might remain in you,"* proclaims the end result of keeping His Commandments and abiding in His Love. It produces *"Joy!"* It is not grievous, burdensome, or hurtful in any respect, but rather the very opposite.

"And that your joy might be full," proclaims the truth that this *"Joy,"* as it is generated by the Holy Spirit, can only come about as His Joy remains in us and as we remain in the Vine. This is *"Joy"* that is not disturbed by circumstances, difficulties, obstacles, or problems. In fact, the Believer is not promised immunity from these things but is, as here, promised *"Joy"* in the midst of these things.

In effect, Jesus is here telling us that He Alone can give what the heart craves. The world attempts to find it in money, power, immorality, and a host of other ways, but all in vain! It is found only in Christ and only in obedience to Christ.

THE CROSS

Actually, the true Joy of the Lord cannot be fully experienced until one understands the Cross of Christ relative to our Sanctification, i.e., *"how we live for God."* Now, some might say, *"If that is the case, why did* not Jesus mention it here?"

He didn't mention it here simply because the time had not yet come. He had not gone to the Cross; consequently, His Disciples would not have known what He was talking about. He did basically state this great Truth in Luke 9:23 and 14:27, but gave precious little explanation about it, and for the obvious reasons.

It would not be until the Lord gave the meaning of the New Covenant to the Apostle Paul, which is the meaning of the Cross, that we were to fully understand the Message of the Cross.

I've been on both sides of this proverbial fence. I know what it is to try to live for God and not understand the Cross of Christ wherein all Victory is, and I also know what it is to live for God by the means of the Cross. There is no comparison between the two.

Jesus Christ is the New Covenant, and the meaning of that New Covenant is the Cross, i.e., *"what Jesus accomplished at the Cross."*

(12) "THIS IS MY COMMANDMENT, THAT YOU LOVE ONE ANOTHER, AS I HAVE LOVED YOU."

The diagram is:

1. Christ raised a moral question with Nicodemus. He immediately stopped a religious discussion by telling this most religious man and professed Believer that he was so sinful and so hopelessly corrupt and fallen as to be incapable of Reformation, and so darkened morally that he could neither recognize nor experience spiritual phenomena unless born from above.

2. This fundamental truth is obnoxious to man, for it humbles him.

3. In this discussion with Nicodemus, the Lord unveiled what man really is. He is a sinner, having responsibility, but no life. He is lost, and he must seek life and pardon outside of himself, that is, in Christ (Jn. 3:1-2).

LOVE ONE ANOTHER

The phrase, *"This is My Commandment,"* constitutes the same as the Father's Commandment had been to Him.

As well, Jesus gave this a short time before as a *"new Commandment"* (Jn. 13:34).

NOTES

"That you love one another, as I have loved you," is the Commandment of which He speaks. It is threefold in meaning:

1. We are to love one another, and we must quickly add, it is not a suggestion.

How can one command love in that love must be free and voluntary, or it is not love?

Jesus is not commanding Believers to love Him, but others!

Consequently, this points to love as the foundation of the New Covenant. If the Believer does not love others or ceases to show that love, this is a sure sign that he is no longer in the Covenant, i.e., *"Vine."*

2. The type of love here spoken is beyond comprehension. We are to love others as He has loved us.

If this is so, it should be obvious that we would do nothing to hurt our brother and sister in the Lord.

3. The type of love of which Jesus speaks had never been enjoyed by humanity, even in the slightest. It can be had and engaged at the present and, in fact, ever since Calvary, because Jesus made it possible for the Holy Spirit to live within us and, consequently, to perfect within us this type of love (agape love). With the Help of the Holy Spirit, anything can be done!

(13) "GREATER LOVE HAS NO MAN THAN THIS, THAT A MAN LAY DOWN HIS LIFE FOR HIS FRIENDS."

The overview is:

1. Unfortunately, the modern church, borrowing the ways of the world, seeks to reform man. It cannot be done!

2. While the message of morality, i.e., *"self-improvement,"* sounds good to the carnal ear and, thereby, appeals to the flesh, such is impossible, even for a Believer.

3. In all of this, by Jesus noting the lifted up serpent in the wilderness, He led Nicodemus, and all others for that matter, to the Cross (Jn. 19:38-42).

GREATER LOVE

The phrase, *"Greater love has no man than this,"* portrays a standard of love far beyond anything the world had ever seen or known. Actually, it only saw it in Jesus, which was one of the reasons they killed Him. His Love showed up their false piety to such an extent that they could only think of ridding themselves of Him. In other words, they knew they did not have what He had, and far from it; therefore, they would remove this which was such a threat to them.

"That a man lay down his life for his friends," shows the very highest love, as evidenced in the word *"greater,"* that one human being can show for another. However, Jesus showed an even greater love in that He died not only for His few Friends but, as well, His Enemies (Jn. 3:16).

This is the standard which the Lord has set for us respecting our love for others. He gave Himself freely for us, and we are to give ourselves freely for others.

How so much of a rebuke this was to His Disciples, especially considering that just hours before, *"There was strife among them, which of them should be accounted the greatest"* (Lk. 22:24).

(14) "YOU ARE MY FRIENDS, IF YOU DO WHATSOEVER I COMMAND YOU."

The exegesis is:

1. Reynolds said of this Command: *"I am showing you the highest possible fruit of My friendship."*

2. *"I am laying down My Life for you."*

3. *"This is how I have loved you: therefore after this manner you are to love one another"*⁹ (Eph. 5:1-2; I Jn. 3:16).

(15) "HENCEFORTH I CALL YOU NOT SERVANTS; FOR THE SERVANT KNOWS NOT WHAT HIS LORD DOES: BUT I HAVE CALLED YOU FRIENDS; FOR ALL THINGS THAT I HAVE HEARD OF MY FATHER I HAVE MADE KNOWN UNTO YOU."

The exposition is:

1. The problem is sin, whether for the unredeemed or the Redeemed.

2. The only answer for sin is the Cross of Christ.

3. Fallen man must be miraculously changed, which can only come about through the Born-Again experience. The Cross made that possible.

SERVANTS?

The phrase, *"Henceforth I called you not servants; for the servant knows not what his lord does,"* presents the theme from Verse 12 of the exercise of mutual love in a realm of Divine Love surrounded by hatred — hatred of the world.

The world would hate them because it hated Him, but they were to live in an atmosphere of love one to another, unaffected by this environment of hate. They were to love one another as He loved them.

However, the sphere or realm of love into which He had brought them was the wondrous Love subsisting between the Father and the Son — a Love of affection based upon relationship.

The Believer is lifted into the enjoyment and dignity of the very Kingdom of Love in which God and Christ mutually exist and subsist. Such knowledge is too wonderful for the poor human heart.

By his very nature, a *"servant"* only does what he is told and has little idea as to why he does such or the reason for it being done. However, as the next phrase proclaims, Jesus lifts the Believer out of this mode of servanthood and elevates him to the place and position of the Friend of God. It is done solely through Grace, for such cannot even remotely be earned.

FRIENDS

The phrase, *"But I have called you friends; for all things that I have heard of My Father I have made known unto you,"* proclaims Believers being made a part of the process, which is of far greater significance than we can ever begin to realize.

Even though we are but adopted children into the Kingdom of God (Rom. 8:15), still, we have been made *"Joint-heirs with Christ,"* and as a result, *"Heirs of God"* (Rom. 8:17).

Making all things known to Believers gives the Believer a tremendous latitude of influence in the world. Of course, as should be obvious, such influence is not in the political, governmental, or economical, but rather in the spiritual. As the Bible sets the Standard, the Believer is to live the Standard. As such, he serves as both *"salt"* and *"Light."*

However, as important as that is, the Believer has the ability and privilege of seeing into the spirit world, and through intercessory prayer, has a tremendous influence on events according to the Will of God as they apply to happenings on Earth (Dan., Chpt. 10; Mat. 16:19; 18:18).

However, this influence is predicated on our being His Friend. This is predicated on our love for others, which means we are keeping His Commandment to love one another.

(16) "YOU HAVE NOT CHOSEN ME, BUT I HAVE CHOSEN YOU, AND ORDAINED YOU, THAT YOU SHOULD GO AND BRING FORTH FRUIT, AND THAT YOUR FRUIT SHOULD REMAIN: THAT WHATSOEVER YOU SHALL ASK OF THE FATHER IN MY NAME, HE MAY GIVE IT YOU."

The structure is:

1. A profession of Faith in Christ, which ignores the question of sin, is worthless.

2. We learn from the Word of God that the Holy Spirit seeks people (Jn. 16:13-15); the Father seeks worshippers (Jn. 4:23); and the Son seeks sinners (Lk. 19:10). The woman who met Jesus at Jacob's well, who had been married five times and who was now living with a man to whom she was not married, became the first Preacher of the Gospel to the Gentiles (Jn. 4:28-29).

I HAVE CHOSEN YOU

The phrase, *"You have not chosen Me, but I have chosen you,"* presents the very opposite of what was normally done at that time.

The Disciple then chose the Master, but Jesus reverses this order. The reasons are obvious:

• *"For the Lord sees not as man sees; for man looks on the outward appearance, but the LORD looks on the heart"* (I Sam. 16:7).

• In choosing His Disciples, and all others, as well, and for all time, such was done from the standpoint of Perfect Knowledge. It was the Heavenly Father Who told Jesus exactly who to choose (Lk. 6:12-13). Consequently, to find fault with the one chosen is to find fault with the One Who does the choosing, i.e., the Heavenly Father.

When the Lord chooses an individual for service, He knows exactly what that person will do, even to the end of his or her life.

NOTES

So, His Choice is predicated, as stated, on Perfect Knowledge.

• The Lord does not really choose on the basis of what the person is presently, but what He can make of that person.

• The Lord does not choose on the premise of good and evil. If He did, He would choose no one because none measure up. That should be obvious from observing the Disciples, and all others, for that matter.

In other words, none are qualified at the beginning. To be sure, being qualified is a Work which only the Holy Spirit can accomplish in the life of the person in question.

• The world looks at individuals in the Work of the Lord as being qualified or disqualified according to their own rules, which are not recognized by the Lord. Regrettably, too much of the modern church has bought into the standards of the world. God sets His Own Rules. For instance, He can qualify one very speedily if that individual meets the Bible criteria of humility and brokenness before the Lord.

• All chosen by the Lord are chosen for life. The Scripture plainly says, *"For the Gifts and Calling of God are without Repentance"* (Rom. 11:29). This simply means that the Lord does not lift the Calling, irrespective of what happens.

THE FAITH

While it is certainly true that some, or even many, may depart from the Faith, they are still responsible for that Calling and will answer to God accordingly.

If they return to the Faith, as many have, they are to immediately begin carrying out the Call of God on their hearts and lives. Paul Rader is a perfect example of this. He built a great work in Chicago; however, there were previous problems.

As a young man, the Lord placed a Call to Ministry upon his life. For a period of time, he was very successful. Then, because of particular situations which arose, he lost his way with God. He quit preaching and actually quit living for God altogether, going into deep sin. However, at a point, the Holy Spirit was able to get through to him, and Paul Rader made his way back to God. As stated, he then built the great work in

Chicago, being mightily used of the Lord. He wrote the song:

"Only believe, only believe,
"All things are possible, only believe.
"Only believe, only believe,
"All things are possible, only believe."

ORDINATION

The phrase, *"And ordained you,"* in the Greek text is *"Tithemi"* and means *"to be appointed to any form of service."* It also means *"I set you,"* referring to the metaphor of *"grafting."*

Even though religious leaders claim to *"ordain"* those who are called into Ministry, in truth, such thinking is incorrect. Really, all that man can do is recognize that which God has already done. Man cannot call, and neither can man ordain!

As well, man cannot rescind or terminate the Calling and Ordination, even though they have repeatedly tried from the very beginning.

The religious leaders in Jerusalem said to Peter and the other Apostles, *"Did not we straightly command you that you should not teach in this Name …?*

"Then Peter and the other Apostles answered and said, We ought to obey God rather then men" (Acts 5:28-29).

FRUIT

The phrase, *"That you should go and bring forth fruit,"* presents the *"Fruit of the Spirit"* (Gal. 5:22-23) as the Highest Achievement of the Spirit of God in the heart and life of the one Called of God, or anyone, for that matter! However, inasmuch as Jesus is speaking here of those who are ordained to Ministry, His Message takes on even greater significance.

One would normally think that the Work of the Holy Spirit in the life of the Believer, helping him to carry out great works for the Lord, even in the winning of many souls, would be the highest achievement, etc. However, here we are told the opposite.

To be sure, these things that we have mentioned are of great significance, as should be obvious. However, the *"Fruit of the Spirit"* is the Highest Achievement of the Spirit of God in the hearts of Believers because such proclaims what a man is, which is even more important than what a man does. What he is will ultimately play out in what he does! As well, the lasting fruit of his work will depend upon the development of the Fruit of the Spirit (love, joy, peace, longsuffering, gentleness, goodness, Faith, meekness, and temperance).

FRUIT THAT REMAINS

The phrase, *"And that your fruit should remain,"* testifies to its validity because, as a result of the Ministry of the Disciples, the multitude of Believers in the world presently proclaims that it does remain.

"That whatsoever you shall ask of the Father in My Name, He may give it you," according to Reynolds says, *"By their fruit they would show themselves to be true Disciples of Christ, and to such the Father can deny nothing."*[10]

Luthardt says, *"If they cause themselves to be found in the right service of Jesus, then will be granted to them what they ask in the Name of Jesus."*[11]

Williams says, *"The argument here is: That as the Father loves the Son, so He loves those whom the Son has chosen; and therefore He will answer their prayer; for how could He withhold anything from them in such a case?"*[12]

Too many in the modern Charismatic community have attempted to force the issue of answered prayer while ignoring the demanded *"Fruit."* *"All hinges on Faith,"* they say! However, the Text does not bear out such. While Faith is certainly required, it is *"Fruit"* that is the subject, which, as well, contains Faith, i.e., *"faithfulness."*

(17) "THESE THINGS I COMMAND YOU, THAT YOU LOVE ONE ANOTHER."

The construction is:

1. As *"Fruit"* is the requirement for answered prayer, *"love"* is the requirement for the bringing forth of *"Fruit."*

2. As stated, the word *"Command"* specifies that this is the order of which all is built, and to ignore or negate one is to ignore or negate all!

3. Love brings forth the keeping of His Commandments, which brings forth Fruit,

which brings forth answered prayer, which answers to all things.

(18) "IF THE WORLD HATE YOU, YOU KNOW THAT IT HATED ME BEFORE IT HATED YOU."

The synopsis is:

1. Jesus said more about the Holy Spirit the last week of His Life than all the balance of His Ministry put together (Jn. 14:16-17).

2. Just before He left, He told His Disciples that He would send back the Holy Spirit, which He did.

3. Before the Cross, the Holy Spirit only dwelt *"with Believers,"* but since the Cross, He now dwells in Believers (Jn. 14:17).

HATE

"If the world hate you," has the sense of a fourfold meaning:

1. The word *"hate"* in the Greek text is *"Miseo."* In this instance, it means *"a malicious and unjustifiable feeling of animosity toward others,"* in this case, the innocent.

2. The word *"if"* speaks of the fact that hatred by the world toward true followers of Christ may not be exhibited in every case. As an example, the Apostle Paul did not meet with animosity in every case from the subjects of the Roman Empire, who, in fact, were pagan, but, of course, at times, he did!

3. If animosity or hatred is exhibited, even as it often is, it will be because of the Righteousness of God that is within the Believer, not because a law has been broken, etc. In truth, the ones exhibiting such animosity will probably little know the reason for their attitude. If asked, they would probably relate something of little consequence.

A PERSONAL STATEMENT

Whenever the Lord began to bless our Ministry, and many people began to be touched by the Power of God, the news media became interested in our efforts. Somewhat naïve in those days, I thought that if we would be completely open with these people, presenting anything to them they asked, they would respond accordingly to our honesty and openness.

However, I came to realize, the hard way, I might quickly add, that they were little

NOTES

interested in the truth, but they only wanted to try to find something which they could twist in order that it appear to be something sinister. The reader must understand: a journalist, that is, if he so desires, can make the Sermon on the Mount appear to be an effort to overthrow the government. These people have by and large already settled it in their minds that Preachers of the Gospel, at least those who are truly Spirit-filled and Spirit-led, are a blot on the landscape which needs to be removed. In all my years, I have had only one newspaper man to write a favorable report of this Ministry. It was in Toronto, Ontario, Canada.

Without going into detail as to what he wrote, suffice to say that his editors were so angry with him that they summarily terminated his employment.

So, the idea that the news media will be fair and objective toward the True Gospel of Christ is wishful thinking!

Then again, we have had government officials in various countries, including America, who have been gracious and kind, for which we were so thankful.

THE APOSTATE CHURCH

4. The greatest hatred of all will come from the apostate church. Even though its very forte is religion, still, it has the spirit of the world plus the spirit of religion, which means that it is Satan's trump card, so to speak.

As I have alluded to Paul, one will find in reading the Book of Acts and his Epistles that the apostate church was his greatest enemy, far surpassing the world per se.

It is obvious what the world is; however, religion is organized by Satan to appear to be like God. In fact, it presents a way of salvation which is very appealing to man but, in reality, is not of God and, therefore, contains no salvation whatsoever! These are the ones who have shed most of the blood of true Christians. These are the ones who, in the past, continued to hinder the Work of God greatly, and continue to do the same presently. Because it claims to be of God and constantly speaks of God, even as the Pharisees of Jesus' Day, many people are deceived.

HATRED

The phrase, *"You know that it hated Me before it hated you,"* refers to the cause of the hatred. It is Jesus!

How in the world could anyone hate One like Jesus Who has never hurt anyone but has helped millions, has never made anyone to be sick but has healed millions, and Who has never brought death but Who has brought Life?

The question is valid because the hatred makes no sense; however, the reason is very obvious:

Jesus was and is God's Son, while the people of the world who do not know God, which makes up the far greater majority, are, in reality, children of the Devil. As such, they have become a part of this age-old conflict, whether they know it or not, of Satan's revolution against God. In other words, he uses them to oppose that which is of God because that is what he does!

Jesus would have drawn the greatest hatred, as should be obvious, simply because He epitomized to the greatest degree all that is Righteous, Holy, and True. Consequently, the unrighteous and self-righteous, and unholy and false, greatly opposed Him.

As well, this same spirit will oppose all who truly follow Christ. To be sure, the closer one is to the Lord and the greater the Hand of God on that particular life and Ministry, the more vicious will be the opposition.

(19) "IF YOU WERE OF THE WORLD, THE WORLD WOULD LOVE HIS OWN: BUT BECAUSE YOU ARE NOT OF THE WORLD, BUT I HAVE CHOSEN YOU OUT OF THE WORLD, THEREFORE THE WORLD HATES YOU."

The diagram is:

1. Because of the Cross and what was effected there by Christ, the Holy Spirit now lives permanently in the hearts and lives of all Believers.

2. However, for the Holy Spirit to accomplish His Desired Purpose in our lives, He requires that our Faith be placed exclusively in Christ and the Cross (Rom. 8:1-11; I Cor. 1:17-18).

3. In effect, the Apostle Paul stated that if the Believer subscribes to laws of any capacity, what Christ did at the Cross will be of no profit for such an individual.

THE WORLD

The phrase, *"If you were of the world, the world would love his own,"* could be translated, *"The world loves its own, and its own loves the world!"*

The word *"world,"* as here used by Jesus, in the Greek is *"Kosmos."* It means *"order"* or *"arrangement"* and pertains to all created things. However, used as a theological term, even as Jesus used it, *"Kosmos"* portrays human society as a system warped by sin and tormented by beliefs, desires, and emotions that surge blindly and uncontrollably.

THE WORLD'S SYSTEM

The world's system, as we speak of it here, is a dark system (Eph. 6:12), operating on basic principles that are not of God but actually of Satan. This is the reason for all of the hunger, war, crime, and trouble in the world, and always has been (Col. 1:13-14).

Its basic hostility to God is often displayed as account after account is given in the Bible, and as continues unto this hour (Jn. 12:31; 15:19; 16:33; 17:14; I Cor. 2:12; 3:19; 11:32; Eph. 2:2; James 1:27; 4:4; I Jn. 2:15-17; 3:1, 13; 5:4-5, 19).

THE RELATIONSHIP OF THE CHRISTIAN TO THE WORLD

Christians live on this Earth and are scattered in every society. Thus, Believers are in each generation's space in time members of their culture's own unique expression of the *"Kosmos,"* i.e., *"world."* In other words, the true Christian is adversely impacted by the culture of his particular society.

The Bible teaches that every human culture is warped and twisted by the impact of sin. The perceptions of each generation, the basic desires that move human beings, and the injustices institutionalized in every society testify to sin's warping power.

CHRISTIAN CULTURE

True Christian culture is a gathering of Believers called to display on Earth a completely different set of values, not based on the cravings, lusts, or boastings of sinful humanity. Rather than being squeezed into the world's mold, we are to be *"transformed by the renewing of our minds"* (Rom. 12:2).

Bluntly put, the Believer is one who *"does not live the rest of his earthly life for evil human desires, but rather for the Will of God"* (I Pet. 4:2).

If we remember that the world represents the systematic expression of human sin in human cultures, we understand why the Believer is not to be of the world though he is in it (Jn. 17:14-18).

We are members of our society, yet the values we display and the structures we create in church, home, and occupation are to be distinctively Christian.

In other words, when the sinner comes to Christ, he is brought out of the culture of this world into the Culture of Christ and the Bible.

A PERSONAL EXPERIENCE

When we were conducting city-wide meetings in foreign countries, some of the missionaries claimed that we could not be effective because we did not understand the *"culture"* of the particular people to whom we were ministering. However, we saw literally tens of thousands brought to a Saving Knowledge of Jesus Christ, irrespective of their culture and my lack of understanding in that realm.

However, this I did and do understand. All cultures, as stated, regardless of their direction, are wicked, ungodly, and have their roots in the powers of darkness. Irrespective of the different inflections, that fact remains.

As well, I knew and know that the hearts of the people do not change no matter the country in which they live or the culture in which they reside. They are sinners who desperately need God.

Also, I knew that sin was the problem, and Jesus Christ was and is the Answer and, in fact, the Only Answer for these people and all people, whomever they may be and wherever they may be. Hence, the Lord gave us a great harvest of souls.

It is simple, irrespective of the part of the world to which one ministers. As stated, the problem is sin, and the solution is *"Jesus Christ and Him Crucified."*

NOTES

WORLDLINESS

As Believers, we need to understand the deadliness of worldliness. Worldliness is not a matter of engaging in those practices that some question. It is unthinkably adopting the perspectives, values, and attitudes of our culture without bringing them under the Judgment of God's Word. It is carrying on our lives as if we did not know Jesus. That is worldliness (Mat. 16:26; Mk. 8:26; Lk. 9:25; I Cor. 5:10; 7:31, 33-34; II Cor. 7:10; I Jn. 2:15-16; 4:17).

The phrase, *"But because you are not of the world,"* means that due to being *"Born-Again,"* Believers are no longer of this world's system. As it is said repeatedly, Believers are in the world but not of the world! The Believer does not dance to its tunes, march to its parades, or make his plans according to its direction. As the Believer is an offense to the world (not because of anything the Believer has adversely done), the world is also an offense to the Believer because of the evil of its culture.

CHOSEN

The phrase, *"But I have chosen you out of the world,"* refers to being chosen by Christ and being brought out of the world's system, although still in the world.

The phrase, *"Therefore the world hates you,"* speaks of animosity which develops and is not caused by the Believer.

When the sinner accepts Christ, instantly, the change in his lifestyle is obvious. His speech changes along with his habits. As a result, friendships change! Even though the Believer says very little, this change is an offense to most of his former friends. The Righteousness within him constantly shows up their evil, which is actually the cause of the animosity.

However, generally the work habits of the Believer change for the better, or at least they surely should! Consequently, he makes a much better employee, neighbor, and associate. This is the *"salt"* and *"Light"* of Believers in the world.

A PERSONAL EXPERIENCE

In 1985, Frances and I, along with others,

were in what was then known as the Soviet Union for a series of Meetings. In speaking to some Russians who had seen much, if not most, of the reign of communism, they spoke to us of an interesting scenario respecting Christians.

At first, Christians, they said, were greatly persecuted. However, after a period of time, the communist leaders began to see that Christians were on time for work, put in an honest day's work, and did not come to work drunk. They also saw that Christians did not steal, nor did they lie. In other words, they were the very best workers in the Soviet Union.

This does not mean that all of the persecution stopped, for it did not, for the hatred of Christ superseded the positive results afforded by His Followers. Nevertheless, it did lessen in its intensity.

If one is to notice, such hatred is not expressed toward the followers of Muhammad or any other religions of the world.

The same can be said for Catholicism and much of that which goes under the heading of Protestant.

Despite the fact that Islam is responsible for most of the terrorist activity in the world, it generates little animosity from the American press, or anywhere else, for that matter.

Why?

It is because the American press and Islam, along with all others of the world's system, actually come from the same source, Satan. So, it loves its own, or at least finds little fault with its activity, irrespective of its destructive nature. True Bible Christianity alone attracts such animosity!

(20) "REMEMBER THE WORD THAT I SAID UNTO YOU, THE SERVANT IS NOT GREATER THAN HIS LORD. IF THEY HAVE PERSECUTED ME, THEY WILL ALSO PERSECUTE YOU; IF THEY HAVE KEPT MY SAYING, THEY WILL KEEP YOURS ALSO."

The overview is:

1. The Gospel does not liberate a man to a life of laziness and self-indulgence but to an unceasing ministry of loving service to humanity.

2. In the Epistle to the Galatians, Paul shows that the Believer has come out from whatever control Divine Law had over him, and in Salvation, has been placed under a superior control, that of the Indwelling Holy Spirit.

3. The Holy Spirit exercises a much stricter supervision over the Believer than Law ever did over the unbeliever.

REMEMBER

The phrase, *"Remember the word that I said unto you, The servant is not greater than his Lord,"* is used in the same sense that it was used in John 13:16. However, as it was used there concerning humility and therefore conduct, it is used here respecting opposition.

"If they have persecuted Me, they will also persecute you," presents a warning of what is to come.

I wonder what was in the minds of the Disciples as they heard Jesus say these words. They were thinking of an earthly kingdom which would commence shortly, and He was speaking of great persecution coming.

Up unto the last few months, they had enjoyed tremendous crowds, with Miracles being performed constantly. It was obvious that the Pharisees were not in sympathy with what Jesus was doing or Who He was, but still, in comparison to all the great things which were happening, this was of no great moment.

THE OPPOSITION

However, in the last few months, the entire situation had begun to change. The animosity of both the Pharisees and Sadducees had increased to such an extent that people were being threatened with excommunication from the synagogue if they continued to follow Christ. Consequently, the crowds began to thin out considerably. As well, there were those constant reminders by Christ of His Coming Death and Resurrection, with Him now speaking strongly of their being hated and persecuted. Such did not fit in with their *"Kingdom Now"* philosophy, as it does not fit presently!

Nevertheless, the Coming of the Holy Spirit would help them to greatly understand that of which He spoke, and, as well, they would begin almost immediately to experience persecution. Actually, it is believed that all 12 of the Apostles, with the exception of John the Beloved, died a martyr's death.

Also, hundreds of thousands, if not millions, have given up their lives for the Cause of Christ down through the centuries, which has literally stained the Earth with blood. It has been exactly as Jesus said it would be.

The only reason that persecution has lessened a great deal in these modern times is because of the tremendous positive impact that Bible Christianity has made upon the world. Nevertheless, the greatest time of persecution is yet to come when the Antichrist makes his debut, literally declaring war on all who name the Name of Jesus, irrespective as to who or where they are.

MY WORD

The phrase, *"If they have kept My Saying, they will keep yours also,"* presents Jesus turning a sentence around, but yet, with it meaning the same.

The truth is, most of the world will not listen to His Message and will oppose the Messenger as well! However, some few will heed the Message, which actually constitutes the Church of all time.

In this Passage, Jesus places the Message and the Messenger on the same par as Himself. In fact, the Message is His Message! As well, there is a veiled warning in this Passage that actually states that if the Messenger is persecuted, it is the same as persecuting Christ, hence, Jesus saying to Paul on the road to Damascus, *"Saul, Saul, why do you persecute Me?"* (Acts 9:4).

(21) "BUT ALL THESE THINGS WILL THEY DO UNTO YOU FOR MY NAME'S SAKE, BECAUSE THEY KNOW NOT HIM WHO SENT ME."

The exegesis is:

1. Paul wrote his last Epistle to Timothy, entrusting him with the greatest Message on Earth, *"Jesus Christ and Him Crucified."*

2. In fact, *"Jesus Christ and Him Crucified"* is the meaning of the New Covenant.

3. Some have said, and rightly so I think, that the Apostle Paul was probably the greatest example for Righteousness ever produced by Christ.

FOR MY NAME'S SAKE

The phrase, *"But all these things will they do unto you for My Name's Sake,"* presents Jesus presenting Himself as the Cause of the persecution and opposition.

It is the Name of Jesus which is hated around the world more so than any other. Millions pray each day, claiming to be addressing their prayer to God, but without the Name of Jesus. They conduct themselves accordingly for varied reasons; however, the main reason is the offense of the Cross. It is with Jesus that the world has a controversy.

Why?

Jesus is the only Representative of the Godhead Who has been seen by men. I speak of the Incarnation. Men have never seen the Father, at least in this fashion, nor have they seen the Holy Spirit. So, Jesus is the One they have touched and therefore rejected. He did not suit them in appearance, in style, in His Manner, or Personality. Therefore, they branded Him as an imposter and blasphemer.

HIS PERFECT RIGHTEOUSNESS

The greatest reason they rejected Christ was because of His Perfect Righteousness, which was a perfect rebuke to their unrighteousness. Being very religious, they did not desire to change their allegiance. Therefore, they rejected Christ and died eternally lost, just as much of the world has died eternally lost.

The phrase, *"Because they know not Him Who sent Me,"* means that despite their claims, the religious leaders of Jesus' Day did not know God and, therefore, did not recognize His Son! Had they known Him, they would have known Jesus!

Reynolds said: *"No fact is more patent in the entire history of human thoughts about God than this, that 'the world by wisdom knows Him not,' nay, it travesties His Name, misrepresents His Character, distrusts, fears, and flees from the Face of God.*

It was left to Christ to reveal the Father. In many ways as well, even Christendom has obscured or denied the Fatherhood."[13]

(22) "IF I HAD NOT COME AND SPOKEN UNTO THEM, THEY HAD NOT HAD SIN: BUT NOW THEY HAVE NO CLOAK FOR THEIR SIN."

The synopsis is:

1. When Paul speaks of *"the Gospel," "the Word," "the Blood," "Redemption," "Salvation," "the Faith,"* etc., he is actually referring to the Cross.

2. The Cross of Christ stands for all of these things and even many things we have not named here.

3. Through the Cross, both Jews and Gentiles are reconciled in one Body to God.

THE WITNESS

The phrase, *"If I had not come and spoken unto them, they had not had sin,"* actually means the sin of rejecting Him, which is the greatest sin of all!

The sin of rejecting Jesus as their Messiah, despite incontrovertible proof, destroyed their Nation, caused them to lose their very souls, and has caused the Jews to be scattered all over the world even as vagabonds. It is all because they rejected Him! As a whole, they do so unto this day!

However, as this pertained to Israel of old, it also pertains to the entirety of the world, for His Coming was because the Father sent Him and was intended for the entirety of mankind (Jn. 3:16).

NO CLOAK FOR SIN

"But now they have no cloak for their sin," means that the world is without excuse.

Before Jesus came and revealed the Father, the world had no understanding of God whatsoever. Despite the Word given to them by the Prophets, even Israel little understood Who He really was. For the most part, their impression was false, resulting in their understanding being skewed. This is proven by their rejection of Christ, Who was a Perfect Representation of the Father.

Jesus revealed the Father to the entirety of the world, hence, the Gospel having gone to the ends of the Earth. So, those who reject Him as the Door and Way to the Father have rejected the Father as well! Consequently, this dooms Islam and all of its followers. The same can be said for the other religions of the world which present other than Christ.

This of which Jesus has just said concerning the *"cloak for sin"* is the very reason that the Great Commission is so important. When one reads the Book of Acts, it immediately becomes crystal clear that priority with God is world Evangelism. This was the thrust of the Early Church, and especially the Apostle Paul, who headed up that thrust.

So, it has been the business of the Church to take this Message to every human being on the face of the Earth in every generation. Sadly, it has by and large failed. However, its failure is not because of the various excuses which it proposes, but rather its lack of dependence on the Holy Spirit.

Without the aid of modern transportation or modern methods of communication, the Early Church evangelized most of the world of its day. It did it by the Power, Authority, Leading, and Anointing of the Holy Spirit.

Consequently, every single person in the world who does not know of Jesus Christ and Who He is, because no one has bothered to take them the Message, in effect, has a cloak for their sin. This does not mean they will be Saved because of their ignorance, but it does mean that the Church will have blood on its hands at the Judgment Bar of God (Ezek. 3:18).

(23) "HE WHO HATES ME HATES MY FATHER ALSO."

The synopsis is:

1. The only way to God is through Jesus Christ (Jn. 14:6).

2. The only way to Jesus Christ is through the Cross (Lk. 14:27).

3. The only way to the Cross is by and through a denial of self (Lk. 9:23).

HATRED OF CHRIST AND THE FATHER

In every conceivable way possible, Jesus repeatedly stated that it was impossible to separate Him from the Father or the Father from Him. Furthermore, the only way, and that means exactly what it says, to the Father is by and through Jesus. As well, anything done to Jesus is done to the Father. Hatred expressed toward Him, as it was by the Jews and so many others from that time until now, is, as well, hatred toward the Father. This is one of the reasons that the preference of Mary over Jesus by the Catholics is such an abomination. Of course, they would argue that they are lifting up Jesus even higher.

What they ignore and where they're wrong is so obvious: it is that anything done toward the Son or the Father must be Scriptural, or it is invalid. The lauding and worship of Mary are not Scriptural! As well, the ignoring of God's Word respecting prayer, claiming that the way to Jesus is through Mary, is grossly unscriptural. In the next Chapter, Jesus will tell us how to pray, and ignoring His Statement is at our own peril.

(24) "IF I HAD NOT DONE AMONG THEM THE WORKS WHICH NONE OTHER MAN DID, THEY HAD NOT HAD SIN: BUT NOW HAVE THEY BOTH SEEN AND HATED BOTH ME AND MY FATHER."

The exposition is:
1. The Cross of Christ is the Way.
2. It only requires Faith.
3. The Object of that Faith must be Christ and the Cross.

SIN

The phrase, *"If I had not done among them the Works which none other man did, they had not had sin,"* proclaims that His Preaching and His Miracles both plainly revealed Who He was. He was God — Love itself in Human Form — and they turned from Him in detestation and in their hatred of Him, crucified Him. Such is man's heart! Hating Him, they hated God, and they hated Him without any reason.

The idea of this Verse is that not only was ample proof given as to Who He was but, actually, abundant proof.

The *"Works"* He did were so astounding that it was impossible for anyone to not know that they were of God. Furthermore, only God could have performed such astounding Miracles.

"They had not had sin," actually says, *"They had not had this sin of rejecting Me."*

The phrase, *"But now have they both seen and hated Both Me and My Father,"* means they hated God as God, and Goodness and Truth just because that God the Father and God the Son were Goodness and Truth.

Reynolds says: *"The awful condemnation is here pronounced that men love darkness rather then light. They positively saw their Father and hated Him. This is the most terrible condemnation that can be pronounced on moral beings."*[14]

So, now Israel is guilty of the supreme sin of rejecting Christ even in the face of incontrovertible proof!

(25) "BUT THIS COMES TO PASS, THAT THE WORD MIGHT BE FULFILLED THAT IS WRITTEN IN THEIR LAW, THEY HATED ME WITHOUT A CAUSE."

The composition is:
1. The words *"the Cross"* and *"the Faith"* could, in fact, be said to be one in the same.
2. The *"good fight of Faith"* is a good fight because it is the *"right fight."*
3. The wonderful thing about this fight, as difficult as it may be at times, is that this is a fight in which we steadily grow stronger while the Evil One steadily grows weaker.

THE FULFILLING OF THE WORD

"But this comes to pass, that the Word might be fulfilled that is written in their Law," does not mean that they were forced to do this thing, but that it was predicted that they would, as God through foreknowledge saw what would happen and gave the prediction to the Prophets.

As well, the phrase as used by Jesus, *"Their Law,"* refers to the Law of Moses and has reference to the fact of their claiming to keep the Law at all times.

It was the Law in which they prided themselves, the Law which was ever in their mouths, and the Law which itself contained the portraiture of their spirit, but which they did not see.

HATRED WITHOUT A CAUSE

The phrase, *"They hated Me without a cause,"* is found in Psalms 35:19; 69:4, and speaks similar words in Psalms 109:3; 119:161.

So, the very *"Law"* they claimed to obey amply predicted their terrible hatred. What irony!

As is plainly obvious, there was no cause whatsoever for hating Him. In truth, He was the only One Who has ever lived Who never gave cause for ill treatment. No other human being can boast of such a thing! And yet, they killed Him, and the apostate church would do the same presently were the time factors changed.

How do I know that?

I know it simply because they attempt to kill those who are truly His. The law of the land does not allow actual murder in this respect, but please believe me, that is the only thing that stops them. Otherwise, they attempt in every way to do the next best thing! They kill the character, reputation, influence, and Ministry in every capacity of the true Disciples of Christ!

It has not changed because it cannot change! The evil in those who killed Christ is the same evil that is in their modern counterparts. Therefore, it reacts accordingly!

(26) "BUT WHEN THE COMFORTER IS COME, WHOM I WILL SEND UNTO YOU FROM THE FATHER, EVEN THE SPIRIT OF TRUTH, WHICH PROCEEDS FROM THE FATHER, HE SHALL TESTIFY OF ME:"

The structure is:

1. When we give of our resources to help take this Message of the Cross to a hurting world, the Holy Spirit through Paul tells us that the Lord places such a gift in the same category as His Cross (Phil. 4:17-19).

2. As well, if we support any ministry that is not of the Cross, whatever it is we are supporting, it is not well-pleasing to God.

3. The great Truth presented is that if we support that which is truly of God, and I continue to speak of the Cross, then we have the Promise of the Lord that *"He shall supply our need according to His Riches in Glory by Christ Jesus."*

THE COMFORTER

The phrase, *"But when the Comforter is come,"* presents the third time that Jesus mentions the Holy Spirit, i.e., Paraclete (Jn. 14:16, 26).

NOTES

Jesus said more about the Holy Spirit the last week of His Ministry than He did the entirety of the previous three and one-half years. It was done in this fashion because He was about to leave. Therefore, He was preparing them for the Advent of the Holy Spirit, and what an Advent it would be! Even as He said: whereas the Holy Spirit had been with them, now He would be in them (Jn. 14:17). He will speak of Him greatly so in the next Chapter as well!

The *"Comforter"* would come about 51 days later.

THE SPIRIT OF TRUTH

The phrase, *"Whom I will send unto you from the Father,"* presents Jesus as the Baptizer with the Holy Spirit (Mat. 3:11; Jn. 1:31-33).

Jesus would ascend 40 days after His Resurrection, and then, some 10 days later on the Day of Pentecost, would send back the Holy Spirit. The Spirit proceeds from the Father and is sent by the Son.

The phrase, *"Even the Spirit of Truth,"* makes the second time the Lord uses this term (Jn. 14:17).

The appellative, *"The Spirit of Truth,"* as used by Jesus, concerns the veracity of the Word of God. The Holy Spirit superintended its writing all the way from Moses, who began with Genesis, to the closing of the Canon of Scripture as given to John on the Isle of Patmos, with the writing of the Book of Revelation. It was about 1,600 years in the process. It began with *"In the Beginning God"* and closed with *"The Grace of our Lord Jesus Christ be with you all. Amen."* As well, every word written between the opening and the close is error free. No other book in the world can make such a claim because it is the Word of God.

Especially considering that a large number of writers contributed to this great Work and lived hundreds of years apart, the Miracle of it being error free all the more points to Deity respecting its inspiration.

While there is an error or two in the translation, there is no error in the original Text. (There are no original Texts in existence presently. However, there are over 10,000 copies, or parts of copies, of

Books of both the Old and New Testaments. Some, especially referring to the New Testament, go back not too distant from the First Century).

FROM THE FATHER

The phrase, *"Which proceeds from the Father,"* proclaims the Father sending the Holy Spirit in the Name of Jesus and by the Authority of Jesus.

Consequently, as should be overly obvious, the Trinity is here plainly delineated. So, one has no excuse in trying to force One into the Other. Again, we state there is One God but manifested in Three Persons, *"God the Father," "God the Son,"* and *"God the Holy Spirit."*

The phrase, *"He shall testify of Me,"* refers to constant and unending Testimony.

In other words, it is the Business of the Holy Spirit to point to Jesus constantly, which He does! He points to Him as Saviour, as Baptizer with the Holy Spirit, as Healer, as our Victory, and as Coming King. Such corresponds to the five derivatives of His Name, *"Wonderful* (Saviour), *Counsellor* (Baptizer with the Holy Spirit), *The Mighty God* (Healer), *The Everlasting Father* (Victory), *The Prince of Peace* (Coming King)" (Isa. 9:6).

(27) "AND YOU ALSO SHALL BEAR WITNESS, BECAUSE YOU HAVE BEEN WITH ME FROM THE BEGINNING."

The construction is:

1. Joel is the Holy Spirit Prophet of the Old Testament.

2. He is the one quoted by Simon Peter on the Day of Pentecost (Acts 2:16-21).

3. Before the Cross, the Holy Spirit, even though working mightily in the world, still was very limited as to what He could do. It was because the blood of bulls and goats could not take away sins (Heb. 10:4). The Cross of Christ took away all sin and thereby changed everything.

THE WITNESS

The phrase, *"And you also shall bear witness,"* referred to the original Twelve who were hand picked for this very purpose.

"Because you have been with Me from the beginning," speaks of them observing all He did and all He said. They would be the embryo of the Early Church as Paul would say, *"And are built upon the Foundation of the Apostles and Prophets, Jesus Christ Himself being the Chief Cornerstone"* (Eph. 2:20).

In fellowship with the Holy Spirit, they were to return love for the hatred that surrounded them, and they were to unite with the Spirit in witnessing for Christ. Only those who know Him and live in communion with Him can testify of Him.

They were not to be stumbled or confounded because they were hated and ill-treated by the chiefs and members of the Hebrew church. Their action resulted from not knowing God in Christ.

That church was of Divine Ordination and was intended as a Light to the world, but it's knowledge of God was sadly carnal. Carnal men can be very zealous for religious truth and use it as an authority for persecuting those who have a true and Spiritual Knowledge of God, as the Disciples would find out, and all since, for that matter!

"Tell me the old, old Story,
"Of unseen things above,
"Of Jesus and His Glory,
"Of Jesus and His Love."

"Tell me the Story simply,
"As to a little child,
"For I am weak and weary,
"And helpless and defiled."

"Tell me the Story slowly,
"That I may take it in,
"That wonderful Redemption,
"God's remedy for sin."

"Tell me the Story often,
"For I forget so soon;
"The early dew of morning,
"Has passed away at noon."

"Tell me the Story softly,
"With earnest tones and grave;
"Remember I'm the sinner,
"Whom Jesus came to save."

"Tell me the Story,
"Always, if you would really be,
"In any time of trouble,
"A comforter to me."

"Tell me the same old Story,
"When you have cause to fear,
"That this world's empty glory,
"Is costing me too dear."

"Yes, and when that world's glory,
"Is dawning on my soul,
"Tell me the old, old Story,
"Christ Jesus makes you whole."

CHAPTER 16

(1) "THESE THINGS HAVE I SPOKEN UNTO YOU, THAT YOU SHOULD NOT BE OFFENDED."

The synopsis is:

1. Before the Crucifixion, it seems that Mary, the sister of Martha and Lazarus, was the only one who actually believed that Jesus would rise from the dead.

2. Somehow, she learned the fact that on the third day, He would rise again. So, the spikenard she had prepared for His dead Body, she now poured *"beforehand"* on His living Body.

3. It is noticeable that Mary was not found at the empty Sepulcher. She was too intelligent to be there. She knew that Jesus wasn't there.

WARNINGS

The phrase, *"These things have I spoken unto you,"* refers to all the warnings of the coming persecution.

It is somewhat ironic. The last thing Jesus told His Disciples before His Crucifixion concerned the coming persecution, which would be severe. As well, I remind the reader that this persecution was not for a lack of faith but because of their Faith.

I wonder how that corresponds to the message given by many modern Christian teachers in telling their followers how to get rich, etc.

"That you should not be offended," in effect, means to not be surprised. It has the same connotation as stumbling over an obstacle of which one was not aware. Jesus is telling them to be aware of what is going to happen.

(2) "THEY SHALL PUT YOU OUT OF THE SYNAGOGUES: YES, THE TIME COMES, THAT WHOSOEVER KILLS YOU WILL THINK THAT HE DOES GOD SERVICE."

The composition is:

1. Putting one's Faith in the Cross of Christ and maintaining one's Faith in that Finished Work will bring about tremendous Blessings.

2. This is the way and, in fact, the only way that one can have a new beginning, irrespective of what the past has been (Jn. 3:16).

3. Jesus Christ is the Source of all things we receive from God while the Cross of Christ is the Means by which all of these things are given.

PERSECUTION

The phrase, *"They shall put you out of the synagogues,"* refers to the religious leaders of Israel and the excommunicating from the fellowship of their country's worship of those who followed Jesus. As the Book of Acts proclaims, they suffered exactly that of which Jesus had spoken.

It should be added here, as the *"Former Rain,"* prophesied by Joel, brought about expulsion from the Jewish church, likewise, the *"Latter Rain,"* as spoken by the same Prophet, will bring about expulsion from the modern institutionalized church (Joel, Chpt. 2).

Such expulsion in these modern times began with Believers, who were members formerly of old-line denominations, being baptized with the Holy Spirit. It has now extended to the Pentecostal and Charismatic varieties. It is sad! That which these denominations and churches once promoted and wore as a badge of honor in the lifting up of Jesus, they now despise! As should be obvious, the persecution of which Jesus speaks comes almost, if not exclusively, from religion.

As we stated in the latter part of Chapter 15, carnal men can be very zealous for religious truth and use it as an authority for persecuting those who have a true and spiritual knowledge of God.

The phrase, *"Yes, the time comes, that whosoever kills you will think that he does*

God service," speaks of terrible religious deception. It began this way, and it will end this way!

The religious leaders of Israel were so deceived during the time of the Early Church that they actually thought their fighting God in the persecution of the Followers of Christ was actually service for God. How deceived can one be!

DECEPTION

It is no different at present. As we have stated, the law of the land does not allow the actual taking of life, at least in religious persecution. Still, for the most part, many modern religious leaders do everything humanly possible to kill the influence and effectiveness of those they deem as deserving such, all the time thinking they are doing God a service.

When one opposes that which is of God, one is opposing God! God has not given the right of discipline or chastisement regarding His Servants to any man. He reserves that right solely to Himself (Rom. 12:19-21; Heb. 12:5-11; James 4:12).

To lay one's hand on that which is of God is a frightful thing! Judgment may be a time in coming, but come it shall!

If a nation sets out to persecute God's People, irrespective as to how rich or powerful that nation may be, it will ultimately be destroyed. The same goes for religious denominations and even individuals. The Scripture plainly says, *"He suffered no man to do them wrong: yes, He reproved kings for their sakes; saying, Touch not My Anointed, and do My Prophets no harm."*

He then said, *"Moreover He called for a famine upon the land: He broke the whole staff of bread"* (Ps. 105:14-16).

If there is a spiritual famine presently, and there definitely is in America and Canada, despite all the religious machinery and wild claims, such can be laid at the doorstep, at least in part, of those who have laid their hands in a negative way on the Lord's Anointed.

(3) "AND THESE THINGS WILL THEY DO UNTO YOU, BECAUSE THEY HAVE NOT KNOWN THE FATHER, NOR ME."

The form is:

NOTES

1. In the First Chapter of Romans, Paul proclaims the entirety of the Gentile world to a man as being spiritually lost, despite all their religion.

2. In the Second and Third Chapters of Romans, the Apostle places the Jews in the same category, i.e., all needing a Redeemer.

3. In the Fourth and Fifth Chapters of Romans, the Holy Spirit through the Apostle proclaims the answer to this dilemma, which is *"Justification by Faith."*

RELIGION

The phrase, *"And these things will they do unto you,"* proclaims the manner of the persecution.

"Because they have not known the Father, nor Me," proclaims not only the fact but the cause of the apostate church's hatred. As should be obvious, religion is the cause of most of the persecution.

As we have stated, religion is Satan's greatest effort. He not only instigates false religions, but he seeks diligently to turn that which is True. He does so by the inserting of the leaven of false doctrine. Most of the time, it is not leaven that is obvious. It is rather subtle and smooth, even parading as an Angel of Light (II Cor. 11:13-15).

Of those who engage in such activity of persecution and opposition to the Gospel, despite their claims, they do not really know God or His Son, the Lord Jesus Christ.

What an indictment!

(4) "BUT THESE THINGS HAVE I TOLD YOU, THAT WHEN THE TIME SHALL COME, YOU MAY REMEMBER THAT I TOLD YOU OF THEM. AND THESE THINGS I SAID NOT UNTO YOU AT THE BEGINNING, BECAUSE I WAS WITH YOU."

The overview is:

1. The Lord can meet man at the Cross and nowhere else.

2. This means that our Faith must be exclusively in Christ and Him Crucified.

3. While the Cross of Christ produces the Righteousness of God, anything and everything else produces self-righteousness.

A PERSONAL EXPERIENCE

The phrase, *"But these things have I told*

you, that when the time shall come, you may remember that I told you of them," tells us several things:

He has told the Church in a collective sense of persecution, which it has encountered from that day until now, at least at certain periods of time. As well, He speaks to those called by Him on an individual basis.

If I remember correctly, it was 1982. As well, I think it was a Saturday morning. I had driven my car on top of the levee, which runs beside the mighty Mississippi River, not far from our home. I did this quite often. There I would have solitude respecting prayer and seeking the Lord. That morning was not to be uneventful.

Generally, I would stay there pretty much all day long, alternating between prayer and the study of the Word. I really do not remember if this was the first or second session of prayer that day; however, at one point, I began to strongly sense the Presence of God. Then, the Lord began to speak to my heart. This is what He said, or words to this effect:

"I will give you the message that I want you to deliver. If you are faithful to what I give you, it will bring great opposition."

He then said, *"The opposition from the Catholics and those of the old-line churches will be strong; however, the greatest opposition will come from your own."*

And finally: *"Your own will turn against you. As a result, you could lose everything! Are you willing to deliver the message I give you?"*

LOSING EVERYTHING?

By losing everything, He meant the extensive outreach of this Ministry, which then had the largest television audience in Gospel in the world. We were televising in some 40 or 50 countries, with the program being translated into various languages. Literally tens of thousands of people were being brought to Christ, and I exaggerate not. As well, our Church, Family Worship Center, would shortly be one of the largest Churches in America at that time, with an attendance of approximately 7,000. As well, the Bible College was just beginning and would experience an almost miraculous growth. The Crusades conducted in countries all over the world saw some of the largest crowds and, especially, some of the largest Altar Calls in history.

I did not answer immediately, continuing to pray, and even being broken before the Lord to such an extent that it is difficult to describe.

After a period of time of attempting to weigh very carefully what the Lord had said to me, I affirmed my resolve to the Lord to do exactly what He wanted. Actually, there was never any doubt about that.

My seeking His Face before giving an answer was to determine if this was really the Lord speaking to me, or was such coming out of my own mind?

To say, *"Yes,"* was not difficult, and yet, I am so thankful that I did not know the extent to which this would come to pass.

THE REASON!

I realize that most think they know the reason religious leaders took a stand against us, which they did; however, what happened was only an excuse. It was not the reason.

The reason was what I preached and the results we were seeing. As the Pharisees of old saw Jesus as a threat, somehow these people were of the same frame of mind. I was very naïve. Having never had any misunderstanding or confrontation with any of these people, and I speak of the leaders of the denomination with which I was then associated, I had no idea of the degree of their hatred for me. However, I was to learn in no uncertain terms!

I am so thankful that I can say, even as I relate this account, that there is no animosity in my heart toward them and, in fact, never has been. To be sure, I grieve, and greatly so, for the tremendous harm done to the Work of God, with certainly some of that my fault, as would be obvious. Of that, I hold myself even more responsible. And yet, I am not responsible for their terrible sin.

Most of those men have gone on now to be with the Lord, but those who took their place are of the same frame of mind, sadly so. Regrettably, as the Laodicean church of Revelation 3:14-22, they see no need for Repentance. Still, it is my prayer that that particular denomination will come back to its first Love. However, the situation presently, I fear, is even much worse than it was in the early 1980s.

THESE THINGS HAVE I TOLD YOU

Yes! The Words of Jesus in Verse 4, *"These things have I told you,"* are very personal to me.

Exactly as He said, *"That time came."* As stated, I am so glad that I did not know at the outset how difficult it would be. In fact, were it not for the Grace of God, it would not have been possible to have stood such a thing. Public humiliation, especially on a worldwide scale, is, without a doubt, at least one of the most difficult things one could face.

Our strength was and is prayer, actually, a continuing of the seeking of the Face of the Lord. We (Frances and I) have literally lain on our faces before God year by year in order that the Holy Spirit may do what He desires. To be sure, there was much in Jimmy Swaggart which needed changing. The wonderful way He has done this, and continues to do so even unto this hour, has drawn me closer to Him than I have ever been in my life. God never gets Glory out of failure, but He does get Glory out of victory over failure.

At this particular time (2013), our network (The SonLife Broadcasting Network) has experienced, and is experiencing, a miraculous growth. At this writing, we are going now into some 60 million homes in America by television, some 25 million in the United Kingdom, and some 25 million in Germany, France, and Spain. We are already translating into Spanish, and I am speaking of translation 24 hours a day, seven days a week. We plan to start translating into Russian in just a few days. By the time you read this, we should be going all over the vast country of Russia with the Gospel of Jesus Christ.

THE ENTIRETY OF THE WORLD

In 2010, the Lord spoke to my heart concerning world Evangelism, and the following is what He said to me:

"In the 1990s, Satan tried to close the door to this Ministry; however, I kept it open about 10 percent compared to what you had been doing in the 1980s. But I am now about to open it wide once again."

And that, He immediately began to do.

The Lord has also spoken to me that a Move of God is coming that is going to touch the entirety of the world and will result in hundreds of thousands, if not millions, being brought into the Kingdom of God. There are many more things the Lord has spoken to my heart, but which I do not feel at liberty to divulge. However, this I do know: what the Lord is going to do is going to be great, and, in fact, it has already begun.

THE MESSAGE OF THE CROSS

The Lord has given this Ministry the privilege of knowing and understanding that which He gave to the Apostle Paul, and I speak of THE MESSAGE OF THE CROSS. In fact, the Church has come full circle.

The Early Church was built on the Foundation of the Cross with the Apostle Paul as the master builder — all under Christ. Regrettably, over the next several centuries, the church began to lose its way and finally morphed into what we now know as the Catholic church. Then, in the early Sixteenth Century, the Reformation took place with the main theme being, *"The Just shall live by Faith."* This was followed in the 1800s by the great Holiness Meetings, and then at the turn of the Twentieth Century, the great Pentecostal Move, which touched the world. And now, the Holy Spirit has brought the Church full circle, and I'm speaking again of the Message of the Cross. In other words, the Lord is taking us back to the Cross. The Bible is clear that the Cross is, in fact, the Gospel (I Cor. 1:17, 18, 23; 2:2). As stated, it's definitely not something new but is the oldest message that man has ever known. It was actually formulated in the mind of the Godhead from before the foundation of the world (I Pet. 1:18-20).

I personally believe that the Message of the Cross is the dividing line between the true Church and the apostate church. In fact, it has always been that way, actually beginning in the Fourth Chapter of Genesis, as it regards Cain and Abel. However, I believe that it is going to be more pronounced now than ever. Martin Luther said, as it regards the Reformation, *"As one viewed the Cross, so one viewed the Reformation."* It's the same thing now. As one views the Cross, so one views the Gospel. It is ever the Cross, the Cross, the Cross!

(5) "BUT NOW I GO MY WAY TO HIM WHO SENT ME; AND NONE OF YOU ASKS ME, WHERE DO YOU GO?"

The diagram is:

1. If there is any great mistake the church makes, it is undervaluing the Holy Spirit.

2. Without the Holy Spirit, the church is no more than any other club or gathering.

3. However, with the Holy Spirit, the Church becomes a living dynamo.

I GO MY WAY

The phrase, *"But now I go My Way to Him Who sent Me,"* speaks of the Ascension, which would take place about 44 days from this moment. However, Jesus would leave only after His Work had been finished in totality. He would now go back to His Father!

The question, *"And none of you asks Me, Where do You go?"* is pointed out for purpose and reason. In fact, why did they not ask Him at this time where He was going inasmuch as they had asked twice before (Jn. 13:36; 14:5)?

(6) "BUT BECAUSE I HAVE SAID THESE THINGS UNTO YOU, SORROW HAS FILLED YOUR HEART."

The exegesis is:

1. The Cross of Christ is the yardstick, the measuring rod, and the plumb line, one might say, for everything that pertains to the Lord and His Word.

2. This is the alarming thing about the modern gospel, which is not the Gospel of the Cross of Christ, but something else altogether.

3. The Purpose Driven Life scheme is a case in point. It has been adopted by almost the entirety of the church world. Its widespread acceptance should be a warning sign that something is wrong. To be sure, something is wrong. The Christ they are promoting is a Crossless Christ.

SORROW!

The Disciples are not asking now simply because it seems they now are beginning to understand what He is saying, at least about leaving.

It seems they now know that He is speaking of going back to Heaven shortly! Therefore, it is beginning to come together for them as to His Crucifixion but, still, only dimly!

Sorrow fills their hearts at the prospect of this, especially considering that He will no longer be with them, at least in the flesh. They have not yet quite understood the Value of the Holy Spirit soon to come, though Jesus has spoken of Him several times, even in this dialogue. Jesus will now give them even greater information respecting the Holy Spirit and what He will do.

If one is to notice, their *"sorrow"* totally left upon the Advent of the Spirit of God (Acts, Chpt. 2).

(7) "NEVERTHELESS I TELL YOU THE TRUTH; IT IS EXPEDIENT FOR YOU THAT I GO AWAY: FOR IF I GO NOT AWAY, THE COMFORTER WILL NOT COME UNTO YOU; BUT IF I DEPART, I WILL SEND HIM UNTO YOU."

The exposition is:

1. The Bible does not teach sinless perfection, but it most definitely does teach that the *"sin nature is not to have dominion over us"* (Rom. 6:14).

2. The only way this dominion can be stopped is by the Believer abiding in God's Prescribed Order of Victory, as given in the Sixth Chapter of Romans.

3. Regrettably, not understanding the Sixth Chapter of Romans, the sin nature rules and reigns in most Christian lives. The only answer for this problem is the Cross of Christ.

THE TRUTH

The phrase, *"Nevertheless I tell you the truth; It is expedient for you that I go away,"* proclaims that the Mission and Ministry of the Holy Spirit to the Body of Christ depended upon the Return of Christ to the Father. This would signify that the great Work of Redemption had been carried out, with the sin debt paid and Heavenly Justice satisfied. This was what Jesus was sent to do, and it was what He did! With it finished, He would go back to the Father.

However, it was the Work and Business of the Holy Spirit to do four things in the world:

1. THE ANOINTING

The Holy Spirit would anoint the Followers of Christ to carry on the Work of Jesus as the Founder of the Church and to destroy the works of Satan. That pertained to the Anointing to preach the Gospel, to heal the sick, to cast out demons, and to destroy the works of the Evil One in general (Acts 1:4).

2. WORLD EVANGELISM

The Holy Spirit was to help the Followers of the Lord to take the Gospel of Jesus Christ to the entirety of the world (Acts 1:8). Jesus died for all of mankind, and all of mankind must know (Mk. 16:15).

That means that Bible Christianity is not a *"western Gospel,"* as some claim, but, in reality, is for the whole world (Jn. 3:16).

3. CONVICTION

The Holy Spirit was to convict the world of sin, Righteousness, and Judgment (Jn. 16:8-11).

The convicting Power of the Holy Spirit is a great part of His Office Work. He Alone can make the sinner aware of his great sin.

4. TO GLORIFY THE LORD JESUS CHRIST

The Holy Spirit will glorify Jesus, i.e., lift Jesus up as the Saviour of mankind, Baptizer with the Holy Spirit, Healer of the sick, Deliverer of those in bondage, and Coming King (Jn. 16:14).

THE COMFORTER

The phrase, *"For if I go not away, the Comforter will not come unto you,"* concerns the respective Office Work of both Jesus and the Holy Spirit — Jesus as Saviour of man and the Holy Spirit as the Power of the Church.

But if I depart, I will send Him unto you," presents a guarantee.

If one is to notice, Jesus uses personal pronouns respecting the Holy Spirit, showing that He is not merely an emanation of the Father, but rather the Third Person of the Divine Trinity (Mat. 28:19; II Cor. 13:14; I Jn. 5:7).

Actually, the Holy Spirit has been sent by both the Father and the Son (Lk. 24:49; Jn. 14:16, 26; 15:26; 16:7; Acts 2:33).

It certainly should be obvious that Jesus arrived in Heaven at the Ascension because the Holy Spirit was sent on the Day of Pentecost in such a glorious manner that it could not be denied. He has been here ever since!

The following Verses give to us His Office Work, at least in part, respecting the world and the Church.

Actually, the balance of the Chapter, especially the next few Verses, gives a compendium of Who the Holy Spirit is and What He does!

(8) "AND WHEN HE IS COME, HE WILL REPROVE THE WORLD OF SIN, AND OF RIGHTEOUSNESS, AND OF JUDGMENT:"

The exposition is:

1. The Story of the Bible is the Story of *"Jesus Christ and Him Crucified."*

2. The Bible, being the Word of God, is the supreme authority as to Faith and Doctrine. Nothing must contradict the Word of God.

3. Its subject is the Sufferings and Glories of Christ — His Sufferings as Sin Bearer (Phil. 2:6-10); His Glories as Sin Purger (Heb. 1:3).

THE COMING OF THE HOLY SPIRIT

The phrase, *"And when He is come,"* referred to the Day of Pentecost. He has remained here ever since.

As we have stated, the Holy Spirit has always been in the Earth. In truth, He has always been in every capacity because He is God. As such, He had no beginning and will have no ending. He is uncaused, unformed, unmade, and uncreated, even in the same capacity and essence as the Father and the Son.

Everything done is carried out by the entirety of the Godhead with perfect unity. But yet, each Member of the Godhead has His Particular Work, at least as it is described in the Word of God. As we have previously stated, perhaps the following simple explanation may shed some light on this extremely complex subject.

• God the Father is over all (Gen. 1:1).

• Jesus Christ, the Son of God, is the Architect of all things (Jn. 1:1-3).

- God the Holy Spirit is the One Who actually carries out the construction or doing of whatever is being addressed (Gen. 1:2).

However, the Coming of the Holy Spirit on the Day of Pentecost presents Him able to function in an entirely different manner due to what Christ did at Calvary and the Resurrection. He now has far greater latitude in which to work because there is now a group of people on Earth, whose number will grow year by year, who have no sin debt against them due to their Faith and trust in what Christ did at Calvary. As a result, the Holy Spirit is able to take up abode within the hearts and lives of each one of these Believers, creating a force and Power heretofore unknown in the world respecting the Work of God. It is that of which Jesus now speaks.

In other words, the entire complexion of all things would change. It would be and is the fulfillment of all the Prophecies of the past. As well, it would signal the beginning of the Church, at least in this fashion.

HE WILL REPROVE THE WORLD

The phrase, *"He will reprove the world,"* actually means that He will *"convict"* the world of certain things. The Greek word for *"reprove"* is *"Elegcho"* and means *"to convince, convict, refute, expose, to bring to shame the person reproved, concerning their sin."* This part of His Office Work is by far the most important. It is the first mention of Jesus, at least in this context, as far as the sinner is concerned.

In this part of His Work, He is not a *"Comforter"* as Jesus has mentioned several times, with that Work being possible only in the hearts and lives of Believers who have already accepted the Lord. So, His Basic Work is twofold, but yet, spreading in several directions.

HE CONVICTS THE WORLD OF SIN, RIGHTEOUSNESS, AND JUDGMENT

Without this, the sinner cannot be saved. In other words, every single person who has ever come to Christ was first convicted of their sin and need for Christ by the Holy Spirit as the Gospel, in some way, was presented to them.

This is what we mean by the statement, *"The convicting Power of the Holy Spirit."* When the Word of God is preached, sung, or presented in some manner, the Holy Spirit anoints that Word to the heart and life of the sinner, with him at that time coming under Conviction. The Holy Spirit pulls back the veil over the sinner's heart, exposing it, with him then seeing himself as he really is, lost without God.

The Conviction can be so powerful that the sinner at times will think if he does not come to God quickly, he will literally drop over into Hell at that very moment. I have seen sinners run down aisles of churches (and I mean literally run) or across grassy corridors in giant stadiums around the world as the Holy Spirit would begin to deal with them, convicting them of their sin. It was so powerful that they could not wait.

Also, as we have already stated, whenever the Christian sins, the Holy Spirit convicts him as well! If and when sin occurs in the life of the Believer, at that moment, fellowship with God stops, and the door of fellowship remains closed until the sin is handled.

At the moment the sin is committed, the Holy Spirit changes from His role as *"Comforter"* (Helper) to the Office Work of *"Conviction"* of sin. At that moment, the Christian is to confess his sin to the Lord (I Jn. 1:9), after which, fellowship will be instantly restored. So, the Holy Spirit not only convicts the world but Believers as well!

PREACHING WHICH DOES NOT BRING CONVICTION

Satan's business is to promote the type of preaching that does not bring any conviction at all. As well, as a part of the Office Work of the Holy Spirit is to convict of sin, likewise, a part of the responsibilities of the Preacher of the Gospel is to preach the Word in a way that it convicts. Many call this *"negative preaching,"* attempting to demean the effort. However, much of the Word of God, even in both Testaments, is in a negative sense even though it may be said in a positive way. Actually, if the preacher of the gospel never preaches the type of message which convicts, the Holy Spirit has little opportunity to convict people of sin, be they Believer or unbeliever. As well, to the one who demeans such preaching, I remind the reader that I have seen literally hundreds of thousands of people brought to a Saving Knowledge of Jesus Christ, and I exaggerate not. Consequently, the fruit of what I am saying, respecting souls being Saved, is obvious all over the world.

THE CHARISMATIC COMMUNITY

Many in the Charismatic community do not even believe in the convicting Power of the Holy Spirit as He convicts of sin, of Righteousness, and of Judgment. Consequently, they do not believe in preaching, which sets the stage for the Holy Spirit to perform this part of His Extremely Important Office Work. They call such preaching and Conviction, *"Condemnation."* As a result, they get very few people Saved in their efforts, by and large, having to practice their doctrine on those whom someone else has brought to Christ. To be frank, the Judaizers did the same thing in the Churches planted by the Apostle Paul. Their erroneous message brought no one to Christ, and they had to practice their wares on people who had already come to the Lord under the preaching of Paul. Actually, the Word of God in its entirety is designed by the Holy Spirit not only to comfort and console but, as well, to convict. To take that out is to deny it's very thrust.

BELIEVERS

Some so-called faith teachers claim that while the Holy Spirit might do this to the world, He does not function in this manner with Believers. However, I remind them, at least those to whom this fits, that even if that were true, which it is not, they would at least see some people Saved in their ministries, which is rarely the case. This tells me, that is, if the Bible is to be the yardstick, that the basic intent and thrust of their message is totally wrong. It convicts precious few, be they sinner or Saint!

I am trying to get the reader to see how important this is and, as well, how much that most churches have veered from this Way of the Spirit.

Some years ago, I was asked to preach one of the services at the National Religious Broadcasters Convention in Washington, D.C. I sought the Lord earnestly as to what I should deliver to these people.

I did my best that day and gave an Altar Call at the end of the message, to which some responded. However, the general consensus among the several thousands of preachers present that day was that such was crude, vulgar, little more than emotionalism, and should not be done.

Of course, there is no way to get people to Christ other than by that method. It is the Bible Way and the Way of the Holy Spirit, as is very obvious in Acts, Chapters 2 through 4.

The question must be asked as to the spiritual condition of the people who attend the churches pastored by such preachers.

THE BIBLE

Inasmuch as the Bible Way is little practiced, which gives the Holy Spirit little or no latitude at all, one can only conclude that most of the people who attend these churches are not really saved but, in fact, have only embraced a Christian philosophy. In other words, they have never been truly *"Born-Again."* They have mentally affirmed Christ, but that is about as far as it goes!

One Preacher said some time ago, *"Holy Spirit Conviction is as scarce as hen's teeth,"* and how right he was! It is scarce because the Gospel is little preached or the Ways of the Lord little subscribed. However, when the Word of God is preached under the Anointing of the Holy Spirit, there will be *"Conviction"* as well as *"comfort."*

A GREAT COMFORT TO BELIEVERS

The Holy Spirit comforts Believers. He does not comfort unbelievers. As Satan has no place in the Believer (or at least should not), likewise, the Holy Spirit has no place in the unbeliever. This means that every iota of strength, Power, Anointing, Leading, Guidance, direction, and provision provided to the Believer comes through the Person and Agency of the Holy Spirit. He helps us in all things, at least as we give Him latitude to do so.

However, I must quickly add that the degree of His Help is predicated solely upon several things. I speak of the desire of the Believer to please the Lord, his communion with the Lord in prayer, his study of the Word of God, and his devotion to the Lord. In truth, the Holy Spirit does not help Believers nearly as much as He desires simply because He is not allowed to do so. With most Believers, even Spirit-filled Believers, too often, there is little consecration or dedication to God. In other words, most are far more carnal than Spiritual. Self-will and the *"flesh"* too often dominate, which greatly hinders the Ability of the Holy Spirit to do what He desires to do and, in fact, has been sent to do!

However, when He is given latitude, there is absolutely nothing He cannot do, irrespective as to whom the Believer may be. He can turn weakness into strength, death into life, poverty into plenty, spiritual anemia into Spiritual Growth, worldliness into Spirituality, and bondage into freedom, in other words, all the things we need. He is there to develop *"Fruit"* in our lives (Gal. 5:22-23).

SIN, RIGHTEOUSNESS, AND JUDGMENT

The phrase, *"Of Sin, and of Righteousness, and of Judgment,"* presents the three great categories of thought, custom, and conduct. Reynolds says: *"These three themes represent the infinite need of the world, with it compelled to see that it is altogether in the wrong."*[1]

This tells us that *"sin,"* inasmuch as it was mentioned first by Jesus, is the root cause and reason for all the problems which beset the human family. Correspondingly, by the use of the word *"Righteousness,"* we are made to know that this is what the world must have but, in reality, is totally bankrupt, at least according to its own ability.

The word *"Judgment"* tells us that ultimately all will be judged by God. So, in simple words, Jesus has told us the cause, which is sin, the cure, which is Righteousness, and the result of not accepting the cure, which is Judgment.

Now, let us look at them one by one.

(9) *"OF SIN, BECAUSE THEY BELIEVE NOT ON ME:"*

The structure is:

NOTES

1. At the Last Supper, the Scripture says that Jesus *"laid aside His Garments"*: this spoke of His Incarnation when He laid aside the expression of His Deity while not losing the possession of His Deity.

2. *"And took a towel"*: this represented the service He would perform for mankind.

3. *"And girded Himself"*: when He laid aside His Garments of Deity, He then *"girded Himself"* with the mantle of humanity, i.e., the Incarnation.

4. *"After that He poured water into a basin"*: this represented the Holy Spirit working through the Master, carrying out the work of obedience regarding the Father's Will (Jn. 13:13-17).

SIN

As stated, the words, *"Of sin,"* proclaim Jesus dealing with this matter first because it is the cause of all problems in the Earth. Before anything can happen that is positive, the question of sin must be dealt with at the very outset. That is first and foremost!

The phrase, *"Because they believe not on Me,"* deals with two things:

1. Jesus is the One Who paid the sin debt at Calvary and, thereby, broke the grip of sin on the human family. As we have repeatedly stated, this problem is so acute, far beyond anything we could comprehend, that it took Jesus dying on Calvary to handle this matter. That is how serious and severe that sin was and is.

Consequently, it is only through Jesus and what He did at the Cross that sin can be addressed and cleansed. This means that all the religions of the world are false. It means that any way other than that which is prescribed in the Word of God, regarding the matter of addressing sin, is doomed to failure. This speaks of psychology or any type of philosophy! It is Jesus Who defeated Satan, thereby, breaking his hold on humanity; consequently, it is Jesus to Whom one must turn!

BELIEVE

2. The word *"believe"* has to do with Faith. However, it speaks totally and conclusively of Faith in Jesus and Jesus Alone!

Since Jesus came and died on Calvary and rose from the dead, the world is confronted with Who He is and What He did! Regrettably, most do not *"believe,"* and most will be eternally lost. However, for those who do believe, they will gain Eternal Life.

When one goes to the very heart of the matter, this Passage tells us that a person's wrong direction is not only the sin he or she commits but, as well, the rejection of Jesus Christ as the Only Solution for sin. So, in the final alternative, it is the sin of *"unbelief!"* Men either believe Christ as to Who He was and What He did and are Saved, or they do not believe Him and are eternally lost. It is on this basis that men will be judged.

The essence of all sin is unbelief, a refusal to surrender the heart and will to the Divine Will and Authority.

In effect, this Passage tells us that of all the wickedness and ungodliness in the world for all time, sin reaches its highest and most willful expression in unbelief toward Jesus Christ.

(10) "OF RIGHTEOUSNESS, BECAUSE I GO TO MY FATHER, AND YOU SEE ME NO MORE."

The construction is:

1. Faith in the Cross of Christ presents the manner in which a person is Born-Again.

2. Faith in the Cross of Christ brings one freedom from the dominion of the sin nature.

3. Faith in the Cross of Christ causes one to be united with Christ, burying one's past life forever.

RIGHTEOUSNESS

The words, *"Of Righteousness,"* proclaim what Christ freely imputes to the believing sinner upon simple Faith in Him. It is *"Righteousness,"* which is totally of God, and which has no origin whatsoever in the world. Actually, that which man must have in order for God to accept him can be found only in Christ.

This *"Righteousness"* is unattainable by obedience to any law, by any merit of man's own, or any other condition than that of Faith in Christ. The man who trusts in Christ becomes *"the Righteousness of God in Him"* (II Cor. 5:21). In Christ, he becomes all that God requires a man to be and all that he could never be in himself.

Abraham made the Word of God his own by the act of the mind and spirit, which is called Faith, and submitted himself to its control. Because Abraham accepted the Word of God by Faith, God accepted him on that basis as one who fulfilled the whole of His Requirements (Rom. 4:3).

WHAT IS THE DEFINITION OF RIGHTEOUSNESS?

The definition of Righteousness, believe it or not, is so simple that even a child can understand it. It simply means that which is *"right."* However, it must be understood, it's God's Definition of what is right instead of man's definition.

God's Definition is found in His Word. In fact, it is His Word all the way from Genesis 1:1 through Revelation 22:21.

Without being Born-Again and one placing one's Faith entirely in Christ and the Cross, the Righteousness of God cannot be had. It is impossible for fallen man to bring about such an attribute — literally impossible! But yet, it can be had, which we will momentarily address.

A lack of the Righteousness of God throughout the entirety of the world is the cause of all war, crime, and man's inhumanity to his fellowman. What little good there is in the world, that which is straight and honest, is there because of the few in the world who are truly Born-Again and, thereby, who truly have the Righteousness of God. Of course, the world does not recognize that at all and would never agree to such, but it is the truth.

HOW DOES ONE OBTAIN THE RIGHTEOUSNESS OF GOD?

There is only one way it can be obtained, and that is by the believing sinner evidencing Faith in Christ and what Christ did for us at the Cross. Upon such Faith, the Lord will impute to such a one a perfect, spotless, pure Righteousness, actually, the *"Righteousness of God"* (Rom. 4:3, 6, 11, 22; 10:6; Gal. 2:20-21; Phil. 3:9). Unfortunately, while correctly believing God for Salvation, in which a perfect, pure Righteousness is imputed to them, far too many Believers seem to forget the manner in which they got in is the manner in which they stay in. In other words, the believing Christian is to continue to place his or her Faith exclusively in Christ and the Cross just as the believing sinner. The Pure, Perfect Righteousness of God cannot be earned or merited, irrespective as to what may be done. It is freely imputed, which means freely given to those who express their Faith in Christ and the Cross. One might say that it's all in the Cross (Rom. 6:1-14; 8:1-11; Gal., Chpt. 5).

RELATIVE RIGHTEOUSNESS

Our Lord outlined this perfectly regarding His Parable of the Pharisee and the Publican (Lk. 18:9-14).

Jesus said that these two men, one a Pharisee and the other a Publican, *"Went up into the Temple to pray."* The Pharisee told the Lord, *"God, I thank You, that I am not as other men are, extortioners, unjust, adulterers, or even as this Publican"* (Lk. 18:10-11). This is what one would call *"relative righteousness."* In other words, *"Relative to this Publican back here, I am a very good man."* To be sure, his prayer did not sit well with the Lord, and neither will such a prayer sit well with the Lord, irrespective as to who prays it. Unfortunately, *"relative righteousness"* is rife in the Christian community. The word oftentimes is, *"Oh I've done some things, but I've never done that."* It is relative righteousness, which God will never honor.

WORKS RIGHTEOUSNESS

This Pharisee also told the Lord, *"I fast twice in the week, I give tithes of all that I possess"* (Lk. 18:12). In other words, he was depending on his *"good works,"* which he thought gave him a place and position with the Lord. It didn't!

IMPUTED RIGHTEOUSNESS

The Lord then said, *"And the Publican, standing afar off, would not lift up so much as his eyes unto Heaven, but smote upon his breast, saying, God be merciful to me a sinner."*

Jesus said, *"I tell you, this man went down to his house justified rather than the other: for every one who exalts himself shall be abased; and he who humbles himself shall be exalted"* (Lk. 18:13-14).

Unfortunately, the relative and works righteousness syndrome did not pass away with the Pharisee of old, but continues to play its havoc in the modern church. Let's say it this way:

THE CROSS AND RIGHTEOUSNESS

Anyone who places his Faith in anything except the Cross of Christ, always and without exception, concludes with self-righteousness, which God hates. In fact, it was self-righteousness that nailed Christ to the Cross.

In the Cross, there is no room for the Law, no room for works, etc. It is simple Faith in Christ and what He did for us at the Cross that got us in and keeps us in. Upon that simple exercise, if one would call it that, the Lord imputes and continues to impute a perfect, spotless Righteousness, the Righteousness of God.

(11) *"OF JUDGMENT, BECAUSE THE PRINCE OF THIS WORLD IS JUDGED."*

The diagram is:

1. Faith in the Cross of Christ causes the Believer to be co-raised with Him and to live in Him.

2. Faith in the Cross of Christ co-quickens or energizes the Believer by the Spirit of God.

3. Faith in the Cross of Christ provides one with forgiveness of all sin, past, present, and future, at least for those who will believe.

JUDGMENT

Part of the Ministry of the Holy Spirit is to convict men of sin. He convinces them of a spotless Righteousness in the Presence of God for them, and He warns them of the Judgment they must suffer if His Testimony is resisted.

The criteria for Judgment are always Christ and the Word of God. Everything, and I mean everything, must pass under the Judgment of the Word. In other words, is it Biblical?

The laws of the land must be made in that respect but, sadly, seldom are! Every ruling in the Church must be accordingly. Everything the Christian believes and every direction taken must be brought under the Judgment of the Word of God. As well,

Jesus is the Living Word, and what He did for us at the Cross determines the Judgment.

THE CROSS

Man's sins were judged at Calvary, at least for those who believe (Jn. 3:16). Upon Faith in Christ and what He did for us at the Cross, such sins can never be brought against the Believer again. They are forever gone, and that means all sin!

However, if the sinner does not avail himself of this privilege, he will ultimately stand at the Great White Throne Judgment and will give account even down to the smallest detail (Rev. 20:11-15).

So, we allow our sins to be judged in Christ, which rids us of them, or else, we will be judged, and without any recourse. All Salvation is in Christ and what He did for us at the Cross.

HUMANISTIC PSYCHOLOGY

Regrettably, the world has been so psychologized that it little believes in a coming Judgment. The idea that man is personally responsible for his wrongdoings is foreign to the psychological way, which claims that man is merely a victim of outward circumstances and, in reality, is morally good. The Bible teaches the very opposite!

Man is morally evil and, in fact, is born that way. It is called original sin. As such, he is not a victim, but rather the cause (Rom., Chpts. 1-3).

Consequently, the only hope for man is for him to be changed in his soul and spirit, which speaks of a wicked heart being made righteous by accepting Christ. As the wicked heart is changed, the external acts of sin begin to cease as well! This can only come about in Christ!

THE PRINCE OF THIS WORLD

The phrase, *"Because the Prince of this world is judged,"* speaks of Satan himself.

This refers to all of Satan's ways, his darkened direction, and his stranglehold on humanity. All have been judged by Christ as to the rightful cause of all the sorrow, sin, and heartache in the world.

The Judgment of the Prince of this world is also a fact lying outside the politics of the world, which may fume and rage as it will. It is beyond the reach of its philosophy or literature, or its courts or armies. Its fashions are the force of this world.

In other words, the sinful prince and spirit of the world is judged by the Lord Jesus and condemned.

As we have already stated, this means that at a point in time, the world and all in it will be judged.

As well, the Holy Spirit is here presently and has been since the Day of Pentecost. He is constantly commenting on this great Truth, which also points out right and wrong. In other words, the Holy Spirit stands as a Witness to Truth and a condemnation of lies.

Hare says: *"The entire conviction of Sin, Righteousness, and Judgment, must be the Work of the Holy Spirit; that all the objective facts, all the teaching of example, all the thunder of Prophecy, all the exposure of sin and wrongdoing, even as it was delineated by the Incarnation and Sacrifice of Christ, must as well be complimented by the Grace of the Holy Spirit on individuals, nations, and humanity at large."*[2]

Consequently, due to the Advent of the Spirit, even though this is the Day of Grace, it will go much harder for unbelievers of this particular time at the Judgment than for any other age. It must never be forgotten, Grace rejected is Judgment guaranteed!

(12) "I HAVE YET MANY THINGS TO SAY UNTO YOU, BUT YE CANNOT BEAR THEM NOW."

The overview is:

1. Noah built an Altar and worshipped. He worshipped God, not the Altar.

2. Paul did not worship the Cross as multitudes do today, but worshipped Him Who died upon it.

3. The *"Altar"* built by Noah and the sacrifices offered upon it were Symbols of Christ and what He would do to redeem the lost sons of Adam's fallen race.

THE NEW COVENANT

The phrase, *"I have yet many things to say unto you,"* pertained to the entirety of the New Covenant, the meaning of which would be given to the Apostle Paul, and the foundation had already been laid by Christ. In fact, Christ is the New Covenant, and the Cross, as stated, is the meaning of that Covenant.

The phrase, *"But you cannot bear them now,"* as stated, points to the foundation being laid, which was necessary, and which He would build thereon with the Advent of the Holy Spirit.

Until the Holy Spirit came, as He would shortly, the capacity of the Apostles to understand these great Truths was limited indeed! So, other than the foundation, there was very little purpose or reason to go further. The Holy Spirit would totally change this spiritual dullness very shortly.

(13) "HOWBEIT WHEN HE, THE SPIRIT OF TRUTH, IS COME, HE WILL GUIDE YOU INTO ALL TRUTH: FOR HE SHALL NOT SPEAK OF HIMSELF; BUT WHATSOEVER HE SHALL HEAR, THAT SHALL HE SPEAK: AND HE WILL SHOW YOU THINGS TO COME."

The exegesis is:

1. Every aspect of the structure of the Tabernacle of the Old Testament presented Christ in His Atoning, Mediatorial, and Intercessory Work.

2. Likewise, the Temple did the same, but with one difference.

3. Just as every whit of the Tabernacle symbolized the Glories attached to Christ and His First Advent, so all the dazzling splendor of the Temple prefigured the Glories of His coming Second Advent.

THE SPIRIT OF TRUTH

The phrase, *"Howbeit when He, the Spirit of Truth, is come, He will guide you into all Truth,"* proclaims the Holy Spirit as being Deity and, as well, along with the Father and the Son, the origin of Truth. However, as a part of His Office Work, He is, as well, the Guarantor of Truth.

In other words, He guides into all Truth, not just some Truth, hence, the inspiration of the entirety of the Word of God, which comes under His Portfolio, so to speak (II Pet. 1:20-21).

So, when one studies the Bible, one is studying that which the Holy Spirit has superintended, not only the genesis of the thought but, in fact, every Word. Of course, that is true if the Bible being used is a word for word translation, such as the King James (Mat. 4:4).

GUIDE

The word *"guide"* in the Greek text is *"Hodegeo"* and means *"to lead the way."* Therefore, we learn from this one word that it is not really possible to properly understand the Word of God without the help of the Holy Spirit. That is the reason the unsaved are bereft of this knowledge.

As well, if a Believer (and that means any Believer) will ask the Lord to give him understanding respecting the Word of God, the Holy Spirit has been obligated by Christ to do that very thing. Knowing this, one must wonder at the plethora of false doctrine that permeates the church! The reason is simple.

It is because the person has not asked the Lord for a proper understanding of the Word, desiring that it mold his thinking and doctrines, rather than his thinking and doctrines attempting to mold the Word. Inasmuch as it is a part of the Office Work of the Holy Spirit to help us understand Truth, there is no excuse for error!

THE HOLY SPIRIT WILL GLORIFY CHRIST

The phrase, *"For He shall not speak of Himself,"* tells us not only What He does but, as well, Whom He represents.

As the Fourteenth Verse proclaims, the Office and Ministry of the Holy Spirit is to glorify Christ. He does not speak of or from Himself, but He unveils to the Believer's heart the Glorious Perfections, Ministries, Offices, Graces, and Fullness of the Lord Jesus Christ.

In effect, all the Attributes of God belong to Christ, and it is the Spirit's Joy to declare and reveal these attributes.

Such being the nature and the limits of the Spirit's Ministry, all pretended revelations of the Spirit which do not throw light upon the Person of Christ as the Incarnate Word, and upon the Bible as the Written Word, are vain. Such pretended revelations are from the spirit of evil, which account for all the false religions of the world, and lead men into darkness, bondage, and death.

THE HOLY SPIRIT WILL SPEAK

The phrase, *"But whatsoever He shall hear, that shall He speak,"* does not pertain to lack of knowledge, as some think, but that He, as God, will *"hear"* only that which is from the Father, which means that it is absolutely certain of perfection. It is not diluted by human thought, thinking, or conjecture; consequently, everything He *"speaks"* is Truth and nothing but the Truth.

He *"speaks"* to the hearts of Believers constantly. All can be absolutely certain that whatever He says is perfectly right. As well, it will always coincide with His Word. If not, or even if there is the slightest variation, one can be certain that the error is not from the Holy Spirit but has come about because the person did not allow himself to be properly led by the Spirit.

Also, He speaks through Prophecy, Tongues and Interpretation, a Word of Knowledge, a Word of Wisdom, etc. He speaks constantly, in fact, in the preaching of the Gospel, at least that which is *"Truth."* As should be obvious, He cannot anoint (verify) error or sin!

HE WILL SHOW YOU THINGS TO COME

The phrase, *"And He will show you things to come,"* pertains to Prophecy, or as one might say, a *"Word of Wisdom,"* which makes up about one-third of the Bible.

These are events, whether predestined or predicted through foreknowledge, which can only be brought about by Deity. To my knowledge, there is no Prophecy whatsoever in any of the other so-called holy books of the major religions of the world.

These books, whatever they may be, are not holy because they are not of God but, in fact, are of Satan. Consequently, the writers of these books were not being inspired, had no semblance of Truth, and above all, could not predict the future. That alone is enough to guarantee the veracity of the Word of God.

When predictions are made concerning the future, the acid test of authenticity is then enjoined. On that premise alone, the Bible must be accepted as the Word of God.

One must consider that about one-half of the Prophecies have been fulfilled, with not one failing relative to its time frame. That within itself is of such outstanding moment that it defies description. Also, due to the fact that about one-half of the Prophecies have been fulfilled, that is a guarantee that the balance will be fulfilled in totality. To give an example on a personal basis, please allow me to relate the following:

THE WORD OF THE LORD

I was saved and baptized with the Holy Spirit at eight years of age. At that time and for several years, I was in a prayer meeting somewhere almost every day. At that tender age, I made an Altar out of an old log in a cope of woods behind our house, where I would frequent very often in seeking the Lord. Also, I would meet with several others at my grandmother's house or the home of my aunt.

During those times, the Lord began to speak to my heart concerning Ministry. He told me I would be an Evangelist and that this Ministry would be worldwide. In effect, He was doing exactly what was said that He would do, *"Showing me things to come!"*

Even as I dictate these notes, I believe the Lord has told me of certain things that are going to happen in the very near future. In fact, some of these things have already begun to happen. If He has spoken to my heart, despite the opposition or what others say, it will come to pass and, as stated, is already beginning to come to pass! All of this is through the Person and Ministry of the Holy Spirit. In fact, it is my belief that He desires to reveal many more things if Believers will only draw closer to the Lord.

(14) "HE SHALL GLORIFY ME: FOR HE SHALL RECEIVE OF MINE, AND SHALL SHOW IT UNTO YOU."

The exposition is:

1. The formula, *"form of Doctrine,"* found in Romans 6:17, is very important. It declares the Christian Faith to have been once for all delivered to Believers as fixed and complete, therefore, neither needing nor accepting additions.

2. Into that *"form,"* as into a mold, the Believers are poured or *"delivered."*

3. The two sides of that mold, so to speak, bring Justification regarding Salvation and Sanctification regarding life and living.

TO GLORIFY JESUS CHRIST

The phrase, *"He shall glorify Me,"* speaks of Jesus. The Greek word for *"glorify"* is *"deoxazo"* and means *"to give glory and honor, and to magnify."*

Why does the Holy Spirit do this?

The reason is simple! Jesus is the One Who paid the price for man's Redemption. He is the One Who went to the Cross; consequently, the entirety of man's Salvation is in Jesus. Inasmuch as He has done these things, He is the One to be glorified. However, there is another reason:

Due to what He did, His Name is above every name and carries the full weight of His Authority in the spirit world. As a result, Satan, every fallen Angel, and every demon spirit respond accordingly to that Name. Therefore, the Holy Spirit, constantly magnifying Him, proclaims to the whole of the spirit world that the entirety of the Godhead stands fully behind Jesus in His Redemption of mankind. Consequently, if the Holy Spirit is constantly glorifying Christ, then the Body of Christ surely should do the same. Jesus is the Epicenter of all! He does not merely contain Salvation, He is Salvation! He does not merely contain Life, He is Life!

All that Jesus has done in His Earthly Ministry is guaranteed by the Holy Spirit; consequently, not a one of these great Victories will ever be lost!

THE HOLY SPIRIT WILL PORTRAY THESE GREAT TRUTHS

The phrase, *"For He shall receive of Mine, and shall show it unto you,"* proclaims these great Victories of which I have just spoken.

If the Believer is sincere before the Lord, the Holy Spirit will show him the wonders of Redemption purchased at Calvary, the glory of Justification and Sanctification by Faith, along with Divine healing and the infilling of the Holy Spirit, in other words, every single Victory that Christ purchased at Calvary and the Resurrection.

(15) *"ALL THINGS THAT THE FATHER HAS ARE MINE: THEREFORE SAID I, THAT HE SHALL TAKE OF MINE, AND SHALL SHOW IT UNTO YOU."*

The exposition is:

1. When Paul said, *"That I may know Him"* (Phil. 3:10), he was speaking of knowing Christ in a particular way — the Way of the Cross.

2. When he spoke of *"the Power of His Resurrection"* (Phil. 3:10), he was not speaking of the coming Resurrection of Life, but rather how to live this Resurrection Life now.

3. When he spoke of *"the fellowship of His Sufferings"* (Phil. 3:10), he was speaking of us entering into the great price that Jesus paid at Calvary, which affords us victory over the world, the flesh, and the Devil. It all pertains to the Cross of Christ.

JESUS CLAIMED ABSOLUTE COMMUNITY WITH GOD THE FATHER

The phrase, *"All things that the Father has are Mine,"* portrays Jesus claiming absolute community with God. Here is a wonderful glimpse into the interrelations of the Godhead.

Reynolds said: *"The 'Mine' of this phrase is declared to embrace something more than the mystery of His Person and Sacrifice. 'All that the Father has,' is a powerful statement indeed! All His fullness of Being, all the treasures of wisdom and knowledge, all the power, all the effulgence of the Glory of the Father, of the human race, and of all things, 'are Mine.'"*[3]

The phrase, *"Therefore said I, that He shall take of Mine, and shall show it unto you,"* proclaims the Holy Spirit communicating heavenly facts to earthly pilgrims. The Disciples had seen the moral Glory of Christ on Earth; the Holy Spirit would unfold to them His Divine Glories in that which belonged to Him as Jehovah's Fellow.

Calvin said concerning Jesus, *"We see how the greater part of men deceive themselves; for they pass by Christ, and go out of the way to seek God by circuitous paths."*[4]

Reynolds said: *"In these Verses we have

a very abundant exhibition of the unity of the Father, Son, and Holy Spirit, coupled with a very remarkable setting forth of the tripersonality."[5]

THE VERACITY OF THE WORDS OF JESUS

The tremendous, even miraculous difference, which is obvious in the Apostles after the Day of Pentecost, portrays to all the veracity of the Words of Jesus. The Holy Spirit has done His Work well, as He will do with any and all who properly consecrate to the Lord.

However, I will warn the reader that Satan will oppose the efforts of the Holy Spirit as nothing else to keep men from receiving from Him. Almost always, He does so through the church, i.e., *"apostate church."*

Religious hierarchy oftentimes claims to be the sole recipient of such truth and will then pass it down to the underlings. Some promote the idea that God no longer speaks to men, while others claim that God may hear some, but not you!

All these claims are pure fabrications. If you will believe Him, irrespective as to whom you may be, the Lord will meet you and will do for you exactly what He said He would do. No Believer has to go through intermediaries, or anyone else, for that matter. You can seek the Lord personally, and He will deal with you personally.

(16) "A LITTLE WHILE, AND YOU SHALL NOT SEE ME: AND AGAIN, A LITTLE WHILE, AND YOU SHALL SEE ME, BECAUSE I GO TO THE FATHER."

The structure is:

1. Under the old Law, there were five great Offerings: the Burnt-Offering, the Meal-Offering, the Trespass-Offering, the Peace-Offering, and the Sin-Offering (Lev., Chpts. 1-7).

2. God only accepted such Offerings as He Himself ordained.

3. The worshipper, imperfect and sinful in himself, was accepted in the perfection of the Offering. In other words, the Priest did not look at the offerer, but rather the Offering. Likewise, God doesn't really look at us, but rather His Son, the Lord Jesus Christ, and our Faith in Him and His Sacrifice.

NOTES

THE ASCENSION

The phrase, *"A little while, and you shall not see Me,"* refers to the Ascension of Christ, which would take place in about 44 days. However, as we shall see, the Disciples did not understand that of which Jesus then spoke.

THE HOLY SPIRIT

The phrase, *"And again, a little while, and you shall see Me,"* refers to the Coming of the Holy Spirit, Who would be sent back by Christ. As well, the Godhead is so much of the same essence that even though Their Office Work may differ, still, to see One is to see the Other.

For instance, Jesus told Philip when he asked to see the Father, *"When you have seen Me, you have seen the Father,"* in other words, *"I am a Perfect Replica of the Father"* (Jn. 14:8-9). In a sense, it is the same with the Holy Spirit.

A part of the Office Work of the Holy Spirit is to so mirror Christ and so glorify Him that Jesus is seen beautifully and perfectly in the Holy Spirit.

I dare say, and I do not think I am wrong, that the Apostles saw Jesus far more perfectly as He was presented by the Holy Spirit than when they were with Him in the flesh. Having the Holy Spirit in them, within itself, proclaims a union similar to the Godhead, and it is actually meant to be. This opens up the possibility of instruction to a degree heretofore unknown. So, the knowledge of Jesus after His Ascension and the Coming of the Holy Spirit greatly exceeded the previous time, which I think is obvious.

As well, please allow me to speak once again of the desired union of the Godhead with the Body of Christ.

THE SIMILARITY

No! In no way is the statement just made meant to proclaim or even hint that Believers will ultimately grow into godhood, as the Mormons teach. That is blatant error!

However, it is meant to proclaim that we are to be so Christlike that when people see us, they actually see Jesus! He is in us for that very purpose (Jn. 14:20).

I GO TO THE FATHER

The phrase, *"Because I go to the Father,"* in essence, proclaims several things:

• His going back to the Father means that this Great Plan of Redemption is completed, at least as it pertains to its inception.

• Having done that, thereby making it possible for man to be totally washed of all sin, the Holy Spirit can now come and, in fact, will now be sent by Both the Father and Christ.

• Actually, the real purpose of the Born-Again experience is that in Jesus, *"We might be built together for an Habitation of God through the Spirit"* (Eph. 2:22).

I think even the Church, which includes all true Believers, does not fully realize the impact the Holy Spirit has had on this world since His Coming on the Day of Pentecost. The *"Former Rain,"* as prophesied by Joel, touched the far greater majority of the civilized world in the time of the Early Church. Regrettably, in the Second Century, the church began to apostatize as the Holy Spirit was given less and less latitude. Due to the fact that all the Apostles and those who knew them had now gone on to Glory, the Holy Spirit was finally pushed out almost altogether, with men gaining preeminence, which ushered in the Dark Ages.

THE BOOK OF ACTS

Let it be ever understood that the Book of Acts is to serve as the criterion for the Church. In other words, we are to imitate it in every respect. If our church does not reflect the Book of Acts experience in totality, then we cannot honestly say that we have a Bible Church. It becomes quite obvious that the apostatized church, which ultimately came to be called the Catholic church, had no similarity whatsoever to the Early Church.

And then, the great Outpouring of the Holy Spirit at the turn of the Twentieth Century ushered in what Joel referred to as the *"Latter Rain"* (Joel 2:23).

At present, which I believe is very near the coming Rapture of the Church, there are approximately 100,000,000 people in the world who have been baptized with the Holy Spirit with the evidence of speaking with other Tongues (Acts 2:4). Regrettably, for the most part, I think it will be found that the churches attended by these people don't have a strong resemblance to the church portrayed in the Book of Acts, but it certainly should! To be sure, the part of the modern church which resembles the Early Church is responsible for most Conversions to Christ, lives changed, sick bodies healed, and demon spirits defeated. However, allow me to quickly say that in no way am I touting particular church denominations, but rather the Holy Spirit and, more perfectly, the Lord Jesus Christ.

THE HOLY SPIRIT

Regrettably, the part of the Christian community that has rejected the example of the Early Church has almost altogether denied the Holy Spirit and, consequently, accomplishes very little for the Cause of Christ. That is blunt, but I believe it to be true!

To be sure, the Holy Spirit having latitude to work in hearts and lives has brought the Kingdom of God to a greater visibility than ever before in history. Even though it will not change the world, that awaiting the Second Coming of the Lord, still, every iota of prosperity and freedom enjoyed anywhere in the world today has come about as a result of the Holy Spirit occupying the hearts and lives of Believers. This has influenced the world greatly in every positive way. Let me give you an example:

At the Rapture, every Born-Again person on the face of the Earth will be taken instantly to be with the Lord. When the true Church is taken away in the Rapture and this powerful influence is gone, society will experience an instantaneous degeneration, which will introduce the Antichrist. To use this nation as an example, America then, minus every Blood-bought Believer, will not even be recognizable as the nation the world once knew. That is how strong, powerful, influential, and effective the Holy Spirit has been (I Thess. 4:16-17).

Some teach that the Holy Spirit will be taken out at the Rapture as well. However, that is completely unscriptural inasmuch as He will continue in this Earth as always, at least since the Day of Pentecost, drawing souls to Jesus Christ (Acts 2:17-21). But yet, considering that the Earth will lose all Born-Again Believers at the Rapture, and do so instantly, one can well imagine the effect that will be instantly felt, despite the fact that other people will continue to be saved.

(17) "THEN SAID SOME OF HIS DISCIPLES AMONG THEMSELVES, WHAT IS THIS THAT HE SAID UNTO US, A LITTLE WHILE, AND YOU SHALL NOT SEE ME: AND AGAIN, A LITTLE WHILE, AND YOU SHALL SEE ME: AND, BECAUSE I GO TO THE FATHER?"

The construction is:

1. The prayer of Jabez was as follows:
2. *"Bless me"*: we learn from all of this that the Lord desires that we ask Him to bless us in every capacity.
3. *"Enlarge my coasts"*: the word *"coasts"* actually means *"borders."* In other words, Jabez was asking the Lord to get him out of this problem into which he had been born.
4. *"That Your Hand might be with me"*: the way this is given speaks of the Right Hand of God, which is the Hand of Blessing and Power.
5. *"That You should keep me from evil, that it may not grieve me"*: this, in effect, is the same prayer that Jesus told us all to pray when He said, *"And lead us not into temptation, but deliver us from evil"* (Mat. 6:13).

THE NECESSITY OF THE HOLY SPIRIT

The phrase, *"Then said some of His Disciples among themselves,"* proclaims their confusion in that they had no idea what He was saying.

Even though every single thing He mentioned is found in the Old Testament, to which they had access, still, not having the Holy Spirit in them, which they would have after the Day of Pentecost, their understanding of the Word of God was weak, to say the least!

Also, they continued to have it in their minds that Jesus was at that time going to *"restore again the Kingdom to Israel"* (Acts 1:6).

THE QUESTION

The question, *"What is this that He said unto us, A little while, and you shall not see Me: and again, a little while, and you shall see Me: and, Because I go to the Father?"* proclaims by their attitude this great thing Jesus was about to do was totally lost unto them at that moment.

Allow us to say it again! Even though these were Saved men, still, without the Holy Spirit, it is easy to see the foolish things they proposed, having absolutely no foundation in the Word of God. Regrettably, their modern counterparts do the same!

While the Born-Again person definitely does have the Holy Spirit within him, still, it is my personal belief, and I think the Scripture backs me up, that without the Baptism with the Holy Spirit according to Acts 2:4, the Spirit of God is pretty well limited to the Regeneration process. Now, that within itself is a Miracle of astounding proportions. However, the Holy Spirit doesn't want to stop with the Regeneration process but desires to do all within our hearts and lives that only He can do. That takes the Baptism with the Holy Spirit, which is always and without exception accompanied by the speaking with other Tongues as the Spirit of God gives the utterance (Acts 1:4; 8:14-17; 9:17; 10:44-47; 19:1-7). It is again my personal belief that without this great Baptism, which is evidenced in the Book of Acts, very little is going to truly be done for the Lord. That is why the Scripture says:

"And, being assembled together with them, Commanded them that they should not depart from Jerusalem, but wait for the Promise of the Father, which, said He, you have heard of Me.

"For John truly baptized with water; but you shall be baptized with the Holy Spirit not many days hence" (Acts 1:4-5).

That command is still incumbent upon Believers presently.

In other words, He was saying, *"Don't go try to witness for Me, try to build Churches, or even have services until you are first baptized with the Holy Spirit."* What the Holy Spirit can do and desires to do within the heart and the life of the Believer can only be brought about by the Holy Spirit Baptism.

(18) "THEY SAID THEREFORE, WHAT IS THIS THAT HE SAID, A LITTLE WHILE? WE CANNOT TELL WHAT HE SAYS."

The diagram is:

1. Men never reject the Cross on theological grounds but always on moral grounds.

2. By using the term, *"Theological grounds,"* we are meaning that it is too difficult to understand. The truth is, the Message of the Cross can be understood by anyone, even little children.

3. One of the reasons that it's hard for most to understand it is simply because they have to unlearn so much error that they have been taught before the Truth can be made real to them.

WE CANNOT TELL WHAT HE SAYS

The question, *"They said therefore, What is this that He said, A little while?"* presents a question which will no longer be asked after the Day of Pentecost. They would then know, not merely by the passing of events, but would have full understanding respecting the entirety of the Plan of God, which the Holy Spirit would make very real to them.

The phrase, *"We cannot tell what He says,"* sadly and regrettably, characterizes most of the modern church as well!

Considering that these men at that time did not have the Holy Spirit within them, whereas those in the modern church do, or else, are supposed to, why don't they understand?

The reason for all error respecting false doctrine, deception, and false Apostles is because the Holy Spirit is given little or no latitude at all. Please bear with the repetition; however, it is so important that I feel it must be said over and over.

ALL THE LIGHT THEY KNEW

There was a time that the Lord used some of the old-line Churches (many years ago), even though they did not believe in the Baptism with the Holy Spirit with the evidence of speaking with other Tongues (Acts 2:4). Actually, they really didn't even know anything about the Baptism with the Holy Spirit. And yet, great Moves of God took place in those particular times, with hundreds of thousands swept into the Kingdom of God. The Lord used them simply because they were walking in all the Light they knew, and they loved the Lord very much. However, at the turn of the Twentieth Century, the Holy Spirit, in response to seeking hearts, began to be poured out all over the world. Even then, and for several decades, the Lord continued to use many of the Preachers who had not been baptized with the Holy Spirit, even though they were definitely Saved.

Nevertheless, as more and more Light was given respecting the Holy Spirit, less and less were those used who opposed the Moving and Operation of the Holy Spirit.

THE CAMPMEETING HOUR

In January, 1969, having felt led of the Lord to do so, we initiated the beginning of our daily radio program, *"The Campmeeting Hour."* This was a program aired Monday through Friday, which was only 15 minutes in duration for each program.

At that time, the Lord gave me instructions to teach on the Holy Spirit, which I did over a network of some 600 radio stations daily. Of course, I was not the only one. There were others being led of the Lord, in whatever capacity, to do the same thing. As a result, literally hundreds of thousands of Baptists, Methodists, Presbyterians, etc., were baptized with the Holy Spirit with the evidence of speaking with other Tongues.

However, at about that time, or even a little before, it seemed as if the Holy Spirit drew the line. Much of the leadership of these old-line denominations took a stand against the Holy Spirit in the most negative ways. Many went so far as to label it as *"of the Devil!"* From that time, these denominations, despite a wealth of religious machinery, have been less and less used by the Lord. At the present time, precious little is being done for the Cause of Christ in those circles. The answer is simple. Light rejected is Light refused and then withdrawn.

As stated at the beginning, there was a time they walked in all the Light they had; however, more Light was given, but many refused to walk in that Light. As a result, most all semblance of the Moving and Operation of the Holy Spirit in any capacity has ceased in those circles.

THE PENTECOSTAL DENOMINATIONS

The Church world is now faced with another dilemma in that some of the major Pentecostal denominations, who once were mightily used of God because of their reliance on the Holy Spirit, are now, sadly and regrettably, forsaking such in favor of the wisdom of men. In other words, they are Pentecostal, at least for the most part, in name only!

As many in the old-line religious denominations refused the Light of the Spirit of God when offered to them, many in the modern Pentecostal denominations have turned away from that Light as well! The results are the same: spiritual stagnation, with almost nothing done for Christ.

Much, if not all, of the time spiritual pride is the culprit. Many in the old-line denominations did not want to admit that there was something more than what they presently had. Many in the modern Pentecostal denominations have become lifted up in pride because of the Blessings of the Lord. In other words, they forgot Who the Author of those Blessings was. Even though it went in different directions, pride is mostly the foundation of cause in both situations.

THE HOLY SPIRIT

When the Saints turn away from the Holy Spirit, and rather seek the wisdom of pitiful men, they lose all that He does. In other words, inasmuch as He is rejected, He cannot lead into all Truth, with the end results being that lies are now embraced. In other words, as the Disciples of old, *"We cannot tell what He* (the Lord) *says!"*

That is the reason for the deception, false doctrine, false apostles, and acceptance of that which is not of the Lord. Little discernment remains.

I will say it again: the Holy Spirit does all things on Earth pertaining to the Godhead, in other words, everything goes through Him. Therefore, when the Holy Spirit is rejected in any capacity, spiritual catastrophe is the result!

The church must come back to dependence on the Holy Spirit, Who will always lead men back to the Bible. This will guarantee His Moving and Operation, with great

NOTES

things being done. Thank God, there is a hunger in the hearts and lives of some for the Truth, which always originates with the Holy Spirit. I want Him! I want what He does! I want to actively seek His Leading and Guidance in all things.

I also know that all things which He gives will be identical to that which was given in the Book of Acts. In other words, the earmarks will be the same. If it is not, then it is not of the Spirit, but rather of man and, consequently, worthless!

THE CROSS OF CHRIST

The first thing that the Spirit of God will do in hearts and lives, who truly desire Him, is to lead the Believer back to the Cross. The Cross of Christ is the Foundation on which all Biblical Truth resides. In fact, it is the Cross which gave and gives the Holy Spirit the latitude to do all that He does (Rom. 6:1-14; 8:1-11). To be sure, the Holy Spirit leading the Church to the Cross is not new. It has always been that way.

Martin Luther said, *"As one viewed the Cross, so they viewed the Reformation."*

The Cross of Christ is the Foundation and if that Foundation be removed or destroyed, what can the righteous do (Ps. 11:3)? In fact, I personally believe that THE MESSAGE OF THE CROSS is what the Holy Spirit is presently saying to the churches (Rev. 3:22).

(19) "NOW JESUS KNEW THAT THEY WERE DESIROUS TO ASK HIM, AND SAID UNTO THEM, DO YOU INQUIRE AMONG YOURSELVES OF THAT I SAID, A LITTLE WHILE, AND YOU SHALL NOT SEE ME: AND AGAIN, A LITTLE WHILE, AND YOU SHALL SEE ME?"

The overview is:

1. The Cross of Christ is the Gospel of Jesus Christ and, in fact, always has been (I Cor. 1:17).

2. As stated, the Cross of Christ is the Foundation of every Bible Doctrine.

3. In fact, this is where all error begins. It is when the Cross of Christ is ignored.

THE CONFUSION OF THE DISCIPLES

The phrase, *"Now Jesus knew that they were desirous to ask Him, and said unto them,"* does not present us with quite enough information to know if He overheard them or was informed by the Holy Spirit regarding their confusion. However, there is a tiny insinuation in the Greek text that the Spirit of the Lord informed Him.

The question, *"Do you inquire among yourselves of that I said, A little while, and you shall not see Me: and again, a little while, and you shall see Me?"* addresses exactly their thoughts. However, Jesus continues to speak to them in a veiled way regarding His Statement.

Why did He not reduce His Terminology to the level they could understand?

ONCE AGAIN, THE HOLY SPIRIT

In effect, He had made it very clear to them concerning His Leaving and the Holy Spirit coming to take His Place. However, due to the fact that the Holy Spirit had not yet come, at least in this fashion, they had little spiritual capacity to really understand much of anything concerning spiritual matters. But yet, and as we have stated several times, that would be remedied shortly.

As well, they were still so taken up with Him immediately restoring Israel that they could little see past their error.

Such is the problem in the hearts and lives of many Believers. In some facet of their Christian experience, many have an erroneous concept of some particular Doctrine, etc. As such, that error clouds everything they think, and to a measure, even dilutes the Truth which they do possess. That is the reason that following the Holy Spirit and allowing Him to have total control within our lives is absolutely imperative, that is, if we are to fully follow Jesus. However, that takes consecration to the Lord, which, regrettably, precious few actually have.

(20) "VERILY, VERILY, I SAY UNTO YOU, THAT YOU SHALL WEEP AND LAMENT, BUT THE WORLD SHALL REJOICE: AND YOU SHALL BE SORROWFUL, BUT YOUR SORROW SHALL BE TURNED INTO JOY."

The exegesis is:

1. The Cross of Christ would change everything for the Disciples and for you and me as well.

NOTES

2. Every Bible Doctrine is built squarely on the Message of the Cross.

3. If any doctrine is not built squarely on the Foundation of the Cross of Christ, then, in some way, it is in error.

THE CRUCIFIXION

The phrase, *"Verily, verily, I say unto you, that you shall weep and lament,"* had to do with His Crucifixion, which would take place the very next day.

The reason for their weeping and lamentation is obvious. However, to a great extent, it would be because of failure to understand what was really being done. Once again, I emphasize that they were still looking for an earthly kingdom, which the Death of Jesus would nullify, with them sinking into a morass of confusion and hurt.

The phrase, *"But the world shall rejoice,"* spoke of the system of the world, which is evil. However, the main point is that Jesus is likening the religious leaders of Israel to the *"world"* and, therefore, not of God.

Pharisaism will exult that this demand for a higher Righteousness than its own is forever hushed. Sadduceeism will rejoice at this troublesome witness to unseen and eternal things being forever silenced, or so they think! The religious hierarchy will boast that now no danger prevails of the Romans taking away their place and Nation.

Actually, the world will applaud this deed of blood; however, they will not applaud long!

THE APOSTATE CHURCH

In a personal way and, of course, very small in comparison to that of Christ, I know what it is for the church to join with the world in their effort of destruction just as they did with Jesus! Consequently, that spirit is not dead but still very much alive. In truth, the apostate church, as Israel was then and many are at present, is of the same spirit as the system of the world because it all comes from the same source, Satan. Actually, there is nothing more wicked, even as the Crucifixion of Christ proved!

The phrase, *"And you shall be sorrowful, but your sorrow shall be turned into joy,"* pertains to His Resurrection, which would bring great *"joy."*

(21) "A WOMAN WHEN SHE IS IN TRAVAIL HAS SORROW, BECAUSE HER HOUR IS COME: BUT AS SOON AS SHE IS DELIVERED OF THE CHILD, SHE REMEMBERS NO MORE THE ANGUISH, FOR JOY THAT A MAN IS BORN INTO THE WORLD."

The exposition is:

1. In the Fifteenth Chapter of I Corinthians, the Apostle proclaims in detail the certitude of the Resurrection.

2. A definition of the Gospel is given us in Verses 3 and 4 of this Fifteenth Chapter of I Corinthians. It is the Atonement and the Resurrection of our Lord Jesus Christ.

3. These two Doctrines, what Jesus accomplished at the Cross and His Resurrection, present the Foundation Stones of the Gospel, so to speak.

TRAVAIL

The phrase, *"A woman when she is in travail has sorrow, because her hour is come,"* speaks of the pain which accompanies the birth of a child.

Jesus uses this analogy to teach a very important lesson.

There is really no way that anything worthwhile for the Lord can be done without this *"travail."*

The Greek word for *"travail"* is *"tikto"* and means *"to beget,"* which is explained by the birthing process. It is an excellent analogy!

The Lord has so designed His Work on Earth in that He allows Believers to have a part in that which He does, a big part, I might quickly add! He first plants the seed in the heart of the one whom He chooses for whatever particular task. Consequently, a burden is given to the individual respecting this particular work, with *"travail"* increasing steadily until, ultimately, the seed is born. This speaks of travailing prayer, even to the point at times of pain. Regrettably, there are not many at the present time who live close enough to the Lord for Him to use in this respect. The Believer must have a strong prayer life, which is not too obvious in many. As a result, very little is done for God, despite all the religious machinery with all its motion, etc.

NOTES

JOY

The phrase, *"But as soon as she is delivered of the child, she remembers no more the anguish, for joy that a man is born into the world,"* tells us two things:

1. Speaking in the spiritual sense, ultimately, the child, i.e., particular Work of God, will be born.

2. When it is born, because it is totally of the Spirit, it will bring great *"joy"* to many. As well, the *"travail"* of the birthing process will be forgotten when the great Work of God comes to fruition.

(22) "AND YOU NOW THEREFORE HAVE SORROW: BUT I WILL SEE YOU AGAIN, AND YOUR HEART SHALL REJOICE, AND YOUR JOY NO MAN TAKES FROM YOU."

The exposition is:

1. In Romans 8:23, we are told that we now have only the *"Firstfruits of the Spirit,"* which refers to the fact that all that Jesus did at the Cross is not available to us yet.

2. We will have the balance at the Resurrection.

3. In Romans 8:23, it tells us that the struggle of Faith is ever with us while we wait for the Redemption of the body, i.e., *"the Resurrection."*

SORROW AND REJOICING

The phrase, *"And you now therefore have sorrow,"* proclaims what was taking place at that very moment in the hearts of the Disciples.

Putting aside His Own Sorrows and Joys in this night of betrayal, He speaks of their sorrows and joys. When He meets His People by-and-by, His Joy will be immeasurably beyond ours, but here, in His Grace, He speaks of their joy in that day. Such is the Perfect and Unselfish Love of that Sinless Bosom.

THE RESURRECTION

The phrase, *"But I will see you again,"* speaks of His Resurrection. However, it seems that during this three days and nights of spiritual blackness while Jesus was in the Tomb, no one remembered these words. This much is certain: no one expected Him to rise from the dead. Therefore, if they remembered this Statement at all, they did not equate it with Resurrection.

The phrase, *"And your heart shall rejoice, and your joy no man takes from you,"* proved to be exactly the case.

Even though He would ascend back to the Father 40 days after His Resurrection, the Scripture plainly projects their joy as not being weakened at all because the Holy Spirit would descend on the Day of Pentecost. This, in effect, would give them a measure of joy they had never experienced before.

(23) "AND IN THAT DAY YOU SHALL ASK ME NOTHING. VERILY, VERILY, I SAY UNTO YOU, WHATSOEVER YOU SHALL ASK THE FATHER IN MY NAME, HE WILL GIVE IT YOU."

The structure is:

1. Jesus died on the Cross not only to address the sins of the sinner but, as well, the failures of the Righteous.

2. If the Believer does sin, we have an Advocate with the Father, Who is Jesus Christ the Righteous (I Jn. 2:1).

3. *"And He is the Propitiation* (satisfaction) *for our sins: and not for ours only, but also for the sins of the whole world"* (I Jn. 2:2).

AND IN THAT DAY

The phrase, *"And in that day,"* speaks of the Day of Pentecost and forward.

This is the reason that Jesus *"Commanded them that they should not depart from Jerusalem, but wait for the Promise of the Father"* (Acts 1:4). That *"day"* continues up to this moment and will continue to the Second Coming.

The phrase, *"You shall ask Me nothing,"* begins the manner of prayer in which Believers must engage, but yet, far, far more!

So, even though it is perfectly proper for Believers to praise Jesus constantly, according to this very Text, it is not proper to pray directly to Jesus. As we shall see, there is a reason for that.

ASK THE FATHER IN THE NAME OF JESUS

The phrase, *"Verily, Verily, I say unto you, Whatsoever you shall ask the Father in My Name, He will give it you,"* spells out exactly how the manner of prayer should be. We are to petition the Father in the Name of Jesus.

However, in these instructions, He placed them, as well as all Believers, in direct relationship with the Father as enjoying the same access as He Himself enjoyed. Further, the Holy Spirit would be so effective a Teacher (I Jn. 2:27) that He would answer all questions, if profitable.

As well, He gives us His Own Name as the Authority through which all needs could be met. However, He pointed out that it would not be necessary for Him to urge the Father to grant our petitions, for neither He nor we would appeal to an unwilling ear.

All Blessing from the Father comes in His (Jesus') Name. It is in His Name that the Holy Spirit has been sent by the Father. In effect, the Father has committed all things unto Him.

"In His Name" means in harmony with His Being and Will in furtherance of His Glory.

(24) "HITHERTO HAVE YOU ASKED NOTHING IN MY NAME: ASK, AND YOU SHALL RECEIVE, THAT YOUR JOY MAY BE FULL."

The synopsis is:

1. There are two ways proposed in the Bible. One is man's way, and the other is God's Way.

2. Man's way is the activity of law and works. God's Way is the hearing of the Gospel and believing it.

3. These two methods are opposed. The Spirit is not received by legal works of any nature but by listening Faith, so to speak.

IN THE NAME OF JESUS

The phrase, *"Hitherto have you asked nothing in My Name,"* simply refers to the fact that while Jesus was with them, they asked Him Personally, which would not have necessitated the use of His Name.

As well, the Disciples at the time of His Earthly sojourn did not fully appreciate or understand the meaning of the Name *"Jesus."* After the Day of Pentecost, their understanding would blossom into full flower because the Holy Spirit would reveal, even in a short time, what that Name actually meant.

In fact, when Peter preached on the Day of Pentecost, which resulted in about 3,000 people being Saved, he would tell them, *"Repent, and be baptized every one of you in the Name* (by the authority of) *of Jesus Christ for the remission of sins* (because your sins have already been remitted), *and you shall receive the Gift of the Holy Spirit"* (Acts 2:38).

A day or so after that when Peter and John went up together into the Temple at the hour of prayer, they were sought after by a lame man for alms.

Peter said to him, *"Silver and gold have I none; but such as I have give I to you: in the Name of Jesus Christ of Nazareth rise up and walk"* (Acts 3:6).

When questioned by the religious authorities concerning this great Healing, Peter answered saying, *"And His Name through Faith in His Name has made this man strong"* (Acts 3:16).

THE POWER OF THE NAME OF JESUS

The Holy Spirit had revealed to Peter in that short period of time just exactly how powerful the Name of Jesus actually was and is. Peter, no doubt, at this time, remembered the things that Jesus had said unto them concerning this very thing. However, it took the Holy Spirit to fully reveal the Power and Glory of what Jesus was actually speaking.

The phrase, *"Ask, and you shall receive, that your joy may be full,"* actually places the Believer in his relationship to the Father on a par with Jesus Christ, God's Only Son. However, it is to always be remembered that this is strictly by Grace, all made possible by the Cross. As well, the Holy Spirit is the One Who empowers us to use that Name, with Him guaranteeing its results.

In all of the Godhead, why is the Name of Jesus so important?

The Lord had referred to Himself in the Old Testament by many different Names, such as *"Jehovah-Elohim,"* which means *"the Eternal Creator"* (Gen. 2:4-25); or *"Jehovah-Jireh,"* which means *"the Lord will provide"* (Gen. 22:8-14); or *"Jehovah-Ropheka,"* which means *"the Lord our Healer"* (Ex. 15:26), to name a few. However, it is the Name of Jesus that is the greatest of all.

THE NAME OF JESUS IS A STATUS NAME

As it relates to the Old Testament Prophesies, the Name Jesus is a status name, declaring the Recipient to be God, born of a Virgin, and the Promised King of David's line. The Name *"Jesus"* means *"Saviour,"* which, within itself, as should be obvious, is the Greatest of all. However, we must remember that Jesus as Saviour is made possible totally and completely by what He did for us at the Cross of Calvary. It is the Cross which makes it possible for Him to be the Saviour.

Whereas the Names used by the Lord in Old Testament times refer to something He would do, such as *"provide"* or *"heal"* etc., the Name *"Jesus"* refers to the greatest act of all, Salvation from sin, i.e., *"the Saviour."*

A FULFILLMENT NAME

It is a significant thing that the First Person named in the New Testament, Who is Jesus, receives not a prediction Name but a fulfillment Name. In other words, the purposes of God are being rounded out to completion.

While the Name of Jesus is also a prediction Name, which looks forward to what He will Himself do, it is more so a fulfillment Name because Jesus is Himself the Fulfillment of what His Name declares.

THE KNOWLEDGE OF THE NAME

Though the Name of Jesus does not confer *"power"* in any magical sense (Acts 19:13), the knowledge of the Name brings people into a whole new relationship with God. They are His Intimates, for this is the significance of *"knowing by Name,"* in this case, Jesus (Ex. 33:12, 18-19; Jn. 17:6). The initiation of the relationship thus described lies on the Divine side: collectively and individually, the People of God are *"called by His Name."*

There are some five aspects of the meaning of the Name of Jesus, and they are as follows:

1. BELIEVING IN THE NAME

John expresses this possibly to a greater extent than any of the other Apostles (Jn. 3:18; 16:23-24; I Jn. 3:23).

It refers to a personal commitment to the Lord Jesus as thus revealed in the Essence of His Person and Work.

2. A STRONG TOWER

Those who are of the people of God are *"kept"* in His Name (Jn. 17:11), which takes up the distinctive Old Testament picture of the Name as a Strong Tower (Prov. 18:10), to which the Believer may run for safety. It means provision and protection.

When Christians are said to be *"Justified in the Name"* (I Cor. 6:11), the implication is the same: the Name, as the unchangeable nature of Jesus and as the summary of all that He is and has done, is the ground of secure possession of all the implied Blessings.

3. THE GLORY OF GOD IS EXPRESSED IN THE NAME OF THE LORD

God's Presence among His People is secured by *"making His Name dwell"* among them (Deut. 12:5, 11, 21; 14:23; 16:2, 6; II Sam. 7:13).

It has sometimes been foolishly pressed that there is a distinction, if not a rift, between a *"Name-theology"* and a *"Glory-theology"* in the Old Testament, but these are two ways of expressing the same thing.

For instance, when Moses sought to see the Glory of God, he found that the Glory had to be verbalized by means of the Name Jehovah (Ex. 33:18; 34:8).

So, the Name of Jesus is also the Glory of God in that it saves men from eternal darkness.

4. THE NAME OF JESUS IS HIS HOLY NAME

Inasmuch as it is Holy, the privilege of its use in no way controls God but is meant to control man, both in worship Godward (Lev. 18:21) and in service toward others (Rom. 1:5). The *"Name"* is thus the motive of service; it is also the message (Acts 9:15) and the Means of Power (Acts 3:16; 4:12).

5. THE NAME OF JESUS IS THE GROUND FOR PRAYER

Actually, this is exactly what we are now studying respecting John 16:23-24.

NOTES

As it is linked to prayer, Water Baptism is associated with the Name of Jesus, either of the Holy Trinity (Mat. 28:19) or the Lord Jesus Personally (Acts 2:38).

The distinction is that the former (the Holy Trinity) stresses the total reality of the Divine Nature and the totality of Blessedness designed for the recipient, whereas the latter stresses the effective means of entry into these things through the sole Meditation of Jesus.

In other words, it is the Name of Jesus and what it means that gives us access to the Father and the Holy Spirit. Once again, it is all made possible by the Cross. This is at least one of the reasons it is so very important.

The Father cannot be reached except through Jesus, and the Holy Spirit cannot indwell a person until his sins have been washed away by the Blood of Jesus.

(25) *"THESE THINGS HAVE I SPOKEN UNTO YOU IN PROVERBS: BUT THE TIME COMES, WHEN I SHALL NO MORE SPEAK UNTO YOU IN PROVERBS, BUT I SHALL SHOW YOU PLAINLY OF THE FATHER."*

The composition is:

1. Five times in the prayer of St. John, Chapter 17, Christ prayed for unity among Believers.

2. Five is the number of Grace, signifying that this unity can be reached only by and through the Grace of God.

3. However, considering that He prayed five times in this one prayer for that petition to be fulfilled, we should then know and realize just how important this is for which He prayed.

PROVERBS

The phrase, *"These things have I spoken unto you in Proverbs,"* concerns the Parables and, as well, His Portraying Truths to them in such a way that even though they would not be able to understand them then, once the Holy Spirit came, He would reveal its meaning even in a fuller way than if Jesus had explained it Personally to them.

I WILL SHOW YOU PLAINLY

The phrase, *"But the time comes, when I*

shall no more speak unto you in Proverbs," refers to the Day of Pentecost and forward.

"But I shall show you plainly of the Father," proclaims Him, through the Holy Spirit, revealing all of these things to His Disciples and, actually, to all of His Followers for all time. The idea is this:

Now that the Holy Spirit has come, there is no excuse for men misunderstanding Who the Father is and the relationship of Jesus to Him. As well, this includes the relationship of the Believer because, as Christ is, so are we (Jn. 14:20).

Jesus used the word *"plainly"* because the Gospel is not something secretive, but does require the service of the Holy Spirit for it to be properly understood.

In the religions of the world, there are all types of secret societies, etc. As such, only a special few know the password, etc. However, in Christianity, all Believers can know all things, with nothing being secretive, if only they will allow the Holy Spirit to *"guide them into all Truth."*

(26) "AT THAT DAY YOU SHALL ASK IN MY NAME: AND I SAY NOT UNTO YOU, THAT I WILL PRAY THE FATHER FOR YOU:"

The pattern is:

1. The Sixth Chapter of Romans reveals the Divine method of Sanctification.

2. The Seventh Chapter of Romans sets out the impossibility under the bondage of law.

3. The sadness is: while every Believer has to go through the Seventh Chapter of Romans regarding daily life and living, most Christians, regrettably, are still there.

ASKING IN THE NAME OF JESUS

The phrase, *"At that day you shall ask in My Name,"* tells us how to pray, but more perfectly, it tells us the access which the Name of Jesus provides.

"And I say not unto you, that I will pray the Father for you," has been misunderstood by many.

The idea is that Jesus does not have to intercede to the Father on behalf of Believers respecting answers to prayer. That is not necessary in that Jesus, by His Death and Resurrection, has reconciled men with God, at least those who believe. His Appearance in the Presence of God for us is the perpetual pledge of the completeness of His Sacrifice. In other words, the Saint has the same access to the Father as Jesus.

What a thought!

THE INTERCESSION OF CHRIST

The word *"intercession"* in Romans 8:26-27, concerning the Holy Spirit, does not speak of pleading one's position, but rather helping us to petition the Father in the right way.

The position of the Believer in Christ and, therefore, guaranteeing access to the Father is never in question. It is only the protocol that is in question.

If the Believer sins, Jesus, at that time, does have to make intercession for the Believer to the Father (Heb. 7:25). However, His Intercession is done by His very Presence. He really does not have to say anything or do anything because His Presence there guarantees the intercession.

Sin separates the Believer from God, as should be obvious! When such does happen, the Holy Spirit ceases to comfort and begins to convict (Jn. 16:8-9). At that time, fellowship with God is broken, for the Lord cannot have fellowship with sin. However, the moment the Believer asks forgiveness (I Jn. 1:9), such is instantly given, with fellowship instantly restored because of the intercession of Christ.

(27) "FOR THE FATHER HIMSELF LOVES YOU, BECAUSE YOU HAVE LOVED ME, AND HAVE BELIEVED THAT I CAME OUT FROM GOD."

The order is:

1. The Holy Spirit through Christ explained the Trinity in the Seventeenth Chapter of the Gospel of John as no other place in the Word of God.

2. While there are Three Personalities in the Godhead, there is but one God. Jesus here explains what He means by *"One."*

3. These Three Personalities are, above all, One in Essence and are manifested in *"God the Father," "God the Son,"* and *"God the Holy Spirit."* All Three, as stated, are God, but there aren't three Gods, just One — One in Unity, One in Purpose, and One in Essence, but not One in Number.

GOD THE FATHER

The phrase, *"For the Father Himself loves you, because you have loved Me,"* proclaims that Jesus is so Dear to the Father that one properly loving Christ guarantees immediate access to the Father on that basis alone. Of course, one cannot love Christ without being *"Born-Again"* (Jn. 3:3). Consequently, exactly as Jesus has just said, He does not have to ask the Father for permission for the Believer to come into the Presence of God because that is guaranteed by one's acceptance of the Sacrifice of Christ at Calvary. So, regarding access, no mediator is required unless, as stated, the Believer sins.

FAITH

The phrase, *"And have believed that I came out from God,"* concerns the Faith of the Believer as it is registered in Christ and what Christ did for us at the Cross. This speaks of the Incarnation, God becoming Man, dwelling with men, and paying the price for man's Redemption. To be Saved and have the Love of the Father, it is absolutely imperative that men believe what Jesus has done for them, which pertains to Both His Humanity and Deity.

(28) "I CAME FORTH FROM THE FATHER, AND AM COME INTO THE WORLD: AGAIN, I LEAVE THE WORLD, AND GO TO THE FATHER."

The form is:

1. We are told in Colossians 2:15 that Jesus totally and completely defeated Satan and all of his minions of darkness at the Cross.

2. It was done by the means of Jesus atoning for all sin. Sin is the legal means by which Satan can hold men in bondage.

3. When Jesus died on the Cross, giving Himself as a Perfect Sacrifice, He and His Sacrifice were accepted by the Father, which atoned for all sin, past, present, and future, at least for all who will believe (Jn. 3:16). All one has to do to accept the benefits of what Christ has done at the Cross is to accept Him as one's personal Saviour.

THE DEITY OF CHRIST

The phrase, *"I came forth from the Father,"* speaks of Christ's Deity. It also speaks of the Mission for which He has been sent. It is something minutely planned and, consequently, proceeds accordingly. To give us an idea as to the degree of such planning, Peter said, *"Who* (speaking of Christ) *verily was foreordained before the foundation of the world* (His Death and Resurrection was foreordained), *but was manifest in these last times for you"* (I Pet. 1:20).

In attempting to understand such planning, the human mind and intellect can only go so far.

"And am come into the world," speaks of coming into a hostile environment, a hostility so pronounced, in fact, that it began at the first Promise of His Coming (Gen. 3:15).

One could probably say that all conflict recorded in the Old Testament, respecting those on whom the Lord had laid His Hand, was ultimately but for one purpose, and that was to stop the Coming of the Redeemer.

DECEPTION

Some may ask the question as to how Satan thought he could stop this process, especially considering that God is Almighty.

Satan is deceived, and grandly so! Sin does that, whether Angel or human. Consequently, he really believes he can foil the predictions of the Word of God, and so do those who follow him, which includes almost the entirety of the world for all time.

"Again, I leave the world, and go to the Father," signifies that despite the hostility, He accomplished the task for which He came, and accomplished it in totality. Consequently, He would go back to the Father in great Victory.

Other than the Holy Spirit, He had no help whatsoever, even to the extent of tacit approval. Even His Disciples were not in sympathy with the Redemption process, even though it was as much for them as it was for the entirety of mankind. Of course, their disapproval was mostly from spiritual and Scriptural ignorance.

As is obvious, the religious hierarchy of Israel was so very opposed to Him that their hatred could be satisfied only by blood lust. He was misunderstood, rejected, disapproved, maligned, ridiculed, and opposed on every hand. So, the question is not to the hostility but to the degree of its expression. Despite that, He did what He came to do!

(29) "HIS DISCIPLES SAID UNTO HIM, LO, NOW YOU ARE SPEAKING PLAINLY, AND SPEAK NO PROVERB."

The diagram is:

1. The Law assured Righteousness to all who perfectly obeyed it (Gal. 3:10), but condemned to death all who failed to give it that perfect obedience.

2. Such an obedience is impossible to man, for he is morally imperfect, and moral imperfection cannot possibly render moral perfection.

3. Christ redeemed the believing sinner from that doom because He suffered in Himself on the Believer's behalf. Thus, at Calvary, He affirmed the authority of that Law and vindicated its justice and goodness.

HIS PURPOSE AND MISSION

The Disciples seemed to have understood what He said and probably had an inkling of what it meant. However, despite their profession, they still little understood His Purpose and Mission. This is proven by their failure to believe that He would rise from the dead after His Crucifixion, although it does seem, as the next Verse proclaims, that they are now more sure of His Person respecting Who He really is. Still, it will take the Holy Spirit to fully reveal Him to them, and all others, for that matter!

(30) "NOW ARE WE SURE THAT YOU KNOW ALL THINGS, AND NEED NOT THAT ANY MAN SHOULD ASK YOU: BY THIS WE BELIEVE THAT YOU CAME FORTH FROM GOD."

The overview is:

1. The ladder (Gen. 28:12), as Jacob saw it, was closed to all but the Angels.

2. In other words, due to the terrible sin debt upon man, even believing man, Heaven was closed to all. Believers who died before the Cross did not go to Heaven, but rather down into Paradise where they were actually held captive by Satan (Eph. 4:8).

3. They were comforted in Paradise, but there was only a gulf which separated Paradise from Hell itself (Lk. 16:19-31). However, when Jesus died on the Cross, the sin debt was forever paid. Now that ladder is open not only to Angels but, also, to all Believers.

JESUS CAME FORTH FROM GOD

The phrase, *"Now are we sure that You know all things,"* seems to have arisen from the fact that they now strongly sensed that nothing in their hearts was hidden from Him.

"And need not that any man should ask You," means that before they would ask particular questions, He, already discerning their thoughts, would begin to answer their proposed inquiry even before it was asked.

"By this we believe that You came forth from God," proclaims their Faith built more so on things He did rather than simply taking His Word.

And yet, I think we judge them too harshly, considering what they were being asked to believe. For certain, we would have done no better and, possibly, not even as well!

He could read their minds, which seemed to impress them greatly; however, He had performed Miracles of far greater magnitude.

I keep saying it because it is true: without the Holy Spirit, it is impossible to have very much spiritual understanding concerning anything.

(31) "JESUS ANSWERED THEM, DO YOU NOW BELIEVE?"

The exegesis is:

1. As it is today, so it was in Paul's day. People demanded that the Gospel should be preached in *"terms of modern thought,"* embellished with scholastic learning, convincing logic, forensic reasoning, and cultured eloquence.

2. The Apostle refused, declared such culture to be the wisdom of this world, and said that preaching according to the Divine Wisdom was preaching in the Power of the Holy Spirit, and that was the only Power which effected the moral result of the New Birth.

3. So, the theme of the preaching of the Apostle, which also should be our theme, and must be our theme, was the Divine Person and Atoning Work of the Great God and Saviour Jesus Christ.

BELIEVE

They had said they now *"believe,"* but did they really?

The Disciples were like children. They hastened to assure Him of their intelligence and of their Faith, but Jesus sorrowfully tells them that every man of them will return to his own home and forsake Him in His Hour of greatest need, as we shall see.

As a Perfect and Sinless Man, Jesus was exquisitely sensitive to sympathy; and yet, He loved them, though they denied Him that human fellowship which His Heart craved.

(32) "BEHOLD, THE HOUR COMES, YES, IS NOW COME, THAT YOU SHALL BE SCATTERED, EVERY MAN TO HIS OWN, AND SHALL LEAVE ME ALONE: AND YET I AM NOT ALONE, BECAUSE THE FATHER IS WITH ME."

The diagram is:

1. Man magnifies sacraments and ceremonies and belittles preaching.
2. God magnifies preaching.
3. It pleases God, by the foolishness of preaching, i.e., preaching the Cross, to save men (I Cor. 1:21).

THE HOUR IS NOW COME

The phrase, *"Behold, the hour comes, yes, is now come,"* is the *"hour"* referred to from before the foundation of the world. Everything pointed to this moment, which proclaims a Love in the Heart of God for depraved humanity that mere man cannot even begin to comprehend.

"That you shall be scattered, every man to his own," proclaims their Faith weakening, as to its power, but not to its essential quality. Their Faith may not stand firm on that awful night, but it will ultimately prevail, and Christ rejoices in the fact that His Words have at last evoked this genuine response. In the prayer which follows (Jn. 17:8), he thanks God *"that they have known verily that I came forth from You, and have believed that You have sent Me."*

SHALL LEAVE ME ALONE

The phrase, *"And shall leave Me Alone,"* proclaims exactly what it says. At the end, He was Alone!

At this time, His Own Family had forsaken Him. The authorities were openly hostile and, in fact, were serving as instruments of Satan to kill Him. Joseph and Nicodemus, and even Lazarus, are silent. Judas is treacherous, with even the Eleven forsaking Him and fleeing exactly as He had predicted.

Reynolds says: *"John and the Mother of Jesus, who follow within earshot of the Cross, are sent away, and there is a moment when He is absolutely alone. He even says, 'My God, My God, why have You forsaken Me?' But yet, in the next phrase, this will change."*[6]

THE FATHER IS WITH ME

The phrase, *"And yet I am not alone, because the Father is with Me,"* is said in this light:

The Father never really left Him at all, with the exception of the horrible time when He became an actual Sin-Offering on the Cross, which was shortly before He died. Bearing the sin of all mankind and about to suffer the curse of the broken Law, His Father would be forced to turn from Him, at least in the realm of Fatherhood. Now He would be the Judge of Jesus Christ, and as such, He judged our sins in Him. He did so by smiting Him with the penalty we should have suffered but that He suffered instead (Isa. 53:4).

He died actually being made a curse by God, which was the plan all along, for this was the only way that man could be redeemed. And yet, He cried in His last Words, *"It is finished"* (Jn. 19:30). And then, with His last Breath, He said, *"Father, into Your Hands I commend My Spirit"* (Lk. 23:46).

Once the price was paid in totality, even as it was by His Death, and even though He died under the Curse of God, one might say, He knew that He would not be received by the Father, so He anticipated the Divine Overshadowing Presence.

Respecting what Jesus had said about the Father being with Him, it had a far greater meaning than mere Presence or Companionship. In effect, it is that of which Paul spoke when the Holy Spirit said through him, *"To wit,* (witness), *that God was in Christ* (concerning all that Christ did, even His Death and Resurrection), *reconciling the world unto Himself"* (II Cor. 5:19).

(33) "THESE THINGS I HAVE SPOKEN

UNTO YOU, THAT IN ME YOU MIGHT HAVE PEACE. IN THE WORLD YOU SHALL HAVE TRIBULATION: BUT BE OF GOOD CHEER; I HAVE OVERCOME THE WORLD."

The exegesis is:

1. When reading the Text (Acts 5:29-31), it becomes overly obvious that Simon Peter subscribed not at all to the modern method espoused by much of the church of embracing all things and saying nothing negative about anything.

2. So, we can follow the modern method, which is totally unscriptural, or we can follow the Bible. We cannot follow both!

3. Peter's use of the titles, *"A Prince"* and *"A Saviour to Israel,"* expresses royalty and Atonement. Not only is the Lord Jesus the Medium of Forgiveness and Life, but He is the Dispenser of both.

PEACE

The phrase, *"These things I have spoken unto you, that in Me you might have peace,"* in effect, says to them, *"Things may look dark; however, despite how they look, everything is under control. Trust what I have said and believe Me!"*

The phrase, *"In the world you shall have tribulation,"* concerns the fundamental condition of Divine Life in this world. The world is totally opposed because its system is solely of Satan.

Notice, He did not say that tribulation possibly would be, but rather, *"You shall have tribulation!"*

"But be of good cheer; I have overcome the world," is spoken of all that is in the world.

As the Last Adam, Jesus had suffered temptation to a degree, in fact, that no human being has ever had to suffer, but yet, failed not at all!

With His Perfect Life, He overcame all the powers of darkness and now stood at the very end totally Victorious. In other words, He kept the Mosaic Law not only in Spirit but down to the letter, which no man had ever done, not even Moses. He did it as a Man filled with the Holy Spirit and not as Deity, even though He was Deity and never ceased to be.

NOTES

OVERCOMING VICTORY

This Statement by Christ is of far greater moment then presently meets the eye.

Jesus lived the Perfect Life, overcoming all, which no man had ever done; however, He did not do this thing for Himself, but rather for fallen man. Now, my Faith in Him and what He did grants to me the overcoming Victory which He gained.

Even though the Law, which told man what was right and what was wrong, is still very much alive in its moral sense, and even demanding that it be kept, still, as a Believer, I am dead to it, even though it is not dead (Rom. 7:4). The reason I, as a Believer, am dead to the Law is because Jesus became my Representative Man and perfectly kept the Law. Consequently, it now has no hold upon me.

This does not mean that I am not responsible as a Believer to keep the moral Law, but it does mean that inasmuch as Jesus has kept it for me, my simple Faith in Him will guarantee me to be an overcomer as well!

TO BE AN OVERCOMER

When reading the Words of Jesus concerning the seven churches of Asia and His Demand that Believers be overcomers, we must understand that there is really nothing we can do to bring about such inasmuch as it already has been done. By having Faith in Him and what He did, we simply enter into His Victory. It is that simple! And yet, it is that wonderful!

When this is understood, it is a cause, and in grand terms, of *"being of good cheer!"*

The problem with many, if not all, Believers, at one time or the other, is that we try to overcome through our own efforts, albeit very religious, and always fail, as fail we must! We fail because man, within himself, is not able to attain the spiritual height. Inasmuch as no human being has ever done such, this abysmal record should tell us something! Actually, that is at least one of the very reasons Jesus came. He would do for us what we could not do for ourselves.

By taking Him as my Saviour, I have become a New Creation in Christ Jesus. At that moment, I am also an overcomer, which came to me simply by Faith and, in fact, can come no other way. One cannot earn such, for *"it is the Gift of God"* (Eph. 2:8). Whatever Jesus is, I am, and thus, all Believers!

"Blessed assurance, Jesus is mine!
"O what a foretaste of Glory Divine!
"Heir of Salvation, purchase of God,
"Born of His Spirit, washed in His Blood."

"This is my story, this is my song,
"Praising my Saviour all the day long;
"This is my story, this is my song,
"Praising my Saviour, all the day long."

CHAPTER 17

(1) "THESE WORDS SPOKE JESUS, AND LIFTED UP HIS EYES TO HEAVEN, AND SAID, FATHER, THE HOUR IS COME; GLORIFY YOUR SON, THAT YOUR SON ALSO MAY GLORIFY YOU."

The composition is:

1. When Jesus came the first time, He was ridiculed, lambasted, and finally crucified. They nailed Him to a Cross and mocked Him while He died — died for them!

2. However, when Jesus comes the second time, it will not be to be beaten, spit upon, or nailed to a tree. He rather will come to this world to take control, and with such power as the world has never known before.

3. I know He's coming the second time simply because He came the first time.

THE WORDS OF JESUS

The phrase, *"These words spoke Jesus,"* and the following, portrays the longest of the Lord's Prayers in the Four Gospels. As well, it is the only one stated to have been prayed with the Disciples.

In Williams' comments, he views this prayer as that of the Lord resuming His Position in Glory as Jehovah's Fellow (Zech. 13:7). As well, He brings up with Him into that Divine Glory His Nature as Man. Also, this prayer regards the Disciples as taking His Place on Earth, and as under the Father's Guardianship, continuing His Work of manifesting the Character of God in Love and Judgment in a world of hatred and sin, and saving men out of it.

The false prophets (Pharisees) thrust themselves forward and claimed reverence and position. He, the Greatest of the Prophets, hid Himself and did not claim to be a professional Prophet — that was not His Mission in coming to Earth — but became a Bond Servant and a Shepherd, which this prayer epitomizes.

SLAVERY

With man having sold himself into slavery, it was necessary that Christ should take that position in order to redeem him.

It was not only sin upon the Sinless Substitute that was smitten at Calvary, but the Substitute Himself, Jehovah's Equal.

He Himself must die in order that man might live, for the curse that rested upon man was the doom of death because of sin. Christ's Death, therefore, was necessary to satisfy that claim and to vindicate and magnify Divine Righteousness.

So, the Shepherd would be smitten and the sheep scattered, but not completely lost, for His Hand, pierced by the flock, shall cause them to return.

This prayer puts the Disciples into an immediate relationship with the Father; commits them to His Love and Care; asks that they may be loved as He Himself was loved; and reveals His Own Indwelling in them by the Holy Spirit, so equipping them for the effectual accomplishment of their Ministry. This efficiency is expressed in the last three mighty Words, *"I in them."*

PRAYER TO THE FATHER

The phrase, *"And lifted up His Eyes to Heaven,"* probably means they were outdoors when this prayer was offered. Some even believe that Jesus had gone to the Temple, and in some of its courts that were open to the skies, there He prayed this prayer. In fact, He may have given there all that is recorded in John, Chapters 14 through 17.

The phrase, *"And said, Father, the hour is come,"* tells us two things:

1. If one is to notice, He did not say, *"My Father"* or *"Our Father,"* but rather, *"Father!"*

God was His Unique Father in a way that He was to no one else. As well, Jesus was the Father's Own Unique Son, as are no others.

Even though God is the Father of all Believers, still, it is in a different sense than the relationship with His Son. While we have all the rights of Jesus freely given to us because of Faith in Him, still, we are *"adopted sons"* (Rom. 8:15).

2. The *"hour"* of which Jesus spoke is the single most important *"hour"* in human history. It was the *"hour"* which would bring about the Redemption of mankind, at least to those who will believe.

The phrase, *"Glorify Your Son,"* presents Christ speaking of Himself in the Third Person.

Reynolds says, *"This is justified by the fact that He here conspicuously rises out of Himself into the consciousness of God, and loses Himself in the Father, which as well is an example for us."*[1]

TO GLORIFY

The *"Glorification"* of which He speaks is of such magnitude that it is beyond compare. It would commence with His Dying, which would usher in Life.

Reynolds said, *"He was crowned with Glory in order that He might taste death for every man. The conflict, the victorious combat with death, was the beginning of His Glory."*[2]

"Glory" refers to something which is beautiful, wonderful, glorious, magnificent, powerful, rich, etc. Considering this, it is difficult for us to understand how Calvary, with its gross humiliation, pain, and sorrow, could in any way be glorious. This is especially true when we consider that He was bearing the sin penalty of the world, which, within itself, is so absolutely wicked and evil that it is beyond compare.

However, as we have previously stated, we find a counterpart for this in the sacrifices of the Old Testament.

A SWEET SAVOR

As gruesome as was the killing of the clean animal, with its blood being poured out on the Altar and then it being burned on the Altar, the Lord referred to it over and over again as a *"sweet savor"* (Gen. 8:21; Ex. 29:18; Lev. 1:9, 13; Num. 15:3).

The act itself was one thing, but what Jesus' Death at Calvary would bring forth, which was the Redemption of mankind, pertains to the actual Glory. The results of that *"Glory"* will not be seen, at least in all of its beauty, until the Resurrection when the Saints will stand Glorified in His Presence because of the price He paid at Calvary (I Cor. 15:51-57).

Of course, Jesus would be beautifully Glorified at the Resurrection.

The phrase, *"That Your Son also may glorify You,"* refers to Him taking upon Himself all the burden of human sorrow and exhausting the poison of the sting of death, which would *"glorify God."*

Carrying out the Will of God by any Believer *"glorifies God!"* However, that which Jesus did is something no other human being could ever do.

(2) "AS YOU HAVE GIVEN HIM POWER OVER ALL FLESH, THAT HE SHOULD GIVE ETERNAL LIFE TO AS MANY AS YOU HAVE GIVEN HIM."

The form is:

1. The Story of the Bible is the Story of Jesus Christ and Him Crucified.

2. Every sacrifice of clean animals in the Old Testament points toward that coming event.

3. In fact, the entirety of the Tabernacle and Temple, with all of its furnishings, ceremonies, and rituals, all and without exception, point to Christ in either His Atoning, Mediatorial, or Intercessory Work.

POWER OVER ALL FLESH

The phrase, *"As You have given Him Power over all flesh,"* presents Him as the Channel through which Eternal Life may be given; however, He would not have this Glory except to glorify the Father.

These opening Words of Jesus reveal the universality and worldwide aspects of the Mission, Authority, and Saving Power of the Son of God. He holds the Keys of the Kingdom and City of God. The Government is upon His Shoulder exactly as prophesied by Isaiah. Through Him, all the nations on Earth are to be blessed.

"*Over all flesh*" speaks to every person on the face of the Earth, and for all time. In other words, there is no other way of Salvation. Jesus Alone provides this Great Gift. When men look elsewhere, even as most do, they are looking at a lie which contains no life, but rather death.

This means that all who follow Muhammad do so to their death. The same goes for Catholicism, Hinduism, Islam, Buddhism, Mormonism, humanism, and even the part of Christianity which is apostate. As should be overly obvious, Salvation is Jesus! It is not a philosophy, church, organization, etc.

ETERNAL LIFE

The phrase, *"That He should give Eternal Life to as many as You have given Him,"* refers to those who meet the conditions laid down in the Scripture concerning Faith. In other words, it is *"whosoever will"* (Jn. 3:16; I Tim. 2:4; II Pet. 3:9; Rev. 22:17)!

No one is arbitrarily chosen by God for Eternal Life to the exclusion of their own participation. In effect, God has chosen all to be Saved. *"For He is not willing that any should perish, but that all may come to Repentance"* (II Pet. 3:9).

"Eternal Life," as here spoken, speaks of Life which comes from Christ to the Believer and is imparted upon Faith.

Such will cause one to know God eternally. Eternal Life is not merely a prolonged existence of eternal continuance of being, for all the wicked have this and will be punished in conscious existence forever (Isa. 66:22-24; Mat. 25:41, 46; Mk. 9:43-49; Rev. 14:9-11; 20:10-15; 21:8).

It is not merely eternal existence, but eternal knowing of God in eternal and perfect correspondence and perfect, eternal, and infinite environment.

This Life is only in God's Son (I Jn. 5:11-12). Thus, Everlasting Life is not merely everlasting existence, but rather an Eternal Life with God.

As well, the *"Eternal Life"* promised by Jesus is extended only by and through His Grace and is accepted by Faith. It is impossible for one to earn such simply because no one even remotely has that capacity.

Such is not necessary inasmuch as Jesus Christ has already purchased this Eternal Life by the giving of His Own Life. So, to attempt to earn such or even to provide part payment, in effect, says that Jesus did not pay it all and that the person must finish out such payment. Such is foolish, but yet, is practiced by most of the world in one way or the other.

(3) "AND THIS IS LIFE ETERNAL, THAT THEY MIGHT KNOW YOU THE ONLY TRUE GOD, AND JESUS CHRIST, WHOM YOU HAVE SENT."

The pattern is:

1. The Gospel does not liberate a man to a life of laziness and self-indulgence, but to an unceasing Ministry of loving service to humanity.

2. The controlling Ministry of the Holy Spirit is the secret of Holy Living, and the only secret for Holy Living.

3. This is the Power of which Paul spoke and the Power we must have to live a victorious life, which is invested in the preaching of the Cross (I Cor. 1:18).

GOD THE FATHER AND
THE LORD JESUS CHRIST

The phrase, *"And this is Life Eternal,"* proclaims the true kernel of what Eternal Life really is.

"That they might know You the Only True God, and Jesus Christ, Whom You have sent," proclaims the condition of Eternal Life. It is twofold:

• To know God is to know Eternal Life, and to know Eternal Life is to know God!

As well, the words *"True God"* tell us that Satan proposes many counterfeits. However, at the same time, the word *"True"* tells us that despite all the claims otherwise, there is only One God.

There is absolutely no way that man can know God in any dimension whatsoever unless he knows Him through Jesus Christ. Apart from Christ, God cannot be understood, recognized, or known in any capacity.

As well, when one knows Him through Christ, one will always know Him as *"the Father!"* Any ideas of God, which deviate from this relationship, proclaim a lack of the true knowledge of God.

God is not the *"force,"* the *"eternal good,"* *"the universal mind,"* or any other such type of foolishness. If He is not known as *"Our Father,"* then it was not the Lord Jesus Christ Who presented Him to us, but rather a spirit of darkness, etc.

THE LORD JESUS CHRIST

The phrase, *"And Jesus Christ, Whom You have sent,"* proclaims Christ associating Himself as such with God, and so claims Deity and Equality; for the knowledge of God in a mere creature could not be or give Eternal Life.

The key word in this Third Verse as made by Christ is *"know"* and in the Greek text is *"ginosko"* and means *"to perceive and understand."* However, this is not mere mental assent, but rather knowledge which has been experienced.

Perhaps the following short diagram will shed more light on the subject.

• The only way to God is through Jesus Christ. There is no other way (Jn. 14:6).

• The only way to Jesus Christ is by the Means of the Cross of Christ (Rom. 6:3-5; I Cor. 1:17; 2:2; Gal. 6:14; Col. 2:10-15).

• The only way to the Cross is by a denial of self (Lk. 9:23).

(4) "I HAVE GLORIFIED YOU ON THE EARTH: I HAVE FINISHED THE WORK WHICH YOU GAVE ME TO DO."

The diagram is:

1. Judges, Chapter 4, may be said to be the women's Chapter.

2. The Faith of Deborah reached out and won a great victory. The Faith of Jael destroyed a great tyrant and saved thousands from certain death.

3. Some would claim that God cannot use women in the preaching and teaching of the Gospel. However, both of these women were raised up and energized by God for their respective Ministries, as were also the great women of the Pauline Epistles.

GOD THROUGH JESUS CHRIST WAS GLORIFIED ON EARTH

The phrase, *"I have glorified You on the Earth,"* proclaims the carrying out of the Will of God in all things. This pertained to the Ministry of Christ in preaching, teaching, healing the sick, and delivering those in bondage to demon spirits, whether by oppression or possession.

"I have finished the Work which You gave Me to do," presents the only statement of its kind in human history.

He had finished the *"Work"* totally and completely, leaving nothing undone, and had, as well, lived a Perfect Life. Consequently, He could present to the Father a Perfect Work and a Perfect Life, which would serve as the Perfect Sacrifice.

(5) "AND NOW, O FATHER, GLORIFY THOU ME WITH THINE OWN SELF WITH THE GLORY WHICH I HAD WITH YOU BEFORE THE WORLD WAS."

The form is:

1. Most preachers boast of their strength, but Paul boasted of his weakness.

2. Paul recognized himself as an earthen vessel. As such, he also realized that nothing could amend the carnal nature, not even the great Revelations and Visions which had been given to him by the Lord.

3. So, to save him from failure and even falling, he was impaled upon a stake, so to speak. Whatever that thorn in the flesh was, the Holy Spirit did not see fit to reveal that to us. However, what is necessary to learn from this experience is the moral purpose of that thorn in Saving the Apostle from destruction.

ALL TRUE GLORY

The phrase, *"And now, O Father, You glorify Me with Your Own Self,"* proclaims that all True Glory exists only in God. When He, as God, became Man, He divested Himself of that Glory.

"With the Glory which I had with You before the world was," presents a request that He would be Glorified as Man with the Glory which is eternally His as God. However, He asked to be reinvested with His Pre-existent Glory, not simply as before, but now in human nature, which was granted in the Resurrection, and which Glory He will wear in human form forever.

It says in this one Scripture that Jesus refers to three experimental estates:

THREE ESTATES

1. Eternal pre-existence as God (Mic. 5:1-2; Jn. 1:1-2; Col. 1:15-18; Rev. 1:8, 11; 2:8; 22:13).

2. Earthly self-emptying in becoming Man (Lk. 2:40, 52; Jn. 1:14; Phil. 2:5-11; Heb. 1:3-9; 2:9-18; 4:14-16; 5:7).

3. Restored Glory but in Human Form (Mat. 28:18; Jn. 17:5; Eph. 1:20-23; Phil. 2:9-11; Heb. 12:2; I Pet. 3:22; Rev. 3:21).

As God, the Glory was automatic. However, as a Human, and that which He, by choice, planned to remain, He had to request such Glory, continuing to set for us an example.

So, in this prayer, we are made to see not only what Jesus did to bring about Redemption, but what He gave up. He will remain in Human Form forever, albeit Glorified, which characterized His Appearances to the Disciples and others after the Resurrection, and His Appearance to John the Beloved on the Isle of Patmos (Rev. 1:10-18).

(6) "I HAVE MANIFESTED YOUR NAME UNTO THE MEN WHICH YOU GAVE ME OUT OF THE WORLD: YOURS THEY WERE, AND YOU GAVE THEM TO ME; AND THEY HAVE KEPT YOUR WORD."

The pattern is:

1. Jude, the half-brother of our Lord (Mat. 13:55; Mk. 6:3), was thinking of writing an Epistle explaining the Way of Salvation, similar to Paul's Epistle to the Romans.

2. However, news reached him of such a nature to cause him to put that project aside and hasten to write the short letter that he did, urging Believers to contend earnestly for the Faith once for all entrusted to them.

THE MANIFESTATION OF THE NAME OF THE LORD

The phrase, *"I have manifested Your Name,"* proclaims that the Name of God was but partially and imperfectly understood before. It speaks of the beginning of the previous Verse, *"O Father,"* and speaks of relationship.

As we have stated, God had manifested Himself in various different Names previously, according to the task or need at hand, but, there was little relationship in those Revelations. However, Jesus opened up the Way to God, which even the greatest Saints had not previously known.

Reynolds said, *"A full Revelation of the Father involves and is involved in a manifestation of His Own Sonship. The relation between the Father and the Son is one of infinite complacency and mutual affection, and the Revelation of it demonstrates the fact of the Eternal and Essential Love of the Divine Being."*[3]

He went on to say, *"Thus the fact that 'God is Love' is manifested in the Life of the Son of Man, Who was in Himself a Revelation of God and because He was and is God."*[4]

THE CHOSEN DISCIPLES

The phrase, *"Unto the men whom You gave Me out of the world,"* proclaims that while the Disciples were yet in the world and ignorant of Jesus, they belonged to Him because they were given to Him by the Father.

However, at the appropriate time, they were drawn out of the world by the Holy Spirit and made a part of the Kingdom of God. In fact, they continued to be in the world but not of the world.

As such, they were privileged to be participants in the greatest Move of God the world had ever known. Miracles were performed of such proportion as to beggar description, even to the raising of the dead! They saw and heard things no man had ever seen or heard in history. This included not only the Twelve but the Seventy also (Lk. 10:1)!

YOU GAVE THEM TO ME

The phrase, *"Yours they were, and You gave them to Me,"* proclaims to us a precondition.

In simple terminology, it means that God had ordained them for this task long before they heard Jesus say, *"Follow Me,"* and, no doubt, long before they were even born.

Understanding the Omniscience of God, at least as far as a human can understand such, the free moral agency of a person is not violated at all with God looking down through time, irrespective of the length, and through foreknowledge, knowing what will or will not be. According to such foreknowledge, the Lord can structure certain things, which I believe He does, in order to carry out His Will.

HE HAS CHOSEN US

Another example is the planting of the Church at Corinth by Paul. Facing terrible opposition, the Lord spoke to him by a Vision. He told him to continue preaching and that He (the Lord) was with him. Then, He said, *"For I have much people in this city"* (Acts 18:9-11).

One must understand that the Lord referred to these people in this manner even before they were Saved!

Paul said, *"According as He has chosen us in Him before the foundation of the world, that we should be holy and without blame before Him in love"* (Eph. 1:4).

Concerning Corinth, this does not speak of predestination respecting the souls of men, but rather foreknowledge. Regarding the statement in Ephesians, such is predestination, but only concerning what the person would be, not who he would be!

The difference in predestination and foreknowledge, as it pertains to God, is that predestination forces the issue, in other words, it leaves the person without a choice. Foreknowledge, at least as it is in the Realm of God, does not tamper at all with one's free moral agency, but rather sees what the individual will do of his own volition and acts accordingly.

The phrase, *"And they have kept Your Word,"* does not at all mean they were perfect in their worship and understanding, but does mean, despite their flaws, they were true to the Light.

As Jesus said this of them, what does He say of us?

(7) "NOW THEY HAVE KNOWN THAT ALL THINGS WHATSOEVER YOU HAVE GIVEN ME ARE OF YOU."

The pattern is:

1. Joel is the Holy Spirit Prophet of the Old Testament, the one quoted by Simon Peter on the Day of Pentecost (Acts 2:16-21).

2. Before the Cross, the Holy Spirit, even though working mightily in the world, still, was very limited as to what He could do because the blood of bulls and goats could not take away sins (Heb. 10:4).

3. This meant that the Holy Spirit could not come into the hearts and lives of Believers at that time to abide permanently as He now can and does.

THE DISCIPLES

It is remarkable that Jesus prays this type of prayer concerning His Disciples when, in a matter of hours, they will all desert Him, with Peter even denying Him.

Actually, the Disciples were insensible and full of faults, and yet, the Grace that loved them spoke of them in the admiring words of Verses 6 through 8.

This should tell us something of the Grace of God. While what one does is very important, as should be obvious, still, the most important thing is the motivation of the heart. When Jesus prayed this prayer, He did not really see them as they were, but what they would ultimately be according to His Grace.

(8) "FOR I HAVE GIVEN UNTO THEM THE WORDS WHICH YOU GAVE ME; AND THEY HAVE RECEIVED THEM, AND HAVE KNOWN SURELY THAT I CAME OUT FROM YOU, AND THEY HAVE BELIEVED THAT YOU DID SEND ME."

The pattern is:

1. Satan and all of his minions of darkness were defeated at the Cross (Col. 2:14-15).

2. For reasons known only to the Lord, the Evil One has been allowed to continue for this last nearly 2,000 years.

3. However, when Jesus comes the second time, Satan and all of his hordes or darkness are going to be placed in the bottomless pit, unable to wreak their torture and horror anymore (Rev. 20:1-3).

THE WORDS WHICH YOU GAVE ME

The phrase, *"For I have given unto them the Words which You gave Me,"* proclaims that Jesus was led by the Father in all that He did, seemingly, even unto the very Words He spoke.

"And they have received them," does not necessarily mean they understood them. In fact, they did not at all understand all He said and did, but despite that, they continued to believe.

"And have known surely that I came out from You," portrays the bedrock of their Faith.

If they did not believe that Jesus came from God and, in fact, was God, such unbelief would have made the foundation faulty, thereby, skewing all else as well! Once again, their understanding of the Incarnation was anything but complete, but the Holy Spirit would handle that shortly! The word *"surely"* proclaims their rock solid belief regarding this great Truth.

"And they have believed that You did send Me," proclaims a core belief not only in His Person but, as well, regarding His Mission, even though that knowledge at this time was imperfect.

(9) "I PRAY FOR THEM: I PRAY NOT FOR THE WORLD, BUT FOR THEM WHICH YOU HAVE GIVEN ME; FOR THEY ARE THINE."

The form is:

1. We find by experience that God tests Faith in order to strengthen and enrich it.

2. Such a test can come at any time, either before a great victory or after a great victory.

3. The tests are always for our benefit. But yet, it is quite possible to fail the test but finish the course.

I PRAY FOR THEM

The phrase, *"I pray for them,"* concerns His Intercession on their behalf and is assured of an answer.

However, we must remember that this petition preceded Him being Glorified, which would take place after Calvary and the Resurrection. Due to the great Victory won there, all Believers now have immediate access to the Father as they come to Him in the Name of Jesus. In other words, even though Jesus serves as our Mediator at Conversion, which is of absolute necessity, such mediation is no longer needed after the individual is *"Born-Again."* Now, all Believers can ask for all Gifts needed, which the Father's Love for them is waiting to supply. There will be no need then that Jesus should pray the Father for them (Jn. 16:26).

However, as Jesus prays this prayer, that time has not yet come, though it was coming and, in fact, did come! So, now He prays for them!

JESUS DID NOT PRAY AT THIS TIME FOR THE WORLD

The phrase, *"I pray not for the world,"* only speaks of this moment, as He had, no doubt, prayed much for the world in days past. Actually, His Entire Ministry was the expression of the Father's Love for the whole world (Jn. 3:16).

He came as Jehovah's Lamb to take away its sin (Jn. 1:29); He bade His Disciples to pray for their enemies (Mat. 5:44); and He even cried at the last for forgiveness for His murderers. In reality, He *"came to seek and save the lost"* and to *"call sinners to Repentance,"* *"not to condemn, but to save the world."*

The simple meaning is that this petition is strictly for His Very Own!

AT THIS TIME, HE PRAYED FOR HIS DISCIPLES, PLUS ALL BELIEVERS, AND FOR ALL TIME

The phrase, *"But for them whom You have given Me,"* presents such Grace as wonderful that reveals these desires and the privileges that flow from His Care for His Own.

Here is heard the Son conversing with the Father respecting Their Common Love for sinful men, and here, the very Heart of the Great Shepherd is laid open. It was so natural and easy for Him to rest His Eyes one moment upon the loved Disciples and then lift them to Heaven to ask precious things for them, and us.

The phrase, *"For they are Yours,"* presents all that Jesus had and did as being first belonging to the Father. What a lesson for us!

If what we do is His Will, and what we have first belongs to Him, we can be assured that whatever is needed, He will supply.

Our problem is: we make our plans and then seek His Blessings. It is best to let Him make the plans, and then we will be assured of His Blessings.

(10) "AND ALL MINE ARE THINE, AND THINE ARE MINE; AND I AM GLORIFIED IN THEM."

The diagram is:

1. There have never been more churches in America than at the present time.

2. However, there has never been less true Word of the Lord preached at any time since the Reformation than now!

3. Regrettably, if the modern church doesn't like the messenger, they reject the message.

ALL MINE ARE YOURS

The phrase, *"And all Mine are Yours,"* proclaims total consecration and that they were the Father's before they were His. As stated, such guarantees the Blessings of God!

The phrase, *"And Yours are Mine,"* presents another picture altogether!

A man can say, *"All mine are Yours,"* but only Jesus could say, *"All Yours are Mine."* This is a claim of Perfect Equality with God.

"And I am Glorified in them," proclaims that all that the Father desired that He do, no matter how despicable, hurtful, humiliating, and injurious, *"Glory"* would be the result, and more perfectly, it would be a *"Glory"* which would be His, hence, *"Glorified!"*

Such is the same for all Believers! Anything truly done for God, which is according to His Will, will ultimately bring Glory, as well, to the Believer.

This is, in part, that of which Jesus spoke concerning Lazarus when He said, *"This sickness is not unto death, but for the Glory of God, that the Son of God might be glorified thereby"* (Jn. 11:4).

This tells us that the sickness and death of Lazarus, at least in this case, constituted a sacrificial ministry on the part of Lazarus. It would glorify the Son of God, which must be the single purpose of every Believer.

We must never seek to glorify ourselves, only Him! And yet, in this single purpose, the Believer will ultimately be glorified also.

As Jesus was ultimately Glorified in His Disciples, He must ultimately be Glorified in us as well! This spoke of their lives lived for Him, with their giving all to His Service, even their very lives.

So, this prayer was wondrously answered in totality.

(11) "AND NOW I AM NO MORE IN THE WORLD, BUT THESE ARE IN THE WORLD, AND I COME TO YOU. HOLY FATHER, KEEP THROUGH YOUR OWN NAME THOSE WHOM YOU HAVE GIVEN ME, THAT THEY MAY BE ONE, AS WE ARE."

The overview is:

1. Paul considered certain individuals to be *"enemies of the Cross of Christ"* (Phil. 3:17-19).

2. He was speaking of the Judaizers, who were Jews who had claimed to accept Christ as the Messiah, but who also insisted that all Believers, both Jews and Gentiles, had to keep the Law.

3. As such, their emphasis was on the Law and not at all on the Cross of Christ.

THE CHARACTER AND NATURE OF GOD

The phrase, *"And now I am no more in the world,"* speaks of His Mission being finished, with Him shortly returning to the Father.

"But these are in the world, and I come to You," speaks of a hostile environment, with God Alone able to keep them.

Respecting Satan's opposition to the Child of God, his subtle ways are so varied and many that one is hard put to properly analyze all. Suffice to say, whatever the temptations, trials, tests, and tribulations, God is able through His Power to keep all who come to Him.

The phrase, *"Holy Father, keep through Your Own Name those whom You have given Me,"* once again points to the *"Name"* as explaining the Character and Nature of God. As we have already stated, this characterizes the Essence of Who He is!

FATHER

Taking the second part last, His Name as *"Father"* pertains to relationship, which should be obvious.

Such relationship can only come about by one being *"Born-Again,"* which, of course, pertains to accepting Jesus and the price He paid as one's Saviour. At that time, relationship with the Father immediately begins, and, in essence, at that moment, He becomes our *"Father."* So, the relationship Christ had with the Father can be had by Believers, as well, at least to a point, and, in fact, is guaranteed, which is the bedrock of Salvation.

Consequently, the little statement used by many, *"The Fatherhood of God and the brotherhood of man,"* although sounding good, is completely erroneous. First of all, God is not the Father of all, only those who are *"Born-Again"* (Jn. 3:3). In truth, Satan is the father of all who do not come to God through Jesus Christ (Jn. 8:42-44).

As well, all men are not brothers, only those who are Saved by the Blood of Jesus! (Eph. 3:14-15).

If it is to be noticed, of all the names Jehovah used concerning Himself, as described in the Old Testament, the name *"Father"* was not used except in a very limited way (Isa. 9:6; 63:16). Even though Believers (those in Covenant) at that time could have a relationship with Him, still, due to the fact that Jesus had not yet come and paid the price at Calvary for man's Redemption, thereby, taking all his sin away, such relationship was limited. However, due to that price now being paid by Christ and man's acceptance by Faith, no sin debt remains. Therefore, the Believer can literally be in Christ and, consequently, in the Father, all made possible by the Cross (Jn. 14:20). As such, God becomes the Believer's Father! Nevertheless, it is not to the degree as He is the Father of Jesus, but he is still granted the same inheritance (Rom. 8:17).

HOLY

Jesus addresses His Father as *"Holy,"* and He appeals to that Holiness as the surest basis of His Petition.

Why did He appeal to His Father's Holiness?

The Kingdom of God is built on *"Holiness and Righteousness!"* As such, it had been imputed to the Disciples, even though they would not be fully cognizant of such until after the Coming of the Holy Spirit.

Nevertheless, the Holiness of God, which, as well, is tied to His Will, guarantees the answer to the petition.

ONE

The phrase, *"That they may be one, as We are,"* proclaims how wonderful is the Grace that reveals these desires and the privileges that flow from His Care for His Beloved People. Here is heard the Son conversing with the Father respecting Their common Love for sinful men, and here the very Heart of the Great Shepherd is laid open.

It was so natural and easy for Him to rest His Eyes one moment upon the loved Disciples and then lift them to Heaven to ask precious things for them.

This prayer concerning the Body of Christ being *"one"* even as the Father and Son are *"One,"* refers to one in essence, in unity, and in purpose. It does not mean one in number. This *"one"* is not for Church unity, as many think, but rather for the taking of the Gospel to the world respecting the Salvation of souls (Vss. 18-21).

As well, to those who try to make the Father the same Person as the Son and vice versa, it is here obvious that this is not what is meant by the word *"One."*

Even though the Church is one Body, it is made up of many members, as is obvious. As well, even as there is One God, He is manifest in Three Persons, *"God the Father, God the Son, and God the Holy Spirit."* So, the word *"One"* does not necessarily have to refer to a number, but can refer to a purpose.

(12) "WHILE I WAS WITH THEM IN THE WORLD, I KEPT THEM IN YOUR NAME: THOSE WHO YOU GAVE ME I HAVE KEPT, AND NONE OF THEM IS LOST, BUT THE SON OF PERDITION; THAT THE SCRIPTURE MIGHT BE FULFILLED."

The exegesis is:

There are three Greek words for *"Redeemed"* or *"Redemption."* They are:

1. *"Agorazo"*: this word means *"to purchase from the slave market"* (I Cor. 6:20).

2. *"Exagorazo"*: this word means *"to purchase out of the slave market, never to be put up for sale again in any slave market."*

3. *"Lutroo"*: this root word means *"ransom money used to liberate a slave."* The idea is, such a price has been paid that demons, devils, Angels, Heaven, or Hell will never be able to say in eternity future that the price was insufficient (I Pet. 1:18; Titus 2:14).

THOSE YOU GAVE, I HAVE KEPT

The phrase, *"While I was with them in the world, I kept them in Your Name,"* proclaims both the Father and the Son in this joint task. As well, He will *"keep them"* who truly follow Him, irrespective of who or where they may be. Here, we have His Promise!

The phrase, *"Those who You gave Me I have kept,"* refers to the fact that Satan had attempted to destroy not only Judas but the entirety of the Disciples.

This included not only the Twelve but, as well, the Seventy, and even others who had come to believe on Him.

JUDAS

The phrase, *"And none of them is lost, but the son of perdition,"* pertains to Judas.

However, it should be clear that Judas was not a *"son of perdition"* (literally, son of destruction; destined to destruction), but became that way after he yielded to Satan near the very close of the Ministry of Christ. In fact, Judas was one of the number given to Jesus by the Father, as is evidenced by the previous phrase. Also, it is impossible to lose something that has never been found.

It should be noted that Judas was not lost because the Power of the Father and the Son was insufficient to keep him, but rather he was lost because of his own self-will. The Lord can only keep those who desire to be kept and will not force one to be kept who does not desire to be so.

The phrase, *"That the Scripture might be fulfilled,"* is found in Psalms 41:9; 69:25-29; 109:8; Acts 1:20-25.

Judas was not lost that Prophecy might come to pass, but Prophecy foretold the fact of his willful sin and lost state. He was lost because he refused to be Saved, and was lost through his own avarice and stubbornness to come back to Christ even after his crime, which he could have done.

This phrase might be paraphrased, *"Which the Scripture foretold!"*

(13) "AND NOW COME I TO YOU; AND THESE THINGS I SPEAK IN THE WORLD, THAT THEY MIGHT HAVE MY JOY FULFILLED IN THEMSELVES."

The exposition is:

1. The beauty of the Twenty-third Psalm knows no comparison. It is called, *"The Shepherd's Psalm."*

NOTES

2. It is written from the position of the sheep that look exclusively to the shepherd for leading and guidance.

3. The Shepherd in Type is the Lord Jesus Christ.

PRAYER

The phrase, *"And now come I to You,"* proclaims the Father as His Teacher, Guide, Leader, Comfort, and Strength. As He set the example relative to prayer, we are meant to follow suit.

It is impossible to have a relationship with the Lord without, at the same time, having a strong prayer life. So, inasmuch as most Christians hardly pray at all, this means, and tragically so, that most have no relationship with the Father.

Considering the Blessings which accrue from such an effort, it is difficult to understand why every Believer would not take total advantage of such a privilege. However, few do!

Believers should pray simply because all of us have great need of Leading and Guidance, as well as other types of petitions. However, the greatest reason to pray is that our relationship with the Lord may be enhanced, which, without prayer, is not possible!

The phrase, *"And these things I speak in the world,"* once again speaks of the hostility registered against Christ and the Disciples, which will exacerbate greatly after the Day of Pentecost. He is praying this prayer in a hostile environment and believes that the Father's Care will protect them in this hostility.

"That they might have My Joy fulfilled in themselves," would be answered on the Day of Pentecost. Then the Holy Spirit came and took up abode in the hearts and lives of Believers and made all things of Jesus real and tangible to them. He continues to do so unto this very hour.

(14) "I HAVE GIVEN THEM YOUR WORD; AND THE WORLD HAS HATED THEM, BECAUSE THEY ARE NOT OF THE WORLD, EVEN AS I AM NOT OF THE WORLD."

The structure is:

1. We are emphatically told in the Word of God that it is *"our Faith"* that gives us

victory over the world (I Jn. 5:4).

2. The type of Faith which the Holy Spirit through John addresses pertains to Faith exclusively in Christ and what He has done for us at the Cross (I Cor. 1:17).

3. Everything hinges on the Cross of Christ!

THE WORD OF GOD

The phrase, *"I have given them Your Word,"* speaks of a permanent endowment.

"Of all that Jesus began to do and teach," is the Word and is the criterion (Acts 1:1).

The phrase, *"And the world has hated them, because they are not of the world, even as I am not of the world,"* proclaims the antagonism because the world is evil, inasmuch as its spirit is ruled by Satan, the Prince of Darkness.

Reynolds said: *"Christ has exposed its hypocrisies and denounced its idols, and inverted its standards, and repudiated its smile, and condemned its Prince, and was now indifferent to its curse."*[5]

As we have previously stated, this *"hatred"* will be evidenced through the apostate church, even as the Pharisees hated Christ. The reason is obvious:

The thrust, direction, purpose, and strength of the apostate church comes from men and not from God, even though it claims to be of God. Anything not born of the Spirit is antagonistic toward God. This has been Satan's greatest thrust from the very beginning and continues unto this hour.

THE HOLY SPIRIT

That which is born of the Spirit is not of this world and has no origination at all in man, even though the Lord uses men to project His Cause. So, it is the age-old conflict between the flesh and the Spirit. It began with Cain killing Abel and continued in the great conflict between Jacob and Esau. Most of that done presently under the guise of *"Gospel,"* in fact, is not gospel but flesh. Sadly, it incorporates most churches and even entire religious denominations.

That which is born of the Spirit bears Fruit unto Christ in the form of souls and the Attributes of the Holy Spirit. It is the true Work of God in the world, and always has been.

That which is of the flesh, at times, is very similar to that which is truly of the Spirit and even uses much of the same terminology. However, it bears no fruit unto the Lord, even though it claims much.

As an example, many if not most, of the modern Pentecostal denominations began of the Spirit. As a result, tremendous things were accomplished for the Cause of Christ. However, many of these have left the Ways of the Spirit, resorting to the flesh, i.e., wisdom of men, and as a result, are presently bringing forth precious little Fruit for the Lord, if any at all! It is sad but these very organizations, which once did so much to take the Gospel to the world, are probably hindering it presently more so now than anything else!

(15) *"I PRAY NOT THAT YOU SHOULD TAKE THEM OUT OF THE WORLD, BUT THAT YOU SHOULD KEEP THEM FROM THE EVIL."*

The construction is:

1. The Doctrine of Luke 17:23-37 strikes against the expectation of many that the world will grow morally better and ultimately become the Kingdom of God.

2. In fact, in this Passage, the Lord gives a fearful picture of the state of the world and the professing Church at the time of His Second Coming.

3. More than once, Jesus pointed to Noah and the state of society in his day (Mat. 24:37) as prefiguring the condition of the nations in these last days.

PROTECTION FROM THE EVIL ONE

Jesus said, *"I pray not that You should take them out of the world."* The following says:

"He does not pray for them to die and leave the world, nor seclude themselves in deserts or segregate themselves from the world in communities and monasteries to escape temptation, but to live as lights and examples of God in the world" (Mat. 5:16; I Cor. 5:10; Phil. 2:15; Titus 2:11-14).

The phrase, *"But that You should keep them from the evil,"* means to keep them from the wiles and machinations of the Evil One, Satan.

The first prayer for the Disciples was that they might be kept; the second prayer asks for protection from the Evil One; the third, as we shall see, asks that their knowledge of the Scriptures should result in separation from all evil (Vs. 17); the fourth, found in Verses 18 through 21, related to oneness with Christ and God in taking the Gospel to the world; and the fifth and last (Vs. 24) concerned their Eternal Home.

(16) "THEY ARE NOT OF THE WORLD, EVEN AS I AM NOT OF THE WORLD."

The synopsis is:

1. The Galatian Christians were putting themselves under Law, guaranteeing their defeat.

2. The reason was, the Holy Spirit, Whom we must have, will help us only if our Faith is exclusively in Christ and the Cross.

3. Paul said that if they placed their Faith elsewhere other than the Cross, they would *"fall from Grace"* (Gal. 5:4). As stated, this refers to the Believer placing his or her faith elsewhere, other than the Cross, which stops the Grace of God. It is a chilling prospect.

THE WORLD

The phrase, *"They are not of the world,"* means that their Calling and Election had absolutely nothing to do with the world and its systems. Everything they had was from God, their Salvation, their Call, their Ministry, their Burden, and their Destination.

As well, even though they were in the world, they were in no way to be like the world. They would not march to its drums, be influenced by its spirit, seek its direction, or be moved by its direction.

To be sure, this short phrase as uttered by Christ should be and, in fact, must be the hallmark of the Child of God. It must never be forgotten! This world or its system holds absolutely nothing for the Believer. His sustenance comes from above, and that means all of his sustenance. He must draw no nourishment from the world or make any attempt to do so. Such is the bane of the ministry and the cause of spiritual anemia.

However, separation, for the Text speaks of this, is not isolation. If we are overtaken by the spirit of the world, we cannot help the world. Our only means to help the world, and that is what we are supposed to do, is to be separate from its influences. We are to be *"salt"* and *"Light!"*

For instance, the Twenty-sixth Chapter of Genesis records some of the struggles of Isaac. When a famine came to Canaan at that time, it seems that Isaac was tempted to go down into Egypt even as his father Abraham had done. He did go to Gerar, which is on the road to Egypt. In fact, Genesis 26:2 says, *"The LORD appeared unto him, and said, Go not down into Egypt; dwell in the land which I shall tell you of."*

The Blessings were not in Egypt (the world), but rather in the Land of Promise.

THE OATH OF THE SEVEN LAMBS

It is disastrous to the Spiritual life for the Christian to go down into *"Egypt."* It is dangerous to go down unto *"Gerar,"* for it is a half-way house to Egypt. A man, like Isaac, may become very rich in *"Gerar,"* but it is not recorded that Jehovah appeared to Isaac in *"Gerar."* He appeared to him before he went there and the very night of the day that he left, but not while there! The Lord wanted him in Beersheba, and only there did the Lord appear to him (Gen. 26:23-24).

"Beersheba" means *"the well or the oath of seven lambs."* Such speaks of the offering up of Christ at Calvary, which would bring a Well of Living Water.

The Believer is only a Blessing to God when he is separate from the world and in the place where God wants him, *"The well of the oath of seven lambs,"* i.e., *"His life modeled after the Sacrifice of Calvary."*

The phrase, *"Even as I am not of the world,"* reflects that the servants should be like their Lord.

The blight of the church is its use of worldly methods, attempting to carry out the Work of the Lord. For instance, the modern Christian contemporary music scene is a case in point. It claims it can win the youth to the Lord by being a carbon copy of the worldly rock groups, etc. Of course, any Believer who has any knowledge at all of the Ways of God sees the absolute stupidity of such direction.

Gabriel told me that many of these so-called Christian rock-rap groups get their inspiration from some of the most notorious groups of the world of this time. How in the world can they think they can bless anyone by receiving their inspiration from the Devil! And yet, they will boldly write on their CDs where their inspiration comes from. God help us!

The truth is, these so-called Christian rock-rap groups need themselves to get Saved. To be sure, the influence they leave in the churches, or wherever it is they put on their act, and an act it is, leaves the young people who associate with such with demon spirits because that's exactly what is guiding the effort.

We must understand that one does not win the alcoholic by drinking with him, the gambler by gambling with him, etc. In fact, the world is not won to Jesus by any of its methods. People are brought to Christ, irrespective of their age, as the Gospel of Jesus Christ is preached under the Anointing of the Holy Spirit, with Him convicting the sinner of *"sin, Righteousness, and Judgment."* How absolutely foolish and how absolutely stupid can we be to even think otherwise!

THE WAYS OF THE WORLD ARE NOT THE WAYS OF GOD

Reynolds said a long time ago, *"How often in our own days has a 'man of the world' filled with its instinct, directed with its purpose, and saturated with its spirit, lauded as the true man and ideal leader of a Christian state?"*

Sometime ago, a so-called Pentecostal leader claimed that President Clinton was a Born-Again Believer simply because Clinton, at that time, had made some right sounding statements in this man's presence.

In fact, such thinking is foolishness gone to seed! Words are cheap! It is the fruit of one's life that counts, and the fruit in that situation just mentioned should be overly obvious.

I keep saying it because it must be said. The ways of the world are not the Ways of God and in no way can be forced into that which is solely of the Spirit. To attempt to do so does not incorporate merely the best of the world but, in fact, causes the Holy Spirit to withdraw, leaving nothing but the world. Sadly, this characterizes most churches and ministries presently! The only Answer is the Spirit of God, and He dwells only in that which is unworldly.

(17) *"SANCTIFY THEM THROUGH YOUR TRUTH: YOUR WORD IS TRUTH."*

The synopsis is:

1. Realizing the Grace of God that had been shown to him, Paul considered himself a *"debtor"* to all men.

2. It did not matter whom the people might be, meaning that he must do his utmost best to take the Gospel to all concerned.

3. Even though Paul couldn't reach all people, still, he felt responsible to all, whether he could reach them or not.

TRUTH

The phrase, *"Sanctify them through Your Truth,"* refers to the Word of God. It alone must ever be the criterion for all things. It alone can set the record straight, and, as a result, it sanctifies the Believer by bringing him into line with its precepts. There is Sanctification in no other!

The word *"sanctify"* means to *"set apart for sacred use."*

The Word of God tells one what is right and what is wrong and the direction one must take to achieve the right. This is the reason the Believer must make the Bible his lifelong project. He not only must study the precepts of its pages but, as well, earnestly seek the Holy Spirit to reveal to him more perfectly these great Truths. In fact, only the Holy Spirit can do such a thing.

While the Lord definitely employs men and women as teachers for this purpose (Eph. 4:11), still, the Word is so important that the Holy Spirit has promised to anoint the Believer so that he or she may know if what they are being taught is right or wrong (I Jn. 2:27). However, such Anointing of the Holy Spirit upon and within the Believer can only come about if the Believer is consecrated to the seeking of Truth. As we have repeatedly stated, too many Believers seek to force the Word of God to verify their erroneous thinking instead of allowing their thinking to be molded by the Word of God. There is a vast difference! The former wants its self-will vindicated, while the latter has his will hidden in Christ in order that the Holy Spirit may reveal these great Truths.

THE WORD OF GOD

It is tragic when Believers allow the Word of God to merely occupy their houses and do not take advantage of its great Truths. The Word of God should be imbibed daily by the Believer. As well, the Believer should read the Word, beginning at Genesis and going straight through to the Book of Revelation.

To skip around in the Bible is to miss what the Holy Spirit is telling us. The Bible is a Story, and it has a beginning and an ending. It should be studied accordingly! As well, it should be studied prayerfully and with diligence, seeking to master its contents, which the Holy Spirit will help one do if one will only be dedicated to such pursuit.

Too often Believers think that such is only for Preachers and not for them as laymen. Nothing could be further from the truth! Its Promises are for the layman as well as for the Preacher of the Gospel. There is to be no distinction!

YOUR WORD IS TRUTH

The phrase, *"Your Word is Truth,"* means that the Bible does not merely contain truth but *"is Truth."*

I have said it so many times in these Volumes and will continue to do so simply because of its magnitude. *"The Bible is the only revealed Truth in the world today and, in fact, ever has been!"* There are many other things which are true, but that is far different than *"Truth."*

Truth by definition cannot be a philosophy because, by its nature, Truth cannot change, while philosophies change almost daily. As well, in its truest form, philosophy is a search for Truth; therefore, it cannot of itself be Truth.

One of the most ridiculous statements made by modern preachers, and it is made very often, is their pontification on the *"psychology of life."* What that is supposed to mean is, of course, anyone's guess! As well, it is understandable that unregenerate men would come up with such foolishness.

NOTES

However, for a man to claim to be a Preacher of the Gospel and to embroil himself into this foolishness of the wisdom of men is, in effect, stupidity gone to seed, especially considering that he has the *"Truth,"* i.e., the Bible, at his fingertips.

Sadly, to a great extent, this is the age of the fundamentalists, Pentecostals, and Charismatics leaving the Word of God, in fact, that which they claim to believe, for the tawdry elements of this present world. What a travesty!

Why?

I suppose there would be many reasons, but perhaps the following just might be the biggest reason of all:

METHODOLOGY

When religious leaders or preachers of any sort, or anyone, for that matter, become overly engrossed in ministry to the exclusion of Jesus, that is where the problem begins.

What do we mean by that?

Ideally, Jesus and Ministry should be one and the same. However, it is very easy to become so engrossed in the particulars of Ministry that, little by little, Jesus becomes smaller and smaller in our lives, which is the road to disaster. We are speaking of things such as how the work is to be done, how it is to be carried out, and what direction to take respecting methodology. If Jesus is Big and Real in one's life, the methods of ministry, to be sure, will take care of themselves. Anyway, it is not our methods as Ministers of the Gospel that help anyone, but rather the Supremacy of Christ within our hearts, Who Alone can meet the needs of man.

The truth is, it is much more fashionable to be big in ministry, with all of its various nuances, than to be big in Jesus. The former is outward while the latter is inward. The former receives the plaudits of men while the latter receives only the opposition of Satan, and greatly so, for that matter!

To have Jesus fill one's heart, the Believer, be he Preacher or otherwise, must have a strong prayer life and a strong attachment to the Word of God. Otherwise, it is literally impossible to have Christ, and we are meaning Christ and the Cross! Jesus, as the *"Living Word,"* makes the *"Written Word"* come alive through the Person and Ministry of the Holy Spirit.

(18) "AS YOU HAVE SENT ME INTO THE WORLD, EVEN SO HAVE I ALSO SENT THEM INTO THE WORLD."

The composition is:

1. I John 5:4 tells us emphatically that it is *"our Faith"* that gives us victory over the world.

2. What exactly does John the Beloved mean by the phrase, *"Our Faith"*?

3. It is to always be Faith in Christ and the Cross, which is the only Faith that God will recognize (I Cor. 1:17, 18; 2:2).

THE WORLD

The phrase, *"As You have sent Me into the world,"* pertains to the Glory which Jesus had with the Father before the world was, and from which He freely divested Himself in order that He might become a Man, The Man Christ Jesus, in which He would deliver mankind. The record is clear that He referred to this quite often (Jn. 10:36; 17:8).

The phrase, *"Even so have I also sent them into the world,"* refers to the Apostolic Commission.

In the Greek text, it is said that the word *"sent"* incorporates the entire ministerial function of all who believe in the Mission of the Son. There is nothing on Earth more important and, in fact, nothing that even comes close.

As well, this not only applied to the original Twelve (minus Judas), but for all who believe on Him through the Word (Mat. 18:18; 28:20; Mk. 16:15-20; Jn. 14:12; 20:21).

To take the Word to the world should be, and, in fact, must be, the single-minded interest of the Church. Sadly, with some few exceptions, that is little the case at present.

THE ASSEMBLIES OF GOD

The Assemblies of God was begun as a fellowship for the very purpose of taking the Gospel to the world, and for many years, God used it tremendously so in this fashion.

However, little by little, this organization ceased to be a fellowship and, more and more, became a denomination. As such, it began to place its faith in the structure of its organization instead of the Word of God. Consequently, men and women in this denomination, who claimed to have a Call of God to particular parts of the world and for particular ministries, were more and more ignored, with the *"system"* sending them to where the system desired, thereby, ignoring the Call of God and it's respective direction. Little by little, the Holy Spirit was replaced with humanistic psychology.

As a result, all prospective missionaries are now subjected to a battery of psychological tests and, in fact, have been for quite some time. These tests pretty much serve as the barometer for acceptance and, as well, if the person is accepted, the tests determine where the new missionary is to be sent. Thus, as stated, the Holy Spirit is pretty much ignored.

In the last two or three years in which I was associated with that particular denomination, I began to notice those who, while claiming to be missionaries, seemed to have little knowledge of the Lord and referred to their *"ministry"* mostly as a *"career."* While I continued to see some few men and women in foreign missions work who I felt were totally sold out to the Lord, thereby, attempting to reach people for Christ, more and more, however, I found that most of these were, in reality, preachers of the gospel not at all, but rather amateur psychologists, etc.

THE HEAVENLY VISION

All of this proclaims a total departure from the very Words of Christ. He sends us into the world, not some foreign missions department. The task of such organizations ideally should be to help and aid such Callings, but not to play God. I will use my own Ministry as an example.

God has called me for a certain task. As Paul said, *"I was not disobedient unto the Heavenly Vision:*

"But showed first unto them of Damascus, and at Jerusalem, and throughout all the coasts of Judaea, and then to the Gentiles, that they should repent and turn to God, and do works meet for Repentance" (Acts 26:19-20).

As a result, it is the business of every Believer, and every other God-called Preacher for that matter, to help me carry out this

Vision. Regrettably, most religious hierarchy has attempted to hinder this Call on my life, despite hundreds of thousands of people, and I exaggerate not, being brought to a Saving Knowledge of Jesus Christ. Sadly, as it was with Paul, it continues unto this very hour. Many in the church hinder instead of help!

(19) "AND FOR THEIR SAKES I SANCTIFY MYSELF, THAT THEY ALSO MIGHT BE SANCTIFIED THROUGH THE TRUTH."

The pattern is:

1. When the Believer sins, and we speak of a sin that he knows he has committed, he is to take that sin to the Lord and confess it before Him (I Jn. 1:9).

2. The Lord has promised to forgive, and that He will do.

3. His Faithfulness is involved because He promised to forgive. His Righteousness is in question, for it would be unjust to punish sin a second time — the penalty of the Believer's sins having been already borne at Calvary.

SANCTIFIED

The phrase, *"And for their sakes I sanctify Myself,"* could be translated:

"I separate Myself unto God to do His Will, even unto death, so that My Disciples may benefit through My Salvation for them and be sanctified continually as they get to know the Word" (I Jn. 1:7; Eph. 5:26).

As a Man, this was necessary on the Part of Christ. Even though God sent Him, and therefore, He came from God, was of God, and, in fact, was God, still, as a Man, it was necessary that He purposely set Himself apart in order that the Holy Spirit might fill every proper vessel. As should be obvious, He set the Example for us.

THROUGH THE TRUTH

The phrase, *"That they also might be sanctified through the Truth,"* proclaims to us several things:

1. It is the Word of God that sanctifies. It Alone proclaims the direction one must travel, and Alone shows a man what he is and how that Jesus is the Only Answer.

2. The meaning of the word *"Sanctification"* is *"to be made not guilty,"* in that one believes in the Finished Work of Christ. It refers to one being set apart solely to Christ and His Cause.

3. To fully understand the Doctrine of Sanctification, one must understand the following:

• Positional Sanctification: this is the position one has in Christ immediately upon Conversion. It is all of Christ and is freely given by Christ the very moment one accepts Him as Lord and Saviour.

In the mind of God, the Believer is *"set apart"* strictly unto Himself (God) and, thereby, from the world and its system. That position does not vacilate, remaining the same irrespective (I Cor. 6:11).

• Conditional Sanctification: primarily, this is what Jesus is addressing. This speaks of our present condition, which is progressive. In other words, one is more and more sanctified as the Truth of the Word of God takes effect in one's heart and life. Hence, it can be referred to as *"progressive Sanctification."* Every Believer is in this mode to one degree or the other.

Whereas *"positional Sanctification"* never varies, *"conditional, or better said, progressive Sanctification,"* varies constantly.

It is the Work of the Holy Spirit to bring the *"condition"* of the Believer up to his *"position,"* consequently, a Work which never ends.

(20) "NEITHER PRAY I FOR THESE ALONE, BUT FOR THEM ALSO WHICH SHOULD BELIEVE ON ME THROUGH THEIR WORD."

The order is:

1. The Lord said in Exodus 12:13, *"When I see the blood,"* not *"When I see your particular church,"* *"your good works,"* etc.

2. The worthiness of the person is not taken into question simply because, in the Eyes of God, there is no worthiness.

3. That which characterizes acceptance by God is that the Blood of His Son, the Lord Jesus Christ, be applied to our hearts and lives, which is done by Faith (Rom. 5:1; Eph. 2:8-9).

THE PRAYER OF CHRIST

The phrase, *"Neither pray I for these alone,"* has reference to Verse 18. Jesus is speaking not only of His Present Disciples, but the multitudes in all ages who would believe their Testimony.

"But for them also which should believe on Me through their Word," has reference to the fact that all must take the Word to others, for that is the method chosen by the Holy Spirit. There is no other way.

This is so very important and, consequently, must not be allowed to lose its significance.

God has devised no other way that the Message of Redemption may be given to a lost world. He calls men and women to this task, and in a sense, all Believers are called. The lost must hear the *"Word,"* and this is the only way it can be heard. This is what makes the *"Kingdom now"* philosophy so ungodly!

This teaching, which goes under various names, is very prominent in the church at present. It is little recognized as error, and gross error at that, but that is what it is.

This teaching pretty well sets aside the Bible Way of Evangelism, which is the preaching of the Gospel of Jesus Christ, in whatever manner. In its place, its adherents have substituted a political way.

KINGDOM NOW

In effect, it teaches that the world is going to become more and more Christianized, consequently, coming to terms with the major religions of the world, such as Islam, Hinduism, Buddhism, etc. The Christianization will take place, they say, as men and women with Christian values, more or less, are elected into high political office. As a result, a great segment of the modern church is very busily engaged in these efforts, thinking to change the nation, and the world, for that matter.

While Believers should definitely be involved in the political process, still, it must be done with the understanding that such, even if successful, will be only of small help.

As a result, their evangelism efforts are pretty well reduced to high political office or trying to convert those who are in these positions.

While every effort definitely should be made to convert any and all, irrespective as to their position, still, such people, even if converted and consecrated to the Cause of Christ, actually can make only a small difference. The reasons should be obvious to the Bible student.

CHURCH

The system of this world is evil; in fact, it is engineered by Satan. As such, it will not change, and as such, the efforts of the church are mostly wasted in making this quest a priority. As stated, the society of the world is evil; consequently, men must be Saved out of that society, not in that society. In effect, that is what the word *"Church"* actually means — *"a Called-out People."*

By attempting to convert political leaders in foreign countries, which certainly should be done, but for the right reason, if successful or thought to be so, such is concluded in the *"Kingdom now"* philosophy to be the winning of that country to Christ. As such, gargantuan numbers are handed out pertaining to sinners accepting Christ. In reality, few have accepted Christ, at least according to these efforts.

A short time ago, while observing a particular religious telecast, the host blatantly announced that his particular *"ministry"* had won over 100,000,000 people to Christ. He then stated, *"Our goal this year is 300,000,000 won to Christ."*

In reality, at least according to the Bible, this effort is not even a ministry, much less the winning of staggering numbers of souls. This *"host"* does not preach and, in fact, little believes in preaching of the Gospel. The reason he uses these staggering numbers is because entire countries, or at least the greater percentage, are concluded to be *"won to Christ"* on the basis of some political leader in that particular country claiming allegiance to Christ.

THE BIBLE WAY

The Bible Way of the Holy Spirit anointing the preached Word of God is totally ignored. Actually, it is frowned upon by the proponents of this philosophy, even though they probably would not admit such. In fact, they use all the right words. However, even though their phraseology is very similar, if not identical, to true Believers, their meaning of these words and phraseology is totally different from Bible Christianity, as we have stated.

The sadness is this gross error is compounded because many Believers, little knowing the Word of God, pretty well fall for whatever they hear. That which is the flashiest and makes the boldest claims is readily accepted, even though there is precious little true Bible substantiation for these claims.

That is the reason the Believer must know the Word and be led by the Spirit of God. Otherwise, false apostles become very attractive.

(21) "THAT THEY ALL MAY BE ONE; AS YOU, FATHER, ARE IN ME, AND I IN YOU, THAT THEY ALSO MAY BE ONE IN US: THAT THE WORLD MAY BELIEVE THAT YOU HAVE SENT ME."

The pattern is:

1. I Samuel 3:1 says, *"The Word of the LORD was precious in those days; there was no open vision."*

2. This means that there was a scarcity of the Word of the Lord in Israel of that day. The Nation and its people were in serious straits, which always is the case when the Word of the Lord is scarce.

3. There have never been more churches in America than at the present time. However, there has never been less True Word of the Lord preached at any time since the Reformation than now!

THAT THEY MAY BE ONE

The phrase, *"That they all may be one,"* is the second of five such petitions in this prayer (Vss. 11, 21-23).

There are three particular unities requested by Christ:

1. Unity in *"Communion,"* in the Fellowship of Christ with the Father — *"One, as We are"* (Vs. 11).

2. Unity in *"Purpose"* with the Father and the Son in the Salvation of sinners (Vss. 18 and 21) — *"One in Us."*

3. Unity in *"Glory"* (Vs. 22) — *"As We are One."*

As we have stated, the type of unity for which Jesus prays concerning Believers is not Church unity, as is popularly supposed, but rather unity in *"Communion," "Purpose,"* and *"Glory."*

While all the different church splinters and factions are not pleasing to the Lord, which is evidenced in I Corinthians 1:10, still, Jesus is calling for a unity of far higher proportions. If achieved, it will automatically bring about the oneness of the Body regarding particular church factions and denominations.

UNITY

The phrase, *"As You, Father, are in Me, and I in You,"* proclaims the foundation of such unity.

In the thoughts of Reynolds, he says that the union between the Father and Son is not a visible manifestation but a Spiritual inference. The common indwelling in the Father and Son, the identity of the Spiritual emotion and purpose in all who have one Lord, one Faith, one Baptism will convince the world by producing a similar inference.[6]

Alford said, *"This unity is not mere outward uniformity, nor can such uniformity produce it. At the same time, its effects are to be real and visible, such that the world may see them."*[7]

The phrase, *"That they also may be one in Us,"* pertains to oneness in *"Purpose"* as Verse 11 pertains to *"Communion."*

As an aside, the pronoun, *"Us,"* proclaims a plurality of Persons in the Godhead, here the Father and the Son, but more particularly, *"Father, Son, and Holy Spirit."*

TO BELIEVE

The phrase, *"That the world may believe that You have sent Me,"* proclaims the Father sending the Son into the world to save the world and the Son sending His Disciples into the world for the same purpose.

This is the *"Glory"* of Verse 22, and this unity in *"Purpose"* will help the world to *"believe."* The Unity in Glory will cause the world to *"know"* that God loved Christ and loved His People, even as Jesus loved His Father.

Such was the foundation of this wondrous prayer. Jesus prayed for the Disciples because they belonged to the Father.

Therefore, He must pray for them, and the Father must be interested in them because Christ was Glorified in them.

The Disciples lost the Companionship of Christ visibly when He ascended, but it was to find themselves put in Christ's Own Relationship with the Father, enjoying all that He enjoyed in that Blessed Fellowship on Earth.

It was in the Power of the enjoyment of this relationship to the Father that the Disciples were enabled to maintain their relationship to the world in love and Testimony, and the rule of that Spiritual Life was to be the Word, i.e., the Scriptures.

The Word was to come first, and then their Mission was to follow. The Word would make it intelligent and effective. The Word was and is opposed to the world. Were they of the world, they would not be sent into it, but they had been taken out of the world, spiritually speaking.

(22) "AND THE GLORY WHICH YOU GAVE ME I HAVE GIVEN THEM; THAT THEY MAY BE ONE, EVEN AS WE ARE ONE."

The form is:

1. The formula, *"form of Doctrine,"* found in Romans 6:17, is very important.

2. It declares the Christian Faith to have been once and for all delivered to Believers as fixed and complete, therefore, neither needing nor accepting additions.

3. Into that form, as into a mold, the Believers are poured or *"delivered."* In other words, such a Believer is subscribing to God's Prescribed Order.

4. This *"form of Doctrine"* can be summed up in the words, *"Jesus Christ and Him Crucified,"* and is the oldest Doctrine, one might say, in the world today, and ever has been. It was formulated in the mind of the Godhead even before the foundation of the world (I Pet. 1:18-20).

THE GLORY

The Phrase, *"And the Glory which You gave Me I have given them,"* pertains to the petition for *"Glory"* as Verse 21 pertained to *"Purpose"* and Verse 11 to *"Communion."* In this we find the totality of ingredients that make up the Christian experience in Christ. Let us look at them one by one:

- *"Communion"*: as Jesus prayed that Believers would have the same type of Communion with the Heavenly Father as He did, we find in this the Source and Strength of all Life as it is lived in Christ. This is the answer for all the vicissitudes of life, stress, or difficulties of every stripe.

If the Believer can have and maintain such Communion (and millions have), everything for which the soul craves can be here found. Such does not mean that all problems instantly go away, but does mean that one can have total peace and security even in the midst of the worst type of difficulties. This is what Communion with the Heavenly Father affords.

Regrettably, the modern church has abandoned this wonderful privilege, at least for the most part, in favor of humanistic psychology. So-called Christian psychologists advise people when frustrated to take a pillow or some such object and beat it, therefore, releasing one's frustrations, anger, etc.

Such would be funny if it were not so ludicrous! No! Such silliness holds no answer for anyone; Communion with our Heavenly Father holds all the answers.

Once again I emphasize the fact that while it is somewhat understandable as to the world taking this direction, it is not understandable at all regarding those who refer to themselves as Believers.

PURPOSE

If one is having proper Communion with the Lord, one will get to know the *"Purpose"* of God relative to His Work on Earth among men.

The other day while looking at a particular gospel telecast (gospel?), the host announced to his audience that his organization had then purchased an entertainment center in a particular city in America. He went on to state how this complex now belonged to the *"Body of Christ."*

Everything in me screamed out against this because I knew it to be at cross purposes with the Will of God. The Purpose of God is not to entertain Christians. To be sure, it is of far higher and more noble purpose.

The *"Purpose"* of the Lord is to take the

greatest Story man has ever known to a hurting, dying world in order that they may be Saved. Whether they accept or not is one thing; however, they must have the opportunity to do one or the other!

CALLED ACCORDING TO HIS PURPOSE

It is Satan's business (and he does it very well) to divert the Body of Christ from its true purpose to other things. While the *"other things"* may be good within themselves, still, they will not, whatever they may be, achieve the Intended Purpose of the Holy Spirit.

As we have repeatedly stated, even to the point of being overly repetitious, the purpose and direction of the Church must, without fail, be the taking of the Gospel to a hurting world. Everything else must be ancillary and supportive of that!

In preaching sometime ago at Family Worship Center, I made mention of a cartoon I had seen a short time before.

It consisted of a huge machine about the size of a room in a house, with hundreds of pulleys, wheels, and moving parts, all clattering at one time, with smoke belching from its several stacks, etc.

As one man stood nearby observing this monstrosity, he turned and asked another man, *"What is it?"*

"It is a giant machine," was the immediate answer as he looked at it in enraptured wonder.

"What does it do?" the first man asked, continuing to stare at the movement of the hundreds of parts and listening to the great racket it was making.

"Do?" the second man remonstrated!

"Yes," the inquirer continued, *"Do?" "What is its function?" "Does It manufacture something or serve some other type of purpose?"*

"No!" the man answered, *"It does not manufacture anything, nor does it serve any purpose or function."*

Then he added, *"But isn't it interesting, all of these mechanical parts functioning at one time?"*

THE MODERN CHURCH

Even though the analogy may be somewhat silly, still, most of the modern church falls into the same category.

It makes a lot of racket and noise, with all types of religious wheels and machinery operating at full capacity. To the carnal mind, it looks like much is taking place, especially considering all the activity.

However, like the machine in the cartoon, it serves no purpose, at least that is devised by the Lord, but because of all the activity, many Believers are lulled into thinking that much is being done for Christ when, in reality, nothing is being done!

The purpose of true Christianity is to carry on *"all that Jesus began both to do and teach"* (Acts 1:1), and in His Exact Manner, should be quickly added.

If it's not Scriptural, it is not His Purpose. As well, if it is not devised by the Holy Spirit, even though it might be right, still, such *"purpose"* not intended by God cannot bring forth proper fruit. It must be *"His Purpose!"*

GLORY

If the *"Communion"* is proper and the *"Purpose,"* in effect, *"His Purpose,"* then the *"Glory of God"* will always garnish the Believer and his efforts.

This *"Glory"* is the privilege of belonging to the Lord in having the distinctive honor of being a part of His glorious Work. This results in the Gospel being preached to the poor, with broken hearts healed and captives set free. It results in spiritual sight being restored and bruises being healed (Lk. 4:17-18).

The phrase, *"That they may be one, even as We are One,"* refers to this *"Glory"* being a fact, even as it is in many hearts and lives.

So, this prayer prayed by Jesus has certainly been answered, and all who have been the beneficiary have reaped untold Spiritual Blessings.

(23) "I IN THEM, AND YOU IN ME, THAT THEY MAY BE MADE PERFECT IN ONE; AND THAT THE WORLD MAY KNOW THAT YOU HAVE SENT ME, AND HAVE LOVED THEM, AS YOU HAVE LOVED ME."

The diagram is:

1. What a Blessing it must have been to have heard Jesus teach!

2. And yet, those whose hearts were not right with God found no substance in His

Words of Life, just as those presently!

3. That's why Jesus was constantly saying, *"He who has ears to hear, let him hear"* (Lk. 8:8).

I IN THEM, AND YOU IN ME

The phrase, *"I in them, and You in Me,"* is spoken distinctly by Christ. The reason it is done thusly is because Jesus distinctly regards Himself as the mediating link of relation between the Father and the Disciples, which He certainly was and is. In this manner alone can this relationship be forged; consequently, Christ, as a Mediating Link of relationship is not optional, but rather an absolute necessity.

PERFECTION?

The phrase, *"That they may be perfect in one,"* actually proclaims the only way such *"perfection"* can be ascertained.

Reynolds said, *"This pertains to each individual Believer reaching the highest perfection of his being, as according to his own capacity and function by the Holy Spirit, he fills his place in the one living Body of the Lord."*[8] Such alone can bring out the full potential of man.

How can this be done?

It can only be done in one way and is the same for all. There must be a hunger and thirst after God, which can only be satisfied by a strong prayer life, as stated, and devotion to the Word of God.

As well, most Believers think if such is brought about, it will be at the Divine Discretion of the Lord. In other words, the individual thinking such becomes a passive instrument. Such is basely incorrect.

One has to stir oneself in order to facilitate such a nearness to the Lord. As we have stated, this is what Jesus meant when He said, *"And for their sakes I sanctify Myself"* (Vs. 19).

The Believer must say within his heart, *"I want to get closer to God,"* and then take the necessary steps to bring this to pass. No! This does not constitute one earning such, for such cannot be earned. It only shows a determination involving a willing mind and an obedient heart. Regrettably, few take it upon themselves to do such.

NOTES

However, for the few who do, they find a Spiritual enrichment such as can be found no place else. The whole thing involves Jesus, the Lord of one's life.

For this to be carried out, one has to make certain that one's Faith is exclusively in Christ and what Christ has done for us at the Cross. That is imperative. As well, as stated, such a Believer desiring to get closer to the Lord must have a strong prayer life. That is where relationship is formed and strengthened.

THAT THE WORLD MAY KNOW

The phrase, *"And that the world may know that You have sent Me,"* proclaims the result of this Perfect Work.

The tragedy is, despite the many who have obeyed Christ in this respect, but yet, considering the whole, the number actually has been comparatively few. Consequently, too many preachers and people spend more time fighting each other than carrying out the Work of God. As such, the Testimony to the world is hardly that of which Jesus here speaks. In fact, it is the very opposite!

The real reason is probably that preachers do not allow Christ to serve as the Chief Shepherd of the Church, but rather usurp authority over Him, which always brings spiritual death.

The phrase, *"And have loved them, as You have loved Me,"* proclaims two distinct things to the world:

1. The unity of Believers in respect to *"Communion, Purpose, and Glory"* proclaims to the world that there is a God.

2. It proclaims to the world that God loves His People! Consequently, there is no greater Testimony. That alone will draw more people to Christ than anything else.

(24) "FATHER, I WILL THAT THEY ALSO, WHOM YOU HAVE GIVEN ME, BE WITH ME WHERE I AM; THAT THEY MAY BEHOLD MY GLORY, WHICH YOU HAVE GIVEN ME: FOR YOU LOVED ME BEFORE THE FOUNDATION OF THE WORLD."

The overview is:

1. If it were possible for *"the natural man"* to do God's Will and to win victories for the Lord, then Saul most definitely would have succeeded, but he didn't succeed. He

rather failed, and failed miserably!

2. He perished at the hands of the very enemies he set out to conquer! Such must ever be the result wherein *"the flesh"* attempts to do battle for God.

3. And yet, most Christians, sadly and regrettably, attempt to live this life in the manner of Saul instead of the manner of David.

THE PRAYER OF CHRIST

The phrase, *"Father, I will that they also, whom You have given Me, be with Me where I am,"* pertains to two things:

1. All the Saints will be with Christ after the Resurrection and, in fact, will help Him rule this Planet in the coming Kingdom Age.

2. Even more importantly, Jesus refers to His Place in the Father and that all Believers follow suit. Once again, this pertains to *"Communion, Purpose, and Glory."*

The phrase, *"That they may behold My Glory, which You have given Me,"* pertains to the exaltation which He will receive in a very short time, but which He had already received when John wrote this.

This corresponds to Paul's statement, *"Wherefore God also has highly exalted Him, and given Him a Name which is above every name:*

"That at the Name of Jesus every knee should bow, of things in Heaven, and things in earth, and things under the earth;

"And that every tongue shall confess that Jesus Christ is Lord, to the Glory of God the Father" (Phil. 2:9-11).

When the Disciples saw Jesus in His Earthly Sojourn, this *"Glory"* was not present except at the *"Transfiguration,"* which was witnessed only by Peter, James, and John. However, such *"Glory"* is now readily obvious and will continue to be forever.

THE FOUNDATION OF THE WORLD

The phrase, *"For You loved Me before the foundation of the world,"* says several things:

• Jesus proclaims here His Preexistence and, therefore, His Deity.

• Love is the foundation of the relationship between the Father and the Son, as *"love"* is the foundation of the entirety of the Work of God on Earth. When it ceases to be of love and, consequently, from Love, it ceases to be of God.

• The word *"foundation"* in the Greek text is *"katabole"* and means *"the disruption, overthrow, and ruin of the social system before Adam."*

In Hebrews 1:10, the Greek word *"themelioo"* is used for *"foundation"* and means *"the founding of the Earth,"* even as it is recorded in Genesis 1:1.

In Genesis 1:2, we have the *"katabole,"* which refers to the overthrow of the social system on the Earth, as stated, by a flood (not Noah's flood).

So, the idea contained in this statement by Jesus is that the Godhead exacted Redemption's Plan even before the fall of Lucifer, which was long before the fall of Adam and Eve. God was able to do this through foreknowledge.

THE PLAN OF REDEMPTION

As well, this great Plan of Redemption for the human family comes from the basis of the Love of God. However, even more particularly, it speaks of the Father asking this of His Only Son even though it would necessitate Him becoming a Man and dying on Calvary. The idea is that the Father asked Him to do such a thing because of His Love for Him, and that Christ would do such because of His Love for the Father. Consequently, when, by Faith, the sinner comes into Christ, the same type of Love is extended by the Father because of the Son.

Reynolds says that this Statement by Jesus is one of the most mysterious of all His Words, one which leads us up to the highest possible conception of the relations between the Father and the Son.[9]

He also said, *"The Eternal Love of which the Godhead Itself is the Source and the Object is that to which we shall be introduced, and which our Lord would have us see and share"* (I Jn. 3:1-3).[10]

(25) "O RIGHTEOUS FATHER, THE WORLD HAS NOT KNOWN YOU: BUT I HAVE KNOWN YOU, AND THESE HAVE KNOWN THAT YOU HAVE SENT ME."

The exegesis is:

1. All sinners are justly doomed by God to eternal death.

2. The Word of God promises eternal safety to anyone who will seek Salvation in the Atoning Saviour.

3. The Believer in Christ knows, therefore, that he shall never perish, and this knowledge is based on two facts outside of himself, which are:

a. The Preciousness of Christ's Blood to God.

b. The Faithfulness of God to His Own Promise (Jn. 3:16).

KNOWING GOD!

The phrase, *"O Righteous Father, the world has not known You,"* proclaims the reason as it is dead in trespasses and sins. This is the spiritual death of which the Lord spoke concerning Adam and Eve.

Consequently, man on his own cannot know God or anything about God.

And yet, because man was created originally in the Image of God, the history of the struggling of the world after God has shown how dense the human darkness is. This struggle takes every conceivable direction that one may think, and all grossly wrong.

There have been signs in the philosophies of the past that men groped after the idea of a Heavenly Father Who should be blind to their faults and indifferent to their follies. However, such is impossible with a Righteous God!

But yet, how many illustrations do the sad and shameless perversions of human intelligence supply?

It has been stated that the Righteousness of God is a more exalted Perfection than His Holiness, that is, if one be permitted to use such terminology. The idea is that God must be Perfectly Righteous, which He is, in order that He be Perfectly Holy.

RIGHTEOUSNESS

Righteousness is the character or quality of being right or just. It was formerly spelled, *"Rightwiseness,"* which clearly expresses the meaning.

It is used to denote an Attribute of God (Rom. 3:5), the context of which shows that *"the Righteousness of God"* means essentially the same as His Faithfulness or Truthfulness, that which is consistent with His Own Nature and Promises.

Romans 3:25-26 speaks of His Righteousness as exhibited in the Death of Christ, which is sufficient to show men that God is neither indifferent to sin nor does He regard it lightly. On the contrary, it demonstrates that quality of Holiness which must find expression in His Condemnation of sin.

As well, the Righteousness which is of God is the only type of Righteousness that God will recognize. It is unattainable by obedience to any law, by any merit of man's own, or any other condition than that of Faith in Christ. In actuality, the man who trusts in Christ becomes *"the Righteousness of God in Him"* (II Cor. 5:21).

In effect, man becomes in Christ all that God requires of man to be, all that he could never be in himself.

FAITH

Because Abraham accepted the Word of God, making it his own by that act of the mind and spirit, which is called Faith, and as the sequel showed, submitting himself to its control, God accepted him as one who fulfilled the whole of His Requirements and, therefore, declared him as *"righteous"* (Rom. 4:3).

This Statement by Christ, *"O Righteous Father,"* sums up the entirety of the basis of Salvation by Faith. It is the *"Blessing of Abraham,"* i.e., *"Justification by Faith."*

God is *"Righteous,"* and as such, can demand no less of His Subjects. At the same time, it is impossible for His Subjects to attain or achieve such, at least on their own. Consequently, He has made it possible for any and all to become perfectly *"Righteous,"* even with His Own Righteousness, by evidencing simple Faith in Christ.

However, the simplicity ends there, with the Plan of Redemption, in fact, an extremely complicated subject that required God finding a way in which man could be declared Righteous. That *"Way"* is Jesus and, more particularly, what He did at the Cross.

RELATIONSHIP

The phrase, *"But I have known You,"* pertains to far more then mere acquaintance.

It speaks of relationship, in fact, a relationship of such extent that it is beyond the pale of human comprehension.

The phrase, *"And these have known that You have sent Me,"* refers to the Mission of Redeeming the world, at least those who will believe (Jn. 3:16).

At that time, His Disciples definitely knew that He was sent from the Father, but more particularly, they would know it in a far more expanded way after the Advent of the Holy Spirit.

(26) "AND I HAVE DECLARED UNTO THEM YOUR NAME, AND WILL DECLARE IT: THAT THE LOVE WHEREWITH YOU HAVE LOVED ME MAY BE IN THEM, AND I IN THEM."

The exposition is:

1. When Paul used the term, *"Christ shall profit you nothing"* (Gal. 5:2), He was speaking to Believers.

2. He is not speaking here of their *"standing in Grace"* as Justified Believers. He is speaking of the method of living the Christian life and of growth in that life.

3. Thus, if the Galatians, or any one, submit to circumcision (this word *"circumcision"* is a catch-all phrase for any type of law), they are putting themselves under law and are depriving themselves of the Ministry of the Holy Spirit, which Christ made possible through His Death and Resurrection, a Ministry which was not provided for under law. One doing such is doomed to failure.

LOVE

The phrase, *"And I have declared unto them Your Name, and will declare it,"* has reference to the fact of what I have just said.

They do now know, but they have more to learn, which the Spirit will teach them. This is proclaimed in the futuristic tense of the phrase, *"And will declare it."*

In fact, due to the magnitude of what Jesus is saying, it is impossible for one to learn everything concerning these things of which Jesus states. It is not that the Holy Spirit is unable to properly instruct or teach, but that the human equation is limited as to its ability to fully grasp an inexhaustible Source.

"That the Love wherewith You have loved Me may be in them, and I in them," proclaims, as stated, that *"Love"* is the foundation of all of which Christ speaks.

He set Himself apart as a Glorified Man to be the One Channel of Truth for the enduement and enrichment of His People, and for their intelligent persistence in separation from the world and its evil.

THE LORD JESUS CHRIST

The Lord is a Perfect Illustration in Glory of separation to God, and His People should be a similar illustration upon Earth. If they will but yield themselves unto Him, He will, by His Holy Spirit, willingly and efficiently live His Life of separation in them.

His Life is to be so identified with our life, His Abode so blended with our being, His Life so repeated in our experience, and His Personality so much entwined and blended with ours that He in us — because He is in us — prolongs and repeats Himself as the Object of an Eternal Love.

Incidentally, scholars of bygone days, and even up to this point, wonder how John the Beloved was able to reproduce so accurately this wondrous discourse as given by Jesus!

However, John practically admits that it was a supernatural process of memory (Jn. 14:25-26).

"Praise the Saviour, you who know Him!
"Who can tell how much we owe Him?
"Gladly let us render to Him all we are and have."

"Trust in Him, you Saints, forever;
"He is Faithful, changing never;
"Neither force nor guile can sever
"Those He loves from Him."

"Then we shall be where we would be,
"Then we shall be what we should be;
"Things that are not now, nor could be,
"Soon shall be our own."

CHAPTER 18

(1) "WHEN JESUS HAD SPOKEN THESE WORDS, HE WENT FORTH WITH

HIS DISCIPLES OVER THE BROOK CEDRON, WHERE WAS A GARDEN, INTO THE WHICH HE ENTERED, AND HIS DISCIPLES."

The diagram is:

1. Paul wrote his last Epistle to Timothy, entrusting him with the greatest Message on Earth, *"Jesus Christ and Him Crucified."*

2. All which that means is, in fact, the entirety of the New Covenant. In other words, the meaning of the New Covenant is the Cross of Christ (I Cor. 1:17, 18, 23; 2:2).

3. It was to the Apostle Paul that this great Truth, the greatest of the ages, was entrusted. Thankfully, he held it faithful unto the very end.

THE WORDS OF CHRIST

The phrase, *"When Jesus had spoken these Words,"* probably refers to everything said in John, Chapters 14 through 17.

In that discourse, He said much about the Holy Spirit, His Deity, and the Believer's position in Christ.

The *"brook Cedron"* in the phrase, *"He went forth with His Disciples over the brook Cedron,"* is referred elsewhere in the Bible as the stream *"Kidron"* (II Sam. 15:23; I Ki. 15:13; II Ki. 23:4). This is where David crossed when he was betrayed by Absalom (II Sam. 15:23).

The brook *"Kidron"* runs in a deep valley between the Mount of Olivet and the city of Jerusalem and, more particularly, the Temple site. Actually, the blood from the offering of thousands of lambs at the Sacrificial Altar in front of the Temple ran through conduits into the brook *"Kidron."*

Josephus, the Jewish historian, said that during Passover time, approximately 250,000 lambs were offered, with the brook, which took off this blood, turning bright red. Now the time had come for the Lamb of God to shed His Life's Blood, which would make unnecessary the continued offering of animals.

GETHSEMANE

The phrase, *"Where was a garden, into the which He entered, and His Disciples,"* spoke of *"Gethsemane."* It seems this was a place where Jesus often went. It was situated on the western side of the Mount of Olivet.

While there sometime ago, we were shown some olive trees that grow abundantly in this garden, which they said could be approximately 2,000 years old. If so, they would've been there at the Time of Christ.

However, some claim that all of the trees were cut when Titus laid siege to Jerusalem, which could well have been the case, but not necessarily so!

We have found in this Gospel according to John that the Godhead of Christ is the Distinctive Feature. Consequently, certain things are omitted which were prominent in the other Gospels, and other things added which are not related elsewhere.

For instance, little if anything is said in this Gospel concerning the apprehensions of the Cross, His Agony in the garden, His Cry, *"Why have You forsaken Me?"*, the darkness of the Cross, the commendation of His Spirit to God, and other features characteristic of His Manhood.

On the other hand, John goes into great detail concerning the Deity of Christ, especially in the last discourse. As well, we see the effect of His *"I Am"* upon His Enemies when they attempted to arrest Him in the garden.

Also, His Triumphant Cry, *"Finish,"* is here made prominent.

This record, therefore, brings out His Personal Glory as Son of God abolishing sin and destroying him who had its power, namely Satan.

(2) "AND JUDAS ALSO, WHICH BETRAYED HIM, KNEW THE PLACE: FOR JESUS OFTTIMES RESORTED THITHER WITH HIS DISCIPLES."

The overview is:

1. The only Way to God is through Jesus Christ (Jn. 14:6).

2. The only Way to Jesus Christ is through the Cross (Lk. 14:27).

3. The only Way to the Cross is a denial of self (Lk. 9:23).

JUDAS

The phrase, *"And Judas also, who betrayed Him, knew the place,"* is related that we may know how Judas knew where to find Him that night.

"For Jesus oftentimes resorted there with His Disciples," seems to be where

He spent most nights while in the city of Jerusalem. In fact, this garden was outside the city limits at that time. So, Judas would have been very familiar not only with the place but, as well, with the Habits of Christ.

(3) "JUDAS THEN, HAVING RECEIVED A BAND OF MEN AND OFFICERS FROM THE CHIEF PRIESTS AND PHARISEES, COMING THITHER WITH LANTERNS AND TORCHES AND WEAPONS."

The exegesis is:

1. We must understand that the entirety of the Bible points to Christ, both Old and New Testaments.

2. The Old Testament points to Christ Who was to come, while the New Testament points to Christ Who has come.

3. Christ and the Cross are ever before the reader in the entirety of the Word of God (Jn. 1:1).

THE CHIEF PRIESTS AND PHARISEES

The phrase, *"Judas then, having received a band of men and officers from the Chief Priests and Pharisees,"* proclaims John completely omitting the Passion of Christ in the garden and cutting straight through to His Arrest.

As stated, this was done because of the manner in which the Holy Spirit desired this Gospel to be written. Presenting Jesus as God, which John powerfully did, of necessity, would have omitted the Passion because such a posture would not be related to God.

"Came there with lanterns and torches and weapons," proclaims the hearts of these people. Being Passover, it was full moon, but treachery and hatred distrusted its pure and gentle light, and, therefore, His Enemies brought their torches and lanterns.

The word *"band"* in the Greek text is *"speira"* and normally refers to approximately 600 men; however, that number varied and could go as low as 200.

Irrespective, there were quite a number of men who came to arrest Jesus.

THE JEWISH SANHEDRIN

Reynolds said, *"The presence of this band of Roman soldiers with the Jewish police gives very great force and impressiveness to the scene of Israel's degradation and of the world's assault upon the Divine Savior."*[1]

The way this is worded concerning the *"Chief Priests"* and *"Pharisees"* tells us that this detachment was under the direction of the Jewish Sanhedrin. Consequently, even though Rome was very much involved, still, it was the *"church"* of that day which spearheaded this evil scene.

Regrettably, Satan's major thrust continues to be in the realm of the *"church."* This he infiltrates and, thereby, controls! As such, he destroys people in two ways:

1. False doctrine

2. Hindrance of the true Work of God, for most all of the opposition comes from this source, i.e., the apostate church. As well, this false church is so near and similar to the true Church at times that only the truly spiritually mature can tell the difference.

(4) "JESUS THEREFORE, KNOWING ALL THINGS THAT SHOULD COME UPON HIM, WENT FORTH, AND SAID UNTO THEM, WHOM SEEK YE?"

The exposition is:

1. Jesus sent a Message to each of the seven churches of Asia. Of these, Laodicea was the last.

2. This particular church constitutes the conclusion of the Church Age and represents the time in which we now live.

3. In other words, the modern church is the Laodicean church, and the Laodicean church is the modern church.

4. The Laodicean church is actually an apostatized church, which means that it has departed from the Truth.

SUPERNATURAL KNOWLEDGE

The phrase, *"Jesus therefore, knowing all things that should come upon Him,"* speaks of being perfectly led by the Father and through the Ministry of the Holy Spirit.

He knew that His Arrest was now imminent, and that He would be crucified very shortly. He knew what the trial would be and how it would be. He knew in detail the animosity and even hatred expressed against Him by the religious leadership of Israel.

This phrase lends credence to the thought that the Holy Spirit had more perfectly described to Jesus exactly what would happen at this time, which probably happened during His Time of Passion in the garden, which John did not mention.

The question, *"Went forth, and said unto them, Whom do you seek?"* speaks of His arrest as He is met by the soldiers and Temple guards. It is probably close to midnight. This was basically the only way they could take Him, for if such had been attempted during the daylight hours, especially in the presence of other people, it could well have caused a riot and, no doubt, would have. So, the religious leadership of Israel would ply their trade of bloodlust at night so as to have the cloak of darkness.

Such is evil, and above all, such is religious evil!

Of course, Jesus knew Whom they were seeking and so made it easy for them.

(5) "THEY ANSWERED HIM, JESUS OF NAZARETH. JESUS SAID UNTO THEM, I AM HE. AND JUDAS ALSO, WHICH BETRAYED HIM, STOOD WITH THEM."

The structure is:

1. We find that God tests Faith in order to strengthen and enrich it.

2. This test can come at any time, either before a great victory or after a great victory.

3. As someone has well said, *"Great Faith must be tested greatly."*

JESUS OF NAZARETH

The phrase, *"They answered Him, Jesus of Nazareth,"* proclaims them speaking the greatest Name in the annals of human history, *"Jesus of Nazareth."*

This *"Name"* has brought peace to untold millions, healing to so much sickness, Salvation from all sin, at least for those who will believe, freedom from all bondage, and Light to push back the darkness.

WHO IS JESUS OF NAZARETH?

In Colossians 1:15, Paul speaks of Him as *"the Image of the Invisible God, the Firstborn of every creature."* We will study the words *"Image"* and *"Firstborn."*

IMAGE

The word *"Image"* has the obvious idea of likeness, but the Greek word does not refer to an accidental likeness, as one egg is like another. It implies an original of which the image is a copy.

However, the Image in this case is not the result of direct imitation as the head of a king on a coin, but is derived like the features of the parent and the child.

In John 3:16, our Lord is the *"Only Begotten Son of God."* John 1:18 refers to Him as the *"Only Begotten Son."* It is a tremendous thought.

The words *"Only Begotten"* do not only mean that our Lord was the only Son of God, but that He as God the Son is alone of His Kind, unique, begotten of God for the purpose of the Redemption of man.

He is the Image of God in the sense that He is a derived Representation of God the Father, coexistent eternally with Him, and possessing the same essence, Deity, Himself.

Being the Representative of God, He is also, therefore, the Manifestation of God. He said to Philip, *"He who has seen Me has seen the Father"* (Jn. 14:9).

However, it must be understood that the Holy Spirit through Paul is speaking of the Incarnation of Christ, i.e., God becoming Man. In this capacity, Jesus is the Son of God and, in essence, the Image of God.

THREE PERSONS OF THE TRINITY

The Christian Doctrine of *"God"* is distinguished by its emphasis on Divine Three-in-one-ness, that is, the eternal coexistence of the Father, Son, and Holy Spirit in the inner personal life of the Godhead. Evangelical theology affirms that the Living, Speaking, and Acting God is a Personal, Divine Trinity of Father, Son, and Holy Spirit in the Eternal Unity of God Himself and in His Work.

The One God, the subject of all Divine Revelation, is self-disclosed — as the Bible authoritatively teaches — as the invisible Father (from Whom all Revelation proceeds), the Son (Who mediates and objectively incarnates that Revelation in a historical manifestation), and the Holy Spirit (Who is Divinely outpoured and subjectively applies that Revelation to men).

CONTROVERSY

The Doctrine of the Trinity or of Divine

Trinity has been at the heart of much theological controversy. The routine objection is that the Doctrine sacrifices monotheism (one God) to *"Tritheism"* (three Gods). However, this objection thrives on a misconception of Divine Personality in attempting to explain God after the definition of man. While there is similarity (man created in the Image of God), it is similarity only. Man is not God, has never been God, and will never be God!

THE REALITY

The Reality and Nature of God, known in the Light of Divine disclosure, yields the historic conviction grounded in the New Testament that God's Being is Father, Son, and Holy Spirit in His Self-manifestation. This insistence on three eternal modes of consciousness in the One God has no parallel in religious philosophy, in other words, that there is One God manifested in Three Persons, God the Father, God the Son, and God the Holy Spirit.

By its very emphasis on the progressive character of historical Revelation, the Scriptural record of the Self-manifestation of the Living God cautions against any notions that the Doctrine of the Trinity was fully understandable in Old Testament times. First and foremost, and as is plainly obvious in the Old Testament, the Revelation presents throughout the truth of monotheism (one God) against the polytheism (many gods) and the practical atheism of the ancient world. God's Unique Transcendent Glory is reflected by the Old Testament's explicit prohibition of all graven images, whether in the similitude of nature or creatures. The Genesis creation narrative emphasizes, however, that God made unfallen man in the Divine Image. In the New Testament, God's Glory is manifested in the Incarnation of the Logos, bearing the express Image of the Divine in human nature. Nowhere does the New Testament emphasis on the Deity of Jesus Christ, or in its Trinitarian statements, deviate in the slightest from the uncompromising monotheism (the worship of one God) of the Old Testament. Both Testaments deplore polytheism (the worship of many gods).

THE TWO HEBREW WORDS FOR *"ONE"*

G. A. F. Knight notes that of the two Hebrew words for *"One ('ehadh' and 'yahidh'),"* the latter means *"unique"* (the only one of its kind), whereas the former does not preclude distinguishable entities (as in Gen. 2:24 where Adam and Eve are said to be one flesh).

However, it must be understood that despite the name, *"Elohim,"* which is a uni-plural noun stressing the potential of more than one, the ancient Hebrews never thought of God in Trinitarian form but always in the singular.

TRINITARIANISM

Explicit Trinitarianism is dependent upon the New Testament Revelation of the *"Sending"* Father, the *"Sent"* Son, and the *"Out poured"* Spirit.

In the experience of the Disciples, the disclosure of the Deity of Christ, ever how it may at first have impressed them, was beyond their understanding. But yet, they knew that Christ was God. They also knew that from the way that Christ spoke of the Father, He was the Son of God. His Assertion of the Unity of Father and Son clearly implied that the oneness of essence was not reducible only to moral and purposive harmony. In other words, the Son was really God, even as the Father was God. This means that the revealed Presence of God demanded recognition, not only of the Person of the Son alongside the Person of the Father, but the Person of the Spirit as well.

THE DOCTRINE OF
THE COEQUAL TRINITY

C. K. Barrett remarks that more than any other New Testament source, the writer of the Fourth Gospel, the Gospel of our study, *"Lays the foundation for a doctrine of a coequal Trinity."*[2] However, the threefold formula is found also in the Great Commission (Mat. 28:19).

Actually, the term, *"Co-Trinity,"* is not a Biblical term, and Scripture gives the Doctrine not in formulated definition but in fragmentary units similar to many other elements of the Christian system of Truth.

B.B. Warfield remarked that the entire New Testament *"is Trinitarian to the core; all its teaching is built on the assumption of the Trinity; and its allusions to the Trinity are frequent, cursory, easy and competent."*[3] There is in the New Testament, as in the Old Testament, only One True and Living God. In its view, Jesus Christ and the Holy Spirit are each God in the fullest sense; and Father, Son, and Spirit stand related to each other as *"I," "Thou,"* and *"He"* (I Cor. 12:4; II Cor. 13:14; Eph. 2:18; 3:2; 4:4; 5:18; I Thess. 1:2-5; II Thess. 2:13; II Tim. 1:3, 13; Titus 3:4).

THE FIRSTBORN OF EVERY CREATURE

The word *"Firstborn,"* as Paul uses it in Colossians 1:15, is from a Greek word that had a certain technical use in the First Century. It is difficult to bring out all its content of meaning in a translation.

It implied priority to all creation. In other words, it does not mean that our Lord was the first created thing to be brought into existence.

The Word declares the absolute pre-existence of the Son of God as God. He existed before any created thing was brought into existence. Therefore, He is not created, and being uncreated, He is Eternal.

In Colossians 1:16, Paul says, *"For by Him were all things created."* Instead of being the first in order of created things, as some claim, He is their Creator. That is what our Lord has reference to in Revelation 3:14 when He speaks of Himself as *"the Beginning of the Creation of God."*

The word *"beginning"* in the Greek has two meanings: *"the first in a series"* or *"the originator"* of something. Our Lord was the Originator of the created Universe in that He was its Creator. Thus, the Greek word translated *"Firstborn"* implies here *"priority to all creation"* and, in effect, refers to the *"Creator!"*

SOVEREIGNTY OVER ALL CREATION

The word *"Firstborn,"* as used here, also speaks of sovereignty over all creation. The *"Firstborn"* is the natural ruler, the acknowledged head. He is also Ruler by right of the fact that He is the Creator.

The words *"every creature"* are more perfectly translated *"all creation."*

Jesus of Nazareth, the Galilean Peasant, the Carpenter, and the Friend of publicans and sinners, is the Image of God, a derived Copy of God the Father, and the Creator of the Universe and its Sovereign Lord.

WHAT JESUS DID FOR LOST SINNERS

He is also the One Who, in Incarnated Form, made peace through the Blood of His Cross. That is, through His Substitutionary Death, He satisfied completely all the claims which the Law of God had against us. We, as lost sinners, violated that Law. The Justice of God demanded that the penalty, death, be paid.

God did not create man out of need. God needs nothing! He created man out of Love; therefore, Love, by its very nature, must redeem man.

So, to effect that Redemption, He, in the Person of His Son, Jesus of Nazareth, stepped down from His Judgment Throne to take upon Himself at Calvary your sin and mine, and your penalty and mine. God's Law being satisfied, He is now free to Righteously bestow Mercy.

Consequently, any and all, who definitely place their trust in the Lord Jesus Christ as Personal Saviour, are immediately granted Eternal Life. It is a Gift of God, purchased by the Blood of the Son of God, and given freely to all who will believe (Jn. 3:16).

(Commentary on the Trinity and Deity of Christ was derived in part from Dr. Kenneth S. Wuest and the Zondervan Encyclopedia of the Bible.)

I AM

The phrase, *"Jesus said unto them, I am He,"* should have been translated, *"I Am,"* for the pronoun *"He"* was added by the translators. As such, He was saying the same thing He said to Moses some 1,600 years before (Ex. 3:14).

Reynolds said, *"In some royal emphasis of tone He said, 'I am,' and the same kind of effect followed, as on various occasions had proved how powerless without His permission the machinations of His foes really were."*[4] In other words, they could only do to Him what He allowed!

The phrase, *"And Judas also, who betrayed Him, stood with them,"* proclaims far and away the most dastardly act ever carried out by a human being.

Judas had a choice to make. He could stand with Jesus or with the religious hierarchy. He could not stand with both!

In a sense, this same choice must be made by all who presently call themselves *"Believers."* The apostate church has the plaudits of the crowd, the favor of the world, the money, and the numbers. To stand with them will stir no opposition, nor will it buck the tide; however, to stand with Jesus is done so at a price — a price, I might quickly add, that most are not willing to pay.

(6) "AS SOON THEN AS HE HAD SAID UNTO THEM, I AM HE, THEY WENT BACKWARD, AND FELL TO THE GROUND."

The exegesis is:

1. The word *"walk,"* as John uses it here (I Jn. 1:7), even as Paul, refers to the manner in which we live this life for the Lord, i.e., our walk with God.

2. The *"fellowship"* of which John speaks in the verse in question is not fellowship with other Christians, as most think, but rather our fellowshipping God and God fellowshipping us.

3. In other words, this Passage takes the Believer to a far higher place and position than mere fellowship with other Believers, as wonderful and necessary as is the latter.

POWER

The phrase, *"As soon then as He had said unto them, I am He,"* describes the Power and Force which were in these words.

"They went backward, and fell to the ground," proclaims the result of His Answer and fulfilled the prediction by David concerning this very moment (Ps. 27:2).

As we have stated, the only thing this small army could do to this Man was that which He allowed them.

(7) "THEN ASKED HE THEM AGAIN, WHOM SEEK YE? AND THEY SAID, JESUS OF NAZARETH."

NOTES

The exposition is:

1. The Moving of the Holy Spirit is the first sign of life (Gen. 1:2).

2. When you, as a Believer, put your Faith exclusively in Christ and what He has done for you at the Cross, the Holy Spirit will then move upon you, even as He did upon the *"face of the waters"* so long, long ago.

3. When the Holy Spirit then moved, the darkness had to lift, which was replaced by Light. It will do the same with any who place their Faith in Christ and what He did for us at the Cross.

JESUS OF NAZARETH

The question, *"Then asked He them again, Whom do you seek?"* is asked for purpose.

He wants them to fully understand what they are doing and exactly Who they are arresting. With this demonstration of His Power, which knocked all of them to the ground, I wonder what thoughts were in their minds. Whatever their mood previously, one can rest assured that it is subdued at present!

"And they said, Jesus of Nazareth," presents the moment, given to them by Christ in His Mercy, in which they could have aborted this dastardly deed. However, despite this display of great Power that they all experienced, they would proceed with their bloodlust. All, no doubt, had excuses to do so!

The Roman soldiers surmised that they had to obey their officers. It was likewise with the Temple guards. In other words, all there that evening had excuses as to why they must go through with this charade, but no real reasons.

Judas had experienced the Power of God countless times during the last three and one-half years. He had seen Jesus perform every type of Miracle. So, beyond the shadow of a doubt, he knew this was the Power of God, but yet, he persisted in pressing forward to his doom and damnation.

He was losing his soul, and they were destroying their Nation!

Any contact with Jesus in any capacity never leaves the person as found. If there is rejection of Christ, the slide downward automatically begins in every way. If there is acceptance, Eternal Life is the result!

(8) "JESUS ANSWERED, I HAVE TOLD YOU THAT I AM HE: IF THEREFORE YOU SEEK ME, LET THESE GO THEIR WAY."

The structure is:

1. Two cities are mentioned in Genesis 12:8. They are *"Beth-el,"* which means *"House of God,"* and *"Hai,"* which means *"garbage dump."*

2. The Altar alone, typifying the Cross, can keep the Believer away from the garbage dump.

3. Other than by the Cross, it is virtually impossible for the Believer to know the difference between the *"House of God"* and the *"garbage dump."*

AUTHORITY

The phrase, *"Jesus answered, I have told you that I am He,"* was said again on behalf of His Disciples. Beyond doubt, they all now know exactly Who Jesus is.

The phrase, *"If therefore you seek Me, let these go their way,"* presents a request, which they dared not disobey.

They had experienced His Almighty Power respecting their coming for His Person. What would He do if they made as if to arrest His Disciples? This demonstration was probably for the very purpose of their protection.

Expositor's say, *"These Words uttered by Jesus were not of weakness and entreaty, but of Authority. 'I give Myself to you voluntarily, but you must not hurt one of My Disciples.*

"I have already given you proof of My Power over you, I will not use it on My behalf, for I lay down My Life for My Sheep; but I will use it if need be to protect My sheep."

He then added, *"It was certainly the Power of Christ that protected them, especially after Peter brandished his sword."*[5]

(9) "THAT THE SAYING MIGHT BE FULFILLED, WHICH HE SPOKE, OF THEM WHICH YOU GAVE ME HAVE I LOST NONE."

The construction is:

1. In the episode of the bitter waters of Marah, we find that the Lord gives a great Promise to Moses, and to you and me.

NOTES

2. It is a Promise of Divine Healing, which addresses itself not only to physical needs, but also to emotional needs, typified by the *"bitter waters"* of Exodus 15:25.

3. But yet, the Promise has a qualification, one which is impossible for us as human beings to meet.

4. We are to *"give ear to His Commandments, and keep all His Statutes."*

5. However, what human being can say that he has always kept all of God's Commandments and Statutes? The answer: none!

6. However, the door is not closed. There is One, only One, Who has always kept all of God's Commandments and Statutes, and that's all that is needed! The *"One"* is the Lord Jesus Christ. Our acceptance of Him gives us His Perfection.

OF THEM WHICH YOU GAVE ME

The phrase, *"That the saying might be fulfilled, which He spoke,"* is an insertion into the narrative given by John.

As he writes these words and the Holy Spirit greatly inspires him, his mind, no doubt, went back to that night so long ago when a few hours earlier, Jesus had said concerning the Disciples, *"While I was with them in the world, I kept them in Your Name: those whom You gave Me I have kept, and none of them is lost, but the son of perdition; that the Scripture might be fulfilled"* (Jn. 17:12).

The phrase, *"Of them which You gave Me have I lost none,"* as John quotes Jesus, as is obvious, is given in an abbreviated form.

Why?

John wrote it this way because the Holy Spirit desired it to be so. The remainder of the Verse concerning Judas was not included here because, by his own wishes and decision, he was no longer a part of Jesus or the other Disciples. So now, the Holy Spirit considers the Eleven to be all, at least of the original Twelve.

(10) "THEN SIMON PETER HAVING A SWORD DREW IT, AND SMOTE THE HIGH PRIEST'S SERVANT, AND CUT OFF HIS RIGHT EAR. THE SERVANT'S NAME WAS MALCHUS."

The synopsis is:

1. We find in the Third Chapter of Judges that idolatry always leads to slavery.

2. Every time that Israel went into idolatry, when they cried for help, the Lord always delivered them, no matter how guilty they were.

3. According to I John 1:9, we find that forgiveness immediately follows true confession.

SIMON PETER

The phrase, *"Then Simon Peter having a sword drew it,"* is in response to the statement made by Jesus some hours earlier, *"and he who has no sword, let him sell his garment, and buy one"* (Lk. 22:36).

No! Jesus was not now advocating they take up the sword. He was teaching them another lesson, which they did not then grasp, and, as well, He did not correct them at this time.

With the Power that Jesus had already evidenced, He had no need of a sword, and neither did His Disciples.

As well, why did Peter think that Jesus now needed help, especially considering that he had just witnessed the entirety of this crowd, that could have numbered several hundreds, falling on their backs at the mere Words of the Master?

THE LAST RECORDED HEALING OF JESUS IN HIS PUBLIC MINISTRY

How so often have all of us, while not doing the same thing, nevertheless, done something similar! We think we are carrying out the Work of God when, in reality, even as Peter, we are only a hindrance, which Jesus has to set straight. It should have been obvious that the Lord did not need any help, and yet, Peter evidently felt that he must do something!

The phrase, *"And smote the High Priest's servant, and cut off his right ear,"* presents Peter, I think, attempting to cleave the man's skull. The Holy Spirit, no doubt, turned aside his aim, with the sword severing the ear only.

"The servant's name was Malchus," was given only by John; however, John did not mention the healing of the man's ear, as did Luke (Lk. 22:51).

NOTES

This is the last recorded Healing of Jesus in His Public Ministry. In some ways, it may have been the most important healing of all.

It was the healing of a wound caused by violence; it was worked on an enemy; it was unasked for; there was no Faith expressed; and there was no thankfulness, at least recorded!

It portrayed the Heart of God, Who would send His Only Son to die for sinners, and not only that, but sinners who hated Him!

(11) **"THEN SAID JESUS UNTO PETER, PUT UP YOUR SWORD INTO THE SHEATH: THE CUP WHICH MY FATHER HAS GIVEN ME, SHALL I NOT DRINK IT?"**

BY THE SWORD—NO!

The phrase, *"Then said Jesus unto Peter, Put up your sword into the sheath,"* presents a truth far greater than the admonition.

In one sentence, Jesus is proclaiming to the Church that the Gospel is not to be spread by the sword and, in fact, cannot be!

As well, the Lord is to be our Defense, as Jesus adequately proved a few moments before Peter extended his sword.

The question, *"The cup which My Father has given Me, shall I not drink it?"* proclaims that which must be done.

His Words have put a stop to all further steps taken for His Defense. He is now of His Own Accord at the disposal of His Enemies.

The *"cup"* that He mentions was the *"cup of suffering,"* which included Calvary. As well, His Death was not just an expiration of Life, but rather a sacrificial death, actually, Jesus would become a Sin-Offering (Ex. 29:14; Lev. 4:3; 6:25; Num. 8:8; Ps. 40:6; II Cor. 5:21; Eph. 5:2). In this, He would suffer the penalty of sin, which was the judgment of God, a penalty that we should have rightly suffered!

The wages of sin is death; therefore, God demanded the death sentence, which was carried out in His Son. Thus, the claims of Divine Justice were satisfied and the accusations of Satan put to rest.

To be sure, this *"cup"* was bitter, so bitter, in fact, that God would turn His Face away from this sordid scene.

After the Passion in the garden, the die was cast. Jesus would drink of this cup because it was the Father's Will (Lk. 22:42).

(12) "THEN THE BAND AND THE CAPTAIN AND OFFICERS OF THE JEWS TOOK JESUS, AND BOUND HIM."

The pattern is:

1. In the Twentieth and Twenty-first Chapters of John's Gospel, the Holy Spirit records four Appearances of the Lord after He rose from the dead.

2. These appearances banished four great enemies of the human heart: *"sorrow," "fear," "doubt,"* and *"care."*

3. Actually, everything that Jesus did was not only for the purpose of helping the individual or people involved but, as well, presented a great lesson for all people and for all time.

THE ROMANS

The phrase, *"Then the band and the Captain,"* speaks of the Roman captain, who was normally a commander of 1,000 men. Actually, a captain was one of six tribunes attached to a legion, showing the importance the Romans attached to the arrest of Jesus, the Jews having represented Him as a dangerous seditionist.

"And officers of the Jews took Jesus, and bound Him," presents the Jewish Temple guards joining with the Romans.

Quite possibly, it was part of Roman law that all prisoners be *"bound,"* thus, not being an indication of Jesus having resisted arrest.

After the exhibition of His Power, they surely knew that binding Him would have little effect if He so desired otherwise. As stated, it was, no doubt, a part of their procedure.

(13) "AND LED HIM AWAY TO ANNAS FIRST; FOR HE WAS FATHER-IN-LAW TO CAIAPHAS, WHICH WAS THE HIGH PRIEST THAT SAME YEAR."

The diagram is:

1. The Holy Spirit through Paul emphatically stated that *"a man is not justified by the works of the Law, but by the Faith of Jesus Christ"* (Gal. 2:16).

2. This automatically places the Believer in one of two places, law or Faith.

3. The True Way, and, in fact, the only Way, is *"the Faith of Jesus Christ."* This refers to what Christ did at the Cross, which demands that the Cross be the Object of our Faith.

THE HIGH PRIEST

The phrase, *"And led Him away to Annas first,"* presents one of the most powerful men in Israel at that time.

He was perhaps the head of the Sanhedrin, the ruling body of Israel.

It is said that he was a man of great capacity and exclusiveness, and being a Sadducee, was charged with fiery passion and bitter hatred of the Pharisees.

He was appointed High Priest in A.D. 7 by Quirinius, governor of Syria. In A.D. 14, he was compelled to retire in favor of his son Ishmael. After him followed Eleazar, and in A.D. 18, Joseph Caiaphas, his son-in-law, was appointed.

Three other sons of Annas held the like position, and it was during the High Priesthood of one bearing his father's name (Ananus) that James the Just was cruelly murdered.

The phrase, *"For he was father-in-law to Caiaphas, which was the High Priest that same year,"* tells us that this office was no longer for life as originally. Now, it was by appointment by Roman authorities.

Luke had spoken of Annas and Caiaphas as both being High Priests; however, he was speaking of some three and one-half years before (Lk. 3:2).

As well, it is not certain if he meant ruling jointly or in turn, with the latter probably being the case.

At any rate, *"Caiaphas"* was now the High Priest but with his father-in-law, Annas, still wielding great power.

Caiaphas was High Priest from A.D. 18 to A.D. 36 when he was deposed by Vitellius, governor of Syria.

(14) "NOW CAIAPHAS WAS HE, WHICH GAVE COUNSEL TO THE JEWS, THAT IT WAS EXPEDIENT THAT ONE MAN SHOULD DIE FOR THE PEOPLE."

The overview is:

1. It is my belief that Paul wrote the Book of Hebrews.

2. Whoever wrote it had to have a

profound knowledge of the Law, the New Covenant, and the Cross.

3. Concerning these subjects, no one had such knowledge as did Paul.

CAIAPHAS

The phrase, *"Now Caiaphas was he, who gave counsel to the Jews,"* presented, in fact, the worst *"counsel"* they had ever received. This *"counsel"* would destroy their Nation and destroy it so completely that it would actually cease to exist.

"That it was expedient that one man should die for the people" means that Caiaphas had already passed sentence on Jesus that He should be killed (Jn. 11:49-52), hence, his presiding over this trial guaranteed its ungodly conclusion. In other words, Jesus need expect no justice or mercy from the decision of this judge.

The truth is, *"Jesus was not tried by rules of justice, or He would not have been crucified, but rather, in essence, by a kangaroo court!"*

To which we have previously alluded, the reader must know and understand that any decision made respecting Christ will always, and without exception, have tremendous results one way or the other. If the decision is opposed to the Word of God, the results can be negative only. According to the Word of God, even though Satan will attempt to greatly hinder, still, there will ultimately be great Blessings.

(15) "AND SIMON PETER FOLLOWED JESUS, AND SO DID ANOTHER DISCIPLE: THAT DISCIPLE WAS KNOWN UNTO THE HIGH PRIEST, AND WENT IN WITH JESUS INTO THE PALACE OF THE HIGH PRIEST."

The form is:

1. While the Bible does not teach sinless perfection, it most definitely does teach that the *"sin nature shall not have dominion over you"* (Rom. 6:14).

2. The sin nature is that which originated with Adam's fall, and it has passed down to every human being since, with the exception of Jesus Christ.

3. When the believing sinner accepts Christ, while the sin nature is not removed, it is made dormant. However, if the Believer places his or her faith in anything other than Christ and the Cross, he will find the sin nature once again ruling within his heart and life. The only answer for sin is the Cross of Christ.

JOHN THE BELOVED

The phrase, *"And Simon Peter followed Jesus, and so did another Disciple,"* refers to John the Beloved, who wrote this account. As he did here, he did elsewhere, as well, referring to himself in the third person (Jn. 13:23; 19:26; 21:7, 20).

"That Disciple was known unto the High Priest, and went in with Jesus into the palace of the High Priest," concerns itself with the first trial or hearing before Annas.

How well that John knew Caiaphas is not known. However, it seems that whatever acquaintance there was, it caused the High Priest to give admittance to both Peter and John and probably allowed John to witness the entirety of the proceedings, at least of the first trial, which was held at night.

(16) "BUT PETER STOOD AT THE DOOR WITHOUT. THEN WENT OUT THAT OTHER DISCIPLE, WHICH WAS KNOWN UNTO THE HIGH PRIEST, AND SPOKE UNTO HER WHO KEPT THE DOOR, AND BROUGHT IN PETER."

The exegesis is:

1. The lame man of Acts 3:6 had, no doubt, heard of Jesus. There is no way that he could not have heard of the Lord.

2. But now, Jesus was dead, having been crucified, or so he thought, and with that, his hopes were dashed to the ground.

3. However, he was to find that Jesus was not dead, and that the Name of Jesus still carried the same Power as when He was on Earth.

PETER

The phrase, *"But Peter stood at the door without,"* probably meant that even though John had permission to enter, Peter did not. Consequently, John would seek admittance for Peter, which was granted, at least into the courtyard immediate to the Judgment Hall, or possibly an anti-room next to the main room itself.

The phrase, *"Then went out that other*

Disciple, who was known unto the High Priest, and spoke unto her who kept the door, and brought in Peter," proclaims permission granted respecting Peter accompanying John.

Incidentally, tradition says that this woman's name, who was the keeper of the door, was Ballila.

(17) "THEN SAID THE DAMSEL THAT KEPT THE DOOR UNTO PETER, ARE YOU NOT ALSO ONE OF THIS MAN'S DISCIPLES? HE SAID, I AM NOT."

The exposition is:

1. How does one crucify the flesh (Gal. 5:24-25)?

2. He does so by looking exclusively to Christ and the Cross.

3. The Cross of Christ is the means of all victory for the Child of God, demanding that it ever be the Object of his Faith. When we speak of the Cross, we aren't speaking of the wooden beam on which Jesus died, but rather what Jesus accomplished at the Cross.

THE DENIAL

The beginning of the question, *"Then said the damsel who kept the door unto Peter,"* gives us a little more information respecting the situation in which Peter now finds himself.

Both Peter and John enter in, but Peter will allow himself to be distracted and, consequently, will erroneously identify himself, as it were, with the captors of the Lord. He tries to pass himself off as an unconcerned spectator.

The question, *"Are not you also one of this Man's Disciples?"* now begins the scenario which will be so hurtful to both Peter and to Jesus.

All of the people, who were warming around this fire at that darkened hour, knew that Jesus had been arrested and had probably seen Him brought through this very area by the soldiers.

The phrase, *"He said, I am not,"* is the very opposite of that said by Jesus when He was arrested.

When the soldiers said they sought Jesus of Nazareth, He said, *"I am He!"*

Considering all the particulars, it was a terrible sin committed by Peter, and, as sin does, the failure would become increasingly worse.

(18) "AND THE SERVANTS AND OFFICERS STOOD THERE, WHO HAD MADE A FIRE OF COALS; FOR IT WAS COLD: AND THEY WARMED THEMSELVES: AND PETER STOOD WITH THEM, AND WARMED HIMSELF."

The construction is:

1. Several things happened at the Birth of Christ that were literally astounding. One of them is as follows:

2. Beginning at about the time that Jesus was born and continuing for approximately thirty-three and one-half years, the great war gates of Janus in Rome were closed, signifying that there was no war anywhere in the Roman Empire during this particular time.

3. Of all the time that Rome ruled, over 1,000 years, this was the only time that those gates had been closed for anything near this period of time.

4. It was because, even though Rome did not know such, the Prince of Peace was in the world. When He left, 33 and one-half years later, war immediately broke out and has continued in the world ever since.

FAITH?

The phrase, *"And the servants and officers stood there, who had made a fire of coals; for it was cold,"* speaks of the physical cold, but the spiritual cold was far worse, of which the literal cold is symbolic.

As well, the *"fire"* was not that of the Spirit but that of man. Regrettably, most churches presently have only man-made fire. As such, they are opposed to Jesus, irrespective of their claims, just as much as the religious leadership of the Israel of long ago.

"And they warmed themselves: and Peter stood with them, and warmed himself," pictures Peter taking up position with the enemies of the Lord.

He had previously entertained the idea that he had great Faith; however, the Faith which he had was mostly misplaced and was in himself and not Christ.

Actually, that is the problem with many

Believers and, possibly, with all of us at one time or the other. Especially considering the tremendous amount of teaching on Faith in the last half century, and looking at the results, one now begins to realize that much of the instruction has been erroneous. This only caused people to have faith in themselves and not God or His Word, despite the claims!

Jesus must always be the Object of our Faith, and most of all, we are speaking of what He did for us at the Cross. Our faith must not be in other things or ourselves, or we will find ourselves in the same situation as Simon Peter (Heb. 12:2).

Faith in ourselves will never really stand the test, while Faith in Christ and What He did for us at the Cross will always stand the test. Peter had Faith in himself, even as he had boldly boasted to Jesus. However, sadly, he would find that his misplaced faith could not even really begin to stand up, as such Faith cannot stand up in any one of us. So, he warmed himself with the enemies of his Lord.

(19) "THE HIGH PRIEST THEN ASKED JESUS OF HIS DISCIPLES, AND OF HIS DOCTRINE."

The synopsis is:

1. We are emphatically told in I John 5:4 that it is *"our Faith"* that gives us victory over the world.

2. This type of Faith must have as its Object the Cross of Christ (I Cor. 1:17, 18, 23; 2:2).

3. The Cross of Christ is the Means, and the only Means, of our walking in victory.

THIS KANGAROO COURT

The phrase, *"The High Priest then asked Jesus of His Disciples,"* refers to all Followers of Christ. In essence, he is accusing Jesus of sedition by such inquiry. As is obvious, he is casting about, trying to find something which will give him occasion to demand the Crucifixion of Christ by Roman authority.

The phrase, *"And of His Doctrine,"* pertained to the things He taught. As we shall see, Jesus will answer them in such a way that shows the silliness of their question.

Jesus had first been taken to Annas,

NOTES

which was at night, and which was illegal according to Jewish law. Consequently, to make legitimate this farce called a trial, they would now repeat the procedure under Caiaphas at about daylight.

The Talmud said, *"Criminal processes can neither commence nor terminate, but during the course of the day."*

As well, if a person was condemned, the sentence could not be until the next day. Also, no judgment could be executed either on the eve of the Sabbath or the eve of any festival.

All of these laws were broken in the Trial of Christ, which was conducted at night on the eve of the Passover and on the eve of the special Sabbath of the Feast.

It had been predicted that justice and judgment would be taken away during His Trial, and so it was (Isa. 53:8; Acts 8:33).

(20) "JESUS ANSWERED HIM, I SPOKE OPENLY TO THE WORLD; I EVER TAUGHT IN THE SYNAGOGUE, AND IN THE TEMPLE, WHITHER THE JEWS ALWAYS RESORT; AND IN SECRET HAVE I SAID NOTHING."

The composition is:

1. Satan has two ways of Salvation: one by sacraments and the other by ethics.

2. Christ's Atonement — possessing infinite moral value — condemns and destroys both these false ways of seeking acceptance with God.

3. Christ is the Measure of the Believer's acceptance. Therefore, that acceptance is perfect, full, and eternal, all based upon Faith in Christ and what He did for us at the Cross.

THE MESSAGE OF CHRIST

The phrase, *"Jesus answered him, I spoke openly to the world,"* means that He had said nothing in secret. Actually, His Message was the most open, revealed, and clearly taught of any message in the history of man.

Everything He did was in the open for all to see. He had no hidden agenda; consequently, not only did the people hear all that He had to say but, as well, so did these religious leaders.

The phrase, *"I ever taught in the synagogue, and in the Temple, where the Jews always resort,"* in essence, says, *"If you are claiming that I preached or taught something wrong, why did not you arrest Me in one of the synagogues or in the Temple?"* *"Why did not you accuse Me before the people?"*

Of course, He knew why they did not act accordingly. They had no grounds on which to arrest Him; therefore, they could not charge Him publicly. Consequently, they had to commit the foul deed at night and away from the people.

"And in secret have I said nothing," was that which they knew to be true.

One of the reasons they were so angry at Him was because of this very thing. He was bold beyond anything they had ever seen or heard, saying exactly what He desired to say, and doing it publicly and openly before all. Therefore, their charges are blatantly false!

(21) "WHY DO YOU ASK ME? ASK THEM WHICH HEARD ME, WHAT I HAVE SAID UNTO THEM: BEHOLD, THEY KNOW WHAT I SAID."

The pattern is:

1. A woman who had been caught in the act of adultery was brought to Jesus by the Pharisees.

2. The Law said to stone her, so what would Jesus do?

3. He would not condemn her but did demand that she sin no more. However, the Law was completely satisfied by Him going to the Cross on her behalf and on our behalf.

THE HYPOCRISY OF THE JEWS

The question, *"Why do you ask Me?"* in effect, punches through their hypocrisy.

If they claim He has preached or taught something unscriptural, why not bring in people who heard Him say these erroneous things because He said everything publicly?

In fact, they did bring in some who attempted to contradict Him, but none of their testimonies agreed (Mk. 14:55-59). However, John did not mention this.

"Ask them who heard Me, what I have said unto them: behold, they know what I said," puts the ball back in their court.

In other words, He is saying that if He has violated the Scripture in any way, there will be people who will have heard Him do so, and they can be brought in. Of course, He did not say anything wrong or unscriptural. So, no reliable witness to such accusations could be found!

TRUMPED UP CHARGES

No! In reality, their charges against Him had nothing to do with supposed erroneous doctrine simply because there was none. Their charges, in fact, were trumped up simply because they hated Him. It was not so much what He taught or preached, or the Healings or Miracles, for that matter. They just plain hated Him. Of course, they attempted to find fault with what He said and did claim that He performed Miracles by the powers of Satan.

The truth is: they hated Him because He was of God and, in fact, was God. They were not of God! He had the Power of God with Him, and they did not! He was Perfectly Righteous, and they were perfectly unrighteous! He was Righteous and Pure while they were unholy and ungodly!

The spirit of darkness in them fought out against the Spirit of Light in Him. Admittedly they were very religious, but in truth, they were religious devils! Therefore, they would kill their Messiah and in the process, destroy themselves and their Nation.

(22) "AND WHEN HE HAD THUS SPOKEN, ONE OF THE OFFICERS WHICH STOOD BY STRUCK JESUS WITH THE PALM OF HIS HAND, SAYING, ANSWEREST THOU THE HIGH PRIEST SO?"

The order is:

1. The Message of the Cross exposes the flesh, false doctrine, and even everything that opposes Christ.

2. Therefore, it arouses the hostility in the natural man, Christian or not!

3. The unkindest cut of all will be Christians opposing Christians, but if you stay the course, the course of the Cross, victory most definitely will be yours — a victory unparalleled.

THE EPITOME OF EVIL

The phrase, *"And when He had thus spoken,"* proclaims the same One Who spoke the worlds into existence. Sadly, He was in their very midst, and they did not know Him. Worse still, they would kill Him!

The phrase, *"One of the officers who stood by struck Jesus with the palm of his hand,"* probably presents him doing this in order to curry favor with the High Priest.

Regrettably so, let not the reader think that such ignoble action ceased with the Crucifixion. I can assure all and sundry that it did not!

How many preachers presently engage in similar pursuits, although not physically, but only because the law of the land prohibits such, and they do so to curry favor with religious leaders?

The correct answer is known only to the Lord; however, from experience of being on the receiving end, I can assure all that the number is staggeringly large.

As I have previously said, one quickly finds out how much of the Love of God is prevalent in the hearts of professing Believers when one is down, and anything negative can be done to him that is desired, and it will not only not be censored, but rather applauded!

THE EVIL HEARTS OF RELIGIOUS MEN

The Trial of Jesus exposed the evil hearts of religious men. They could do anything to Him they so desired, as stated, with no fear of reprisal, but rather commendation. Consequently, this scene will portray in living color exactly what they are. The truth is, even though they thought Jesus was on trial, in fact, they were on trial before the Judge of all Creation.

The question, *"Saying, Do You answer the High Priest so?"* answers to the fact that they were looking for a reason to strike Him. He had not said anything wrong, sarcastic, or belligerent. He had simply answered their question.

This is one of the reasons that religious denominations can become so wicked. Inasmuch as such an organization is unscriptural anyway, the leaven, without fail, will take its deadly toll until the whole is leavened. Consequently, many of those who occupy these unscriptural positions of so-called religious leadership take upon themselves a God-like aura. As such, whatever they say is right simply because they say it, whether it has any validity or not. As well, whatever is said to them, exactly as here, is treated as if the person is speaking to God. Hence, this officer would strike Jesus! Regrettably, this scene has been played out tens of thousands of times from then until now.

The tragedy is that the people of Israel little knew or understood how ungodly their religious leaders actually were! Regrettably, with some few exceptions, it is the same presently. How blessed the people are if they have godly leadership.

GODLY!

I have preached all over the world for over 50 years. During this particular time, I have had the privilege of meeting a few men and women in places of high leadership in the Work of God who were godly, but not many. Most of the time, the political structure of religious organizations is such that godly men cannot or will not participate.

How many of the people of Israel would have thought that their leadership would not only not accept the true Messiah, but actually would kill Him, and in the most brutal way possible? I am sure that a few did know because of their Spiritual maturity and godliness. However, not many!

It is the same presently!

It is ironic that the High Priest was supposed to be a Type of Christ. Ideally, that was his role in the Law of Moses. However, Israel had so strayed from the Law of God, actually inserting their own law, that they little knew anymore what was right or wrong. As we have stated, the office of the High Priest was no longer according to the Aaronic lineage, but rather was a political appointment governed by Rome. How the mighty have fallen. Instead of this High Priest representing Christ, he represented Satan!

(23) *"JESUS ANSWERED HIM, IF I HAVE SPOKEN EVIL, BEAR WITNESS OF THE EVIL: BUT IF WELL, WHY DO YOU SMITE ME?"*

The form is:

1. It is incumbent upon us to have the Blessing which the Cross of Christ affords (I Cor. 1:17-18).

2. It is done simply by Faith, which pertains to placing our Faith exclusively in

Christ and What He did for us at the Cross (I Cor. 2:2).

3. We must not allow our Faith to be moved elsewhere. That is the secret of all Blessing (Col. 2:10-15).

JESUS ANSWERED HIM

The phrase, *"Jesus answered him,"* presents a quiet appeal to the conscience of the wretched upstart who dared to insult and even strike the Lord of Glory.

"If I have spoken evil, bear witness of the evil," is not only addressed to the man who has struck Him but, as well, to the High Priest and the entirety of this assemblage. In other words, He is saying, *"If I have spoken or committed some type of evil, tell me what it is!"*

The question, *"But if well, why do you smite Me?"* in effect, says, *"What have I said or done to deserve this?"*

This one Statement and Question by Jesus sums up not only those of that moment, but actually for all time. Has Jesus Christ ever done evil to anyone? The answer to that, of course, is an obvious, *"No!"*

Has He done well and good for us? The answer to that is an obvious, *"Yes!"*

WHY THE HATRED OF CHRIST?

This being true, why the animosity and hatred against Him as is registered by most?

That answer is obvious as well! Their deeds are dark, so they reject His Light simply because it shows up their evil deeds!

It is pointed out with great force that the Chief Priests, who were mostly Sadducees and Pharisees, had great difficulty in formulating any specific charge because of their animosities toward each other.

If the Pharisee party made too much of a point of His Doctrine and practice concerning the Sabbath, the Sadducees, who had little regard for such things, would have argued against this approach.

As well, the Sadducees, who desired to call into question His Cleansing of the Temple, did not dare do so because the Pharisees, who, as well, deplored the buying and the selling, would immediately have justified the act.

Consequently, Caiaphas limits his inquiries to the supposed character of some

NOTES

private teachings to his initiated Disciples — a charge that was refuted by the continual publicity and openness of all His Teaching.

(24) *"NOW ANNAS HAD SENT HIM BOUND UNTO CAIAPHAS THE HIGH PRIEST."*

The order is:

1. The Red Sea and the Jordan River typify the Death and Resurrection of Christ.

2. The Red Sea pictures death to sin; the Jordan, death to self, i.e., the Baptism with the Holy Spirit.

3. The one separates from Egypt, i.e. the world, the other from cold, dead, dry religion.

CAIAPHAS

Verse 24 is spoken in the past tense and, therefore, speaks of Jesus being sent from Annas, to whom He had been sent first (Vs. 13), to Caiaphas, which account commences with the Nineteenth Verse.

Some claim that this account was Annas and not Caiaphas; however, upon my investigation, this does not seem to be the case. Every evidence, I think, points to this account of John as being the main trial with Caiaphas sitting in judgment.

John refers to the *"High Priest"* in Verse 19 without calling him by name; however, he did point out Caiaphas as High Priest in Verse 13.

Some say that both Annas and Caiaphas were serving as High Priests that year, but such does not seem to be the case.

(25) *"AND SIMON PETER STOOD AND WARMED HIMSELF. THEY SAID THEREFORE UNTO HIM, ARE YOU NOT ALSO ONE OF HIS DISCIPLES? HE DENIED IT, AND SAID, I AM NOT."*

The diagram is:

1. Whoever these individuals were of Philippians 3:17-19, the Apostle concluded them to be *"enemies of the Cross of Christ."*

2. He didn't say, *"Enemies of Christ,"* but rather, *"Enemies of the Cross of Christ."*

3. He was speaking of the Judaizers, whom he mentioned at the beginning of the Third Chapter of Philippians.

SIMON PETER

The phrase, *"And Simon Peter stood and warmed himself,"* now picks up the account of this Apostle as it ended in Verse 18. Actually, while the trial was taking place, the scenario with Peter was unfolding outside the door.

The question, *"They said therefore unto him, Are you not also one of His Disciples?"* presents others taking up the accusation along with the damsel of Verse 17. They, no doubt, had heard her, along with Peter's first denial.

The phrase, *"He denied it, and said, I am not,"* presents the second denial, and emphatically so!

(26) "ONE OF THE SERVANTS OF THE HIGH PRIEST, BEING HIS KINSMAN WHOSE EAR PETER CUT OFF, SAID, DID NOT I SEE YOU IN THE GARDEN WITH HIM?"

The overview is:

1. The manner and way that one can tell if one is truly following Christ is that his Faith is totally and completely in Christ and the Cross.

2. The only way that the Believer is going to be free from the *"works of the flesh"* is by Faith in Christ and the Cross.

3. If one resorts to law in any measure, and we speak of rules, regulations, etc., such a Believer is going to fail the Lord.

SATAN'S FELL SWOOP

The phrase, *"One of the servants of the High Priest, being his kinsman whose ear Peter cut off,"* identifies the last accuser. He had been in the garden at the arrest of Jesus and now recognizes Peter as the one who had cut off the ear of his relative.

The question, *"Said, did not I see you in the garden with Him?"* presents the occasion for the third denial.

(27) "PETER THEN DENIED AGAIN: AND IMMEDIATELY THE ROOSTER CROWED."

The exegesis is:

1. Job is the oldest Book in the Bible and, thereby, the oldest Book in the world.

2. It was written by Moses (Lk. 24:27, 44).

3. It explains the problem of why good men are afflicted. It is in order to bring about their Sanctification.

4. It is interesting that this difficult question should be the first taken up and answered in the Bible.

THE THIRD DENIAL

The phrase, *"Peter then denied again,"* presents the third lie and denial of Jesus.

Matthew recorded that he said, *"Then began he to curse and to swear, saying, I know not the Man"* (Mat. 26:74).

The cursing and swearing did not refer to profanity but probably even worse. He was calling curses upon himself if what he said was untrue. As well, he was swearing by the Name of God that he did not know Jesus; consequently, I think it is obvious as to how serious this was that Peter did.

"And immediately the rooster crowed," proclaims the fulfillment of the prediction of Jesus (Lk. 22:34).

It was at this moment that Jesus looked at Peter, as Jesus was being led from the first trial of sorts before Annas to the main trial before Caiaphas and the Sanhedrin. Luke recorded that when this happened, *"Peter remembered the Word of the Lord, how He had said unto him, Before the rooster crows, you shall deny Me three times."*

PETER'S REACTION

Luke then said, *"And Peter went out, and wept bitterly"* (Lk. 22:61-62).

It was at this moment that Peter repented. What must he have felt when, upon uttering the last denial with cursing and swearing, he looks up and stares into the bloated, beaten Face of Jesus as the Lord is being led past him. Despite His Grief and Pain, the Eyes of Jesus must have looked kindly toward the fisherman, but yet, it was a look that pierced the very depths of Peter's soul. No doubt, it would be a moment he would never forget! What he had done would then overwhelm him, with him stumbling from this place to some point of seclusion, where great racking sobs shook his body.

It was at this moment, no doubt, that Satan made his greatest bid for Peter's soul. The despair and the grief must have been overwhelming. As well, Satan must have fed him, telling him that all was now lost. He had failed Jesus so miserably, and at a time when the Master needed him more than ever.

However, whatever happened that early morning hour, as bad as it must have been, did not cause Peter to quit, which was, no doubt, Satan's intention. Despite his terrible failure, and terrible it was, the fisherman determined that if Jesus would have him, he would remain by His Side.

Tradition says that ever after, when Peter would hear the sound of a rooster crowing, he would fall to his knees, shaking with bitter sobs.

If our chronology is right concerning John's account, this would have happened with Peter immediately following Verse 18 and preceding Verse 19.

(28) "THEN LED THEY JESUS FROM CAIAPHAS UNTO THE HALL OF JUDGMENT: AND IT WAS EARLY; AND THEY THEMSELVES WENT NOT INTO THE JUDGMENT HALL, LEST THEY SHOULD BE DEFILED; BUT THAT THEY MIGHT EAT THE PASSOVER."

The form is:

1. The Law of Moses assured Righteousness to all who perfectly obeyed it (Gal. 3:10), but condemned to death all who failed to give it that perfect obedience.

2. Such an obedience was impossible to man, for he, born in sin, is morally imperfect, and moral imperfection cannot possibly render moral perfection.

3. Christ redeemed the believing sinner from that doom because He suffered it Himself on the Believer's behalf. Thus, at Calvary, He affirmed the authority of that Law and vindicated its justice and goodness.

THE HALL OF JUDGMENT

The phrase, *"Then led they Jesus from Caiaphas unto the hall of judgment,"* speaks of Pilate's judgment hall. It was supposed to be a court of justice but, in this case, would be a court of injustice of the grossest kind.

Due to Israel being under the yoke of Rome, they were somewhat restricted respecting certain things.

While Roman law did allow the Jewish Sanhedrin (the ruling body) to have certain latitude in criminal cases, that which involved capital punishment required the confirmation of the Roman procurator, in this case, Pilate.

In special cases where a Gentile passed the barrier which divided the inner court of the Temple from that of the Gentiles, the Sanhedrin, as thought by some, was granted the power of death by Roman administrators (Acts 21:28). This concession may have extended to other offenses against the Temple, whether in fact or supposed, as with Stephen (Acts 6:13). However, the case of Stephen seems to have had some features of an illegal mob act.

In the case of Jesus, the Sanhedrin would have a difficult time proving that He had actually transgressed the Temple in any way. While it was true that He had cleansed it by driving out the money changers, still, as we have previously stated, if certain members of the Sanhedrin, who were Sadducees, had brought up this occasion, the Pharisees, who were also members of the Sanhedrin, would not have lent their support because they too felt that the activity of the moneychangers was little short of blasphemy.

MOSAIC LAW

However, the Jews really did not desire to try Jesus according to Mosaic Law, not only because there was no charge they could successfully bring against Him from that source, but because they wanted Rome to carry out this foul deed so as to make the people think that Jesus was guilty of some heinous crime, or else, Rome would not have demanded jurisdiction. To carry this out, they would claim that Jesus was committing high treason against Rome by claiming to be a King, etc.

As well, by doing this, they felt that the tens, if not hundreds, of thousands of people in the city who had come for the Passover, and who were Friends of Jesus, would have no recourse against Rome. They had formulated their plan well.

The phrase, *"And it was early,"* no doubt, represents the fourth watch of the night, which was between three and six o'clock in the morning, but closer to six.

The trumped up trial by Caiaphas had just ended and was, no doubt, conducted immediately at daylight in order to satisfy Jewish Law, which stated that a man could not be tried at night.

DEFILED?

The phrase, *"And they themselves went not into the judgment hall,"* presents an ironic turn of events. They could murder the Lord of Glory, but their religion forbade them to enter the house of a Gentile. Such is self-righteousness!

The phrase, *"Lest they should be defiled,"* actually had nothing to do with Mosaic Law but was a purely rabbinic observance. In other words, it was another one of those made-up laws, which had no relativity to Scripture. As well, self-righteousness abounds in such activity.

John, in his own quiet way, here allows us to see the religious hierarchy holding strong to the stupendous spectacle of malicious ritualism and of unscrupulous antagonism to the Holiest One. Such is religion!

In their jaded, demented, and perverted minds, they thought they would be *"defiled"* by entering into this Gentile presence while, all the time, plotting diligently to murder Jesus.

Here we observe the niceties of outward formalities which occasion religion and self-righteousness while, all the time, the heart is black and evil. That is the reason that religion is such a horrifying spectacle. It deals not at all with the true problem of man, which is an evil, wicked heart. It rather busies itself with myriad rules, which it thinks affords some type of Righteousness. I would hope the reader can fully see the awfulness of this spectacle, which characterizes, as well, so much of the world presently! Sadly, most church activity falls into this category.

THE PASSOVER?

The phrase, *"But that they might eat the Passover,"* has reference to the idea that cleansing from such defilement would take a period of time, and, therefore, they would not be able to partake of the Passover that day. They did not even remotely realize that they were killing the True Passover, actually, the One to Whom the ritual Passover had always pointed.

Jesus and His Disciples had eaten the Passover a day early, actually, the evening before, in order that Jesus might die at the exact time of the offering of the Paschal sacrifice, which was at 3 p.m. This was the day of the Passover, which was a Wednesday and not Friday, as many suppose. Jesus would stay in the grave three full days and nights, rising from the dead shortly after sunset on Saturday evening, which began the new day of Sunday in Jewish reckoning of that time. Days are now reckoned as beginning at midnight whereas, then, the new day began at sunset.

(29) "PILATE THEN WENT OUT UNTO THEM, AND SAID, WHAT ACCUSATION BRING YOU AGAINST THIS MAN?"

The diagram is:

1. Judgment always begins with Believers and pertains to our Faith, whether in the Cross or otherwise (I Pet. 4:17-18).
2. The Cross alone is spared judgment, for there Jesus was judged in our place.
3. If God will judge His Own, how much more will He judge the unredeemed? The Cross alone stays the judgment of God. That must ever be understood.

PONTIUS PILATE

The phrase, *"Pilate then went out unto them,"* has reference to paying deference to their religious taboo. They would not come into the building because it was Gentile, so he would go out to them. This was probably on a porch-type affair with the courtyard spread out in front, where this crowd had gathered as they brought Jesus. Pilate is here introduced by John without fanfare. Due to the fact that John's Gospel was written last (after the other three), it is taken for granted that all by now are well acquainted with Pilate.

He was the fifth governor of Judaea under the Romans and held that office from A.D. 26-36. He was represented in Rome by Philo.

THE TEMPERAMENT OF PILATE

Philo speaks of Pilate's *"ferocious passions,"* and says that he was given to fits of furious wrath, and that he had reason to fear the complaints laid before Tiberius, the Roman Caesar. This was because of *"his acts of insolence, his habit of insulting people, for his cruelty, and murders of people untried and uncondemned, and his never-ending inhumanity."* These complaints might bring upon him the rebuke, which ultimately the emperor gave him, in consequence of his endeavor to force from the Jews assent to his placing gilded shields in the palace of Herod.

Josephus, the Jewish historian, gives a better account of Pilate. He shows that a portion of his administration was not without beneficent purpose, and that he would have done more respecting benefits but was thwarted by the fanatical opposition of the Jews.

Irrespective, this will prove to be the most momentous day of his life. He will stand in judgment concerning the Son of God but, in reality, will himself be judged.

WHAT ACCUSATION BRING YOU AGAINST THIS MAN?

The question of our heading shows that something had conspired to provoke certain sympathy on his part with Jesus and to excite additional suspicion of the Jews.

There seems to be some small evidence that Pilate had already been told of these proceedings and had agreed to hear the case at that early morning hour. In other words, their coming was not a surprise.

To be frank, this question, *"What accusation do you bring against this Man?"* could be asked of any and all! In fact, no truthful accusation can be brought against Him because He is the Only Truly Good Thing that has ever happened to this world.

Every single freedom, prosperity, and benefit that has ever come to the human family in any form has come by, of, and through the Lord Jesus Christ and What He did for us at Calvary's Cross.

(30) "THEY ANSWERED AND SAID UNTO HIM, IF HE WERE NOT A MALEFACTOR, WE WOULD NOT HAVE DELIVERED HIM UP TO YOU."

The overview is:

1. If Paul had not rebuked Peter publicly (Gal. 2:11-13), the entire Message of Grace could have been compromised, and most likely would have been!

2. Satan carries on his greatest work, not from outside the church, but from inside the church.

3. The Holy Spirit through Paul characterized their actions as hypocrisy. In other words, they knew better!

NO ACCUSATION

The phrase, *"They answered and said unto him,"* actually records no answer at all simply because they had no case against Jesus.

"If He were not a malefactor, we would not have delivered Him up to you," proclaims Him as an evildoer, but they do not say what evil He has done!

In reality, they did not want Pilate to judge but to execute the sentence they had already illegally passed. However, he was not willing to execute a Man Whom he had not tried and Who was not guilty, so he offered to turn Jesus over to them for execution.

(31) "THEN SAID PILATE UNTO THEM, TAKE YOU HIM, AND JUDGE HIM ACCORDING TO YOUR LAW. THE JEWS THEREFORE SAID UNTO HIM, IT IS NOT LAWFUL FOR US TO PUT ANY MAN TO DEATH."

The overview is:

1. What are the weapons of our warfare (II Cor. 10:3-5)?

2. Paul says they aren't *"carnal,"* which means they aren't anything we think up or that we can do as a human being.

3. The weapons of our warfare are Faith in Christ and What He did for us at the Cross, and that exclusively.

PILATE

The phrase, *Then said Pilate unto them, You take Him, and judge Him according to your Law,"* proclaims him desiring to rid himself of this matter.

There was probably a twofold reason for Pilate's answer:

1. He knew Jesus had done nothing wrong and was brought here because of the evildoing of the religious hierarchy (Mat. 27:18).

2. Hating the Jews as he did, Pilate would use this occasion to once again let them know that they could do very little without him.

"The Jews therefore said unto him, It is not lawful for us to put any man to death," automatically lets us know that they had no

desire for justice to be served, but that they had already condemned Him in their hearts. They wanted Him dead!

In fact, as we have stated, it is thought that they did have the right to apply capital punishment in some cases, but, of course, this did not apply to Jesus. So, they were really saying that they could not put Him to death according to Mosaic Law based on the flimsy charges they had leveled against Him. However, they hated Him so much that they would go to any length to see that the death sentence was carried out. This is from the *"church"* of that day!

(32) "THAT THE SAYING OF JESUS MIGHT BE FULFILLED, WHICH HE SPOKE, SIGNIFYING WHAT DEATH HE SHOULD DIE."

The exegesis is:

1. If the Believer subscribes to laws in any capacity, what Christ did at the Cross will be of no profit for such an individual.

2. Although the Holy Spirit continues to reside in the Believer, He is curtailed in His Efforts to help.

3. What is the reason? Such a Believer failing to place his or her faith exclusively in Christ and the Cross, but rather something else, is committing spiritual adultery. As it should be obvious, this ties the hands, so to speak, of the Holy Spirit.

THE DEATH HE SHOULD DIE

The phrase, *"That the saying of Jesus might be fulfilled,"* proclaims that the Mind of God had long since settled this question (I Pet. 1:19-20).

Jesus had foretold this in John 3:14, 8:28, and in 12:32.

In the synopsis, He had repeatedly spoken of the type of death He would die (Mat. 10:38; 16:24; Mk. 8:34; Lk. 14:27). In Matthew 20:19 and Luke 9:22-23, He clearly predicted His Crucifixion by the Gentiles.

The phrase, *"Which He spoke, signifying what death He should die,"* is of such magnitude, not only proclaiming that He would die, but even more particularly, what type of death He would experience. In other words, a certain type of death was necessary in order that Jesus fully satisfy the claims of Heavenly Justice.

NOTES

THE RELIGIOUS HIERARCHY

Consequently, what the religious hierarchy would do, even though it was the most wicked act in human history, still would play into the Hands of God. This is more remarkable when one realizes that even though He was predestined to die in this manner, it was not predestined that the religious hierarchy would do what it did. They did it out of their own free will, which made it even more wicked and vile.

Not realizing they were fulfilling Prophecy (Deut. 21:23; Isa., Chpt. 53), they withdrew from stoning Him for fear of the multitude. As well, their hatred for Him was such that they thought death by stoning too painless. Consequently, they determined to bring Him into the power of the Roman governor, which they did; for against Pilate, the people could do nothing, and so the priests would secure the punishment of Crucifixion.

As well, the political order in which this was carried out involved the entirety of the world. Judaea had become a Roman province, which, by its very act, joined with Gentile and Jew together. Consequently, they both would offer up the awful Sacrifice, and all the world would stand guilty of the Death of our Lord.

The manner or kind of death was full of significance. To satisfy the claims of Heavenly Justice and to satisfy the sin debt against man, Jesus had to come under the penalty of the broken Law. The curse of the Law was death (Deut. 11:28; 21:22-23).

THE CURSE OF
THE BROKEN LAW

Paul said, *"Christ has redeemed us from the curse of the Law, being made a curse for us: for it is written, Cursed is everyone who hangs on a tree"* (Gal. 3:13).

So, to be made a Curse in our place, thereby, suffering the penalty of the broken Law in our stead, Jesus had to die by Crucifixion. That alone would satisfy the claims of Heavenly Justice.

All came under the curse of the broken Law because all had broken the Law. As well, due to being polluted by sin and, consequently, an unworthy sacrifice, it would have done man no good to have died for his sin, for such would not have saved him because such a sacrifice could not be accepted by God. For the Sacrifice to be accepted, it had to be a Perfect Life in a Perfect Body, untainted by sin and pollution, which alone could be accepted by God. This is the very reason that God became Man: in order that such a Sacrifice could be provided (Isa. 7:14).

He did for us what we could not do for ourselves, in effect, dying by being made a Curse because this is what the broken Law demanded.

CURSED BY GOD?

In essence, Christ was not cursed by God. He was made a Curse, which is far, far different. This means that He had to suffer the penalty of the broken Law even though He had not broken it Himself, not in the slightest, and because every human being had, in fact, broken the Law, which demanded death. The death of which we speak is eternal separation from God, which refers to Hellfire forever and forever.

Some teach that Christ became a sinner on the Cross, died and went to Hell as all sinners do, and was Born-Again in Hell after three days and nights of suffering. Nothing could be further from the Truth. You won't find a shred of that anywhere in the Bible, and you won't find it because it never happened.

When Jesus died, the last Words that He said were, *"Father, into Your Hands I commend My Spirit: and having said thus, He gave up the ghost"* (Lk. 23:46).

If Jesus became a sinner on the Cross, as some teach, and was dying and going to Hell even as sinners do, He could not have commended His Spirit unto His Father. No, His Death was the payment for all sin. In fact, Jesus never went into the burning side of Hell. He went down into Paradise where He *"led captivity captive,"* meaning that He took all of these souls out of that place, with them then going to Heaven. This could be done now because He had atoned for all sin, past, present, and future, at least for all who will believe (Jn. 3:16).

NOTES

JUSTIFICATION BY FAITH

By Faith in Christ, God awards to the believing sinner the fact that all sin debt has been paid, resulting in no claims left upon him which can be exercised by Satan. In other words, upon having Faith in Christ, the sinner is now declared, *"Not guilty,"* by the God of Heaven. It is called, *"Justification by Faith"* or *"Righteousness freely imputed to the believing sinner."*

As such, the sinner now becomes a New Creation in Christ Jesus, and all by Faith. So, it was important not only that He die but, as well, that He die a certain death, which He did!

WHY THE CROSS?

The Mosaic Law said: *"And if a man have committed a sin worthy of death, and he be to be put to death, and you hang him on a tree:*

"His body shall not remain all night upon the tree, but you shall in any wise bury him that day; (for he who is hanged is accursed of God;) that your land be not defiled, which the LORD your God gives you for an inheritance" (Deut. 21:22-23).

This is the reason that the religious leaders of Israel demanded that Jesus be put on the Cross (Mat. 27:23). They knew that one put on the tree was accursed of God, and so they reasoned that the people would then think, *"Were He really the Messiah, God would never allow Him to be put on a Cross."* They did not realize that the Lord had foretold the event of the Cross some 1,500 years earlier, as it concerned the brazen serpent on the pole (Num. 21:8-9). It was necessary that Jesus go to the Cross in order that He might atone for all the sins of mankind, and I mean the worst sins, at least for all who would believe (Jn. 3:16). So, Jesus was made a Curse on the Cross, not because of His Sins, for He had none, but for the sin of the whole world and for all time (Jn. 1:29; Gal. 3:13).

CHRIST THE KING

Whenever the Jews formulated a charge against Jesus to present to the Roman governor, they claimed that they found Him perverting the Nation and forbidding to give tribute to Caesar, *"Saying that He Himself is Christ a King"* (Lk. 23:2).

They felt this would move Pilate against Him.

However, this probably seemed ludicrous to Pilate in that these bigoted and rebellious priests, who perpetually resisted the claims of Roman governors to enforce tribute, should now hypocritically pretend that a Prophet-Leader of their own had been guilty of such a charge.

Pilate knew that these priests regarded any action that cheated Rome not as a crime, but as something patriotic. So, he, no doubt, saw with shrewdness that the Jews had merely cloaked their real antagonism by presenting an incrimination which, under ordinary circumstances, they would have treated as a crowning virtue.

(33) "THEN PILATE ENTERED INTO THE JUDGMENT HALL AGAIN, AND CALLED JESUS, AND SAID UNTO HIM, ARE YOU THE KING OF THE JEWS?"

The overview is:

1. Realizing the Grace of God that had been shown to him, Paul considered himself as a *"debtor"* to all men.

2. It really didn't matter who they were, he must do his utmost to take the Gospel to all concerned.

3. While Paul couldn't reach all people, however, he felt responsible to all, whether he could reach them or not, and so should we!

THE KING OF THE JEWS!

The phrase, *"Then Pilate entered into the judgment hall again, and called Jesus,"* refers to him calling Jesus to his side. Out of hearing of the crowd, he begins to question Jesus.

John did not mention it, but Luke gives a little fuller account, relating that the religious hierarchy, plus others who had brought Jesus to the judgment hall, had claimed before Pilate that Jesus was *"saying that He Himself is Christ a King"* (Lk. 23:2).

In fact, Jesus had not made any statements of this nature. While He definitely was the King, actually, *"The King of kings,"* this was not the time to fill that position. In reality, Jesus claiming Kingship is what

NOTES

the Disciples desired, but He repeatedly told them otherwise. He pointed instead to His Coming Death. So, the accusations of the Jews were baseless (Mat. 16:21-23).

As the mob (for they had turned into a mob) made their loud accusations and bitter charges, spearheaded by *"the Chief Priests and Elders"* (Mat. 27:11-12; Mk. 15:3-4), Jesus stood before Pilate. Reynolds said, *"His solemn and accusing silence caused the Governor to marvel greatly"*[6] (Mat. 27:14; Mk. 15:5).

PILATE AND JESUS

As Pilate looks at Jesus, he is observed through the eyes of a Roman man of the world, who has never learned to rule his policy by any notions of Righteousness and truth and, consequently, is utterly unable to appreciate the spiritual claims of this Nazarene. Yet, he was shrewd enough to see that so far as Roman authority was concerned, this Prisoner was utterly harmless.

The question, *"And said unto Him, Are You the King of the Jews?"* is an answer to their baseless charge.

He expected a negative reply.

I doubt that anything that happened concerning the Person of Jesus that morning was ludicrous to the governor, yet he must have pondered this abused and rejected Prisoner who stood before him. The Man who stood before him was this bound and bleeding Sufferer, who had no apparent followers around Him. He was actually betrayed by one of His Intimate Friends and deserted by the rest. As well, He was hounded to death by the fierce cries of Pharisees and Sadducees, Chief Priests and Elders!

Should He answer in the affirmative, it might easily suggest itself to Pilate that He must be under some futile hallucination.

(34) "JESUS ANSWERED HIM, DO YOU SAY THIS THING OF YOURSELF, OR DID OTHERS TELL IT TO YOU OF ME?"

The overview is:

1. The last two Chapters of Revelation portray a world that is totally free of sin of any type of description, totally free of Satan, all demon spirits, and all fallen Angels, and totally free of those who will not serve the Lord.

2. Sadly and regrettably, all those in that capacity are in the Lake of Fire where they will remain forever and forever (Rev. 20:10-15).

3. God the Father will then actually change His Headquarters from Planet Heaven to Planet Earth.

THE QUESTION ASKED BY JESUS

This question of Verse 34, as asked by Jesus, is meant to take the governor beyond the hurled accusations of those who were thirsty for blood.

Irrespective of the Appearance of Jesus, which, at the time, was anything but kingly, there had to have been something about Him, an aura or Presence, especially now, which took Him out of the ordinary. As well, the question He asked Pilate had to be freighted with Conviction. I do not feel it left Pilate as it found him.

I have no doubt in my mind that in the coming months and even years, Pilate pondered his question to Jesus over and over and, more than all, the Answer that Jesus gave. I do not believe that the Sight of this Bedraggled Figure ever left his mind. And then, the question probes deep into Pilate's heart.

He, no doubt, knew of the Jewish claims of a coming Messiah. Undoubtedly, he had attempted to acquaint himself with the customs of these strange people he had been sent to govern. As well, it is almost a certainty that he had heard of the great Miracles performed by Christ and especially the gigantic crowds. Something of this nature was bound to come to the ears of the Roman governor. Now, Jesus stands before him and asks of him a question concerning kingship.

(35) "PILATE ANSWERED, AM I A JEW? YOUR OWN NATION AND THE CHIEF PRIESTS HAVE DELIVERED YOU UNTO ME: WHAT HAVE YOU DONE?"

The exegesis is:

1. In Galatians 3:2-3, two methods are proposed here. One is man's way, and the other is God's Way.

2. Man's way is the activity of law and works.

NOTES

3. God's Way is the hearing of the Gospel and believing it, i.e., *"Jesus Christ and Him Crucified."*

THE ANSWER OF PILATE

The question, *"Pilate answered, Am I a Jew?"* is asked with some sarcasm and is actually more of a statement than a question.

In effect, he is saying that he has little interest in the internal affairs of the Jews as long as such does not threaten the authority of Rome. As well, his question is said as much to himself as it was to Jesus. He considers himself to be far above these conquered people, and, as a Roman, he recognizes no king except Caesar and those appointed by Caesar.

"Your Own Nation and the Chief Priests have delivered You unto me," in effect, says, *"I am not making the charge, they are!"* As well, he is saying that personally, he has no reason of his own to assume that Jesus was a political aspirant.

The Roman governor was right! He had in no way instigated the arrest of Christ, nor had he brought any charge against Jesus. All of this was strictly the doing of the religious hierarchy of Israel.

WHAT HAVE YOU DONE?

Little did he know or realize the extent of what he had said! In all of his efforts to govern these strange people, he little realized that what happened here today would be heralded all over the world, never to be forgotten, even down to the most minute detail. At this moment, he has little idea as to the magnitude of these proceedings. Regrettably, he will learn too late!

The question, *"What have You done?"* is as much asked of himself as it is of Jesus.

This very question poses the confusion that is in the governor's mind. He knows Jesus is Innocent of these charges, and, as well, he realizes that Jesus is Different than anyone he has ever seen.

The answer to Pilate's question is easy. *"What have You done?"*

Jesus has healed countless thousands of every disease imaginable. He has even raised the dead. He has loosed untold numbers from demonic bondage that have made life hell on Earth. He has spoken the greatest Words that man has ever heard. He has given men hope beyond this mortal coil. He has lifted their eyes from the struggle of this life to a better land and a better place. He called it *"Eternal Life!"*

He has made statements such as no man had ever made before. He is the Door to the Father. He is the Way to God, and, in fact, He is God! Furthermore, He would and did redeem man from the awful clutches of sin, thereby, breaking Satan's grip and hold over the human race.

What have You done?

He is Saviour, Healer, Baptizer with the Holy Spirit, and Giver of Eternal Life. He is God, Who came down to this Earth in the form of Man in order to redeem man. That He did! And He did it so well that it need never be done again.

(36) "JESUS ANSWERED, MY KINGDOM IS NOT OF THIS WORLD: IF MY KINGDOM WERE OF THIS WORLD, THEN WOULD MY SERVANTS FIGHT, THAT I SHOULD NOT BE DELIVERED TO THE JEWS: BUT NOW IS MY KINGDOM NOT FROM HENCE."

The exposition is:

1. The fountain of which Zechariah speaks (Zech. 13:1) was historically opened at Calvary but will be consciously opened to repentant Judah in the future day of her Repentance.

2. However, the fact and function of that fountain only becomes conscious to the awakened sinner.

3. A true sense of sin and guilt, in relationship to God, awakens the sense of the need of cleansing. So, the shed and cleansing Blood of the Lamb of God becomes precious to the convicted conscience.

THE KINGDOM

The phrase, *"Jesus answered, My Kingdom is not of this world,"* in no way denies His Kingship but does claim that the origin of His Kingdom and Kingship is not of this world. Neither now nor at any future period will it derive its origin from this source.

In fact, His Royal Power and State are not furnished by earthly force or fleshly ordinances, physical energies, material wealth, or imperial armies. In truth, He is a *"King,"* and He has a *"Kingdom."* However, it is a Kingdom over hearts and lives alone.

At that particular time, His Kingdom consisted of only a few hundred people; however, from then until now, hundreds of millions have become a part of that *"Kingdom."* Its entrance is by being *"Born-Again,"* which means to accept Jesus as one's personal Saviour and making Him the Lord of one's life (Jn. 3:3).

To be sure, this *"Kingdom,"* with Him as *"King,"* is responsible, as we have previously stated, for all freedom, prosperity, and Salvation in the world, in fact, everything that is good.

THIS KINGDOM OF GOD

The mighty Roman Empire kingdom, which ruled the world of Jesus' Day, is no more. It is only a memory in the history books. However, the *"Kingdom"* which Jesus founded is even today the largest, most powerful, and most influential Kingdom on the face of the Earth. As well, there is coming an hour when this *"Kingdom"* will not only rule within the hearts and lives of select men and women, boys and girls, but, in fact, over the entirety of the Earth. It alone is the past, the present, and the future. All other kingdoms will ultimately bow to this *"Kingdom"* (Dan. 2:44).

However, it must ever be remembered that the Strength and Power of this *"Kingdom"* is its *"King,"* our Lord and Saviour, Jesus Christ.

The phrase, *"If My Kingdom were of this world,"* plainly tells Pilate, and all concerned, for that matter, that He (Jesus) is not an earthly king as people think of kings. He is no threat to Caesar, or anyone, for that matter, except Satan and his kingdom of darkness.

In fact, Jesus actually did have a political following and could have commanded it in a moment's time. Actually, not only His Disciples but multiple thousands of others in Israel desired that He use His Great Power in a political manner, thereby, overthrowing Rome. However, this was not the type of kingdom which He had come to establish. Man's root problem was not political, physical, or economic. Man's real problem was spiritual, and it was that which Jesus addressed.

THE KINGDOM OF DARKNESS

In fact, as stated, He was using His Power against a kingdom, but it was a kingdom of darkness in the spiritual realm, which was and is the cause of all the problems and difficulties on Earth.

The phrase, *"Then would My Servants fight, that I should not be delivered to the Jews,"* says to the governor that were He what they claimed Him to be, a usurper over Rome and a hurtful seditionist to Israel, His Followers would have long since been incited to use force. However, inasmuch as none of that has ever happened, not even in the slightest, such, within itself, was proof enough that He was no threat to anyone in a political or military sense. In effect, He is saying that such should be obvious to the governor!

"But now is My Kingdom not from hence," does tell us something about the future.

In effect, He is saying that even though His Kingdom is spiritual only at present, there will come a day when it will fill the Earth in every capacity, be it spiritual, physical, economic, or material. The Prophet said, *"For the Earth shall be filled with the knowledge of the Glory of the LORD, as the waters cover the sea"* (Hab. 2:14; Rev., Chpt. 19).

So, He is saying, *"Not now, but ultimately it shall!"*

(37) *"PILATE THEREFORE SAID UNTO HIM, ARE YOU A KING THEN? JESUS ANSWERED, YOU SAY THAT I AM A KING. TO THIS END WAS I BORN, AND FOR THIS CAUSE CAME I INTO THE WORLD, THAT I SHOULD BEAR WITNESS UNTO THE TRUTH. EVERY ONE WHO IS OF THE TRUTH HEARS MY VOICE."*

The exposition is:

1. Two priests, one destined to be High Priest, recorded in Leviticus 10:1-2, suffered the judgment of God because they ignored Calvary.

2. Coals of fire were to be taken from the Brazen Altar, which typified Calvary, and placed on the Golden Altar in the Tabernacle.

3. However, they took *"strange fire,"* which came from some ignition other than the Altar, and placed that on the Golden Altar. They were stricken dead immediately for their action.

ARE YOU A KING?

The question, *"Pilate therefore said unto Him, Are You a King then?"* is not exactly known as to whether it is asked in sarcasm or sincerity. Quite probably, there is a little of both!

Pilate, a product of the Roman way, thought of kings in an entirely different light than what he was observing here in Jesus. Kings had authority and power, even as he as governor had such. And yet, Jesus carried no appearance of such whatsoever. This instigated the scorn. In other words, *"This is a joke,"* as Pilate would have thought!

And yet, there is something about Jesus that is regal despite His Appearance. In fact, Pilate had never dealt with a Man such as Jesus, and neither had anyone else, for that matter. Jesus, being the only Perfect Human being Who has ever lived and, in fact, the Son of God, was in truth, *"Very Man"* and *"Very God."*

THE PERFECT MAN

When one dealt with Jesus, even as Pilate here did, he was dealing with a Perfect Man, Who had no prejudice or bias regarding race, color, nationality, or position. He was dealing with One Who did not merely contain love, but, in fact, was Love! As such, He hated nothing but sin, while all the time loving the sinner.

In His Character and Nature, which were obvious to all, at least if they would admit such, Pilate surely sensed this regal bearing and, as such, surely addressed Jesus with some sincerity.

The phrase, *"Jesus answered, You say that I am a King,"* is the same way as saying, *"Yes, it is so!"*

The phrase, *"To this end was I born,"* addresses the Incarnation, God becoming Man (Isa. 7:14).

And yet, He was *"born"* as no other human being has ever been born.

All of the human family had been born, and continues to be born, as a result of procreation. This speaks of the union of man and woman, which God intended! However, due to Adam being the bearer of the seed of procreation, when he fell in the Garden of Eden, the whole of the human family from him forward, with no exceptions, would be born in sin, even as David said. *"Behold, I was shaped in iniquity; and in sin did my mother conceive me"* (Ps. 51:5). So, instead of Adam and Eve bringing sons and daughters of God into the world and their seed doing the same, as was originally intended by God, due to the Fall, offspring can be brought into the world only *"in His* (Adam's) *own likeness,"* after *"his* (Adam's) *image"* (Gen. 5:3). Consequently, all, even from then until now, are born in a fallen state, which is called *"original sin."*

THE PERFECTION OF CHRIST

As a result, man is hopelessly lost with no means or ways to save himself. Therefore, God became Man, but in a different manner than any other. Even though He was born of woman, His Conception was not the result of the union of man with woman, in this case, Mary. His Conception was decreed by God and brought about by the Holy Spirit (Lk. 1:34-35). In other words, the conception of Jesus in Mary's womb was brought about exactly as God brought about light, *"And God said"* (Gen. 1:3). To say it in a different way: there was no physical union of any nature concerning His Conception.

Consequently, as Jesus had no earthly father, He was not born in a fallen state as all others, but without sin or its nature. As a result, He would be the Representative Man for all who would believe, thereby, succeeding as the Last Adam where the first Adam failed (I Cor. 15:22, 45).

In this Perfect, Sinless Body, He walked in Perfection for the entirety of His Life, thereby, keeping and fulfilling the Law of Moses in every respect. Now, this Perfect Body and Perfect Life would be offered up to God as a Sin-Offering on behalf of others. Such would satisfy the claims of Heavenly Justice, thereby, removing the enmity between God and man. He satisfied the curse of the broken Law, which was death, even though He had never broken that Law. All of it was done for humanity. *"That whosoever believes in Him should not perish, but have Everlasting Life"* (Jn. 3:16).

This is the reason He was *"born!"*

FOR THIS CAUSE

The phrase, *"And for this cause came I into the world,"* referred to two things:

1. He is to be King in the hearts of all who believe Him. Westcott said that the word *"coming"* in the Greek implies that His Coming is permanent in its effect and not simply a past historical fact. In other words, as Jesus was King in the hearts of His Followers then, as few as they were, He is to be King in the hearts of all who believe Him now and, in fact, in this respect, all who have ever lived.

2. At the Second Coming (Rev., Chpt. 19), He will come back *"King of kings and Lord of lords,"* referring to the entirety of the Earth and for all people. At that time, He will Personally reign from Jerusalem. It is referred to as the *"Kingdom Age,"* with Christ ruling and reigning in this Earth for a thousand years, which will show the world what it could have been all along (Rev., Chpt. 20).

At the end of the 1,000 years, the Lord will refurbish Heaven and Earth, thereby, removing all traces of sin, totally fulfilling the Prophecy of John the Baptist, *"Whose fan is in His Hand, and He will thoroughly purge His Floor, and gather His Wheat into the garner; but He will burn up the chaff with unquenchable fire"* (Mat. 3:12).

WITNESS UNTO THE TRUTH

The phrase, *"That I should bear witness unto the Truth,"* carries in its statement the entirety of the embodiment of the Ways of God.

Before the High Priest, Jesus declared that He was the Son of God, and before the Roman governor, He claimed to be the King of the Jews.

However, He declared to Pilate, and to all, for that matter, that His Kingdom is not of human origination or appointment. It was and is a Divine Institution.

Until the Kingdom comes, and come it shall, His Present Kingdom is the moral Kingdom of Truth. There is but One Teacher in that Kingdom, and every Spirit-taught heart listens to that Voice.

Even though others, such as the Prophets of old, had spoken fearlessly and clearly about this *"Truth,"* Jesus not only declared it but, in fact, was and is *"the Truth"* (Jn. 14:6).

The idea is that the Prophets spoke of the *"Truth,"* as is God's Word, but Jesus proclaimed that Truth in His Person, which means that nothing was concealed. To say it in another way: all Truth is revealed in Jesus and Jesus Alone! This means, as we have repeatedly stated, that there is no *"truth"* in any of the religions of the world or philosophies of man. All Truth originates and is characterized by the Person of Jesus Christ. He Alone is the *"Witness"* of this Way.

THE WITNESS

As well, the word *"witness"* in the Greek text is *"martureo"* and has reference to *"martyr,"* which means *"one who bears witness by his death."* Truth would die that Truth might live. To say it in another way: *"Truth"* would die in order that the *"lie"* would be defeated and broken, that *"Truth"* may live free of this deadly encumbrance.

The *"Kingdom of God"* is *"Truth,"* while all other kingdoms are lies.

"Every one who is of the Truth hears My Voice" means *"to obey as a supreme authority."* This *"Truth"* is the *"Written Word"* and the *"Living Word,"* Who is Truth.

In effect, Jesus is saying, *"Every one who is of the Truth hears the Voice of Christ and will accept His Authority as final and supreme."*

Notice that He said, *"My Voice!"* We cannot know *"Truth"* or anything about Truth by listening to Muhammad, Confucius, Gautama of Buddhism, Joseph Smith of Mormonism, or the Pope, for that matter, or any other fake luminary. As well, *"His Voice"* will always coincide with *"His Word."*

(38) "PILATE SAID UNTO HIM, WHAT IS TRUTH? AND WHEN HE HAD SAID THIS, HE WENT OUT AGAIN UNTO THE JEWS, AND SAID UNTO THEM, I FIND IN HIM NO FAULT AT ALL."

The exegesis is:

1. The idea of I John 4:1-3 is that Believers are to stop believing every spirit.

2. Paul finds the source of false doctrine in demons who actuate the false teachers who propound heresy (I Tim. 4:1).

3. Thus, these are human beings actuated either by demons or by the Holy Spirit, whichever side they are on.

WHAT IS TRUTH?

The question, *"Pilate said unto Him, What is Truth?"* tells us something about the philosophical quests of that day.

At that time, discussions about Truth were constant. The Roman world was excellent at borrowing the philosophies of others and then incorporating them into Roman thought and dogma. This basically pointed toward the Greeks, who gave the world the great thinkers, such as Socrates, Plato, Aristotle, etc. However, these men, and thousands of others like them, did not know God and, as a result, staggered from one presumption to the next, with no actual knowledge of Truth.

In fact, the only people on the face of the Earth at that time who had any knowledge of Truth were the Jews, and that was because of the Word of God being given to them. However, they had, by now, so corrupted the Word by their subtractions and additions that precious few of them had any true knowledge of God. This was evidenced in their treatment of Christ!

So, Pilate, in hearing most of his life these philosophical arguments and noting their vast contradictions, felt that no one knew what *"Truth"* actually was and, consequently, had succumbed to the role of a cynic. To be frank, cynicism plagues a great percentage of humanity at present, and always has.

CYNICISM

Pilate, as many others, was utterly unable to believe in the existence of a world or region where any higher reality than force prevailed. Actually, this was the strong suit of the Romans. Even though they strongly looked at the philosophical ideas of their day, all error, we might quickly add, such was only a slight excursion, with force being their long suit.

In view of that, Pilate did not equate Jesus with any type of force or power in that regard. No doubt, the thought entered his mind as to how a philosophical argument over Truth had anything to do with plots against Caesar. What has Truth to do with Kingship?

So, he dismissed all of this out of hand as being inconsequential, respecting the charges brought against Jesus by the Jews.

He had no idea at all at the moment that this Forlorn, Bedraggled Human Being standing before him was actually the Creator of all things, the very Personification of Truth, and, in fact, Truth itself, actually God in Human Form. And yet, there is some small evidence that he would never forget this moment, with its significance growing larger by the day until, ultimately, it weighed on his mind constantly. Some years after this time, tradition says that Pilate committed suicide.

PILATE'S DILEMMA

The phrase, *"And when he had said this, he went out again unto the Jews, and said unto them,"* is done so in the midst of tumult, even as the other three Evangelists proclaim (Mat. 27:12-14; Mk. 15:3-5; Lk. 23:4-12).

The phrase, *"I find in Him no fault at all,"* was proclaimed for two reasons:

1. In dealing with Jesus Personally, even though only for a short period of time, it was obvious that Jesus was not guilty of treason against Rome, or any other type of infraction. Even in a few minutes, this fact became crystal clear; consequently, there was nothing to these charges!

2. The attitude of the religious hierarchy and those with them, which spelled of hatred, proclaimed instantly to any honest heart, at least in this matter, that their problem was personal and not some actual crime He had committed. They had a personal animosity against Him, which quickly became very obvious to the governor, and which had nothing to do with the charges.

NOTES

It was hatred, pure and simple, and for reasons that Pilate did not understand!

At this point, as the Jews began to scream their accusations, it seems that Pilate then came to the knowledge that Jesus was a Galilean, therefore, in Herod's jurisdiction, who was in Jerusalem at that very time. Consequently, Jesus was sent to Herod, with Pilate, no doubt, hoping that he could rid himself of this very troublesome affair. However, such was not to be, with Jesus being brought back to Pilate very shortly!

John does not mention this, and actually, Luke is the only one who gives that particular account (Lk. 23:6-12).

(39) "BUT YOU HAVE A CUSTOM, THAT I SHOULD RELEASE UNTO YOU ONE AT THE PASSOVER: WILL YOU THEREFORE THAT I RELEASE UNTO YOU THE KING OF THE JEWS?"

The structure is:

1. Much of the world, spiritually speaking, is controlled by demon spirits.

2. According to the Scripture, when the demoniac of Mark 5:6 saw Jesus, he ran and worshipped Him. However, it was out of fear and not out of love.

3. This tells us that demon spirits worship the Lord more than many who call themselves *"Christians."*

SHOULD I RELEASE THE KING OF THE JEWS?

The phrase, *"But you have a custom, that I should release unto you one at the Passover,"* seems to have taken place immediately upon Jesus being returned to Pilate from Herod.

Where this *"custom"* originated of a criminal being released at every Passover is not known; however, from the statement, *"You have a custom,"* it seems that it was of the Jews and not Rome. Some claimed that the Jews originated such in order to symbolize their Deliverance from Egypt as slaves.

Others claimed it was a custom of Rome even practiced in other countries, but on a different basis, inasmuch as the Passover was conducted only in Jerusalem. However, there is no proof in any of these claims.

The question, *"Will you therefore that I release unto you the King of the Jews?"*

is said with some sarcasm, but yet, as an appeal to the absurdity of these charges. In other words, *"Look at Jesus. Does He look like a King?"*

Pilate believed that Jesus may have had some friends in this crowd who would now stand up for Him. As Mark describes it, there is some evidence that the crowd wavered at that moment (Mk. 15:11). However, Mark said, *"But the Chief Priests moved the people,"* meaning that they began to tell all who would listen to rather ask for the release of Barabbas. Their word prevailed, with the crowd quickly rallying to their demands (Mat. 27:20).

(40) "THEN CRIED THEY ALL AGAIN, SAYING, NOT THIS MAN, BUT BARABBAS. NOW BARABBAS WAS A ROBBER."

The construction is:

1. Jesus said more about the Holy Spirit the last week of His Life than all the balance of His Ministry put together.

2. He is now about to leave His Disciples. So, now He will tell them how the Holy Spirit will be sent back to them in a completely new dimension, a dimension, in fact, that Believers had not heretofore known.

3. Before the Cross, the Holy Spirit only dwelt *"with Believers,"* but beginning with the Day of Pentecost, He would come into the hearts and lives of Believers to dwell permanently. It was because the Cross lifted the sin debt, at least for all who will believe.

BARABBAS

The phrase, *"Then cried they all again, saying, Not this Man, but Barabbas,"* foils the hope of Pilate. He thought maybe he could get off the hook, thinking, surely, they would not prefer a robber over Jesus! He was to be sadly disappointed!

"Now Barabbas was a robber," simply means they chose a *"robber"* above Christ. In the words of Williams, he said, *"And ever since they have been mercilessly robbed."*[7]

"Not this Man, but Barabbas!" was their verdict.

According to some manuscripts, the full name of this robber was *"Jesus Barabbas."* If that, in fact, was the case, they had a choice between *"Jesus Christ,"* the Saviour of humanity, the Healer of the sick, the Deliverer of mankind, and the Son of God, or *"Jesus Barabbas,"* the robber, son of Satan!

Reynolds said, *"Human power and popular feeling and corporate conscience reached the bottomless abyss of degradation with this decision."*[8]

He went on to say, *"Even human nature itself must bear the shame which by this cry for vengeance against goodness was branded upon its brow forever."*[9]

In fact, almost the entirety of the world for all time has chosen its mortals, branding their champions with some type of Deity, while, at the same time, it has said, *"Not this Man,"* referring to Jesus.

As Israel tragically and sadly learned her mistake too late, billions have followed suit. There is no other choice. It is either *"this Man,"* i.e., the Lord Jesus Christ, or that produced by Satan.

But as for me:

"My Faith has found a resting place,
"Not in device nor creed;
"I trust the Ever-living One,
"His Wounds for me shall plead."

"I need no other argument,
"I need no other plea,
"It is enough that Jesus died,
"And that He died for me."

CHAPTER 19

(1) "THEN PILATE THEREFORE TOOK JESUS, AND SCOURGED HIM."

The construction is:

1. A false message has been circulated in the modern church that if a person is in the very center of the Will of God, there will be no problems.

2. If there are problems, so it is erroneously claimed, that means the person is out of the Will of God. Nothing could be further from the truth!

3. The more directly that one is in the Will of God, just as Paul and Silas were when they were preaching the Gospel in Philippi, the more that Satan is going to do everything within his power to hinder. As

it was with them, so it is with everyone in that capacity.

THE SCOURGING

Reynolds said concerning this *"scourging,"* *"The utter meanness and cowardice of his offer to add ignominious pain and insult to the brutal mockeries of Herod and his soldiers, brands Pilate with eternal shame."*[1]

Reynolds went on to say, *"He obviously fancied that the sight of their Victim's utter humiliation, His reduction to the lowest possible position, would sate their burning rage. Scourging was the ordinary preliminary of Crucifixion, and in Pilate's mind, was to be the conclusion of the whole matter."*[2]

However, He was to find that the bloodlust of the Jews, and especially the religious hierarchy, would not be satisfied with anything less than His Life. They wanted Him dead but would not be displeased at all at the torture He was to suffer in the meantime.

Pilate, accustomed to the gladiator shows and the fickleness of the crowds in quickly changing from one mood to the other, possibly thought that this crowd would do likewise. However, he did not understand the depth of Jewish fanaticism, nor did he at all understand the people he had been ordered to govern. However, it does seem that even he, who was jaded, to say the least, was somewhat shaken by the depths of their brutality and the demands of their bloodlust.

SPIRITUAL DEPRAVITY

Pilate, being a pagan, did not understand, nor could he understand, the depths of spiritual depravity. When people who have once known God, or at least who profess to have known Him, then turn from Him, their situation exacerbates to an alarming degree. Especially considering that this was the religious hierarchy of Israel and the spiritual guides of the people, the depths of their depravity were undoubtedly of greater magnitude than any other group of people in the world. In fact, these people, or at least many of them, had blasphemed the Holy Spirit; therefore, they were totally turned over to Satan, despite the fact that they constantly talked about God. In truth, they did not know God at all, for if they had known Him, they would have known His Son. As such, as we have stated, their plight was worse than the Romans simply because they had the Word of God at their disposal whereas Rome had no such Light.

ROMAN SCOURGING

The Roman practice of *"scourging"* inflicted hideous torture. It was executed upon slaves with thin elm rods or straps having leaden balls or sharply-pointed bones attached, and was delivered on the bent, bare, and tense back of the victim.

For this purpose, the victim, in this case Jesus, was probably fastened to a pillar.

The beating usually brought blood with the first stroke and reduced the back to a fearful state of raw and quivering flesh. Strong men often succumbed under it, with the *"scourging"* being so severe that many died under its blows.

It was to this sickening scene that the Prophet Isaiah cried some 800 years before, *"But He was wounded for our transgressions, He was bruised for our iniquities: the chastisement of our peace was upon Him; and with His Stripes we are healed"* (Isa. 53:5).

The word *"healed"* as used here in Isaiah, from the Hebrew text means *"to be made thoroughly whole,"* which speaks to the spiritual, physical, and mental attributes of man.

(2) "AND THE SOLDIERS PLATTED A CROWN OF THORNS, AND PUT IT ON HIS HEAD, AND THEY PUT ON HIM A PURPLE ROBE."

The pattern is:

1. Before the Cross, animal sacrifices served as a substitute until the Substance would eventually come, Who would be Christ.

2. However, the blood of animal sacrifices was woefully insufficient to retire the sin debt (Heb. 10:4).

3. But, since the Cross, where the price was paid for sin — past, present, and future — and in every capacity, at least for all who will believe (Jn. 3:16), man can be saved by evidencing Faith in Christ and what Christ did at the Cross. In other words, he can be clean in every capacity.

THE CROWN OF THORNS

The phrase, *"And the soldiers platted a crown of thorns,"* has been addressed by many as to the kind of thorns here mentioned.

Some have said these were victor's thorns, which grew to about six inches in length. If so, they would have made a horrifying crown when pressed down and pierced the scalp.

Others have suggested that this crown could have been made from a particular type of palm leaves, which were readily available, and which had very sharp spines.

Irrespective, one can be certain that the soldiers not only intended to greatly humiliate Christ but, as well, to inflict as much pain as possible.

Jesus was now, as described in street parlance, *"fair game."* In other words, He had no protection from anyone or anything, at least on Earth. The soldiers, or anyone, for that matter, could do anything to Him they so desired without any fear of reprisal.

The phrase, *"And put it on His Head,"* implies force and means the false crown was driven into the flesh and produced great agony.

"And they put on Him a purple robe," was probably the one placed on Him by Herod.

All was done, not only to inflict pain but, as well, to make fun or sport of Him as a King.

(3) "AND SAID, HAIL, KING OF THE JEWS! AND THEY SMOTE HIM WITH THEIR HANDS."

The form is:

1. At approximately the turn of the Twentieth Century, the great *"latter rain"* outpouring of the Holy Spirit began. The *"former rain"* took place during the time of the Early Church, as recorded in the Book of Acts (Joel 2:23).

2. The mainline denominations rejected this latter rain outpouring. They attempted to preach the Cross without the Holy Spirit, which presented a *"perverted gospel,"* which the Lord could never accept. As a result, they are no longer preaching the Cross or the Holy Spirit.

3. The Full Gospel Churches, which were born out of this great latter rain outpouring, tried to preach the Holy Spirit without the Cross. As the former would not suffice, neither would the latter. Now, most so-called Full Gospel churches are not preaching either one.

KING OF THE JEWS!

The phrase, *"And said, Hail, King of the Jews!"* was meant to insult not only Him but the Nation of Israel as well! In other words, *"This is your King?"*

The phrase, *"And they smote Him with their hands,"* means that they continued hitting Him in the Face with their open palms or doubled-up fists. As well, Matthew mentions that they had put a reed in His Hand, symbolic of a scepter, and if He refused to hold it, they could have taken it from Him, smiting Him with it (Mat. 27:29).

Reynolds said, *"The representatives of the outside world as it applied to the Romans thus share expressly in the shame and ban by which the Hebrew theocracy is crushed, and the prince of this world is judged. 'They know not what they do'; but Jew and Roman are equally guilty before God."*[3]

(4) "PILATE THEREFORE WENT FORTH AGAIN, AND SAID UNTO THEM, BEHOLD, I BRING HIM FORTH TO YOU, THAT YOU MAY KNOW THAT I FIND NO FAULT IN HIM."

The pattern is:

1. Without a doubt, Romans 8:2 is one of the most important Scriptures in the entirety of the Bible.

2. It tells how the Holy Spirit works in our lives, and there could be little more important than that.

3. To have His Help, It is required that we place our Faith exclusively in the Cross of Christ, from which the Holy Spirit works.

I FIND NO FAULT IN HIM

The phrase, *"Pilate therefore went forth again, and said unto them, Behold, I bring Him forth to you,"* proclaims another fruitless appeal to the perverted humanity and justice of the maddened mob.

Reynolds said, *"But what a revelation of Pilate's own weakness and shame! He can find no fault, but has connived at, nay, ordered the worst part of this atrocious punishment."*[4]

"That you may know that I find no fault in Him," proclaims his decision, but yet, as stated, he would beat Him unmercifully!

Evidently, he must have thought that Jesus, standing before them scourged, bleeding, crowned, and with this cast-off robe thrown over Him, would satisfy their bloodlust. However, he was to find that religious persecutors have no love for, or mercy on, their victims. In fact, down through the centuries, the Earth has been soaked with blood, all because of the heartless hatred of religion. It is the scourge of the Earth! It is that which claims to be of God, but is rather of its author, Satan.

APOSTATE CHRISTIANITY

To be sure, the worst kind of all is that which goes under the guise of Christendom but, in fact, is apostate. Regrettably, that makes up most, if not all, of the Catholic church, as well as much of its Protestant counterpart. The only thing that stops persecution from these sources is the law of the land, and not the lack of desire on the part of the hearts of these modern apostates.

Shockingly enough, the percentage of those who fall into this category would be higher, even far higher, than most would ever dare think!

In the Catholic Inquisition of the Middle Ages, the Catholic church controlled many countries. Consequently, much of the torture was done under the guise of the state when, in reality, it had its birth in the *"church."*

(5) "THEN CAME JESUS FORTH, WEARING THE CROWN OF THORNS, AND THE PURPLE ROBE. AND PILATE SAID UNTO THEM, BEHOLD THE MAN!"

The diagram is:

1. Why is Christ Crucified a stumblingblock to the Jews?

2. The Jews knew that anyone who was hung on a tree for committing a dastardly crime was cursed by God (Deut. 21:22-23).

3. Jesus was hung on a Cross. So, in the mind of Jews, He was cursed by God. Consequently, He could not be the Messiah, or so they thought. Christ was, however, not cursed by God, but rather was made a curse, which is altogether different (Gal. 3:13).

NOTES

BEHOLD THE MAN!

The phrase, *"Then came Jesus forth, wearing the crown of thorns, and the purple robe,"* was meant somehow, at least Pilate hoped, to mitigate their ferocity. Regrettably, it only whetted their appetite for more!

The phrase states, *"And Pilate said unto them, Behold the Man,"* rather than, *"The King."*

However, the appeal to humanity was vain, and Pilate's momentary sentiment failed of its end. Not a voice in Jesus' Favor broke the silence.

Reynolds said, *"As Caiaphas did not know the enormous significance of his own decision regarding the Crucifixion of Christ (Jn. 11:50), so Pilate from his purely secular position, did not appreciate the worldwide meaning of his own words.*

"He did not know that he had at his side the Man of men, the perfect veritable Man, the unattainable ideal of all humanity realized.

"He did not anticipate that the crown of thorns, the robe of simulated royalty, the sign of blood agony, and the insults borne with sublime patience and ineffable love, were even then lifting Jesus to the Throne of eternal memory and universal dominion; nor how His Own Words would be enshrined in art, and continued to the end of time a crystallization of the deepest emotion of the people of God.

"Behold The Man!"

(6) "WHEN THE CHIEF PRIESTS THEREFORE AND OFFICERS SAW HIM, THEY CRIED OUT, SAYING, CRUCIFY HIM, CRUCIFY HIM. PILATE SAID UNTO THEM, TAKE YE HIM, AND CRUCIFY HIM: FOR I FIND NO FAULT IN HIM."

The pattern is:

1. Some Christians have the erroneous idea that if they embrace Christ and the Cross, making that the sole Object of their Faith, then they will never again be tempted.

2. That is not true!

3. Bluntly and plainly, the Holy Spirit through Simon Peter here tells us (I Pet. 4:12-13) that that's not the case at all. In fact, we are not to even think it out of the

ordinary, or *"strange,"* concerning the *"fiery trial which is to try you."*

CRUCIFY HIM!

The phrase, *"When the Chief Priests therefore and officers saw Him,"* did not bring about the hoped-for results planned by Pilate. I wonder what his thoughts were.

This pagan, who knows not God, is moved to pity by this sight, but he sees these who claim to know God, even the religious leadership who actually took the lead in inciting the mob, showing no pity at all!

The phrase, *"They cried out, saying, Crucify Him, crucify Him,"* registers the most hideous words that ever came out of the mouths of any human beings at any time.

This one cry would bring upon Israel the total destruction of their Nation and their children being scattered over the entirety of the world for now about some 1,900 years.

As well, it must be remembered that it was not the drunks, drug addicts, or any such people who clamored for the Life of Jesus, but rather the leadership of the church of that day!

Were the time factors to be changed and this scene transported to the present moment, sadly, I have no doubt that the cry presently would be the same and the monsters of the same identification.

RELIGION

The reader may think my words to be overly strong. However, it must be remembered that I am only portraying what is here written and according to what happened. The truth is, such modern *"religious leaders"* of exactly the same stripe as those who crucified Christ are leading more people to Hell than all the vice and sins of passion put together a thousand times over.

The phrase, *"Pilate said unto them, You take Him, and crucify Him: for I find no fault in Him,"* proclaims the governor once again attempting to absolve himself of blame.

However, he was not man enough to do the right thing. Regrettably, the majority of the world, and for all time, follows in Pilate's footsteps.

To do the right thing, one generally has to go against conventional wisdom and prevailing opinion. It is impossible, even as Pilate would find out, to please both God and Satan at the same time.

Millions would like to live for God simply because they know that Jesus Christ is the Son of God and the Saviour of men. As well, they know they are sinners in desperate need of redemption. However, they are not man enough, nor do they have courage enough, to buck the tide of prevailing opinion against Christ. So, in their vacillation, they make no decision at all, seemingly not realizing that indecision is a decision, but in the wrong way.

Was Pilate giving them permission to take the law into their own hands by telling the Jews to take Christ and crucify Him, irrespective of his court and against his will?

No! He was pretty much daring them to attempt such! He would then have recourse against them and could unleash the praetorian guard; however, they did not rise to the bait.

(7) "THE JEWS ANSWERED HIM, WE HAVE A LAW, AND BY OUR LAW HE OUGHT TO DIE, BECAUSE HE MADE HIMSELF THE SON OF GOD."

The construction is:

1. When Jesus comes back the second time, setting up His Kingdom, which will be worldwide, *"The Earth shall be full of the knowledge of the LORD, as the waters cover the sea"* (Hab. 2:14).

2. The government of the world will then be upon His Shoulder.

3. For the first time in its history, the world will then know Righteousness, peace, prosperity, and freedom as never before.

THE SON OF GOD

The phrase, *"The Jews answered him, We have a law, and by our law He ought to die,"* speaks of the Jewish Sanhedrin, the ruling body of Israel, both civil and religious.

There was no separation of church and state in Israel, both being one and the same. So, they are now informing Pilate that the highest Jewish court has passed the death sentence upon Christ.

"Because He made Himself the Son of God," proclaims their excuse; however, it was wrong in that Jesus did not make

Himself such but, in fact, was such!

The truth is, Jesus had made no secret of His Divine claims before the Sanhedrin. As well, the proof of these claims was readily available. In fact, the proof was abundant! I speak of His Perfect Genealogy, which was of absolute necessity, His Miracles, His Fulfillment of Scripture in every capacity, and His Introduction by John the Baptist, who was raised up specifically for this purpose.

THE SANHEDRIN

Did the Sanhedrin investigate these claims?

The proof positive was of such abundance that it was obvious to all without much investigation. To be sure, they knew He was the *"Son of David,"* meaning that had the Davidic lineage of Throne rights continued, Jesus would now be King. This knowledge was so abundantly widespread that even a blind beggar by the name of Bartimaeus was to address Him as *"Son of David"* (Mk. 10:47).

As well, His Miracles were so abundant and beyond reproach that they could not be denied! Consequently, they could only claim that He was doing such by the power of Satan, which, within itself, was blasphemy. Also, He constantly presented Scripture as a foundation, not only concerning what He preached and taught but, as well, referring to His Person.

So, it was not really a matter of investigating His Claims simply because the proof was so abundant in every description that they really could not be denied.

So, the only charge they could find was His Claim as Messiah. Even then, they twisted the charge, claiming He was a Professing King in order to fit the Roman definition of treason. Trying that first, they now fell back on their earlier charge concerning His Earlier Claims of Deity; however, it would not be delightful to the ears of Pilate.

(8) "WHEN PILATE THEREFORE HEARD THAT SAYING, HE WAS THE MORE AFRAID."

The exegesis is:

1. As stated, in other accounts, every Miracle of Healing that Jesus performed was not only for the person or persons involved but, also, was meant to teach a great Spiritual Truth.

2. For instance, when Jesus delivered the demoniac of Gadara, the Gadarenes took no interest in the Salvation of this man. They were only interested in the loss of their property, i.e., the hogs, which the demons had destroyed. They have many successors today.

3. The Deliverance of people from the powers of darkness, be it alcohol, drugs, etc., excites no one in the world, but the destruction of a distillery by fire causes much excitement, etc.

FEAR

The phrase, *"When Pilate therefore heard that saying,"* presents the governor being shaken, to say the least!

Every evidence is that Pilate's *"wife* (had already) *sent unto him, saying, Have nothing to do with that Just Man: for I have suffered many things this day in a dream because of Him"* (Mat. 27:19).

Her name was Claudia Procula.

This, no doubt, unnerved Pilate, especially considering the strange demeanor of Jesus, which was unlike any other man he had ever known.

The phrase, *"He was the more afraid,"* presents him torn between two fears:

1. He was fearful of offending the Sanhedrin, with the possibility that they would file formal charges against him to Caesar if he did not do as they desired. As well, he was concerned respecting a potential rebellion. He little knew at this time that the general populace, at least as a whole, loved Jesus, with the opposition coming mainly from the religious hierarchy. Consequently, there would have been no rebellion!

Actually, the very reason Jesus was arrested at night and tried during those hours is because the Sanhedrin feared the people. So, Pilate had no concern from that sector, but this, at the present, he hardly knew.

2. When they mentioned that Jesus had claimed to be *"the Son of God,"* this struck a deep fear within his heart. The word *"afraid"* as used here, in the Greek text is *"phobeo"* and means *"to be exceedingly afraid."*

The word *"more"* shows that he had feared something like this all along, but now, due to their statement and the warning given to him by his wife, he sensed that he was in the midst of something that was far, far bigger than he had ever known. In truth, it was bigger than anything any human being in history had ever known, at least Judgment being passed upon a Man, and in this case, *"God!"*

It flashed through his mind, and exceedingly so, that he was on the verge of killing an Innocent Man — a Miracle-Worker, and even One Who claimed to be *"the Son of God."*

This was an appeal by the Holy Spirit to Pilate's heart. The Lord gave this dream to his wife in order to serve as a warning. It was not God's Will that Pilate be guilty of this monstrous sin and ultimately lost. In fact, God is *"not willing that any should perish, but that all should come to Repentance"* (II Pet. 3:9).

Of course, the question could be asked that if Pilate had done the right thing and released Jesus, how would Prophecy be fulfilled in that Christ had to be crucified in order to redeem humanity?

To answer that question, several things should be noted:

God is Omnipotent (all-powerful) and Omniscient (all-knowing).

• We must understand that God has never and, in fact, shall never predestine anyone to be lost. As we have just stated, the Will of God is that all men should come to Repentance and that none would perish. So, Pilate was not predestined to do this thing. He had a choice with which both the Holy Spirit and Satan dealt.

• It was not predicted in the Word of God through foreknowledge that Pilate would be the one who would serve as the judge of Jesus Christ. In fact, even that which is predicted does not necessarily mean that it was predestined, but only that God through foreknowledge looked down into the future and saw what would happen respecting man's own choice. However, that does not mean the will of the people was tampered with in any way.

• The actual Crucifixion, in fact, was predestined (I Pet. 1:19-20), but how it was carried out was not predestined at all! In other words, while it was a certainty that Jesus was going to die on a Cross, who the players would be in this awful scenario, such as Pilate, were not predestined.

• God being Omnipotent (all-powerful), Omniscient (all-knowing), and Omnipresent (everywhere), could have worked out the situation in numberless ways in order that this foul thing be done, which was an absolute necessity, that is, if man was to be redeemed, and without violating anyone's free moral agency.

(9) "AND WENT AGAIN INTO THE JUDGEMENT HALL, AND SAID UNTO JESUS, WHO ARE YOU? BUT JESUS GAVE HIM NO ANSWER."

The diagram is:

1. When the Apostle said, *"That I may know Him"* (Phil. 3:10), he was speaking of knowing Christ in a particular way.

2. The first way was *"the Power of His Resurrection."* This was not speaking of the coming Resurrection of the dead, etc., but rather living this Resurrection Life (Rom. 6:3-5).

3. *"The fellowship of His Sufferings,"* had to do with all the benefits that we can accrue from the Cross.

4. *"Being made conformable unto His Death,"* has to do with the great pivot point of the Plan of God. We are to base our lives strictly and totally on what He did for us at the Cross, which is the Intention here of the Holy Spirit (Rom. 8:2).

FROM WHERE DO YOU COME?

The phrase, *"And went again into the judgment hall,"* pictures Pilate leaving the porch, or area which opened to the courtyard where these accusers had gathered, and now coming back into the hall to question Jesus further. However, he came in a shaken man!

The question, *"And said unto Jesus, Who are You?"* pertains to Jesus being *"the Son of God."* Pilate was asking Jesus if He was God.

The idea that Jesus was a Supernatural Being Whom no Cross could destroy — some mysterious half-human, half-Divine, in fact, that which filled popular literature of that day — had lurked in his mind for the entirety of this period and, even now, exacerbates.

JESUS GAVE NO ANSWER

The phrase, *"But Jesus gave him no answer,"* pictures the fulfillment of Prophecy. The prophetic picture had foretold of Him that like *"a sheep before her shearers is dumb, so He opened not His Mouth"* (Isa. 53:7). But yet, there was a reason for this!

Pilate's fear stemmed far more from what could happen to him if Jesus, in reality, was Deity than any desire to accept Him as Saviour and, consequently, to serve Him. In fact, Jesus never attempted to prove His Deity except to relate the fact of His Relationship with the Father, and in such a way as to be unmistakable as to Who He was (Jn. 14:1, 6-11, 20).

Jesus little responded to idle curiosity, sarcasm, doubt, or unbelief. He responded to Faith, as He always responds to Faith. Pilate did not ask in faith; consequently, he received no answer and neither will anyone else in this capacity (Heb. 11:6).

(10) "THEN SAID PILATE UNTO HIM, DO YOU REFUSE TO SPEAK UNTO ME? DO YOU NOT KNOW THAT I HAVE POWER TO CRUCIFY YOU, AND HAVE POWER TO RELEASE YOU?"

The overview is:

1. The opposition of the world is bitter to the Believer, but the opposition of the Church, believe it or not, is more bitter.

2. For instance, Samson's own people were quite ready to hand him over to a cruel death in order to maintain their so-called peace (Judg. 15:11-12)!

3. This condition of spiritual degradation marks, and has marked, the history, sad to say, of the Christian Church.

AUTHORITY?

The question, *"Then said Pilate unto Him, Why do you refuse to speak unto me?"* proclaims the Roman governor as being irritated in that Jesus did not answer him. In fact, the pronoun, *"Me,"* speaking of Pilate, is emphatic! In other words, he feels his importance. He probably does not wonder at all that Jesus would remain silent before the maligning mob, but considering the power that he (Pilate) has, even the power of life and death, or so he thinks, he not at all understands Jesus being silent before him, and will say so!

The question, *"Do you not know that I have power to crucify You, and have power to release You?"* proclaims Pilate, in his impatient anger, forgetting the possibility of Who Jesus really is. To be sure, we will learn something from this exchange.

The word *"power"* as it is used, speaks of *"authority."* The authority of which he speaks comes from Caesar. Under certain rules and guidelines, he can wield this *"power."* Men struggle for this type of power and, at times, will even sell their souls to obtain such.

(11) "JESUS ANSWERED, YOU COULD HAVE NO POWER AT ALL AGAINST ME, EXCEPT IT WERE GIVEN YOU FROM ABOVE: THEREFORE HE WHO DELIVERED ME UNTO YOU HAS THE GREATER SIN."

The exposition is:

1. The great principle that God cannot give victory *"to the flesh"* appears in this night scene, as recorded in Genesis 32:24.

2. It is the broken heart that begins to experience what Divine Power means.

3. Better for the sun to rise upon a limping Israel than to set upon a lying Jacob.

GOD CONTROLS ALL

The phrase, *"Jesus answered, You could have no power at all against Me, except it were given you from above,"* tells us to the degree of control exercised by God. From this, we learn several things:

• God ordains government, which Pilate represents. However, those in government, who discharge their responsibilities wrongly, will ultimately answer to God.

• God exercises control as to who serves in government down to the lowest functionary. If the people are evil, much of the time, the Lord will appoint officials of like caliber.

• Even though these individuals, as Pilate, think their authority comes from a senior official or a constitution and bylaws, in reality, all authority ultimately comes from God.

- God is ever mindful as to how this authority is exercised, but especially against those who bear His Name.
- Nothing can happen to a Believer unless the Lord causes such or allows it. By virtue of the price He has paid for man's Redemption, the Believer becomes an object of special attention (I Cor. 6:20; 7:23).
- The Believer is to pray *"for all who are in authority,"* in the realm of earthly government (I Tim. 2:2). This means that proper intercession can change things respecting political leaders.
- This tells us that even though Believers are citizens of a particular country and, therefore, subject to the authority of that country, unless the authority violates the Word of God, more particularly, Believers are citizens of the Kingdom of God, which always takes preeminence.

THE GREATER SIN

The phrase, *"Therefore he who delivered Me unto you has the greater sin,"* as well, tells us several things:

- We learn from this that some sins are worse than others, i.e., *"greater sin."* In this case, Jesus is saying that even though Pilate is committing sin by failing to conduct his office responsibly regarding our Lord, the far greater sin is committed by the religious hierarchy of Israel who has trumped up these charges.
- We learn, as well, that those who have access to a greater degree of Spiritual Light and knowledge of the Word of God are held more responsible than those who have little or no access to such.
- In this, we actually see two kingdoms: First of all, we see the political system of the world, which is by and large controlled by Satan, but who has to answer to God.

Second, we see the Kingdom of God on Earth in the midst of the kingdom of this world. Sadly, God's Kingdom at this time, which was ensconced in Israel, was, for all practical purposes, nonexistent. That which was supposed to be His *"Kingdom,"* in reality, was in league with the kingdom of darkness.

So, even though Jesus, the Lord of Glory, was then present on Earth, God's Kingdom, at best, would have numbered a few thousand people.

These two kingdoms continue to exist to this present hour, but thankfully, God's True Kingdom is now much larger, numbering into the millions.

However, the day is coming when only the Kingdom of God will remain. This will take place at the Second Coming (Rev., Chpt. 19). Then, the suffering, pain, sickness, sorrow, war, and disease will, for all practical purposes, come to an end.

TWO KINGDOMS

Of these two kingdoms, God judges the sins committed by those in His Kingdom with much more severity, and we speak of those who refuse to repent. Of these things, erroneous spiritual direction, which speaks of a violation of the Word of God, is judged the harshest of all. This speaks of those who claim to be in His Kingdom going the opposite direction of the Word of God, which speaks of hypocrisy, acute self-righteousness, and a false way of salvation — exactly as the Israel of Jesus' Day! That is why Jesus said to the religious leadership of Israel, *"That the publicans* (tax-collectors, who were thought of as committing high treason against Israel) *and the harlots go into the Kingdom of God before you"* (Mat. 21:31).

Even though all of Israel who did not truly know God was held responsible, at least in a sense, for what was done to Christ, with the religious hierarchy and especially the Sanhedrin taking the lion's share of the blame, the greatest responsibility of all was leveled at Caiaphas, the High Priest. This is proven by Jesus using the pronoun, *"He,"* in referring to this man, in the statement made to Pilate when referring to the *"greater sin."*

(12) "AND FROM THENCEFORTH PILATE SOUGHT TO RELEASE HIM: BUT THE JEWS CRIED OUT, SAYING, IF YOU LET THIS MAN GO, YOU ARE NOT CAESAR'S FRIEND: WHOSOEVER MAKES HIMSELF A KING SPEAKS AGAINST CAESAR."

The structure is:

1. We are told in Colossians 2:15 that

Jesus totally and completely defeated Satan and all of his minions of darkness at the Cross.

2. Just exactly how was this done?

3. Sin is the legal means by which Satan holds man in bondage. However, with all sin removed, which it was at the Cross, Satan has lost that legal right.

4. So, if any man, redeemed or otherwise, is in bondage to sin, it is because his faith is in something other than Christ and the Cross (Rom. 8:2).

INFAMY

The phrase, *"And from thenceforth Pilate sought to release Him,"* does not tell us exactly how he sought to bring this about. At any rate, the one thing he needed in order to do the right thing was courage, and that he did not have. So, he would go down in infamy as the man who crucified Christ.

"But the Jews cried out, saying, If you let this Man go, you are not Caesar's friend," is ironic because they hated Caesar. However, they hated their own Messiah more!

Now seeing that their present ploys have not worked, the religious leadership of Israel will result to unscrupulous abandonment of all their patriotic boasts. These men, who hated Rome and were perpetually plotting against the imperial power, will now stoop to the level of claiming loyalty to Caesar.

CAESAR?

The phrase, *"Whosoever makes himself a king speaks against Caesar,"* hits at Pilate's weakest spot.

It was known that Tiberius, the stepson of Augustus Caesar, was insecure to the point of being jealous of his own authority. Consequently, no charge was as fatal to a Roman procurator as the charge of even a hint of disloyalty to the emperor. Especially considering that the relations of Pilate with the emperor were not very satisfactory anyway, the Jews had hit a nerve. He knew these brigands, who were demanding the Death of Christ, would prefer charges against him of disloyalty to Caesar at the drop of a hat, so to speak.

Now, he is more afraid of the Jews than He is of Jesus. Even though not nearly as public as Pilate, in one way or the other, all must come to this place of decision, and in one way or the other, all do! As with Pilate, it will never be easy to side with Jesus and take His Part. It was not then, and it is not now! One must understand that to accept Jesus, it must be done at the expense of all else, and we mean all else! That means friends, family, position, place, and status, whatever that may be. Regrettably and sadly, most go the way of Pilate, with only a few standing against the tide saying, "Yes," to the King of kings and Lord of lords. But to those who do, they are immediately granted Eternal Life.

(13) "WHEN PILATE THEREFORE HEARD THAT SAYING, HE BROUGHT JESUS FORTH, AND SAT DOWN IN THE JUDGMENT SEAT IN A PLACE THAT IS CALLED THE PAVEMENT, BUT IN THE HEBREW, GABBATHA."

The synopsis is:

1. Joshua was instructed by the Lord to take 12 stones from the wilderness side of the Jordan and put those stones in the riverbed (Josh. 4:8-9).

2. These stones signified their wilderness wanderings.

3. When the Jordan came back to its original position, the wilderness stones would be forever covered, which was the idea.

4. Unfortunately, far too many Christians seek to dive down into those murky waters and bring up a stone, which is a great insult to Christ, to say the least. Why? What the Lord has forgiven is forever gone and is not to be brought up again.

THE JUDGMENT SEAT

The phrase, *"When Pilate therefore heard that saying, he brought Jesus forth,"* presents Jesus brought out of the judgment hall to stand before this mob. What the purpose of Pilate was at this time is not quite clear. In some way, it seems that even he does not know what to do, but with the charge against him of not being Caesar's friend, his protest is tepid at best!

"And sat down in the judgment seat in a place that is called the Pavement, but in the Hebrew, Gabbatha," actually speaks of a stone platform in the open court in front of the praetorium, the place of final sentence.

It was a *"judgment seat"* alright, but not as they thought. Before the Tribunal of Heaven, Pilate, along with the entirety of Israel, was on trial. Sadly, they all would be *"found wanting."* In a few years, Pilate would be dead, some say by suicide. Some 37 years later, this very spot would be a smoking ruin with Jerusalem leveled to the ground and tens of thousands of Jews impaled on Crosses, with over 1 million killed in various ways. Israel at that time would literally cease to be a Nation. They thought they were judging Jesus, but, in reality, they were judging themselves.

(14) "AND IT WAS THE PREPARATION OF THE PASSOVER, AND ABOUT THE SIXTH HOUR: AND HE SAID UNTO THE JEWS, BEHOLD YOUR KING!"

The composition is:

1. According to Exodus 17:9, while the Lord did not destroy Amalek, He did determine to have war with him from generation to generation.

2. Amalek is a type of the flesh.

3. Amalek was to dwell in the land but not to reign in it.

4. Likewise, while the sin nature dwells in us, of whom Amalek was a type, it is not to rule and reign (Rom. 6:12).

THE PREPARATION FOR THE PASSOVER

The phrase, *"And it was the preparation of the Passover,"* was actually a Wednesday instead of Friday as supposed by most. Of the approximately 1,600 years of Passovers since instituted by Moses in Egypt as given to him by God, little did they realize that this would be the greatest Passover of all. The greatest of all Jewish Feasts typified the Lamb of God, Who would give His Life, thereby, taking away the sin of the world. On this day, Jesus would fulfill this most sacred type by literally becoming the Passover Himself, which He was! However, even though He stood before them, even at the judgment seat, they did not know Him, despite enough proof to satisfy a thousand courts of law 10 times over. Of the millions who have died in previous centuries looking forward to the coming of the Promise, when He actually came, He was rejected but, yet, accepted by God.

Such is the tragedy! Men reject what God accepts, and God accepts what men reject!

THE TIME HAD COME

The phrase, *"And about the sixth hour,"* proclaims John using Roman time, which was similar to our present-day reckoning, which meant six o'clock in the morning.

The Jewish manner of reckoning time then was totally different than ours presently and would have put it at noon, which was the sixth hour of the day.

However, we know from Mark's account, who did use Jewish time in his reckoning, that Jesus was crucified on the third hour of the day, which would have been 9 a.m. (Mk. 15:25), which was the time of the morning sacrifice, and had been such for some 1,600 years. We also know that Jesus died at the ninth hour, which was 3 p.m., having spent six hours on the Cross, which was the time of the evening sacrifice (Mk. 15:34).

To say it again, Jesus was crucified at the time of the morning sacrifice and died at the time of the evening sacrifice, fulfilling that type completely.

From that account, we know this *"sixth hour,"* as spoken by John, referred to Roman time and actually 6 a.m., or rather *"about"* that time, as John said.

The remainder of the things which happened, such as securing the Cross and other particulars, with Jesus carrying the Cross to Golgotha, would have easily consumed the three hours from 6 a.m. to 9 a.m. when He was crucified.

BEHOLD YOUR KING

The phrase, *"And he (Pilate) said unto the Jews, Behold your King!"* sounds like a resignation on the part of Pilate, realizing his tepid efforts to save Christ will not be realized. Wavering between the favor of Tiberius and the claims of justice, he will put what he thinks is self-interest first but will prove to be the very opposite.

To proclaim Jesus as *"King"* at this stage to the mob only incenses them further, which Pilate surely knew would happen.

(15) "BUT THEY CRIED OUT, AWAY WITH HIM, AWAY WITH HIM, CRUCIFY HIM. PILATE SAID UNTO THEM, SHALL

I CRUCIFY YOUR KING? THE CHIEF PRIESTS ANSWERED, WE HAVE NO KING BUT CAESAR."

The synopsis is:

1. According to Exodus 30:7 and 30:10, there can be no acceptable worship apart from Atonement.

2. In the matter of Atonement, all worshippers stand on one common ground, and that is the Sacrifice of Christ.

3. In the Old Testament, which, of course, was before the Cross, *"Atonement"* was the best that could be done as it regards sins, which means to cover them. Under the New Covenant, since the Cross, sins are not merely covered but completely taken away (Jn. 1:29).

CRUCIFY HIM!

The phrase, *"But they cried out, Away with Him, away with Him, crucify Him,"* presented their answer concerning Jesus as *"King,"* or anything else, for that matter! That was done by the church of that day!

Once again, they were not satisfied to simply do away with Him; they must *"crucify Him!"* Knowing that Rome alone could crucify, they felt that the general populace would think that Jesus had committed some type of treason against Rome, hence, the Crucifixion. Their plan was well laid out, and they would go to any length to ensure its completion.

The question, *"Pilate said unto them, Shall I crucify your King?"* was exactly what they wanted while denying that He was their *"King."*

The phrase, *"The Chief Priests answered, We have no king but Caesar,"* presents them denying the Lord Jesus while accepting lord Caesar.

As before, they had shouted, *"Not this Man, but Barabbas!"* so now, *"Not the Lord of Glory but the demon lord of Rome; not this King of kings but Tiberius Augustus!"*

THE PRINCE OF THIS WORLD

In renouncing Christ by the lips of their Chief Priests, they put themselves under the power of the prince of this world, and they answered terribly for their crime.

"They elected Caesar to be their king, by Caesar they were destroyed."

NOTES

Reynolds said: *"Their Theocracy fell by their mad rage against the Perfect Embodiment of the Highest Righteousness and purest Love."*[6]

Very shortly, they found that their choice of Caesar, which was the conclusion of a long line of bad choices, to be the worst they ever made. They would find that Caesar was a very hard taskmaster; however, they would find out too late!

In truth, they have been ruled by Caesar ever since, which has resulted in the Jewish people being the most vilified on the face of the Earth. Down through the centuries, as quickly as they would attempt to find solace in some particular country, *"Caesar"* would begin his persecution, causing them to flee to another.

Then, the worst of all was surely the Hitler holocaust, with this *"Caesar"* attempting to decimate these strange people from the face of the Earth. He would be successful in slaughtering some 6,000,000.

It all stems back to the throated roar of that early morning hour in Jerusalem nearly 2,000 years ago. They made their choice, and it has been a choice which has paid in blood millions of times over.

KING?

Sadder still, untold hundreds of millions of others have followed in their footsteps. They say either literally or by their actions, *"We have no king but fashion!"* *"We have no king but mammon!"* *"We have no king but politics!"* *"We have no king but money!"* *"We have no king but pleasure!"* *"We have no king but our royal selves!"*

To be sure, the decision of these hundreds of millions fares no better than that of Israel of old and following. All bring destruction, for Satan's very business is to *"steal, kill, and destroy"* (Jn. 10:10).

The Holy Spirit is emphatic that the *"Chief Priests,"* in reality, the religious leadership of Israel, stand as the most culpable.

Of the hundreds of thousands of preachers in the world today respecting Christendom, how many of them are really preaching the Gospel?

I am afraid the true number would be shockingly small. As a result, all those who sit under these portrayers of a false way are doomed just as surely as the people of Israel of so long ago!

Sadder still, if the people only knew the Word of God, much false direction could be avoided.

(16) "THEN DELIVERED HE HIM THEREFORE UNTO THEM TO BE CRUCIFIED. AND THEY TOOK JESUS, AND LED HIM AWAY."

The overview is:

1. It is the Holy Spirit, the Third Person of the Trinity, so to speak, Who has always carried out the Work of God on Earth.

2. Regarding the Godhead, the only thing the Spirit of God didn't do on this Earth was the glorious Redemption process of Christ in coming to this world and dying on a Cross.

3. But yet, the Holy Spirit most definitely superintended that great Event, the greatest Work of the Ages, from beginning to end.

THE DEATH OF CHRIST AND THE JEWS

The phrase, *"Then delivered he Him therefore unto them to be crucified,"* means that he acquiesced to their wishes.

Even though Pilate carried out this dastardly deed, actually, the most horrifying of all the ages, still, the Holy Spirit lays the Death of Christ at the doorstep of the Jews.

Peter said, *"You killed Him, crucifying Him by the hands of lawless men"* (Acts 2:23). He then said, *"You killed the Prince of Life"* (Acts 3:15).

"And they took Jesus, and led Him away," proclaims that which they wanted and which they got. Consequently, they would now have *"Caesar,"* but let us say it again: Caesar down through the centuries has proven to be a most horrible taskmaster.

However, Pilate was not without guilt, as should be obvious. He said in Verse 4, *"I find no fault in Him,"* and then turned around and *"delivered he Him to be crucified"* (Jn. 19:16). Thus, as predicted in Isaiah 53:8, He was taken from judgment, i.e., He was refused justice.

(17) "AND HE BEARING HIS CROSS WENT FORTH INTO A PLACE CALLED THE PLACE OF A SKULL, WHICH IS CALLED IN THE HEBREW GOLGOTHA."

NOTES

The exegesis is:

1. The word *"walk"* as used in Galatians 5:16-18, as used here, refers to the act of conducting oneself or ordering one's manner of life or behavior.

2. The word *"lust"* refers to a strong desire, impulse, or passion, the context indicating whether it is a good or an evil one.

3. The word *"flesh"* refers here to the totally depraved nature of the person, which is indicative of a human being.

THE CROSS

The phrase, *"And He bearing His Cross,"* presents Him bearing a terrible humiliation.

At this time, the purple robe was taken from Him, with His bleeding Form once more clothed with His own Garments (Mat. 27:31; Mk. 15:20).

Even though John does not relate such, the full Text shows that the terrible torture had taken its toll on Jesus, with Him unable to carry the Cross the entirety of the distance. Consequently, one called Simon of Cyrene was made to bear the Cross, that is, when Jesus could carry it no further (Lk. 23:26).

Even as I write these words, I find it difficult to carry on, realizing that He did all of this for you and me. Only Love, and to be sure, a Love such as man had never known, could carry out such an act. He was not dying for good men because, in a sense, none existed. He was dying for all, even those who hated Him, as is here obvious! What He suffered, none of us will ever fully know.

THE RELIGIOUS LEADERS

On the other side of the ledger, to observe the unutterable cruelty practiced by the religious leaders of Israel portrays a depth of depravity that borders the unexplainable. How could people talk about God so much and be so far from Him? How could people be so cruel, so inhuman, and so devoid of feelings?

This entire scenario portrays the spiritual guides of Israel as being exceedingly more wicked than Pilate who was a pagan, consequently, knowing nothing about God!

In truth, Israel had long since departed from God. Religion had become a business, with its leaders using and abusing the people. They cloaked their wickedness under hypocrisy, thereby, presenting a face of emphasized religion while, in reality, knowing God not at all! However, all the religious activity fooled the people, at least most of them. It is no different presently!

Great amounts of religious activity fool Scriptural illiterates, making them think the false is true; consequently, untold millions are deceived, with most even losing their souls as a result. In fact, the most dangerous places in town are the churches. Of course, there are some few good Churches where the Gospel is preached and the Spirit of God is real, however, only a few! The far greater majority lull their adherents to sleep but, sadly, a sleep of death.

GOLGOTHA

The phrase, *"Went forth into a place called the place of a skull, which is called in the Hebrew Golgotha,"* undoubtedly speaks of that which is referred to presently as *"Gordon's Calvary,"* named for the British general who discovered the place of Crucifixion and the Tomb.

It is almost certain that this spot is the actual place and not the Catholic claim of the *"Church of the Holy Sepulchre."* This *"church"* is located in the heart of Jerusalem, and it is very difficult to imagine or trace any line of wall which could have run in such a way as to seclude the supposed site of the Tomb from the city, which was demanded by Jewish Law.

In addition, the site discovered by General Gordon bears the resemblance of a *"skull,"* with the excavated Tomb of Joseph nearby, where, undoubtedly, Jesus was buried.

As well, John will say in Verse 20, *"For the place where Jesus was crucified was near to the city."* This referred to the demands of the Law that Crucifixion or burial places must not be in the city.

The English keepers of the Tomb claim that Jesus was probably crucified at the base of the hill instead of on its top. Their argument is that Rome always executed criminals in a public place, in this case, outside the city but along a major thoroughfare, where the gruesome scene could be observed by all. This spoke of Roman power and served as a warning to other would-be criminals.

WHERE JESUS WAS CRUCIFIED

That possibility is logical; however, this one thing I think is certain, whether on top of the hill or at its base, undoubtedly, this is where Jesus was crucified.

Of course, this site is now within the city limits and actually has one of, if not the, major bus stations of the city at its base.

Irrespective, *"Golgotha"* will always be the site where Jesus paid the price for dying humanity. It was there that He redeemed mankind from the terrible clutches of darkness. It was there where He paid the terrible sin debt and satisfied the claims of Heavenly Justice. It was there where His Blood was poured out from His Perfect Body, which served as a Sin-Offering. It was there where He bruised the head of Satan (Gen. 3:15).

(18) *"WHERE THEY CRUCIFIED HIM, AND TWO OTHER WITH HIM, ON EITHER SIDE ONE, AND JESUS IN THE MIDST."*

The exposition is:

1. The words *"through ignorance"* of Leviticus 4:2, prove that man, whether he be a Chief Priest or a *"common person,"* cannot know, at least in totality, what sin is.

2. This reveals the efficacy of Christ's Atonement for sin, which is not to be measured by man's consciousness of sin but by God's Measurement of it.

3. To believe this fact fills the heart with a Divine peace.

THE CRUCIFIXION

The phrase, *"Where they crucified Him,"* proclaims the religious hierarchy of Israel having their way. They were successful in pressuring Pilate to carry out this dark deed, actually, the darkest in human history.

Crucifixion was the most hideous form of death that the tortured mind of man could ever begin to conceive. It was a type of death which no Roman citizen could suffer, and which was reserved for the most ignominious and degraded of mankind — for traitors, brigands, and condemned slaves.

The way the Crucifixion was carried out varied in different places and with different executioners; however, the following is probably the way Jesus was crucified:

Generally, the victim did not carry the entirety of the Cross but only the crossbar, which, within itself, could have weighed as much as 50 to 100 pounds. The vertical beam or shaft was normally left standing in the ground.

When the victim arrived carrying the crossbeam, normally he would be laid on the ground with his shoulders on the crossbeam, each arm extended out to its full length on either side, and tied with ropes. Then the hands would be fastened with huge iron nails to the wood. It is almost certain that the nails were driven through the wrists immediately in back of the hand, so the weight of the body would not strip out the nails. At any rate, Jews considered the wrists as a part of the hand. If that is correct, then the nail prints will be in His Wrists instead of the Palm of His Hands as normally thought.

JESUS OF NAZARETH THE KING OF THE JEWS

Sometimes, the center beam was taken out of the ground, with the crossbar fastened across its top and the victim fastened thereon. However, most probably, in this case, it was left in the ground, with Jesus fastened to the crossbar only at the beginning.

He would then have been lifted up, crossbar and all, with it resting on top of the central beam.

A small piece of wood or settle was arranged at the middle portion of the central beam. When the victim was laid against that beam, it helped bear a portion of the weight of the body that could not normally be sustained by the gaping wounds in the hands. The feet were then nailed as the hands had been!

On top of the cross, at least on the central beam, was normally fastened another piece of wood at its top, on which was listed the crime of the individual. In Jesus' Case, Pilate wrote, *"Jesus of Nazareth the King of the Jews."*

This extended piece of wood is what gave the cross a *"T"* appearance.

CRUCIFIED THE LORD OF GLORY

Despite the excruciating pain and the thirst which accompanied such pain due to the loss of blood, there was nothing in this in human torture necessarily to occasion a quick death. The sufferers often lingered, sometimes for several days, finally dying at the last of thirst, starvation, and utterly intolerable agony. The Romans generally left the bodies to be devoured by birds of prey; however, the Jews normally buried their corpses.

This form of death was ultimately outlawed by Constantine I, and has never been renewed, at least as a legitimate form of execution.

There, these Jews, by the hands of lawless men, by Roman executioners, *"crucified the Lord of Glory."* By their hideous insensibility to goodness and by judicial blindness, bigotry, envy, and pride, seemingly not knowing the infinite crime they were committing, they offered up this Sacrifice, slaying the Lamb of God, in effect, a Passover of transcendent price.

That torture-tree has become His Throne and the very symbol of all that is most sacred and all-inspiring in the entire region of human thought.

TWO OTHERS CRUCIFIED WITH HIM

The phrase, *"And two other with Him, on either side one, and Jesus in the midst,"* proclaims such being designed purposely, placing Him in the midst of two criminals. Consequently, they added to their inconceivable wickedness by this gross insult!

And yet, little did these reprobates know that by doing this, they were fulfilling Prophecy given by Isaiah some 800 years previously. He said, *"And He made His Grave* (place of death) *with the wicked"* (Isa. 53:9).

As well, even at this awful scene, one of these thieves would accept Jesus as his Saviour. So, that which they thought to be so humiliating was really the reason for which He came — to save sinners.

Little did the thief know when he was taken for Crucifixion that day that he would hang immediately by the Lord of Glory. Such a wonder he could hardly have surmised or even understood. But yet, despite the horror of this scene, it would turn out to be the greatest day this man had ever known, for he would meet Jesus, and meet Him as Saviour.

Tragically and sadly, the other thief allowed this all-inspiring moment to slip by, consequently, dying eternally lost.

There is a possibility that a number of others were crucified that day, as well, but only these two are mentioned simply because they were placed near Jesus, one on either side.

(19) "AND PILATE WROTE A TITLE, AND PUT IT ON THE CROSS. AND THE WRITING WAS, JESUS OF NAZARETH THE KING OF THE JEWS."

The structure is:

1. The Holy Spirit through the Apostle Paul tells us in II Timothy 3:1-5 what the condition of the world will be in the *"last days."*

2. Actually, the Holy Spirit was speaking of the days in which we presently live.

3. These are the last days of the Church, meaning that its Dispensation is about over, which means that the Righteous will soon be raptured.

JESUS OF NAZARETH THE KING OF THE JEWS

The phrase, *"And Pilate wrote a title, and put it on the Cross,"* is mentioned in this manner because the governor did not normally engage in such activity. However, Pilate personally wrote this title himself, or else, had someone near to him to do so, with the command that his soldiers would attach it to the top of the Cross, which was normally used for this purpose. It was done to spite the Jews.

The phrase, *"And the writing was, 'JESUS OF NAZARETH THE KING OF THE JEWS,'"* even though intended as sarcasm toward the Jews, nevertheless, was exactly the Truth and, accordingly, was engineered by the Holy Spirit.

Expositors say the inscription named the only crime for which He was Crucified. It was a true statement, for He was and will always be, King of the Jews, and will be so acknowledged by them at the Second Advent (Isa. 9:6-7; Zech. 12:10-13:1; Mat. 23:39; Lk. 1:32-33; Rev. 1:7).

(20) "THIS TITLE THEN READ MANY OF THE JEWS: FOR THE PLACE WHERE JESUS WAS CRUCIFIED WAS NIGH TO THE CITY: AND IT WAS WRITTEN IN HEBREW, AND GREEK, AND LATIN."

The construction is:

1. When Aaron and his sons were anointed, with the description given in the Twenty-ninth Chapter of Exodus, the sons were anointed with him and not he with them. Everything is connected with Jesus, of which Aaron was a Type.

2. The Precious Blood of Christ had first to be poured out before the Spirit could be poured forth.

3. Sinners must first be washed from their sins in that Precious Blood before they can be baptized with the Holy Spirit (Jn. 14:17).

JERUSALEM

The phrase, *"This title then read many of the Jews,"* served its purpose exactly as Pilate hoped it would.

"For the place where Jesus was crucified was near to the city," means it was immediately outside the city limits of Jerusalem and alongside a major highway. Consequently, hundreds read this inscription during the first three hours Jesus hung on the Cross (darkness covered the city the last three hours). As the city was glutted with Jews from all over the Roman Empire who had come in for the Passover, many of these would take the inscription back with them, which, no doubt, caused much discussion.

The phrase, *"And it was written in Hebrew, and Greek, and Latin,"* speaks of three different languages, which probably accounts for what seems to be slight inconsistencies respecting the exact wording as recorded in all four Gospels.

At any rate, there have been very few attacks made by the skeptics concerning the accuracy of the inscription, which they most certainly would have done if, in fact, there were actual discrepancies.

As a result of the manner in which Pilate wrote this inscription (three languages), such proclaimed Christ's Royalty to the three great divisions of the civilized world as a providential fact of supreme interest.

I think one cannot help but see that this was part of the preparation made by Divine

Providence for announcing to the whole world the Kingdom of Jesus Christ. Since the Cross, from the very first, it thus became a Throne and the Crucifixion an installation into the Kingdom. We learn thence the meaning of the Christian principle, *"If we suffer with Him, we shall also reign with Him."*

(21) "THEN SAID THE CHIEF PRIESTS OF THE JEWS TO PILATE, WRITE NOT, THE KING OF THE JEWS; BUT THAT HE SAID, I AM KING OF THE JEWS."

The synopsis is:

1. What did Jesus mean when He said on the Cross, *"It is finished"*?

2. It was the great Plan of God, which had been formulated in the Mind of the Godhead from before the foundation of the world (I Pet. 1:18-20).

3. The Story of Jesus Christ and Him Crucified is, in fact, the emphasis of the entirety of the Bible. All of eternity marched toward this one great happening.

THE INSCRIPTION

The phrase, *"Then said the Chief Priests of the Jews to Pilate,"* tells us that the inscription did exactly what Pilate thought it would do. The hierarchy would scramble to Pilate, demanding that it be changed. It is interesting that the Holy Spirit caused John to write the phrase, *"The Chief Priests of the Jews,"* which spoke of the very ones who should have welcomed Jesus with open arms. In truth, the Priesthood of Israel will have a very close association with the Kingship of theocratic Israel during the coming Kingdom Age (Ezek., Chpts. 40-47). Consequently, inasmuch as they refused so glorious a place alongside the King as provided by the Holy Spirit, their rebellion could do nothing but intensify, which ultimately took them to destruction.

CAESAR

The phrase, *"Write not, The King of the Jews; but that He said, I am King of the Jews,"* seems somewhat ironic!

Had they not already declared that they had no king but Caesar? So, why should they care?

These Priests knew perfectly well that Jesus had altogether refused being an Heir of David at this time, although that's exactly what He was. He would not entertain the Kingship of Israel in any fashion, even though demanded by His Disciples. So, this was not His Claim, even though He, in fact, was a King, i.e., *"The King!"*

These self-righteous bigots not only did not want Him as King but, as well, did not desire that anyone think, even in the slightest way, that this One Whom they hated could be thought by anyone to be *"The King of the Jews."* So, they insisted the inscription be changed!

(22) "PILATE ANSWERED, WHAT I HAVE WRITTEN I HAVE WRITTEN."

The composition is:

1. It can be said, I think, that the Holy Spirit through Christ explained the Trinity in the Seventeenth Chapter of the Gospel of John as no place else in the Word of God.

2. While there are Three Personalities in the Godhead, there is but One God.

3. They are one in essence, in unity, and in purpose, but not one in number. Jesus used the word *"One"* six times in the Seventeenth Chapter. The word as He used it was not as a number, but rather as essence, unity, and purpose.

PILATE AND THE RELIGIOUS LEADERS OF ISRAEL

Pilate is determined to have the last say, despite the fact that he was not man enough to do the right thing regarding Jesus. He knew our Lord was innocent of any wrongdoing whatsoever. He knew how baseless were the charges leveled against Him concerning treason against Caesar by these reprobates. To be sure, he hates them now even more than he ever had. He sees their hypocrisy, even their evil, although he is a pagan.

Consequently, they can feel free to complain as much as they like respecting his decision. What he had written, he had written, and it would stand.

In effect, he was saying, *"You have falsely charged Him with rebelling against Caesar, and you know that you have lied to my face."*

And then, *"He is your King, and so perish all your futile attempts to shatter the arm that holds you now in its grasp."*

So, in Pilate's anger against the religious leaders of Israel, he had proclaimed the Truth about Jesus, even answering his own question posed to Jesus a short time earlier, *"What is Truth!"*

(23) "THEN THE SOLDIERS, WHEN THEY HAD CRUCIFIED JESUS, TOOK HIS GARMENTS, AND MADE FOUR PARTS, TO EVERY SOLDIER A PART; AND ALSO HIS COAT: NOW THE COAT WAS WITHOUT SEAM, WOVEN FROM THE TOP THROUGHOUT."

The pattern is:

1. Without a doubt, Romans 8:2 is one of the most important Scriptures in the entirety of the Bible.

2. It sums up all that Paul has been teaching as it regards the meaning of the New Covenant.

3. It tells us how the Holy Spirit works in our lives, and there could be little more important than that.

THE COAT

The phrase, *"Then the soldiers, when they had crucified Jesus,"* as is obvious, pertains to the gruesome work being completed of nailing Him to the Cross.

Little did they realize that the One in Whom they were driving the nails was actually the Creator of all things. They had probably served this extremely undesirable duty many times; however, they were to see things this day they had never seen before.

"Took His Garments, and made four parts, to every soldier a part," means that four soldiers were employed in the Crucifixion.

What these particular garments were, we are not actually told. However, they, no doubt, included His Sandals, the sash which went around the outer robe, and the outer robe itself. Some have concluded that there was also a type of headdress. At any rate, the soldiers divided these items.

"And also His Coat: now the coat was without seam, woven from the top throughout," probably does not refer to the outer robe, as many have believed, but rather that which was worn immediately under that outer garment, reaching down to the knees and sometimes even to the ankles. It would have had sleeves as well.

It seems the value of this particular garment was that it was without seam, meaning it was all of one piece of cloth.

This one piece of cloth forming the coat was typical of our Lord. He was One with the Father in essence, in purpose, and union.

(24) "THEY SAID THEREFORE AMONG THEMSELVES, LET US NOT REND IT, BUT CAST LOTS FOR IT, WHOSE IT SHALL BE: THAT THE SCRIPTURE MIGHT BE FULFILLED, WHICH SAID, THEY PARTED MY RAIMENT AMONG THEM, AND FOR MY VESTURE THEY DID CAST LOTS. THESE THINGS THEREFORE THE SOLDIERS DID."

The order is:

1. In II Peter 2:20-22, he is saying the same thing that Paul said in Hebrews 6:4-6 and 10:26-29.

2. He is speaking of Believers, that is, people who have truly been Born-Again, who have now ceased to believe Christ and what He did at the Cross.

3. While they may claim to believe Christ, they have actually divorced Him from the Cross, hence, the Apostle saying that they are *"denying the Lord Who bought them,"* which means they were denying what Christ did for them at the Cross.

CASTING LOTS

The phrase, *"They said therefore among themselves, Let us not rend it, but cast lots for it, whose it shall be,"* presents that which John saw and heard with his own eyes and ears. Actually, it seems he was the only Disciple to stand near the Cross at this time.

Inasmuch as the *"coat"* or garment was without seam, there was no way they could rightly divide it among themselves without it being ruined. Consequently, they would *"cast lots for it,"* meaning they gambled for it.

It seems it was the custom that whatever belongings or scraps the condemned had were to go to the soldiers who took part in the Crucifixion. No doubt, Mary, His Mother, would have greatly desired these items, but due to this unwritten rule, the soldiers would take these garments instead.

THE FULFILLMENT OF SCRIPTURE

The phrase, *"That the Scripture might be fulfilled, which said, They parted My Raiment among them, and for My Vesture they did cast lots,"* pertains to Psalms 22:18.

Jesus was conscious throughout all these proceedings and, no doubt, watched the soldiers parting His Garments and casting lots for His Vesture. As well, He heard what they were saying to one another, and He thought of and possibly prayed the whole of Psalms 22.

The minuteness of this prediction as given by David, and its detailed fulfillment approximately 1,000 years later by Roman soldiers, is one of the many overwhelming proofs of Inspiration. How little these soldiers thought that in sharing the Lord's Clothing and making an exception of the tunic, and casting lots for it, they were fulfilling a Prophecy given so long ago.

THE SOLDIERS

The phrase, *"These things therefore the soldiers did,"* is said in this fashion because it was an eyewitness account by John.

Other things happened at this time, recorded by Matthew, Mark, and Luke, which John did not mention, such as the revolting scene of brutal mockery by the religious leaders, who ridiculed the Dying Lord with His seeming Helplessness. They charged Him with hypocrisy, scoffed at His having boasted of His Divine Sonship, and taunted Him to *"come down from the Cross!"*

Some have suggested that this was even a greater temptation and provocation than that which the Devil had suggested in the wilderness.

Of course, He had the Power to do so, but that was not the Will of the Father, and the Father's Will was His Will as well!

Had He done so, sin and death would still have been inseparably linked, the curse would not have been broken, nor the Sacrifice completed. Consequently, if He was to redeem man, and this is the very reason for which He came, He had to drink that cup down to the final dregs. He must bear the death penalty itself of the broken Law, and that He did!

NOTES

(25) "NOW THERE STOOD BY THE CROSS OF JESUS HIS MOTHER, AND HIS MOTHER'S SISTER, MARY THE WIFE OF CLEOPHAS, AND MARY MAGDALENE."

The diagram is:

1. The Conversion of the thief who was crucified with Jesus is peculiar to Luke (Lk. 23:42-43).

2. It is one of the most remarkable Conversions in the Bible. In one flash of Light, the Holy Spirit revealed Christ to this man and taught him of the Lord's Future Kingdom of Glory, though at the moment, He was hanging in shame and agony on the Tree.

3. The thief did not ask for any physical relief to his pain but only for a remembrance in the future Kingdom. It was granted!

MARY THE MOTHER OF JESUS

The phrase, *"Now there stood by the Cross of Jesus His Mother,"* spoke of Mary. It was actually pronounced *"Miriam."*

The suffering she must have endured as she watched this spectacle is, no doubt, beyond comprehension! And yet, I know she would be very grieved if she knew the manner in which the Catholic church addresses her as the Mother of God and as an intercessor between Jesus and man.

As well, I think the Scriptural indication is that Believers, upon dying and going to be with Jesus, are, at that time, shut off regarding knowledge of happenings on Earth. Were this not so, great sorrow would plague many, if not all, concerning loved ones back on Earth who are going astray, or other particulars which bring grief. We know there is no sorrow or grief in Heaven; therefore, that, of necessity, demands that particular barriers be placed, the one in Heaven and those on Earth.

MARY MAGDALENE

The phrase, *"And His Mother's sister, Mary the wife of Cleophas, and Mary Magdalene,"* perhaps was speaking of that particular moment because Matthew says that many women stood afar off beholding these things, which included Salome, John's mother (Mat. 27:55; Mk. 15:40-41).

As well, we learn that *"Mary the wife of Cleophas,"* was the sister of Mary, the Mother of Jesus. However, this Mary and Mary Magdalene were actually pronounced *"Maria."* So, Mary, the Mother of Jesus, was actually named *"Miriam"* and her sister *"Maria."*

Also, this means that James the less and Joseph were cousins of the Lord.

As well, it is believed by many that Salome was also a sister of Mary, the Mother of Jesus, which would have made James and John cousins, also, of our Lord.

James, the brother of John, is different than the other Disciple, *"James the son of Alphaeus,"* (Mat. 10:3), sometimes called, *"James the less"* (Mk. 15:40).

"Mary Magdalene" seems to have not been a relative of the others but had been delivered by Jesus from the possession of seven demons; consequently, she would be the very first person to herald the Resurrection of Christ (Mk. 16:9).

(26) "WHEN JESUS THEREFORE SAW HIS MOTHER, AND THE DISCIPLE STANDING BY, WHOM HE LOVED, HE SAID UNTO HIS MOTHER, WOMAN, BEHOLD YOUR SON!"

The diagram is:

1. The example of Ruth is the example of true Salvation (Ruth 1:16-17).

2. Millions who have never been Born-Again presently clog the churches.

3. Sinners are saved, not so much by their acceptance of Christ, although that is imperative, but by God's Acceptance of Christ on their behalf.

JOHN THE BELOVED

The phrase, *"When Jesus therefore saw His Mother, and the Disciple standing by, whom He loved,"* spoke of John the Beloved. It seems as if John was standing near the Mother of Jesus, attempting to console her in every way he could.

"He said unto His Mother, Woman, Behold your son!" was addressed to Mary and to John the Beloved.

The term, *"Woman,"* as it was used then, was not an expression of coldness, but rather an honorific title of endearment.

Joseph, the foster father of Jesus, was now dead, and, as well, as stated in John 7:5, it seems that His own Half-brothers did not believe in Him.

Due to this factor and upcoming events, Jesus would place the care of Mary into the hands of John the Beloved.

And yet, very shortly after the Resurrection, He would appear to His Half-brother James, who would then accept Him and actually become the leader of the Church in Jerusalem (Gal. 1:19). Jude, another half-brother, would also accept the Lord as the Saviour of mankind, with both these men writing the short Epistles in the New Testament which bear their names.

So, whatever problem there had been in the family caused by unbelief, it would be corrected very shortly after the Resurrection of Christ.

(27) "THEN SAID HE TO THE DISCIPLE, BEHOLD YOUR MOTHER! AND FROM THAT HOUR THAT DISCIPLE TOOK HER UNTO HIS OWN HOME."

The overview is:

1. The Apostle John did not portray his statements on forgiveness in order that Believers keep sinning, but rather that we stop sinning.

2. However, if the Believer does sin, thank God, we have an Advocate, Who is the Righteous One and, at the same time, one might say, the Mercy Seat.

3. The Work of our Lord, His Person, and His Action all unite in maintaining the Believer in the enjoyment of conscious fellowship with God.

BEHOLD YOUR MOTHER

The phrase, *"Then said He to the Disciple, Behold your mother!"* told John that from that moment on, he was to look at Mary exactly as his own mother.

The phrase, *"And from that hour that Disciple took her unto his own home,"* proclaims John speaking of himself in the third person, as he often did.

There are some who think that Zebedee and his wife Salome, and John, also, had homes both in Jerusalem and Capernaum, which seems to have been the case.

We do know that Zebedee, the father of James and John, was not a poor man but, in fact, possessed boats, fishing equipment, and had day laborers working for him (Mk. 1:20). As well, it seems that Salome (Mat. 27:55; Lk. 8:3) traveled extensively with Jesus and ministered of her substance to Him and to the Twelve.

JERUSALEM

It is known that Jerusalem at that time contained a large fish market in order to supply the many thousands who came in for the great Feast Days. So, being in the fishing business, it stands to reason that they well could have had a domicile there also.

James and Jude, the Lord's Half-brothers, soon became Followers of Christ, and even possibly the other half-brothers, also, which would have changed the situation of animosity in the home that had been against Jesus. Still, from this one Passage, it seems that John, and possibly his mother, Salome, carried out the Master's Command in totality.

Reynolds said, *"We must ever think of John and his mother Salome ever by the Mother of the Lord, whether at Jerusalem, Capernaum, or Ephesus."*[7] And then he said, *"The few words given here by John speak volumes, and his reticence as elsewhere, gives an unutterable grandeur to his words."*[8]

(28) "AFTER THIS, JESUS KNOWING THAT ALL THINGS WERE NOW ACCOMPLISHED, THAT THE SCRIPTURE MIGHT BE FULFILLED, SAID, I THIRST."

The exegesis is:

1. According to James 5:14-15, Divine Healing is a part and parcel of the great Gospel of Faith.

2. While the Lord does not heal all of the time, He most definitely still heals.

3. When I say the Lord heals, I'm saying it on the authority of His Word. However, I'm also saying it on the authority that Word has had in my life in effecting Healing for me when I was some 10 years old.

HIS CONCERN FOR OTHERS

The two words *"after this"* portray Christ as He always was, even in His dying Agony, seeing to His Mother. To the end, His Concern was for others!

"Jesus knowing that all things were now accomplished," speaks of the last minutes before His Death.

NOTES

The significance of this moment is absolutely incomprehensible. This, which had been planned from eternity past, was now about to be fulfilled in totality. All that the Prophets had said and done for this 4,000 previous years led up, in one way or the other, to this very moment. That to Whom the hundreds of millions of sacrifices pointed was about to make sacrifices unnecessary. This was the moment that the Courts of Heaven would be satisfied respecting the terrible sin debt of man. It would be paid in full! The grip of Satan would be broken, with every bondage of darkness shattered, with Satan having no more hold upon humanity, at least those who would trust Jesus as Saviour.

ACCOMPLISHED

The word *"accomplished"* in the Greek text is *"teleo"* and means to *"complete and finish, and discharge a debt."* However, it should be quickly said that it was a debt that He did not owe but would pay because He was the only One Who could pay this monstrous debt, and would do so, even as He did, at a fearful price.

The phrase, *"That the Scripture might be fulfilled, said, I thirst,"* is taken from Psalms 69:21.

There were many happenings at the Cross that John did not record, such as the supernatural darkness, the rending of the Veil in the Temple, the Visions of the Resurrected Saints, and the Testimony of the Centurion (Mat. 27:45-56; Mk. 15:33-39; Lk. 23:44-49). He didn't even mention the cry of Jesus, *"Eloi, Eloi, Lama Sabachthani"* (Ps. 22:1). Even though John did not record many of the happenings at the Cross, he did record two words of the Lord, which the others omitted, *"I thirst!"*

Physically, His Thirst was caused by the terrible loss of body fluids, such as sweat and blood.

Spiritually, it was caused by His Separation from His Father because He was bearing the sin penalty of the world — a picture, I might add, on which God could not look!

As well, from noon till three o'clock in the afternoon when He died, *"There was darkness over all the land,"* signifying the terrible darkness of sin and the hiding of the Face of God (Mat. 27:45), and, as well, *"The earth did quake, and the rocks rent"* (Mat. 27:51).

(29) "NOW THERE WAS SET A VESSEL FULL OF VINEGAR: AND THEY FILLED A SPONGE WITH VINEGAR, AND PUT IT UPON HYSSOP, AND PUT IT TO HIS MOUTH."

The exposition is:

1. The *"Intercession"* the Holy Spirit makes for us is not the same as the Intercession made by Christ for us (Rom. 8:26-27).

2. The intercession made by Christ concerns sin (Heb. 7:25).

3. The type of Intercession made for us by the Holy Spirit concerns the help that we need in order to do what we need to do and live as we need to live (Jn. 16:13-15).

A VESSEL FULL OF VINEGAR

The phrase, *"Now there was set a vessel full of vinegar,"* presents a type of wine but not an intoxicant.

He had been offered this type of wine sometime earlier. It was mixed with an intoxicant, of which He would not partake (Mat. 27:34), because He would bear the full brunt of His Suffering.

This *"vinegar,"* as spoken by John, was probably little more than grape juice.

"And they filled a sponge with vinegar, and put it upon hyssop," speaks of a plant, which produces stems three or four feet long, and grew at random, even in the crevices of rocks. It was that which was used to put the blood on the doorposts in Egypt at the first Passover.

In a sense, it is symbolic of the Humanity of Christ. It is strange and yet beautiful that the Holy Spirit would so construct this awful scene in the Dying Moments of Christ that the same plant would be used again in basically the same manner.

At the first, it applied the blood which had been shed by the innocent victim, in that case, a lamb. At the latter, the Blood from the innocent Victim was applied to it, in this case, the Blood of Christ, for the wounds on His Head and Face were still shedding blood. Neither did the soldiers realize, nor whoever it may have been who offered the vinegar, even in the slightest, what all of this meant.

The phrase, *"And put it to His Mouth,"* is the last thing He received before His Death.

(30) "WHEN JESUS THEREFORE HAD RECEIVED THE VINEGAR, HE SAID, IT IS FINISHED: AND HE BOWED HIS HEAD, AND GAVE UP THE GHOST."

The structure is:

1. When David offered to fight the giant, not for money or for the hand of the king's daughter, every man he spoke to had no higher thought than that (I Sam. 17:45).

2. However, David knew that the matter was more noble and more serious than this. He was to bring the Philistine giant and the Living God face-to-face. What had a woman and her money to do with that?

3. Saul tried to get David to use his armor, but David knew that God could not give victories to *"the flesh,"* and neither can Faith use such.

THE LAST MOMENTS OF CHRIST ON EARTH

The phrase, *"When Jesus therefore had received the vinegar,"* pertained to the moistening of the lips and tongue, which had dried up because of the loss of body fluid. More than likely, He asked for this in order that He might speak the last words.

When all of this was happening, even though it was only three o'clock in the afternoon, darkness filled the land. Consequently, the soldiers probably had to use a torch in order that there be light enough to apply the hyssop soaked with vinegar to the Lips of the Master. Even though we are given little information, it stands to reason that, due to the darkness and that which was happening, this moment was one quite possibly of eerie silence. This was only moments before the price was paid in full!

IT IS FINISHED

The phrase, *"He said, It is finished,"* proclaims the greatest Words, albeit of great price, that any sinner could ever hear.

The world's debt was paid; the types and symbolism of the Old Covenant had been adequately fulfilled. Every iota and tittle of the Law had been magnified. The reality, of which the Temple and the Sabbath were shadows, and the Priesthood and the offerings innumerable, which were figures, had all been realized.

The sin of humanity is branded with an eternal curse, deeper than any previous Manifestation of the Divine Justice could have produced; and yet, it loses its sting. God reconciled the world to Himself by the Death of His Son by this curse thus falling upon His Only Begotten. The earthly judges were condemned by their Victim. The great and last enemy was itself wounded unto death. The Seed of the Woman (Jesus) bruised the serpent's head (Satan) when that Seed received the bruise in His Own Heel, which was death. The Paschal (Passover) Lamb was slain. The Lamb of God took away the sin of the world. The prince of this world, Satan himself, had his power broken and was cast out. The sin debt being paid, the High Courts of Heavenly Justice were now satisfied.

THE SEVEN SAYINGS ON THE CROSS

The seven sayings on the Cross were probably uttered by Jesus in the following order; however, it is only speculative at best, for it is not certain as to the correct order:

Before the darkness:

1. *"Woman, Behold your Son! . . . Behold your Mother"* (Jn. 19:26-27)!

2. *"Father, forgive them; for they know not what they do"* (Lk. 23:34).

3. *"Verily I say unto you, Today shall you be with Me in Paradise"* (Lk. 23:43).

During the darkness:

4. *"I thirst"* (Jn. 19:28).

5. *"My God, My God, why have You forsaken Me"* (Ps. 22:1; Mat. 27:46; Mk. 15:34)?

6. *"Father, into Your Hands I commend My Spirit"* (Lk. 23:46).

7. *"It is finished"* (Jn. 19:30).

Quite possibly, six and seven should be reversed, but again, the order of these sayings is only speculative at best.

WHAT DID *"IT IS FINISHED"* MEAN?

When Jesus cried, *"It is finished,"* exactly what did He mean?

Let's go to the Word of God. Paul said, and I quote from THE EXPOSITOR'S STUDY BIBLE:

"And you, being dead in your sins and the uncircumcision of your flesh (*speaks of spiritual death [i.e., 'separation from God'], which sin does!*), **has He quickened together with Him** (*refers to being made spiritually alive, which is done through being 'Born-Again'*), **having forgiven you all trespasses** (*the Cross made it possible for all manner of sins to be forgiven and taken away*);

"Blotting out the handwriting of Ordinances that was against us (*pertains to the Law of Moses, which was God's Standard of Righteousness that man could not reach*), **which was contrary to us** (*Law is against us, simply because we are unable to keep its precepts, no matter how hard we try*), **and took it out of the way** (*refers to the penalty of the Law being removed*), **nailing it to His Cross** (*the Law with its decrees was abolished in Christ's Death, as if Crucified with Him*);

"*And* having spoiled principalities and powers (*Satan and all of his henchmen were defeated at the Cross by Christ Atoning for all sin; sin was the legal right Satan had to hold man in captivity; with all sin atoned, he has no more legal right to hold anyone in bondage*), **He (Christ) made a show of them openly** (*what Jesus did at the Cross was in the face of the whole universe*), **triumphing over them in it.** (*The triumph is complete and it was all done for us, meaning we can walk in power and perpetual Victory due to the Cross*)" **(Col. 2:13-15).**

The Cross of Christ satisfied the demands of a thrice-Holy God in that the sin debt was paid there, and paid in totality, referring to sins, past, present, and future, at least for all who will believe (Jn. 3:16).

THE CROSS AND SATAN

Jesus didn't go to the Cross to satisfy any demand by Satan. God owes Satan nothing. Jesus went to the Cross to satisfy the demands of Almighty God. God could not allow sin to go unpunished, and yet, had He demanded that man pay the price, man could not have done so. So, if the price was to be paid and humanity salvaged, God would have to become Man, which He did, and pay the price Himself, which He wondrously and gloriously did!

"It is finished!"

The last Words He uttered were said *"with a loud Voice,"* showing that He did not die of physical weakness, but rather breathed out His Own Life (Lk. 23:46).

The phrase, *"And He bowed His Head, and gave up the ghost,"* would have probably been better translated *"Gave up His Spirit."*

The Greek word for *"ghost"* is *"Ekpneo"* and means *"to breathe out."*

JESUS YIELDED UP HIS SPIRIT

It is interesting that in Matthew 27:50 and John 19:30, which give the same account, two different verbs are used.

Both refer to the fact and stress that such is done of His Own volition. In other words, He did not die from His Wounds or from anything else. He simply gave up His Own Life.

The expression in Matthew means that *"Jesus yielded up His Spirit,"* and in John, *"He gave up His Spirit."* Both mean the same thing but stress the fact that He gave up His Life freely and no man took it from Him.

Also, it should be noted that no one saw Jesus die. He died in total darkness, with His last Words heard but His facial Expressions unseen. Even though the darkness represented the hidden face of God, still, despite Jesus bearing the sin penalty for all of humanity and for all time, this moment was so Holy that it was not proper for any one to look upon the Countenance of God's Perfect Sacrifice.

All certainly knew that He had died by that which followed, but no one saw Him die! As well, no one saw Him rise from the dead, but His Appearances proved beyond the shadow of a doubt that He did.

(31) "THE JEWS THEREFORE, BECAUSE IT WAS THE PREPARATION, THAT THE BODIES SHOULD NOT REMAIN UPON THE CROSS ON THE SABBATH DAY, (FOR THAT SABBATH DAY WAS AN HIGH DAY,) BESOUGHT PILATE THAT THEIR LEGS MIGHT BE BROKEN, AND THAT THEY MIGHT BE TAKEN AWAY."

The diagram is:

NOTES

1. If we properly love the Lord and know that He loves us, which He most definitely does, then we know that He is working everything according to our benefit.

2. Everything that happens to a Child of God is either *"caused"* by the Lord or *"allowed"* by the Lord.

3. While the Lord definitely does not cause sin, as should be obvious, He does allow it, but with consequences.

ON WHAT DAY WAS JESUS CRUCIFIED?

The phrase, *"The Jews therefore, because it was the preparation,"* concerned the preparation of the Passover meal (Jesus and His Disciples had eaten it a day early).

"That the bodies should not remain upon the Cross on the Sabbath Day, (for that Sabbath Day was an high day)," does not speak of the regular Jewish Sabbath of Saturday, but rather the *"High Day"* of the Passover, also called a Sabbath, but which took place on a Thursday.

Actually, this is what confuses many people. It's simply because they think the writer is speaking of the regular weekly Sabbath of the Jews; consequently, they erroneously place the Crucifixion of Christ on Friday, which is wrong. As is here obvious, Jesus was crucified on a Wednesday. He had to remain in the Tomb three full days and three nights in order to fulfill His own Words (Mat. 12:40).

THE RULES OF RELIGION

The phrase, *"Besought Pilate that their legs might be broken, and that they might be taken away,"* had to do with violating this special Passover Sabbath, with which the Jews were concerned. They were always concerned about their rules of religion, but had little concern about the things that really mattered, such as the murdering of their Messiah.

However, whatever their reasons, what they did fulfilled the Word of God in another way, of which they were little concerned.

The Scripture says, *"And if a man have committed a sin worthy of death, and he be to be put to death, and you hang him on a tree* (crucified): *his body shall not remain all night upon the tree, but you shall in any wise bury him that day; (for he who is hanged* [crucified] *is accursed of God)"* (Deut. 21:22-23).

Even though Jesus had committed no sin whatsoever, still, He died for all, *"For all have sinned ... and the wages of sin is death"* (Rom. 3:23; 6:23).

As such, as previously explained, He had to be crucified because that is what the Law demanded (Deut. 21:22).

As well, all who suffered this type of death, at least in Israel, and legitimately so, were *"accursed of God,"* i.e., eternally lost. As such, they had to be buried before night.

THE SCRIPTURE MUST BE FULFILLED

Consequently, if the Law was to be upheld, and it was in every respect, Jesus could not remain on the Cross that night. He had to be taken down and buried, which He was.

This should be understood in the context that the Jews would very much have enjoyed leaving Him on the Cross for days, which it normally took for one to die from this type of execution. However, due to the Passover, all must be removed from the crosses. Therefore, they fulfilled the Word of God without realizing they were doing so.

Some may wonder as to how Jesus could be cursed by God and not be eternally lost!

He was not cursed so much as He was *"made a curse,"* which is altogether different (Gal. 3:13). He could not be cursed by God in the sense that we think of such because He had never sinned, so, He had to be *"made a curse,"* which is altogether different. In other words, He was made to be a Sacrifice.

Even though He did experience the curse of the broken Law, which was death, thereby, suffering its dread penalty, still, Satan had no claim on Him because He had never sinned and, in fact, had kept the Law in every respect. Therefore, the twin champions of Satan (sin and death) could not hold Him, with Him forever breaking sin's grip upon humanity and toppling death from his gory throne.

As One Who was perfect, in fact, the Only Perfect Man Who ever lived, He paid the price

NOTES

we could not pay ourselves and, thereby, set us free, that is, if we will express Faith in Him and What He did for us at the Cross.

As such, death could not hold Him because, as stated, it had no claim upon Him. Therefore, He broke its bonds and walked out of that Tomb. Every Angel in Heaven must have shouted, *"He lives!"*

And then, the Word of God shouts for all to hear, *"Because He lives, I shall live also."*

(32) "THEN CAME THE SOLDIERS, AND BROKE THE LEGS OF THE FIRST, AND OF THE OTHER WHICH WAS CRUCIFIED WITH HIM."

The overview is:

1. When Paul preached to Felix, the governor of that region, the Holy Spirit anointed Paul greatly, and Felix came under great Conviction and literally *"trembled"*!

2. Evidently, Paul knew nothing about the now so widely acclaimed modern method of preaching to the unsaved, which states that such unsettling subjects should not be approached.

3. As well, the Holy Spirit also knew nothing about it either. Telling some jokes and spreading some religious pablum would have had no spiritual effect on Felix, and neither will it have any spiritual effect on anyone else.

PARADISE

From the way the Scripture reads, it seems of the four soldiers attending this Crucifixion, two went to one side and two to the other, using a short axe to break both legs of each victim. The shock of such an act, added to what had already taken place, normally brought death very shortly.

Even though John did not mention the following, one of these men being crucified, who was guilty of specific crimes, observed very closely the Son of God being crucified very near him. Matthew said that both thieves at the beginning vilified Jesus (Mat. 27:44).

However, one of these men ceased his blasphemy and began to speak favorably of the Lord of Glory. And then he turned and said, *"Lord, remember me when You come into Your Kingdom."*

"And Jesus said unto him, Verily I say

unto you, Today shall you be with Me in Paradise" (Lk. 23:40-43).

So, at least for one of these former thieves, a day which had begun so horribly would end so gloriously!

(33) "BUT WHEN THEY CAME TO JESUS, AND SAW THAT HE WAS DEAD ALREADY, THEY BROKE NOT HIS LEGS."

The exposition is:

1. Beginnings are one thing while endings are another!

2. On the first day of every new year, many people make resolutions, with very few of them being kept.

3. However, there is a way that a brand new beginning can be made, irrespective as to what the past has been. That Way is the Lord Jesus Christ.

THE PERSON OF THE LORD JESUS CHRIST

The phrase, *"But when they came to Jesus,"* portrays them coming to Him last because of His Cross being in the middle.

"And saw that He was dead already," presents something extremely unusual!

Crucifixion was normally a very slow death, with the victim, at times, hanging on the cross for several days until he ultimately died from shock, thirst, and starvation. However, Jesus was already dead, not because He died of causes, but rather that He breathed out His Own Life purposely. Consequently, I think one could say that His Death was totally unlike the death of anyone else who has ever lived.

In fact, having never sinned and, therefore, not having a sin nature, Jesus would never have been sick, would never have aged (regarding old age), and unless voluntarily, as it actually did happen, never would have died. In fact, the Holy Spirit told Him exactly when He could die, which was 3 p.m., the time of the evening sacrifice (Heb. 9:14).

As the Last Adam, He came exactly as the first Adam. As well, Adam and Eve would not have died had they not sinned and, therefore, suffered the Fall. It was sin that brought on death. I do not speak of particular acts of sin, but rather the very figure or principle of sin, which we refer to as original sin, which kills everything it touches.

THE HUMAN BODY

Even then, the human body was so wonderfully made, even though only of dust, that it took nearly a thousand years after the Fall to wear it down in order that it would ultimately die. Consequently, when you read in Genesis, Chapter 5, of the longevity of these individuals, such as Adam living 930 years before he died, Seth living 912 years before he died, and Enos living 905 years before he died, plus all others who lived at that time, these are not fables. They actually lived that long.

After those of that time finally died, it seems as if death began to speed up the aging process, with Abraham living 175 years before he died (Gen. 25:7-8). Abraham lived about 400 years after the Flood.

Moses lived about 400 years after Abraham and died at the age of 120 years old (Deut. 34:7).

David lived about 600 years after Moses and died at 70 years old, with that probably being the average lifespan for much of the world at present, despite the wonder drugs, etc.

So, death has taken its deadly toll, but Jesus has defeated death, and one day soon, it will be no more (I Cor. 15:54-57).

PARADISE, A PART OF HELL?

The phrase, *"They broke not His Legs,"* referred to the lack of necessity, but more importantly, the fulfillment of Scripture, as we shall see!

When Jesus died, His Soul and Spirit left His Body and went down into Paradise. There He liberated all who were in that place, thereby, taking them to Heaven (Ps. 16:10; Mat. 12:40; Eph. 4:8-10; Heb. 2:14-15).

Before Jesus paid the price for man's Redemption at Calvary, all Believers, which included all the Old Testament Saints, went down into Paradise upon death. This was actually a part of Hell, but not the burning side; however, they were held captive there by Satan. Satan still had a claim against all of these even though they were Saved.

His claim was their sins, which were not taken away, although covered by Atonement. The writer of Hebrews tells us that the blood of bulls and goats could not take away sins (Heb. 10:4). Therefore, as stated, Satan still had a claim against these.

However, when Jesus died on Calvary, paying the eternal price, the sin of all Believers was not merely covered but was taken away (Jn. 1:29). Consequently, Satan now had no more claim, and these souls could be liberated from this place and taken to Heaven. From that moment on, upon death, every Saint immediately goes to be with Jesus in Heaven (Phil. 1:23).

WHAT HAPPENED THE SEVENTY-TWO HOURS WHEN JESUS DIED?

Not only did He deliver all those who were in Paradise, as stated, taking them with Him to Heaven, but He also *"preached unto the spirits in prison"* (I Pet. 3:19).

These were not human beings, for such are never called spirits in the Bible. Where human spirits are referred to, it is always qualified and clarified by speaking of them as *"spirits of men"* (Heb. 12:23); *"spirits of all flesh"* (Num. 16:22; 27:16); and *"spirits of the Prophets"* (I Cor. 14:32).

Man is a living soul and has a spirit, but we are not spirits. Where the word *"spirit"* is used without such qualifications, it refers to spirit beings, such as Angels, etc. (Ps. 104:4; Heb. 1:7, 14).

These spirits to whom Jesus preached were fallen Angels (II Pet. 2:4; Jude 6-7).

As well, the word *"preached"* as it is here used by Peter, is not the same as preaching the Gospel, but simply means *"to announce something whether good or bad."* What He said to them is not known!

As well, the Gospel is never preached to human beings after they die.

THE JESUS DIED SPIRITUALLY DOCTRINE

All of this completely destroys the erroneous *"Jesus Died Spiritually"* doctrine. This doctrine teaches that Jesus died as a sinner on the Cross, consequently, going to Hell, and we mean the burning side of the pit, where He suffered for three days and three nights and then was Born-Again in Hell, signifying the Firstborn among many, etc. However, there is not a shred of Scriptural evidence to support such, with the entirety of the tenor of the Bible saying the opposite. Jesus did not die as a sinner. In fact, He was a Sin-Offering, which satisfied the claims of Heavenly Justice. Even though He took the penalty for our sins, He did not sin Himself. As well, to be a sinner, one must sin, and Jesus never sinned. Therefore, He could not have died as a sinner because He never was a sinner. Such teaching that Jesus died spiritually and had to be Born-Again in Hell shows a complete misunderstanding of Who He was and What He did!

(34) "BUT ONE OF THE SOLDIERS WITH A SPEAR PIERCED HIS SIDE, AND FORTHWITH CAME THERE OUT BLOOD AND WATER."

The construction is:

1. Aaron, the brother of Moses, was the first Great High Priest of Israel, a symbol of the Lord Jesus Christ, Who is forever our High Priest (Heb. 7:26-27).

2. Aaron, as the Great High Priest, wore a crown of sorts, which was to bear on its front a golden plate bearing the words *"Holiness to the Lord."*

3. Believer, look away from your 10,000 failures and look upon the Lord Jesus Christ, Who is Holiness Personified, symbolized by Aaron. Realize that your Holiness is, and ever shall be, altogether in Christ.

THE PIERCED SIDE

The phrase, *"But one of the soldiers with a spear pierced His Side,"* along with the remainder of the Verses of this Chapter, are fundamentally valuable as affirming beyond controversy the actual Death of Jesus Christ.

The added Testimony of the centurion, which John did not relate (Mat., Chpt. 27), is also most valuable. For the doom to which the sinner is justly sentenced to death under the Wrath of God, and if Christ did not really die and suffer that Wrath, as many claim, then the Divine Sentence has not been satisfied, and the sinner is not released.

However, even though some in later centuries, and even unto the modernists of this hour, may attempt to claim that He did not die but merely went unconscious and then revived in the Tomb, no one at the time of His Death, even His Most Strident Enemies, doubted that He died. There was too much proof by too many different individuals, even including, as stated, the Roman centurion.

BLOOD AND WATER

The phrase, *"And forthwith came there out blood and water,"* is proclaimed by some to be the result of a broken or ruptured heart. Some even claim that this is what caused His Death, the grief over what was being done to Him by His Very Own, and above all, knowing that it would destroy them as it did!

However, even though His Heart may definitely have ruptured, and though it may definitely have been caused by grief, still, this is not what killed Him, even though such may have happened moments afterward.

He fully gave up His Own Life, actually breathing it out. As well, when He died, He *"cried with a loud Voice, He said, Father, into Your Hands I commend My Spirit"* (Lk. 23:46), and then cried, *"It is finished,"* or else, made that statement before the giving of His Spirit to His Father.

So, if He had died from a broken heart, He could not have loudly cried accordingly, as would be obvious.

No! He died by simply giving up His Life because the Holy Spirit at that time told Him to die (Heb. 9:14). As stated, the heart could have burst immediately thereafter, which, according to medical science, would have produced the *"blood and water."*

(35) "AND HE THAT SAW IT BEAR RECORD, AND HIS RECORD IS TRUE: AND HE KNOWS WHAT HE SAYS IS TRUE, THAT YOU MIGHT BELIEVE."

The synopsis is:

1. How does one crucify the flesh (Gal. 5:24-25)?

2. The flesh, as the word is used by Paul, refers to the human being. In other words, it refers to our personal ability, talent, ambition, education, motivation, etc., in other words, what a human being can do.

3. Even though these things mentioned are not sin within themselves, it is impossible to live for God by the means of the flesh.

NOTES

4. We overcome the flesh by placing our Faith exclusively in Christ and What Christ did for us at the Cross, which then gives the Holy Spirit latitude to work within our lives (I Cor. 1:17, 18, 23; 2:2).

HIS RECORD IS TRUE

The phrase, *"And He who saw it bear record, and his record is true,"* refers to John speaking of himself as an eyewitness.

"And he knows what he says is true, that you might believe," pertains to the Death of Christ.

In effect, John is saying, *"He died, and I know it because I was there, and of that, you can believe."*

Of this moment, Toplady wrote:

*"Let the water and the blood,
"From Your Riven Side which flowed,
"Be of sin the double cure,
"Saved from wrath and make me pure."*

(36) "FOR THESE THINGS WERE DONE, THAT THE SCRIPTURE SHOULD BE FULFILLED, A BONE OF HIM SHALL NOT BE BROKEN."

The composition is:

1. Most children never climb out over a negative childhood. In other words, if they are abused at an early age, it scars them for life.

2. However, Jabez (I Chron. 4:9-10) turned to the one Source Who could change the situation, and it was the Lord. That Source is available to all, even you and me!

3. Jabez asked of the Lord that he would be *"blessed."* He then said, *"Enlarge my borders,"* and then, *"That Your Hand might be with me,"* and finally, *"That You would keep me from evil, that it may not grieve me."*

4. The Lord heard and answered his prayer just as He will yours, if you will only turn to Him.

A BONE OF HIM SHALL NOT BE BROKEN

The phrase, *"For these things were done,"* in this case, pertains to something predestined. In other words, inasmuch as Jesus was serving as the Lamb of God Who would take away the sin of the world, it was necessary that He totally fulfill the type respecting the lamb offered to God in Old

Testament times, which was to be shielded from unnecessary mutilation (Ex. 12:46; Num. 9:12; Ps. 34:20).

The phrase, *"That the Scripture should be fulfilled, A Bone of Him shall not be broken,"* refers to *"Christ our Passover is sacrificed for us"* (I Cor. 5:7).

Actually, at this very time, the Jews were hurrying to eat their paschal lamb, not a bone of which could be legally broken.

(37) "AND AGAIN ANOTHER SCRIPTURE SAID, THEY SHALL LOOK ON HIM WHOM THEY PIERCED."

The pattern is:

1. In brief form, Exodus 17:12 gives us the blueprint for victory. It says:

2. *"But Moses' hands were heavy."* When Moses *"held up his hands,"* Israel prevailed. Otherwise, Amalek prevailed. The hands growing weary symbolizes the flesh, which quickly wearies.

3. *"And they took a stone, and put it under him, and he sat thereon."* The *"stone"* is a Type of Christ. In Him, we rest, and only in Him can we rest.

4. *"And Aaron and Hur stayed up his hands, the one on the one side, and the other on the other side:"* Aaron is a Type of Christ as our Great High Priest, the Lord Jesus Christ, ever making Intercession for us. *"Hur"* is a Type of the Holy Spirit. With the Intercessor and the Holy Spirit holding up our hands, they will then be *"steady."*

THE SCRIPTURE

The phrase, *"And again another Scripture said,"* proclaims that everything that happened to Jesus had been foretold in Scripture. Once again, as the Word of God was the criterion then, the Word of God is the criterion now.

"They shall look on Him Whom they pierced," is derived from Psalms 22:16 and Zechariah 12:10. In these Passages is a double thrust:

1. David prophesied in Psalms 22:16 that the Jews would look upon our Lord's pierced Body, which John related.

2. Zechariah, the great Prophet who ministered to Israel after returning from the dispersion, looked forward to the Second Coming when Israel, in a repentant state, will look upon the Lord Whom they pierced.

This will be fulfilled in that coming glad day when every eye shall see Him, and the full Revelation of His Majesty shall smite the whole world with penitence or despair. In effect, both Jews and Gentiles pierced His Side. The Roman soldier literally carried out the foul deed, while the Jews, by their insistence upon Him being crucified, held the greater responsibility. At any rate, both, or rather all, were guilty!

(38) "AND AFTER THIS JOSEPH OF ARIMATHAEA, BEING A DISCIPLE OF JESUS, BUT SECRETLY FOR FEAR OF THE JEWS, BESOUGHT PILATE THAT HE MIGHT TAKE AWAY THE BODY OF JESUS: AND PILATE GAVE HIM LEAVE. HE CAME THEREFORE, AND TOOK THE BODY OF JESUS."

The pattern is:

1. Men can only believe in God by believing in the Lamb of God.

2. It is not by means of the Creation that they believe, although that is proof of the Creator, for such cannot give rest to the conscience.

3. Man can only believe in God by the means of Jesus, the Lamb of God Who redeemed them to God, and did so by going to the Cross.

JOSEPH OF ARIMATHAEA

The phrase, *"And after this Joseph of Arimathaea,"* refers to all of the above things having been done, with Joseph now entering the picture, but he had probably been there all the time.

He was a member of the Jewish Sanhedrin along with Nicodemus. This signified that these men were rich and powerful, holding great sway over the entirety of Israel of that day.

Even though it was the Sanhedrin who demanded the Death of Jesus, these two did not vote for such a thing, with the possibility that they were not even present at this early morning gathering.

A DISCIPLE OF JESUS

The phrase, *"Being a Disciple of Jesus,"* presents a simple statement, but as we shall see, it is laden with difficulties.

Joseph, being very wealthy, plus being a member of the Sanhedrin, the ruling body of Israel, was one of the most powerful and influential men of that time, and, of course, we speak of the Jews.

To be a *"Disciple"* refers to one being a learner and a follower, in this case, a Follower of Christ. Consequently, there are three particulars which should be addressed respecting this man.

1. THE SANHEDRIN

Being a member of the Sanhedrin, he knew firsthand of the tremendous opposition toward Jesus by the religious leaders of the Nation, with him being one of those leaders. He had, no doubt, been a part of countless conversations when Jesus was ridiculed, lampooned, maligned, and verbally raped. But yet, as the next phrase will portray, while not joining in the opposition, he did not oppose it either. In other words, he kept his positive thoughts about Jesus to himself.

He, no doubt, quickly learned that his public acceptance of Christ would entail an instant dismissal from the Sanhedrin and, as well, every effort would be made to destroy him in every way, be it financial, social, material, or spiritual. So, it was a decision he had to make respecting his public acceptance of Christ, and one which, incidentally, did not come easily.

Regrettably, many, and maybe all, in one way or the other, face the same situation. What will it cost to publicly accept Christ?

2. JESUS CHRIST

On the other hand, he had come face-to-face with Jesus Christ. For the first time in his life, he had truly and wondrously sensed God, and in a way he had never sensed Him before. Jesus was so unlike the Pharisees and religious leaders of Israel. There was no spiritual life in what they did but great Spiritual Life in what Jesus did! For the first time in his life, he was coming to know God in a way he had never known Him before. In truth, this was the first time he had ever really known what God was actually like. Jesus had made God so real, so near, so ever present, and so wonderful! By contrast, Judaism, at least as it was now, was freighted with rules and regulations which seemed to be unending, and which satisfied not at all the longing of the heart.

In fact, Who was this Man Jesus Christ? Was He really the Messiah? Of course, all the members of the Sanhedrin denied this, with the exception of Nicodemus and himself. But yet, he knew what he had felt, had experienced, and had gained since coming to know Jesus.

3. A DECISION

Ultimately, he was going to have to make a decision between the two. He had come to know that it was impossible to accept Christ and the Sanhedrin also. One or the other had to go. This was becoming more and more obvious and a decision he was going to be forced to make. As events will prove, the Holy Spirit would force those events by the Crucifixion of Christ.

The phrase, *"But secretly for fear of the Jews,"* speaks of fear of what others would say and what they would do. If he, as a member of the Sanhedrin, accepted Christ, he would be excommunicated from the religious life of Israel. Inasmuch as both the secular and religious were combined, they would seek to destroy him in every way. This is the reason for his *"secrecy,"* but a reason which the Lord would not accept.

The very tenor of the Text proclaims the Holy Spirit pushing Joseph to a place of decision, which would be brought to a head when he saw Jesus hanging on the Cross.

Was the price demanded, the leaving all to follow Christ, too much to ask?

IS THE PRICE TOO HIGH?

No! It is the price demanded of all; however, to not accept Christ causes one to pay even a higher price, a much, much higher price, the loss of one's soul. Millions try to have it both ways, but such is not possible. Actually, this very spirit of compromise is the spirit which characterizes this modern age.

For the most part, entertainers are now told they can continue in their present lifestyle and still be Saved at the same time. To be frank, this pretty well characterizes the whole of modern Christendom. The bartender accepts Christ, and he is by and large told that he can continue to tend bar. The dance instructor accepts the Lord, and he is led to believe he can continue in this vein. The Hollywood actor accepts the Lord, and he is encouraged to remain in that lifestyle.

As well, Catholics truly come to Christ, and they are encouraged to remain in that same church. To be frank, the list is endless.

SEPARATION

While the Lord does not demand or even ask for isolation, He does demand separation. While we are in the world, we are not of the world. The spirit of the world must not be a part of the Child of God. If the Word of God is followed, which the Holy Spirit always does, that which is of the world and its system, which pertains to its culture and its spirit, will have to be shed by the new Believer in Christ. To be sure, if the person follows the Holy Spirit, this is always what happens (II Cor. 6:14-18; 7:1).

It is not a question of rules and regulations or things one can do or cannot do. It has a far higher principle than that. It is being led by the Spirit of God, which will always be according to the Word of God.

However, at the same time, the Spirit of the Lord will not tell a person to remain in something that is obviously not of the Lord, but rather of the world. One of the great Ministries of the Spirit is to lead the person away from the spirit of the world toward the Spirit of Christ. To be blunt, there is no such thing as a secret Disciple of Christ, at least for very long!

PILATE

The phrase, *"Besought Pilate that he might take away the Body of Jesus,"* proclaims Joseph of Arimathaea now boldly taking a stand for Christ.

Joseph was a secret Disciple and Nicodemus a midnight Disciple, but God used them to honor the Dead Body of His Beloved Son. Up to the moment of His Death, shame and suffering were appointed to Him. However, from the moment He died, Honor and Glory were destined to Him, so Angels, soldiers, and counselors honored and guarded His Sacred Body.

And yet, as these two, it has often been the case in history that men honor dead Saints with whom, when living, they were ashamed to associate. To follow Christ in His Path of shame and to daily compromise oneself on His Account is a very different thing from association with His Cause upon some great occasion, which does not, in itself, demand this shame and loss.

The phrase, *"And Pilate gave him leave,"* entertains much more detail than John here mentions.

Mark mentioned that Pilate marveled that Jesus was already dead. He even questioned the centurion who was in charge of this detail, *"Whether He had been any while dead"* (Mk. 15:43-45). It was against Roman law for one to be removed from a cross until it was certain that the person had expired.

So, we now have the Testimony of a Roman centurion that Jesus was indeed dead, which he had verified himself. This puts to rest any speculation that He really did not die but only went unconscious, etc.

THE BODY OF JESUS

The phrase, *"He came therefore, and took the Body of Jesus,"* circumvented the plans of the Jews to remove the Corpse to the Valley of the Son of Hinnom, which, in reality, was a garbage dump. As well, it was even used by some of the Old Testament Prophets to symbolize Hell itself.

However, it had been prophesied that He would be buried *"with the rich in His Death"* (Isa. 53:9).

It is almost positive that Joseph did not know of this Prophecy but for this event. Therefore, I wonder how he felt when he realized eventually that by giving Jesus his new Tomb, he fulfilled that spoken by Isaiah nearly 800 years before. What a privilege was his that the Son of God would have use of such in the greatest happening of human history, the Redemption of mankind!

And yet, all Believers, in one way or the other, fall into the same category. How privileged we are to be able to support the Work of God in any capacity. How wonderful it will be when we stand before Him, and He will tell us of lives changed and souls Saved because of our giving of money to take the Gospel to the world, or our supplication in prayer that sinners may be Saved.

(39) "AND THERE CAME ALSO NICODEMUS, WHICH AT THE FIRST CAME TO JESUS BY NIGHT, AND BROUGHT A MIXTURE OF MYRRH AND ALOES, ABOUT AN HUNDRED POUND WEIGHT."

The form is:

1. The great Brazen Altar, which sat in front of the Tabernacle, represented Jesus and Calvary.

2. The copper pictured Judgment and the enduring strength of His Atoning Sacrifice.

3. Its polished surface pictured His Sinlessness, and its measurements, three by five, pictured His Deity and His Grace.

4. Its shape, foursquare, expressed its provision and sufficiency for the four corners of the Earth. Its position, in front of the entrance to the House, pictured the fact that the Crucified Lamb of Calvary is the One and Only Way to God.

NICODEMUS

The phrase, *"And there came also Nicodemus, who at the first came to Jesus by night,"* tells us two things:

1. Nicodemus was also a member of the Sanhedrin and very rich as well! Evidently, the same struggles faced by Joseph of Arimathaea were faced also by this man.

2. The Holy Spirit through the Apostle reminds the reader that Nicodemus had come to Jesus at night at the very beginning of the Ministry of the Master. This would have been about three and one-half years earlier. So, the struggle had continued from then until now. How far he had come in his spiritual quest from then unto now is anyone's guess. However, this one thing is certain:

It took Calvary to bring both men to an open Confession.

WHY CALVARY?

It would seem that this would have had the very opposite effect. Jesus dying in total disgrace and humiliation, and not using His Power at all to save Himself, would seemingly have disillusioned these men.

Some three and one half years earlier, when Jesus had explained to Nicodemus what it meant to be Born-Again, He also told him the means by which this would be accomplished. He had said, *"And as Moses lifted up the serpent in the wilderness, even so must the Son of Man be lifted up"* (Jn. 3:14).

I doubt very seriously that Nicodemus understood what Jesus was talking about at that particular time. However, as the months wore on, I believe the Holy Spirit took those words to his heart, and that he, no doubt, discussed this with Joseph many, many times. And now, as they both see Jesus on this Cross, despite the humiliation and the shame, it begins to come together. They now know what He was talking about when He spoke of being *"lifted up."* Even though it would take the Day of Pentecost to complete their understanding, they now knew enough to realize and understand somewhat Who Jesus really was and what He actually was doing. Hence, they looked at Calvary now in an entirely different way, not as defeat, but as Victory. So now, they are no longer secret Disciples but take an open stand on the Side of Jesus Christ, which all ultimately must do.

THE EMBALMING

The phrase, *"And brought a mixture of myrrh and aloes, about an hundred pound weight,"* pertained to the embalming process as it was then done by wealthy Jews.

This was not embalming as practiced by the Egyptians (Gen. 50:2-3). Jews simply anointed the body and wrapped it in fine linen, putting the spices and ointments in the folds.

In Christ's Case, the operation was not completed due to the coming of the High Sabbath (Passover). However, as soon as they could legally do so, which was the coming Sunday morning, the women came back to complete the work (Mk. 16:1). The linen was bound around each leg and arm and a napkin placed over the face.

As well, the *"hundred pounds"* of these spices would have been very costly, but which these men could well afford.

(40) "THEN TOOK THEY THE BODY OF JESUS, AND WOUND IT IN LINEN CLOTHES WITH THE SPICES, AS THE MANNER OF THE JEWS IS TO BURY."

The diagram is:

1. A particular Prophet died, and his wife was left penniless (II Ki. 4:3).

2. Her situation was so acute that the creditors were about to come and take her sons away, forcing them into servitude. When it comes to the world, *"The creditor is come."* Satan is that creditor, and he will take all, steal all, and destroy all (Jn. 10:10).

3. The woman, however, took her problem to Elisha, i.e., *"the Lord."* Unfortunately, the modern church has come to the place that it advocates taking our problems to the psychologist. What a sorry trade!

4. The Lord met her need in a great way. My grandmother taught me a long time ago, *"Jimmy, God is a big God, so ask big!"* I have never forgotten that, and it has helped me to touch this world for Christ.

TAKING CHRIST DOWN FROM THE CROSS

The phrase, *"Then took they the Body of Jesus,"* is of far greater portent than meets the eye.

They would have taken Him down from the Cross in one of two ways:

1. They would have first pulled the nails from His Feet and then lifted Him up, crossbeam and all, gently laying Him on the ground, which is probably what happened.

2. Or else, they could have pulled all the nails from His Feet and Hands, then taking Him down, leaving the crossbeam nailed to the upright centerpiece, called the stipe.

With no one else to help them, except maybe the centurion, they would have done their best to clean the blood from His Hands and Feet, as well as His Side and Face. However, due to the manner in which His Face was disfigured due to the pulling out of His Beard, there would have been very little they could have done in that respect.

I wonder what their thoughts were as they handled His Body, knowing that this was the very Body prepared for Him in order to redeem mankind (Heb. 10:5).

Irrespective of what their thoughts were at the moment, it is positive that in later years, they would come more fully to realize how special and wonderful was that moment and how privileged they were!

LINEN CLOTHES

The phrase, *"And wound it in linen clothes with the spices,"* would have been done painstakingly.

As they applied the spices to His Body, gently wrapping the linen around Him, as special as this was, it also has a negative connotation.

Whatever their thoughts were to this time as to Who He actually was, they did not believe He would rise from the dead, hence, the embalming process. In fact, no one, not even His Choice Disciples, believed that He would be resurrected.

Why?

They had heard Him several times refer to His Coming Death and, as well, to His Resurrection. Of course, the record is clear that they really did not think this was going to happen, or else, they thought He was speaking of something Spiritual and not of actual death. But now, He was dead!

As much as they loved Him, none believed, as stated, that He would rise from the dead. I think at this juncture, they were totally confused in their minds and spirits. That which they felt could not happen had happened! As well, His Death had been so traumatic that they could not see past the present circumstances.

THE BURIAL

The phrase, *"As the manner of the Jews is to bury,"* proclaims, as stated, their lack of faith in His coming Resurrection.

And yet, there was another situation at hand which, no doubt, had an effect on what they did.

Importance was attached to a splendid funeral (Lk. 16:22), and this costly interment was not without its deep significance.

The manner of burial regarding the spices, etc., in effect, made a statement regarding the importance of the person in question. Were the deceased poverty-stricken, it would be obvious that such would not be done. As well, if the deceased had no friends, no care or concern would be extended.

So, Joseph and Nicodemus are making a statement by their action that they were Friends of Christ and considered Him to be One of Greatness. Hence, they would go to all of this trouble, which not only showed their feelings, but was a rebuke to the religious hierarchy of Israel, who would have buried Him in the potter's field had not someone, such as Joseph, intervened.

(41) "NOW IN THE PLACE WHERE HE WAS CRUCIFIED THERE WAS A GARDEN; AND IN THE GARDEN A NEW SEPULCHRE, WHEREIN WAS NEVER MAN YET LAID."

The overview is:

1. The only way to have victory over sin is through what the Holy Spirit taught us through Paul in the Sixth Chapter of Romans.

2. The first place that the great Apostle took us was straight to the Cross, as outlined in Verses 3 through 5.

3. The Believer is to understand that every single thing he receives comes to him by virtue of what Christ did at the Cross, all on our behalf.

THE GARDEN

The phrase, *"Now in the place where He was crucified there was a garden,"* has John alone mentioning the *"garden."*

We are not told by John, however, that this Sepulchre was Joseph's own (Matthew gives this explanation), that it was cut out of a rock, or the nature or quality of it. Matthew, Luke, and John remark that it was new in the sense of being as yet unused.

Consequently, this prevented the possibility of any confusion or the Lord's Sacred Body coming into contact with corruption.

"And in the garden a new sepulchre, wherein was never man yet laid," pertains to this Tomb containing the Body of Jesus only, and that just for three days and nights. It is extremely doubtful, however, that this Tomb was ever used again after the Resurrection. The Prince of Life had lain here, and I hardly think that Joseph would have allowed it to be used ever again, even to contain his remains upon his death.

(42) "THERE LAID THEY JESUS THEREFORE BECAUSE OF THE JEWS' PREPARATION DAY; FOR THE SEPULCHRE WAS NEAR AT HAND."

The exegesis is:

1. The Apostle John in I Jn. 1:8 emphatically states that the Christian continues to have the sin nature.

NOTES

2. Paul explains this in Romans, Chapter 6, proclaiming the fact that while the Believer is to be dead to the sin nature, the sin nature itself is not dead in the Believer and will not be removed until the first Resurrection of Life (I Cor. 15:53).

3. The Christian who believes he has no sin nature, that it is completely eradicated, is deceiving himself and nobody else.

JESUS

The phrase says, *"There laid they Jesus,"* not *"the Body of Jesus,"* for it was not a corpse, although dead. It was *"Jesus"* Who lay in that rock Tomb. Such language could not be used of a mere man. It could only be true of Him Who was Ever-Living.

So, He rode upon a colt upon which man had never ridden, and He reposed in a Tomb wherein man had never yet lain.

THE PREPARATION DAY

The phrase, *"Therefore because of the Jews' preparation day,"* spoke of the Passover, which would commence at sundown.

As we have stated, the beginning of a new day in the manner which Jews then reckoned such did not begin at midnight, as we now do, but rather at the going down of the sun. Therefore, when the sun set that evening, which was Wednesday, the day Jesus was crucified, the new day of Thursday began.

Jesus died at exactly the time the Passover lamb was offered, which was at three o'clock in the afternoon. The Passover meal was to be prepared that day and eaten that night, which began the High Sabbath, i.e., the Passover Sabbath, and not the regular Saturday Sabbath.

THE SEPULCHRE

The phrase, *"For the sepulchre was near at hand,"* meant it was near the place of Crucifixion.

They would have carried over the Body of Jesus, placing it gently in the Tomb.

That *"garden"* is still there today, and the Tomb can still be seen.

The last time Frances and I were in Israel, we had somewhat over 100 people with us and conducted a Service in the *"garden."* Each in turn went into the Sepulchre, which

I had visited several times previously; however, this was to be a special time for both Frances and me.

As I crouched down, walking into the Tomb, looking at the place where His Body had lain, and from where He had been raised from the dead, all of a sudden, I began to sense the Presence of God. Frances related as to how it moved upon her in the same manner.

For a few moments, I think I saw what He had done for me and what it all meant, at least to a degree greater than I had known previously.

I think that which the Holy Spirit impressed upon me to such a degree was that all of this was done for sinners. None was done for Himself or on the part of Heaven, but it was all for sinners! Then we realize that He did not fail, but rather did everything He came to do. As a result, no one need ever be lost, and no one need ever lack for Spiritual Victory.

"Holy, Holy, Holy!
"Lord God Almighty!
"Early in the morning
"Our song shall rise to Thee;
"Holy, Holy, Holy!
"Merciful and Mighty!
"God in Three Persons,
"Blessed Trinity!"

"Holy, Holy, Holy!
"Tho' the darkness hide Thee,
"Tho' the eye of sinful man
"Your Glory may not see,
"Only You are Holy!
"There is none beside You;
"Perfect in Power, Love, and Purity."

CHAPTER 20

(1) "THE FIRST DAY OF THE WEEK COMES MARY MAGDALENE EARLY, WHEN IT WAS YET DARK, UNTO THE SEPULCHRE, AND SEES THE STONE TAKEN AWAY FROM THE SEPULCHRE."

The exposition is:

1. The Miracle mentioned, beginning with II Kings 2:19, would be the second Miracle performed by the Prophet Elisha, with the opening of Jordan being the first (II Ki. 2:14).

2. The Elders of the City of Jericho told the Prophet that the place was pleasant, but the ground was barren because the water was poisoned.

3. The Holy Spirit told Elisha to bring him a *"new cruse."* It was made of clay and symbolized the Humanity of Christ, i.e., *"His Incarnation."*

4. Elisha then told the men to *"put salt therein,"* which was a type of the incorruptible Word of God.

5. The Scripture says that Elisha *"took the new cruse"* to the *"spring of the waters"* and *"cast the salt in there."*

6. The waters were instantly healed and remain pure and clear unto this day.

THE FIRST DAY OF THE WEEK

The phrase, *"The first day of the week,"* was the day of His Resurrection. Actually, it had begun at sundown the day before, which was Saturday, according to the manner in which Jews reckoned time. So, Jesus was, no doubt, raised from the dead very shortly after the sun had set and night had settled in. The Father would not leave His Son in the Tomb one minute longer than was necessary.

The Resurrection of Jesus Christ is the greatest event in the history of the world. Without the Resurrection, Calvary, as would be obvious, would have been in vain.

Heathen and foes admit the fact of the Death of Jesus. The evidence is overwhelming, multiform, and sufficient to establish itself to the ordinary reason of mankind. It is a matter of indubitable history. The proof was given to the entire world; however, many, if not most, doubt the Resurrection.

THE FOUR ACCOUNTS

Some would claim that the four accounts of the Resurrection do not correspond. As such, they claim a discrepancy in the Sacred Text. However, the four different accounts prove the authenticity of the Text rather than the opposite. Had the Text been *"doctored"* or *"edited,"* they would have all read the same. So, the differences, not discrepancies or contradictions, we might quickly add, only verify the Inspiration.

The four different accounts only portray what the eyewitnesses saw or the writer heard, as in the case of Luke. They are not contradictions, only different accounts.

Any four people could witness a graphic situation, and upon investigation, four different accounts would be given. One or two would add things the others did not say, for whatever reason; however, such does not mean a contradiction, as stated, only a different account.

WORSHIP

As well, if one is to notice, inasmuch as Jesus rose from the dead on *"the first day of the week,"* this day was ever after celebrated as a day of worship, consequently, taking the place of the old Jewish Sabbath (Jn. 20:1, 19, 26-29; Acts 20:6-12; I Cor. 16:1-2).

The Outpouring of the Holy Spirit was on the first day of the week, the day after seven Jewish Sabbaths (Acts 2:1).

After Christ's Ascension, the first Gospel Sermon was preached on the first day; and the first Conversions (about 3,000) took place on the first day, i.e., Sunday (Acts 2:1-42).

Also, it must be understood that no recognition was given by Christ or any Apostle to the old Jewish Seventh-Day Sabbath after the Resurrection. In fact, Sunday, the first day, as stated, became known as *"The Lord's Day"* (Rev. 1:10).

MARY MAGDALENE

The phrase, *"Comes Mary Magdalene early, when it was yet dark, unto the sepulchre,"* probably referred to about five o'clock in the morning.

John only mentioned Mary Magdalene, but Matthew, Mark, and Luke all speak of other women being with her as well. However, John did not say the others were not present; he just failed to mention them at all, for whatever reason.

The reason was probably because Mary Magdalene seems to have been the first one to tell Peter and John that the stone had been rolled away from the mouth of the Sepulchre and that the Body of Jesus was missing. It seems the other women also said the same thing to Peter and John, but with Mary Magdalene possibly arriving first (Lk. 24:9-10).

As well, Luke stated that the women plus Mary Magdalene had seen two Angels at the Tomb, who had even spoken to them (Lk. 24:1-8). However, John did not mention this either.

It seems that all the women were thrown somewhat into a state of shock upon meeting with these events, with all running to tell the Disciples, and Mary Magdalene, as stated, possibly arriving first.

Even though John does not mention the fact, the women had come early that morning, bringing more spices to complete the embalming process. Many have scoffed at this, claiming that Joseph and Nicodemus had already placed about 100 pounds of spices on His Body when He was placed in the Tomb three days before (Jn. 19:39). However, the skeptics err because they do not understand that these women desired to place spices on the Body of Jesus, not so much that they were needed, but because they loved Him. Consequently, they wanted to do something, and this was all they could do.

As well, this tells us that not a single one of His Followers, even those who were the closest to Him, believed that He would rise from the dead. The only possible exception is Mary and Martha, the sisters of Lazarus whom Jesus had raised from the dead.

But He did!

THE STONE WAS ROLLED AWAY

The phrase, *"And sees the stone taken away from the sepulchre,"* proclaims something these women did not expect to find. Actually, the detailed accounts of all the circumstances surrounding the Resurrection of Christ, which registered shock and surprise regarding all parties, preclude the hypothesis that these people stole the Body of Jesus away, as circulated by the Jews of that day. To be sure, if such a thing had happened, the stories would have been told in an entirely different way, as should be obvious!

As well, how could someone have stolen the Body of Jesus from the Tomb when four Roman soldiers were constantly on guard all the time, changing the guard every three hours (Mat. 27:65-66)?

(2) "THEN SHE RAN, AND CAME TO SIMON PETER, AND TO THE OTHER DISCIPLE, WHOM JESUS LOVED, AND SAID UNTO THEM, THEY HAVE TAKEN AWAY THE LORD OUT OF THE SEPULCHRE, AND WE KNOW NOT WHERE THEY HAVE LAID HIM."

The synopsis is:

1. The words *"chastened"* and *"chastisement"* of Hebrews 12:6-8 do not carry the idea of punishment, but rather of corrective measures.

2. It is meant to drive the person to the Lord, with the Holy Spirit then correcting the situation, which He Alone can do.

3. The problem is sin, even as the problem always is sin (Heb. 12:4). To be sure, the Holy Spirit will not rest until the problem is solved, ever how long it takes, and ever how severe the chastening has to be.

4. The Believer is not to despise *"the chastening of the Lord,"* but rather understand its necessity.

THE WORDS OF MARY MAGDALENE

The phrase, *"Then she ran, and came to Simon Peter, and to the other Disciple, whom Jesus loved,"* speaks of John, for he referred to himself in this manner (Jn. 13:23; 19:26; 20:2; 21:7, 20-25).

As well, with him relating that she was running, this probably explains her arriving a little sooner than the others.

Also, it should be noted that John, who wrote this account, it is believed, over 50 years after the event, gives Simon Peter first place in recognition.

"And said unto them, They have taken away the Lord out of the sepulchre," proclaims her still thinking of the Lord as dead, despite the fact that two Angels had plainly said to them, *"He is not here, but is risen: remember how He spoke unto you when He was yet in Galilee, saying, The Son of Man must be delivered into the hands of sinful men, and be crucified, and the third day rise again"* (Lk. 24:6-7).

Quite possibly, she and the others did not recognize them as Angels and, therefore, did not quite believe or, most likely, did not really understand what the Angels had said.

"And we know not where they have laid Him," probably referred to her thinking that Joseph and Nicodemus had moved the Body of Jesus to some other place. As is obvious, she is not thinking of Resurrection.

(3) "PETER THEREFORE WENT FORTH, AND THAT OTHER DISCIPLE, AND CAME TO THE SEPULCHRE."

The exegesis is:

1. Due to what Christ did at the Cross, the Mosaic Legislation had been fulfilled and set aside.

2. In fact, while Peter was at the home of Simon the Tanner, the Lord had given him a Vision showing him all of this. After this, Peter was willing to go to the home of Cornelius, a Gentile, and preach the Gospel to him and his house (Acts, Chpt. 10).

3. So, when Peter came to the Church at Antioch, he acknowledged no difference between Gentiles and Jews regarding the Gospel, which is the way he should have conducted himself.

4. However, certain Jewish preachers came from Jerusalem, actually sent by James, who, even though they are not identified, evidently were men of distinction.

5. These individuals saw Peter eating with the Gentiles, which was opposed by Mosaic Law. They contended that he was going against Levitical Legislation.

6. Paul stepped up and resisted Peter and thus showed that he not only refused to take orders from Jerusalem Apostles, whomever these might have been, but on the other hand, felt that his apostolic position gave him the right to stand openly against them in matters of wrong conduct, which he definitely did.

PETER AND JOHN

Exactly where Peter and John were staying in Jerusalem at this time of the Passover is not known. As we have suggested, there is a possibility that Zebedee even owned a second home in Jerusalem; however, that is only conjecture.

Irrespective, whether Peter and John were staying together with all the other Disciples or whether they were apart, Mary

Magdalene brought the news of the empty Tomb first to Peter and John.

"Peter therefore went forth," refers to him going speedily because the story had seemed incredulous to him.

"And that other Disciple, and came to the sepulchre," refers to John, as stated!

Had they believed the Lord concerning His Resurrection, they would, no doubt, have been at the Tomb when the three days and nights expired. They were not there because of unbelief; consequently, they missed being personal witnesses of the greatest Miracle ever recorded in the annals of human history.

(4) "SO THEY RAN BOTH TOGETHER: AND THE OTHER DISCIPLE DID OUTRUN PETER, AND CAME FIRST TO THE SEPULCHRE."

The exposition is:

1. Any number of times, Jesus told His Disciples that He would go to Jerusalem, be killed, and raised again the third day (Mat. 16:21).

2. They seemed to understand not at all what He was saying, despite the several times He related this to them.

3. In their thinking, there was no place in the picture for a *"Cross."* This meant that they really did not understand, at least at this time, the Mission of Christ. They would understand after the Day of Pentecost.

PETER AND JOHN COME TO THE TOMB

The phrase, *"So they ran both together,"* seems to indicate that the other Disciples were not with them at this particular time. As well, this portrays the desire to examine that which Mary Magdalene had portrayed. Also, wherever they were staying in Jerusalem must not have been very far from the Tomb.

"And the other Disciple did outrun Peter, and came first to the sepulchre," speaks of John, who wrote this account. Even though it does not say so in these Passages, from Verse 11, we know that Mary followed them back to the Tomb but lagged somewhat behind due to their running.

Some have assumed from this that Peter was an old man; however, there is nothing in Scripture to verify such or even hint accordingly.

Others have suggested, as well, that Peter's heart and conscience were weighted down because of his denial of Christ some three days before. This well could have been and, no doubt, continued to rest heavily upon Peter's heart. However, at the same time, some people just run faster than others, which is probably the case in this instance.

(5) "AND HE STOOPING DOWN, AND LOOKING IN, SAW THE LINEN CLOTHES LYING; YET WENT HE NOT IN."

The pattern is:

1. It is believed that Saul, the first king of Israel, was 20 years old when he was crowned king. He reigned 40 years; therefore, he would be 60 years old at the time of his death.

2. The sunny morning of his beginning ended in a black night of horror and death.

3. It must be said that self-will wrecked his life and his reign (I Chron. 10:13-14). In that self-will, he found himself opposing God at every turn of his life.

THE EMPTY TOMB

The phrase, *"And he stooping down, and looking in,"* refers to John, who arrived at the Tomb a few moments before Peter.

"Saw the linen clothes lying," referred to the *"linen cloth"* of John 19:40, which had been used by Joseph and Nicodemus to wrap the Body of Jesus with the spices.

The word *"lying"* in this instance refers to something neatly folded and orderly arranged. Of course, if someone had stolen the Body of Jesus, such would not have been done. They would not have taken the time to remove the cloth.

"Yet went he not in," refers to John, for whatever reason, not going into the Tomb but standing in the doorway where the huge stone covering had sat and looking in. Respecting the Death and Resurrection of Christ, the following might prove helpful.

The moment Jesus died, which was on the Cross, His Soul and Spirit left His Body and went down into the nether regions for particular purposes.

As we have already stated, He preached to the spirits in prison, which referred to fallen Angels, and He delivered the Saints in Paradise. However, the preaching was not Good News, but rather an announcement. It is not revealed to us simply because it evidently had to do only with Angels, fallen Angels at that, and not men. All the time His Spirit and Soul were doing this, His Body was in the Tomb.

THE GLORIFIED BODY

However, when He was Resurrected three days and nights after His Death, His Soul and Spirit were reunited with His Body, which was then Glorified. Consequently, in that Glorified State, He came out of the Tomb. He has remained in that State ever since and, in fact, will ever remain in the Glorified State.

His Resurrection was the foundation and prelude for the coming Resurrection of every Saint of God who has ever lived.

One of the reasons that John may not have gone into the Tomb is because of the prohibition by the Law of Moses of touching a dead human body. If this was done, the *"man shall be unclean seven days."* He would then have to go through a purification process, which was quite extensive (Num., Chpt. 19).

This Law was enacted in order that Israel would understand the terrible consequences of sin, which is death.

However, these prohibitions were forever ended when Jesus died on Calvary, which cleansed from all sin, at least for all who will believe, and, therefore, destroyed the effect of its wages, which is death.

So, there would be no defilement by going into the Tomb of Jesus, or such defilement anymore or in any place, at least in this fashion.

(6) "THEN CAME SIMON PETER FOLLOWING HIM, AND WENT INTO THE SEPULCHRE, AND SAW THE LINEN CLOTHES LIE."

The order is:

1. There were five great offerings in the Levitical Law.

2. They were the Burnt-Offering, the Meal-Offering, the Trespass-Offering, the Peace-Offering, and the Sin-Offering (Lev., Chpts. 1-7).

3. God only accepted such offerings as He Himself ordained. The worshipper, imperfect and sinful in himself, was accepted in the perfection of the offering, and so it is presently. We are saved by accepting Christ and His Sacrifice.

SIMON PETER

The phrase, *"Then came Simon Peter following him,"* is due to the obvious fact that John simply outran him.

However, something must have been on Peter's mind far different than that of John. The last time Peter had seen Jesus, at least close enough to where he could see His Face, was when Jesus looked at him right after the denial (Lk. 22:61).

Peter probably saw Him hanging on the Cross, but that was at a distance and, therefore, not much discernable (Lk. 23:49).

Of course, exactly what Peter was thinking at this time, only God knows! However, the denial had been so traumatic that I cannot believe that he came to the Tomb without it weighing heavily upon his mind. Would he get to look upon that Face one more time? To end his three and one-half years of public association with Jesus in this manner was a burden not easily borne. Knowing that the last time he saw Him, Jesus looked intently at him at the time of gross failure was a hard thing to bear. However, this would be rectified very shortly, but Peter, at the time, was not aware of that.

THE SEPULCHRE

The phrase, *"And went into the Sepulchre,"* proclaims that which John did not do. Whatever defilement the Law of Moses addressed concerning the dead was not on Peter's mind at present. Did he think that Jesus was possibly risen from the dead?

Every evidence, as we shall see, seems to indicate that, at this time, none thought of Resurrection but only that something had happened that they did not now understand. Maybe someone had stolen the Body of Jesus, but who, especially considering that this Tomb was guarded for the last 72 hours by four Roman soldiers, changing shifts every three hours.

However, there were now no soldiers in sight.

THE LINEN CLOTHES

"And saw the linen clothes lie," is once again brought out by the Holy Spirit in order for us to realize its significance.

If Joseph or Nicodemus had moved His Body, as possibly Mary and others suspected, they would not have taken the linen cloth from His Body. As well, if the soldiers had moved Him somewhere else, or anyone, for that matter, they would not have removed this material, for such would not have been plausible.

No! Those linen items neatly folded and lying on the place where Jesus had lain in death represented His Resurrection.

Either they were removed by the Angels at the Resurrection, or they simply fell off His Glorified Body at that moment, which is probably what happened. Either Jesus or the Angels then neatly folded these items and laid them on the burial slab.

(7) "AND THE NAPKIN, THAT WAS ABOUT HIS HEAD, NOT LYING WITH THE LINEN CLOTHES, BUT WRAPPED TOGETHER IN A PLACE BY ITSELF."

The form is:

1. The Holy Spirit, Who resides in the heart and life of every Believer (I Cor. 3:16), doesn't require much of us, but He does require one thing.

2. He requires Faith! However, the Faith which He requires must be placed in the correct Object.

3. That correct Object is always Christ and the Cross. It was at the Cross where the Lord Jesus atoned for all sin. Consequently, the power of sin was broken, which means that Satan there lost his right to hold man in captivity and bondage.

RESURRECTION

The phrase, *"And the napkin, that was about His Head, not lying with the linen clothes,"* presents that which is extremely interesting simply because Jesus' Head and Face had been so maltreated that He was hardly recognizable.

"But wrapped together in a place by itself," speaks of something which had

NOTES

fallen off by itself or had been removed. At any rate, it was neatly folded and probably laid where His Head had been.

Once again we state, in the stealing of a body, such would not have been done. None of these actions spoke of haste, which would have accompanied the moving or stealing of a body, but rather something done deliberately and with precision.

These items neatly folded and placed conspicuously shouted *"Resurrection!"* The items themselves, plus the way they were handled, proclaimed Victory over sin and death.

As well, the manner in which these things were done proclaimed to all that the Resurrected Jesus was not a spirit, but capable of activity and physical exertion. In other words, He is a Living Person, not an abstract principle or vague force.

These are evident proofs that however great the change which had passed over Him, the Living One was the same Man that He had ever been, but yet, in a greatly expanded way.

(8) "THEN WENT IN ALSO THAT OTHER DISCIPLE, WHICH CAME FIRST TO THE SEPULCHRE, AND HE SAW, AND BELIEVED."

The overview is:

1. The main purpose of the Holy Spirit giving us, through Paul, Chapters 9 through 11 of Romans was not, as stated, for prophetic analysis, even though that in measure was given, but rather to warn the Church.

2. If the church follows in Israel's footsteps by being ignorant of God's Righteousness or by refusing God's Righteousness, attempting, as Israel, to establish its own righteousness, the church will be cut off just as Israel was cut off.

3. God's Righteousness is gained totally and completely by one's Faith in Christ and the Cross and no other way (I Cor. 1:17, 18, 23; 2:2; Col. 2:10-15).

JOHN THE BELOVED

The phrase, *"Then went in also that other Disciple, who came first to the sepulchre,"* speaks of John also now entering the Tomb with Peter.

"And he saw, and believed," refers to what

Mary reported, and not that Jesus had risen from the dead, as the next Scripture reveals.

In their minds, Jesus was still dead, even though His Body had been removed elsewhere. How they accounted for the linen wrappings is anyone's guess!

The truth is, despite being the Disciples of Christ, they were in a state of unbelief and, thereby, could not see the obvious before their eyes.

(9) "FOR AS YET THEY KNEW NOT THE SCRIPTURE, THAT HE MUST RISE AGAIN FROM THE DEAD."

The exegesis is:

1. In the jaded world of Pilate's day, the governor had grown cynical.

2. So, he asked Christ, *"What is Truth?"* He really did not expect an answer, but the answer had already been given.

3. Some have claimed that *"all truth is God's Truth."* They are trying to justify the foray of the church into humanistic psychology, claiming that God gave this *"truth"* to Sigmund Freud. In fact, nothing could be further from the truth!

4. Truth is not a philosophy or a culture. Truth is a Person, the Lord Jesus Christ (Jn. 14:6).

THE SCRIPTURE

Verse 9 is evidently speaking of Psalms 16:10-11, *"For You will not leave My Soul in Hell* (the Paradise side of Hell)*; neither will You suffer Your Holy One to see corruption.*

"You will show Me the Path of Life: in Your Presence is fullness of joy; at Your right Hand there are pleasures for evermore."

Why is it that they did not know this Passage in Psalms?

(10) "THEN THE DISCIPLES WENT AWAY AGAIN UNTO THEIR OWN HOME."

The exposition is:

1. Concerning Jesus speaking with the woman at Jacob's Well, we find that the Holy Spirit seeks people (Jn. 16:13-15); the Father seeks worshippers (Jn. 4:23); and the Son seeks sinners (Lk. 19:10).

2. Jesus did not pointedly reveal Himself to Nicodemus, but He did reveal Himself to this Samaritan woman.

3. Why didn't he reveal Himself to Nicodemus?

4. The sinner, exampled by the woman, accepts such, but self-righteousness, exampled by Nicodemus, could never accept such! Merit in the one case did not admit into Eternal Life, and demerit in the other did not exclude from it.

JERUSALEM

Verse 10 simply refers to the place they were temporarily residing, respecting their coming to Jerusalem to keep the Passover.

As they left that early morning hour, going back to where they were staying, no doubt, there were untold questions which filled their hearts and minds. To be frank, still not believing in His Resurrection, they could not put all of these situations together. Nothing made sense to them because nothing could make sense to them due to their unbelief.

(11) "BUT MARY STOOD WITHOUT AT THE SEPULCHRE WEEPING: AND AS SHE WEPT, SHE STOOPED DOWN, AND LOOKED INTO THE SEPULCHRE,"

The construction is:

1. The correct name of king Ahaz, king of Judah, was *"Jehoahaz,"* which means *"the possession of Jehovah."*

2. The man was so ungodly that the Spirit of God strikes the Jehovah-syllable out of his name, invariably calling him *"Ahaz,"* which simply means *"possession."*

3. Such was his life. He was led, influenced, and possessed by anyone or anything except God (II Ki. 16:10-11).

WEEPING

The phrase, *"But Mary* (Mary Magdalene) *stood without at the sepulchre weeping,"* presents her staying after Peter and John had gone.

Mary did not know where Jesus was, and still believing that somebody had taken His Body but not knowing where, she remained near the only place she could identify with Him. Although very little is known about Mary Magdalene before this time, Mark tells us that Jesus had delivered her of *"seven demons"* (Mk. 16:9).

JESUS GAVE HER BACK HER LIFE

Even though no information is given

other than that, one can well imagine the suffering she endured before she met Jesus. How she came to be demon possessed, we are not told! Neither are we told what type of woman she was that would have brought about this terrible bondage. We are actually given no account at all of how she met Jesus and experienced this great Deliverance. This we do know:

Jesus gave her back her life, and for that, she would love Him in such a way that it makes understandable her actions respecting these events. She would rather be close to where His Body had been than to go anywhere else.

She knew how her life had changed. The fact that the religious hierarchy of Israel, who professed to know God, would murder Him was beyond her comprehension or understanding. She stood there *"weeping"* with a broken heart!

Jesus was Her Life, and without Him, life would lose its meaning and purpose. So it is with all who truly know Him and His Power to save!

"And as she wept, she stooped down, and looked into the sepulchre," evidently represents the second time she had done this (Mat. 28:1-7; Mk. 16:1-7; Lk. 24:1-11).

(12) "AND SAW TWO ANGELS IN WHITE SITTING, THE ONE AT THE HEAD, AND THE OTHER AT THE FEET, WHERE THE BODY OF JESUS HAD LAIN."

The synopsis is:

1. Israel first permitted to remain in their midst the inhabitants of the land, who were heathen. Then, very soon, they became insensible to the existence of these sources of evil and misery.

2. Such is the sad history presently of many Christians.

3. We learn from Judges that the *"Promise"* is different than the *"Possession."* The *"Promise"* does not contain a *"Possession"* free of the enemy, but, most of the time, it is filled with the enemy. However, as Faith claims the Promise, likewise, it must claim the Possession of the Promise.

TWO ANGELS

The phrase, *"And saw two Angels in white sitting,"* apparently represents the second appearance of Angels.

It seems that she did not really understand at the time that these were Angels. Actually, regarding the first appearance, Luke calls them *"two men."* However, the Scripture often interchanges the two descriptions because Angels look very much like men.

One must understand that all of these people, especially Mary Magdalene, were grief-stricken and somewhat in a state of shock, and, therefore, probably did not evaluate things quite as they should, as anyone does under such circumstances.

She knew that the religious hierarchy of Israel had masterminded the murder of Jesus, and that the Roman governor had carried out their request in performing the foul deed. As well, she knew that Joseph and Nicodemus, two powerful men in Israel, had prepared Jesus for the burial. As a result, Mary Magdalene really did not know what was happening. I doubt very seriously that she knew, as stated, at least at that time, that these beings were Angels.

The phrase, *"The one at the head, and the other at the feet, where the Body of Jesus had lain,"* in a sense of the word, represents the true Mercy Seat, with the Angels representing the Cherubim. The Angels sat, but the Cherubim had stood, for expiation was now accomplished (Ex. 25:19).

Williams said, *"Most probably these Angels were Princes; for the dignity and importance of the Resurrection demanded the Ministry of the highest Angels"*[1] (Dan. 9:21; 10:21; 12:1; Lk. 1:19, 26).

(13) "AND THEY SAY UNTO HER, WOMAN, WHY DO YOU WEEP? SHE SAID UNTO THEM, BECAUSE THEY HAVE TAKEN AWAY MY LORD, AND I KNOW NOT WHERE THEY HAVE LAID HIM."

The composition is:

1. There are three things that must be done if the Believer is to walk in victory. They are:

2. The individual must deny himself. This speaks of denying one's personal strength, ability, education, motivation, etc.

3. The individual must take up the Cross: this means that one must places one's Faith exclusively in Christ and what Christ has

done for us at the Cross. It means that every Blessing comes to us by the Means of the Cross.

4. This must be done daily: it is somewhat like our Faith being renewed in the Cross of Christ on a daily basis (Lk. 9:23).

WHY DO YOU WEEP?

The question, *"And they say unto her, Woman, why do you weep?"* is somewhat more personal than the statement the Angels had made upon the first appearance. Then they said, *"Fear not: for I know that you seek Jesus, which was crucified.*

"He is not here: for He is risen, as He said. Come, see the place where the Lord lay" (Mat. 28:5-6).

The other three accounts of this first appearance are each a little different in wording but with the same meaning. Quite possibly, the Angels said other things which were not reported at all!

In the second appearance to Mary Magdalene, they spoke directly to her as to why she was weeping. Actually, their question was a mild rebuke.

None had believed Jesus when He spoke of being crucified and then rising from the dead. Now, no one believed the Angels; however, all of this was about to change.

WHERE IS HE?

He is alive, even as the Angels were proclaiming, which should be an occasion for great joy; however, unbelief hindered the reception of this Message, actually, the greatest in human history. Jesus is not dead; He is alive!

The phrase, *"She said unto them, Because they have taken away my Lord,"* proclaims, in a sense, the heart of Mary. Jesus is *"my Lord,"* which speaks volumes. He had changed her life, and she had given Him her heart. In her mind, there would never be another because of what He did for her and, in fact, so many, many others as well.

"And I know not where they have laid Him," in essence, says, *"Wherever He is, even though it is only a Dead Body, there I want to be."*

Inasmuch as she and other women had come earlier in order to bring spices to add to that which had already been done by Joseph and Nicodemus, such action only portrays their desire to do something, as little as it may have been. In other words, love had to express itself in some way.

(14) "AND WHEN SHE HAD THUS SAID, SHE TURNED HERSELF BACK, AND SAW JESUS STANDING, AND KNEW NOT THAT IT WAS JESUS."

The synopsis is:

1. Jesus Christ is our *"Advocate with the Father."*

2. If the Saint loses fellowship with Christ through sin, and the Believer properly confesses that sin, the Lord, in a sense, pleads our cause on the basis of His Precious Blood and, thereby, brings us back into fellowship again.

3. However, when we say *"plead,"* we are not really meaning that Jesus says or does anything. His very Presence before the Father guarantees that the Intercession will be accepted, at least for those who will believe (I Jn. 2:1-2).

SHE DIDN'T KNOW IT WAS JESUS

The phrase, *"And when she had thus said, she turned herself back,"* would have been better translated, *"She was caused to turn back."*

There is no record that the Angels said anything else to her, and perhaps she noticed the Angels looking behind her, and it was that which caused her to turn around.

To a wounded heart seeking Christ Himself, Angels, however glorious, have little interest. This fact demonstrates the idolatry and the folly of modern Angel adoration. All righteous Angels will direct attention to the Lord Jesus.

"And saw Jesus standing, and knew not that it was Jesus," portrays Him in His Glorified Form, but yet, looking a little different than any other man. He could have appeared in Transfiguration Glory as He had done some time past, but this was not to be.

In fact, there is no record that anyone recognized Jesus after He had risen from the dead, at least immediately (Lk. 24:16; Jn. 21:4)!

RECOGNITION!

Why?

Concerning His Walk with the two Disciples on the road to Emmaus, which took place on the day of His Resurrection, the Scripture says, *"But their eyes were holden that they should not know Him"* (Lk. 24:16). The idea is that He purposely caused them to not recognize Him, at least until He was ready for them to do so!

Even though we are not specifically told, their lack of recognition seemed to have something to do with their lack of faith. He would ultimately reveal Himself to all who were His closer Followers, but the evidence is that a test of Faith was enjoined upon all of them in one way or the other.

He wanted them to know and understand that He had risen from the dead, and that was easy enough to prove. However, He wanted their Faith and confidence to rest more so on the Word of God than what merely their eyes could see. While it certainly was important that they see Him after the Resurrection, which they did, it was even more important that they know this was in fulfillment of the Word of God (Ps. 16:10-11). As well, the cleansing of the leper in the Law of Moses was in portrayal of the Death and Resurrection of Christ, which they should have known!

THE DEATH AND RESURRECTION OF CHRIST

Regarding the cleansing of the leper, two birds were chosen, with one being sacrificed, representing the Crucifixion of Christ. The other was turned loose, representing the Resurrection of Christ through which sin, sickness, and the entire curse would be removed from mankind (Lev., Chpt. 14).

If Christ had died and remained dead, His Atoning Work would have been in vain. It was the Resurrection that ratified what His Death had accomplished (Rom. 4:25; I Cor. 15:1-23; Col. 3:1; Heb. 4:14-16; 6:20; 7:11, 17, 25; 9:24-28; I Pet. 1:3; 3:21-22).

But yet, it should be made abundantly clear that the entire Work of Redemption was finished at the Cross. While the Resurrection did ratify what had been done, really, there was no question about Him rising from the dead. However, if Jesus had failed to atone for even one sin, past, present, or future, due to the fact that the wages of sin is death, He could not have risen from the dead. However, the fact that He arose proclaims the fact of a total Atonement.

If the Apostles and Mary Magdalene, along with others, had known the Bible as they should, His Death and Resurrection would not have been a shock or surprise. But yet, in their defense, the Holy Spirit had not yet been given, at least in the capacity He would come on the Day of Pentecost. After this Advent, which was made possible by the Death and Resurrection of Christ, understanding these things became much easier (Jn. 7:37-39).

(15) "JESUS SAID UNTO HER, WOMAN, WHY DO YOU WEEP? WHOM DO YOU SEEK? SHE, SUPPOSING HIM TO BE THE GARDENER, SAID UNTO HIM, SIR, IF YOU HAVE BORNE HIM HENCE, TELL ME WHERE YOU HAVE LAID HIM, AND I WILL TAKE HIM AWAY."

The composition is:

1. The fire of Exodus 30:7 and the Blood of Exodus 30:10 teach that there can be no acceptable worship apart from Atonement.

2. In the matter of Atonement, all worshippers stand on one common ground, and that is the Sacrifice of Christ.

3. The Brazen Altar of the Tabernacle was for the sinner and the Brazen Laver for the Saint. The former testified of the Blood of Christ, the latter, of the Word of God. The former cleansed the conscience; the latter, the conduct.

WHY DO YOU WEEP?

The question, *"Jesus said unto her, Woman, why do you weep?"* is identical to that asked by the Angels.

Of course, Jesus knew the answers to all of these questions, but I think He was testing her Faith.

If we look at these incidents in the realm of one passing or failing these tests of Faith, I think we will misunderstand what Jesus was doing.

While it was a test of Faith, even in every occurrence, it was tendered in order to teach them, rather than whether they would pass or fail. Were it judged on the latter basis, all failed; however, Jesus wanted this to be a lesson. So, it was a test of Faith but tendered in order that they may understand that all things which pertain to God must be anchored on the principle of Faith, which stands on the Foundation of the Word of God (Rom. 10:17).

WHOM DO YOU SEEK?

The question, *"Whom do you seek?"* presents the second question asked by Jesus and really gets to the heart of the matter.

So, the first said by Jesus to His Followers after the Resurrection was in the form of two questions. They are very significant and, consequently, hold much greater meaning than something merely said to Mary Magdalene.

1. *"Woman, why do you weep?"* In effect, by virtue of His Death and Resurrection, Jesus has taken away the cause of weeping relative to the great difficulties and unknowns of life. He will be with us in all trials and difficulties and, as well, has defeated sin, death, and the grave. Therefore, man can be free and not have any fear of death.

So, in respect to these great problems, which have plagued humanity from the very beginning, they were victoriously addressed and answered at a Hill called Calvary and from the Tomb of Resurrection.

2. *"Whom do you seek?"* To know that these grand and glorious things have been done presents a Truth of monumental proportions. However, that they were done is one thing, but the main thing is, the One Who did it all, i.e., *"the Lord Jesus Christ."*

Many want the solution without the Saviour! Such is not to be!

If one wants the tears wiped from his eyes, one will have to embrace not only Bible Christianity but, as well, the *"Author and Finisher"* of what Christianity really is. To divorce Christianity from Jesus is to leave Christianity as little more than hollow mockery, a philosophy, if you please! And yet, tens of millions attempt to do this very thing.

Tens of millions have embraced the church, which contains no Salvation. As such, Jesus is just a part of the mix, and an elementary part at that! Then, the individual only has religion.

However, Bible Christianity is not a religion but a relationship. That relationship is with Jesus Christ. He is All in All!

"Whom do you seek?"

A LACK OF RECOGNITION

The phrase, *"She, supposing Him to be the gardener,"* evidently means that she thought this man worked for Joseph of Arimathaea, who owned this garden. Still there is no thought of Resurrection!

How many times do we, as Believers, fail to recognize Jesus, thinking Him to be someone else? As this was because of unbelief in Mary, it is because of unbelief in all the rest of us as well!

As a Believer having Faith in God and His Word, we must understand that Jesus is literally in everything, in one way or the other, that happens to us. Of course, He is not in sin or failure in any way, but He is definitely there to bring us out of that dilemma, should such occur.

Look for Jesus! Look for Him in our trials. Look for Him in the Blessings and that which seems not to be Blessings. Look for Him in our adversities, even in that which looks like reverses. In fact, every single thing that happens to the Child of God is either caused by the Lord or allowed by Him. So, if we understand that, we will not mistake Him for the *"gardener."*

OVERWHELMING GRIEF

The question, *"Said unto Him, Sir, if You have borne Him hence, tell me where you have laid Him,"* proclaims again that she had absolutely no notion of Resurrection.

She was utterly overwhelmed with one bitter, cruel thought. The Sacred Body was to be embalmed with the precious spices, which, quite possibly, she had spent her all to buy.

She probably knew that the Jews wanted to take His Body and place it in the valley of Hinnom, which, in actuality, was a garbage dump, and she maybe feared this was what had happened.

The phrase, *"And I will take Him away,"*

simply means that if they would allow her, she would give Him a proper burial.

The beautiful thing about this entire scenario is that Jesus appeared first to a woman, which carries deep significance (Mk. 16:9).

Due to Eve being the first to fall in the Garden of Eden, from that moment, women were treated somewhat with disdain. She had few, if any, rights whatsoever. Most of the time, her husband was chosen for her by her parents, with her wishes being entertained not at all. As well, all the mundane labor and chores of the household were her responsibilities in every manner, even to the point of negating all common courtesy. In other words, if something had to be carried from one place to the other, and the man was standing there unencumbered, it would not even enter his mind to perform this task himself. His wife would be expected to do such.

THE CURSE ON THE FEMALE GENDER

Because of the Fall, the Lord had said to Eve: *"I will greatly multiply your sorrow and your conception; in sorrow you shall bring forth children; and your desire shall be to your husband, and he shall rule over you"* (Gen. 3:16).

Thereafter, the idea seemed to be, at least as man considered the situation, that he would make certain that the curse upon the female gender was carried out to its utter conclusion and harm.

No! The fault was not that of God for leveling such a curse, for, in reality, He had no choice. The fault was in man because of his ungodly attitude.

Sin, as in the case of Eve, and Adam, as well, who actually received the greatest curse of all (Gen. 3:17-19), always wreaks its deadly toll! However, Adam, and most all men who followed him, took it upon themselves to add to the sorrow which had come to women.

Considering how Jesus conducted Himself toward women, and especially the equality He gave them with men, we learn that it is never pleasing to God, and actually downright sinful, for any Believer in any capacity to take it upon himself to punish another. Such lies in the domain of God altogether and never in the realm of man (Rom. 12:19).

FAITH

James, in effect, said, *"Who do you think you are, thinking you are qualified to judge another?"* (James 4:12).

By the Example of Christ, we find that the Lord paid the penalty of the curse that had been placed on woman, thereby, restoring her, at least all who will believe. Naturally, the curse was lifted on Adam, as well, and once again, to those who believe.

It is true that man does not yet have all the benefits of what Jesus did at Calvary, our now having only the firstfruits, and yet, in spirit, we do have it!

Not only was it vastly significant that Jesus appeared first of all to a woman, the reason, as well, is of vast significance. That reason is *"Faith!"*

This tells all and sundry that God honors Faith on the part of women the same as He does men. In other words, everything is based solely upon the principle of Faith, and we are speaking of Faith in Christ and what Christ did for us at the Cross, and not because of gender, wealth, education, position, race, etc.

So, it was not because He arbitrarily showed deference to Mary Magdalene by appearing to her first of all, but simply because she evidenced more Faith than anyone else.

PERFECT FAITH?

As well, we must learn that even though this was true on her part, still, as is glaringly obvious, her Faith, in fact, was extremely weak. But yet, Jesus honored her Faith where it was, even as weak as it was, and built thereon. There is a great principle here which we should learn.

In fact, no one has perfect Faith. To be frank, even though the Faith of some is much greater than others, if we are to be honest, all of us would probably fall into the category of the man who brought his demon possessed son to Jesus and then was told by the Lord, *"If you can believe, all things are possible to him who believes."*

The man answered and said, *"Lord, I believe; please help my unbelief"* (Mk. 9:23-24).

Exactly as with that man, Jesus will always reward our Faith and will, as well, help us in our unbelief, which seems to reside in all, at least in some measure.

Last of all, Jesus appeared first to this woman, even though she had formerly been possessed by *"seven demons"* (Mk. 16:9).

JUSTIFICATION BY FAITH

Of course, Jesus delivered her, but the moral and great Truth found in this speaks of *"Justification by Faith."* In other words, her past was not her present, with the past, in fact, having been totally wiped away by Christ. As someone has well said, *"The Child of God has no past while the Devil has no future."*

It is sad, but many, if not most, Believers do not really understand *"Justification by Faith,"* which means they really do not understand the Grace of God. This means they really do not understand the Cross of Christ, which also means that they really do not understand the New Covenant.

When Jesus forgives someone, it is totally forgiven and forgotten. It is never to be brought up again, at least by those who would accuse. To do such a thing is an abomination in the Eyes of God, which, in effect, actually insults and does despite to the Spirit of Grace (Heb. 10:29). In fact, it ridicules the great Price that Jesus paid at Calvary's Cross. We must always remember the following:

While Jesus most definitely died for the sins of the sinner, He also died for the failures of the Saints.

(16) "JESUS SAID UNTO HER, MARY. SHE TURNED HERSELF, AND SAID UNTO HIM, RABBONI; WHICH IS TO SAY, MASTER."

The synopsis is:

1. As the Tabernacle in every aspect of its structure presented Christ in His Atoning, Mediatorial, and Intercessory Work, likewise, the Temple did the same, but with one difference.

2. Just as every whit of the Tabernacle symbolized the Glories attaching to Christ in His First Advent, so all the dazzling splendor of the Temple prefigured the Glories of His Coming Second Advent.

3. Both buildings were designed by God. Nothing was left to the religious feeling, taste, or imagination of Moses, David, or Solomon (Heb. 8:5; I Chron. 28:19).

JESUS NOW REVEALS HIMSELF

The phrase, *"Jesus said unto her, Mary,"* proclaims the individual response which the Lord always gives to Faith.

The first expression of *"woman"* makes her the representative of the whole of suffering humanity. The second expression of *"Mary"* proclaims the individuality of the Gospel and the manner in which He deals with all who come to Him.

In other words, followers of Christ are not nameless, faceless statistics, but rather personal recipients of His Grace.

This is extremely important in that the Salvation of each Believer is a personal Salvation, rendered Personally by Jesus, and received personally by the believing sinner.

Psalms 147:4 says, *"He tells the number of the stars; He calls them all by their names."*

Even though in a direct sense this speaks of the planetary bodies, as well, it speaks of each individual Believer. John said in Revelation 1:16, *"And He had in His Right Hand Seven Stars,"* which refers to the Pastors of the seven Churches of Asia and, in reality, all Pastors and all Churches and for all time.

So, He calls every Believer by name.

The phrase, *"She turned herself,"* refers to her recognizing His Voice.

MASTER

The phrase, *"And said unto Him, Rabboni; which is to say, Master,"* in the Greek Text says, *"My Master!"*

However, the manner in which she addressed Jesus tells us that she still did not have the full picture as to Who He really is, *"The Messiah, the Son of God, the Lord of Glory!"*

Reynolds said, *"Her joy knew no bounds, but her conception of the reality of that which was revealed to her was most imperfect. It was the realization of Love rather than the perception afforded only by Revelation."*[2]

In this Fourth Gospel, the Holy Spirit records four Appearances of the Lord after He rose from the dead, and these Appearances banished four great enemies of the human heart.

They are *"sorrow, fear, doubt, and care."*

Mary was weeping (Jn. 20:11); the Disciples were trembling, as we shall see (Jn. 20:19); Thomas was doubting (Jn. 20:25); and the Apostles were despairing (Jn. 21:3). So, the dread darkness of *"sorrow"* was addressed here by Jesus, not only for Mary, but all others as well!

However, in each case, the Appearance of Jesus sufficed to dismiss the enemy and to fill his place with joy, courage, Faith, and contentment. Many other priceless effects also resulted from these Appearances — for these were not the only ones — but the Spirit, with design, mentions no others at this time.

(17) "JESUS SAID UNTO HER, TOUCH ME NOT; FOR I AM NOT YET ASCENDED TO MY FATHER: BUT GO TO MY BRETHREN, AND SAY UNTO THEM, I ASCEND UNTO MY FATHER, AND YOUR FATHER; AND TO MY GOD, AND YOUR GOD."

The composition is:

1. Abraham is referred to as the *"Altar builder"* (Gen. 12:7). Why did he build so many Altars?

2. Whenever the Lord spoke to Abraham, which was the moment of his Conversion, ever how it happened, the Lord made it very clear to the Patriarch as to the manner in which man was to approach God. It could only be through the sacrifice of a clean animal, which necessitated the shedding of blood, all which symbolized Christ.

3. God accepts nothing from humanity except it comes by the way of the Cross (I Cor. 1:17).

DON'T DETAIN ME

In a sense, Mary Magdalene represents the people of Israel.

Cleansed from the evil spirit of idolatry, Israel returned from Babylon swept and garnished, but empty. Seven other spirits more wicked took possession of her, typified by the seven demons which were cast out of Mary by Jesus. As well, on that coming Glad Day, Jesus will rid Israel of all evil spirits, which will take place at the Second Coming, as is described in Zechariah 13:2.

"Jesus said unto her, Touch Me not," in effect, says, *"Do not hold onto Me; do not try to detain Me."*

Evidently, Mary was so literally overwrought with gladness of heart that Jesus was really alive that she clutched Him in such a way that speaks of her fear that He might be lost to her again.

"For I am not yet ascended to My Father," is believed by some that Jesus meant that He was about to go to the Father in Heaven where His Shed Blood would be applied to the Mercy Seat in Heaven.

Investigating this as thoroughly as I can, I really do not believe that's what Jesus was addressing. Were that the case, that would mean that the Redemption Plan was not finished at Calvary, whereas Jesus plainly said, *"It is finished."* When Jesus died on the Cross, nothing was left undone, no sin left unatoned, no power of darkness left undefeated, and no process of Redemption left incomplete.

When He addressed Mary in this fashion, I believe that He was speaking of His Coming Ascension, which would take place in just a few days. As we've already stated, Mary was so overwrought by seeing Him that she was clinging to Him, not wanting to let go, and He gently reminded her that she should not do that. I don't think that Jesus then went to Heaven, offered up His Blood on Heaven's Mercy Seat, and then came back, etc. Jesus Christ is the Mercy Seat. In other words, the Mercy Seat that sat on the Ark of the Covenant in the Holy of Holies in the Tabernacle first, and the Temple second, was a replica, if you will, of Who Jesus really is. If He is the Mercy Seat, and He most definitely was and is, then the Blood was applied when He shed such at Calvary's Cross.

As well, if one is to notice, Jesus did not say, *"Our Father,"* but rather *"My Father."*

Reynolds said: *"He Who is Father of Christ and Father of men, is so in different ways. He is Father of Christ by nature and of men by Grace."*[3]

His *"Father"* was in Heaven, which has every indication of being a Planet. From the description given in Revelation, Chapters 21 and 22, no other conclusion can be drawn than that Heaven is a real and tangible place.

As well, it seems the mode of travel carried out by Christ, which will be available to all Glorified Saints at the Resurrection, is carried out by the speed of thought. In other words, some of the Planets of the Universe are so distant from Earth that even if one were able to travel at the speed of light (186,000 miles a second), still, it would take far too long to capture such a vast distance. Consequently, during the coming Kingdom Age, and then forever, I believe every Saint of God will have access to Heaven and will come and go between Heaven and Earth, and do so at the speed of thought, and the travel will be instant.

MY BRETHREN

The phrase, *"But go to My Brethren,"* speaks not of those who were His Halfbrothers in the flesh, but rather His Chosen Disciples (minus Judas, who was now dead).

"And say unto them, I ascend unto My Father, and your Father; and to My God, and your God," once again emphasizes the fact of the unique personal relationship between Christ and the Father, which no Believer has, at least to that degree!

However, this statement, as given by Christ, definitely does portray a relationship, and a great one at that, between the Believer and the Heavenly Father. Actually, the very purpose of Calvary and the Resurrection was to establish this relationship through Redemption, which it did!

The Proclamation of Jesus concerning His *"Ascension"* tells us several things:

• He is God and, as stated, has a unique relationship with the Father that is held by no other.

• The Ascension on all accounts, which would take place shortly, specified that the Work Jesus came to do was completed in its totality, leaving nothing undone.

(18) "MARY MAGDALENE CAME AND TOLD THE DISCIPLES THAT SHE HAD SEEN THE LORD, AND THAT HE HAD SPOKEN THESE THINGS UNTO HER."

The pattern is:

NOTES

1. The lessons of the Fifteenth Chapter of Leviticus are:
2. The first is the Holiness of God and of His Dwelling Place.
3. Second is the loving and minute interest that He takes in the habits of His Children. Nothing is too small or too private for Him. Even their clothing and their health concern Him deeply.
4. The third is the corruption of fallen nature. It is defiled. By walking, sleeping, sitting, standing, or lying, its every touch conveyed pollution — a painful lesson for proud humanity.
5. The fourth is the cleansing power of the shed Blood and the sanctifying virtue of the Word of God. They are the only ways of cleansing and Holiness.

UNBELIEF

The phrase, *"Mary Magdalene came and told the Disciples that she had seen the Lord,"* regrettably, presents that her account was met with unbelief (Mk. 16:9-11).

Unbelief is a deadly thing, keeping all of us from so much of what the Lord desires to do. As we have stated, this is one of the very reasons that the Disciples did not recognize Jesus when He appeared after the Resurrection.

Even His closest Ones had misinterpreted His Mission on Earth, despite Him telling them several times exactly what He was to do. In their minds, He was going to use His great Power to overthrow Rome, once again making Israel the premier Nation in the world. Of course, they would have powerful positions in this Kingdom.

Believing this error, they believed nothing else! Consequently, they could not recognize Him, and neither can anyone who is saddled with unbelief.

This is the reason that some Believers, who are registering unbelief, can be right in the middle of a Move of the Spirit of God, actually, with the Spirit moving mightily at times, and yet, not see or understand what is going on. There is no faith, so they do not see! Unbelief blinds while Faith enlightens!

"And that He had spoken these things unto her," portrays her telling them exactly what Jesus had said.

They probably would not have accused her of lying but, obviously, they did believe that, in her grief, she was hallucinating.

(19) "THEN THE SAME DAY AT EVENING, BEING THE FIRST DAY OF THE WEEK, WHEN THE DOORS WERE SHUT WHERE THE DISCIPLES WERE ASSEMBLED FOR FEAR OF THE JEWS, CAME JESUS AND STOOD IN THE MIDST, AND SAID UNTO THEM, PEACE BE UNTO YOU."

The order is:

1. *"My Sabbath you shall keep"* (Ex. 31:14). What distinguishes God's People is participation in God's Rest.

2. Christ is God's Rest (Heb., Chpt. 4).

3. The honor or dishonor done to the Sabbath was the test under the Law. The honor or dishonor done to Christ was the test under Grace.

4. Death was the penalty for dishonoring the Sabbath of the Old Testament. A similar penalty attaches to dishonoring Christ, i.e., spiritual death.

THE FIRST DAY OF THE WEEK

The phrase, *"Then the same day at evening, being the first day of the week,"* proclaims the first gathering on a Sunday. It is clear that Christ honored this day two times to meet with His Disciples. Then, too, Pentecost came about on the first day of the week, and they had gathered at least one other first day during the 10 days of waiting for the Holy Spirit (Lk. 24:49; Acts 1:1-8; 2:1). Christians have been gathering ever since on the first day or Sunday (Acts 20:7; I Cor. 16:1-2).

"When the doors were shut where the Disciples were assembled for fear of the Jews," is believed by some to point to others who were present, along with the original Eleven. If, in fact, that were true, and it probably was, Joseph and Nicodemus would probably have been there as well. It is even possible that James and Jude, the Lord's Half-brothers, were present also, for, at some point in time, Jesus had appeared to James. Whatever happened at this meeting, we are not told, but it made an instant Believer out of the Lord's Brother in the flesh (I Cor. 15:7).

The *"fear"* here expressed pertained to the idea or thought that the religious authorities, having now murdered Jesus, may very well seek to do the same to His closest Followers. However, the Day of Pentecost would take away this *"fear"* and would instead present to them a boldness, which was the very opposite of their present experience.

JESUS CAME

The phrase, *"Came Jesus and stood in the midst,"* proclaims no instruction as to how this was done. From the Text, it seems that He just simply appeared before them without coming through a door, etc. Actually, the doors were locked, as the Scripture indicates, and He could appear or disappear at will.

Here we have a Revelation made to prepared minds of a new order of existence. This means that the Spiritual body, which Glorified Saints will have, becomes possessed with additional senses and powers of which we presently have no conception or experience. Therefore, the person clothed with such a body is alive to properties of matter and dimensions of space and active forces, all of which would be supernatural to us, considering how confined we are now and here (Reynolds).

What Christ manifested after the Resurrection is the kind of physical body and life that will eventually be the condition of all the Redeemed.

The phrase, *"And said unto them, Peace be unto you,"* presents a common salutation used by most all at that time.

However, whereas it was merely a form on the part of others as it was used, with Jesus, it was something else entirely. In other words, when He used the word *"peace,"* it meant something (Jn. 14:27; 16:33).

(20) "AND WHEN HE HAD SO SAID, HE SHOWED UNTO THEM HIS HANDS AND HIS SIDE. THEN WERE THE DISCIPLES GLAD, WHEN THEY SAW THE LORD."

The form is:

1. Whenever the people of Israel were numbered, in other words, a census taken, every person from 20 years old and above had to give a half shekel of silver, which was, in a sense, a tax. Silver was a symbol of Redemption.

2. All, whether rich or poor, had to give the same amount, signifying that Redemption, of which all of this was a Type, was the same for all.

3. This, no doubt, is one of the reasons the Lord grew incensed with David when he numbered the people. Every evidence is that David ignored the census tax, which meant that he, in effect, was ignoring the very basis of Israel's existence — the shed Blood of the Lamb.

HIS HANDS, HIS SIDE, HIS FEET

The phrase, *"And when He had so said, He showed unto them His Hands and His Side,"* had to do with His Wounds, which proved He was not a spirit, but rather a Human with a Human Body while, at the same time, God.

Luke added, *"His Hands and His Feet"* (Lk. 24:39). John calls attention to the special Wound in His Sacred Side, the making of which he had so closely described and verified (Jn. 19:33-35).

As well, Jesus portraying to them these Wounds was not only to prove that He was Resurrected, Real, and Alive before them but, as well, that He had died for them, paying the price for man's Redemption. These Wounds would ever testify to its veracity. He is the Living One Who was dead and is alive forevermore.

HIS SACRIFICIAL DEATH

Actually, John would later write concerning his Vision of the Throne of God, *"And in the midst of the Elders, stood a Lamb as it had been slain"* (Rev. 5:6). Thus, in His Greatest Glory, neither does He, nor can His People, forget His Sacrificial Death.

The phrase, *"Then were the Disciples glad, when they saw the Lord,"* means that the *"peace"* which they had not had, they now have. Jesus is alive!

THE GLADNESS

The *"gladness"* here mentioned is of such consequence that mere words fail to describe its complexity.

The greatest loss to any person is the loss of one's faith. It is somewhat like an earthquake. When such happens, and the ground begins to shake, nothing else is stable. Likewise it is with one's Faith!

Their Faith had been greatly tested and, in fact, had been found wanting. However, what little spark was left, and there definitely was some that remained, would now be greatly enhanced and strengthened by the Appearance of Christ. To be frank, He is still appearing through His Word and through the Person, Agency, Office, and Ministry of the Holy Spirit.

How many times have all of us been imprisoned by fear, as these locked doors represented, and then have the Lord to move within our hearts and lives with, all of a sudden, everything changing instantly. Maybe the problems did not leave, but the care of those problems was given to Him, which is where they belonged in the first place.

So, this appearance by Christ was meant to serve as a banishment of *"fear,"* even as His appearance to Mary Magdalene banished *"sorrow."* In other words, these appearances were not just for the people in question, but for any and all, and performed a great work of overcoming power in the hearts and lives of all who will believe.

(21) "THEN SAID JESUS TO THEM AGAIN, PEACE BE UNTO YOU: AS MY FATHER HAS SENT ME, EVEN SO SEND I YOU."

The diagram is:

1. *"And he believed in the LORD; and He counted it to him for Righteousness"* (Gen. 15:6). If one understands this Passage, then one has a working knowledge of the Bible.

2. *"He believed in the LORD."* What does that mean?

3. It means that Abraham believed that God ultimately would send a Redeemer into this world and would do so through his (Abraham's) offspring.

PEACE

The phrase, *"Then said Jesus to them again, Peace be unto you,"* is said by design.

The first *"Peace"* gave to all who were assembled a new Revelation.

The second *"Peace"* was a summons to service, as we shall see.

"As My Father has sent Me, even so

send I you," pertains to the Great Commission of taking the Gospel of Jesus Christ to the world.

In other words, the Father had sent Him on a special Commission, which He had carried out to the letter, and now He is sending us on a special Commission, which we are to carry out as well.

(22) "AND WHEN HE HAD SAID THIS, HE BREATHED ON THEM, AND SAID UNTO THEM, RECEIVE YE THE HOLY SPIRIT."

The overview is:

1. Leviticus, Chapter 16, describes the Great Day of Atonement.

2. It occurred once a year. There was no other day like it. It dealt with the sins of the whole Nation for 12 months. It foreshadowed the Lamb of God taking away the sin of the world (Jn. 1:29).

3. Abel's lamb redeemed one man; the Paschal lamb, one family; the Day of Atonement lamb, one Nation; the Lamb of Calvary, the whole world.

RECEIVE THE HOLY SPIRIT

The phrase, *"And when He had said this, He breathed on them,"* presents the same act performed in Genesis 2:7. There He breathed Life, both physical and spiritual, into lifeless man.

Now, He breathes Spiritual Life into those who are powerless. Into Adam, He breathed the Breath of Life, and now, upon His Sons and Daughters, He breathes the Holy Spirit.

"And said unto them, Receive the Holy Spirit," has reference to the fact that the Spirit was to be their Guard and their Teacher for the Mission on which He sent them. He Himself, as sent by the Father, had received the same Spirit, but without measure (Lk. 4:18-19).

They did not, in fact, receive the Holy Spirit at this time but were made ready to receive Him on the Day of Pentecost, which they did. In essence, Jesus was saying to them that what He did at Calvary and the Resurrection would now make it possible for them, and all Believers for that matter, to *"receive,"* or to be baptized with the Holy Spirit (Jn. 7:39; Acts 2:4).

NOTES

(23) "WHOSE SOEVER SINS YOU REMIT, THEY ARE REMITTED UNTO THEM; AND WHOSE SOEVER SINS YOU RETAIN, THEY ARE RETAINED."

The exegesis is:

1. The darkness that was here prevalent (Gen. 1:2) was taken away only by the *"Spirit of God"* as He *"moved upon the face of the waters."*

2. As someone has well said, *"The Moving of the Holy Spirit is the first sign of Life."*

3. There is a darkness in the heart and life of every unbeliever. Regrettably, there is also a *"darkness"* in the hearts and lives of many Believers because of wrong direction, erroneous doctrine, or failing to take advantage of God's Prescribed Order of Victory.

SINS

The Prophets of old were stated to personally perform that which they were commissioned to declare, which, in reality, was performed by the Lord. Ignorance of this Hebraism originated the huge edifice of auricular confession and priestly absolution performed by Catholic priests.

The phrase, *"Whose soever sins you remit, they are remitted unto them,"* in its simplest form means that when the Gospel of Jesus Christ is preached and then accepted by sinners, the Preacher of the Gospel, or any Believer, for that matter, can announce unequivocally to the new Believer that all his sins are *"remitted,"* i.e., *"forgiven."*

THE RETAINING OF SINS

The phrase, *"And whose soever sins you retain, they are retained,"* is the same as the former, but exactly opposite. In other words, if the Gospel is refused, the Believer has the obligation and responsibility to inform the Christ-rejecter that despite whatever else he might do, he is still in his sins and barring Repentance, will suffer the consequences.

This means that every Preacher of the Gospel and, in fact, all Believers, as stated, are obligated to point out false doctrine. It is not pleasant to say, nor is it pleasant to hear, but the Catholic must be told that his church cannot save him, and all of the sins he has confessed to the priests are, in fact, not forgiven, *"but retained."* The same would go for Mormonism and all other false religions of the world.

As well, all Church members must be informed that the Church, irrespective of its association, cannot save. Faith in Christ alone saves! Unequivocally, that speaks of one having a personal relationship with Christ and not something that is done by proxy, such as joining a church. Such, in fact, offers no salvation simply because individuals have mistaken the church for Christ.

At the same time, the obligation and privilege of telling one that upon Faith in Christ, his sins are forgiven, also draws strong opposition in many religious circles. The idea that one can have all sins washed away by simple Faith in Christ without works or merit and, as well, have the Righteousness of God freely imputed is offensive to some!

(24) "BUT THOMAS, ONE OF THE TWELVE, CALLED DIDYMUS, WAS NOT WITH THEM WHEN JESUS CAME."

The exposition is:

1. Genesis 3:15 presents the first mention of the Cross, although in shadow.

2. The Lord told Satan through the serpent that Victory would come by the *"Seed of the woman."* Ironically, woman has no seed, with the exception of One Who was and is the Lord Jesus Christ.

3. Christ bruised the head of Satan and did so at Calvary's Cross. That's where Satan was totally and completely defeated (Col. 2:14-15).

THOMAS

The phrase, *"But Thomas, one of the Twelve, called Didymus,"* simply means he was a twin.

Many refer to him as *"doubting Thomas"* because he doubted, but, on the same basis, we can call all the Apostles doubters and unbelievers (Mat. 28:17; Mk. 16:11-14; Lk. 24:11, 25, 41; Jn. 20:27).

He simply had not been with the others when Christ had appeared. He lost out by not being faithful together with the rest, and so it is today (Heb. 10:25).

Thomas is supposed to have labored in India and left many Christian Converts. Here, idol priests tortured him with red-hot plates and then cast him, it is said, into an oven, which had no effect on him. They then pierced him with spears while in the furnace until he died. Saint Jerome says that his body, unconsumed, was buried at a town called Calamina.

TWELVE

As well, the number *"Twelve"* is important. Of course, Judas had long since been replaced by Matthias by the time John wrote this Gospel.

"Twelve," in effect, stands for God's Government.

The phrase, *"Was not with them when Jesus came,"* should present a lesson to all!

The lesson of Thomas should teach all of us how important it is for each and every Believer to be in church every single time its doors are open, at least when and where possible. With the understanding that particular types of employment do not allow some to be in every Service, still, as stated, when and where possible, every Service should be attended.

The reason is obvious, exactly as portrayed in the experience of Thomas. The very time he was not there, Jesus appeared, which was of supreme significance.

As well, one never knows what the Holy Spirit will do in any and each Service; therefore, every Service must be attended. To not do so, at least where possible, portrays a lack of concern or regard for the Spiritual needs within our lives.

I must come to the conclusion that Believers who do not take advantage of every Service, at least where possible, are not as concerned about their Spiritual welfare as they should be.

FOUR GROUPS

In reality, a Church has four groups of people attending its Services:

1. The person who calls himself a Believer but pretty much attends when he feels like it, which probably refers to a couple of times a month, if that!

2. The Believer who comes only on Sunday mornings, completely ignoring all other Services.

3. The Believer who comes to Sunday morning Services and mid-week Services but sees no need to come on Sunday nights. At times, it is reversed, with the individual coming on Sunday nights but not to the mid-week Services.

4. The Believer who faithfully attends every Service.

Please understand, if a Believer who has a problem in his or her life will evidence Faith, the Lord will tailor-make a special Service just for that Believer. However, if the Believer is absent. . . .

(25) "THE OTHER DISCIPLES THEREFORE SAID UNTO HIM, WE HAVE SEEN THE LORD. BUT HE SAID UNTO THEM, EXCEPT I SHALL SEE IN HIS HANDS THE PRINT OF THE NAILS, AND PUT MY FINGER INTO THE PRINT OF THE NAILS, AND THRUST MY HAND INTO HIS SIDE, I WILL NOT BELIEVE."

The structure is:

1. Immediately after the Fall, Adam and Eve lost the light which had enswathed them before the Fall. They were now naked and, more than all, naked to the Judgment of God (Gen. 3:7).

2. As a result, they *"sewed fig leaves together and made themselves aprons."*

3. Regrettably, man has been trying to cover his Spiritual nakedness with fig leaves from then until now.

WE HAVE SEEN THE LORD

The phrase, *"The other Disciples therefore said unto him, We have seen the Lord,"* was, in fact, the greatest announcement that had ever been made.

"But he said unto them, Except I shall see in His Hands the print of the nails, and put my finger into the print of the nails, and thrust my hand into His Side," proclaims a very harsh and ugly position on the part of Thomas. To speak of the terrible wounds suffered by our Lord at Calvary in such a cavalier fashion presents the results of unbelief. As it was in Thomas at that time, so it is in all who fail to believe what God is doing.

The phrase, *"I will not believe,"* is presented as *"unreasonable, obstinate, rebellious, prejudicial, presumptuous, insolent, stubborn, self-willed, boastful, insensible, hardening, and deceitful."*

(26) "AND AFTER EIGHT DAYS AGAIN HIS DISCIPLES WERE WITHIN, AND THOMAS WITH THEM: THEN CAME JESUS, THE DOORS BEING SHUT, AND STOOD IN THE MIDST, AND SAID, PEACE BE UNTO YOU."

The pattern is:

1. When Adam and Eve had to answer to the Lord for their failure, the Bible tells us that the Lord God *"made coats of skins, and clothed them."* For this to be done, the Lord had to kill one or more animals, which necessitated blood being shed.

2. The skins were then taken from these animals and used to supply clothing or a covering for Adam and Eve.

3. The death of the animal or animals was the First Symbol of Christ, Who would give His Life in order to cover the sins of man.

4. Anything man attempts to use to cover his sins, other than the precious shed Blood of the Lord Jesus Christ, is looked at by God as *"fig leaves,"* rating it totally unacceptable.

5. The Blood of Jesus Christ alone can cleanse from all sin, which then makes possible the Righteousness of God as a covering — all made possible by the Cross (I Jn. 1:7).

THE FIRST DAY OF THE WEEK

The phrase, *"And after eight days again His Disciples were within, and Thomas with them,"* presents Jesus meeting with them again on Sunday, the first day of the week, the day of His Resurrection.

Six more Sundays after this eighth day after the Resurrection made 50 days, the Day of Pentecost. His Time on the other four Sundays while He remained on Earth with them was spent in teaching (Acts 1:3).

The fortieth day or Thursday, He ascended (Acts 1:11). This left 10 days until the second Sunday after His Ascension, and the seventh Sunday after His Resurrection, which was the fiftieth day or Pentecost (Lev. 23:15-16; Acts 2:1).

What Christ did between Sundays is not known. He might have used part of this to teach also; however, we know that He did not teach the first week between Sundays.

"Then came Jesus, the doors being shut, and stood in the midst," proclaims His Entrance exactly as at the first. He just simply appeared before them in the room, seemingly without coming through the door, the walls, etc.

The phrase, *"And said, Peace be unto you,"* presents, once again, the familiar greeting.

(27) "THEN SAID HE TO THOMAS, REACH HITHER YOUR FINGER, AND BEHOLD MY HANDS; AND REACH HITHER YOUR HAND, AND THRUST IT INTO MY SIDE: AND BE NOT FAITHLESS, BUT BELIEVING."

The form is:

1. There was no difference between the two brothers, Cain and Abel, but an eternal difference between their sacrifices.

2. They were both corrupt branches of a decayed tree, both born outside of Eden, both guilty, both sinners, no moral difference, and both sentenced to death.

3. The words *"By Faith"* in Hebrews 11:4 teach us that God had revealed a way of approach to Himself (Rom. 10:17). Abel accepted this way, which is the way of the Cross, but Cain rejected it.

ANOTHER APPEARANCE OF CHRIST

The phrase, *"Then said He to Thomas,"* seems as if He made this Appearance solely for Thomas.

What Love!

"Reach here your finger, and behold My Hands; and reach here your hand, and thrust it into My Side," presents Jesus, at least in the latter phrase, using the same words that Thomas had used, showing that He knew exactly what Thomas had said.

"And be not faithless," presents Thomas coming close to this darkness, which, if continued, could have resulted in the loss of his soul.

How many alleged Believers today are, in fact, *"faithless,"* and, therefore, *"unbelievers"*?

Millions who claim Salvation are presently *"faithless"* respecting the Acceptance of Jesus Alone regarding Redemption. In fact, these people are not saved but only religious.

FAITHLESS

Others are genuinely Saved but are *"faithless"* respecting the mighty Baptism with the Holy Spirit (Acts 2:4). Consequently, there is no growth in the Lord on their part, and, in fact, *"faithlessness,"* as leaven, if not rooted out, will ultimately corrupt the whole.

It was not possible for Thomas to not believe that Jesus had been raised from the dead and retain his Salvation. So, that which Jesus said is so very, very important.

The phrase, *"But believing,"* simply means, *"Have Faith!"*

Every evidence is that Thomas did exactly that!

Faith begets Faith while unbelief begets unbelief!

As well, this Appearance of Christ addressed the life problem of *"doubt."*

(28) "AND THOMAS ANSWERED AND SAID UNTO HIM, MY LORD AND MY GOD."

The order is:

1. Abel's Altar was beautiful to God's Eye and repulsive to man's. Cain's altar was beautiful to man's eye but repulsive to God's.

2. These *"altars"* exist today. Around the one, that is, Christ and His Atoning Work, few are gathered; around the other, many.

3. God accepts the slain lamb and rejects the offered fruit. With the offering being rejected, of necessity, so is the offerer.

4. The only Sacrifice that God will accept is *"Jesus Christ and Him Crucified"* (I Cor. 1:17).

MY LORD AND MY GOD

There is no evidence that Thomas touched the Wounds of the Master; however, that which Jesus did and said brought out the greatest proclamation of Faith recorded to date of the Disciples.

This is not a mere exclamation but one of the plainest and most irresistible Testimonies of the Deity of Jesus Christ.

Respecting the phrase, *"My Lord and my God,"* Thomas was the first to give this title to Jesus, other than the Prophets predicting these events (Isa. 9:6-7; Ps. 45:6-7).

Thomas here prefigures the unbelieving

Hebrew Nation who will not believe until they look upon Him Whom they have pierced. In rebuking Him, the Lord gave a Precious Promised Blessing to those who, having not seen Him, yet love Him.

Christ accepted Divine Worship from Thomas, who confessed Him as Jehovah and Elohim, the Mighty and One God of Genesis, Chapters 1 and 2.

Had Jesus been only conscious of humanity, He would have rebuked Thomas: however, He accepted these Titles and the worship. As we shall see, the words of Verse 29 disprove the assertion that Thomas' exclamation was only that common to man when greatly surprised — such an expression of astonishment as *"O! My God."*

No, it was not that, but it was Thomas giving Jesus the Title, which He most definitely deserved.

(29) "JESUS SAID UNTO HIM, THOMAS, BECAUSE YOU HAVE SEEN ME, YOU HAVE BELIEVED: BLESSED ARE THEY WHO HAVE NOT SEEN, AND YET HAVE BELIEVED."

The form is:

1. The only way to God is through Jesus Christ (Jn. 14:6).

2. The only way to Jesus Christ is through the Cross (Lk. 14:27).

3. The only way to the Cross is by an abnegation of self (Lk. 9:23).

BELIEVING

The phrase, *"Jesus said unto him, Thomas, because you have seen Me, you have believed,"* presents the lowest form of Faith. Regrettably, the other Disciples fell into the same category, and yet, all had gone through a great trauma. They had seen Him brutally murdered, and now it was hard to believe that He was gloriously alive.

"Blessed are they who have not seen, and yet have believed," concerns the entirety of the Church through all ages. Only a few actually saw Him, at least in comparison to the hundreds of millions who have accepted Him since but yet have not seen Him! This is a higher type of Faith, as should be obvious.

And yet, millions of Christians actually have the same attitude as Thomas. They demand to see some type of sign before they will ultimately believe. Actually, most probably fall into this category.

The criterion must always be the Word of God and not particular signs or things one can observe with the eye. Lest we are too hard on the Disciples, we should take a close look at ourselves. With most of us, unless the Lord continues to reinforce His Word, we soon lose courage, with our Faith getting weaker and weaker.

(30) "AND MANY OTHER SIGNS TRULY DID JESUS IN THE PRESENCE OF HIS DISCIPLES, WHICH ARE NOT WRITTEN IN THIS BOOK."

The pattern is:

1. The Lord *"smells a sweet savor"* only as it regards our Faith in Christ and what He did for us at the Cross.

2. This means that everything else is repugnant to Him, coming up rather as a *"stink"* in His Nostrils.

3. That rules out every fad and every scheme, anything and everything, for that matter, which is not anchored solely in *"Jesus Christ and Him Crucified"* (I Cor. 1:23).

SIGNS

The phrase, *"And many other signs truly did Jesus in the presence of His Disciples,"* covers several areas.

In fact, Jesus performed many Miracles, which are recorded by the other Evangelists, but not John. As well, no doubt, He performed many Miracles which were not recorded at all!

For instance, there are only three incidents recorded of Jesus raising the dead. However, Augustine, who lived about 350 years after Christ, proclaimed that Jesus raised many others from the dead, as well, which He, no doubt, did!

"Which are not written in this Book," refers to the Gospel of John.

Now, referring to this statement by John, this was the chance for the writers of the apocryphal gospels, which, incidentally, are not valid, of which they were not slow to avail themselves.

(31) "BUT THESE ARE WRITTEN, THAT YOU MIGHT BELIEVE THAT JESUS IS THE CHRIST, THE SON OF GOD; AND

THAT BELIEVING YOU MIGHT HAVE LIFE THROUGH HIS NAME."

The composition is:

1. The only way that one can converse with the Lord is that his or her Faith be anchored squarely in Christ and the Cross.

2. That's the reason that Abraham had to build a new Altar everywhere he went. There was no other way to converse with the Lord.

3. It has not changed even unto this moment. Man can come to God only by the way of the Cross (I Cor. 2:2).

THAT YOU MIGHT BELIEVE

The phrase, *"But these are written, that you might believe that Jesus is the Christ, the Son of God,"* pertains to the fact that John did not feel led of the Holy Spirit to record great numbers of Miracles, but that his Book is to make prominent the Eternal Life, which all who believe in Him apart from Miracles and material vision, receive.

The phrase, *"And that believing you might have Life through His Name,"* proclaims that the Holy Spirit desires that Faith accept the Testimony of the Scripture that Jesus of Nazareth is the Messiah officially, and the Son of God essentially, and that whoever believes in Him shall live Eternally in ever-enduring bliss.

> *"Far dearer than all that the world can impart,*
> *"Was the Message that came to my heart;*
> *"How that Jesus Alone for my sin did atone,*
> *"And Calvary covers it all."*
>
> *"Calvary covers it all,*
> *"My past with its sin and stain.*
> *"My guilt and despair Jesus took on Him there,*
> *"And Calvary covers it all."*

CHAPTER 21

(1) "AFTER THESE THINGS JESUS SHOWED HIMSELF AGAIN TO THE DISCIPLES AT THE SEA OF TIBERIAS; AND ON THIS WISE SHOWED HE HIMSELF."

The structure is:

1. *"These things"* refer to the happenings with Thomas and the other Disciples.

2. Now our Lord will make another appearance to these men, which will be at the Sea of Galilee.

3. The manner in which He will reveal Himself will address another acute life problem.

AFTER THESE THINGS

The phrase, *"After these things Jesus showed Himself again to the Disciples,"* proclaims the fact that Jesus only appeared, it seems, to those who were His Followers. Believers in Him were those alone who could see His Spiritual Body.

However, as we have stated, these, at best, only had weak Faith, at least as regarded the Resurrection of Christ, but, still, there was some Faith! Actually, the principle is the same.

The Lord reveals Himself to hungry, searching hearts. To be sure, He definitely will reveal Himself to the unsaved, which, in fact, He does constantly. It is done in a variety of ways, such as the preaching of the Gospel, the witnessing of a friend, or any number of other ways. Still, it is to a searching heart, irrespective as to how sinful and wicked that individual may be.

PROFESSORS OF RELIGION!

However, it seems that the Scripture is clear that the Lord little reveals Himself to the professor of religion, one who has opted for his own righteousness instead of that provided by the Lord. A perfect case in point is the Pharisees. That door was shut! They did not desire Christ because they did not actually desire reality within their lives. As well, they saw no need for the Righteousness provided for by God but were satisfied with their own self-righteousness. In truth, this is the hardest group of people in the world to reach for Christ.

They fall into the category of saying, *"I am rich, and increased with goods, and have need of nothing."*

Jesus said of them, *"And knowest not that you are wretched, and miserable, and poor, and blind, and naked."*

He then said, *"I counsel you to buy of Me gold tried in the fire, that you may be rich; and white raiment, that you may be clothed, and that the shame of your nakedness do not appear; and anoint your eyes with eyesalve, that you may see"* (Rev. 3:17-18).

SELF-RIGHTEOUSNESS AND THE CROSS OF CHRIST

If one places one's faith in anything other than the Cross of Christ, irrespective as to how correct and right the other thing might be in its own way, still, such direction will lead to self-righteousness every single time. In fact, the only cure for self-righteousness is the Cross of Christ.

The very term, *"Self-righteousness,"* speaks of an effort being made to obtain Righteousness in a way other than the Cross of Christ.

The phrase, *"At the Sea of Tiberias,"* refers to the Sea of Galilee and occasions the only time this name is used in the Gospels.

In fact, by the time John wrote his Gospel, which was about A.D. 90, Israel had been pretty much destroyed by the Romans. Jerusalem was now a smoking ruin. The Temple was no more. As well, the familiar cities around the Sea of Galilee were all but destroyed, with the exception of Tiberias.

In truth, all of this was a fulfillment of what Jesus had said about these cities, which had experienced the greatest display of the operation of the power of God of any place in the world and for all time. In fact, the greater majority of the Ministry of Christ was carried out in these little cities, with Capernaum actually serving as His Headquarters (Mat. 11:21).

The city of Tiberias was the only town left on the lake, and it seems this body of water came to be known by that name.

There is no record that Jesus ever visited the city of Tiberias.

TIBERIAS

The city of Tiberias was founded by Herod Antipas about A.D. 20 and named after the emperor Tiberias. Actually, Herod made the city his capital.

Some of the buildings of the city were built on ground that included a former graveyard and so rendered the city unclean in Jewish eyes, which may be the reason Jesus did not visit there, if, in fact, He did not. It was a thoroughly Gentile city, and He seems to have avoided it in favor of the numerous Jewish towns on the lakeshore.

However, after the destruction of Jerusalem in A.D. 70, Tiberias became a chief seat of Jewish learning, with many great Jewish works, such as the Talmud, compiled there.

I have personally been to this city many times and have stood on the balcony of the hotel room where we were staying, looking out over the Sea of Galilee, I suppose, for hours on end. Tiberias sits on the western shore of that lake, about two-thirds distance toward its southern extremity.

THE FOURTH APPEARANCE OF CHRIST

The phrase, *"And on this wise showed He Himself,"* represents the fourth appearance of the Lord, at least in the context of His great Victories over various life problems.

As we shall see, seven Apostles were present at this appearance, Apostles, we might add, who, in that early morning hour, were tired, dejected, friendless, and without sustenance. They were filled with care, anxiety, and perplexity, despite the previous appearances by Christ.

It was a desperate position. However, this fourth appearance of the Lord dismissed their *"care"* and provided them with an abundant breakfast, with the fellowship of Him Who brought with Himself all Heaven in its fullness and the cattle on a thousand hills for their sustenance. Thus, these four apparitions banished four enemies, as we have stated, i.e., *"sorrow"* (the appearance to Mary Magdalene), *"fear"* (the appearance to all the Apostles in Jerusalem, with the exception of Thomas), *"doubt"* (the appearance the following Sunday to all the Disciples including Thomas), and now, Jesus would address the problem of *"care."*

SPIRITUAL LIFE

As we shall see, Jesus does not now appear to visible eyesight inasmuch as they did not recognize Him on the Galilee shore.

Consequently, He first manifested Himself to the spiritual consciousness, and such appearances have the same moral power to all at present as it did that day so long ago. Actually, this is that of which we spoke regarding Jesus revealing Himself presently, and for all time, to hungry hearts.

Spiritual Life originates in a manifestation of the Lord Jesus Christ to the soul (Mat. 11:27), and that Life is sustained by a repetition of such manifestations. As well, these manifestations are not confined to houses of prayer and worship but may be enjoyed in the ordinary places of daily toil, as represented by this great happening by the Sea of Tiberias.

The word *"showed"* would have probably been better translated *"manifested."* It means not only to reveal Himself but also His Power. In fact, He loves to manifest Himself *"again"* and *"again"* to His Disciples.

(2) "THERE WERE TOGETHER SIMON PETER, AND THOMAS CALLED DIDYMUS, AND NATHANAEL OF CANA IN GALILEE, AND THE SONS OF ZEBEDEE, AND TWO OTHER OF HIS DISCIPLES."

The pattern is:

1. *"Beth-el"* means *"House of God." "Hai"* means *"garbage dump."*
2. The Altar alone, typifying the Cross, can keep the Believer away from the garbage dump.
3. It is virtually impossible for the Believer to know the difference between the *"House of God"* and the *"garbage dump,"* other than by the Cross.

HIS DISCIPLES

The phrase, *"There were together Simon Peter,"* represents, I think, that even though having failed, Peter had not lost his Faith. Actually, Jesus had told him that He would pray that his Faith fail not, and one can be assured that this prayer was answered (Lk. 22:31-32).

As well, I think we can derive from this description concerning Peter being named first that he still stood at the head of the company. The man who was a rock and the man of impetuous energy was recognized thus so by the Holy Spirit. This should proclaim to us the grace of God in that the losing of a battle is not the loss of the war.

The phrase, *"And Thomas called Didymus,"* portrays to us his new-found solid position in Christ. His faithlessness had vanished, with his love emerging from the depths of despondency to the loftiest Faith, and had come to feel and say that the risen Christ was both Lord and God. Thomas, who had formerly shrunk from the society of his fellow Apostles, was now closely united with them, more than he ever previously had seemed to be.

"And Nathanael of Cana in Galilee," places this Apostle, at least regarding his hometown, in the little city where Jesus had performed His First Miracle by changing the water to wine.

The phrase, *"And the sons of Zebedee,"* pointed to James and John.

"And two other of His Disciples," gives us no clue as to their identity.

(3) "SIMON PETER SAID UNTO THEM, I GO A FISHING. THEY SAY UNTO HIM, WE ALSO GO WITH YOU. THEY WENT FORTH, AND ENTERED INTO A SHIP IMMEDIATELY; AND THAT NIGHT THEY CAUGHT NOTHING."

The structure is:

1. Without an understanding of the Cross of Christ, there is absolutely no discernment regarding false doctrine.
2. The Holy Spirit tells us (I Tim. 4:1) that in the last days there would be a *"departure from the Faith."*
3. *"The Faith"* constitutes *"Christ and Him Crucified,"* i.e., *"the Cross of Christ."*

FISHING

The phrase, *"Simon Peter said unto them, I go a fishing,"* presents such as being carried out without prayer, or so it seems. As a result, they caught nothing.

A Christian ministry originating in the energy of the carnal will, which secures the cooperation of others by its effect and sympathy, is sunless and fruitless. However, when it is under the governance of the Head of the Church, it is full of sunshine and rich in fruit.

Even though the Scripture is not clear, it seems this fishing expedition was not for pleasure but because of the necessity of making a living for their families.

JESUS

For the past three and one-half years, Jesus had met their every single need. Thousands were flocking to His Side constantly, at least the first two and one-half years, with every type of Miracle being performed. This, no doubt, caused many to give liberally of their means respecting finances, etc. At any rate, there is no hint whatsoever that any of the families connected with Jesus were lacking in any manner respecting money. This is considerable when one realizes that the party which sometimes traveled with Jesus was quite large, considering that, at one time, He sent out 70 men other than the original Twelve.

Even though the Twelve stayed with Him constantly, it is not clear if the Seventy were there all the time. At any rate, considering that all of the Twelve were breadwinners, with even possibly some of the others being full-time, as well, one must come to the conclusion that the expenses were quite high, considering all of these families.

Despite all the traumatic events which had taken place in the last few days, and considering that Jesus was now alive, still, it, no doubt, entered Peter's mind, as well as others, as to how they would now make a living. Consequently, the life problem of *"care"* now loomed large in front of them. So, this is the reason, I believe, that he was fishing this night, along with the others, on the Sea of Galilee. He was trying, as stated, to make a living for his family.

THEY CAUGHT NOTHING

The phrase, *"They say unto him, We also go with you,"* presents the other six Disciples. Where the other four were at this time, we are not told.

"They went forth, and entered into a ship immediately," probably referred to one of the vessels formerly used by Peter and the sons of Zebedee in their former fishing business.

"And that night they caught nothing," points to the fact that they were doing this for income and not for pleasure. Had it been for pleasure, they would not have stayed

NOTES

that long, considering that the fish did not seem to be running.

It is easy for us to criticize them for a lack of faith, but due to the events, I am certain, as stated, that they were now wondering as to how they could make a living. Actually, at this stage, they really did not know what they were going to do.

The way the Text reads, or rather hints, in their minds, they somewhat thought that it was all over. If that were their thoughts, they were in for a great surprise!

(4) "BUT WHEN THE MORNING WAS NOW COME, JESUS STOOD ON THE SHORE: BUT THE DISCIPLES KNEW NOT THAT IT WAS JESUS."

The composition is:

1. Thank God, the morning will come, even after a dark night.

2. Jesus was now on the scene.

3. But yet, the Disciples did not recognize Him at first.

THE MORNING HAS NOW COME

The phrase, *"But when the morning was now come, Jesus stood on the shore,"* presents the beginning of one of the most valuable lessons the Disciples would ever learn.

"But the Disciples knew not that it was Jesus," once again portrays the same experience as held by others.

In all the post-Resurrection appearances, with possibly the exception of the times Jesus suddenly appeared in the room where the Disciples had gathered, He was not recognizable. Mary thought He was a gardener, with the two Disciples on the way to Emmaus thinking He was a stranger (Lk. 24:13-32). Now He appears again, with them not knowing Who He is, at least at the outset.

As I have already alluded, I feel that this was done by Christ for reason and purpose. It was a test of Faith, as everything that happens to the Believer is a test of Faith in one way or the other. They must learn to take Him at His Word and not demand that which they can see with the eyes or touch with the hands.

While it was necessary that certain people see Him after the Resurrection, for the obvious reasons, still, the greatest lesson must be that of Faith.

He had told them that He would *"be killed, and be raised again the third day,"* which had obviously happened (Mat. 16:21). However, most of that which would happen from here forward would be on the basis solely of the Word of God. Consequently, their Faith must be anchored in the Word, which they were now being taught.

(5) "THEN JESUS SAID UNTO THEM, CHILDREN, HAVE YOU ANY MEAT? THEY ANSWERED HIM, NO."

The overview is:

1. The effect of the birth of Isaac was to make manifest the character of Ishmael (Gen. 21:9-10).

2. The birth of Isaac, which was a work of the Holy Spirit that filled Sarah's heart with joy, filled Hagar's, who was a work of the flesh, with murder.

3. Isaac and Ishmael symbolize the new and the old natures in the Believer.

JESUS SPEAKS TO THE DISCIPLES

The question, *"Then Jesus said unto them, Children, have you any meat?"* was meant to draw them out. In effect, He was asking them if they had any food for breakfast as it was now early morning. They had fished all night but without success.

Also, some think that His Question may have suggested that they thought He was attempting to purchase fish. Actually, the word *"meat"* was used in this fashion and could refer to fish or lambs, or any type of food for that matter.

The phrase, *"They answered Him, No!"* presents a somewhat listless answer and showed their lack of success for a night's work.

(6) "AND HE SAID UNTO THEM, CAST THE NET ON THE RIGHT SIDE OF THE SHIP, AND YOU SHALL FIND. THEY CAST THEREFORE, AND NOW THEY WERE NOT ABLE TO DRAW IT FOR THE MULTITUDE OF FISHES."

The diagram is:

1. In your Bible, Hagar and Sarah typify the two covenants of works and Grace, of bondage and liberty (Gal., Chpt. 4).

2. The birth of the New Nature demands the expulsion of the old.

3. It is impossible, in fact, to improve the old nature.

4. How foolish, therefore, appears the doctrine of moral evolution!

5. Man's way of holiness is to improve the *"old man,"* that is, to improve Ishmael. The effort is both foolish and hopeless.

THE SUPERNATURAL POWER OF GOD

The phrase, *"And He said unto them, Cast the net on the right side of the ship, and you shall find,"* gives us no hint if they knew this was Jesus at this stage. There is indication in the Fifth Verse that they did by now recognize Him and some indication in the Seventh Verse that could go either way.

Being professional fishermen, it seems unlikely they would have placed any credence in the simple instructions of a stranger to cast the net on the right side of the ship, especially considering the assurance given that it would result in a great catch! They had toiled all night and had taken nothing, and the mere suggestion of throwing the net a few yards from their present location must have seemed ludicrous!

And yet, is it possible that the cadence of His Words and the authority of His Command caused them to suspect that this just might be Jesus? The next Verse says, *"No,"* and at the same time, *"Yes!"* The recognition factor in the phrase, *"It is the Lord,"* even though after the fact, seems to contain a suspicion as well!

I personally think they obeyed so quickly simply because John suspected it was Jesus.

THE MULTITUDE OF FISH

The phrase, *"They cast therefore,"* seems to indicate that they had confidence in what He had instructed and, therefore, quickly obeyed.

"And now they were not able to draw it for the multitude of fish," presents the results of their obedience.

All night long and working tirelessly had produced nothing, but one Word from Jesus and the complexion changed entirely.

This appearance of Jesus addressed the life problem of *"care!"*

There is every evidence that they were fearful of being able to make a living for their families, that is, if they continued in the Ministry, especially considering that Jesus would no longer be with them. However, He was here telling them that He would, in fact, be with them and that every need would be met. He had shown them that His Miracle-working Power would still be available even though He, at least in a physical sense, would be gone. After the advent of the Holy Spirit, they would come to know this in a far grander and more expectant manner.

In fact, this catch was so large that they were unable to get the net containing the fish into the ship, and had to get the net to the shore by the use of a smaller vessel, as Verse 8 proclaims.

This is the manner in which God is able to answer prayer. This is the manner in which He will answer prayer, at least for all those who show Faith in His Word.

(7) "THEREFORE THAT DISCIPLE WHOM JESUS LOVED SAID UNTO PETER, IT IS THE LORD. NOW WHEN SIMON PETER HEARD THAT IT WAS THE LORD, HE GIRDED HIS FISHER'S COAT UNTO HIM, (FOR HE WAS NAKED,) AND DID CAST HIMSELF INTO THE SEA."

The exegesis is:

1. The name, *"Jehovah-jireh"* (Gen. 22:13-14) means *"the Lord will see"* or *"provide."*

2. What will He provide?

3. He will provide a Redeemer, which all of this represented, as it regards the proposed offering up of Isaac as a sacrifice.

SIMON PETER

The phrase, *"Therefore that Disciple whom Jesus loved said unto Peter, It is the Lord,"* referred to John the Beloved.

What had just happened was characteristic of Jesus. He was a Miracle Worker! He is a Miracle Worker! He ever shall be a Miracle Worker! *"Jesus Christ the same yesterday, and today, and forever"* (Heb. 13:8).

"Now when Simon Peter heard that it was the Lord," implies tremendous joy and anticipation on his part. In spite of the Miracle-working power of Christ that had produced the tremendous catch of fish, the Text will show that even though he was the one who instigated the fishing expedition, all interest was lost in these things, with Jesus now the primary Focus of the one referred to as the *"big fisherman!"*

NOTES

WITHOUT JESUS, NOTHING GOES RIGHT

The phrase, *"He girded his fisher's coat unto him, (for he was naked),"* does not refer to a total lack of clothing, for he was still dressed in a tunic. Evidently he had laid aside his outer garment in order that it not be soiled, etc.

"And did cast himself into the sea," proclaims such being done, not to aid regarding the overburdened net, but rather to come quickly to Jesus.

As we have stated, the only thing that mattered to him now was Jesus. Consequently, we should not be too hard on him for the fishing expedition for the simple reason that he little knew what to do at this stage. But now, all is well because Jesus is near.

This should be a lesson to all! Without the Lord, nothing goes right. Without Him, life has no purpose or meaning. However, with Him, with His Involvement and with His Participation, nothing anymore is mundane. With Him, mundane things are miraculously increased, such as the great catch of fish, when Jesus comes upon the scene. The idea is that one's eyes not become focused on those things which are incidental, but that we allow God's Blessings to perform the intended, which is to draw us closer to Christ.

(8) "AND THE OTHER DISCIPLES CAME IN A LITTLE SHIP; (FOR THEY WERE NOT FAR FROM LAND, BUT AS IT WERE TWO HUNDRED CUBITS,) DRAGGING THE NET WITH FISH."

The synopsis is:

1. The great test of Faith which the Lord required of Abraham, as it regards the proposed offering up of his son Isaac, was for the purpose of telling the great Patriarch how mankind would be delivered.

2. It would be by and through the Death of God's only Son, of which Isaac was a type.

3. However, as the Lord told Abraham of the manner of Redemption, which would be by death, He did not tell him how this death would be brought about, which would be by the Cross. That information would be given to Moses some 400 years later (Num. 21:8-9).

THE ABILITY OF CHRIST

The phrase, *"And the other Disciples came in a little ship,"* evidently refers to a smaller boat or dingy, which was often towed behind a larger vessel for whatever the need.

Due to the fact of the net being so laden with fish that these seven men could not get it into the main ship, the smaller vessel would come in handy.

"For they were not far from land, but as it were two hundred cubits," represented approximately 100 yards.

"Dragging the net with fish," represents a tremendous catch, which took only a few minutes, versus their night-long efforts, which had produced only an empty net. Such is the effort without Christ, and such is the effort with Christ!

Even though financial prosperity is not the goal and purpose of the great Ministry of Christ, with Salvation being that purpose and principle, still, as a peripheral work, Jesus Christ grandly and gloriously prospers His Followers economically, at least if they will believe Him. However, there is a danger in this, which we have seen in the last few years, relative to the modern *"greed gospel."*

THE PERSON OF CHRIST

The main focus must always be the Person of Christ, not only what He can do. Sadly, millions get their eyes on the great catch of fish, losing sight of Jesus, with Him only being used in this capacity, which is a corruption of the Gospel.

However, if one will studiously keep one's eyes upon Jesus, ever seeking to be like Him, the other things will follow, just as this great net full of fish.

Actually, whenever a person comes to Christ, that person enters into God's Economy. This is what Jesus was speaking of when He said, *"Take no thought for your life, what you shall eat, or what you shall drink; nor yet for your body, what you shall put on. Is not the life more than meat, and the body than raiment?"*

He then said, *"Behold the fowls of the air: for they sow not, neither do they reap, nor gather into barns; yet your Heavenly Father feeds them. Are you not much better than they?"* (Mat. 6:25-26).

GOD'S ECONOMY

Regarding the Scriptures just quoted, the Lord is saying that these creatures, irrespective of the simplicity of their creation, are in God's Economy, which guarantees their sustenance. Correspondingly, when the individual comes to Christ, he too, as stated, enters into God's Economy, which is the lesson Jesus is here teaching.

The reason there is so much starvation, hunger, privation, poverty, and want in the world is because the far greater majority of the world does not enjoy this privilege, rather saying that they can handle this task much better themselves. Of course, the fallacy of such an idea is obvious for all to see.

However, when a person turns to Christ, not only is Salvation from sin his due, which is the very ingredient of what Jesus has done simply because this is man's greatest need, but, as well, peripheral Blessings, such as economic prosperity, healing for the physical body, and the great Peace of God are also a part of this great economy. That is the reason Jesus said, *"Seek you first the Kingdom of God, and His Righteousness; and all these things shall be added unto you"* (Mat. 6:33).

JESUS, THE PRIMARY OBJECTIVE

Thank God, one day, and very soon we pray, God's Economy will rule and reign over the entirety of the world, which will eliminate poverty, sickness, sorrow, heartache, and everything that steals, kills, and destroys. Sin was handled at Calvary, but all the Fruit of what was done at Calvary has not yet been realized, but one day shall, and very soon!

However, as we have already stated, one must not get one's eyes on the peripheral Blessings at the expense of Christ. Jesus must ever be the Focal Point, the Primary Objective, and the Seeking of the soul.

So, the Disciples had caught absolutely nothing all night long, except their efforts and experience respecting the fishing business. However, now, due to the arrival of Jesus, they had so many fish in their net that they could not lift it into the ship, but rather had to drag it to land.

What a scene, a very wonderful scene this must have been!

(9) "AS SOON THEN AS THEY WERE COME TO LAND, THEY SAW A FIRE OF COALS THERE, AND FISH LAID THEREON, AND BREAD."

The synopsis is:

1. The birthright was to go to the firstborn. In this case, it was Esau. It pertained to the father's blessings involving supremacy. It also included a double portion of the family estate. Last of all, it concerned the domestic Priesthood.

2. The domestic Priesthood meant that the oldest son acted as Priest for the family and offered up sacrifices, which God had commanded Adam and his sons to offer.

3. Officiating the sacrifices meant that the firstborn knew and understood that this was a Symbol of the coming Redeemer. However, the Scripture says that Esau had no regard for any coming Redeemer. He was interested only in the now and present.

WHERE DID JESUS GET THE BREAD AND THE FISH?

The phrase, *"As soon then as they were come to land,"* represents only a short period of time to drag the heavily laden net the approximate 100 yards.

They now came to the shore with the net laden with fish, whereas if Jesus had not come, their net would have been empty.

"They saw a fire of coals there, and fish laid thereon, and bread," causes one to immediately ask the question as to where Jesus had secured this bread and fish. The next Verse proclaims that such did not come from the miraculous catch recently enjoyed.

One must remember that during those times of long ago, there were no ready provisions of supplies on every corner, as it basically is in many places presently. Anyway, it was only a little bit after daylight, which made it highly improbable that Jesus could have secured these provisions from a commercial outlet.

Some three and one-half years earlier, Jesus was tempted by Satan but would not, at the Evil One's suggestion, turn the stones to bread because that would have been a misuse of His Power. Now, I personally

NOTES

believe that He did exactly that. Whereas He would not use His Power for Himself, He used it constantly for others, even as He now did.

I see no corruption of the Scripture, but rather validation, to believe that Jesus actually turned stones into bread and fish. He had multiplied five loaves and two fish into enough food to feed well over 10,000 people. So, why not believe that this breakfast which He prepared was produced on the same Miracle-working basis?

So, the provision, which was thus made in advance for the need of the Disciples, becomes symbolic of Christ's Power to meet all the wants and needs of this dying world.

(10) "JESUS SAID UNTO THEM, BRING OF THE FISH WHICH YOU HAVE NOW CAUGHT."

The exposition is:

1. Jacob, deplorable as was his character, valued Divine and eternal Blessings.

2. So, he tried to purchase the birthright; however, he found to his dismay that such could not be done. God has nothing for sale. Everything He has is a *"Gift"* (Jn. 3:16).

3. Had Jacob placed himself in God's Hands at the beginning, the Prophecy made to his mother before he was born (Gen. 25:23) would have been fulfilled to him without the degradation and suffering that his own scheming brought upon him.

BRING THE FISH

We are not told what was done with the fish. However, the indication of the Command, *"Bring of the fish which you have now caught,"* implies that they were to be properly handled and prepared for sale through a commercial outlet. Why not!

As we shall see, this was far too many fish for the Disciples and their families to eat, for it seems that each fish was quite large, with the selling of them, or even giving them away, the only other course.

(11) "SIMON PETER WENT UP, AND DREW THE NET TO LAND FULL OF GREAT FISH, AN HUNDRED AND FIFTY AND THREE: AND FOR ALL THERE WERE SO MANY, YET WAS NOT THE NET BROKEN."

The form is:

1. God had a controversy with Jacob because of his faulty life.

2. As a consequence, he found himself in deadly peril. When he realized that God Himself was behind that peril, and it really was not with Esau, his brother, that he had to contend, but rather with the Angel of Jehovah Himself, he then learned a valuable lesson.

3. When sore broken by that Mighty Hand, and when he ceased to wrestle and clung instead with weeping and supplication to the very God Who wounded him, it was then he got the victory and the glorious name of *"Israel."*

THE GREAT CATCH

The phrase, *"Simon Peter went up, and drew the net to land full of great fish,"* presents him having arrived at the shore before the others, and now going back out a little ways and helping them to drag the net to land. He had come as quickly as possible to see Jesus, which he evidently did, but of which the Scripture is silent. Now he helps the others pull the net the last few yards.

As well, the Scripture uses the term, *"Great fish,"* which insinuates that each fish was far larger than normal.

The phrase, *"An hundred and fifty and three,"* represents several things:

• This was not an estimate, but rather an exact count. As well, the exact count speaks of individual souls brought to Christ, with that number, whatever it may be, surely known to God.

As the Lord told the Prophet, *"Yet I have left Me seven thousand in Israel, all the knees which have not bowed unto Baal, and every mouth which has not kissed him"* (I Ki. 19:18).

• The catch was symbolic of the Disciples being fishers of men. The harvest would be great, even as the Book of Acts would portray.

• The order by which this was carried out and directed thusly by Jesus portrays Him as the Head of the Church and not some poor mortal. He Alone can give command for direction, as evidenced by the net being thrown on the right side of the ship, and for organization, which concerned the net with the fish being brought to land, and He tallies the results, hence, 153 fish.

THE NET HELD

So, He tells us how to get souls Saved, how to properly teach and instruct them after Salvation, and with precision, exactly how many there were, noting the preciousness of each individual soul.

"And for all there were so many, yet was not the net broken," presents a contrast with the miraculous catch given in Luke 5:6, where the net did break.

Symbolically speaking, that net then broke because the Holy Spirit had not yet come. Consequently, of all that which Jesus gave to the amassed thousands during His public Ministry, much, if not most, was little understood and, thereby, lost, at least at that particular time.

However, by this net not breaking despite its load, Jesus was pointing to the advent of the Holy Spirit, Who would *"bring all things to your remembrance, whatsoever I have said unto you"* (Jn. 14:26). In other words, the net will not break!

(12) "JESUS SAID UNTO THEM, COME AND DINE. AND NONE OF THE DISCIPLES DID ASK HIM, WHO ARE YOU? KNOWING THAT IT WAS THE LORD."

The synopsis is:

1. The great principle that God cannot give victory *"to the flesh"* appears in this night scene with Jacob wrestling with the Lord.

2. It is the broken heart that begins to experience what Divine Power means. Better for the sun to rise upon a limping Israel than to set upon a lying Jacob.

3. God had to cripple the *"flesh"* in Jacob, as He has to cripple the flesh in us. It can only be done one way. It is the Holy Spirit alone Who can subdue the flesh.

COME AND DINE

The phrase, *"Jesus said unto them, Come and dine,"* presents Him, as usual, and even in His Glorified State, functioning as a Servant. He had prepared the meal for them, showing them that He would ever do so for the rest of their lives. They would not starve, as Satan, no doubt, had attempted to make them believe, but would rather *"dine."* It was a meal, one must quickly add, prepared by none other than the Lord of Glory Himself.

What a Promise!

The question, *"And none of the Disciples did ask Him, Who are You?"* presents to us a great meaning.

IT WAS THE LORD

The phrase, *"Knowing that it was the Lord,"* presents them knowing such because Jesus had just performed several Miracles, all on their behalf.

Concerning religious phenomenon of one type or the other, millions are presently asking, *"Who are you?"* meaning that the earmarks of the True Gospel are not present.

Of this one can be certain: where Jesus is, there will be Miracles. They may come in varied and different ways, such as the Salvation of souls, which one could probably say is the greatest Miracle of all, bondages being broken, the sick being healed, etc. The moral is: if Jesus is there, things will happen!

Sadly, in most churches, nothing is happening, and I mean nothing, at least as far as the moving and operation of the Holy Spirit are concerned. To be frank, most people, including preachers, do not even believe in the Holy Spirit, at least as this subject is taught in the Word of God. Consequently, there may be much religious machinery generating much activity, but as far as something being done for the Lord is concerned, nothing is happening. To be frank, if the Holy Spirit in any capacity is ignored, Jesus will be little present either!

There was no need for the Disciples to question Jesus regarding the guaranteeing of His Identity. They knew Who He was, even though in a Glorified State, by the things He did.

(13) *"JESUS THEN COMES, AND TAKES BREAD, AND GIVES THEM, AND FISH LIKEWISE."*

The exposition is:

1. In Hebrews 11:21, the Holy Spirit points to Jacob's action in Genesis, Chapter 49, as the great Faith action of his life.

2. Feeble, dying, and having nothing, except the staff on which he leaned and worshipped, he had bestowed vast and unseen possessions on his grandsons.

3. The double portion given to Joseph as the firstborn was a conquered portion (Gen. 49:22). The possession given by God to the Divine Firstborn among many brethren, the Lord Jesus Christ, is also a conquered possession, i.e., it was done at the Cross, and it redeemed His People out of the land of the enemy — the Amorite, one might say.

EATING HIS FLESH AND DRINKING HIS BLOOD, I.E., THE CROSS

The phrase, *"Jesus then comes,"* once more presents Christ in the Servant role.

"And takes bread, and gives them, and fish likewise," portends a far greater meaning than merely food for breakfast.

The *"bread"* was symbolic of Himself, with the *"meat"* being symbolic of His Word. This is all that is needed, Jesus and the Word!

However, the mere knowledge of Jesus is not enough; we have to *"eat His Flesh and drink His Blood"* (Jn. 6:53-58).

This speaks of His Word becoming a part of one's being, with Him being accepted in totality. This is what is meant by His Statement, *"At that day* (time) *you shall know that I am in My Father, and you in Me, and I in you"* (Jn. 14:20).

(14) *"THIS IS NOW THE THIRD TIME THAT JESUS SHOWED HIMSELF TO HIS DISCIPLES, AFTER THAT HE WAS RISEN FROM THE DEAD."*

The exposition is:

1. He said, *"When I see the Blood"* (Ex. 12:13), not *"When I see your particular Church,"* *"your good works,"* *"your particular denomination,"* or whatever!

2. Its *"When I see the Blood, I will pass over you."*

3. The worthiness of the person is not taken into question simply because in the Eyes of God, there is no worthiness. The goodness of the person is also not taken into question simply because in the Eyes of God, no one can really be called *"good."*

4. That which characterizes acceptance by God is that the Blood of His Son, the Lord Jesus Christ, be applied to our hearts and lives. Applying the Blood of Jesus Christ

refers to what He did for us at the Cross of Calvary and is done by Faith (Rom. 5:1; Eph. 2:8-9).

THE APPEARANCES OF CHRIST AFTER THE RESURRECTION

This was the third time for Him to reveal Himself to the majority of His Disciples, but it was the seventh appearance since the Resurrection.

Up to this time, He had appeared to the following:

- Mary Magdalene (Mk. 16:9; Jn. 20:15-16).
- Women at the Tomb (Mat. 28:9).
- Two Disciples on the road to Emmaus (Lk. 24:13-31).
- Peter (Lk. 24:34; I Cor. 15:5).
- The Ten (Jn. 20:19).
- The Eleven (Jn. 20:26).
- The Seven (Jn. 21:1-22). This was after the second Sunday. After this, it seems He appeared according to the following:
- The Eleven on a certain mountain in Galilee (Mat. 28:16).
- The Twelve, including Matthias (Acts 1:26; I Cor. 15:5).
- Above 500 brethren (I Cor. 15:6).
- James, the Lord's Brother (I Cor. 15:7; Gal. 1:19).

Some feel the following constitutes a twelfth appearance, which it probably did.

- All of the Apostles (Mk. 16:19-20; Lk. 24:50-53; Acts 1:2-12, 26; I Cor. 15:7).

(15) "SO WHEN THEY HAD DINED, JESUS SAID TO SIMON PETER, SIMON, SON OF JONAH, DO YOU LOVE ME MORE THAN THESE? HE SAID UNTO HIM, YES, LORD; YOU KNOW THAT I LOVE YOU. HE SAID UNTO HIM, FEED MY LAMBS."

The construction is:

1. The Holy Spirit states in I Corinthians 5:7 that the Passover pictured Christ's Sacrifice of Himself in order to save sinners sentenced to die.

2. Two great facts appear in the first Passover: the certain doom of the firstborn and his certain Salvation. He was doomed to death by God, not because of his conduct, but because of his birth.

3. This latter fact, he could not alter. He was, therefore, hopelessly lost. He was, however, absolutely Saved because of the value of the life sacrificed for him. He knew he was Saved because God had pledged Himself to most certainly save all who sprinkled the shed blood upon the doorpost. This was all a Type of the price Jesus would pay on Calvary's Cross in order that we might be Saved (Jn. 3:16).

MIRACLE FOOD

The phrase, *"So when they had dined,"* gives every indication that it was Miracle food. In other words, it was that which Jesus had spoken into being.

As such, this *"food,"* no doubt, had the same effect on them, but in a spiritual sense, as the meal prepared by the Angel had on Elijah in a physical sense (I Ki. 19:5-8).

"Jesus said to Simon Peter," presents the fourth personal address to Peter and portrays Spiritual Growth, despite the negative connotations:

- In the first instance, the Grace of God selected Simon of Jonah to be a *"Rock"* and was instituted at His Calling (Jn. 1:42).
- In the second, *"Not flesh and blood,"* but the Father's Grace revealed the mystery of the Divine Sonship to him and won for him the name of *"Peter"* (Mat. 16:17).
- In the third, the utter weakness of Simon's own flesh reveals the power of the prayer of Jesus for him that his Faith fail not (Lk. 22:32).
- In this instance after the Resurrection, Jesus portrays *"Love"* as the foundation of the Apostolic Commission. As well, the three questions posed to Peter, and with his answers, cancelled out the three denials.

The idea is that this great Christian Message is based on love and not strength, as Peter had boasted at first, but which he now renounces.

PETER, DO YOU LOVE ME MORE THAN THESE?

The question, *"Simon, son of Jonah, do you love Me more than these?"* is actually referring to Peter's boasts immediately before the Crucifixion that he loved Jesus more than the other Disciples (Mat. 26:31-35; Mk. 14:29).

Concerning love, Jesus used the Greek verb *"agapao,"* which means *"ardent, supreme, and perfect."*

The phrase, *"He said unto Him, Yes, Lord; You know that I love You,"* presents Peter using the Greek verb *"phileo,"* which means *"to like, be fond of, to feel friendship for another."*

The type of *"love"* here expressed by Peter was of far less dimension than that expressed by Jesus. However, Peter was not being trite. He well remembered the boasts he had previously made concerning his love for Jesus and the terrible failure which had come to him. Consequently, he did not want to make this mistake again. Therefore, he used a word for love that was not boastful, but yet, at the same time, strangely enough, portrayed the exact opposite of what he was saying. In other words, he really loved Jesus, ardently, supremely, and perfectly, at least as best he knew, but would never again boast of such.

FEED MY LAMBS

The phrase, *"He said unto him, Feed My Lambs,"* presents two things:

1. Love to Christ is the first, high, and main condition of faithful service. Consequently, Peter would have this as his prime, chief, and most laudable foundation.

2. Peter was here assured by the Lord of his Commission.

Regrettably, if Peter had lived presently and had been a member of some particular Pentecostal denominations, he would not have been able to *"feed My Lambs,"* i.e., to preach and teach the Gospel for at least two years. Therefore, he would not have been able to preach the inaugural Message on the Day of Pentecost, which resulted in some 3,000 people being Saved (Acts, Chpt. 2).

Actually, if these denominations had existed then, and he had been associated with them, much of the Book of Acts would have been completely rewritten. Of course, such only speaks of hypocrisy and self-righteousness. When one adds to or takes from the Word of God, one has done despite to the Spirit of Grace (Heb. 10:29).

As well, the use of the word *"lambs"* by Jesus refers to the newest type of Converts, who need special attention and will be entrusted to Peter.

(16) "HE SAID TO HIM AGAIN THE SECOND TIME, SIMON, SON OF JONAH, DO YOU LOVE ME? HE SAID UNTO HIM, YES, LORD; YOU KNOW THAT I LOVE YOU. HE SAID UNTO HIM, FEED MY SHEEP."

The construction is:

1. As one reads II Samuel, Chapter 12, one must come to the conclusion that it testifies to the inspiration of the Bible, for only the Holy Spirit could have (would have) recorded so faithfully its infamy and horror.

2. It gives a true insight into man's nature as sinful and fallen.

3. It teaches the reader the humbling lesson that such is the nature he possesses, and that if Divine restraints are withheld and temptations sufficiently attractive and skillfully offered, there is no depth of evil, shame, and falsehood to which he will not fall.

4. Uriah, the husband of Bath-sheba, was one of David's 37 mighty men (II Sam. 23:39). To make him the bearer of the letter arranging for his murder was a depth of infamy which is appalling. Worse yet, it was committed by one of the godliest men who ever lived — David.

JESUS AGAIN THE SECOND TIME . . .

The question, *"He said to him again the second time, Simon, son of Jonah, do you love Me?"* presents Jesus leaving off the words *"more than these."* However, He did continue to use the strong Greek word *"Agapao"* for love.

By Jesus leaving off the words *"more than these,"* He was drawing Peter away from the boastful attitude of comparing his love to that of others. Actually, such can never stand the test. It speaks of self-righteousness and hypocrisy.

Jesus was saying that true love is not expressed by attempting to outdo others, which is the very opposite of what love ought to be. In fact, Paul wrote regarding love, that it *"seeks not her own"* (I Cor. 13:5).

THE WORDS OF PETER

The phrase, *"He said unto Him, Yes, Lord; You know that I love You,"* presents Peter using the same Greek verb *"phileo"* for love as he did the first time.

Despite the pressure, Peter would not succumb to his old weakness!

Despite the third question asked of Peter, as we shall see, I do not feel that Jesus was displeased with Peter's answers. Conversely, I think He was rather pleased instead! It showed Peter no longer depending on himself, which meant that he realized the weakness of the flesh and was determined not to succumb again.

"He said unto him, Feed My Sheep," this time, speaks of strong, mature Believers. So, Peter would not only have the patience and love to deal with young Converts, he would also have the strength and power to deal with mature Believers.

As well, had Jesus been displeased with Peter's answers, He would not have continued to grant him these able Commissions.

The word *"feed"* in all cases means *"to provide pasture, take care of, guide, lead, defend, govern, and shepherd the flock."*

(17) "HE SAID UNTO HIM THE THIRD TIME, SIMON, SON OF JONAH, DO YOU LOVE ME? PETER WAS GRIEVED BECAUSE HE SAID UNTO HIM THE THIRD TIME, DO YOU LOVE ME? AND HE SAID UNTO HIM, LORD, YOU KNOW ALL THINGS; YOU KNOW THAT I LOVE YOU. JESUS SAID UNTO HIM, FEED MY SHEEP."

The pattern is:

1. David's effort to shield Bath-sheba is the one redeeming feature in this sad history. However, his plans were his own, and unfortunately, they succeeded. Bitter fruit usually follows from successful human plans.

2. Had David, directly he had sinned against God, Uriah, and Bath-sheba, cast himself with anguish of heart upon God, the Lord would have made a way of escape and forgiveness consistent with Himself and morally instructive to David.

3. David's anger in Verse 5 of II Samuel, Chapter 12, concerning the lamb is a remarkable instance of how sensitive the moral judgment may be at the very time when the heart is blinded by sin! This fact illustrates the deceitfulness of sin (Heb. 3:13).

4. And yet, David had a true knowledge of God. When his sin was pointed out by Nathan the Prophet with the awful words, *"You are the man,"* David's first thoughts were not the punishment that would follow but the injury done to God.

THE THIRD TIME

The question, *"He said unto him the third time, Simon, son of Jonah, Do you love Me?"* presents Jesus now using *"phileo"* as Peter had used.

I think that Jesus used this word as a way of telling Peter that he need not be afraid to use the stronger word for love. It is obvious by now that Peter was no longer trusting in his own strength and, in fact, placed no trust in it at all. This is obvious! Therefore, the lesson had been taught and learned well!

Consequently, the greater kind of love, or anything else for that matter, can be used by the Believer, providing he knows and understands that within himself, such cannot be, but definitely can be if one is faithfully looking to Jesus for provision.

While boasting within oneself is deadly, as by now should be obvious, still, the idea is not self-destruction, but rather self hidden in Christ. If that is properly done, in effect, one can boast of great things, with it being obvious that the boast is in Christ and not self or others. Jesus does not desire that Peter, or any other Believer for that matter, stifle his Faith, but rather that the Faith be properly placed, which is not in self but Christ.

GRIEF

The phrase, *"Peter was grieved because He said unto him the third time, Do you love Me?"* reminded Peter so strongly of the three denials.

However, the Lord only wounded his heart in order to train and fit him for the high honor of shepherding that which was most precious to Himself, i.e., the Sheep of John, Chapter 10.

The phrase, *"And he said unto Him, Lord, You know all things,"* is a different answer now than Peter had given the last two times.

He now knew that Jesus knew all things about him, that which he did, thought, and felt, all of his bewilderment, all of his mistakes, all of his impulsiveness and mixture of motive, all of his self-assertion, and all of his weakness and disloyalty. He also knew that the Lord knew all the inner springs and lines of his nature and that he had played the fool. He was a hypocrite in his denials.

However, he now knew that the Lord also knew that his Faith did not really fail, though his courage did.

LOVE

The phrase, *"You know that I love You,"* in essence, says, *"Lord, You know exactly what type of love I have for You!"* Consequently, he now knew what he had not previously known. Jesus knew everything about him, even as He does concerning all, which makes our silly boastings and false faith so trite and foolish!

The phrase, *"Jesus said unto him, Feed My Sheep,"* expresses total and complete confidence.

Even though in Peter's mind the three Commandments concerning the tending of the spiritual flock may have referred to his denials, with Jesus, it had no such connotation. It rather expressed total and complete trust and confidence in Peter, which, upon future contemplation, must have been tremendously encouraging to the Disciple.

As well, many expositors have conjectured that these three Commands of Christ to Peter constituted a recommission; however, such is unscriptural!

The original Commission given by Christ concerning Peter, or anyone for that matter, once in force is never abrogated, at least by the Lord. The Holy Spirit through Paul plainly tells us, *"For the Gifts and Calling of God are without Repentance"* (Rom. 11:29).

While the individual may not live up to the Call, still, the Call remains. In fact, the Holy Spirit is ever seeking, even as Jesus did with Peter, to bring the person up to the level of the High and Holy Calling placed on his or her life.

IT WAS NOT A RECOMMISSION

So, as stated, these Statements by Jesus are not a recommission, but rather of assurance. Such is always necessary simply because Satan takes full advantage of any failure, telling the person, even as he, no doubt, told Peter, that his Call was now abrogated. Consequently, the assurance given by Jesus was not only for Peter, but rather for all.

Too often, men, especially religious men, seek to find ways to stop one from carrying out the Call of God upon one's life, while the Lord does the very opposite. Religious men love to say, *"You cannot preach,"* while the Lord loves to say, *"Feed My Sheep!"*

(18) "VERILY, VERILY, I SAY UNTO YOU, WHEN YOU WERE YOUNG, YOU GIRDED YOURSELF, AND WALKED WHERE YOU WOULD: BUT WHEN YOU SHALL BE OLD, YOU SHALL STRETCH FORTH YOUR HANDS, AND ANOTHER SHALL GIRD YOU, AND CARRY YOU WHERE YOU WOULD NOT."

The diagram is:

1. The rebellion and violent death of Absalom was, without a doubt, the greatest trial of David's life, more so because he felt that he was to blame. David was now 56 years old; Absalom 24; and Solomon six years of age.

2. Absalom easily deceived the people by a profession of devotion to them (II Sam. 15:2-6), and as easily deceived his father by a profession of devotion to God (II Sam. 15:7-8).

3. Because man has fallen from God's moral Image, he can readily deceive and be deceived (II Tim. 3:13).

PETER

The phrase, *"Verily, verily, I say unto you,"* presents the twenty-fifth and last occurrence of this double Amen.

"When you were young, you girded yourself, and walked where you would," refers to the time when he was but a lad. The word *"young"* in no way supports the popular belief that Peter was at this time an aged man, or at least in his middle years. Even though it is only a guess, Peter at this time was probably about 25 years old.

The idea in this statement has far more than the mere suggestion of former years, but rather that Peter now belonged to Christ and, as such, was no longer his own man.

In truth, this is the battleground for most. Man loathes to give up control of his life, even to the Lord of Glory. Actually, even after Conversion, this remains the chief battlefield.

However, man cannot make his own way, even converted man. The entire tenor of the spirit of the world is in the opposite direction of the Ways of God. As well, the Fall has left the mind of man somewhat twisted and perverted. As such, he will automatically gravitate toward the wrong. Despite repeated failure, he feels the next effort will solve the problem regarding direction, which it never does. At times, man is able to achieve certain things, whether wealth, status, or position. However, these things tend only to deceive him further, making him think that this is the sought-for goal, but he finds after arriving that the thirst remains!

SUBDUING THE FLESH

To subdue the flesh is what Peter had to do and what all must do, at least if God is to use us. Such is not an easy or pleasant task.

The discovery of the worthlessness of self, such as the experience of Peter, is the first step in Christian experience, with the Worthfulness of Christ being the last step.

Peter had to be brought to the place and position, as we all do, that he *"abhorred himself."* To be sure, it is not a pleasant trip, but yet, a journey that must be taken, that is, if we are to obey God. The flesh dies hard while the Spirit invigorates slowly.

The phrase, *"But when you shall be old, you shall stretch forth your hands, and another shall gird you,"* proclaims the prediction of Peter's faithfulness unto death, which undoubtedly comforted and strengthened his pierced heart and, as well, prevented the other Disciples from scornfully reminding him of his former cowardice.

BLUSTER!

This statement, as given by Christ to Peter, is so thoughtful and beautiful because Satan, no doubt, had filled Peter's mind with fear that on some distant day, he might repeat this terrible scenario. When one thinks very highly of himself, as Peter evidently had done, it is a rude shock to awaken to the fact that what one thought was strength is, in reality, mere bluster. All confidence is then gone; however, this is the very purpose of the Holy Spirit, but only partially so.

It is not so much the loss of confidence which the Holy Spirit seeks, as that of the confidence being properly placed. I speak of a transfer from self to Christ. Peter's confidence would now be in the Lord, and said by none other than the Lord Jesus Christ.

So, the One Who predicted the denial now predicts faithfulness. As stated, how this must have warmed the heart of the Apostle.

SELF-WILL

The phrase, *"And carry you where you would not,"* refers to the time at a distant day when Peter would die. Another would take him to where he would not desire to go — to death and the grave. This tells us something else about ourselves as well.

The old self-will, though it be indeed mastered, will not have utterly vanished. If it be not so, where would be the Sacrifice? Even the Blessed Lord Himself said, *"Not My Will, but Yours be done."*

Verily, even the Sanctified Nature of the Sinless Man, prepared in the spotless womb of the Blessed Virgin by the Holy Spirit, anointed by the Spirit, and in living in absolute union with the Only Begotten Son, was in human consciousness disposed to cry, *"If it be possible, let this cup pass from Me."*

Concerning Peter in his old age, *"Being carried to where he would not,"* Tertullian and Eusebius said that the Apostle, upon facing death, preferred crucifixion with his head downwards on the plea that to be crucified as his Master was too great an honor for one who had denied his Lord.

(19) "THIS SPOKE HE, SIGNIFYING BY WHAT DEATH HE SHOULD GLORIFY GOD. AND WHEN HE HAD SPOKEN THIS, HE SAID UNTO HIM, FOLLOW ME."

The overview is:

1. Deception and rebellion are grievous in any case. However, for such to lodge in the heart of one's own son, and we speak of Absalom against David, presents injury of the highest sort.

2. Absalom reasoned that inasmuch as David had sinned with Bath-sheba and had planned the murder of her husband (actions that were heinous indeed), he could take the throne. Most of the people of Israel agreed with him!

3. However, God had not selected Absalom to take the throne. God had selected David. Even though David had sinned terribly, the Lord had not deposed him as king. If

Absalom had succeeded in his plan, it would have destroyed Israel.

PETER DIED BY CRUCIFIXION

The phrase, *"This spoke He, signifying by what death he should glorify God,"* was written by John after Peter had died.

To which we have already eluded, tradition says that Peter died by crucifixion. Many have felt that the phrase in the previous Verse, *"You shall stretch forth your hands,"* as predicted by Jesus, speaks of this type of most cruel death.

However, whatever type of death it was, it glorified God!

As well, Peter would know from the statement given by Jesus, *"But when you shall be old,"* that he would not die an early death.

This reached forward to the time that Peter, along with some or all of the other Apostles, were put in the common prison in Jerusalem for preaching the Gospel of Jesus Christ. The Scripture says that the *"Sadducees were filled with indignation"* against them (Acts 5:17-18).

There seemed to be every indication that the Sanhedrin had planned to execute some, if not all, and especially Peter, who was the leader. However, I do not think that Peter was concerned at all. He remembered what Jesus had said a few months earlier. He was not old, so he was not going to die as of now.

That night, *"The Angel of the Lord opened the prison doors, and brought them forth,"* which proclaims a miraculous escape (Acts 5:19-26).

FOLLOW ME

The phrase, *"And when He had spoken this, He said unto him, Follow Me,"* proclaims that he would do, when strengthened by Christ's Resurrection, what in his weakness he had promised prematurely.

The needful order was that Christ should first die for Peter's Salvation, which He had accomplished, and then that Peter should die for his faithfulness to Christ.

As well, Jesus had used the same words, *"Follow Me,"* to Peter and to others some three and one-half years earlier, but this Command, and a Command it was, had special connotations for the Apostle, even beyond that originally given by Christ. As stated, which these instructions entail, Peter would die for the Lord!

Peter's devotion was intense and at times passionate, but it was marked with a striking disposition, from first to last, to lead as well as *"follow,"* to advise as well as to be guided, to stretch forth his hands, and to gird himself for his own enterprises.

However, with all of his extraordinary peculiarities, he never relinquished his Faith. And now, the Lord in one Word corrected every one of his failings anew and instituted him into his sublime mission by the Call, *"Follow Me."*

(20) "THEN PETER, TURNING ABOUT, SEEING THE DISCIPLE WHOM JESUS LOVED FOLLOWING; WHICH ALSO LEANED ON HIS BREAST AT SUPPER, AND SAID, LORD, WHICH IS HE WHO BETRAYS YOU?"

The exegesis is:

1. David, one of the greatest Men of God who ever lived, now came to the place that he must die. The giant-killer could not evade death. Because of Adam's fall, death is passed on all men.

2. Thank God, the enemy called death was defeated at Calvary. Even though its effect will be the last to be destroyed, that day will come for certain (I Cor. 15:26, 54-57).

3. The Lord had promised David that He would give him a son whom God would raise up to him, God being His Father and He being His Son, Who should build the Temple of Jehovah and reign forever and ever. This was the Promise, and David himself knew it referred to Christ (II Sam., Chpt. 7).

THE FLESH

The phrase, *"Then Peter, turning about, seeing the Disciple whom Jesus loved following,"* spoke of John and once more, even this soon, presents Peter's extraordinary characteristic to guide rather than to follow. Old habits die hard!

This is the reason that the great battle for the Child of God is ever the flesh. As well, we must remember that the *"flesh"* in the Child of God, even Peter, is just as hateful to God as the *"flesh"* in the ungodly. Both stem from the same source!

One would think, would not one, that the self-will in Peter would now be broken, especially now? However, even in the very Shadow of Christ, self-will dies hard.

The learning comes slow and, most of the time, is accompanied by tribulation, which seems to be the only vehicle able to throttle this opposite direction of man.

The phrase, *"Which also leaned on His Breast at supper, and said, Lord, which is he who betrays You?"* presents John speaking of himself and taking us back to the Last Supper.

(21) "PETER SEEING HIM SAID TO JESUS, LORD, AND WHAT SHALL THIS MAN DO?"

The synopsis is:

1. The word *"Pentecost"* in the Hebrew means *"Fifty"* or *"Fiftieth."* It refers to 50 days after the Passover.

2. The *"Day of Pentecost"* was one of the great Feast Days of the Jews. It probably occurred in late May.

3. It was on this *"Day"* that the Holy Spirit came to this world in a completely new dimension, all made possible by the Cross.

PETER AND JOHN

The phrase, *"Peter seeing him said to Jesus,"* proclaims Peter about to inquire concerning John the Beloved.

The question, *"Lord, and what shall this man do?"* presents Peter asking something for which he will be rebuked.

It should be a lesson to us, with one quickly asking as to how many lessons Peter has provided for us. And yet, have we done any better?

One may wonder at the wisdom of Jesus choosing someone such as Simon Peter! Then again, one may wonder at Jesus choosing any of us!

However, the Lord does not choose those whom He will use on the merit of their present disposition, but He chooses them because of what He can make of them. No one is ready at the time of the Call. As well, one does not get ready easily or quickly even after the Call. But yet, when the Lord calls us, He does so knowing everything about us, even from the beginning to the finish. And still, He calls us, which can only speak of Grace.

(22) "JESUS SAID UNTO HIM, IF I WILL THAT HE TARRY TILL I COME, WHAT IS THAT TO YOU? YOU FOLLOW ME."

The overview is:

1. Whoever these individuals were whom Paul addressed in Philippians 3:17-19, the Apostle concluded them to be *"enemies of the Cross of Christ."*

2. He didn't say *"enemies of Christ,"* but rather *"enemies of the Cross of Christ."* He was speaking of the Judaizers, whom he mentioned at the beginning of this Third Chapter of Philippians.

A MILD REBUKE

The question, *"Jesus said unto him, If I will that he tarry till I come, what is that to you?"* presents one prediction and one particular.

Peter represents the Church, whether earthly or Heavenly, crucified with Christ.

John represents the Church living on Earth up to the Coming of Christ. Each Believer should, in this sense, be as Peter or John.

In fact, John would *"tarry"* long, living to near the end of that Century. As well, Jesus came to him while he was on the *"Isle that is called Patmos, for the Word of God, and for the Testimony of Jesus Christ"* (Rev. 1:9).

At that time, which is believed to be about A.D. 97, Jesus gave to John the Book we now know as *"The Revelation,"* or as it is called in the Greek, *"The Apokalupsis,"* which means *"to unveil or uncover."* It implies the lifting of a curtain so all can see alike what is uncovered.

THE PARTICULAR

As well, as the prediction was given, the particular is now addressed, proclaiming that it was none of Peter's business as to what Jesus' Will was for John. In other words, Peter had enough on his plate without involving himself in that which pertained to his fellow Apostle.

How so much stronger the Church would be if each member in particular attended to his or her own business and stayed out of the business of others! Jesus here plainly tells us not to involve ourselves respecting others, at least in this fashion. He could not be clearer or plainer.

The phrase, *"You follow Me,"* presents *"you"* as emphatic. In other words, He was telling Peter to attend to his own business, with the assurance that there would be plenty there to keep him busy.

The lesson we should learn from this is that the great theme of the Gospel by John is not the Glory of any Church, but the Personal Glory of the Lord Jesus. His Person and the Eternal Life that is in Him formed the Foundation of Faith. As well, no matter how human Testimony to His Sufficiency and Preciousness may fail, He Himself remains in all of His Perfection and Faithfulness as the Sustainer of Faith.

So, John presents God to us in Him, and Paul, as we shall see in his Epistles, presents us in Him to God.

(23) "THEN WENT THIS SAYING ABROAD AMONG THE BRETHREN, THAT THAT DISCIPLE SHOULD NOT DIE: YET JESUS SAID NOT UNTO HIM, HE SHALL NOT DIE; BUT, IF I WILL THAT HE TARRY TILL I COME, WHAT IS THAT TO YOU?"

The form is:

1. The Parable of the Prodigal Son portrays the only time in Scripture that God, personified in this Parable by the Father, is pictured running.

2. In that, for which and to which He ran, provides a fitting example of Who God is and What God is. He is Love!

3. This Parable, in fact, destroys the argument that no Atoning and Mediating Saviour is needed between God and the sinner.

MISINTERPRETATION

The phrase, *"Then went this saying abroad among the brethren, that that Disciple should not die,"* proclaims the manner in which Scripture can be misinterpreted. To be frank, too much of this goes on even in the modern church. Error has a tendency to multiply itself. In other words, if *"leaven"* is not rooted out, it will ultimately corrupt the whole (I Cor. 5:6).

"Yet Jesus said not unto him, He shall not die," refers to John setting the record straight as to what Jesus had actually said to him.

As we have stated, it is believed that John wrote his Gospel about A.D. 90. If that is correct, this would have been after all the original Apostles had died. Paul had already gone on to be with the Lord as well. John the Beloved was the only one left of the original Twelve.

About six years later, he would write the Book of Revelation, which would close out the Canon of Scripture.

IF I WILL

By this time (about A.D. 90) much of the civilized world of that day had been evangelized respecting the Gospel of Jesus Christ. So, when John mentioned the word *"brethren,"* this would have involved quite a large number, stretching all the way from Rome in Italy to Alexandria in Egypt, a distance of nearly a thousand miles by sea.

By the end of the next Century, the Gospel would have reached all the way to Germany. It is remarkable considering that this was done without the aid of modern transportation or communication.

It was done because of the power, working, and anointing of the Holy Spirit!

The question, *"But, if I will that he tarry till I come, what is that to you?"* presents Jesus in the words, *"If I will,"* as the absolute disposal of human life and reveals His Godhead. As should be obvious, He knows the total future of all men. Recognizing and understanding One of such Power and Omniscience should portray to all the fallacy of attempting to circumvent His Will. While such certainly can be done and, in fact, is done constantly, the end results are never good. In all things, we must desire His Will.

(24) "THIS IS THE DISCIPLE WHICH TESTIFIES OF THESE THINGS, AND WROTE THESE THINGS: AND WE KNOW THAT HIS TESTIMONY IS TRUE."

The overview is:

1. Sin is the problem, whether it's an unbeliever or a Believer.

2. The Cross is the only answer for sin. There is no other!

3. When Jesus died on the Cross, He atoned for all sin and all sins, past, present, and future, at least for those who will believe (Jn. 3:16).

JOHN THE BELOVED

The phrase, *"This is the Disciple who testifies of these things,"* presents John as an eyewitness of all he relates.

"And wrote these things," verifies John as the author of this Book.

"And we know that his Testimony is true," verifies the inspiration of the Holy Spirit upon these accounts in that which we refer to as *"The Gospel according to John."*

(25) "AND THERE ARE ALSO MANY OTHER THINGS WHICH JESUS DID, THE WHICH, IF THEY SHOULD BE WRITTEN EVERY ONE, I SUPPOSE THAT EVEN THE WORLD ITSELF COULD NOT CONTAIN THE BOOKS THAT SHOULD BE WRITTEN. AMEN."

The order is:

1. Some Christians have the erroneous idea that if they embrace Christ and the Cross, making that the sole Object of their Faith, then they will never again be tempted, never have another problem, etc.

2. Bluntly and plainly, the Holy Spirit through Simon Peter (I Pet. 4:12-13) here tells us that that's not the case at all.

3. Whenever a person accepts Christ and the Cross, making that the sole Object of his Faith, which will automatically cause him to throw aside all false doctrine, many times, the opposition from the religious sector will be fierce. Sometimes, even our own families will oppose us.

THE MANY THINGS THAT JESUS DID

The phrase, *"And there are also many other things which Jesus did,"* speaks, no doubt, of the many Miracles He performed, some of which are not recorded in any of the Four Gospels. However, that which the Holy Spirit wanted us to have was given.

"The which, if they should be written every one," lends credence to the idea that there were far more Miracles and Happenings performed by Jesus that are not recorded than those which were recorded.

"I suppose that even the world itself could not contain the books that should be written. Amen," is not meant to promote the idea that the physical world could not support on its surface the number of books that could be written about the Lord Jesus Christ. Instead, it means that human intelligence, in its totality, is incapable of receiving and accepting all that could be written about Him. The idea is that the subject is inexhaustible simply because Christ is God and, as such, is totally beyond the pale of human comprehension.

CHRIST, THE INFINITE

Already, millions of volumes have been written down through the Centuries. Countless millions more, no doubt, will be written even in the coming Kingdom Age. Were the world to last for millions of years, the day would never come that would exhaust the Gospel Story.

Christ is Infinite, the Earth finite; hence, the supposition of the Verse is most reasonable.

This Book written by John the Beloved presents the Gospel as a Feast. As well, the very purpose of its being is to invite all to the Feast. In truth, many come, accepting its Gifts, but do not love the Giver. So, true Conversion is to truly love Him.

John portrays the idea that the Christian is Saved to serve. Feeding others successfully depends on frequent *"dining,"* i.e., Communion.

Each Disciple had to keep going to Jesus for food for the multitude. Personal obedience in following is more important than curiosity in knowing what this or that man may do, even as Jesus in this last Chapter explained to Peter.

Matthew, in presenting Jesus as King, closed his Book with the Words, *"I am with you always, even unto the end of the world. Amen."*

Mark, presenting Jesus as a Servant, closed with the Words, *"And confirming the Word with signs following. Amen."*

Luke, presenting Jesus as the Man, closed with the Word, *"And were continually in the Temple, praising and blessing God. Amen."*

John, presenting Jesus as God, closed with the Words, *"I suppose that even the world itself could not contain the books that should be written. Amen."*

Tradition says that John died in Ephesus and was there buried.

Browning wrote this of the Apostle:

"If I live yet, it is for good, more Love,
"Through me to men: be nought but ashes here
"That keep awhile my semblance, who was John–
"Still, when they scatter, there is left on Earth,
"No one alive who knew (consider this!)
"–Saw with his eyes and handled with his hands.
"That which was from the first, the Word of Life.
"How will it be when none more says, 'I saw'?
"Such ever was Love's Way: to rise, it stoops.
"Since I, whom Christ's Mouth taught,
"Was bidden teach,
"I went, for many years, about the world,
"Saying 'It was so; so I heard and saw,'
"Speaking as the case asked: and men believed."

"To me that Story–ay, that Life and Death
"Of which I wrote 'it was'–to me, it is;
"–Is, here and now: I apprehend nought else."

"Yea, and the Resurrection and Uprise
"To the right hand of the Throne ...
"I saw the Power; I see the Love, once weak,
"Resume the Power: and in this Word 'I See,'
"Lo, there is recognized the Spirit of both
"That moving o'er the spirit of man, unblinds
"His eye and bids him look . . .
"Then stand before that fact, that Life and death,
"Stay there at gaze, till it dispart, dispread,
"As though a star should open out, all sides,
"Grow the world on you, as it is my world."

NOTES

BIBLIOGRAPHY

CHAPTER 1

George Williams, *The Student's Commentary on the Holy Scriptures*, Grand Rapids, Kregel Publications, 1949, pg. 777.

H. D. M. Spence, *The Pulpit Commentary: Vol. I*, Grand Rapids, Eerdmans Publishing Company, 1978.

George Williams, *The Student's Commentary on the Holy Scriptures*, Grand Rapids, Kregel Publications, 1949, pg. 777.

H. D. M. Spence, *The Pulpit Commentary: Vol. I*, Grand Rapids, Eerdmans Publishing Company, 1978.

George Williams, *The Student's Commentary on the Holy Scriptures*, Grand Rapids, Kregel Publications, 1949, pg. 777.

H. W. Robertson, *Inspiration and Revelation in the Old Testament*.

E. Jacob, *Old Testament Theology*.

G. A. F. Knight, *A Christian Theology of the Old Testament*.

H. D. M. Spence, *The Pulpit Commentary: Vol. I*, Grand Rapids, Eerdmans Publishing Company, 1978.

Ibid.

George Williams, *The Student's Commentary on the Holy Scriptures*, Grand Rapids, Kregel Publications, 1949, pg. 780.

Ibid.

Frederic Louis Godet, *Commentary on the Gospel of John*, Funk & Wagnalls, New York, 1886, pg. 335.

Ibid.

CHAPTER 2

George Williams, *The Student's Commentary on the Holy Scriptures*, Grand Rapids, Kregel Publications, 1949, pg. 781.

Vine's Expository Dictionary.

Albert Barnes, *Notes on the New Testament: Volume II, Luke & John*, London, Blackie & Sons, pg. 193.

George Williams, *The Student's Commentary on the Holy Scriptures*, Grand Rapids, Kregel Publications, 1949, pgs. 781-782.

NOTES

CHAPTER 3

C. H. Mackintosh, *Notes on the Book of Leviticus*, Loizeaux Brothers, New York, 1880, pg. 219.

Kenneth S. Wuest, *The New Testament: An Expanded Translation*, Wm. B. Eerdmans Publishing Company, 1961, pg. 215.

CHAPTER 4

George Williams, *The Student's Commentary on the Holy Scriptures*, Grand Rapids, Kregel Publications, 1949, pg. 784.

CHAPTER 5

Paul C. Vitz, *Psychology as Religion, the Cult of Self-Worship*, Wm. B. Eerdmans Publishing Company, Grand Rapids, Michigan, 1977, pg. xiii.

E. Brooks Holifield, *A History of Pastoral Care in America*, Wipf & Stock Publishers, 2005, pg. 263.

Martin L. Gross, *The Psychological Society*, Random House, 1978.

George Williams, *The Student's Commentary on the Holy Scriptures*, Grand Rapids, Kregel Publications, 1949, pg. 787.

Kenneth S. Wuest, *Great Truths to Live By*, William B. Eerdmans Publishing Company, Grand Rapids, Michigan.

H. D. M. Spence, *The Pulpit Commentary: Vol. I*, Grand Rapids, Eerdmans Publishing Company, 1978.

CHAPTER 6

H. D. M. Spence, *The Pulpit Commentary: Vol. I*, Grand Rapids, Eerdmans Publishing Company, 1978.

Ibid.

Ibid.

J. H. Thayer, *A Greek-English Lexicon of the New Testament*, Zondervan, Grand Rapids, Michigan, 1963, pg. 50.

H. D. M. Spence, *The Pulpit Commentary: Vol. I*, Grand Rapids, Eerdmans Publishing Company, 1978.

Ibid.

CHAPTER 7

George Williams, *The Student's Commentary on the Holy Scriptures*, Grand Rapids, Kregel Publications, 1949, pg. 793.

H. D. M. Spence, *The Pulpit Commentary: Vol. I*, Grand Rapids, Eerdmans Publishing Company, 1978.

CHAPTER 8

Joseph Augustus Seiss, *Holy Types*, Smith English & Co., New York, 1866, pg. 148.

H. D. M. Spence, *The Pulpit Commentary: Vol. I*, Grand Rapids, Eerdmans Publishing Company, 1978.

Ibid.

Ibid.

CHAPTER 9

Reinhold Niebuhr, *An Interpretation of Christian Ethics*, Meridian Books, 1958.

Charles Henry Mackintosh, *Notes on the Book of Leviticus*, Loizeaux Brothers, New York, 1880, pg. 16.

H. D. M. Spence, *The Pulpit Commentary: Vol. II*, Grand Rapids, Eerdmans Publishing Company, 1978.

Ibid.

CHAPTER 10

Charles Henry Mackintosh, *Notes on the Book of Leviticus*, George Morrish, London, pgs. 31-32.

H. D. M. Spence, *The Pulpit Commentary: Vol. II*, Grand Rapids, Eerdmans Publishing Company, 1978.

Ibid.

CHAPTER 11

H. D. M. Spence, *The Pulpit Commentary: Vol. II*, Grand Rapids, Eerdmans Publishing Company, 1978.

Ibid.

C. H. Mackintosh, *Notes on the Book of Leviticus*, George Morrish Publishing, London, pg. 93.

H. D. M. Spence, *The Pulpit Commentary: Vol. II*, Grand Rapids, Eerdmans Publishing Company, 1978.

Ibid.

CHAPTER 12

H. D. M. Spence, *The Pulpit Commentary: Vol. II*, Grand Rapids, Eerdmans Publishing Company, 1978.

NOTES

CHAPTER 13

George Williams, *Williams' Complete Bible Commentary*, Grand Rapids, Kregel Publications, 1994, pg. 804.
Ibid.
Ibid.
Ibid.
H. D. M. Spence, *The Pulpit Commentary: Vol. II*, Grand Rapids, Eerdmans Publishing Company, 1978.
Ibid.
Ibid.
Ibid.
Ibid.
Ibid.
Ibid.

CHAPTER 14

The Pulpit Commentary, Wm. B. Eerdmans Publishing Company, Grand Rapids, 1897, Book of John.

CHAPTER 15

H. D. M. Spence, *The Pulpit Commentary: St. John Vol. II*, Grand Rapids, Eerdmans Publishing Company, 1978.
George Williams, *Williams' Complete Bible Commentary*, Grand Rapids, Kregel Publications, 1994, pg. 274.
Ibid.
Ibid.
Ibid.
Ibid.
H. D. M. Spence, *The Pulpit Commentary: St. John Vol. II*, Grand Rapids, Eerdmans Publishing Company, 1978.
Ibid.
Ibid.
Ibid.
George Williams, *Williams' Complete Bible Commentary*, Grand Rapids, Kregel Publications, 1994, pg. 808.
H. D. M. Spence, *The Pulpit Commentary: St. John Vol. II*, Grand Rapids, Eerdmans Publishing Company, 1978.
Ibid.

CHAPTER 16

H. D. M. Spence, *The Pulpit Commentary: St. John Vol. II*, Grand Rapids, Eerdmans Publishing Company, 1978.
Archdeacon Hare, *Mission of the Comforter*, 1900s.
H. D. M. Spence, *The Pulpit Commentary: St. John Vol. II*, Grand Rapids, Eerdmans Publishing Company, 1978.
Ibid.
Ibid.
Ibid.

CHAPTER 17

H. D. M. Spence, *The Pulpit Commentary: St. John Vol. II*, Grand Rapids, Eerdmans Publishing Company, 1978.
Ibid.
Ibid.
Ibid.
Ibid.
Ibid.
Ibid.
Ibid.
Ibid.

CHAPTER 18

H. D. M. Spence, *The Pulpit Commentary: St. John Vol. II*, Grand Rapids, Eerdmans Publishing Company, 1978.
C. K. Barrett, *The Gospel According to St. John*, Philadelphia, The Westminster Press, 1978, pg. 98.
B. B. Warfield, *The Biblical Doctrine of the Trinity*, Grand Rapids: Baker, 1991.
H. D. M. Spence, *The Pulpit Commentary: St. John Vol. II*, Grand Rapids, Eerdmans Publishing Company, 1978.
Expositor's Commentary.
H. D. M. Spence, *The Pulpit Commentary: St. John Vol. II*, Grand Rapids, Eerdmans Publishing Company, 1978.
George Williams, *Williams' Complete Bible Commentary*, Grand Rapids, Kregel Publications, 1994, pg. 813.
H. D. M. Spence, *The Pulpit Commentary: St. John Vol. II*, Grand Rapids, Eerdmans Publishing Company, 1978.
Ibid.

CHAPTER 19

H. D. M. Spence, *The Pulpit Commentary: St. John Vol. II: 19:1*, Grand Rapids, Eerdmans Publishing Company, 1978.

Ibid.

H. D. M. Spence, *The Pulpit Commentary: St. John Vol. II: 19:3*, Grand Rapids, Eerdmans Publishing Company, 1978.

H. D. M. Spence, *The Pulpit Commentary: St. John Vol. II: 19:4*, Grand Rapids, Eerdmans Publishing Company, 1978.

H. D. M. Spence, *The Pulpit Commentary: St. John Vol. II: 19:5*, Grand Rapids, Eerdmans Publishing Company, 1978.

H. D. M. Spence, *The Pulpit Commentary: St. John Vol. II: 19:15-16*, Grand Rapids, Eerdmans Publishing Company, 1978.

H. D. M. Spence, *The Pulpit Commentary: St. John Vol. II: 19:27*, Grand Rapids, Eerdmans Publishing Company, 1978.

Ibid.

CHAPTER 20

George Williams, *Williams' Complete Bible Commentary*, Grand Rapids, Kregel Publications, 1994, pg. 816.

H. D. M. Spence, *The Pulpit Commentary: St. John Vol. II*, Grand Rapids, Eerdmans Publishing Company, 1978.

Ibid.

REFERENCE BOOKS

Atlas Of The Bible — Rogerson

Expository Dictionary of Bible Words — L. O. Richards

Matthew Henry Commentary On The Holy Bible — Matthew Henry

New Bible Dictionary — Tyndale

Strong's Exhaustive Concordance Of The Bible

The Complete Word Study Dictionary

The Essential Writings — Josephus

The Interlinear Greek — English New Testament — George Ricker Berry

The International Standard Bible Encyclopedia

The Pulpit Commentary — H. D. M. Spence

The Student's Commentary On The Holy Scriptures — George Williams

The Zondervan Pictorial Encyclopedia Of The Bible

Vine's Expository Dictionary Of New Testament Words

Webster's New Collegiate Dictionary

Word Studies In The Greek New Testament, Volume I — Kenneth S. Wuest

Young's Literal Translation Of The Holy Bible

INDEX

The index is listed according to subjects. The treatment may include a complete dissertation or no more than a paragraph. But hopefully it will provide some help.

As well, even though extended treatment of a subject may not be carried in this Commentary, one of the other Commentaries may well include the desired material.

ABIDE IN ME, AND I IN YOU 503
ABIDING IN JESUS 517
ABILITY OF CHRIST 678
A BONE OF HIM SHALL NOT BE BROKEN 643
ABOUT FIVE THOUSAND MEN 201
ABRAHAM 106
ABRAHAM'S SEED? 292
A CATEGORICAL NEGATIVE 30
ACCEPTANCE 218
ACCOMPLISHED 636
ACCUSATION OF THE JEWS AGAINST JESUS 303
A COMMON ANCESTOR 5
A COVETED POSITION 454
ADAM 337
ADDICTION TREATMENT INDUSTRY 506
A DECISION 423
A DISAGREEMENT? 305
A DISCIPLE OF JESUS 644
ADULTERY 269
A FEAST OF THE JEWS 154
A FINISHED WORK 291
AFTER ITS KIND 5
AFTER THESE THINGS 672
A FULFILLMENT NAME 557
A GLORIOUS PRESENT AND A GLORIOUS FUTURE 398
A GOOD MAN! 246
A GREAT COMFORT TO BELIEVERS 541
A HARD SAYING? 232
A KING 204
A LACK OF RECOGNITION 660
A LACK OF UNDERSTANDING 458
ALL MINE ARE YOURS 571
ALL THE LIGHT THEY KNEW 552

ALL THE TRUTH 287
ALL TRUE GLORY 567
ALL TRUTH CONCERNING BEHAVIOR IS FOUND IN THE BIBLE 470
ALL TRUTH IS GOD'S TRUTH? 469
ALONE 14
ALWAYS THE FATHER'S SON? 101
A LYING MURDERER 297
A MAN SENT FROM GOD 13
A MASTER OF ISRAEL 82
A MILD REBUKE 688
A MIRACLE OF UNPRECEDENTED PROPORTIONS 333
AN ANALYSIS OF THIS GOSPEL vi
AN ANGEL 156
AN ANTHROPOMORPHISM? 138
A NATIONALISTIC SALVATION? 179
AN AWFUL UTTERANCE 438
AND I IN YOU 488
AND THE WORD WAS GOD 2
AND THE WORD WAS WITH GOD 1
AN EARTHLY KINGDOM 457
AN ETHICAL CULT 88
A NEW COMMANDMENT 461
A NEW RELIGION? 515
AN EXPLANATION! 56
ANGELS AND HUMAN BEINGS 157
AN HONOR 331
ANIMOSITY AGAINST CHRIST 245
AN OFFENSE 233
ANOINTING 318, 407
AN ORDERLY PROCESSION 201
ANOTHER APPEARANCE OF CHRIST 670
ANOTHER COMFORTER 482

695

ANOTHER JESUS, ANOTHER SPIRIT, ANOTHER GOSPEL 312
ANSWER 31
ANSWER GIVEN BY CHRIST 76, 491
ANSWER IS THE CROSS OF CHRIST 489
ANSWER OF PILATE 610
ANTICHRIST 194
AN UNBIASED TESTIMONY 58
ANYTHING? 481
A PARTICULAR MORNING 266
A PART OF EVERYTHING 61
A PEASANT 44
A PERSONAL EXAMPLE 7, 489
A PERSONAL EXPERIENCE 11, 16, 125, 144, 247, 263, 277, 288, 301, 304, 323, 331, 338, 379, 387, 410, 422, 424, 527, 535
A PERSONAL STATEMENT 525
A PICTURE OF HUMANITY 159
APOSTATE CHRISTIANITY 619
APOSTATE CHURCH 525, 554
APOSTLE PAUL 477
APPEARANCE OF DEATH 310
APPEARANCES OF CHRIST AFTER THE RESURRECTION 682
A PROPER UNDERSTANDING 85, 364
A PROPHET? 129
ARE WE SAVED AND KEPT BY WORKS OR BY FAITH? 98
ARE YOU A KING? 612
ARE YOU ELIJAH? 30
ARE YOU GREATER THAN ABRAHAM? 304
ASCENDING UP TO HEAVEN 86
ASCENSION 549
ASKING AND RECEIVING 518
ASKING IN THE NAME OF JESUS 559
ASK THE FATHER IN THE NAME OF JESUS 556
ASSEMBLIES OF GOD 578
AS THE SCRIPTURE HAS SAID 259
ASTONISHMENT 453
AS WE ARE JUDGING OURSELVES 270
A SWEET SAVOR 565
A TROUBLED HEART? 464
ATTEMPTING TO EARN SALVATION 120
AT THAT DAY 486
AT THIS TIME, HE PRAYED FOR HIS DISCIPLES, PLUS ALL BELIEVERS, AND FOR ALL TIME 570
AUTHORITY 183, 594
AUTHORITY? 623
AUTHORITY OF THE BELIEVER 478
A VESSEL FULL OF VINEGAR 637
BAPTISM WITH THE HOLY SPIRIT 484
BAPTIST PREACHER 364

BARABBAS 616
BAROMETER OF FAITH? 203
BASIS OF JUDGMENT 108
BEARING FRUIT? 504
BEARING MUCH FRUIT 519
BEARING WITNESS OF THE LIGHT 15
BECAUSE HE KNEW ALL MEN 71
BECAUSE I LIVE, YOU SHALL LIVE ALSO 486
BEFORE PROHIBITION 51
BEGINNING OF MIRACLES 60
BEGINNING OF THE MINISTRY OF CHRIST 38
BEGINNING OF THE OPPOSITION 69
BEHOLD THE MAN! 619
BEHOLD YOUR KING 626
BEHOLD YOUR MOTHER 635
BELIEF IN HIS NAME 71
BELIEVE 542, 561
BELIEVE IN HIM 90
BELIEVE IN THE LIGHT 430
BELIEVE ME 131
BELIEVE ON ME 389
BELIEVERS 541
BELIEVE THE WORKS 374
BELIEVING 259, 451, 497, 671
BELIEVING CHRIST 435
BELIEVING ON HIM 107
BELIEVING ON JESUS 220
BEST WAS SAVED UNTIL THE LAST 59
BETHANY 377
BETRAYAL 442, 447
BIBLE 5, 469, 541
BIBLE CHRISTIANITY 475
BIBLE WAY 580
BIBLE WAY IN BRIEF 515
BIBLICAL PROOF 375
BLASPHEMY 301
BLESSED CONSISTENCY! 332
BLIND 340
BLINDED EYES AND HARDENED HEARTS 432
BLOOD AND WATER 643
BLUSTER! 686
BODILY PRESENCE 138
BODY OF JESUS 646
BONDAGE? 288
BOOK OF ACTS 236, 550
BORN OF THE FLESH 80
BORN OF THE SPIRIT 80
BORN OF WATER AND OF THE SPIRIT 79
BOTH OR NONE 180
BRANCH BEARS FRUIT OR ELSE IT WILL BE TAKEN AWAY 501
BREAD OF LIFE 203

BREAD WHICH CAME DOWN FROM HEAVEN 230
BRIDEGROOM 112
BRING THE FISH 679
BROTHERS OF CHRIST 245
BUDDHISM 175
BURIAL 648
BURNED 517
BUT 123
BUT, ISN'T THAT WHERE FAITH ALWAYS TAKES US? 334
BUT WHAT DO YOU SAY? 272
BUT YOU KNOW HIM 485
BY FAITH 435
BY THE SWORD, NO! 595
CAESAR 632
CAESAR? 625
CAIAPHAS 597, 602
CALL 454
CALLED ACCORDING TO HIS PURPOSE 583
CAMPMEETING HOUR 552
CAN A SAVED PERSON BE LOST? 95
CAPERNAUM 62
CASTING LOTS 633
CENTRAL FOCUS OF DIVINE REVELATION 284
CEPHAS 43
CEREMONIES? 136
CHARACTER AND NATURE OF GOD 571
CHARISMATIC COMMUNITY 541
CHIEF PRIESTS 413
CHIEF PRIESTS AND PHARISEES 589
CHILDREN OF GOD? 293
CHOSEN 450, 527
CHOSEN DISCIPLES 568
CHRISTIAN CULTURE 526
CHRISTIAN EXPERIENCE 230
CHRISTIANITY 141
CHRISTIANITY IS REST 230
CHRISTIAN PSYCHOLOGY IS AN EXCELLENT CASE IN POINT 160
CHRISTIAN RESURRECTION 185
CHRIST IS THE SOURCE WHILE THE CROSS IS THE MEANS 476
CHRIST, THE INFINITE 690
CHRIST THE KING 608
CHURCH 12, 161, 191, 283, 430, 580
CIRCUMCISION 251
CIRCUMCISION OF THE HEART 78
CLAIMS OF CHRIST 283
COAT 633
CODEPENDENCY: A PLAGUE UPON THE LAND 506
CODEPENDENCY FOR ALL 506

COME AND DINE 680
COME AND SEE 45
COME UNTO ME 258
COMFORTER 493, 532, 539
COMING OF THE HOLY SPIRIT 539
COMMANDMENT GIVEN TO CHRIST 499
COMMANDMENTS 520
COMMANDMENTS? 482
COMMISSION 146
COMPARING JESUS WITH ANGELS 157
CONDEMNATION 107
CONFUCIANISM 175
CONFUSION OF THE DISCIPLES 553
CONQUEST OF SIN BY JESUS CHRIST 315
CONSCIENCE 313
CONSEQUENCES FOR CREATION 310
CONSEQUENCES FOR THE HUMAN RACE 310
CONSEQUENCES OF REJECTING CHRIST AND THE CROSS 360
CONSEQUENCES OF SIN 310
CONSTRUCTION OF THE TEMPLE 70
CONTINUING IN THE WORD OF GOD 287
CONTRADICITONS AND DECEPTIONS 514
CONTRADICTION 7
CONTRAST BETWEEN THE CARNAL NATURE AND THE HOLY SPIRIT 51
CONTROVERSY 590
CONVICTION 274
CORN OF WHEAT 421
CORRECT OBJECT OF FAITH 476
CREATION 4
CREATION CANNOT PRODUCE SOMETHING GREATER THAN ITSELF 5
CREATOR 3
CROSS 88, 228, 257, 363, 421, 459, 464, 498, 520, 545, 628
CROSS AND RIGHTEOUSNESS 544
CROSS AND SATAN 638
CROSS OF CHRIST 104, 163, 362, 428, 477, 478, 553
CROSS OF CHRIST ALONE IS THE ANSWER 508
CROSS OF CHRIST AND SANCTIFYING PEACE 495
CROSS OF CHRIST AND THE LOVE OF GOD 482
CROSS OF CHRIST AND THE MODERN CHURCH 346
CROWN OF THORNS 618
CRUCIFIED THE LORD OF GLORY 630
CRUCIFIXION 554, 629
CRUCIFY HIM! 620, 627
CURSED BY GOD? 608
CURSE OF THE BROKEN LAW 607
CURSE ON THE FEMALE GENDER 661
CYNICISM 614
DARKNESS 278
DARKNESS COMPREHENDED IT NOT 12

DAUGHTER OF ZION 415
DAVID 271
DEAD MATTER 5
DEATH? 303
DEATH AND BELIEVERS 395
DEATH AND RESURRECTION OF CHRIST 659
DEATH AS A DESCRIPTION 395
DEATH HE SHOULD DIE 607
DEATH OF CHRIST 88
DEATH OF CHRIST AND THE JEWS 628
DEATH OF CHRIST AT CALVARY 428
DEATH OF JESUS 396
DECEPTION 73, 102, 166, 535, 560
DEFECTIVE FAITH? 153
DEFILED? 605
DEFINITION OF SIN 309
DEGENERATION 6
DEITY 174, 221
DEITY OF CHRIST 443, 560
DENIAL 463, 598
DEPENDENT ON THE SPIRIT 38
DEPRAVITY OF MAN 311
DIFFERENCE IN BELIEVERS AND HIMSELF 176
DIFFERENCES vi
DIFFERENCES? 27
DIFFICULT! 423
DIRE CIRCUMSTANCES 436
DISCIPLES 140, 232, 569
DISCIPLES OF THE LORD 519
DISPENSATION OF GRACE 365
DISTRIBUTION 202
DIVINE DEGREE 487
DIVINE ENTANGLEMENT 487
DIVINE NATURE 101, 508
DOCTRINAL IMPLICATIONS OF THE RESURRECTION 186
DOCTRINE OF THE COEQUAL TRINITY 591
DOCTRINE OF UNCONDITIONAL ETERNAL SECURITY 94
DOES GOD USE EVIL? 451
DOMINION GIVEN TO MAN 479
DON'T DETAIN ME 663
DON'T UNDERSTAND . . . 102
DO YOU BELIEVE? 335, 474
DO YOU BELIEVE THIS? 390
DO YOU KNOW WHAT I HAVE DONE TO YOU? 448
DO YOU MARVEL? 81
DO YOU NOT KNOW THESE THINGS? 83
DRINK 123, 258
DROPPED THE STONES 274
DWELLING IN THE LORD 228
DWELLING WITH THE LORD 492

DWELT AMONG US 23
DYING IN ONE'S SINS 282
EARTHLY THINGS 84
EATING HIS FLESH AND DRINKING HIS BLOOD, I.E., THE CROSS 681
EATING THE FLESH AND DRINKING THE BLOOD 225
ELDERS OF THE LOCAL CHURCH 270
EMBALMING 647
EMPHASIS OF THE EARLY CHURCH REGARDING THE RESURRECTION 184
EMPTY TOMB 653
END OF SATAN'S DOMINION IS NEAR 480
END OF THE APPEAL 456
ENTIRETY OF THE WORLD 537
ENTRANCE OF CHRIST 415
EPITOME OF EVIL 600
ERRONEOUS THINKING 473
ERROR OF UNCONDITIONAL ETERNAL SECURITY 358
ETERNAL 94
ETERNAL LIFE 90, 357, 566
ETERNALLY LOST 106
ETERNAL SECURITY 105, 362
ETERNAL TRUTH 299
EVERLASTING LIFE 94, 123, 220
EVERY MAN 17
EVERYTHING SHOULD BE TAKEN TO JESUS 419
EVERYTHING THAT JESUS DID 381
EVIL 297
EVIL ANGELS 156
EVIL HEARTS OF RELIGIOUS MEN 601
EVIL WORKS 244
EVOLUTION: FACT OR FICTION 4
EXAMPLE 449
EXAMPLES 95
EXAMPLES! 328
EXCOMMUNICATION 328
EXPATIATION 226
EXPRESSION OF HIS DEITY 369
EXTERNAL 516
FAITH 21, 62, 167, 206, 291, 334, 422, 467, 476, 523, 560, 586, 661
FAITH? 598
FAITH IN ACTION 151
FAITH IN CHRIST 465
FAITH IN THE FATHER 181
FAITHLESS 670
FAKE LUMINARIES 175
FALL 10, 162, 309
FALSE PROPHETS 161
FAMILY OF CHRIST 63

FAMILY WORSHIP CENTER MEDIA CHURCH 345
FATHER 178, 472, 571
FATHER DRAWS SINNERS TO JESUS 222
FATHER IS WITH ME 562
FATHERS 130
FATHER'S WILL 219
FATHER WHO SENT ME 439
FEAR 206, 621
FEAST OF TABERNACLES 241
FEAST OF THE PASSOVER 440
FEED MY LAMBS 683
FELLOWSHIP 454
FILL THEM UP TO THE BRIM 56
FIRSTBORN OF EVERY CREATURE 592
FIRST DAY OF THE WEEK 650, 665, 669
FIRST MIRACLE OF JESUS 50
FISHING 674
FIVE GODS 128
FIVE HUSBANDS 128
FLEEING FROM FALSE SHEPHERDS 343
FLESH 236, 687
FOLLOWING JESUS 197, 424
FOLLOW ME 687
FOOLISHNESS OF EVOLUTION 7
FORFEITING SALVATION? 105
FORMALITY 154
FORMER BLIND MAN WAS TEACHING ISRAEL 335
FOR MY NAME'S SAKE 529
FOR THE HOLY SPIRIT WAS NOT YET GIVEN 260
FOR THIS CAUSE 425, 613
FOR YOUR SAKE 426
FOUNDATION 428
FOUNDATION OF THE GOSPEL 363
FOUNDATION OF THE WORLD 585
FOUR ACCOUNTS 650
FOUR GROUPS 668
FOURTH APPEARANCE OF CHRIST 673
FOURTH WATCH OF THE NIGHT 206
FOUR WITNESSES 188
FOUR WORDS IN THE GREEK LANGUAGE FOR LOVE 91
FREE! 289
FREE MORAL AGENCY 362
FREE WILL OF HUMAN BEINGS 101
FRIENDS 522
FROM THE FATHER 533
FROM WHERE DID IT COME? 57
FROM WHERE DO YOU COME? 622
FRUIT 524
FRUITLESS EXERCISES 211
FRUITS OF THE DOCTRINE OF UNCONDITIONAL ETERNAL SECURITY 104
FRUIT THAT REMAINS 524
FRUSTRATING THE GRACE OF GOD 367
FULFILLING OF THE SCRIPTURES 451
FULFILLING OF THE WORD 531
FULFILLMENT? 124
FULFILLMENT OF SCRIPTURE 634
GARDEN 649
GENTILE CHURCH 352
GENTILES 256
GEOLOGY 6
GETHSEMANE 588
GIFT 123
GIFT OF GOD 119
GIRDED HIMSELF 443
GIVE ME THIS WATER 124
GIVING THANKS 201
GLADNESS 666
GLORIFIED 35, 378, 420, 459
GLORIFIED BODY 654
GLORIFY HIM 459
GLORIFYING THE NAME OF THE HEAVENLY FATHER 426
GLORY 582, 583
GLORY OF GOD 381
GOD 26
GOD AS THE FATHER 27
GOD AS THE FATHER OF JESUS 28
GOD-CONSCIOUSNESS AND SELF-CONSCIOUSNESS 159
GOD CONTROLS ALL 623
GOD IS A SPIRIT 137
GOD IS OUR FATHER 28
GOD KIND OF LOVE 462
GODLY! 601
GOD MANIFEST IN THE FLESH 174
GOD'S ATTITUDE TO MAN 310
GOD'S CONCERN 158
GOD'S ECONOMY 678
GOD'S PRESCRIBED ORDER OF VICTORY 290
GOD THE FATHER 560
GOD THE FATHER AND GOD THE SON 399
GOD THE FATHER AND THE LORD JESUS CHRIST 566
GOD THROUGH JESUS CHRIST WAS GLORIFIED ON EARTH 567
GOD WORKS THROUGH INDIVIDUALS 304
GOLGOTHA 629
GOOD WINE 50
GOOD WORKS 369
GOSPEL AND THE CROSS OF CHRIST 363
GOSPEL OR 12-STEPS? 514
GRACE AND TRUTH 26

GREAT CATCH 680
GREAT DAY OF ATONEMENT 68
GREAT DAY OF THE FEAST 257
GREATER LOVE 521
GREATER SIN 624
GREAT HARVEST OF SOULS 11
GREAT WIND 206
GREED MESSAGE 160, 210
GREEKS 418
GREEK SCHOLAR 97
GRIEF 684
GROANING IN HIMSELF 394
GUIDE 546
HALL OF JUDGMENT 604
HARVEST 145
HATE 525
HATERS OF THE LIGHT 109
HATING ONE'S LIFE 422
HATRED 526
HATRED AGAINST CHRIST 243
HATRED OF CHRIST 172
HATRED OF CHRIST AND THE FATHER 530
HATRED WITHOUT A CAUSE 531
HEAD OF EACH MEMBER INDIVIDUALLY 347
HEADSHIP OF CHRIST 17
HEARING CHRIST 112
HEARING THE WORD 181
HEAVENLY FATHER CAN ONLY BE SEEN IN JESUS 473
HEAVENLY THINGS 85
HEAVENLY VISION 578
HEBREWS 97
HE BROUGHT HIM TO JESUS 42
HE CAME DOWN FROM HEAVEN 86
HE CAN MAKE SOMETHING OF NOTHING 61
HE CONVICTS THE WORLD OF SIN, RIGHTEOUSNESS, AND JUDGMENT 540
HE DROVE THEM OUT 67
HE HAS CHOSEN US 569
HE MADE ALL THINGS 4
HENCEFORTH 472
HEREAFTER 445
HE SAW A MAN WHO WAS BLIND FROM HIS BIRTH 307
HE WASHED AND CAME SEEING 319
HE WHO BAPTIZES WITH THE HOLY SPIRIT 39
HE WHO EATS THIS BREAD SHALL LIVE FOREVER 231
HE WHO HAS SENT ME 286
HE WHO IS WITHOUT SIN AMONG YOU . . . 273
HE WILL REPROVE THE WORLD 540
HE WILL SHOW YOU THINGS TO COME 547

HIGH PRIEST 596
HINDERING THE WORK OF GOD 267
HIRELING 350
HIRELINGS 351, 374
HIS BRETHREN 63
HIS CONCERN FOR OTHERS 636
HIS DIET 14
HIS DISCIPLES 68, 416, 674
HIS DISCIPLES REMEMBERED 70
HIS GLORY 23
HIS HANDS, HIS SIDE, HIS FEET 666
HIS HOUR 440
HIS MESSAGE 14
HIS PERFECT RIGHTEOUSNESS 529
HIS PURPOSE AND MISSION 561
HIS RAIMENT 14
HIS RECORD IS TRUE 643
HIS SACRIFICIAL DEATH 666
HISTORY OF MANKIND 311
HOLY 572
HOLY FLESH OF CHRIST 224
HOLY SPIRIT 36, 114, 125, 143, 235, 259, 268, 308, 431, 457, 549, 550, 553, 574
HOLY SPIRIT AND WORSHIP 137
HOLY SPIRIT IN THE BELIEVER 494
HOLY SPIRIT WILL GLORIFY CHRIST 546
HOLY SPIRIT WILL PORTRAY THESE GREAT TRUTHS 548
HOLY SPIRIT WILL SPEAK 547
HORROR OF ALL HORRORS 256
HOSTILITY v
HOSTILITY TO GOD 313
HOUR COMES AND NOW IS 134
HOUR IS COME 420
HOUR IS NOW COME 562
HOW CAN A MAN BE BORN AGAIN? 78
HOW CAN THESE THINGS BE? 82
HOW DID JESUS DEFEAT SATAN AT THE CROSS? 104
HOW DOES ONE OBTAIN THE RIGHTEOUSNESS OF GOD? 543
HOW DOES THE HOLY SPIRIT WORK? 312
HOW GOD WORKS 503
HOW TO LIVE FOR GOD 85
HUMAN BODY 641
HUMANISTIC PSYCHOLOGY 545
HUMANITY OF CHRIST 187
HUMILITY 370
HUSBANDMAN 500
HYPOCRISY 31
HYPOCRISY OF THE JEWS 600
I AM 592

I AM NOT OF THIS WORLD 283
I AM THE BREAD OF LIFE 215
I AM THE DOOR 348
I AM THE DOOR OF THE SHEEP 346
I AM THE RESURRECTION AND THE LIFE 389
I AM THE SON OF GOD 373
IDENTIFICATION 455
IF ANY MAN 258
IF ANY MAN THIRST, LET HIM COME UNTO ME AND DRINK 257
I FIND NO FAULT IN HIM 618
IF I WILL 689
IF WE LOVE CHRIST, THE FATHER WILL LOVE US 490
IF YOU KNOW ME, YOU KNOW THE FATHER 470
I GO AWAY, BUT I WILL COME AGAIN UNTO YOU 496
I GO MY WAY 538
I GO TO THE FATHER 550
I HAVE CHOSEN YOU 523
I IN THEM, AND YOU IN ME 584
IMAGE 590
IMMEDIATELY 208
IMPOSSIBLE? 362
IMPOTENCY OF MAN 165
IMPOTENT MAN 164
IMPUTATION OF SIN 310
IMPUTED RIGHTEOUSNESS 544
INABILITY OF MAN 314
INCARNATION 23, 221
IN CHRIST 8
INFAMY 625
IN HIM WAS LIFE 9
IN POWER AND WORKS 177
INSCRIPTION 632
INSTANT RIGHTEOUSNESS 302
INSTRUCTIONS OF THE HOLY SPIRIT 383
INSUFFICIENT RESOLVE? 463
INTERCESSION 361
INTERCESSION OF CHRIST 559
IN THAT DAY 556
IN THE BEGINNING WAS THE WORD 1
IN THE NAME OF JESUS 556
ISAIAH THE PROPHET 431
IS CLEAN EVERY WHIT 447
IS IT WHO HE WAS OR WHAT HE DID? 75
IS IT WHO HE WAS OR WHAT HE DID? 75
ISLAM 93
ISRAEL'S RESPONSE TO CHRIST 301
IS THE PRICE TOO HIGH? 645
IS THIS NOT THE BEGGAR? 320

IT IS FINISHED 637
IT IS THE HOLY SPIRIT WHO MAKES ALIVE 234
IT IS THE HOLY SPIRIT WHO MAKES ALIVE 234
ITS CENTRAL MESSAGE 191
IT WAS NIGHT 458
IT WAS NOT A RECOMMISSION 685
IT WAS THE LORD 681
I WILL NOT LEAVE YOU COMFORTLESS 485
I WILL SHOW YOU PLAINLY 558
JACOB AND ISRAEL 43
JACOB'S WELL 118
JEHOVAH OF THE OLD TESTAMENT WAS JESUS 433
JERUSALEM 130, 154, 196, 631, 636, 656
JESUS 34, 207, 335, 396, 489, 649, 675
JESUS AGAIN THE SECOND TIME . . . 683
JESUS AND DEMON SPIRITS 3
JESUS AND HIS DISCIPLES 109
JESUS AND JERUSALEM 64
JESUS AND NATHANAEL 46
JESUS AND RESURRECTION POWER 179
JESUS AND THE JEWS 20
JESUS AND THE RELIGIOUS STRUCTURE 344
JESUS ANSWERED 69
JESUS ANSWERED HIM 602
JESUS ANSWERED THEM 210, 369
JESUS AS THE LIGHT OF THE WORLD 318
JESUS AS TRUTH 468
JESUS CAME 665
JESUS CAME FORTH FROM GOD 561
JESUS CAME NOT TO JUDGE 437
JESUS CHRIST 293
JESUS CHRIST AND SIN 299
JESUS CHRIST AND THE BIBLE 2
JESUS CHRIST IS THE ANSWER 200
JESUS CHRIST SETS PEOPLE FREE 515
JESUS CLAIMED ABSOLUTE COMMUNITY WITH GOD THE FATHER 548
JESUS DID NOT COMMIT HIMSELF 71
JESUS DID NOT PRAY AT THIS TIME FOR THE WORLD 570
JESUS DIED SPIRITUALLY DOCTRINE 642
JESUS FOUND HIM 335
JESUS GAVE HER BACK HER LIFE 656
JESUS GAVE NO ANSWER 623
JESUS GLORIFIED 261
JESUS IS COMING AGAIN 78
JESUS IS THE INTERSECTION 93
JESUS IS THE LIGHT 436
JESUS NOW REVEALS HIMSELF 662
JESUS OF NAZARETH 174, 590, 593

JESUS OF NAZARETH THE KING OF
   THE JEWS 630, 631
JESUS OF NAZARETH, THE SON OF JOSEPH 44
JESUS PASSED BY 307
JESUS SAID UNTO THEM 55
JESUS SPEAKS TO THE DISCIPLES 676
JESUS STANDS ALONE 177
JESUS STOOD AND CRIED 258
JESUS, THE ONLY WAY TO THE FATHER 470
JESUS, THE PRIMARY OBJECTIVE 678
JESUS WAS ABOUT TO LEAVE 486
JESUS WEARY? 118
JESUS WROTE ON THE GROUND 272
JESUS YIELDED UP HIS SPIRIT 639
JEWISH SABBATH AND THE PRESENT DAY 169
JEWISH SANHEDRIN 589
JEWS 133, 168, 340
JEWS AND JESUS 176
JEWS' PASSOVER 64
JOB 502
JOHN, A DISCIPLE OF JOHN THE BAPTIST v
JOHN THE BAPTIST 110
JOHN THE BELOVED 597, 635, 655, 690
JOHN WAS A FISHERMAN v
JOSEPH OF ARIMATHAEA 644
JOY 520, 555
JUDAS 573, 588
JUDAS ISCARIOT 409, 441
JUDAS WAS A THIEF 410
JUDGMENT 338, 544
JUDGMENT AND RECREATION 6
JUDGMENT OF THIS WORLD 427
JUDGMENT SEAT 625
JUSTIFICATION BY FAITH 608, 662
JUST SHALL LIVE BY FAITH 132
KEY BIBLE PASSAGES RELATING TO DEATH 397
KING? 627
KINGDOM 611
KINGDOM NOW 580
KINGDOM OF DARKNESS 612
KINGDOM OF GOD 78
KING OF ISRAEL 414
KING OF KINGS AND LORD OF LORDS 205
KING OF THE JEWS! 609, 618
KNOWING GOD! 586
KNOWING JESUS AND KNOWING
   THE FATHER 471
KNOWLEDGE OF THE NAME 557
LABOUR NOT FOR THE MEAT WHICH
   PERISHES 211
LACK OF DISCERNMENT 457
LACK OF FAITH IN CHRIST AND THE CROSS 359

LACK OF LOVE FOR GOD ALSO IGNORES HIS
   WORD 492
LAID ASIDE HIS GARMENTS 443
LAMB OF GOD 34
LARGE SUMS OF MONEY 410
LAST DAYS OF OUR LORD 406
LAST GREAT MOVE 59
LAST MOMENTS OF CHRIST ON EARTH 637
LAST ONE v
LAST RECORDED HEALING OF JESUS IN HIS
   PUBLIC MINISTRY 595
LAW? 429
LAW AND THE LIFE OF ISRAEL 25
LAW OF MOSES 24, 271
LAZARUS 377, 406
LAZARUS CAME FORTH 401
LEARN THE LESSON? 52
LEAVING THE PRINCIPLES OF THE DOCTRINE
   OF CHRIST 358
LED BY MEN 39
LEFTOVER FRAGMENTS 203
LET HIM 258
LIARS 298
LIE OF PSYCHOLOGY 505
LIFE 10, 470
LIFE EVERLASTING 440
LIFE-GIVING FATHER 229
LIFE OF CHRIST WAS NOT TAKEN BY ANY
   MAN 353
LIFE WAS THE LIGHT OF MEN 9
LIFTING UP OF THE SERPENT IN THE
   WILDERNESS 87
LIFT UP HOLY HANDS 135
LIFT UP YOUR EYES AND
   LOOK ON THE FIELDS 146
LIFT UP YOUR EYES AND LOOK ON THE
   FIELDS 146
LIGHT 13, 15, 287, 339, 363, 429
LIGHT OF LIFE 278
LIGHT OF MAN 15
LIGHT OF MEN 10
LIGHT OF THE WORLD 276
LINEN CLOTHES 648, 655
LIVING BREAD 224
LIVING BY CHRIST 229
LIVING WATER 120
LIVING WATER THAT IS WITHIN 123
LOGOS 152
LOOK ON THE FIELDS 145
LOOK WHAT THE LORD HAS DONE 380
LORD AND MASTER 449
LORD, HOW LONG? 490

LORD, I BELIEVE 337
LORD, WHO IS IT? 455
LOSING EVERYTHING? 536
LOVE 91, 158, 441, 481, 519, 587, 685
LOVE FOR THE LORD 491
LOVE ONE ANOTHER 521
LOVING ONE'S LIFE 422
LOVING THE LORD 488
LOWLY CLAY 318
MAN ADMITTING WHAT HE IS 232
MAN AND BIBLICAL CREATION 7
MAN FEAR 328, 434
MAN IS FALLEN 217
MAN IS INCURABLY RELIGIOUS 93
MAN'S ATTITUDE TO GOD 310
MANSIONS 465
MAN'S PRETENTION TO BE GOD 309
MAN'S TERRIBLE DILEMMA 9
MANY BELIEVED ON JESUS 413
MANY PEOPLE 413
MARRIAGE BETWEEN A MAN AND A WOMAN 61
MARTHA 386, 407
MARVEL! 183
MARY 57
MARY AND ISRAEL 52
MARY BELIEVED 411
MARY, BY HER OWN ACTION DISPROVES THE CATHOLIC DOCTRINES 51
MARY MAGDALENE 634, 651
MARY THE MOTHER OF JESUS 634
MASTER 662
MASTER AND LORD 448
MASTER, WHO DID SIN ... ? 308
MEAT WHICH PERISHES 212
MERCY 269
MERCY AND GRACE 276
METHODOLOGY 577
MINIMIZING THE PROBLEMS? 507
MIRACLE FOOD 682
MIRACLES 75
MIRACLES! 56
MISINTERPRETATION 689
MONEY CHANGERS 66
MORALLY AND SPIRITUALLY BLIND 308
MORE ABUNDANT LIFE 349
MORE IS BETTER? 55
MORE THIEVES AND ROBBERS 349
MOSAIC LAW 604
MOSES 332
MUCH FRUIT 505
MURDEROUS INTENT IN THEIR HEARTS 387
MURMURING 233, 246

MY BRETHREN 664
MY FATHER IS GREATER THAN I 497
MY FATHER'S HOUSE 68
MY FATHER'S NAME 194
MY HOUR IS NOT YET COME 53
MY JUDGMENT IS JUST 188
MY LORD AND MY GOD 670
MY WORD 529
MY WORDS WHICH I SPEAK UNTO YOU 474
NAILING IT TO HIS CROSS 511
NAZARETH 45
NEITHER DO I CONDEMN YOU 275
NEVER PERISH 357
NICODEMUS 74, 647
NICODEMUS CAME TO JESUS BY NIGHT 74
NO ACCUSATION 606
NO CEREMONIAL RITE 80
NO CLOAK FOR SIN 530
NO CONDEMNATION 98, 105, 181
NO FEAR 496
NO FERMENTATION 227
NO LIGHT 436
NO LIGHT IN HIM 382
NONE WHO COME TO HIM WILL BE LOST 219
NONE WHO COME TO HIM WILL BE LOST 219
NO SALVATION IN THE LAW 271
NOT ABIDE IN DARKNESS 437
NOT A PROPER EXEGESIS OF SCRIPTURE 361
NOT AS THE WORLD GIVES 495
NOT FOR SALVATION 25
NOT YOUR HUSBAND 129
NOW IS THE SON OF MAN GLORIFIED 458
OBEDIENCE 55
OBJECTIVE TRUTH VERSUS SUBJECTIVE TRUTH 468
OF THEM WHICH YOU GAVE ME 594
ONCE AGAIN, THE HOLY SPIRIT 554
ONE 572
ONE CANNOT SEE THE FATHER UNTIL ONE HAS SEEN JESUS 473
ONE FOLD AND ONE SHEPHERD 352
ONE GOD 28
ONE HERE IS NOT CLEAN 447
ONE OF TWO CAMPS 294
ONLY BELIEVE 153
ONLY JESUS 176
ONLY THE CROSS OF CHRIST 226
ONLY THE LORD KNOWS THE HEART OF MAN 73
ON WHAT DAY WAS JESUS CRUCIFIED? 639
ORDINATION 524
ORIGINAL SIN 76

OUR RELATIONSHIP WITH GOD 29
OUR REPRESENTATIVE MAN 88
OVERCOMING SIN 228
OVERCOMING VICTORY 563
OVERWHELMING GRIEF 660
OXEN, SHEEP, AND DOVES 66
PARABLE 344
PARADISE 401, 640
PARADISE, A PART OF HELL? 641
PASSED FROM DEATH UNTO LIFE 181
PASTURE 348
PAUL 96, 100
PAUL AND PETER 97
PAUL AND THIS VERY SITUATION OF THE SINFUL NATURE 100
PAUL IS WRITING TO BELIEVERS 365
PEACE 494, 563, 666
PENALTY 271
PERFECT FAITH? 661
PERFECTION? 584
PERSECUTION 534
PETER 597, 685
PETER AND JOHN 652, 688
PETER AND JOHN COME TO THE TOMB 653
PETER DIED BY CRUCIFIXION 687
PETER, DO YOU LOVE ME MORE THAN THESE? 682
PETER'S REACTION 603
PETERS REPLY 446
PETTY RULES WHICH HAVE NO SCRIPTURAL FOUNDATION 324
PHILIP AND ANDREW 419
PHILIP FINDS NATHANAEL 44
PILATE 606, 646
PILATE AND JESUS 609
PILATE AND THE RELIGIOUS LEADERS OF ISRAEL 632
PILATE'S DILEMMA 615
PONTIUS PILATE 605
POWER 21, 354, 454, 593
POWER! 417
POWER OVER ALL FLESH 565
PRAISING GOD TO WHOM THEY NO LONGER PRAY 235
PRAYER 573
PRAYER TO THE FATHER 564
PREACHING WHICH DOES NOT BRING CONVICTION 540
PREDESTINATION? 217, 433
PREJUDICE 140
PREPARATION 466
PRIDE AND HUMILITY 411

PRINCIPALITIES AND POWERS 511
PROFESSORS OF RELIGION! 672
PROFOUND vi
PROPER RELATIONSHIP GUARANTEES WORSHIP OF GOD 137
PROPER RESPONSE 75
PROTECTION FROM THE EVIL ONE 574
PROVERBS 558
PROVING THE BELIEVER 198
PSYCHOLOGY 127
PUNISHMENT? 273
PURPOSE 582
RABBI? 74
RADIO, TELEVISION, AND CITYWIDE CRUSADES 423
RAISED FOR OUR JUSTIFICATION 186
RAISED FROM THE DEAD 412
RANK AND DESIGNATIONS 156
REASONS CHRISTIANS LOOK ELSEWHERE 512
RECEIVE THE HOLY SPIRIT 667
RECEIVING 452
RECEIVING CHRIST 21
RECEIVING JESUS 208
RECOGNITION 36
RECOGNITION! 659
REDEMPTION 242
REJECTION 20
REJOICE? 497
RELATIONSHIP 454, 586
RELATIVE RIGHTEOUSNESS 544
RELIGION 126, 299, 339, 535, 620
RELIGION AT WORK 262
RELIGIOUS BONDAGE 289
RELIGIOUS FLESH 237
RELIGIOUS HIERARCHY 168, 344
RELIGIOUS THINGS 126
RELIGIOUS WOLVES 351
REMEMBER 528
REMEMBRANCE 493
REPEATED INSPECTION BY THE WORD, WHICH ALSO CLEANSES 446
REPENTANCE 96
REPRODUCTION 5
RESTORATION 269
RESURRECTION 70, 655
RESURRECTION OF LIFE AND RESURRECTION OF DAMNATION 185
RIGHTEOUSNESS 543, 586
RIGHT OR WRONG 247
RISE 166
RIVALRY? 183
RIVERS OF LIVING WATER 259

ROMANS, CHAPTER 6 100
ROMANS, CHAPTER SEVEN 291
ROMAN SCOURGING 617
RULES 169
SACRIFICES? 77
SACRIFICIAL MINISTRY 379
SALVATION 106
SALVATION IS OF THE JEWS 133
SAMARITANS 129
SANCTIFIED 579
SATAN 455
SATAN HAS NOTHING IN JESUS 499
SATAN IS YOUR FATHER 293
SATAN'S FELL SWOOP 603
SAVIOUR TODAY, JUDGE TOMORROW 437
SEARCH THE SCRIPTURES 191
SECULAR AND CHRISTIAN HUMANISM 160
SEE, HEAR, AND UNDERSTAND 432
SEEKING THE GLORY OF GOD 249
SELF RIGHTEOUSNESS 302
SELF-RIGHTEOUSNESS AND THE CROSS OF CHRIST 673
SELF-WILL 456, 686
SEPARATION 646
SERIOUS PROBLEMS WITH PROBLEM SOLUTIONS 507
SERVANTS? 522
SHALL LEAVE ME ALONE 562
SHALL NEVER DIE 390
SHALL NEVER HUNGER 215
SHALL NEVER THIRST 123, 216
SHE DIDN'T KNOW IT WAS JESUS 658
SHEEP HAVING NO SHEPHERD 387
SHOULD I RELEASE THE KING OF THE JEWS? 615
SHOULD NOT PERISH 90, 94
SHOW US THE FATHER 472
SHOW US THE FATHER? 474
SIGNS 671
SIMON PETER 445, 453, 462, 595, 602, 654, 677
SIMON THE SON OF JONAH 43
SIN 127, 277, 289, 531, 542
SIN AND BONDAGE 371
SIN, RIGHTEOUSNESS, AND JUDGMENT 542
SINS 667
SIX WATERPOTS OF STONE 54
SLAVERY 564
SOME THINGS UNIQUELY THE FATHER'S 27
SON OF JOSEPH? 45
SONS OF THUNDER v
SORROW! 538
SORROW AND REJOICING 555
SOUL SLEEP? 383

SOVEREIGNTY OVER ALL CREATION 592
SPIRIT, SOUL, AND BODY 8
SPIRITUAL DEPRAVITY 617
SPIRITUAL GROWTH 199
SPIRITUAL IMMATURITY 461
SPIRITUAL INSIGHT 455
SPIRITUAL LEADERSHIP! 326
SPIRITUAL LIFE 673
SPIRITUAL REALITIES 142
STANDING AND STATE 98
STRAIGHTWAY 460
STRANGERS 343
SUBDUING THE FLESH 686
SUBSTITUTION AND IDENTIFICATION 371
SUCCESS? 162
SUFFICIENT PROOF 51
SUPERNATURAL KNOWLEDGE 589
SUPPORT? 172
TAKE UP YOUR BED 166
TAKE UP YOUR BED AND WALK 170
TAKING CHRIST DOWN FROM THE CROSS 648
TAKING THE GOSPEL TO THE WORLD 120
TEACHING THE MULTITUDES 267
TESTING EVERY MAN'S WORK 198
THADDAEUS 490
THAT HE MAY ABIDE WITH YOU FOREVER 483
THAT I THIRST NOT . . . 125
THAT THE WORLD MAY KNOW 584
THAT THEY MAY BELIEVE 400
THAT THEY MAY BE ONE 581
THAT WE MAY SEE AND BELIEVE 213
THAT WHICH IS NOT SCRIPTURAL 342
THAT WHICH IS SOON TO COME 131
THAT WHICH THE FATHER DID TO REDEEM THE WORLD 92
THAT WHICH WAS WRITTEN vi
THAT YOU MIGHT BELIEVE 672
THE BREAD FROM HEAVEN 230
THE LIVING IMAGE OF GOD 8
THE LORD JESUS CHRIST 331, 366, 567, 587
THE LORD KNOWS WHAT TO DO 199
THE LORD OF THE COVENANT 337
THE LORD OF WHO? 282
THE LOST SOUL COMING TO CHRIST 319
THE LOVE OF DARKNESS 108
THE LOVE OF GOD 193, 491
THE MAIN CONCERN 508
THE MANIFESTATION OF THE NAME OF THE LORD 568
THE MANIFESTING OF HIS GLORY 62
THE MAN WAS MADE WHOLE 167
THE MANY THINGS THAT JESUS DID 690

THE MASK OF REVERENCE FOR ANOTHER VIRTUE 409
THE MATTER OF PURIFYING 111
THE MEANING OF THE SECOND DREAM 59
THE MEAT THAT ENDURES UNTO EVERLASTING LIFE 211
THE MEAT THAT ENDURES UNTO EVERLASTING LIFE 211
THE MESSAGE OF CHRIST 599
THE MESSAGE OF THE CROSS 234, 537
THE MESSIAH 129, 281
THE METHOD OF THE LORD 122
THE MINISTRY WORKS OF CHRIST 370
THE MIRACLE 202
THE MIRACLES 197, 373
THE MIRACULOUS CHANGE 319
THE MODERN CHURCH 583
THE MONEY CHANGERS 67
THE MORAL QUESTION 77
THE MORE IT WILL BE OPPOSED 387
THE MORNING HAS NOW COME 675
THE MOST COMPLEX SUBJECTS 184
THE MOTHER OF CHRIST 53
THE MULTITUDE OF FISH 676
THE NAME OF JESUS 493
THE NAME OF JESUS IS A STATUS NAME 557
THE NAME OF THE LORD 414
THE NATURE OF DEATH 394
THE NATURE OF THE RESURRECTED BODY 185
THE NECESSITY OF REGENERATION 314
THE NECESSITY OF THE HOLY SPIRIT 551
THE NEED! 150
THE NET HELD 680
THE NEW BIRTH 76
THE NEW COVENANT 461, 487, 545
THE NEW CREATION IN CHRIST 8
THE NEW NATURE 92
THE NEW TESTAMENT 96
THE NOBLEMAN 149
THEN YOU SHALL KNOW 285
THE OATH OF THE SEVEN LAMBS 575
THE ODOUR OF THE OINTMENT 408
THE OFFENCE OF THE CROSS 234
THE OINTMENT 407
THE OLD TESTAMENT 509
THE ONE INGREDIENT IS FAITH 360
THE ONE WHOM GOD HAS SENT 114
THE ONLY BEGOTTEN OF THE FATHER 23
THE ONLY BEGOTTEN SON OF GOD 107
THE OPPOSITION 528
THE ORIGIN OF SIN 309
THE PARTICIPATION OF ALL IN ADAM'S SIN 311

THE PARTICULAR 688
THE PASSOVER 64, 71
THE PASSOVER? 605
THE PATH 46
THE PENTECOSTAL DENOMINATIONS 553
THE PERFECTION OF CHRIST 613
THE PERFECT MAN 612
THE PERSON OF CHRIST 678
THE PERSON OF THE LORD JESUS CHRIST 641
THE PHARISEES 74, 264, 323, 417
THE PIERCED SIDE 642
THE PLACE OF REDEMPTION AND THE MANNER OF REDEMPTION 87
THE PLAIN TALK OF JESUS 132
THE PLAN OF REDEMPTION 585
THE POOR 412
THE POWER OF HIS RESURRECTION 187
THE POWER OF THE CROSS 509
THE POWER OF THE HOLY SPIRIT 510
THE POWER OF THE NAME OF JESUS 557
THE POWER TO CHANGE THINGS 61
THE PRACTICING OF SIN 290
THE PRAISE OF MEN 434
THE PRAYER OF CHRIST 579, 585
THE PRECIOUS BLOOD OF JESUS CHRIST 271
THE PREPARATION DAY 649
THE PREPARATION FOR THE PASSOVER 626
THE PRESENT ROLE OF ANGELS 157
THE PRICE TAG 434
THE PRINCE OF THIS WORLD 498, 545, 627
THE PRINCE OF THIS WORLD CAST OUT 427
THE PRIORITIES OF THIS MINISTRY 145
THE PRISONER IS NOW FREE 167
THE PROGRESSIVE ORDER 471
THE PROOF OF THE RAISING OF LAZARUS 416
THE PSYCHOLOGICAL WAY OR THE SPIRITUAL WAY 512
THE PURGED BRANCH 501
THE PURGING 502
THE PURIFYING OF THE JEWS 54
THE PURPOSE 504
THE PURPOSE OF SEEKING GOD 382
THE QUESTION 110, 551
THE QUESTION ASKED BY JESUS 610
THE REALITY 591
THE REALITY OF THE WRATH OF GOD 315
THE REASON! 536
THE RECORD 37, 279
THE REJECTION OF CHRIST 359
THE RELATIONSHIP BETWEEN THE FATHER AND THE SON 28
THE RELATIONSHIP OF THE CHRISTIAN TO THE

WORLD 526
THE RELIGIOUS HIERARCHY 607
THE RELIGIOUS LEADERS 628
THE RELIGIOUS LEADERS EXCOMMUNICATE THE FORMER BLIND MAN 335
THE RELIGIOUS LEADERS OF ISRAEL 345
THE RELIGIOUS LEADERS REVILED THE FORMER BLIND MAN 330
THE REST 251
THE RESURRECTION 179, 408, 555
THE RESURRECTION AND THE ASCENSION 440
THE RESURRECTION OF BELIEVERS 185
THE RETAINING OF SINS 667
THE REVELATION 139
THE REVELATION AND CONDEMNATION OF EVERY EVIL WAY 109
THERE YOU MAY BE 466
THE RIGHT WAY AND THE WRONG WAY 439
THE ROMANS 596
THE RULES OF RELIGION 639
THE SABBATH 167
THE SABBATH DAY 173, 322
THE SACRIFICE FOR SIN 87
THE SACRIFICE OF CHRIST 260
THE SAMARITANS 117
THE SANHEDRIN 92, 621
THE SCOURGE 66
THE SCOURGING 617
THE SCRIPTURE 644, 656
THE SCRIPTURE MUST BE FULFILLED 640
THE SEAL 212
THE SEA OF GALILEE 196
THE SECOND COMING 415
THE SECRET 248
THE SEEKING FATHER 136
THESE HYPOCRITES 322
THE SELF-EMPTYING OF CHRIST 370
THE SELF-RIGHTEOUS? 139
THE SEPULCHRE 649, 654
THE SERVANT 450
THE SERVANT OF SIN 290
THE SERVANT PRINCIPLE 444
THESE THINGS HAVE I TOLD YOU 537
THE SEVEN SAYINGS ON THE CROSS 638
THE SHED BLOOD OF THE LORD JESUS CHRIST 318
THE SHINING LIGHT 10
THE SHIP OF LIFE 208
THE SIGN 69
THE SIMILARITY 549
THE SIN NATURE 99, 229
THE SITUATION HAS LITTLE CHANGED 344
THE SOLDIERS 634

THE SONLIFE BROADCASTING NETWORK 58
THE SONLIFE BROADCASTING NETWORK 11, 18
THE SON OF GOD 620
THE SON OF MAN 212, 286, 420
THE SON OF MAN LIFTED UP 87
THE SON OF MAN WHICH IS IN HEAVEN 86
THE SOURCE OF DEATH 394
THE SPIRIT DESCENDING 37
THE SPIRIT-FILLED LIFE 135
THE SPIRIT NOT BY MEASURE 114
THE SPIRIT OF SATAN 294
THE SPIRIT OF TRUTH 483, 532, 546
THE SPIRITUAL REBIRTH 77
THE STATE OF THE DECEASED BELIEVER 383
THE STONE 398
THE STONE WAS ROLLED AWAY 651
THE STORM 146
THE STRANGER 342
THE SUPERIORITY OF JESUS TO ANGELS 157
THE SUPERNATURAL POWER OF GOD 676
THE SUPPER 407, 443
THE SYSTEM OF THIS WORLD 243
THE TABERNACLE 135
THE TEACHER 493
THE TEMPERAMENT OF PILATE 605
THE TEMPLE 65
THE TEMPTING OF THE PHARISEES 272
THE TERRIBLE LIABILITY OF SIN 315
THE TESTIMONY 84, 142
THE THIEF 349
THE THIRD DENIAL 603
THE THIRD TIME 684
THE TIME HAD COME 626
THE TOWEL 444
THE TRAP 165
THE TRINITY 27, 448
THE TROUBLING OF THE WATER 158
THE TRUE CHURCH 264
THE TRUE LIGHT 17
THE TRUE VINE 500
THE TRUTH 188, 467, 538
THE TURN OF EVENTS 58
THE TWISTING AND PERVERTING OF THE SCRIPTURES 300
THE TWO HEBREW WORDS FOR "ONE" 591
THE UNION OF CHRIST AND THE FATHER 475
THE VERACITY OF THE WORDS OF JESUS 549
THE VINE AND THE BRANCHES 504
THE VOICE FROM HEAVEN 426
THE WASHING 447
THE WASHING OF THE FEET 446

THE WATER A SYMBOLISM 123
THE WAYS OF THE WORLD ARE NOT THE WAYS OF GOD 576
THE WAY, THE TRUTH, AND THE LIFE 467
THE WELL IS DEEP 121
THE WHOLE WORLD 222
THE WHOLE WORLD IS INCLUDED 92
THE WICKEDNESS OF RELIGION 324
THE WILDERNESS 14
THE WILL OF GOD 143, 219, 400, 423
THE WILL OF MAN 22
THE WILL OF THE FLESH 21
THE WIND? 81
THE WINE OF SALVATION 58
THE WISDOM OF MAN AND THE WORSHIP OF FALSE GODS 507
THE WITHERED BRANCH 516
THE WITNESS 14, 530, 533, 614
THE WITNESS OF SCRIPTURE 312
THE WOLF 350
THE WOMAN 268, 275
THE WOMAN OF SAMARIA 119
THE WOMAN TAKEN IN ADULTERY 267
THE WORD 232
THE WORD OF GOD 83, 96, 160, 204, 237, 270, 277, 293, 300, 429, 488, 492, 574, 577
THE WORD OF GOD TESTIFIES OF JESUS 192
THE WORD OF THE LORD 11, 248, 547
THE WORD OF THE LORD TO THEM WHO SOLD DOVES 67
THE WORD OF THE LORD TO THEM WHO SOLD DOVES 67
THE WORDS OF CHRIST 180, 588
THE WORDS OF GOD 438
THE WORDS OF JESUS 166, 564
THE WORDS OF MARY MAGDALENE 652
THE WORDS OF PETER 683
THE WORDS OF THE APOSTLE PAUL, i.e., THE WORD OF GOD 358
THE WORDS WHICH YOU GAVE ME 569
THE WORD WAS MADE FLESH 22, 363
THE WORD WILL SUFFICE 151
THE WORLD 91, 526, 575, 578
THE WORLD DOESN'T SEE THE HOLY SPIRIT, NEITHER KNOWS HIM 485
THE WORLD'S SYSTEM 526
THEY BELIEVED 70
THEY CAUGHT NOTHING 675
THEY DID WHAT HE TOLD THEM TO DO 57
THEY MARVELLED 247
THEY WERE FILLED 202
THEY WHO BELIEVE ON HIM SHOULD RECEIVE 260
THEY WOULD STONE JESUS 371
THE ZEAL OF YOUR HOUSE 69
THIEVES AND ROBBERS 347
THIRST 122, 258
THIS FELLOW? 332
THIS IS THE WORK OF GOD 213
THIS KANGAROO COURT 599
THIS KINGDOM OF GOD 611
THIS MIRACLE 417
THIS SICKNESS IS NOT UNTO DEATH 378
THOMAS 668
THOSE WHOM THE FATHER GIVES TO CHRIST 217
THOSE YOU GAVE, I HAVE KEPT 572
THOUGHTS OF GOD 512
THREE ESTATES 567
THREE PERSONS OF THE TRINITY 590
THREE PURPOSES OF THE LAW 231
THROUGH HIM 15
THROUGH THE TRUTH 579
TIBERIAS 673
TO BAPTIZE WITH WATER 38
TO BE AN OVERCOMER 563
TO BELIEVE 475, 581
TO BE WHOLE 170
TO GLORIFY 565
TO GLORIFY JESUS CHRIST 548
TO KILL JESUS 172
TOOK A TOWEL 443
TO SPEAK FAVORABLY OF JESUS 246
TO STONE JESUS 369
TO TAKE AWAY THE SIN OF THE WORLD 35
TOTAL CORRUPTION 106
TO THE GLORY OF GOD 249
TO ULTIMATELY DIE 517
TRAVAIL 555
TRINITARIANISM 591
TRODDING UNDERFOOT THE SON OF GOD 360
TROUBLED IN SPIRIT 453
TRUE FAITH 72
TRUE WORSHIP 134
TRUMPED UP CHARGES 600
TRUSTING CHRIST 97
TRUTH 79, 297, 298, 308, 576
TRUTH AS TRUE INTELLECTUALISM 468
TRUTH IS NOT A PHILOSOPHY BUT A MAN 468
TWELVE 668
TWO ANGELS 657
TWO GREAT PRINCIPLES, FIRST THE CENTER 46
TWO KINGDOMS 624
TWO LIES 513

TWO OTHERS CRUCIFIED WITH HIM 630
TWO RESURRECTIONS 184
TWO TYPES OF UNRIGHTEOUSNESS 31
ULTIMATELY TO CHRIST 425
UNBELIEF 85, 192, 213, 256, 279, 326, 432, 509, 513, 664
UNDENIABLE 360
UNDENIABLE EVIDENCE 361
UNITY 581
UNITY AND CONFORMITY 162
UNPRODUCTIVE! 501
UPON WHOM YOU SHALL SEE THE SPIRIT DESCENDING 39
VICTORY 460
VICTORY OVER DEATH 397
VISIBLE MANIFESTATION 114
WAIT FOR THE PROMISE OF THE FATHER 40
WALK 166
WALKING AFTER THE FLESH AND WALKING AFTER THE SPIRIT 236
WALKING IN DARKNESS 430
WALKING IN THE NIGHT 382
WARNINGS 534
WARPED, TWISTED THINKING 334
WASHING THE FEET OF THE DISCIPLES 444
WAS PETER SINCERE? 463
WAS THE INTERCESSION OF MARY HELPFUL? 51
WAS THERE EVER A MIRACLE OF THIS SORT? 334
WAS THE WINE OF THIS MIRACLE ALCOHOLIC WINE? 49
WATER BAPTISM 14, 79, 109
WE ARE NOT IN THE KINGDOM AGE YET 518
WE ARE TO BE LIKE OUR FATHER 29
WE CANNOT TELL WHAT HE SAYS 552
WEEPING 656
WE HAVE FOUND HIM 44
WE HAVE SEEN THE LORD 669
WE KNOW WHAT WE WORSHIP 133
WE SHALL BE LIKE HIM 186
WE SPEAK THAT WE DO KNOW 83
WE WOULD SEE JESUS . . . 418
WHAT ABOUT THE CHRISTIAN WHO IS STRUGGLING WITH A CONTINUOUS SIN? 102
WHAT ABOUT THOSE WHO HAVE NEVER HEARD THE GOSPEL? 18
WHAT ABOUT THOSE WHO HAVE NEVER HEARD THE GOSPEL? 18
WHAT ACCUSATION BRING YOU AGAINST THIS MAN? 606
WHAT ARE THE QUALIFICATIONS FOR THE USE OF THE NAME OF JESUS? 478
WHAT ARE THE WAYS OF THE LORD? 365
WHAT COMMANDMENTS? 489, 520

WHAT DID HE MEAN BY LIGHT? 277
WHAT DID JESUS DO? 57
WHAT DID JESUS DO AT THE CROSS? 236
WHAT DID JESUS SAY? 52
WHAT DID JESUS SAY TO HIM? 166
WHAT DID JESUS WRITE? 273
WHAT DOES IT MEAN TO BELIEVE ON THE SON OF GOD? 336
WHAT DOES IT MEAN TO BE WHOLE? 162
WHAT DOES IT MEAN TO WALK AFTER THE SPIRIT? 80
WHAT DOES THE NAME OF JESUS MEAN IN THE SPIRIT WORLD? 479
WHAT HAPPENED THE SEVENTY-TWO HOURS WHEN JESUS DIED? 642
WHAT HAPPENS WHEN A BELIEVER SINS? 98
WHAT HAVE YOU DONE? 610
WHAT HE SEES THE FATHER DO 178
WHAT IS GOD'S METHOD OF VICTORY? 163
WHAT IS GOD'S PRESCRIBED ORDER? 366
WHAT IS SPIRITUAL AUTHORITY? 16
WHAT IS THE DEFINITION OF RIGHTEOUSNESS? 543
WHAT IS THE FLESH? 22, 312
WHAT IS THE MEANS OF GRACE? 367
WHAT IS THE REASON FOR THIS NETWORK? 144
WHAT IS THE WORD OF THE CROSS? 509
WHAT IS THIS FRUIT? 502
WHAT IS TRUTH? 614
WHAT JESUS DID AT THE CROSS 371
WHAT JESUS DID FOR LOST SINNERS 592
WHAT KIND OF FAITH? 361
WHAT SIGN DO YOU SHOW US? 213
WHAT THE BIBLE SAYS! 395
WHAT THE CHILD OF GOD IS FACING 510
WHAT THE LAW COULD NOT DO 158
WHAT THE LAW INCLUDED 25
WHAT WAS THE FRUIT OF THE MINISTRY OF JESUS? 325
WHEN JESUS BEHELD HIM 42
WHEN THE PEOPLE HEARD . . . 414
WHERE DID JESUS GET THE BREAD AND THE FISH? 679
WHERE DO DEMON SPIRITS COME FROM? 156
WHERE DO YOU GET THIS LIVING WATER? 121
WHERE DO YOU GET THIS LIVING WATER? 121
WHERE I GO 466
WHERE IS HE? 658
WHERE JESUS WAS CRUCIFIED 629
WHERE WILL HE GO? 255
WHITE ALREADY TO HARVEST 145

WHO ARE YOU? 31
WHO IS JESUS? 221
WHO IS JESUS CHRIST? 369
WHO IS JESUS OF NAZARETH? 590
WHOM DO YOU SEEK? 660
WHOM THE WORLD CANNOT RECEIVE 484
WHOSE NAME WAS JOHN 13
WHOSOEVER 89, 123
WHOSOEVER WILL 36
WHY? 323
WHY CALVARY? 647
WHY DID JESUS USE THE APPELLATIVE *"THIEVES AND ROBBERS"*? 347
WHY DID NOT HIS BRETHREN BELIEVE IN HIM? 63
WHY DID THE HOLY SPIRIT THROUGH CHRIST CHOOSE THE CHANGING OF WATER TO WINE AS HIS FIRST MIRACLE? 61
WHY DOES GOD DEMAND WORSHIP? 136
WHY DO SOME COME AND BELIEVE, AND MOST DO NOT? 217
WHY DO YOU WEEP? 658, 659
WHY IS THE PREACHING OF THE CROSS SO IMPORTANT? 480
WHY THE CROSS? 608
WHY THE HATRED OF CHRIST? 602
WILL NOT COME TO THE LIGHT 109
WILLPOWER 103
WILL YOU BE MADE WHOLE? 159
WILL YOU RAISE IT UP IN THREE DAYS? 70
WINE IN BIBLICAL TIMES 50
WITHOUT GUILE 46
WITHOUT JESUS, NOTHING GOES RIGHT 677
WITHOUT ME YOU CAN DO NOTHING 505
WITNESS UNTO THE TRUTH 613
WOMAN 119
WOMAN, WHAT HAVE I TO DO WITH YOU? 53
WORKS OF THE FATHER 374
WORKS RIGHTEOUSNESS 544
WORLD EVANGELISM 146
WORLDLINESS 527
WORSHIP 338, 651
WORSHIPPING HIM IN SPIRIT AND IN TRUTH 138
YOU! 12
YOU ARE FROM BENEATH 283
YOU CANNOT COME 282
YOU GAVE THEM TO ME 568
YOU HAVE SEEN ME AND BELIEVE NOT 216
YOU IN ME 487
YOUR FATHER THE DEVIL 297
YOUR WORD IS TRUTH 577
YOU WORSHIP YOU KNOW NOT WHAT 131

For information concerning the *Jimmy Swaggart Bible Commentary,* please request a Gift Catalog.

You may inquire by using Books of the Bible.

- Genesis (639 pages) (11-201)
- Exodus (639 pages) (11-202)
- Leviticus (435 pages) (11-203)
- Numbers
  Deuteronomy (493 pages) (11-204)
- Joshua
  Judges
  Ruth (329 pages) (11-205)
- I Samuel
  II Samuel (528 pages) (11-206)
- I Kings
  II Kings (560 pages) (11-207)
- I Chronicles
  II Chronicles (528 pages) (11-226)
- Ezra
  Nehemiah
  Esther (288 pages) (11-208)
- Job (320 pages) (11-225)
- Psalms (672 pages) (11-216)
- Proverbs (311 pages) (11-227)
- Ecclesiastes
  Song Of Solomon (238 pages) (11-228)
- Isaiah (688 pages) (11-220)
- Jeremiah
  Lamentations (456 pages) (11-070)
- Ezekiel (508 pages) (11-223)
- Daniel (403 pages) (11-224)
- Hosea
  Joel
  Amos (496 pages) (11-229)
- Obadiah
  Jonah
  Micah
  Nahum
  Habakkuk
  Zephaniah (545 pages) (11-230)
- Haggai
  Zechariah
  Malachi (449 pages) (11-231)

- Matthew (888 pages) (11-073)
- Mark (606 pages) (11-074)
- Luke (736 pages) (11-075)
- John (532 pages) (11-076)
- Acts (697 pages) (11-077)
- Romans (536 pages) (11-078)
- I Corinthians (632 pages) (11-079)
- II Corinthians (589 pages) (11-080)
- Galatians (478 pages) (11-081)
- Ephesians (550 pages) (11-082)
- Philippians (476 pages) (11-083)
- Colossians (374 pages) (11-084)
- I Thessalonians
  II Thessalonians (498 pages) (11-085)
- I Timothy
  II Timothy
  Titus
  Philemon (687 pages) (11-086)
- Hebrews (831 pages) (11-087)
- James
  I Peter
  II Peter (730 pages) (11-088)
- I John
  II John
  III John
  Jude (377 pages) (11-089)
- Revelation (602 pages) (11-090)

For telephone orders you may call 1-800-288-8350 with bankcard information. All Baton Rouge residents please use (225) 768-7000.

For mail orders send to:
Jimmy Swaggart Ministries
P.O. Box 262550
Baton Rouge, LA 70826-2550

Visit our website: www.jsm.org

NOTES

NOTES

NOTES

NOTES

NOTES

NOTES

NOTES

NOTES

NOTES

NOTES

NOTES